COMMENT

By Stuart Barnes

It goes without saying that the return of spectators in the new season is the most fervent wish of players, managers, referees and, not least, club officials desperately in need of income to go some way to balancing the books. Football has soldiered on the best it could in the past six months – a soulless time for the game at all levels which none of us want to experience again. The Government has signalled a partial return of fans in October, depending on whether Covid-19 can be kept under control, with hopefully a bigger proportion to follow. There is obviously no guarantee, but let's hope the worst is over and a start can be made to address some of the deep-seated problems affecting the game before and after lockdown. Top of the list must be a commitment from the Premier League and its clubs for more financial support for lower league teams, particularly those genuinely in trouble. Sustainable competition across all divisions is essential. Without it, there is an imbalance which not only threatens local sides but harms local communities. Massive, six-figure weekly salaries, in some cases paid to players happy to sit on the sidelines, can no longer be acceptable. Huge sums paid to agents must be curbed. Lowering ticket prices should be on the agenda. All this will not happen overnight. It could be months, even years, as long as the wheels are set in motion. The thorny subject of VAR also has to be addressed. Fractions and centimetres have no place in football. A pragmatic approach to decision-making makes much more sense. Referees must be allowed to consult pitchside monitors. And why not have former players, with a deep insight into what happens on the pitch, offering their opinion alongside officials in the VAR bunker? There would surely be fewer wrong calls and less controversy.

Television delivered one of the few benefits of lockdown by delving into the archives and giving us the chance to see again some of the game's greatest moments. None more so than England's 1966 World Cup triumph which remains a vivid reminder of a different era. There was Gordon Banks, goalkeeper supreme, yet still four years away from the save that, more than anything, defined his career – from Pele's downward, goal-bound header in the tournament in Mexico. At the heart of the defence, cultured captain Bobby Moore had the perfect foil in the no-nonsense Jack Charlton. Alongside them, Ray Wilson made every effort to compensate for the early misplaced clearing header which enabled Helmut Haller to put West Germany ahead. Galloping down the right flank with a seemingly inexhaustible amount of energy was Alan Ball. On the opposite side was Martin Peters, scorer of England's second goal and the player Sir Alf Ramsey deemed to be 'ten years ahead of his time.' Sadly, none of those six players are still with us, with Peters and Charlton having passed away during the course of last season. That leaves George Cohen, perhaps the most underrated member of the team; Nobby Stiles, who danced a jig of delight with the Jules Rimet Trophy in one hand and his dentures in the other; Roger Hunt, who wheeled away in celebration, convinced Geoff Hurst's second goal HAD bounced down over the line from the crossbar; Bobby Charlton, whose two semi-final goals against Portugal paved the way for his side to become world champions; and Hurst whose hat-trick clincher was accompanied by the never-to-be-forgotten words of commentator Kenneth Wolstenholme. Memories are certainly made of this.

Will the present-day England be able to make the same use of home advantage when the rescheduled European Championship goes ahead – hopefully – next summer? And how is Gareth Southgate's side likely to line up for a tournament spread initially across the Continent, with the semi-finals and finals at Wembley? After an enforced ten-month international break, Southgate will have to re-evaluate his choices. So much can change over the season, with some players falling by the wayside and others making the breakthrough. Currently, form and fitness permitting, there would seem to be four and possibly five definites – Harry Maguire, Jordan Henderson, Harry Kane, Raheem Sterling and Marcus Rashford. Trent Alexander-Arnold and Declan Rice had fine seasons with Liverpool and West Ham respectively and should be strong contenders, along with Ben Chilwell. Elsewhere, Jordan Pickford faces a strong challenge from Nick Pope for the goalkeeper's jersey, while the youthful enterprise of Mason Mount and Jadon Sancho is expected to be a factor. So, too, will the emergence of Phil Foden, who could be the one to make the biggest impact.

A SEASON LIKE NO OTHER

It was the season like no other, caused by a disease like no other. It forced football into hibernation and left clubs with severe financial consequences. When the top ones in England were able to resume, the sound of silence echoed around empty grounds. Points-per-game became the new norm, settling promotion and relegation issues. The royal box was ruled out of bounds on FA Cup Final day. And the country's top manager was told, to his obvious bemusement, that success might have to be accompanied by an asterisk in the record books. It was also the year that one England player forced the Government into an embarrassing U-turn and another was applauded for his efforts to raise money for the NHS. With the new season under way, less than a month after Manchester City and Manchester United were still contesting European honours from the old one, everyone is asking what the future holds for the game. The FA warned that COVID-19 'presented economic challenges beyond the wildest imagination.' One chairman delivered a worst-case scenario of many clubs going to the wall. Already, it has taken its toll in Scotland, with all three divisions below the Premiership deciding on a 27-match campaign, nine fewer than normal, and not kicking-off until the middle of October. By then, the Government has indicated there could be some spectators allowed back, unless the virus returns to the levels experienced in the UK and all around the world.

Their absence took the shine of some outstanding performance in 2019-20, notably Liverpool's first domestic title for 30 years, which under normal circumstances would have been celebrated by a joyful, full house at Anfield but which had to be restricted to an emotional presentation by Sir Kenny Dalglish, who was manager the last time the club were champions. Nonetheless, Jurgen Klopp, who followed up Champions League and Club World Cup success, was in buoyant mood, if a little puzzled about the use of the asterisk, which he promised to google to understand its significance. Arsenal, whose new manager Mikel Arteta was an early victim of the virus, also celebrated on the pitch in a deserted stadium, this time Wembley after their FA Cup victory, instead of having the usual formalities. Their delight was no less pronounced, even if two-goal matchwinner Pierre-Emerick Aubameyang made a hash of lifting the trophy from the presentation table and dropping it before he was able to hoist it in front of team-mates. Wolves had nothing to show from a marathon season, but their staying power won many admirers after losing to Sevilla in the quarter-finals of the Europa League 383 days on from starting out in a qualifying tie. Leeds, once part of the English game's elite, finally made it back to the Premier League after an absence of 16 years with an enterprising young team skilfully led by the shrewd Argentine Marcelo Bielsa, who succeeded where many previous Elland Road managers had failed. Gareth Ainsworth is from a different managerial mould, spending his spare time playing in a rock band, but he too delivered eye-catching success by leading little Wycombe into the Championship via the play-offs.

Among the players, Jordan Henderson captained Liverpool to the title impressively and was named Footballer of the Year by the football writers. He also made a big impression off the field during lockdown by launching a charitable fund for the NHS .and raising more money with a raffle for signed shirts. Manchester United's Marcus Rashford was involved in helping to raise £20m for a charity providing meals for vulnerable people, then pressuring the Government into reversing a decision not to provide free school meals over the summer. England manager Gareth Southgate also did his bit early in the pandemic with an emotional open letter to supporters (see below) urging them not to worry about the postponement of Euro 2020 – which now goes ahead in the summer of 2021 while retaining its original title for marketing purposes – but concentrate on each other to come through the pandemic. Sadly, some of the game's biggest names were lost. Martin Peters and Jack Charlton became the fifth and sixth members of England's 1966 World Cup-winning team to pass away. Harry Gregg was a fine goalkeeper for club and country who achieved hero status in the 1958 Munich air disaster when pulling three Manchester United team-mates Bobby Charlton, Jackie Blanchflower and Dennis Viollet, manager Matt Busby and a mother and her child, from the

burning wreckage. We also saw the demise, after 125 years, of newly-promoted but financially-stricken Bury, the first club to drop out since 1992. All their opening five League One fixtures were postponed and, when talk of a rescue bid came to nothing, they were expelled for what the EFL called failing to provide evidence of financial viability.
STUART BARNES

MESSAGE FROM GARETH SOUTHGATE

For everyone in our country, the primary focus of the present – and the coming months – is undoubtedly to look after our families, support our communities and work together to come through what is clearly the most extreme test we've faced collectively in decades. On behalf of all the team and staff, I would like to take this opportunity to send our sympathies to those who have lost loved ones already. Our thoughts are with you and those who sadly will suffer similarly in the coming period. In the way you've all come together to support our team, we must now work together to combat a virus that is causing physical and emotional issues to so many. So, please continue to follow the guidelines for hygiene and sensible precautions put in place to control the spread of the virus in order to protect those most vulnerable to its impact. The responsibility lies with us all.

We are also conscious of the economic uncertainty affecting so many businesses and, consequently, virtually every family. Coupled with the unique challenges of self-isolation, the loss of routine to normal working and social life, we face real challenges to our mental wellbeing. Our children may feel anxious with uncertainty. It's not normal for any of us and it's going to challenge us all. Look out for each other. Please don't suffer alone and remember that our great country has come through these enormous challenges before. Together, we will do so again.

We were due to play next week and to represent you all this summer, but now is clearly not the moment for us to take centre stage. The heroes will be the men and women who continue working tirelessly in our hospitals and medical centres to look after our friends and families. They won't receive the individual acclaim, but we all know their importance is beyond anything we do on the pitch. When we play again as an England team, it will be at a time when not only our country but the rest of the world as well is on the road to recovery. Hopefully, we will be closer to each other than ever and ready for the beautiful distraction that football can bring. To play in a European Championship next summer will still be possible for all our squad. So we shouldn't spend another moment thinking about the postponement of the competition. I feel sure that when the moment comes I will never have been prouder to be the leader. Again, on behalf of us all, I wish you and your families strength and love to thrive through the challenges ahead.

(Issued in late March, 2020)

WHAT THEY SAID ABOUT COVID-19 ...

'Football faces economic challenges beyond the wildest imagination of those who run it. In the face of this adversity, all stakeholders in the game, from players, fans, clubs, owners and administrators, need to step up and share the pain to keep the game alive. We face the danger of losing clubs as finances collapse' – **Greg Clarke**, chairman of the FA, spelling out the threat posed by the pandemic.

'We need the address the long term, otherwise we will be back in this situation in three years. We need hope. We need a plan. We need clarity. We can't go on from one bailout to another' – **Rick Parry**, chairman of the English Football League, warning that clubs face a £200m loss.

'Football has to look outwards. It has to do something quite spectacular so it sets the tone for the rest of the country' – **Gary Neville**, former Manchester United and England defender and an influential voice in the game.

"There is a real, stark probability that if something isn't agreed now within football to ensure all clubs can pay their bills and get through to the point where income is resumed, you will be looking at 50 or 60 clubs ceasing to exist. Genuinely, I am talking about that many' – **Phil Hodgkinson**, Huddersfield owner.

'I cannot help feeling that speculation around transfers of individual players for millions of pounds this summer seems to ignore the realities that face the sport' – **Ed Woodward**, Manchester United's executive vice-chairman warns that days of big-money moves could be over.

'We shouldn't spend another moment thinking about the postponement of the competition' – **Gareth Southgate**, England manager, in a message to supporters urging them not to worry about the postponement of Euro 2020 but concentrate on each other to come through the pandemic.

'There needs to be a point where enough is enough and we say let's finish it'– **Harry Kane**, England captain, says the Premier League season will have to be cancelled if it cannot be completed by the end of June.

'Thank you NHS' – **Wembley** paying tribute to health service workers with an illuminated message on the stadium arch.

'I have spent nearly 20 years growing this club and there have been many hurdles along the way. The pandemic is the most serious of them all'– **Daniel Levy**, Tottenham chairman.

'We believe we came to the wrong conclusion and are truly sorry for that' – **Liverpool** reverse their decision to use the Government's furlough scheme to pay non-playing staff.

'It's inconsequential where Luton finish, or what division we are in next season, if there isn't a next season. We have to keep football intact' – **Gary Sweet**, chief executive of Lutyon.

'It reminded me of walking up Mount Kilimanjaro. I could hardly walk' – **Brendan Rodgers**, Leicester manager, on contracting COVID-19.

DAY BY DAY DIARY 2019–20

JULY 2019

17 West Ham pay a club-record £42.5m for Eintracht Frankfurt's French striker Sebastien Haller. Stevenage are fined £5,000 by the FA for sexist chanting by supporters towards fourth official Lisa Rashid during the home game against Bury.

18 Newly-promoted Bury have a 12-point deduction imposed by an English Football League ruling that the club's rescue bid is an 'insolvency event.' Kilmarnock are knocked out of the Europa League by Welsh part-timers Connah's Quay in the first qualifying round.

19 Daniel Sturridge, released by Liverpool, is fined £75,000 and banned for six weeks – four of them suspended – for breaching betting rules.

20 David de Gea agrees a new six-year contract with Manchester United.

21 Sheffield United break their transfer record for the third time in the summer transfer window with the £10m signing of Bournemouth's Lys Mousset.

22 Newcastle sign Brazilian striker Joelinton from the German club Hoffenheim for a club-record £40m.

23 Nathaniel Clyne is ruled out for up to six months with a knee ligament injury, sustained during Liverpool's close season tour of the United States.

24 Notts County, relegated from the Football League for the first time, are taken over by a Danish consortium.

25 Arsenal's Mesut Ozil and Sead Kolasinac escape unhurt from an attempted carjacking in a London street.

26 Tottenham sign a new eight-year shirt sponsorship deal with insurance company AIA worth around £360m.

27 Former England striker Darren Bent, who played for nine clubs, announces his retirement at the age of 35.

28 Micah Richards, former Manchester City and England defender, retires at 31 because of a chronic knee injury.

29 Bury's opening League One fixture against MK Dons is postponed by the English Football League after the club fail to provide evidence of financial viability. Walsall director Leigh Pomlett takes over the club from chairman Jeff Bonser, the main shareholder for 28 years.

30 Patrice Evra, former Manchester United defender and winner of 81 caps for France, announces his retirement at 38.

31 Sheffield Wednesday's Fernando Forestieri is banned for six matches and fined £25,000 by the FA for racist language towards Mansfield player Krystian Pearce during a pre-season game in July 2018.

AUGUST 2019

1 Arsenal sign Ivory Coast winger Nicolas Pepe from Lille for a club-record £72m.

2 For the fourth time, Sheffield United break their transfer record, this time signing Swansea's Oliver McBurnie for £20m. Bury have their second fixture, against Accrington, postponed.

3 Celtic open their defence of the Scottish Premiership title by beating St Johnstone 7-0. Football League newcomers Salford start with a 2-0 victory over Stevenage. On an emotional afternoon in east London, Leyton Orient beat Cheltenham 1-0 with a goal from Josh Wright, the late Justin Edinburgh's final signing for the club.

4 Manchester City defeat Liverpool 5-4 on penalties after a 1-1 scoreline in the Community Shield, curtain-raiser to the new Premier League season.

5 Harry Maguire becomes the world's most expensive defender when joining Manchester United from Leicester for £80m, eclipsing the £75m Liverpool paid for Virgil van Dijk in January 2018. Brighton sign Brentford's Neal Maupay for a club-record £20m.

6 In the most high-profile signing of the transfer window, Wayne Rooney joins Derby as player-coach from Washington-based DC United – a move taking effect in January 2019. Chelsea's board apologise unreservedly for the grooming and abuse of young players by former chief scout Eddie Heath in the 1970s. An independent report by Charles Geekie QC is also critical of former assistant manager Dario Gradi for not doing more to stop it.

7 John McGinn signs a new five-year contract with Aston Villa. The FA launch a free streaming platform dedicated to women's football, including Super League matches.

8 Watford become the tenth Premier League club to break their transfer record in the summer window, paying Rennes £31m for Senegal winger Ismaila Sarr. Biggest deal on deadline day takes Romelu Lukaku from Manchester United to Inter Milan for £74m. Arsenal's £25m acquisition of Kieran Tierney from Celtic is a Scottish record. Total spending during the summer of £1.41bn is slightly down on the 2018 total of £1.43bn.

9 Liverpool launch the new Premier League season by beating promoted Norwich 4-1. Bury are threatened with expulsion from the English Football League after having a third match, a League Cup tie against Sheffield Wednesday, called off. Manchester City's Leroy Sane is ruled out for six months with a knee ligament injury sustained in the Community Shield match. City's Ilkay Gundogan signs a new four-year contract.

10 Manchester City begin their defence of the title by beating West Ham 5-0, with the newly introduced VAR system used several times. Queens Park Rangers rename their Loftus Road ground the Kiyan Prince Foundation Stadium after the academy player stabbed to death aged 15.

11 Arsenal leave out Mesut Ozil and Sead Kolasinac from their squad to play Newcastle because of continued security worries over the attempted carjacking.

12 Bury have a fourth fixture, against Gillingham, called off as staff use the club's website to urge owner Steve Dale to sell up.

13 Manchester City avoid a transfer ban after admitting breaching rules on signing youth players. FIFA fine the club £315,000. Celtic are knocked out of the Champions League in the third qualifying round after conceding four goals at home to the Romanian side CFR Cluj.

14 Liverpool defeat Chelsea 5-4 on penalties after a 2-2 scoreline in the European Super Cup in Istanbul. The match is refereed by Stephanie Frappart, of France, the first woman to take charge of a major European men's match. Along with her assistants, Michelle O'Neill (Ireland) and Manuela Nicolosi (Italy), she wins widespread praise.

15 Sol Campbell, who led Macclesfield's escape from relegation, leaves the cash-strapped club after nine months as manager by mutual agreement. Aberdeen are knocked out of the Europa League by the Croatian club Rijeka in a third qualifying round tie. Bury's midweek fixture against Rotherham is postponed.

16 Jan Siewert, manager of Huddersfield for seven months, is sacked after a single victory in 19 matches.

17 Ashley Cole, 38, confirms his retirement after winning 13 major titles with Arsenal and Chelsea and 107 England caps.

18 Daryl McMahon, former manager of National League club Ebbsfleet, takes charge at Macclesfield.

19 Bolton postpone their midweek fixture against Doncaster because of 'welfare concerns' about having to play too many young players. Sheffield United's Oliver Norwood retires from international football after winning 57 Northern Ireland caps.

20 Bury are expelled from the League Cup and have a sixth fixture called off, against Tranmere.

21 Phil Parkinson resigns after three years as Bolton manager, adding to the turmoil at the club.

22 Alex Oxlade-Chamberlain signs a 12-month contract extension with Liverpool through to 2023.

23 The English Football League offer Bury a lifeline via a possible takeover of the club. Rangers are ordered by UEFA to close a section of Ibrox for their play-off tie against Legia Warsaw after racist behaviour by supporters in a previous Europa League game. Swindon manager Richie Wellens is given a two-match ban and £1,000 fine by the FA for improper conduct.

24 Nice, the French club managed by former Arsenal midfielder Patrick Vieira, are bought by Ineos, a company founded by British billionaire Sir Jim Ratcliffe.

25 Charlie Daniels sustains a knee injury in Bournemouth's match against Manchester City and is ruled out for the season.

27 Bury, elected to the Football League in 1894, are expelled after the proposed takeover falls through. The League Two runners-up become the first club to drop out since Maidstone's demise in 1992. EFL chief Debbie Jevans calls it 'a dark day.' League One continues with 23 clubs, with three teams relegated instead of four and one relegated from League Two instead of two.

28 Fellow crisis club Bolton are saved by a takeover by Football Ventures, a private limited company.

29 The English Football League refuse to reconsider Bury's expulsion after pleas from local MPs and supporters' groups. Wolves, Celtic and Rangers win play-off matches to reach the group stage of the Europa League. The Irish club Linfield are beaten. Liverpool's Virgil van Dijk is voted Europe's best player. England full-back Lucy Bronze wins the women's award. Millwall manager Neil Harris is fined £2,000 by the FA for misconduct.

30 West Ham's Manuel Lanzini signs a new contract through to 2023. Rangers are ordered to close a section of Ibrox for their opening Europa League group game against Feyenoord after being found guilty of a second UEFA charge of sectarian chanting. The FA fine West Bromwich Albion manager Slaven Bilic £2,000 for misconduct.

31 Former Rochdale and Barnsley manager Keith Hill takes charge at Bolton and signs nine new free transfer, unattached and loan players.

SEPTEMBER 2019

2 Europe's top five leagues spent a record £5bn in the summer transfer window, according to figures by the Deloitte sport business group.

3 Manchester City's Aymeric Laporte has knee surgery after being carried off against Brighton and is ruled out for five months.

4 Huddersfield are fined £50,000 for breaching FA advertising regulations with a spoof, sash-style shirt bearing the logo of a bookmaker for a pre-season friendly.

5 David McGoldrick's 85th minute header, his first international goal, gives the Republic of Ireland a 1-1 draw with Switzerland in a Euro 2020 qualifier. Northern Ireland need an own goal to defeat Luxembourg 1-0 in a friendly.

6 Scotland lose their first qualifier of the season 2-1 against Russia after John McGinn puts them ahead with his first international goal. Wales defeat Azerbaijan 2-1 with an 84th minute Gareth Bale header. Garry Monk is appointed Sheffield Wednesday's new manager – his fifth club in four years. Kevin Bond, manager of Southend for four months, resigns after six successive league defeats.

7 Harry Kane scores a hat-trick, including two penalties, and sets up Raheem Sterling for another goal as England defeat Bulgaria 4-0 in their qualifying group. Watford sack Javi Gracia after a single point gained from the opening four matches, the tenth managerial change since the Pozzo family bought the club in June 2012. Quique Sanchez Flores returns for a second spell in charge. A record crowd for a Women's Super League game, 31,213, watch Manchester City defeat Manchester United 1-0 at the Etihad.

8 Stevenage manager Dino Maamria is sacked with his team second from bottom after seven matches.

9 Steven Davis becomes Northern Ireland's most capped outfield player with his 113th appearance in the Euro 2020 qualifier against Germany – a 2-0 defeat which ends his side 100 per cent record in their group. Scotland's chances of automatic qualification are effectively ended by a 4-0 home defeat by Belgium. Wales defeat Belarus 1-0 in a friendly. Lincoln manager Danny Cowley takes over at Huddersfield after initially rejecting the job.

10 England trail after 34 seconds, lead 5-1 at half-time and are then pegged back to 5-3 by Kosovo in a see-saw match in which exciting attacking play is undermined by defensive deficiencies. Jadon Sancho scores his first two international goals and there is a rare penalty miss by Harry Kane. James Collins, one of five new Republic of Ireland caps, scores in a 3-1 friendly match win over Bulgaria. Alan Browne and Kevin Long are also on the mark for the first time.

11 Jordan Stevens, 19-year-old Leeds midfielder, is banned for six weeks and fined £1,200 for

breaching FA betting regulations. Everton's Yerry Mina receives a £10,000 fine for appearing in a TV advert with a Colombian betting company.

12 A crowd of more than 51,000 watch former Manchester City captain Vincent Kompany's testimonial match at the Etihad in aid of a charity for the homeless.

13 Referees' chief Mike Riley admits at a Premier League meeting to four incorrect VAR decisions in the first month of the season.

15 David de Gea ends long-standing speculation about his future by signing a new contract with Manchester United through to 2023.

16 The High Court awards full control of Sheffield United to Prince Abdullah in his case against co-owner Kevin McCabe.

17 Birmingham are fined £42,500 by the FA for the attack by a supporter on Aston Villa captain Jack Grealish last season.

18 Victor Lindelof signs a new contract with Manchester United through to 2024.

19 Former Newcastle academy coach Peter Beardsley is suspended from football for seven months after being found guilty of an FA charge of racially abusing young players. Callum Hudson-Odoi, 18, signs a new five-year contract with Chelsea. Laurent Banide, manager of Oldham for three months, is sacked after a single win in nine league games and replaced by Dino Maamria, ten days after his own dismissal by Stevenage. Rick Parry, former chief executive of the Premier League and Liverpool, is appointed chairman of the Football League.

20 Celtic are fined £11,000 by UEFA for fans setting off flares and throwing objects during their Europa League play-off victory over AIK in Stockholm – the 17th time since 2007 the club have been fined by Europe's governing body. Michael Appleton, former Oxford, Blackburn, Blackpool and Portsmouth manager, takes over at Lincoln.

22 Jurgen Klopp, Liverpool's Champions League-winning manager, is named FIFA's coach of the year. Barcelona's Lionel Messi wins the top player award. Leeds manager Marcelo Bielsa wins the fair play trophy for ordering his team to allow Aston Villa to score an uncontested equaliser.

23 Manchester United manager Ole Gunnar Solskjaer is given a vote of confidence after his side's indifferent start to the season. United announce record annual revenues of £627m. Tottenham are knocked out of the League Cup on penalties by Colchester.

24 West Ham lose 4-0 to Oxford in their third round tie.

25 AFC Wimbledon suspend manager Wally Downes after he is charged by the FA with breaching betting regulations.

26 Football League clubs reject a move for Bury to return in League Two in season 2020-21. One team, rather than two, will be relegated from this division at the end of the current season.

27 Derby captain Richard Keogh is ruled out for the rest of the season with a knee injury, sustained in a car crash involving team-mates Tom Lawrence and Mason Bennett.

29 Ollie Watkins scores a hat-trick of headers in Brentford's 3-1 Championship victory over Barnsley.

30 Cardiff are ordered by FIFA to pay Nantes £5.3m as the first instalment of the £15m transfer fee for Emiliano Sala, who died in a plane crash before playing for his new club.

OCTOBER 2019

1 Tottenham are humbled 7-2 by Bayern Munich in the Champions League – the biggest margin of defeat for an English team at home in any European competition. Former Arsenal winger Serge Gnabry scores four goals.

2 The English Football League fine Liverpool £200,000, half of which is suspended, for fielding an ineligible player, Pedro Chirivella, in their League Cup win over MK Dons. David Pemsel, chief executive of the Guardian Media Group, is named the Premier League's new chief executive.

3 England manager Gareth Southgate leaves out four of his World Cup players, Dele Alli, Eric Dier, Jesse Lingard and Kyle Walker for Euro 2020 qualifiers against the Czech Republic and Bulgaria.

4 Millwall's Neil Harris, appointed in April 2015 and the Championship's longest-serving manager, resigns after a run of eight matches without a win.

5   Derby's Tom Lawrence and Mason Bennett are fined six weeks' wages by the club after being charged with drink-driving – and later banned by magistrates.

6   Aaron Connolly, 19, is called into the Republic of Ireland squad for Euro 2020 qualifiers against Georgia and Switzerland after scoring twice on his full Premier League debut for Brighton against Tottenham.

7   Barnsley manager Daniel Stendel is sacked after a 5-1 defeat by Preston leaves his side second from bottom. Dario Gradi, suspended by the FA in 2016, retires after a 36-year association with Crewe, included three spells as manager.

8   Sunderland dismiss their manager Jack Ross following a 2-0 defeat at Lincoln. Aaron Cresswell signs a new contract through to 2023 with West Ham.

9   Another Championhip manager leaves – Jose Gomes sacked after ten months at Reading with his side third from bottom.

10 Scotland concede four goals in 27 second-half minutes, lose 4-0 to Russia and must rely on qualifying for Euro 2020 via the play-offs after winning their Nations League group. Northern Ireland's chances diminish after a 3-1 defeat by Holland. Kieffer Moore's first international goal keeps alive Welsh hopes in a 1-1 draw against Slovakia.

11 England lose a qualifying game for the first time for ten years, beaten 2-1 in the Czech Republic after leading with Harry Kane's fifth minute penalty. The Premier League's youngest-ever player, 16-year-old Liverpool midfielder Harvey Elliott, is banned for two weeks by the FA for mocking Harry Kane on social media.

12 The Republic of Ireland stay on top of their qualifying group after a goalless draw against Georgia.

13 John McGinn becomes the first Scotland player to score a first-half-hat-trick since 1952. It comes in a 6-0 win over San Marino in which Lawrence Shankland and Stuart Findlay mark their full debuts with a goal each.

14 England's 6-0 win over Bulgaria is overshadowed by racist abuse against Tyrone Mings, making his international debut, Raheem Sterling and Marcus Rashford. Referee Ivan Bebek halts play twice to initiate new UEFA anti-racism protocol and Gareth Southgate's side consider walking off. Sterling scores a hat-trick and Ross Barkley nets twice. Northern Ireland's Paddy McNair also scores two goals as Northern Ireland win a friendly match away from home for the first time for 13 years – 3-2 against the Czech Republic, who show ten changes from their victory over England. Mark Bowen, Reading's sporting director and a former Wales full-back, is appointed the club's fourth manager in 19 months.

15 The events in Sofia have immediate ramifications. UEFA charge the Bulgaria Football Union on four separate counts, its president Borislav Mihaylov is forced to resign and team captain Ivelin Popov issues an apology. The Republic of Ireland lose 2-0 to Switzerland and have captain Seamus Coleman sent off for a second yellow card. West Ham's Robert Snodgrass retires from international football after winning 28 Scotland caps.

16 Charlton manager Lee Bowyer is given a three-match touchline ban and £4,000 fine by the FA for improper conduct after the home defeat by Swansea. Carl Fletcher, former Wales midfielder and Plymouth manager, takes over at Leyton Orient, who make a permanent appointment four months after the death of Justin Edinburgh, during which time Ross Embleton was interim manager.

17 Manchester United manager Ole Gunnar Solskjaer is given a vote of confidence by executive vice-chairman Ed Woodward after the club's worst start to a season in 30 years. UEFA fine Manchester City £13,600 for supporters throwing objects during the Champions League match against Dinamo Zagreb. Liverpool are fined £8,600 for a pitch invasion after their game against Salzburg. Celtic are given a £10,400 fine for flares set off during the Europa League games against CFR Cluj. Former Bolton manager Phil Parkinson takes over at Sunderland.

18 Wally Downes, the suspended AFC Wimbledon manager, is banned for 28 days and fined £3,000 for breaching FA betting rules.

19 Jadon Sancho is fined £86,000 by Borussia Dortmund for reporting back for training late after international duty with England. An FA Cup fourth qualifying round tie is abandoned midway

through the second-half after Haringey Borough walk off complaining of racist abuse by Yeovil supporters.

20 AFC Wimbledon sack Wally Downes. Aaron Ramsdale signs a new, undisclosed long-term contract with Bournemouth.

21 Research funded by the FA and players' union shows that former footballers are more than three-and-a-half times more likely to die of dementia than members of the public in the same age range. Millwall appoint Gary Rowett, formerly in charge of Stoke, Derby and Birmingham, as their new manager.

22 Sol Campbell, who left Macclesfield after saving the club from going out of the Football League, is appointed Southend manager – hours before his new team lose 7-1 at home to Doncaster.

23 Raheem Sterling scores a hat-trick in 11 second-half minutes against Atalanta in the Champions League. Wycombe supporters vote to approve the takeover of the club by American lawyer Rob Couhig.

24 Glyn Hodges, assistant to Wally Downes, is appointed AFC Wimbledon's new manager. Newcastle goalkeeper Martin Dubravka signs a new six-year contract.

25 Leicester score a record-breaking 9-0 win over Southampton – the biggest away from home in top-flight football, equalling Manchester United's 9-0 Premier League victory over Ipswich in 1995 and inflicting Southampton's worst-ever defeat.

27 Arsenal captain Granit Xhaka reacts angrily to taunts from his own fans after being substituted against Crystal Palace at the Emirates.

28 Jim Bentley, appointed in May 2011 and the longest-serving manager in the top four divisions, resigns at bottom-of-the table Morecambe and takes over at National League club AFC Fylde.

29 The Bulgarian Football Union are ordered to play two internationals behind closed doors – one suspended for two years – and fined £65,000 for the racist abuse in Sofia. The punishment is criticised as being too soft by anti-racist groups. UEFA fine the English FA £4,300 for supporters disrupting the national anthem. Brentford and Millwall are both fined £14,000 by the FA for a players' confrontation. Yeovil win their replayed FA Cup tie with Haringey 3-0.

30 Derby sack captain Richard Keogh for his involvement in the car crash which led to court convictions for two teammates. Liverpool and Arsenal draw their League Cup fourth round tie 5-5, with Liverpool winning 5-4 on penalties.

31 Hearts manager Craig Levein is sacked after a single Scottish Premiership win. Levein, who also loses his role as director of football, stays at the club until the end of the season developing backroom and youth operations. Bristol City manager Lee Johnson is given a one-match touchline ban and £2,000 fine by the FA for abusive language after the defeat by Luton.

NOVEMBER 2019

1 Nathan Jones is sacked after nine months as Stoke manager with his side second from bottom.

2 MK Dons dismiss manager Paul Tisdale immediately after a 3-1 home defeat by Tranmere leaves them third from bottom.

3 Everton's Andre Gomes is ruled out for four months with a dislocated fracture of his right ankle after a challenge from Tottenham's Son Heung-min, who is sent off.

4 Former Scotland defender Russell Martin is appointed the new manager of MK Dons and gives up playing to concentrate in his new role. Granit Xhaka is stripped of the Arsenal captaincy following his fall out with supporters. Charlton are fined £12,500 and Bristol City £10,000 by the FA for a players' confrontation. Paul Heckingbottom is sacked after nine months as Hibernian manager with his side third from bottom of the Scottish Premiership and beaten 5-2 by Celtic in their League Cup semi-final.

5 The FA clear Son Heung-min from blame for the injury to Andre Gomes and uphold Tottenham's appeal against the South Korean's red card.

6 Liverpool face having to field two teams for matches in successive days after confirmation of their League Cup quarter-final against Aston Villa on December 17, 24 hours before a Club World Cup semi-final in Qatar – 4,000 miles away.

7 Manchester United and Celtic qualify for the knockout stage of the Europa League. Former

Plymouth manager Derek Adams takes over at Morecambe.

8 Michael O'Neill is appointed Stoke's new manager, while continuing to take charge of Northern Ireland's bid to qualify for Euro 2020. Burnley's Chris Wood signs a new contract through to 2023.

9 The FA Cup first-round tie between Accrington and Crewe lasts for more than three hours after referee Neil Hair and his replacement, fourth official Alan Clayton, are both injured and assistant referee Danny Gratton takes over. A record crowd of more than 77,000 at Wembley see England women lose 2-1 to Germany in a friendly international.

10 Liverpool open up a lead of nine points over Manchester City at the top of the Premier League after defeating the defending champions 3-1.

11 Raheem Sterling is dropped from England's Euro 2020 qualifier against Montenegro after scuffling with team-mate Joe Gomez at their St George's Park base – the day after the players' confrontation during Liverpool's match against Manchester City. Manager Neil Warnock leaves Cardiff by mutual consent with his side in the bottom half of the table.

12 Raheem Sterling apologises to Joe Gomez and his England team-mates for his behaviour. The FA fine Birmingham £7,500 and Cardiff £5,000 for a players' fracas.

13 Bernardo Silva is fined £50,000 and banned for one match by the FA for an offensive social media message sent to Manchester City team-mate Benjamin Mendy. Steven Pressley, manager of Carlisle for ten months, is sacked with his side 19th. Former Arsenal manager Arsene Wenger is appointed FIFA's chief of global football development.

14 In their 1,000th international, England confirm a place in Euro 2020 by beating Montenegro 7-0 with the youngest starting line-up for 60 years – 23 years and 255 days. Harry Kane scores a first-half hat-trick and Tammy Abraham nets his first goal for the senior team. Joe Gomez is booed after coming off the bench and manager Gareth Southgate criticises those responsible. Derrick Williams, Sean Maguire and Callum Robinson score for the first time for an experimental Republic of Ireland side, who defeat New Zealand 3-1 in a friendly. Carl Fletcher, manager of Leyton Orient for 29 days, is dismissed following an FA Cup defeat by Isthmian League side Maldon and Tiptree. The club say he did not fit into their coaching unit.

15 Former Millwall manager Neil Harris takes charge at Cardiff. Another League Two manager is sacked – Grimsby's Michael Jolley after a single point in five matches. BT Sport retain rights for coverage of Champions League and Europa League matches in a £1.2bn deal from 2021–24.

16 Northern Ireland captain Steven Davis has a bitter-sweet night against Holland. On his 116th international appearance, Davis overtakes David Beckham as the most-capped Home Nations midfield player, but fires a penalty over the bar in a goalless draw which ends their chances of automatic qualification for Euro 2020. Wales defeat Azerbaijan 2-0 to keep their hopes alive. Scotland also win away, 2-1 against Cyprus.

17 England complete a record-breaking run in their group. A 4-0 victory over Kosovo takes their tally to an unrivalled 37 goals, while Harry Kane becomes the first England player to score in every qualifying match. Harry Winks and Mason Mount also have a night to remember, scoring their first international goals.

18 The Republic of Ireland are held 1-1 by Denmark, Matt Doherty scoring his first international goal, and, like Scotland and Northern Ireland, have to rely on victory in the play-offs to reach the finals.

19 Mauricio Pochettino is sacked after five-and-a-half-years as Tottenham manager, with his side in the bottom half of the table after 12 games, 20 points behind leaders Liverpool and 11 off a top-four place. Wales reach the European Championship Finals for the second successive time by beating Hungary 2-0 with two goals from Aaron Ramsey. Scotland defeat Cyprus 2-1 in their final group match, John McGinn's brace taking his tally to six goals in three games. Michael Smith's first international goal puts Northern Ireland ahead in Frankfurt, but his side are then overwhelmed by Germany, whose 6-1 win includes a hat-trick by former Arsenal winger Serge Gnabry.

20 Hours after announcing Mauricio Pochettino's departure, Tottenham appoint Jose Mourinho as his successor on a four-year contract. Manchester City post a record season's revenue of £535m. Gerhard Struber, coach of the Austrian club Wolfsberger, is named Barnsley's new manager.

21 Bolton are given a five-point penalty, suspended for 18 months, for failing to fulfill fixtures against Brentford and Doncaster. Half of a £70,000 fine is also suspended.

22 Referees' chief Mike Riley admits at a meeting of Premier League clubs to four cases of VAR wrongly overturning correct decisions by on-field referees. Celtic are fined £13,000 by UEFA for supporters' chanting and banners in the home Europa League match against Lazio.

23 Joao Moutinho signs a new contract with Wolves through to 2022.

24 Carlisle appoint Rochdale's No 2, Chris Beech, as their new manager.

25 Brighton manager Graham Potter signs a contract extension until 2025 after six months in the job.

26 Tottenham retrieve a 2-0 deficit to defeat Olympiacos 4-2 and reach the Champions League knockout stage. Manchester City go through as group winners, despite being held 1-1 at home by Shakhtar Donetsk.

27 Manchester City's parent company acquire a majority stake in their eighth football club – India's Mumbai City.

28 Wolves qualify for the Europa League's knockout stage. Manchester United, already through, field their youngest-ever side in Europe – an average age of 22 years, 26 days. Alfredo Morelos breaks former Celtic striker Henrik Larsson's scoring record for a Scottish club in a European season with his 12th and 13th goals in a 2-2 draw with Feyenoord.

29 Arsenal sack manager Unai Emery after seven games without a win in all competitions. The Spaniard, in charge for 18 months following Arsene Wenger's departure, is replaced by coach Freddie Ljungberg on a temporary basis. David Pemsel resigns as the Premier League's new chief executive, before starting the job, over allegations of sending inappropriate text messages.

DECEMBER 2019

1 Quique Sanchez Flores is sacked after 85 days of his second spell as Watford manager, with a single victory in ten Premier League matches.

2 Lionel Messi is voted the world's best player for a record sixth time, with Virgil van Dijk the runner-up. Crawley dismiss Gabriele Cioffi after ten defeats in 14 matches in all competitions.

3 Pep Clotet is appointed Birmingham's permanent manager after six months as caretaker.

4 Richarlison signs a new five-year contract with Everton. John Yems, former manager of football operations at Bournemouth, takes over at Crawley.

5 Marco Silva, manager of Everton for 18 months, is sacked with his side third from bottom after a 5-2 defeat by Liverpool.

6 Former Leicester manager Nigel Pearson takes over at Watford until the end of the season, the club's seventh appointment in five years. Brendan Rodgers signs a new five-and-a-half-year contract with Leicester. Chelsea's transfer ban, imposed by FIFA, is halved on appeal to the Court of Arbitration for Sport, enabling the club to conduct transfer in the January 2020 window. A fine of £460,000 is also halved.

7 Daniel Stendel, formerly in charge of Barnsley, is appointed the new Hearts manager. Macclesfield's match against Crewe is postponed after their squad refuse to play because of non-payment of wages.

8 Celtic, playing with ten men for the final 30 minutes after the dismissal of Jeremie Frimpong, win the Scottish League Cup for the fourth successive season, beating Rangers 1-0 with a goal from Christopher Jullien.

9 Russia are banned by the World Anti-Doping Agency from competing in the 2022 World Cup in Qatar as part of a four-year suspension from major international competitions. Daryl Murphy, Bolton's former Republic of Ireland striker, admits to serving a six-week FA ban last season for taking cocaine on a night out while at Nottingham Forest.

10 Liverpool, 2-0 winners in Salzburg, and Chelsea, who beat Lille 2-1, qualify for the Champions League knockout stage.

11 Wigan manager Paul Cook serves a one-match touchline ban after receiving four yellow cards.

12 Arsenal and Rangers qualify for the knockout stage of the Europa League. Richard Masters, the Premier League's interim chief executive since Richard Scudamore's departure in November

2018, is given the job on a permanent basis. Chelsea's Fikayo Tomori signs a new five-year contract.

13 Liverpool manager Jurgen Klopp signs a new contract through to 2024. Midfielder James Milner pens a deal to 2022. Steven Gerrard, manager of Rangers, extends his contract to 2024.

14 John Dempster, manager of Mansfield for seven months, is sacked with his side 18th after a single win in eight matches.

15 China's state broadcaster scraps live coverage of Arsenal v Manchester City following social media comments by Mesut Ozil critical of the treatment of the country's Muslim Uigur community. Arsenal say it is the player's personal opinion. Graham Westley is appointed manager of Stevenage for the fourth time, with caretaker Mark Sampson reverting to first-team coach.

16 The Chinese foreign ministry claim Mesut Ozil has been 'blinded and misled' and invite him to visit the region. David Baldwin, Burnley's chief executive, is appointed CEO of the Football League. UEFA fine Celtic £13,375 for supporters setting off fireworks during the Europa League match against Lazio in Rome – the club's fourth punishment by Europe's governing body this season. Fulham are fined £5,000 by the FA for misconduct by players against Bristol City.

17 With the senior team in Qatar for the World Club Cup, Liverpool field their youngest-ever starting line-up for a League Cup quarter-final against Aston Villa – 19 years and 182 days. Under 23 coach Neil Critchley takes charge for the tie which Villa win 5-0. Graham Coughlan leaves Bristol Rovers, fourth in League One, to become manager of League Two Mansfield, citing his new club's ambitions and the chance to be closer to his Sheffield home. Angelo Alessio, manager of Kilmarnock for six months, is sacked after a single win in eight games.

18 A stoppage-time goal by Roberto Firmino gives Liverpool a 2-1 win over the Mexican side Monterrey and a place in the World Club Cup Final.

19 Macclesfield are deducted six points by the Football League for non-payment of wages and failing to fulfil a fixture against Crewe. A further four-point penalty is suspended.

20 Mikel Arteta, Pep Guardiola's assistant at Manchester City and a former captain at the Emirates, is appointed Arsenal's new manager. Carlo Ancelotti, three times a Champions League winner and a former Chelsea manager, takes over at Everton – the club's fifth permanent appointment in six years. Tottenham's Toby Alderweireld signs a new contract through to 2023.

21 Martin Peters, a member of England's World Cup-winning side of 1966 and a scorer in the 4-2 win over West Germany in the final, dies aged 76. Liverpool become world club champions by beating Flamengo, of Brazil, 1-0 with an extra-time goal from Roberto Firmino.

22 Referee Anthony Taylor halts the Tottenham-Chelsea game in the second-half after Chelsea defender Antonio Rudiger complains of racist abuse from the crowd.

23 Ben Garner, former West Bromwich Albion and Crystal Palace coach, is appointed the new manager of Bristol Rovers.

24 Alan Pardew, out of football since leaving West Bromwich Albion in April 2018, is appointed coach to the Dutch side Den Haag until the end of the season.

26 Liverpool move 13 points clear at the top of the Premier League with a 4-0 victory over Leicester.

27 Manchester City manager Pep Guardiola concedes the title, at the half-way point of the season, after a 3-2 defeat by Wolves.

28 West Ham's Manuel Pellegrini becomes the season's sixth Premier League manager to be sacked, immediately after a home defeat by Leicester leaves his side one place above the relegation zone.

29 David Moyes, who kept West Ham up during six months in charge during the 2017-18 season, returns to the club to replace Manuel Pellegrini.

30 Former Northern Ireland captain Aaron Hughes is made an MBE. Jill Scott, winner, of 146 England caps, receives the same award in the New Year Honours. Caretaker Alex Dyer is appointed Kilmarnock manager until the end of the season.

31 Chelsea post an annual loss of £96.6m. Ian Holloway, out of management since leaving

Queens Park Rangers in May 2018, takes over at Grimsby, fifth from bottom of League Two and without a win in 11 games. Joey Barton is given a one-match touchline ban by the FA after being sent to the stands during Fleetwood's match against Bristol Rovers.

JANUARY 2020

1 After a controversial five-year ownership, Roland Duchatelet sells Charlton for £1 to a consortium, headed by Syrian businessman Tahnoon Nimer who pledges investment in the club. Goalkeeper Tom Heaton and Brazil striker Wesley sustain knee ligament injuries in Aston Villa's win over Burnley and are ruled out for the rest of the season.

2 Liverpool complete a calendar year without losing a Premier League match. Wayne Rooney makes his first appearance as Derby's player-coach, captaining the side and having a hand in both their goals in a 2-1 win over Barnsley. Daryl McMahon resigns as manager of troubled Macclesfield after four-and-a-half-months in the job.

3 Arsenal's Calum Chambers is ruled out for nine months with a knee ligament injury sustained against Chelsea. All the weekend's FA Cup third round ties kick-off a minute later than normal as part of a campaign to promote mental health, backed by the Duke of Cambridge, president of the FA.

5 Sunderland owner Stewart Donald puts the club up for sale following pressure from supporters' groups.

6 Sadio Mane is named African Player of the Year, with his Liverpool team-mate Mohamed Salah runner-up. Celtic's Ryan Christie is given a three-match ban by the Scottish FA for grabbing Alfredo Morelos's testicles during the defeat by Rangers.

7 Tottenham close an investigation into alleged racist abuse from the crowd against Chelsea's Antonio Rudiger after the club and the Metropolitan Police find no evidence 'to corroborate or contradict' the claim. The FA give Oxford manager Karl Robinson a one-match touchline ban and £4,000 fine for verbally abusing referee Craig Hicks during the game against Shrewsbury.

8 The FA reject calls from Government to withdraw from a deal with gambling companies for streaming of FA Cup ties. Leyton Orient appoint Ross Embleton manager on a 12-month rolling contract after a second spell as caretaker.

9 A hamstring injury requiring surgery rules out Tottenham's Harry Kane until April – two months before the start of Euro 2020. Gambling firms waive their exclusive rights and allow the FA to stream FA Cup ties for free.

10 Manager Chris Wilder extends his contract with Sheffield United through to 2024.

11 Liverpool achieve a record start to the season for Europe's top five leagues with 61 points from 21 games.

12 Manchester City's Sergio Aguero overtakes Thierry Henry's total of 175 goals to become the Premier League's highest overseas scorer.

13 Oliver McBurnie, Sheffield United's record signing, is 'reminded of his responsibilities' by the FA after being photographed making a gesture towards Cardiff fans while supporting his former team Swansea.

14 Everton declare a record annual loss of £111.8m. Jordan Henderson and Lucy Bronze are named England supporters' Players of the Year for 2019.

15 Bobby Brown, Scotland's first full-time manager, dies aged 96. Five Liverpool players, Alisson, Trent Alexander-Arnold, Virgil van Dyke, Andrew Robertson and Sadio Mane, along with Manchester City's Kevin De Bruyne, are named in UEFA's Team of the Year, voted for by fans.

16 Chelsea's Reece James signs a new five-and-a-half-year contract. Former Republic of Ireland winger Mark Kennedy is appointed Macclesfield's new manager until the end of the season.

17 Premier League referees are told to make more use of pitchside monitors for red card decisions.

18 Mike Dean becomes the first referee to take charge of 500 Premier League matches when he officiates at Arsenal v Sheffield United.

19 Manchester United's Marcus Rashford joins Harry Kane as a fitness concern for club and country with a double stress fracture of his back, ruling him out for up to three months.

20 Manchester City manager Pep Guardiola calls for one of the cup competitions – by implication

the League Cup – to be scrapped to ease the pressure on top players. Brighton's Dan Burn signs a new contract through to 2023.

21 Liverpool manager Jurgen Klopp also urges fewer matches by having penalty shoot-outs, instead of replays, in the FA Cup.

22 Wycombe's Scott Kashket is banned for six months, with four months suspended, and fined £3,400 for breaking FA betting rules.

23 Watford, beaten FA Cup finalists last season, lose 2-1 to Tranmere in a third round replay.

24 Manchester United are fined £20,000 by the FA for players surrounding referee Craig Pawson in protest during the defeat by Liverpool.

25 Leyton Orient rename their West Stand after former manager Justin Edinburgh, who died in June 2019.

26 Jurgen Klopp promises to field a team entirely of youngsters in the replay after Liverpool are held 2-2 by Shrewsbury in the fourth round of the FA Cup.

27 Christian Eriksen, one of Tottenham's longest-serving players with 305 appearances for the club, gets his wish for a new challenge with a £16m move to Inter Milan.

28 A stoppage-time goal by Egypt striker Trezeguet against Leicester puts Aston Villa into the League Cup Final 3-2 on aggregate.

29 Manchester City win the second semi-final by the same scoreline, despite losing the return leg 1-0 to Manchester United. Tottenham secure two £27m signings, making midfielder Giovani Lo Celso's loan from Real Betis permanent and bringing in striker Steven Bergwijn from PSV Eindhoven. Two League Two managers are sacked. Cambridge's Colin Calderwood pays the price for back-to-back 4-0 home defeats and a single win in ten games. Paul Hurst, in charge at Scunthorpe for eight months, leaves after one win in eight matches.

30 Sheffield United pay a club-record fee of £22m for Genk's Norway midfield player Sander Berge. Manchester United sign Portugal midfielder Bruno Fernandes from Sporting Lisbon for £47m.

31 Premier League clubs spend £25m on a subdued winter transfer deadline day – the lowest total since 2010. West Ham pay the biggest single fee – £20m for Hull striker Jarrod Bowen. Total spending for the month is £230m.

FEBRUARY 2020

2 Sky Sports apologise to West Ham owners David Sullivan and David Gold for 'any factual inaccuracies' on their football discussion programme.

3 Glenn Murray, 36, signs a new one-year contract with Brighton after scoring their equaliser in a 3-3 draw against West Ham. Gary Bowyer, manager of Bradford for 11 months, is sacked after seven games without a victory leave his side outside the play-off positions.

4 With his senior players ordered to rest during the Premier League's winter break and Jurgen Klopp himself missing the tie, Liverpool field their youngest-ever side – average age 19 years and 102 days – for the club's FA Cup fourth round replay. Under 23 manager Neil Critchley takes charge of the 1-0 win over Shrewsbury, watched by an Anfield crowd of 52,000.

5 Stuart McCall is appointed Bradford's new manager – his third spell in charge at the club.

7 Brighton's Davy Propper signs a new contract through to 2023.

8 Tottenham's Dele Alli apologises for a social media post joking about COVID-19, admitting he let himself and his club down.

9 Manchester City face a fixture backlog after their Premier League game against West Ham is postponed because of extreme weather conditions caused by Storm Ciara.

10 World Cup winner Sir Geoff Hurst, Premier League record-scorer Alan Shearer and Westminster politicians back a campaign by the *Daily Mail* for Jimmy Greaves, all-time leading marksmen in English top-flight football, to be honoured.

11 Simon Grayson, manager of Blackpool for seven months, is sacked after a single win in 12 League One and FA Cup matches.

12 Chelsea agree a £37.8m fee with Ajax to sign Morocco winger Hakim Ziyech in the summer. Referee Bobby Madley, sacked as a Premier League referee in August 2018 for making a joke about a disabled person, is given permission to take charge of League One and League Two matches next season.

13 Rangers manager Steven Gerrard questions the 'mental strength' of his team as they fall ten points behind Celtic in the Scottish Premiership after going into the winter break two points adrift with a game in hand.

14 Manchester City are banned from European competition for the next two seasons for 'serious breaches' of UEFA's financial fair play regulations between 2012 and 2016. The club are also fined £25m for overstating sponsorship revenue in their accounts. City express 'disappointment but not surprise' and announce an appeal to the Court of Arbitration for Sport against a 'prejudicial' punishment.

15 Amid speculation that Manchester City may also be deducted Premier League points, manager Pep Guardiola is reported to be telling friends he is staying at the club.

16 Harry Gregg, hero of the 1958 Munich air disaster for rescuing Manchester United team-mates from the burning plane, dies aged 87.

17 Graham Westley parts company with Stevenage, two months into his fourth spell as manager, after a sixth successive defeat leaves the club seven points adrift at the bottom of League Two. Birmingham's Marc Roberts is fined £2,000 for breaching FA betting rules.

18 Tottenham's Champions League prospects take another blow when Harry Kane is joined on the injured list by Son Heung-min with a fractured arm.

19 Manager Pep Guardiola publicly predicts that Manchester City will win their appeal against UEFA's two-year European ban and says he will be staying at the club. The Scottish FA fine Rangers £15,000, with £5,000 suspended, for misconduct by players and staff in matches against Celtic and Hibernian.

20 Diogo Jota becomes the first Wolves player to score back-to-back hat-tricks in Europe, his treble against Espanyol in the Europa League following the one against Besiktas in December.

21 Wycombe are taken over by American businessman Rob Couhig. Barnsley are fined £20,000 by the FA for fans' sectarian abuse directed at Stoke's James McClean. Wigan manager Paul Cook is given a one-match touchline ban and £4,000 fine for abusive language towards referee Oliver Langford after the game against Middlesbrough.

22 Justin Fashanu, the first English professional to come out as gay while still playing, is posthumously inducted into the National Football Museum's Hall of Fame.

23 Ten venues are announced for the 2021 Women's European Championship in England, including Old Trafford where the host nation will open the tournament on July 7. Wembley hosts the final on August 1.

24 Liverpool equal Manchester City's all-time record of 18 successive top-flight wins by beating West Ham 3-2.

25 Former Arsenal striker Serge Gnabry, scorer of four goals in Bayern Munich's 7-2 win at Tottenham in a group match, nets twice in their 3-0 first leg victory over Chelsea at Stamford in the first knockout round. Fleetwood manager Joey Barton is given a two-match touchline ban and £2,000 fine by the FA for abusive language towards a match official during the game against Wycombe.

26 Manchester City lodge their official appeal to the Court of Arbitration for Sport against UEFA's European ban. Rangers complete a fine comeback to reach the last 16 of the Europa League, defeating Braga 1-0 in Portugal after retrieving a 2-0 deficit to win the first leg at Ibrox 3-2.

27 Arsenal, 2019 beaten finalists, are knocked out in the last 32 of the Europa League by Olympiacos, who score in the 119th minute at the Emirates to win on away goals. Celtic also go out, 4-2 to Copenhagen over the two legs. Manchester United beat Bruges 6-1 and Wolves overcome Espanyol 6-3.

28 Leeds goalkeeper Kiko Casilla is banned for eight matches and fined £60,000 by the FA for racially abusing Charlton's Jonathan Leko. Two days before Aston Villa's League Cup Final against Manchester City, the club post an annual loss of £68.9m.

29 Liverpool's unbeaten run of 44 unbeaten Premier League matches, stretching back to January 2019, ends with a 3-0 defeat at Watford.

MARCH 2020

1 Manchester City win the League Cup for the third successive season, and the fifth time in

seven years, beating Aston Villa 2-1 in the final.

2   The FA, Premier League and English Football League meet Government and health officials to discuss possible contingency measures for the COVID-19 outbreak. Former England striker Daniel Sturridge is banned for four months for breaching betting rules after the FA appeal against his original six-week ban by an independent commission, with four weeks suspended. Sturridge has his fined doubled to £150,000 and leaves the Turkish club Trabzonspor. Neil Critchley, manager of the Liverpool under-23 team, is appointed Blackpool's new manager.

3   England draw Belgium, Denmark and Iceland in their top group for the next UEFA Nations League. In League B, Wales and the Republic of Ireland are paired alongside Bulgaria and Finland. Scotland face Israel, Slovakia and the Czech Republic. Northern Ireland play Romania Norway and Austria. Everton's Mason Holgate signs a new five-year-contract.

4   Tottenham's Eric Dier climbs into the stand to confront an abusive spectator after an FA Cup fifth-round defeat on penalties by Norwich.

5   Everton manager Carlo Ancelotti is fined £8,000 by the FA for confronting referee Chris Kavanagh and receiving a red card after his side's disallowed stoppage-time goal against Manchester United. Crystal Palace manager Roy Hodgson signs a one-year contract extension. Newcastle's Matt Ritchie and Jonjo Shelvey sign new deals through to 2023.

6   The Premier League and English Football League ban pre-match handshakes until further notice because of COVID-19. Burton goalkeeper Kieran O'Hara is banned for six matches and fined £2,500 by the FA for biting Peterboough's Sammie Szmodics. Everton's Dominic Calvert-Lewin signs a new five-year-contract. England's women lose 2-0 to the USA in the SheBelieves Cup four-team tournament in Orlando.

7   Across Europe, the COVID-19 outbreak causes matches to be suspended. Birmingham are cleared of a charge of misconduct for failing to stick to an agreed business plan.

8   Ellen White comes off the bench to give England a 1-0 win over Japan in their second SheBelieves Cup match in New Jersey.

9   The English Football League express 'concern' over a boardroom dispute at Charlton involving majority shareholder Tahnoon Nimer and chairman Matt Southall. Cambridge appoint Mark Bonner manager after four wins out of seven as caretaker.

10 Tottenham, beaten finalists in 2019, lose 4-0 on aggregate to Leipzig in the Champions League's first knockout round.

11 Holders Liverpool are knocked out. They lead Atletico Madrid 2-1 on aggregate in extra-time at Anfield, then concede three goals to lose 4-2. Manchester City's rearranged Premier League match against Arsenal is postponed after Olympiacos owner Evengelos Marinakis, in contact with Arsenal players after the clubs' Europa League tie at the Emirates, contracts the virus. Bristol Rovers manager Ben Garner is fined £500 by the FA for questioning the integrity of referee Ben Toner after the match against Sunderland. England women lose their final match 1-0 to Spain in the SheBelieves Cup in Texas.

12 Arsenal announce that manager Mikel Arteta has tested positive for coronavirus. Manchester United, in Austria, and Wolves, in Greece, play Europa League round 16 matches behind closed doors. Sheffield United's Enda Stevens signs a new three-year-contract.

13 The Premier League and English Football League are shut down until April 3 at the earliest following talks between the two governing bodies and the FA. All Scottish football is suspended. So are the Champions League and Europa League. Chelsea announce that winger Callum Hudson-Odoi has tested positive for the virus.

14 Karren Brady, vice-chairman of relegation-threatened West Ham, says the season should be declared void. Half the scheduled National League games go ahead, along with most of those in the North and South Divisions.

15 With coronavirus now a pandemic, pressure builds on UEFA to postpone Euro 2020, which embraces matches across Europe including Wembley, Hampden Park and the Aviva Stadium. Italy become the first federation to call for the postponement.

16 The National League suspend fixtures until at least April 3. Chelsea remind Mason Mount of his 'responsibilities' after he is pictured having a kickabout, despite being told to self-isolate for 14 days.

17 UEFA announce the postponement of Euro 2020 and reschedule the tournament for the summer of 2021. Qualifying play-offs featuring Scotland, Northern Ireland and the Republic of Ireland are put on hold. The European Under-21 Championship, scheduled for 2021, is delayed for a year. So, too, is the women's European Championship in England. Macclesfield's six-point deduction is cut to four points on appeal.

18 The English Football League deliver a £50m short-term relief fund to help clubs with cash flow problems. It includes the early release of award payments and interest-free loan facilities. The EFL Trophy Final between Portsmouth and Salford, scheduled for April 5, is postponed. Hearts announce a 50 per cent pay cut for all players and staff. Gary Neville and former Manchester United team-mate Ryan Giggs open the two hotels they own in the city free of charge to NHS workers. Chelsea offer their hotel at Stamford Bridge to hospital staff.

19 The suspension of all English and Scottish matches is put back to April 30 at least.

20 In an emotional open letter to supporters, England manager Gareth Southgate urges them not to waste time worrying about the postponement of Euro 2020 but concentrate on supporting each other to come through the pandemic. England team doctor Rob Chakraverty leaves the FA following scrutiny of his previous role as chief medical officer of UK Athletics. Chairman Matt Southall is removed from the Charlton board over the dispute with majority shareholder Tahnoon Nimer.

21 *Match of the Day* returns on BBC with Gary Lineker, Alan Shearer and Ian Wright debating the best captains of the Premier League era. Scotland's Highland League clubs decide to finish the season early, with Brora, 13 points ahead at the top, declared champions

23 Trials of concussion substitutes are delayed following the postponement of the Tokyo Olympics.

24 Manchester City manager Pep Guardiola donates one million euros (£921,000) to fighting coronavirus in his native Spain. Three of Europe's top players, Lionel Messi, Cristiano Ronaldo and Robert Lewandowski, are reported to have pledged the same amount.

25 Watford offer their Vicarage Road stadium, next to the town's General Hospital, to the NHS for meetings and induction courses.

26 All football in England below the three divisions that make up the National League ends immediately with results expunged. The same applies to the women's game below the Super League and Championship.

27 The Premier League, English Football League and the players' union the PFA admit in a joint statement that 'difficult decisions' must be taken to counter the financial impact of coronavirus.

28 Republic of Ireland winger James McClean is fined two weeks' wages by Stoke for posting on social media a picture of himself wearing a black paramilitary-style balaclava in front of his children.

29 England captain Harry Kane says the Premier League season will have to be cancelled if it cannot be completed by the end of June. Manchester City make the Etihad Stadium available to the NHS during the pandemic.

30 Aston Villa captain Jack Grealish is fined and disciplined by the club after ignoring Government stay-at-home guidelines by attending a party and being pictured near the scene of a car accident.

31 The National League's top three divisions are suspended indefinitely as officials decide how best to end the season.

APRIL 2020

1 Bournemouth's Eddie Howe becomes the first Premier League manager to take a pay cut amid the COVID-19 crisis. UEFA suspend Champions League and Europa League matches until further notice and all international matches until at least the end of June.

2 Health Secretary Matt Hancock's call for Premier League players to take a pay cut is rejected by PFA chief executive Gordon Taylor. The Belgian League becomes the first major European casualty of the crisis, abandoned with Club Bruges declared champions.

3 A resumption of domestic matches is ruled out by governing bodies 'until it is safe to do so.' The Premier League ask players to take a 30 per cent wage cut, bring forward payment

of £125m to EFL and National League clubs to help with cash flow and donate £20m to the NHS. Mick McCarthy is replaced as Republic of Ireland manager by under-21 manager Stephen Kenny earlier than planned, following the postponement of Euro 2020 play-off matches and the tournament itself.

4 In an unprecedented video conference call, Premier League players insist on having greater control over any wage cuts, with the money to go to the NHS, support lower-league football and enable non-playing staff to be paid in full.

5 England team managers Gareth Southgate and Phil Neville take 30 per cent pay cuts as two of the FA's highest earners. Manchester City's Kyle Walker apologises for breaching Government lockdown instructions by holding a party at his house and is later fined by the club.

6 Liverpool reverse their decision to use the Government's furlough scheme to pay non-playing staff and apologise to supporters for coming to 'the wrong conclusion.'

7 Greg Clarke, chairman of the FA, warns that the COVID-19 crisis presents football with 'economic challenges beyond the wildest imagination.' FIFA approve plans for the extension of players' contracts and the summer transfer window.

8 Premier League captains, led by Liverpool's Jordan Henderson, launch a charitable fund to raise money for the NHS.

9 Tottenham manager Jose Mourinho admits he flouted Government lockdown measures by holding a training session with record-signing Tanguy Ndombele. Three other players, Serge Aurier, Davinson Sanchez and Ryan Sessegnon are filmed out running together.

10 Talks continue to stall over Premier League players taking pay cuts, with their union, the PFA, calling for financial breakdowns of all clubs.

11 Southampton become the first top-flight club to announce wage deferrals for players.

12 Scottish football is left in limbo after a crucial vote by one club – Dundee – on a proposal by the SPFL to end the season immediately for teams in the Championship and Leagues One and Two is not registered on time.

13 Tottenham are reported to be ready to sell Harry Kane. The club follow Liverpool by reversing their decision to furlough non-playing staff following criticism from supporters.

14 Bournemouth say they, too, listened to supporters for the club's U-turn on the furlough scheme.

15 The season ends for Scotland's three divisions below the Premiership after Dundee vote for the SPFL proposal. Dundee United (Championship), Raith Rovers (League One) and Cove Rangers (League Two) are declared champions. Partick are relegated from the second tier and Stranraer demoted from the third. The vote authorises the SPFL to determine the outcome of the Premiership season and form a task force to consider reconstructing the four divisions.

16 Rangers manager Steven Gerard calls the SPFL vote an 'absolute mess' and needs investigating.

17 Norman Hunter, winner of six major trophies with Leeds and a member of England's World Cup squads in 1966 and 1970, dies aged 76 after contracting coronavirus. The Premier League remain committed to completing the season.

18 The SPFL advance a £1.8m payment to lower league clubs following the decision to end their season.

19 The English Football League launch an investigation into January's takeover of Charlton. Accrington's Sam Finley is banned for eight matches and fined £850 by the FA for abusing Paul McShane in their game against Rochdale.

20 Arsenal become the first Premier League club to agree a wage cut with their players – most taking a 12.5 per cent reduction, along with manager Mikel Arteta. Brighton's Amex Stadium is converted into a coronavirus testing centre.

21 National League clubs vote to end the season, with promotion and relegation issues to be decided later. Tottenham remind squad players of their 'responsibilities' for a second time after Serge Aurier and Moussa Sissoko are pictured training together.

22 Michael O'Neill, appointed Northern Ireland manager in 2011, leaves the job to concentrate on managing Stoke. Leagues One and Two clubs ask the EFL for salary cuts next season.

23 Arsenal remind players of their 'responsibilities' after four are pictured ignoring social-

21

distancing measures – Alexandre Lacazette, David Luiz, Nicolas Pepe and Granit Xhaka. The FA announce that Phil Neville will step down as manager of the England women's team at the end of his contract in July 2021. UEFA decide that the European Championship, put back to 2021, will still be known as Euro 2020 because of large amounts of merchandise already produced. Leeds decide to name their South Stand after Norman Hunter.

24 Liverpool City Council announce an investigation into the impact of Liverpool's Champions League tie against Atletico Madrid at Anfield – attended by 3,000 Spanish fans – on the spread of COVID-19. Luton manager Graeme Jones and three of his coaching staff are sacked in cost-cutting measures by the club. Investment banker Gary Hoffman is appointed the Premier League's new chairman.

25 The Dutch Eredivisie season is abandoned with no champions declared. Coach Alan Pardew and his assistant Chris Powell leave Den Haag by mutual consent after their struggling team escape being relegated. FIFA release £120m to national associations hit financially by the pandemic, with 211 member countries receiving at least £400,000

26 Everton describe as 'appalling' Moise Kean's flouting of lockdown restrictions by partying at his flat and discipline the Italian striker.

27 Arsenal become the first Premier League club to reopen their training ground, with players working out in strictly controlled sessions.

28 Runaway leaders Paris Saint-Germain are declared champions after France's Ligue 1 season is abandoned.

29 FIFA's medical chief, Michel d'Hooghe, warns against restarting the season amid the pandemic and says clubs should be focusing on the next campaign.

30 Former Sheffield United, Stoke and Reading striker Dave Kitson launches a campaign to overhaul the Professional Footballers' Association and remove long-serving chief executive Gordon Taylor.

MAY 2020

1 Manchester City's Sergio Aguero becomes the highest-profile player to voice worries over a resumption of the season.

2 In the Premier League's latest conference call, clubs remain committed to completion, with matches earmarked at a number of neutral grounds.

3 Liverpool's Jordan Henderson is instrumental in another drive to raise money for the NHS – Premier League players signing shirts for a raffle.

4 Marcos Rojo, Manchester United defender on loan at Estudiantes, is filmed flouting lockdown rules in Argentina.

5 EFL chairman Rick Parry warns that clubs face losing £200m because of COVID-19 and some may go out of business.

6 FIFA agree to teams making five substitutions when matches resume.

7 Macclesfield have more points deducted, this time effectively losing five for an unfulfilled fixture against Plymouth and non-payment to players.

8 Manchester City accept Kyle Walker's explanation for another breach of distancing guidelines, citing compassionate grounds for the defender travelling to see family.

9 Opposition grows among some Premier League clubs to completing the season on neutral grounds.

10 The EFL consider how best to award promotion and relegation places if Leagues One and Two are abandoned.

11 Premier League clubs are told that relegation will be enforced, even if the season is not completed.

12 Scottish clubs reject calls, led by Rangers, for an independent investigation into the vote to end the lower-league season.

13 Harry Kane pledges sponsorship for shirts worn in the 2020-21 season by Leyton Orient, the club where he made his first professional start, with three good causes benefiting.

14 The Government gives the green light for a resumption of the season in England at a meeting with the FA, Premier League and EFL.

15 League Two clubs abandon the season because continuing behind closed doors is considered not financially viable. They agree to a points-per-game system to decide positions, with play-offs as normal. Swindon are declared champions.

16 Germany's Bundesliga becomes the first major European league to resume. UEFA express confidence that the season's Champions League and UEFA League will be completed.

17 A second, successful programme of Bundesliga matches boosts the Premier League's plans for 'Project Restart.'

18 Celtic, 13 points ahead of Rangers, are declared champions for a record-equalling ninth successive year as the Scottish Premiership season is terminated. Hearts are relegated.

19 Premier League clubs resume training in small groups. Burton manager Nigel Clough steps down to help ease the club's financial position and is replaced by club captain Jake Buxton.

20 Olivier Giroud and Willy Caballero sign 12-month contract extensions at Chelsea.

23 Premier League figures show that of 1,744 initial tests at clubs for COVID-19, eight were positive among players and staff.

24 Huddersfield owner Phil Hodgkinson warns that in the worst case scenario 50 or 60 clubs could go to the wall as a result of COVID-19. Championship players return to their first phase of training after two positives in 1,014 tests.

25 The Women's Super League and Championship seasons are abandoned, with final positions to be decided later.

26 Elliott Whitehouse is banned for six matches and fined £2,000 by the FA for abusing an opponent in Grimsby's match against Northampton.

27 Nathan Jones is appointed Luton manager for the second time, 16 months after leaving the club to take over at Stoke, where he was sacked in November 2019. The FA fine Women's Super League club Arsenal £50,000 for 'an act of discrimination' when dismissing an autistic coach in 2014.

28 The Premier League announce the season will restart on June 17, featuring matches between clubs with a fixture in hand – Manchester City v Arsenal and Aston Villa v Sheffield United. The final weekend is scheduled for July 25-26. All 92 remaining matches will be televised live. The announcement comes as players return to partial contact training.

29 Leicester manager Brendan Rodgers reveals that he became the second manager, after Arsenal's Mikel Arteta, to contract COVID-19.

31 The EFL announce that the Championship season, including play-off matches, will restart on June 20 behind closed doors.

JUNE 2020

1 Premier League clubs start returning to contact training. Southampton manager Ralph Hasenhuttl signs a new four-year contract.

2 Southend are given a suspended three-point deduction and fined £7,500 by the EFL for late payments to players and fielding an ineligible player against Lincoln.

3 Manchester City's Phil Foden is reminded of his responsibilities by the club after being pictured having a kickabout on a beach.

4 Businessman Au Yeung Wai Kay takes over Wigan from another Hong Kong-based organisation, the International Entertainment Corporation. Shane Long signs a two-year contract extension at Southampton.

5 Chelsea are declared champions of the abandoned Women's Super League, overtaking Manchester City on a points-per-game ratio.

7 Charlton's majority shareholder, Tahnoon Nimer, agrees to sell the club to a consortium headed by businessman Paul Elliott.

8 Manchester City's Raheem Sterling, appearing on the BBC *Newsnight* programme, calls for more black managers in English football. His club appoint Juanma Lillo, one of Pep Guardiola's Spanish mentors, as assistant manager to replace Mikel Arteta. Birmingham announce that their manager, Pep Clotet, will leave the club in July to explore further coaching opportunities.

9 League One clubs follow those in League Two in voting to curtail the season, with promotion, relegation and play-off positions decided on a points-per-game system. Champions Coventry and runners-up Rotherham go up automatically, with Tranmere, Southend and Bolton relegated.

10 Businessman James Anderson donates £3m to help Scottish clubs through COVID-19. Ben Foster, 37, agrees a new two-year contract with Watford. Stuart Kettlewell takes sole charge of Ross County after his co-manager, Steven Ferguson, becomes the Scottish Premiership club's chief executive.

11 Tottenham's Dele Alli is fined £50,000 and banned for one match for a 'poorly-judged' social media post about COVID-19. FA Cup sponsor Emirates donate title rights to this season's final to mental health campaign Heads Up. Matches resume in Spain's La Liga. Sheffield United captain Billy Sharp signs a two-year contract extension and vice-captain Oliver Norwood pens a three-year deal.

12 Premier League clubs face a £1bn reduction in revenue for the season, according to financial services company Deloitte. Birmingham avoid a potential points deduction after the EFL win their appeal against an independent disciplinary commission decision to clear the club of misconduct by breaching an agreed business plan. The EFL declare the matter closed.

13 Bolton decide not to offer manager Keith Hill a new contract when it expires at the end of June.

14 Odsonne Edouard, Celtic's leading marksmen, is named Footballer of the Year by the Scottish football writers.

15 Scottish clubs decide against a proposed restructuring of the league with an extended Premiership of 14 teams and three lower divisions of ten each. Championship clubs vote for a shortened 2020–21 season of 27 matches – nine fewer than normal – because of the effects of COVID-19. Caretaker Alex Dyer is given the Kilmarnock manager's job on a permanent basis.

16 Having helped raise £20m for a charity providing meals for vulnerable people, Manchester United's Marcus Rashford forces the Government to reverse a decision not to provide free school meals over the summer. Premier League clubs prepare to resume the season in a whole new setting – no spectators, no pre-match handshakes, artificial crowd noise, pitchside social distancing, five substitutions instead of three and drinks breaks. For the early fixtures, players will hold a minute's silence for victims of the pandemic, pay tribute to NHS staff and to the Black Lives Matter movement

17 One hundred days after the last top-flight match, Aston Villa and Sheffield United share a goalless draw, with United denied the chance of victory by the failure, for the first time, of goal-line technology after the ball clearly crosses Villa's line. Later, Manchester City defeat Arsenal 3-0. UEFA announce the return of international football in September and confirm the same 12 venues, including Wembley, Hampden Park and the Aviva Stadium, for the rearranged Euro 2020 next summer. Barrow are declared champions of the abandoned National League and return to the Football League after a 48-year absence.

18 Chelsea agree a £47.5m fee for Timo Werner, Leipzig's Germany striker. Bristol Rovers' Jordanian president, Wael Al-Qadi, takes full control of the club. Callum Davidson, former Scotland defender who finished his playing career at the club, is appointed St Johnstone's new manager.

19 Macclesfield retain their Football League place by a hair's breadth – despite a third points deduction of the season. They lose two more points for non-payment of wages, taking the total surrendered to 13, but finish with a points-per-game average of 0.62, compared to the 0.61 of Stevenage, who drop into the National League.

20 Matches resume in the EFL Championship and in Italy's Serie A.

21 Robbie Neilson leaves promoted Dundee United to begin a second spell as manager of relegated Hearts.

22 Burnley condemn, and apologise for, a plane trailing a banner with the message 'white lives matter' before the start of the club's match against Manchester City at the Etihad Stadium. Scottish League One and Two clubs follow the Championship and vote for a shortened 2020-21 season of 27 fixtures.

23 Middlesbrough manager Jonathan Woodgate is sacked with his team fourth from bottom after a

3-0 home defeat by Swansea. He is replaced immediately by Neil Warnock, who takes charge of his 15th league club.

24 Premier League clubs paid £263m to agents during 2019-20, according to figures from the FA – an increase of nearly £3m on the previous year. They show Liverpool (£30.3m), Manchester City (£29m) and Manchester United (£27.6m) the biggest spenders, with Burnley (£3.9m) the lowest. Scott McTominay signs a contract extension through to 2025 with Manchester United. Arsenal's David Luiz signs on for another year.

25 Liverpool are crowned champions for the first time since 1990, with a record seven games still to play, after Manchester City's defeat at Chelsea leaves the title holders 23 points behind. Andy Carroll signs a one-year contract extension with Newcastle.

26 Manager Jurgen Klopp sets Liverpool's sights on surpassing Manchester United's 20 League titles after their 19th success.

26 Ian Baraclough is named the new Northern Ireland manager, following England's Gareth Southgate and the Republic of Ireland's Stephen Kenny in being promoted from the under-21 team role.

27 Watford investigate reports that striker Andre Gray held a party at his home in breach of COVID-19 lockdown rules.

28 Andre Gray, Nathaniel Chalobah and Domingos Quina are left out of Watford's squad for the home game against Southampton.

29 Northampton beat Exeter 4-0 in the League Two play-off Final – Wembley's first competitive match played behind closed doors. Aleksdandar Mitrovic is banned for three matches by the FA after being caught on camera elbowing Ben White in Fulham's match against Leeds. Scottish Premiership clubs resume full contact training ahead of the new season.

30 Sol Campbell leaves relegated Southend by mutual agreement after eight months as manager.

JULY 2020

1 A month after a change of ownership, Wigan go into administration and incur a 12-point deduction. A Premier League statement stresses that support for the Black Lives Matter campaign is about eradicating racial prejudice and not an endorsement of a political movement. A fortnight after Barrow's promotion to the EFL, manager Ian Evatt leaves the club to take charge at Bolton.

2 Manchester City's Leroy Sane joins Bayern Munich for an initial fee of £44.7m. Bukayo Saka, 18-yearold Arsenal midfielder, is rewarded for an impressive first season in the Premier League with a new long-term contract.

3 Wigan's administrators launch an investigation into claims that the club's plight is linked to a bet in the Philippines on the club being relegated.

4 Lee Johnson, appointed in February 2016 and the longest serving manager in the Championship, is sacked by Bristol City after a run of two points from nine matches.

6 Manchester United's Nemanja Matic signs a new contract through to 2023. Micky Mellon leaves Tranmere to become manager of Dundee United, newly promoted to the Scottish Premiership.

7 Eric Dier is banned for four matches and fined £40,000 by the FA for confronting a spectator in the stand after Tottenham's FA Cup defeat by Norwich. Wigan appeal against their 12-point deduction.

8 Birmingham manager Pep Clotet leaves the club earlier than planned, following a 3-1 home defeat by Swansea.

9 Former Blackburn midfielder and Oldham manager David Dunn takes charge at Barrow.

10 Jack Charlton, centre-half in England's 1966 World Cup-winning team, dies aged 85.

11 Norwich are the first club to be relegated, down after a single season in the Premier League.

13 Manchester City's two-season European ban, imposed by UEFA, is quashed on appeal by the Court of Arbitration for Sport in Lausanne, Switzerland. The club's fine of £25m for not complying with UEFA's initial investigation, is reduced to £9m. Wycombe reach the game's second tier for the first time by beating Oxford 2-1 in the League One Play-off Final.

14 Pep Guardiola, Manchester City manager, rejects criticism of the court's decision by Liverpool's Jurgen Klopp and Tottenham's Jose Mourinho.

15 Colchester's John McGreal, appointed in May 2016 and the longest-serving manager in League Two, is sacked following the club's defeat by Exeter in the play-offs.

16 Manchester City chairman Khaldoon Al Mubarak is revealed to have had clear-the-air talks with the president of UEFA, Aleksander Ceferin. Gabriel Martinelli, Arsenal's Brazilian midfielder, is ruled out until the end of 2020 with a knee injury.

17 Leeds are promoted to the Premier League, ending the club's 16-year absence from the top-flight. The Government signals a partial return of spectators to Premier League matches in October. Former player and assistant manager Mike Jackson takes charge at Tanmere.

18 Mikel Arteta gets the better of his managerial mentor Pep Guardiola as Arsenal defeat Manchester City 2-0 to reach the FA Cup Final for a record 21st time.

19 Manchester United goalkeeper David de Gea is blamed for mistakes contributing to two of the goals in their 3-1 defeat by Chelsea in the second semi-final. Watford, with two games left to retain their Premier League status, sack manager Nigel Pearson following a reported disagreement with owner Gino Pozzo. Huddersfield manager Danny Cowley is also dismissed, two days after keeping the club in the Championship.

20 Birmingham's Jude Bellingham becomes the world's most expensive 17-year-old when signing for Borussia Dortmund for an initial £25m.

21 Merseyside police warn Liverpool fans not to congregate outside Anfield while the Premier League trophy is presented.

22 Captain Jordan Henderson receives the trophy from Sir Kenny Dalglish, who signed him from Sunderland during his second spell as manager.

23 Carlos Corberan, Marcelo Bielsa's assistant at title-winning Leeds, is named Huddersfield's new manager.

24 The Premier League and EFL announce September 12 as the start of the 2020–21 season.

25 Port Vale striker Tom Pope is banned for six matches and fined £3,500 by the FA for posting a message deemed to be anti-Semitic on social media.

26 On the final day of the Premier League season, Bournemouth and Watford are relegated alongside Norwich. Chelsea and Manchester United join Liverpool and Manchester City in next season's Champions League, with Leicester missing out. Jamie Vardy, scorer of 23 goals for Leicester, wins the Golden Boot award, with Ederson's 16 clean sheets for City earning him the Golden Glove.

28 The Court of Arbitration for Sport, in a 93-page report, names nine clubs who objected to Manchester City's European ban being lifted – Arsenal, Burnley, Chelsea, Leicester, Liverpool, Manchester United, Newcastle, Tottenham and Wolves.

29 Neal Warnock agrees to continue as Middlesbrough manager for the 2020–21 season. Steve Ball, former player and assistant manager, is given the Colchester job.

30 A Saudi Arabian-backed consortium pulls out of a £300m bid to buy Newcastle from Mike Ashley.

31 Sheffield Wednesday are deducted 12 points for the 2020–21 season for breaking spending rules. Former Nottingham Forest manager Aitor Karanka takes charge at Birmingham. Oldham manager Dino Maamria is sacked after a 19th place finish in the curtailed League Two season.

AUGUST 2020

1 Arsenal come from behind to beat Chelsea 2-1 in the FA Cup Final. Eddie Howe leaves Bournemouth by mutual consent after 25 years at the club as player and manager. Harry Kewell, former Leeds and Liverpool winger, becomes Oldham's sixth manager in under two years.

2 Celtic open their bid for a record tenth successive title with a hat-trick by Odsonne Edouard in a 5-1 win over Hamilton. Harrogate Town reach the Football League for the first time by beating Notts County 3-1 in the National League Play-off Final.

3 Wigan lose their appeal against a 12-point deduction and are relegated from the Championship.

4 Fulham make an immediate return to the Premier League with a 2-1 extra-time victory over Brentford in the Championship Play-off Final. Harrogate prepare to play opening home matches in League Two at Doncaster's Keepmoat Stadium after replacing their artificial pitch with a grass one.

5 Manchester United ease through to the quarter-finals of the Europa Lague by beating Austrian team LASK 7-1 on aggregate. Arsenal announce 55 staff redundancies because of the impact of COVID-19.

6 Wolves reach the Europa League's last eight with a hard-earned 2-1 victory over Olympiacos over the two legs. Rangers go out 4-1 to Bayer Leverkusen. Premier League clubs vote against continuing with five substitutes.

7 Manchester City reach the last eight of the Champions League with a 4-2 success against Real Madrid. EFL clubs vote through landmark salary caps of £2.5m per squad a year in League One and £1.5m in League Two. The proposed takeover of Charlton by a consortium headed by businessman Paul Elliott is rejected by the EFL. Neil Cox, Notts County's assistant manager, takes charge at Scunthorpe, where he started his playing career.

8 Eight Aberdeen players apologise for breaking lockdown rules by visiting a bar and causing the postponement of the club's match against St Johnstone. Jason Tindall, Eddie Howe's long-serving assistant, steps up to become Bournemouth's new manager.Chelsea go out of the Champions League, beaten 7-1 on aggregate by Bayern Munich.

9 Dean Holden steps up from assistant manager to take charge at Bristol City.

10 Bruno Fernandes converts Manchester United's 21st penalty of the season in all competitions for a 1-0 win over Copenhagen in Cologne in the quarter-finals of the Europa League at the start of a series of single-leg ties in German cities.

11 Raul Jimenez has a penalty saved as Wolves go out of the Europa League in Duisburg, beaten 1-0 by an 88th minute goal by Sevilla. Aberdeen are ordered to postpone two more fixtures, against Hamilton and Celtic. The defending champions are told to cancel another game, against St Mirren, after defender Boli Bolingoli flew to Spain and failed to quarantine. Celtic manager Neil Lennon accuses him of 'a total betrayal of trust.'

12 Mark Molesley, manager of National League South club Weymouth, takes over at Southend.

13 FA Cup replays are scrapped and prizemoney reduced to 2017-18 levels for the new season. League Cup semi-finals will be one leg, not two, and there will no Premier League winter break.

14 Holland women's manager Sarina Wiegman replaces Phil Neville in charge of the England team.

15 Manchester City bow out of the Champions League at the quarter-final stage for the third success season, beaten 3-1 by Lyon in the single leg tie. Watford, who had three different managers in their relegation season, give the job to former Serbian international and Maccabi Tel Aviv coach Vladimir Ivic on a one-year-contract.

16 Manchester United are beaten 2-1 by Sevilla in the semi-finals of the Europa League.

17 Southampton captain James Ward-Prowse signs a new five-year contract.

18 Arsenal's FA Cup match-winner Pierre-Emerick Aubameyang agrees a new contract.

20 Manchester United captain Harry Maguire is arrested after an alleged incident on the Greek holiday island of Mykonos. He denies an altercation with police.

21 Former Manchester United striker Romelu Lukaku puts Inter Milan ahead with a penalty in the Europa League Final, then concedes an own goal to give Sevilla a 3-2 win – the club's fourth in the competition in the last seven years.

23 Bayern Munich are crowned champions of Europe for the sixth team with a 1-0 win over Paris Saint-Germain in the Champions League Final in Lisbon, delivered by a 59th minute header from Kingsley Coman.

ENGLISH TABLES 2019–2020

PREMIER LEAGUE

		P	W	D	L	F	A	W	D	L	F	A	GD	Pts
			Home						**Away**					
1	Liverpool	38	18	1	0	52	16	14	2	3	33	17	52	99
2	Man City	38	15	2	2	57	13	11	1	7	45	22	67	81
3	Man Utd	38	10	7	2	40	17	8	5	6	26	19	30	66
4	Chelsea	38	11	3	5	30	16	9	3	7	39	38	15	66
5	Leicester	38	11	4	4	35	17	7	4	8	32	24	26	62
6	Tottenham	38	12	3	4	36	17	4	8	7	25	30	14	59
7	Wolves	38	8	5	4	27	19	7	7	5	24	21	11	59
8	Arsenal	38	10	6	3	36	24	4	8	7	20	24	8	56
9	Sheffield Utd	38	10	3	6	24	15	4	9	6	15	24	0	54
10	Burnley	38	8	4	7	24	23	7	5	7	19	27	-7	54
11	Southampton	38	6	3	10	21	35	9	4	6	30	25	-9	52
12	Everton	38	8	7	4	24	21	5	3	11	20	35	-12	49
13	Newcastle	38	6	8	5	20	21	5	3	11	18	37	-20	44
14	Crystal Palace	38	6	5	8	15	20	5	5	9	16	30	-19	43
15	Brighton	38	5	7	7	20	27	4	7	8	19	27	-15	41
16	West Ham	38	6	4	9	30	33	4	5	10	19	29	-13	39
17	Aston Villa	38	7	3	9	22	30	2	5	12	19	37	-26	35
18	Bournemouth	38	5	6	8	22	30	4	1	14	18	35	-25	34
19	Watford	38	6	6	7	22	27	2	4	13	14	37	-28	34
20	Norwich	38	4	3	12	19	37	1	3	15	7	38	-49	21

Liverpool, Manchester City, Manchester United, Chelsea all into Champions League group stage; Leicester, Arsenal into Europa League group stage, Tottenham into second qualifying round.

Prize money/TV revenue (league position = amount received)
1 £174m, 2 168m, 3 £166m, 4 £160m, 5 £147m, 6 £155m, 7 £141m, 8 £148m, 9 £132m, 10 £127m, 11 £123m, 12 £128m, 13 £126m, 14 £115m, 15 £113m, 16 £113m, 17 £106m, 18 £100.m, 19 £97m, 20 £94m

Biggest win: Southampton 0 Leicester 9
Highest aggregate score: Southampton 0 Leicester 9
Highest attendance: 73,737 Manchester Utd v Liverpool
Lowest attendance: 10,020 Bournemouth v Burnley
Player of Year: Kevin De Bruyne (Manchester City)
Manager of Year: Jurgen Klopp (Liverpool)
Golden Boot: 23 goals Jamie Vardy (Leicester
Golden Glove: 16 clean sheets Ederson (Manchester City)
Leading league scorers: 23 Vardy (Leicester), 22 Aubameyang (Arsenal), Ings (Southampton); 20 Sterling (Manchester City); 19 Salah (Liverpool); 18 Kane (Tottenham), Mane (Liverpool); 17 Martial (Manchester Utd), Rashford Manchester Utd); Raul Jimenez (Wolves); 16 Aguero (Manchester City); 15 Abraham (Chelsea); 14 Gabriel Jesus (Manchester City), Wood (Burnley); 13 Calvert-Lewin (Everton), De Bruyne (Manchester City); Richarlison (Everton),; 11 Mahrez (Manchester City), Pukki (Norwich), Son Heung-min (Tottenham)

SKY BET CHAMPIONSHIP

			Home					Away						
		P	W	D	L	F	A	W	D	L	F	A	GD	Pts
1	Leeds	46	15	5	3	40	14	13	4	6	37	21	42	93
2	WBA	46	10	10	3	44	27	12	7	4	33	18	32	83
3	Brentford	46	14	5	4	44	18	10	4	9	36	20	42	81
4	Fulham**	46	15	2	6	40	26	8	10	5	24	22	16	81
5	Cardiff	46	11	9	3	35	21	8	7	8	33	37	10	73
6	Swansea	46	10	5	8	27	23	8	11	4	35	30	9	70
7	Nottm Forest	46	10	5	8	27	27	8	11	4	31	23	8	70
8	Millwall	46	10	8	5	33	25	7	9	7	24	26	6	68
9	Preston	46	12	4	7	39	29	6	8	9	20	25	5	66
10	Derby	46	11	8	4	33	21	6	5	12	29	43	-2	64
11	Blackburn	46	10	9	4	33	24	7	3	13	33	39	3	63
12	Bristol City	46	8	7	8	30	33	9	5	9	30	32	-5	63
13	QPR	46	9	5	9	42	42	7	5	11	25	34	-9	58
14	Reading	46	7	4	12	26	34	8	7	8	33	24	1	56
15	Stoke	46	11	3	9	36	36	5	5	13	26	42	-6	56
16	Sheffield Wed	46	7	7	9	19	30	8	4	11	39	36	-8	56
17	Middlesbrough	46	6	8	9	20	29	7	6	10	28	32	-13	53
18	Huddersfield	46	6	8	9	26	30	5	6	12	26	40	-18	51
19	Luton	46	8	7	8	33	37	6	2	15	21	45	-28	51
20	Birmingham	46	6	7	10	33	42	6	7	10	21	33	-21	50
21	Barnsley	46	7	9	7	29	33	5	4	14	20	36	-20	49
22	Charlton	46	8	6	9	28	27	4	6	13	22	38	-15	48
23	Wigan*	46	10	7	6	33	23	5	7	11	24	33	1	47
24	Hull	46	7	3	13	29	37	5	6	12	28	50	-30	45

*Wigan deducted 12 pts due to administration ** also promoted
Biggest win: Wigan 8 Hull 0
Highest aggregate score: Birmingham 4 Leeds 5
Highest attendance: 36,514 Leeds v Huddersfield
Lowest attendance: 8,965 Wigan v Reading
Manager of Year: Marcelo Bielsa (Leeds)
Leading league scorers: 26 Mitrovic (Fulham); 25 Watkins (Brentford); 20 Grabban (Nottm Forest); 19 Grant (Huddersfield); 17 Benrahma (Brentford); 16 Armstrong (Blackburn), Bamford (Leeds), Bowen (Hull); 15 Ayew (Swansea); Jutkiewicz (Birmingham); Mbuemo (Brentford); 14 Collins (Luton), Eze (QPR), Woodrow (Barnsley); 13 Fletcher (Sheffield Wed), Hugill (QPR), Meite (Reading), Smith (Millwall). Also: 18 Wells (13 QPR, 5 Bristol City)

SKY BET LEAGUE ONE

			Home					Away							
		P	W	D	L	F	A	W	D	L	F	A	GD	Pts	PPG
1	Coventry	34	11	5	1	22	11	7	8	2	26	19	18	67	1.97
2	Rotherham	35	8	5	4	31	16	10	3	5	30	22	23	62	1.77
3	Wycombe**	34	13	3	2	34	20	4	5	7	11	20	5	59	1.73
4	Oxford Utd	34	11	3	3	33	13	6	6	5	28	24	24	60	1.71
5	Portsmouth	35	12	6	0	36	15	5	3	9	17	21	17	60	1.71
6	Fleetwood	35	10	7	1	25	13	6	5	6	26	25	13	60	1.71
7	Peterborough	35	12	3	2	41	13	5	5	8	27	27	28	59	1.68
8	Sunderland	36	10	8	1	35	13	6	3	8	13	19	16	59	1.63
9	Doncaster	34	10	5	4	30	19	5	4	6	21	14	18	54	1.58
10	Gillingham	35	9	3	5	27	17	3	12	3	15	17	8	51	1.45
11	Ipswich	36	6	5	6	23	18	8	5	6	23	18	10	52	1.44
12	Burton	35	6	8	3	19	14	6	4	8	31	36	0	48	1.37
13	Blackpool	35	9	2	6	27	23	2	10	6	17	20	1	45	1.28
14	Bristol Rov	35	7	6	5	23	19	5	3	9	15	30	-11	45	1.28
15	Shrewsbury	34	6	5	6	21	24	4	6	7	10	18	-11	41	1.20
16	Lincoln	35	10	3	4	28	18	2	3	13	16	28	-2	42	1.20
17	Accrington	35	7	2	8	33	27	3	8	7	14	26	-6	40	1.14
18	Rochdale	34	5	4	7	19	22	5	2	11	20	35	-18	36	1.05
19	MK Dons	35	9	1	8	20	21	1	6	10	16	26	-11	37	1.05
20	AFC Wimbledon	35	5	9	4	18	18	3	2	12	21	34	-13	35	1.00
21	Tranmere	34	3	6	8	19	26	5	2	10	17	34	-24	32	0.94
22	Southend	35	2	4	11	18	42	2	3	13	21	43	-46	19	0.54
23	Bolton*	34	4	8	5	17	23	1	3	13	10	43	-39	14	0.41

Season curtailed – COVID-19. Positions decided on points-per-game
Bury expelled; *Bolton deducted 12 pts; ** also promoted

Biggest win: Accrington 7 Bolton 1; Lincoln 0 Oxford 6; Peterborough 6 Rochdale 0; Southend 1 Doncaster 7
Highest aggregate score: Accrington 7 Bolton 1; Lincoln 5 Ipswich 3; Southend 1 Doncaster 7
Highest attendance: 33,821 Sunderland v Bolton
Lowest attendance: 1,816 Accrington v Peterborough
Manager of Year: Mark Robins (Coventry)

Leading league scorers: 24 Toney (Peterborough); 15 Gnanduillet (Blackpool), Henderson (Rochdale), Madden (Fleetwood); 14 Eisa (Peterborough), Godden (Coventry), Ladapo (Rotherham), Walker (Lincoln); 13 Clarke-Harris (Bristol Rov), Taylor (Oxford); 12 Henry (Oxford); 11 Curtis (Portsmouth), Forss (AFC Wimbledon), Gooch (Sunderland), Healey (MK Dons), Jackson (Ipswich), Norwood (Ipswich), Sadlier (Doncaster)

SKY BET LEAGUE TWO

		Home					Away							
		P	W	D	L	F	A	W	D	L	F	A	GD	Pts	PPG
1	Swindon	36	13	2	4	34	17	8	4	5	28	22	23	69	1.91
2	Crewe	37	13	3	3	38	17	7	6	5	29	26	24	69	1.86
3	Plymouth	37	12	5	2	38	16	8	3	7	23	23	22	68	1.83
4	Cheltenham	36	11	5	2	35	17	6	8	4	17	10	25	64	1.77
5	Exeter	37	10	7	1	31	15	8	4	7	22	28	10	65	1.75
6	Colchester	37	9	5	4	28	17	6	8	5	24	20	15	58	1.56
7	Northampton **	37	11	2	6	31	14	6	5	7	23	26	14	58	1.56
8	Port Vale	37	9	8	1	28	15	5	7	7	22	29	6	57	1.54
9	Bradford	37	11	5	2	29	14	3	7	9	15	26	4	54	1.45
10	Forest Green	36	5	4	8	16	22	8	6	5	27	18	3	49	1.36
11	Salford	37	5	6	8	20	24	8	5	5	29	22	3	50	1.35
12	Walsall	36	6	5	8	21	26	7	3	7	19	23	-9	47	1.30
13	Crawley	37	10	4	4	30	19	1	10	7	21	28	4	48	1.29
14	Newport	36	9	7	3	20	13	3	3	11	12	26	-7	46	1.27
15	Grimsby	37	6	5	7	22	27	6	6	7	23	24	-6	47	1.27
16	Cambridge	37	7	3	8	23	27	5	6	8	17	21	-8	45	1.21
17	Leyton Orient	36	5	8	6	26	30	5	4	8	21	25	-8	42	1.16
18	Carlisle	37	5	7	7	17	26	5	5	8	22	30	-17	42	1.13
19	Oldham	37	6	7	5	28	21	3	7	9	16	36	-13	41	1.10
20	Scunthorpe	37	6	6	7	24	25	4	4	10	20	31	-12	40	1.08
21	Mansfield	36	4	5	8	27	29	5	6	8	21	26	-7	38	1.05
22	Morecambe	37	4	8	6	20	23	3	3	13	15	37	-25	32	0.86
23	Stevenage	36	2	6	9	10	22	1	7	11	14	28	-26	22	0.61
24	Macclesfield *	37	5	9	4	19	17	2	6	11	13	30	-15	23	0.51

Season curtailed – COVID-19. Positions decided on points-per-game
*Macclesfield deducted 17pts; ** also promoted

Biggest win: Crewe 5 Morecambe 0; Mansfield 6 Oldham 1; Oldham 5 Newport 0
Highest aggregate score: Grimsby 5 Port Vale 2; Mansfield 6 Oldham 1; Mansfield 3 Forest Green 4
Highest attendance: 17,668 Bradford v Grimsby
Lowest attendance: 1,389 Macclesfield v Exeter
Manager of Year: David Artell (Crewe)
Leading league scorers: 25 Doyle (Swindon); 14 Maynard (Mansfield); 13 Bowman (Exeter), Yates (Swindon); 12 Lubala (Crawley), Palmer (Crawley), Porter (Crewe); 11 Robinson (Colchester), Rose (Mansfield), Vaughan (Bradford); 10 Sarcevic (Plymouth), Van Veen (Scunthorpe); 9 Gordon (Walsall), Hanson (Grmsby), Norris (Colchester), Powell (Crewe), Smith (Oldham)

PREMIER LEAGUE RESULTS 2019–2020

	Arsenal	Aston Villa	Bournemouth	Brighton	Burnley	Chelsea	Crystal Palace	Everton	Leicester	Liverpool	Man City	Man Utd	Newcastle	Norwich	Sheffield Utd	Southampton	Tottenham	Watford	West Ham	Wolves
Arsenal	–	3-2	1-0	1-2	2-1	1-2	2-2	3-2	1-1	2-1	0-3	2-0	4-0	4-0	1-1	2-2	2-2	3-2	1-0	1-1
Aston Villa	1-0	–	1-2	2-1	2-2	1-2	2-0	2-0	1-4	1-2	1-6	0-3	2-0	1-0	0-0	1-3	2-3	2-1	0-0	0-1
Bournemouth	1-1	2-1	–	3-1	0-1	2-2	0-1	3-1	4-1	0-3	1-3	1-0	1-4	0-0	1-1	0-2	0-0	0-3	2-2	1-2
Brighton	2-1	2-1	2-0	–	1-1	1-1	0-1	3-2	0-0	1-3	0-5	0-3	0-0	2-0	1-1	0-2	3-0	1-1	1-1	2-2
Burnley	0-0	1-2	3-0	1-1	–	2-4	0-2	1-0	2-1	0-3	1-4	0-2	1-0	2-0	1-1	3-0	1-1	1-0	3-0	1-1
Chelsea	2-2	2-1	0-1	2-0	3-0	–	2-0	4-0	1-1	1-2	2-1	0-2	1-0	1-0	2-2	0-2	2-1	3-0	0-1	2-0
Crystal Palace	1-1	1-0	1-0	1-1	0-1	2-3	–	0-0	0-2	1-2	0-2	1-1	0-1	1-0	0-1	0-2	1-1	1-0	2-1	1-1
Everton	0-0	1-1	1-3	1-0	0-1	1-3	3-1	–	2-1	0-0	1-3	1-1	2-2	2-0	0-2	0-2	1-1	1-0	2-0	3-2
Leicester	2-0	4-0	3-1	0-0	2-1	2-2	3-0	2-1	–	0-4	0-1	0-2	5-0	1-1	2-0	9-0	2-1	1-0	4-1	0-0
Liverpool	3-1	2-1	2-1	2-1	1-1	5-3	4-0	5-2	2-1	–	3-1	2-0	3-1	4-1	2-0	4-0	2-1	2-0	3-2	1-0
Man City	3-0	3-0	2-1	4-0	5-0	2-1	2-0	2-1	0-1	4-0	–	1-2	5-0	2-0	2-0	2-1	2-0	8-0	2-0	2-0
Man Utd	1-1	2-2	5-2	3-1	0-2	4-0	1-2	1-1	1-0	1-1	2-0	–	4-1	4-0	3-0	2-2	2-1	3-0	1-1	0-0
Newcastle	0-1	1-1	2-1	0-0	0-0	0-1	1-0	1-2	0-3	1-3	2-2	1-0	–	0-0	0-2	2-1	1-0	1-1	2-3	1-1
Norwich	2-2	1-5	1-0	1-1	1-2	2-3	1-1	2-0	1-1	0-1	3-2	1-3	1-1	–	1-2	0-1	2-2	1-2	1-1	1-2
Sheffield Utd	1-0	2-0	2-1	1-1	3-0	3-0	1-0	0-1	0-1	0-1	0-1	3-3	0-0	1-0	–	1-0	3-1	1-1	1-0	1-0
Southampton	1-0	1-1	1-3	1-1	1-2	1-4	1-1	1-2	0-9	1-2	1-0	1-1	0-1	2-1	1-1	–	1-0	1-1	1-3	1-2
Tottenham	2-1	3-1	3-2	2-1	5-0	0-2	4-0	1-0	3-0	0-1	2-0	1-1	2-1	2-1	1-1	2-1	–	2-1	2-0	2-3
Watford	2-2	3-0	0-0	0-3	0-3	1-2	0-0	2-3	1-1	3-0	0-4	2-0	2-1	2-1	1-1	3-1	0-0	–	1-3	2-1
West Ham	1-3	1-1	4-0	3-3	0-1	3-2	1-2	1-1	1-2	0-2	0-5	2-0	2-0	2-0	1-1	3-1	2-3	3-1	–	0-2

SKY BET CHAMPIONSHIP RESULTS 2019–2020

Home \ Away	Barnsley	Birmingham	Blackburn	Brentford	Bristol City	Cardiff	Charlton	Derby	Fulham	Huddersfield	Hull	Leeds	Luton	Middlesbrough	Millwall	Nottm Forest	Preston	QPR	Reading	Sheffield Wed	Stoke	Swansea	WBA	Wigan
Barnsley	–	0-1	1-1	1-2	1-0	0-2	2-2	2-2	1-0	2-1	3-1	0-2	1-3	1-0	0-0	1-0	0-3	5-3	1-1	1-1	2-4	1-1	1-1	0-0
Birmingham	2-0	–	1-1	0-1	1-3	1-1	0-1	3-2	1-1	2-1	3-3	4-5	1-2	1-0	1-1	1-1	0-1	0-2	1-3	3-3	2-1	1-3	1-1	2-3
Blackburn	3-2	1-0	–	1-0	2-2	0-0	0-2	0-2	0-2	0-1	1-1	2-1	1-2	1-0	2-0	0-1	2-1	2-1	4-3	2-1	0-0	2-1	2-3	3-0
Brentford	1-2	0-4	2-2	–	0-4	0-4	1-2	1-0	3-0	0-1	1-1	1-1	7-0	3-2	3-2	1-0	0-1	2-1	1-0	5-0	0-0	1-0	1-0	0-0
Bristol City	1-0	1-3	0-2	1-1	–	1-1	2-1	3-2	5-2	0-1	3-0	1-1	3-0	2-0	1-2	0-0	1-0	3-1	1-0	1-2	1-1	3-1	1-0	3-0
Cardiff	3-2	4-2	2-1	0-0	0-1	–	2-2	1-1	1-1	2-1	2-0	1-3	3-1	1-0	1-1	1-1	2-0	1-2	1-0	1-0	1-0	0-0	0-3	2-2
Charlton	2-1	0-1	0-2	1-2	2-1	2-2	–	3-0	1-1	3-2	2-2	1-0	3-1	0-1	1-1	1-0	0-1	2-1	1-2	1-3	0-0	1-2	2-2	2-2
Derby	2-1	3-2	0-2	1-3	3-0	3-0	0-0	–	3-2	3-0	0-3	1-3	2-0	2-0	0-1	1-1	0-0	1-0	2-1	1-1	3-1	0-0	2-2	1-0
Fulham	0-3	1-1	0-2	3-0	0-1	0-1	1-1	0-0	–	1-2	3-2	2-0	3-2	1-0	1-1	0-1	0-1	3-0	1-2	5-3	4-0	1-0	1-1	2-2
Huddersfield	0-1	2-1	2-0	0-3	0-1	0-3	3-2	1-1	4-1	–	0-3	2-1	0-1	0-1	0-1	1-1	2-1	1-0	0-5	1-0	0-0	1-0	1-1	2-2
Hull	0-1	3-0	2-1	1-1	1-1	2-0	2-2	0-3	3-1	3-0	–	0-4	2-0	2-0	0-1	0-3	0-0	0-3	3-0	1-4	2-5	0-1	2-1	2-2
Leeds	1-0	1-0	2-1	1-2	0-1	2-3	0-4	0-1	2-0	0-2	1-4	–	1-1	4-0	3-2	1-2	2-1	1-2	2-0	1-0	1-1	2-2	0-1	1-0
Luton	1-0	1-1	3-2	3-2	3-0	1-0	0-1	2-0	3-1	1-1	2-0	2-1	–	3-3	1-1	2-2	1-1	0-1	1-1	0-4	2-1	0-3	1-0	1-0
Middlesbrough	1-0	1-1	1-1	0-1	1-3	1-0	0-1	2-2	0-1	4-0	0-1	0-4	3-3	–	2-0	3-3	1-1	1-2	2-0	0-2	2-0	1-1	1-2	2-2
Millwall	1-2	0-0	0-1	1-0	1-1	2-2	4-0	1-2	1-1	3-2	0-1	3-2	0-1	1-1	–	0-2	1-1	0-0	0-1	0-3	3-1	2-2	0-2	2-2
Nottm Forest	5-1	3-2	2-0	1-0	2-2	0-1	1-1	2-2	2-2	2-2	2-2	0-1	2-2	2-2	2-2	–	2-2	0-4	1-2	1-3	4-2	1-3	1-2	0-1
Preston	0-1	2-2	3-2	1-1	0-1	2-0	4-0	1-2	1-0	4-0	1-1	1-1	0-1	1-1	1-1	1-1	–	2-0	0-2	0-3	1-1	1-4	1-0	0-2
QPR	2-0	2-3	4-2	6-1	0-1	6-1	2-0	1-3	1-2	2-0	1-0	0-2	2-1	0-2	4-3	1-3	1-3	–	1-3	3-2	1-0	2-2	0-2	2-2
Reading	2-0	2-1	1-3	0-1	2-2	3-0	1-0	3-0	2-0	2-2	2-1	0-3	3-0	0-2	1-2	1-1	1-0	1-3	–	1-3	1-2	2-0	1-3	1-0
Sheffield Wed	1-1	1-1	2-0	0-1	0-1	1-2	1-0	1-3	1-2	5-3	1-0	1-4	1-0	1-0	1-4	1-0	1-4	1-2	2-2	–	3-2	3-2	2-1	1-1
Stoke	4-0	1-2	1-2	3-1	0-0	2-5	4-0	1-0	1-0	2-5	5-0	0-3	0-1	1-1	2-1	2-3	1-0	1-2	0-0	3-2	–	1-2	0-0	2-1
Swansea	0-0	3-0	1-1	1-0	3-1	0-3	0-0	2-3	2-0	4-4	0-3	1-0	2-0	2-2	0-0	1-1	2-0	0-0	1-1	2-1	1-2	–	0-0	2-1
WBA	2-2	0-0	2-0	1-0	1-0	1-1	2-2	1-1	2-2	2-1	0-1	0-2	1-0	1-0	0-0	1-2	1-2	1-0	1-3	2-1	0-0	5-1	–	0-1
Wigan	0-0	1-0	2-3	0-0	3-0	2-2	1-0	2-2	1-0	2-2	2-2	2-0	1-0	2-2	1-0	2-1	0-3	2-1	1-0	2-1	3-0	1-1	1-1	–

SKY BET LEAGUE ONE RESULTS 2019–2020

	Acc	AFC	Bla	Bol	BRo	Bur	Cov	Don	Fle	Gil	Ips	Lin	MK	Oxf	Pet	Por	Roc	Rot	Shr	Sou	Sun	Tra	Wyc
Accrington	–	2-1	1-1	7-1	–	2-0	–	2-1	–	–	2-0	4-3	2-1	2-2	0-2	4-1	1-2	1-2	2-3	1-2	1-3	1-2	0-0
AFC Wimbledon	1-1	–	2-0	2-2	1-2	1-0	1-4	2-1	0-1	1-2	0-0	2-1	0-3	1-2	2-0	3-2	3-2	1-2	2-3	1-1	3-1	–	0-1
Blackpool	0-1	2-0	–	2-1	2-0	3-4	0-0	–	3-1	2-3	2-1	2-1	0-3	2-1	4-3	1-1	1-3	1-2	0-1	2-1	–	1-2	1-1
Bolton	0-0	0-0	0-2	–	1-1	–	1-2	0-2	1-0	1-1	0-5	5-1	1-0	0-0	0-0	0-1	3-1	6-1	3-2	4-2	2-0	–	0-2
Bristol Rov	3-3	1-2	1-0	0-2	–	–	0-2	2-1	1-0	0-0	0-1	2-2	1-0	3-1	1-1	2-2	3-1	0-1	1-1	1-1	2-0	4-2	0-0
Burton	1-1	0-0	3-2	2-2	2-0	–	1-2	2-1	2-2	1-1	1-1	0-2	1-0	2-2	1-1	2-2	3-1	0-1	0-0	1-1	1-2	4-2	–
Coventry	0-0	1-0	1-2	2-1	2-0	–	–	–	3-2	1-0	0-1	2-1	1-0	1-0	1-0	1-0	0-1	1-2	0-0	1-0	1-2	–	3-1
Doncaster	1-1	2-1	0-1	2-2	4-1	–	0-0	–	–	1-2	2-1	2-1	1-0	1-1	2-0	1-2	2-1	0-3	3-1	3-1	1-2	0-1	3-1
Fleetwood	2-0	0-1	2-2	5-0	0-0	1-2	0-2	3-2	–	1-2	0-1	2-1	1-0	1-1	1-2	1-0	2-1	2-2	2-0	3-1	1-0	–	1-1
Gillingham	–	1-2	2-2	–	1-2	4-1	2-1	–	1-1	–	0-0	1-1	3-1	1-1	1-2	1-1	1-0	0-3	3-0	3-1	1-0	2-0	2-0
Ipswich	4-1	2-1	2-2	5-1	3-0	3-2	0-1	1-7	3-3	0-0	–	1-0	1-0	0-6	1-4	0-2	3-0	0-1	5-3	4-0	0-1	1-3	0-0
Lincoln	2-0	2-1	1-0	1-0	3-0	1-0	0-0	0-1	0-1	1-0	1-0	–	3-1	1-1	1-2	1-1	1-1	1-3	0-0	2-1	1-1	3-0	–
Milton Keynes	–	5-0	2-1	1-0	3-0	2-4	3-3	3-0	0-1	0-1	3-0	2-0	–	1-0	0-4	0-1	3-0	1-3	3-0	4-0	0-1	1-3	2-0
Oxford	3-0	3-2	–	1-0	–	1-0	2-2	0-3	1-3	3-0	4-0	2-0	4-0	–	0-0	2-0	6-0	3-2	2-0	4-0	3-0	2-0	4-0
Peterborough	4-0	–	3-2	1-0	–	2-2	3-3	–	2-2	0-0	2-2	2-0	3-1	1-1	–	2-0	3-0	3-2	2-0	4-1	3-0	2-0	4-0
Portsmouth	2-1	–	0-0	1-0	2-2	1-0	1-2	2-3	2-2	2-2	1-0	1-1	2-0	1-1	0-3	–	3-0	3-1	0-0	–	1-2	–	0-3
Rochdale	–	1-2	0-0	2-0	1-2	3-0	1-2	1-0	1-0	2-2	1-0	0-2	1-1	1-2	0-3	0-3	–	3-1	2-0	2-1	0-2	1-1	0-3
Rotherham	1-0	3-1	2-0	3-4	3-1	0-2	0-2	1-7	0-3	1-1	1-3	2-1	2-2	0-4	1-0	2-1	3-0	–	1-2	2-2	2-2	–	0-1
Shrewsbury	0-2	3-1	3-0	0-0	3-4	3-2	0-2	1-0	0-3	2-2	0-2	1-1	1-1	1-2	1-0	1-0	2-2	1-2	–	0-0	1-0	1-1	0-0
Southend	–	1-4	1-3	2-3	3-1	0-2	0-2	1-7	3-3	0-1	1-3	2-1	2-2	0-4	1-0	0-3	0-3	2-2	1-2	–	0-1	0-0	4-3
Sunderland	–	3-1	1-1	0-0	3-0	1-2	1-1	0-0	1-2	2-2	1-0	3-1	2-1	1-1	2-1	1-1	3-0	1-1	1-0	1-0	–	5-0	4-0
Tranmere	1-1	–	2-1	5-0	3-1	2-0	1-4	0-3	–	2-1	1-2	3-1	3-2	2-2	2-2	0-2	2-3	1-0	0-1	4-3	0-0	–	3-1
Wycombe	1-1	–	2-1	2-0	3-1	–	1-4	1-0	0-1	0-1	1-1	3-1	3-2	3-3	1-0	1-0	2-1	1-0	0-0	4-3	1-0	3-1	–

SKY BET LEAGUE TWO RESULTS 2019–2020

The following grid gives results with home teams listed across the bottom axis and away teams listed down the right axis. A dash (—) indicates a fixture that was not played.

Home \ Away	Walsall	Swindon	Stevenage	Scunthorpe	Salford	Port Vale	Plymouth	Oldham	Northampton	Newport	Morecambe	Mansfield	Macclesfield	Leyton Orient	Grimsby	Forest Green	Exeter	Crewe	Crawley	Colchester	Cheltenham	Carlisle	Cambridge	Bradford
Bradford	2-1	3-1	—	2-2	1-1	1-2	2-1	3-0	2-1	1-0	0-1	2-3	2-2	2-3	1-1	—	2-0	—	2-1	—	1-1	—	0-0	—
Cambridge	—	0-0	—	3-2	—	—	2-0	1-2	0-2	2-0	1-0	0-2	2-1	—	—	0-1	4-0	—	2-1	2-1	0-1	1-2	—	3-1
Carlisle	2-1	1-1	2-0	4-1	0-4	—	1-0	1-0	2-1	2-0	2-2	1-0	3-0	2-1	0-0	0-1	1-3	2-4	2-1	0-3	0-1	—	0-0	0-0
Cheltenham	3-1	2-2	4-1	1-0	2-2	0-0	0-3	3-0	—	—	2-1	1-0	2-1	2-1	—	1-2	—	1-1	1-1	1-1	3-0	2-0	3-0	1-0
Colchester	—	3-1	—	3-1	—	—	0-1	—	4-0	3-1	0-1	—	2-1	—	2-3	—	2-2	—	2-2	—	1-2	0-0	1-2	0-0
Crawley	—	—	2-0	2-2	1-0	0-0	—	3-0	—	—	1-1	1-0	—	2-0	3-2	2-2	2-2	1-1	—	2-1	1-1	—	2-3	2-1
Crewe	—	0-4	3-1	—	—	0-1	3-0	2-1	—	1-0	5-0	1-1	2-0	2-2	—	0-2	0-1	—	1-2	—	1-1	2-0	—	2-1
Exeter	—	—	—	3-1	2-0	—	2-2	—	—	0-2	—	2-0	1-0	0-4	1-3	2-0	1-1	1-2	—	0-0	1-0	4-1	2-0	2-1
Forest Green	1-0	3-1	1-0	1-1	4-1	—	0-3	5-1	3-2	4-2	0-2	1-1	1-0	—	1-0	—	0-1	—	2-2	1-0	0-0	1-4	2-0	—
Grimsby	3-3	3-1	—	—	—	—	—	1-0	0-3	2-1	1-0	2-2	1-1	1-3	—	2-3	—	—	—	1-0	—	—	2-0	1-1
Leyton Orient	1-2	1-1	1-0	—	1-2	2-3	1-0	—	1-1	—	4-1	0-1	—	—	1-1	2-4	2-0	—	2-0	1-0	0-0	1-1	2-1	1-1
Macclesfield	—	—	0-0	0-2	—	5-2	—	2-2	2-2	2-1	3-1	0-0	—	2-0	0-1	2-1	2-3	1-2	2-2	1-1	1-1	2-2	1-0	—
Mansfield	3-1	2-2	3-1	0-1	0-2	3-3	4-0	1-1	—	—	5-0	—	1-0	2-2	0-2	2-1	0-1	1-2	1-2	0-1	1-1	2-2	1-1	1-2
Morecambe	—	—	—	2-0	1-2	2-2	2-2	6-1	—	2-1	—	2-2	0-1	3-0	2-0	3-4	2-3	1-1	1-1	—	0-0	1-1	1-1	1-2
Newport	—	—	3-1	2-1	2-0	2-1	1-0	1-2	2-2	—	3-0	2-2	1-0	4-0	2-2	—	2-3	1-1	—	2-1	1-1	—	2-0	2-1
Northampton	0-1	0-3	—	2-1	—	2-1	—	0-1	—	1-1	3-0	2-2	0-1	1-1	3-0	0-2	1-1	4-1	—	0-0	0-2	1-0	0-1	2-1
Oldham	0-0	1-3	0-2	1-1	1-4	1-0	—	—	2-2	1-2	—	1-3	2-2	0-3	5-0	—	—	—	—	—	1-0	—	1-0	3-0
Plymouth	0-1	—	3-0	0-2	1-0	1-0	—	—	1-1	2-3	3-0	3-1	0-0	0-3	3-1	2-1	1-1	—	—	1-0	1-0	0-1	2-0	2-1
Port Vale	2-0	—	0-1	1-2	2-0	—	1-1	2-3	1-2	1-3	1-0	3-1	3-0	1-1	1-1	2-1	—	3-1	—	0-3	—	3-2	1-1	2-0
Salford	3-0	2-2	1-1	3-0	—	1-2	1-2	0-0	3-0	2-1	1-0	2-2	2-0	1-0	2-0	—	2-3	—	—	0-0	—	—	—	1-1
Scunthorpe	0-1	0-0	1-1	—	2-1	1-0	1-3	0-0	0-1	0-2	0-2	1-0	1-0	1-1	2-2	1-1	2-2	2-2	2-2	2-2	1-2	2-3	1-1	1-1
Stevenage	2-0	2-3	1-1	1-1	2-2	3-0	1-1	1-1	0-1	0-1	0-0	2-2	0-1	2-2	3-2	2-0	—	—	—	—	—	3-2	4-0	1-1
Swindon	2-1	—	2-0	2-1	—	2-2	—	2-0	3-2	0-1	0-2	1-0	0-0	3-1	—	—	2-3	1-2	1-0	—	0-2	3-2	—	2-1
Walsall	—	0-0	0-0	2-0	2-0	0-2	1-1	2-0	0-1	1-2	0-2	1-0	1-0	1-1	—	—	—	—	2-1	0-1	—	—	—	0-1

HIGHLIGHTS OF THE PREMIER LEAGUE SEASON 2019–20

AUGUST 2019

9 Liverpool kick off the new season with a 4-1 win over promoted Norwich, all their goals coming in the first-half.

10 Raheem Sterling scores a hat-trick, amid a flurry of decisions by VAR, as Manchester City open their defence of the title by crushing West Ham 5-0 at the London Stadium. The newly-introduced system rules out a goal from Gabriel Jesus by the narrowest margin and delivers a retaken penalty for encroachment which Sergio Aguero converts after his first effort is saved by Lukasz Fabianski. John McGinn marks his new five-year contract by putting Aston Villa ahead at Tottenham, who respond with a debut goal from new-signing Tanguy Ndombele, followed by two from Harry Kane in the final four minutes. The third promoted side, Sheffield United, earn a point at Bournemouth, with Billy Sharp's 88th minute goal cancelling out Chris Mepham's first for the home side. Graham Potter gets off to a flying start as Brighton manager with two productive substitutions at Watford – Florin Andone scoring with his first touch and record-buy Neal Maupay rounding off a 3-0 success. Burnley match that scoreline against Southampton, Ashley Barnes netting twice. Everton's Morgan Schneiderlin is sent off for a second yellow card in a goalless draw at Crystal Palace.

11 Two goals from Marcus Rashford, his first a penalty, and one on his debut by Daniel James point Manchester United to a 4-0 victory over Frank Lampard's Chelsea. Pierre-Emerick Aubameyang's strike is enough for Arsenal to take the points at St James' Park and spoil Steve Bruce's first game in charge of Newcastle. Leander Dendoncker falls victim to the new handball law, having his effort disallowed by VAR's ruling against team-mate Willy Boly, and Wolves having to be satisfied with a goalless draw at Leicester.

17 Another hat-trick and more VAR controversy make the headlines for the second successive Saturday. Teemu Pukki's treble fires Norwich to a 3-1 victory over Newcastle. Gabriel Jesus is denied a stoppage-time 3-2 winner for Manchester City against Tottenham for handball by Aymeric Laporte. Stand-in goalkeeper Adrian, whose penalty save in midweek won the European Super Cup for Liverpool against Chelsea, is left red-faced after gifting Danny Ings a goal by passing the ball straight to the Southampton striker. But his side hold on for a 2-1 win. Bournemouth prevail by the same scoreline at Villa Park, where Liverpool loanee Harry Wilson is on the mark 12 minutes into his debut. Another summer arrival, Douglas Luiz, scores for the home side, while Leandro Trossard's first for Brighton in a 1-1 draw against West Ham comes after he has one ruled out by VAR for offside. Arsenal defeat Burnley 2-1 for the club's first six-point haul from the opening two fixtures since season 2009-10.

18 Bramall Lane welcomes back Premier League football after a dozen years and celebrates as Sheffield United's John Lundstram scores the only goal of the game against Crystal Palace. Mason Mount nets his first for Chelsea in a 1-1 draw with Leicester.

19 Paul Pogba pulls rank on Marcus Rashford, then takes some stick after having his penalty saved by Rui Patricio in Manchester United's 1-1 draw at Wolves.

23 Record-signing Wesley sets Aston Villa on the way to a 2-0 success against Everton with his first goal for the club.

24 Another record buy, West Ham's Sebastien Haller, opens his account with a brace in their 3-1 success at Watford. So does Tammy Abraham for Chelsea with two in the 3-2 win at Norwich, Frank Lampard's first in charge. Summer-signings Moussa Djenepo and Oliver McBurnie have mixed fortune after their first goals. Two minutes after coming off the bench, the Mali winger puts Southampton on course for a 2-0 victory at Brighton, who have Florin Andone shown a straight red card for a high tackle on Yan Valery. McBurnie's header for Sheffield United is not enough to prevent a 2-1 defeat by Leicester. Crystal Palace deliver the day's best all-round performance with the club's first league victory over Manchester United since 1991 – 2-1 courtesy of Patrick van Aanholt's 93rd minute strike at Old Trafford. Two for

Mohamed Salah, one a penalty in the 3-1 defeat of Arsenal, maintain Liverpool's 100 per cent start – the only one after three matches.

25 Steve Bruce secures his first three points as Newcastle manager – 1-0 at Tottenham thanks to a first goal from another record-signing, Joelinton. Manchester City's 3-1 win at Bournemouth features two by Sergio Aguero.

31 Sheffield United take pride of place for their recovery against Chelsea at Stamford Bridge after falling behind to two Tammy Abraham goals. Callum Robinson pulls one back, then forces Kurt Zouma to concede an own goal in the 89th minute. Jamie Vardy's brace includes a 30-yard volley as Leicester defeat Bournemouth 3-1 in one of three matches producing VAR controversy, with team-mate Youri Tielemans escaping action for a late tackle on Callum Wilson. Henri Lansbury's equaliser for ten-man Aston Villa seconds from the end at Crystal Palace is ruled out by a booking for Jack Grealish for diving in the build-up. And Fabian Schar's equaliser for Newcastle against Watford is later shown to have involved an incident of handball. Villa's Egyptian midfielder Trezeguet is sent off for a second yellow card. So, too, is Kevin Danso in Southampton's 1-1 draw against Manchester United at St Mary's, where Jannik Vestergaard heads his first goal for the club. Manchester City ease past Brighton 4-0 with Sergio Aguero on the mark twice, while Roberto Firmino becomes the first Brazilian to score 50 Premier League goals as Liverpool win 3-0 at Burnley.

SEPTEMBER 2019

1 Arsenal retrieve a 2-0 deficit to earn a point against Tottenham. Richarlison scores twice in Everton's 3-2 victory over Wolves, who have Willy Boly sent off in stoppage-time for a second yellow card.

14 Injury-hit Norwich end Manchester City's 18-match unbeaten Premier League run. Rodri scores his first goal for the defending champions; but they are punished for defensive mistakes as Kenny McLean, Todd Cantwell and Teemu Pukki give Daniel Farke's side a notable 3-2 victory. Liverpool trail to on-loan Jetro Willems's first goal for Newcastle, but open up an early five-point lead at the top by beating Newcastle 3-1, Sadio Mane netting twice. Tammy Abraham, 21, becomes the youngest Chelsea player to score a Premier League hat-trick – and the first in the competition to also concede an own goal in the same match. Fellow academy products Fikayo Tomori, with his first for the club, and Mason Mount are also on the mark in a 5-2 win away to Wolves, who have Patrick Cutrone on the scoresheet for the first time. Two by Son Heung-min put Tottenham on the way to a 4-0 success against Crystal Palace, while Burnley's Jeff Hendrick marks his 100th Premier League appearance with a stoppage-time equaliser at Brighton. Billy Sharp is shown a straight red card for lunging at Stuart Armstrong in Sheffield United's 1-0 home defeat by Southampton.

15 Watford, with Quique Sanchez Flores beginning a second spell as manager after the dismissal of Javi Gracia, retrieve a two-goal half-time deficit, established by Pierre-Emerick Aubameyang, for a 2-2 draw against Arsenal. Callum Wilson also gets two as Bournemouth see off Everton 3-1.

16 West Ham's Arthur Masuaku is sent off for a second yellow card in the goalless draw at Villa Park.

20 Bournemouth climb to third ahead of the weekend games by winning for the first time at Southampton – 3-1.

21 Manchester City score five times in the opening 18 minutes on the way to an 8-0 drubbing of Watford – the club's biggest win in top-flight football. David Silva delivers the fastest goal of the season after 52 seconds and Bernardo Silva goes on to complete the first hat-trick of his career. Watford beaten 6-0 by City in the FA Cup Final, suffer their worst-ever league defeat. Lys Mousset opens his account for Sheffield United in a 2-0 success away to Everton, a scoreline matched by Burnley against Norwich, courtesy of a brace from Chris Wood.

22 A spectacular free-kick by Trent Alexander-Arnold puts Liverpool on the way to a hard-earned 2-1 victory at Chelsea. West Ham's 2-0 defeat of Manchester United enables Manuel Pellegrini to become the first to beat four United managers in the Premier League – David Moyes, Louis van Gaal, Jose Mourinho and now Ole Gunnar Solskjaer. Record-signing Nicolas Pepe opens his account from the penalty spot for Arsenal, who overcome the dismissal of Ainsley Maitland-Niles to defeat Aston Villa 3-2. Romain Saiss is also shown two yellow cards, but Wolves earn a point at Crystal Palace with a 95th minute equaliser from Diogo Jota.

28 Two glaring goalkeeping errors have contrasting consequences. Sheffield United's Dean Henderson allows a shot from Georginio Wijnaldum to slip through his grasp, enabling Liverpool to prevail at Bramall Lane and maintain a five-point lead at the top. Tottenham's Hugo Lloris is also left red-faced when dispossessed inside his own six-yard area by Danny Ings, who puts Southampton on level terms. But his team overcome that setback, and a second yellow card for Serge Aurier, to win 2-1 with a goal from Harry Kane. Two goalkeepers make their Premier League debuts for Norwich at Selhurst Park, where Ralf Fahrmann, deputising for the injured Tim Krul, is forced off after 22 minutes and replaced by Michael McGovern. Crystal Palace win 2-0, Luka Milivojevic marking his 100th appearance for the club by converting a penalty. Raheem Sterling's 100th club goal rounds off Manchester City's 3-1 victory at Everton, while Wolves register their first three points of the season by beating Watford 2-0.

29 Jamie Vardy scores twice as Leicester record their biggest Premier League win – 5-0 against Newcastle, who have Isaac Hayden shown a straight red card for a reckless challenge on Dennis Praet.

OCTOBER 2019

5 Aston Villa deliver a Royal Command Performance at Carrow Road. The Duke of Cambridge takes his family to watch his favourite team against Norwich and cheers on a 5-1 victory, launched by two goals from the Brazilian striker Wesley, who also has a penalty saved by Michael McGovern. Josip Drmic's consolation is his first for Norwich. Aaron Connolly, 19, scores twice on his full Premier League debut for Brighton against Tottenham, whose 3-0 defeat follows a 7-2 Champions League drubbing by Bayern Munich. A dislocated elbow sustained by captain Hugo Lloris completes a miserable week for Mauricio Pochettino and his team. Sadio Mane celebrates his 100th league appearance for Liverpool by opening the scoring against Leicester and winning the penalty which James Milner converts in the 95th minute for a 2-1 victory. Jordan Ayew also strikes late as Crystal Palace climb to fourth ahead of Sunday's matches, his 87th minute goal securing a 2-1 success at West Ham. Everton's Seamus Coleman is sent off for two yellow cards in a 1-0 loss at Burnley.

6 Manchester City, badly missing injured central defenders Aymeric Laporte and John Stones, lose to 2-0 at home to two Adama Traore goals in the final 15 minutes for buoyant Wolves and fall eight points behind leaders Liverpool. The red half of the city also has problems as United's worst start for 30 years continues with a 1-0 defeat at Newcastle. Steve Bruce, for his 400th Premier League game as a manager, gives a debut to Matty Longstaff, alongside older brother Sean in midfield, and the 19-year-old caps an impressive performance with the only goal. David Luiz heads his first for Arsenal, who beat Bournemouth by the same scoreline, while Chelsea's youngsters continue to make an impact, Tammy Abraham taking his top-flight tally to eight so far and Mason Mount registering his fourth in a 4-1 victory at Southampton.

19 England manager Gareth Southgate sees Aston Villa captain Jack Grealish enhance his claim for international recognition with an impressive performance against Brighton. Grealish opens the scoring and sets up a stoppage-time winner for Matt Targett, his first goal for the club. Adam Webster also nets his first for Brighton, who have Aaron Mooy sent off for a second yellow card. Amid VAR confusion, another late strike earns Tottenham a 1-1 draw against Watford, with Dele Alli's 86th minute effort shown on the scoreboard as 'No goal' despite having been awarded. Controversy, too, at Leicester, where Burnley protest at having a second goal ruled out in a 2-1 defeat after Jonny Evans bundles the ball into his own net under pressure from Chris Wood. Everton, pointless in the previous four games, move out of the bottom three with a 2-0 victory over West Ham, rounded off by substitute Gylfi Sigurdsson's classy finish, while Manchester City win by the same scoreline away to Crystal Palace to cut Liverpool's lead at the top.

20 VAR also impacts on the end to Liverpool's run of Premier League wins, one short of Manchester City's record of 18, at Old Trafford. They protest that Marcus Rashford's goal for Manchester United should have been disallowed for a foul on Divock Origi and need substitute Adam Lallana's first in the league in 29 appearances, after 85 minutes, to avoid defeat.

21 Lys Mousset, the third of Sheffield United's four summer club-record signings, scores the only goal of the game for a notable victory over Arsenal.

25 Leicester mark the first anniversary of the death of chairman Vichai Srivaddhanaprabha in a helicopter crash with a record-breaking performance against Southampton at St Mary's. A 9-0 win is the biggest away from home in top-flight football, equals Manchester United's 9-0 Premier League victory over Ipswich in 1995 and inflicts Southampton's worst-ever defeat after they have Ryan Bertrand shown a straight red card after 12 minute for his challenge on Ayoze Perez. Jamie Vardy and Perez both score hat-tricks, with Ben Chilwell, Youri Tielemans and James Maddison also on the mark.

26 Christian Pulisic opens his account for Chelsea with the 'perfect' hat-trick – left-foot, right-foot, header- in a 4-2 success at Burnley, becoming the second American to score three goals in the Premier League after Fulham's Clint Dempsey in 2012. Brighton come from behind to defeat Everton 3-2 thanks to VAR's first penalty award, converted by Neal Maupay, and Lucas Digne's stoppage-time own goal. Lys Mousset is on the mark again for Sheffield United to earn a 1-1 draw at West Ham. Manchester City have Fernandinho shown a second yellow card against Aston Villa, but by then are closing out a 3-0 victory.

27 Manchester United become the first club to score 2,000 Premier League goals on an eventful afternoon at Carrow Road. They defeat Norwich 3-1, despite Marcus Rashford and Anthony Martial having VAR-awarded penalties kept out by Tim Krul, who also produces one of the saves of the season from Martial's point-blank header. Arsenal fans turn on their substituted captain Granit Xhaka as Crystal Palace recover for a point after conceding two goals inside the first 10 minutes. Liverpool, too, come from behind, seeing off Tottenham 2-1 after conceding a goal to Harry Kane after 47 seconds. They end the month six points ahead of Manchester City and eight clear of Leicester and Chelsea . Newcastle's Sean Longstaff receives a straight red card for his challenge on Ruben Neves in a 1-1 draw with Wolves.

NOVEMBER 2019

2 Sadio Mane comes to Liverpool's rescue with their unbeaten record under threat at Villa Park. He crosses for Andrew Robertson to head an 87th minute equaliser, then makes it 2-1 with a header of his own four minutes into added-time. Manchester City also come from behind to defeat stubborn Southampton by the same scoreline, Kyle Walker scoring the winner in the 86th minute. Sheffield United climb to sixth as two John Lundstram goals set up a 3-0 victory over Burnley. Federico Fernandez nets his first for Newcastle who win 3-2 at West Ham, scoring more than one goal in a match for the first time this season. Goalkeepers Kepa Arrizabalaga and Ben Foster embrace at the end of the game at Vicarage Road after Chelsea's record-signing saves a stoppage-time header from his Watford counterpart to protect a 2-1 advantage.

3 The weekend programme is overshadowed by a horrific injury sustained by Everton's Andre Gomes during the 1-1 draw with Tottenham. The Portugal midfielder is ruled out for four months with a dislocated fracture of his right ankle caused by the freak combination of Son Heung-min's challenge, Gomes planting his foot in the turf and the impact from Serge Aurier. Son, in tears, is shown a red card by Martin Atkinson which is later rescinded. In the other game, Leicester win 2-0 away to Crystal Palace, with Caglar Soyuncu scoring his first goal for the club.

8 Gerard Deulofeu scores after 76 seconds and sets up a second goal for Andre Gray as Watford net their first three points of the season with a 2-0 win at fellow-strugglers Norwich, despite the dismissal of Christian Kabasele for a second yellow card.

9 Leicester climb to second after Jamie Vardy takes his tally to eight in six games in a 2-0 victory over Arsenal. They are bracketed on 26 points with Chelsea, who overcome Crystal

Palace by the same scoreline with their youngest-ever Premier League starting line up – an average age of 24 years and 88 days. Newcastle continue to rely on defenders for goals, with seven of their last nine having come from that department after DeAndre Yedlin and Ciaran Clark secure a 2-1 scoreline against Bournemouth. Chris Wood celebrates a new contract by scoring Burnley's second goal in a 3-0 success against faltering West Ham. Wood has another chalked off by VAR, which also rules out David McGoldrick's effort for Sheffield United, who nevertheless maintain an unbeaten away record in a 1-1 draw at Tottenham – Mauricio Pochettino's last match before his sacking.

10 Liverpool overcome Manchester City 3-1 to go nine points clear of the defending champions in another match riddled with VAR controversy. City are denied a sixth minute penalty – and a possible decisive advantage – when the ball strikes Trent Alexander-Arnold's arm and 22 seconds later Fabinho puts Liverpool ahead from 25 yards. Wolves win the West Midlands derby 2-1 against Aston Villa, who are forced to field third-choice goalkeeper Orjan Nyland after injuries to Tom Heaton and Jed Steer.

23 Jose Mourinho gets off to a flying start on his return to the Premier League. Tottenham score three goals in 49 minutes before having to settle for a 3-2 victory at West Ham, whose manager Manuel Pellegrini comes under pressure after a single point in six games. Three other managers feel the heat. Unai Emery's Arsenal need a 96th equaliser from Alexandre Lacazette, his second goal of the game, after James Ward-Prowse scores from the rebound, after his penalty is saved bv Bernd Leno, to put Southampton in sight of all three points at the Emirates. Emery is sacked six days later. Marco Silva's Everton are beaten 2-0 at home by Norwich, who end a run of one point in seven matches. And Quique Sanchez Flores, two months into his second spell at Watford, sees his side replace Norwich at the foot of the table when conceding three second-half goals to Burnley for a 3-0 home defeat. In sharp contrast, Brendan Rodgers is riding high after Leicester's 2-0 victory at Brighton, confirmed by Jamie Vardy's twice-taken penalty. His first attempt, saved by Mat Ryan, then headed in on the rebound by James Maddison, is ruled out for by VAR for encroachment. His second is confidently put away. At the top, Roberto Firmino's 85th minute strike gives Liverpool a 2-1 win at Crystal Palace, while Manchester City come from behind to defeat Chelsea by the same scoreline. Bournemouth captain Simon Francis, making his first start since Boxing Day after a knee injury, is sent off for a second yellow card in the 2-1 home defeat by Wolves.

24 Brandon Williams, 19, scores his first goal for the club and Mason Grreeenwood, 18, nets his first in the Premier League goals as Manchester United retrieve a two-goal deficit to lead 3-2 at Bramall Lane. But Sheffield United have the final say – Oliver McBurnie's 90th minute equaliser.

30 Liverpool extend their lead over Manchester City to 11 points, courtesy of two headed goals from Virgil van Dijk. But they are left clinging on after Alisson is sent off for handling outside the penalty box and Brighton reduce the arrears through Lewis Dunk. City drop more points in a 2-2 draw at Newcastle, who level the match for a second time with Jonjo Shelvey's 22-yard drive in the 88th minute. Another late goal and more VAR controversy seal the fate of Quique Sanchez Flores, who is sacked after Watford's 2-1 defeat at Southampton. James Ward-Prowse settles it in the 83rd minute, five minutes after his side's equaliser from Danny Ings stands amid a questionable handball in the build-up. The pressure eases somewhat on Manuel Pellegrini, thanks to full-back Aaron Cresswell finishing like a striker to secure West Ham's 1-0 victory at Chelsea. Third-choice goalkeeper David Martin, son of club legend Alvin Martin, also plays a key role on his Premier League debut at the age of 33, then breaks down his tears in his father's arms at the final whistle. A revitalised Dele Alli is on the mark twice as Tottenham make it ten Premier League and Champions League goals in Jose Mourinho's first three games with a 3-2 victory over Bournemouth, for whom Harry Wilson replies twice.

DECEMBER 2019

1 Leicester remain in second place, eight points behind Liverpool, as Kelechi Iheanacho makes a match-winning first Premier League appearance of the season against Everton. The substitute sets up Jamie Vardy's equaliser, then scores himself in the third minute of stoppage-time. Arsenal, with Freddie Ljungberg in temporary change, scramble a 2-2 draw at Norwich, thanks to two from Pierre-Emerick Aubameyang, his first a retaken penalty after Tim Krul's save proves in vain because of encroachment. Lys Mousset is on the mark after 63 seconds for Sheffield United, who maintain their unbeaten away record by holding Wolves to 1-1.

3 A brace by Gabriel Jesus puts Manchester City on the way to a 4-1 success at Burnley. Crystal Palace overcome the loss of Mamadou Sakho, shown a straight red card for a high challenge on Adam Smith after 19 minutes, to defeat Bournemouth 1-0.

4 Liverpool have Alisson suspended, Fabinho injured and rest Mohamed Salah and Roberto Firmino. But they still crush Everton 5-2 in a club-record 32nd unbeaten league match which is followed by the dismissal of Everton manager Marco Silva. Divock Origi delivers two of the goals. Jamie Vardy scores for a seventh straight league game to set Leicester on the way to a 2-0 victory over Watford, converting a penalty after being denied one earlier and receiving a yellow card for diving. Jose Mourinho tastes defeat with Tottenham for the first time on his return to Old Trafford, where two Marcus Rashford goals, one a penalty, give Manchester United the verdict 2-1. John Terry's return to Stamford Bridge, as part of Aston Villa's coaching team, also ends in defeat by the same scoreline against Chelsea.

5 Arsenal's problems mount in a ninth game in all competitions without a win, the club's worst run since 1977. Brighton prevail 2-1 at the Emirates, Neal Maupay netting the winner in the 80th minute.

7 Manchester City's title defence looks to be over after a 2-1 home defeat by Manchester United, who score twice in seven minutes through Marcus Rashford's penalty and Anthony Martial. The match is overshadowed by racial abuse directed at United players and objects thrown from the crowd. Liverpool, with Jurgen Klopp continuing to rotate his players impressively, are 3-0 winners at Bournemouth, whose injury problems mount when Nathan Ake and Callum Wilson limp off. Son Heung-min delivers a strong contender for goal of the season when running with the ball for 80 yards from the edge of his own penalty to score Tottenham's third in a 5-0 victory over Burnley. Harry Kane nets twice with thumping drives, while Dominic Calvert-Lewin, wearing interim manager Duncan Ferguson's jersey No 9 jersey, also gets two as Everton answer Ferguson's rallying call to overcome Chelsea 3-1.

8 Two more goals for Jamie Vardy and a club-record eighth successive win in top-flight football for Leicester – 4-1 away to Aston Villa, who face a £25,000 fine for six bookings. Diogo Jota also gets two as Wolves extend their unbeaten Premier League run to 11 matches in a 2-2 draw at Brighton. Sheffield United's Chris Basham becomes the first player to have a red card rescinded by VAR, with referee Simon Hooper's punishment for the defender's challenge on Kenny McLean downgraded to a yellow during United's 2-1 win at Norwich.

9 Arsenal end their lean spell with three second-half goals in nine minutes for a 3-1 success at West Ham.

14 Leicester's winning run is ended in a 1-1 draw against Norwich. So is Jamie Vardy's eight-match scoring streak after his header is ruled to be going wide until Tim Krul palms it into his own net. Bournemouth, with nine players injured, end their five-match losing sequence, courtesy of Dan Gosling 84th minute strike on his first start of the season at Chelsea. West Ham's Sebastien Haller also scores the only goal, at Southampton, to ease the pressure on Manuel Pellegrini. Two by Mohamed Salah earn Liverpool a 2-0 win over Watford, who miss several chances to embarrass the leaders. Two from Sheffield United's John Fleck account for Aston Villa by the same scoreline after Villa captain Jack Grealish hits the bar with a penalty.

15 Kevin De Bruyne delivers one of the season's finest individual performances in the first 45 minutes at the Emirates. The Belgian scores twice with sweetly-struck shots, is denied a hat-trick by goalkeeper Bernd Leno and sets up a goal for Raheem Sterling in the 3-0 victory over Arsenal. Tottenham also win away – 2-1 against Wolves with Jan Vertonghen's stoppage-time header.

21 No-one celebrates a goal more joyfully than Newcastle's Paraguayan midfielder Miguel Almiron, who scores his first for the club on his 27th appearance for a 1-0 victory over

Crystal Palace. Record-signing Oliver McBurnie also gets the only goal as Sheffield United prevail at Brighton to stretch their unbeaten away record to nine games – the best start for a promoted team since Burnley's ten in season 1947-48. Danny Ings continues as Southampton's best hope of survival, a brace in the 3-1 win at Villa Park taking his tally to ten goals in 12 games. Villa lose John McGinn for up to three months with a fractured ankle. With Liverpool involved in the World Club Cup, Manchester City make up some ground, coming from behind to end Leicester's nine-match unbeaten run 3-1. At Goodison Park, there is the rare sight of two incoming managers, Carlo Ancelotti and Mikel Arteta, sizing up their new teams from the directors' box as Everton and Arsenal share a goalless draw.

22 Frank Lampard outsmarts his one-time mentor Jose Mourinho as two goals by Willian, the second a penalty, give Chelsea a 2-0 away win over Tottenham, who have Son Heung-min shown a straight red card for raising his boot at Antonio Rudiger. The performance is overshadowed when Rudiger complains of racist abuse from the crowd and referee Anthony Taylor halts the game. Watford provide Nigel Pearson with his first three points – and end a club-record run of 12 Premier League home matches without a win – by overcoming Manchester United 2-0.

26 Liverpool look every inch champions-elect when overwhelming Leicester 4-0 at the King Power Stadium. Roberto Firmino, their match-winner against Flamengo in the Club World Cup, scores twice, James Milner converts a penalty and the outstanding Trent Alexander-Arnold rounds off the victory, having had a hand in the three other goals. Southampton make light of the absence of the prolific Danny Ings, rested ahead of the weekend match against Crystal Palace, to produce their best performance of the season for a 2-0 success away at Chelsea. Palace come from behind to defeat West Ham 2-1 with Cheikhou Kouyate's first goal for the club followed by a brilliant solo effort from Jordan Ayew in the 90th minute. Anthony Martial is on the mark twice as Manchester United see off Newcastle 4-1, while new managers Carlo Ancelotti, and Mikel Arteta both make satisfactory starts. Dominic Calvert-Lewin heads the only goal of the game for Ancelotti's Everton against Burnley. Arsenal, under their former captain Arteta, draw 1-1 at Bournemouth.

27 Pep Guardiola concedes the title with Manchester City 14 points behind after a dramatic fifth defeat of the season at Molineux. Despite having goalkeeper Ederson sent off in the 12th minute for bringing down Diogo Jota, they lead with two goals from Raheem Sterling, the first from the rebound after Rui Patricio again saves a twice-taken penalty, the second kick awarded for encroachment. Adama Traore and Raul Jimenez level for Wolves, who then score a third from Matt Doherty after 89 minutes.

28 Manuel Pellegrini is sacked as West Ham manager immediately after a 2-1 home defeat by Leicester leaves his side a single point above the relegation zone. Leicester take the points despite making nine changes and wasting a penalty when Lukasz Fabianski saves from Demarai Gray. Iran striker Alireza Jahanbakhsh and on-loan Australia midfielder Aaron Mooy score their first goals for Brighton, who defeat Bournemouth 2-0 and have another from Dan Burn chalked off for offside. VAR rules out two more by millimetres – Teemu Pukki's as Norwich draw 2-2 with Tottenham and Max Meyer's in Crystal Palace's 1-1 result at Southampton. A brace by captain Troy Deeney, including a penalty, helps Watford overcome the dismissal of Adrian Mariappa for two yellow cards by defeating Aston Villa 3-0. Dominic Calvert-Lewin is also on the mark twice for Everton, who win 2-1 at Newcastle.

29 Another day of controversy. Sheffield United surrender their unbeaten away record 2-0 against Manchester City after Lys Mousset has a goal ruled out by VAR for offside, then John Fleck is impeded by referee Chris Kavanagh, enabling Kevin De Bruyne to send Sergio Aguero through for 1-0. At Anfield, Wolves feel aggrieved after Sadio Mane's match-winner for Liverpool is allowed to stand after initially being disallowed, while Pedro Neto is denied an equaliser by offside. Mikel Arteta is seven minute plus stoppage-time away from victory in his first Arsenal home match until influential substitute Jorginho and Tammy Abraham turn things around for a 2-1 win by Chelsea. Liverpool lord it on 55 points, ahead of Leicester (42), Manchester City (41) and Chelsea (35).

JANUARY 2020

1 David Moyes makes the perfect start to his second spell as West Ham manager. Mark Noble leads by example with two goals, one a penalty, in a 4-0 victory over Bournemouth and his side also escape a red card for Aaron Cresswell's challenge on Ryan Fraser, with VAR instructing Graham Scott to change his red card to yellow. Watford's Christian Kabasele is not so fortunate after denying Wolves substitute Diogo Jota a goalscoring chance, having his yellow card from Andrew Madley upgraded to red. But they hold on for a 2-1 win, making it ten points from four games under Nigel Pearson, and there is also New Year cheer for Mikel Arteta as Arsenal overcome Manchester United 2-0 for his first success as manager. Aston Villa have mixed fortunes, a 2-1 success at Burnley clouded by injuries to goalkeeper Tom Heaton and striker Wesley, who are ruled out for the rest of the season. For Newcastle, it's all gloom, losing Jetro Willems, Javier Manquillo, Jonjo Shelvey and Fabian Schar, finishing with ten men after using all their substitutes and going down 3-0 at home to Leicester, for whom Hamza Choudhury scores his first goal for the club. Harry Kane limps off during Tottenham's 1-0 defeat at Southampton, adding to concern expressed by some managers at the demands placed on players by a four-match Christmas and New Year programme.

2 Liverpool complete a calendar year without losing a Premier League match by beating Sheffield United 2-0.

11 Revenge is a dish best served cold and Southampton achieve exactly that in the biting wind and rain of the King Power Stadium. They trail to Dennis Praet's first goal for Leicester, then make a mockery of that record 9-0 defeat at St Mary's with a 2-1 victory to climb towards mid-table after taking 13 points from five matches. Danny Ings and Stuart Armstrong are their scorers. Roberto Firmino's strike at Tottenham takes Liverpool to 61 points from 21 fixtures – a record start to the season for Europe's top five leagues. Marcus Rashford marks his 200th game for Manchester United with two goals, one from the penalty spot, in the 4-0 defeat of Norwich. In sharp contrast, Arsenal's leading marksman Pierre-Emerick Aubameyang is sent off after scoring against Crystal Palace. Paul Tierney delivers a yellow card for the captain's lunge on Max Meyer, but is instructed by VAR to upgrade it to a straight red. The game ends 1-1.

12 Sergio Aguero reaches two Premier League milestones in Manchester City's 6-1 victory at Villa Park, overtaking Thierry Henry (175) as the highest overseas scorer and replacing Alan Shearer at the top of the table of hat-tricks with his 12th for the club. Riyad Mahrez nets City's first two goals. Watford, with Troy Deeney's successful return from injury complementing the impact made by Nigel Pearson, climb out of the bottom three for the first time with a 3-0 success at Bournemouth, who slip deeper into trouble after a single point and a single goal in five fixtures.

18 Wolves, on the receiving end of some disputed VAR verdicts, take advantage of decisions in their favour to produce a fine comeback at St Mary's and put the brake on Southampton's surge. Trailing 2-0 at half-time, they reply through Pedro Neto, then two goals from Raul Jimenez, the first a penalty, bring a 3-2 victory. Two more for Sergio Aguero, overtaking a first for Crystal Palace from Everton loanee Cenk Tosun, look to have given Manchester City three points, until Wilfried Zaha forces Fernandinho into conceding an 89th minute own goal for 2-2. Another late one rewards Newcastle for a backs-to-the-wall performance against Chelsea, Isaac Hayden's header coming in the fourth minute of stoppage-time. The meeting of the bottom two also ends 1-0 after Teemu Pukki's penalty for Norwich against Bournemouth. There are two dismissals – Bournemouth's Steve Cook for handling new-signing Ondrej Duda's goal-bound shot and the home side's Ben Godfrey when Paul Tierney upgrades yellow to red after watching the player's challenge on Callum Wilson on the pitchside monitor. Troy Deeney has a penalty saved by Paulo Gazzaniga and is grateful that Watford's new boy, Ignacio Pussetto, comes off the bench in the 89th minute to clear off the line from Erik Lamela, preserving a 0-0 scoreline against Tottenham. Referee Mike Dean takes charge of his 500th Premier League game – Arsenal's 1-1 draw with Sheffield United.

19 Goalkeeper Alisson delivers the most memorable celebration of the season as Liverpool complete a 2-0 victory over Manchester United. After his long clearance sends Mohamed Salah away for their second goal in stoppage-time, the Brazilian runs the length of the pitch to celebrate with his team-mate. Burnley, boosted by Nick Pope's penalty save from Jamie Vardy, come from behind to defeat Leicester 2-1.

21 Newcastle find the spirit and stamina for another stoppage-time surge – this time after going 2-0 down at Everton. Florian Lejeune, without a goal for the club, comes off the bench to break his duck and 60 seconds later scrambles another to earn a point. Everton have Moise Kean on the mark for the first time. Aston Villa also celebrate in added time as Tyrone Mings unwittingly deflects Ezri Konsa's shot into the net for 2-1 against Watford, having previously escaped a second yellow card for handling. And there is another decisive late goal for a defender when injury-dogged Hector Bellerin scores ten-man Arsenal's second equaliser after 87 minutes against Chelsea, David Luiz having received a straight red card on his return to Stamford Bridge for bringing down Tammy Abraham. Bournemouth enjoy a much-needed boost after a single point and just one goal from six games, defeating Brighton 3-1, with Harry Wilson and Callum Wilson both on the scoresheet, while Sergio Aguero makes it six goals in three matches with the only one of the game for Manchester City away to Sheffield United.

22 Burnley defeat Manchester United at Old Trafford for the first time since 1962, Chris Wood and Jay Rodriguez, with a tremendous angled drive, delivering a 2-0 scoreline. Ayoze Perez scores twice in the final ten minutes of normal time, his second goal a penalty, to confirm Leicester's 4-1 defeat of West Ham.

23 A midweek clutch of late goals continues at Molineux, where Roberto Firmino gives Liverpool a 2-1 win over Wolves in the 84th minute.

29 Liverpool win their game in hand, 2-0 at West Ham, to reach 70 points and extend their lead ahead of Manchester City (51), Leicester (48) and Chelsea (40). At the bottom, Norwich have 17, with Watford, Bournemouth and West Ham all on 23.

FEBRUARY 2020

1 Watford are on course to boost their chances of beating the drop when leading 2-0 against Everton, with Adam Masina's opener his first goal for the club. Instead, two in first-half stoppage-time from central defender Yerry Mina level the match. Then, despite having Fabian Delph sent off for a second yellow card, Carlo Ancelotti's side win it with Theo Walcott's 90th minute strike. Brighton's powers of recovery are also evident. They trail 2-0 and 3-1 after two deflected Robert Snodgrass goals for West Ham, but earn a point at 3-3, sealed by Glenn Murray's first of the season in the league. Bournemouth, too, show resilience, overcoming a second yellow card for Jefferson Lerma six minutes into the second-half to defeat Aston Villa 2-1. Mbwana Samatta, the first Tanzanian to play in the Premier League, scores on his Villa debut. Antonio Rudiger, on his 100th appearance for Chelsea, delivers both their goals in a 2-2 draw at Leicester, while Mohamed Salah fires a brace for Liverpool, who survive a testing first-half against Southampton to score four times without reply in the second period and go 22 points clear. Joel Ward's red card for his challenge on Enda Stevens is changed to yellow after referee Andy Madley consults the pitchside monitor. But there is no escape for his side as Crystal Palace go down 1-0 at home to Sheffield United.

2 Steven Bergwijn, Tottenham's new signing from PSV Eindhoven, makes a dream debut, volleying their first goal in a 2-0 victory over Manchester City, who have Oleksandr Zinchenko dismissed for a second yellow card.

8 As the Premier League enters its first winter break, staggered over two weeks, Everton make it five wins in eight matches under Carlo Ancelotti, defeating Crystal Palace 3-1, to close in on a place in Europe. Brighton salvage a point against Watford with a 79th minute own goal from Adrian Mariappa.

9 Substitute John Lundstram fires an 84th minute winner as Sheffield United come from behind to defeat Bournemouth 2-1. Manchester City face a fixture pile-up after their game against West Ham is postponed because of extreme weather caused by Storm Ciara.

14 Leicester's Hamza Choudhury is sent off for a second booking in a goalless draw against Wolves.

15 Sadio Mane comes off the Liverpool bench to score the only goal of the game at Norwich – his 100th in all competitions, with 25 for Southampton and 75 for the champions-in-waiting. Another substitute, Matej Vydra, nets his first in the Premier League since September 2018 to give Burnley a 2-1 victory at Southampton.

16 Son Heung-min, shouldering Tottenham's main goal threat in the absence of Harry Kane, strikes in the fourth minute of stoppage-time to give Tottenham a 3-2 success at Villa Park – his second of the afternoon after converting the rebound when Pepe Reina saves his penalty. In an eventful match, team-mate Toby Alderweireld scores at both ends, while Villa's Bjorn Engels nets his first for the club, concedes the penalty and commits the mistake leading to Son's winner. Arsenal record their biggest win of the season, 4-0 against Newcastle, with all the goals coming in the second-half.

17 The race for Champions League places hots up as Manchester United defeat faltering Chelsea 2-0 at Stamford Bridge with goals from Anthony Martial and Harry Maguire, who escapes a red card for kicking out at Michy Batshuayi.

19 In their first match since a having two-year European ban imposed by UEFA, Manchester City are 2-0 winners over West Ham, who remain in the bottom three.

22 On another day of VAR controversy, Eddie Howe, Frank Lampard and Brendan Rodgers are critical of decisions in their teams' matches. Howe fumes over Bournemouth's 3-0 defeat by Burnley after Harry Wilson's equaliser on the break is ruled out and play recalled to the other end where the home side are awarded a penalty for handball, converted for 2-0 by Jay Rodriguez. Lampard protests after Chelsea's 2-1 win over Tottenham about Giovani Lo Celso staying on the pitch for stamping on Cesar Azpilicueta – and officials later admit the error. Chelsea's goals come from two players out of favour for much of the season – Olivier Giroud and Marcos Alonso. Leicester manager Rodgers calls for consistency on handball decisions after one in favour for Manchester City and another refused for his own team. Sergio Aguero has his spot-kick saved by Kasper Schmeichel – City's fifth miss from their last seven – but they prevail with an 80th minute goal by substitute Gabriel Jesus. Newcastle have Valentino Lazaro shown a straight red card and face a fine for six bookings in a 1-0 defeat at Crystal Palace.

23 Diogo Jota, hat-trick hero of Wolves' 4-0 Europa League win over Espanyol, caps a memorable week with two more goals in a 3-0 victory over Norwich. Manchester United match that scoreline against Watford as Bruno Fernandes wins and converts a penalty his first for the club. Dominic Calvert-Lewin puts Everton ahead after 49 seconds at the Emirates, but two by Pierre Emerick-Aubameyang, his second 26 seconds after the interval, point Arsenal to a 3-2 success.

24 Liverpool equal Manchester City's all-time record of 18 successive top-flight wins by beating West Ham 3-2 with an 81st minute goal from Sadio Mane.

28 Full-back Jamal Lewis offers Norwich a glimmer of hope with his first league goal – an eye-catching volley for a 1-0 win over Leicester.

29 Liverpool's run of 44 unbeaten Premier League matches, stretching back to January 2019, ends in a 3-0 defeat at Watford, who score three times in 18 minutes in the second-half through Ismaila Sarr (2) and Troy Deeney. Their victory is clouded by a knee ligament injury which threatens to put Gerard Deulofeu out for the remainder of the season. West Ham, without a win in seven games, boost their chances of staying up as new-signing Jarrod Bowen opens his account in a 3-1 success against Southampton. Crystal Palace move towards safety with the only goal of the game at Brighton in Roy Hodgson's 100th Premier League game as manager of the club. But Bournemouth are denied all three points by Marcos Alonso's 85th minute equaliser for Chelsea – his second of the match – in a 2-2 scoreline. With Manchester City playing in the League Cup Final against Aston Villa, Liverpool's lead remains at 22 points. They have 79, City 57, Leicester 50, Chelsea 45 and Manchester United and Wolves 42. Norwich stay bottom on 21, with Villa 25, and three teams on 27 – Bournemouth, Watford and West Ham.

MARCH 2020

1 A red face for David de Gea and a red card for Carlo Ancelotti at Goodison Park. Manchester United's goalkeeper is left embarrassed as Dominic Calvert-Lewin charges down his attempted clearance, the ball flying back into the net. Ancelotti confronts referee Chris Kavanagh after Calvert-Lewin's deflected stoppage-time shot for 2-1 is disallowed and becomes the first Premier League manager to see red since the introduction of new powers for match officials. Wolves, through to the last 16 of the Europa League, complete another successful week by twice coming from behind against Tottenham – now without Son Heung-min as well as Harry Kane – then scoring the winner through Raul Jimenez.

7   Liverpool set a top-flight record of 22 successive home wins, surpassing the mark set by Bill Shankly's Anfield side in 1972. Mohamed Salah scores on his 100th Premier League appearance for the club and James Milner preserves a 2-1 scoreline against Bournemouth with a superb goalline clearance from Ryan Fraser. Roy Hodgson celebrates his contract extension as Jordan Ayew delivers another 1-0 victory, against Watford, which takes Crystal Palace to a secure-looking 39 points. Matt Ritchie has a penalty saved by Alex McCarthy at Southampton, but Allan Saint-Maximin is on the on the mark for Newcastle's 1-0 win which ends their run of four games with a goal. The home side have Moussa Djenepo's yellow card for stamping on Isaac Hayden upgraded to red after referee Graham Scott consults the pitch-side monitor.

8   Manchester United complete their first Premier League double over Manchester City since season 2009-10 with a 2-0 victory at Old Trafford, rounded off when Scott McTominay returns Ederson's misdirected clearance back over the goalkeeper from 35 yards. Chelsea follow up a midweek FA Cup success over Liverpool with their biggest victory of the season – 4-0 against Everton.

9   Jamie Vardy, without a goal for nearly three months, scores twice as Leicester win in the league for the first time since January 22. They beat Aston Villa 4-0, with Vardy's first goal a penalty and Harvey Barnes also netting twice. It proves to be the last match before the big shutdown.

JUNE 2020

17 Exactly 100 days after the season's suspension, Aston Villa and Sheffield United launch its resumption in an empty stadium with a goalless draw clouded in controversy. Chris Wilder's side celebrate after Villa goalkeeper Orjan Nyland carries Oliver Norwood's free-kick over the line. But goal-line technology fails for the first time and referee Michael Oliver has no alternative but to rule it out. Later in the evening, Raheem Sterling scores the summer's first goal to put Manchester City on the way to a 3-0 win over Arsenal, who have substitute David Luiz shown a straight red card for pulling back Riyad Mahrez and conceding the penalty which Kevin De Bruyne converts for his side's second goal.

19 Injury-dogged Paul Pogba comes off the bench for his first Manchester United appearance since Boxing Day and wins the penalty which Bruno Fernandes converts for a point at Tottenham. Danny Ings registers his 16th league goal of the season, then sets up Stuart Armstrong as Southampton score twice in five minutes on the way to a 3-0 success at Norwich.

20 Neal Maupay strikes in the fifth minute of stoppage-time as Brighton come from behind to defeat Arsenal 2-1 and boost their chances of staying up. Watford salvage a point when Craig Dawson delivers his first goal for the club with an overhead kick in the 93rd minute to cancel out Ben Chilwell's thunderous cross-shot for Leicester three minutes earlier. But Bournemouth struggle after conceding another spectacular goal – a free-kick from Luka Milivojevic – and go down 2-0 to Crystal Palace in the BBC's first-ever live Premier League match. And West Ham lose by the same scoreline at home to Wolves where influential substitute Adama Traore has a hand in goals for Raul Jimenez and Pedro Neto.

21 Joelinton scores in the Premier League for the first time since August to complete Newcastle's 3-0 win over Sheffield United, who have John Egan sent off for a second booking with the game goalless. Steve Bruce's biggest victory since taking over leaves his side 11 points clear of the relegation zone, but Aston Villa remain in trouble, beaten 2-1 at home by Chelsea after leading through a first Premier League goal for Kortney Hause. The Merseyside derby at Goodison Park ends goalless, leaving Liverpool waiting a little longer to be crowned champions.

22 Burnley, the last club to return to action, weakened by injuries and embarrassed by an offensive banner flown over the Etihad Stadium, are beaten 5-0 by Manchester City, who have Phil Foden and Riyad Mahrez both on the mark twice, with Mahrez's second goal a penalty.

23 Brighton are denied the chance to move further away from trouble by Kasper Schmeichel's penalty save from Neal Maupay at Leicester and have to settle for a goalless draw. David Moyes rages at VAR after West Ham's 2-0 defeat at Tottenham, arguing that an own goal by Tomas Soucek should have been disallowed for a handling offence.

24 Liverpool move to within touching distance of the title with a 4-0 win over Crystal Palace, highlighted by Fabinho's 30-yard piledriver. Anthony Martial delivers a 3-0 success for Manchester United against Sheffield United with the club's first Premier League hat-trick since Robin van Persie's treble in Sir Alex Ferguson's final season seven years ago.

25 Jurgen Klopp and his side celebrate after watching Manchester City finally concede the title in a 2-1 defeat by Chelsea. Liverpool become champions for the first time since 1990, 23 points in the clear with a record seven games still to play. City have Fernandinho sent off for handling on the line at Stamford Bridge. Southampton's Jack Stephens is also shown a straight red, for denying Pierre-Emerick Aubameyang a scoring opportunity, in a 2-0 home defeat by Arsenal, who have Joe Willock on the mark for the first time in the Premier League.

28 Danny Ings nets twice as Southampton complete their climb away from the relegation zone by winning 3-1 at Watford and reaching 40 points.

29 Burnley captain Ben Mee marks his 300th league appearance for the club with the only goal of the game against Crystal Palace – his first since January 2017.

30 Bruno Fernandes, fast becoming the signing of the season, scores twice as Manchester United close in on a Champions League place with a 3-0 victory at Brighton. They climb to within two points of fourth-place Chelsea and three behind Leicester in third.

JULY 2020

1 An 89th minute goal by substitute Andriy Yarmolenko gives West Ham much-needed breathing space. They defeat Chelsea 3-2 – Tomas Souceck scoring his first for the club – while two relegation rivals struggle. Norwich, seven points adrift, look doomed after a 4-0 defeat by Arsenal, with Cedric Soares making a scoring debut and Pierre-Emerick Aubameyang on the mark twice. Bournemouth are beaten 4-1 at home by Newcastle, for whom Valentino Lazaro opens his first Premier League account.

2 Manchester City players form a guard of honour at the Etihad to greet Liverpool, then hand the new champions a 4-0 beating – their biggest Premier League defeat since losing 5-0 with ten men at the same stadium in September 2017. Phil Foden scores one, has a hand in two other goals and continues to look the natural replacement for the departing David Silva. Record-signing Sander Berge puts Sheffield United on the way to a 3-1 success against Tottenham, whose protests about Harry Kane's disallowed equaliser again highlights calls for a revision of the handball rule.

4 Jamie Vardy reaches a personal milestone and 18-year-olds Mason Greenwood and Bukayo Saka continue their impressive progress. Vardy, scores his 100th Premier League goal, is the first to reach 20 for the season and adds another in the 3-0 defeat of Crystal Palace. Greenwood is hailed by his manager Ole Gunnar Solskjaer as the best young finisher he has seen with two eye-catching strikes as Manchester United add to Bournemouth's woes with a 5-2 victory. Three days after signing a new long-term contract, Saka puts Arsenal on the way to a 2-0 win at Wolves with his first in the league. Willian's third penalty in successive matches helps Chelsea overcome Watford 3-0, while Brighton all-but secure their place for next season with the only goal at Norwich from Leandro Trossard.

5 Che Adams scores spectacularly to give Southampton a 1-0 win over Manchester City. His first for the club, in 30 appearances in all competitions, is launched from 45 yards over stranded goalkeeper Ederson after Stuart Armstrong disposses Oleksandr Zinchenko. Curtis Jones, 19, fresh from signing a new five-year contract with Liverpool, celebrates his first in the Premier League, rounding off a 2-0 victory over Aston Villa.

7   Danny Welbeck's first in the league since August 2018 – an overhead kick – gives Watford a 2-1 victory over Norwich. Jamie Vardy's 84th minute equaliser earns Leicester a point at the Emirates, but they lose third place to Chelsea, 3-2 winners at Crystal Palace. Arsenal have substitute Eddie Nketiah shown a straight red card for a dangerous tackle on James Justin.

8   West Ham continue to look over their shoulder after losing to a Jay Rodriguez header for Burnley. Sheffield are also 1-0 winners, against Wolves, courtesy of John Egan's header three minutes into stoppage-time. Two by Mohamed Salah point Liverpool to their 30th win of the season, 3-1 at Brighton, while Manchester City crush Newcastle 5-0.

9   Manchester United and Bournemouth benefit from controversial VAR penalty rulings. Bruno Fernandes puts United on the way to a 3-0 scoreline at Villa Park after Ezri Konsa is ruled to have tripped the Portuguese midfielder. Bournemouth hold on to a goalless draw against Tottenham after a two-handed shove by Josh King on Harry Kane in the area goes unpunished.

11 Michail Antonio scores all four goals in a 4-0 success at Carrow Road to relegate Norwich and boost West Ham's chances of staying up. Watford also do well, coming from behind to defeat Newcastle with two penalties from Troy Deeney. David McGoldrick, without a Premier League goal all season, nets twice as Sheffield United undermine Chelsea's Champions League chances 3-0. Raheem Sterling completes his third hat-trick of the season in comical fashion at Brighton, the ball bouncing in off his head with the Manchester City player on the ground. City win 5-0, scoring five or more in the campaign for the sixth time. But Liverpool stumble at Anfield for the first time since January 2019, an equaliser by Burnley's Jay Rodriguez ending their bid to become the first team to go through a season with a perfect home record.

12 Bournemouth and Aston Villa end lean runs to revive their chances of staying up. Dominic Solanke, without a Premier League goal in 38 appearances for Eddie Howe's team, is on the mark twice as they come from behind for a 4-1 win against Leicester, who have Caglar Soyuncu dismissed for kicking out at Callum Wilson with the score 2-1. Bournemouth acquire three points for the first time in ten matches, while Villa are successful for the first time in 11. Two goals by Trezeguet give them a 2-0 victory over Crystal Palace, who have Christian Benteke dismissed, also for a straight red, after the final whistle for kicking out at Ezri Konsa. Tottenham recover from conceding first to defeat Arsenal 2-1 thanks to an 81st minute header from Toby Alderweireld.

13 Manchester United, with David de Gea making his 400th appearance for the club, miss the chance to go third above Chelsea when substitute Michael Obafemi's 96th minute goal gives Southampton a 2-2 draw at Old Trafford.

14 Chelsea take advantage by beating Norwich 1-0 with a goal from Olivier Giroud to consolidate their position.

15 Liverpool's pursuit of Manchester City's record points total of 100 is ended when mistakes by Virgil van Dijk and Alisson are punished by Alexandre Lacazette and Reiss Nelson as Arsenal come from behind beat them 2-1. Harry Kane passes 200 club goals with a brace in Tottenham's 3-1 victory at Newcastle. Bournemouth have more shots on goal than Manchester City, but miss chances and lose 2-1 at the Etihad.

16 At Goodison Park, Aston Villa lead through Ezri Konsa's first Premier League goal for the club until the 87th minute when Theo Walcott earns Everton a point. With Manchester City's European ban lifted and Pep Guardiola's side guaranteed Champions League football next season, the race for the two other places hots up. Manchester United, 2-0 winners at Crystal Palace, and Leicester, who defeat Sheffield United by the same scoreline, close in on Chelsea, with a single point separating the three teams.

17 Mark Noble makes his 500th appearance for the club as West Ham effectively make sure of staying up at the expense of Watford, who are back in trouble after a 3-1 defeat and have manager Nigel Pearson sacked two days later.

18 Norwich complete their home fixtures on a sour note. Emiliano Buendia is sent off for elbowing Ashley Westwood, Josip Drmich also receives a straight red, for lunging at Erik Pieters, and Ben Godfrey concedes an own goal in a record ninth successive defeat, 2-0 by Burnley, who equal their highest Premier League points total of 54.

19 Two goals by Harry Kane point Tottenham towards a Europa League place, leaving Leicester's top-four prospects in the balance after a 3-0 defeat. Bournemouth are on the brink of going down, losing 2-0 at home to Southampton, for whom Danny Ings scores his 21st goal of the season, then has a penalty saved by Aaron Ramsdale.

20 Sheffield United's bid to cap an impressive first season back in the top-flight with a Europa League place is ended by a 1-0 home defeat by Everton. Daniel Podence scores his first Wolves goal in a 2-0 win over Crystal Palace.

21 Aston Villa climb out of the bottom three in their penultimate fixture, courtesy of the evening's only goal from Trezeguet against Arsenal. They move above Watford, who also surrender a superior goal difference after another drubbing by Manchester City. Raheem Sterling nets twice, the second goal from the rebound after his penalty is saved by Ben Foster, in City's 4-0 victory which takes their tally to 18 in the last three matches against Watford.

22 On the night the title trophy is presented, Liverpool and Chelsea deliver a goal feast – Jurgen Klopp's side winning 5-3, with Roberto Firmino scoring his first Anfield goal of the season. Manchester United are held 1-1 by West Ham, for whom Michail Antonio's penalty is his eighth goal in six matches.

26 Aston Villa, Manchester United and Chelsea take pride of place on the final day of the season. Villa complete a great escape with captain Jack Grealish's goal for a 1-1 draw at West Ham, having taken eight points from their final four fixtures. Bournemouth are relegated, despite an impressive 3-1 victory at Everton. So, too, are Watford, beaten 3-2 at Arsenal, for whom Kieran Tierney scores his first goal, alongside Pierre-Emerick Aubameyang's brace. United's record 14th penalty of the campaign, converted by Bruno Fernandes, sets up a 2-0 victory in a Champions League decider at Leicester. The home side miss out on a top-four place and have Jonny Evans sent off for lunging at Scott McTominay. Jamie Vardy's Gold Boot award for 23 goals provides some consolation. Chelsea hold on to fourth place by beating Wolves 2-0, Mason Mount and Olivier Giroud scoring in first-half stoppage-time. Tottenham join Leicester in the Europa League, courtesy of a 1-1 draw at Crystal Palace, who end a seven-match losing streak. At the top, Liverpool trail after 23 seconds to Dwight Gayle's strike for Newcastle, but win 3-1 to finish on a club-record 99 points. David Silva bids farewell to the Premier League after ten years at Manchester City, who top 100 goals for the second time in three seasons. Kevin De Bruyne scores twice in the 5-0 drubbing of Norwich, while Che Adams gets two for Southampton, 3-1 winners against a tired Sheffield United. Brighton also finish on a high, a 2-1 victory at Burnley bringing their highest Premier League points tally of 41.

HOW LIVERPOOL BECAME CHAMPIONS

AUGUST 2019

9   Liverpool 4 (Hanley 7 og, Salah 19, Van Dijk 28, Origi 42) Norwich 1 (Pukki 64). Att: 53,333

17   Southampton 1 (Ings 83) Liverpool 2 (Mane 45, Firmino 71). Att: 31,712

24   Liverpool 3 (Matip 41, Salah 49 pen, 58) Arsenal 1 (Torreira 85). Att: 53,298

31   Burnley 0 Liverpool 3 (Wood 33 og, Mane 37, Firmino 80). Att: 21,762

SEPTEMBER 2019

14   Liverpool 3 (Mane 28, 40, Salah 72) Newcastle 1 (Willems 7). Att: 51,430

22   Chelsea 1 (Kante 71) Liverpool 2 (Alexander-Arnold 14, Firmino 30). Att: 40,638

28   Sheffield Utd 0 Liverpool 1 (Wijnaldum 70). Att: 31,774

OCTOBER 2019

5   Liverpool 2 (Mane 40, Milner 90+5 pen) Leicester 1 (Maddison 80). Att: 51,400

20   Manchester Utd 1 (Rashford 36) Liverpool 1 (Lallana 85). Att: 73,737

27   Liverpool 2 (Henderson 52, Salah 75 pen) Tottenham 1 (Kane 1). Att: 53,222

NOVEMBER 2019

2   Aston Villa 1 (Trezeguet 21) Liverpool 2 (Robertson 87, Mane 90). Att: 41,878

10   Liverpool 3 (Fabinho 6, Salah 13, Mane 51) Manchester City 1 (Bernardo Silva 78). Att: 53,324

23   Crystal Palace 1 (Zaha 82) Liverpool 2 (Mane 49, Firmino 85). Att: 25,486

30   Liverpool 2 (Van Dijk 18, 24) Brighton 1 (Dunk 79). Att: 53,319

DECEMBER 2019

4   Liverpool 5 (Origi 6, 31, Shaqiri 17, Mane 45, Wijnaldum 90) Everton 2 (Keane 21, Richarlison 45). Att: 53,094

7   Bournemouth 0 Liverpool 3 (Oxlade-Chamberlain 35, Keita 44, Salah 54). Att: 10,832

14   Liverpool 2 (Salah 38, 90) Watford 0. Att: 53,311

26   Leicester 0 Liverpool 4 (Firmino 31, 74, Milner 71 pen, Alexander-Arnold 78). Att: 32,211

29   Liverpool 1 (Mane 42) Wolves 0. Att: 53,326

JANUARY 2020

2   Liverpool 2 (Salah 4, Mane 64) Sheffield Utd 0. Att: 53,321

11   Tottenham 0 Liverpool 1 (Firmino 37). Att: 61,023

19   Liverpool 2 (Van Dijk 14, Salah 90+3) Manchester Utd 0. Att: 52,916

23   Wolves 1 (Raul Jimenez 51) Liverpool 2 (Henderson 8, Firmino 84). Att: 31,746

29   West Ham 0 Liverpool 2 (Salah 35 pen, Oxlade-Chamberlain 52). Att: 59,959

FEBRUARY 2020

1   Liverpool 4 (Oxlade-Chamberlain 47, Henderson 60, Salah 72, 90) Southampton 0. Att: 53,291

14   Norwich 0 Liverpool 1 (Mane 78). Att: 27,110

24   Liverpool 3 (Wijnaldum 9, Salah 68, Mane 81) West Ham 2 (Diop 12, Fornals 54). Att: 53,313

29   Watford 3 (Sarr 54, 60, Deeney 72) Liverpool 0. Att: 21,634

MARCH 2020

7   Liverpool 2 (Salah 24, Mane 33) Bournemouth 1 (C Wilson 9). Att: 53,323

JUNE 2020

(All matches from here behind closed doors)

21   Everton 0 Liverpool 0

24   Liverpool 4 (Alexander-Arnold 23, Salah 44, Fabinho 55, Mane 69) Crystal Palace 0

25   Liverpool clinched title after Manchester City lost at Chelsea. Liverpool 23 pts ahead with 7 games left

JULY 2020

2   Manchester City 4 (De Bruyne 25 pen, Sterling 35, Foden 45, Oxlade-Chamberlain 66 og) Liverpool 0

5   Liverpool 2 (Mane 71, Jones 89) Aston Villa 0

8   Brighton 1 (Trossard 45) Liverpool 3 (Salah 6, 76, Henderson 8)

11   Liverpool 1 (Robertson 34) Burnley 1 (Rodriguez 69)

15   Arsenal 2 (Lacazette 32, Nelson 44) Liverpool 1 (Mane 20)

22   Liverpool 5 (Keita 23, Alexander-Arnold 38, Wijnaldum 43, Firmino 55, Oxlade-Chamberlain 84) Chelsea 3 (Giroud 45, Abraham 61, Pulisic 73)

26   Newcastle 1 (Gayle 1) Liverpool 3 (Van Dijk 38, Origi 59, Mane 89)

ENGLISH FOOTBALL LEAGUE PLAY-OFFS 2020

Scott Parker's homework paid big dividends in the Championship final against Brentford. Having identified a potential weakness in goalkeeper David Raya, the **Fulham** manager instructed Joe Bryan to shoot, rather than cross, when his side were awarded a free-kick with the game still goalless into extra-time. Bryan did just that, a low, skidding delivery catching Raya unawares, and the left-back scored again to seal the club's return to the Premier League at the first attempt. This time, he combined with Aleksandar Mitrovic after another productive example of Parker's tactical awareness, Mitrovic, whose 26 goals achieved a top-six place, was only half-fit after missing the semi-final against Cardiff with a hamstring injury. But his manager asked for half-an-hour off the bench and the Serbian striker's presence was enough to make a difference. Brentford's reply in stoppage-time, Henrik Dalsgaard's header, was no more than a token gesture at the end of a season in which their dream of taking top-flight football to the club's new stadium died in an empty Wembley. They passed up the chance of automatic promotion after a superb regular campaign with a nervous finish, which raised the possibility of losing key players in the transfer window. By contrast, unfancied **Wycombe** were smiling all the way to the Championship after defeating Oxford 2-1 in a tight League One decider in which two more defenders proved the key. Anthony Stewart put Gareth Ainsworth's side ahead from Joe Jacobson's corner, with the aid of a deflection off goalkeeper Simon Eastwood. Jacobson's penalty from the penalty spot settled it ten minutes from the end of normal time after Eastwood brought down Fred Onyedinma. **Northampton** defeated ten-man Exeter 4-0 in the League Two Final, leading through Ryan Watson's deflected shot and West Bromwich Albion loanee Callum Morton, then adding late goals from Sam Hoskins and Andy Williams after Dean Moxey was shown a straight red card for his challenge on Watson. **Harrogate** reached the Football League for the first time when goals by George Thomson, Connor Hall and Jack Diamond delivered a 3-1 success against Notts County.

ELIMINATORS (one match)

NATIONAL LEAGUE
Boreham Wood 2 (Smith 54, Rhead 80) Halifax 1 (Sho-Silva 19). Yeovil 0 Barnet 2 (McCallum 53, Vilhete 86)

SEMI-FINALS
(one match)
NATIONAL LEAGUE
Harrogate 1 (Muldoon 65) Boreham Wood 0. Notts Co 2 (Dennis 37, Roberts 59) Barnet 0

SEMI-FINALS, FIRST LEG

CHAMPIONSHIP
Cardiff 0 **Fulham** 2 (Onomah 49, Kebano 90+1). **Swansea** 1 (Ayew 81) **Brentford** 0
LEAGUE ONE
Portsmouth 1 (Curtis 32) **Oxford** 1 (Browne 43). Fleetwood 1 (Evans 4 pen) **Wycombe** 4 (Ofoborh 2, Cairns 7 og, Wheeler 45, Samuel 57)
LEAGUE TWO
Colchester 1 (Bramall 81) **Exeter** 0. Northampton 0 **Cheltenham** 2 (Raglan 26, Thomas 86)

SEMI-FINALS, SECOND LEG

CHAMPIONSHIP
Brentford 3 (Watkins 11, Marcondes 15, Mbeumo 46) **Swansea** 1 (Brewster 78) – Brentford won 3-2 on aggregate. **Fulham** 1 (Kebano 9) **Cardiff** 2 (Nelson 8, Tomlin 47) – Fulham won 3-2 on agg
LEAGUE ONE
Oxford 1 (Harrison 45 og) **Portsmouth** 1 (Harness 38) – aet, agg 2-2, Oxford won 5-4 on pens.

Wycombe 2 (Onyedinma 47, 90) **Fleetwood** 2 (Andrew 22, Evans 60 pen) — Wycombe won 6-3 on agg
LEAGUE TWO
Cheltenham 0 **Northampton** 3 (Oliver 9, Morton 57, 77) - Northampton won 3-2 on agg.
Exeter 3 (Martin 10, Richardson 58, Bowman 111) **Colchester** 1 (Senior 78) — aet, Exeter won 3-2 on agg

FINALS

CHAMPIONSHIP – TUESDAY, AUGUST 4, 2020
Brentford 1 (Dalsgaard 120+4) **Fulham 2** (Bryan 105,118) — aet, Wembley
Brentford (4-3-3): Raya, Dalsgaard, Jansson (capt), Pinnock, Henry (Fosu-Henry 105), Jensen (Dervisoglu 105), Norgaard, Dasilva (Canos 83), Mbuemo (Marcondes 61), Watkins, Benrahma. **Subs not used**: Daniels, Valencia, Jeanvier, Zamburek, Roerslev. **Booked**: Jensen, Norgaard. **Manager**: Thomas Frank.
Fulham (4-2-3-1): Rodak, Odoi (Christie 110), Hector, Ream, Bryan, Reed, Cairney (capt), Kebano (Knockaert 81), Onomah (Le Marchand 110), De Cordova-Reid (Mitrovic 92), Kamara (Ivan Cavaleiro 105). **Subs not used**: Bettinelli, McDonald, Johansen, Sessegnon. **Booked**: Reed, Cairney, Hector, Knockaert, Mitrovic, Ivan Cavaleiro, Rodak. **Manager**: Scott Parker
Referee: M Atkinson (Yorks). **Half-time**: 0-0

LEAGUE ONE – MONDAY, JULY 13, 2020
Oxford United 1 (Sykes 57) **Wycombe Wanderers 2** (Stewart 9, Jacobson 79 pen) - Wembley
Oxford United (4-3-3): Eastwood, Long (Forde 80), Dickie (capt), Moore, Ruffels, Sykes, Gorrin (Kelly 46), Brannagan, Henry (Agyei 80), Taylor, Browne (Woodburn 89). **Subs not used**: Stevens, Mousinho, Mackie, Hanson, Atkinson. **Booked**: Gorrin. **Manager**: Karl Robinson
Wycome Wanderers (4-4-2): Allsop, Grimmer, Stewart, Charles, Jacobson, Wheeler, Gape, Ofoborh (Thompson 62), Bloomfield (capt) (Pattison 46), Samuel (Akinfenwa 62), Onyedinma (Freeman 90+3). **Subs not used**: Stockdale, Jombati, Kashket, Phllips, Parker. **Booked**: Thompson. **Manager**: Gareth Ainsworth
Referee: R Jones (Northumberland). **Half-time**: 0-1

LEAGUE TWO – MONDAY, JUNE 29, 2020
Exeter City 0 **Northampton Town** 4 (Watson 11, Morton 31, Hoskins 80, A Williams 89) - Wembley
Exeter City (3-5-2): Maxted, Sweeney (Dickenson 82), A Martin, Moxey, R Williams, Taylor (capt), Atangana (Sparkes 61), Richardson, Law, Bowman, Fisher (Collins 52). **Subs not used**: Ward, L Martin, Ajose, Jay, Seymour. **Booked**: A Martin. **Sent off**: Moxey (59). **Manager**: Matt Taylor
Northampton Town (3-5-2): Arnold, Goode (capt), Turnbull, Wharton, Adams (Marshall 31), McCormack (Olayinka 74), Hoskins, Harriman, Watson (Anderson 88), Oliver (Smith 74), Morton (A Williams 88). **Subs not used**: Cornell, J Martin, Lines, Warburton. **Booked**: Wharton, Watson. **Manager**: Keith Curle
Referee: M Salisbury (Lancs). **Half-time**: 0-2

NATIONAL LEAGUE – SUNDAY, AUGUST 2, 2020
Harrogate Town 3 (Thomson 5, Hall 28, Diamond 71) **Notts County** 1 (Roberts 46) - Wembley
Harrogate Town (4-4-2): Belshaw, Fallowfield, Smith, Hall, Burrell, Thomson, Falkingham (capt), Kerry, Diamond, Muldoon (Beck 87), Martin (Stead 61). **Subs not used**: Cracknell, Emmett, Leesley, Harrat. **Booked**: Hall, Kerry. **Manager**: Simon Weaver
Notts County (4-4-2): Slocombe, Brindley (Kelly-Evans 87), Lacey, Turner, Bagan, Roberts, Rose, Doyle, (capt), O'Brien (Thomas 46), Dennis (Boldewijn 46), Wootton. **Subs not used**: McDonnell, Rawlinson, Crawford. **Booked**: Bagan, Roberts. **Manager**: Neal Ardley
Referee: J Bell (Yorks). **Half-time**: 2-0

PLAY-OFF FINALS – HOME & AWAY

1987: Divs 1/2: Charlton beat Leeds 2-1 in replay (Birmingham) after 1-1 agg (1-0h, 0-1a). Charlton remained in Div 1 Losing semi-finalists: Ipswich and Oldham. **Divs 2/3: Swindon** beat Gillingham 2-0 in replay (Crystal Palace) after 2-2 agg (0-1a, 2-1h). Swindon promoted to Div 2. Losing semi-finalists: Sunderland and Wigan; Sunderland relegated to Div 3. **Divs 3/4: Aldershot** beat Wolves 3-0 on agg (2-0h, 1-0a) and promoted to Div 3. Losing semi-finalists: Bolton and Colchester; Bolton relegated to Div 4

1988: Divs 1/2: Middlesbrough beat Chelsea 2-1 on agg (2-0h, 0-1a) and promoted to Div 1; Chelsea relegated to Div 2. Losing semi-finalists: Blackburn and Bradford City. **Divs 2/3: Walsall** beat Bristol City 4-0 in replay (h) after 3-3 agg (3-1a, 0-2h) and promoted to Div 2. Losing semi-finalists: Sheffield Utd and Notts County; Sheffield Utd relegated to Div 3. **Divs 3/4: Swansea** beat Torquay 5-4 on agg (2-1h, 3-3a) and promoted to Div 3. Losing semi-finalists: Rotherham and Scunthorpe.; Rotherham relegated to Div 4

1989: Div 2: Crystal Palace beat Blackburn 4-3 on agg (1-3a, 3-0h). Losing semi-finalists: Watford and Swindon. **Div 3: Port Vale** beat Bristol Rovers 2-1 on agg (1-1a, 1-0h). Losing semi-finalists: Fulham and Preston **Div.4: Leyton Orient** beat Wrexham 2-1 on agg (0-0a, 2-1h). Losing semi-finalists: Scarborough and Scunthorpe

PLAY-OFF FINALS AT WEMBLEY

1990: Div 2: Swindon 1 Sunderland 0 (att: 72,873). Swindon promoted, then demoted for financial irregularities; Sunderland promoted. Losing semi-finalists: Blackburn and Newcastle Utd **Div 3: Notts County** 2 Tranmere 0 (att: 29,252). Losing semi-finalists: Bolton and Bury. **Div 4: Cambridge Utd** 1 Chesterfield 0 (att: 26,404). Losing semi-finalists: Maidstone and Stockport County

1991: Div 2: Notts County 3 Brighton 1 (att: 59,940). Losing semi-finalists: Middlesbrough and Millwall. **Div 3: Tranmere** 1 Bolton 0 (att: 30,217). Losing semi-finalists: Brentford and Bury. **Div 4: Torquay** 2 Blackpool 2 – Torquay won 5-4 on pens (att: 21,615). Losing semi-finalists: Burnley and Scunthorpe

1992: Div 2: Blackburn 1 Leicester 0 (att: 68,147). Losing semi-finalists: Derby and Cambridge Utd. **Div 3: Peterborough** 2 Stockport 1 (att: 35,087). Losing semi-finalists: Huddersfield and Stoke. **Div 4: Blackpool** 1 Scunthorpe 1 aet, Blackpool won 4-3 on pens (att: 22,741). Losing semi-finalists: Barnet and Crewe

1993: Div 1: Swindon 4 Leicester 3 (att: 73,802). Losing semi-finalists: Portsmouth and Tranmere. **Div 2: WBA** 3 Port Vale 0 (att: 53,471). Losing semi-finalists: Stockport and Swansea. **Div 3: York** 1 Crewe 1 aet, York won 5-3 on pens (att: 22,416). Losing semi-finalists: Bury and Walsall

1994: Div 1: Leicester 2 Derby 1 (att: 73,671). Losing semi-finalists: Millwall and Tranmere. **Div 2: Burnley** 2 Stockport 1 (att: 44,806). Losing semi-finalists: Plymouth Argyle and York. **Div 3: Wycombe** 4 Preston 2 (att: 40,109). Losing semi-finalists: Carlisle and Torquay

1995: Div 1: Bolton 4 Reading 3 (att: 64,107). Losing semi-finalists: Tranmere and Wolves. **Div 2: Huddersfield** 2 Bristol Rov 1 (att: 59,175). Losing semi-finalists: Brentford and Crewe. **Div 3: Chesterfield** 2 Bury 0 (att: 22,814). Losing semi-finalists: Mansfield and Preston

1996: Div 1: Leicester 2 Crystal Palace 1 aet (att: 73,573). Losing semi-finalists: Charlton and Stoke. **Div 2: Bradford City** 2 Notts Co 0 (att: 39,972). Losing semi-finalists: Blackpool and Crewe. **Div 3: Plymouth Argyle** 1 Darlington 0 (att: 43,431). Losing semi-finalists: Colchester and Hereford

1997: Div 1: Crystal Palace 1 Sheffield Utd 0 (att: 64,383). Losing semi-finalists: Ipswich and Wolves. **Div 2: Crewe** 1 Brentford 0 (att: 34,149). Losing semi-finalists: Bristol City and Luton. **Div 3: Northampton** 1 Swansea 0 (att: 46,804). Losing semi-finalists: Cardiff and Chester

1998: Div 1: Charlton 4 Sunderland 4 aet, Charlton won 7-6 on pens (att: 77, 739). Losing semi-finalists: Ipswich and Sheffield Utd. **Div 2: Grimsby** 1 Northampton 0 (att: 62,988). Losing semi-finalists: Bristol Rov and Fulham. **Div 3: Colchester** 1 Torquay 0 (att: 19,486). Losing semi-finalists: Barnet and Scarborough

1999: Div 1: Watford 2 Bolton 0 (att: 70,343). Losing semi-finalists: Ipswich and Birmingham. **Div 2: Manchester City** 2 Gillingham 2 aet, Manchester City won 3-1 on pens (att: 76,935). Losing semi-finalists: Preston and Wigan. **Div 3: Scunthorpe** 1 Leyton Orient 0 (att: 36,985). Losing semi-finalists: Rotherham and Swansea

2000: Div 1: Ipswich 4 Barnsley 2 (att: 73,427). Losing semi-finalists: Birmingham and Bolton. **Div 2: Gillingham** 3 Wigan 2 aet (att: 53,764). Losing semi-finalists: Millwall and Stoke. **Div 3: Peterborough** 1 Darlington 0 (att: 33,383). Losing semi-finalists: Barnet and Hartlepool

PLAY-OFF FINALS AT MILLENNIUM STADIUM

2001: Div 1: Bolton 3 Preston 0 (att: 54,328). Losing semi-finalists: Birmingham and WBA. **Div 2: Walsall** 3 Reading 2 aet (att: 50,496). Losing semi-finalists: Stoke and Wigan. **Div 3: Blackpool** 4 Leyton Orient 2 (att: 23,600). Losing semi-finalists: Hartlepool and Hull

2002: Div 1: Birmingham 1 Norwich 1 aet, Birmingham won 4-2 on pens, (att: 71,597). Losing semi-finalists: Millwall and Wolves. **Div 2: Stoke** 2 Brentford 0 (att: 42,523). Losing semi-finalists: Cardiff and Huddersfield. **Div 3: Cheltenham** 3 Rushden & Diamonds 1 (att: 24,368). Losing semi-finalists: Hartlepool and Rochdale

2003: Div 1: Wolves 3 Sheffield Utd 0 (att: 69,473). Losing semi-finalists: Nott'm Forest and Reading. **Div 2: Cardiff** 1 QPR. 0 aet (att: 66,096). Losing semi-finalists: Bristol City and Oldham. **Div 3: Bournemouth** 5 Lincoln 2 (att: 32,148). Losing semi-finalists: Bury and Scunthorpe

2004: Div 1: Crystal Palace 1 West Ham 0 (att: 72,523). Losing semi-finalists: Ipswich and Sunderland. **Div 2: Brighton** 1 Bristol City 0 (att: 65,167). Losing semi-finalists: Hartlepool and Swindon. **Div 3: Huddersfield** 0 Mansfield 0 aet, Huddersfield won 4-1 on pens (att: 37,298). Losing semi-finalists: Lincoln and Northampton

2005: Championship: West Ham 1 Preston 0 (att: 70,275). Losing semifinalists: Derby Co and Ipswich. **League 1: Sheffield Wed** 4 Hartlepool 2 aet (att: 59,808). Losing semi-finalists: Brentford and Tranmere **League 2: Southend** 2 Lincoln 0 aet (att: 19532). Losing semi-finalists: Macclesfield and Northampton

2006: Championship: Watford 3 Leeds 0 (att: 64,736). Losing semi-finalists: Crystal Palace and Preston. **League 1: Barnsley** 2 Swansea 2 aet (att: 55,419), Barnsley won 4-3 on pens. Losing semi-finalists: Huddersfield and Brentford. **League 2: Cheltenham** 1 Grimsby 0 (att: 29,196). Losing semi-finalists: Wycombe and Lincoln

PLAY-OFF FINALS AT WEMBLEY

2007: Championship: Derby 1 WBA 0 (att: 74,993). Losing semi-finalists: Southampton and Wolves. **League 1: Blackpool** 2 Yeovil 0 (att: 59,313). Losing semi-finalists: Nottm Forest and Oldham. **League 2: Bristol Rov** 3 Shrewsbury 1 (att: 61,589). Losing semi-finalists: Lincoln and MK Dons

2008: Championship: Hull 1 Bristol City 0 (att: 86,703). Losing semi-finalists: Crystal Palace and Watford. **League 1: Doncaster** 1 Leeds 0 (att: 75,132). Losing semi-finalists: Carlisle and Southend. **League 2: Stockport** 3 Rochdale 2 (att: 35,715). Losing semi-finalists: Darlington and Wycombe

2009: Championship: Burnley 1 Sheffield Utd 0 (att: 80,518). Losing semi-finalists: Preston and Reading. **League 1: Scunthorpe** 3 Millwall 2 (att: 59,661). Losing semi-finalists: Leeds and MK Dons. **League 2: Gillingham** 1 Shrewsbury 0 (att: 53,706). Losing semi-finalists: Bury and Rochdale

2010: Championship: Blackpool 3 Cardiff 2 (att: 82,244). Losing semi-finalists: Leicester and Nottm Forest. **League 1: Millwall** 1 Swindon 0 (att:73,108). Losing semi-finalists: Charlton and Huddersfield. **League 2: Dagenham & Redbridge** 3 Rotherham 2 (att: 32,054). Losing semi-finalists: Aldershot and Morecambe.

2011: Championship: Swansea 4 Reading 2 (att: 86,581). Losing semi-finalists: Cardiff and Nottm Forest. **League 1: Peterborough** 3 Huddersfield 0 (Old Trafford, att:48,410). Losing semi-finalists: Bournemouth and MK Dons. **League 2: Stevenage** 1 Torquay 0 (Old Trafford, att: 11,484. Losing semi-finalists: Accrington and Shrewsbury

2012: Championship: West Ham 2 Blackpool 1 (att: 78,523). Losing semi-finalists: Birmingham and Cardiff. **League 1: Huddersfield** 0 Sheffield Utd 0 aet, Huddersfield won 8-7 on pens (att: 52,100). Losing semi-finalists: MK Dons and Stevenage. **League 2: Crewe** 2 Cheltenham 0 (att: 24,029). Losing semi-finalists: Southend and Torquay

2013: Championship: Crystal Palace 1 Watford 0 (att: 82,025). Losing semi-finalists: Brighton and Leicester. **League 1: Yeovil** 2 Brentford 1 (att: 41,955). Losing semi-finalists: Sheffield Utd and Swindon. **League 2: Bradford** 3 Northampton 0 (att: 47,127). Losing semi-finalists: Burton and Cheltenham

2014: Championship: QPR 1 Derby 0 (att: 87,348). Losing semi-finalists: Brighton and Wigan. **League 1: Rotherham** 2 Leyton Orient 2 aet, Rotherham won 4-3 on pens (att: 43,401). Losing semi-finalists: Peterborough and Preston. **League 2: Fleetwood** 1 Burton 0 (att: 14,007). Losing semi-finalists: Southend and York

2015: Championship: Norwich 2 Middlesbrough 0 (att: 85,656). Losing semi-finalists: Brentford and Ipswich. **League 1: Preston** 4 Swindon 0 (att: 48,236). Losing semi-finalists: Chesterfield and Sheffield Utd. **League 2: Southend** 1 Wycombe 1 aet, Southend won 7-6 on pens (att: 38,252). Losing semi-finalists: Stevenage and Plymouth

2016: Championship: Hull 1 Sheffield Wed 0 (att: 70,189). Losing semi-finalists: Brighton and Derby. **League 1: Barnsley** 3 Millwall 1 (att 51,277). Losing semi-finalists: Bradford and Walsall. **League 2: AFC Wimbledon** 2 Plymouth 0 (att 57,956). Losing semi-finalists: Accrington and Portsmouth)

2017: Championship: Huddersfield 0 Reading 0 aet, Huddersfield won 4-3 on pens (att 76,682). Losing semi-finalists: Fulham and Sheffield Wed. **League 1: Millwall** 1 Bradford 0 (att 53,320. Losing semi-finals: Fleetwood and Scunthorpe. **League 2: Blackpool** 2 Exeter 1 (att 23,380). Losing semi-finalists: Carlisle and Luton

2018: Championship: Fulham 1 Aston Villa 0 (att 85,243). Losing semi-finalists: Derby and Middlesbrough. **League 1: Rotherham** 2 Shrewsbury 1 (att 26,218). Losing semi-finalists: Charlton and Scunthorpe. **League 2: Coventry** 3 Exeter 1. Losing semi-finalists: Lincoln and Notts Co

2019: Championship: Aston Villa 2 Derby 1 (85,826). Losing semi-finalists: Leeds and WBA. **League 1: Charlton** 2 Sunderland 1 (76,155). Losing semi-finalists: Doncaster and Portsmouth. **League 2: Tranmere** 1 Newport 0, aet (25,217 Losing semi-finalists: Forest Green and Mansfield

HISTORY OF THE PLAY-OFFS

Play-off matches were introduced by the Football League to decide final promotion and relegation issues at the end of season 1986-87. A similar series styled 'Test Matches' had operated between Divisions One and Two for six seasons from 1893-98, and was abolished when both divisions were increased from 16 to 18 clubs.

Eighty-eight years later, the play-offs were back in vogue. In the first three seasons (1987-88-89), the Finals were played home-and-away, and since they were made one-off matches in 1990, they have featured regularly in Wembley's spring calendar, until the old stadium closed its doors and the action switched to the Millennium Stadium in Cardiff in 2001.

Through the years, these have been the ups and downs of the play-offs:

1987: Initially, the 12 clubs involved comprised the one that finished directly above those relegated in Divisions One, Two and Three and the three who followed the sides automatically promoted in each section. Two of the home-and-away Finals went to neutral-ground replays, in which **Charlton** clung to First Division status by denying Leeds promotion while **Swindon** beat Gillingham to complete their climb from Fourth Division to Second in successive seasons, via the play-offs, Sunderland fell into the Third and Bolton into Division Four, both for the first time. **Aldershot** went up after finishing only sixth in Division Four; in their Final, they beat Wolves, who had finished nine points higher and missed automatic promotion by one point.

1988: Chelsea were relegated from the First Division after losing on aggregate to **Middlesbrough**, who had finished third in Division Two. So Middlesbrough, managed by Bruce Rioch, completed the rise from Third Division to First in successive seasons, only two years after their very existence had been threatened by the bailiffs. Also promoted via the play-offs: **Walsall** from Division Three and **Swansea** from the Fourth. Relegated, besides Chelsea: Sheffield Utd (to Division Three) and Rotherham (to Division Four).

1989: After two seasons of promotion-relegation play-offs, the system was changed to involve the four clubs who had just missed automatic promotion. That format has remained. Steve Coppell's **Crystal Palace**, third in Division Two, returned to the top flight after eight years, beating Blackburn 4-3 on aggregate after extra time. Similarly, **Port Vale** confirmed third place in Division Three with promotion via the play-offs. For **Leyton Orient**, promotion seemed out of the question in Division Four when they stood 15th on March 1. But eight wins and a draw in the last nine home games swept them to sixth in the final table, and two more home victories in the play-offs completed their season in triumph.

1990: The play-off Finals now moved to Wembley over three days of the Spring Holiday week-end. On successive afternoons, **Cambridge Utd** won promotion from Division Four and **Notts Co** from the Third. Then, on Bank Holiday Monday, the biggest crowd for years at a Football League fixture (72,873) saw Ossie Ardiles' **Swindon** beat Sunderland 1-0 to reach the First Division for the first time. A few weeks later, however, Wembley losers **Sunderland** were promoted instead, by default; Swindon were found guilty of "financial irregularities" and stayed in Division Two.

1991: Again, the season's biggest League crowd (59,940) gathered at Wembley for the First Division Final in which **Notts Co** (having missed promotion by one point) still fulfilled their ambition, beating Brighton 3-1. In successive years, County had climbed from Third Division to First via the play-offs – the first club to achieve double promotion by this route. Bolton were denied automatic promotion in Division Three on goal difference, and lost at Wembley to an extra-time goal by **Tranmere**. The Fourth Division Final made history, with Blackpool beaten 5-4 on penalties by **Torquay** – first instance of promotion being decided by a shoot-out. In the table, Blackpool had finished seven points ahead of Torquay.

1992: Wembley that Spring Bank Holiday was the turning point in the history of **Blackburn.** Bolstered by Kenny Dalglish's return to management and owner Jack Walker's millions, they beat Leicester 1-0 by Mike Newell's 45th-minute penalty to achieve their objective – a place in the new Premier League. Newell, who also missed a second-half penalty, had recovered from a broken leg just in time for the play-offs. In the Fourth Division Final **Blackpool** (denied by penalties the previous year) this time won a shoot-out 4-3 against Scunthorpe., who were unlucky in the play-offs for the fourth time in five years. **Peterborough** climbed out of the Third Division for the first time, beating Stockport County 2-1 at Wembley.

1993: The crowd of 73,802 at Wembley to see **Swindon** beat Leicester 4-3 in the First Division Final was 11,000 bigger than that for the FA Cup Final replay between Arsenal and Sheffield Wed Leicester rallied from three down to 3-3 before Paul Bodin's late penalty wiped away **Swindon**'s bitter memories of three years earlier, when they were denied promotion after winning at Wembley. In the Third Division Final, **York** beat Crewe 5-3 in a shoot-out after a 1-1 draw, and in the Second Division decider, **WBA** beat Port Vale 3-0. That was tough on Vale, who finished third in the table with 89 points – the highest total never to earn promotion in any division. They had beaten Albion twice in the League, too.

1994: Wembley's record turn-out of 158,586 spectators at the three Finals started with a crowd of 40,109 to see Martin O'Neill's **Wycombe** beat Preston 4-2. They thus climbed from Conference to Second Division with successive promotions. **Burnley's** 2-1 victory in the Second Division Final was marred by the sending-off of two Stockport players, and in the First Division decider **Leicester** came from behind to beat Derby Co and end the worst Wembley record of any club. They had lost on all six previous appearances there – four times in the FA Cup Final and in the play-offs of 1992 and 1993.

1995: Two months after losing the Coca-Cola Cup Final to Liverpool, Bruce Rioch's **Bolton** were back at Wembley for the First Division play-off Final. From two goals down to Reading in front of a crowd of 64,107, they returned to the top company after 15 years, winning 4-3 with two extra-time goals. **Huddersfield** ended the first season at their new £15m. home with promotion to the First Division via a 2-1 victory against Bristol Rov – manager Neil Warnock's third play-off success (after two with Notts Co). Of the three clubs who missed automatic promotion by one place, only **Chesterfield** achieved it in the play-offs, comfortably beating Bury 2-0.

1996: Under new manager Martin O'Neill (a Wembley play-off winner with Wycombe in 1994), **Leicester** returned to the Premiership a year after leaving it. They had finished fifth in the table, but in the Final came from behind to beat third-placed Crystal Palace by Steve Claridge's shot in the last seconds of extra time. In the Second Division **Bradford City** came sixth, nine points behind Blackpool (3rd), but beat them (from two down in the semi-final first leg) and then clinched promotion by 2-0 v Notts County at Wembley. It was City's greatest day since they won the Cup in 1911. **Plymouth Argyle** beat Darlington in the Third Division Final to earn promotion a year after being relegated. It was manager Neil Warnock's fourth play-off triumph in seven seasons after two with Notts County (1990 and 1991) and a third with Huddersfield in 1995.

1997: High drama at Wembley as **Crystal Palace** left it late against Sheffield Utd in the First Division play-off final. The match was scoreless until the last 10 seconds when David Hopkin lobbed Blades' keeper Simon Tracey from 25 yards to send the Eagles back to the Premiership after two seasons of Nationwide action. In the Second Division play-off final, **Crewe** beat Brentford 1-0 courtesy of a Shaun Smith goal. **Northampton** celebrated their first Wembley appearance with a 1-0 victory over Swansea thanks to John Frain's injury-time free-kick in the Third Division play-off final.

1998: In one of the finest games ever seen at Wembley, **Charlton** eventually triumphed 7-6 on penalties over Sunderland. For Charlton, Wearside-born Clive Mendonca scored a hat-trick and Richard Rufus his first career goal in a match that lurched between joy and despair for both sides as it ended 4-4. Sunderland defender Michael Gray's superb performance ill deserved to end with his weakly struck spot kick being saved by Sasa Ilic. In the Third Division, the penalty spot also had a role to play, as **Colchester's** David Gregory scored the only goal to defeat Torquay, while in the Second Division a Kevin Donovan goal gave **Grimsby** victory over Northampton.

1999: Elton John, watching via a personal satellite link in Seattle, saw his **Watford** side overcome Bolton 2-0 to reach the Premiership. Against technically superior opponents, Watford prevailed with application and teamwork. They also gave Bolton a lesson in finishing through match-winners by Nick Wright and Allan Smart. **Manchester City** staged a remarkable comeback to win the Second Division Final after trailing to goals by Carl Asaba and Robert Taylor for Gillingham. Kevin Horlock and Paul Dickov scored in stoppage time and City went on to win on penalties. A goal by Spaniard Alex Calvo-Garcia earned **Scunthorpe** a 1-0 success against Leyton Orient in the Third Division Final.

2000: After three successive play-off failures, **Ipswich** finally secured a place in the Premiership. They overcame the injury loss of leading scorer David Johnson to beat Barnsley 4-2 with goals by 36-year-old Tony Mowbray, Marcus Stewart and substitutes Richard Naylor and Martijn Reuser. With six minutes left of extra-time in the Second Division Final, **Gillingham** trailed Wigan 2-1. But headers by 38-year-old player-coach Steve Butler and fellow substitute Andy Thomson gave them a 3-2 victory. Andy Clarke, approaching his 33rd birthday, scored the only goal of the Third Division decider for **Peterborough** against Darlington.

2001: Bolton, unsuccessful play-off contenders in the two previous seasons, made no mistake at the third attempt. They flourished in the new surroundings of the Millennium Stadium to beat Preston 3-0 with goals by Gareth Farrelly, Michael Ricketts – his 24th of the season – and Ricardo Gardner to reach the Premiership. **Walsall**, relegated 12 months earlier, scored twice in a three-minute spell of extra time to win 3-2 against Reading in the Second Division Final, while **Blackpool** capped a marked improvement in the second half of the season by overcoming Leyton Orient 4-2 in the Third Division Final.

2002: Holding their nerve to win a penalty shoot-out 4-2, **Birmingham** wiped away the memory of three successive defeats in the semi-finals of the play-offs to return to the top division after an absence of 16 years. Substitute Darren Carter completed a fairy-tale first season as a professional by scoring the fourth spot-kick against Norwich. **Stoke** became the first successful team to come from the south dressing room in 12 finals since football was adopted by the home of Welsh rugby, beating Brentford 2-0 in the Second Division Final with Deon Burton's strike and a Ben Burgess own goal. Julian Alsop's 26th goal of the season helped **Cheltenham** defeat League newcomers Rushden & Diamonds 3-1 in the Third Division decider.

2003: Wolves benefactor Sir Jack Hayward finally saw his £60m investment pay dividends when the club he first supported as a boy returned to the top flight after an absence of 19 years by beating Sheffield Utd 3-0. It was also a moment to savour for manager Dave Jones, who was forced to leave his previous club Southampton because of child abuse allegations, which were later found to be groundless. **Cardiff**, away from the game's second tier for 18 years, returned with an extra-time winner from substitute Andy Campbell against QPR after a goalless 90 minutes in the Division Two Final. **Bournemouth**, relegated 12 months earlier, became the first team to score five in the end-of-season deciders, beating Lincoln 5-2 in the Division Three Final.

2004: Three tight, tense Finals produced only two goals, the lowest number since the Play-offs were introduced. One of them, scored by Neil Shipperley, gave **Crystal Palace** victory over West Ham, the much-travelled striker tapping in a rebound after Stephen Bywater parried Andy Johnson's shot. It completed a remarkable transformation for Crystal Palace, who were 19th in the table when Iain Dowie left Oldham to become their manager. **Brighton** made an immediate return to Division One in a poor game against Bristol City which looked set for extra-time until Leon Knight netted his 27th goal of the campaign from the penalty spot after 84 minutes. **Huddersfield** also went back up at the first attempt, winning the Division Three Final in a penalty shoot-out after a goalless 120 minutes against Mansfield.

2005: Goals were few and far between for Bobby Zamora during **West Ham**'s Championship season – but what a difference in the Play-offs. The former Brighton and Tottenham striker scored three times in the 4-2 aggregate win over Ipswich in the semi-finals and was on the mark again with the only goal against Preston at the Millennium Stadium. **Sheffield Wed** were eight minute away from defeat against Hartlepool in the League One decider when Steven MacLean made it 2-2 from the penalty spot and they went on to win 4-2 in extra-time. **Southend**, edged out of an automatic promotion place, won the League Two Final 2-0 against Lincoln, Freddy Eastwood scoring their first in extra-time and making the second for Duncan Jupp. **Carlisle** beat Stevenage 1-0 with a goal by Peter Murphy in the Conference Final to regain their League place 12 months after being relegated.

2006: From the moment Marlon King scored his 22nd goal of the season to set up a 3-0 win over Crystal Palace in the semi-final first leg, **Watford** had the conviction of a team going places. Sure enough, they went on to beat Leeds just as comfortably in the final. Jay DeMerit, who was playing non-league football 18 months earlier, headed his side in front. James Chambers fired in a shot that hit a post and went in off goalkeeper Neil Sullivan. Then Darius Henderson put away a penalty after King was brought down by Shaun Derry, the man whose tackle had ended Boothroyd's playing career at the age of 26. **Barnsley** beat Swansea on penalties in the League One Final, Nick Colgan making the vital save from Alan Tate, while Steve Guinan's goal earned **Cheltenham** a 1-0 win over Grimsby in the League Two Final. **Hereford** returned to the Football League after a nine-year absence with Ryan Green's extra-time winner against Halifax in the Conference Final.

2007: Record crowds, plenty of goals and a return to Wembley for the finals made for some eventful and entertaining matches. Stephen Pearson, signed from Celtic for £650,000 in the January transfer window, took **Derby** back to the Premier League after an absence of five seasons with a 61st minute winner, his first goal for the club, against accounted for West Bromwich Albion. It was third time lucky for manager Billy Davies, who had led Preston into the play-offs, without success, in the two previous seasons. **Blackpool** claimed a place in the game's second tier for the first time for 30 years by beating Yeovil 2-0 – their tenth successive victory in a remarkable end-of-season run. Richard Walker took his tally for the season to 23 with two goals for **Bristol Rov**, who beat Shrewsbury 3-1 in the League Two Final. Sammy McIlroy, who led Macclesfield into the league in 1997, saw his Morecambe side fall behind in the Conference Final against Exeter, but they recovered to win 2-1.

2008: Wembley has produced some unlikely heroes down the years, but rarely one to match 39-year-old Dean Windass. The **Hull** striker took his home-town club into the top-flight for the first time with the only goal of the Championship Final against Bristol City – and it was a goal fit to grace any game. In front of a record crowd for the final of 86,703, Fraizer Campbell, his 20-year-old partner up front, picked out Windass on the edge of the penalty box and a sweetly-struck volley flew into the net. **Doncaster**, who like Hull faced an uncertain future a few years earlier, beat Leeds 1-0 in the League One Final with a header by James Hayer from Brian Stock's corner. Jim Gannon had lost four Wembley finals with **Stockport** as a player, but his first as manager brought a 3-2 win against Rochdale in the League Two Final with goals by Anthony Pilkington and Liam Dickinson and a Nathan Stanton own goal. Exeter's 1-0 win over Cambridge United in the Conference Final took them back into the Football League after an absence of five years.

2009: Delight for Burnley, back in the big time after 33 years thanks to a fine goal from 20 yards by Wade Elliott, and for their town which became the smallest to host Premier League football. Despair for Sheffield Utd, whose bid to regain a top-flight place ended with two players, Jamie Ward and Lee Hendrie, sent off by referee Mike Dean. Martyn Woolford capped a man-of-the match performance with an 85th minute winner for Scunthorpe, who beat Millwall 3-2 to make an immediate return to the Championship, Matt Sparrow having scored their first two goals. Gillingham also went back up at the first attempt, beating Shrewsbury with Simeon Jackson's header seconds from the end of normal time in the League Two Final. Torquay returned to the Football League after a two-year absence by beating Cambridge United 2-0 in the Conference Final.

2010: Blackpool, under the eccentric yet shrewd Ian Holloway, claimed the big prize two years almost to the day after the manager was sacked from his previous job at Leicester. On a scorching afternoon, with temperatures reaching 106 degrees, they twice came back from a goal down to draw level against Cardiff through Charlie Adam and Gary Taylor-Fletcher, then scored what proved to be the winner through Brett Ormerod at the end of a pulsating first half. **Millwall**, beaten in five previous play-offs, reached the Championship with the only goal of the game against Swindon from captain Paul Robinson. **Dagenham & Redbridge** defeated Rotherham 3-2 in the League Two Final, Jon Nurse scoring the winner 20 minutes from the end. **Oxford** returned to the Football League after an absence of four years with a 3-1 over York in the Conference Final.

2011: Scott Sinclair scored a hat-trick as **Swansea** reached the top flight, just eight years after almost going out of the Football League. Two of his goals came from the penalty spot as Reading were beaten 4-2 in the Championship Final, with Stephen Dobbie netting their other goal. The day after his father's side lost to Barcelona in the Champions League Final, Darren Ferguson led **Peterborough** back to the Championship at the first attempt with goals by Tommy Rowe, Craig Mackail-Smith and Grant McCann in the final 12 minutes against Huddersfield. John Mousinho scored the only one of the League Two Final for **Stevenage**, who won a second successive promotion by beating Torquay. **AFC Wimbledon**, formed by supporters in 2002 after the former FA Cup-winning club relocated to Milton Keynes, completed their rise from the Combined Counties to the Football League by winning a penalty shoot-out against Luton after a goalless draw in the Conference Final.

2012: West Ham were third in the Championship and second best to Blackpool in the final. But they passed the post first at Wembley, thanks to an 87th minute goal from Ricardo Vaz Te which gave Sam Allardyce's side a 2-1 victory. Allardyce brought the Portuguese striker to Upton Park from Barnsley for £500,000 – a fee dwarfed by the millions his goal was worth to the club. Goalkeepers took centre stage in the League One Final, with **Huddersfield** and Sheffield United still locked in a marathon shoot-out after a goalless 120 minutes. Alex Smithies put the 21st penalty past his opposite number Steve Simonsen, who then drove over the crossbar to give

Huddersfield victory by 8-7. Nick Powell, 18, lit up the League Two Final with a spectacular volley as **Crewe** beat Cheltenham 2-0. **York** regained a Football League place after an absence of eight years by beating Luton 2-1 in the Conference decider.

2013: Veteran Kevin Phillips, a loser in three previous finals, came off the bench to fire **Crystal Palace** into the Premier League with an extra-time penalty. Wilfried Zaha was brought down by Marco Cassetti and 39-year-old Phillips showed nerves of steel to convert the spot-kick. A goalline clearance by Joel Ward then denied Fernando Forestieri as Watford sought an equaliser. **Yeovil** upset the odds by reaching the Championship for the first time. They defeated Brentford 2-1, Paddy Madden scoring his 23rd goal of the season and on-loan Dan Burn adding the second. **Bradford**, back at Wembley three months after their Capital One Cup adventure, swept aside Northampton 3-0 in the League Two Final with goals from James Hanson, Rory McArdle and Nahki Wells. **Newport** returned to the Football League after a 25-year absence by defeating Wrexham 2-0 in the Conference Final.

2014: An immediate return to the Premier League for **Queens Park Rangers** seemed unlikely when Gary O'Neil was sent off for bringing down Derby's Johnny Russell. There was still more than half-an-hour to go of a match Derby had dominated. But Rangers held on and with 90 minutes nearly up Bobby Zamora punished a mistake by captain Richard Keogh to score the only goal. **Rotherham** retrieved a 2-0 deficit against Leyton Orient with two goals by Alex Revell in the League One Final and won the eventual penalty shoot-out 4-3 for a second successive promotion. **Fleetwood** achieved their sixth promotion in ten seasons with a 1-0 victory over Burton, courtesy of a free-kick from Antoni Sarcevic in the League Two Final. Liam Hughes and Ryan Donaldson were on the mark as **Cambridge United** returned to the Football League after a nine-year absence by beating Gateshead 2-1 in the Conference Final, two months after winning the FA Trophy at Wembley

2015: **Norwich** were rewarded for a flying start with a return to the Premier League at the first attempt. Cameron Jerome put them ahead against Middlesbrough after 12 minutes of the Championship Final and Nathan Redmond made it 2-0 three minutes later, a scoreline they maintained without too many problems. Jermaine Beckford's hat-trick put **Preston** on the way to a record 4-0 victory over Swindon in the League One Final. **Southend**, who like Preston were denied automatic promotion on the final day of the regular season, beat Wycombe 7-6 on penalties after the League Two Final ended 1-1. **Bristol Rovers** were also penalty winners, by 5-3 against Grimsby in the Conference decider, so making an immediate return to the Football League.

2016: A goal worthy of winning any game took Hull back to the Premier League at the first attempt. Mohamed Diame, their French-born Senegal international midfielder, curled a 25-yard shot into the top corner after 72 minues for a 1-0 win over Sheffield Wednesday. Another spectacular goal, by Adam Hammill, helped Barnsley beat Millwall 3-1 on their return to Wembley for the League One Final after winning the Johnstone's Paint Trophy. AFC Wimbledon achieved their sixth promotion since being formed by supporters in 2002, defeating favourites Plymouth 2-0 in the League Two Final. Grimsby ended a six-year absence from the Football League with a 3-1 victory over Forest Green in the National League decider

2017: David Wagner transformed **Huddersfield** from relegation candidates into a Premier League club – with the help of German penalty-taking expertise. After a goalless Championship Play-off Final, they beat Reading 4-3 in a shoot-out clinched by Christopher Schindler'spot-kick. Steve Morison followed up his two goals in **Millwall's** League One semi-final against Scunthorpe with the only one against Bradford, in the 85th minute at Wembley. Brad Potts and Mark Cullen were on the mark to give **Blackpool** a 2-1 victory over Exeter in the League Two Final. **Forest Green** beat Tranmere 3-1 in the National League Final, on-loan Kaiyne Woolery scoring twice.

2018: **Fulham** overcame the sending-off of central defender Denis Odoi after 70 minutes for a second yellow card to reach the Premier League. They protected the lead established by a goal from captain Tom Cairney, set up by the Championship's Player of the Year, 18-year-old Ryan Sessegnon, to defeat Aston Villa 1-0. There was another captain's performance in the League One Final, Richard Wood scoring both goals in **Rotherham's** 2-1 win over Shrewsbury. **Coventry** ended years of decline by beating Exeter 3-1 in the League Two Final with goals from Jordan Willis, Jordan Shipley and Jack Grimmer. **Tranmere** had Liam Ridehalgh dismissed after 48 seconds for a two-footed challenge, but were 2-1 winners over Boreham Wood in the National League Final (Andy Cook and James Norwood).

2019: **Aston Villa** made a royal return to the Premier League after a three-year absence by defeating Derby 2-1. Prince William, a supporter of the club, joined the celebrations at Wembley after loanee Anwar El Ghazi and bargain-buy John McGinn scored the goals to complete the club's renaissance under former Brentford manager Dean Smith. **Charlton** recovered from Naby Sarr's bizarre own goal – a back-pass missed by goalkeeper Dillon Phillips – to equalise through Ben Purrington and beat Sunderland with captain Patrick Bauer's goal seconds from time. **Tranmere** made a successful return to the national stadium after winning the National League decider in 2018, scoring the only goal against Newport through Connor Jennings. **Salford**, co-owned by six former Manchester United players, defeated AFC Fylde 3-0 in the National League decider to reach the Football League for the first time.

Play-off attendances

1987	20	310,000	2004	15	388,675
1988	19	305,817	2005	15	353,330
1989	18	234,393	2006	15	340,804
1990	15	291,428	2007	15	405,278
1991	15	266,442	2008	15	382,032
1992	15	277,684	2009	15	380,329
1993	15	319,907	2010	15	370,055
1994	15	314,817	2011	15	310,998
1995	15	295,317	2012	15	332,930
1996	15	308,515	2013	15	346,062
1997	15	309,085	2014	15	307,011
1998	15	320,795	2015	15	367,374
1999	15	372,969	2016	15	393,145
2000	15	333,999	2017	15	323,727
2001	15	317,745	2018	15	373,295
2002	15	327,894	2019	15	430,025 (record)
2003	15	374,461	2020		No attendances – Covid 19

THE THINGS THEY SAY ...

'We are champions of England, Europe and the world. I know how that sounds, but it's the truth. I'm not a person who has a pictures with things, but I will make sure I have all these pictures' – **Jurgen Klopp** on the night Liverpool received the Premier League trophy.

'Getting 97 points last season and not winning it was hard to take. We had unfinished business' – **Jordan Henderson**, Liverpool captain.

'This was never about me and you, never about politics. This was a cry out for help from vulnerable parents all over the country to feed the nation's poorest children' – **Marcus Rashford**, Manchester United striker, after his campaign forced Ministers to reverse their decision not to provide free school meals over the summer.

'I woke up even earlier than usual, then I realised it was my first day. It felt like the first day at school' – **Jurgen Klopp**, Liverpool manager, on the return to training.

ENGLISH HONOURS LIST

PREMIER LEAGUE

	First	Pts	Second	Pts	Third	Pts
1992–3a	Manchester Utd	84	Aston Villa	74	Norwich	72
1993–4a	Manchester Utd	92	Blackburn	84	Newcastle	77
1994–5a	Blackburn	89	Manchester Utd	88	Nottm Forest	77
1995–6b	Manchester Utd	82	Newcastle	78	Liverpool	71
1996–7b	Manchester Utd	75	Newcastle	68	Arsenal	68
1997–8b	Arsenal	78	Manchester Utd	77	Liverpool	65
1998–9b	Manchester Utd	79	Arsenal	78	Chelsea	75
1999–00b	Manchester Utd	91	Arsenal	73	Leeds	69
2000–01b	Manchester Utd	80	Arsenal	70	Liverpool	69
2001–02b	Arsenal	87	Liverpool	80	Manchester Utd	77
2002–03b	Manchester Utd	83	Arsenal	78	Newcastle	69
2003–04b	Arsenal	90	Chelsea	79	Manchester Utd	75
2004–05b	Chelsea	95	Arsenal	83	Manchester Utd	77
2005–06b	Chelsea	91	Manchester Utd	83	Liverpool	82
2006–07b	Manchester Utd	89	Chelsea	83	Liverpool	68
2007–08b	Manchester Utd	87	Chelsea	85	Arsenal	83
2008–09b	Manchester Utd	90	Liverpool	86	Chelsea	83
2009–10b	Chelsea	86	Manchester Utd	85	Arsenal	75
2010–11b	Manchester Utd	80	Chelsea	71	Manchester City	71
2011–12b	Manchester City*	89	Manchester Ud	89	Arsenal	70
2012–13b	Manchester Utd	89	Manchester City	78	Chelsea	75
2013–14b	Manchester City	86	Liverpool	84	Chelsea	82
2014–15b	Chelsea	87	Manchester City	79	Arsenal	75
2015–16b	Leicester	81	Arsenal	71	Tottenham	70
2016–17b	Chelsea	93	Tottenham	86	Manchester City	78
2017–18b	Manchester City	100	Manchester Utd	81	Tottenham	77
2018–19b	Manchester City	98	Liverpool	97	Chelsea	72
2019–20b	Liverpool	99	Manchester City	81	Manchester Utd	66

* won on goal difference. Maximum points: a, 126; b, 114

FOOTBALL LEAGUE

FIRST DIVISION

1992–3	Newcastle	96	West Ham	88	††Portsmouth	88
1993–4	Crystal Palace	90	Nottm Forest	83	††Millwall	74
1994–5	Middlesbrough	82	††Reading	79	Bolton	77
1995–6	Sunderland	83	Derby	79	††Crystal Palace	75
1996–7	Bolton	98	Barnsley	80	††Wolves	76
1997–8	Nottm Forest	94	Middlesbrough	91	††Sunderland	90
1998–9	Sunderland	105	Bradford City	87	††Ipswich	86
1999–00	Charlton	91	Manchester City	89	Ipswich	87
2000–01	Fulham	101	Blackburn	91	Bolton	87
2001–02	Manchester City	99	WBA	89	††Wolves	86
2002–03	Portsmouth	98	Leicester	92	††Sheffield Utd	80
2003–04	Norwich	94	WBA	86	††Sunderland	79

CHAMPIONSHIP

2004–05	Sunderland	94	Wigan	87	††Ipswich	85
2005–06	Reading	106	Sheffield Utd	90	Watford	81
2006–07	Sunderland	88	Birmingham	86	Derby	84
2007–08	WBA	81	Stoke	79	Hull	75
2008–09	Wolves	90	Birmingham	83	††Sheffield Utd	80

2009–10	Newcastle	102	WBA	91	††Nottm Forest	79
2010–11	QPR	88	Norwich	84	Swansea	80
2011–12	Reading	89	Southampton	88	West Ham	86
2012–13	Cardiff	87	Hull	79	††Watford	77
2013–14	Leicester	102	Burnley	93	††Derby	85
2014–15	Bournemouth	90	Watford	89	Norwich	86
2015–16	Burnley	93	Middlesbrough	89	††Brighton	89
2016–17	Newcastle	94	Brighton	93	††Reading	85
2017–18	Wolves	99	Cardiff	90	Fulham	88
2018–19	Norwich	94	Sheffield Utd	89	††Leeds	83
2019–20	Leeds	93	WBA	83	††Brentford	81

Maximum points: 138 ††Not promoted after play–offs

SECOND DIVISION

1992–3	Stoke	93	Bolton	90	††Port Vale	89
1993–4	Reading	89	Port Vale	88	††Plymouth Argyle	85
1994–5	Birmingham	89	††Brentford	85	††Crewe	83
1995–6	Swindon	92	Oxford Utd	83	††Blackpool	82
1996–7	Bury	84	Stockport	82	††Luton	78
1997–8	Watford	88	Bristol City	85	Grimsby	72
1998–9	Fulham	101	Walsall	87	Manchester City	82
1999–00	Preston	95	Burnley	88	Gillingham	85
2000–01	Millwall	93	Rotherham	91	††Reading	86
2001–02	Brighton	90	Reading	84	††Brentford	83
2002–03	Wigan	100	Crewe	86	††Bristol City	83
2003–04	Plymouth Argyle	90	QPR	83	††Bristol City	82

LEAGUE ONE

2004–05	Luton	98	Hull	86	††Tranmere	79
2005–06	Southend	82	Colchester	79	††Brentford	76
2006–07	Scunthorpe	91	Bristol City	85	Blackpool	83
2007–08	Swansea	92	Nottm Forest	82	Doncaster	80
2008–09	Leicester	96	Peterborough	89	††MK Dons	87
2009–10	Norwich	95	Leeds	86	Millwall	85
2010–11	Brighton	95	Southampton	92	††Huddersfield	87
2011–12	Charlton	101	Sheffield Wed	93	††Sheffield Utd	90
2012–13	Doncaster	84	Bournemouth	83	††Brentford	79
2013–14	Wolves	103	Brentford	94	††Leyton Orient	86
2014–15	Bristol City	99	MK Dons	91	Preston	89
2015–16	Wigan	87	Burton	85	††Walsall	84
2016–17	Sheffield Utd	100	Bolton	86	††Scunthorpe	82
2017–18	Wigan	98	Blackburn	96	††Shrewsbury	87
2018–19	Luton	94	Barnsley	91	Charlton	88
2019–20a	Coventry	67	Rotherham	62	Wycombe	59

a season abandoned – Covid-19; points-per-game decided final positions
Maximum points: 138 †† Not promoted after play–offs

THIRD DIVISION

1992–3a	Cardiff	83	Wrexham	80	Barnet	79
1993–4a	Shrewsbury	79	Chester	74	Crewe	73
1994–5a	Carlisle	91	Walsall	83	Chesterfield	81
1995–6b	Preston	86	Gillingham	83	Bury	79
1996–7b	Wigan	87	Fulham	87	Carlisle	84
1997–8b	Notts Co	99	Macclesfield	82	Lincoln	75
1998–9b	Brentford	85	Cambridge Utd	81	Cardiff	80
1999–00b	Swansea	85	Rotherham	84	Northampton	82
2000–01b	Brighton	92	Cardiff	82	*Chesterfield	80
2001–02b	Plymouth Argyle	102	Luton	97	Mansfield	79

2002–03b	Rushden & D	87	Hartlepool Utd	85	Wrexham	84
2003–04b	Doncaster	92	Hull	88	Torquay	81

* Deducted 9 points for financial irregularities

LEAGUE TWO

2004–05b	Yeovil	83	Scunthorpe	80	Swansea	80
2005–06b	Carlisle	86	Northampton	83	Leyton Orient	81
2006–07b	Walsall	89	Hartlepool	88	Swindon	85
2007–08b	MK Dons	97	Peterborough	92	Hereford	88
2008–09b	Brentford	85	Exeter	79	Wycombe	78
2009–10b	Notts Co	93	Bournemouth	83	Rochdale	82
2010–11b	Chesterfield	86	Bury	81	Wycombe	80
2011–12b	Swindon	93	Shrewsbury	88	Crawley	84
2012–13b	Gillingham	83	Rotherham	79	Port Vale	78
2013–14b	Chesterfield	84	Scunthorpe	81	Rochdale	81
2014–15b	Burton	94	Shrewsbury	89	Bury	85
2015–16b	Northampton	99	Oxford	86	Bristol Rov	85
2016–17b	Portsmouth	87	Plymouth	87	Doncaster	85
2017–18b	Accrington	93	Luton	88	Wycombe	84
2018–19b	Lincoln	85	Bury	79	MK Dons	79
2019–20c	Swindon	69	Crewe	69	Plymouth	68

 c season abandoned – Covid 19; points-per-game decided final positions
Maximum points: a, 126; b, 138

FOOTBALL LEAGUE 1888–1992

1888–89a	Preston	40	Aston Villa	29	Wolves	28
1889–90a	Preston	33	Everton	31	Blackburn	27
1890–1a	Everton	29	Preston	27	Notts Co	26
1891–2b	Sunderland	42	Preston	37	Bolton	36

OLD FIRST DIVISION

1892–3c	Sunderland	48	Preston	37	Everton	36
1893–4c	Aston Villa	44	Sunderland	38	Derby	36
1894–5c	Sunderland	47	Everton	42	Aston Villa	39
1895–6c	Aston Villa	45	Derby	41	Everton	39
1896–7c	Aston Villa	47	Sheffield Utd	36	Derby	36
1897–8c	Sheffield Utd	42	Sunderland	39	Wolves	35
1898–9d	Aston Villa	45	Liverpool	43	Burnley	39
1899–1900d	Aston Villa	50	Sheffield Utd	48	Sunderland	41
1900–1d	Liverpool	45	Sunderland	43	Notts Co	40
1901–2d	Sunderland	44	Everton	41	Newcastle	37
1902–3d	The Wednesday	42	Aston Villa	41	Sunderland	41
1903–4d	The Wednesday	47	Manchester City	44	Everton	43
1904–5d	Newcastle	48	Everton	47	Manchester City	46
1905–6e	Liverpool	51	Preston	47	The Wednesday	44
1906–7e	Newcastle	51	Bristol City	48	Everton	45
1907–8e	Manchester Utd	52	Aston Villa	43	Manchester City	43
1908–9e	Newcastle	53	Everton	46	Sunderland	44
1909–10e	Aston Villa	53	Liverpool	48	Blackburn	45
1910–11e	Manchester Utd	52	Aston Villa	51	Sunderland	45
1911–12e	Blackburn	49	Everton	46	Newcastle	44
1912–13e	Sunderland	54	Aston Villa	50	Sheffield Wed	49
1913–14e	Blackburn	51	Aston Villa	44	Middlesbrough	43
1914–15e	Everton	46	Oldham	45	Blackburn	43
1919–20f	WBA	60	Burnley	51	Chelsea	49
1920–1f	Burnley	59	Manchester City	54	Bolton	52

Season	1st	Pts	2nd	Pts	3rd	Pts
1921–2f	Liverpool	57	Tottenham	51	Burnley	49
1922–3f	Liverpool	60	Sunderland	54	Huddersfield	53
1923–4f	*Huddersfield	57	Cardiff	57	Sunderland	53
1924–5f	Huddersfield	58	WBA	56	Bolton	55
1925–6f	Huddersfield	57	Arsenal	52	Sunderland	48
1926–7f	Newcastle	56	Huddersfield	51	Sunderland	49
1927–8f	Everton	53	Huddersfield	51	Leicester	48
1928–9f	Sheffield Wed	52	Leicester	51	Aston Villa	50
1929–30f	Sheffield Wed	60	Derby	50	Manchester City	47
1930–1f	Arsenal	66	Aston Villa	59	Sheffield Wed	52
1931–2f	Everton	56	Arsenal	54	Sheffield Wed	50
1932–3f	Arsenal	58	Aston Villa	54	Sheffield Wed	51
1933–4f	Arsenal	59	Huddersfield	56	Tottenham	49
1934–5f	Arsenal	58	Sunderland	54	Sheffield Wed	49
1935–6f	Sunderland	56	Derby	48	Huddersfield	48
1936–7f	Manchester City	57	Charlton	54	Arsenal	52
1937–8f	Arsenal	52	Wolves	51	Preston	49
1938–9f	Everton	59	Wolves	55	Charlton	50
1946–7f	Liverpool	57	Manchester Utd	56	Wolves	56
1947–8f	Arsenal	59	Manchester Utd	52	Burnley	52
1948–9f	Portsmouth	58	Manchester Utd	53	Derby	53
1949–50f	*Portsmouth	53	Wolves	53	Sunderland	52
1950–1f	Tottenham	60	Manchester Utd	56	Blackpool	50
1951–2f	Manchester Utd	57	Tottenham	53	Arsenal	53
1952–3f	*Arsenal	54	Preston	54	Wolves	51
1953–4f	Wolves	57	WBA	53	Huddersfield	51
1954–5f	Chelsea	52	Wolves	48	Portsmouth	48
1955–6f	Manchester Utd	60	Blackpool	49	Wolves	49
1956–7f	Manchester Utd	64	Tottenham	56	Preston	56
1957–8f	Wolves	64	Preston	59	Tottenham	51
1958–9f	Wolves	61	Manchester Utd	55	Arsenal	50
1959–60f	Burnley	55	Wolves	54	Tottenham	53
1960–1f	Tottenham	66	Sheffield Wed	58	Wolves	57
1961–2f	Ipswich	56	Burnley	53	Tottenham	52
1962–3f	Everton	61	Tottenham	55	Burnley	54
1963–4f	Liverpool	57	Manchester Utd	53	Everton	52
1964–5f	*Manchester Utd	61	Leeds	61	Chelsea	56
1965–6f	Liverpool	61	Leeds	55	Burnley	55
1966–7f	Manchester Utd	60	Nottm Forest	56	Tottenham	56
1967–8f	Manchester City	58	Manchester Utd	56	Liverpool	55
1968–9f	Leeds	67	Liverpool	61	Everton	57
1969–70f	Everton	66	Leeds	57	Chelsea	55
1970–1f	Arsenal	65	Leeds	64	Tottenham	52
1971–2f	Derby	58	Leeds	57	Liverpool	57
1972–3f	Liverpool	60	Arsenal	57	Leeds	53
1973–4f	Leeds	62	Liverpool	57	Derby	48
1974–5f	Derby	53	Liverpool	51	Ipswich	51
1975–6f	Liverpool	60	QPR	59	Manchester Utd	56
1976–7f	Liverpool	57	Manchester City	56	Ipswich	52
1977–8f	Nottm Forest	64	Liverpool	57	Everton	55
1978–9f	Liverpool	68	Nottm Forest	60	WBA	59
1979–80f	Liverpool	60	Manchester Utd	58	Ipswich	53
1980–1f	Aston Villa	60	Ipswich	56	Arsenal	53
1981–2g	Liverpool	87	Ipswich	83	Manchester Utd	78

1982–3g	Liverpool	82	Watford	71	Manchester Utd	70
1983–4g	Liverpool	80	Southampton	77	Nottm Forest	74
1984–5g	Everton	90	Liverpool	77	Tottenham	77
1985–6g	Liverpool	88	Everton	86	West Ham	84
1986–7g	Everton	86	Liverpool	77	Tottenham	71
1987–8h	Liverpool	90	Manchester Utd	81	Nottm Forest	73
1988–9j	††Arsenal	76	Liverpool	76	Nottm Forest	64
1989–90j	Liverpool	79	Aston Villa	70	Tottenham	63
1990–1j	Arsenal	83	Liverpool	76	Crystal Palace	69
1991–2g	Leeds	82	Manchester Utd	78	Sheffield Wed	75

Maximum points: *a*, 44; *b*, 52; *c*, 60; *d*, 68; *e*, 76; *f*, 84; *g*, 126; *h*, 120; *j*, 114

*Won on goal average †Won on goal diff ††Won on goals scored No comp 1915–19 –1939–46

OLD SECOND DIVISION 1892–1992

1892–3a	Small Heath	36	Sheffield Utd	35	Darwen	30
1893–4b	Liverpool	50	Small Heath	42	Notts Co	39
1894–5c	Bury	48	Notts Co	39	Newton Heath	38
1895–6c	*Liverpool	46	Manchester City	46	Grimsby	42
1896–7c	Notts Co	42	Newton Heath	39	Grimsby	38
1897–8c	Burnley	48	Newcastle	45	Manchester City	39
1898–9d	Manchester City	52	Glossop	46	Leicester Fosse	45
1899–1900d	The Wednesday	54	Bolton	52	Small Heath	46
1900–1d	Grimsby	49	Small Heath	48	Burnley	44
1901–2d	WBA	55	Middlesbrough	51	Preston	42
1902–3d	Manchester City	54	Small Heath	51	Woolwich Arsenal	48
1903–4d	Preston	50	Woolwich Arsenal	49	Manchester Utd	48
1904–5d	Liverpool	58	Bolton	56	Manchester Utd	53
1905–6e	Bristol City	66	Manchester Utd	62	Chelsea	53
1906–7e	Nottm Forest	60	Chelsea	57	Leicester Fosse	48
1907–8e	Bradford City	54	Leicester Fosse	52	Oldham	50
1908–9e	Bolton	52	Tottenham	51	WBA	51
1909–10e	Manchester City	54	Oldham	53	Hull	53
1910–11e	WBA	53	Bolton	51	Chelsea	49
1911–12e	*Derby	54	Chelsea	54	Burnley	52
1912–13e	Preston	53	Burnley	50	Birmingham	46
1913–14e	Notts Co	53	Bradford PA	49	Woolwich Arsenal	49
1914–15e	Derby	53	Preston	50	Barnsley	47
1919–20f	Tottenham	70	Huddersfield	64	Birmingham	56
1920–1f	*Birmingham	58	Cardiff	58	Bristol City	51
1921–2f	Nottm Forest	56	Stoke	52	Barnsley	52
1922–3f	Notts Co	53	West Ham	51	Leicester	51
1923–4f	Leeds	54	Bury	51	Derby	51
1924–5f	Leicester	59	Manchester Utd	57	Derby	55
1925–6f	Sheffield Wed	60	Derby	57	Chelsea	52
1926–7f	Middlesbrough	62	Portsmouth	54	Manchester City	54
1927–8f	Manchester City	59	Leeds	57	Chelsea	54
1928–9f	Middlesbrough	55	Grimsby	53	Bradford City	48
1929–30f	Blackpool	58	Chelsea	55	Oldham	53
1930–1f	Everton	61	WBA	54	Tottenham	51
1931–2f	Wolves	56	Leeds	54	Stoke	52
1932–3f	Stoke	56	Tottenham	55	Fulham	50
1933–4f	Grimsby	59	Preston	52	Bolton	51
1934–5f	Brentford	61	Bolton	56	West Ham	56
1935–6f	Manchester Utd	56	Charlton	55	Sheffield Utd	52
1936–7f	Leicester	56	Blackpool	55	Bury	52

1937–8f	Aston Villa	57	Manchester Utd	53	Sheffield Utd	53
1938–9f	Blackburn	55	Sheffield Utd	54	Sheffield Wed	53
1946–7f	Manchester City	62	Burnley	58	Birmingham	55
1947–8f	Birmingham	59	Newcastle	56	Southampton	52
1948–9f	Fulham	57	WBA	56	Southampton	55
1949–50f	Tottenham	61	Sheffield Wed	52	Sheffield Utd	52
1950–1f	Preston	57	Manchester City	52	Cardiff	50
1951–2f	Sheffield Wed	53	Cardiff	51	Birmingham	51
1952–3f	Sheffield Utd	60	Huddersfield	58	Luton	52
1953–4f	*Leicester	56	Everton	56	Blackburn	55
1954–5f	*Birmingham	54	Luton	54	Rotherham	54
1955–6f	Sheffield Wed	55	Leeds	52	Liverpool	48
1956–7f	Leicester	61	Nottm Forest	54	Liverpool	53
1957–8f	West Ham	57	Blackburn	56	Charlton	55
1958–9f	Sheffield Wed	62	Fulham	60	Sheffield Utd	53
1959–60f	Aston Villa	59	Cardiff	58	Liverpool	50
1960–1f	Ipswich	59	Sheffield Utd	58	Liverpool	52
1961–2f	Liverpool	62	Leyton Orient	54	Sunderland	53
1962–3f	Stoke	53	Chelsea	52	Sunderland	52
1963–4f	Leeds	63	Sunderland	61	Preston	56
1964–5f	Newcastle	57	Northampton	56	Bolton	50
1965–6f	Manchester City	59	Southampton	54	Coventry	53
1966–7f	Coventry	59	Wolves	58	Carlisle	52
1967–8f	Ipswich	59	QPR	58	Blackpool	58
1968–9f	Derby	63	Crystal Palace	56	Charlton	50
1969–70f	Huddersfield	60	Blackpool	53	Leicester	51
1970–1f	Leicester	59	Sheffield Utd	56	Cardiff	53
1971–2f	Norwich	57	Birmingham	56	Millwall	55
1972–3f	Burnley	62	QPR	61	Aston Villa	50
1973–4f	Middlesbrough	65	Luton	50	Carlisle	49
1974–5f	Manchester Utd	61	Aston Villa	58	Norwich	53
1975–6f	Sunderland	56	Bristol City	53	WBA	53
1976–7f	Wolves	57	Chelsea	55	Nottm Forest	52
1977–8f	Bolton	58	Southampton	57	Tottenham	56
1978–9f	Crystal Palace	57	Brighton	56	Stoke	56
1979–80f	Leicester	55	Sunderland	54	Birmingham	53
1980–1f	West Ham	66	Notts Co	53	Swansea	50
1981–2g	Luton	88	Watford	80	Norwich	71
1982–3g	QPR	85	Wolves	75	Leicester	70
1983–4g	†Chelsea	88	Sheffield Wed	88	Newcastle	80
1984–5g	Oxford Utd	84	Birmingham	82	Manchester City	74
1985–6g	Norwich	84	Charlton	77	Wimbledon	76
1986–7g	Derby	84	Portsmouth	78	††Oldham	75
1987–8h	Millwall	82	Aston Villa	78	Middlesbrough	78
1988–9j	Chelsea	99	Manchester City	82	Crystal Palace	81
1989–90j	†Leeds	85	Sheffield Utd	85	†† Newcastle	80
1990–1j	Oldham	88	West Ham	87	Sheffield Wed	82
1991–2j	Ipswich	84	Middlesbrough	80	†† Derby	78

Maximum points: a, 44; b, 56; c, 60; d, 68; e, 76; f, 84; g, 126; h, 132; j, 138 * Won on goal average † Won on goal difference †† Not promoted after play–offs

THIRD DIVISION 1958–92

1958–9	Plymouth Argyle	62	Hull	61	Brentford	57
1959–60	Southampton	61	Norwich	59	Shrewsbury	52
1960–1	Bury	68	Walsall	62	QPR	60

1961–2	Portsmouth	65	Grimsby	62	Bournemouth	59
1962–3	Northampton	62	Swindon	58	Port Vale	54
1963–4	*Coventry	60	Crystal Palace	60	Watford	58
1964–5	Carlisle	60	Bristol City	59	Mansfield	59
1965–6	Hull	69	Millwall	65	QPR	57
1966–7	QPR	67	Middlesbrough	55	Watford	54
1967–8	Oxford Utd	57	Bury	56	Shrewsbury	55
1968–9	*Watford	64	Swindon	64	Luton	61
1969–70	Orient	62	Luton	60	Bristol Rov	56
1970–1	Preston	61	Fulham	60	Halifax	56
1971–2	Aston Villa	70	Brighton	65	Bournemouth	62
1972–3	Bolton	61	Notts Co	57	Blackburn	55
1973–4	Oldham	62	Bristol Rov	61	York	61
1974–5	Blackburn	60	Plymouth Argyle	59	Charlton	55
1975–6	Hereford	63	Cardiff	57	Millwall	56
1976–7	Mansfield	64	Brighton	61	Crystal Palace	59
1977–8	Wrexham	61	Cambridge Utd	58	Preston	56
1978–9	Shrewsbury	61	Watford	60	Swansea	60
1979–80	Grimsby	62	Blackburn	59	Sheffield Wed	58
1980–1	Rotherham	61	Barnsley	59	Charlton	59
†1981–2	**Burnley	80	Carlisle	80	Fulham	78
†1982–3	Portsmouth	91	Cardiff	86	Huddersfield	82
†1983–4	Oxford Utd	95	Wimbledon	87	Sheffield Utd	83
†1984–5	Bradford City	94	Millwall	90	Hull	87
†1985–6	Reading	94	Plymouth Argyle	87	Derby	84
†1986–7	Bournemouth	97	Middlesbrough	94	Swindon	87
†1987–8	Sunderland	93	Brighton	84	Walsall	82
†1988–9	Wolves	92	Sheffield Utd	84	Port Vale	84
†1989–90	Bristol Rov	93	Bristol City	91	Notts Co	87
†1990–1	Cambridge Utd	86	Southend	85	Grimsby	83
†1991–2	Brentford	82	Birmingham	81	††Huddersfield	78

* Won on goal average ** Won on goal difference † Maximum points 138 (previously 92) †† Not promoted after play-offs

FOURTH DIVISION 1958–92

1958–9	Port Vale	64	Coventry	60	York	60	Shrewsbury	58
1959–60	Walsall	65	Notts Co	60	Torquay	60	Watford	57
1960–1	Peterborough	66	Crystal Palace	64	Northampton	60	Bradford PA	60
1961–2	Millwall	56	Colchester	55	Wrexham	53	Carlisle	52
1962–3	Brentford	62	Oldham	59	Crewe	59	Mansfield	57
1963–4	*Gillingham	60	Carlisle	60	Workington	59	Exeter	58
1964–5	Brighton	63	Millwall	62	York	62	Oxford Utd	61
1965–6	*Doncaster	59	Darlington	59	Torquay	58	Colchester	56
1966–7	Stockport	64	Southport	59	Barrow	59	Tranmere	58
1967–8	Luton	66	Barnsley	61	Hartlepool Utd	60	Crewe	58
1968–9	Doncaster	59	Halifax	57	Rochdale	56	Bradford City	56
1969–70	Chesterfield	64	Wrexham	59	Swansea	60	Port Vale	59
1970–1	Notts Co	69	Bournemouth	60	Oldham	59	York	56
1971–2	Grimsby	63	Southend	60	Brentford	59	Scunthorpe	57
1972–3	Southport	62	Hereford	58	Cambridge Utd	57	Aldershot	56
1973–4	Peterborough	65	Gillingham	62	Colchester	60	Bury	59
1974–5	Mansfield	68	Shrewsbury	62	Rotherham	58	Chester	57
1975–6	Lincoln	74	Northampton	68	Reading	60	Tranmere	58
1976–7	Cambridge Utd	65	Exeter	62	Colchester	59	Bradford City	59
1977–8	Watford	71	Southend	60	Swansea	56	Brentford	59
1978–9	Reading	65	Grimsby	61	Wimbledon	61	Barnsley	61
1979–80	Huddersfield	66	Walsall	64	Newport	61	Portsmouth	60
1980–1	Southend	67	Lincoln	65	Doncaster	56	Wimbledon	55
†1981–2	Sheffield Utd	96	Bradford City	91	Wigan	91	Bournemouth	88
†1982–3	Wimbledon	98	Hull	90	Port Vale	88	Scunthorpe	83

68

†1983–4	York	101	Doncaster	85	Reading	82	Bristol City	82
†1984–5	Chesterfield	91	Blackpool	86	Darlington	85	Bury	84
†1985–6	Swindon	102	Chester	84	Mansfield	81	Port Vale	79
†1986–7	Northampton	99	Preston	90	Southend	80	††Wolves	79
†1987–8	Wolves	90	Cardiff	85	Bolton	78	††Scunthorpe	77
†1988–9	Rotherham	82	Tranmere	80	Crewe	78	††Scunthorpe	77
†1989–90	Exeter	89	Grimsby	79	Southend	75	††Stockport	74
†1990–1	Darlington	83	Stockport	82	Hartlepool Utd	82	Peterborough	80
1991–2a	Burnley	83	Rotherham	77	Mansfield	77	Blackpool	76

* Won on goal average Maximum points: †, 138; a, 126; previously 92 †† Not promoted after play–offs

THIRD DIVISION – SOUTH 1920–58

1920–1a	Crystal Palace	59	Southampton	54	QPR	53
1921–2a	*Southampton	61	Plymouth Argyle	61	Portsmouth	53
1922–3a	Bristol City	59	Plymouth Argyle	53	Swansea	53
1923–4a	Portsmouth	59	Plymouth Argyle	55	Millwall	54
1924–5a	Swansea	57	Plymouth Argyle	56	Bristol City	53
1925–6a	Reading	57	Plymouth Argyle	56	Millwall	53
1926–7a	Bristol City	62	Plymouth Argyle	60	Millwall	56
1927–8a	Millwall	65	Northampton	55	Plymouth Argyle	53
1928–9a	*Charlton	54	Crystal Palace	54	Northampton	52
1929–30a	Plymouth Argyle	68	Brentford	61	QPR	51
1930–31a	Notts Co	59	Crystal Palace	51	Brentford	50
1931–2a	Fulham	57	Reading	55	Southend	53
1932–3a	Brentford	62	Exeter	58	Norwich	57
1933–4a	Norwich	61	Coventry	54	Reading	54
1934–5a	Charlton	61	Reading	53	Coventry	51
1935–6a	Coventry	57	Luton	56	Reading	54
1936–7a	Luton	58	Notts Co	56	Brighton	53
1937–8a	Millwall	56	Bristol City	55	QPR	53
1938–9a	Newport	55	Crystal Palace	52	Brighton	49
1946–7a	Cardiff	66	QPR	57	Bristol City	51
1947–8a	QPR	61	Bournemouth	57	Walsall	51
1948–9a	Swansea	62	Reading	55	Bournemouth	52
1949–50a	Notts Co	58	Northampton	51	Southend	51
1950–1d	Nottm Forest	70	Norwich	64	Reading	57
1951–2d	Plymouth Argyle	66	Reading	61	Norwich	61
1952–3d	Bristol Rov	64	Millwall	62	Northampton	62
1953–4d	Ipswich	64	Brighton	61	Bristol City	56
1954–5d	Bristol City	70	Leyton Orient	61	Southampton	59
1955–6d	Leyton Orient	66	Brighton	65	Ipswich	64
1956–7d	*Ipswich	59	Torquay	59	Colchester	58
1957–8d	Brighton	60	Brentford	58	Plymouth Argyle	58

THIRD DIVISION – NORTH 1921–58

1921–2b	Stockport	56	Darlington	50	Grimsby	50
1922–3b	Nelson	51	Bradford PA	47	Walsall	46
1923–4a	Wolves	63	Rochdale	62	Chesterfield	54
1924–5a	Darlington	58	Nelson	53	New Brighton	53
1925–6a	Grimsby	61	Bradford PA	60	Rochdale	59
1926–7a	Stoke	63	Rochdale	58	Bradford PA	57
1927–8a	Bradford PA	63	Lincoln	55	Stockport	54
1928–9a	Bradford City	63	Stockport	62	Wrexham	52
1929–30a	Port Vale	67	Stockport	63	Darlington	50
1930–1a	Chesterfield	58	Lincoln	57	Wrexham	54
1931–2c	*Lincoln	57	Gateshead	57	Chester	50
1932–3a	Hull	59	Wrexham	57	Stockport	54
1933–4a	Barnsley	62	Chesterfield	61	Stockport	59
1934–5a	Doncaster	57	Halifax	55	Chester	54

69

1935–6a	Chesterfield	60	Chester	55	Tranmere	54
1936–7a	Stockport	60	Lincoln	57	Chester	53
1937–8a	Tranmere	56	Doncaster	54	Hull	53
1938–9a	Barnsley	67	Doncaster	56	Bradford City	52
1946–7a	Doncaster	72	Rotherham	64	Chester	56
1947–8a	Lincoln	60	Rotherham	59	Wrexham	50
1948–9a	Hull	65	Rotherham	62	Doncaster	50
1949–50a	Doncaster	55	Gateshead	53	Rochdale	51
1950–1d	Rotherham	71	Mansfield	64	Carlisle	62
1951–2d	Lincoln	69	Grimsby	66	Stockport	59
1952–3d	Oldham	59	Port Vale	58	Wrexham	56
1953–4d	Port Vale	69	Barnsley	58	Scunthorpe	57
1954–5d	Barnsley	65	Accrington	61	Scunthorpe	58
1955–6d	Grimsby	68	Derby	63	Accrington	59
1956–7d	Derby	63	Hartlepool Utd	59	Accrington	58
1957–8d	Scunthorpe	66	Accrington	59	Bradford City	57

Maximum points: a, 84; b, 76; c, 80; d, 92 * Won on goal average

TITLE WINNERS

PREMIER LEAGUE
Manchester Utd 13
Chelsea 5
Manchester City 4
Arsenal 3
Blackburn 1
Leicester 1
Liverpool 1

CHAMPIONSHIP
Newcastle 2
Reading 2
Sunderland 2
Wolves 2
Bournemouth 1
Burnley 1
Cardiff 1
Leeds 1
Leicester 1
Norwich 1
QPR 1
WBA 1

DIV 1 (NEW)
Sunderland 2
Bolton 1
Charlton 1
Crystal Palace 1
Fulham 1
Manchester City 1
Middlesbrough 1
Newcastle 1
Norwich 1
Nottm Forest 1
Portsmouth 1

DIV 1 (ORIGINAL)
Liverpool 18
Arsenal 10
Everton 9
Aston Villa 7
Manchester Utd 7

Sunderland 6
Newcastle 4
Sheffield Wed 4
Huddersfield 3
Leeds 3
Wolves 3
Blackburn 2
Burnley 2
Derby 2
Manchester City 2
Portsmouth 2
Preston 2
Tottenham 2
Chelsea 1
Ipswich 1
Nottm Forest 1
Sheffield Utd 1
WBA 1

LEAGUE ONE
Luton 2
Wigan 2
Brighton 1
Bristol City 1
Charlton 1
Coventry 1
Doncaster 1
Leicester 1
Norwich 1
Scunthorpe 1
Sheffield Utd 1
Southend 1
Swansea 1
Wolves 1

DIV 2 (NEW)
Birmingham 1
Brighton 1
Bury 1
Chesterfield 1
Fulham 1
Lincoln 1

Millwall 1
Plymouth 1
Preston 1
Reading 1
Stoke 1
Swindon 1
Watford 1
Wigan 1
Notts Co 1

DIV 2 (ORIGINAL)
Leicester 6
Manchester City 6
Sheffield Wed 5
Birmingham 4
Derby 4
Liverpool 4
Ipswich 3
Leeds 3
Middlesbrough 3
Notts County 3
Preston 3
Aston Villa 2
Bolton 2
Burnley 2
Chelsea 2
Grimsby 2
Manchester Utd 2
Norwich 2
Nottm Forest 2
Stoke 2
Tottenham 2
WBA 2
West Ham 2
Wolves 2
Blackburn 1
Blackpool 1
Bradford City 1
Brentford 1
Bristol City 1
Bury 1

Coventry	1	QPR	1	Carlisle	1
Crystal Palace	1	Sheffield Utd	1	Gillingham	1
Everton	1	Sunderland	1	Lincoln	1
Fulham	1			MK Dons	1
Huddersfield	1	**LEAGUE TWO**		Northampton	1
Luton	1	Chesterfield	2	Notts County	1
Millwall	1	Swindon	2	Portsmouth	1
Newcastle	1	Accrington	1	Walsall	1
Oldham	1	Brentford	1	Yeovil	1
Oxford Utd	1	Burton	1		

APPLICATIONS FOR RE-ELECTION (System discontinued 1987)

14	Hartlepool	4	Norwich	2	Oldham
12	Halifax	3	Aldershot	2	QPR
11	Barrow	3	Bradford City	2	Rotherham
11	Southport	3	Crystal Palace	2	Scunthorpe
10	Crewe	3	Doncaster	2	Southend
10	Newport	3	Hereford	2	Watford
10	Rochdale	3	Merthyr	1	Blackpool
8	Darlington	3	Swindon	1	Brighton
8	Exeter	3	Torquay	1	Bristol Rov
7	Chester	3	Tranmere	1	Cambridge Utd
7	Walsall	2	Aberdare	1	Cardiff
7	Workington	2	Ashington	1	Carlisle
7	York	2	Bournemouth	1	Charlton
6	Stockport	2	Brentford	1	Mansfield
5	Accrington	2	Colchester	1	Port Vale
5	Gillingham	2	Durham	1	Preston
5	Lincoln	2	Gateshead	1	Shrewsbury
5	New Brighton	2	Grimsby	1	Swansea
4	Bradford PA	2	Millwall	1	Thames
4	Northampton	2	Nelson	1	Wrexham

RELEGATED CLUBS (TO 1992)

1892–3	In Test matches, Darwen and Sheffield Utd won promotion in place of Accrington and Notts Co
1893–4	Tests, Liverpool and Small Heath won promotion Darwen and Newton Heath relegated
1894–5	After Tests, Bury promoted, Liverpool relegated
1895–6	After Tests, Liverpool promoted, Small Heath relegated
1896–7	After Tests, Notts Co promoted, Burnley relegated
1897–8	Test system abolished after success of Burnley and Stoke, League extended Blackburn and Newcastle elected to First Division

Automatic promotion and relegation introduced

FIRST DIVISION TO SECOND DIVISION

1898–9	Bolton, Sheffield Wed
1899–00	Burnley, Glossop
1900–1	Preston, WBA
1901–2	Small Heath, Manchester City
1902–3	Grimsby, Bolton
1903–4	Liverpool, WBA
1904–5	League extended Bury and Notts Co, two bottom clubs in First Division, re-elected
1905–6	Nottm Forest, Wolves
1906–7	Derby, Stoke
1907–8	Bolton, Birmingham
1908–9	Manchester City, Leicester Fosse
1909–10	Bolton, Chelsea
1910–11	Bristol City, Nottm Forest
1911–12	Preston, Bury
1912–13	Notts Co, Woolwich Arsenal
1913–14	Preston, Derby
1914–15	Tottenham, *Chelsea
1919–20	Notts Co, Sheffield Wed
1920–1	Derby, Bradford PA
1921–2	Bradford City, Manchester Utd
1922–3	Stoke, Oldham
1923–4	Chelsea, Middlesbrough
1924–5	Preston, Nottm Forest
1925–6	Manchester City, Notts Co
1926–7	Leeds, WBA
1927–8	Tottenham, Middlesbrough
1928–9	Bury, Cardiff

1929–30	Burnley, Everton
1930–1	Leeds, Manchester Utd
1931–2	Grimsby, West Ham
1932–3	Bolton, Blackpool
1933–4	Newcastle, Sheffield Utd
1934–5	Leicester, Tottenham
1935–6	Aston Villa, Blackburn
1936–7	Man§chester Utd, Sheffield Wed
1937–8	Manchester City, WBA
1938–9	Birmingham, Leicester
1946–7	Brentford, Leeds
1947–8	Blackburn, Grimsby
1948–9	Preston, Sheffield Utd
1949–50	Manchester City, Birmingham
1950–1	Sheffield Wed, Everton
1951–2	Huddersfield, Fulham
1952–3	Stoke, Derby
1953–4	Middlesbrough, Liverpool
1954–5	Leicester, Sheffield Wed
1955–6	Huddersfield, Sheffield Utd
1956–7	Charlton, Cardiff
1957–8	Sheffield Wed, Sunderland
1958–9	Portsmouth, Aston Villa
1959–60	Luton, Leeds
1960–61	Preston, Newcastle
1961–2	Chelsea, Cardiff
1962–3	Manchester City, Leyton Orient
1963–4	Bolton, Ipswich
1964–5	Wolves, Birmingham
1965–6	Northampton, Blackburn
1966–7	Aston Villa, Blackpool
1967–8	Fulham, Sheffield Utd
1968–9	Leicester, QPR
1969–70	Sheffield Wed, Sunderland
1970–1	Burnley, Blackpool
1971–2	Nottm Forest, Huddersfield
1972–3	WBA, Crystal Palace
1973–4	Norwich, Manchester Utd, Southampton
1974–5	Chelsea, Luton, Carlisle
1975–6	Sheffield Utd, Burnley, Wolves
1976–7	Tottenham, Stoke, Sunderland
1977–8	Leicester, West Ham, Newcastle
1978–9	QPR, Birmingham, Chelsea
1979–80	Bristol City, Derby, Bolton
1980–1	Norwich, Leicester, Crystal Palace
1981–2	Leeds, Wolves, Middlesbrough
1982–3	Manchester City, Swansea, Brighton
1983–4	Birmingham, Notts Co, Wolves
1984–5	Norwich, Sunderland, Stoke
1985–6	Ipswich, Birmingham, WBA
1986–7	Leicester, Manchester City, Aston Villa
1987–8	Chelsea**, Portsmouth, Watford, Oxford Utd
1988–9	Middlesbrough, West Ham, Newcastle
1989–90	Sheffield Wed, Charlton, Millwall
1990–1	Sunderland, Derby
1991–2	Luton, Notts Co, West Ham

* Subsequently re-elected to First Division when League extended after the war
** Relegated after play-offs

SECOND DIVISION TO THIRD DIVISION

1920–1	Stockport
1921–2	Bradford City, Bristol City
1922–3	Rotherham, Wolves
1923–4	Nelson, Bristol City
1924–5	Crystal Palace, Coventry
1925–6	Stoke, Stockport
1926–7	Darlington, Bradford City
1927–8	Fulham, South Shields
1928–9	Port Vale, Clapton Orient
1929–30	Hull, Notts County
1930–1	Reading, Cardiff
1931–2	Barnsley, Bristol City
1932–3	Chesterfield, Charlton
1933–4	Millwall, Lincoln
1934–5	Oldham, Notts Co
1935–6	Port Vale, Hull
1936–7	Doncaster, Bradford City
1937–8	Barnsley, Stockport
1938–9	Norwich, Tranmere
1946–7	Swansea, Newport
1947–8	Doncaster, Millwall
1948–9	Nottm Forest, Lincoln
1949–50	Plymouth Argyle, Bradford PA
1950–1	Grimsby, Chesterfield
1951–2	Coventry, QPR
1952–3	Southampton, Barnsley
1953–4	Brentford, Oldham
1954–5	Ipswich, Derby
1955–6	Plymouth Argyle, Hull
1956–7	Port Vale, Bury
1957–8	Doncaster, Notts Co
1958–9	Barnsley, Grimsby
1959–60	Bristol City, Hull
1960–1	Lincoln, Portsmouth
1961–2	Brighton, Bristol Rov
1962–3	Walsall, Luton
1963–4	Grimsby, Scunthorpe
1964–5	Swindon, Swansea
1965–6	Middlesbrough, Leyton Orient
1966–7	Northampton, Bury
1967–8	Plymouth Argyle, Rotherham
1968–9	Fulham, Bury
1969–70	Preston, Aston Villa
1970–1	Blackburn, Bolton
1971–2	Charlton, Watford
1972–3	Huddersfield, Brighton
1973–4	Crystal Palace, Preston, Swindon
1974–5	Millwall, Cardiff, Sheffield Wed
1975–6	Portsmouth, Oxford Utd, York
1976–7	Carlisle, Plymouth Argyle, Hereford
1977–8	Hull, Mansfield, Blackpool
1978–9	Sheffield Utd, Millwall, Blackburn
1979–80	Fulham, Burnley, Blackpool
1980–1	Preston, Bristol City, Bristol Rov
1981–2	Cardiff, Wrexham, Orient
1982–3	Rotherham, Burnley, Bolton
1983–4	Derby, Swansea, Cambridge Utd
1984–5	Notts Co, Cardiff, Wolves

1985–6	Carlisle, Middlesbrough, Fulham
1986–7	Sunderland**, Grimsby, Brighton
1987–8	Sheffield Utd**, Reading, Huddersfield
1988–9	Shrewsbury, Birmingham, Walsall
1989–90	Bournemouth, Bradford City, Stoke
1990–1	WBA, Hull
1991–2	Plymouth Argyle, Brighton, Port Vale
** Relegated after play–offs	

THIRD DIVISION TO FOURTH DIVISION

1958–9	Rochdale, Notts Co, Doncaster, Stockport
1959–60	Accrington, Wrexham, Mansfield, York
1960–1	Chesterfield, Colchester, Bradford City, Tranmere
1961–2	Newport, Brentford, Lincoln, Torquay
1962–3	Bradford PA, Brighton, Carlisle, Halifax
1963–4	Millwall, Crewe, Wrexham, Notts Co
1964–5	Luton, Port Vale, Colchester, Barnsley
1965–6	Southend, Exeter, Brentford, York
1966–7	Doncaster, Workington, Darlington, Swansea
1967–8	Scunthorpe, Colchester, Grimsby, Peterborough (demoted)
1968–9	Oldham, Crewe, Hartlepool Utd, Northampton
1969–70	Bournemouth, Southport, Barrow, Stockport
1970–1	Gillingham, Doncaster, Bury, Reading
1971–2	Mansfield, Barnsley, Torquay, Bradford City
1972–3	Scunthorpe, Swansea, Brentford, Rotherham
1973–4	Cambridge Utd, Shrewsbury, Rochdale, Southport
1974–5	Bournemouth, Watford, Tranmere, Huddersfield
1975–6	Aldershot, Colchester, Southend, Halifax
1976–7	Reading, Northampton, Grimsby, York
1977–8	Port Vale, Bradford City, Hereford, Portsmouth
1978–9	Peterborough, Walsall, Tranmere, Lincoln
1979–80	Bury, Southend, Mansfield, Wimbledon
1980–1	Sheffield Utd, Colchester, Blackpool, Hull
1981–2	Wimbledon, Swindon, Bristol City, Chester
1982–3	Reading, Wrexham, Doncaster, Chesterfield
1983–4	Scunthorpe, Southend, Port Vale, Exeter

1984–5	Burnley, Orient, Preston, Cambridge Utd
1985–6	Lincoln, Cardiff, Wolves, Swansea
1986–7	Bolton**, Carlisle, Darlington, Newport
1987–8	Doncaster, York, Grimsby, Rotherham**
1988–9	Southend, Chesterfield, Gillingham, Aldershot
1989–90	Cardiff, Northampton, Blackpool, Walsall
1990–1	Crewe, Rotherham, Mansfield
1991–2	Bury, Shrewsbury, Torquay, Darlington
** Relegated after plays–offs	

DEMOTED FROM FOURTH DIVISION TO CONFERENCE

1987	Lincoln
1988	Newport
1989	Darlington
1990	Colchester
1991	No demotion
1992	No demotion

DEMOTED FROM THIRD DIVISION TO CONFERENCE

1993	Halifax
1994–6	No demotion
1997	Hereford
1998	Doncaster
1999	Scarborough
2000	Chester
2001	Barnet
2002	Halifax
2003	Exeter, Shrewsbury
2004	Carlisle, York

DEMOTED FROM LEAGUE TWO TO CONFERENCE/NATIONAL LEAGUE

2005	Kidderminster, Cambridge Utd
2006	Oxford Utd, Rushden & Diamonds
2007	Boston, Torquay
2008	Mansfield, Wrexham
2009	Chester Luton
2010	Grimsby, Darlington
2011	Lincoln, Stockport
2012	Hereford, Macclesfield
2013	Barnet, Aldershot
2014	Bristol Rov, Torquay
2015	Cheltenham, Tranmere
2016	Dagenham, York
2017	Hartlepool, Leyton Orient
2018	Barnet, Chesterfield
2019	Notts Co, Yeovil
2020	Macclesfield

RELEGATED CLUBS (SINCE 1993)

1993
Premier League to Div 1: Crystal Palace, Middlesbrough, Nottm Forest
Div 1 to Div 2: Brentford, Cambridge Utd, Bristol Rov
Div 2 to Div 3: Preston, Mansfield, Wigan, Chester

1994
Premier League to Div 1: Sheffield Utd, Oldham, Swindon
Div 1 to Div 2: Birmingham, Oxford Utd, Peterborough
Div 2 to Div 3: Fulham, Exeter, Hartlepool Utd, Barnet

1995
Premier League to Div 1: Crystal Palace, Norwich, Leicester, Ipswich
Div 1 to Div 2: Swindon, Burnley, Bristol City, Notts Co
Div 2 to Div 3: Cambridge Utd, Plymouth, Cardiff, Chester, Leyton Orient

1996
Premier League to Div 1: Manchester City, QPR, Bolton
Div 1 to Div 2: Millwall, Watford, Luton
Div 2 to Div 3: Carlisle, Swansea, Brighton, Hull

1997
Premier League to Div 1: Sunderland, Middlesbrough, Nottm Forest
Div 1 to Div 2: Grimsby, Oldham, Southend
Div 2 to Div 3: Peterborough, Shrewsbury, Rotherham, Notts Co

1998
Premier League to Div 1: Bolton, Barnsley, Crystal Palace
Div 1 to Div 2: Manchester City, Stoke, Reading
Div 2 to Div 3: Brentford, Plymouth, Carlisle, Southend

1999
Premier League to Div 1: Charlton, Blackburn, Nottm Forest
Div 1 to Div 2: Bury, Oxford Utd, Bristol City
Div 2 to Div 3: York, Northampton, Lincoln, Macclesfield

2000
Premier League to Div 1: Wimbledon, Sheffield Wed, Watford
Div 1 to Div 2: Walsall, Port Vale, Swindon
Div 2 to Div 3: Cardiff, Blackpool, Scunthorpe, Chesterfield

2001
Premier League to Div 1: Manchester City, Coventry, Bradford City
Div 1 to Div 2: Huddersfield, QPR, Tranmere

Div 2 to Div 3: Bristol Rov, Luton, Swansea, Oxford Utd

2002
Premier League to Div 1: Ipswich, Derby, Leicester
Div 1 to Div 2: Crewe, Barnsley, Stockport
Div 2 to Div 3: Bournemouth, Bury, Wrexham, Cambridge Utd

2003
Premier League to Div 1: West Ham, WBA, Sunderland
Div 1 to Div 2: Sheffield Wed, Brighton, Grimsby
Div 2 to Div 3: Cheltenham, Huddersfield, Mansfield, Northampton

2004
Premier League to Div 1: Leicester, Leeds, Wolves
Div 1 to Div 2: Walsall, Bradford City, Wimbledon
Div 2 to Div 3: Grimsby, Rushden & Diamonds, Notts Co, Wycombe

2005
Premier League to Championship: Crystal Palace, Norwich, Southampton
Championship to League 1: Gillingham, Nottm Forest, Rotherham
League 1 to League 2: Torquay, Wrexham, Peterborough, Stockport

2006
Premier League to Championship: Birmingham, WBA, Sunderland
Championship to League 1: Crewe, Millwall, Brighton
League 1 to League 2: Hartlepool Utd, MK Dons, Swindon, Walsall

2007
Premier League to Championship: Sheffield Utd, Charlton, Watford
Championship to League 1: Southend, Luton, Leeds
League 1 to League 2: Chesterfield, Bradford City, Rotherham, Brentford

2008
Premier League to Championship: Reading, Birmingham, Derby
Championship to League 1: Leicester, Scunthorpe, Colchester
League 1 to League 2: Bournemouth, Gillingham, Port Vale, Luton

2009
Premier League to Championship: Newcastle, Middlesbrough, WBA
Championship to League 1: Norwich, Southampton, Charlton
League 1 to League 2: Northampton, Crewe, Cheltenham, Hereford

2010

Premier League to Championship: Burnley, Hull, Portsmouth

Championship to League 1: Sheffield Wed, Plymouth, Peterborough

League 1 to League 2: Gillingham, Wycombe, Southend, Stockport

2011

Premier League to Championship: Birmingham, Blackpool, West Ham

Championship to League 1: Preston, Sheffield Utd, Scunthorpe

League 1 to League 2: Dagenham & Red bridge, Bristol Rov, Plymouth, Swindon

2012

Premier League to Championship: Bolton, Blackburn, Wolves

Championship to League 1: Portsmouth, Coventry, Doncaster

League 1 to League 2: Wycombe, Chesterfield, Exeter, Rochdale

2013

Premier League to Championship: Wigan, Reading, QPR

Championship to League 1: Peterborough, Wolves, Bristol City

League 1 to League 2: Scunthorpe, Bury, Hartlepool, Portsmouth

2014

Premier League to Championship: Norwich, Fulham, Cardiff

Championship to League 1: Doncaster, Barnsley, Yeovil

League 1 to League 2: Tranmere, Carlisle, Shrewsbury, Stevenage

2015

Premier League to Championship: Hull, Burnley QPR

Championship to League 1: Millwall, Wigan, Blackpool

League 1 to League 2: Notts Co, Crawley, Leyton Orient, Yeovil

2016

Premier League to Championship: Newcastle, Norwich, Aston Villa

Championship to League 1: Charlton, MK Dons, Bolton

League 1 to League 2: Doncaster, Blackpool, Colchester, Crewe

2017

Premier League to Championship: Hull, Middlesbrough, Sunderland

Championship to League 1: Blackburn, Wigan, Rotherham

League 1 to League 2: Port Vale, Swindon, Coventry, Chesterfield

2018

Premier League to Championship: Swansea, Stoke, WBA

Championship to League 1: Barnsley, Burton, Sunderland

League 1 to League 2: Oldham, Northampton, MK Dons, Bury

2019

Premier League to Championship: Cardiff, Fulham, Huddersfield

Championship to League 1: Rotherham, Bolton, Ipswich

League 1 to League 2: Plymouth, Walsall, Scunthorpe, Bradford

2020

Premier League to Championship: Bournemouth, Watford, Norwich

Championship to League 1: Charlton, Wigan, Hull

League 1 to League 2: Tranmere, Southend, Bolton

ANNUAL AWARDS

FOOTBALL WRITERS' ASSOCIATION

Footballer of the Year: 1948 Stanley Matthews (Blackpool); **1949** Johnny Carey (Manchester Utd); **1950** Joe Mercer (Arsenal); **1951** Harry Johnston (Blackpool); **1952** Billy Wright (Wolves); **1953** Nat Lofthouse (Bolton); **1954** Tom Finney (Preston); **1955** Don Revie (Manchester City); **1956** Bert Trautmann (Manchester City); **1957** Tom Finney (Preston) **1958** Danny Blanchflower (Tottenham); **1959** Syd Owen (Luton); **1960** Bill Slater (Wolves); **1961** Danny Blanchflower (Tottenham); **1962** Jimmy Adamson (Burnley); **1963** Stanley Matthews (Stoke); **1964** Bobby Moore (West Ham); **1965** Bobby Collins (Leeds); **1966** Bobby Charlton (Manchester Utd); **1967** Jack Charlton (Leeds); **1968** George Best (Manchester Utd); **1969** Tony Book (Manchester City) & Dave Mackay (Derby) – shared; **1970** Billy Bremner (Leeds); **1971** Frank McLintock (Arsenal); **1972** Gordon Banks (Stoke); **1973** Pat Jennings (Tottenham); **1974** Ian Callaghan (Liverpool); **1975** Alan Mullery (Fulham); **1976** Kevin Keegan (Liverpool); **1977** Emlyn Hughes (Liverpool); **1978** Kenny Burns (Nott'm Forest); **1979** Kenny Dalglish (Liverpool); **1980** Terry McDermott (Liverpool); **1981** Frans Thijssen (Ipswich); **1982** Steve Perryman (Tottenham); **1983** Kenny Dalglish (Liverpool); **1984** Ian Rush (Liverpool); **1985** Neville Southall (Everton); **1986** Gary Lineker (Everton); **1987** Clive Allen (Tottenham); **1988** John Barnes (Liverpool); **1989** Steve Nicol (Liverpool); Special award to the Liverpool players for the compassion shown to bereaved families after the Hillsborough Disaster; **1990** John Barnes (Liverpool); **1991** Gordon Strachan (Leeds); **1992** Gary Lineker (Tottenham); **1993** Chris Waddle (Sheffield Wed); **1994** Alan Shearer (Blackburn); **1995** Jurgen Klinsmann (Tottenham); **1996** Eric Cantona (Manchester Utd); **1997** Gianfranco Zola (Chelsea); **1998** Dennis Bergkamp (Arsenal); **1999** David Ginola (Tottenham); **2000** Roy Keane (Manchester Utd); **2001** Teddy Sheringham (Manchester Utd); **2002** Robert Pires (Arsenal); **2003** Thierry Henry (Arsenal); **2004** Thierry Henry (Arsenal); **2005** Frank Lampard (Chelsea); **2006** Thierry Henry (Arsenal); **2007** Cristiano Ronaldo (Manchester Utd); **2008** Cristiano Ronaldo (Manchester Utd); **2009** Steven Gerrard (Liverpool); **2010** Wayne Rooney (Manchester Utd); **2011** Scott Parker (West Ham); **2012** Robin van Persie (Arsenal); **2013** Gareth Bale (Tottenham); **2014** Luis Suarez (Liverpool); **2015** Eden Hazard (Chelsea); **2016** Jamie Vardy (Leicester); **2017** N'Golo Kante (Chelsea); **2018** Mohamed Salah (Liverpool); **2019** Raheem Sterling (Manchester City); **2020** Jordan Henderson (Liverpool)

PROFESSIONAL FOOTBALLERS' ASSOCIATION

Player of the Year: 1974 Norman Hunter (Leeds); **1975** Colin Todd (Derby); **1976** Pat Jennings (Tottenham); **1977** Andy Gray (Aston Villa); **1978** Peter Shilton (Nott'm Forest); **1979** Liam Brady (Arsenal); **1980** Terry McDermott (Liverpool); **1981** John Wark (Ipswich); **1982** Kevin Keegan (Southampton); **1983** Kenny Dalglish (Liverpool); **1984** Ian Rush (Liverpool); **1985** Peter Reid (Everton); **1986** Gary Lineker (Everton); **1987** Clive Allen (Tottenham); **1988** John Barnes (Liverpool); **1989** Mark Hughes (Manchester Utd); **1990** David Platt (Aston Villa); **1991** Mark Hughes (Manchester Utd); **1992** Gary Pallister (Manchester Utd); **1993** Paul McGrath (Aston Villa); **1994** Eric Cantona (Manchester Utd); **1995** Alan Shearer (Blackburn); **1996** Les Ferdinand (Newcastle); **1997** Alan Shearer (Newcastle); **1998** Dennis Bergkamp (Arsenal); **1999** David Ginola (Tottenham); **2000** Roy Keane (Manchester Utd); **2001** Teddy Sheringham (Manchester Utd); **2002** Ruud van Nistelrooy (Manchester Utd); **2003** Thierry Henry (Arsenal); **2004** Thierry Henry (Arsenal); **2005** John Terry (Chelsea); **2006** Steven Gerrard (Liverpool); **2007** Cristiano Ronaldo (Manchester Utd); **2008** Cristiano Ronaldo (Manchester Utd); **2009** Ryan Giggs (Manchester Utd); **2010** Wayne Rooney (Manchester Utd); **2011** Gareth Bale (Tottenham); **2012** Robin van Persie (Arsenal); **2013** Gareth Bale (Tottenham); **2014** Luis Suarez (Liverpool); **2015** Eden Hazard (Chelsea); **2016** Riyad Mahrez (Leicester); **2017** N'Golo Kante (Chelsea); **2018** Mohamed Salah (Liverpool); **2019** Virgin van Dijk (Liverpool)

Young Player of the Year: 1974 Kevin Beattie (Ipswich); **1975** Mervyn Day (West Ham); **1976** Peter Barnes (Manchester City); **1977** Andy Gray (Aston Villa); **1978** Tony Woodcock (Nott'm Forest);

1979 Cyrille Regis (WBA); 1980 Glenn Hoddle (Tottenham); 1981 Gary Shaw (Aston Villa); 1982 Steve Moran (Southampton); 1983 Ian Rush (Liverpool); 1984 Paul Walsh (Luton); 1985 Mark Hughes (Manchester Utd); 1986 Tony Cottee (West Ham); 1987 Tony Adams (Arsenal); 1988 Paul Gascoigne (Newcastle); 1989 Paul Merson (Arsenal); 1990 Matthew Le Tissier (Southampton); 1991 Lee Sharpe (Manchester Utd); 1992 Ryan Giggs (Manchester Utd); 1993 Ryan Giggs (Manchester Utd); 1994 Andy Cole (Newcastle); 1995 Robbie Fowler (Liverpool); 1996 Robbie Fowler (Liverpool); 1997 David Beckham (Manchester Utd); 1998 Michael Owen (Liverpool); 1999 Nicolas Anelka (Arsenal); 2000 Harry Kewell (Leeds); 2001 Steven Gerrard (Liverpool); 2002 Craig Bellamy (Newcastle); 2003 Jermaine Jenas (Newcastle); 2004 Scott Parker (Chelsea); 2005 Wayne Rooney (Manchester Utd); 2006 Wayne Rooney (Manchester Utd); 2007 Cristiano Ronaldo (Manchester Utd); 2008 Cesc Fabregas (Arsenal); 2009 Ashley Young (Aston Villa); 2010 James Milner (Aston Villa); 2011 Jack Wilshere (Arsenal); 2012 Kyle Walker (Tottenham); 2013 Gareth Bale (Tottenham); 2014 Eden Hazard (Chelsea); 2015 Harry Kane (Tottenham); 2016 Dele Alli (Tottenham); 2017 Dele Alli (Tottenham); 2018 Leroy Sane (Manchester City); 2019 Raheem Sterling (Manchester City)

Merit Awards: 1974 Bobby Charlton & Cliff Lloyd; 1975 Denis Law; 1976 George Eastham; 1977 Jack Taylor; 1978 Bill Shankly; 1979 Tom Finney; 1980 Sir Matt Busby; 1981 John Trollope; 1982 Joe Mercer; 1983 Bob Paisley; 1984 Bill Nicholson; 1985 Ron Greenwood; 1986 England 1966 World Cup-winning team; 1987 Sir Stanley Matthews; 1988 Billy Bonds; 1989 Nat Lofthouse; 1990 Peter Shilton; 1991 Tommy Hutchison; 1992 Brian Clough; 1993 Manchester Utd; 1968 European Champions; Eusebio; 1994 Billy Bingham; 1995 Gordon Strachan; 1996 Pele; 1997 Peter Beardsley; 1998 Steve Ogrizovic; 1999 Tony Ford; 2000 Gary Mabbutt; 2001 Jimmy Hill; 2002 Niall Quinn; 2003 Sir Bobby Robson; 2004 Dario Gradi; 2005 Shaka Hislop; 2006 George Best; 2007 Sir Alex Ferguson; 2008 Jimmy Armfield; 2009 John McDermott; 2010 Lucas Radebe; 2011 Howard Webb; 2012 Graham Alexander; 2013 Eric Harrison/Manchester Utd Class of '92; 2014 Donald Bell (posthumously; only footballer to win Victoria Cross; World War 1); 2015 Steven Gerrard & Frank Lampard; 2016 Ryan Giggs; 2017 David Beckham; 2018 Cyrille Regis (posthumously); 2019 Steph Houghton

MANAGER OF THE YEAR 1

(chosen by media and sponsors)

1966 Jock Stein (Celtic); 1967 Jock Stein (Celtic); 1968 Matt Busby (Manchester Utd); 1969 Don Revie (Leeds); 1970 Don Revie (Leeds); 1971 Bertie Mee (Arsenal); 1972 Don Revie (Leeds); 1973 Bill Shankly (Liverpool); 1974 Jack Charlton (Middlesbrough); 1975 Ron Saunders (Aston Villa); 1976 Bob Paisley (Liverpool); 1977 Bob Paisley (Liverpool); 1978 Brian Clough (Nott'm Forest); 1979 Bob Paisley (Liverpool); 1980 Bob Paisley (Liverpool); 1981 Ron Saunders (Aston Villa); 1982 Bob Paisley (Liverpool); 1983 Bob Paisley (Liverpool); 1984 Joe Fagan (Liverpool); 1985 Howard Kendall (Everton); 1986 Kenny Dalglish (Liverpool); 1987 Howard Kendall (Everton); 1988 Kenny Dalglish (Liverpool); 1989 George Graham (Arsenal); 1990 Kenny Dalglish (Liverpool); 1991 George Graham (Arsenal); 1992 Howard Wilkinson (Leeds); 1993 Alex Ferguson (Manchester Utd); 1994 Alex Ferguson (Manchester Utd); 1995 Kenny Dalglish (Blackburn); 1996 Alex Ferguson (Manchester Utd); 1997 Alex Ferguson (Manchester Utd); 1998 Arsene Wenger (Arsenal); 1999 Alex Ferguson (Manchester Utd); 2000 Sir Alex Ferguson (Manchester Utd); 2001 George Burley (Ipswich); 2002 Arsene Wenger (Arsenal); 2003 Sir Alex Ferguson (Manchester Utd); 2004 Arsene Wenger (Arsenal); 2005 Jose Mourinho (Chelsea); 2006 Jose Mourinho (Chelsea); 2007 Sir Alex Ferguson (Manchester Utd); 2008 Sir Alex Ferguson (Manchester Utd); 2009 Sir Alex Ferguson (Manchester Utd); 2010 Harry Redknapp (Tottenham); 2011 Sir Alex Ferguson (Manchester Utd); 2012: Alan Pardew (Newcastle); 2013 Sir Alex Ferguson (Manchester Utd); 2014 Tony Pulis (Crystal Palace); 2015 Jose Mourinho (Chelsea); 2016 Claudio Ranieri (Leicester); 2017 Antonio Conte (Chelsea); 2018 Pep Guardiola (Manchester City); 2019 Pep Guardiola (Manchester City); 2020 Jurgen Klopp (Liverpool)

MANAGER OF THE YEAR 2

(Chosen by the League Managers' Association)

1993 Dave Bassett (Sheffield Utd); **1994** Joe Kinnear (Wimbledon); **1995** Frank Clark (Nott'm Forest); **1996** Peter Reid (Sunderland); **1997** Danny Wilson (Barnsley); **1998** David Jones (Southampton); **1999** Alex Ferguson (Manchester Utd); **2000** Alan Curbishley (Charlton Athletic); **2001** George Burley (Ipswich); **2002** Arsene Wenger (Arsenal); **2003** David Moyes (Everton); **2004** Arsene Wenger (Arsenal); **2005** David Moyes (Everton); **2006** Steve Coppell (Reading); **2007** Steve Coppell (Reading); **2008** Sir Alex Ferguson (Manchester Utd); **2009** David Moyes (Everton); **2010** Roy Hodgson (Fulham); **2011** Sir Alex Ferguson (Manchester Utd); **2012:** Alan Pardew (Newcastle); **2013** Sir Alex Ferguson (Manchester Utd); **2014** Brendan Rodgers (Liverpool); **2015** Eddie Howe (Bournemouth); **2016** Claudio Ranieri (Leicester); **2017** Antonio Conte (Chelsea); **2018** Pep Guardiola (Manchester City); **2019** Chris Wilder (Sheffield Utd); **2020** Jurgen Klopp (Liverpool)

SCOTTISH FOOTBALL WRITERS' ASSOCIATION

Footballer of the Year: 1965 Billy McNeill (Celtic); **1966** John Greig (Rangers); **1967** Ronnie Simpson (Celtic); **1968** Gordon Wallace (Raith); **1969** Bobby Murdoch (Celtic); **1970** Pat Stanton (Hibernian); **1971** Martin Buchan (Aberdeen); **1972** David Smith (Rangers); **1973** George Connelly (Celtic); **1974** World Cup Squad; **1975** Sandy Jardine (Rangers); **1976** John Greig (Rangers); **1977** Danny McGrain (Celtic); **1978** Derek Johnstone (Rangers); **1979** Andy Ritchie (Morton); **1980** Gordon Strachan (Aberdeen); **1981** Alan Rough (Partick Thistle); **1982** Paul Sturrock (Dundee Utd); **1983** Charlie Nicholas (Celtic); **1984** Willie Miller (Aberdeen); **1985** Hamish McAlpine (Dundee Utd); **1986** Sandy Jardine (Hearts); **1987** Brian McClair (Celtic); **1988** Paul McStay (Celtic); **1989** Richard Gough (Rangers); **1990** Alex McLeish (Aberdeen); **1991** Maurice Malpas (Dundee Utd); **1992** Ally McCoist (Rangers); **1993** Andy Goram (Rangers); **1994** Mark Hateley (Rangers); **1995** Brian Laudrup (Rangers); **1996** Paul Gascoigne (Rangers); **1997** Brian Laudrup (Rangers); **1998** Craig Burley (Celtic); **1999** Henrik Larsson (Celtic); **2000** Barry Ferguson (Rangers); **2001** Henrik Larsson (Celtic); **2002** Paul Lambert (Celtic); **2003** Barry Ferguson (Rangers); **2004** Jackie McNamara (Celtic); **2005** John Hartson (Celtic); **2006** Craig Gordon (Hearts); **2007** Shunsuke Nakamura (Celtic); **2008** Carlos Cuellar (Rangers); **2009** Gary Caldwell (Celtic); **2010** David Weir (Rangers); **2011** Emilio Izaguirre (Celtic); **2012** Charlie Mulgrew (Celtic); **2013** Leigh Griffiths (Hibernian); **2014** Kris Commons (Celtic); **2015** Craig Gordon (Celtic); **2016** Leigh Griffiths (Celtic); **2017** Scott Sinclair (Celtic); **2018** Scott Brown (Celtic); **2019** James Forrest (Celtic); **2020** Odsonne Edouard

PROFESSIONAL FOOTBALLERS' ASSOCIATION SCOTLAND

Player of the Year: 1978 Derek Johnstone (Rangers); **1979** Paul Hegarty (Dundee Utd); **1980** Davie Provan (Celtic); **1981** Mark McGhee (Aberdeen); **1982** Sandy Clarke (Airdrieonians); **1983** Charlie Nicholas (Celtic); **1984** Willie Miller (Aberdeen); **1985** Jim Duffy (Morton); **1986** Richard Gough (Dundee Utd); **1987** Brian McClair (Celtic); **1988** Paul McStay (Celtic); **1989** Theo Snelders (Aberdeen); **1990** Jim Bett (Aberdeen); **1991** Paul Elliott (Celtic); **1992** Ally McCoist (Rangers); **1993** Andy Goram (Rangers); **1994** Mark Hateley (Rangers); **1995** Brian Laudrup (Rangers); **1996** Paul Gascoigne (Rangers); **1997** Paolo Di Canio (Celtic) **1998** Jackie McNamara (Celtic); **1999** Henrik Larsson (Celtic); **2000** Mark Viduka (Celtic); **2001** Henrik Larsson (Celtic); **2002** Lorenzo Amoruso (Rangers); **2003** Barry Ferguson (Rangers); **2004** Chris Sutton (Celtic); **2005** John Hartson (Celtic) and Fernando Ricksen (Rangers); **2006** Shaun Maloney (Celtic); **2007** Shunsuke Nakamura (Celtic); **2008** Aiden McGeady (Celtic); **2009** Scott Brown (Celtic); **2010** Steven Davis (Rangers); **2011** Emilio Izaguirre (Celtic); **2012** Charlie Mulgrew (Celtic); **2013** Michael Higdon (Motherwell); **2014** Kris Commons (Celtic); **2015** Stefan Johansen (Celtic); **2016** Leigh Griffiths (Celtic); **2017** Scott Sinclair (Celtic); **2018** Scott Brown (Celtic); **2019** James Forrest (Celtic); **2020** No Award

Young Player of the Year: 1978 Graeme Payne (Dundee Utd); **1979** Ray Stewart (Dundee Utd); **1980** John McDonald (Rangers); **1981** Charlie Nicholas (Celtic); **1982** Frank McAvennie (St Mirren); **1983** Paul McStay (Celtic); **1984** John Robertson (Hearts); **1985** Craig Levein (Hearts);

1986 Craig Levein (Hearts); **1987** Robert Fleck (Rangers); **1988** John Collins (Hibernian); **1989** Billy McKinlay (Dundee Utd); **1990** Scott Crabbe (Hearts); **1991** Eoin Jess (Aberdeen); **1992** Phil O'Donnell (Motherwell); **1993** Eoin Jess (Aberdeen); **1994** Phil O'Donnell (Motherwell); **1995** Charlie Miller (Rangers); **1996** Jackie McNamara (Celtic); **1997** Robbie Winters (Dundee Utd); **1998** Gary Naysmith (Hearts); **1999** Barry Ferguson (Rangers); **2000** Kenny Miller (Hibernian); **2001** Stilian Petrov (Celtic); **2002** Kevin McNaughton (Aberdeen); **2003** James McFadden (Motherwell); **2004** Stephen Pearson (Celtic); **2005** Derek Riordan (Hibernian); **2006** Shaun Maloney (Celtic); **2007** Steven Naismith (Kilmarnock); **2008** Aiden McGeady (Celtic); **2009** James McCarthy (Hamilton); **2010** Danny Wilson (Rangers); **2011:** David Goodwillie (Dundee Utd); **2012** James Forrest (Celtic); **2013** Leigh Griffiths (Hibernian): **2014** Andy Robertson (Dundee Utd); **2015** Jason Denayer (Celtic); **2016** Kieran Tierney (Celtic); **2017** Kieran Tierney (Celticl); **2018** Kieran Tierney (Celtic); **2019** Ryan Kent (Rangers); **2020** No Award

SCOTTISH MANAGER OF THE YEAR

1987 Jim McLean (Dundee Utd); **1988** Billy McNeill (Celtic); **1989** Graeme Souness (Rangers); **1990** Andy Roxburgh (Scotland); **1991** Alex Totten (St Johnstone); **1992** Walter Smith (Rangers); **1993** Walter Smith (Rangers); **1994** Walter Smith (Rangers); **1995** Jimmy Nicholl (Raith); **1996** Walter Smith (Rangers); **1997** Walter Smith (Rangers); **1998** Wim Jansen (Celtic); **1999** Dick Advocaat (Rangers); **2000** Dick Advocaat (Rangers); **2001** Martin O'Neill (Celtic); **2002** John Lambie (Partick Thistle); **2003** Alex McLeish (Rangers); **2004** Martin O'Neill (Celtic); **2005** Alex McLeish (Rangers); **2006** Gordon Strachan (Celtic); **2007** Gordon Strachan (Celtic); **2008** Billy Reid (Hamilton); **2009** Csaba Laszlo (Hearts); **2010** Walter Smith (Rangers); **2011:** Mixu Paatelainen (Kilmarnock); **2012** Neil Lennon (Celtic); **2013** Neil Lennon (Celtic); **2014** Derek McInnes (Aberdeen); **2015** John Hughes (Inverness); **2016** Mark Warburton (Rangers); **2017** Brendan Rodgers (Celtic); **2018** Jack Ross (St Mirren); **2019** Steve Clarke (Kilmarnock); **2020** Neil Lennon (Celtic)

EUROPEAN FOOTBALLER OF THE YEAR

1956 Stanley Matthews (Blackpool); **1957** Alfredo di Stefano (Real Madrid); **1958** Raymond Kopa (Real Madrid); **1959** Alfredo di Stefano (Real Madrid); **1960** Luis Suarez (Barcelona); **1961** Omar Sivori (Juventus); **1962** Josef Masopust (Dukla Prague); **1963** Lev Yashin (Moscow Dynamo); **1964** Denis Law (Manchester Utd); **1965** Eusebio (Benfica); **1966** Bobby Charlton (Manchester Utd); **1967** Florian Albert (Ferencvaros); **1968** George Best (Manchester Utd); **1969** Gianni Rivera (AC Milan); **1970** Gerd Muller (Bayern Munich); **1971** Johan Cruyff (Ajax); **1972** Franz Beckenbauer (Bayern Munich); **1973** Johan Cruyff (Barcelona); **1974** Johan Cruyff (Barcelona); **1975** Oleg Blokhin (Dynamo Kiev); **1976** Franz Beckenbauer (Bayern Munich); **1977** Allan Simonsen (Borussia Moenchengladbach); **1978** Kevin Keegan (SV Hamburg); **1979** Kevin Keegan (SV Hamburg); **1980** Karl-Heinz Rummenigge (Bayern Munich); **1981** Karl-Heinz Rummenigge (Bayern Munich); **1982** Paolo Rossi (Juventus); **1983** Michel Platini (Juventus); **1984** Michel Platini (Juventus); **1985** Michel Platini (Juventus); **1986** Igor Belanov (Dynamo Kiev); **1987** Ruud Gullit (AC Milan); **1988** Marco van Basten (AC Milan); **1989** Marco van Basten (AC Milan); **1990** Lothar Matthaus (Inter Milan); **1991** Jean-Pierre Papin (Marseille); **1992** Marco van Basten (AC Milan); **1993** Roberto Baggio (Juventus); **1994** Hristo Stoichkov (Barcelona); **1995** George Weah (AC Milan); **1996** Matthias Sammer (Borussia Dortmund); **1997** Ronaldo (Inter Milan); **1998** Zinedine Zidane (Juventus); **1999** Rivaldo (Barcelona); **2000** Luis Figo (Real Madrid); **2001** Michael Owen (Liverpool); **2002** Ronaldo (Real Madrid); **2003** Pavel Nedved (Juventus); **2004** Andriy Shevchenko (AC Milan); **2005** Ronaldinho (Barcelona); **2006** Fabio Cannavaro (Real Madrid); **2007** Kaka (AC Milan); **2008** Cristiano Ronaldo (Manchester United); **2009** Lionel Messi (Barcelona)

WORLD FOOTBALLER OF YEAR

1991 Lothar Matthaus (Inter Milan and Germany); **1992** Marco van Basten (AC Milan and Holland); **1993** Roberto Baggio (Juventus and Italy); **1994** Romario (Barcelona and Brazil); **1995** George

Weah (AC Milan and Liberia); **1996** Ronaldo (Barcelona and Brazil); **1997** Ronaldo (Inter Milan and Brazil); **1998** Zinedine Zidane (Juventus and France); **1999** Rivaldo (Barcelona and Brazil); **2000** Zinedine Zidane (Juventus and France); **2001** Luis Figo (Real Madrid and Portugal); **2002** Ronaldo (Real Madrid and Brazil); **2003** Zinedine Zidane (Real Madrid and France); **2004** Ronaldinho (Barcelona and Brazil); **2005** Ronaldinho (Barcelona and Brazil); **2006** Fabio Cannavaro (Real Madrid and Italy); **2007** Kaka (AC Milan and Brazil); **2008** Cristiano Ronaldo (Manchester United and Portugal); **2009** Lionel Messi (Barcelona and Argentina)

FIFA BALLON D'OR
(replaces European and World Footballer of the Year)

2010: Lionel Messi (Barcelona). **2011** Lionel Messi (Barcelona); **2012** Lionel Messi (Barcelona); **2013** Cristiano Ronaldo (Real Madrid); **2014:** Cristiano Ronaldo (Real Madrid); **2015** Lionel Messi (Barcelona)

FIFA BEST PLAYER
2016 Cristiano Ronaldo (Real Madrid); **2017** Cristiano Ronaldo (Real Madrid); **2018** Luka Modric (Real Madrid) ; **2019** Lionel Messi (Barcelona and Argentina)

FIFA WORLD COACH OF THE YEAR
2010: Jose Mourinho (Inter Milan). **2011** Pep Guardiola (Barcelona); **2012** Vicente del Bosque (Spain); **2013** Jupp Heynckes (Bayern Munich); **2014** Joachim Low (Germany); **2015** Luis Enrique (Barcelona); **2016** Claudio Ranieri (Leicester), **2017** Zinedine Zidane (Real Madrid); **2018** Didier Deschamps (France); **2019** Jurgen Klopp (Liverpool)

THE THINGS THEY SAY...

'Manchester City committed serious breaches of the club licensing and financial fair play regulations by overstating sponsorship revenue in its accounts and in the break-even information submitted to UEFA between 2012 and 2016' – **UEFA** ban City from European competition for two years.

'This is a case initiated by UEFA, prosecuted by UEFA and judged by UEFA. With this prejudicial process now over, the club will pursue an impartial judgment' – **Manchester City** responding to the ban and £25m fine.

'Most of the alleged breaches were either not established or time-barred' – **Court of Arbitration for Sport** quashing the ban and reducing the fine to £9m.

'I am happy that City can play Champions League, but I don't think it was a good day for football, to be honest. I think FFP is a good idea. It is there for protecting teams, protecting the competition' – **Jurgen Klopp**, Liverpool manager.

'It's a disgraceful decision, a bad day for football. It would now be better to open the circus door and allow clubs to spend whatever they like' – **Jose Mourinho**, Tottenham manager.

'I tell Jose and Jurgen that it was a good day for football, a very good day. We played with the same rules as everyone. If we broke them we would have been punished' – **Pep Guardiola**, Manchester City manager.

REVIEWS APPEARANCES, SCORERS 2019–20

(figures in brackets denote appearances as substitute; average attendances before lockdown)

PREMIER LEAGUE

ARSENAL

Mikel Arteta came through a testing first taste of management with a victory in the FA Cup Final which could open up a new chapter at the Emirates under the 38-year-old Spaniard. Arsenal, a club on the way down after the Arsene Wenger era and Unai Emery's spell in charge, experienced their worst Premier League season for 25 years, down in eighth place They also faced missing out on a place in Europe for the first time in that long. Instead, Arteta engineered a 2-1 victory over Chelsea at Wembley, courtesy of two goals from Pierre-Emerick Aubameyang, with some shrewd decision-making, both in terms of selection and in tactical awareness on the day. There was no place in the squad for either Mesut Ozil or Matteo Guendouzi, players now regarded as high maintenance. By contrast, the key roles played by David Luiz and Granit Xhaka illustrated how these two were rehabilitated under Arteta after earlier problems. The former captain, who also had to himself with contracting COVID-19, took over a struggling team when Emery was sacked midway through the season and had some early success – 2-0 against Manchester United and a point earned at Stamford Bridge. Later, Arsenal came from behind to interrupt Liverpool's title celebrations. But despite the improvement, their form remained inconsistent, while defeat by Olympiacos in the Europa League was a setback.

Aubameyang P-E 3	Maitland-Niles A 15 (5)	Pepe N..................... 22 (9)
Bellerin H 13 (2)	Mari P.............................2	Saka B 19 (7)
Chambers C 13 (1)	Martinelli G 6 (8)	Smith Rowe E........... 1 (1)
Ceballos D 18 (6)	Martinez E.............. 8 (1)	Soares C..................... 3 (2)
Guendouzi M........... 19 (5)	Mkhitaryan H.............. 1 (2)	Sokratis 19
Holding R 6 (2)	Monreal N 3	Tierney K 12 (3)
Kolasinac S............. 19 (7)	Mustafi S 13 (2)	Torreira L................ 17 (12)
Lacazette A 22 (8)	Nelson R 7 (10)	Willock J 8 (21)
Leno B 30	Nketiah E 7 (6)	Xhaka G 30 (1)
Luiz D 32 (1)	Ozil M........................18	

League goals (56): Aubameyang 22, Lacazette 10, Pepe 5, Martinelli 3, Nketiah 2, Luiz 2, Sokratis 2, Bellerin 1, Chambers 1, Nelson 1, Ozil 1, Saka 1, Soares 1, Tierney 1, Torreira 1, Willock 1, Xhaka 1.
FA Cup goals (11): Aubameyang 4, Nketiah 2, Ceballos 1, Nelson 1, Saka 1, Pepe 1,Sokratis 1.
League Cup goals (10): Martinelli 4, Willock 2, Holding 1, Maitland-Niles 1, Nelson 1, Torreira 1
Europa League goals (16): Aubameyang 3, Martinelli 3, Lacazette 2, Pepe 2, Saka 2, Willock 2, Ceballos 1,Mustafi 1
Average home league attendance: 60,279. **Player of Year**: Pierre Emerick Aubameyang

ASTON VILLA

A £140m investment in new players was about to turn sour as Villa went ten matches without a victory, fell four points adrift and looked set for an immediate return to the Championship. Instead, a commendable recovery by Dean Smith's side brought safety on a nerve-shredding final day of the season. Amid growing claims that the club signed players ill-equipped for the demands of the Premier League, two of those brought in made notable contributions. Egypt international Trezeguet scored twice for a 2-0 victory over Crystal Palace and the only one of the game against Arsenal. Former Brentford defender Ezri Konsa netted his first in the league against Everton and only an 87th minute equaliser by Theo Walcott denied them another three points. Throughout this difficult campaign, however, captain Jack Grealish had done most to keep his side afloat and it was fitting that his goal at West Ham in the final round of fixtures proved crucial. Although the lead last barely a minute, another1-1 scoreline enabled Villa to stay up, a point ahead of Bournemouth in the third relegation place. Major injuries had played a significant part in the struggle. Goalkeeper Tom Heaton and £22m record-signing Wesley sustained knee ligament damage early in the New Year and played no further part. Then, influential midfielder John McGinn was ruled out for three months with an ankle injury. Smith was also unhappy that Villa were the only club asked to play four matches in 11 days immediately after lockdown. Away from the pressures, they flourished in the League Cup, reaching the final and making Manchester City work hard for a 2-1 success.

Borja	(2)	Heaton T	20	Reina P	12
Davis K	4 (14)	Hourihane C	18 (9)	Samatta M	11 (3)
Douglas Luiz	28 (8)	Jota	4 (6)	Steer J	1
Drinkwater D	4	Kodjia J	- (6)	Targett M	27 (1)
El Ghazi A	26 (8)	Konsa E	24 (1)	Taylor N	11 (3)
Elmohamady A	11 (7)	Lansbury H	2 (8)	Trezeguet	20 (14)
Engels B	15 (2)	McGinn J	27 (1)	Vassilev I	- (4)
Grealish J	36	Mings T	33	Wesley	21
Guilbert F	22 (3)	Nakamba M	19 (10)		
Hause K	17 (1)	Nyland O	5 (2)		

League goals (41): Grealish 8, Trezeguet 6, Wesley 5, El Ghazi 4, Douglas Luiz 3, Hourihane 3, McGinn 3, Mings 2, Elmohamady 1, Engels 1, Hause 1, Konsa 1, Samatta 1, Targett 1, Opponents 1
FA Cup goals (1): El Ghazi 1. **League Cup goals** (20): Hourihane 4, Grealish 2, Guilbert 2, Kodjia 2, Davis 1, El Ghazi 1, Elmohamady 1, Jota 1, Kodija 1, Samatta 1, Targett 1, Trezeguet 1, Wesley 1, Opponents 1
Average home league attendance: 41,661. **Player of Year**: Jack Grealish

BOURNEMOUTH

The end of a five-year Premier League adventure was followed by the end of an era when Eddie Howe left the club after a 25-year association as player and manager. Howe, who led Bournemouth from the brink of extinction into English football's high society, went by mutual consent after what he described in an emotional statement as 'an incredible journey.' Fittingly, his final match was in keeping with the standards he had insisted on during his time as manager – an enterprising 3-1 victory at Everton in the final round of fixtures. But that performance, along with a 4-1 success against Leicester in the penultimate home game, failed to paper over season-long weaknesses which enabled Aston Villa to escape the drop by a single point gained in their final match against West Ham. Bournemouth won three of the opening six against Villa, Everton and Southampton, with Callum Wilson on the mark four times and on-loan Harry Wilson looking like another promising point of attack. But that threat diminished, alongside a spate of injuries which ravaged the defence, and after losing to Norwich early in the New Year they scored just twice in nine games and won once – ironically 1-0 at Chelsea with a goal by Dan Gosling. The return of Wales midfielder David Brooks, out for a year with torn ankle ligaments, offered a lifeline. So did Dominic Solanke's first league goals in 38 appearances for the team. Instead, a 2-0 home defeat by Southampton highlighted all the problems and left them with too much to do.

Ake N	29	Cook S	28 (1)	Fraser R	21 (7)
Billing P	29 (5)	Daniels C	2	Gosling D	14 (10)
Brooks D	8 (1)	Danjuma A	6 (8)	Ibe J	- (2)
Cook L	14 (13)	Francis S	10 (5)	Kelly L	7 (1)

.ing J................. 24 (2)	Simpson J.................. 1 (3)	Surman A 2 (3)
erma J 31 (2)	Smith A...................24	Surridge S.................. - (4)
1epham C 10 (2)	Solanke D 17 (15)	Travers M........................1
.amsdale A...................37	Stacey J.................. 17 (2)	Wilson C 32 (3)
.ico D.......................27	Stanislas J 7 (8)	Wilson H................. 20 (11)

eague goals (40): Wilson C 8, Wilson H 7, King 6, Gosling 3, Solanke 3, Stanislas 3, Ake 2, Billing 1, Brooks 1, Cook S 1, Fraser 1, Lerma 1, Mepham 1, Opponents 2
A Cup goals (5): Billing 2, Solanke 1, Surridge 1, Wilson C 1. **League Cup goals**: None
average home league attendance: 10,510. **Player of Year**: Aaron Ramsdale

BRIGHTON AND HOVE ALBION

Graham Potter justified an early vote of confidence by leading Brighton away from relegation trouble. Six months into the manager's job as Chris Hughton's successor, he was handed a two-year contract extension through to 2025 by a satisfied chairman Tony Bloom. His side were keeping their distance from the bottom three, helped by record-signing Neal Maupay's 80th minute winner at the Emirates. But they came under pressure going into lockdown, two points away from trouble after eight matches without a victory. It eased immediately on the resumption when the former Brentford striker scored in the fifth minute of stoppage-time to add to Lewis Dunk's equaliser as Brighton came from behind to complete a notable double over Arsenal. Then, they all but secured their position for next season with the only goal at Norwich from Leandro Trossard. After conceding eight in matches against Liverpool and Manchester City, they finished on a high with a stunning 25-yard strike by Mali international Yves Bissouma for his first in the Premier League. It came in a 2-1 win at Burnley which brought the club's best top-flight points total of 41, one more than in 2017–18.

.lzate S.................. 12 (7)	Gross P.................. 22 (7)	Murray G..................7 (16)
ndone F.................... 1 (2)	Jahanbakhsh A 3 (7)	Propper D.................32 (3)
ernardo.................... 7 (7)	Lamptey T.................. 7 (1)	Ryan M..........................38
Bissouma Y 15 (7)	Locadia J 1 (1)	Schelotto E.................. 4 (4)
.ong G .... - (4)	MacAllister A.............. 4 (5)	Stephens D.................28 (5)
urn D 33 (1)	March S 11 (8)	Trossard L.................22 (9)
onnolly A 14 (10)	Maupay N.................. 30 (7)	Webster A......................31
uffy S 12 (7)	Montoya M 23 (4)	
unk L.......................36	Mooy A....................25 (6)	

eague goals (39): Maupay 10, Trossard 5, Dunk 3, Connolly 3, Webster 3, Cross 2, Jahanbakhsh , Mooy 2, Andone 1, Bissouma 1, Duffy 1, Murray 1, Propper 1, Opponents 4.
A Cup goals: None. **League Cup goals** (3): Connolly 1, Murray 1, Roberts H 1
average home league attendance: 30, 376. **Player of Year**: Lewis Dunk

BURNLEY

Burnley matched their highest Premier League points total of 54 to finish a satisfying season the top half of the table. They also recorded the most number of wins, 15, alongside two quality individual performances. Chris Wood scored 14 goals and Nick Pope was runner-up for the league's Golden Glove award, one behind Ederson's tally of 16 clean sheets for Manchester City. In doing so, Pope put himself in line to add to his two England caps in the new campaign which concludes with the rescheduled European Championship finals. Wood and strike partner ay Rodriguez, with a spectacular angled drive, gave Burnley their first victory over Manchester nited at Old Trafford since 1962. Another notable performance came at Anfield, where an qualiser by Rodriguez ended Liverpool's chances of a 100 per cent home record. The season ad its controversy, with manager Sean Dyche speaking publicly about his dissatisfaction ith the club running down players' contracts and leaving him with a selection problem for a resumption of the season after lockdown. Burnley lost 5-0 to Manchester City in the first game back, then went seven unbeaten before going down 2-1 at home by Brighton in the final fixture

Bardsley P 21	Lennon A 4 (12)	Tarkowski J 38
Barnes A.............. 17 (2)	Long K 6 (2)	Taylor C 22 (2)
Brady R 5 (12)	Lowton M 17	Thompson M.................- (1)
Brownhill J............. 9 (1)	McNeil D.....................38	Vydra M..............7 (12)
Cork J.........................30	Mee B.........................32	Westwood A 35
Drinkwater D 1	Pieters E 21 (3)	Wood C 29 (3)
Gudmundsson J B..... 6 (6)	Pope N.........................38	
Hendrick J 22 (2)	Rodriguez J 20 (16)	

League goals (43): Wood 14, Rodriguez 8, Barnes 6, Hendrick 2, McNeil 2, Tarkowski 2, Vydra 2, Westwood 2, Brady 1, Gudmundsson 1, Mee 1, Opponents 2
FA Cup goals (5): Pieters 2, Rodriguez 2, Hendrick 1. **League Cup goals** (1): Rodriguez 1
Average home league attendance: 20,260. **Player of Year**: Nick Pope

CHELSEA

Frank Lampard graced Stamford Bridge as a player for a dozen years and his return as manager suggested he could make a major impact in that role, too. Defeat by Arsenal in the FA Cup and by Bayern Munich in the Champions League did nothing to undermine reaching a Wembley final and retaining place in Europe's premier club competition in a demanding season with a team refreshingly influenced by youth. Lampard had to face up to the loss of the club's best player, Eden Hazard and a transfer ban, alongside all the high expectation that comes with this particular job. There was also the little matter of a 4-0 defeat by Manchester United in his first match which shone the spotlight even more. That was quickly overtaken by a record-equalling run of seven straight away wins in all competitions, together with a top-four place secured then maintained for the rest of the campaign. It was not all plain sailing, particularly during a mid-winter run of four defeats in five, including one at home to Bournemouth, and a sequence of four games without a win early in the New Year. But Chelsea regained momentum each time while transfer business also resumed after the ban was halved on appeal, with fees agreed for Morocco winger Hakim Ziyech and Germany striker Timo Werner ahead of the summer window. More signings were promised after the loss at Wembley, where Lampard declared he had no complaints about the result, despite injuries to Christian Pulisic, Cesar Azpilicueta and Pedro and a questionable second yellow card for Mateo Kovacic.

Abraham T.............. 25 (9)	Emerson..................... 13 (2)	Loftus-Cheek R 2 (5)
Anjorin F..................... - (1)	Gilmour B.................. 2 (4)	Marcos Alonso 15 (3)
Arrizabalaga K................33	Giroud O 12 (6)	Mount M 32 (5)
Azpilicueta C..................36	Hudson-Odoi C 7 (15)	Pedro..........................8 (3)
Barkley R.............. 13 (8)	James R 16 (8)	Pulisic C 19 (6)
Batshuayi M............. 1 (15)	Jorginho 27 (4)	Rudiger A 19 (1)
Broja A..................... - (1)	Kante N'Golo 20 (7)	Tomori F.......................15
Caballero W....................5	Kovacic M 23 (8)	Willian 29 (7)
Christensen A..................21	Lamptey T .... - (1)	Zouma K 25 (3)

League goals (69): Abraham 15, Pulisic 9, Willian 9, Giroud 8, Mount 7, Marcos Alonso 4, Jorginho 4, Kante 3, Azpilicueta 2, Rudiger 2, Barkley 1, Batshuayi 1, Hudson-Odoi 1, Kovacic 1, Pedro 1, Tomori 1
FA Cup goals (11): Barkley 3, Batshuayi 1, Giroud 1, Hudso-Odoi 1, Mount 1, Pulisic 1, Tomori 1, Willian 1, Opponents 1. **League Cup goals** (8): Batshuayi 3, Barkley 1, Hudson-Odoi 1, James 1, Pedro 1, Zouma 1
Champions League goals (12): Abraham 3, Azpilicueta 2, Jorginho 2, Batshuayi 1, James 1, Kovacic 1, Pulisic 1, Willian 1

CRYSTAL PALACE

A rollercoaster season seemed to be turning Roy Hodgson's way before and immediately after its enforced suspension. Amid an injury list, with eight players out of action at one time, Palace had dropped into the lower reaches of the table after a single win in 11 matches. But with the casualty list easing, they were on the move again with successive 1-0 victories over Newcastle, Brighton and Watford. Then, when play resumed, a 2-0 victory at Bournemouth, in the first top-flight English league game to be shown live on the *BBC* since 1988, took them ahead of Arsenal and level on points with Tottenham. The revival hinted at a challenge for a Europa League place. Instead, a 4-0 defeat by Liverpool sparked another slide, prolonged at Villa Park when Mamadou Sakho' s early goal, with the aid of his shoulder, was ruled out by VAR – the latest in a lengthy run of controversial handball decisions. Palace lost seven successive matches in all and were goalless in six of them, before breaking the sequence in the final match of the season when Jeffrey Schlupp cancelled out Harry Kane's early strike for Tottenham. It didn't prevent Palace from having the worst scoring record, apart from relegated Norwich, of 31. Hodgson admitted the problem had to be solved in the transfer market 'with someone who can score goals like Kane.'

Ayew J	37	Kouyate C	29 (6)	Schlupp J	11 (6)
Benteke C	13 (11)	McArthur J	37	Tomkins J	18
Cahill G	25	McCarthy J	16 (17)	Townsend A	14 (10)
Camarasa V	1	Meyer M	6 (11)	Van Aanholt P	29
Cenk Tosun	2 (3)	Milivojevic L	28 (3)	Ward J	27 (2)
Dann S	14 (2)	Mitchell T	2 (2)	Wickham C	- (6)
Guaita V	35	Pierrick B	- (2)	Zaha W	37 (1)
Hennessey W	3	Riedewald J	7 (10)		
Kelly M	17 (2)	Sakho M	11 (3)		

League goals (31): Ayew 9, Zaha 4, Milivojevic 3, Schlupp 3, Van Aanholt 3, Benteke 2, Cenk Tosun 1, Kouyate 1, Tomkins 1, Townsend 1, Wickham 1, Opponents 2
FA Cup goals: None. League Cup goals: None
Average home league attendance: 25,060. Player of Year: Jordan Ayew

EVERTON

Everton experienced their worst season since finishing one place above the relegation zone in 2003-04. David Moyes declared himself 'embarrassed' on that occasion. This time, Carlo Ancelotti called for more 'ambition, motivation and passion' to improve on 12th position which left his team completely in the shadow of their next-door neighbours. The club's fifth manager in six years, replaced Marco Silva, sacked after 18 months in the job in the wake of a 5-2 defeat by Liverpool approaching the midway point of the campaign. After coach Duncan Ferguson lifted spirits in a caretaker role, notably by a 3-1 Goodison Park success against Chelsea achieved with two goals from Dominic Calvert-Lewin, Ancelotti took over a side fifth from bottom. The three-times Champions League winner led them away from the threat of going down and into the top half before back-to-back victories over Watford and Crystal Palace. But Everton remained inconsistent through to the final fixture when a 3-1 home defeat by relegated Bournemouth reflected much of what had gone before. Leighton Baines made his final appearance off the bench in that match, announcing afterwards his retirement at the age of 35 after making 420 appearances in 13 years at the club and winning 30 England caps.

Baines L	4 (4)	Branthwaite J	2 (2)	Cenk Tosun	2 (3)
Bernard	15 (12)	Calvert-Lewin D	30 (6)	Coleman S	21 (6)

Davies T 23 (7)	Holgate M 24 (3)	Pickford J 38
Delph F 13 (3)	Iwobi A 19 (6)	Richarlison 36
Digne L 35	Kean M 6 (23)	Schneiderlin M 12 (3)
Gbamin J-P 1 (1)	Keane M 28 (3)	Sidibe D 18 (7)
Gomes A 17 (2)	Mina Y 25 (4)	Sigurdsson G 28 (7)
Gordon A 4 (7)	Niasse O .... - (3)	Walcott T 17 (8)

League goals (44): Calvert-Lewin 13, Richarlison 13, Bernard 3, Kean 2, Keane 2, Mina 2, Sigurdsson 2, Walcott 2, Cenk Tosun 1, Davies 1, Iwobi 1, Opponents 2
FA Cup goals: None. **League Cup goals** (10): Calvert-Lewin 2, Richarlison 2, Baines 1, Davies 1, Digne 1, Holgate 1, Iwobi 1, Sigurdsson 1
Average home league attendance: 39,150. **Player of Year**: Dominic Calvert-Lewin

LEICESTER CITY

Leicester lost key players, lost confidence and surrendered what looked like a cast-iron Champions League place. They were overtaken by fast-finishing Manchester United and had to be satisfied with a Europa League spot as manager Brendan Rodgers admitted his side were 'still a work in progress.' Leicester went into lockdown with an-eight point cushion after beating Aston Villa 4-0 in the final Premier League game before the season was interrupted. Rodgers had signed a new five-and-a-half-year contract. But his side emerged without the services of Ricardo Pereira, then lost James Maddison and Ben Chilwell to further injuries. By the time of Turkish defender Caglar Soyuncu's suspension for a red card at Bournemouth, they were holding on to fourth place on goal difference. After just two wins in eight matches since the resumption, Leicester were not best prepared for a last-day decider against United and a 2-0 home defeat came as no real surprise. Jamie Vardy provided some consolation, having reached 100 Premier League goals, then claiming the season's Golden Boot award for 23, which included a hat-trick in the 9-0 demolition of Southampton. Vardy was one ahead of Arsenal's Pierre-Emerick Aubameyang and Southampton's Danny Ings.

Albrighton M 9 (11)	Gray D 3 (18)	Ndidi W 29 (3)
Perez A 26 (7)	Hirst G .... - (2)	Pereira R 28
Barnes H 24 (12)	Iheanacho K 12 (8)	Praet D 12 (15)
Bennett R 3 (2)	James M .... - (1)	Schmeichel K 38
Chilwell B 27	Justin J 11 (2)	Soyuncu C 34
Choudhury H 9 (10)	Maddison J 29 (2)	Thomas L 3
Evans J 38	Mendy N 4 (3)	Tielemans Y 32 (5)
Fuchs C 8 (3)	Morgan W 4 (7)	Vardy J 34 (1)

League goals (67): Vardy 23, Perez 8, Barnes 6, Maddison 6, Iheanacho 5, Chilwell 3, Pereira 3, Tielemans 3, Gray 2, Ndidi 2, Choudhury 1, Evans 1, Praet 1, Soyuncu 1, Opponents 2
FA Cup goals (4): Barnes 1, Iheanacho 1, Pereira 1, Opponents 1. **League Cup goals** (12): Iheanacho 4, Maddison 3, Tielemans 2, Evans 1, Gray 1, Justin 1.
Average home league attendance: 32,061. **Player of Year**: Jamie Vardy

LIVERPOOL

World champions, European champions, English champions – Jurgen Klopp belted out Liverpool's achievements without a hint of glorification, just pure delight, after the title Anfield prized most of all arrived 30 years on from the last one. They ran Manchester City so close the previous season. This time they ran away from City, and everyone else, in a season-long display of class and consistency. In the three summers from 2016-18, Klopp made significant, expensive additions to a squad he knew was not ready. This time there were no major signings – he felt their time had come. Pre-season results were not great; international demands on Sadio Mane, Mohamed Salah and Roberto Firmino considerable; goalkeeper Alisson was ruled out for two months with a calf injury sustained in the second match. Even so, Liverpool proved unstoppable, leaving City in their slipstream by the end of the year when Pep Guardiola had conceded, 13 points adrift. They paused from domestic issues to lift the Club World Cup against Brazil champions Flamengo, resuming normal service at home with a 4-0 win over Leicester. Liverpool went on to equal City's all-time record of 18 successive top-flight wins with an 81st minute winner from Mane, before a run of 44 unbeaten Premier League matches, stretching back to January 2019, came to an end in a 3-0 defeat at Watford. The club's Champions League defence was then ended by Atletico Madrid before lockdown. When the season resumed, they were crowned champions on June 25 – the latest ever and also the earliest with seven games still to play. Liverpool fell one short of City's Premier League record of 100 points and their winning margin of 19. Klopp also acknowledged how difficult it was for supporters not to be able to pack Anfield for the trophy presentation. But it was still one to remember, with Jordan Henderson receiving it from Sir Kenny Dalglish – the last Liverpool manager to finish top in 1990.

Adrian	9 (2)	Jones C	1 (5)	Origi D	7 (21)
Alexander-Arnold T	35 (3)	Keita N	9 (9)	Oxlade-Chamberlain A	17 (13)
Alisson	29	Lallana A	3 (12)	Robertson A	34 (2)
Elliott H	- (2)	Lovren D	9 (1)	Salah M	33
Fabinho	22 (6)	Mane S	31 (4)	Shaqiri X	2 (5)
Firmino R	34 (4)	Matip J	8 (1)	Wijnaldum G	35 (2)
Gomez J	22 (6)	Milner J	9 (13)	Williams N	3 (3)
Henderson J	26 (4)	Minamino T	2 (8)	Van Dijk V	38

League goals (85): Salah 19, Mane 18, Firmino 9, Van Dijk 5, Wijnaldum 4, Henderson 4, Origi 4, Oxlade-Chamberlain 4, Wijnaldum 4, Fabinho 2, Keita 2, Milner 2, Robertson 2, Jones 1, Lallana 1, Matip 1, Shaqiri 1, Opponents 2
FA Cup goals (4): Jones 2, Opponents 2. **League Cup goals** (7): Milner 2, Origi 2, Hoever K-J 1, Oxlade-Chamberlain 1, Opponents1
Champions League goals (15): Salah 4, Oxlade-Chamberlain 3, Mane 2, Wijnaldum 2, Firmino 1, Keita 1, Lovren 1, Robertson 1
Club World Cup goals (3): Firmino 2, Keita 1 **European Super Cup goals** (2): Mane 2. **Community Shield goals** (1): Matip 1
Average home league attendance: 53,143. **Player of Year**: Jordan Henderson

MANCHESTER CITY

Outpaced in the Premier League, knocked out of the FA Cup by his 'apprentice' and second best again in the Champions League. Rarely has Pep Guardiola faced a bleaker set of results at the end of a season in which his side's continued dominance of the League Cup offered limited consolation. The club's biggest achievement, it could be argued, was overturning at the Court of Arbitration for Sport a two-year European ban imposed by UEFA for breaching financial fair play rules. Failure to invest in a defence weakened by the departure of Vincent Kompany, was laid bare when Aymeric Laporte sustained a knee injury early on and did not play again for five months. Well before his return, Guardiola had handed the title to Liverpool, who were 14 points ahead by the end of the year and continued to stretch their lead. John Stones failed to impose his authority, midfield protector Fernandinho was uncomfortable in a stop-gap role at the back and the whole team were unbalanced. There was still an abundance of goals, notably from Raheem Sterling's most productive campaign. But by the time Liverpool clinched top spot with a record seven matches still to play after a single defeat, their rivals had been second best eight times. City then lost to Arsenal, managed by Guardiiola's former assistant Mikel Arteta, with another Wembley appearance beckoning after the defeat of Aston Villa had delivered a hat-trick of League Cup success. Finally, and probably the biggest blow of all, came with a third straight quarter-final defeat, by Lyon, in the Champions League after the normally reliable Sterling had missed horribly the chance to level the match at 2-2.

Aguero S............... 18 (6)	Fernandinho 26 (4)	Mendy B 18 (1)
Angelino 4 (2)	Foden P 9 (14)	Otamendi N............. 18 (6)
Bernardo Silva 23 (11)	Gabriel Jesus.......... 21 (13)	Rodri 29 (6)
Bravo C.................... 3 (1)	Garcia E................... 8 (5)	Sane L....................- (1)
David Silva............. 22 (5)	Gundogan I 21 (10)	Sterling R................ 30 (3)
De Bruyne K............ 32 (3)	Joao Cancelo J 13 (4)	Stones J.................. 12 (4)
Doyle T ....- (1)	Laporte A 14 (1)	Walker K 28 (1)
Ederson 35	Mahrez R 21 (12)	Zinchenko O 13 (6)

League goals (102): Sterling 20, Aguero 16, Gabriel Jesus 14, De Bruyne 13, Mahrez 11, Bernardo Silva 8, David Silva 6, Foden 5, Rodri 3, Gundogan 2, Otamendi 2, Laporte 1, Walker 1, Opponents 2
FA Cup goals (11): Aguero 2, Gabriel Jesus 2, Bernardo Silva 1, De Bruyne 1, Foden 1, Gundogan 1, Harwood-Bellis T 1, Sterling 1, Zinchenko 1 **League Cup goals** (14): Aguero 3, Sterling 3, Bernardo Silva 1, Gabriel Jesus 1, Joao Cancelo 1, Mahrez 1, Otamendi 1, Rodri 1, Opponents 2
Champions League goals (21): Gabriel Jesus 6, Sterling 6, Aguero 2, De Bruyne 2, Foden 2, Gundogan 2, Mahrez 1
Community Shield goals (1): Sterling 1
Average home league attendance: 54,391. **Player of Year**: Kevin De Bruyne

MANCHESTER UNITED

Ole Gunnar Solskjaer acknowledged the progress made after a dreadful start to the season had left Old Trafford in turmoil and his own position under threat. United recovered to regain a Champions League place and were knocking on the door of three knockout competitions. But Solskjaer admitted his side were not the finished article. And as if to validate that verdict, he added: 'Nowhere near.' Domestically, the Premier League table highlighted the manager's reservations – 33 points adrift of champions Liverpool and 15 away from runners-up Manchester City. So did the FA Cup when two errors by David de Gea and Harry Maguire's own goal presented Chelsea with a 3-1 semi-final victory. Wembley beckoned again, this time in the League Cup, until a 3-1 home defeat by their neighbours in the first leg left them with too much to do in the return. Abroad, United were left to rue missed chances against Sevilla in the Europa League which cost a third semi-final setback. So, at the end of a marathon campaign, United had to be satisfied with forcing their way into the league's top four in the penultimate fixture and remaining there in a make-or-break final match against Leicester. Another nerveless penalty by Bruno Fernandes, followed in stoppage-time by substitute Jesse Lingard's first league goal of a season spent mostly in the shadows, did the trick. It was the Portuguese midfielder's eighth in eight attempts since he arrived in the winter transfer window, settled into an elegant stride straight away and now looks a key figure in Solskjaer's plans to take United a step further.

Bailly E..................... 1 (3)	Ighalo O ....- (11)	Pereira A 18 (7)
Bruno Fernandes 14	James D................... 26 (7)	Pogba P 13 (3)
Chong T.....................- (3)	Jones P.........................2	Rashford M....................31
Dalot D..................... 1 (3)	Lindelof V.....................35	Rojo M 1 (2)
De Gea D...................38	Lingard J................. 9 (13)	Shaw L..................... 20 (4)
Fred 23 (6)	Maguire H 38	Tuanzebe A.................. 2 (3)
Fosu-Mensah T........... 2 (1)	Martial A 31 (1)	Wan-Bissaka A 34 (1)
Garner J.....................- (1)	Mata J 8 (11)	Williams B................. 11 (6)
Gomes A ....- (2)	Matic N................... 18 (3)	Young A 10 (2)
Greenwood M 12 (19)	McTominay S 20 (7)	

League goals (66): Martial 17, Rashford 17, Greenwood 10, Bruno Fernandes 8, McTominay 4, James 3, Lindelof 1, Lingard 1, Maguire 1, Pereira 1, Pogba 1, Williams 1, Opponents 1
FA Cup goals (13): Ighalo 3, Maguire 2, Bruno Fernandes 1, Dalot 1, Greenwood 1, Jones 1,

Lingard 1, Martial 1, Mata 1, Shaw 1 **League Cup goals** (7): Rashford 4, Greenwood 1, Martial 1, Opponents 1
Europa League goals (25): Greenwood 5, Martial 4, Bruno Fernandes 3, Fred 2, Ighalo 2, Lingard 2, Mata 2, James 1, McTominay 1, Pereira 1, Rashford 1, Young 1
Average home league attendance: 73,393. **Player of Year**: Bruno Fernandes

NEWCASTLE UNITED

It was a case of as you were at the end of the season for owner Mike Ashley and manager Steve Bruce. A long-mooted takeover of the club fell through when a Saudi Arabian-backed consortium withdrew an agreed £300m offer. On the field, there was a repeat of the 13th place in 2019, this time with Bruce in charge after the departure of Rafael Benitez for the riches of Chinese football. Nothing changed either in Newcastle's search for a proven goalscorer. A record £40m was paid to the German club Hoffenheim for the Brazilian striker Joelinton, who scored the winner against Tottenham in his third Premier League match, then had to wait another 27 for the next, in a 3-0 victory over Sheffield United in the first match after lockdown. Midfielder Jonjo Shelvey's total of six as leading scorer told its own story. At least supporters had their money's worth watching French winger Allan Saint-Maximin, a £17m purchase from Nice whose driving runs and sublime skills made him one of the season's best value for money buys. One of the season's best performances, 4-1 at Bournemouth, left Newcastle three points off a place in the top half. But a failure to win any of the final six matches left them well short.

Almiron M	35 (1)	Joelinton	32 (6)	Ritchie M	14 (4)
Atsu C	6 (13)	Ki Sung-Yueng	1 (2)	Rose D	10 (1)
Bentaleb N	8 (4)	Krafth E	11 (6)	Saint-Maximin A	23 (3)
Carroll A	4 (15)	Lascelles J	24	Schar F	18 (4)
Clark C	14	Lazaro V	4 (9)	Shelvey J	25 (1)
Dubravka M	38	Lejeune F	4 (2)	Watts K	- (1)
Dummett P	14 (2)	Longstaff M	6 (3)	Willems J	18 (1)
Fernandez F	29 (3)	Longstaff S	14 (9)	Yedlin D	10 (6)
Gayle D	10 (10)	Manquillo J	18 (3)		
Hayden I	26 (3)	Muto Y	2 (6)		

League goals (38): Shelvey 6, Almiron 4, Gayle 4, Saint-Maximin 3, Clark 2, Fernandez 2, Joelinton 2, Lejeune 2, Longstaff M 2, Ritchie 2, Schar 2, Willems 2, Hayden 1, Lascelles 1, Lazaro 1, Longstaff S 1, Yedlin 1
FA Cup goals (11): Almiron 4, Joelinton 2, Lazaro 1, Longstaff M 1, Longstaff S 1, Saint-Maximin 1, Opponents 1. **League Cup goals** (1): Muto 1
Average home league attendance: 48,248. **Player of Year**: Martin Dubravka

NORWICH CITY

A season that turned stale after an encouraging start ended with Norwich out of their depth and making an immediate return to the Championship. 'Men against boys' was manager Daniel Farke's stark assessment when relegation was confirmed by a 4-0 home defeat by West Ham. Throughout, the club never veered from a safety-first financial policy, making only modest additions to the squad that won promotion. At first, Farke's young side looked as if they might be capable of holding their own. Teemu Pukki, whose 29 goals had done most to deliver the title, scored a hat-trick against Newcastle and was on the mark again in the 3-2 defeat of defending champions Manchester City. Pukki had six strikes to his credit from the opening five matches before the first worrying signs came with a 5-1 home defeat by Aston Villa. The goals dried up, a crop of injuries took its toll and once Norwich had dropped into the bottom the bottom three two months into the campaign, they never looked like escaping. Some relief from a long, hard winter came with a run to the sixth round of the FA Cup. But by the time

Michail Antonio scored all four of West Ham's goals, they had managed just two in 11 league matches. The final straw came in the final home match when Emiliano Buendia and Josip Drmich were sent off and Ben Godfrey conceded an own goal in a record tenth successive defeat, 2-0 by Burnley.

Aarons M 36	Hanley G 14 (1)	Pukki T 33 (3)
Amadou I 8 (3)	Hernandez O........... 14 (12)	Roberts P ....- (3)
Buendia E............... 28 (8)	Idah A..................... 1 (11)	Rupp L....................8 (4)
Byram S 15 (2)	Klose T 7	Srbeny D ....- (8)
Cantwell T............... 30 (7)	Krul T 36	Stiepermann M 14 (10)
Drmic J.................. 5 (16)	Leitner M 7 (2)	Tettey A...................28 (2)
Duda O 9 (1)	Lewis J................... 25 (3)	Thomas J...................- (1)
Fahrmann R 1	Martin J .... - (4)	Trybull T..................14 (2)
Famewo A .... - (1)	McGovern M 1 (1)	Vrancic M...............6 (14)
Godfrey B 30	McLean K 32 (5)	Zimmermann C..........16 (1)

League goals (26): Pukki 11, Cantwell 6, Buendia 1, Drmic 1, Hernandez 1, Lewis 1, McLean 1, Srbeny 1, Tettey 1, Vrancic 1, Opponents 1
FA Cup goals (8): Idah 3, Drmic 2, Cantwell 1, Hanley 1. Hernandez 1. **League Cup goals**: None.
Average home league attendance: 27,025. **Player of Year**: Tim Krul

SHEFFIELD UNITED

Chris Wilder's team exceeded all expectations on their return to the Premier League after a 12-year absence. There were no inhibitions, no safety-first measures to guard against a quick return to the Championship. Instead, they were organised, disciplined and brimming with confidence to such an extent that a European place remained alive until the penultimate game. The club prepared well – breaking their transfer record four times without breaking the bank and doing so again during the winter window. An unbeaten away record stretching to nine matches was the best start for a promoted side since Burnley's ten in season 1947-48. It eventually fell to Manchester City after Lys Mousset had a goal ruled out by VAR for offside and John Fleck was impeded by referee Chris Kavanagh, enabling Kevin De Bruyne to send Sergio Aguero through for City's first goal. Wilder's contract extension through to 2024 coincided with sixth in the table, a position undermined when United returned from lockdown short on goals. But 3-1 against Tottenham, then 3-0 against Chelsea as David McGoldrick broke his duck with two goals restored hopes of a Europa League spot. Instead, with relentless running and pressing used up, there were weary defeats against Leicester, Everton and Southampton, resulting in a still-commendable ninth position.

Baldock G 38	Henderson D....................36	O'Connell J...............32 (1)
Basham C 38	Jagielka P 2 (4)	Osborn B 6 (7)
Berge S 12 (2)	Lundstram J 26 (8)	Robinson C.................9 (7)
Besic M 2 (7)	McBurnie O 24 (12)	Robinson J 6
Clarke L .... - (2)	McGoldrick D........... 22 (6)	Rodwell J ....- (1)
Egan J 36	Moore S 2	Sharp B 10 (15)
Fleck J 28 (2)	Morrison R .... - (1)	Stevens E.....................38
Freeman K .... - (2)	Mousset L 11 (19)	Zivkovic R ....- (5)
Freeman L 3 (8)	Norwood O 37 (1)	

League goals (39): McBurnie 6, Mousset 6, Fleck 5, Lundstram 5, Sharp 3, Baldock 2, Egan 2, McGoldrick 2, Stevens 2, Berge 1, Norwood 1, Robinson C 1, Opponents 3
FA Cup goals (7): McGoldrick 2, Besic 1, Clarke 1, Norwood 1, Robinson C 1, Sharp 1. **League Cup goals** (2): Norwood 1, Stearman R 1
Average home league attendance: 30,869. **Player of Year**: Chris Basham

SOUTHAMPTON

Ralph Hasenhuttl led his team away from the wreckage of a record 9-0 home defeat by Leicester towards mid-table respectability and was rewarded with a new four-year contract. It came ahead of lockdown with their Premier League status still not assured. After play resumed, lingering doubts were eased by the 3-0 defeat of Norwich, then the 40-point mark reached when Danny Ings scored twice in a 3-1 success against Watford. The two performances underlined Southampton's record on their travels, with nine wins – three more than at St Mary's – bettered only by Liverpool and Manchester City. The most notable came in the return against Leicester – a 2-1 victory courtesy of goals from Ings and Stuart Armstrong. Frustrating home form was lifted for a moment by a spectacular winner from Che Adams against Manchester City. His first for the club, in 30 appearances in all competitions, was launched from 45 yards over stranded goalkeeper Ederson after Armstrong dispossessed Oleksandr Zinchenko. Southampton also finished well, beating Sheffield United 3-1 with Ings taking his tally to 22 from the penalty spot. He shared second place, alongside Arsenal's Pierre-Emerick Aubameyang, behind Golden Boot winner Jamie Vardy of Leicester.

Adams C 12 (18)	Ings D 32 (6)	Tella N ....- (1)
Armstrong S 19 (11)	Long S 15 (11)	Valery Y 10 (1)
Bednarek J.................34	McCarthy A.....................28	Vestergaard J 17 (2)
Bertrand R 31 (1)	Obafemi M 8 (13)	Vokins J 1
Boufal S 8 (12)	Redmond N....................32	Walker-Peters K 7 (3)
Danso K 3 (3)	Romeu O 20 (10)	Ward-Prowse J 38
Djenepo M 10 (8)	Smallbone W 4 (5)	Yoshida M 6 (2)
Gunn A.................10	Soares C.....................16	
Hojbjerg P.............. 30 (3)	Stephens J 27 (1)	

League goals (51): Ings 22, Armstrong 5, Ward-Prowse 5, Adams 4, Redmond 4, Obafemi 3, Djenepo 2, Long 2, Bednarek 1, Bertrand 1, Stephens 1, Vestergaard 1
FA Cup goals (5): Boufal 1, Ings 1, Long 1, Smallbone 1, Vokins 1. **League Cup goals** (6): Ings 2, Obafemi 1, Redmond 1, Soares 1, Stephens 1
Average home league attendance: 29,675. **Player of Year:** Danny Ings

TOTTENHAM HOTSPUR

Tottenham finished a see-saw season with a flourish to claim a place in the Europa League under Jose Mourinho. They went into lockdown on the back of a catalogue of injuries, including Harry Kane and Son Heung-Min, indifferent results and trailing in the table. They emerged refreshed and at full strength, with Mourinho grateful for what he called 'a second chance.' Momentum built as Toby Alderweireld's 81st minute header settled the north London derby. Kane passed 200 goals with a brace at Newcastle and scored two more to undermine Leicester's Champions League chances. Another, in a 1-1 draw at Crystal Palace in the final fixture, enabled his side to overtake Wolves for sixth place. Tottenham had started the season with Mauricio Pochettino insisting that a top-four spot was no longer enough – the club had to win something. But a third of the way through they were in the bottom half and had been humbled 7-2 at home by Bayern Munich in a Champions League group match. Pochettino was sacked after five-and-a-half-years in charge. Hours after his departure was announced, Mourinho came in on a four-year contract. Tottenham went through in Europe as group runners-up, but fell to Leipzig in the first knockout round 4-0 on aggregate.

Alderweireld T 33	Dier E..................... 15 (4)	Kane H..........................29
Alli D........................ 21 (4)	Eriksen C 10 (10)	Lamela E 12 (13)
Aurier S................... 31 (2)	Gedson Fernandes .... - (7)	Lloris H 21
Bergwijn S 8 (6)	Foyth J 1 (3)	Lo Celso G 15 (13)
Davies B 16 (2)	Gazzaniga P 17 (1)	Lucas Moura 25 (10)

Ndombele T 12 (9)	Sessegnon R 4 (2)	Vertonghen J 19 (4)
Nkoudou G-K .... - (1)	Sissoko M 28 (1)	Walker-Peters K 3
Parrott T .... - (2)	Skipp O 1 (6)	Wanyama V .... - (2)
Rose D 10 (2)	Son Heung-min 28 (2)	Winks H 26 (5)
Sanchez D 27 (2)	Tanganga J 6	

League goals (61): Kane 18, Son Heung-min 11, Alli 8, Lucas Moura 4, Bergwijn 3, Alderweireld 2, Eriksen 2, Lamela 2, Ndombele 2, Sissoko 2, Aurier 1, Vertonghen 1, Opponents 5
FA Cup goals (8): Lucas Moura 2, Son Heung-min 2, Lamela 1, Lo Celso 1, Vertonghen 1, Opponents 1. **League Cup goals:** None
Champions League goals (18): Kane 6, Son Heung-min 5, Alli 1, Aurier 1, Eriksen 1, Lamela 1, Lo Celso 1, Lucas Moura 1, Sessegnon 1
Average home league attendance: 59,384. **Player of Year:** Son Heung-Min

WATFORD

Watford gambled for the highest stakes when sacking Nigel Pearson with two games of the season remaining. The shock move did not pay off and the club were relegated after five continuous seasons in the Premier League. Pearson, attempting the fourth rescue act of his managerial career, argued with owner Gino Pozzo after a 3-1 defeat at West Ham, having described some of his players as 'passengers.' It left his side still three points clear of trouble, but facing tough opposition in their remaining fixtures. With coach Hayden Mullins in temporary charge, Watford lost 4-0 at home to Manchester City, then 3-2 away to Arsenal, after trailing 3-0, to fall one point adrift of Aston Villa. Pearson had answered the call having previously steered Leicester from the bottom of the table, six points adrift at Christmas, to safety, preserved Southampton's Championship status and in his first job kept Carlisle in the Football League. He became the season's third man in charge at Vicarage Road after Javi Gracia and Quique Sanchez Flores were both dismissed. Watford's winless home run stretched to a record 12 games for the first time in their history and they suffered a record 8-0 defeat away to Manchester City. Under Pearson, they inflicted Liverpool's first defeat with two goals from record-signing Ismaila Sarr, overcame Norwich thanks to Danny Welbeck's spectacular overhead kick and defeated Newcastle courtesy of two nerveless penalties by captain Troy Deeney – performances which suggested they might stay up.

Capoue E 30	Foster B 38	Masina A..................20 (6)
Cathcart C.............. 28 (1)	Foulquier D 1 (2)	Pereyra R 17 (11)
Chalobah N 10 (12)	Gray A...................... 7 (16)	Prodl S............................1
Cleverley T 11 (7)	Holebas J 11 (3)	Pussetto I......................- (7)
Dawson C................. 26 (3)	Hughes W................ 27 (3)	Quina.......................- (4)
Deeney T 26 (1)	Janmaat D................ 7 (1)	Sarr I 22 (6)
Deulofeu G............. 25 (3)	Joao Pedro .... - (3)	Success I ....- (5)
Doucoure A 36 (1)	Kabasele C 26 (1)	Welbeck D................8 (10)
Femenia K 26 (2)	Mariappa A.............. 15 (5)	

League goals (36): Deeney 10, Sarr 5, Deulofeu 4, Doucoure 4, Pereyra 3, Dawson 2, Gray 2, Welbeck 2, Cleverley 1, Hughes 1, Masina 1, Opponents 1
FA Cup goals (4): Chalobah 1, Dele-Bashiru T 1, Hinds K 1, Pereyra 1. **League Cup goals** (5): Janmaat 1, Penaranda A 1, Pereyra 1, Sarr 1, Welbeck 1
Average home league attendance: 20,839. **Player of Year:** Ben Foster

WEST HAM UNITED

David Moyes led West Ham to safety for the second time in three seasons – with the help of an impressive scoring burst from Michail Antonio. Moyes returned to the club he lifted during a short-term contract in 2017-18 after Manuel Pellegrini was sacked midway through when a home defeat by Leicester left his side a point above the relegation zone. The former Everton and Manchester United manager started with a 4-0 victory over Bournemouth, captain Mark Noble scoring twice. But the failure to defend winning leads proved a continuing problem, with 22 points dropped as a result by the time matches were suspended. An 89th minute winner by substitute Andriy Yarmolenko against Chelsea gave West Ham some much-needed breathing space. Antonio was also on the mark and scored again when a point was forthcoming at Newcastle. Then, he delivered all four in a 4-0 victory at Norwich – a first for the club since David Cross in 1981. With work still to be done, Jarrod Bowen and Tomas Soucek continued to prove influential signings. Noble made his 500th appearance and his side, effectively reached the safety of 37 points by beating Watford 3-1 as Antonio took his tally to seven in four games.

Ajeti A .... - (9)	Haller S 24 (8)	Randolph D 2
Antonio M 19 (5)	Hernandez J 1 (1)	Rice D 38
Balbuena F 13 (4)	Holland N .... - (2)	Roberto 7 (1)
Bowen J 11 (2)	Johnson B 3	Sanchez C 1 (5)
Cresswell A 31	Lanzini J 14 (10)	Snodgrass R 17 (7)
Diop I 31 (1)	Martin D 4 (1)	Soucek T 12 (1)
Fabianski L 25	Masuaku A 10 (7)	Wilshere J 2 (6)
Felipe Anderson 20 (5)	Ngakia J 5	Yarmolenko A 10 (13)
Fornals P 24 (12)	Noble M 32 (1)	Zabaleta P 6 (4)
Fredericks R 25 (2)	Ogbonna A 31	

League goals (49): Antonio 10, Haller 7, Snodgrass 5, Yarmolenko 5, Noble 4, Cresswell 3, Diop 3, Soucek 3, Fornals 2, Ogbonna 2, Balbuena 1, Bowen 1, Felipe Anderson 1, Hernandez 1, Rice 1
FA Cup goals (2): Fornals 1, Zabaleta 1. **League Cup goals** (2): Fornals 1, Wilshere 1
Average home league attendance: 59,925. **Player of Year**: Declan Rice

WOLVERHAMPTON WANDERERS

Wolves missed out by tiny margins and had nothing tangible to show from a marathon season. They were also left to reflect on a penalty miss by their most reliable goalscorer which could have changed the complexion on another enterprising campaign. In 2019, Nuno Espirito Santo's side were applauded throughout the game for one of the best performances by Premier League newcomers. This time, they matched that seventh place, with an extra two points to show for it, but it was not enough for another Europa League place, which went to Tottenham on goal difference, alongside FA Cup winners Arsenal. Wolves lost their last match 2-0 to Chelsea, one of three defeats in the final six league matches when tiredness was beginning to take its toll. They soldiered on in the resumed Europa League campaign, reaching the last eight in the delayed tie against Olympiacos, ironically as it turned out, with a Raul Jimenez penalty. It delivered a one-off tie against Sevilla, 383 days after launching their campaign against the Northern Irish team Crusaders. Wolves had a golden opportunity to strike an early blow in their 59th match at the start of what amounted to a mini-tournament in Germany. Adama Traore won a penalty after a typical surging run, but Raul had his spot-kick saved, amid claims that the goalkeeper had moved off his line and defenders were guilty encroaching. Sevilla then went through to a semi-final against Manchester United with an 88th minute header from Lucas Ocampos, leaving bereft opponents with little time to respond.

Bennett R 7 (4)	Doherty M 32 (4)	Podence D .... 3(6)
Boly W 22	Gibbs-White M 1 (6)	Raul Jimenez 37 (1)
Bruno Jordao .... - (1)	Jesus Vallejo 1 (1)	Ruben Neves 35 (3)
Coady C 38	Joao Moutinho 34 (4)	Ruben Vinagre 6 (10)
Cutrone P 3 (9)	Jonny 33 (2)	Rui Patricio 38
Dendoncker L 32 (6)	Kilman M 2 (1)	Saiss R 31 (2)
Diogo Jota 27 (7)	Pedro Neto 9 (20)	Traore A 27 (10)

League goals (51): Raul Jimenez 17, Diogo Jota 7, Dendoncker 4, Doherty 4, Traore 4, Pedro Neto 3, Cutrone 2, Jonny 2, Ruben Neves 2, Saiss 2, Joao Moutinho 1, Podence 1, Opponents 2
FA Cup goals: None. League Cup goals (2): Bruno Jordao 1, Cutrone 1. **Europa League goals** (38): Raul Jimenez 10, Diogo Jota 9, Doherty 3, Dendoncker 2, Pedro Neto 2, Ruben Neves 2, Ruben Vinagre 2, Traore 2, Bennett 1, Boly 1, Gibbs-White 1, Saiss 1, Opponents 2
Average home league attendance: 31,360. **Player of Year**:

SKY BET CHAMPIONSHIP

BARNSLEY

Barnsley survived a dreadful start to beat the drop against all the odds in a dramatic finish to the season. They stayed up by defeating promotion-chasing Nottingham Forest and Brentford in the last two fixtures to condemn Charlton to League One instead. A single win in the opening 18 matches was accompanied by Daniel Stendel's dismissal after a 5-1 defeat at Preston. He was replaced by Gerhard Struber, coach of the Austrian club Wolfsberger, who managed to put a second victory on the board – 3-1 against Hull in his third match in charge. Conor Chaplin then scored a hat-trick in a 5-3 success against Queens Park Rangers and his seven goals in seven games were instrumental in lifting his side off the bottom. Cauley Woodrow later chipped in with five in six as Barnsley put together their most productive run, beating Fulham, Middlesbrough and Hull in successive matches without conceding a goal. But they were unable to make up sufficient ground on the tightly-packed bunch of teams above them. And what looked like their last chance went begging when successive games against three of them – Stoke, Luton and Wigan – netted only two points. Instead, they beat Forest 1-0, followed by a 2-1 success at Griffin Park, courtesy of first goals or the club from Callum Styles, then substitute Clarke Oduor in stoppage-time.

Andersen M	37 (1)	McGeehan C	10 (3)	Simoes E	6 (11)
Bahre M-S	20 (6)	Miller G	- (1)	Styles C	5 (12)
Brown J	39 (1)	Mowatt A	44	Thiam M	3 (5)
Cavare D	11	Odour R	12 (4)	Thomas L	24 (15)
Chaplin C	36 (8)	Palmer R	3	Walton J	9
Collins B	19	Panillos D	2 (2)	Wilks M	8 (7)
Diaby B	21	Radlinger S	18	Williams B	16 (4)
Dougall K	9 (3)	Ritzmaier M	13 (2)	Williams J	29 (1)
Green J	- (2)	Schmidt P	2 (27)	Wolfe M	- (1)
Halme A	26 (6)	Sibbick T	17 (1)	Woodrow C	37 (3)
Ludewig K	13 (5)	Sollbauer M	17		

League goals (49): Woodrow 14, Chaplin 11, Halme 4, Brown 3, Mowatt 3, Schmidt 3, McGeehan 2, Simoes 2, Bahre 1, Diaby 1, Odour 1, Styles 1, Thomas 1, Wilks 1, Opponents 1
FA Cup goals (5): Chaplin 2, Brown 1, Thomas 1, Woodrow 1. **League Cup goals**: None
Average home league attendance: 14,061. **Player of Year**: Alex Mowatt

BIRMINGHAM CITY

For the fourth successive season, Birmingham lived dangerously before continuing renewing their Championship status. This time it was a stoppage-time goal from Lukas Jutkiewicz in the penultimate home match which finally calmed nerves. His productive strike partnership with Aston Villa loanee Scott Hogan looked to have established mid-table stability during a ten-match unbeaten run before the season was suspended. Instead, the team struggled when it resumed, losing to Huddersfield and Stoke and requiring Gary Gardner's 88th minute header, his second goal of the game, for a point against Hull after twice trailing. Manager Pep Clotet, scheduled to leave the club at the end of the campaign, departed after a home defeat by

Swansea. And when Hogan had a penalty saved in a 'six-pointer' against Charlton, Birmingham were up against it. But with 93 minutes on the clock Jutkiewicz delivered the equaliser which took his side to the 50-point safety mark. Clotet was succeeded by former Nottingham Forest manager Aitor Karanka.

Agus.................... - (1)	Crowley D............... 29 (9)	Miguel Fernandez..........- (1)
Alvaro 12 (12)	Davis D..................... 13 (2)	Montero J..................2 (12)
Bailey O..................... - (6)	Dean H..................... 34 (5)	Mrabti K..................... 12 (3)
Bajrami G 2	Gardner G................. 27 (8)	Pedersen K..................... 44
Bela J...................... 22 (8)	Gordon N 1 (1)	Reid J.......................- (4)
Bellingham J........... 32 (9)	Harding W 7 (8)	Roberts M 33 (1)
Boyd-Munce C........... - (6)	Hogan S 16 (1)	Seddon S 3 (1)
Burke R .... - (1)	Jutkiewicz L 42 (4)	Sunjic I..................37 (3)
Camp L....................36	Kieftenbeld M........... 2 (6)	Trueman C..................... 10
Clarke-Salter J............19	Maghoma J............. 7 (11)	Villalba F............... 15 (2)
Colin M..........................44	McEachran J............... 5 (3)	

League goals (54): Jutkiewicz 15, Hogan 7, Bellingham 4, Gardner 4, Pedersen 4, Alvaro 3, Sunjic 3, Bela 2, Mrabti 2, Bailey 1, Clarke-Salter 1, Colin 1, Crowley 1, Dean 1, Maghoma 1, Villalba 1, Opponents 3
FA Cup goals (4): Bela 2, Crowley 1, Dean 1. **League Cup goals:** None
Average home league attendance: 20,412. **Player of Year**: Lukas Jutkiewicz

BLACKBURN ROVERS

Blackburn overcame the mid-season loss of leading scorer Bradley Dack with a knee ligament injury to remain on the fringes of a play-off place. Four wins out of six early in the New Year included a 5-0 away success against Sheffield Wednesday, their biggest in the league for 19 years. And they came out of lockdown with a 3-1 win over Bristol City to close to within a point of Preston in sixth place. Northern Ireland midfielder Corry Evans marked his return from a fractured skull and broken nose to score his first goal since 2015. Unluckily, a broken toe in that game put him out of action again and three successive defeats proved costly for his side. Rovers lost at Wigan and Barnsley and were beaten 3-1 at home by leaders Leeds to fall eight points behind. Adam Armstrong's spectacular 45-yard winner at Cardiff, followed by a point against West Bromwich Albion, offered a glimmer of hope. But defeat by Millwall was an anti-climax and they finished seven points adrift after a campaign undermined by repeatedly conceding goals from set pieces.

Armstrong A............. 40 (6)	Davenport J .... - (9)	Nyambe R 30 (1)
Bell A..................... 19 (2)	Downing S................ 38 (3)	Rankin-Costello J........8 (3)
Bennett E 29 (12)	Evans C 11 (2)	Rothwell J 21 (15)
Brereton B 7 (8)	Gallagher S............. 28 (14)	Samuel D 7 (8)
Buckley J 5 (15)	Graham D 14 (24)	Tosin Adarabioyo 33 (1)
Carter H..................2	Holtby L 16 (11)	Travis L.....................41 (2)
Chapman H................. - (5)	Johnson B 25 (9)	Vale J..........................- (1)
Cunningham G 8	Lenihan B 37	Walton C 46
Dack, B 22	Mulgrew C 2	Williams D..................... 17

League goals (66): Armstrong 16, Dack 9, Gallagher 6, Graham 4, Holtby 3, Johnson 3, Lenihan 3, Tosin Adarabioyo 3, Williams 3, Buckley 2, Downing 2, Rothwell 2, Samuel 2, Travis 2, Brereton 1, Evans 1, Opponents 4
FA Cup goals (1): Armstrong 1. **League Cup goals** (4): Dack 1, Downing 1, Gallagher 1, Rothwell 1
Average home league attendance: 13,873. **Player of Year**: Adam Armstrong

BRENTFORD

Brentford were left pondering what might have been after their bid to bring Premier League football to a new stadium faltered at the final hurdle. Last-game nerves cost them the chance of automatic promotion, while a goalkeeping error presented neighbours Fulham with the upper hand in the Play-off Final. But this was still a memorable season for Thomas Frank and his players, whose football was at times as good anything the Championship had to offer. Eight successive wins, commencing with 5-0 against Sheffield Wednesday in the last game before the season was suspended, had bridged a nine-point deficit to second place with two fixtures remaining. In the first, they were refused what looked like blatant penalty when Ethan Pinnock had his shirt grabbed by Stoke's Bruno Martins Indi and lost to the only goal. Then, a home 'banker' against Barnsley in the last match at Griffin Park proved anything but as their struggling opponents scored a stoppage-time winner for 2-1. Brentford, left two points adrift of second-place West Bromwich Albion, regrouped to overcome Swansea in the second leg of their semi-final after goals from Ollie Watkins and Emiliano Marcondes in the opening 15 minutes. A league double over Fulham offered confidence going into the Wembley decider, which proved a cagey affair until extra-time when David Raya misjudged a 40-yard free-kick from Joe Bryan, who added a second before Henrik Dalsgaard pulled one back in added time.

Baptiste S.................. 3 (9)	Jansson P.....................34	Racic L 3 (1)
Benrahma S............. 39 (4)	Jeanvier J................. 25 (1)	Raya D........................... 46
Canos S 11 (2)	Jensen M 30 (9)	Roersley M 5 (6)
Clarke J .... - (1)	Karelis N.................... 1 (3)	Sorensen M B .... - (1)
Dasilva J 34 (8)	Marcondes E.......... 13 (12)	Thompson D .... - (2)
Dalsgaard H 42 (1)	Mbeumo B 36 (6)	Valencia J.................. 1 (18)
Dervisoglu H .... - (4)	Mokotjo K................. 14 (11)	Watkins O.................... 46
Forss M .... - (2)	Norgaard C 40 (2)	Yearwood D.................. - (2)
Fosu-Henry T............. 2 (8)	Oksanen J .... - (1)	Zamburek J 1 (15)
Henry R........................46	Pinnock E................. 34 (2)	

Play-offs – appearances: Benrahma 3, Dalsgaard 3, Henry 3, Jansson 3, Jensen 3, Mbeumo 3, Norgaard 3, Pinnock 3, Raya 3, Watkins 3, Dasilva 2 (1), Marcondes 1 (2), Canos – (2), Baptiste – (1), Dervisoglu – (1), Fosu-Henry – (1), Roersley – (1),
League goals (80): Watkins 25, Benrahma 17, Mbeumo 15, Dasilva 10, Marcondes 2, Pinnock 2, Dalsgaard 2, Fosu-Henry 1, Jeanvier 1, Jensen 1, Mokotjo 1, Racic 1, Valencia 1, Opponents 2. **Play-offs – goals** (4): Dalsgaard 1, Marcondes 1, Mbeumo 1, Watkins 1
FA Cup goals (1): Marcondes 1. **League Cup goals** (1): Forss 1
Average home league attendance: 11,699. **Player of Year:** Said Benrahma

BRISTOL CITY

Lee Johnson looked to be leading his side back into contention for a play-off place when a lean spell going into the New Year was transformed by a purple patch of five wins in six match. It culminated in a 3-2 victory over Derby with first goals for the club from winter signings Nahki Wells and Filip Benkovic. City were within goal difference of the top-six and just three points away from Leeds in second position. Then it all turned sour, before and immediately after the season was suspended. Seven defeats and two draws in nine matches put them out of the promotion picture. Johnson, appointed in February 2016 and the longest-serving manager in the Championship, was sacked after the latest defeat, 1-0 at home to Cardiff which left City nine points adrift. Caretaker Dean Holden won his first two games, against Hull and Middlesbrough, but a modest finish left his team in mid-table. Holden was later confirmed in the job.

Afobe B 8 (4)	Bentley D................. 42 (1)	Diedhiou F 29 (12)
Baker N 33 (1)	Brownhill J.....................28	Eliasson N 18 (19)
Benkovic F 6 (4)	Dasilva J 22 (2)	Henriksen M 4

Hunt J	29 (6)	Palmer K	11 (14)	Taylor M	- (1)
Kalas T	23	Paterson J	15 (6)	Vyner Z	4 (4)
Maenpaa N	4	Pereira P	14 (7)	Watkins M	5 (4)
Massengo H-N	23 (2)	Rodri	1 (5)	Weimann A	42 (3)
Moore T	16 (5)	Rowe T	24 (5)	Wells N	13 (4)
Nagy A	16 (7)	Semenyo A	3 (6)	Williams A	32
O'Dowda C	17 (15)	Smith K	19 (3)	Wright B	3
Pack M	1	Szmodics S	1 (2)		

League goals (60): Diedhiou 12, Weimann 9, Paterson 6, Brownhill 5, Wells 5, Afobe 3, Eliasson 3, Benkovic 2, Pereira 2, Rowe 2, Williams 2, Baker 1, Moore 1, Nagy 1, O'Dowda 1, Palmer 1, Watkins 1, Opponents 3
FA Cup goals (1): Diedhiou 1. **League Cup goals (3):** Diedhiou 1, Hunt 1, Walsh 1 L
Average home league attendance: 21,548. **Player of Year:** Famara Diedhiou

CARDIFF CITY

Neil Harris raised hopes of an immediate return to the Premier League after replacing Neil Warnock, who left by mutual consent with his side in the bottom half of the table a third of the way into the season. The former Millwall manager lifted them in the play-offs, but they paid the price for not taking chances when on top during the opening half of the first leg against Fulham. Cardiff were outplayed after the interval, took a two-goal deficit to Craven Cottage and came up just short after a commendable 2-1 victory, courtesy of goals from Curtis Nelson and Lee Tomlin, which left Fulham hanging on to a 3-2 aggregate scoreline. Harris had repaired the damage of a 6-1 defeat by Queens Park Rangers at the start of the New Year with successive victories over West Bromwich Albion, Reading, Luton and Huddersfield. Cardiff broke into the top-six by winning 3-1 at Preston with late goals by substitutes Nathaniel Mendez-Laing and Robert Glatzel. By then they had scored more goals – 15 – by players coming off the bench than any other team in the Championship.

Adomah A	9	Madine G	5 (3)	Richards A	10 (1)
Bacuna L	35 (6)	Mendez-Laing N	21 (6)	Sanderson D	9 (1)
Bamba S	1 (5)	Morrison S	35 (1)	Smith B	- (3)
Bennett J	44	Murphy J	16 (11)	Smithies A	30
Bogle O	2 (9)	Nelson C	31 (2)	Tomlin L	24 (9)
Day J	- (1)	Pack M	32 (5)	Vassell I	- (2)
Etheridge N	16	Paterson C	18 (18)	Vaulks W	18 (9)
Flint A	26	Peltier L	24 (1)	Ward D	7 (21)
Glatzel R	23 (7)	Ralls J	25 (2)	Whyte G	15 (9)
Hoilett J	29 (12)	Reid B	1		

Play-offs – appearances: Bacuna 2, Bennett 2, Hector 2, Morrison 2, Nelson 2, Pack 2, Ralls 2, Smithies 2, Glatzel 1 (1), Mendez-Laing 1 (1), Tomlin 1 (1), Murphy 1 (1), Vaulks 1 (1), Ward 1 (1), Paterson – (1), Whyte – (1)
League goals (68): Tomlin 8, Glatzel 7, Hoilett 7, Ralls 7, Ward 7, Murphy 5, Paterson 5, Morrison 4, Vaulks 4, Flint 3, Mendez-Laing 3, Pack 2, Bacuna 1, Bogle 1, Nelson 1, Vassell 1, Opponents 2. **Play-offs – goals (2):** Nelson 1, Tomlin 1
FA Cup goals (10): Murphy 3, Flint 2, Paterson 2, Glatzel 1, Ward 1, Whyte 1. **League Cup goals:** None
Average home league attendance: 22,822. **Player of Year:** Sean Morrison

CHARLTON ATHLETIC

Considering a catalogue of problems on and off the pitch, Charlton deserved some credit for taking their survival bid to the final game of the season before dropping into the bottom three and returning immediately to League One. A club with one of the smallest budgets in the division lost players after promotion, including captain Patrick Bauer, whose goal seconds from the end decided the Play-off Final against Sunderland. They also lost Lyle Taylor for three months with a knee injury after scoring five goals in the opening six games which netted 14 points. After resuming his role as leading marksman into lockdown, Taylor then refused to carry on in case injury denied him a possible move in the summer. Chris Solly and on-loan David Davis joined him, against the background of a chaotic ownership struggle, which followed the revelation that the club were under a transfer embargo. Lee Bowyer's side stayed afloat on goal difference after salvaging a 2-2 draw in the penultimate fixture against Wigan with Macauley Bonne's 93rd minute goal. But while their defeat by champions Leeds on the final evening came as no surprise, no-one expected Barnsley to succeed at Brentford – a result which left Charlton a point adrift.

Aneke C.................. 2 (18)	Green A..................... 8 (5)	Oshilaja A................. 19 (6)
Bonne M.................. 26 (7)	Hemed T.................... 9 (9)	Oztumer E 11 (3)
Cullen J..........................34	Kayal B 2 (4)	Pearce J................... 35 (4)
Davis D..........................5	Lapslie G................. 4 (6)	Phillips D 46
Davison J 5 (4)	Ledley J 1	Pratley D............... 30 (6)
Dempsey B .... 3(1)	Leko J 19 (2)	Purrington B........... 24 (7)
Dijksteel A........................1	Lockyer T 43	Sarr N...................... 26 (3)
Doughty A.............. 20 (9)	Smith M................... - (2)	Solly C 12 (2)
Field S 10 (7)	Matthews A 28 (1)	Taylor L.................. 17 (5)
Forster-Caskey J 7 (4)	McGeady A 8 (2)	Vennings J...................- (3)
Gallagher C 25 (1)	Morgan A 11 (10)	Williams J 15 (11)

League goals (50): Bonne 11, Taylor 11, Gallagher 6, Leko 5, Sarr 3, Doughty 2, Green 2, Pratley 2, Purrington 2, Aneke 1, Cullen 1, Davison 1, Lapslie 1, Lockyer 1, Pearce 1
FA Cup goals: None. **League Cup goals** None
Average home league attendance: 18,017. **Player of Year**: Dillan Phillips

DERBY COUNTY

Derby continued to search unsuccessfully for the key to a return to the Premier League. Frank Lampard couldn't manage it in 2019 when the club lost in the play-offs for the fourth time in six years. This time, they turned to Wayne Rooney, appointed player-coach and captain, alongside Phillip Cocu, who succeeded Lampard. The pair had to contend with early problems on and off the field – a single win from the opening eight games and three players involved in a car crash, after which captain Richard Keogh was sacked and Tom Lawrence and Mason Bennett fined. Derby drifted along in mid-table until well into the New Year before a hint of improvement accompanied back-to-back wins over Stoke and Swansea. Then, the season finally took off with five successive victories either side of lockdown, including a hat-trick by 18-year-old Louie Sibley at Millwall. Derby seemed poised, a point behind sixth-place Cardiff. Instead, there were defeats by West Bromwich Albion and Brentford, followed by costly mistakes by Rooney and Jason Knight which gifted goals to Cardiff, whose victory took them out of Derby's reach.

Bennett M.................. 2 (5)	Hamer B 24 (1)	Martin C................. 25 (10)
Bielik K 19 (1)	Hector-Ingram J .... - (1)	Paterson J...........5 (5)
Bird M................... 21 (1)	Holmes D 29 (4)	Rooney W 20
Bogle J 33 (4)	Huddlestone T..............11	Roos K 22
Brown J .... - (1)	Jozefzoon F 6 (8)	Shinnie G................ 12 (11)
Buchanan L 3 (2)	Keogh R..........................8	Sibley L 9 (2)
Clarke M 34 (1)	Knight J 20 (11)	Waghorn M 36 (7)
Davies C 25 (7)	Lawrence T...................37	Whittaker M 1 (15)
Dowell K 8 (2)	Lowe M 24 (5)	Wisdom A............... 16 (2)
Evans G 11 (6)	Malone S 15 (3)	
Forsyth C 20 (2)	Marriott J 10 (22)	

League goals (62): Waghorn 12, Martin 11, Lawrence 10, Knight 6, Rooney 5, Sibley 5, Holmes 2, Marriott 2, Shinnie 2, Bogle 1, Clarke 1, Huddlestone 1, Malone 1, Paterson 1, Whittaker 1, Opponents 1
FA Cup goals (5): Holmes 1, Marriott 1, Martin 1, Rooney 1, Wisdom 1. **League Cup goals** (1) Buchanan 1
Average home league attendance: 26,727. **Player of Year**: Matt Clarke

FULHAM

Leading marksman Aleksandar Mitrovic and occasional scorer Joe Bryan fired Fulham back to the Premier League at the first attempt. The Serbian striker netted 26 goals – more than anyone in the four divisions – as Scott Parker's side overcame some patchy form at Craven Cottage to finish fourth in the regular season. A hamstring injury ruled him out of the play-off semi-finals in which they won 2-0 at Cardiff in the first leg, then reverted to type by losing the return 2-1 to edge through. And Mitrovic admitted he was only half-fit when coming off the bench in extra-time at Wembley with the final against west London neighbours Brentford goalless. But his presence was enough make a difference and he teed up left-back Bryan for the second of his two goals which settled the match 2-1.Bryan had scored only once previously , against Wigan in a victory which paved the way for a return to the leading grounp after dropped points forced them down to mid-table. Mitrovic scored a hat-trick against Luton to accelerate the climb and once established Fulham were always comfortable. There was a brief wobble immediately after lockdown, a sixth home defeat, this one by Brentford who completed the double over their rivals, followed by one at Leeds which ruled out any prospect of automatic promotion. But 17 points accumulated from the final seven games sealed their position.

Arter H 21 (7)	Jasper S...................... - (2)	O'Riley M ....- (1)
Ayite F........................ - (1)	Johansen S............. 19 (14)	Odoi D 30 (4)
Bettinelli M.............. 13 (1)	Kamara A................. 8 (17)	Onomah J.............. 20 (11)
Bryan J 39 (4)	Kebano N............... 5 (11)	Ream T 44
Cairney T 38 (1)	Knockaert A........... 32 (10)	Reed H 21 (4)
Christie C 13 (11)	Kongolo T.................. - (1)	Rodak M 33
De Cordova-Reid B.. 30 (11)	Le Marchand M........... 3 (9)	Sessegnon S............ 9 (5)
De La Torre L .... - (2)	Mawson A................. 25 (2)	Stansfield J ....- (1)
Hector M 20	McDonald K 7 (9)	
Ivan Cavaleiro 36 (7)	Mitrovic A....................40	

Play-offs – appearances: Bryan 3, Cairney 3, De Cordova-Reid 3, Hector 3, Kebano 3, Onomah 3, Ream 3, Reed 3, Rodak 3, Christie 2 (1), Knockaert 2 (1), Kamara 1 (2), Odoi 1 (2), Le Marchand – (2), Ivan Cavaleiro – (1), Mitrovic – (1)
League goals (64): Mitrovic 26, Cairney 8, De Cordova-Reid 6, Ivan Cavaleiro 6, Kamara 5, Kebano 5, Knockaert 3, Onomah 3, Arter 2, Bryan 1 Christie 1, Opponents 1. **Play-offs – goals** (5): Bryan 2, Kebano 2, Onomah 1
FA Cup goals (2): Arter 1, Knockaert 1. **League Cup goals**: None
Average home league attendance: 18,204. **Player of Year**: Aleksandar Mitrovic

HUDDERSFIELD TOWN

Danny Cowley might have expected a pat on the back for steering Huddersfield away from the threat of a second successive relegation. Instead, two days after a crucial victory over Premier League-bound West Bromwich Albion, he was sacked by chairman Phil Hodgkinson, who said the club 'had a different vision for how our ambitions can be achieved'. Hodgkinson replaced him with Spanish coach Carlos Corberan, fresh from his role alongside Marcelo Bielsa in returning Leeds to the top-flight after a 16-year absence. Cowley, whose brother Nicky also left his role at the club, was thought to have wanted to build a side with more English players in it. He had succeeded Jan Siewert – dismissed after seven months in charge – after initially turning down the job and lifted Huddersfield from second from bottom to seven points clear of trouble going into the New Year. That shrunk to two points during the course of a tough run of fixtures against leading teams. But defensively they tightened up after the season's enforced break and were rewarded when Arsenal loanee Emile Smith Rowe scored an 86th minute winner against Albion to bring up the safety mark of 51 points.

Bacuna J 25 (13)	Harratt K .... - (1)	Pyke R ....- (1)
Brown J 12 (3)	High S .... - (1)	Quaner C .... - (5)
Campbell F 21 (12)	Hogg J 37	Rowe A 1
Chalobah T 30 (6)	Kachunga E 30 (6)	Schindler C 46
Coleman J 2 (1)	King A 6 (8)	Schofield R 1
Daly M .... - (4)	Kongolo T 10 (1)	Simpson D 23 (1)
Diakhaby A 9 (9)	Koroma J 3 (4)	Smith Rowe E 13 (6)
Duhaney D 4 (2)	Lossl J 15	Stankovic J G 13 (6)
Edmonds-Green R .... 1(1)	Mbenza I 1 (4)	Stearman R 17
Elphick T 14	Mooy A 1	Toffolo H 19
Grabara K 28	Mounie S 12 (18)	Willock C 8 (6)
Grant K 42 (1)	O'Brien L 36 (2)	Van La Parra R 3 (1)
Hadergjonaj F 14 (7)	Pritchard A 10 (8)	

League goals (52): Grant 19, Mounie 8, Bacuna 6, Campbell 3, Kachunga 3, O'Brien 2, Schindler 2, Smith Rowe 2, Willock 2, Chalobah 1, Daly 1, Gorenc-Stankovic 1, Toffolo 1, Opponents 1
FA Cup goals: None. **League Cup goals**: None.
Average home league attendance: 21,748. **Player of Year**: Lewis O'Brien

HULL CITY

Hull lost their two best players in the winter transfer window, dropped like a stone into the relegation zone and stayed there after the club's worst league defeat of modern times. They went into the New Year two points off a play-off place with Jarrod Bowen's winner against Sheffield Wednesday, his 16th goal of the season. But everything changed after Bowen moved to West Ham for £20m and Polish winger Kamil Grosicki joined West Bromwich Albion for £800,000 after he, too, turned down a new contract. Hull were also hit injuries, including Scotland under-21 forward James Scott in one of his first training sessions after signing from Motherwell. Then, captain Eric Lichaj and vice-captain Jackson Irvine failed to agree terms to carry on after lockdown and did not feature again. Hull conceded five goals to Brentford and Stoke and four to Swansea, Leeds and West Bromwich Albion. Then came an 8-0 drubbing by Wigan, with seven goals conceded in the first-half, accompanied by an apology to supporters from manager Grant McCann. With little separating a cluster of teams struggling to survive, there was still a way out. But further defeats by Luton and Cardiff meant they finished bottom after a single win in 20 matches, so will be playing third-tier football for the first time since 2005

Balogh N .... - (3)	Grosicki K 28	Magennis J 20 (9)
Batty D 19 (11)	Honeyman G 21 (21)	McKenzie R 8
Berry J .... - (1)	Ingram M 1	McLoughlin S 5 (2)
Bowen J 29	Irvine J 34 (1)	Pennington M 13 (1)
Bowler J 11 (17)	Kane H 6 (1)	Samuelsen M 3 (4)
Burke R 36	Kingsley S 7 (1)	Scott J 4 (3)
Da Silva Lopes L 33 (7)	Lewis-Potter K 1 (20)	Stewart K 21 (6)
Dicko N 1 (1)	Lichaj E 29	Tafazolli R 7 (8)
Eaves T 22 (18)	Long G 45	Toral J-M 8 (6)
Elder C 30	MacDonald A 5	Wilks M 16 (2)
Fleming B 4	Maddison M 4 (3)	De Wijs J 35

League goals (57): Bowen 16, Grosicki 6, Eaves 5, Wilks 5, Magennis 4, Stewart 3, Da Silva Lopes 2, Irvine 2, Kane 2, Lewis-Potter 2, Tafazolli 2, De Wijs 2, Batty 1, Bowler 1, Honeyman 1, Maddison 1, Scott 1, Opponents 1
FA Cup goals (4): Eaves 3, Grosicki 1. **League Cup goals** (5): Bowen 1, Magennis 1, Milinkovic M 1, Tafazolli 1, Toral 1
Average home league attendance: 11,614. **Player of Year**: Jarrod Bowen

LEEDS UNITED

Premier League football returned to Elland Road after an absence of 16 years for one of the former heavyweights of the English game. Almost as many managers had tried and failed to repair the damage of the 2003-04 season when Leeds were relegated alongside Leicester and Wolves. The latest, Marcelo Bielsa, succeeded at the second attempt after a high-profile coaching career at international level, with Argentina and Chile, and at clubs in Spain, Italy and France. His side squandered their chance in 2019 with a single point from the final four games, then defeat by Derby in the play-off semi-finals. This time they made no mistake and went up as champions after eventually shaking off the challenge of West Bromwich Albion. Only once did Leeds look vulnerable. Following a crazy 5-4 win at Birmingham, settled by a 95th minute own goal, they surrendered a nine-point advantage over third-place Fulham. Five successive wins, without conceding a goal, put them back in charge. When the Championship resumed, they forced Fulham out of contention with a 3-0 victory, defeated Blackburn 3-1 and prepared to party after crushing Stoke 5-0. Leeds won all their last six games to claim the title ten points ahead of Albion in second place.

Alioski E	21 (18)	Davis L	- (3)	Nketiah E	2 (15)
Augustin J-K	- (3)	Douglas B	6 (9)	Phillips K	37
Ayling L	35 (2)	Forshaw A	6 (1)	Poveda I	1 (3)
Bamford P	43 (2)	Gotts R	- (1)	Roberts T	12 (11)
Berardi G	13 (9)	Harrison J	45 (1)	Shackleton J	5 (17)
Bogusz M	- (1)	Helder Costa	33 (10)	Stevens J	- (4)
Casey O	- (1)	Hernandez P	27 (9)	Struijk P	2 (3)
Clarke J	- (1)	Kiko Casilla	36	White B	46
Cooper L	36 (2)	Klich M	45		
Dallas S	45	Meslier L	10		

League goals (77): Bamford 16, Hernandez 9, Harrison 6, Klich 6, Alioski 5, Dallas 5, Ayling 4, Helder Costa 4, Roberts 4, Nketiah 3, Cooper 2, Phillips 2, Shackleton 2, Opponents 8
FA Cup goals: None. **League Cup goals** (5): Nketiah 2, Berardi 1, Helder Costa 1, Klich 1
Average home league attendance: 35,321. **Player of Year**: Ben White

LUTON TOWN

Nathan Jones returned to Kenilworth Road aiming to regain the respect of supporters he admitted he betrayed when leaving to the club midway through their 2018-19 promotion campaign. The Welsh manager, reappointed on his 47th birthday during the enforced Championship break, admitted the manner and timing of his departure for an ill-fated spell in charge at Stoke were poor. Two months later, he had succeeded in the eyes of most by steering the club away from the threat of an immediate return to League One. Jones, brought back after his successor Graeme Jones lost his job, along with three of the coaching staff, in cost-cutting measures, took over a side second from bottom, six points from safety. The deficit was halved by James Collins's winner at Swansea and Harry Cornick's eye-catching strike for a point away to leaders Leeds. Luton then failed to take advantage of two home games in four days, losing 5-0 to Reading, for whom Yakou Meite scored four times, and conceding an 84th minute equaliser against relegation rivals Barnsley. But they finished with a flourish, defeating Huddersfield, Hull and Blackburn to finish three points clear of trouble.

Berry L	15 (6)	Bradley S	39 (1)	Brown I	17 (8)
Bolton L	10 (14)	Bree J	34 (5)	Butterfield J	11 (4)

Carter-Vickers C 15 (1)	Kioso, P .... - (1)	Ruddock P 40 (4)
Collins J 44 (2)	Lee E 8 (3)	O'Shea J 13
Cornick H 37 (8)	LuaLua K 15 (14)	Sheehan A 2 (2)
Cranie M 19 (5)	McManaman C 10 (13)	Shinnie A 16 (5)
Daniels D 2 (1)	Moncur G 1 (16)	Sluga S 33
Galloway B .... - (3)	Pearson M 41 (1)	Tunnicliffe R 37 (3)
Hylton D 2 (9)	Potts D 31 (2)	
Jones L 1 (3)	Rea G 13 (2)	

League goals (54): Collins 14, Cornick 9, McManaman 4, Bradley 3 LuaLua 3, Ruddock 3, Cranie 2, Pearson 2, Berry 1, Brown 1, Butterfield 1, Daniels 1, Lee 1, Moncur 1, Potts 1, Shinnie 1, Tunnlicliffe 1, Opponents 5
FA Cup goals: None. **League Cup goals** (6): Jervis J 1, Jones 1, Lee 1, Sheehan 1, Shinnie 1, Opponents 1
Average home league attendance: 10,048. **Player of Year**: James Collins

MIDDLESBROUGH

Neil Warnock reached another milestone in a long managerial career after answering the call to save Middlesbrough from the threat of relegation. Forty years after the first of his 16 club appointments, he supervised three victories in his first six matches to take them to the 50-point safety mark. All three were achieved away from home – against fellow-strugglers Stoke, promotion-hopefuls Millwall and mid-table Reading, where Patrick Roberts, on loan from Manchester City, set up the equaliser for Ashley Fletcher and scored the 82nd minute winner himself, his first for the club. For good measure, another three points were collected on their travels – 2-1 against Sheffield Wednesday on the final day of the season. Warnock was brought in to replace Jonathan Woodgate, sacked after a 3-0 home defeat by Swansea in the first match of the season's resumption with only goal difference separating his side from the bottom three. It was a continuation of Middlesbrough's poor form at the Riverside which started, ironically, after Wodgate was named the Championship's December manager of the month for 13 points achieved. Warnock agreed to stay on for the 2020-21 season.

Assombalonga B 27 (8)	Gestede R 5 (14)	Randolph D 14
Ayala D 23 (2)	Howson J 41	Roberts P 8 (2)
Bola M 6 (1)	Johnson M 29 (9)	Saville G 31 (6)
Browne M 5 (8)	Liddle B .... - (1)	Shotton R 20 (1)
Clayton A 21 (6)	McNair P 36 (5)	Spence D 18 (4)
Coulson H 20 (9)	Morrison R 3	Stojanovic D 8
Dijksteel A 12 (4)	Moukoudi H 8	Tavernier M 27 (10)
Fletcher A 37 (6)	Nmecha L 4 (7)	Walker S 1 (6)
Friend G 14	O'Neill T .... - (1)	Wing L 28 (12)
Fry D 36	Pears A 24	Wood N ....- (1)

League goals (48): Assombalonga 11, Fletcher 11, Wing 7, McNair 6, Tavernier 3, Ayala 2, Gestede 2, Coulson 1, Johnson 1, Roberts 1, Saville 1, Spence 1, Opponents 1
FA Cup goals (2): Fletcher 1, Saville 1. **League Cup goals** (2): Bola 1, Fletcher 1
Average home league attendance: 19,933. **Player of Year**: Jonny Howson

MILLWALL

Gary Rowett stabilised the fortunes of his new club, then led a spirited bid for a play-off place. It stretched to the penultimate fixture before faltering amid a clutch of teams aiming for the final top-six place. Millwall flirted with relegation in 2019 and experienced early season problems this time – a run of eight matches without a victory, followed by the resignation of Neil Harris, the Championship's longest-serving manager with four-and-a-half-years behind him. Rowett made a winning start, 2-0 against former club Stoke, and supervised steady progress towards the leading group. His side went into lockdown on the back of Matt Smith's hat-trick in 13 first-half minutes for a 3-0 success against Nottingham Forest at the City Ground and within striking distance of the leading group. They came out of it on the receiving end of a treble scored by Derby teenager Louie Sibley and took a while to restore momentum. It came with three wins in four matches – Charlton, Hull and Blackburn – but then a 4-3 defeat by Queens Park Rangers ended their chances.

Bennett M.............. 7 (2)	Hutchinson S................36	Romeo M 43
Bialkowski B 45 (1)	Leonard R 13 (4)	Skalak J..................... 4 (8)
Bodvarsson J D...... 13 (18)	Mahoney C 14 (24)	Smith M................20 (21)
Bradshaw T........... 29 (16)	McCarthy J.............. 1 (1)	Thompson B........20 (8)
Brown J 1	Mitchell B 1 (6)	Wallace J.....................43
Burey T .... - (1)	Molumby J 31 (5)	Wallace M 38 (5)
Cooper J 46	Muller H.................. - (1)	Williams S..............28 (4)
Ferguson S............. 19 (10)	O'Brien A 8 (10)	Woods R.................17 (1)
Fielding F 1	Pearce A 28 (1)	

League goals (57): Smith 13, Wallace J 10, Bradshaw 8, Hutchinson 6, Bodvarsson 4, Cooper 3, O'Brien 3, Bennett 2, Mahoney 2, Williams 2, Leonard 1, Molumby 1, Skalak 1, Thompson 1 **FA Cup goals** (3): Bradshaw 1, Mahoney 1, Smith 1. **League Cup goals** (4): Bodvarsson 2, Bradshaw 1, O'Brien 1
Average home league attendance: 13,734. **Player of Year**: Bartosz Bialkowski

NOTTINGHAM FOREST

Forest's season-long promotion challenge imploded in the final round of fixtures: They were on the receiving end of a remarkable six-goal swing which enabled Swansea to claim the last play-off place. Sabri Lamouchi's side had looked odds on to go forward when establishing a six-point cushion, together with a superior goal difference, with two games remaining. That advantage was halved in the first of them after conceding a 93rd minute winner to struggling Barnsley. Four days later, nerves were calmed when Tobias Figueiredo equalised against Stoke at the City Ground. But Forest conceded three times in the final 20 minutes to lose 4-1 after a 96th minute own goal by Nuno da Costa. At the same time, Swansea sealed a 4-1 win of their own in added time against ten-man Reading to go above their rivals with a one-goal advantage. Ironically, Lamouchi had signed a new contract on the eve of the season's resumption, becoming the club's first manager since Billy Davies in his first spell nine years ago to lead the club through an entire campaign.

Adomah A.................. 5 (19)	Grabban L................ 43 (2)	Robinson J 16 (2)
Ameobi S................. 37 (8)	Jenkinson C............ 7 (1)	Samba B....................40
Benalouane Y............. - (1)	Joao Carvalho 9 (14)	Semedo A..............10 (14)
Bong G 1	Johnson B 2 (2)	Smith J..........................2
Bostock J 1 (6)	Lolley J................ 37 (5)	Sow S 22 (3
Cash M.................. 40 (2)	Mighten A .... - (8)	Tiago Silva 34 (10)
Chema 7 (1)	Mir A 2 (9)	Walker T......................1 (6)
Dawson M 16 (2)	Muric A....................4	Watson B....................45
Diakhaby A 2 (12)	Nuno Da Costa............ 4 (6)	Worrall J....................46
Figueiredo T............30	Ribeiro Y........................27	Yates R 16 (11)

League goals (58): Grabban 20, Lolley 9, Ameobi 5, Cash 3, Figueiredo 3, Tiago Silva 3, Watson 3, Yates 3, Adomah 2, Semedo 2, Dawson 1, Joao Carvalho 1, Walker 1, Worrall 1, Opponents 1 **FA Cup goals**: None. **League Cup goals** (4): Adomah 1, Joao Carvalho 1, Lolley 1, Tiago Silva 1
Average home league attendance: 27,748. **Player of Year**: Matty Cash

PRESTON NORTH END

Preston were knocking at the promotion door throughout the first half of the season, notably when going top, ahead of the eventual champions Leeds on goal difference, after Paul Gallagher's penalty winner at Charlton. With Alex Neil reaffirming his commitment to the club amid interest from managerless Stoke, his side remained in contention well into the New Year. But they were found wanting in a run of matches against leading rivals just before the season was suspended, then immediately it resumed. Defeats away to West Bromwich Albion and Fulham were followed by further back-to-back reversals, this time at home against Cardiff and Derby. Preston were also second best at Deepdale to Queens Park Rangers, leaving them six points adrift and running out of fixtures. They came from behind to end seven games without a win by beating Sheffield Wednesday at Hillsborough before points dropped against two more leading teams, Nottingham Forest and Brentford, forced them out of contention.

Barkhuizen T............ 35 (9)	Ginnelly J.................... - (1)	Nugent D 11 (13)
Bauer P 41	Green A..................... - (4)	Pearson B.....................38
Bayliss T.................... - (1)	Harrop J 15 (17)	Potts B 14 (18)
Bodin B 11 (7)	Hughes A 28	Rafferty J 28 (1)
Browne A 35 (8)	Huntington P 8 (1)	Rudd D 46
Clarke T...................... 7 (3)	Johnson D 32 (1)	Sinclair S 11 (7)
Davies B 36	Ledson R 8 (5)	Stockley J...............9 (23)
Fisher D 26 (2)	Maguire S 36 (8)	Storey J.....................7 (3)
Gallagher P 22 (11)	Moult L 2	

League goals (59): Johnson 12, Barkhuizen 9, Gallagher 6, Harrop 5, Maguire 5, Browne 4, Stockley 4, Bauer 3, Sinclair 3, Bodin 2, Potts 2, Moult 1, Nugent 1, Pearson 1, Rafferty 1
FA Cup goals (2): Bodin 1, Harrop 1. **League Cup goals (6):** Barkhuizen 2, Harrop 2, Green 1, Huntington 1
Average home league attendance: 13,579. **Player of Year:** Daniel Johnson

QUEENS PARK RANGERS

Rangers lost three influential players and with them an outside chance of challenging for a place in the play-offs. Nahki Wells, on loan from Burnley, scored a hat-trick in a 6-1 New Year victory over Cardiff and netted the only goal against high-riding Leeds, taking his tally to 13. He was then recalled by the Premier League club and sold to Bristol City. Three successive defeats followed his departure, before Rangers fired again with maximum points against Stoke, Derby and Preston, the latter after falling behind and having Geoff Cameron sent off, But, as finances became stretched like many other clubs because of Covid-19, the club were unable to agree new contracts with captain Grant Hall and midfielder Marc Pugh, who left Loftus Road during the break in the season. On resumption, points in the bank provided insurance against five defeats in six, while any chance of making up ground on the leading group was lost. Rangers, nevertheless, went on to secure a modest improvement after three finishes in the lower reaches of the table. They settled into 13th place after 4-3 victory over Millwall in the final home game which brought Conor Masterson and Todd Kane their first goals for the club.

Amos L....................... 26 (8)	Hugill J 30 (9)	Osayi-Samuel B 34 (3)
Ball D.......................30 (1)	Kakay O 7	Oteh A 1 (8)
Barbet Y 27	Kane T...................21 (11)	Pugh M...................12 (15)
Bettache F .... - (3)	Kelly L.........................19	Rangel A 21
Cameron G...................36	Leistner T 20 (2)	Scowen J....................8 (10)
Chair I 26 (15)	Lumley J 27	Shodipo O 2 (10)
Clarke J .... - (6)	Manning R 41	Wallace L 10 (1)
Eze E............................46	Masterson C 10 (2)	Wells N 20 (6)
Gubbins J .... - (1)	Smith M..................... 2 (6)	
Hall G............................30	Mlakar J .... - (6)	

League goals (67): Eze 14, Hugill 13, Wells 13, Hall 5, Osayi-Samuel 5, Chair 4, Manning 4, Amos 2, Pugh 2, Ball 1, Cameron 1, Kane 1, Masterson 1, Opponents 1
FA Cup goals (6): Hugill 2, Osayi-Samuel 1, Scowen 1, Wallace 1. Wells 1. **League Cup goals** (3): Chair 1, Manning 1, Wells 1
Average home league attendance: 13,721. **Player of Year:** Eberechi Eze

READING

An improved season was illuminated by eye-catching scoring feats from record-signing George Puscas and Ivory Coast international Yakou Meite. Romania striker Puscas, a £9m buy from Inter Milan, scored a hat-trick in five minutes (79 pen, 80, 84) in a 3-1 win at Wigan. Meite netted three times in 18 first-half minutes against Luton and added another after the interval to become to first Reading player to hit four since Kerry Dixon in 1982. That 5-0 victory at Kenilworth Road was the club's biggest away from home since the 1989-90 campaign. It enabled Mark Bowen's side to return to winning ways after a single point gained in the first three fixtures after lockdown. Meite went on to reach 17 for the season in all competitions and although his side won only one of the five remaining fixtures, they finished 14th after being down in 20th in each of the two previous campaigns. Bowen, Reading's sporting director and a former Wales full-back, became their fourth manager in 19 months after Jose Gomes was sacked ten months into the job when a decent start was followed by a single point from six matches.

Adam C 8 (13)	Joao Virginia 2	Obita J 14 (7)
Aluko S...................... - (2)	Loader D 1 (6)	Olise M 13 (6)
Araruna F................... 2 (1)	Lucas Joao 12 (7)	Osho G..................... 4 (1)
Baldock S 12 (12)	Masika A .... - (5)	Pele 26 (5)
Barrett J 2 (3)	McCleary G.............. 2 (17)	Puscas G................. 30 (8)
Barrow M........................1	McIntyre T................ 9 (1)	Richards O 23 (5)
Blackett T............... 16 (4)	Meite Y 32 (8)	Rinomhota A............. 28 (9)
Boye L................ 5 (14)	Miazga M 19 (1)	Swift J 40 (1)
Cabral R.......................44	Moore L 40 (3)	Yiadom A................... 24
Ejaria O 36	Morrison M 43 (1)	
Gunter C.................. 18 (2)	Novakovich A............... - (1)	

League goals (59): Meite 13, Puscas 12, Lucas Joao 6, Swift 6, Baldock 5, Ejaria 3, Adam 2, Miazga 2, Morrison 2, Obita 2, McCleary 1, Moore 1, Pele 1, Obita 1, Rinomhota 1, Yiadom 1, Opponents 1
FA Cup goals (9): Meite 2, Baldock 1, Boye 1, Loader 1, Obita 1, Puscas 1, Richards 1, Rinomhota 1, **League Cup goals** (6): Barrett 2, Meite 2, Boye 1, Puscas 1
Average home league attendance: 14,407. **Player of Year:** Rafael Cabral

SHEFFIELD WEDNESDAY

A nasty sting in the tail awaited the club after another season of modest achievement. They had 12 points deducted from the start of 2020–21 for breaching financial rules by including the sale of Hillsborough in accounts for 2017–18, despite the stadium being sold a year later. The penalty followed a campaign in which Wednesday were riding high approaching the midway point when Jordan Rhodes ended a 20-month wait for a goal for the team with the perfect hat-trick – left-foot, header, right-foot – in a 4-0 win at Nottingham Forest. A week later, Barry Bannan's 85th minute penalty against Bristol City lifted them to third behind West Bromwich Albion and Leeds. Promotion talk was in the air. Instead, Rhodes went off the boil, the goals dried up for leading scorer Steven Fletcher and a single win in 11 matches – albeit at Elland Road – resulted in a fall into mid-table, nine points adrift. That lean run included a 5-0 beating at home by Blackburn and another by the same scoreline at Brentford in the final match before lockdown. There was no sign of a resurgent when the season resumed, Wednesday finishing in the bottom half under Garry Monk, his fifth managerial job in five years after spells at Swansea, Leeds, Middlesbrough and Birmingham.

Bannan B 42 (2)	Iorfa D 40 (1)	Reach A 26 (11)
Borner J.................. 34 (3)	Lee K..................... 20 (8)	Rhodes J 7 (9)
Da Cruz A 8 (6)	Lees T 24 (3)	Shaw L...................... 1 (1)
Dawson C................ 23 (1)	Lucas Joao ....– (1)	Urhoghide O 3
Fletcher S 23 (4)	Luongo M 17 (10)	Westwood K 14
Forestieri F 8 (9)	Murphy J................ 24 (15)	Wickham C.................8 (5)
Fox M..................... 24 (3)	Nuhiu A 14 (24)	Wildsmith J 9
Harris K 40 (3)	Odubajo M 19 (3)	Windass J 6 (3)
Hunt A 2 (4)	Palmer L....................33	Winnall S 6 (7)
Hutchinson S 20 (3)	Pelupessy J 11 (6)	

League goals (58): Fletcher 13; Murphy 9, Nuhiu 6, Harris 3, Luongo 3, Rhodes 3, Windass 3, Bannan 2, Forestieri 2, Fox 2, Iorfa 2, Lees 2, Wickham 2, Borner 1, Hutchinson 1, Lucas Joao 1, Reach 1, Winnall 1, Opponents 1
FA Cup goals (3): Fox 1, Reach 1, Winnall 1. **League Cup goals** (1): Nuhiu 1
Average home league attendance: 23,733. **Player of Year**: Dominic Iorfa

STOKE CITY

Michael O'Neill had a turbulent introduction to club football after eight years as an international manager with Northern Ireland. He stepped straight into a relegation struggle which stretched until the 44th fixture when the accepted safety mark of 50 points was reached and the prospect of a second drop in three seasons averted. O'Neill, appointed when Nathan Jones was sacked after nine months in the wake of a club-record 11 home games without a victory, made a good start with maximum points against Barnsley and Wigan. And Stoke moved out of the bottom three for the first time when Tyrese Campbell and Sam Vokes scored in stoppage-time for a 3-2 win over Sheffield Wednesday on Boxing Day. But their inconsistency continued through to the season's suspension – during which O'Neill gave up his then part-time international role – with five goals scored against Huddersfield and Hull and four conceded to Derby and Queens Park Rangers. It was again evident after the break, until victory over Birmingham and a point away to Bristol City lifted the pressure. With no worries, Stoke finished by beating Nottingham Forest 4-1 and forcing them out of the play-offs.

Afobe B 1	Duffy M...................... 1 (5)	Etebo P.....................8 (3)
Allen J 34 (1)	Edwards T 13	Powell N 22 (7)
Batth D.................... 40 (3)	Federici A....................7	Shawcross R................... 5
Biram Diouf M........... - (8)	Gregory L 22 (18)	Smith T................... 27 (3)
Butland J....................35	Hogan S 4 (9)	Sorenson J................. 2 (4)
Campbell T 18 (15)	Ince T...................... 31 (7)	Thompson J.................8 (7)
Carter-Vickers C.............12	Lindsay L 17 (3)	Tymon J 1 (1)
Chester J 13 (3)	Martins Indi B 31 (2)	Verlinden T................- (5)
Clucas S....................44	McClean J 33 (3)	Vokes S 18 (18)
Collins N 6 (8)	Ndiaye B 10 (3)	Ward S..................... 15
Cousins J 15 (5)	Ngoy J .... - (1)	Woods R........................ 8
Davies A 4	Oakley-Boothe T.......... 1 (1)	

League goals (62): Clucas 11, Campbell 9, McClean 7, Gregory 6, Powell 5, Vokes 4, Allen 4. Batth 4, Hogan 3, Ince 3, Biram Diouf 1, Lindsay 1, Opponents 3
FA Cup goals: None. **League Cup goals** (4): Vokes 3, Batth 1
Average home league attendance: 22,828. **Player of Year**: James McClean

SWANSEA CITY

Swansea lost manager Graham Potter, leading scorer Oli McBurnie and influential midfielder Daniel James from the previous season. They gained Steve Cooper, who led England to the World

Under-17 Cup in 2017 and here took his new team into the play-offs in a remarkable finish to the regular season. With two matches remaining, they were six points behind and had an inferior goal difference to Nottingham Forest, who looked certain to continue their promotion bid. Instead, Forest imploded and Swansea achieved a six-goal swing in the final round of fixtures after beating Reading 4-1, then hearing Forest's defeat by Stoke by the same scoreline. Strikes in the final eight minutes by Liam Cullen and Wayne Routledge, his second of the game in stoppage-time, lifted Swansea to sixth place, ahead of their rivals by a one-goal difference. Andre Ayew then gave them the advantage in the semi-final first leg against Brentford, who responded with two goals in the opening quarter-of-an-hour of the return and a third straight after the restart. Liverpool loanee Rhian Brewster pulled one back, but Cooper admitted his side had left themselves with too much to do.

Ayew A 43 (1)	Dyer N 7 (3)	Naughton K 28 (4)
Bidwell J................. 36 (1)	Fulton J 29 (7)	Peterson K 4 (3)
Borja 15 (5)	Gallagher C.................19	Roberts C 32 (6)
Brewster R 19 (1)	Garrick J 1 (10)	Rodon J 20 (1)
Byers G 22 (3)	Grimes M 46	Routledge W 10 (11)
Cabango B 19 (2)	Guehi M 11 (1)	Surridge S 7 (13)
Carroll T 5 (3)	John D .... - (1)	Wilmot B 16 (5)
Celina B 28 (7)	Kalulu A 7 (4)	Woodman F 43
Cullen L................... - (6)	McKay B .... - (4)	Van der Hoorn M 27 (1)
Dhanda Y................. 9 (7)	Mulder E 3 (1)	

Play-offs – appearances: Ayew 2, Bidwell 2, Brewster 2, Fulton 2, Gallagher 2, Grimes 2, Guehi 2, Mulder 2, Roberts 2, Van der Hoorn 2, Cabango 1 (1), Naughton 1, Celina – (1), Dhanda – (1)
League goals (62): Ayew 15, Brewster 10, Borja 6, Routledge 4, Surridge 4, Dhanda 3, Fulton 3, Naughton 3, Byers 2, Celina 2, Garrick 2, Wilmot 2, Cabango 1, Cullen 1, Dyer 1, Roberts 1, Van der Hoorn 1, Opponents 1. **Play-offs – goals (2)**: Brewster 1, Ayew 1
FA Cup goals (1): Byers 1. **League Cup goals** (10): Surridge 3, Ayew 2, Byers 2, Garrick 1, Peterson 1, Routledge 1
Average home league attendance: 16,150. **Player of Year**: Andre Ayew

WEST BROMWICH ALBION

Former West Ham manager Slaven Bilic successfully rebuilt his new team and restored Premier League football to The Hawthorns after an absence of two seasons. Jay Rodriguez and Dwight Gaye, with 45 goals between them, were among those who left the club after a play-off semi-final defeat by Aston Villa. This time, Albion had no-one to match that tally, but remained a potent attacking force, with Charlie Austin and Hal Robson-Kanu heading a list of 19 different scorers. The capacity to salvage points from losing positions proved another significant asset as Albion went toe-to-toe with Leeds at the top of the table. The two sides established a ten-point cushion over their nearest rivals approaching the midway point. Albion came under pressure after seven matches without a win into the New Year, but regained momentum with 16 points and 13 goals from the next six. They also responded to defeat by a surging Brentford when the Championship returned after a three-month break, beating Sheffield Wednesday, Hull and Derby. It then became hard work, with pressure building to a peak in the final round of fixtures. Albion's nervy 2-2 draw against Queens Park Rangers proved enough for the runners-up spot behind Leeds – but only because of Brentford's shock home defeat by Barnsley.

Ajayi S................... 42 (1)	Burke O .... - (2)	Gibbs K 14
Austin C 18 (16)	Diangana G 23 (7)	Grosicki K 4 (10)
Barry G 1 (2)	Edwards K 9 (17)	Harper R 4 (6)
Bartley K 37 (1)	Ferguson N 21	Hegazi A 14 (2)
Brunt C...................... - (7)	Furlong D................ 22 (9)	Johnstone S 46

Krovinovic F 24 (16)	Phillips M 30 (9)	Townsend C.............. 19 (8)
Livermore J 43 (2)	Robinson C 10 (6)	Zohore K 5 (12)
O'Shea D 16 (1)	Robson-Kanu H 24 (15)	
Pereira M................. 38 (4)	Sawyers R 42	

League goals (77): Austin 10, Robson-Kanu 10, Diangana 8, Pereira 8, Phillips 7, Ajayi 5, Krovinovic 5, Livermore 3, O'Shea 3, Robinson 3, Zohore 3, Bartley 2, Edwards 2, Furlong 2, Hegazi 1, Ferguson 1, Gibbs 1, Grosicki 1, Sawyers 1, Opponents 3
FA Cup goals (4): Zohore 2, Phillips 1, Townsend 1. **League Cup goals** (1): Austin 1
Average home league attendance: 24,053. **Player of Year**: Matheus Pereira

WIGAN ATHLETIC

Paul Cook and his side delivered one of the game's great 'escapes' – then had it ruled out by a 12-point deduction. Wigan were penalised for going into administration and went down as a result, having lost just once in the final 15 matches while completing the season with the rarity of a positive goal difference. With two fixtures remaining, it looked as if the deduction might be clawed back. They had just swamped Hull 8-0, a league record score for the club with Everton loanee Kieran Dowell scoring a hat-trick, to reduce their relegation zone deficit to two points. But conceding a stoppage-time equaliser against struggling Charlton proved costly and another draw in the final fixture with promotion-chasing Fulham, after leading through Kieffer Moore, was not enough. The two matches underlined a season-long weakness – dropping points from winning positions. Cook declared himself 'proud' of the efforts of the players, before resigning amid speculation about taking charge at another Championship club.

Balogun L 10 (1)	Jacobs M................. 19 (13)	Morsy S.......................... 43
Byrne N 39	Jones J........................... 7	Mulgrew C 12
Dobre A .... - (1)	Kipre C 32 (4)	Naismith K 22 (15)
Dowell K 12	Lang C .... - (1)	Pearce T..................... 4 (3)
Dunkley C 22 (4)	Lowe J 40 (6)	Pilkington A.............. 9 (7)
Enobakhare B............. - (2)	MacLeod L 11 (1)	Roberts G 3 (6)
Evans L 18 (14)	Marshall D................... 39	Robinson A................... 38
Fox D 9 (2)	Massey G 21 (10)	Sterling D................ 7 (1)
Garner J.................. 9 (19)	Mlakar J .... - (1)	Williams J 34 (4)
Gelhardt J 2 (16)	Moore K 32 (4)	Windass J................ 12 (3)

League goals (57): Moore 10, Dunkley 6, Lowe 6, Dowell 5, Windass 4, Jacobs 3, Morsy 3, Naismith 3, Pilkington 3, Evans 2, Garner 2, Kipre 2, Byrne 1, Gelhardt 1, Robinson 1, Williams 1, Opponents 4
FA Cup goals: None. **League Cup goals**: None
Average home league attendance: 10,592. **Player of Year**: Sam Morsy

SKY BET LEAGUE ONE

ACCRINGTON STANLEY

Accrington overcame a sticky start – one win in nine – and a New Year slump to keep their distance from the relegation zone. In between, there were some eye-catching results, including the division's joint biggest win – 7-1 against Bolton. Colby Bishop scored two of those goals and netted another brace in a 4-1 success against promotion-minded Portsmouth two games later. Then, after his side managed a single point in the first five fixtures of 2020, they reeled off straight victories over AFC Wimbledon, Shrewsbury and Lincoln, the latter a 4-3 success against Lincoln, courtesy of Sam Finley's 95th minute winner after his side came from behind three times. Before kick-off against Wimbledon, supporters made a presentation to Billy Kee following his retirement for health reasons. Two spells at the club were also marked by his No

29 shirt being retired. In season 2017-18, Kee scored 25 goals as Accrington were promoted as League Two champions.

Alese A 6 (4)	Diallo S..................... 6 (3)	McConville S 15 (3)
Ashley-Seal B............ 3 (2)	Edwards P .... - (4)	Opoku J 19 (2)
Baker-Richardson C 2	Evtimov D....................19	Pritchard J 20 (10)
Barclay B.....................8	Finley S 29 (2)	Rodgers H 5 (1)
Bishop C.................. 24 (3)	Francis-Angol Z................5	Sherif L.....................2 (6)
Bursik J.....................16	Grant R 3 (2)	Simpson C.................. 1 (1)
Charles D................ 26 (7)	Hughes M....................31	Sykes R 31
Clark J.......................34	Johnson C 32 (1)	Wilson Carvalho 1 (7)
Conneely S.............. 30 (1)	Maguire J 10 (1)	Zanzala O.................7 (17)

League goals (47): Bishop 10, Charles 8, Clark 6, Zanzala 6, McConville 5, Finley 2, Pritchard 2, Conneely 1, Grant 1, Hughes 1, Sykes 1, Opponents 4
FA Cup goals: None. **League Cup goals** (1): Bishop 1. **League Trophy goals** (15): Clark 2, Sykes 2, Zanzala 2, Baker-Richardson 1, Bishop 1, Charles 1, Diallo 1, Finley 1, McConville 1, Pritchard 1, Simpson 1, Wilson Carvalho 1
Average home league attendance: 2,862

AFC WIMBLEDON

For the third successive season, Wimbledon lived on their nerves before escaping relegation by the tightest of margins. This time it was by 0.06 of a goal after it was abandoned and places decided on a points-per-game basis. They finished just ahead of Tranmere, one of the clubs arguing unsuccessfully that the campaign should be completed. Despite a 5-0 beating at Oxford, Glyn Hodges' side looked to have sufficient points in the bank, with their rivals on a run of 11 matches without a win. Instead, Tranmere reeled off three successive victories to close the gap to three points, with a game in hand, and put a whole new complexion on the struggle to stay up. Assistant manager Hodges had taken over when Wally Downes, a fellow member of the old club's 'Crazy Gang' was sacked two days after being banned and fined for breaching FA betting regulations. Wimbledon were then already facing hard times after their worst start to a league seasons – 11 matches without a win.

Appiah K 9 (10)	Madelin J ....– (1)	Roscrow A ....- (11)
Connolly D .... - (3)	McDonald R 11 (4)	Rudoni J 8 (3)
Day J.........................9	McDonnell J 1	Sanders M................. 18 (2)
Delaney R 13 (1)	McLoughlin S 14 (9)	Sorensen M 9
Folivi M 6 (4)	Nightingale W 8 (1)	Thomas T 31
Forss M 17 (1)	O'Neill L 30 (1)	Trott N 23
Guinness-Walker N ... 19 (4)	Osew P................. 15 (3)	Tzanev N 2
Hartigan A 20 (7)	Pigott J 31 (3)	Wagstaff S 23 (3)
Kalambayi P..................16	Pinnock M 17 (8)	Wood T ....- (2)
Lamy J 1 (1)	Reilly C 28 (2)	Wordsworth A.............6 (4)

League goals (39): Forss 11, Pigott 7, Appiah 4, Reilly 4, Pinnock 3, Delaney 1, Guinness-Walker 1, McLoughlin 1, O'Neill 1, Osew 1, Sanders 1, Thomas 1, Wagstaff 1, Wordsworth 1, Opponents 1
FA Cup goals (1): Pigott 1. **League Cup goals** (2): O'Neill 1, Wagstaff 1. **League Trophy goals** (4): Folivi 1, Pigott 1, Reilly 1, Wood 1
Average home league attendance: 4,383

BLACKPOOL

Boosted by attendances at Bloomfield Road up by nearly 60 per cent in the first full season since the removal of the controversial Oyston family as owners, Blackpool were well positioned for a promotion challenge approaching the halfway point of the season. Simon Grayson, back as manager nearly ten years after his first spell in charge, led his side up to fourth with a 3-1 local derby victory over Fleetwood, watched by a crowd of more than 10,000. But the margin for error was so slim in such a competitive division, with eight other clubs having similar ambitions, that a run of eight matches without a win proved costly. Blackpool dropped into the bottom half of the table and Grayson was sacked after seven months in charge. His replacement, Liverpool Under-23 team manager Neil Critchley, had little opportunity to regain momentum, with the campaign curtailed following a goalless draw in the return against Fleetwood, his first match, and a 2-1 defeat by Tranmere. They were then 13th.

Alnwick J......................22	Heneghan B 24 (2)	Ronan C...................... 10
Anderton N 1 (1)	Howard M..........................4	Scannell S...................3 (5)
Bola M 5	Husband J......................28	Sims J .... - (1)
Bushiri R 2 (2)	Kaikai S 17 (5)	Spearing J.................28 (2)
Delfouneso N 21 (7)	MacDonald C 9 (3)	Thompson J.............15 (3)
Dewsbury-Hall K......... 9 (1)	Madine G 9 (1)	Thorniley J 2
Edwards R 19 (2)	Maxwell C..........................9	Tilt C........................17 (3)
Feeney L 33 (2)	Moore T..........................8	Turton O..................26 (4)
Gnanduillet A 25 (5)	Nottingham M.......... - (3)	Virtue M 20 (4)
Guy C 6 (9)	Nuttall J 9 (18)	Ward G......................2 (3)
Hardie R 2 (5)	Pritchard H.............. - (2)	

League goals (44): Gnanduillet 15, Dewsbury-Hall 4, Kaikai 4, Delfouneso 3, Heneghan 2, Madine 2, Nuttall 2, Spearing 2, Virtue 2, Edwards 1, Feeney 1, Ronan 1, Scannell 1, Thompson 1, Opponents 3
FA Cup goals (9): Delfouneso 4, Gnanduillet 2, Kaikai 1, Virtue 1, Opponents 1. **League Cup goals** (2): Gnanduillet 1, Turton 1. **League Trophy goals** (8): Nuttall 2, Bushiri 1, Hardie 1, Heneghan 1, Kaikai 1, Nottingham 1, Opponents 1
Average home league attendance: 8,770. **Player of Year**: Liam Feeney

BOLTON WANDERERS

While neighbours Bury went under, Bolton survived their financial crisis, thanks to a takeover by Football Ventures, a private limited company. But they had to start with a 12-point deduction, imposed for going into administration, lost several senior players and a failure to win any of the opening 11 games, pointed to a second successive relegation. Keith Hill, Bolton-born former Rochdale and Barnsley manager, maintained a cheery countenance after taking over when Phil Parkinson resigned. He signed nine free transfer, unattached and loan players, who broke their duck by beating Bristol Rovers 2-0 away from home with goals from two of his experienced men, Luke Murphy and Daryl Murphy. Wins over Fleetwood and MK Dons followed immediately, putting points on the board for the first time, but that surge was never repeated. When the season was abandoned, Bolton were bottom, 14 points in credit, and the club decided not to award Hill a new contract. He was replaced by Ian Evatt, fresh from taking Barrow into the Football League.

Alexander M......................1	Darcy R 14 (5)	Hamilton E 12
Boon J 1 (2)	Delaney R 2 (2)	Hobbs J......................11
Bridcutt L 11	Dodoo J 16 (8)	Hurford-Lockett F .... - (2)
Brockbank H 5 (1)	Earl J 9	King-Harmes C...........3 (2)
Brown E 4 (1)	Edwards L..........................6	Lowe J 28 (1)
Brown-Sterling D 1 (1)	Emmanuel J............. 25 (2)	Matthews R......................33
Bryan K 6	Faal M .... - (2)	Mellis J.................... 1 (5)
Buckley W 3 (2)	Fleming B..........................10	Murphy D................. 23 (1)
Bunney J 1 (1)	Georgiou A .... - (2)	Murphy L 26 (3)
Chicksen A.............. 14 (2)	Graham S 6 (7)	Nsiala A......................12
Crawford A......................12	Hall C...................... - (1)	O'Grady C 10 (10)

Oztumer E	1	Senior A	1(1)	White J	3 (1)
Politic D	19 (5)	Verlinden T	12 (3)	Wright J	11
Riley R	- (1)	Weir J	7 (1)	Zouma Y	14 (3)

League goals (27): Murphy D 8, Dodoo 4, Politic 3, Verlinden 3, Murphy L 2, O'Grady 2, Bryan 1, Darcy 1, Delaney 1, Hamilton 1, Hobbs 1
FA Cup goals: None. **League Cup goals** (2): Darcy 1, Politic 1. **League Trophy goals** (5): Crawford 2, O'Grady 2, Politic 1
Average home league attendance: 11,511

BRISTOL ROVERS

Rovers lost manager Graham Coughlan, lost momentum and lost the chance of maintaining a promotion challenge. They were fourth, and on a high, after winning at Ipswich when Coughlan left to join Mansfield, 18th in League Two, citing the club's ambitions and the chance to be closer to his Sheffield home. Ben Garner, former West Bromwich Albion and Crystal Palace coach who succeeded him six days later, had to wait 11 matches for his first victory. Rovers, with just four points and four goals in that spell, dropped to 13th before coming from behind to defeat Blackpool 2-1 with goals from Alfie Kilgour and Josh Ginnelly. Garner's second success, 2-0 against Sunderland courtesy of two goals from Jonson Clarke-Harris, was not enough for a top-half finish, although it knocked their opponents out of the play-offs. Mansfield, meanwhile, finished 21st

Abraham T	- (4)	Hare J	7 (3)	Nichols T	12 (7)
Adeboyejo V	6 (12)	Hargreaves C	3 (3)	Ogogo A	25 (2)
Barrett J	3 (4)	Harries C	2 (1)	Reilly G	1 (3)
Bennett K	2 (10)	Holmes-Dennis T	2 (2)	Rodman A	23 (6)
Blackman J	10	Jaakkola A	21	Sercombe L	20 (2)
Clarke O	26 (1)	Kelly M	2 (3)	Smith T	11 (9)
Clarke-Harris J	24 (2)	Kilgour A	33	Tomlinson L	- (1)
Craig T	34	Leahy L	31 (1)	Upson E	32 (1)
Daly J	1 (2)	Little M	9 (2)	Van Stappershoef J	4 (1)
Davies T	18 (1)	Menayesse R	10 (3)		
Ginnelly J	5 (4)	Mitchell-Lawson J	8 (2)		

League goals (38): Clarke-Harris 13, Ogogo 3, Smith 3, Craig 2, Kilgour 2, Mitchell-Lawson 2, Nichols 2, Rodman 2, Upson 2, Adeboyejo 1, Clarke 1, Davies 1, Ginnelly 1, Sercombe 1, Opponents 2
FA Cup goals (6): Clarke-Harris 2, Craig 1, Leahy 1, Rodman 1, Sercombe 1. **League Cup goals** (4): Smith 2, Clarke-Harris 1, Nichols 1. **League Trophy goals** (5): , Adebayejo 1, Kilgour 1, Little 1, Nichols 1, Sercombe 1
Average home league attendance: 7,397

BURTON ALBION

Nigel Clough stepped down as manager after a season in which his side flirted with a play-off spot before falling away. A run of five victories in six matches, including four-goal performances against Tranmere and Bolton and three scored against Rochdale, lifted them briefly to sixth place. But they lost leading scorer Liam Boyce to Hearts in the winter transfer window and despite Jamie Murphy's productive loan spell from Rangers, won just once in ten matches before the campaign was cut short and finished 12th. Clough left to ease the club's financial burden caused by the COVID-19 crisis. Brother Simon, the chief scout, and long-standing assistant Gary Crosby also departed. Clough, who took Burton into the Championship during his four-and-a-half-year second spell in charge, was replaced by club captain Jake Buxton.

Akins L.................35	Fraser S 25 (5)	Quinn S 27 (2)
Anderson J................. - (1)	Garratt B 2 (1)	Sarkic O.................24 (4)
Boyce L.................`17 (8)	Hart B.................. - (3)	Sbarra J.................6 (16)
Brayford J.................29 (3)	Hutchinson R 8 (9)	Shaughnessy J............6 (2)
Broadhead N.............12 (7)	Murphy J.................10	Templeton D.............7 (11)
Buxton J.................20 (4)	Nartey R................. 20 (5)	Thomas K.................- (2)
Daniel C 19 (5)	O'Hara K.................33	Wallace K.................20 (6)
Dyer L ....- (5)	O'Toole J-J.................25	
Edwards R 33	Powell J 7 (3)	

League goals (50): Akins 9, Boyce 8, Murphy 7, Edwards 5, Fraser 5, Powell 3, Sarkic 3, Templeton 3, Brayford 2, Broadhead 2, Buxton 1, Sbarra 1, Wallace 1
FA Cup goals (8): Fraser 2, Akins 1, Boyce 1, Brayford 1, Edwards 1, Sarkic 1, Templeton 1.
League Cup goals (9): Boyce 5, Broadhead 1, Edwards 1, Fraser 1, Sarkic 1. **League Trophy goals** (4): Akins 1, Fraser 1, Quinn 1, Templeton 1
Average home league attendance: 2,986

BURY

League football died at Gigg Lane after 125 years, Instead of preparing for a return to the game's third tier after winning promotion the previous season, financial mismanagement finally caught up with this old club. All the opening five fixtures, against MK Dons Accrington, Gillingham, Rotherham and Tranmere, were postponed, along with a League Cup tie against Sheffield Wednesday. Repeated talk of a rescue bid came to nothing and Bury were expelled for what the EFL called failing to provide evidence of financial viability. 'It was a dark day in our history,' said the governing body of the first club to drop out since Maidstone's demise in 1992.

COVENTRY CITY

Mark Robins's side made light of having to concede home advantage after the failure to agree a deal to remain at the Ricoh Arena. They delivered a second promotion in three years, crowned by the title, in a highly competitive division that took its toll of some of the more fancied clubs. Coventry adapted immediately to life at St Andrew's in Birmingham, losing just once there in 17 matches. They were also formidable in 'routine' away games, none more so than in back-to-back 4-1 wins over Wycombe and Tranmere which cemented a place among the leading group. Matt Godden, without a goal for four months, scored a hat-trick in both and enjoyed another productive spell at the end of his side's 14-match unbeaten run which put them five points clear at the top when the season was cut short. During that spell they took maximum points against Portsmouth, Sunderland and Ipswich and shared the honours with Rotherham, who finished runners-up.

Allen J.................... 7 (4)	Hiwula J................... 14 (1)	O'Hare C 18 (11)
Bakayoko A 11 (12)	Hyam D................. 28 (1)	Pask J......................- (2)
Bapaga W .... - (1)	Jobello W 10	Rose M 30 (1)
Biamou M 5 (13)	Kastaneer G 1 (9)	Shipley J.................24 (7)
Dabo F.................32	Kelly L 25 (2)	Wakefield C ....- (1)
Drysdale D 1	Marosi M.................34	Walsh L 25 (1)
Eccles J.................. 1 (2)	Mason B 10 (1)	Watson T.................1 (2)
Giles R .... - (1)	McCallum S 25 (1)	Westbrooke E.............22 (3)
Godden M 22 (4)	McFadzean K............ 28 (2)	

League goals (48): Godden 14, Shipley 5, Bakayoko 4, Biamou 4, Westbrooke 4, O'Hare 4, Walsh 3, Hiwula 2, Hyam 2, McCallum 2, Rose 2, Allen 1, Jobello 1, Kastaneer 1
FA Cup goals (12): Biamou 4, Shipley 2, Bakayoko 1, McCallum 1, O'Hare 1, Pask 1, Walsh 1, Opponents 1. **League Cup goals** (4): Hiwula 2, Bakayoko 1, Godden 1. **League Trophy goals** (3): Biamou 3
Average home league attendance (at St Andrew's , Birmingham): 6,677. **Player of Year**: Fankaty Dabo

DONCASTER ROVERS

Darren Moore's side spent much of the abbreviated season on the fringes of a play-off place without managing to do quite enough to make the breakthrough. Twice, there were hints that Moore's first season at the Keepmoat after being sacked by West Bromwich Albion might prove a productive one. The first accompanied a 7-1 victory over nine-man Southend, the joint biggest score of the season, which took them to within goal difference of sixth-place Oxford, with a game in hand. Then, after failing to win any of the next five fixtures, Doncaster restored momentum with their best performance of the season – 3-0 at Peterborough – and this time built on the result to close to within two points of the top six. But with the division proving so competitive and leaving little room for error, back-to-back defeats by Gillingham and Shrewsbury left them adrift again

Amos D..........................2	Ennis N..................22 (7)	Ramsey J 6 (1)
Anderson T 32	Gomes M.............13 (10)	Sadlier K................28 (5)
Baptiste A.....................2	Halliday B 34	Sheaf B................29 (3)
Bingham R............ 3 (5)	James R 26 (1)	Sterling K.......................1 (2)
Blair M 3 (9)	John C 17 (1)	Taylor J 22 (6)
Cole D 5 (4)	Kiwomya A ....- (1)	Thomas K.............5 (5)
Coppinger J...........24 (5)	Lawlor I........................7	Watters M..................- (5)
Crawford A................- (1)	Lokilo J ....- (1)	Whiteman B 33
Daniels D.................. 8 (2)	May A 7 (8)	Wright J 16 (4)
Dieng T.......................27	Okenabirhie F............. 2 (3)	

League goals (51): Sadlier 11, Ennis 6, Taylor 6, Whiteman 5, Coppinger 3, Ramsey 3, Thomas 3, James 2, John 2, Okenabirhie 2, Anderson 1, Bingham 1, May 1, Sheaf 1, Opponents 4
FA Cup goals (3): Anderson 1, Bingham 1, Coppinger 1. **League Cup goals:** None. **League Trophy goals** (6): May 2, John 1, Sadlier 1, Sterling 1, Wright 1
Average home league attendance: 8,252. **Player of Year:** Tom Anderson

FLEETWOOD TOWN

Fleetwood's dream of Championship football turned into a nightmare in the first leg of their play-off semi-final at Highbury. A solid season's work unravelled in the first seven minutes against Wycombe when they conceded two goals, the second when goalkeeper Alex Cairns flapped a corner into his own net. Joey Barton's side then had Lewis Coyle sent off for a reckless challenge after half-an-hour, Paddy Madden dismissed for a second yellow card late on and lost 4-1. Commendably, they delivered a more disciplined performance in the return match, goals from Danny Andrew and Ched Evans from the penalty spot looking set to bring a moral victory until a Wycombe equaliser four minutes into stoppage-time for 2-2. Fleetwood's best start to a Football League campaign had netted 26 points from 14 games. They faltered early in the New Year, but regrouped with experienced midfielder Glenn Whelan on board to accumulate 19 points from seven matches, five of them against promotion rivals, to book a top-six place.

Andrew D......................35	Dunne J 9	Morris J..................23 (10)
Biggins H............... 5 (5)	Eastham A 5 (4)	Rossiter J 15
Burns W 31 (3)	Evans C..................19 (9)	Saunders H ....- (6)
Cairns A........................25	Gibson L.....................9	Southam M...................- (1)
Clarke P 11 (1)	Gilks M 5	Souttar H 33 (1)
Connolly C...................13	Hunter A 1 (13)	Sowerby J............13 (11)
Coutts P 28 (4)	Madden P 25 (10)	Thorvaldsson I ....- (2)
Coyle L...........................34	McAleny C 4 (8)	Wallace R ....- (3)
Crellin W........................5	McKay B 7 (1)	Whelan G 11
Dempsey K 19 (2)	Mooney D ....- (1)	

Play-offs – appearances: Burns 2, Cairns 2, Connolly 2, Coutts 2, Evans 2, Gibson 2, McKay 2, Morris 2, Souttar 2, Whelan 2, Andrew 1 (1), Coyle 1, Dempsey – (2), Saunders – (2), Madden – (1), Southam – (1)
League goals (51): Madden 15, Evans 9, Morris 7, Souttar 3, Andrew 2, Burns 2, Connolly 2, Dempsey 2, McAleny 2, McKay 2, Clarke 1, Coyle 1, Dunne 1, Opponents 2. **Play-offs – goals** (3): Evans 2, Andrew 1
FA Cup goals (5): Evans 1, Hunter 1, Madden 1, McAleny 1, Morris 1. **League Cup goals:** None. **League Trophy goals:** (13): Madden 3, Andrew 2, Burns 2, Clarke 2, Morris 2, Coutts 1, Sowerby 1
Average home league attendance: 3,130

GILLINGHAM

Steve Evans delivered a top-half finish for a club who had flirted with the threat of relegation in each of the previous three seasons. In his seventh Football League job, Evans made a new-look side difficult to beat, as evidenced during a 15-match unbeaten run starting in early December with a 1-0 victory over Sunderland, secured by Connor Ogilvie's 89th minute goal. The sequence embraced seven wins and eight draws which, at the time, offered an outside chance of breaking into a play-off position. A home defeat by struggling AFC Wimbledon, inflicted in stoppage time, put paid to that. But at least there was the satisfaction of another strong performance against Sunderland in their final match before the campaign was abandoned. Mikael Mandron scored twice against his old club for a point, his second coming six minutes into stoppage-time. Previously, Gillingham earned an FA Cup first round replay at the Stadium of Light and won the replay with Brandon Hanlan's extra-time goal.

Akinde J 7 (2)	Hanlan B 31 (4)	Ndjoli M 7 (5)
Bonham J 35	Hodson L 4 (3)	O'Connor T 26 (2)
Byrne M 16 (2)	Jakubiak A 12 (12)	Ogilvie C 33
Charles-Cook R 5 (10)	Jones A 30	O'Keefe S 26 (4)
Cisse O 2	Lee O 22 (6)	Pringle B 6 (4)
Ehmer M 35	List E 1 (3)	Roberts J 10
Fuller B 30	Mandron M 13 (10)	Tucker J 26 (2)
Graham J 2 (5)	Marshall M 3 (15)	Willock M 3 (4)

League goals (42): Jakubiak 6, Mandron 5, Hanlan 4, Lee 4, Ogilvie 4, Charles-Cook 3, O'Keefe 3, Jones 2, Ndjoli 2, Roberts 2, Akinde 1, Cisse 1, Ehmer 1, O'Connor 1, Opponents 3
FA Cup goals (5): Hanlan 2, Lee 2, Byrne 1. **League Cup goals** (2): Hanlan 1, Ndjoli 1. **League Trophy goals** (4): Jakubiak 1, Mandron 1, O'Keefe 1, Tucker 1
Average home league attendance: 5,148. **Player of Year:** Connor Ogilvie

IPSWICH TOWN

Paul Lambert's side were strongly fancied for an immediate return to the Championship and their odds shortened further with an unbeaten 11-match run to start the season. It was the club's best since 1980-81, yet masked what was to prove their achilles heel – matches against their many promotion rivals in a tough division. The cracks appeared during a run of eight games without a win, accompanied by a fall to fifth. Lambert signed a new contract through to the summer of 2025 and his side broke the sequence by beating Accrington, then regained top spot when overcoming Lincoln. After that it was downhill all the way – seven defeats, one draw and a single success, against Burton. It meant that when the season was abandoned, Ipswich were eight points off the play-offs, having recorded a single victory, over Fleetwood, against the top eight teams.

Bishop E 2 (7)	Dobra A .... - (3)	Downes F 29
Chambers L 31	Donacien J 12 (1)	Dozzell A 8 (2)

Earl J 5 (2)	Judge A 21 (9)	Roberts J .... - (1)
Edwards G 22 (5)	Keane W 14 (9)	Rowe D..................... 9 (5)
El Mizouni I 1 (2)	Kenlock M 8 (1)	Sears F..................... 2 (9)
Garbutt L....................28	McGavin B 1	Simpson T .... - (3)
Georgiou A .... - (10)	Nolan J.................... 17 (5)	Skuse C 25 (4)
Holy T.......................21	Norris W....................15	Vincent-Young K 9
Huws E.................... 11 (6)	Norwood J 22 (6)	Wilson J.................. 21 (2)
Jackson K 28 (4)	Nsiala A............................3	Woolfenden L 31

League goals (46): Jackson 11, Norwood 11, Garbutt 5, Judge 3, Keane 3, Downes 2, Edwards 2, Nolan 2, Vincent-Young 2, Chambers 1, Rowe 1, Sears 1, Woolfenden 1, Opponents 1
FA Cup goals (4): Dozzell 1, Garbutt 1, Judge 1, Keane 1. **League Cup goals** (1): Dobra 1. **League Trophy goals** (8): Roberts 3, Keane 2, El Mizouni 1, Huws 1, Opponents 1
Average home league attendance: 19,549

LINCOLN CITY

Another successful season under Danny Cowley beckoned when a flying start brought maximum against Accington, Rotherham and Southend. Instead, the manager who delivered two promotions in three years, agreed to take over at Huddersfield, after initially rejecting the job, and was joined by his assistant, brother Nicky. Cowley's replacement, former Oxford manager Michael Appleton, watched from the stands before officially taking over and saw the effect on the team in a 6-0 home defeat by Oxford. Appleton had a single victory to show from his first seven games before Lincoln cemented a mid-table position with five-goal performances against Ipswich and Bolton during a run of 10 points from five games in which Tyler Walker scored six goals. Walker returned to parent club Nottingham Forest in the winter transfer window and there was another seven-match lean spell until Josh Vickers saved a penalty to preserve a 3-2 success in their final match against Burton.

Akinde J 3 (20)	Edun T............................6	Payne J.................. 18 (5)
Anderson H............. 24 (6)	Elbouzedi Z 1 (4)	Pett T 1 (1)
Andrade B 11 (6)	Grant J.................... 29 (3)	Scully A 3 (2)
Bolger C 25 (3)	Hesketh J 14 (6)	Shackell J 26
Bostwick M 16 (2)	Hopper T................. 5 (3)	Sheehan A...................... 1
Bridcutt L......................5	John-Jules T 7	Toffolo H 26
Chapman E 5 (6)	Lewis A .... - (2)	Vickers J 35
Connolly C 9 (2)	Melbourne M 6 (2)	Walker T.................. 26 (3)
Coventry C 5 (2)	Morrell J.....................29	
Eardley N....................35	O'Connor M 14 (3)	

League goals (44): Walker 14, Akinde 5, Anderson 5, Grant 2, Hopper 2, Payne 2, Scully 2, Shackell 2, Andrade 1, Bostwick 1, Bridcutt 1, Hesketh 1, John-Jules 1, Lewis 1, O'Connor 1, Toffolo 1, Opponents 2
FA Cup goals (1): Walker 1. **League Cup goals** (3): Anderson 2, Andrade 1. **League Trophy goals** (4): Akinde 3, Walker 1
Average home league attendance: 8,986

MILTON KEYNES DONS

Rhys Healey returned from injury to play a leading role in Dons easing clear of the threat of an immediate return to League Two. Healey, out for three-and-a-half-months with thigh trouble, scored nine goals in 13 games, including a run of five in succession, to lift his side from third from bottom under new manager Russell Martin. The former Norwich and Scotland central defender, who was in the Dons line-up that clinched promotion on the final day of the previous season, replaced Paul Tisdale. He immediately retired from playing to concentrate on his new role. Tisdale started the season with four league wins out of seven and two Carabao Cup victories, but was sacked after a single point and two goals from a run of nine games. The League Cup wins brought a third round tie against Liverpool (0-2) which attracted a club-record crowd of 28,521 to Stadium MK.

Agard K 11 (8)	Harley R..................... 2 (1)	Morris C 9 (1)
Asonganyi D .... - (3)	Healey R 15 (4)	Nicholls L......................35
Boateng H.................. 14 (6)	Houghton J...................30	Nombe S 11 (10)
Bowery J.................. 10 (6)	Kasumu D 14 (7)	Poole R 17 (2)
Brittain C.................. 28 (3)	Lewington D 32 (1)	Reeves B................ 4 (13)
Cargill B 7 (5)	Martin R..................11	Thompson L 7 (2)
Dickenson B.............. 2 (5)	Mason J 10 (3)	Walsh J 23 (1)
Gilbey A.................. 27 (3)	McGrandles C 25 (6)	Williams G..................... 28
Gladwin B .... - (9)	Moore-Taylor J 13 (1)	

League goals (36): Healey 11, Gilbey 5, Mason 3, Agard 2, Bowery 2, Houghton 2, Morris 2, Nombe 2, Brittain 1, Gladwin 1, Kasumu 1, Martin 1, McGrandles 1, Reeves 1 Williams 1
FA Cup goals: None. **League Cup goals** (6): Boateng 1, Brittain 1, Healey 1, Kasumu 1, McGrandles 1, Nombe 1. **League Trophy goals** (7): Agard 2, Nombe 2, Dickenson 1, Mason 1, McGrandles 1
Average home league attendance: 9,246. **Player of Year**: Alex Gilbey

OXFORD UNITED

Oxford lost the chance of a shot at automatic promotion when the season came to a halt – and were then left deflated after losing the Play-off Final to Wycombe. Five successive wins and 14 goals scored, six by Matt Taylor, lifted them to within two points of second-place Rotherham, with every chance of going higher until the suspension. Oxford and Portsmouth were bracketed together when points-per-game determined-final positions and there was nothing to separate the teams when they met in the semi-finals. Both legs finished 1-1 before Simon Eastwood made the decisive shoot-out save from Cameron McGeehan, followed by Cameron Brannagan's conversion for 5-4. Eastwood made a less successful intervention at Wembley, where he brought down Fred Onyedinma to concede the 79th minute penalty that gave Wycombe a 2-1 success. Mark Sykes had put Oxford level and they were on top for much of the match without accepting further chances. Previously, the club reached the quarter-finals of the League Cup for the first time since season 1987-88 and made Manchester City work for a 3-1 victory.

Agyei D.................... 1 (12)	Fosu T 21 (4)	Moore E 12 (8)
Archer J.......................6	Gorrin A 29 (2)	Mousinho J............. 25 (1)
Baptiste S................ 9 (8)	Hall R 3 (10)	Ruffels J 35
Brannagan C 29 (1)	Hanson J.................... 2 (3)	Sykes M 17 (6)
Browne M 8 (3)	Henry J...................30	Taylor M 20 (6)
Cadden C..................21	Holland N.................. 7 (3)	Thorne G................... 1 (3)
Dickie R 34	Kelly L 1 (2)	Woodburn B...............11
Eastwood S..................29	Long S 10 (6)	
Forde A 9 (9)	Mackie J 15 (17)	

Play-offs – appearances: Brannagan 3, Browne 3, Dickie 3, Eastwood 3, Gorrin 3, Henry 3, Long 3, Moore 3, Ruffels 3, Sykes 2 (1), Taylor 2 (1), Woodburn 1 (2), Mackie 1 (1), Agyei – (3), Forde – (3), Hanson – (1), Kelly – (1), Mousinho – (1)
League goals (61): Taylor 13, Henry 12, Fosu 8, Brannagan 5, Browne 4, Agyei 3, Ruffels 3, Holland 2, Mackie 2, Baptiste 1, Forde 1, Long 1, Moore 1, Sykes 1, Woodburn 1, Opponents 3.
Play-offs – goals (3): Browne 1, Sykes 1, Opponents 1

FA Cup goals (9): Hall 2, Baptiste 1, Fosu 1, Henry 1, Holland 1, Kelly 1, Long 1, Taylor 1. **League Cup goals** (9): Taylor 2, Baptiste 1, Brannagan 1, Fosu 1, Hall 1, Henry 1, Moore 1, Sykes 1. **League Trophy goals** (8): Hall 3, Baptiste 1, Brannagan 1, Dickie 1, Forde 1, Taylor 1. **Average home league attendance**: 7,636. **Player of Year**: Rob Dickie

PETERBOROUGH UNITED

Peterborough narrowly missed out on the play-offs for the second year running, this time in a dispute over whether the season should be completed. Chairman Darragh MacAnthony led a six-club campaign to resume matches after a two-month interruption caused by COVID-19. But his proposal was defeated and a points-per-game system used to determine final positions. It meant Peterborough, in sixth place with 59 points from 35 games for an average of 1.68, were overtaken by Wycombe, whose tally of 59 came from one fewer fixture gave them an average of 1.73. Darren Ferguson's side had regained momentum after a difficult spell leading up to Christmas and into the New Year, with just two points and one goal in six matches. Ivan Toney regained his scoring touch as they delivered four-goal performances against Wycombe, Ipswich, Oxford and Southend. Toney was also on the mark against another promotion-chasing side, Portsmouth, and finished the division's top marksman on 24.

Beevers M	32	Eisa M	27 (2)	Reed L	23 (1)
Bennett R	7 (6)	Jade-Jones R	2 (9)	Szmodics S	10
Blake-Tracy F	11 (3)	Kanu I	1 (5)	Tasdemir S	1 (9)
Boyd G	17 (5)	Kent F	28	Taylor J	11
Brown R	10	Knight J	16 (8)	Thompson N	12 (3)
Burrows H	2 (2)	Maddison M	19 (3)	Toney I	32
Butler D	26 (3)	Mason N	25 (5)	Ward J	18 (10)
Dembele S	12 (13)	Pym C	35	Woodyard A	8 (6)

League goals (68): Toney 24, Eisa 14, Maddison 9, Dembele 5, Szmodics 4, Knight 3, Ward 3, Butler 2, Taylor 2, Kent 1, Reed 1 **FA Cup goals** (8): Eisa 2, Jade-Jones 2, Toney 2, Kent 1, Maddison 1. **League Cup goals**: None. **League Trophy goals** (6): Jade-Jones 2, Ward 2, Dembele 1, Kanu 1
Average home league attendance: 7,371. **Player of Year**: Ivan Toney

PORTSMOUTH

The weight of expectation continued to haunt Portsmouth. For the second successive season – and the third time in five years – they lost in the semi-finals of the play-offs after starting the campaign as firm favourites to go up. This time, they went ahead in both legs, at home through Ronan Curtis, then with a Marcus Harness goal. Twice Oxford levelled, in the return through an Ellis Harrison own goal, and went through 5-4 on penalties after former Portsmouth goalkeeper Simon Eastwood saved from Cameron McGeehan. Some consolation came with the team's defence of the EFL Trophy – another final reached, against Salford, and now scheduled for the new season after the original Wembley date was one of the victims of the pandemic. There was also the division's only unbeaten home record to show when play was halted. It embraced ten successive wins at Fratton Park – seven in the league, one FA Cup tie and two Trophy matches – the best since Alan Ball was manager in season 1986-87.

Bass A	15	Evans G	10 (7)	McGeehan C	10 (2)
Bolton J	20 (3)	Harness M	16 (9)	Naylor T	33
Brown L	16	Harrison E	17 (11)	Pitman B	4 (7)
Burgess C	31 (1)	Haunstrup B	7 (3)	Raggett S	26
Cannon A	13 (5)	Hawkins O	5 (2)	Seddon S	10 (2)
Close B	27 (2)	MacGillivray C	20	Walkes A	10 (1)
Curtis R	31 (2)	Marquis J	25 (8)	Whatmough J	1
Downing P	6	McCrorie R	12 (5)	Williams R	20 (6)

Play-offs – appearances: Bass 2, Burgess 2, Curtis 2, Harness 2, Harrison 2, McGeehan 2, Morris 2, Raggett 2, Bolton 1 (1), Brown 1 (1), Cannon 1 (1), Williams 1 (1), McCrorie 1, Seddon 1, Marquis – (2), Evans – (1), Hawkins – (1)
League goals (53): Curtis 11, Marquis 8, Evans 5, Harness 5, Harrison 5, Burgess 3, Close 3, Williams 3, Pitman 2, Raggett 2, Bolton 1, Brown 1, Cannon 1, Naylor 1, Seddon 1, Opponents 1. **Play-offs – goals** (2): Curtis 1, Harness 1
FA Cup goals (10): Close 2, Curtis 2, Marquis 2, Bolton 1, Burgess 1, Haunstrup 1, Pitman 1. **League Cup goals** (5): Harrison 2, Close 1, Harness 1, Marquis 1. **League Trophy goals** (15): Harrison 3, Marquis 3, Harness 2, McGeehan 2, Flint J 1, Lethbridge B 1, Maloney L 1, Pitman 1, Walkes 1
Average home league attendance: 17,804. **Player of Year**: Christian Burgess

ROCHDALE

Ian Henderson reached a personal milestone while continuing to play a leading role in preserving his team's League One status. The evergreen striker scored his 100th league goal for the club in some style, rounding off a 16-pass move with a typical predatory finish in a 3-0 victory at Southend. For the seventh successive season, 35-year-old Henderson reached double figures, this time with 15 to his name, including two-goal performances on four occasions – against Tranmere in the opening fixture, Rotherham in the final one and AFC Wimbledon and Accrington in between. Another veteran, along with a teenage prospect, shared Rochdale's other major moments. An equaliser by Luke Matheson, 16, took their League Cup tie at Old Trafford to a penalty shoot-out, which Manchester United won 5-3. Later in the season, Matheson, now 17, set up 40-year-old Aaron Wilbraham for an FA Cup equaliser at St James' Park against Newcastle, who won the replay 4-1.

Andrew C 3 (17)	Lund M 5	Pyke R 11 (2)
Baah K 4 (3)	Lynch J 8	Rathbone O 19 (5)
Bradley L .... - (2)	Magloire T 2	Ryan J 16 (8)
Camps C 28	Matheson L 18 (2)	Sanchez R 26
Done M 14 (10)	McLaughlin R .... - (3)	Smith T 2 (2)
Dooley S 19 (3)	McNulty J 13 (1)	Tavares R 1 (13)
Gillam M .... - (2)	McShane P............. 15 (1)	Wilbraham A..............11 (8)
Henderson I 29 (2)	Morley A.................. 18 (5)	Williams J 28
Hopper H .... - (1)	Norrington-Davies R 27	
Keohane J 26 (2)	O'Connell E 31	

League goals (39): Henderson 15, Camps 6, Dooley 3, Wilbraham 3, Rathbone 2, Lund 1, Matheson 1, Norrington-Davies 1, Pyke 1, Ryan 1, Smith 1, Tavares 1
FA Cup goals (5): McShane 1, Morley 1, Wilbraham 1, Williams 1, Opponents 1. **League Cup goals** (8): Camps 2, Done 1, Henderson 1, Matheson 1, Morley 1, Pyke 1, Rathbone 1. **League Trophy goals** (3): Pyke 1, Tavares 1, Wilbraham 1
Average home league attendance: 3,632. **Player of Year**: Eoghan O'Connell

ROTHERHAM UNITED

For the second time in three seasons, Rotherham rebounded immediately and impressively from relegation from the Championship. They more than compensated for patchy form at their New York Stadium with the best away record in the toughest of divisions to claim the runners-up spot behind Coventry. Paul Warne's side went into the Christmas and New Year programme in eighth place, having suffered a fourth home defeat – by lowly Rochdale with the first half of the scheduled campaign not yet complete. They came out of it with four straight victories, seven goals scored against promotion rivals Peterborough and Oxford and momentum restored. Paul Warne's side also overcame Ipswich, while delivering a 10th victory on their travels at Accrington. There was a stumble at Rochdale, but not enough to forfeit a two-point advantage over three teams – Oxford, Portsmouth and Fleetwood – when the season was abandoned.

Adelakun H	8 (1)	Ladapo F	20 (11)	Proctor J	- (3)
Barlaser D	24 (3)	Lamy J	- (3)	Robertson C	17
Clarke T	4 (4)	Lindsay J	14 (8)	Smith M	26 (8)
Crooks M	31 (2)	MacDonald S	3 (10)	Thompson A	9 (1)
Hastie J	10 (4)	Mattock J	22 (2)	Tilt C	
Ihiekwe M	33	Morris C	11 (10)	Vassell K	13 (7)
Iversen D	34	Ogbene C	19 (6)	Wiles B	28 (5)
Jones B	9 (1)	Olosunde M	27 (5)	Wood R	21 (2)
Koroma J	- (5)	Price L	1	Yates J	- (1)

League goals (61): Ladapo 14, Crooks 9, Smith 9, Vassell 4, Hastie 3, Morris 3, Wiles 3, Wood 3, Barlaser 2, Ihiekwe 2, Robertson 2, Lindsay 1, Mattock 1, Ogbene 1, Opponents 4
FA Cup goals (9): Smith 3, Ihiekwe 2, Ladapo 2, Crooks 1, Vassell 1. **League Cup goals** (4): Crooks 1, Ladapo 1, Vassell 1, Wood 1. **League Trophy goals** (3): Clarke 1, Morris 1, Opponents 1
Average home league attendance: 8,906. **Player of Year**: Michael Ihiekwe

SHREWSBURY TOWN

Shrewsbury struggled for points during an eventful FA Cup run – but had sufficient in the bank to avoid being drawn into a relegation struggle. They overcame Bristol City in a round three replay with an 89th minute goal struck from 25 yards by defender Aaron Pierre, after Sean Goss equalised at Ashton Gate. In round four, two by substitute Jason Cummings, his first a penalty, retrieved a 2-0 deficit against Liverpool, who brought on Alex Oxlade-Chamberlain, Mohamed Salah and Roberto Firmino late on in a unsuccessful bid for the winner. For the replay at Anfield, Jurgen Klopp rested all his senior players and missed the game himself, leaving Under-23 manager Neil Critchley to supervise a 1-0 victory, decided by an own goal by Ro-Shaun Williams. Before, during and after that run, Shrewsbury failed to win any of their ten league matches, finally returning to winning ways by beating Doncaster with a goal by captain Dave Edwards, his first for the club.

Beckles O	25 (3)	Lang C	14 (2)	Pierre A	29 (1)
Cummings J	13 (11)	Laurent J	30 (1)	Ramsay K	3 (2)
Ebanks-Landell E	28	Love D	26 (2)	Sears R	2
Edwards D	24 (5)	McAleny C	5	Thompson L	1 (9)
Eisa A	- (1)	McCormick L	4 (1)	Udoh D	12 (13)
Giles R	15 (4)	Morison S	6 (1)	Vela J	4
Golbourne S	14 (1)	Murphy J	4	Vincelot R	2
Goss J	15 (7)	Norburn O	17	Walker B	4 (11)
Hart S	2 (2)	O'Leary M	30	Whalley S	15 (8)
John-Lewis L	- (2)	Okenabirhie F	6 (11)	Williams R-S	24 (1)

League goals (31): Cummings 4, Udoh 4, Beckles 3, Lang 3, Norburn 3, Pierre 3, Laurent 2, Okenabirhie 2, Whalley 2, Ebanks-Landell 1, Edwards 1, Giles 1, Golbourne 1, Opponents 1
FA Cup goals (8): Cummings 2, Laurent 2, Edwards 1, Goss 1, Pierre 1, Walker 1. **League Cup goals**: None. **League Trophy goals** (8): Edwards 2, Cummings 1, Golbourne 1, Okenabirhie 1, Thompson 1, Walker 1, Opponents 1
Average home league attendance: 6,059. **Player of Year**: Aaron Pierre

SOUTHEND UNITED

Sol Campbell defied the odds to keep Macclesfield in the Football League the previous season, but was unable to work the same magic at Roots Hall. Southend turned to the former England defender following a club-record six successive defeats to start the season and an unsuccessful move for former Celtic striker Henrik Larsson. Succeeding Kevin Bond, who resigned after four months as manager, Campbell watched from the stands as his new team crashed 7-1 at home to Doncaster and had two players sent off. He then had to wait nearly three months for a first league win – 2-1 against Accrington courtesy of Charlie Kelman and Jason Demetriou's penalty. It was followed by a first at home by the same scoreline, with Kelman again on the mark and Elvis Bwomono heading a 96th minute decider. But his youthful side, with several senior players having departed, were still 12 points adrift and six more straight defeats ended any hopes of making further inroads into that deficit. They eventually finished 16 points adrift and Campbell left the club by mutual consent, along with his coaching staff.

Acauah E	- (7)	Hamilton E	12 (2)	Ndukwu L	- (7)
Barratt S	3 (6)	Hopper T	12 (2)	Oxley M	19
Bishop N	12	Humphrys S	14 (7)	Phillips H	2
Blackman A	1 (2)	Hutchinson I	12 (10)	Ralph N	17
Bwomono E	34	Hyam L	2 (3)	Ridgewell L	1
Clifford T	8	Kelman C	12 (6)	Robinson T	1 (2)
Coker K	- (2)	Kiernan R	17 (2)	Rush M	1 (6)
Cox S	16 (3)	Kinali E	3 (3)	Seaden H	1
Demetriou J	15 (5)	Kyprianou H	1	Shaughnessy J	14 (2)
Dieng T	21	Lennon H	15 (1)	Taylor R	2
Egbri T	6	Mantom S	21 (1)	Taylor C	- (1)
Gard L	2	McLaughlin S	27	White J	9 (2)
Goodship B	14 (9)	Milligan M	30		
Gunnarsson P	3	Mitchell-Nelson M	5 (1)		

League goals (39): Humphrys 5, Kelman 5, McLaughlin 4, Demetriou 3, Goodship 3, Cox 2, Dieng 2, Hopper 2, Mantom 2, Acauah 1, Bwomono 1, Egbri 1, Gard 1, Hutchinson 1, Kiernan 1, Lennon 1, Phillips 1, Opponents 3
FA Cup goals: None. **League Cup goals (3):** Kelman 2, Goodship 1. **League Trophy goals (3):** Hamilton 1, Hopper 1, Ralph 1
Average home league attendance: 6,192. **Player of Year:** Elvis Bwomono

SUNDERLAND

Faltering in the final furlong for the second successive season, Sunderland saw another promotion chance slip away. In 2019, under Jack Ross, two points from the last four fixtures ended their chances of going up automatically and was followed by defeat from Charlton in the Play-off Final. This time, a run of four successive wins without conceding a goal put Phil Parkinson's side within striking distance of the top two. But an identical finish of two draws and two defeats, before the campaign was abandoned, left them out of the top six. Sunderland joined five clubs pressing for a resumption of the season, but the move was defeated. Ross was sacked two months into the season following a 2-0 defeat at Lincoln. Parkinson, who resigned two months previously at crisis club Bolton, replaced him immediately. He won just two of his first nine league games, but Sunderland were on the march in the New Year, with Parkinson named manager of the month for a productive January.

Burge L	5	Leadbitter G	11 (3)	O'Nien L	35
De Bock L	4 (1)	Lynch J	14 (2)	Ozturk A	20 (2)
Dobson G	26 (3)	Maguire C	28 (7)	Power M	30 (3)
Embleton E	1 (2)	Mbunga B	- (4)	Scowen J	1 (3)
Flanagan T	16 (2)	McGeady A	13 (2)	Semenyo A	1 (6)
Gooch L	28 (2)	McGeouch D	5 (3)	Watmore R	6 (11)
Grigg W	8 (12)	McLaughlin J	31 (1)	Willis J	35
Hume D	30 (2)	McLaughlin C	12 (3)	Wright B	5
Lafferty K	2 (9)	McNulty M	7 (8)	Wyke C	22 (5)

League goals (48): Gooch 11, Maguire 10, Wyke 5, McGeady 4, O'Nien 4, Lafferty 2, McNulty 2, Power 2, Willis 2, Flanagan 1, Grigg 1, Hume 1, Mbunga 1, Watmore 1, Opponents 1
FA Cup goals (1): McGeady 1. **League Cup goals** (8): McNulty 2, Dobson 1, Flanagan 1, Grigg 1, McGeady 1, Power 1, Wyke 1. **League Trophy goals** (4): Grigg 1, Maguire 1, McNulty 1, Whatmore 1
Average home league attendance: 30,118

TRANMERE ROVERS

Tranmere breathed new life into their bid to stay up, then had it cut short when the season was abandoned. A run of 11 games without a win, before, during and after a notable Cup run, left them eight points adrift, with seemingly little chance of avoiding an immediate return to League Two. Instead, successive away victories over Shrewsbury, Accrington and Blackpool cut the deficit to three, with a fixture in hand. Under the points-per-game system to determine final positions, the club finished 0.06 of a goal behind AFC Wimbledon. Chairman Mark Palios argued that a margin of error should be applied to such a tiny amount, but lost a majority vote. So the abiding memory of the season had to be an FA Cup third round tie against Watford. Tranmere retrieved a 3-0 deficit at Vicarage Road with goals by Connor Jennings, Manny Monthe and Paul Mullin and won the replay 2-1, with Monthe again on the mark, followed by substitute Mullin's extra-time decider, earning a plum tie against Manchester United (0-6). Micky Mellon left during the summer to become Dundee United manager. He was replaced by assistant-manager Mike Jackson.

Banks O	8 (3)	Ferrier M	15 (5)	Pilling L	- (1)
Blackett-Taylor C	13 (11)	Gilmour H	2 (2)	Ponticelli J	1
Borthwick-Jackson C	1 (2)	Hepburn-Murphy R	8 (9)	Potter D	11 (1)
Caprice J	19 (1)	Jennings C	23 (6)	Ray G	15
Chapman A	6	McCullough L	6	Ridehalgh L	27 (2)
Clarke P	6	Monthe E	30 (1)	Vaughan J	8
Cook A	5	Morris K	33 (1)	Wilson K	13
Danns N	13 (5)	Mullin P	9 (11)	Woods C	9 (4)
Davies S	28	Nelson S	16 (3)	Woodyard A	11
Ellis M	3	Payne S	11 (4)		
Feeney M	1	Perkins D	23 (4)		

League goals (36): Ferrier 5, Hepburn-Murphy 4, Jennings 4, Payne 4, Banks 3, Mullin 3, Vaughan 3, Blackett-Taylor 2, Ellis 2, Morris 2, Monthe 1, Ridehalgh 1, Woodyard 1, Opponents 1
FA Cup goals (14): Ferrier 4, Morris 3, Blackett-Taylor 2, Monthe 2, Mullin 2, Jennings 1. **League Cup goals:** None. **League Trophy goals** (6): Jennings 2, Blackett-Taylor 1, Gilmour 1, Hepburn-Murphy 1, Ray 1
Average home league attendance: 6,776

WYCOMBE WANDERERS

Gareth Ainsworth led his side into the Championship against all the odds. In a remarkable season which many expected to be a struggle to avoid relegation, Wycombe reached the second tier for the first time in the club's history with a 2-1 victory over Oxford in the Play-off Final. Anthony Stewart scored with a far-post header from Joe Jacobson's first corner and Jacobson got the winner from the penalty spot 11 minutes from the end after Fred Onyedinma was brought down by goalkeeper Simon Eastwood. It was their second promotion in three seasons under Ainsworth, the longest serving manager in the Football League but the antithesis of every other with his long hair and love of playing in a rock band in his spare time. Wycombe spent much of the campaign in the top two until two defeats in the last four matches before the season was suspended left them outside the play-offs. They rose to third when places were determined on a points-per-game basis, then defeated Fleetwood 6-3 on aggregate in the semi-finals after winning the first leg away from home 4-1. Ainsworth, appointed in November 2012 after ending his playing career at the club, lost his two previous appearances at Wembley – the 2015 League Two Final against Southend and the 1994 Division Three Final – to Wycombe – when playing for Preston.

Aarons R.................. 5 (5)	Jacobson J 30	Phillips G 10 (1)
Akinfenwa A........... 20 (12)	Jombati S.................. 6 (1)	Samuel A 15 (6)
Allsop R......................32	Kashket S................ 11 (8)	Smyth P 13 (6)
Bloomfield M........... 22 (5)	Mascoll J................. 2 (2)	Stewart A 34
Charles D......................25	McCarthy J.....................9	Stockdale D 2
El-Abd A......................2	Ofoborh N 7 (11)	Thompson C 20 (1)
Freeman N 16 (10)	Onyedinma F 11 (2)	Wheeler D 25 (6)
Gape D 28	Parker J 3 (10)	
Grimmer J......................18	Pattison A 8 (9)	

Play-offs – appearances: Allsop 3, Bloomfield 3, Charles 3, Gape 3, Grimmer 3, Jacobson 3, Ofoborh 3, Onyedinma 3, Samuel 3, Stewart 3, Wheeler 3, Akinfenwa – (3), Pattison – (3), Thompson – (3), Freeman – (2), Kashket – (1)
League goals (45): Akinfenwa 10, Jacobson 9, Kashket 4, Onyedinma 4, Wheeler 3, Bloomfield 2, Charles 2, Freeman 2, Stewart 2, Aarons 1, McCarthy 1, Samuel 1, Smyth 1, Opponents 3.
Play-offs – goals (8): Onyedinma 2, Jacobson 1, Ofoborh 1, Samuel 1, Stewart 1, Wheeler 1, Opponents 1
FA Cup goals (3): Jacobson 1,Samuel 1, Stewart 1. **League Cup goals** (1): Samuel 1. **League Trophy goals (3)**: Aarons 1, Ofoborh 1, Parker 1.
Average home league attendance: 5,653

SKY BET LEAGUE TWO

BRADFORD CITY

A new-look squad entertained high hopes of taking the club back to League One at the first attempt. They figured prominently among the favourites for promotion and looked well placed when entering the New Year a point behind Crewe in third place. But eight matches without a win, yielding just five points, proved costly. The run coincided with leading scorer James Vaughan being allowed to join Tranmere on loan in the winter transfer window. Gary Bowyer, manager for 11 months, was sacked after a 3-0 defeat at Oldham, and replaced by Valley Parade favourite Stuart McCall, taking charge for the third time after spells from 2007-10 and 2016-18. His side returned to winning ways against Stevenage and also overcame promotion-chasing Plymouth. It proved not enough amid further defeats by Cambridge, Newport and Salford ,which meant that when the season was abandoned, Bradford were four points adrift of the play-offs.

Akpan H 13 (6)	Henley A 22 (2)	O'Donnell R 33
Anderson J................. 3 (2)	Ismail Z 6 (5)	Omari P ....- (2)
Connolly D 22 (5)	Longridge J.................. - (1)	Oteh A 8 (10)
Cooke C.................. 18 (7)	McCartan S 8 (13)	Palmer M 17 (1)
Devine A 6 (7)	McGee L.....................4	Pritchard H...............14 (7)
Devitt J 3 (2)	Mellor K 22 (3)	Reeves J...................17 (1)
Donaldson C.............. 18 (2)	Middleton G 2 (1)	Richards-Everton B 32
Doyle E......................6	Mottley Henry D 4 (3)	Scannell S................. 2 (3)
French T.................. - (2)	Novak L......................6	Taylor C................. 9 (5)
Gibson J 3 (3)	O'Connor A.............. 34 (2)	Vaughan J 23 (2)
Guthrie K.................. 1 (1)	O'Connor P 16 (3)	Wood C......................35

League goals (44): Vaughan 11, Donaldson 4, McCartan 4, Oteh 4, Akpan 3, Pritchard 3, Novak 2, O'Connor 2, Richards-Everton 2, Anderson 1, Connolly 1, Devine 1, Ismail 1, Mellor 1, Reeves 1, Scannell 1, Opponents 2
FA Cup goals (1): Oteh 1. **League Cup goals**: None. **League Trophy goals** (3): Akpan 1, French 1, O'Connor P 1
Average home league attendance: 14,255

CAMBRIDGE UNITED

Mark Bonner introduced some much-needed momentum at the Abbey Stadium after the dismissal of manager Colin Calderwood in the wake of back-to-back 4-0 home defeats by Stevenage and Salford, along with one victory in ten matches. Bonner, formerly academy manager and first-team coach, took charge on a caretaker basis and won his first four games against Colchester, Newport, Scunthorpe and Bradford. The next three, against Plymouth, Carlisle and Leyton Orient delivered a single point, but he was given the job permanently, with owner Paul Barry praising the way he had 'motivated everyone and galvanised the club.' Four days after he signed a two-year contract, the season was shut down and later called off with Cambridge 16th, an improvement of five places on 2019.

Adeboyejo V	7 (1)	Ibehre J 2 (2)	Norville-Williams J .... - (5)
Burton C	10	Jones D 10 (4)	O'Neil L 23 (5)
Carruthers S	7 (3)	Knibbs H 12 (12)	Richards M 14 (4)
Dallas A	2 (20)	Knoyle K 26	Roles J 12 (11)
Darling H	23 (1)	Lambe R 14 (9)	Smith S 25 (3)
Davies L	14 (2)	Lewis P 35 (1)	Taft G 25 (2)
Dunk H	20 (9)	Maris G 24 (6)	Taylor G 29 (1)
El Mizouni I	5 (2)	Mitov D 27	Ward E 13
Hannant L	23 (4)	Mullin P 5 (1)	

League goals (40): Smith 7, Knibbs 6, Lewis 5, Roles 5, Dallas 2, Darling 2, Lambe 2, Mullin 2, Richards 2, El Mizouni 1, Hannant 1, Knoyle 1, Maris 1, O'Neil 1, Taft 1, Taylor 1
FA Cup goals (1): Smith 1. **League Cup goals** None. **League Trophy goals** (2): Knibbs 2
Average home league attendance: 4,178

CARLISLE UNITED

After four successive top-half finishes, Carlisle had a largely disappointing season. Worries about being sucked into the relegation zone, with a third of the campaign gone, cost Steven Pressley his job after ten months as manager. His successor, Rochdale's No 2 Chris Beech, had little joy – apart from a rousing FA Cup tie against Cardiff – until back-to-back victories delivered a much-needed cushion. Carlisle defeated Walsall 2-1, then won 4-1 at Forest Green with a hat-trick from Nathan Thomas, completed from the penalty spot. They went on to beat Cambridge and Newport in two of their three final matches before the abandonment had them in 18th place. Round three of the Cup offered the chance of an upset when Jack Bridge and Harry McKirdy established a 2-0 advantage at Cardiff, before the Championship side came back to level. McKirdy scored two more in a thrilling replay, which his side lost 4-3 when it could have gone either way.

Alessandra L	10	Hope H 13 (10)	Sagaf M 11 (6)
Anderton N	10	Hunt M 3 (1)	Olomola O 14 (13)
Branthwaite J	9	Iredale J 18 (4)	Omari P 6 (1)
Bridge J	20 (8)	Jones G 30	Scougall S 14 (6)
Carroll C	6 (3)	Jones M 37	Sorensen E 1 (7)
Charters T	- (7)	Kayode J 3 (2)	Thomas N 31 (2)
Collin A	37	Knight-Percival N ... 14 (1)	Watt E 12
Elliott C	13 (3)	Loft R 9 (17)	Webster B 32
Guy C	2 (1)	McKirdy H 21 (7)	
Hayden A	18	Mellish J 13 (2)	

League goals (39): McKirdy 5, Olomola 5, Thomas 5, Loft 4, Kayode 3, Anderton 2, Hayden 2, Hope 2, Iredale 2, Omari 2, Scougall 2, Alessandra 1, Elliott 1, Sagaf 1, Watt 1, Webster 1
FA Cup goals (12): McKirdy 5, Thomas 3, Bridge 1, Hayden 1, Jones M 1, Olomola 1. **League Cup goals** (4): Bridge 2, McKirdy 1, Thomas 1. **League Trophy goals** (5): Loft 2, Branthwaite 1, Carroll 1, Hope 1
Average home league attendance: 4,140

CHELTENHAM TOWN

Michael Duff's side let slip a golden opportunity to carry a much-improved season through to Wembley. They won the first leg of their play-off semi-final 2-0 at Northampton with goals from Charlie Raglan and Conor Thomas, along with impressive goalkeeping from Owen Evans, who saved a penalty with the scoresheet blank. The performance set things up perfectly for the return leg. Instead, Cheltenham trailed early on, conceded two more goals after the interval to lose 3-2 on aggregate and Duff admitted: 'We were beaten up.' After three successive finishes in the lower reaches of the table, they were up to fourth on the back of the best defensive record in the division – just 27 goals conceded – accompanied by a run of five successive victories before the campaign was curtailed, one of which came against Northampton. Duff, the former Northern Ireland international, signed a new contract through to June 2023.

Addai A	7 (18)	Flinders S	25	Nichols T	1 (4)
Bowry D	- (1)	Greaves J	29	Raglan C	35
Boyle W	11 (2)	Horton G	- (1)	Reid R	5 (4)
Broom R	33 (1)	Hussey C	31 (2)	Reilly G	18 (3)
Campbell T	6 (5)	Ince R	1 (8)	Sheaf M	14 (5)
Clements C	16 (6)	Lloyd G	3 (10)	Smith J	2 (10)
Debayo J	3 (4)	Long S	31 (3)	Thomas C	22 (4)
Doyle-Hayes J	28 (2)	Lovett R	- (1)	Tozer B	34
Evans O	11	May A	12	Varney L	18 (3)

Play-offs – appearances: Boyle 2, Broom 2, Doyle-Hayes 2, Evans 2, Hussey 2, Long 2, Raglan 2, Thomas 2, Tozer 2, May 1 (1), Nichols 1 (1), Reid 1 (1), Smith 1 (1), Ince – (2), Addai – (1), **League goals** (52): Broom 8, Varney 7, May 6, Thomas 6. Addai 4,, Reilly 4, Reid 3, Tozer 3, Boyle 2, Hussey 2, Sheaf 2, Doyle-Hayes 1, Long 1, Raglan 1, Smith 1, Opponents 1. **Play-offs – goals** (2): Raglan 1, Thomas 1
FA Cup goals (3): Addai 2, Reid 1. **League Cup goals**: None. **League Trophy goals** (8): Smith 3, Addai 1, Lloyd 1, Long 1, Sheaf 1, Tozer 1
Average home league attendance: 3,203. **Player of Year**: Ryan Broom

COLCHESTER UNITED

After being squeezed out of the play-offs in two of the previous three seasons, Colchester broke through this time in what proved to be the final game before play the division was halted. They won 3-0 at Carlisle with goals from Kwame Poku (2) and Luke Norris to overtake Port Vale. Both regular fixtures against semi-final opponents Exeter had been drawn and both legs proved tight affairs. An 81st minute free-kick from full-back Cohen Bramall gave them the advantage, but it was Exeter who went through in extra-time of the return 3-2 on aggregate. Colchester had forced their way into contention with an unbeaten run of 16 matches, seven wins and nine draws. They also enjoyed a long run in the League Cup, defeating Crystal Palace and Tottenham on penalties, alongside victories over Swindon and Crawley, to earn a quarter-final tie at Old Trafford, where Manchester United were held for 45 minutes before winning 3-0. Manager John McGreal was sacked during the summer and replaced by assistant Steve Ball.

Bramall C	24	Clampin R	13	Cowan-Hall P	2 (3)
Brown J	5 (6)	Comley B	22 (2)	Eastman T	35 (1)

Gambin L	9 (19)	Norris L	19 (13)	Sarpong-Wiredu B	5 (2)
Gerken D	36	Nouble F	30 (6)	Senior C	19 (10)
Harriott C	17 (5)	Ogedi-Uzokwe J	- (2)	Sowunmi O	5 (2)
Hasanally A	- (2)	Pell H	21 (10	Stevenson B	24 (4)
Jackson R	33 (1)	Poku K	23 (6)	Moore T	1
James C	- (3)	Prosser L	35	Vincent-Young K	2
Kensdale O	- (1)	Robinson T	19 (9)		
Lapslie T	7 (10)	Ross E	1		

Play-offs – appearances: Bramall 2, Eastman 2, Gerken 2, Jackson 2, Norris 2, Nouble 2, Pell 2, Poku 2, Prosser 2, Stevenson 2, Gambin 1 (1), Senior 1 (1), Cowan-Hall – (2), Lapslie – (2), Robinson – (2), Welch-Hayes M – (1)

League goals (52): Robinson 11, Norris 9, Nouble 5, Poku 5, Harriott 3, Pell 3, Prosser 3, Eastman 2, Jackson 2, Senior 2, Stevenson 2, Bramall 1, Comley 1, Gambin 1, Opponents 2.

Play-offs – goals (2): Bramall 1, Senior 1

FA Cup goals: None. **League Cup goals (6):** Comley 1, Eastman 1, Gambin 1, Norris 1, Senior 1, Opponents 1. **League Trophy goals (6):** Cowan-Hall 2, Clampin 1, Norris 1, Robinson 1, Opponents 1

Average home league attendance: 3,634. **Player of Year:** Tom Eastman

CRAWLEY TOWN

A solid start laid the foundation for Crawley's best showing since their return to League Two in 2016. They accumulated 16 points from the opening ten fixtures and a continuation of productive home form ensured a top-half finish. Ten victories on their own ground compensated for just one – at Leyton Orient – on their travels, although ten draws away from home showed they were often a difficult side to beat. The season's one major lean spell accounted for manager Gabriele Cioffi, sacked in early December after a run of ten defeats in 14 games – four of them in cup ties. He was replaced by John Yems, former manager of football operations at Bournemouth, whose first victory – 4-0 against Northampton – sparked a return to form, notable for the marksmanship of Ollie Palmer, whose two-goal performances against Bradford, Grimsby and Plymouth earned him a nomination for January's Player of the Month award.

Adebowale E	1	Francomb G	10 (5)	Palmer O	22 (6)
Allarakhia T	7 (12)	German R	1 (7)	Payne J	1 (1)
Bloomfield M	10 (11)	Grego-Cox R	24 (4)	Powell J	- (6)
Bulman D	28 (1)	Lubala B	32 (2)	Sendles-White J	12 (2)
Camara P	23 (6)	McNerney J	6	Sesay D	18 (7)
Dacres-Cogley J	15 (1)	Morais F	2 (3)	Tunnicliffe J	37
Dallison T	20 (1)	Morris G	37	Van Velzen G	(4)
Doherty J	30 (1)	Nadesan A	22 (3)	Young L	13 (2)
Ferguson N	29 (2)	Nathaniel-George A	7 (9)		

League goals (51): Palmer 13, Lubala 12, Ferguson 5, Nadesan 5, Grego-Cox 4, Bloomfield 3, Nathaniel-George 3, Camara 1, German 1, Payne 1, Tunnicliffe 1, Young 1, Opponents 1.

FA Cup goals (5): Grego-Cox 2, Nadesan 1, Nathaniel-George 1, Palmer 1. **League Cup goals (6):** Bulman 1, Dallison 1, Ferguson 1, Lubala 1, Morais 1, Nadesan 1. **League Trophy goals (2):** Bloomfield 1, Nathaniel-George 1

Average home league attendance: 2,232

CREWE ALEXANDRA

David Artell completed a promotion double as Crewe finished runners-up to Swindon. In 2012, he captained the club to victory in the League Two Play-off Final against Cheltenham. This time, as manager, he supervised the division's highest-scoring team, featuring five-goal performances against Morecambe and Stevenage and four netted against Carlisle (twice) and Salford. After the club's best start for 24 years – 26 points accumulated from 13 matches – Crewe tracked their rivals for much of the season until what proved to be the final outing for both. Artell's side went top on goal difference by winning the return fixture against Stevenage 3-1, while Swindon lost 2-0 at home to Forest Green. But the positions were reversed because of the points-per-game system used to finalise positions, with Crewe having played one game more.

Adebisi R.................. 1 (1)	Johnson T.................. - (1)	Nottingham M.............. 12
Ainley C.................. 6 (19)	Jones J.................. 13 (10)	Offord L.................. 9
Anene C.................. 12 (16)	Kirk C.................. 35 (1)	Pickering H.................. 35
Dale O.................. 7 (20)	Lancashire O.................. 7 (2)	Porter C.................. 25 (1)
Finney O.................. 11 (7)	Lowery T.................. 28 (1)	Powell D.................. 24 (6)
Green P.................. 22 (4)	Mbulu C.................. 3 (1)	Richards D.................. 2
Hunt N.................. 22 (3)	Ng P.................. 36	Walker S.................. 6
Jaaskelainen W.................. 35	Nolan E.................. 19	Wintle R.................. 37

League goals (67): Porter 12, Powell 9, Anene 7, Kirk 7, Finney 5, Lowery 5, Nolan 3, Pickering 3, Wintle 3, Ainley 2, Green 2, Jones 2, Ng 2, Hunt 1, Nottingham 1, Walker 1, Opponents 2
FA Cup goals (7): Anene 2, Dale 1, Green 1, Kirk 1, Porter 1, Opponents 1. **League Cup goals** (3): Kirk 1, Porter 1, Wintle 1. **League Trophy goals** (4): Ainley 1, Dale 1, Finney 1, Green 1
Average home league attendance: 4,580 **Player of Year**: Ryan Wintle

EXETER CITY

More Wembley disappointment for Exeter, who lost the divisional Play-off Final for the third time in four years. This time, they were unable to cope with the aerial threat posed by Northampton, who scored twice from long throws and once from a free-kick in a 4-0 victory. Manager Matt Taylor admitted his side were dominated physically. Dean Moxey's red card for lunging at Ryan Watson, with an hour played, ruled out any chance of retrieving a two-goal deficit and they conceded twice more in the final ten minutes. Exeter, who defeated Colchester 3-2 on aggregate in their semi-final with an extra-time goal from Ryan Bowman, topped the table early on with 22 points from ten games. They maintained one of the division's best defensive records well into the New Year and were still neck-and-neck with eventual champions Swindon until losing 2-0 to Northampton in the regular season's return fixture, then dropping points to Crawley, Crewe and Walsall to finish fifth.

Ajose N.................. 10 (3)	Martin A.................. 32 (3)	Sweeney P.................. 35 (1)
Atangana N.................. 18 (4)	Martin L.................. 21 (7)	Taylor J.................. 24 (9)
Bowman R.................. 36 (1)	Maxted J.................. 17	Tillson J.................. - (2)
Chrisene B.................. - (1)	Moxey D.................. 21 (3)	Ward L.................. 20
Collins A.................. 33 (3)	Parkes T.................. 25 (6)	Warren G.................. - (1)
Dickenson B.................. 8 (2)	Randall J.................. - (2)	Williams R.................. 33 (4)
Fisher A.................. 3 (13)	Richardson J.................. 10 (8)	Woodman C.................. 4 (2)
Jay M.................. 9 (5)	Seymour B.................. 3 (8)	
Law N.................. 28 (4)	Sparkes J.................. 17	

Play-offs – appearances: Bowman 3, Law 3, Martin A 3, Moxey 3, Sweeney 3, Taylor 3, Williams 3, Atangana 2 (1), Fisher 2, Maxted 2, Richardson 2, Collins 1 (2), Sparkes 1 (1), Martin L 1, Ward 1, Dickenson – (3), Parkes – (3), Jay – (1), Seymour – (1)
League goals (53): Bowman 13, Law 7, Martin L 6, Williams 5, Jay 4, Ajose 2, Dickenson 2, Martin A 2, Moxey 2, Parkes 2, Sweeney 2, Taylor 2, Atangana 1, Collins 1, Fisher 1, Richardson 1. **Play-offs – goals** (3): Bowman 1, Martin A 1, Richardson 1
FA Cup goals (4): Fisher 2, Atangana 1, Bowman 1. **League Cup goals** (1): Sweeney 1. **League Trophy goals** (13): Jay 4, Ajose 3, Randall 2, Martin L 1, Taylor 1, Tillson 1, Opponents 1
Average home league attendance: 4,847. **Player of Year**: Randell Williams

FOREST GREEN ROVERS

Forest Green fell away in the second half of the season and missed out on the chance of a second successive play-off place. They built on a solid start to go top of the fourth tier for the first time after back-to-back wins over Salford (4-0) and Crawley (3-1). There was another brief spell there following a 2-1 local derby success at Cheltenham. And heading into the New Year, Rovers still held down a place in the leading group. But five successive home defeats put the brake on, with a 4-3 win at Mansfield – achieved by Aaron Collins's stoppage-time goal after his side trailed 2-0 – proving a brief respite. Their only other victory in the final 12 matches came away to leaders Swindon, where Matty Stevens and Ebou Adams delivered a 2-0 success. Any prospect of building on that performance, and using the fixture in hand to start bridging a nine-point deficit, disappeared when League Two was abandoned with ten matches remaining.

Adams E. 30 (4)	Grubb D 3 (4)	Rawson F 28 (2)
Aitchison J 23 (5)	Hall R 3 (3)	Shephard L 17 (2)
Allen T 2 (3)	Kitching L 27 (2)	Smith A 8
Bailey O. 5	Logan C 5	Stevens M 21 (8)
Bernard D 25 (3)	March J 7 (3)	Stokes C 5
Brown J 5	McCoulsky S 4 (2)	Taylor K 5 (1)
Collins A 14 (14)	McGinley N 14 (6)	Thomas L 14 (1)
Covil V .... - (2)	Mills J 24	Williams G 2 (1)
Dawson K 12 (3)	Mills M 17 (2)	Winchester C 35
Frear E 7 (7)	Mondal J 7 (14)	Wollacott J 9 (1)
Godwin-Malife U 11 (1)	Morton J 7 (5)	

League goals (43): Mills J 7, Aitchison 5, Winchester 5, Adams 4, Collins 4, Stevens 4, Rawson 3, March 2, Mondal 2, Allen 1, Bailey 1, Frear 1, Shephard 1, Williams 1, Opponents 2.
FA Cup goals (6): Aitchison 1, Collins 1, Mills J 1, Shephard 1, Stevens 1, Opponents 1. **League Cup goals**: None. **League Trophy goals** (3): Stevens 2, Grubb 1
Average home league attendance: 2,541

GRIMSBY TOWN

Ian Holloway breathed new life into this old club after the season's most surprising managerial appointment. Along with transforming results and boosting attendances, he became a shareholder at Blundell Park, while insisting he was there for 'a long-term project.' When majority shareholder John Fenty later announced he was stepping back from day-to-day involvement, Holloway effectively became director of football. Out of management since leaving Queens Park Rangers in May 2018, he succeeded the sacked Michael Jolley, taking over a side without a win in 11 league games, just three goals scored and sliding into trouble. Grimsby put aside that threat by scoring 20 in the next 11 fixtures, including a 3-2 win at Colchester in which Charles Vernam completed a hat-trick by beating four players in a dazzling run from inside his own half. Vernam was also on the mark in a 2-0 success against local rivals Scunthorpe – their last match before the premature end to the season. By then, Grimsby were up to mid-table.

Benson J 8 (3)	Green M 19 (10)	Robson R 11 (5)
Cardwell H .... - (2)	Hanson J 26 (3)	Rose A 7 (11)
Clarke B 10 (3)	Hendrie L 32	Russell S 1
Clifton H 22 (3)	Hessenthaler J 28	Tilley L 3 (7)
Cook J 10 (4)	Hewitt E. 18 (2)	Vernam C 19 (8)
Davis H. 19 (2)	McKeown J 36	Waterfall L 30
Driscoll-Glennon A 11 (1)	Ogbu M 11 (9)	Whitehouse E 25 (8)
Garmston B 3 92)	Ohman L 14 (1)	Wright M 12 (13)
Gibson L 16 (1)	Pollock M 11 (8)	
Grandin E 4 (1)	Ring S 1 (1)	

League goals (45): Hanson 9, Vernam 7, Robson 3, Whitehouse 3, Benson 2, Clarke 2, Cook 2, Green 2, Ogbu 2, Rose 2, Waterfall 2, Wright 2, Driscoll-Glennon 1, Garmston 1, Hendrie 1, Hessenthaler 1, Ohman 1, Opponents 2
FA Cup goals (1): Waterfall 1. **League Cup goals** (2): Cook 1, Green 1. **League Trophy goals** (4): Ogbu 2, Cardwell 1, Green 1
Average home league attendance: 4,599. **Player of Year**: James Hanson

LEYTON ORIENT

The death of manager Justin Edinburgh from a cardiac arrest in June 2019, six weeks after leading the club back to the Football League as National League champions, cast a shadow over the season. As a tribute, the club renamed their West Stand after him. Ross Embleton, Edinburgh's assistant, took over on an interim basis, which continued into the season and on for four months until the appointment of Carl Fletcher, former Wales midfielder and Plymouth manager. Fletcher was sacked after 29 days in the wake of an FA Cup first round home defeat by non-league Maldon. He failed to win any of his five games in charge and the club said he did not fit into their coaching unit. Embleton returned as caretaker, then signed a 12-month rolling contract. Orient spent most of the abbreviated campaign in the lower reaches of the table, finishing 17th.

Alabi J...................... - (10)	Ekpiteta M 26 (1)	Marsh G 23 (3)
Angol L..................... 20 (6)	Gorman D.................. 7 (6)	McAnuff J ....- (1)
Brill D 19	Happe D........................32	Sargeant S 11 (1)
Brophy J 29 (5)	Harrold M................. 9 (15)	Sotiriou R................... 7 (3)
Cisse O....................... 9 (1)	Johnson D 4 (2)	Turley J 8
Clay C....................... 30 (5)	Judd M 15	Vigouroux L 6
Coulson J................. 26 (2)	Kyprianou H 3 (3)	Widdowson J.............. 14 (2)
Dayton J 8 (3)	Ling S.............................15	Wilkinson C 23 (3)
Dennis L 7 (9)	Maguire-Drew J....... 21 (12)	Wright J 33 (2)

League goals (47): Wright 8, Maguire-Drew 7, Sotiriou 5, Wilkinson 5, Angol 4, Brophy 2, Harrold 2, Johnson 2, Alabi 1, Cisse 1, Coulson 1, Dayton 1, Dennis 1, Happe 1, Turley 1, Widdowson 1, Opponents 4
FA Cup goals (1): Dayton 1. **League Cup goals**: None. **League Trophy goals** (4): Angol 1, Dennis 1, Gorman 1, Happe 1
Average home league attendance: 5,504

MACCLESFIELD TOWN

Another traumatic season looked to have ended with Macclesfield clinging to their Football League status. When a points-per-game formula was used to determine final positions after it was cut short by COVID-19, they had 0.62 to show for 23rd position, one ahead of Stevenage (0.61). But with the new campaign just a month away, the EFL won an appeal against the club's suspended four-point deduction, imposed by an independent disciplinary commission, for breaching regulations. The sanction was applied immediately, Macclesfield were relegated to the National League with 0.51and Stevenage survived. The EFL said the decision was 'final and binding'. Over the course of the season, failing to pay wages and to fulfil fixtures cost them 17 points in all. On the field, they would have comfortably avoided the bottom spot because of Stevenage's failings despite managerial upheavals. Sol Campbell, who supervised their great escape in 2019, left three matches in after nine months in charge, reportedly by mutual agreement. His successor, Daryl McMahon, former manager of National League Ebbsfleet, resigned after four-and-a-half months, bringing in former Republic of Ireland winger Mark Kennedy.

Archibald T 23 (5)	Cameron N............... 12 (4)	Clarke E..................... 5 (1)
Blyth J...................... - (19)	Charles-Cook R.................2	Evans O 24

Fitzpatrick D 17 (4)	Kirby C 29 (5)	Tollitt B 4 (1)
Gnahoua A 26 (3)	McCourt J 18 (3)	Tracey S 6 (1)
Gomis V 4 (7)	Mitchell J 11	Vassell T 17
Hamblin H 3 (1)	Ntambwe B .... - (3)	Welch-Hayes M 24
Harris J 25	O'Keefe C 28 (3)	Whitehead D 10
Horsfall F 21 (5)	Osadebe E 22 (3)	Wilson D 1 (4)
Ironside J 25 (8)	Rose M .... - (1)	
Kelleher F 37	Stephens B 13 (10)	

League goals (32): Ironside 6, Archibald 4, Gnahoua 4, Osadebe 4, Stephens 3, McCourt 2, Vassell 2, Blyth 1, Harris 1, Kelleher 1, Kirby 1, Tracey 1, Welch-Hayes 1, Opponents 1
FA Cup goals: None. **League Cup goals** (2): Gomis 1, Opponents 1. **League Trophy goals** (5): Archibald 2, Fitzpatrick 1, Gomis 1, Ironside 1
Average home league attendance: 1,998. **Player of Year**: Fiacre Kelleher

MANSFIELD TOWN

Two Nicky Maynard hat-tricks were rare highlights in another season of under-achievement. Mansfield were again among the favourites for promotion, but won only four times at home, had no back-to-victories to show and finished fourth from bottom. Maynard's first treble came in a 6-1 victory over Oldham. His second delivered a 3-2 win at Cambridge, Graham Coughlan's first as manager after replacing John Dempster, who was sacked seven months into the job in the wake of a single win in eight league games. That performance was followed by successive home defeats by Grimsby and Forest Green, highlighting their inconsistency. Coughlan left Bristol Rovers, fourth in League One, citing his new club's ambitions and the chance to be close to his Sheffield home. For the new season, he will be working alongside the club's new director of football, former Wigan chairman David Sharpe.

Afolayan O .... - (6)	Knowles J .... - (5)	Shaughnessy C 14 (1)
Benning M 30 (3)	Logan C 22	Smith A 1 (4)
Bishop N 27 (1)	MacDonald A 27 (2)	Sterling-James O 1 (7)
Charsley H 7 (2)	Maynard N 29 (4)	Stone A 3
Clarke J 6 (6)	Mellis J 9 (4)	Sweeney R 32 (1)
Cook A 10 (13)	Olejnik B 11	Tomlinson W 15 (3)
Davies C .... - (5)	Pearce K 28 (1)	Watts K 7
Gordon K 17 (1)	Preston M 20 (2)	White H 9 (1)
Hamilton C 25 (9)	Riley J 6	
Khan O 12 (9)	Rose D 28 (3)	

League goals (48): Maynard 14, Rose 11, Cook 7, Hamilton 2, Pearce 2, Afolayan 1, Gordon 1, Khan 1, Knowles 1, MacDonald 1, Preston 1, Riley 1, Sterling-James 1, Sweeney 1, Tomlinson 1, Watts 1, Opponents 1
FA Cup goals (1): Maynard 1. **League Cup goals** (2): Pearce 1, Sterling-James 1. **League Trophy goals** (6): Sterling-James 2, Hamilton 1, Knowles 1, Rose 1, Sweeney 1
Average home league attendance: 4,419

MORECAMBE

Derek Adams returned to management in one of the toughest jobs in the game and steered Morecambe away from the bottom of the table. The former Plymouth boss came in when Jim Bentley called time on eight-and-a-half-years in charge – longest tenure in the Football League – to take over at AFC Fylde. There was no immediate change of fortune to the club's worst start to a league season, with a 3-0 defeat by Adams's former team and a 5-0 beating by Crewe, exposing their problems. But they drew encouragement when coming from behind to beat Newport 2-1 with goals from Cole Stockton and John O'Sullivan. The New Year brought maximum points against Port Vale, Walsall and Macclesfield, putting Morecambe eight points clear of bottom-of-the-table Stevenage. And with their rivals showing no sign of a similar improvement, that was enough to be safe.

Alessandra L 21 (1)	Howard M.................... - (1)	Old S 37
Bradbury H .... - (3)	Kenyon A 22 (5)	Phillips A 11
Brewitt T.................. 17 (5)	Lavelle S 31	Roche B 16
Buxton A.................... 9 (4)	Leitch-Smith AJ........ 8 (15)	Slew J 9 (2)
Conlan L.................. 19 (1)	Mafoumbi C...................9	Stockton C 23 (7)
Cooney R 11	Mbulu C 1 (2)	Sutton R 11 (4)
Cranston J 12 (12)	Mendes Gomes C 15 (1)	Tanner G 23
Diagouraga T.................12	Miller S 10 (8)	Tutte A 10 (2)
Ellison K.................. 8 (13)	O'Sullivan J................ 27 (7)	Wildig A...................21 (7)
Halstead M 12	Oates R 2 (3)	

League goals (35): Alessandra 5, Stockton 5, Phillips 4, O'Sullivan 3, Wildig 3, Leitch-Smith 2, Mendes Gomes 2, Miller 2, Old 2, Brewitt 1, Buxton 1, Diagouraga 1, Ellison 1, Kenyon 1, Lavelle 1, Sutton 1
FA Cup goals (1): Stockton 1. **League Cup goals** (2): Old 2. **League Trophy goals** (6): Brewitt 1, Conlan 1, Ellison 1, Howard 1, Tutte 1, Wildig 1
Average home league attendance: 2,264

NEWPORT COUNTY

Early season optimism faded as a shortage of goals took its toll and resulted in a modest finish in the bottom half. A single defeat in the opening 13 matches lifted Newport to third, raising hopes of a repeat of the previous campaign when they reached the Play-off Final and came so close to defeating Tranmere. Instead, they failed to win any of the next ten league games. Completing the double over Scunthorpe and eventual champions Swindon in back-to-back games, followed closely by a victory against Macclesfield, suggested a rally. But the goals dried up again, with Padraig Amond and Jamille Matt unable to reproduce their productive form of the previous campaign. Only Stevenage scored fewer than Newport's eventual tally of 32. They fared better in the League Trophy, reaching the semi-finals before Salford denied them of the chance of a fifth visit to Wembley in eight years on penalties.

Abrahams T............ 17 (16)	Haynes R 32	McNamara D 20 (1)
Amond P............... 26 (7)	Howkins K 10 (6)	Nurse G 9 (8)
Baker A 4	Inniss R 21 (1)	O'Brien M...................... 21
Bennett S 25 (3)	Khan O 4 (1)	Poleon D .... - (5)
Collins L .... - (6)	King T...........................31	Sheehan J 33
Demetriou M 21	Labadie J 24 (3)	Townsend N 5
Dolan M................ 13 (9)	Leadbitter D 3	Waters B 2 (4)
Gorman D 7 (1)	Maloney T 5 (5)	Whitely C 3 (7)
Green J.................... 8 (3)	Matt J...................... 26 (7)	Willmott R................ 26 (1)

League goals (32): Amond 8, Matt 6, Abrahams 4, Labadie 3, Sheehan 2, Bennett 1, Gorman 1, Green 1, Haynes 1, Howkins 1, Inniss 1, Nurse 1, O'Brien 1, Opponents 1
FA Cup goals (4): Amond 3, Labadie 1. **League Cup goals** (2): Abrahams 1, Amond 1. **League Trophy goals** (15): Abrahams 5, Maloney 3, Amond 1, Bennett 1, Collins 1, Dolan 1, Hillier R 1, Whiteley 1, Opponents 1
Average home league attendance: 3,867. **Player of Year**: Scott Bennett

NORTHAMPTON TOWN

Keith Curle's side returned to League One with an impressive blend of character and power in the play-offs. A 2-0 home defeat by Cheltenham in the first semi-final leg looked to have put paid to their chances. But two goals by Callum Morton, on loan from West Bromwich Albion, and one from Vadaine Oliver turned the tables in the return and they swept aside Exeter at Wembley. Northampton matched the biggest-ever win in a final, 4-0 by Preston against Swindon in 2015, with captain Charlie Goode playing a key role. Two of his long throws led to goals for Ryan Watson and Andy Williams. His free-kick paved the way for Morton to score for the eighth time in 12 appearances for the club. Sam Hoskins was also on the mark to complete Curle's first promotion as a manager. His side forced their way into the division's leading group with five wins out of six starting in the New Year. Then, after three successive defeats, they were back on track after defeating Exeter 2-0 in the return fixture of the regular season.

Adams N................37	Kaja E.................. - (4)	Pollock S...................3 (8)
Anderson P 17 (1)	Lines C 25 (6)	Roberts M ....- (1)
Arnold S 4	Marshall M 5 (2)	Smith M 7 (12)
Bunney J 3 (1)	Martin J 13 (4)	Turnbull J.................31
Goode C.................36	McCormack A 11 (4)	Warburton M...........8 (10)
Cornell D 33 (1)	McWilliams S 13 (4)	Waters B 2 (5)
Hall-Johnson R.........4 (1)	Morias J .... - (2)	Watson R 21 (4)
Harriman M 15 (6)	Morton C.................7 (2)	Wharton S 30 (2)
Hoskins S 36 (1)	Olayinka J 1	Williams A...............20 (12)
Jones L 6 (1)	Oliver V 19 (11)	

Play-offs – appearances: Adams 3, Arnold 3, Goode 3, Harriman 3, McCormack 3, Morton 3, Oliver 3, Turnbull 3, Wharton 3, Watson 3, Hoskins 2, Olayinka 1 (2), Smith – (3), Anderson – (2), Williams – (2), Marshall – (1), Martin – (1)

League goals (54): Hoskins 8, Williams 8, Morton 5, Turnbull 5, Watson 5, Oliver 4, Smith 4, Goode 3, Wharton 3, Lines 2, Adams 1, Anderson 1, McWilliams 1, Pollock 1, Warburton 1, Opponents 2. **Play-offs – goals (7)**: Morton 3, Hoskins 1, Oliver 1, Watson 1, Williams 1
FA Cup goals (12): Oliver 3, Adams 2, Hoskins 2, Smith 2, Goode 1, Watson 1, Wharton 1.
League Cup goals (1): Warburton 1. **League Trophy goals (3)**: Harriman 1, Hoskins 1, Smith 1
Average home league attendance: 5,101

OLDHAM ATHLETIC

Boundary Park has seen more managerial upheaval than any other club in recent seasons and there was more this time. Three months after being appointed, former Monaco coach Laurent Banide was sacked in the wake of a single win in the opening nine league games. He was replaced immediately by Dino Maamria, who became the club's sixth manager in two years, ten days after his own dismissal by Stevenage. The Tunisian started with a 3-1 win over Morecambe, but the size of the task was soon evident in a 6-1 beating at Mansfield and that contrast in fortunes continued for much of the abbreviated season. Oldham conceded five goals to Exeter and four to Salford, while overcoming Newport 5-0 and delivering back-to-back three-goal performances against Mansfield, in the return fixture, and Bradford. They managed to stay clear of trouble, although finishing five places worse off than the previous season's 14th. Maamria was sacked and replaced by former Leeds and Liverpool winger Harry Kewell.

Adams K...................- (1)	Hamer T..................36 (1)	Piergianni C..............11
Akpa Akpro J-L.............3	Iacovitti A...............24	Rowe D....................10
Borthwick-Jackson C.......6	Jones D....................6	Sefil S.....................3 (1)
Branger J 9 (7)	Maouche M 20 (11)	Segbe Azankpo D 22 (6)
Dearnley Z 6 (2)	McCann C 15 (1)	Smith J..................25 (3)
De la Paz Z 22 (1)	McHale D ....- (1)	Smith-Brown A 5 (1)
Dieseruvwe E............1 (3)	McKinney L ....- (2)	Stott J.....................8 (1)
Eagles C 5 (10)	Mills Z 19 (6)	Sylla M 25 (5)
Egert T 3 (3)	Missilou C 27 (3)	Vera U....................3 (2)
Emmerson Z ....- (2)	Morais F 14 (2)	Wheater D 34
Fage D 7 (5)	N'Guessan C 3 (5)	Wilson S.................8 (13)
Gaskell R ....- (1)	Nepomuceno G 12 (3)	Woods G 15

League goals (44): Smith 9, Dearnley 4, Segbe Azankpo 4, Wheater 4, Hamer 3, Maouche 3, Missilou 3, Rowe 3, Branger 2, Morais 2, Nepomuceno 2, Wilson 2, Mills 1, Sylla 1, Vera 1
FA Cup goals (2): Morais 1, Smith 1. **League Cup goals** (2): Maouche 1, Nepomuceno 1. **League Trophy goals** (5): Segbe Azankpo 2, Iacovitti 1, Smith 1, Stott 1.
Average home league attendance: 3,466

PLYMOUTH ARGYLE

Ryan Lowe led Argyle straight back to League One in his first season as manager – with the help of five players signed from his former club Bury. A new-look side were on the fringes of an automatic promotion place for much of the campaign before four successive wins and 11 goals scored lifted them to third, 19-year-old Luke Jephcott making an immediate impact on his return from a loan spell at Truro with four of them. That advantage was surrendered when dropping points to lowly Macclesfield and Cambridge, then regained courtesy of 3-0 victories over Grimsby and in the return against Macclesfield. When the season ended prematurely, Argyle were just a point behind the top two, Swindon and Crewe. Accompanying this success was completion of the new Mayflower Stand, officially opened at Home Park in front of a 15,000 crowd for the match against Swindon. It completed the redevelopment of a stadium now fully geared to the aim of the club to work towards Championship football.

Aimson W	5	Grant Joel	14 (10)	Randell A	- (4)
Bakinson T	12 (2)	Grant Joshua	17 (5)	Riley J	11 (4)
Baxter J	3 (6)	Hardie R	5 (8)	Rudden Z	7 (7)
Canavan N	32 (1)	Jephcott L	13 (1)	Sarcevic A	30 (2)
Clarke B	2 (7)	Lolos K	- (4)	Sawyer G	28
Cleal J	- (1)	Mayor D	31 (3)	Taylor R	7 (10)
Cooper G	21 (6)	McFadzean C	24 (1)	Telford D	7 (12)
Edwards J	31 (3)	Moore B	26 (4)	Wootton S	34 (1)
Grant Conor	10 (7)	Palmer A	37		

League goals (61): Sarcevic 10, Hardie 7, Jephcott 7, Moore 5, Grant Joel 4, Cooper 3, Edwards 3, McFadzean 3, Aimson 2, Bakinson 2, Canavan 2, Grant Conor 2, Rudden 2, Taylor 2, Telford 2, Mayor 1, Riley 1, Wootton 1, Opponents 2
FA Cup goals (2): McFadzean 1, Sarcevic 1. **League Cup goals** (4): Baxter 1, McFadzean 1, Taylor 1, Telford 1. **League Trophy goals** (4): Grant Joel 1, Moore 1, Riley 1, Rudden 1
Average home league attendance: 10,338. **Player of Year**: Antoni Sarcevic

PORT VALE

A major improvement in fortunes was tempered by a sense of frustration at Vale Park. John Askey, backed by new owners Carol and Kevin Shanahan, led his side to within a single point of the play-offs when League Two was abandoned. It was a sharp contrast to the struggle to stay afloat in the previous three seasons. But it would have been even more rewarding had Vale managed to find a cure to dropping points from winning positions, particularly in the first half of the campaign. The second half was better - a productive run of six wins in nine including three goals scored against promotion contenders Exeter and Colchester. Ultimately, however, a 90th minute equaliser conceded at home to Scunthorpe in the penultimate fixture proved decisive. Even though nine games remained, Vale voted to cancel for what the club described as 'the greater good.'

Amoo D	30 (2)	Browne R	6 (5)	Cullen M	7 (11)
Archer J	- (3)	Burgess S	23 (1)	Evans C	1 (4)
Atkinson W	7 (4)	Campbell-Gordon R	- (1)	Gibbons J	31 (1)
Bennett R	17 (9)	Clark M	4	Joyce L	36
Brisley S	6 (3)	Conlon T	19 (3)	Kennedy K	1
Brown S	37	Crookes A	14	Legge L	37

132

Lloyd R	1 (5)	Pope T	15 (17)	Worrall D	34
Montano C	29 (1)	Smith N	33 (1)		
Oyeleke E	3 (3)	Taylor J	16 (2)		

League goals (50): Bennett 6, Pope 6, Cullen 5, Smith 5, Taylor 5. Amoo 4, Legge 4, Worrall 4, Burgess 3, Atkinson 1, Brisley 1, Conlon 1, Gibbons 1, Joyce 1, Opponents 3
FA Cup goals (5): Pope 4, Worrall 1. **League Cup goals (1):** Cullen 1. **League Trophy goals (9):** Cullen 2, Taylor 2, Amoo 1, Archer 1, Bennett 1, Browne 1, Burgess 1
Average home league attendance: 4,862

SALFORD CITY

A place in the top half of the table and a return ticket booked to Wembley represented a satisfying introduction to league football for the club part-owned by six former Manchester United players. Graham Alexander's team overcame patchy home form, and a tendency to drop points from winning positions, with an excellent away record which offered a slim chance of making the play-offs until the season ended prematurely with nine matches remaining. No team in the division bettered eight victories on their travels. There were three fewer at the Peninsula Stadium, with a 2-0 success against Bradford in the final fixture the first there since Boxing Day. Salford, who defeated AFC Fylde to win the National League Play-off Final in 2019 at Wembley, qualified for a repeat appearance in the EFL Trophy Final by beating Newport on penalties. But the April date against Portsmouth, for which 50,000 tickets had already been sold, was another victim of COVID-19.

Andrade B	6 (1)	Howard M	3	Rodney D	1 (2)
Armstrong L	12 (9)	Hughes S	4 (4)	Rooney A	24 (8)
Baldwin J	10 (3)	Hunter A	9 (2)	Shelton M	5
Beesley J	4 (3)	Jervis J	19 (1)	Smith M	3 (1)
Burgess C	26 (3)	Jones D	3	Thomas-Asante B	15 (5)
Conway C	15 (5)	Jones J	15 (5)	Threlkeld O	12 (6)
Dieseruvwe E	10 (10)	Letheren K	19	Touray I	35
Doyle A	- (1)	Lloyd D	4 (5)	Towell R	22 (4)
Eastham A	4	Maynard L	21 (1)	Walker T	- (4)
Elliott T	3 (5)	Neal C	15	Whitehead D	7 (5)
Gaffney R	1 (1)	O'Connor M	8	Wilson J	4 (1)
Gibson D	2 (1)	Piergianni C	11 (2)	Wiseman S	25
Hogan L	11 (1)	Pond N	19 (3)		

League goals (49): Rooney 8, Thomas-Asante 6 Hunter 5, Jervis 4, Touray 4, Dieseruvwe 3, Towell 3, Beesley 2, Burgess 2, Lloyd 2, Wilson 2, Armstrong 1, Baldwin 1, Elliott 1, Maynard 1, O'Connor 1, Shelton 1, Whitehead 1, Opponents 1
FA Cup goals (2): Touray 1, Towell 1. **League Cup goals:** None. **League Trophy goals (12):** Armstrong 3, Burgess 2, Elliott 1, Hogan 1, Jervis 1, Lloyd 1, Rooney 1, Threlkeld 1, Towell 1
Average home league attendance: 2,997. **Player of Year:** Ibou Touray

SCUNTHORPE UNITED

Another poor season for relegated Scunthorpe, who extended their run without a win from the end of the previous campaign to a club-record 16 when taking a single point from the opening seven games. The sequence was broken by a 3-0 victory over Morecambe and a gradual improvement delivered a run of eight games without defeat, accompanied by a climb to mid-table by Christmas. But form lapsed again – one win in eight – leading to the dismissal of Paul Hurst after eight months in charge. It meant the club were looking for their ninth manager in six years. Russ Wilcox returned to the role of caretaker and five players came in during the January transfer window. Scunthorpe, however, continued to concede more second-half goals than any team in the division right to the end when a 2-0 home defeat by local rivals Grimsby left them fifth from bottom. Hurst's replacement was Notts County's assistant manager Neil Cox.

Bedeau J 11	Green D .... - (2)	Perch J 30
Beestin A .... - (3)	Hammill A 3	Proctor J 4 (9)
Ben El-Mhanni Y .... - (1)	Lawlor I 4	Pugh T .... - (1)
Brown J 20	Lawrence-Gabriel J 8 (1)	Rowe J 1
Butler A 16 (2)	Liddle B 2 (2)	Slater R 7 (5)
Butroid L 4	Lund M 22	Songo'o Y 16
Clarke J 11 (1)	McArdle R 26	Sutton L 13 (3)
Colclough R 8 (12)	McAtee J 11 (8)	Ward J 3 (3)
Dales A .... - (3)	McGahey H 31 (1)	Watson R 23
Eastwood J 10 (1)	Miller G 7 (8)	Wootton K 4 (1)
Eisa A 24 (4)	Novak L 18 (1)	Van Veen K 23 (4)
Gillieard A 33 (2)	Ntlhe K 14 (4)	

League goals (44): Van Veen 10, Gillieard 6, Eisa 5, Novak 5, Lund 4, McArdle 3, McAtee 3, Ward 2, Bedeau 1, Miller 1, Ntlhe 1, Perch 1, Proctor 1, Opponents 1
FA Cup goals (1): Colclough 1. **League Cup goals:** None. **League Trophy goals (13):** Van Veen 5, Eisa 4, Novak 2, Colclough 1, Lund 1.
Average home league attendance: 3,546. **Player of Year:** Kevin van Veen

STEVENAGE

Ten seasons in the Football League seemed to have come to an end by the tiniest of margins. When this one ended prematurely, and final positions were decided on a points-per-game system, the club went down with an average of 0.61, while second-from-bottom Macclesfield stayed up on 0.62. But the EFL won an appeal against Macclesfield's suspended four-point deduction, imposed by an independent disciplinary commission, for the latest on a series of misdemeanours. The sanction was applied immediately, Macclesfield were relegated to the National League with 0.51 and Stevenage survived. The EFL said the decision was 'final and binding. On performances, Stevenage had nothing to complain about – just three victories and a club-record eight successive defeats at the end as managers came and went – Dino Maamria, Mark Sampson as caretaker, Graham Westley for a fourth spell in charge which lasted 63 days, then finally coach Alex Revell. Chairman Phil Wallace acknowledged his team's failings while arguing against what he called a 'forced and artificial relegation.'

Bastien S 1	Folami B .... - (2)	Parrett D 11 (6)
Byrom J 5 (1)	Guthrie K 18 (4)	Reading P 1
Carroll C 2 (2)	Husin N 6 (4)	Revell A .... - (2)
Carter C 25 (4)	Iontton A 4 (3)	Rollinson J .... - (1)
Cassidy J 8 (1)	Jackson S 2 (2)	Smith J .... - (1)
Cowley J 11 (7)	Kemp D 5 (1)	Smyth L .... - (1)
Cuthbert S 21	Kennedy B 12 (6)	Soares T 14 (1)
Dabo D 8	Lakin C 18 (2)	Sonupe E 5 (4)
Denton T 13 (2)	Leesley J 7 (1)	Stokes C 25
Digby P 16 (1)	List E 19 (2)	Taylor P 5 (5)
El-Abd A 1 (1)	Mackail-Smith C 6 (12)	Timlin M 11 (6)
Farman P 35	Newton D 6 (4)	VanCouten T 12 (4)
Fernandez L 2 (2)	Nugent B 23	Watts K 14 (2)
Fielding J 1 (2)	Parkhouse D 2 (2)	Wildin L 21

League goals (24): Carter 5, Guthrie 5, Cowley 2, Cuthbert 2, Lakin 2, List 2, Newton 2, Cassidy 1, Kemp 1, Sonupe 1, Wildin 1
FA Cup goals (1): List 1. **League Cup goals (1):** Parrett 1. **League Trophy goals (5):** Cowley 3, Carter 1, Mackail-Smith 1.
Average home league attendance: 2,914

SWINDON TOWN

Eoin Doyle and Jerry Yates formed a free-scoring partnership to fire Swindon to the title. Doyle, on loan from Bradford, was on the mark in 11 successive league games before being recalled by his parent club in the winter transfer window. Three weeks later, he rejoined the leaders, this time on a permanent basis, and so did Yates for another loan period after his brief recall by Rotherham. Richie Wellens's side went top in mid-November and stayed there for nearly four months until losing at home to Forest Green in what proved to be their final game. Crewe took over the leadership on goal difference after beating Stevenage in their last fixture, but had played one more match than Swindon, who were crowned champions on the points-per-game system used to finalise positions. Wellens signed a new three-and-a-half-year contract shortly before the season was curtailed.

Anderson K 17 (3)	Edmonds-Green R 9	McGilp C ....- (2)
Ballard D .... - (1)	Fryers Z..........................22	Muskwe A...................- (5)
Baudry M......................24	Grant A 29 (1)	Palmer M ....- (1)
Benda S 24	Hope H 4 (1)	Reid T.........................1 (3)
Broadbent T 3 (6)	Hunt R 33 (1)	Rose D 10 (9)
Caddis P 18 (1)	Iandolo E 10 (3)	Twine S ....- (6)
Conroy D........................11	Isgrove L 24 (5)	Woolery K..............20 (14)
Curran T .... - (2)	Jaiyesimi D.............. 15 (6)	Yates J....................30 (1)
Donohue D.......................5	Lyden J 17 (4)	Zakuani G..................5 (1)
Doughty M 24 (7)	May A 1 (8)	
Doyle E..........................28	McCormick L 12	

League goals (62): Doyle 25, Yates 13, Anderson 6, Jaiyesimi 5, Hope 2, Woolery 2, Doughty 1, Edmonds-Green 1, Fryers 1, Hunt 1, Lyden 1, Rose 1, Opponents 3
FA Cup goals (1): Yates 1. **League Cup goals**: None. **League Trophy goals** (2): Ballard 1, May 1.
Average home league attendance: 7,788. **Player of Year**: Anthony Grant

WALSALL

A new manager and a mass clearout of players following relegation meant Walsall were pretty much starting from scratch on the club's return to the fourth tier after 12 seasons of League One football. Darrell Clarke's new-look line-up struggled for goals early on before building some momentum with back-to-back wins over Morecambe, Scunthorpe and Crawley. Losing a 3-0 lead against Exeter and having to settle for a point was damaging, but the longer the campaign the greater the consistency achieved. They retrieved a two-goal deficit to beat Northampton 3-2 with goals by Josh Gordon, Danny Guthrie and Rory Holden in stoppage-time and were on a run of 11 points from five matches when the campaign came to an end with ten fixtures remaining. Walsall, then 14th, moved up two places above Grimsby and Crawley with the points-per-game system used to decide final positions.

Adebayo E.............. 15 (15)	Holden R.................. 23 (6)	Pring C....................20 (1)
Bates A.......................9 (4)	Jules Z.................. 13 (4)	Roberts K 1 (1)
Clarke J.......................27	Kiersey J 1 (1)	Roberts L 32
Cockerill-Mollett C 6 (3)	Kinsella L.............. 28 (3)	Rose J..........................4
Facey S 12 (1)	Lavery C 22 (5)	Sadler M 24 (3)
Gaffney R 11 (4)	Liddle G 10 (2)	Scarr D 32 (1)
Gordon J 26 (8)	McDonald W 21 (7)	Sheron N...................6 (1)
Guthrie D 17 (8)	Nolan J .... - (4)	Sinclair S 22 (4)
Hardy J.......................2 (9)	Norman C................ 12 (6)	

League goals (40): Gordon 9, Adebayo 8, McDonald 5, Lavery 4, Clarke 3, Holden 2, Sadler 2, Sinclair 2, Bates 1, Gaffney 1, Guthrie 1, Hardy 1, Opponents 1
FA Cup goals (3): Lavery 2, Bates 1. **League Cup goals** (2): Lavery 2. **League Trophy goals** (11): Gordon 3, Lavery 2, McDonald 2, Scarr 2, Kinsella 1, Norman 1.
Average home league attendance: 4,664. **Player of Year**: Josh Gordon

LEAGUE CLUB MANAGERS 2020–21

Figure in brackets = number of managerial changes at club since the War. †Second spell at club

PREMIER LEAGUE

Arsenal (13)	Mikel Arteta	December 2019
Aston Villa (27)	Dean Smith	October 2018
Brighton (34)	Graham Potter	May 2019
Burnley (24)	Sean Dyche	October 2012
Chelsea (31)	Frank Lampard	July 2019
Crystal Palace (43)	Roy Hodgson	September 2017
Everton (21)	Carlo Ancelotti	December 2019
Fulham (34)	Scott Parker	May 2019
Leeds (33)	Marcelo Bielsa	June 2018
Leicester (31)	Brendan Rodgers	February 2019
Liverpool (14)	Jurgen Klopp	October 2015
Manchester City (30)	Pep Guardiola	May 2016
Manchester Utd (12)	Ole Gunnar Solskjaer	April 2019
Newcastle (28)	Steve Bruce	July 2019
Sheffield Utd (38)	Chris Wilder	May 2016
Southampton (29)	Ralph Hasenhuttl	December 2018
Tottenham (24)	Jose Mourinho	November 2019
WBA (35)	Slaven Bilic	June 2019
West Ham (17)	David Moyes+	December 2019
Wolves (27)	Nuno Espirito Santo	May 2017

+Second spell as manager

CHAMPIONSHIP

Barnsley (28)	Gerhard Struber	November 2019
Birmingham (31)		
Blackburn (31)	Tony Mowbray	February 2017
Bournemouth (25)	Jason Tindall	August 2020
Brentford (34)	Thomas Frank	October 2018
Bristol City (27)	Neil Holden	August 2020
Cardiff (32)	Neil Harris	November 2019
Coventry (35)	Mark Robins	March 2017
Derby (28)	Phillip Cocu	July 2019
Huddersfield (31)	Carlos Corberan	July 2020
Luton (4)	Nathan Jones +	May 2020
Middlesbrough (24)	Neil Warnock	June 2020
Millwall (32)	Gary Rowett	October 2019
Norwich (29)	Daniel Farke	May 2017
Nottm Forest (27)	Sabri Lamouchi	June 2019
Preston (29)	Alex Neil	July 2017
QPR (36)	Mark Warburton	May 2019
Reading (25)	Mark Bowen	October 2019
Rotherham (28)	Paul Warne	April 2017
Sheffield Wed (32)	Garry Monk	September 2019
Stoke (27)	Michael O'Neill	November 2019
Swansea (38)	Steve Cooper	June 2019
Watford (38)	Vladimir Ivic	August 2020
Wycombe (10)	Gareth Ainsworth	November 2012

Number of changes since elected to Football League: Wycombe 1993. Since returning: Luton 2014. + Second spell as manager

LEAGUE ONE

Accrington (4)	John Coleman	September 2014
AFC Wimbledon (3)	Glyn Hodges	October 2019

Blackpool (34)	Neil Critchley	March 2020
Bristol Rov (2)	Ben Garner	December 2019
Burton (4)	Jake Buxton	May 2020
Charlton (25)	Lee Bowyer	September 2018
Crewe (22)	David Artell	January 2017
Doncaster (7)	Darren Moore	July 2019
Fleetwood (5)	Joey Barton	June 2018
Gillingham (27)	Steve Evans	May 2019
Hull (31)	Grant McCann	June 2019
Ipswich (15)	Paul Lambert	October 2018
Lincoln (1)	Michael Appleton	September 2019
MK Dons (19)	Russell Martin	November 2019
Northampton (36)	Keith Curle	October 2018
Oxford (4)	Karl Robinson	March 2018
Peterborough (32)	Darren Ferguson+	January 2019
Plymouth (35)	Ryan Lowe	June 2019
Portsmouth (34)	Kenny Jackett	June 2017
Rochdale (33)	Brian Barry-Murphy	April 2019
Shrewsbury (7)	Sam Ricketts	December 2018
Sunderland (33)	Phil Parkinson	October 2019
Swindon (33)	Richie Wellens	November 2018
Wigan (25)		

+Third spell as manager. Number of changes since elected to Football League: Peterborough 1960, Wigan 1978, Burton 2009, AFC Wimbledon 2011, Fleetwood 2012. Since returning: Doncaster 2003, Shrewsbury 2004, Accrington 2006, Oxford 2010, Bristol Rov 2015, Lincoln 2017

LEAGUE TWO

Barrow (-)	David Dunn	July 2020
Bolton (25)	Ian Evatt	July 2020
Bradford (39)	Stuart McCall++	March 2020
Cambridge (4)	Mark Bonner	March 2020
Carlisle (8)	Chris Beech	November 2019
Cheltenham (1)	Michael Duff	September 2018
Colchester (29)	Steve Ball	July 2020
Crawley (9)	John Yems	December 2019
Exeter (1)	Matt Taylor	June 2018
Forest Green (-)	Mark Cooper	May 2016
Grimsby (4)	Ian Holloway	December 2019
Harrogate (-)	Simon Weaver	May 2009
Leyton Orient (2)	Ross Embleton+	January 2020
Mansfield (5)	Graham Coughlan	December 2019
Morecambe (2)	Derek Adams	November 2019
Newport (5)	Mike Flynn	May 2017
Oldham (37)	Harry Kewell	August 2020
Port Vale (28)	John Askey	February 2019
Salford (-)	Graham Alexander	May 2018
Scunthorpe (32)	Neil Cox	August 2020
Southend (32)	Mark Molesley	August 2020
Stevenage (7)	Alex Revell	February 2020
Tranmere (1)	Mike Jackson	July 2020
Walsall (37)	Darrell Clarke	May 2019

+Second spell as manager. ++Third spell as manager. Number of changes since elected to Football League: Morecambe 2007, Stevenage 2010, Crawley 2011, Forest Green 2017, Salford 2019, Harrogate 2020. Since returning: Colchester 1992, Carlisle 2005, Exeter 2008, Mansfield 2013, Newport 2013, Cambridge 2014, Cheltenham 2016, Grimsby 2016, Tranmere 2018, Leyton Orient 2019, Barrow 2020

MANAGERIAL CHANGES 2019–20

PREMIER LEAGUE

Arsenal: Out – Unai Emery (Nov 2019); In – Mikel Arteta
Bournemouth: Out – Eddie Howe (Aug 2020); In – Jason Tindall
Everton: Out – Marco Silva (Dec 2019); Carlo Ancelotti
Tottenham: Out – Mauricio Pochettino (Nov 2019); In – Jose Mourinho
Watford: Out – Javi Gracia (Sep 2019); In – Quique Sanchez Flores; (Out Nov 2019);
    In – Nigel Pearson (Out Jul 2020); In – Vladimir Ivic
West Ham: Out – Manuel Pellegrini (Dec 2019); In – David Moyes

CHAMPIONSHIP

Barnsley: Out – Daniel Stendel (Oct 2019); In – Gerhard Struber
Birmingham: Out – Pep Clotet (Jul 2020);
Bristol City: Out – Lee Johnson (Jul 2020); In – Neil Holden
Cardiff: Out – Neil Warnock (Nov 2019); In – Neil Harris
Huddersfield: Out – Jan Siewert (Aug 2019); In – Danny Cowley (Out Jul 2020);
    In – Carlos Corberan
Luton: Out – Graeme Jones (Apr 2020); In – Nathan Jones
Middlesbrough: Out – Jonathan Woodgate (Jun 2020); In – Neil Warnock
Millwall: Out – Neil Harris (Oct 2019); In – Gary Rowett
Reading: Out – Jose Gomes (Oct 2019); In – Mark Bowen
Stoke: Out – Nathan Jones (Nov 2019); In – Michael O'Neill

LEAGUE ONE

AFC Wimbledon: Out – Wally Downes (Oct 2019); In – Glyn Hodges
Blackpool: Out – Simon Grayson (Feb 2020); In – Neil Critchley
Bolton: Out – Phil Parkinson (Aug 2019); In – Keith Hill; (Out Jun 2020); In – Ian Evatt
Bristol Rovers: Out – Graham Coughlan (Dec 2019); In – Ben Garner
Burton: Out – Nigel Clough (May 2020); In – Jake Buxton
Lincoln: Out – Danny Cowley (Sep 2019); In – Michael Appleton
MK Dons: Out – Paul Tisdale (Nov 2019); In – Russell Martin
Southend   Out – Kevin Bond (Sep 2019); In – Sol Campbell (out Jun 2020); In – Mark
Moseley
Sunderland: Out – Jack Ross (Oct 2019); In – Phil Parkinson

LEAGUE TWO

Bradford: Out – Gary Bowyer (Feb 2020); In – Stuart McCall
Cambridge: Out – Colin Calderwood (Jan 2020); in – Mark Bonner
Carlisle: Out – Steven Pressley (Nov 2019); In – Chris Beech
Colchester: Out – John McGreal (Jul 2020); In – Steve Ball
Crawley: Out – Gabriele Cioffi (Nov 2019); In – John Yems
Grimsby: Out – Michael Jolley (Nov 2019); In – Ian Holloway
Leyton Orient: Out – Ross Embleton (Oct 2019); In – Carl Fletcher; Out (Nov 2019);
    In – Ross Embleton
Macclesfield: Out – Sol Campbell (Aug 2019); In – Daryl McMahon (Out Jan 2020);
    In – Mark Kennedy (Out Aug 2020)
Mansfield: Out – John Dempster (Dec 2019); In – Graham Coughlan
Morecambe: Out – Jim Bentley (Oct 2019); In – Derek Adams
Oldham: Out – Laurent Banide (Sep 2019); In – Dino Maamria (Out Jul 2020);
    In – Harry Kewell
Scunthorpe: Out – Paul Hurst (Jan 2020); In – Neil Cox
Stevenage: Out – Dino Maamria (Sep 2019); In – Graham Westley; Out (Feb 2020);
    In – Alex Revell

FOOTBALL'S CHANGING HOMES

Brentford's dream of bringing Premier League football to their new home ended with defeat by Fulham in the play-offs, but owner Matthew Benham believes the 17,250-seater Community Stadium still promises an exciting future for the club. More than 10,000 seats were sold by mid-summer and Benham said: 'I am absolutely confident that the unique nature of the site has resulted in a stadium that is different to the majority of new ones – small enough to create a fantastic atmosphere, yet big enough to enable the continued growth of our supporter base while offering a brilliant match-day experience for all.' After playing at Griffin Park since 1904, the club have moved less than a mile away to near Kew Bridge, where the £70m arena, incorporating 900 new homes, will be shared with London Irish rugby club, who are leaving Reading's Madejski Stadium after 20 years. It will be one of the venues for the European Women's Championship finals in England, now scheduled for July 2022 after being put back a year because of COVID-19.

Among Brentford's opponents for the new season are newly-promoted **Coventry City**, who have announced plans to build a new stadium in partnership with the University of Warwick on a site on the south-west edge of the city, owned by the university. A joint statement from both parties promised 'a visionary, environmentally friendly arena in terms of materials, energy, noise, building and access.' They also envisage supporters arriving at a new light rail station running alongside a new link road. Coventry left the Ricoh Arena in 2019 after a long-running dispute with the owners. They played home matches last season at St Andrew's in Birmingham and signed an agreement to continue to groundshare in 2020-21. **Forest Green Rovers** – the self-styled 'greenest club of all,' have received government-backed planning consent for a new wooden stadium at an eco park next to junction 13 of the M5. Opponents claiming it was not part of the local plan failed to have the scheme 'called in' for further investigation.

AFC Wimbledon are back on course to return to their roots in Plough Lane in season 2021-22 after signing their new stadium's final construction contract with investment from local businessman Nick Robertson and a crowdfunding campaign. The scheme was delayed when the club said a further £11m was needed for completion. Wimbledon have been playing at Kingsmeadow in Kingston upon Thames since being found by supporters of the old club. **Luton Town** cleared a hurdle towards moving to a new home a mile from Kenilworth Road , funded by a new shopping and leisure park, when a challenge to the park plan was rejected by the High Court. Another club wanting to move, **Southend United**, have agreed a deal with the local council and a social housing provider to build it, along with 1,300 homes, at Fossetts Farm.

In the Premier League, **Liverpool** have delayed plans to extend the Anfield Road stand because of COVID-19. It would increase capacity by 7,000 to over 60,000 at an estimated cost of £60m. **Manchester United** have also put on hold proposal to increase capacity at Old Trafford. **Manchester City** have looked into extending the North stand with a third tier which woud take capacity of the Etihad to 61,000. Other clubs who have examined increasing attendances include **Leeds United, Newcastle United, Sheffield United** and **West Bromwich Albion**.

THE THINGS THEY SAY ...

'I was born and brought up only a couple of miles from the stadium and I am really happy to have the opportunity to give back to the club that gave me my first professional start' – **Harry Kane** pledges sponsorship for shirts worn in the 2020-21 season by Leyton Orient, with three good causes benefiting.

'We score three times at home for the first time this season and there's no-one here to see it' – **Steve Bruce**, Newcastle manager, sees the irony of a 3-0 win over Sheffield United.

'The game in a heartbeat has changed. I don't know where it is going. It is sucking the life out of me and the supporters' – **Chris Wilder**, Sheffield United manager, on the VAR controversies.

EMIRATES FA CUP 2019–20

FIRST ROUND

A marathon tie at the Wham Stadium lasts three hours and features three referees. The first, Neil Hair, limps off midway through the first half. His replacement, fourth official Alan Clayton is also injured and half-time lasts more than half-an-hour as Accrington and Crewe officials discuss how to continue. Managers John Coleman and David Artell agree the match should continue, with assistant referee Danny Gratton taking over in the middle, only one assistant, Conor Brown, running the line, a toss of the coin deciding on which side he operates and Clayton reverting to fourth official. Gratton sends off Accrington's Mark Hughes for bringing down Owen Dale and Crewe go through 2-0 with goals from Charlie Kirk and Chris Porter (pen). Three teams are beaten by non-league opposition, including Southend, whose new manager Sol Campbell lifted the trophy as a player with Arsenal. They lose to an 84th minute goal for Dover by Ruel Sotiriou. Leyton Orient are knocked out 2-1 at home by Maldon and Tiptree, who have Danny Parish and Jorome Slew on the mark, with Parish later sent off for a second yellow card. Macclesfield, fielding a youthful side with senior players on strike over unpaid wages, go down 4-0 at home to Kingstonian, whose scorers are Louie Theophanous (2), Dan Hector and Dan Bennett.

Accrington 0 Crewe 2	Nantwich 0 AFC Fylde 1
AFC Wimbledon 1 Doncaster 1	Oxford City 1 Solihull 5
Barnet 0 Fleetwood 2	Salford 1 Burton 1
Blackpool 4 Morecambe 1	Shrewsbury 1 Bradford 1
Bolton 0 Plymouth 1	Stevenage 1 Peterborough 1
Bristol Rov 1 Bromley 1	Stourbridge 2 Eastleigh 2
Cambridge 1 Exeter 1	Sunderland 1 Gillingham 1
Carshalton 1 Boston 4	Tranmere 2 Wycombe 2
Cheltenham 1 Swindon 1	Walsall 2 Darlington 2
Chippenham 0 Northampton 3	Wrexham 0 Rochdale 0
Colchester 0 Coventry 2	Yeovil 1 Hartlepool 4
Crawley 4 Scunthorpe 1	York 0 Altrincham 1
Dover 1 Southend 0	**Replays**
Dulwich Hamlet 1 Carlisle 4	Bradford 0 Shrewsbury 1
Ebbsfleet 2 Notts Co 3	Bromley 0 Bristol Rov 1
Forest Green 4 Billericay 0	Burton 4 Salford 1
Gateshead 1 Oldham 2	Darlington 0 Walsall 1
Grimsby 1 Newport 1	Doncaster 2 AFC Wimbledon 0
Harrogate 1 Portsmouth 2	Eastleigh 3 Stourbridge 0
Hayes 0 Oxford Utd 2	Exeter 1 Cambridge 0
Ipswich 1 Lincoln 1	Gillingham 1 Sunderland 0 (aet)
Leyton Orient 1 Maldon and Tiptree 2	Lincoln 0 Ipswich 1
Macclesfield 0 Kingstonian 4	Newport 2 Grimsby 0
Maidenhead 1 Rotherham 3	Peterborough 2 Stevenage 0
Maidstone 1 Torquay 0	Rochdale 1 Wrexham 0
Mansfield 1 Chorley 0	Swindon 0 Cheltenham 1
MK Dons 0 Port Vale 1	Wycombe 1 Tranmere 2 (aet)

SECOND ROUND

Two quick-fire hat-tricks and two comebacks provide the highlights of the round. Tom Pope scores all three Port Vale goals in the space of nine second-half minutes for victory at Cheltenham. Morgan Ferrier is not far behind with three in 11 minutes in Tranmere's 5-1 win over Chichester. Rotherham trail Solihull 3-0 after 75 minutes, then hit back to go through with goals by Freddie

Ladapo, Michael Ihiekwe and two headers from Michael Smith, the second in stoppage-time. Hartlepool also recover when trailing 2-0 at Exeter, Nicky Featherstone from 25 yards and Nicke Kabamba earning a replay. This goes to extra-time when Josh Hawkes is on on the mark to give the non-league side the verdict. They are joined in round three by AFC Fylde, who reach this stage for the first time, defeating Kingstonian courtesy of two Jordan Williams goals.

Blackpool 3 Maidstone 1	Portsmouth 2 Altrincham 1
Bristol Rov 1 Plymouth 1	Rochdale 0 Boston 0
Cheltenham 1 Port Vale 3	Shrewsbury 2 Mansfield 0
Coventry 1 Ipswich 1	Solihull 3 Rotherham 4
Crawley 1 Fleetwood 2	Tranmere 5 Chichester 1
Eastleigh 1 Crewe 1	Walsall 0 Oxford 1
Exeter 2 Hartlepool 2	**Replays**
Forest Green 2 Carlisle 2	Boston 1 Rochdale 2
Gillingham 3 Doncaster 0	Carlisle 1 Forest Green 0
Kingstonian 0 AFC Fylde 2	Crewe 3 Eastleigh 1
Maldon and Tiptree 0 Newport 1	Hartlepool 1 Exeter 0 (aet)
Northampton 3 Notts Co 1	Ipswich 1 Coventry 2
Oldham 0 Burton 1	Plymouth 0 Bristol Rov 1
Peterborough 3 Dover 0	

THIRD ROUND

Tranmere take pride of place by overcoming Watford to earn a plum tie against Manchester United. The Premier League side, their sights set on trying to avoid relegation, make wholesale changes for the tie, but that takes nothing away from Tranmere's recovery from a 3-0 half-time deficit at Vicarage Road with goals by Connor Jennings, Manny Monthe and Paul Mullin's 87th minute penalty. Nor does it detract from victory in the replay, with Cameroon defender Monthe again on the mark, followed by substitute Mullin's extra-time decider. Teenagers Curtis Jones and Adam Idah, alongside evergreen Aaron Wilbraham, also make headlines. Jones, 18, gives a youthful Liverpool side showing nine changes victory over near full-strength Everton with a spectacular finish from 22 yards. Idah, also 18, scores a hat-trick as Norwich win 4-2 at Preston, his third goal coming from the penalty spot. Wilbraham, aged 40 and playing for his tenth club, comes off the bench to earn Rochdale another chance against Newcastle with an equaliser set up by 17-year-old Luke Matheson. Wilbraham starts the replay, but an own goal by Eoghan O'Connell puts his side up against it and they go down 4-1. Briefest appearance of the round is made by Birmingham substitute Ivan Sunjic, who is on for just 98 seconds before a straight red card for bringing down Blackburn's Sam Gallagher.

Arsenal 1 Leeds 0	Gillingham 0 West Ham 2
Bournemouth 4 Luton 0	Leicester 2 Wigan 0
Birmingham 2 Blackburn 1	Liverpool 1 Everton 0
Brentford 1 Stoke 0	Manchester City 4 Port Vale 1
Brighton 0 Sheffield Wed 1	Middlesbrough 1 Tottenham 1
Bristol City 1 Shrewsbury 1	Millwall 3 Newport 0
Bristol Rov 2 Coventry 2	Oxford Utd 4 Hartlepool 1
Burnley 4 Peterborough 2	Preston 2 Norwich 4
Burton 2 Northampton 4	QPR 5 Swansea 1
Cardiff 2 Carlisle 1	Reading 2 Blackpool 2
Charlton 0 WBA 1	Rochdale 1 Newcastle 1
Chelsea 2 Nottm Forest 0	Rotherham 2 Hull 3
Crewe 1 Barnsley 3	Sheffield Utd 2 AFC Fylde 1
Crystal Palace 0 Derby 1	Southampton 2 Huddersfield 0
Fleetwood 1 Portsmouth 2	Watford 3 Tranmere 3
Fulham 2 Aston Villa 1	Wolves 0 Manchester Utd 0

Replays

Blackpool 0 Reading 2
Carlisle 3 Cardiff 4
Coventry 3 Bristol Rov 0
Manchester Utd 1 Wolves 0

Newcastle 4 Rochdale 1
Shrewsbury 1 Bristol City 0
Tottenham 2 Middlesbrough 1
Tranmere 2 Watford 1 (aet)

FOURTH ROUND

Two goals by substitute Jason Cummings, his first a penalty, enable Shrewsbury to retrieve a 2-0 deficit against Liverpool, who bring on Alex Oxlade-Chamberlain, Mohamed Salah and Roberto Firmino late on in a bid for the winner. For the replay, Jurgen Klopp rests all his senior players and misses the game himself. Under 23 manager Neil Critchley takes charge of the club's youngest-ever side – average age 19 years and 102 days – and they win 1-0 with an own goal by Ro-Shaun Williams. Nine changes made by both Brentford and Leicester for their tie also reflect the growing trend for clubs to concentrate on league matters. But there is still plenty to savour, none more so than Oxford holding Newcastle to a goalless draw at St James' Park and coming from 2-0 down in the replay to level through Liam Kelly's 84th minute free-kick and Nathan Holland's equaliser in the fourth minute of stoppage-time. But Steve Bruce's team prevail in extra-time with a goal from Allan Saint-Maximin. Slaven Bilic returns to West Ham, the club that sacked him, and engineers a 1-0 success, courtesy of Conor Townsend's ninth minute goal and his side's ability to preserve the advantage after losing Semi Ajayi to a second yellow card with 20 minutes remaining. Tranmere's run ends with a 6-0 defeat by Manchester United, who have six different scorers.

Bournemouth 1 **Arsenal** 2
Brentford 0 Leicester 1
Burnley 1 Norwich 2
Coventry 0 Birmingham 0
Hull 1 **Chelsea** 2
Manchester City 4 Fulham 0
Millwall 0 Sheffield Utd 2
Newcastle 0 Oxford 0
Northampton 0 Derby 0
Portsmouth 4 Barnsley 2
QPR 1 Sheffield Wed 2
Reading 1 Cardiff 1
Shrewsbury 2 Liverpool 2

Southampton 1 Tottenham 1
Tranmere 0 Manchester Utd 6
West Ham 0 WBA 1
Replays
Birmingham 2 Coventry 2
(aet, Birmingham won 4-1 on pens)
Cardiff 3 Reading 3
(aet, Reading won 4-1 on pens)
Derby 4 Northampton 2
Liverpool 1 Shrewsbury 0
Oxford 2 Newcastle 3
Tottenham 3 Southampton 2

FIFTH ROUND

There is no storybook reunion with Manchester United for Wayne Rooney. Derby's player-coach receives a warm welcome from fans of his former club and has two trademark free-kicks kept out by Sergio Romero. But two goals by the former Watford striker Odion Ighalo, on loan from Chinese club Shanghai Shenhua, point United to a 3-0 victory, with a booking for bringing down Fred all Rooney has to show from an emotional night. Miguel Almiron is also on the mark twice as Newcastle prevail 3-2 at The Hawthorns to reach the quarter-finals for the first time since 2006. Norwich put their Premier League problems aside to go through at Tottenham, courtesy of Tim Krul saving from Troy Parrott and Gedson Fernandes in a penalty shoot-out. On its conclusion, Tottenham's Eric Dier climbs into the stand to confront an abusive supporter. Liverpool's bid for a domestic double ends at Stamford Bridge, where a fine solo goal from Ross Barkley highlights Chelsea's 2-0 success. Wins for Arsenal, Leicester, Manchester City and Sheffield United complete all-Premier League line-up in the last eight.

Chelsea 2 Liverpool 0
Derby 0 Manchester Utd 3
Leicester 1 Birmingham 0
Portsmouth 0 **Arsenal** 2
Reading 1 Sheffield Utd 2 (aet)

Sheffield Wed 0 Manchester City 1
Tottenham 1 Norwich 1
(aet, Norwich won 3-2 on pens)
WBA 2 Newcastle 3

SIXTH ROUND

Harry Maguire and Dani Ceballos score late goals to put Manchester United and Arsenal into the semi-finals. Skipper Maguire strikes two minutes from the end of extra-time, with ten-man Norwich's resistance set to take the tie to penalties following a straight red card for Timm Klose for wrestling Odion Ighalo to the ground. Manager Ole Gunnar Solskjaer makes history with six substitutions – the first time in English football. At Bramall Lane, David McGoldrick equalises for Sheffield United in the 87th minute, but Arsenal substitute Ceballos has the final say a minute into stoppage-time. Chelsea's Ross Barkley also comes off the bench to deliver the only goal at Leicester, while holders Manchester City overcome blanket Newcastle defending for a 2-0 victory, completed by Raheem Sterling's sublime finish from 20 yards.

Norwich 1 **Manchester Utd 2** (aet)
Leicester 0 **Chelsea 1**

Newcastle 0 **Manchester City 2**
Sheffield Utd 1 **Arsenal 2**

SEMI-FINALS (both at Wembley)

Pierre-Emerick Aubameyang scores both goals as Arsenal defeat Manchester City as Mikel Arteta gets the better of his managerial mentor Pep Guardiola. Olivier Giroud and Mason Mount punish mistakes by David de Gea and Chelsea make sure of victory against Manchester United with an own goal by Harry Maguire.

Arsenal 2 Manchester City 0

Manchester United 1 **Chelsea** 3

FINAL

The fledgling manager and his master marksman upheld Arsenal's proud FA Cup tradition in a final which also did full justice to Wembley, despite an unprecedented, unnerving empty stadium. Mikel Arteta's preparation and match-day tactical awareness reflected his learning experience as a player under Arsene Wenger and working alongside Pep Guardiola at Manchester City. Pierre-Emerick Aubameyang matched his two goals in the semi-finals against Guardiola's team with as emphatic a penalty as you would ever see, then the winner with a trademark world-class finish. The combination enabled their team to overcome a testing start, gradually douse Chelsea's fire and establish superiority. The reward was a record 25th successive season in Europe, albeit in the Europa League and not the Champions League to which Arteta aspires. Frank Lampard had no complaints about the result, unhappy with the way his side failed to maintain their enterprising start. But he had every right to argue that fortune did favour them, notably when the impressive Christian Pulisic sliced the chance of a second goal at the start of the second-half while collapsing with a pulled a hamstring and leaving the pitch in some distress. Lampard had already lost his captain, Cesar Azpilicueta, with a similar injury and finally saw Pulisic's replacement, Pedro, carried off holding a damaged shoulder. In between, Chelsea had Mateo Kovacvic sent off for a debatable second yellow card which effectively ended their chances. Lampard, like Arteta at the end of his first season in charge, had a guaranteed Champions League place to compensate. Like the Spaniard he looks to have a bright future ahead.

ARSENAL 2 (Aubameyang 28 pen, 67) **CHELSEA 1** (Pulisic 5)
Wembley (behind closed doors); Saturday, Auguest 1, 2020
Arsenal (3-4-3): Martinez, Holding, Luiz (Sokratis 88), Tierney (Kolasinac 90+13), Bellerin, Ceballos, Xhaka, Maitland-Niles, Pepe, Lacazette (Nketiah 82), Aubameyang (capt). **Subs not used**: Macey, Torreira, Nelson, Willock, Smith, Saka. **Booked**: Ceballos. **Manager**: Mikel Arteta
Chelsea (3-4-2-1): Caballero, Azpilicueta (capt) (Christensen 35), Zouma, Rudiger (Hudson-Odoi 78), James, Jorginho, Kovacic, Marcos Alonso, Mount (Barkley 78), Pulisic (Pedro 49), Giroud (Abraham 78). **Subs not used**: Arrizabalaga, Kante, Tomori, Emerson. **Booked**: Kovacic, Azpilicueta, Mount, Rudiger, Barkley. **Sent off**: Kovacic (73). **Manager**: Frank Lampard
Referee: A Taylor (Cheshire). **Half-time**: 1-1

HOW THEY REACHED THE FINAL

Arsenal
Round 3: 1-0 home to Leeds (Nelson)
Round 4: 2-1 away to Bournemouth (Saka, Nketiah)
Round 5: 2-0 away to Portsmouth (Sokratis, Nketiah)
Round 6: 2-1 away to Sheffield Utd (Pepe, Ceballos)
Semi-final: 2-0 v Manchester City (Aubameyang 2)

Chelsea
Round 3: 2-0 home to Nottm Forest (Hudson Odoi, Barkley)
Round 4: 2-1 away to Hull (Batshuayi, Tomori)
Round 5: 2-0 home to Liverpool (Willian, Barkley)
Round 6: 1-0 away to Leicester (Barkley)
Semi-final: 3-1 v Manchester Utd (Giroud, Mount, Maguire og)

Leading scorers: 5 Ball (Solihull), McKirdy (Carlisle); 4 Almiron (Newcastle), Aubameyang (Arsenal), Biamou (Coventry), Delfouneso (Blackpool), Ferrier (Tranmere), Pope (Port Vale)

FINAL FACTS AND FIGURES

- Arsenal have an unprecedented record of seven wins in their last seven FA Cup Finals, dating back to 2002. Four of those have come in the last seven seasons.

- Mikel Arteta became the first to captain and manage the club to victory in the competition, having lifted the trophy after a 3-2 extra-time victory over Hull in 2014. He was also the first manager to be shown a yellow card, following a touchline confrontation with Antonio Rudiger.

- Pierre-Emerick Aubameyang was the first Arsenal player to score twice in a final since Reg Lewis in the 2-0 win over Liverpool in 1950. In his last full season with Borussia Dortmund before joining Arsenal for a then club-record £56m, Aubameyang scored the winner from the penalty spot against Eintracht Frankfurt in the 2017 German Cup Final. He was also top scorer in the Bundesliga that season with 31 goals.

- With the Royal Box out of bounds, Aubameyang collected the trophy on the pitch – and promptly dropped it before hoisting it in front of celebrating team-mates.

- Chelsea have won seven of their last ten finals in the competition, with all three defeats coming against Arsenal.

- Christian Pulisic became the first American player to score in the showpiece match.

- Willy Caballero (38) became the oldest to play for Chelsea in the final. Substitute Callum Hudson-Odoi (19) was the youngest.

- Mateo Kovacic was the sixth player to be sent off, after Kevin Moran (Manchester Utd), Jose Reyes (Arsenal), Pabo Zabaleta (Manchester City), Chris Smalling (Manchester Utd) and Victor Moses (Chelsea)

- Anthony Taylor showed Victor Moses a second yellow card for diving in 2017 when Chelsea were also beaten 2-1 by Arsenal. This time, Taylor became the first referee since 1901 to take charge of a second final in the competition The FA deemed it unfair to appoint a first-time official and not have his family and friends able to attend.

- The match was renamed the Heads Up FA Cup Final to raise mental health awareness. Prince William, president of the FA, appeared by video link from Sandringham to promote the initiative. Emirates, the competition sponsor, agreed to the change.

FA CUP FINAL SCORES & TEAMS

1872 Wanderers 1 (Betts) Bowen, Alcock, Bonsor, Welch; Betts, Crake, Hooman, Lubbock, Thompson, Vidal, Wollaston. Note: Betts played under the pseudonym 'AH Chequer' on the day of the match **Royal Engineers 0** Capt Merriman; Capt Marindin, Lieut Addison, Lieut Cresswell, Lieut Mitchell, Lieut Renny-Tailyour, Lieut Rich, Lieut George Goodwyn, Lieut Muirhead, Lieut Cotter, Lieut Bogle

1873 Wanderers 2 (Wollaston, Kinnaird) Bowen; Thompson, Welch, Kinnaird, Howell, Wollaston, Sturgis, Rev Stewart, Kenyon-Slaney, Kingsford, Bonsor **Oxford University 0** Kirke-Smith; Leach, Mackarness, Birley, Longman, Chappell-Maddison Dixon, Paton, Vidal, Sumner, Ottaway. March 29; 3, 000; A Stair

1874 Oxford University 2 (Mackarness, Patton) Neapean; Mackarness, Birley, Green, Vidal, Ottaway, Benson, Patton, Rawson, Chappell-Maddison, Rev Johnson **Royal Engineers 0** Capt Merriman; Major Marindin, Lieut W Addison, Gerald Onslow, Lieut Oliver, Lieut Digby, Lieut Renny-Tailyour, Lieut Rawson, Lieut Blackman Lieut Wood, Lieut Von Donop. March 14; 2, 000; A Stair

1875 Royal Engineers 1 (Renny-Tailyour) Capt Merriman; Lieut Sim, Lieut Onslow, Lieut (later Sir) Ruck, Lieut Von Donop, Lieut Wood, Lieut Rawson, Lieut Stafford, Capt Renny-Tailyour, Lieut Mein, Lieut Wingfield-Stratford **Old Etonians 1** (Bonsor) Thompson; Benson, Lubbock, Wilson, Kinnaird, (Sir) Stronge, Patton, Farmer, Bonsor, Ottaway, Kenyon-Slaney. March 13; 2, 000; CW Alcock. aet **Replay – Royal Engineers 2** (Renny-Tailyour, Stafford) Capt Merriman; Lieut Sim, Lieut Onslow, Lieut (later Sir) Ruck, Lieut Von Donop, Lieut Wood, Lieut Rawson, Lieut Stafford, Capt Renny-Tailyour, Lieut Mein, Lieut Wingfield-Stratford **Old Etonians 0** Capt Drummond-Moray; Kinnaird, (Sir) Stronge, Hammond, Lubbock, Patton, Farrer, Bonsor, Lubbock, Wilson, Farmer. March 16; 3, 000; CW Alcock

1876 Wanderers 1 (Edwards) Greig; Stratford, Lindsay, Chappell-Maddison, Birley, Wollaston, C Heron, G Heron, Edwards, Kenrick, Hughes **Old Etonians 1** (Bonsor) Hogg; Rev Welldon, Lyttleton, Thompson, Kinnaird, Meysey, Kenyon-Slaney, Lyttleton, Sturgis, Bonsor, Allene. March 11; 3, 500; WS Rawson aet **Replay – Wanderers 3** (Wollaston, Hughes 2) Greig; Stratford, Lindsay, Chappel-Maddison, Birley, Wollaston, C Heron, G Heron, Edwards, Kenrick, Hughes **Old Etonians 0** Hogg; Lubbock, Lyttleton, Farrer, Kinnaird, (Sir) Stronge, Kenyon-Slaney, Lyttleton, Sturgis, Bonsor, Allene. March 18; 1, 500; WS Rawson

1877 Wanderers 2 (Kenrick, Lindsay) Kinnaird; Birley, Denton, Green, Heron, Hughes, Kenrick, Lindsay, Stratford, Wace, Wollaston **Oxford University 1** (Kinnaird og) Allington; Bain, Dunnell, Rev Savory, Todd, Waddington, Rev Fernandez, Otter, Parry, Rawson. March 24; 3, 000; SH Wright, aet

1878 Wanderers 3 (Kinnaird, Kenrick 2) (Sir) Kirkpatrick; Stratford, Lindsay, Kinnaird, Green, Wollaston, Heron, Wylie, Wace, Denton, Kenrick **Royal Engineers 1** (Morris) Friend; Cowan, (Sir) Morris, Mayne, Heath, Haynes, Lindsay, Hedley, (Sir) Bond, Barnet, Ruck. March 23; 4, 500; SR Bastard

1879 Old Etonians 1 (Clerke) Hawtrey; Edward, Bury, Kinnaird, Lubbock, Clerke, Pares, Goodhart, Whitfield, Chevalier, Beaufoy **Clapham Rovers 0** Birkett; Ogilvie, Field, Bailey, Prinsep, Rawson, Stanley, Scott, Bevington, Growse, Keith-Falconer. March 29; 5, 000; CW Alcock

1880 Clapham Rovers 1 (Lloyd-Jones) Birkett; Ogilvie, Field, Weston, Bailey, Stanley, Brougham, Sparkes, Barry, Ram, Lloyd-Jones **Oxford University 0** Parr; Wilson, King, Phillips, Rogers, Heygate, Rev Childs, Eyre, (Dr) Crowdy, Hill, Lubbock. April 10; 6, 000; Major Marindin

1881 Old Carthusians 3 (Page, Wynyard, Parry) Gillett; Norris, (Sir) Colvin, Prinsep, (Sir) Vintcent, Hansell, Richards, Page, Wynyard, Parry, Todd **Old Etonians 0** Rawlinson; Foley, French, Kinnaird, Farrer, Macauley, Goodhart, Whitfield, Novelli, Anderson, Chevallier. April 9; 4, 000; W Pierce-Dix

1882 Old Etonians 1 (Macauley) Rawlinson; French, de Paravicini, Kinnaird, Foley, Novelli, Dunn, Macauley, Goodhart, Chevallier, Anderson **Blackburn Rov 0** Howarth; McIntyre, Suter, Hargreaves, Sharples, Hargreaves, Avery, Brown, Strachan, Douglas, Duckworth. March 25; 6, 500; JC Clegg

1883 Blackburn Olympic 2 (Matthews, Costley) Hacking; Ward, Warburton, Gibson, Astley, Hunter, Dewhurst, Matthews, Wilson, Costley, Yates **Old Etonians 1** (Goodhart) Rawlinson; French, de Paravicini, Kinnaird, Foley, Dunn, Bainbridge, Chevallier, Anderson, Goodhart, Macauley. March 31; 8, 000; Major Marindin, aet

1884 Blackburn Rov 2 (Sowerbutts, Forrest) Arthur; Suter, Beverley, McIntyre, Forrest, Hargreaves, Brown, Inglis Sowerbutts, Douglas, Lofthouse **Queen's Park 1** (Christie) Gillespie; MacDonald, Arnott, Gow,

Campbell, Allan, Harrower, (Dr) Smith, Anderson, Watt, Christie. March 29; 4, 000; Major Marindin

1885   Blackburn Rov 2 (Forrest, Brown) Arthur; Turner, Suter, Haworth, McIntyre, Forrest, Sowerbutts, Lofthouse, Douglas, Brown, Fecitt **Queen's Park 0** Gillespie; Arnott, MacLeod, MacDonald, Campbell, Sellar, Anderson, McWhammel, Hamilton, Allan, Gray. April 4; 12, 500; Major Marindin

1886   Blackburn Rov 0 Arthur; Turner, Suter, Heyes, Forrest, McIntyre, Douglas, Strachan, Sowerbutts, Fecitt, Brown **WBA 0** Roberts; Green, Bell, Horton, Perry, Timmins, Woodhall, Green, Bayliss, Loach, Bell. April 3; 15, 000; Major Marindin **Replay – Blackburn Rov 2** (Sowerbutts, Brown) Arthur; Turner, Suter, Walton, Forrest, McIntyre, Douglas, Strachan, Sowerbutts, Fecitt, Brown **WBA 0** Roberts; Green, Bell, Horton, Perry, Timmins, Woodhall, Green, Bayliss, Loach, Bell. April 10; 12, 000; Major Marindin

1887   Aston Villa 2 (Hodgetts, Hunter) Warner; Coulton, Simmonds, Yates, Dawson, Burton, Davis, Albert Brown, Hunter, Vaughton, Hodgetts **WBA 0** Roberts; Green, Aldridge, Horton, Perry, Timmins, Woodhall, Green, Bayliss, Paddock, Pearson. April 2; 15, 500; Major Marindin

1888   WBA 2 (Bayliss), Woodhall) Roberts; Aldridge, Green, Horton, Perry, Timmins, Woodhall, Bassett, Bayliss, Wilson, Pearson **Preston 1** (Dewhurst) Mills-Roberts; Howarth, Holmes, Ross, Russell, Gordon, Ross, Goodall, Dewhurst, Drummond, Graham. March 24; 19, 000; Major Marindin

1889   Preston 3 (Dewhurst, Ross, Thomson) Mills-Roberts; Howarth, Holmes, Drummond, Russell, Graham, Gordon, Goodall, Dewhurst, Thompson, Ross **Wolves 0** Baynton; Baugh, Mason, Fletcher, Allen, Lowder, Hunter, Wykes, Brodie, Wood, Knight. March 30; 22, 000; Major Marindin

1890   Blackburn Rov 6 (Lofthouse, Jack Southworth, Walton, Townley 3) Horne; James Southworth, Forbes, Barton, Dewar, Forrest, Lofthouse, Campbell, Jack Southworth, Walton, Townley **Sheffield Wed 1** (Bennett) Smith; Morley, Brayshaw, Dungworth, Betts, Waller, Ingram, Woolhouse, Bennett, Mumford, Cawley. March 29; 20, 000; Major Marindin

1891   Blackburn Rov 3 (Dewar, Jack Southworth, Townley) Pennington; Brandon, Forbes, Barton, Dewar, Forrest, Lofthouse, Walton, Southworth, Hall, Townley **Notts Co 1** (Oswald) Thraves; Ferguson, Hendry, Osborne, Calderhead, Shelton, McGregror, McInnes Oswald, Locker, Daft. March 21; 23, 000; CJ Hughes

1892   WBA 3 (Geddes, Nicholls, Reynolds) Reader; Nicholson, McCulloch, Reynolds, Perry, Groves, Bassett, McLeod, Nicholls, Pearson, Geddes **Aston Villa 0** Warner; Evans, Cox, Devey, Cowan, Baird, Athersmith, Devey, Dickson, Hodgetts, Campbell. March 19; 32, 810; JC Clegg

1893   Wolves 1 (Allen) Rose; Baugh, Swift, Malpass, Allen, Kinsey, Topham, Wykes, Butcher, Griffin, Wood **Everton 0** Williams; Kelso, Howarth, Boyle, Holt, Stewart, Latta, Gordon, Maxwell, Chadwick, Milward. March 25; 45, 000; CJ Hughes

1894   Notts Co 4 (Watson, Logan 3) Toone; Harper, Hendry, Bramley, Calderhead, Shelton, Watson, Donnelly, Logan Bruce, Daft **Bolton 1** (Cassidy) Sutcliffe; Somerville, Jones , Gardiner, Paton, Hughes, Tannahill, Wilson, Cassidy, Bentley, Dickenson. March 31; 37, 000; CJ Hughes

1895   Aston Villa 1 (Chatt) Wilkes; Spencer, Welford, Reynolds, Cowan, Russell, Athersmith Chatt, Devey, Hodgetts, Smith **WBA 0** Reader; Williams, Horton, Perry, Higgins, Taggart, Bassett, McLeod, Richards, Hutchinson, Banks. April 20; 42, 560; J Lewis

1896   Sheffield Wed 2 (Spikesley 2) Massey; Earp, Langley, Brandon, Crawshaw, Petrie, Brash, Brady, Bell, Davis, Spikesley **Wolves 1** (Black) Tennant; Baugh, Dunn, Owen, Malpass, Griffiths, Tonks, Henderson, Beats, Wood, Black. April 18; 48, 836; Lieut Simpson

1897   Aston Villa 3 (Campbell, Wheldon, Crabtree) Whitehouse; Spencer, Reynolds, Evans, Cowan, Crabtree, Athersmith, Devey, Campbell, Wheldon, Cowan **Everton 2** (Bell, Boyle) Menham; Meechan, Storrier, Boyle, Holt, Stewart, Taylor, Bell, Hartley, Chadwick, Milward. April 10; 65, 891; J Lewis

1898   Nottm Forest 3 (Capes 2, McPherson) Allsop; Ritchie, Scott, Forman, McPherson, Wragg, McInnes, Richards, Benbow, Capes, Spouncer **Derby 1** (Bloomer) Fryer; Methven, Leiper, Cox, Goodall, Bloomer, Boag, Stevenson, McQueen. April 16; 62, 017; J Lewis

1899   Sheffield Utd 4 (Bennett, Beers, Almond, Priest) Foulke; Thickett, Boyle, Johnson, Morren, Needham, Bennett, Beers, Hedley, Almond, Priest **Derby 1** (Boag) Fryer; Methven, Staley, Cox, Paterson, May, Arkesden, Bloomer, Boag, McDonald, Allen. April 15; 73, 833; A Scragg

1900   Bury 4 (McLuckie 2, Wood, Plant) Thompson; Darroch, Davidson, Pray, Leeming, Ross, Richards,

Wood, McLuckie, Sagar, Plant **Southampton 0** Robinson; Meechan, Durber, Meston, Chadwick, Petrie, Turner, Yates, Farrell, Wood, Milward. April 21; 68, 945; A Kingscott

1901 Tottenham 2 (Brown 2) Clawley; Erentz, Tait, Morris, Hughes, Jones, Smith, Cameron, Brown, Copeland, Kirwan **Sheffield Utd 2** (Priest, Bennett) Foulke; Thickett, Boyle, Johnson, Morren, Needham, Bennett, Field, Hedley, Priest, Lipsham. April 20; 110, 820; A Kingscott **Replay – Tottenham 3** (Cameron, Smith, Brown) Clawley; Erentz, Tait, Morris, Hughes, Jones, Smith, Cameron, Brown, Copeland, Kirwan. **Sheffield Utd 1** (Priest) Foulke; Thickett, Boyle, Johnson, Morren, Needham, Bennett, Field, Hedley, Priest, Lipsham. April 27; 20, 470; A Kingscott

1902 Sheffield Utd 1 (Common) Foulke; Thickett, Boyle, Needham, Wilkinson, Johnson, Bennett, Common, Hedley, Priest, Lipsham **Southampton 1** (Wood) Robinson; Fry, Molyneux, Meston, Bowman, Lee, Turner, Wood Brown, Chadwick, Turner. April 19; 76, 914; T Kirkham. **Replay – Sheffield Utd 2** (Hedley, Barnes) Foulke; Thickett, Boyle, Needham, Wilkinson, Johnson, Barnes, Common, Hedley, Priest, Lipsham **Southampton 1** (Brown) Robinson; Fry, Molyneux, Meston, Bowman, Lee, Turner, Wood, Brown, Chadwick, Turner. April 26; 33, 068; T Kirkham

1903 Bury 6 (Leeming 2, Ross, Sagar, Wood, Plant) Monteith; Lindsey, McEwen, Johnston, Thorpe, Ross, Richards, Wood, Sagar Leeming, Plant **Derby 0** Fryer; Methven, Morris, Warren, Goodall, May, Warrington, York, Boag, Richards, Davis. April 18; 63, 102; J Adams

1904 Manchester City 1 (Meredith) Hillman; McMahon, Burgess, Frost, Hynds, Ashworth, Meredith, Livingstone, Gillespie, Turnbull, Booth **Bolton 0** Davies; Brown, Struthers, Clifford, Greenhalgh, Freebairn, Stokes, Marsh, Yenson, White, Taylor. April 23; 61, 374; AJ Barker

1905 Aston Villa 2 (Hampton 2) George; Spencer, Miles, Pearson, Leake, Windmill, Brawn, Garratty, Hampton, Bache, Hall **Newcastle 0** Lawrence; McCombie, Carr, Gardner, Aitken, McWilliam, Rutherford, Howie, Appleyard, Veitch, Gosnell. April 15; 101, 117; PR Harrower

1906 Everton 1 (Young) Scott; Crelley, Walter Balmer, Makepeace, Taylor, Abbott, Sharp, Bolton, Young, Settle, Hardman **Newcastle 0** Lawrence; McCombie, Carr, Gardner, Aitken, McWilliam, Rutherford, Howie, Orr, Veitch, Gosnell. April 21; 75, 609; F Kirkham

1907 Sheffield Wed 2 (Stewart, Simpson) Lyall; Layton, Burton, Brittleton, Crawshaw, Bartlett, Chapman, Bradshaw, Wilson, Stewart, Simpson **Everton 1** (Sharp) Scott; Walter Balmer, Bob Balmer, Makepeace, Taylor, Abbott, Sharp, Bolton, Young, Settle, Hardman. April 20; 84, 594; N Whittaker

1908 Wolves 3 (Hunt, Hedley, Harrison) Lunn; Jones, Collins, Rev Hunt, Wooldridge, Bishop, Harrison, Shelton, Hedley, Radford, Pedley **Newcastle 1** (Howie) Lawrence; McCracken, Pudan, Gardner, Veitch, McWilliam, Rutherford, Howie, Appleyard, Speedie, Wilson. April 25; 74, 697; TP Campbell

1909 Manchester Utd 1 (Sandy Turnbull) Moger; Stacey, Hayes, Duckworth, Roberts, Bell, Meredith, Halse, J Turnbull, S Turnbull, Wall **Bristol City 0** Clay; Annan, Cottle, Hanlin, Wedlock, Spear, Staniforth, Hardy, Gilligan, Burton, Hilton. April 24; 71, 401; J Mason

1910 Newcastle 1 (Rutherford) Lawrence; McCracken, Whitson, Veitch, Low, McWilliam, Rutherford, Howie, Higgins, Shepherd, Wilson **Barnsley 1** (Tufnell) Mearns; Downs, Ness, Glendinning, Boyle, Utley, Tufnell, Lillycrop, Gadsby, Forman, Bartrop. April 23; 77, 747; JT Ibbotson **Replay – Newcastle 2** (Shepherd 2, 1pen) Lawrence; McCracken, Carr, Veitch, Low, McWilliam, Rutherford, Howie, Higgins, Shepherd, Wilson **Barnsley 0** Mearns; Downs, Ness, Glendinning, Boyle, Utley, Tufnell, Lillycrop, Gadsby, Forman, Bartrop. April 28; 69, 000; JT Ibbotson

1911 Bradford City 0 Mellors; Campbell, Taylor, Robinson, Gildea, McDonald, Logan, Speirs, O'Rourke, Devine, Thompson **Newcastle 0** Lawrence; McCracken, Whitson, Veitch, Low, Willis, Rutherford, Jobey, Stewart, Higgins, Wilson. April 22; 69, 068; JH Pearson **Replay – Bradford City 1** (Speirs) Mellors; Campbell, Taylor, Robinson, Torrance, McDonald, Logan, Speirs, O'Rourke, Devine, Thompson **Newcastle 0** Lawrence; McCracken, Whitson, Veitch, Low, Willis, Rutherford, Jobey, Stewart, Higgins, Wilson. April 26; 58, 000; JH Pearson

1912 Barnsley 0 Cooper; Downs, Taylor, Glendinning, Bratley, Utley, Bartrop, Tufnell, Lillycrop, Travers, Moore **WBA 0** Pearson; Cook, Pennington, Baddeley, Buck, McNeal, Jephcott, Wright, Pailor, Bowser, Shearman. April 20; 54, 556; JR Shumacher **Replay – Barnsley 1** (Tufnell) Cooper; Downs, Taylor, Glendinning, Bratley, Utley, Bartrop, Harry, Lillycrop, Travers, Jimmy Moore **WBA 0** Pearson; Cook, Pennington, Baddeley, Buck, McNeal, Jephcott, Wright, Pailor, Bowser, Shearman. April 24; 38, 555; JR Schumacher. aet

1913 Aston Villa 1 (Barber) Hardy; Lyons, Weston, Barber, Harrop, Leach, Wallace, Halse, Hampton, Stephenson, Bache **Sunderland 0** Butler; Gladwin, Ness, Cuggy, Thomson, Low, Mordue, Buchan,

Richardson, Holley, Martin. April 19; 120, 081; A Adams

1914 **Burnley 1** (Freeman) Sewell; Bamford, Taylor, Halley, Boyle, Watson, Nesbit, Lindley, Freeman, Hodgson, Mosscrop **Liverpool 0** Campbell; Longworth, Pursell, Fairfoul, Ferguson, McKinley, Sheldon, Metcalfe, Miller, Lacey, Nicholl. April 25; 72, 778; HS Bamlett

1915 **Sheffield Utd 3** (Simmons, Fazackerly, Kitchen) Gough; Cook, English, Sturgess, Brelsford, Utley, Simmons, Fazackerly, Kitchen, Masterman, Evans **Chelsea 0** Molyneux; Bettridge, Harrow, Taylor, Logan, Walker, Ford, Halse, Thomson, Croal, McNeil. April 24; 49, 557; HH Taylor

1920 **Aston Villa 1** (Kirton) Hardy; Smart, Weston, Ducat, Barson, Moss, Wallace, Kirton, Walker, Stephenson, Dorrell **Huddersfield 0** Mutch; Wood, Bullock, Slade, Wilson, Watson, Richardson, Mann, Taylor, Swann, Islip. April 24; 50, 018; JT Howcroft. aet

1921 **Tottenham 1** (Dimmock) Hunter; Clay, McDonald, Smith, Walters, Grimsdell, Banks, Seed, Cantrell, Bliss, Dimmock **Wolves 0** George; Woodward, Marshall, Gregory, Hodnett, Riley, Lea, Burrill, Edmonds, Potts, Brooks. April 23; 72, 805; S Davies

1922 **Huddersfield 1** (Smith pen) Mutch; Wood, Wadsworth, Slade, Wilson, Watson, Richardson, Mann, Islip, Stephenson, Billy Smith **Preston 0** Mitchell; Hamilton, Doolan, Duxbury, McCall, Williamson, Rawlings, Jefferis, Roberts, Woodhouse, Quinn. April 29; 53, 000; JWP Fowler

1923 **Bolton 2** (Jack, JR Smith) Pym; Haworth, Finney, Nuttall, Seddon, Jennings, Butler, Jack, JR Smith, Joe Smith, Vizard **West Ham 0** Hufton; Henderson, Young, Bishop, Kay, Tresadern, Richards, Brown, Watson, Moore, Ruffell. April 28; 126, 047; DH Asson

1924 **Newcastle 2** (Harris, Seymour) Bradley; Hampson, Hudspeth, Mooney, Spencer, Gibson, Low, Cowan, Harris, McDonald, Seymour **Aston Villa 0** Jackson; Smart, Mort, Moss, Milne, Blackburn, York, Kirton, Capewell, Walker, Dorrell. April 26; 91, 695; WE Russell

1925 **Sheffield Utd 1** (Tunstall) Sutcliffe; Cook, Milton, Pantling, King, Green, Mercer, Boyle, Johnson, Gillespie, Tunstall **Cardiff 0** Farquharson; Nelson, Blair, Wake, Keenor, Hardy, Davies, Gill, Nicholson, Beadles, Evans. April 25; 91, 763; GN Watson

1926 **Bolton 1** (Jack) Pym; Haworth, Greenhalgh, Nuttall, Seddon, Jennings, Butler, JR Smith, Jack, Joe Smith, Vizard **Manchester City 0** Goodchild; Cookson, McCloy, Pringle, Cowan, McMullan, Austin, Browell, Roberts, Johnson, Hicks. April 24; 91, 447; I Baker

1927 **Cardiff 1** (Ferguson) Farquharson; Nelson, Watson, Keenor, Sloan, Hardy, Curtis, Irving, Ferguson, Davies, McLachlan **Arsenal 0** Lewis; Parker, Kennedy, Baker, Butler, John, Hulme, Buchan, Brain, Blythe, Hoar. April 23; 91, 206; WF Bunnell

1928 **Blackburn 3** (Roscamp 2, McLean) Crawford; Hutton, Jones, Healless, Rankin, Campbell, Thornewell, Puddefoot, Roscamp, McLean, Rigby **Huddersfield 1** (Jackson) Mercer; Goodall, Barkas, Redfern, Wilson, Steele, Jackson, Kelly, Brown, Stephenson, Smith. April 21; 92, 041; TG Bryan

1929 **Bolton 2** (Butler, Blackmore) Pym; Haworth, Finney, Kean, Seddon, Nuttall, Butler, McClelland, Blackmore, Gibson, Cook **Portsmouth 0** Gilfillan; Mackie, Bell, Nichol, McIlwaine, Thackeray, Forward, Smith, Weddle, Watson, Cook. April 27; 92, 576; A Josephs

1930 **Arsenal 2** (James, Lambert) Preedy; Parker, Hapgood, Baker, Seddon, John, Hulme, Jack, Lambert, James, Bastin **Huddersfield 0** Turner; Goodall, Spence, Naylor, Wilson, Campbell, Jackson, Kelly, Davies, Raw, Smith. April 26; 92, 488; T Crew

1931 **WBA 2** (WG Richardson 2) Pearson; Shaw, Trentham, Magee, Bill Richardson, Edwards, Glidden, Carter, WG Richardson, Sandford, Wood **Birmingham 1** (Bradford) Hibbs; Liddell, Barkas, Cringan, Morrall, Leslie, Briggs, Crosbie, Bradford, Gregg, Curtis. April 25; 92, 406; AH Kingscott

1932 **Newcastle 2** (Allen 2) McInroy; Nelson, Fairhurst, McKenzie, Davidson, Weaver, Boyd, Richardson, Allen, McMenemy, Lang **Arsenal 1** (John) Moss; Parker, Hapgood, Jones, Roberts, Male, Hulme, Jack, Lambert, Bastin, John. April 23; 92, 298; WP Harper

1933 **Everton 3** (Stein, Dean, Dunn) Sagar; Cook, Cresswell, Britton, White, Thomson, Geldard, Dunn, Dean, Johnson, Stein **Manchester City 0** Langford; Cann, Dale, Busby, Cowan, Bray, Toseland, Marshall, Herd, McMullan, Eric Brook. April 29; 92, 950; E Wood

148

1934 **Manchester City 2** (Tilson 2) Swift; Barnett, Dale, Busby, Cowan, Bray, Toseland, Marshall, Tilson, Herd, Brook **Portsmouth 1** (Rutherford) Gilfillan; Mackie, Smith, Nichol, Allen, Thackeray, Worrall, Smith, Weddle, Easson, Rutherford. April 28; 93, 258; Stanley Rous

1935 **Sheffield Wed 4** (Rimmer 2, Palethorpe, Hooper) Brown; Nibloe, Catlin, Sharp, Millership, Burrows, Hooper, Surtees, Palethorpe, Starling, Rimmer **WBA 2** (Boyes, Sandford) Pearson; Shaw, Trentham, Murphy, Bill Richardson, Edwards, Glidden, Carter, WG Richardson, Sandford, Wally. April 27; 93, 204; AE Fogg

1936 **Arsenal 1** (Drake) Wilson; Male, Hapgood, Crayston, Roberts, Copping, Hulme, Bowden, Drake, James, Bastin **Sheffield Utd 0** Smith; Hooper, Wilkinson, Jackson, Johnson, McPherson, Barton, Barclay, Dodds, Pickering, Williams. April 25; 93, 384; H Nattrass

1937 **Sunderland 3** (Gurney, Carter, Burbanks) Mapson; Gorman, Hall, Thomson, Johnston, McNab, Duns, Carter, Gurney, Gallacher, Burbanks **Preston 1** (Frank O'Donnell) Burns; Gallimore, Andy Beattie, Shankly, Tremelling, Milne, Dougal, Beresford, Frank O'Donnell, Fagan, Hugh O'Donnell. May 1; 93, 495; RG Rudd

1938 **Preston 1** (Mutch pen) Holdcroft; Gallimore, Andy Beattie, Shankly, Smith, Batey, Watmough, Mutch, Maxwell, Bob Beattie, Hugh O'Donnell **Huddersfield 0** Hesford; Craig, Mountford, Willingham, Young, Boot, Hulme, Issac, MacFadyen, Barclay, Beasley. April 30; 93, 497; AJ Jewell. aet

1939 **Portsmouth 4** (Parker 2, Barlow, Anderson) Walker; Morgan, Rochford, Guthrie, Rowe, Wharton, Worrall, McAlinden, Anderson, Barlow, Parker **Wolves 1** (Dorsett) Scott; Morris, Taylor, Galley, Cullis, Gardiner, Burton, McIntosh, Westcott, Dorsett, Maguire. April 29; 99, 370; T Thompson

1946 **Derby 4** (Stamps 2. Doherty, Bert Turner og) Woodley; Nicholas, Howe, Bullions, Leuty, Musson, Harrison, Carter, Stamps, Doherty, Duncan **Charlton Athletic 1** (Bert Turner) Bartram; Phipps, Shreeve, Bert Turner, Oakes, Johnson, Fell, Brown, Arthur Turner, Welsh, Duffy. April 27; 98, 000; ED Smith. aet

1947 **Charlton Athletic 1** (Duffy) Bartram; Croker, Shreeve, Johnson, Phipps, Whittaker, Hurst, Dawson, Robinson, Welsh, Duffy **Burnley 0** Strong; Woodruff, Mather, Attwell, Brown, Bray, Chew, Morris, Harrison, Potts, Kippax. April 26; 99, 000; JM Wiltshire. aet

1948 **Manchester Utd 4** (Rowley 2, Pearson, Anderson) Crompton; Carey, Aston, Anderson, Chilton, Cockburn, Delaney, Morris, Rowley, Pearson, Mitten **Blackpool 2** (Shimwell pen, Mortensen) Robinson; Shimwell, Crosland, Johnston, Hayward, Kelly, Matthews, Munro, Mortensen, Dick, Rickett. April 24; 99, 000; CJ Barrick

1949 **Wolves 3** (Pye 2, Smyth) Williams; Pritchard, Springthorpe Crook, Shorthouse, Wright, Hancocks, Smyth, Pye, Dunn, Mullen **Leicester 1** (Griffiths) Bradley; Jelly, Scott, Walter Harrison, Plummer, King, Griffiths, Lee, Jimmy Harrison, Chisholm, Adam. April 30; 99, 500; RA Mortimer

1950 **Arsenal 2** (Lewis 2) Swindin; Scott, Barnes, Forbes, Les Compton, Mercer, Cox, Logie, Goring, Lewis, Denis Compton **Liverpool 0** Sidlow; Lambert, Spicer, Taylor, Hughes, Jones, Payne, Baron, Stubbins, Fagan, Liddell. April 29; 100, 000; H Pearce

1951 **Newcastle 2** (Milburn 2) Fairbrother; Cowell, Corbett, Harvey, Brennan, Crowe, Walker, Taylor, Milburn, Jorge Robledo, Mitchell **Blackpool 0** Farm; Shimwell, Garrett, Johnston, Hayward, Kelly, Matthews, Mudie, Mortensen, Slater, Perry. April 28; 100, 000; W Ling

1952 **Newcastle 1** (George Robledo) Simpson; Cowell, McMichael, Harvey, Brennan, Ted Robledo, Walker, Foulkes, Milburn, George Robledo, Mitchell **Arsenal 0** Swindin; Barnes, Smith, Forbes, Daniel Mercer, Cox, Logie, Holton, Lishman, Roper. May 3; 100, 000; A Ellis

1953 **Blackpool 4** (Mortensen 3, Perry) Farm; Shimwell, Garrett, Fenton, Johnston, Robinson, Matthews, Taylor, Mortensen, Mudie, Perry **Bolton 3** (Lofthouse, Moir, Bell) Hanson; Ball, Ralph Banks, Wheeler, Barrass, Bell, Holden, Moir, Lofthouse, Hassall, Langton. May 2; 100, 000; M Griffiths

1954 **WBA 3** (Allen 2 [1pen], Griffin) Sanders; Kennedy, Millard, Dudley, Dugdale, Barlow, Griffin, Ryan, Allen, Nicholls, Lee **Preston 2** (Morrison, Wayman) Thompson; Cunningham, Walton, Docherty, Marston, Forbes, Finney, Foster, Wayman, Baxter, Morrison. May 1; 100, 000; A Luty

1955 **Newcastle 3** (Milburn, Mitchell, Hannah) Simpson; Cowell, Batty, Scoular, Stokoe, Casey, White, Milburn, Keeble, Hannah, Mitchell **Manchester City 1** (Johnstone) Trautmann; Meadows, Little, Barnes, Ewing, Paul, Spurdle, Hayes, Revie, Johnstone, Fagan. May 7; 100, 000; R Leafe

1956 **Manchester City 3** (Hayes, Dyson, Johnstone) Trautmann; Leivers, Little, Barnes, Ewing, Paul, Johnstone, Hayes, Revie, Dyson, Clarke **Birmingham 1** (Kinsey) Merrick; Hall, Green, Newman, Smith, Boyd, Astall, Kinsey, Brown, Murphy, Govan. May 5; 100, 000; A Bond

1957 **Aston Villa 2** (McParland 2) Sims; Lynn, Aldis, Crowther, Dugdale, Saward, Smith, Sewell, Myerscough, Dixon, McParland **Manchester Utd 1** (Tommy Taylor) Wood; Foulkes, Byrne, Colman, Blanchflower, Edwards, Berry, Whelan, Tommy Taylor, Charlton, Pegg. May 4; 100, 000; F Coultas

1958 **Bolton 2** (Lofthouse 2) Hopkinson; Hartle, Tommy Banks, Hennin, Higgins, Edwards, Birch, Stevens, Lofthouse, Parry, Holden **Manchester Utd 0** Gregg; Foulkes, Greaves, Goodwin, Cope, Crowther, Dawson, Ernie Taylor, Charlton, Viollet, Webster. May 3; 100, 000; J Sherlock

1959 **Nottingham Forest 2** (Dwight, Wilson) Thomson; Whare, McDonald, Whitefoot, McKinlay, Burkitt, Dwight, Quigley, Wilson, Gray, Imlach **Luton Town 1** (Pacey) Baynham; McNally, Hawkes, Groves, Owen, Pacey, Bingham, Brown, Morton, Cummins, Gregory. May 2; 100, 000; J Clough

1960 **Wolves 3** (McGrath og, Deeley 2) Finlayson; Showell, Harris, Clamp, Slater, Flowers, Deeley, Stobart, Murray, Broadbent, Horne **Blackburn 0** Leyland; Bray, Whelan, Clayton, Woods, McGrath, Bimpson, Dobing, Dougan, Douglas, McLeod. May 7; 100, 000; K Howley

1961 **Tottenham 2** (Smith, Dyson) Brown; Baker, Henry, Blanchflower, Norman, Mackay, Jones, White, Smith, Allen, Dyson **Leicester 0** Banks; Chalmers, Norman, McLintock, King, Appleton, Riley, Walsh, McIlmoyle, Keyworth, Cheesebrough. May 6; 100, 000; J Kelly

1962 **Tottenham 3** (Greaves, Smith, Blanchflower pen) Brown; Baker, Henry, Blanchflower, Norman, Mackay, Medwin, White, Smith, Greaves, Jones **Burnley 1** (Robson) Blacklaw; Angus, Elder, Adamson, Cummings, Miller, Connelly, McIlroy, Pointer, Robson, Harris. May 5; 100, 000; J Finney

1963 **Manchester Utd 3** (Law, Herd 2) Gaskell; Dunne, Cantwell, Crerand, Foulkes, Setters, Giles, Quixall, Herd, Law, Charlton **Leicester 1** (Keyworth) Banks; Sjoberg, Norman, McLintock, King, Appleton, Riley, Cross, Keyworth, Gibson, Stringfellow. May 25; 100, 000; K Aston

1964 **West Ham 3** (Sissons, Hurst, Boyce) Standen; Bond, Burkett, Bovington, Brown, Moore, Brabrook, Boyce, Byrne, Hurst, Sissons **Preston 2** (Holden, Dawson) Kelly; Ross, Lawton, Smith, Singleton, Kendall, Wilson, Ashworth, Dawson, Spavin, Holden. May 2; 100, 000; A Holland

1965 **Liverpool 2** (Hunt, St John) Lawrence; Lawler, Byrne, Strong, Yeats, Stevenson, Callaghan, Hunt, St John, Smith, Thompson **Leeds 1** (Bremner) Sprake; Reaney, Bell, Bremner, Charlton, Hunter, Giles, Storrie, Peacock, Collins, Johanneson. May 1; 100, 000; W Clements. aet

1966 **Everton 3** (Trebilcock 2, Temple) West; Wright, Wilson, Gabriel, Labone, Harris, Scott, Trebilcock, Young, Harvey, Temple **Sheffield Wed 2** (McCalliog, Ford) Springett; Smith, Megson, Eustace, Ellis, Young, Pugh, Fantham, McCalliog, Ford, Quinn. May 14; 100, 000; JK Taylor

1967 **Tottenham 2** (Robertson, Saul) Jennings; Kinnear, Knowles, Mullery, England, Mackay, Robertson, Greaves, Gilzean, Venables, Saul. Unused sub: Jones **Chelsea 1** (Tambling) Bonetti; Allan Harris, McCreadie, Hollins, Hinton, Ron Harris, Cooke, Baldwin, Hateley, Tambling, Boyle. Unused sub: Kirkup. May 20; 100, 000; K Dagnall

1968 **WBA 1** (Astle) Osborne; Fraser, Williams, Brown, Talbut, Kaye, Lovett, Collard, Astle Hope, Clark Sub: Clarke rep Kaye 91 **Everton 0** West; Wright, Wilson, Kendall, Labone, Harvey, Husband, Ball, Royle, Hurst, Morrissey. Unused sub: Kenyon. May 18; 100, 000; L Callaghan. aet

1969 **Manchester City 1** (Young) Dowd: Book, Pardoe, Doyle, Booth, Oakes, Summerbee, Bell, Lee, Young, Coleman. Unused sub: Connor **Leicester 0** Shilton; Rodrigues, Nish, Roberts, Woollett, Cross, Fern, Gibson, Lochhead, Clarke, Glover. Sub: Manley rep Glover 70. April 26; 100, 000; G McCabe

1970 **Chelsea 2** (Houseman, Hutchinson) Bonetti; Webb, McCreadie, Hollins, Dempsey, Ron Harris, Baldwin, Houseman, Osgood, Hutchinson, Cooke. Sub: Hinton rep Harris 91 **Leeds 2** (Charlton, Jones) Sprake; Madeley, Cooper, Bremner, Charlton, Hunter, Lorimer, Clarke, Jones, Giles, Gray Unused sub: Bates. April 11; 100, 000; E Jennings. aet **Replay – Chelsea 2** (Osgood, Webb) Bonetti; Webb, McCreadie, Hollins, Dempsey, Ron Harris, Baldwin, Houseman, Osgood, Hutchinson, Cooke. Sub: Hinton rep Osgood 105 **Leeds 1** (Jones) Harvey; Madeley, Cooper, Bremner, Charlton, Hunter, Lorimer, Clarke, Jones, Giles, Gray Unusued sub: Bates. April 29; 62, 078; E Jennings. aet

1971 Arsenal 2 (Kelly, George) Wilson; Rice, McNab, Storey, McLintock Simpson, Armstrong, Graham, Radford, Kennedy, George. Sub: Kelly rep Storey 70 **Liverpool 1** (Heighway) Clemence; Lawler, Lindsay, Smith, Lloyd, Hughes, Callaghan, Evans, Heighway, Toshack, Hall. Sub: Thompson rep Evans 70. May 8; 100, 000; N Burtenshaw. aet

1972 Leeds 1 (Clarke) Harvey; Reaney, Madeley, Bremner, Charlton, Hunter, Lorimer, Clarke, Jones, Giles, Gray. Unused sub: Bates **Arsenal 0** Barnett; Rice, McNab, Storey, McLintock, Simpson, Armstrong, Ball, George, Radford, Graham. Sub: Kennedy rep Radford 80. May 6; 100, 000; DW Smith

1973 Sunderland 1 (Porterfield) Montgomery; Malone, Guthrie, Horswill, Watson, Pitt, Kerr, Hughes, Halom, Porterfield, Tueart. Unused sub: Young **Leeds 0** Harvey; Reaney, Cherry, Bremner, Madeley, Hunter, Lorimer, Clarke, Jones, Giles, Gray. Sub: Yorath rep Gray 75. May 5; 100, 000; K Burns

1974 Liverpool 3 (Keegan 2, Heighway) Clemence; Smith, Lindsay, Thompson, Cormack, Hughes, Keegan, Hall, Heighway, Toshack, Callaghan. Unused sub: Lawler **Newcastle 0** McFaul; Clark, Kennedy, McDermott, Howard, Moncur, Smith, Cassidy, Macdonald, Tudor, Hibbitt. Sub: Gibb rep Smith 70. May 4; 100, 000; GC Kew

1975 West Ham 2 (Alan Taylor 2) Day; McDowell, Tommy Taylor, Lock, Lampard, Bonds, Paddon, Brooking, Jennings, Alan Taylor, Holland. Unused sub: Gould **Fulham 0** Mellor; Cutbush, Lacy, Moore, Fraser, Mullery, Conway, Slough, Mitchell, Busby, Barrett. Unused sub: Lloyd. May 3; 100, 000; P Partridge

1976 Southampton 1 (Stokes) Turner; Rodrigues, Peach, Holmes, Blyth, Steele, Gilchrist, Channon, Osgood, McCalliog, Stokes. Unused sub: Fisher **Manchester Utd 0** Stepney; Forsyth, Houston, Daly, Brian Greenhoff, Buchan, Coppell, McIlroy, Pearson, Macari, Hill. Sub: McCreery rep Hill 66. May 1; 100, 000; C Thomas

1977 Manchester Utd 2 (Pearson, J Greenhoff) Stepney; Nicholl, Albiston, McIlroy, Brian Greenhoff, Buchan, Coppell, Jimmy Greenhoff, Pearson, Macari, Hill. Sub: McCreery rep Hill 81 **Liverpool 1** (Case) Clemence; Neal, Jones, Smith, Kennedy, Hughes, Keegan, Case, Heighway, Johnson, McDermott. Sub: Callaghan rep Johnson 64. May 21; 100, 000; R Matthewson

1978 Ipswich Town 1 (Osborne) Cooper; Burley, Mills, Talbot, Hunter, Beattie, Osborne, Wark, Mariner, Geddis, Woods. Sub: Lambert rep Osborne 79 **Arsenal 0** Jennings; Rice, Nelson, Price, Young, O'Leary, Brady, Hudson, Macdonald, Stapleton, Sunderland. Sub: Rix rep Brady 65. May 6; 100, 000; D Nippard

1979 Arsenal 3 (Talbot, Stapleton, Sunderland) Jennings; Rice, Nelson, Talbot, O'Leary, Young, Brady, Sunderland, Stapleton, Price, Rix. Sub: Walford rep Rix 83 **Manchester Utd 2** (McQueen, McIlroy) Bailey; Nicholl, Albiston, McIlroy, McQueen, Buchan, Coppell, Jimmy Greenhoff, Jordan, Macari, Thomas. Unused sub: Brian Greenhoff. May 12; 100, 000; R Challis

1980 West Ham 1 (Brooking) Parkes; Stewart, Lampard, Bonds, Martin, Devonshire, Allen, Pearson, Cross, Brooking, Pike. Unused sub: Brush **Arsenal 0** Jennings; Rice, Devine, Talbot, O'Leary, Young, Brady, Sunderland, Stapleton, Price, Rix. Sub: Nelson rep Devine 61. May 10; 100, 000; G Courtney

1981 Tottenham 1 (Hutchison og) Aleksic; Hughton, Miller, Roberts, Perryman, Villa, Ardiles, Archibald, Galvin, Hoddle, Crooks. Sub: Brooke rep Villa 68. **Manchester City 1** (Hutchison) Corrigan; Ranson, McDonald, Reid, Power, Caton, Bennett, Gow, Mackenzie, Hutchison Reeves. Sub: Henry rep Hutchison 82. May 9; 100, 000; K Hackett. aet Replay – **Tottenham 3** (Villa 2, Crooks) Aleksic; Hughton, Miller, Roberts, Perryman, Villa, Ardiles, Archibald, Galvin, Hoddle, Crooks. Unused sub: Brooke **Manchester City 2** (Mackenzie, Reeves pen) Corrigan; Ranson, McDonald, Reid, Power, Caton, Bennett, Gow, Mackenzie, Hutchison Reeves. Sub: Tueart rep McDonald 79. May 14; 92, 000; K Hackett

1982 Tottenham 1 (Hoddle) Clemence; Hughton, Miller, Price, Hazard, Perryman, Roberts, Archibald, Galvin, Hoddle, Crooks. Sub: Brooke rep Hazard 104 **Queens Park Rangers 1** (Fenwick) Hucker; Fenwick, Gillard, Waddock, Hazell, Roeder, Currie, Flanagan, Allen, Stainrod, Gregory. Sub: Micklewhite rep Allen 50. May 22; 100, 000; C White. aet Replay – **Tottenham 1** (Hoddle pen) Clemence; Hughton, Miller, Price, Hazard, Perryman, Roberts, Archibald, Galvin, Hoddle, Crooks. Sub: Brooke rep Hazard 67 **Queens Park Rangers 0** Hucker; Fenwick, Gillard, Waddock, Hazell, Neill, Currie, Flanagan, Micklewhite, Stainrod, Gregory. Sub: Burke rep Micklewhite 84. May 27; 90, 000; C White

1983 Manchester Utd 2 (Stapleton, Wilkins) Bailey; Duxbury, Moran, McQueen, Albiston, Davies, Wilkins, Robson, Muhren, Stapleton, Whiteside. Unused sub: Grimes **Brighton 2** (Smith, Stevens) Moseley; Ramsey, Gary A Stevens, Pearce, Gatting, Smillie, Case, Grealish, Howlett, Robinson, Smith. Sub: Ryan rep Ramsey 56. May 21; 100, 000; AW Grey, aet **Replay – Manchester Utd 4** (Robson 2, Whiteside, Muhren pen) Bailey; Duxbury, Moran, McQueen, Albiston, Davies, Wilkins, Robson, Muhren, Stapleton, Whiteside. Unused sub: Grimes **Brighton 0** Moseley; Gary A Stevens, Pearce, Foster, Gatting, Smillie, Case, Grealish, Howlett, Robinson, Smith. Sub: Ryan rep Howlett 74. May 26; 100, 000; AW Grey

1984 **Everton 2** (Sharp, Gray) Southall; Gary M Stevens, Bailey, Ratcliffe, Mountfield, Reid, Steven, Heath, Sharp, Gray, Richardson. Unused sub: Harper **Watford 0** Sherwood; Bardsley, Price, Taylor, Terry, Sinnott, Callaghan, Johnston, Reilly, Jackett, Barnes. Sub: Atkinson rep Price 58. May 19; 100, 000; J Hunting

1985 **Manchester Utd 1** (Whiteside) Bailey; Gidman, Albiston, Whiteside, McGrath, Moran, Robson, Strachan, Hughes, Stapleton, Olsen. Sub: Duxbury rep Albiston 91. Moran sent off 77. **Everton 0** Southall; Gary M Stevens, Van den Hauwe, Ratcliffe, Mountfield, Reid, Steven, Sharp, Gray, Bracewell, Sheedy. Unused sub: Harper. May 18; 100, 000; P Willis. aet

1986 **Liverpool 3** (Rush 2, Johnston) Grobbelaar; Lawrenson, Beglin, Nicol, Whelan, Hansen, Dalglish, Johnston, Rush, Molby, MacDonald. Unused sub: McMahon **Everton 1** (Lineker) Mimms; Gary M Stevens, Van den Hauwe, Ratcliffe, Mountfield, Reid, Steven, Lineker, Sharp, Bracewell, Sheedy. Sub: Heath rep Stevens 65. May 10; 98, 000; A Robinson

1987 **Coventry City 3** (Bennett, Houchen, Mabbutt og) Ogrizovic; Phillips, Downs, McGrath, Kilcline, Peake, Bennett, Gynn, Regis, Houchen, Pickering. Sub: Rodger rep Kilcline 88. Unused sub: Sedgley **Tottenham 2** (Clive Allen, Mabbutt) Clemence; Hughton Thomas, Hodge, Gough, Mabbutt, Clive Allen, Paul Allen, Waddle, Hoddle, Ardiles. Subs: Gary A Stevens rep Ardiles 91; Claesen rep Hughton 97. May 16; 98, 000; N Midgley. aet

1988 **Wimbledon 1** (Sanchez) Beasant; Goodyear, Phelan, Jones, Young, Thorn, Gibson Cork, Fashanu, Sanchez, Wise. Subs: Cunningham rep Cork 56; Scales rep Gibson 63 **Liverpool 0** Grobbelaar; Gillespie, Ablett, Nicol, Spackman, Hansen, Beardsley, Aldridge, Houghton, Barnes, McMahon. Subs: Johnston rep Aldridge 63; Molby rep Spackman 72. May 14; 98, 203; B Hill

1989 **Liverpool 3** (Aldridge, Rush 2) Grobbelaar; Ablett, Staunton, Nichol, Whelan, Hansen, Beardsley, Aldridge Houghton, Barnes, McMahon. Subs: Rush rep Aldridge 72; Venison rep Staunton 93. **Everton 2** (McCall 2) Southall; McDonald, Van den Hauwe, Ratcliffe, Watson, Bracewell, Nevin, Steven, Cottee, Sharp, Sheedy. Subs: McCall rep Bracewell 58; Wilson rep Sheedy 77. May 20; 82, 500; J Worrall. aet

1990 **Manchester Utd 3** (Robson, Hughes 2) Leighton; Ince, Martin, Bruce, Phelan, Pallister, Robson, Webb, McClair, Hughes, Wallace. Subs: Blackmore rep Martin 88; Robins rep Pallister 93. **Crystal Palace 3** (O'Reilly, Wright 2) Martyn; Pemberton, Shaw, Gray, O'Reilly, Thorn, Barber, Thomas, Bright, Salako, Pardew. Subs: Wright rep Barber 69; Madden rep Gray 117. May 12; 80, 000; A Gunn. aet **Replay – Manchester Utd 1** (Martin) Sealey; Ince, Martin, Bruce, Phelan, Pallister, Robson, Webb, McClair, Hughes, Wallace. Unused subs: Robins, Blackmore **Crystal Palace 0** Martyn; Pemberton, Shaw, Gray, O'Reilly, Thorn, Barber, Thomas, Bright, Salako, Pardew. Subs: Wright rep Barber 64; Madden rep Salako 79. May 17; 80, 000; A Gunn

1991 **Tottenham 2** (Stewart, Walker og) Thorstvedt; Edinburgh, Van den Hauwe, Sedgley, Howells, Mabbutt, Stewart, Gascoigne, Samways, Lineker, Paul Allen. Subs: Nayim rep Gascoigne 18; Walsh rep Samways 82. **Nottingham Forest 1** (Pearce) Crossley; Charles, Pearce, Walker, Chettle, Keane, Crosby, Parker, Clough, Glover, Woan. Subs: Hodge rep Woan 62; Laws rep Glover 108. May 18; 80, 000; R Milford. aet

1992 **Liverpool 2** (Thomas, Rush) Grobbelaar; Jones, Burrows, Nicol, Molby, Wright, Saunders, Houghton, Rush, McManaman, Thomas. Subs: Marsh, Walters **Sunderland 0** Norman; Owers, Ball, Bennett, Rogan, Rush, Bracewell, Davenport, Armstrong, Byrne, Atkinson. Subs: Hardyman rep Rush 69; Hawke rep Armstrong 77. May 9; 80, 000; P Don

1993 **Arsenal 1** (Wright) Seaman; Dixon, Winterburn, Linighan, Adams, Jensen, Davis, Parlour, Merson, Campbell, Wright. Subs: Smith rep Parlour 66; O'Leary rep Wright 90. **Sheffield Wed 1** (Hirst) Woods; Nilsson Worthington, Palmer, Hirst, Anderson, Waddle, Warhurst, Bright, Sheridan, Harkes. Subs: Hyde rep Anderson 85; Bart-Williams rep Waddle 112. May 15; 79, 347; K Barratt. aet **Replay – Arsenal 2** (Wright, Linighan) Seaman; Dixon, Winterburn, Linighan, Adams, Jensen, Davis, Smith, Merson, Campbell, Wright. Sub: O'Leary rep Wright 81. Unused sub: Selley **Sheffield Wed 1** (Waddle) Woods; Nilsson, Worthington, Palmer, Hirst, Wilson, Waddle, Warhurst, Bright, Sheridan, Harkes. Subs: Hyde rep Wilson 62; Bart-Williams rep Nilsson 118. May 20; 62, 267; K Barratt. aet

1994   Manchester Utd 4 (Cantona 2 [2pens], Hughes, McClair) Schmeichel; Parker, Bruce, Pallister, Irwin, Kanchelskis, Keane, Ince, Giggs, Cantona, Hughes. Subs: Sharpe rep Irwin 84; McClair rep Kanchelskis 84. Unused sub: Walsh (gk) **Chelsea 0** Kharine; Clarke, Sinclair, Kjeldberg, Johnsen, Burley, Spencer, Newton, Stein, Peacock, Wise Substitutions Hoddle rep Burley 65; Cascarino rep Stein 78. Unused sub: Kevin Hitchcock (gk) May 14; 79, 634; D Elleray

1995   Everton 1 (Rideout) Southall; Jackson, Hinchcliffe, Ablett, Watson, Parkinson, Unsworth, Horne, Stuart, Rideout, Limpar. Subs: Ferguson rep Rideout 51; Amokachi rep Limpar 69. Unused sub: Kearton (gk) **Manchester Utd 0** Schmeichel; Gary Neville, Irwin, Bruce, Sharpe, Pallister, Keane, Ince, Brian McClair, Hughes, Butt. Subs: Giggs rep Bruce 46; Scholes rep Sharpe 72. Unused sub: Gary Walsh (gk) May 20; 79, 592; G Ashby

1996   Manchester Utd 1 (Cantona) Schmeichel; Irwin, Phil Neville, May, Keane, Pallister, Cantona, Beckham, Cole, Butt, Giggs. Subs: Scholes rep Cole 65; Gary Neville rep Beckham 89. Unused sub: Sharpe **Liverpool 0** James; McAteer, Scales, Wright, Babb, Jones, McManaman, Barnes, Redknapp, Collymore, Fowler. Subs: Rush rep Collymore 74; Thomas rep Jones 85. Unused sub: Warner (gk) May 11; 79, 007; D Gallagher

1997   Chelsea 2 (Di Matteo, Newton) Grodas; Petrescu, Minto, Sinclair, Lebouef, Clarke, Zola, Di Matteo, Newton, Hughes, Wise. Sub: Vialli rep Zola 89. Unused subs: Hitchcock (gk), Myers **Middlesbrough 0** Roberts; Blackmore, Fleming, Stamp, Pearson, Festa, Emerson, Mustoe, Ravanelli, Juninho, Hignett. Subs: Beck rep Ravanelli 24; Vickers rep Mustoe 29; Kinder, rep Hignett 74. May 17; 79, 160; S Lodge

1998   Arsenal 2 (Overmars, Anelka) Seaman; Dixon, Winterburn, Vieira, Keown, Adams, Parlour, Anelka, Petit, Wreh, Overmars. Sub: Platt rep Wreh 63. Unused subs: Manninger (gk); Bould, Wright, Grimandi **Newcastle 0** Given; Pistone, Pearce, Batty, Dabizas, Howey, Lee, Barton, Shearer, Ketsbaia, Speed. Subs: Andersson rep Pearce 72; Watson rep Barton 77; Barnes rep Ketsbaia 85. Unused subs: Hislop (gk); Albert. May 16; 79, 183; P Durkin

1999   Manchester Utd 2 (Sheringham, Scholes) Schmeichel; Gary Neville, Johnsen, May, Phil Neville, Beckham, Scholes, Keane, Giggs, Cole, Solskjaer. Subs: Sheringham rep Keane 9; Yorke rep Cole 61; Stam rep Scholes 77. Unused subs: Blomqvist, Van Der Gouw **Newcastle 0** Harper; Griffin, Charvet, Dabizas, Domi, Lee, Hamann, Speed, Solano, Ketsbaia, Shearer. Subs: Ferguson rep Hamann 46; Maric rep Solano 68; Glass rep Ketsbaia 79. Unused subs: Given (gk); Barton. May 22; 79, 101; P Jones

2000   Chelsea 1 (Di Matteo) de Goey; Melchiot Desailly, Lebouef, Babayaro, Di Matteo, Wise, Deschamps, Poyet, Weah, Zola. Subs: Flo rep Weah 87; Morris rep Zola 90. Unused subs: Cudicini (gk); Terry , Harley **Aston Villa 0** James; Ehiogu, Southgate, Barry, Delaney, Taylor, Boateng, Merson, Wright, Dublin, Carbone. Subs: Stone rep Taylor 79; Joachim rep Carbone 79; Hendrie rep Wright 88. Unused subs: Enckelman (gk); Samuel May 20; 78, 217; G Poll

2001   Liverpool 2 (Owen 2) Westerveld; Babbel, Henchoz, Hyypia, Carragher, Murphy, Hamann, Gerrard, Smicer, Heskey, Owen. Subs: McAllister rep Hamann 60; Fowler rep Smicer 77; Berger rep Murphy 77. Unused subs: Arphexad (gk); Vignal **Arsenal 1** (Ljungberg) Seaman; Dixon, Keown, Adams, Cole, Ljungberg, Grimandi, Vieira, Pires, Henry, Wiltord. Subs: Parlour rep Wiltord 76; Kanu rep Ljungberg 85; Bergkamp rep Dixon 90. Unused subs: Manninger (gk); Lauren. May 12; 72, 500; S Dunn

2002   Arsenal 2 (Parlour, Ljungberg) Seaman; Lauren, Campbell, Adams, Cole, Parlour, Wiltord, Vieira, Ljungberg, Bergkamp, Henry Subs: Edu rep Bergkamp 72; Kanu rep Henry 81; Keown rep Wiltord 90. Unused subs: Wright (gk); Dixon **Chelsea 0** Cudicini; Melchiot, Desailly, Gallas, Babayaro, Gronkjaer, Lampard, Petit, Le Saux, Floyd Hasselbaink, Gudjohnsen. Subs: Terry rep Babayaro 46; Zola rep Hasselbaink 68; Zenden rep Melchiot 77. Unused subs: de Goey (gk); Jokanovic. May 4; 73, 963; M Riley

2003   Arsenal 1 (Pires) Seaman; Lauren, Luzhny, Keown, Cole, Ljungberg, Parlour, Gilberto, Pires, Bergkamp, Henry. Sub: Wiltord rep Bergkamp 77. Unused subs: Taylor (gk); Kanu, Toure, van Bronckhorst **Southampton 0** Niemi; Baird, Svensson, Lundekvam, Bridge, Telfer, Svensson, Oakley, Marsden, Beattie, Ormerod. Subs: Jones rep Niemi 66; Fernandes rep Baird 87; Tessem rep Svensson 75. Unused subs: Williams, Higginbotham. May 17; 73, 726; G Barber

2004   Manchester Utd 3 (Van Nistelrooy [2, 1 pen], Ronaldo) Howard; Gary Neville, Brown, Silvestre, O'Shea, Fletcher, Keane, Ronaldo, Scholes, Giggs, Van Nistelrooy. Subs: Carroll rep Howard, Butt rep Fletcher, Solskjaer rep Ronaldo 84. Unused subs: P Neville, Djemba-Djemba **Millwall 0** Marshall; Elliott, Lawrence, Ward, Ryan, Wise, Ifill, Cahill, Livermore, Sweeney, Harris. Subs: Cogan rep Ryan, McCammon rep Harris 74 Weston rep Wise 88. Unused subs: Gueret (gk); Dunne. May 22; 71, 350; J Winter

2005 Arsenal 0 Lehmann; Lauren, Toure, Senderos, Cole, Fabregas, Gilberto, Vieira, Pires, Reyes, Bergkamp Subs: Ljungberg rep Bergkamp 65, Van Persie rep Fabregas 86, Edu rep Pires 105. Unused subs: Almunia (gk); Campbell. Reyes sent off 90. **Manchester Utd 0** Carroll; Brown, Ferdinand, Silvestre, O'Shea, Fletcher, Keane, Scholes, Rooney, Van Nistelrooy, Ronaldo. Subs: Fortune rep O'Shea 77, Giggs rep Fletcher 91. Unused subs: Howard (gk); G Neville, Smith. **Arsenal** (Lauren, Ljungberg, van Persie, Cole, Vieira) beat Manchester Utd (van Nistelrooy, Scholes [missed], Ronaldo, Rooney, Keane) 5-4 on penalties. May 21; 71, 876; R Styles

2006 Liverpool 3 (Gerrard 2, Cisse) Reina; Finnan, Carragher, Hyypiä, Riise, Gerrard, Xabi, Sissoko, Kewell, Cisse, Crouch. Subs: Morientes rep Kewell 48, Kromkamp rep Alonso 67, Hamman rep Crouch 71. Unused subs: Dudek (gk); Traoré **West Ham 3** (Ashton, Konchesky, Carragher (og)) Hislop; Scaloni, Ferdinand, Gabbidon, Konchesky, Benayoun, Fletcher, Reo-Coker, Etherington, Ashton, Harewood. Subs: Zamora rep Ashton 71, Dailly rep Fletcher, Sheringham rep Etherington 85. Unused subs: Walker (gk); Collins. **Liverpool** (Hamann, Hyypiä [missed], Gerrard, Riise) beat **West Ham** (Zamora [missed], Sheringham, Konchesky [missed], Ferdinand [missed]) 3-1 on penalties. May 13; 71, 140; A Wiley

2007 Chelsea 1 (Drogba) Cech, Ferreira, Essien, Terry, Bridge, Mikel, Makelele, Lampard, Wright-Phillips, Drogba, Joe Cole Subs: Robben rep J Cole 45, Kalou rep Wright-Phillips 93, A Cole rep Robben 108. Unused subs: Cudicini (gk); Diarra. **Manchester Utd 0** Van der Sar, Brown, Ferdinand, Vidic, Heinze, Fletcher, Scholes, Carrick, Ronaldo, Rooney, Giggs Subs: Tevez rep Fletcher 92, O'Shea rep Carrick, Solskjaer rep Giggs 112. Unused subs: Kuszczak (gk); Evra. May 19; 89, 826; S Bennett

2008 Portsmouth 1 (Kanu) James; Johnson, Campbell, Distin, Hreidarsson, Utaka, Muntari, Mendes, Diarra, Kranjcar, Kanu. Subs: Nugent rep Utaka 69, Diop rep Mendes 78, Baros rep Kanu 87. Unused subs: Ashdown (gk); Pamarot. **Cardiff 0** Enckelman; McNaughton, Johnson, Loovens, Capaldi, Whittingham, Rae, McPhail, Ledley, Hasselbaink, Parry. Subs: Ramsey rep Whittingham 62, Thompson rep Hasselbaink 70, Sinclair rep Rae 87. Unused subs: Oakes (gk); Purse. May 17; 89, 874; M Dean

2009 Chelsea 2 (Drogba, Lampard) Cech; Bosingwa, Alex, Terry, Ashley Cole, Essien, Mikel, Lampard, Drogba, Anelka, Malouda. Subs: Ballack rep Essien 61. Unused subs: Hilario (gk), Ivanovic, Di Santo, Kalou, Belletti, Mancienne. **Everton 1** (Saha) Howard; Hibbert, Yobo, Lescott, Baines, Osman, Neville, Cahill, Pienaar, Fellaini, Saha. Subs: Jacobsen rep Hibbert 46, Vaughan rep Saha 77, Gosling rep Osman 83. Unused subs: Nash, Castillo, Rodwell, Baxter. May 30; 89, 391; H Webb

2010 Chelsea 1 (Drogba) Cech; Ivanovic, Alex, Terry, Ashley Cole, Lampard, Ballack, Malouda, Kalou, Drogba, Anelka. Subs: Belletti rep Ballack 44, J Cole rep Kalou 71, Sturridge rep Anelka 90. Unused subs: Hilario (gk), Zhirkov, Paulo Ferreira, Matic. **Portsmouth 0** James; Finnan, Mokoena, Rocha, Mullins, Dindane, Brown, Diop, Boateng, O'Hara, Piquionne. Subs: Utaka rep Boateng 73, Belhadj rep Mullins 81, Kanu rep Diop 81. Unused subs: Ashdown (gk), Vanden Borre, Hughes, Ben Haim. May 15; 88, 335; C Foy

2011 Manchester City 1 (Y Toure) Hart; Richards, Kompany, Lescott, Kolarov, De Jong, Barry, Silva, Y Toure, Balotelli, Tevez. Subs: Johnson rep Barry73, Zabaleta rep Tevez 87, Vieira rep Silva 90. Unused subs: Given (gk), Boyata, Milner, Dzeko. **Stoke 0** Sorensen; Wilkinson, Shawcross, Huth, Wilson, Pennant, Whelan, Delap, Etherington, Walters, Jones. Subs: Whitehead rep Etherington 62, Carew rep Delap 80, Pugh rep Whelan 84. Unused subs: Nash (gk); Collins, Faye, Diao. May 14; 88, 643; M Atkinson

2012 Chelsea 2 (Ramires, Drogba) Cech; Bosingwa, Ivanovic, Terry, Ashley Cole, Mikel, Lampard, Ramires, Mata, Kalou, Drogba. Subs: Meireles rep Ramires76, Malouda rep Mata 90. Unused subs: Turnbull (gk), Paulo Ferreira, Essien, Torres, Sturridge. **Liverpool 1** (Carroll) Reina; Johnson, Skrtel, Agger, Luis Enrique, Spearing, Bellamy, Henderson, Gerrard, Downing, Suarez. Subs Carroll rep Spearing 55, Kuyt rep Bellamy 78. Unused subs: Doni (gk), Carragher, Kelly, Shelvey, Rodriguez. May 5; 89, 102; P Dowd

2013 Wigan 1 (Watson) Robles; Boyce, Alcaraz, Scharner, McCarthy, McArthur, McManaman, Maloney, Gomez, Espinoza, Kone. Subs: Watson rep Gomez 81. Unused subs: Al Habsi (gk), Caldwell, Golobart, Fyvie, Henriquez, Di Santo. **Manchester City 0** Hart; Zabaleta, Kompany, Nastasic, Clichy, Toure, Barry, Silva, Tevez, Nasri, Aguero. Subs: Milner rep Nasri 54, Rodwell rep Tevez 69, Dzeko rep Barry 90. Unused subs: Pantilimon (gk), Lescott, Kolarov, Garcia. Sent off Zabaleta (84). May 11; 86, 254; A Marriner

2014 Arsenal 3 (Cazorla, Koscielny, Ramsey) Fabianski; Sagna, Koscielny, Mertesacker, Gibbs, Arteta, Ramsey, Cazorla, Ozil, Podolski, Giroud. Subs: Sanogo rep Podolski 61, Rosicky rep Cazorla 106, Wilshire rep Ozil 106. Unused subs: Szczesny (gk), Vermaelen, Monreal, Flamini. **Hull 2** (Chester, Davies) McGregor; Davies, Bruce, Chester, Elmohamady, Livermore, Huddlestone, Meyler, Rosenior,

Quinn, Fryatt. Subs: McShane rep Bruce 67, Aluko rep Quinn 71, Boyd rep Rosenior 102. Unused subs: Harper (gk), Figueroa, Koren, Sagbo. May 17; 89, 345; L Probert. aet

2015 **Arsenal 4** (Walcott, Sanchez, Mertesacker, Giroud) Szczesny; Bellerin, Koscielny, Mertesacker, Monreal, Coquelin, Cazorla, Ramsey, Ozil, A Sanchez, Walcott. Subs: Wilshere rep Ozil 77, Giroud rep Walcott 77, Oxlade-Chamberlain rep A Sanchez 90. Unused subs: Ospina (gk), Gibbs, Gabriel, Flamini. **Aston Villa 0** Given; Hutton, Okore, Vlaar, Richardson, Cleverley, Westwood, Delph, N'Zogbia, Benteke, Grealish. Subs: Agbonlahor rep N'Zogbia 53, Bacuna rep Richardson 68, C Sanchez rep Westwood 71. Unused subs: Guzan (gk), Baker, Sinclair, Cole. May 30; 89, 283; J Moss

2016 **Manchester Utd 2** (Mata, Lingard) De Gea, Valencia, Smalling, Blind, Rojo, Carrick, Rooney, Fellaini, Mata, Martial, Rashford. Subs: Darmian rep Rojo 65, Young rep Rashford 71, Lingard rep Mata 90. Unused subs: Romero, Jones, Herrera, Schneiderlin. Smalling sent off 105 . **Crystal Palace 1** (Puncheon) Hennessey, Ward, Dann, Delaney, Souare, Cabaye, Jedinak, Zaha, McArthur, Bolasie, Wickham. Unused subs: Speroni, Adebayor, Sako, Kelly. Subs: Puncheon rep Cabaye 72, Gayle rep Wickham 86, Mariappa rep Dann 90 May 21; 88, 619; M Clattenburg

2017 **Arsenal 2** (Sanchez, Ramsey) Ospina, Holding, Mertesacker, Monreal, Bellerin, Ramsey, Xhaka, Oxlade-Chamberlain, Sanchez, Ozil, Welbeck. Subs: Giroud rep Welbeck78, Coquelin rep Oxlade-Chamberlain 83, Elneny rep Sanchez 90. Unused subs: Cech (gk), Walcott, Iwobi, Lucas Perez. **Chelsea 1** (Diego Costa) Courtois, Azpilicueta, Luiz, Cahill, Moses, Kante, Matic, Alonso, Pedro, Diego Costa, Hazard. Subs Fabregas rep Matic 62, Willian rep Pedro 72, Batshuayi rep Diego Costa 88. Unused subs: Begovic (gk), Terry, Zouma, Ake, Moses sent off 68. May 27; 89, 472; A Taylor

2018 **Chelsea 1** (Hazard pen) Courtois, Azpilicueta, Cahill, Rudiger, Moses, Fabregas, Kante, Bakayoko, Alonso, Hazard, Giroud. Subs: Morata rep Giroud 89, Willian rep Hazard 90. Unused subs: Caballero (gk), Barkley, Pedro, Zappacosta, Chalobah. **Manchester Utd 0** De Gea, Valencia, Smalling, Jones, Young, Herrera, Matic, Pogba, Lingard, Sanchez, Rashford. Subs: Martial rep Lingard 73, Lukaku rep Rashford 73, Mata rep Jones 87. Unused subs: Romero (gk), Bailly, Darmian, McTominay. May 19, 87, 647; M Oliver

2019 **Manchester City 6** (Gabriel Jesus 2, Sterling 2, David Silva, De Bruyne) Ederson, Walker, Kompany, Laporte, Zinchenko, Gundogan, David Silva, Bernardo Silva, Mahrez, Gabriel Jesus, Sterling. Subs: De Bruyne rep Mahrez 55, Sane rep Gundogan 73, Stones rep Davi Silva 79. Unused subs: Muric (gk), Danilo, Otamendi, Aguero. **Watford 0** Gomes, Femenia, Mariappa, Cathcart, Holebas, Hughes, Capoue, Doucoure, Pereyra, Deulofeu, Deeney, Subs: Success rep Pereyra 65, Gray rep Deulofeu 65, Cleverley rep Hughes 73. Unused subs: Foster (gk), Janmaat, Masina, Kabasele. May 18; 85, 854; K Friend

VENUES

Kennington Oval 1872; **Lillie Bridge** 1873; **Kennington Oval** 1874–1892 (1886 replay at the **Racecourse Ground, Derby**); **Fallowfield**, Manchester, 1893; **Goodison Park** 1894; **Crystal Palace** 1895–1914 (1901 replay at **Burnden Park**; 1910 replay at **Goodison Park**; 1911 replay at **Old Trafford**; 1912 replay at **Bramall Lane**);; **Old Trafford** 1915; **Stamford Bridge** 1920–1922; **Wembley** 1923–2000 (1970 replay at **Old Trafford**; all replays from 1981 at **Wembley**); **Millennium Stadium** 2001–2006; **Wembley** 2007–2019

ROONEY DAMPENS PRESTON PRIDE

Wayne Rooney put a damper on Preston's milestone match at Deepdale last season. The club became the first in English football to reach 5,000 league matches and were also involved in the first to be played in July, having kicked-off ahead of the other fixtures on that evening. But they were denied a victory over Derby to mark the occasion when player-coach Rooney scored the only goal from a free-kick. Two factors placed the club on top of this table – being among founder members of the league and playing for many years in divisions with 46-game seasons. Notts County's relegation in 2019 cost them the chance to be first to 5,000. They remain on 4,986, Preston's record going into the match was 4,999, won 1,940, drawn 1,284, lost 1,775, goals for 7,400, goals against 6,968.

SUMMARY OF FA CUP WINS

Arsenal	14	Sheffield Wed	3	Clapham Rov	1
Manchester Utd	12	West Ham	3	Coventry	1
Tottenham	8	Bury	2	Derby	1
Chelsea	8	Nottm Forest	2	Huddersfield	1
Aston Villa	7	Old Etonians	2	Ipswich	1
Liverpool	7	Portsmouth	2	Leeds	1
Blackburn Rov	6	Preston	2	Notts Co	1
Manchester City	6	Sunderland	2	Old Carthusians	1
Newcastle	5	Barnsley	1	Oxford University	1
Everton	5	Blackburn Olympic	1	Royal Engineers	1
The Wanderers	5	Blackpool	1	Southampton	1
WBA	5	Bradford City	1	Wigan	1
Bolton	4	Burnley	1	Wimbledon	1
Sheffield Utd	4	Cardiff	1		
Wolves	4	Charlton	1		

APPEARANCES IN FINALS (Figures do not include replays)

Arsenal	21	The Wanderers*	5	Notts Co	2
Manchester Utd	20	West Ham	5	Queen's Park (Glasgow)	2
Chelsea	14	Derby	4	Watford	2
Liverpool	14	Leeds	4	Blackburn Olympic*	1
Everton	13	Leicester	4	Bradford City*	1
Newcastle	13	Oxford University	4	Brighton	1
Aston Villa	11	Royal Engineers	4	Bristol City	1
Manchester City	11	Southampton	4	Coventry*	1
WBA	10	Sunderland	4	Fulham	1
Tottenham	9	Blackpool	3	Hull	1
Blackburn Rov	8	Burnley	3	Ipswich*	1
Wolves	8	Cardiff	3	Luton	1
Bolton	7	Nottm Forest	3	Middlesbrough	1
Preston	7	Barnsley	2	Millwall	1
Old Etonians	6	Birmingham	2	Old Carthusians*	1
Sheffield Utd	6	Bury*	2	QPR	1
Sheffield Wed	6	Charlton	2	Stoke	1
Huddersfield	5	Clapham Rov	2	Wigan	1
Portsmouth	5	Crystal Palace	2	Wimbledon*	1

(* Denotes undefeated)

APPEARANCES IN SEMI-FINALS (Figures do not include replays)

31 Manchester Utd; **30** Arsenal; **26** Everton; **24** Chelsea; Liverpool; **21** Aston Villa, Tottenham; **20** WBA; **18** Blackburn; **17** Newcastle; **16** Sheffield Wed; **15** Manchester City, Wolves; **14** Bolton, Sheffield Utd; **13** Derby; **12** Nottm Forest, Southampton, Sunderland; **10** Preston; **9** Birmingham; **8** Burnley, Leeds; **7** Huddersfield, Leicester, Portsmouth, Watford, West Ham; **6** Fulham, Newcastle Old Etonians, Oxford University; **5** Millwall, Notts Co, The Wanderers; **4** Cardiff, *Crystal Palace, Luton, Queen's Park (Glasgow), Royal Engineers, Stoke; **3** Barnsley, Blackpool, Clapham Rov, Ipswich, Middlesbrough, Norwich, Old Carthusians, Oldham, The Swifts; **2** Blackburn Olympic, Brighton, Bristol City, Bury, Charlton, Grimsby, Hull, Reading, Swansea, Swindon, Wigan, Wimbledon; **1** Bradford City, Cambridge University, Chesterfield, Coventry, Crewe, Darwen, Derby Junction, Marlow, Old Harrovians, Orient, Plymouth Argyle, Port Vale, QPR, Rangers (Glasgow), Shropshire Wand, Wycombe, York

(*A previous and different Crystal Palace club also reached the semi-final in season 1871–72)

CARABAO EFL CUP 2019–20

FIRST ROUND

AFC Wimbledon 2 MK Dons 2
(MK Dons won 4-2 on pens)
Accrington 1 Sunderland 3
Barnsley 0 Carlisle 3
Blackburn 3 Oldham 2
Blackpool 2 Macclesfield 2
(Macclesfield won 4-2 on pens)
Bradford 0 Preston 4
Brentford 1 Cambridge 1
(Cambridge won 5-4 on pens)
Bristol Rov 3 Cheltenham 0
Charlton 2 Forest Green 0
(Forest Green won 5-3 on pens)
Colchester 3 Swindon 0
Coventry 4 Exeter 1
Gillingham 2 Newport 2
(Newport won 4-1 on pens)
Grimsby 1 Doncaster 0
Huddersfield 0 Lincoln 1
Luton 3 Ipswich 1
Mansfield 2 Morecambe 2
(Morecambe won 6-5 on pens)
Middlesbrough 2 Crewe 2

(Crewe won 4-2 on pens)
Nottm Forest 1 Fleetwood 0
Oxford 1 Peterborough 0
Plymouth 2 Leyton Orient 0
Portsmouth 3 Birmingham 0
Port Vale 1 Burton 0
QPR 3 Bristol City 3
(QPR won 5-4 on pens)
Rochdale 5 Bolton 2
Salford 0 Leeds 3
Scunthorpe 0 Derby 1
Shrewsbury 1 Rotherham 4
Stevenage 1 Southend 2
Swansea 3 Northampton 1
Tranmere 1 Hull 3
Walsall 2 Crawley 3
WBA 1 Millwall 2
Wigan 0 Stoke 1
Wycombe 1 Reading 1
(Reading won 4-2 on pens)
Not played
Sheffield Wed v Bury
(Sheffield Wed go through)

SECOND ROUND

Bournemouth 0 Forest Green 0
(Bournemouth won 3-0 on pens)
Bristol Rov 1 Brighton 2
Burnley 1 Sunderland 3
Burton 4 Morecambe 0
Cardiff 0 Luton 3
Crawley 1 Norwich 0
Crewe 1 **Aston Villa** 6
Crystal Palace 0 Colchester 0
(Colchester won 5-4 on pens)
Fulham 0 Southampton 1
Grimsby 0 Macclesfield 0
(Grimsby won 5-4 on pens)
Leeds 2 Stoke 2
(Stoke won 5-4 on pens)
Lincoln 2 Everton 4

Newcastle 1 Leicester 1
(Leicester won 4-2 on pens)
Newport 0 West Ham 2
Nottm Forest 3 Derby 0
Oxford 2 Millwall 2
(Oxford won 4-2 on pens)
Plymouth 2 Reading 4
Preston 2 Hull 2
(Preston won 5-4 on pens)
QPR 0 Portsmouth 2
Rochdale 2 Carlisle 1
Rotherham 0 Sheffield Wed 1
Sheffield Utd 2 Blackburn 1
Southend 1 MK Dons 4
Swansea 6 Cambridge 0
Watford 3 Coventry 0

THIRD ROUND

Arsenal 5 Nottm Forest 0
Brighton 1 **Aston Villa** 3
Burton 0 Bournemouth 0
Chelsea 7 Grimsby 1
Colchester 0 Tottenham 0
(Colchester won 4-3 on pens)

Crawley 1 Stoke 1
(Crawley won 5-3 on pens)
Luton 0 Leicester 4
Manchester Utd 1 Rochdale 1
(Manchester Utd won 5-3 on pens)
MK Dons 0 Liverpool 2

Oxford 4 West Ham 0
Portsmouth 0 Southampton 4
Preston 0 **Manchester City** 3
Sheffield Utd 0 Sunderland 1

Sheffield Wed 0 Everton 2
Watford 2 Swansea 1
Wolves 1 Reading 1
(Wolves won 4-2 on pens)

FOURTH ROUND

Aston Villa 2 Wolves 1
Burton 1 Leicester 3
Chelsea 1 Manchester Utd 2
Crawley 1 Colchester 3
Everton 2 Watford 0

Liverpool 5 Arsenal 5
(Liverpool won 5-4 on pens)
Manchester City 3 Southampton 1
Oxford 1 Sunderland 0
(Oxford won 4-2 on pens)

QUARTER-FINALS

Aston Villa 5 Liverpool 0
Everton 2 Leicester 2
(Leicester won 4-2 on pens)

Manchester Utd 3 Colchester 0
Oxford 1 **Manchester City** 3

SEMI-FINALS (two legs)

Leicester 1 **Aston Villa** 1
Aston Villa 2 Leicester 1
(Aston Villa won 3-2 on agg)

Manchester Utd 1 **Manchester City** 3
Manchester City 0 Manchester Utd 1
(Manchester City won 3-2 on agg)

FINAL

Pep Guardiola achieved a record-equalling victory in the competition he has insisted should be sacrificed to ease the fixture burden on players. Lifting the League Cup after an absorbing final ranked him alongside Liverpool's Bob Paisley as a three-time winner in successive seasons after beating Arsenal in 2018 and Chelsea 12 months later. His club closed in on another record, one behind Liverpool with their seventh success overall – five of them coming in the last seven seasons. But the Manchester City manager believes one trophy should be scrapped – by implication the League Cup – to allow for a more balanced Premier League programme and a reduction in injuries. Goals by Sergio Aguero and Rodri, alongside a man-of-the-match performance from the maturing Phil Foden, outweighed a commendable performance from Villa, who made a game of it after conceding twice in the opening half-hour. Mbwana Samatta made his own piece of history by becoming the first Tanzanian player to grace Wembley with a goal – a spectacular diving header from Anwar El Ghazi's cross before half-time. Overall, City were good value for their success, but Dean Smith's side took plenty of optimism into their fight for Premier League survival with this performance against team a who crushed them 6-1 in the Premier League at Villa Park seven weeks earlier.

ASTON VILLA 1 (Samatta 41) MANCHESTER CITY 2 (Aguero 20, Rodri 30)
Wembley (82, 149); Sunday, March 1, 2020
Aston Villa (4-2-3-1): Nyland, Guilbert, Engels, Mings, Targett, Marvelous Nakamba, Douglas Luiz, Elmohamady (Trezeguet 70), Grealish (capt), El Ghazi (Hourihane 70), Samatta (Davis 79). **Subs not used**: Reina, Taylor, Lansbury, Konsa. **Booked**: Elmohamady, Marvelous Nakamba, Mings. **Manager**: Dean Smith
Manchester City (4-3-3): Claudio Bravo, Walker, Stones, Fernandinho, Zinchenko, Gundogan (De Bruyne 58), Rodri, David Silva (capt) (Bernardo Silva 76), Foden, Aguero (Gabriel Jesus 83, Sterling. **Subs not used**: Ederson, Mendy, Mahrez, Otamendi. **Booked**: Sterling, Rodri.
Manager: Pep Guardiola
Referee: L Mason. **Half-time**: 1-2

HOW THEY REACHED THE FINAL
Aston Villa
Round 2: 6-1 away to Crewe (Hourihane 2, Konsa, Davis, Guilbert, Grealish)
Round 3: 3-1 away to Brighton (Jota, Hourihane, Grealish)
Round 4: 2-1 home to Wolves (El Ghazi, Elmohamady)

Quarter-final: 5-0 home to Liverpool (Kodjia 2, Hourihane, Wesley, Boyes og)
Semi-final v Leicester – first leg, 1-1 away (Guilbert); second leg, 2-1 home (Targett, Trezeguet)

Manchester City
Round 3: 3-0 away to Preston (Sterling, Gabriel Jesus, Ledson og)
Round 4: 3-1 home to Southampton (Aguero 2, Otamendi)
Quarter-final: 3-1 away to Oxford (Sterling 2, Joao Cancelo)
Semi-final v Manchester Utd – first leg, 3-1 away (Bernardo Silva, Mahrez, Pereira og); second leg, 0-1 home

LEAGUE CUP – COMPLETE RESULTS

LEAGUE CUP FINALS

1961*	Aston Villa beat Rotherham 3-2 on agg (0-2a, 3-0h)
1962	Norwich beat Rochdale 4-0 on agg (3-0a, 1-0h)
1963	Birmingham beat Aston Villa 3-1 o agg (3-1h, 0-0a)
1964	Leicester beat Stoke 4-3 on agg (1-1a, 3-2h)
1965	Chelsea beat Leicester 3-2 on agg (3-2h, 0-0a)
1966	WBA beat West Ham 5-3 on agg (1-2a, 4-1h)

AT WEMBLEY

1967	QPR beat WBA (3-2)
1968	Leeds beat Arsenal (1-0)
1969*	Swindon beat Arsenal (3-1)
1970*	Man City beat WBA (2-1)
1971	Tottenham beat Aston Villa (2-0)
1972	Stoke beat Chelsea (2-1)
1973	Tottenham beat Norwich (1-0)
1974	Wolves beat Man City (2-1)
1975	Aston Villa beat Norwich (1-0)
1976	Man City beat Newcastle (2-1)
1977†*	Aston Villa beat Everton (3-2 after 0-0 and 1-1 draws)
1978††	Nottm Forest beat Liverpool (1-0 after 0-0 draw)
1979	Nottm Forest beat Southampton (3-2)
1980	Wolves beat Nottm Forest (1-0)
1981†††	Liverpool beat West Ham (2-1 after 1-1 draw)

MILK CUP

1982*	Liverpool beat Tottenham (3-1)
1983*	Liverpool beat Man Utd (2-1)
1984**	Liverpool beat Everton (1-0 after *0-0 draw)
1985	Norwich beat Sunderland (1-0)
1986	Oxford Utd beat QPR (3-0)

LITTLEWOODS CUP

1987	Arsenal beat Liverpool (2-1)
1988	Luton beat Arsenal (3-2)
1989	Nottm Forest beat Luton (3-1)
1990	Nottm Forest beat Oldham (1-0)

RUMBELOWS CUP

1991	Sheffield Wed beat Man Utd (1-0)
1992	Man Utd beat Nottm Forest (1-0)

COCA-COLA CUP

1993	Arsenal beat Sheffield Wed (2-1)
1994	Aston Villa beat Man Utd (3-1)
1995	Liverpool beat Bolton (2-1)
1996	Aston Villa beat Leeds (3-0)
1997***	Leicester beat Middlesbrough (*1-0 after *1-1 draw)
1998	Chelsea beat Middlesbrough (2-0)

WORTHINGTON CUP (at Millennium Stadium from 2001)

1999	Tottenham beat Leicester (1-0)
2000	Leicester beat Tranmere (2-1)
2001	Liverpool beat Birmingham (5-4 on pens after *1-1 draw)
2002	Blackburn beat Tottenham (2-1)
2003	Liverpool beat Man Utd (2-0)

CARLING CUP (at Wembley from 2008)

2004	Middlesbrough beat Bolton (2-1)
2005*	Chelsea beat Liverpool (3-2)
2006	Man Utd beat Wigan (4-0)
2007	Chelsea beat Arsenal (2-1)
2008*	Tottenham beat Chelsea (2-1)
2009	Man Utd beat Tottenham (4-1 on pens after *0-0 draw)
2010	Man Utd beat Aston Villa (2-1)
2011	Birmingham beat Arsenal (2-1)
2012	Liverpool beat Cardiff (3-2 on pens after *2-2 draw)

CAPITAL ONE CUP (at Wembley from 2013)

2013	Swansea beat Bradford (5-0)
2014	Manchester City beat Sunderland (3-1)
2015	Chelsea beat Tottenham (2-0)
2016	Manchester City beat Liverpool (3-1 on pens after *1-1 draw)

* After extra time. † First replay at Hillsborough, second replay at Old Trafford. †† Replayed at Old Trafford. ††† Replayed at Villa Park. ** Replayed at Maine Road. *** Replayed at Hillsborough

EFL CUP (at Wembley from 2017)

2017	Manchester Utd beat Southampton (3-2)

CARABAO CUP (at Wembley from 2018)

2018	Manchester City beat Arsenal (3-0)
2019	Manchester City beat Chelsea (4-3 on pens after *0-0 draw)
2020	Manchester City beat Aston Villa (2-1)

SUMMARY OF LEAGUE CUP WINNERS

Liverpool	8	Arsenal	2	Oxford Utd	1
Manchester City	7	Birmingham	2	QPR	1
Aston Villa	5	Norwich	2	Sheffield Wed	1
Chelsea	5	Wolves	2	Stoke	1
Manchester Utd	5	Blackburn	1	Swansea	1
Nottm Forest	4	Leeds	1	Swindon	1
Tottenham	4	Luton	1	WBA	1
Leicester	3	Middlesbrough	1		

LEAGUE CUP FINAL APPEARANCES

12 Liverpool; **9**, Aston Villa, Chelsea, Manchester Utd; **8** Arsenal, Manchester City, Tottenham; **6** Nottm Forest; **5** Leicester; **4** Norwich; **3** Birmingham, Middlesbrough, WBA; **2** Bolton, Everton, Leeds, Luton, QPR, Sheffield Wed, Southampton, Stoke, Sunderland, West Ham, Wolves; **1** Blackburn, Bradford, Cardiff, Newcastle, Oldham, Oxford Utd, Rochdale, Rotherham, Swansea, Swindon, Tranmere, Wigan (Figures do not include replays)

LEAGUE CUP SEMI-FINAL APPEARANCES

17 Liverpool, Tottenham; **15** Arsenal, Aston Villa, Manchester Utd **14** Chelsea, ; **12** Manchester City; **9** West Ham; **6** Blackburn, Leicester, Nottm Forest; **5** Birmingham, Everton, Leeds, Middlesbrough, Norwich; **4** Bolton, Burnley, Crystal Palace, Ipswich, Sheffield Wed, Sunderland, WBA; **3** Bristol City, QPR, Southampton, Stoke, Swindon, Wolves; **2** Cardiff, Coventry, Derby, Luton, Oxford Utd, Plymouth, Sheffield Utd, Tranmere, Watford, Wimbledon; **1** Blackpool, Bradford, Burton, Bury, Carlisle, Chester, Huddersfield, Hull, Newcastle, Oldham, Peterborough, Rochdale, Rotherham, Shrewsbury, Stockport, Swansea, Walsall, Wigan, Wycombe (Figures do not include replays)

THE THINGS THEY SAY...

'Not often do you get the chance to call a Prince a villain' – Gary Lineker, *Match of the Day* presenter, after an excited Prince George sees Aston Villa win 5-1 at Norwich, along with his parents, the Duke and Duchess of Cambridge.

'I want to express my surprise after completing the best season in Watford's history' – **Javi Gracia** on his dismissal four games into the new campaign.

OTHER COMPETITIONS 2019–20

FA COMMUNITY SHIELD

LIVERPOOL 1 (Matip 77) MANCHESTER CITY 1 (Sterling 12)
(Manchester City won 5-4 on pens)
Wembley (77,565); Sunday, August 4, 2019

Liverpool (4-3-3): Alisson, Alexander-Arnold (Matip 67), Gomez, Van Dijk, Robertson, Henderson (capt) (Lallana 79), Fabinho (Keita 67), Wijnaldum, Salah, Firmino (Shaqiri 79), Origi (Oxlade-Chamberlain 79). **Subs not used:** Mignolet, Lovren. **Manager:** Jurgen Klopp
Manchester City (4-3-3): Bravo, Walker, Stones, Otamendi, Zinchenko, De Bruyne (Foden 89), Rodri, David Silva (capt) (Gundogan 61), Bernardo Silva, Sterling, Sane (Gabriel Jesus 13). **Subs not used:** Ederson, Aguero, Angelino, Garcia. **Booked:** De Bruyne. **Manager:** Pep Guardiola
Penalty shoot-out: Liverpool – scored: Shaqiri, Lallana, Oxlade-Chamberlain, Salah; missed: Wijnaldum. **Manchester City** – scored: Gundogan, Bernardo Silva, Foden, Zinchenko, Gabriel Jesus
Referee: M Atkinson (Yorks). **Half-time:** 0-1

LEASING.COM EFL TROPHY

(Three points for a group match win. One point for a drawn game after 90 minutes, then penalties with winners awarded one additional point. Group winners and runners-up through to knockout stage)

NORTHERN SECTION

GROUP A

	P	W	D	L	F	A	Pts
Leicester U21	3	2	1	0	5	3	8
Scunthorpe	3	2	1	0	6	2	7
Sunderland	3	1	0	2	4	7	3
Grimsby	3	0	0	3	4	7	0

GROUP B

Accrington	3	3	0	0	10	3	9
Fleetwood	3	1	1	1	7	5	5
Oldham	3	1	0	2	5	10	3
Liverpool U21	3	0	1	2	5	9	1

GROUP C

Salford	2	2	0	0	4	0	6
Tranmere	2	1	0	1	2	3	3
Aston Villa U21	2	0	0	2	1	4	0

GROUP D

Port Vale	3	3	0	0	7	4	9
Shrewsbury	3	2	0	1	7	3	6
Macclesfield	3	1	0	2	5	7	3
Newcastle U21	3	0	0	3	2	7	0

GROUP E

Everton U21	3	1	2	0	5	3	6
Mansfield	3	1	2	0	4	3	5

Crewe	3	0	2	1	4	6	4
Burton	3	1	0	2	4	5	3

GROUP F

Man City U21	3	2	0	1	5	4	6
Bolton	3	1	2	0	5	3	5
Rochdale	3	1	1	3	4	5	
Bradford	3	0	1	2	3	5	2

GROUP G

Blackpool	3	2	0	1	7	3	6
Wolves U21	3	1	1	1	6	5	5
Morecambe	3	1	1	1	6	8	4
Carlisle	3	1	0	2	5	8	3

GROUP H

Man Utd U21	3	3	0	0	5	1	9
Doncaster	3	1	0	2	6	6	3
Lincoln	3	1	0	2	4	4	3
Rotherham	3	1	0	2	3	7	3

SOUTHERN SECTION

GROUP A

Colchester	3	2	1	0	5	3	7
Ipswich	3	2	0	1	6	2	6
Gillingham	3	1	0	2	4	7	3
Tottenham U21	3	0	1	2	5	2	2

GROUP B

Portsmouth	3	2	1	0	6	3	8
Oxford	3	2	1	0	8	4	7
Norwich U21	3	1	2	0	4	6	3
Crawley	3	0	0	3	2	7	0

GROUP C

	P	W	D	L	F	A	Pts
Brighton U21	3	2	1	0	5	1	7
Leyton Orient	3	1	1	1	3	4	5
AFC Wimbledon	3	1	0	2	4	5	3
Southend	3	1	0	2	3	5	3

GROUP D

	P	W	D	L	F	A	Pts
Walsall	3	2	1	0	7	0	7
Coventry	3	1	2	0	3	2	6
Forest Green	3	1	1	1	3	8	5
Southampton U21	3	0	0	3	4	7	0

GROUP E

	P	W	D	L	F	A	Pts
Exeter	3	3	0	0	6	1	9
Newport	3	1	0	2	11	11	3
West Ham U21	3	1	0	2	9	11	3
Cheltenham	3	1	0	2	8	11	3

GROUP F

	P	W	D	L	F	A	Pts
Bristol Rov	3	2	1	0	4	2	7
Chelsea U21	3	2	0	1	5	4	6
Plymouth	3	1	1	1	4	2	5
Swindon	3	0	0	3	2	7	0

GROUP G

	P	W	D	L	F	A	Pts
MK Dons	3	2	0	1	5	2	6
Stevenage	3	1	1	1	2	4	5
Fulham U21	3	1	1	1	3	3	4
Wycombe	3	1	0	2	3	4	3

GROUP H

	P	W	D	L	F	A	Pts
Portsmouth	3	3	0	0	5	1	9
Northampton	3	1	1	1	2	3	5
Arsenal U21	3	0	2	1	2	3	3
Cambridge	3	0	1	2	2	4	1

SECOND ROUND

North: Accrington 2 Bolton 0; Blackpool 1 Scunthorpe 3; Doncaster 0 Leicester U21 3; Everton U21 0 Fleetwood 4; Port Vale 2 Mansfield 2 (Port Vale won 4-2 on pens); Salford 3 Wolves U21 0; Shrewsbury 1 Manchester City U21 1 (Manchester City U21 won 6-5 on pens); Tranmere 3 Manchester Utd U21 2

South: Brighton U21 0 Newport 0 (Newport won 5-4 on pens); Bristol Rov 1 Leyton Orient 1 (Bristol Rov won 4-2 on pens); Colchester 1 Stevenage 2; Exeter 0 Oxford 0 (Exeter won 3-0 on pens); MK Dons 2 Coventry 0; Peterborough 1 Ipswich 1 (Ipswich won 6-5 on pens); Portsmouth 2 Northampton 1; Walsall 3 Chelsea U21 2

THIRD ROUND

Bristol Rov 0 Stevenage 1; Exeter 2 Ipswich 1; Fleetwood 2 Accrington 2 (Accrington won 5-3 on pens); Newport 3 MK Dons 0; Salford 3 Port Vale 0; Scunthorpe 3 Manchester City U21 1; Tranmere 1 Leicester U21 2; Walsall 1 Portsmouth 2

FOURTH ROUND

Exeter 3 Stevenage 0; Newport 1 Leicester U21 0; Portsmouth 2 Scunthorpe 1; Salford 2 Accrington 1

SEMI-FINALS

Newport 0 Salford 0 (Salford won 6-5 on pens); Portsmouth 3 Exeter 2

FINAL

Portsmouth v Salford – cancelled (COVID-19)

BUILDBASE FA TROPHY

FIRST ROUND: AFC Fylde 1 Curzon Ashton 0; AFC Telford 0 Leamington 5; Atherton 2 Barrow 2; Barnet 2 Weymouth 1; Bath 2 Sholing 0; Bradford PA 2 Halesowen 2; Carshalton 3 Aveley 3; Chelmsford 2 Havant 1; Chesterfield 0 Notts Co 1; Dorking 3 Bromley 0; Eastbourne 2 Salisbury 2; Eastleigh 6 Yate 1; Enfield 0 Ebbsfleet 2; Farsley 2 Altrincham 2; FC United 2 Kettering 1; Halifax 4 Wrexham 0; Harrogate 3 Hartlepool 2; Hednesford 0 Chester 0; Hornchurch 1 Dulwich Hamlet 0; King's Lynn 2 Dover 2 (aet, King's Lynn won 4-2 on pens);

Kingstonian 3 Woking 1; Maidenhead 4 Hemel Hempstead 2; Maidstone 2 Concord 3; Matlock 2 Chorley 2; Royston 2 Boreham Wood 0; Solihull 2 Darlington 2; South Shields 2 Southport 2; Stockport 4 Blyth 2; Sutton 1 Dagenham 1; Tombridge 2 Hampton 2; Torquay 5 Aldershot 1; Yeovil 3 Welling 1. **Replays:** Altrincham 1 Farsley 2 (aet); Aveley 2 Carshalton 0; Barrow 2 Atherton 0; Chester 2 Hednesford 1; Chorley 1 Matlock 2 (aet, Matlock won 4-3 on pens); Halesowen 2 Bradford PA 0; Hampton 2 Tonbridge 0; Salisbury 1 Eastbourne 0; Southport 3 South Shields 1

SECOND ROUND: AFC Fylde 4 Southport 1; Barrow 7 FC United 0; Chelmsford 4 Salisbury 0; Concord 1 Bath 1; Darlington 0 Harrogate 2; Dorking 1 Stockport 1; Eastleigh 2 Matlock 1; Ebbsfleet 1 King's Lynn 0; Farsley 1 Barnet 1; Halesowen 2 Maidenhead 2; Hornchurch 1 Aveley 2; Kingstonian 1 Leamington 1; Notts Co 2 Dagenham 1; Royston 3 Chester 0; Torquay 1 Halifax 2; Yeovil 4 Hampton 0. **Replays:** Barnet 2 Farsley 0; Bath 1 Concord 2; Leamington 1 Kingstonian 0; Maidenhead 1 Halesowen 3; Stockport 0 Dorking 4

THIRD ROUND: Aveley 3 Chelmsford 1; Barnet 3 Barrow 0; Concord 2 Leamington 2 (aet, Concord won 4-3 on pens); Dorking 2 AFC Fylde 4; Ebbsfleet 0 Royston 2 (aet); Halifax 0 Halesowen 1; Harrogate 2 Eastleigh 0; Yeovil 1 Notts Co 2

FOURTH ROUND: AFC Fylde 2 Harrogate 3 (aet); Barnet 1 Halesowen 2 (aet); Concord 2 Royston 1 (aet); Notts Co 5 Aveley 0
Competition abandoned – COVID 19

FINALS – RESULTS
Associated Members' Cup
1984   (Hull) Bournemouth 2 Hull 1

Freight Rover Trophy – Wembley
1985   Wigan 3 Brentford 1
1986   Bristol City 3 Bolton 0
1987   Mansfield 1 Bristol City 1
         (aet; Mansfield won 5-4 on pens)

Sherpa Van Trophy – Wembley
1988   Wolves 2 Burnley 0
1989   Bolton 4 Torquay 1

Leyland Daf Cup – Wembley
1990   Tranmere 2 Bristol Rov 1
1991   Birmingham 3 Tranmere 2

Autoglass Trophy – Wembley
1992   Stoke 1 Stockport 0
1993   Port Vale 2 Stockport 1
1994   Huddersfield 1 Swansea 1
         (aet; Swansea won 3-1 on pens)

Auto Windscreens Shield – Wembley
1995   Birmingham 1 Carlisle 0
         (Birmingham won in sudden-death overtime)
1996   Rotherham 2 Shrewsbury 1
1997   Carlisle 0 Colchester 0
         (aet; Carlisle won 4-3 on pens)
1998   Grimsby 2 Bournemouth 1
         (Grimsby won with golden goal in extra-time)
1999   Wigan 1 Millwall 0
2000   Stoke 2 Bristol City 1

LDV Vans Trophy – Millennium Stadium
2001   Port Vale 2 Brentford 1
2002   Blackpool 4 Cambridge Utd 1
2003   Bristol City 2 Carlisle 0
2004   Blackpool 2 Southend 0
2005   Wrexham 2 Southend 0

Football League Trophy – Millennium Stadium
2006   Swansea 2 Carlisle 1

Johnstone's Paint Trophy – Wembley
2007   Doncaster 3 Bristol Rov 2 (aet)
         (Millennium Stadium)
2008   MK Dons 2 Grimsby 0
2009   Luton 3 Scunthorpe 2 (aet)
2010   Southampton 4 Carlisle 1
2011   Carlisle 1 Brentford 0
2012   Chesterfield 2 Swindon 0
2013   Crewe 2 Southend 0
2014   Peterborough 3 Chesterfield 1
2015   Bristol City 2 Walsall 0
2016   Barnsley 3 Oxford 2

Checkatrade Trophy – Wembley
2017   Coventry 2 Oxford 1
2018   Lincoln 1 Shrewsbury 0
2019   Portsmouth 2 Sunderland 2
         (aet, Portsmouth won 5-4 on pens)

FINALS – AT WEMBLEY
Full Members' Cup (Discontinued after 1992)

| 1985–86 | Chelsea 5 Man City 4 |
| 1986–87 | Blackburn 1 Charlton 0 |

Simod Cup
| 1987–88 | Reading 4 Luton 1 |
| 1988–89 | Nottm Forest 4 Everton 3 |

Zenith Data Systems Cup
1989–90	Chelsea 1 Middlesbrough 0
1990–91	Crystal Palace 4 Everton 1
1991–92	Nottm Forest 3 Southampton 2

Anglo-Italian Cup (Discontinued after 1996
* Home club)
1970	*Napoli 0 Swindon 3
1971	*Bologna 1 Blackpool 2 (aet)
1972	*AS Roma 3 Blackpool 1
1973	*Fiorentina 1 Newcastle 2
1993	Derby 1 Cremonese 3 (at Wembley)
1994	Notts Co 0 Brescia 1 (at Wembley)
1995	Ascoli 1 Notts Co 2 (at Wembley)
1996	Port Vale 2 Genoa 5 (at Wembley)

FA Vase

At Wembley (until 2000 and from 2007)
1975	Hoddesdon 2 Epsom & Ewell 1
1976	Billericay 1 Stamford 0*
1977	Billericay 2 Sheffield 1 (replay Nottingham after a 1-1 at Wembley)
1978	Blue Star 2 Barton Rov 1
1979	Billericay 4 Almondsbury Greenway 1
1980	Stamford 2 Guisborough Town 0
1981	Whickham 3 Willenhall 2*
1982	Forest Green 3 Rainworth MF Welfare 0
1983	VS Rugby 1 Halesowen 0
1984	Stansted 3 Stamford 2
1985	Halesowen 3 Fleetwood 1
1986	Halesowen 3 Southall 0
1987	St Helens 3 Warrington 2
1988	Colne Dynamoes 1 Emley 0*
1989	Tamworth 3 Sudbury 0 (replay Peterborough after a 1-1 at Wembley)
1990	Yeading 1 Bridlington 0 (replay Leeds after 0-0 at Wembley)
1991	Guiseley 3 Gresley Rov 1 (replay Bramall Lane Sheffield after a 4-4 at Wembley)
1992	Wimborne 5 Guiseley 3
1993	Bridlington 1 Tiverton 0
1994	Diss 2 Taunton 1*
1995	Arlesey 2 Oxford City 1
1996	Brigg Town 3 Clitheroe 0
1997	Whitby Town 3 North Ferriby 0
1998	Tiverton 1 Tow Law 0
1999	Tiverton 1 Bedlington 0

2000	Deal 1 Chippenham 0
2001	Taunton 2 Berkhamsted 1 (Villa Park)
2002	Whitley Bay 1 Tiptree 0* (Villa Park)
2003	Brigg 2 AFC Sudbury 1 (Upton Park)
2004	Winchester 2 AFC Sudbury 0 (St Andrews)
2005	Didcot 3 AFC Sudbury 2 (White Hart Lane)
2006	Nantwich 3 Hillingdon 1 (St Andrews)
2007	Truro 3 AFC Totton 1
2008	Kirkham & Wesham (Fylde) 2 Lowestoft 1
2009	Whitley Bay 2 Glossop 0
2010	Whitley Bay 6 Wroxham 1
2011	Whitley Bay 3 Coalville 2
2012	Dunston 2 West Auckland 0
2013	Spennymoor 2 Tunbridge Wells 1
2014	Sholing 1 West Auckland 0
2015	North Shields 2 Glossop North End 1*
2016	Morpeth 4 Hereford 1
2017	South Shields 4 Cleethorpes 0
2018	Thatcham 1 Stockton 0
2019	Chertsey 3 Cray Valley 1*
* After extra-time

FA Trophy Finals
At Wembley
1970	Macclesfield 2 Telford 0
1971	Telford 3 Hillingdon 2
1972	Stafford 3 Barnet 0
1973	Scarborough 2 Wigan 1*
1974	Morecambe 2 Dartford 1
1975	Matlock 4 Scarborough 0
1976	Scarborough 3 Stafford 2*
1977	Scarborough 2 Dag & Red 1
1978	Altrincham 3 Leatherhead 1
1979	Stafford 2 Kettering 0
1980	Dag & Red 2 Mossley 1
1981	Bishop's Stortford 1 Sutton 0
1982	Enfield 1 Altrincham 0*
1983	Telford 2 Northwich 1
1984	Northwich 2 Bangor 1 (replay Stoke after a 1-1 at Wembley)
1985	Wealdstone 2 Boston 1
1986	Altrincham 1 Runcorn 0
1987	Kidderminster 2 Burton 0 (replay WBA after a 0-0 at Wembley)
1988	Enfield 3 Telford 2 (replay WBA after a 0-0 at Wembley)
1989	Telford 1 Macclesfield 0*
1990	Barrow 3 Leek 0
1991	Wycombe 2 Kidderminster 1
1992	Colchester 3 Witton 1
1993	Wycombe 4 Runcorn 1
1994	Woking 2 Runcorn 1

1995 Woking 2 Kidderminster 1
1996 Macclesfield 3 Northwich 1
1997 Woking 1 Dag & Red & Redbridge 0*
1998 Cheltenham 1 Southport 0
1999 Kingstonian 1 Forest Green 0
2000 Kingstonian 3 Kettering 2

At Villa Park
2001 Canvey 1 Forest Green 0
2002 Yeovil 2 Stevenage 0
2003 Burscough 2 Tamworth 1
2004 Hednesford 3 Canvey 2
2005 Grays 1 Hucknall 1* (Grays won 6-5 on pens)

At Upton Park
2006 Grays 2 Woking 0

At Wembley
2007 Stevenage 3 Kidderminster 2
2008 Ebbsfleet 1 Torquay 0
2009 Stevenage 2 York 0
2010 Barrow 2 Stevenage 1*
2011 Darlington 1 Mansfield 0 *
2012 York 2 Newport 0
2013 Wrexham 1 Grimsby 1 * Wrexham won 4-1 on pens)
2014 Cambridge Utd 4 Gosport 0
2015 North Ferriby 3 Wrexham 3* (North Ferriby won 5-4 on pens)
2016 Halifax 1 Grimsby 0
2017 York 3 Macclesfield 2
2018 Brackley 1 Bromley 1
2019 AFC Fylde 1 Leyton Orient 0
(* Brackley won 5-4 on pens)
(*After extra-time)

FA Youth Cup Winners

Year	Winners	Runners-up	Agg
1953	Man Utd	Wolves	9-3
1954	Man Utd	Wolves	5-4
1955	Man Utd	WBA	7-1
1956	Man Utd	Chesterfield	4-3
1957	Man Utd	West Ham	8-2
1958	Wolves	Chelsea	7-6
1959	Blackburn	West Ham	2-1
1960	Chelsea	Preston	5-2
1961	Chelsea	Everton	5-3
1962	Newcastle	Wolves	2-1
1963	West Ham	Liverpool	6-5
1964	Man Utd	Swindon	5-2
1965	Everton	Arsenal	3-2
1966	Arsenal	Sunderland	5-3
1967	Sunderland	Birmingham	2-0
1968	Burnley	Coventry	3-2
1969	Sunderland	WBA	6-3
1970	Tottenham	Coventry	4-3
1971	Arsenal	Cardiff	2-0
1972	Aston Villa	Liverpool	5-2
1973	Ipswich	Bristol City	4-1
1974	Tottenham	Huddersfield	2-1
1975	Ipswich	West Ham	5-1
1976	WBA	Wolves	5-0
1977	Crystal Palace	Everton	1-0
1978	Crystal Palace	Aston Villa	*1-0
1979	Millwall	Man City	2-0
1980	Aston Villa	Man City	3-2
1981	West Ham	Tottenham	2-1
1982	Watford	Man Utd	7-6
1983	Norwich	Everton	6-5
1984	Everton	Stoke	4-2
1985	Newcastle	Watford	4-1
1986	Man City	Man Utd	3-1
1987	Coventry	Charlton	2-1
1988	Arsenal	Doncaster	6-1
1989	Watford	Man City	2-1
1990	Tottenham	Middlesbrough	3-2
1991	Millwall	Sheffield Wed	3-0
1992	Man Utd	Crystal Palace	6-3
1993	Leeds	Man Utd	4-1
1994	Arsenal	Millwall	5-3
1995	Man Utd	Tottenham	†2-2
1996	Liverpool	West Ham	4-1
1997	Leeds	Crystal Palace	3-1
1998	Everton	Blackburn	5-3
1999	West Ham	Coventry	9-0
2000	Arsenal	Coventry	5-1
2001	Arsenal	Blackburn	6-3
2002	Aston Villa	Everton	4-2
2003	Man Utd	Middlesbrough	3-1
2004	Middlesbrough	Aston Villa	4-0
2005	Ipswich	Southampton	3-2
2006	Liverpool	Man City	3-2
2007	Liverpool	Man Utd	††2-2
2008	Man City	Chelsea	4-2
2009	Arsenal	Liverpool	6-2
2010	Chelsea	Aston Villa	3-2
2011	Man Utd	Sheffield Utd	6-3
2012	Chelsea	Blackburn	4-1
2013	Norwich	Chelsea	4-2
2014	Chelsea	Fulham	7-6
2015	Chelsea	Man City	5-2
2016	Chelsea	Man City	4-2
2017	Chelsea	Man City	6-2
2018	Chelsea	Arsenal	7-1
2019	Liverpool	Man City	*†††1-1

†††Liverpool won 5-3 on pens
(*One match only; †Manchester Utd won 4-3 on pens, ††Liverpool won 4-3 on pens)

CHARITY/COMMUNITY SHIELD RESULTS (POST WAR)
[CHARITY SHIELD]

1948	Arsenal	Manchester Utd	4-3
1949	Portsmouth	Wolves	*1-1
1950	England World Cup XI	FA Canadian Tour Team	4-2
1951	Tottenham	Newcastle	2-1
1952	Manchester Utd	Newcastle	4-2
1953	Arsenal	Blackpool	3-1
1954	Wolves	WBA	*4-4
1955	Chelsea	Newcastle	3-0
1956	Manchester Utd	Manchester City	1-0
1957	Manchester Utd	Aston Villa	4-0
1958	Bolton	Wolves	4-1
1959	Wolves	Nottm Forest	3-1
1960	Burnley	Wolves	*2-2
1961	Tottenham	FA XI	3-2
1962	Tottenham	Ipswich Town	5-1
1963	Everton	Manchester Utd	4-0
1964	Liverpool	West Ham	*2-2
1965	Manchester Utd	Liverpool	*2-2
1966	Liverpool	Everton	1-0
1967	Manchester Utd	Tottenham	*3-3
1968	Manchester City	WBA	6-1
1969	Leeds	Manchester City	2-1
1970	Everton	Chelsea	2-1
1971	Leicester	Liverpool	1-0
1972	Manchester City	Aston Villa	1-0
1973	Burnley	Manchester City	1-0
1974	Liverpool	Leeds	1-1
	(Liverpool won 6-5 on penalties)		
1975	Derby Co	West Ham	2-0
1976	Liverpool	Southampton	1-0
1977	Liverpool	Manchester Utd	*0-0
1978	Nottm Forest	Ipswich	5-0
1979	Liverpool	Arsenal	3-1
1980	Liverpool	West Ham	1-0
1981	Aston Villa	Tottenham	*2-2
1982	Liverpool	Tottenham	1-0
1983	Manchester Utd	Liverpool	2-0
1984	Everton	Liverpool	1-0
1985	Everton	Manchester Utd	2-0
1986	Everton	Liverpool	*1-1
1987	Everton	Coventry	1-0
1988	Liverpool	Wimbledon	2-1
1989	Liverpool	Arsenal	1-0
1990	Liverpool	Manchester Utd	*1-1
1991	Arsenal	Tottenham	*0-0
1992	Leeds	Liverpool	4-3
1993	Manchester Utd	Arsenal	1-1
	(Manchester Utd won 5-4 on penalties)		
1994	Manchester Utd	Blackburn	2-0
1995	Everton	Blackburn	1-0
1996	Manchester Utd	Newcastle	4-0
1997	Manchester Utd	Chelsea	1-1
	(Manchester Utd won 4-2 on penalties)		
1998	Arsenal	Manchester Utd	3-0
1999	Arsenal	Manchester Utd	2-1

| 2000 | Chelsea | Manchester Utd | 2-0 |
| 2001 | Liverpool | Manchester Utd | 2-1 |

COMMUNITY SHIELD

2002	Arsenal	Liverpool	1-0
2003	Manchester Utd	Arsenal	1-1
	(Manchester Utd won 4-3 on penalties)		
2004	Arsenal	Manchester Utd	3-1
2005	Chelsea	Arsenal	2-1
2006	Liverpool	Chelsea	2-1
2007	Manchester Utd	Chelsea	1-1
	(Manchester Utd won 3-0 on penalties)		
2008	Manchester Utd	Portsmouth	0-0
	(Manchester Utd won 3-1 on pens)		
2009	Chelsea	Manchester Utd	2-2
	(Chelsea won 4-1 on pens)		
2010	Manchester Utd	Chelsea	3-1
2011	Manchester Utd	Manchester City	3-2
2012	Manchester City	Chelsea	3-2
2013	Manchester Utd	Wigan	2-0
2014	Arsenal	Manchester City	3-0
2015	Arsenal	Chelsea	1-0
2016	Manchester Utd	Leicester	2-1
2017	Arsenal	Chelsea	1-1
	(Arsenal won 4-1 on pens)		
2018	Manchester City	Chelsea	2-0
2019	Manchester City	Liverpool	1-1
	(Manchester City won 5-4 on pens)		

(Fixture played at Wembley 1974–2000 and from 2007); Millennium Stadium 2001–06; Villa Park 2012) * Trophy shared

THE THINGS THEY SAY...

'Racism has won. They never get punished. In the end, I'm the scapegoat' – **Antonio Rudiger**, Chelsea defender, on the decision to close an investigation into alleged racist chants against him from the Tottenham crowd after the club and the Metropolitan Police found no evidence 'to corroborate or contradict' it.

'It was hard for me to see my team-mate get booed for something that was my fault' – **Raheem Sterling**.

'Raheem is a very important player for us, but I felt it was the right thing to do. We are like a family and all families have disagreements. The important thing is that you communicate and work through those disagreements' – **Gareth Southgate**, England manager, after dropping Raheem Sterling for the Euro 2020 qualifier against Montenegro for scuffling with team-mate Joe Gomez at St George's Park.

'I've taken full responsibility and accepted the consequences' – **Raheem Sterling** admits he was in the wrong.

'No England player in an England shirt should be booed. I'm hugely disappointed for Joe, but he has the support of the dressing room' – **Gareth Southgate** after Joe Gomez was booed when on as a substitute.

SCOTTISH TABLES 2019–2020

(Season curtailed – COVID-19. Final positions determined by points-per-game)

LADBROKES PREMIERSHIP

		P	Home					Away					Gd	Pts	PPG
			W	D	L	F	A	W	D	L	F	A			
1	Celtic	30	14	0	1	50	7	12	2	1	39	12	70	80	2.67
2	Rangers	29	11	1	2	33	7	10	3	2	31	12	45	67	2.31
3	Motherwell	30	7	1	7	23	23	7	3	5	18	15	3	46	1.53
4	Aberdeen	30	7	3	5	23	19	5	6	4	17	17	4	45	1.50
5	Livingston	30	8	4	2	19	8	2	5	9	22	31	2	39	1.30
6	St Johnstone	29	5	6	5	19	26	3	6	4	9	20	-18	36	1.24
7	Hibernian	30	5	7	3	26	22	4	3	8	16	27	-7	37	1.23
8	Kilmarnock	30	6	5	4	20	15	3	1	11	11	26	-10	33	1.10
9	St Mirren	30	4	6	4	13	13	2	2	11	11	28	-17	29	0.97
10	Ross Co	30	5	3	6	17	23	2	5	9	12	37	-31	29	0.97
11	Hamilton	30	4	3	9	16	26	2	6	6	14	24	-20	27	0.90
12	Hearts	30	2	7	6	19	23	2	4	9	12	29	-21	23	0.77

Celtic champions, Hearts relegated. Celtic into Champions League first qualifying round; Rangers into Europa League second qualifying round: Aberdeen and Motherwell into first qualifying round.
Leading scorers: 22 Edouard (Celtic); 13 Defoe (Rangers); 12 Doidge (Hibernian), Morelos (Rangers); 11 Christie (Celtic), Cosgrove (Aberdeen); 10 Forrest (Celtic); 9 Brophy (Kilmarnock), Dykes (Livingston), Griffiths (Celtic), McGregor (Celtic); 8 Lawless (Livingston), Obika (St Mirren)

LADBROKES CHAMPIONSHIP

		P	Home			Away			F	A	Gd	Pts	PPG
			W	D	L	W	D	L					
1	Dundee Utd	28	10	3	1	8	2	4	52	22	30	59	2.11
2	Inverness	27	8	2	3	6	1	7	39	32	7	45	1.67
3	Dundee	27	7	2	4	4	6	4	32	31	1	41	1.52
4	Ayr	27	6	3	5	6	1	6	38	35	3	40	1.48
5	Arbroath	26	6	4	3	4	2	7	24	26	-2	36	1.38
6	Dunfermline	28	7	3	5	3	4	6	41	36	5	37	1.32
7	Morton	28	6	5	3	4	1	9	45	52	-7	36	1.29
8	Alloa	28	4	4	6	3	6	6	33	43	-10	31	1.11
9	Queen of South	28	4	2	8	3	5	6	28	40	-12	28	1.00
10	Partick	27	2	4	7	4	6	6	32	47	-15	26	0.96

Dundee Utd champions and promoted, Partick relegated
Leading scorers: 24 Shankland (Dundee Utd); 18 Nisbet (Dunfermline); 10 Forrest (Ayr), Hemmings (Dundee), O'Hara (Alloa); 8 Dobbie (Queen of South), McHugh (Morton), Trouten (Alloa); 7 Clark (Dundee Utd), White (Inverness)

LADBROKES LEAGUE ONE

		Home			Away							
		P	W	D	L	W	D	L	F	A	Gd	Pts	PPG
1	Raith	28	9	4	1	6	4	4	49	33	+16	53	1.89
2	Falkirk	28	10	2	2	4	8	2	54	18	+36	52	1.86
3	Airdrieonians| 28	7	4	4	4	7	2	44	38	+11	48	1.71
4	Montrose	28	9	0	5	6	2	6	48	38	+10	47	1.68
5	East Fife	28	6	6	2	6	3	5	44	36	+8	45	1.61
6	Dumbarton	28	6	3	5	5	2	7	35	44	-9	38	1.36
7	Clyde	28	7	4	3	2	3	9	35	43	-8	34	1.21
8	Peterhead	27	5	4	5	2	1	10	30	44	-14	26	0.96
9	Forfar	28	4	3	7	2	3	9	26	47	-21	24	0.86
10| Stranraer	27	2	4	6	0	6	9	28	57	-29	16	0.59

Raith champions and promoted, Stranraer relegated

Leading scorers: 20 Goodwillie (Clyde); 19 McManus (Falkirk); 12 Carrick (Airdrieonians); 11 Gallagher (Airdrieonians); 10 Lyons (Montrose); 9 Agnew (East Fife), Gullan (Raith), Webster (Montrose); 8 Brown (Peterhead); Layne (Dumbarton)

LADBROKES LEAGUE TWO

		Home			Away							
		P	W	D	L	W	D	L	F	A	Gd	Pts	PPG
1	Cove	28	14	0	0	8	2	4	76	34	42	68	2.43
2	Edinburgh City	27	10	2	2	7	4	4	49	28	21	55	2.04
3	Elgin	28	7	2	5	5	5	4	48	34	14	43	1.54
4	Cowdenbeath	27	10	2	2	2	3	8	37	35	2	41	1.52
5	Queen's Park	28	6	5	3	5	2	7	37	35	2	40	1.43
6	Stirling	28	3	3	7	7	3	5	34	35	-1	36	1.29
7	Annan	27	6	4	4	3	0	10	33	54	-21	31	1.15
8	St'housemuir	28	3	4	8	4	4	5	32	48	-16	29	1.04
9	Albion	26	5	2	5	1	4	9	37	51	-14	24	0.92
10| Brechin	27	2	3	8	2	2	10	31	60	-29	17	0.63

Cove champions and promoted, no relegation

Leading scorers: 24 Megginson (Cove); 16 Sutherland (Elgin); 15 Masson (Cove); 13 Kouider-Aissa (Queen's Park); 11 Byrne (Albion); 10 Duffy (Stirling), Handling (Edinburgh City), Hester (Elgin); 8 Hopkirk (Stenhousemuir)

LADBROKES SCOTTISH LEAGUE RESULTS
2019–2020

PREMIERSHIP

	Aberdeen	Celtic	Hamilton	Hearts	Hibernian	Kilmarnock	Livingston	Motherwell	Rangers	Ross Co	St Johnstone	St Mirren
Aberdeen	–	0-4	1-0	3-2	1-1	3-0	2-1	0-1	2-2	3-0	1-1	2-1
	–	1-2			3-1					1-2	0-1	
Celtic	2-1	–	2-1	3-1	2-0	3-1	4-0	2-0	1-2	6-0	7-0	2-0
		–	5-0		3-1					3-0		5-0
Hamilton	0-1	0-1	–	2-1	1-1	2-0	2-1	1-3	1-3	2-2	0-1	0-1
	1-3	1-4	–			1-0	2-4	2-0				
Hearts	1-1	0-2	2-2	–	0-2	0-1	1-1	2-3	1-1	0-0	0-1	5-2
			2-2	–		2-3		1-1	2-1			
Hibernian	3-0	1-1	2-1	1-2	–	2-2	2-2	3-1	0-3	2-2	2-2	1-0
				1-3	–		1-1			3-0		2-2
Kilmarnock	0-0	1-3	2-2	3-0	2-0	–	2-1	0-1	1-2	0-0	0-0	1-0
	2-2				1-2	–				2-1	3-1	
Livingston	0-2	2-0	0-0	0-0	2-0	3-0	–	0-0	0-2	4-0	1-0	2-1
		2-2					–	1-0				2-1
Motherwell	0-3	2-5	1-2	1-0	3-0	2-1	2-1	–	0-2	1-2	4-0	2-0
		0-4			0-0			–		4-1		1-2
Rangers	5-0	0-2	5-0	5-0	6-1	1-0	3-1	2-1	–	2-0	–	1-0
	0-0		0-1		2-1		1-0		–			
Ross Co	1-3	1-4	3-0	0-0	2-1	1-0	1-4	1-2	0-4	–	2-2	2-1
							2-0		0-1	–	1-1	
St Johnstone	1-1	0-3	3-2	1-0	1-4	0-1	2-2	0-1	0-4	1-1	–	0-0
			3-3			2-1	1-0	2-1	2-2		–	
St Mirren	1-0	1-2	0-0	0-0	1-2	1-0	3-3	0-3	0-1	2-1	2-0	–
	0-0		1-1	1-0							0-0	–

CHAMPIONSHIP

	Alloa	Arbroath	Ayr	Dundee	Dundee Utd	Dunfermline	Inverness	Morton	Partick	Queen of South
Alloa	–	0-1	1-4	0-3	1-0	2-1	0-2	0-2	1-1	2-2
	–	2-0	0-2		0-0		2-0		1-1	
Arboath	2-1	–	0-3	1-1	0-1	1-0	3-0	1-0	1-1	0-0
		–				0-0	1-2	2-1		2-0
Ayr	2-1	1-1	–	1-2	2-0	0-1	0-2	4-2	4-1	1-0
			–	0-0	0-0		1-0	1-2		1-2
Dundee	2-1	2-0	1-0	–	0-2	4-3	0-0	2-1	1-3	1-2
	0-0		2-0	–			0-2		2-0	
Dundee Utd	2-1	2-1	4-0	6-2	–	2-0	4-1	6-0	1-0	3-0
		0-1		1-1	–		2-1	1-1	1-1	
Dunfermline	1-1	2-0	3-2	2-2	0-2	–	0-1	3-1	5-1	2-0
	1-3		0-1	2-0	2-0	–	1-2			1-1
Inverness	2-2	2-1	2-0	1-0	0-3	2-0	–	5-0	1-3	2-0
	1-1	0-1					–	3-2		3-1
Morton	4-1	1-0	2-3	1-0	1-2	1-1	2-1	–	3-2	2-2
	4-4	1-1		1-1			3-2	–	1-2	
Partick	1-1	1-3	2-3	0-1	1-2	0-3	3-1	2-1	–	0-1
		1-1			1-4	1-1			–	0-0
Queen of South	0-1	2-0	3-1	1-1	4-0	1-1	0-2	1-0	1-2	–
	2-3			0-1	0-1	2-3		0-4		–

	Airdrieonians	Clyde	Dumbarton	East Fife	Falkirk	Forfar	Montrose	Peterhead	Raith	Stranraer
Airdrieonians	–	3-1	3-1	4-0	0-0	0-2	1-3	2-1	0-1	2-2
	–	2-0		1-0	1-1	1-0			0-1	0-0
Clyde	3-1	–	1-2	1-1	1-0	0-0	0-2	1-2	2-2	6-1
		–	2-0	2-1	3-2		2-1			3-3
Dumbarton	0-1	1-2	–	2-4	1-1	3-1	0-2	1-0	0-1	3-1
	0-0	1-0	–			2-0			1-0	1-1
East Fife	4-1	0-0	2-2	–	0-0	1-0	0-1	1-1	4-2	1-1
	2-2		4-2	–				1-0	3-5	4-2
Falkirk	1-2	0-1	6-0	0-0	–	3-0	2-1	4-0	1-1	3-0
			3-0	2-0	–	6-0	1-0	3-0		
Forfar	1-4	0-0	3-4	1-2	0-2	–	2-0	2-1	1-2	1-0
		2-1		0-1		–	2-3		1-1	1-1
Montrose	0-1	4-0	1-2	1-3	2-3	3-0	–	4-3	0-1	2-1
	1-0		2-1	1-0			–	4-3		4-1
Peterhead	1-2	1-1	2-3	1-2	0-0	1-0	0-0	–	2-0	3-0
	0-2	2-0	1-0		1-3	1-1		–		
Raith	1-0	5-2	0-2	1-1	2-2	0-0	3-0	4-0	–	3-1
		1-0			1-1	2-1	4-3	2-1	–	
Stranraer	0-2	3-0	0-0	0-2	0-3	2-4	2-2	1-2	3-2	–
					1-1		0-1		1-1	–

LEAGUE TWO

	Albion	Annan	Brechin	Cove	Cowdenbeath	Edinburgh City	Elgin	Queen's Park	Stenhousemuir	Stirling
Albion	–	4-2	0-1	4-4	–	1-3	1-3	2-0	2-1	2-1
	–		4-1	2-2			1-2			0-3
Annan	3-2	–	5-2	6-1	1-0	0-2	1-1	3-2	1-1	0-0
	2-1				0-0		0-4		0-3	2-3
Brechin	0-0	0-1	–	2-4	2-1	2-3	2-1	0-3	1-2	1-1
				1-5			1-2	0-0		0-2
Cove	3-0	3-0	3-0	–	3-2	5-0	2-0	3-0	2-1	1-0
		2-0	3-2		3-1	2-1		2-0		
Cowdenbeath	1-0	3-1	2-1	1-3	–	1-0	0-0	1-0	3-1	1-0
	2-1	3-1	3-2				1-1			1-4
Edinburgh City	3-2	4-0	2-1	2-1	2-0	–	1-1	2-1	4-0	1-0
	3-0	3-0	0-0					1-2		0-1
Elgin	2-2	4-0	3-1	0-2	3-0	3-3	–	3-1	0-1	1-2
					3-0	3-2		0-1	2-3	3-1
Queen's Park	1-1	1-2	5-2	1-3	0-3	2-1	0-0	–	1-1	1-1
	2-2	2-0			1-0		2-0		2-1	
Stenhousemuir	2-3	1-2	1-0	3-2	0-3	1-3	2-2	0-3	–	0-2
	1-0		2-2	0-3	2-2	1-2	0-0			
Stirling	3-0	2-0	2-4	1-2	0-0	0-1	1-0	0-1	1-1	–
				1-7			1-2	1-3	0-3	

CELTIC TARGET RECORD TENTH TITLE

Neil Lennon set his sights on a record tenth successive title after a threat by Rangers to his side's supremacy petered out. Going into the winter break, their rivals closed to within two points, with a game in hand, after goals by Ryan Kent and Nikola Katic delivered a 2-1 victory at Celtic Park. But defeats by Hearts, Kilmarnock and Hamilton ended their challenge, prompting manager Steven Gerrard to question his team's 'mental strength.' Celtic had extended their advantage to 13 points when the season was curtailed and were declared champions when a points-per-game average was used to determine final positions. Lennon, who has been involved in five of those successful campaigns in two spells as manager, now wants to emulate Jock Stein's nine-in-a-row titles between 1966-74 and the same dominance Rangers enjoyed between 1989-1997. He said: 'I grew up on stories of that Celtic team. To be able to match it is very special. We can go for ten because I know it's what our supporters want.'

HOW THEY CONTINUED TO REIGN SUPREME

AUGUST 2019

3	Celtic 7 (Johnston 9, Christie 26, 30, 67, Ntcham 72, Edouard 80, Griffths 86) St Johnstone 0. Att: 58,877
10	Motherwell 2 (Donnelly 12, 90+2) Celtic 5 (Ajer 14, Griffiths 41, Forrest 66, Edouard 76, Christie 86 pen). Att: 8,822
25	Celtic 3 (Berra 29 og, McGregor 54, Halkett 60 og) Hearts 1 (Washington 81). Att: 58,763

SEPTEMBER 2019

1	Rangers 0 Celtic 2 (Edouard 32, Hayes 90+3). Att: 49,873
14	Hamilton 0 Celtic 1 (Forrest 4). Att: 5,300
22	Celtic 3 (Edouard 44, 53, Christie 57) Kilmarnock 1 (Brophy 33). Att: 57,137
28	Hibernian 1 (Ajer 8 og) Celtic 1 (Christie 24). Att: 18,339

OCTOBER 2019

6	Livingston 2 (Robinson 47, Dykes 73) Celtic 0. Att: 8,196
19	Celtic 6 (Elyounoussi 4, 72, Edouard 46, McGregor 49, Fontaine 50 og, Forrest 55) Ross Co 0. Att: 58,566
27	Aberdeen 0 Celtic 4 (Edouard 10, Frimpong 15, Forrest 37, Elyounoussi 45). Att: 15,079
30	Celtic 2 (Elyounoussi 49, Forrest 54) St Mirren 0. Att: 56,127

NOVEMBER 2019

| 10 | Celtic 2 (Edouard 9, Tait 54 og) Motherwell 0. Att: 57,137 |
| 23 | Celtic 4 (Edouard 19, Brown 57, Forrest 64, 90+1) Livingston 0. Att: 58,247 |

DECEMBER 2019

1	Ross Co 1 (Stewart 24) Celtic 4 (Christie 11, 38, Rogic 67, Johnston 73). Att: 6,512
4	Celtic 2 (Christie 13, Brown 90+2) Hamilton 1 (Ogboe 90). Att: 54,584
15	Celtic 2 (Frimpong 39, Edouard 66) Hibernian 0. Att: 57,598
18	Hearts 0 Celtic 2 (Christie 28, Ntcham 40). Att: 17,297
21	Celtic 2 (Jullien 7, Edouard 66) Aberdeen 1(Cosgrove 35). Att: 59,131
26	St Mirren 1 (MacPherson 89) Celtic 2 (McGregor 22, Forrest 32). Att: 6,7978

29   Celtic 1 (Edouard 42) Rangers 2 (Kent 36, Katic 56). Att: 58,922

JANUARY 2020

22   Kilmarnock 1 (Kabamba 66) Celtic 3 (Edouard 25, Griffiths 51, Jullien 73).
Att: 8,307

25   Celtic 3 (Edouard 65, 68, McGregor 37 pen) Ross Co 0. Att: 58,785

29   St Johnstone 0 Celtic 3 (Ntcham 6, Forrest 20, Griffiths 26). Att: 8,743

FEBRUARY 2020

2   Hamilton 1 (Ogboe 27) Celtic 4 (Edouard 35, 81, Jullien 78, Forrest 90+1).
Att: 4,708

5   Motherwell 0 Celtic 4 (Edouard 9, 80, Griffiths 51, McGregor 75). Att: 8,534

12   Celtic 5 (Ntcham 30, Jullien 46, McGregor 52, Christie 67, Simunovic 80) Hearts 0.
Att: 57,431

15   Aberdeen 1 (Taylor 27) Celtic 2 (McGregor 10, Ajer 81). Att: 14,135

22   Celtic 3 (Ajer 28, Edouard 33, Griffiths 62) Kilmarnock 1 (Brophy 6 pen). Att: 58,883

MARCH 2020

4   Livingston 2 (Guthrie 24, Robinson 46) Celtic 2 (McGregor 16, Rogic 90+1).
Att: 8,640

7   Celtic 5 (Griffiths 18, 44, 74, Edouard 54, McGregor 90 pen) St Mirren 0.
Att: 58,998

Season terminated – Covid-19. Celtic confirmed as champions, 13 points ahead of Rangers
from an extra match played

THE THINGS THEY SAY...

'For the supporters, for whom the club is part of the community and a real senses of identity, it's a tragic story. It worries me and I think it could be something we see a bit more frequently' – **Gareth Southgate**, England manager, on Bury's demise.

'This has to be one of the darkest days in the league's history. It will be felt across the entire football family' – **Debbie Jevans**, executive chair of the EFL.

'There will be a nine or ten out there soon' – **Ben Foster**, Watford goalkeeper, predicts Manchester City will one day hit double figures after his side are beaten 8-0.

'I literally became a head on a stick. I felt degraded'– **Peter Crouch**, the Premier League's record scorer of 51 headers, on his final season before retiring after 21 years with nine clubs.

'I've had some mad nights and some bad nights, but I don't think I've been in a game like that' – **Frank Lampard**, Chelsea manager, after his side recovered from trailing 4-1 to draw 4-4 with Ajax in a Europa League game of two sendings-off, two own goals and two penalties.

SCOTTISH HONOURS LIST

PREMIER DIVISION

	First	Pts	Second	Pts	Third	Pts
1975–6	Rangers	54	Celtic	48	Hibernian	43
1976–7	Celtic	55	Rangers	46	Aberdeen	43
1977–8	Rangers	55	Aberdeen	53	Dundee Utd	40
1978–9	Celtic	48	Rangers	45	Dundee Utd	44
1979–80	Aberdeen	48	Celtic	47	St Mirren	42
1980–81	Celtic	56	Aberdeen	49	Rangers	44
1981–2	Celtic	55	Aberdeen	53	Rangers	43
1982–3	Dundee Utd	56	Celtic	55	Aberdeen	55
1983–4	Aberdeen	57	Celtic	50	Dundee Utd	47
1984–5	Aberdeen	59	Celtic	52	Dundee Utd	47
1985–6	*Celtic	50	Hearts	50	Dundee Utd	47
1986–7	Rangers	69	Celtic	63	Dundee Utd	60
1987–8	Celtic	72	Hearts	62	Rangers	60
1988–9	Rangers	56	Aberdeen	50	Celtic	46
1989–90	Rangers	51	Aberdeen	44	Hearts	44
1990–1	Rangers	55	Aberdeen	53	Celtic	41
1991–2	Rangers	72	Hearts	63	Celtic	62
1992–3	Rangers	73	Aberdeen	64	Celtic	60
1993–4	Rangers	58	Aberdeen	55	Motherwell	54
1994–5	Rangers	69	Motherwell	54	Hibernian	53
1995–6	Rangers	87	Celtic	83	Aberdeen	55
1996–7	Rangers	80	Celtic	75	Dundee Utd	60
1997–8	Celtic	74	Rangers	72	Hearts	67

PREMIER LEAGUE

	First	Pts	Second	Pts	Third	Pts
1998–99	Rangers	77	Celtic	71	St Johnstone	57
1999–2000	Rangers	90	Celtic	69	Hearts	54
2000–01	Celtic	97	Rangers	82	Hibernian	66
2001–02	Celtic	103	Rangers	85	Livingston	58
2002–03	*Rangers	97	Celtic	97	Hearts	63
2003–04	Celtic	98	Rangers	81	Hearts	68
2004–05	Rangers	93	Celtic	92	Hibernian	61
2005–06	Celtic	91	Hearts	74	Rangers	73
2006–07	Celtic	84	Rangers	72	Aberdeen	65
2007–08	Celtic	89	Rangers	86	Motherwell	60
2008–09	Rangers	86	Celtic	82	Hearts	59
2009–10	Rangers	87	Celtic	81	Dundee Utd	63
2010–11	Rangers	93	Celtic	92	Hearts	63
2011–12	Celtic	93	**Rangers	73	Motherwell	62
2012–13	Celtic	79	Motherwell	63	St Johnstone	56

Maximum points: 72 except 1986–8, 1991–4 (88), 1994–2000 (108), 2001–10 (114)
* Won on goal difference. **Deducted 10 pts for administration

PREMIERSHIP

	First	Pts	Second	Pts	Third	Pts
2013–14	Celtic	99	Motherwell	70	Aberdeen	68
2014–15	Celtic	92	Aberdeen	75	Inverness	65
2015–16	Celtic	86	Aberdeen	71	Hearts	65
2016–17	Celtic	106	Aberdeen	76	Rangers	67
2017–18	Celtic	82	Aberdeen	73	Rangers	70
2018–19	Celtic	87	Rangers	78	Kilmarnock	67
2019–20C	Celtic	80	Rangers	67	Motherwell	46

C Season curtailed – COVID-19

FIRST DIVISION (Scottish Championship until 1975–76)

	First	Pts	Second	Pts	Third	Pts
1890–1a	††Dumbarton	29	Rangers	29	Celtic	24
1891–2b	Dumbarton	37	Celtic	35	Hearts	30
1892–3a	Celtic	29	Rangers	28	St Mirren	23
1893–4a	Celtic	29	Hearts	26	St Bernard's	22
1894–5a	Hearts	31	Celtic	26	Rangers	21
1895–6a	Celtic	30	Rangers	26	Hibernian	24
1896–7a	Hearts	28	Hibernian	26	Rangers	25
1897–8a	Celtic	33	Rangers	29	Hibernian	22
1898–9a	Rangers	36	Hearts	26	Celtic	24
1899–1900a	Rangers	32	Celtic	25	Hibernian	24
1900–1c	Rangers	35	Celtic	29	Hibernian	25
1901–2a	Rangers	28	Celtic	26	Hearts	22
1902–3b	Hibernian	37	Dundee	31	Rangers	29
1903–4d	Third Lanark	43	Hearts	39	Rangers	38
1904–5a	†Celtic	41	Rangers	41	Third Lanark	35
1905–6a	Celtic	46	Hearts	39	Rangers	38
1906–7f	Celtic	55	Dundee	48	Rangers	45
1907–8f	Celtic	55	Falkirk	51	Rangers	50
1908–9f	Celtic	51	Dundee	50	Clyde	48
1909–10f	Celtic	54	Falkirk	52	Rangers	49
1910–11f	Rangers	52	Aberdeen	48	Falkirk	44
1911–12f	Rangers	51	Celtic	45	Clyde	42
1912–13f	Rangers	53	Celtic	49	Hearts	41
1913–14g	Celtic	65	Rangers	59	Hearts	54
1914–15g	Celtic	65	Hearts	61	Rangers	50
1915–16g	Celtic	67	Rangers	56	Morton	51
1916–17g	Celtic	64	Morton	54	Rangers	53
1917–18f	Rangers	56	Celtic	55	Kilmarnock	43
1918–19f	Celtic	58	Rangers	57	Morton	47
1919–20h	Rangers	71	Celtic	68	Motherwell	57
1920–1h	Rangers	76	Celtic	66	Hearts	56
1921–2h	Celtic	67	Rangers	66	Raith	56
1922–3g	Rangers	55	Airdrieonians	50	Celtic	46
1923–4g	Rangers	59	Airdrieonians	50	Celtic	41
1924–5g	Rangers	60	Airdrieonians	57	Hibernian	52
1925–6g	Celtic	58	Airdrieonians	50	Hearts	50
1926–7g	Rangers	56	Motherwell	51	Celtic	49
1927–8g	Rangers	60	Celtic	55	Motherwell	55
1928–9g	Rangers	67	Celtic	51	Motherwell	50
1929–30g	Rangers	60	Motherwell	55	Aberdeen	53
1930–1g	Rangers	60	Celtic	58	Motherwell	56
1931–2g	Motherwell	66	Rangers	61	Celtic	48
1932–3g	Rangers	62	Motherwell	59	Hearts	50
1933–4g	Rangers	66	Motherwell	62	Celtic	47
1934–5g	Rangers	55	Celtic	52	Hearts	50
1935–6g	Celtic	68	Rangers	61	Aberdeen	61
1936–7g	Rangers	61	Aberdeen	54	Celtic	52
1937–8g	Celtic	61	Hearts	58	Rangers	49
1938–9f	Rangers	59	Celtic	48	Aberdeen	46
1946–7f	Rangers	46	Hibernian	44	Aberdeen	39
1947–8g	Hibernian	48	Rangers	46	Partick	46
1948–9i	Rangers	46	Dundee	45	Hibernian	39
1949–50i	Rangers	50	Hibernian	49	Hearts	43
1950–1i	Hibernian	48	Rangers	38	Dundee	38
1951–2i	Hibernian	45	Rangers	41	East Fife	37
1952–3i	*Rangers	43	Hibernian	43	East Fife	39
1953–4i	Celtic	43	Hearts	38	Partick	35

	First		Second		Third	
1954–5f	Aberdeen	49	Celtic	46	Rangers	41
1955–6f	Rangers	52	Aberdeen	46	Hearts	45
1956–7f	Rangers	55	Hearts	53	Kilmarnock	42
1957–8f	Hearts	62	Rangers	49	Celtic	46
1958–9f	Rangers	50	Hearts	48	Motherwell	44
1959–60f	Hearts	54	Kilmarnock	50	Rangers	42
1960–1f	Rangers	51	Kilmarnock	50	Third Lanark	42
1961–2f	Dundee	54	Rangers	51	Celtic	46
1962–3f	Rangers	57	Kilmarnock	48	Partick	46
1963–4f	Rangers	55	Kilmarnock	49	Celtic	47
1964–5f	*Kilmarnock	50	Hearts	50	Dunfermline	49
1965–6f	Celtic	57	Rangers	55	Kilmarnock	45
1966–7f	Celtic	58	Rangers	55	Clyde	46
1967–8f	Celtic	63	Rangers	61	Hibernian	45
1968–9f	Celtic	54	Rangers	49	Dunfermline	45
1969–70f	Celtic	57	Rangers	45	Hibernian	44
1970–1f	Celtic	56	Aberdeen	54	St Johnstone	44
1971–2f	Celtic	60	Aberdeen	50	Rangers	44
1972–3f	Celtic	57	Rangers	56	Hibernian	45
1973–4f	Celtic	53	Hibernian	49	Rangers	48
1974–5f	Rangers	56	Hibernian	49	Celtic	45

*Won on goal average †Won on deciding match ††Title shared. Competition suspended 1940–46 (Second World War)

SCOTTISH TITLE WINS

Rangers	*54	Hibernian	4	Kilmarnock	1
Celtic	51	Dumbarton	*2	Motherwell	1
Aberdeen	4	Dundee	1	Third Lanark	1
Hearts	4	Dundee Utd	1	(*Incl 1 shared)

FIRST DIVISION (Since formation of Premier Division)

	First	Pts	Second	Pts	Third	Pts
1975–6d	Partick	41	Kilmarnock	35	Montrose	30
1976–7j	St Mirren	62	Clydebank	58	Dundee	51
1977–8j	*Morton	58	Hearts	58	Dundee	57
1978–9j	Dundee	55	Kilmarnock	54	Clydebank	54
1979–80j	Hearts	53	Airdrieonians	51	Ayr	44
1980–1j	Hibernian	57	Dundee	52	St Johnstone	51
1981–2j	Motherwell	61	Kilmarnock	51	Hearts	50
1982–3j	St Johnstone	55	Hearts	54	Clydebank	50
1983–4j	Morton	54	Dumbarton	51	Partick	46
1984–5j	Motherwell	50	Clydebank	48	Falkirk	45
1985–6j	Hamilton	56	Falkirk	45	Kilmarnock	44
1986–7k	Morton	57	Dunfermline	56	Dumbarton	53
1987–8k	Hamilton	56	Meadowbank	52	Clydebank	49
1988–9j	Dunfermline	54	Falkirk	52	Clydebank	48
1989–90j	St Johnstone	58	Airdrieonians	54	Clydebank	44
1990–1j	Falkirk	54	Airdrieonians	53	Dundee	52
1991–2k	Dundee	58	Partick	57	Hamilton	57
1992–3k	Raith	65	Kilmarnock	54	Dunfermline	52
1993–4k	Falkirk	66	Dunfermline	65	Airdrieonians	54
1994–5l	Raith	69	Dunfermline	68	Dundee	68
1995–6l	Dunfermline	71	Dundee Utd	67	Morton	67
1996–7l	St Johnstone	80	Airdrieonians	60	Dundee	58
1997–8l	Dundee	70	Falkirk	65	Raith	60
1998–9l	Hibernian	89	Falkirk	66	Ayr	62
1999–2000l	St Mirren	76	Dunfermline	71	Falkirk	68
2000–01l	Livingston	76	Ayr	69	Falkirk	56
2001–02l	Partick	66	Airdie	56	Ayr	52

	Pts		Pts		Pts
002-03l Falkirk	81	Clyde	72	St Johnstone	67
003-04l Inverness	70	Clyde	69	St Johnstone	57
004-05l Falkirk	75	St Mirren	60	Clyde	60
005-06l St Mirren	76	St Johnstone	66	Hamilton	59
006-07l Gretna	66	St Johnstone	65	Dundee	53
007-08l Hamilton	76	Dundee	69	St Johnstone	58
008-09l St Johnstone	65	Partick	55	Dunfermline	51
009-10l Inverness	73	Dundee	61	Dunfermline	58
010-11l Dunfermline	70	Raith	60	Falkirk	58
011-12l Ross	79	Dundee	55	Falkirk	52
012-13l Partick	78	Morton	67	Falkirk	53

HAMPIONSHIP

First	Pts	Second	Pts	Third	Pts
013-14l Dundee	69	Hamilton	67	Falkirk	66
014-15l Hearts	91	Hibernian	70	Rangers	67
015-16l Rangers	81	Falkirk	70	Hibernian	70
016-17l Hibernian	71	Falkirk	60	Dundee Utd	57
017-18l St Mirren	74	Livingston	62	Dundee Utd	61
018-19l Ross Co	71	Dundee Utd	65	Inverness	56
019-20C Dundee Utd	59	Inverness	45	Dundee	41

Season curtailed – COVID-19
aximum points: a, 36; b, 44; c, 40; d 52; e, 60; f, 68; g, 76; h, 84; i, 60; j, 78; k, 88; l, 108
Won on goal difference

ECOND DIVISION

First	Pts	Second	Pts	Third	Pts
921-2a Alloa	60	Cowdenbeath	47	Armadale	45
922-3a Queen's Park	57	Clydebank	52	St Johnstone	50
923-4a St Johnstone	56	Cowdenbeath	55	Bathgate	44
924-5a Dundee Utd	50	Clydebank	48	Clyde	47
925-6a Dunfermline	59	Clyde	53	Ayr	52
926-7a Bo'ness	56	Raith	49	Clydebank	45
927-8a Ayr	54	Third Lanark	45	King'sPark	44
928-9b Dundee Utd	51	Morton	50	Arbroath	47
929-30a *LeithAthletic	57	East Fife	57	Albion	54
930-1a Third Lanark	61	Dundee Utd	50	Dunfermline	47
931-2a *E Stirling	55	St Johnstone	55	Stenhousemuir	46
932-3c Hibernian	55	Queen of South	49	Dunfermline	47
933-4c Albion	45	Dunfermline	44	Arbroath	44
934-5c Third Lanark	52	Arbroath	50	St Bernard's	47
935-6c Falkirk	59	St Mirren	52	Morton	48
936-7c Ayr	54	Morton	51	St Bernard's	48
937-8c Raith	59	Albion	48	Airdrieonians	47
938-9c Cowdenbeath	60	Alloa	48	East Fife	48
946-7d Dundee Utd	45	Airdrieonians	42	East Fife	31
947-8e East Fife	53	Albion	42	Hamilton	40
948-9e *Raith	42	Stirling	42	Airdrieonians	41
949-50e Morton	47	Airdrieonians	44	St Johnstone	36
950-1e *Queen of South	45	Stirling	45	Ayr	36
951-2e Clyde	44	Falkirk	43	Ayr	39
952-3 E Stirling	44	Hamilton	43	Queen's Park	37
953-4e Motherwell	45	Kilmarnock	42	Third Lanark	36
954-5e Airdrieonians	46	Dunfermline	42	Hamilton	39
955-6b Queen's Park	54	Ayr	51	St Johnstone	49
956-7b Clyde	64	Third Lanark	51	Cowdenbeath	45
957-8b Stirling	55	Dunfermline	53	Arbroath	47
958-9b Ayr	60	Arbroath	51	Stenhousemuir	46

1959–60b	St Johnstone	53	Dundee Utd	50	Queen of South	49
1960–1b	Stirling	55	Falkirk	54	Stenhousemuir	50
1961–2b	Clyde	54	Queen of South	53	Morton	44
1962–3b	St Johnstone	55	E Stirling	49	Morton	48
1963–4b	Morton	67	Clyde	53	Arbroath	46
1964–5b	Stirling	59	Hamilton	50	Queen of South	45
1965–6b	Ayr	53	Airdrieonians	50	Queen of South	47
1966–7b	Morton	69	Raith	58	Arbroath	57
1967–8b	St Mirren	62	Arbroath	53	East Fife	49
1968–9b	Motherwell	64	Ayr	53	East Fife	48
1969–70b	Falkirk	56	Cowdenbeath	55	Queen of South	50
1970–1b	Partick	56	East Fife	51	Arbroath	46
1971–2b	*Dumbarton	52	Arbroath	52	Stirling	50
1972–3b	Clyde	56	Dunfermline	52	Raith	47
1973–4b	Airdrieonians	60	Kilmarnock	58	Hamilton	55
1974–5b	Falkirk	54	Queen of South	53	Montrose	53

SECOND DIVISION (MODERN)

	First	Pts	Second	Pts	Third	Pts
1975–6d	*Clydebank	40	Raith	40	Alloa	35
1976–7f	Stirling	55	Alloa	51	Dunfermline	50
1977–8f	*Clyde	53	Raith	53	Dunfermline	48
1978–9f	Berwick	54	Dunfermline	52	Falkirk	50
1979–80f	Falkirk	50	E Stirling	49	Forfar	46
1980–1f	Queen's Park	50	Queen of South	46	Cowdenbeath	45
1981–2f	Clyde	59	Alloa	50	Arbroath	50
1982–3f	Brechin	55	Meadowbank	54	Arbroath	49
1983–4f	Forfar	63	East Fife	47	Berwick	43
1984–5f	Montrose	53	Alloa	50	Dunfermline	49
1985–6f	Dunfermline	57	Queen of South	55	Meadowbank	49
1986–7f	Meadowbank	55	Raith	52	Stirling	52
1987–8f	Ayr	61	St Johnstone	59	Queen's Park	51
1988–9f	Albion	50	Alloa	45	Brechin	43
1989–90f	Brechin	49	Kilmarnock	48	Stirling	47
1990–1f	Stirling	54	Montrose	46	Cowdenbeath	45
1991–2f	Dumbarton	52	Cowdenbeath	51	Alloa	50
1992–3f	Clyde	54	Brechin	53	Stranraer	53
1993–4f	Stranraer	56	Berwick	48	Stenhousemuir	47
1994–5g	Morton	64	Dumbarton	60	Stirling	58
1995–6g	Stirling	81	East Fife	67	Berwick	60
1996–7g	Ayr	77	Hamilton	74	Livingston	64
1997–8g	Stranraer	61	Clydebank	60	Livingston	59
1998–9g	Livingston	77	Inverness	72	Clyde	53
1999–2000g	Clyde	65	Alloa	64	Ross Co	62
2000–01g	Partick	75	Arbroath	58	Berwick	54
2001–02g	Queen of South	67	Alloa	59	Forfar Athletic	53
2002–03g	Raith	59	Brechin	55	Airdrie	54
2003–04g	Airdrie	70	Hamilton	62	Dumbarton	60
2004–05g	Brechin	72	Stranraer	63	Morton	62
2005–06g	Gretna	88	Morton	70	Peterhead	57
2006–07g	Morton	77	Stirling	69	Raith	62
2007–08g	Ross	73	Airdrie	66	Raith	60
2008–09g	Raith	76	Ayr	74	Brechin	62
2009–10g	*Stirling	65	Alloa	59	Cowdenbeath	59
2010–11g	Livingston	82	*Ayr	59	Forfar	59
2011–12g	Cowdenbeath	71	Arbroath	63	Dumbarton	58
2012–13g	Queen of South	92	Alloa	67	Brechin	61

LEAGUE ONE

	First	Pts	Second	Pts	Third	Pts
2013–14g	Rangers	102	Dunfermline	63	Stranraer	51
2014–15g	Morton	69	Stranraer	67	Forfar	66
2015–16g	Dunfermline	79	Ayr	61	Peterhead	59
2016–17g	Livingston	81	Alloa	62	Airdrieonians	52
2017–18g	Ayr	76	Raith	75	Alloa	60
2018–19g	Arbroath	70	Forfar	63	Raith	60
2019–20C	Raith	53	Falkirk	52	Airdrieonians	48

C Season curtailed – COVID-19

Maximum points: a, 76; b, 72; c, 68; d, 52e, 60; f, 78; g, 108 *Won on goal average/goal difference

THIRD DIVISION (MODERN)

1994–5	Forfar	80	Montrose	67	Ross Co	60
1995–6	Livingston	72	Brechin	63	Caledonian Th	57
1996–7	Inverness	76	Forfar	67	Ross Co	77
1997–8	Alloa	76	Arbroath	68	Ross Co	67
1998–9	Ross Co	77	Stenhousemuir	64	Brechin	59
1999–2000	Queen's Park	69	Berwick	66	Forfar	61
2000–01	*Hamilton	76	Cowdenbeath	76	Brechin	72
2001–02	Brechin	73	Dumbarton	61	Albion	59
2002–03	Morton	72	East Fife	71	Albion	70
2003–04	Stranraer	79	Stirling	77	Gretna	68
2004–05	Gretna	98	Peterhead	78	Cowdenbeath	51
2005–06	*Cowdenbeath	76	Berwick	76	Stenhousemuir	73
2006–07	Berwick	75	Arbroath	70	Queen's Park	68
2007–08	East Fife	88	Stranraer	65	Montrose	59
2008–09	Dumbarton	67	Cowdenbeath	63	East Stirling	61
2009–10	Livingston	78	Forfar	63	East Stirling	61
2010–11	Arbroath	66	Albion	61	Queen's Park	59
2011–12	Alloa	77	Queen's Park	63	Stranraer	58
2012–13	Rangers	83	Peterhead	59	Queen's Park	56

LEAGUE TWO

	First	Pts	Second	Pts	Third	Pts
2013–14	Peterhead	76	Annan	63	Stirling	58
2014–15	Albion	71	Queen's Park	61	Arbroath	56
2015–16	East Fife	62	Elgin	59	Clyde	57
2016–17	Arbroath	66	Forfar	64	Annan	58
2017–18	Montrose	77	Peterhead	76	Stirling	55
2018–19	Peterhead	79	Clyde	74	Edinburgh City	67
2019–20C	Cove	68	Edinburgh City	55	Elgin	43

C Season curtailed – COVID-19

Maximum points: 108 * Won on goal difference

RELEGATED FROM PREMIER DIVISION/PREMIER LEAGUE/PREMIERSHIP

1975–6	Dundee,	St Johnstone	1985–6	No relegation
1976–7	Kilmarnock,	Hearts	1986–7	Clydebank, Hamilton
1977–8	Ayr,	Clydebank	1987–8	Falkirk, Dunfermline, Morton
1978–9	Hearts,	Motherwell	1988–9	Hamilton
1979–80	Dundee,	Hibernian	1989–90	Dundee
1980–1	Kilmarnock,	Hearts	1990–1	No relegation
1981–2	Partick,	Airdrieonians	1991–2	St Mirren, Dunfermline
1982–3	Morton,	Kilmarnock	1992–3	Falkirk, Airdrieonians
1983–4	St Johnstone,	Motherwell	1993–4	St J'stone, Raith, Dundee
1984–5	Dumbarton,	Morton	1994–5	Dundee Utd

1995–6	Falkirk, Partick	2009–10	Falkirk
1996–7	Raith	2010–11	Hamilton
1997–8	Hibernian	2011–12	Dunfermline, *Rangers
1998–9	Dunfermline	2012–13	Dundee
1999–2000	No relegation	2013–14	Hibernian, **Hearts
2000–01	St Mirren	2014–15	St Mirren
2001–02	St Johnstone	2015–16	Dundee Utd
2002–03	No relegation	2016–17	Inverness
2003–04	Partick	2017–18	Partick, Ross Co
2004–05	Dundee	2018–19	Dundee
2005–06	Livingston	2019–20	Hearts
2006–07	Dunfermline		*Following administration, liquidation and new club
2007–08	Gretna		formed. **Deducted 15 points for administration
2008–09	Inverness		

RELEGATED FROM FIRST DIVISION/CHAMPIONSHIP

1975–6	Dunfermline, Clyde	1998–9	Hamilton, Stranraer
1976–7	Raith, Falkirk	1999–2000	Clydebank
1977–8	Alloa, East Fife	2000–01	Morton, Alloa
1978–9	Montrose, Queen of South	2001–02	Raith
1979–80	Arbroath, Clyde	2002–03	Alloa Athletic, Arbroath
1980–1	Stirling, Berwick	2003–04	Ayr, Brechin
1981–2	E Stirling, Queen of South	2004–05	Partick, Raith
1982–3	Dunfermline, Queen's Park	2005–06	Brechin, Stranraer
1983–4	Raith, Alloa	2006–07	Airdrie Utd, Ross Co
1984–5	Meadowbank, St Johnstone	2007–08	Stirling
1985–6	Ayr, Alloa	2008–09	*Livingston, Clyde
1986–7	Brechin, Montrose	2009–10	Airdrie, Ayr
1987–8	East Fife, Dumbarton	2010–11	Cowdenbeath, Stirling
1988–9	Kilmarnock, Queen of South	2011–12	Ayr, Queen of South
1989–90	Albion, Alloa	2012–13	Dunfermline, Airdrie
1990–1	Clyde, Brechin	2013–14	Morton
1991–2	Montrose, Forfar	2014–15	Cowdenbeath
1992–3	Meadowbank, Cowdenbeath	2015–16	Livingston, Alloa
1993–4	Dumbarton, Stirling, Clyde,	2016–17	Raith, Ayr
	Morton, Brechin	2017–18	Dumbarton, Brechin
1994–5	Ayr, Stranraer	2018–19	Falkirk
1995–6	Hamilton, Dumbarton	2019–20	Partick
1996–7	Clydebank, East Fife		*relegated to Division Three for breaching insolvency
1997–8	Partick, Stirling		rules

RELEGATED FROM SECOND DIVISION/LEAGUE ONE

1993–4	Alloa, Forfar, E Stirling,	2005–06	Dumbarton
	Montrose, Queen's Park,	2006–07	Stranraer, Forfar
	Arbroath, Albion,	2007–08	Cowdenbeath, Berwick
	Cowdenbeath	2008–09	Queen's Park, Stranraer
1994–5	Meadowbank, Brechin	2009–10	Arbroath, Clyde
1995–6	Forfar, Montrose	2010–11	Alloa, Peterhead
1996–7	Dumbarton, Berwick	2011–12	Stirling
1997–8	Stenhousemuir, Brechin	2012–13	Albion
1998–9	East Fife, Forfar	2013–14	East Fife, Arbroath
1999–2000	Hamilton	2014–15	Stirling
2000–01	Queen's Park, Stirling	2015–16	Cowdenbeath, Forfar
2001–02	Morton	2016–17	Peterhead, Stenhousemuir
2002–03	Stranraer, Cowdenbeath	2017–18	Queen's Park, Albion
2003–04	East Fife, Stenhousemuir	2018–19	Stenhousemuir, Brechin
2004–05	Arbroath, Berwick	2019–20	Stranraer

RELEGATED FROM LEAGUE TWO

| 2015–16 | East Stirling | 2019–20 | No relegation |
| 2018–19 | Berwick | | |

SCOTTISH PREMIERSHIP 2019–2020

(appearances and scorers for season curtailed by Covid-19 with teams having eight or nine fixtures remaining)

ABERDEEN

Anderson B	1 (10)	Hedges R 14 (8)
Bryson C 5 (3)	Hernandez R............. 1 (1))
Campbell D............. 6 (9)	Kennedy M 7 (1)
Considine A............. 25 (2)	Leigh G 18
Cosgrove S 22 (3)	Lewis J........................30
Devlin M 11 (3)	Logan S 23 (3)
Ferguson L...................28	Main C 12 (6)
Gallagher J............. 11 (11)	McGeouch D............. 6 (1)
Gleeson S .... - (1)	McGinn N................ 22 (6)

McKenna S....................24
McLennan C............. 9 (9)
Ojo F 16
Ross E 1 (1)
Taylor A 14
Vyner Z 15 (1)
Wilson J 7 (4)
Wright S....................2 (1)

League goals (40): Cosgrove 11, McGinn 6, Considine 4, Hedges 4, Main 4, McLennan 3, Anderson 1, Ferguson 1, Gallagher 1, Leigh 1, McKenna 1, Taylor 1, Vyner 1, Opponents 1
Scottish Cup goals (7): Cosgrove 3, Considine 1, Ferguson 1, Kennedy 1, Opponents 1. **League Cup goals (4):** Cosgrove 3, Considine 1
Europa League goals (10): Cosgrove 6, Ferguson 1, Leigh 1, McGinn 1, Wright 1
Average home league attendance: 13,836. **Player of Year:** Andrew Considine

CELTIC

Ajer K........................28	Elhamed H A 3 (2)	McGregor C 30
Bain S 2	Elyounoussi M 7 (3)	Morgan L...............3 (2)
Bauer M 6 (3)	Forrest J.......................28	Ntcham O............. 17 (6)
Bayo V 1 (7)	Forster B....................28	Ralston A .... - (2)
Bitton N 9 (6)	Frimpong J 12 (2)	Rogic T 6 (10)
Bolingoli-Mbombo B 14	Griffiths L 10 (11)	Shved M................... - (1)
Brown S.......................29	Hayes J 5 (9)	Simunovic J................6
Christie R 17 (7)	Johnston M................. 4 (7)	Sinclair S .... - (2)
Dembele K................. - (1)	Jullien C......................28	Taylor G................ 11 (1)
Edouard O 25 (2)	Klimala P .... - (2)	Welsh S......................1

League goals (89): Edouard 22, Christie 11, Forrest 10, Griffiths 9, McGregor 9, Elyounoussi 4, Jullien 4, Ntcham 4, Ajer 3, Brown 2, Frimpong 2, Johnston 2, Rogic 2, Hayes 1, Simunovic 1, Opponents 3
Scottish Cup goals (6): Bayo 1, Brown 1, Christie 1, Griffiths 1, McGregor 1, Ntcham 1. **League Cup goals (13):** Brown 2, Elyounoussi 2, Ntcham 2, Bayo 1, Forrest 1, Johnston 1, Jullien 1, McGregor 1, Rogic 1, Sinclair 1
Champions League goals (16): Christie 4, Edouard 2, Forrest 2, McGregor 2, Ajer 1, Griffiths 1, Johnston 1, Shved 1, Sinclair 1, Opponents 1
Europa League goals (18): Edouard 4, Christie 3, Forrest 3, Johnston 2, Jullien 2, Morgan 2, Elyounoussi 1, Ntcham 1
Average home league attendance: 57.944. **Player of Year:** Odsonne Edouard

HAMILTON ACADEMICAL

Alston B 14 (5)	Davies S 5 (8)	Hamilton J............... 11 (1)
Beck A 2 (4)	Easton B 17 (1)	Hughes R................. 5 (3)
Collar W................. 14 (2)	Fjortoft M 5 (2)	Hunt J..................... 10 (6)
Cunningham R 6 (3)	Fon Williams O...............15	MacKinnon D 3 (3)
Dales A......................1 (1)	Gogic A..........................29	Martin S 18 (2)

183

McGowan A...................22	Oakley G..................... 17 (4)	Templeton D............... 3 (3)
McKenna C............... 2 (1)	Ogkmpoe M............. 16 (7)	Want S 9 (2)
McMann S 27	Smith L................. 17 (6)	Winter A .... - (3)
Miller M................. 16 (5)	Southwood L..................15	Woods S 3
Mimnaugh R .... - (1)	Stanger G 1	
Moyo D.................. 8 (12)	Stubbs S.......................19	

League goals (30): Ogkmpoe 6, Oakley 4, Cunningham 3, Miller 3, Smith 3, Davies 2, Moyo 2, Alston 1, Collar 1, Gogic 1, McGowan 1, Templeton 1, Want 1, Woods 1
Scottish Cup goals (6): Dales 1, Martin 1, McMann 1, Miller 1, Smith 1, Winter 1. **League Cup goals** (8): Cunningham 4, Alston 1, McMann 1, Ogkmboe 1, Smith 1
Average home league attendance: 2,565

HEART OF MIDLOTHIAN

Avdijaj D.................... 1 (2)	Hickey A 22	Pereira J........................20
Berra C..................... 18 (1)	Ikpeazu U................. 15 (8)	Sibbick T 2
Boyce L 6 (2)	Irving A 14 (4)	Smith M.........................23
Bozanic O................. 13 (5)	Keena A 1 (4)	Souttar J 7
Brandon J................... 6 (3)	Langer M................. 1 (1)	Walker J................. 10 (5)
Clare S 24 (2)	MacLean S................. 8 (3)	Washington C............. 7 (8)
Damour L................. 13 (5)	McDonald A....................1	Whelan D................. 13 (2)
Dikamona C 8 (3)	Meshino R 9 (10)	White A................... 12 (2)
Doyle C.............................2	Moore L 6 (1)	Wighton C 1 (1)
Garuccio B.............. 2 (2)	Morrison C................. 2 (2)	Zlamal Z......................... 8
Halkett C 24	Mulraney J 12 (5)	
Henderson E 5 (6)	Naismith S 14 (3)	

League goals (31): Clare 4, Naismith 4, Bozanic 3, Meshino 3, Walker 3, Washington 3, Boyce 2, Halkett 2, Ikpeazu 2, Berra 1, Hickey 1, MacLean 1, Mulraney 1, Opponents 1.
Scottish Cup goals (7): Clare 2, Bozanic 1, Halkett 1, Henderson 1, Irving 1, Naismith 1. **League Cup goals** (10): Halkett 4, Irving 1, MacLean 1, McDonald 1, Smith 1, Walker 1, Washington 1
Average home league attendance: 16,751

HIBERNIAN

Allan S 28 (2)	James T..........................6	Murray F ....- (7)
Boyle M 15 (5)	Kamberi F 16 (4)	Naismith J.....................13
Docherty G................ 5 (1)	Mackie S................. 1 (1)	Newell J................. 13 (6)
Doidge C................. 25 (3)	Mallan S 14 (6)	Omeonga S................ 4 (4)
Gray D.................... 3 (1)	Marciano O.....................19	Porteous R 14
Gullan J................... 1 (4)	Maxwell C.............. 11 (1)	Shaw O ....- (4)
Hallberg M 18 (2)	McGinn P 6 (1)	Slivka V................. 12 (4)
Hanlon P 30	McGregor D 4 (2)	Stevenson L............. 26 (1)
Horgan D 12 (16)	McNulty M 4 (2)	Vela J............................. 9
Jackson A 12 (2)	Middleton G 4 (2)	Whittaker S 5 (2)

League goals (42): Doidge 12, Allan 5, Boyle 5, Horgan 3, Jackson 3, Kamberi 3, Mallan 3, Hanlon 2, Docherty 1, Hallberg 1, McNulty 1, Naismith 1, Porteous 1, Opponents 1
Scottish Cup goals (15): Doidge 4, McNulty 3, Allan 2, Docherty 2, Boyle 1, Gullan 1, Jackson 1, Omeonga 1. **League Cup goals** (15): Kamberi 5, Allan 3, Doidge 2, Hallberg 1, James 1, Murray 1, Newell 1, Vela 1
Average home league attendance: 16,747

KILMARNOCK

Branescu L 26
Broadfoot K.............. 6 (3)
Brophy E.................. 24 (4)
Bruce A 11 (5)
Bunn H...................... 2 (1)
Burke C 20 (6)
Cameron I.................. - (1)
Connell K.................. - (1)
Del Fabro D............. 21 (1)
Dicker G.......................30

El Makrini M............. 19 (2)
Findlay S.......................18
Hamalainen N........... 27 (1)
Hendrie S.................. 1 (1)
Jackson S................... 1 (3)
Johnson C 3 (1)
Kabamba N 9
Kiltie G 2 (8)
Koprivec J 4 (1)
McKenzie R 24 (3)

Millar L....................14 (6)
Millen R.......................2 (2)
O'Donnell S 28
Power A 28
Sow O 2 (6)
St Clair H .... - (2)
Taylor A.......................- (1)
Taylor G.......................2
Thomas D................3 (17)
Wilson I...................3 (1)

League goals (31): Brophy 9, Burke 5, O'Donnell 3, Dicker 2, El Makrini 2, Kabamba 2, Bruce 1, Del Fabro 1, Findlay 1, Kiltie 1, McKenzie 1, Millar 1, Thomas 1, Opponents 1
Scottish Cup goals (9): Findlay 2, Kabamba 2, Brophy 1, Bruce 1, El Makrini 1, Johnson 1, Kiltie 1. **League Cup goals** (1): Thomas 1. **Europa League goals** (2): Brophy 1, Findlay 1
Average home league attendance: 5,856

LIVINGSTON

Ambrose E......................3
Bartley M.................. 27 (1)
Brown C..........................9
Crawford R............. 13 (7)
Devlin N 11
Dykes L.......................25
Erskine C 3 (7)
Guthrie J.......................28
Jacobs K 14 (10)
Lamie R 19 (3)

Lawless S 29 (1)
Lawson S 13 (6)
Lithgow A 9 (3)
McCrorie R 8
McMillan J 19 (2)
Menga D .... - (3)
Miller L .... - (3)
Odofin H 3 (4)
Pepe C .... - (2)
Pittman S.......................23

Robinson S............. 13 (9)
Sarkic M 14
Savane I.......................- (1)
Schofield R.......................1
Sibbald C 14 (4)
Souda A 11 (6)
Stewart R 7
Stobbs J...................1 (3)
Taylor-Sinclair A........ 12 (2)
Tiffoney S..................1 (7)

League goals (41): Dykes 9, Lawless 8, Guthrie 5, Pittman 3, Taylor-Sinclair 3, Lithgow 2, Robinson 2, Sibbald 2, Souda 2, Bartley 1, Lamie 1, Stobbs 1, Opponents 2
Scottish Cup goals (3): Lawless 2, Dykes 1. **League Cup goals** (12): Lamie 3, Dykes 2, Sibbald 2, Souda 2, Lawless 1, Lithgow 1, Pittman 1
Average home league attendance: 3,542. **Player of Year:** Jon Guthrie

MOTHERWELL

Aarons R..........................6
Campbell A 30
Carroll J.......................21
Cole D 12 (7)
Donnelly L 22
Dunne C..........................3
Gallagher D....................30
Gillespie M 30
Grimshaw L....................25

Hartley P 23 (2)
Hylton J 18 (10)
Ilic C 3 (5)
Long C 21 (4)
MacIver R................... 1 (6)
Maguire B 4 (3)
Manzinga C .... - (6)
Mugabi B 6 (4)
Ndjoli M.......................- (1)

O'Hara M 9 (8)
Polworth L...................28 (2)
Scott J 15 (7)
Seedorf S 9 (13)
Tait R 12 (2)
Turnbull D ....- (2)
Watt T.........................2 (2)

League goals (41): Donnelly 7, Long 7, Campbell 5, Cole 4, Scott 3, Carroll 2, Gallagher 2, Hylton 2, Seedorf 2, Hartley 1, MacIver 1, Manzinga 1, O'Hara 1, Polworth 1, Watt 1, Opponents 1

Scottish Cup goals (8): Long 3, Aarons 1, Campbell 1, O'Hara 1, Polworth 1, Watt 1. **League Cup goals** (14): Donnelly 4, Scott 3, Hylton 2, Hartley 1, Ilic 1, Long 1, Polworth 1, Seedorf 1
Average home league attendance: 5,575. **Player of Year:** Allan Campbell

RANGERS

Arfield S 22 (4)	Goldson C 29	Kent R 18 (3)
Aribo J 25 (2)	Hagi I 6 (1)	King A ....- (2)
Barisic B 22	Halliday A 4 (2)	McGregor A 27
Barker B 2 (4)	Helander F 8	Morelos A 18 (8)
Davis S 20 (4)	Jack R 19	Murphy J ....- (2)
Defoe J 11 (9)	Jones J 2 (5)	Ojo S 9 (10)
Edmundson G 4 (3)	Kamara G 18 (1)	Polster M 3 (3)
Flanagan J 5	Kamberi F 1 (5)	Stewart G 3 (13)
Foderingham W 2	Katic N 17 (2)	Tavernier J 24

League goals (64): Defoe 13, Morelos 12, Kent 7, Arfield 5, Jack 4, Aribo 3, Goldson 3, Stewart 3, Tavernier 3, Barisic 2, Katic 2, Barker 1, Edmundson 1, Hagi 1, Helander 1, Kamberi 1, Ojo 1, Opponents 1

Scottish Cup goals (6): Arfield 3, Aribo 1, Defoe 1, Morelos 1. **League Cup goals** (7): Helander 2, Morelos 2, Aribo 1, Defoe 1, Kamara 1

Europa League goals (33): Morelos 14, Aribo 4, Ojo 4, Defoe 2, Hagi 2, Arfield 1, Davis 1, Edmudson 1, Goldson 1, Jack 1, Katic 1, Kent 1

Average home league attendance: 49,238. **Player of Year**: Ryan Jack

ROSS COUNTY

Baxter N 13	Gardyne M 13 (1)	Paton H 11 (8)
Chalmers J 6 (8)	Graham B 5 (13)	Power S ....- (1)
Cowie D 7 (2)	Grivosti T 5 (1)	Shaw O 2 (5)
Donaldson C 7	Henderson E 6 (3)	Spence L 10 (5)
Draper R 8 (3)	Kelly S 18	Spittal B 10 (10)
Erwin L 11 (6)	Laidlaw R 17	Stewart R 19 (2)
Fontaine L 22	McKay B 22 (5)	Tillson J 5 (2)
Foster R 20 (1)	Morris C 17	Vigurs I 16
Fraser M 25 (1)	Mullin J 21 (6)	Watson K 14 (3)

League goals (29): McKay 7, Stewart 7, Graham 4, Chalmers 3, Spittal 2, Vigurs 2, Erwin 1, Fontaine 1, Fraser 1, Mullin 1

Scottish Cup goals: None. **League Cup goals** (14): McKay 4, Stewart 4, Graham 2, Spittal 2, Mullin 1, Paton 1

Average home league attendance: 4,664. **Player of Year**: Ross Stewart

ST JOHNSTONE

Booth C 12 (1)	Gordon L 16	McCart J 7 (1)
Butcher M 3 (3)	Hendry C 5 (15)	O'Halloran M 14 (10)
Callachan R 1 (1)	Holt J 15 (2)	Ralston A 21 (1)
Clark Z 29	Kane C 11 (12)	Swanson D 3 (4)
Craig L 9 (6)	Kennedy M 16 (2)	Tanser S 19 (2)
Davidson M 17	Kerr J 29	Vihmann M 2 (2)
Duffy W 11	May S 20 (4)	Wotherspoon D 15 (6)
Foster R 2	McCann A 26 (3)	Wright D 16 (6)

League goals (28): Hendry 7, May 6, McCann 4, Kennedy 3, Wotherspoon 3, O'Halloran 2, Kane 1, Kerr 1, Opponents 1

Scottish Cup goals (5): Booth 1, Davidson 1, Hendry 1, May 1, Opponents 1. **League Cup goals** (6): Kennedy 2, Tanser 2, Hendry 1, Kane 1

Average home league attendance: 4,091. **Player of Year**: Ali McCann

ST MIRREN

Andreu T................ 16 (12)	Glover S 1	McGinn S 7 (2)
Breadner C.................. - (2)	Hladky V 30	McGrath J 4 (3)
Broadfoot K................ 7 (1)	Hodson L 5 (2)	McLoughlin S 21
Chabbi S.................... - (2)	Jakubiak A 4 (3)	Morias J 14 (12)
Cooke C .... - (6)	MacKenzie G 9 (1)	Mullen D 7 (10)
Djorkaeff O ....-(2)	MacPherson C.......... 15 (1)	Obika J 26 (4)
Durmus I 21 (7)	Magennis K 22	Wallace R 2 (1)
Famewo A.......................9	McAllister K 4 (11)	Waters C 27
Flynn R.......................22	McCarthy C......................9	
Foley S 27	McGinn P................. 21 (1)	

League goals (24): Obika 8, Durmus 4, Andreu 2, MacPherson 2, Morias 2, Mullen 2, Foley 1, Magennis 1, McCarthy 1, McLoughlin 1
Scottish Cup goals (8): Obika 4, Foley 1, Jakubiak 1, Mullen 1, Opponents 1. **League Cup goals** (3): Cooke 1, Djorkaeff 1, Mullen 1
Average home league attendance: 5,376. **Player of Year**: Sam Foley

TUNNOCK'S CARAMEL WAFER SCOTTISH CHALLENGE CUP 2019–20

First round: Albion 1 Hearts U21 4; Berwick 1 Rangers U21 2; Brora 6 Aberdeen U21 0; Fraserburgh 2 Ross Co U21 3; Hamilton U21 4 BSC Glasgow 0; Hibernian U21 3 Elgin 4; Kelty 4 Kilmarnock U21 0; Livingston U21 1 Formartine 3; Motherwell U21 1 Spartans 0; Queen's Park 2 Celtic U21 2 (Celtic U21 won 4-3 on pens); St Johnstone U21 1 Cove 4; St Mirren U21 1 East Kilbride 0

Second round: Annan 1 Kelty 1 (Kelty won 6-5 on pens); Brechin 4 Elgin 5; Brora 1 Cove 2'; Clyde 4 Motherwell U21 0; Dumbarton 0 St Mirren U21 1; East Fife 0 Stirling 2; Falkirk 1 Celtic U21 1 (Falkirk won 6-5 on pens); Hamilton U21 0 Airdrieonians 1; Hearts U21 3 Cowdenbeath 1; Montrose 2 Forfar 1; Peterhead 0 Formartine 0 (Formartine won 7-6 on pens); Ross Co U21 2 Raith 3; Stenhousemuir 2 Edinburgh City 1; Stranraer 0 Rangers U21 2

Third round: Airdrieonians 3 Bohemians 2; Ballymena 0 Rangers U21 1; Clyde 3 Queen of South 2; Connah's Quay 1 Cove 0; Dundee 1 Elgin 2; Dundee Utd 0 Arbroath 0 (Arbroath won 4-3 on pens); Dunfermline 1 Alloa 2; Formartine 0 Glenavon 3; Kelty 1 Solihull 1 (Solihull won 4-2 on pens); Inverness 3 Morton 1; Montrose 0 Partick 2; Raith 2 Falkirk 0; Stenhousemuir 1 New Saints 1 (Stenhousemuir won 3-1 on pens); St Mirren U21 1 Stirling 0; Waterford 3 Hearts U21 1; Wrexham 1 Ayr 1 (Wrexham won 6-5 on pens)

Fourth round: Airdrieonians 0 Elgin 2; Arbroath 0 Clyde 2; Inverness 3 Alloa 0; Partick 2 Connah's Quay 0; Raith 3 Glenavon 1; Solihull 3 Rangers U21 3 (Rangers U21 won 4-3 on pens); Stenhousemuir 3 Waterford 2; Wrexham 4 St Mirren U21 1

Quarter-finals: Inverness 0 Clyde 0 (Inverness won 4-2 on pens); Raith 3 Elgin 2; Rangers U21 2 Wrexham 0; Stenhousemuir 1 Partick 4

Semi-finals: Inverness 2 Rangers U21 1; Partick 1 Raith 2

Final: postponed – COVID-19

BETFRED SCOTTISH LEAGUE CUP 2019–20

Teams awarded three points for a win, one point for a drawn match after 90 minutes, then penalties with winners awarded one additional point. Eight group winners and four best runners-up through to knockout stage to join four sides competing in Europe – Aberdeen, Celtic, Kilmarnock and Rangers

GROUP A

	P	W	D	L	F	A	Pts
Hearts Q	4	2	2	0	6	3	9
East Fife Q	4	2	1	1	5	3	8
Dundee Utd	4	2	1	1	6	4	7
Stenhousemuir	4	1	0	3	4	6	3
Cowdenbeath	4	1	0	3	2	7	3

GROUP B

	P	W	D	L	F	A	Pts
Ross Co Q	4	4	0	0	12	2	12
Forfar Q	4	3	0	1	9	4	9
Montrose	4	1	1	2	4	9	5
St Johnstone	4	1	0	3	6	5	3
Brechin	4	0	1	3	1	12	1

GROUP C

	P	W	D	L	F	A	Pts
Hibernian Q	4	3	1	0	8	1	11
Alloa	4	2	1	1	8	8	7
Arbroath	4	2	0	2	10	8	6
Elgin	4	1	1	2	7	7	5
Stirling	4	0	1	3	3	12	1

GROUP D

	P	W	D	L	F	A	Pts
Dundee Q	4	2	2	0	4	0	10
Inverness	4	2	1	1	7	4	7
Peterhead	4	1	2	1	3	4	6
Cove	4	1	1	2	6	5	4
Raith	4	1	0	3	4	11	3

GROUP E

	P	W	D	L	F	A	Pts
Motherwell Q	4	4	0	0	13	0	12
Morton Q	4	2	1	1	14	8	8
Queen of South	4	1	2	1	10	10	6
Dumbarton	4	1	0	3	3	12	3
Annan	4	0	1	3	3	13	1

GROUP F

	P	W	D	L	F	A	Pts
Partick Q	4	3	0	1	8	5	10
Hamilton Q	4	2	2	0	8	5	9
Airdrieonians	4	1	1	2	7	8	5
Queen's Park	4	0	3	1	4	5	5
Clyde	4	0	1	3	6	10	1

GROUP G

	P	W	D	L	F	A	Pts
Livingston Q	4	3	1	0	10	3	11
Ayr	4	2	1	1	12	5	7
Falkirk	4	2	1	1	6	3	7
Stranraer	4	1	1	2	9	5	5
Berwick	4	0	0	4	0	21	0

GROUP H

	P	W	D	L	F	A	Pts
Dunfermline Q	4	3	0	1	13	3	9
Albion	4	2	1	1	3	7	7
St Mirren	4	1	2	1	3	3	6
East Kilbride	4	1	1	2	1	5	5
Edinburgh City	4	1	0	3	2	4	3

SECOND ROUND: Celtic 2 Dunfermline 1 (aet); Dundee 1 Aberdeen 2 (aet); East Fife 0 Rangers 3; Forfar 1 Livingston 2; Hibernian 5 Morton 3 (aet); Motherwell 1 Hearts 2; Kilmarnock 1 Hamilton 0; Partick 3 Ross Co 2 (aet); **QUARTER-FINALS:** Celtic 5 Partick 0; Hearts 2 Aberdeen 2 (aet, Hearts won 3-0 on pens); Kilmarnock 0 Hibernian 0 (aet, Hibernian won 5-4 on pens); Livingston 0 Rangers 1; **SEMI-FINALS:** Hibernian 2 Celtic 5 (Hampden Park); Rangers 3 Hearts 0 (Hampden Park)

FINAL
RANGERS 0 CELTIC 1 (Jullien 60)
Hampden Park (51,117); Sunday, December 8, 2019

Rangers (4-5-1): McGregor, Tavernier (capt), Goldson, Helander (Katic 84), Barisic, Aribo (Barker 74), Jack, Kamara (Defoe 71), Arfield, Kent, Morelos. **Subs not used:** Foderingham, Ojo, Flanagan, Stewart. **Booked:** Kamara, Arfield, Aribo. **Manager:** Steven Gerrard
Celtic (4-2-3-1): Forster, Frimpong, Ajer, Jullien, Hayes, Brown (capt), McGregor, Forrest (Bitton 66), Christie, Elyounoussi (Johnston 46), Morgan (Edouard 59). **Subs not used:** Gordon, Rogic, Ntcham, Bolingoli-Mbombo. **Booked:** Ajer, McGregor. **Sent off:** Frimpong (63). **Manager:** Neil Lennon
Referee: W Collum. **Half-time:** 0-0

SCOTTISH LEAGUE CUP FINALS

1946	Aberdeen beat Rangers (3-2)
1947	Rangers beat Aberdeen (4-0)
1948	East Fife beat Falkirk (4-1 after 0-0 draw)
1949	Rangers beat Raith Rov (2-0)
1950	East Fife beat Dunfermline Athletic (3-0)
1951	Motherwell beat Hibernian (3-0)
1952	Dundee beat Rangers (3-2)
1953	Dundee beat Kilmarnock (2-0)
1954	East Fife beat Partick (3-2)
1955	Hearts beat Motherwell (4-2)
1956	Aberdeen beat St Mirren (2-1)
1957	Celtic beat Partick (3-0 after 0-0 draw)
1958	Celtic beat Rangers (7-1)
1959	Hearts beat Partick (5-1)
1960	Hearts beat Third Lanark (2-1)
1961	Rangers beat Kilmarnock (2-0)
1962	Rangers beat Hearts (3-1 after 1-1 draw)
1963	Hearts beat Kilmarnock (1-0)
1964	Rangers beat Morton (5-0)
1965	Rangers beat Celtic (2-1)
1966	Celtic beat Rangers (2-1)
1967	Celtic beat Rangers (1-0)
1968	Celtic beat Dundee (5-3)
1969	Celtic beat Hibernian (6-2)
1970	Celtic beat St Johnstone (1-0)
1971	Rangers beat Celtic (1-0)
1972	Partick beat Celtic (4-1)
1973	Hibernian beat Celtic (2-1)
1974	Dundee beat Celtic (1-0)
1975	Celtic beat Hibernian (6-3)
1976	Rangers beat Celtic (1-0)
1977†	Aberdeen beat Celtic (2-1)
1978†	Rangers beat Celtic (2-1)
1979	Rangers beat Aberdeen (2-1)
1980	Dundee Utd beat Aberdeen (3-0 after 0-0 draw)
1981	Dundee Utd beat Dundee (3-0)
1982	Rangers beat Dundee Utd (2-1)
1983	Celtic beat Rangers (2-1)
1984†	Rangers beat Celtic (3-2)
1985	Rangers beat Dundee Utd (1-0)
1986	Aberdeen beat Hibernian (3-0)
1987	Rangers beat Celtic (2-1)
1988†	Rangers beat Aberdeen (5-3 on pens after 3-3 draw)
1989	Rangers beat Aberdeen (3-2)
1990†	Aberdeen beat Rangers (2-1)
1991†	Rangers beat Celtic (2-1)
1992	Hibernian beat Dunfermline Athletic (2-0)
1993†	Rangers beat Aberdeen (2-1)
1994	Rangers beat Hibernian (2-1)
1995	Raith Rov beat Celtic (6-5 on pens after 2-2 draw)
1996	Aberdeen beat Dundee (2-0)
1997	Rangers beat Hearts (4-3)
1998	Celtic beat Dundee Utd (3-0)
1999	Rangers beat St Johnstone (2-1)
2000	Celtic beat Aberdeen (2-0)
2001	Celtic beat Kilmarnock (3-0)
2002	Rangers beat Ayr (4-0)
2003	Rangers beat Celtic (2-1)
2004	Livingston beat Hibernian (2-0)
2005	Rangers beat Motherwell (5-1)
2006	Celtic beat Dunfermline Athletic (3-0)
2007	Hibernian beat Kilmarnock (5-1)
2008	Rangers beat Dundee Utd (3-2 on pens after 2-2 draw)
2009†	Celtic beat Rangers (2-0)
2010	Rangers beat St Mirren (1-0)
2011†	Rangers beat Celtic (2-1)
2012	Kilmarnock beat Celtic (1-0)
2013	St Mirren beat Hearts (3-2)
2014	Aberdeen beat Inverness Caledonian Thistle (4-2 on pens after 0-0 draw)
2015	Celtic beat Dundee Utd (2-0)
2016	Ross Co beat Hibernian (2-1)
2017	Celtic beat Aberdeen (3-0)
2018	Celtic beat Motherwell (2-0)
2019	Celtic beat Aberdeen (1-0)
2020	Celtic beat Rangers (1-0)

(† After extra time; Skol Cup 1985–93, Coca-Cola Cup 1995–97, Co-operative Insurance Cup 1999 onwards)

SUMMARY OF SCOTTISH LEAGUE CUP WINNERS

Rangers	27	East Fife	3	Motherwell	1
Celtic	19	Hibernian	3	Partick	1
Aberdeen	7	Dundee Utd	2	Raith	1
Hearts	4	Kilmarnock	1	Ross Co	1
Dundee	3	Livingston	1	St Mirren	1

WILLIAM HILL SCOTTISH FA CUP 2019–20

FIRST ROUND

Broxburn 3 East Stirling 2
Buckie 4 Civil Service 1
Caledonian 3 Rothes 4
Cumbernauld 1 Penicuik 5
Dalbeattie 1 Gala 3
Edinburgh Univ 1 Lochee 3
Forres 1 Banks O'Dee 4
Fort William 5 Vale of Leithen 0
Fraserburgh 0 Bonnyrigg 1
Gretna 1 Hill of Beath 0
Inverurie 3 Wick 2

Keith 2 Univ of Stirling 3
Kelty 0 Auchinleck 3
Linlithgow 1 Huntly 0
Nairn 0 Clachcuddin 0
Strathspey 2 Lossiemouth 1
Spartans 1 Deveronvale 1
Turriff 1 Formartine 5
Replays
Clachcuddin 2 Nairn 1
Deveronvale 1 Spartans 2
Albion 0 Formartine 2

SECOND ROUND

Albion 1 Fort William 1
Annan 2 Brechin 2
Auchinleck 1 Cove 0
Bonnyrigg 2 Buckie 0
Clachnacuddin 0 Brora 7
Cowdenbeath 1 Broxburn 1
East Kilbride 3 Gretna 1
Edinburgh City 3 Banks O'Dee 1
Elgin 3 Berwick 1
Formartine 2 Gala 2
Lochee 1 BSC Glasgow 1

Penicuik 3 Stenhousemuir 0
Rothes 1 Inverurie 3
Spartans 0 Queen's Park 2
Stirling Alb 2 Strathspey 0
Stirling Univ 0 Linlithgow 2
Replays
Brechin 0 Annan 2
Broxburn 3 Cowdenbeath 0
BSC Glasgow 2 Lochee 1
Fort William0 Albion 5
Gala 1 Formartine 2

THIRD ROUND

Albion 1 Airdrieonians 4
Auchinleck 1 Arbroath 1
Bonnyrigg 2 Montrose 1
Dumbarton 3 Forfar 1
East Fife 3 BSC Glasgow 4
Edinburgh City 4 Annan 1
Elgin 1 Alloa 3
Formartine 0 East Kilbride 4
Inverurie 0 Broxburn 1
Linlithgow 1 Falkirk 4

Morton 1 Brora 1
Partick 1 Penicuik 1
Queen of South 1 Queen's Park 2
Raith 1 Peterhead 0
Stirling 0 Clyde 2
Stranraer 1 Dunfermline 0
Replays
Arbroath 3 Auchinleck 0
Brora 1 Morton 3
Aberdeen 2 Stenhousemuir 1

FOURTH ROUND

Aberdeen 1 Dumbarton 0
Alloa 2 Inverness 3
Arbroath 0 Falkirk 0
Ayr 1 Ross Co 0
Bonnyrigg 0 Clyde 1
Dundee 0 Motherwell 3
Dundee Utd 2 Hibernian 2
East Kilbride 1 BSC Glasgow 3
Hamilton 5 Edinburgh City 0
Hearts 5 Airdrieonians 0

Kilmarnock 6 Queen's Park 0
Livingston 3 Raith 1
Partick 1 Celtic 2
Rangers 2 Stranraer 0
St Johnstone 3 Morton 0
St Mirren 3 Broxburn 0
Replays
Falkirk 2 Arbroath 0
Hibernian 4 Dundee Utd 2

FIFTH ROUND

Aberdeen 0 Kilmarnock 0
Ayr 1 St Johnstone 2
BSC Glasgow 1 Hibernian 4
Clyde 0 Celtic 3

Falkirk 0 Hearts 1
Hamilton 1 Rangers 4
Inverness 1 Livingston 0
St Mirren 1 Motherwell 1

Replays
Kilmarnock 3 Aberdeen 4 (aet)

Motherwell 4 St Mirren 4
(aet, St Mirren won 3-2 on pens)

SIXTH ROUND

Hearts 1 Rangers 0
Hibernian 5 Inverness 2

St Mirren 0 Aberdeen 2
St Johnstone 0 Celtic 1

SEMI-FINALS

Celtic v Aberdeen, Hibernian v Hearts – postponed, Covid-19; to be played Oct-Nov 2020

FINAL

Sunday, December 20, 2020

SCOTTISH FA CUP FINALS

1874	Queen's Park beat Clydesdale (2-0)	**1907**	Celtic beat Hearts (3-0)
1875	Queen's Park beat Renton (3-0)	**1908**	Celtic beat St Mirren (5-1)
1876	Queen's Park beat Third Lanark (2-0 after 1-1 draw)	**1909**	Cup withheld because of riot after two drawn games in final between Celtic and Rangers (2-2, 1-1)
1877	Vale of Leven beat Rangers (3-2 after 0-0, 1-1 draws)	**1910**	Dundee beat Clyde (2-1 after 2-2, 0-0 draws)
1878	Vale of Leven beat Third Lanark (1-0)	**1911**	Celtic beat Hamilton (2-0 after 0-0 draw)
1879	Vale of Leven awarded Cup (Rangers withdrew after 1-1 draw)	**1912**	Celtic beat Clyde (2-0)
1880	Queen's Park beat Thornlibank (3-0)	**1913**	Falkirk beat Raith (2-0)
1881	Queen's Park beat Dumbarton (3-1)	**1914**	Celtic beat Hibernian (4-1 after 0-0 draw)
1882	Queen's Park beat Dumbarton (4-1 after 2-2 draw)	**1915–19**	No competition (World War 1)
1883	Dumbarton beat Vale of Leven (2-1 after 2-2 draw)	**1920**	Kilmarnock beat Albion (3-2)
1884	Queen's Park awarded Cup (Vale of Leven withdrew from Final)	**1921**	Partick beat Rangers (1-0)
1885	Renton beat Vale of Leven (3-1 after 0-0 draw)	**1922**	Morton beat Rangers (1-0)
		1923	Celtic beat Hibernian (1-0)
1886	Queen's Park beat Renton (3-1)	**1924**	Airdrieonians beat Hibernian (2-0)
1887	Hibernian beat Dumbarton (2-1)	**1925**	Celtic beat Dundee (2-1)
1888	Renton beat Cambuslang (6-1)	**1926**	St Mirren beat Celtic (2-0)
1889	Third Lanark beat Celtic (2-1)	**1927**	Celtic beat East Fife (3-1)
1890	Queen's Park beat Vale of Leven (2-1 after 1-1 draw)	**1928**	Rangers beat Celtic (4-0)
		1929	Kilmarnock beat Rangers (2-0)
1891	Hearts beat Dumbarton (1-0)	**1930**	Rangers beat Partick (2-1 after 0-0 draw)
1892	Celtic beat Queen's Park (5-1)	**1931**	Celtic beat Motherwell (4-2 after 2-2 draw)
1893	Queen's Park beat Celtic (2-1)	**1932**	Rangers beat Kilmarnock (3-0 after 1-1 draw)
1894	Rangers beat Celtic (3-1)		
1895	St Bernard's beat Renton (2-1)	**1933**	Celtic beat Motherwell (1-0)
1896	Hearts beat Hibernian (3-1)	**1934**	Rangers beat St Mirren (5-0)
1897	Rangers beat Dumbarton (5-1)	**1935**	Rangers beat Hamilton (2-1)
1898	Rangers beat Kilmarnock (2-0)	**1936**	Rangers beat Third Lanark (1-0)
1899	Celtic beat Rangers (2-0)	**1937**	Celtic beat Aberdeen (2-1)
1900	Celtic beat Queen's Park (4-3)	**1938**	East Fife beat Kilmarnock (4-2 after 1-1 draw)
1901	Hearts beat Celtic (4-3)		
1902	Hibernian beat Celtic (1-0)	**1939**	Clyde beat Motherwell (4-0)
1903	Rangers beat Hearts (2-0 after 0-0, 1-1 draws)	**1940–6**	No competition (World War 2)
1904	Celtic beat Rangers (3-2)	**1947**	Aberdeen beat Hibernian (2-1)
1905	Third Lanark beat Rangers (3-1 after 0-0 draw)	**1948†**	Rangers beat Morton (1-0 after 1-1 draw)
1906	Hearts beat Third Lanark (1-0)	**1949**	Rangers beat Clyde (4-1)
		1950	Rangers beat East Fife (3-0)
		1951	Celtic beat Motherwell (1-0)
		1952	Motherwell beat Dundee (4-0)
		1953	Rangers beat Aberdeen (1-0 after 1-1 draw)

1954	Celtic beat Aberdeen (2-1)	1988	Celtic beat Dundee Utd (2-1)
1955	Clyde beat Celtic (1-0 after 1-1 draw)	1989	Celtic beat Rangers (1-0)
1956	Hearts beat Celtic (3-1)	1990†	Aberdeen beat Celtic (9-8 on pens after 0-0 draw)
1957†	Falkirk beat Kilmarnock (2-1 after 1-1 draw)	1991†	Motherwell beat Dundee Utd (4-3)
1958	Clyde beat Hibernian (1-0)	1992	Rangers beat Airdrieonians (2-1)
1959	St Mirren beat Aberdeen (3-1)	1993	Rangers beat Aberdeen (2-1)
1960	Rangers beat Kilmarnock (2-0)	1994	Dundee Utd beat Rangers (1-0)
1961	Dunfermline beat Celtic (2-0 after 0-0 draw)	1995	Celtic beat Airdrieonians (1-0)
1962	Rangers beat St Mirren (2-0)	1996	Rangers beat Hearts (5-1)
1963	Rangers beat Celtic (3-0 after 1-1 draw)	1997	Kilmarnock beat Falkirk (1-0)
1964	Rangers beat Dundee (3-1)	1998	Hearts beat Rangers (2-1)
1965	Celtic beat Dunfermline (3-2)	1999	Rangers beat Celtic (1-0)
1966	Rangers beat Celtic (1-0 after 0-0 draw)	2000	Rangers beat Aberdeen (4-0)
1967	Celtic beat Aberdeen (2-0)	2001	Celtic beat Hibernian (3-0)
1968	Dunfermline beat Hearts (3-1)	2002	Rangers beat Celtic (3-2)
1969	Celtic beat Rangers (4-0)	2003	Rangers beat Dundee (1-0)
1970	Aberdeen beat Celtic (3-1)	2004	Celtic beat Dunfermline (3-1)
1971	Celtic beat Rangers (2-1 after 1-1 draw)	2005	Celtic beat Dundee Utd (1-0)
1972	Celtic beat Hibernian (6-1)	2006†	Hearts beat Gretna (4-2 on pens after 1-1 draw)
1973	Rangers beat Celtic (3-2)	2007	Celtic beat Dunfermline (1-0)
1974	Celtic beat Dundee Utd (3-0)	2008	Rangers beat Queen of the South (3-2)
1975	Celtic beat Airdrieonians (3-1)	2009	Rangers beat Falkirk (1-0)
1976	Rangers beat Hearts (3-1)	2010	Dundee Utd beat Ross Co (3-0)
1977	Celtic beat Rangers (1-0)	2011	Celtic beat Motherwell (3-0)
1978	Rangers beat Aberdeen (2-1)	2012	Hearts beat Hibernian (5-1)
1979†	Rangers beat Hibernian (3-2 after two 0-0 draws)	2013	Celtic beat Hibernian (3-0)
1980†	Celtic beat Rangers (1-0)	2014	St Johnstone beat Dundee Utd (2-0)
1981	Rangers beat Dundee Utd (4-1 after 0-0 draw)	2015	Inverness beat Falkirk (2-1)
1982†	Aberdeen beat Rangers (4-1)	2016	Hibernian beat Rangers (3-2)
1983†	Aberdeen beat Rangers (1-0)	2017	Celtic beat Aberdeen (2-1)
1984†	Aberdeen beat Celtic (2-1)	2018	Celtic beat Motherwell (2-0)
1985	Celtic beat Dundee Utd (2-1)	2019	Celtic beat Hearts (2-1)
1986	Aberdeen beat Hearts (3-0)	† After extra time
1987†	St Mirren beat Dundee Utd (1-0)	

SUMMARY OF SCOTTISH CUP WINNERS

Celtic 39, Rangers 33, Queen's Park 10, Hearts 8, Aberdeen 7, Clyde 3, Hibernian 3, Kilmarnock 3, St Mirren 3, Vale of Leven 3, Dundee Utd 2, Dunfermline 2, Falkirk 2, Motherwell 2, Renton 2, Third Lanark 2, Airdrieonians 1, Dumbarton 1, Dundee 1, East Fife 1, Inverness 1, Morton 1, Partick 1, St Bernard's 1, St Johnstone 1

THE THINGS THEY SAY...

'It just didn't fit into what we had as a coaching unit and the ethos of the football club' – **Martin Ling**, Leyton Orient's director of football, on the sacking of Carl Fletcher after 29 days as manager.

'The feeling was I was back where I belong. This is my natural habitat' – **Jose Mourinho** on his return to the Premier League with Tottenham.

'I've scored goals and been to Cup finals, but that was an incredible feeling, something that can never be taken away from me' – **Duncan Ferguson**, former Everton centre-forward, on the 3-1 win over Chelsea in his first match as interim manager following the dismissal of Marco Silva.

VANARAMA NATIONAL LEAGUE 2019–2020

	P	W	D	L	F	A	GD	Pts	PPG
Barrow	37	21	7	9	68	39	29	70	(1.89)
Harrogate	37	19	9	9	61	44	17	66	(1.78)
Notts Co	38	17	12	9	61	38	23	63	(1.66)
Yeovil	37	17	9	11	61	44	17	60	(1.62)
Boreham Wood	37	16	12	9	55	40	15	60	(1.62)
Halifax	37	17	7	13	50	49	1	58	(1.57)
Barnet	35	14	12	9	52	42	10	54	(1.54)
Stockport	39	16	10	13	51	54	-3	58	(1.49)
Solihull	38	15	10	13	48	37	11	55	(1.45)
Woking	38	15	10	13	50	55	-5	55	(1.45)
Dover	38	15	9	14	49	49	0	54	(1.42)
Hartlepool	39	14	13	12	56	50	6	55	(1.41)
Bromley	38	14	10	14	57	52	5	52	(1.37)
Torquay	36	14	6	16	56	61	-5	48	(1.33)
Sutton	38	12	14	12	47	42	5	50	(1.32)
Eastleigh	37	11	13	13	43	55	-12	46	(1.24)
Dag & Red	37	11	11	15	40	44	-4	44	(1.19)
Aldershot	39	12	10	17	43	55	-12	46	(1.18)
Wrexham	37	11	10	16	46	49	-3	43	(1.16)
Chesterfield	38	11	11	16	55	65	-10	44	(1.16)
Maidenhead	38	12	5	21	44	58	-14	41	(1.08)
Ebbsfleet	39	10	12	17	47	68	-21	42	(1.08)
AFC Fylde	37	9	12	16	44	60	-16	39	(1.05)
Chorley	38	4	14	20	31	65	-34	26	(0.68)

(Season terminated early – Covid-19. Final positions decided on points-per-game basis)
Barrow champions and promoted to EFL; Harrogate also promoted; Ebbsfleet, AFC Fylde,
Chorley relegated. Play-off Final: Harrogate 3 Notts Co 1

Leading scorers: 20 Quigley (Barrow); 18 Kabongo (Boreham Wood), Reid (Torquay); 17
Murphy (Yeovil), Rooney (Barrow); 16 Effiong (Dover), Hyde (Woking); 15 Akinola (Barnet),
Beautyman (Sutton); 14 Marsh (Boreham Wood)

CHAMPIONS

1979–80	Altrincham	1995–96	Stevenage	2011–2012*	Fleetwood
1980–81	Altrincham	1996–97*	Macclesfield	2012–13*	Mansfield
1981–82	Runcorn	1997–98*	Halifax	2013–14*	Luton
1982–83	Enfield	1998–99*	Cheltenham	2014–15*	Barnet
1983–84	Maidstone	1999–2000*	Kidderminster	2015–16*	Cheltenham
1984–85	Wealdstone	2000–01*	Rushden	2016–17*	Lincoln
1985–86	Enfield	2001–02*	Boston	2017–18*	Macclesfield
1986–87*	Scarborough	2002–03*	Yeovil	2018–19*	Leyton Orient
1987–88*	Lincoln	2003–04*	Chester	2019–20*	Barrow
1988–89*	Maidstone	2004–05*	Barnet	*Promoted to Football League
1989–90*	Darlington	2005–06*	Accrington	Conference – Record
1990–91*	Barnet	2006–07*	Dagenham	*attendance: 11,085 Bristol*
1991–92*	Colchester	2007–08*	Aldershot	*Rov v Alfreton, April 25, 2015*
1992–93*	Wycombe	2008–09*	Burton	
1993–94	Kidderminster	2009–10*	Stevenage	
1994–95	Macclesfield	2010–11*	Crawley	

VANARAMA NATIONAL LEAGUE RESULTS 2019–2020

Home \ Away	Aldershot	Barnet	Barrow	Boreham-W	Bromley	Chesterfield	Chorley	Dag & R	Dover	Eastleigh	Ebbsfleet	FC Halifax	Fylde	Harrogate	Hartlepool	Maidstone	Notts Co	Solihull	Stockport	Sutton	Torquay	Woking	Wrexham	Yeovil
Aldershot	–	1-2	0-0	3-2	0-1	2-2	3-3	0-1	4-0	3-1	7-0	1-2	1-2	1-0	0-3	2-0	2-1	0-3	0-3	1-1	1-1	1-0	1-0	1-3
Barnet	2-1	–	3-1	0-0	1-2	2-2	2-2	2-1	1-0	2-0	5-2	1-2	1-1	2-1	0-1	2-0	0-2	3-0	2-0	1-2	2-1	4-2	1-3	1-0
Barrow	2-0	0-3	–	2-2	0-3	2-2	2-1	1-1	2-1	1-3	0-2	0-2	1-1	0-2	2-2	1-0	2-1	2-2	3-2	1-1	2-2	2-0	1-1	1-0
Boreham-W	0-0	0-0	1-1	–	1-0	2-2	2-1	3-0	3-0	2-3	5-2	5-0	0-2	4-2	2-1	1-0	1-2	2-2	1-2	1-0	2-2	2-2	2-2	1-0
Bromley	1-2	1-2	2-2	1-0	–	2-1	2-3	1-1	1-2	1-2	3-1	2-3	2-2	0-0	1-1	2-1	2-2	2-2	0-0	1-0	1-0	1-0	0-2	1-1
Chesterfield	2-1	1-2	2-2	2-1	2-1	–	2-3	3-0	1-2	1-2	4-0	5-0	2-2	2-1	1-5	2-1	2-2	1-6	2-2	1-0	3-3	1-0	3-2	1-2
Chorley	0-0	1-3	0-2	0-0	0-0	1-2	–	0-0	1-2	2-0	0-4	2-3	1-2	0-2	0-0	1-2	2-0	3-0	2-2	1-0	1-0	1-2	0-2	1-2
Dag & R	6-1	0-2	2-1	0-2	1-1	1-2	0-0	–	3-1	3-1	1-1	0-1	5-1	4-2	3-1	1-2	2-0	1-1	0-0	0-0	0-0	0-2	0-2	3-2
Dover	2-0	1-1	2-1	3-0	3-0	1-1	1-1	1-2	–	3-1	1-1	0-2	2-2	1-1	1-1	3-4	2-0	0-1	0-0	0-0	3-2	1-2	2-1	0-1
Eastleigh	0-0	1-2	3-0	2-0	1-3	0-2	1-1	1-2	3-1	–	1-1	0-2	1-2	0-2	2-2	2-1	2-0	1-1	0-1	1-1	2-4	1-2	0-2	1-3
Ebbsfleet	1-2	1-1	0-3	2-1	0-2	2-2	0-0	1-0	4-2	1-1	–	1-4	5-1	0-2	2-0	1-2	2-2	0-0	2-1	1-0	2-4	2-0	2-1	0-1
FC-Halifax	1-0	1-1	1-0	1-1	2-1	1-3	1-1	3-0	0-1	1-1	1-1	–	4-1	0-0	2-2	1-0	2-1	0-1	2-0	1-1	2-3	1-4	2-1	2-2
Fylde	1-2	1-1	1-1	1-2	2-1	3-1	1-1	1-0	0-1	3-1	0-1	0-1	–	1-1	2-2	1-0	0-2	1-2	2-0	1-1	2-1	1-2	0-2	3-0
Harrogate	1-0	2-1	0-4	1-2	0-0	2-0	1-1	2-3	0-2	3-0	1-0	2-2	2-2	–	4-1	1-0	2-0	2-2	2-0	2-0	2-1	1-1	0-2	2-2
Hartlepool	1-0	2-2	0-4	0-0	2-3	1-1	0-0	1-0	1-2	0-1	0-1	0-1	1-1	0-1	–	0-0	0-0	1-0	2-0	1-3	2-4	2-3	4-2	2-1
Maidstone	1-2	0-4	1-4	0-1	1-2	1-2	4-1	5-1	1-2	2-0	1-3	0-1	1-1	1-1	0-2	–	0-0	1-0	1-2	1-1	0-0	1-1	0-2	0-2
Notts Co	3-1	0-3	1-2	2-2	3-0	3-0	4-0	2-1	2-0	4-0	2-3	1-0	2-0	0-0	2-2	3-0	–	0-0	2-0	1-1	2-0	2-3	3-2	3-0
Solihull	2-1	0-0	3-2	2-1	2-1	2-1	4-2	1-0	3-0	2-0	2-1	5-1	3-1	3-1	0-1	0-2	1-4	–	3-0	0-0	3-0	1-1	0-2	2-1
Stockport	1-2	3-2	2-2	1-3	0-2	1-0	2-2	0-2	1-2	0-1	1-1	0-1	3-1	4-2	1-1	0-3	1-1	1-0	–	0-4	2-0	6-2	3-1	3-2
Sutton	2-0	1-1	2-2	0-2	0-0	0-3	2-0	2-3	1-2	2-3	2-3	5-1	3-1	3-1	2-2	0-2	1-1	0-0	1-5	–	2-0	4-1	1-2	0-1
Torquay	2-0	4-2	2-2	2-1	0-3	1-1	2-0	1-0	1-2	2-3	0-0	0-1	2-0	4-2	2-0	0-2	0-1	1-2	1-5	0-2	–	2-3	2-0	0-2
Woking	0-1	3-2	2-2	0-1	1-0	0-1	1-1	0-2	1-1	1-1	1-3	1-0	3-1	1-0	2-2	2-2	0-0	1-0	1-2	1-2	1-1	–	3-0	1-0
Wrexham	1-1	1-1	1-1	1-0	3-1	0-1	1-1	2-0	4-2	1-0	2-3	2-0	0-1	1-1	2-2	2-2	0-0	1-2	1-2	1-1	0-1	3-0	–	3-3
Yeovil	2-2	1-3	2-2	3-0	2-1	1-2	1-1	1-0	0-1	1-0	2-0	2-0	3-2	1-2	2-2	2-1	3-1	0-0	1-1	1-0	6-2	3-1	3-0	–

VANARAMA NATIONAL LEAGUE NORTH

	P	W	D	L	F	A	GD	Pts	PPG
King's Lynn	32	19	7	6	63	39	24	64	(2.00)
York	34	19	9	6	52	28	24	66	(1.94)
Boston	32	17	7	8	46	32	14	58	(1.81)
Brackley	34	16	12	6	61	25	36	60	(1.76)
Altrincham	33	16	9	8	62	40	22	57	(1.72)
Chester	32	15	9	8	58	38	20	54	(1.68)
Gateshead	31	14	10	7	47	31	16	52	(1.67)
Spennymoor	34	15	10	9	63	45	18	55	(1.61)
Guiseley	33	14	8	11	52	41	11	50	(1.51)
Darlington	33	14	6	13	43	50	-7	48	(1.45)
Farsley	34	14	6	14	50	45	5	48	(1.41)
Southport	32	12	7	13	40	41	-1	43	(1.34)
Alfreton	32	12	4	16	48	55	-7	40	(1.25)
AFC Telford	34	11	9	14	51	56	-5	42	(1.24)
Kidderminster	33	10	8	15	39	43	-4	38	(1.15)
Hereford	35	9	12	14	39	56	-17	39	(1.11)
Gloucester	30	9	6	15	39	57	-18	33	(1.11)
Leamington	32	9	8	15	39	51	-12	35	(1.09)
Kettering	31	7	11	13	36	46	-10	32	(1.03)
Curzon Ashton	33	8	10	15	34	42	-8	34	(1.03)
Blyth	33	6	5	22	32	78	-46	23	(0.70)
Bradford PA	33	5	5	23	25	80	-55	20	(0.61)

King's Lynn champions and promoted; no relegation. Altrincham also promoted.
Play-off Final: Boston 0 Altrincham 1

VANARAMA NATIONAL LEAGUE SOUTH

	P	W	D	L	F	A	GD	Pts	PPG
Wealdstone	33	22	4	7	69	35	34	70	(2.12)
Havant	34	19	10	5	64	37	27	67	(1.97)
Weymouth	35	17	12	6	60	35	25	63	(1.80)
Bath	35	18	9	8	50	37	13	63	(1.80)
Slough	35	17	9	9	51	38	13	60	(1.71)
Dartford	34	16	8	10	60	46	14	56	(1.65)
Dorking	35	14	8	13	58	56	2	50	(1.43)
Hampton & R	33	14	5	14	51	50	1	47	(1.42)
Maidstone	33	12	9	12	48	44	4	45	(1.36)
Chelmsford	34	11	11	12	55	56	-1	44	(1.29)
Hemel H	34	12	8	14	36	43	-7	44	(1.29)
Welling	34	12	6	16	38	46	-8	42	(1.24)
Oxford City	34	11	9	14	47	60	-13	42	(1.24)
Chippenham	35	10	12	13	39	45	-6	42	(1.20)
Tonbridge	31	9	9	13	46	54	-8	36	(1.16)
Concord	32	10	7	15	44	48	-4	37	(1.16)
Billericay	32	8	13	11	46	55	-9	37	(1.16)
Eastbourne	33	8	14	11	38	54	-16	38	(1.15)
Dulwich Hamlet	35	9	10	16	51	50	1	37	(1.06)
St Albans	35	9	10	16	41	54	-13	37	(1.06)
Braintree	35	10	5	20	44	67	-23	35	(1.00)
Hungerford	33	8	4	21	38	64	-26	28	(0,85)

Wealdstone champions and promoted; no relegation. Weymouth also promoted.
Play-off Final: Weymouth 0 Dartford 0 (Weymouth won 3-0 on pens)

OTHER LEAGUES 2019–20

JD WELSH PREMIER

	P	W	D	L	F	A	GD	Pts
Connah's Quay	26	16	8	2	47	19	28	56
New Saints	26	16	4	6	69	27	42	52
Bala	26	15	4	7	53	23	30	49
Barry	25	12	6	7	35	29	6	42
Caernarfon	26	11	5	10	36	38	-2	38
Newtown	25	10	5	10	25	30	-5	35
Cardiff MU	25	9	8	8	30	29	1	35
Cefn Druids	25	10	5	10	37	39	-2	35
Aberystwyth	26	7	6	13	36	55	-19	27
Penybont	25	5	6	14	29	48	-19	21
Carmarthen	25	4	6	15	28	49	-21	18
Airbus	26	4	5	17	28	67	-39	17

Remaining fixtures cancelled. Connah's Quay declared champions. **League Cup Final:** Connah's Quay 3 STM Sport 0

BETVICTOR PREMIER

	P	W	D	L	F	A	GD	Pts
Worthing	34	21	8	5	72	41	31	71
Cray	33	18	10	5	63	45	18	64
Hornchurch	33	17	11	5	62	28	34	62
Folkestone	32	18	8	6	60	34	26	62
Carshalton	34	18	8	8	59	38	21	62
Horsham	33	17	6	10	51	35	16	57
Enfield	32	16	8	8	61	51	10	56
Bognor Regis	32	16	5	11	58	46	12	53
Leatherhead	31	15	7	9	48	42	6	52
Kingstonian	31	11	14	6	42	36	6	47
East Thurrock	30	14	4	12	47	40	7	46
Margate	33	11	10	12	47	54	-7	43
Potters Bar	32	11	8	13	47	56	-9	41
Bowers & Pitsea	33	11	7	15	49	42	7	40
Haringey	30	11	6	13	44	47	-3	39
Lewes	34	8	7	19	35	55	-20	31
Bishop's Stortford	32	8	4	20	37	63	-26	28
Cheshunt	31	8	3	20	39	59	-20	27
Corinthian Cas	31	6	8	17	33	44	-11	26
Wingate & Finchley	33	5	10	18	34	58	-24	25
Merstham	33	6	7	20	34	70	-36	25
Brightlingsea	33	5	9	19	24	62	-38	24

All results expunged – no promotion or relegation

BETVICTOR NORTH

	P	W	D	L	F	A	GD	Pts
South Shields	33	21	6	6	64	34	30	69
FC United	32	16	9	7	73	51	22	57
Warrington	32	14	13	5	57	44	13	55
Basford	32	16	7	9	49	39	10	55
Lancaster	34	15	8	11	58	46	12	53
Nantwich	31	15	7	9	55	39	16	52
Whitby	31	14	8	9	54	42	12	50
Scarborough	35	14	8	13	44	47	-3	50
Morpeth	27	14	6	7	48	37	11	48
Hyde	33	12	7	14	55	55	0	43
Gainsborough	32	11	9	12	53	50	3	42
Stalybridge	33	12	6	15	42	50	-8	42
Bamber Bridge	33	12	4	17	53	64	-11	40
Witton	31	10	9	12	40	43	-3	39
Mickleover	29	11	5	13	42	52	-10	38
Radcliffe	32	11	5	16	34	50	-16	38
Ashton *	29	10	7	12	40	45	-5	36
Buxton	32	8	11	13	56	52	4	35
Grantham	32	7	9	16	38	71	-33	30
Matlock	28	8	5	15	36	43	-7	29
Atherton	26	8	4	14	36	49	-13	28
Stafford	33	4	11	18	29	53	-24	33

*Deducted 1 pt. All results expunged – no promotion or relegation

BETVICTOR SOUTH

	P	W	D	L	F	A	GD	Pts
Truro	31	21	4	6	65	30	35	67
Chesham	33	21	3	9	70	44	26	66
Hayes & Yeading	32	17	6	9	65	42	23	57
Swindon Super	32	17	6	9	50	41	9	57
Tiverton	29	16	7	6	69	41	28	55
Taunton	31	15	8	8	63	53	10	53
Salisbury	29	14	8	7	55	40	15	50
Gosport	33	13	10	10	35	32	3	49
Poole	27	14	6	7	46	28	18	48
Weston SM	29	13	6	10	54	45	9	45
Met Police	30	13	4	13	46	48	-2	43
Farnborough	30	13	3	14	41	43	-2	42
Merthyr	31	9	11	11	37	37	0	38
Hendon	31	10	8	13	47	51	-4	38
Wimborne	33	10	7	16	39	52	-13	37
Hartley Wintney	27	10	6	11	38	39	-1	36
Harrow	33	9	8	16	42	60	-18	35
Blackfield & Langley	31	8	9	14	33	50	-17	33
Yate	31	8	5	18	38	56	-18	29
Walton Cas	33	7	6	20	40	71	-31	27
Beaconsfield	32	6	7	19	29	54	-25	25
Dorchester	32	4	6	22	36	81	-45	18

All results expunged – no promotion or relegation

BETVICTOR SOUTH CENTRAL

	P	W	D	L	F	A	GD	Pts
Peterborough Spts	33	19	8	6	90	46	44	65
Tamworth	30	21	2	7	63	27	36	65
Royston	30	19	6	5	62	28	34	63
Bromsgrove	32	17	6	9	80	43	37	57
Rushall	33	15	8	10	58	43	15	53
Stourbridge	32	16	5	11	53	52	1	53
Banbury	32	14	10	8	48	31	17	52
Coalville	30	14	9	7	51	32	19	51
Nuneaton	33	14	8	11	57	46	11	50
Kings Langley	30	15	5	10	51	41	10	50
Rushden & D	30	14	7	9	50	45	5	49
Barwell	32	14	6	12	58	54	4	48
Needham Market	33	13	9	11	43	40	3	48
Hednesford	32	14	5	13	50	44	6	47
Biggleswade	30	13	4	13	45	46	-1	43
Lowestoft	33	13	2	18	48	62	-14	41
Hitchin	32	10	9	13	43	49	-6	39
Stratford	33	8	4	21	42	74	-32	28
Leiston	32	6	8	18	39	87	-48	26
St Ives	33	6	5	22	33	76	-43	23
Alvechurch	30	4	5	21	25	58	-33	17
Redditch	33	3	3	27	24	89	-65	12

All results expunged – no promotion or relegation

BREEDON HIGHLAND LEAGUE

	P	W	D	L	F	A	GD	Pts
Brora	26	24	0	2	96	14	82	72
Inverurie	28	19	2	7	80	40	40	59
Fraserburgh	23	17	4	2	79	23	56	55
Rothes	23	17	2	4	53	22	31	53
Buckie	24	17	2	5	64	35	29	53
Formartine	23	14	2	7	62	21	41	44
Forres	27	13	4	10	67	49	18	43
Nairn	22	12	3	7	39	41	-2	39
Keith	27	10	4	13	50	65	-15	34
Wick	25	9	5	11	38	47	-9	32
Deveronvale	27	9	4	14	42	56	-14	31
Huntly	27	6	6	15	35	73	-38	24
Strathspey	22	6	1	15	29	54	-25	19
Turriff	27	5	3	19	33	83	-50	18
Clachnacuddin	27	4	4	19	27	63	-36	16
Lossiemouth	28	4	1	23	22	87	-65	13
Fort William	20	3	1	16	18	61	-43	10

Remaining fixtures cancelled. Brora declared champions

LOWLAND LEAGUE

	P	W	D	L	F	A	GD	Pts
Kelty	25	22	2	1	95	17	78	68
Bonnyrigg	24	20	2	2	70	22	48	62
East Stirling	26	17	2	7	77	29	48	53
BSC	22	16	3	3	58	21	37	51
Spartans	25	16	1	8	49	32	17	49
Civil Service	23	12	3	8	40	38	2	39
East Kilbride	23	11	4	8	43	24	19	37
Caledonian	26	11	3	12	57	55	2	36
Cumbernauld	27	10	6	11	49	50	-1	36
Stirling Univ	25	9	4	12	28	44	-16	31
Gala	25	7	6	12	39	55	-16	27
Berwick	24	6	6	12	32	41	-9	24
Gretna	24	2	6	16	21	62	-41	12
Edinburgh Univ	25	2	6	17	18	66	-48	12
Dalbeattie	23	3	2	18	19	68	-49	11
Vale of Leithen	23	2	2	19	18	89	-71	8

Remaining fixtures cancelled. Kelty declared champions

PREMIER LEAGUE UNDER 23
DIVISION ONE

	P	W	D	L	F	A	GD	Pts
Chelsea	18	10	8	0	34	20	14	38
Leicester	18	10	5	3	36	21	15	35
Brighton	18	10	1	7	36	26	10	31
Derby	18	7	6	5	33	32	1	27
Liverpool	17	7	5	5	34	34	0	26
Arsenal	18	6	7	5	32	32	0	25
Everton	18	5	7	6	32	33	-1	22
Manchester City	18	6	3	9	30	29	1	21
Blackburn	17	6	3	8	27	26	1	21
Tottenham	18	6	3	9	31	34	-3	21
Southampton	18	4	3	11	23	47	-24	15
Wolves	18	2	5	11	21	35	-14	11

Remaining fixtures cancelled

DIVISION TWO

	P	W	D	L	F	A	GD	Pts
West Ham	18	14	4	0	58	21	37	46
Manchester Utd	17	14	1	2	45	17	28	43
WBA	16	11	1	4	38	22	16	34
Stoke	18	8	3	7	32	27	5	27
Middlesbrough	18	8	2	8	34	43	-9	26
Newcastle	18	8	1	9	29	32	-3	25
Aston Villa	17	6	4	7	27	28	-1	22
Swansea	17	6	3	8	22	32	-10	21
Reading	18	6	2	10	35	37	-2	20
Fulham	18	6	2	10	26	32	-6	20
Norwich	17	5	2	10	23	35	-12	17
Sunderland	18	0	1	17	10	53	-43	1

Remaining fixtures cancelled

WOMEN'S FOOTBALL 2019–20
CHELSEA'S TITLE ON POINTS-PER-GAME

Unbeaten Chelsea were declared champions after the Women's Super League season was abandoned because of Covid-19. At the time, they trailed Manchester City by a single point, but had a game in hand and were elevated to the top spot on a points-per-game ratio. The FA board's majority decision was determined 'on sporting merit.' Liverpool were relegated and replaced by Championship winners Aston Villa. It was Chelsea's second title in three seasons and their third overall after success in 2015. Manager Emma Hayes's side also won the League Cup, defeating Arsenal 2-1 in the final with two goals from Beth England, her second in stoppage-time, in front of a record crowd for the competition of 6,743 at the City Ground, Nottingham. 'We would have preferred to play the remaining games,' said Hayes. 'But player welfare was always our priority. This was the best and fairest outcome.' In the FA Cup, Chelsea defeated Charlton and Liverpool and were due to play Everton in the quarter-finals when the campaign was terminated. They will join Manchester City in next season's Champions League. City lost to Atletico Madrid in the round of 16 this time. Arsenal defeated Slavia Prague and were drawn against Paris Saint-Germain in the quarter-finals.

BARCLAYS FA SUPER LEAGUE

	P	W	D	L	F	A	GD	Pts	PPG
Chelsea	15	12	3	0	47	11	36	39	(2.60)
Manchester City	16	13	1	2	39	9	30	40	(2.50)
Arsenal	15	12	0	3	40	13	27	36	(2.40)
Manchester Utd	14	7	2	5	24	12	12	23	(1.64)
Reading	14	6	3	5	21	24	-3	21	(1.50)
Everton	14	6	1	7	21	21	0	19	(1.36)
Tottenham	15	6	2	7	15	24	-9	20	(1.33)
West Ham	14	5	1	8	19	34	-15	16	(1.14)
Brighton	16	3	4	9	11	30	-19	13	(0.81)
Bristol City	14	2	3	9	9	38	-29	9	(0.64)
Birmingham	13	2	1	10	5	23	-18	7	(0.53)
Liverpool	14	1	3	10	8	20	-12	6	(0.42)

Finishing positions on points-per-game ratio. Chelsea champions, Liverpool relegated

CHAMPIONSHIP

	P	W	D	L	F	A	GD	Pts	
Aston Villa	14	13	1	0	39	11	28	40	(2.86)
Sheffield Utd	14	11	1	2	46	16	30	34	(2.43)
Durham	14	10	2	2	33	10	23	32	(2.29)
London City	15	8	2	5	25	24	1	26	(1.73)
London Bees	12	4	3	5	16	19	-3	15	(1.25)
Leicester	15	4	3	8	22	35	-13	15	(1.00)
Blackburn	12	3	1	8	13	25	-12	10	(0.83)
Lewes	12	2	3	7	10	18	-8	9	(0.75)
Crystal Palace	14	2	4	8	15	33	-18	10	(0.71)
Coventry Utd	14	2	3	9	19	35	-16	9	(0.64)
Charlton	12	0	7	5	9	21	-12	7	(0.58)

Finishing positions on points per game-ratio. Aston Villa champions and promoted. No relegation

NATIONAL LEAGUE NORTH

	P	W	D	L;	F	A	GD	Pts
Sunderland	14	13	1	0	53	10	43	40
Derby	15	9	2	4	46	17	29	29
Nottm Forest	13	9	1	3	27	19	8	28
Stoke	14	8	1	5	32	17	15	25
Burnley	11	7	1	3	19	13	6	22
Huddersfield	12	5	3	4	35	22	13	18
WBA	11	5	2	4	31	20	11	17
Middlesbrough	15	4	2	9	27	52	-25	14
Fylde	14	3	4	7	15	24	-9	13
Loughborough	15	4	1	10	24	42	-18	13
Hull	14	2	0	12	23	64	-41	6
Sheffield	10	1	0	9	7	39	-32	3

All results expunged. No promotion or relegation

NATIONAL LEAGUE SOUTH

	P	W	D	L	F	A	GD	Pts
Crawley	14	12	1	1	36	9	27	37
Watford	11	9	1	1	40	14	26	28
Oxford Utd	14	9	0	5	44	20	24	27
Plymouth	14	9	0	5	42	18	24	27
Yeovil	13	8	2	3	46	17	29	26
Cardiff	13	8	1	4	23	9	14	25
Portsmouth	9	5	0	4	28	15	13	15
MK Dons	14	4	1	9	18	30	-12	13
Gillingham	11	3	2	6	12	27	-15	11
Keynsham	12	2	1	9	9	39	-30	7
Hounslow	14	0-	3	11	4	73	-69	3
Chichester	13	0	2	11	6	37	-31	2

All results expunged. No promotion or relegation

THE THINGS THEY SAY...

'I got the ball and tried to pass it to Dele (Alli), but I couldn't find him, so I just kept going' – **Son Heung-min** on racing 80 yards with the ball to score the Premier League's goal of the season in Tottenham's 5-0 win over Burnley.

'In 20 years in management I don't think I've known a crazy 15 minutes like that' – **Steve Bruce**, Newcastle manager, after his side had four players injured and conceded two goals in the space of a quarter-of-an-hours of a 3-0 home defeat by Leicester, their fourth game in 11 days over Christmas and New Year.

'A volley with his right foot is like seeing Halley's Comet or Lord Lucan riding Shergar' – **Mark Warburton**, Queens Park Rangers manager, on Lee Wallace's goal in the 5-1 FA Cup third round win over Swansea.

'It's a wacky game football for sure. It just shows you shouldn't leave a game early' – **Steve Bruce**, Newcastle manager, after two stoppage time goals earned a 2-2 draw against Everton.

IRISH FOOTBALL 2019–20

SSE AIRTRICITY LEAGUE OF IRELAND

PREMIER DIVISION

	P	W	D	L	F	A	Pts
Dundalk	36	27	5	4	73	18	86
Shamrock Rov	36	23	6	7	62	21	75
Bohemians	36	17	9	10	47	28	60
Derry City	36	15	12	9	56	34	57
St Patrick's	36	14	10	12	29	35	52
Waterford	36	12	7	17	46	53	43
Sligo	36	10	12	14	38	47	42
Cork City	36	9	10	17	29	49	37
Finn Harps	36	7	7	22	26	64	28
UCD	36	5	4	27	25	82	19

Leading scorer: 14 Junior Ogedi-Uzokwe (Derry). **Player of Year:** Jack Byrne (Shamrock Rov). **Young Player of Year:** Danny Mandroiu (Bohemians). **Goalkeeper of Year:** Gary Rogers (Dundalk). **Personality of Year:** Vinnie Perth (Dundalk)

FIRST DIVISION

	P	W	D	L	F	A	Pts
Shelbourne	27	19	3	5	50	19	60
Drogheda	27	16	3	8	59	36	51
Longford	27	16	3	8	41	23	51
Cabinteely	27	14	8	5	39	28	50
Bray Wdrs	27	14	4	9	44	26	46
Cobh	27	8	7	12	38	51	31
Galway	27	7	5	15	36	42	26
Athlone	27	4	6	17	30	61	18
Wexford	27	2	5	20	22	65	11
Limerick *	27	10	6	11	33	41	10

* deducted 26 pts

Leading scorer: 17 Robert Manley (Cabinteely). **Player of Year:** Robert Manley

Extra.ie CUP FINAL

Shamrock Rovers 1 (McEneff (pen) **Dundalk** 1 (Duffy). (Shamrock Rovers won 4-2 on pens), Aviva Stadium, November 3, 2019
Shamrock Rovers: Mannus, O'Brien, Lopes, Grace, Kavanagh (Farrugia), Finn, McEneff, O'Neill, Byrne, Greene (Lafferty), Burke (Bolger)
Dundalk: Rogers, Gannon, Gartland, Cleary, Massey, Hoare (G Kelly), Benson (Mountney), McGrath, Murray (D Kelly), Duffy, Hogan (Flores)
Referee: D. Tomney (Dublin)

EA SPORTS LEAGUE CUP FINAL

Derry City 2 (Parkhouse, Ogedi-Uzokwe) **Dundalk** 2 (Duffy, Gannon), aet, Dundalk won 6-5 on pens. Brandywell Stadium, Derry, September 14, 2019

DANSKE BANK PREMIERSHIP

	P	W	D	L	F	A	Pts
Linfield	31	22	3	6	71	24	69
Coleraine	31	19	8	4	64	24	65
Crusaders	31	17	8	6	66	30	59
Cliftonville	31	18	5	8	48	22	59
Glentoran	31	17	7	7	60	33	58
Larne	31	16	8	7	59	29	56
Glenavon	31	10	5	16	46	71	35
Carrick	31	10	2	19	34	47	32
Dungannon	31	8	6	17	36	76	30
Ballymena	31	7	6	18	34	54	27
Warrenpoint	31	5	3	23	26	85	18
Institute	31	2	9	20	23	72	15

Remaining fixtures cancelled. Linfield champions, Institute relegated
Leading scorer: 18 Joe Gormley (Cliftonville). No awards

BLUEFIN SPORT

	P	W	D	L	F	A	Pts
Portadown	31	20	6	5	72	30	66
Ballinamallard	30	19	3	8	71	34	60
Loughall	31	18	4	9	64	45	58
Ards	31	16	6	9	68	44	54
Newry	30	15	6	9	55	32	51
Dundela	31	13	7	11	43	49	46
Ballyclare	30	11	7	12	53	49	40
H&W Welders	31	10	5	16	52	63	35
Queens	31	11	1	19	59	69	34
Dergview	30	8	5	17	38	54	29
Knockbreda	30	7	4	19	36	84	25
PSNI	30	7	2	21	40	98	23

Remaining fixtures cancelled. Portadown promoted
Leading scorer: 25 Ryan Campbell (Ballinamallard)

SADLER'S PEAKY BLINDER IRISH CUP FINAL

Glentoran 2 (O'Neill, McDaid) **Ballymena Utd** 1 (Friel), aet, Windsor Park, July 31, 2020
Glentoran: Morris, Kane, Gallagher, McDaid, McClean, Nasseri, Crowe (O'Connor), O'Neill (Fraser), Cowan, Van Overbeek (Smyth), Donnelly (Peers)
Ballymena Utd: Glendinning, Addis (Burns), Whiteside, Friel (K Kane), McCullough, McGrory (T Kane), Balmer), Winchester (Knowles), Ervin, Lecky, Millar, Kelly
Referee: T. Marshall (Irvinestown)

BETMCLEAN LEAGUE CUP FINAL

Coleraine 2 (Lowry (pen), McLaughlin) **Crusaders** 1 (McGonigle), Windsor Park, February, 15, 2020

TOALS COUNTY ANTRIM SHIELD FINAL

Ballymena Utd 1 (Millar) **Cliftonville** 2 (Maguire, R Curran), Windsor Park, January 20, 2020

UEFA CHAMPIONS LEAGUE 2019–20

FIRST QUALIFYING ROUND, FIRST LEG

Dundalk 0 Riga 0. Att: 3,100. **Linfield** 0 Rosenborg 2 (Jensen 22, Soederland 69). Att: 2,710. **New Saints** 2 (Draper 49 pen, Edwards 77) Feronikeli 2 (Zeka 89, Fazliu 90+3). Att: 1,140. Sarajevo 1 (Oremus 29) **Celtic** 3 (Johnston 35, Edouard 51, Sinclair 85). Att: 24,723

SECOND LEG

Celtic 2 (Christie 26, McGregor 76) Sarajevo 1 (Tatar 62). Att: 58,662 (Celtic won 5-2 on agg). Feronikeli 0 **New Saints** 1 (Ebbe 67). Att: 7,800 (New Saints won 3-2 on agg). Riga 0 **Dundalk** 0. Att: 6,050 (agg 0-0, Dundalk won 5-4 on pens). Rosenborg 4 (Konradsen 20, 51, Akintola 69, Helland 85) **Linfield** 0 Att: 11,904 (Rosenborg won 6-0 on agg)

ON AGGREGATE

AIK 4 Ararat 3; BATE Borisov 3 Piast Gliwice 2; CFR Cluj 3 Astana 2; Ferencvaros 5 Ludogorets 3; HJK Helsinki 5 HB Torshavn 2; Maribor 5 Valur 0; Nomme Kalju 2 Shkendija 2 (Nomme Kalju won on away goals); Qarabag 2 Partizan Tirana 0; Red Star Belgrade 2 Suduva 1; Saburtalo 4 Sheriff Tiraspol 3; Sutkeska 2 Slovan Bratislava 2 (aet, Sutjeska won 3-2 on pens) Valletta 3 Dudelange 3 (Valletta won on away goals)

SECOND QUALIFYING ROUND, FIRST LEG

Celtic 5 (Ajer 36, Christie 44 pen, 65, Griffiths 45, McGregor 77) Nomme Kalju 0. Att: 41,872. **Dundalk** 1 (Hoban 78) Qarabag 1 (Emrell 4). Att: 3,100. **New Saints** 0 Copenhagen 2 (Soteriou 18, Skov 61 pen). Att: 1,230

SECOND LEG

Copenhagen 1 (Zeca 52) **New Saints** 0. Att: 12,523 (Copenhagen won 3-0 on agg). Nomme Kalju 0 **Celtic** 2 (Kulinits 10 og, Shved 90+3). Att: 4,014 (Celtic won 7-0 on agg). Qarabag 3 (Romero 12, 87, Ailton 76) **Dundalk** 0. Att: 5,832 (Qarabag won 4-1 on agg)

ON AGGREGATE

Apoel Nicosia 4 Sutjeska 0; Basle 4 PSV Eindhoven 4 (Basle won on away goals); CFR Cluj 3 Maccabi Tel Aviv 2; Dinamo Zagreb 5 Saburtalo 0; Ferencvaros 4 Valletta 2; Maribor 4 AIK 4 (Maribor won on away goals); Olympiacos 4 Viktoria Plzen 0; Red Star Belgrade 3 HJK Helsinki 2; Rosenborg 3 BATE Borisov 2

THIRD QUALIFYING ROUND, FIRST LEG

CFR Cluj 1 (Rondon 28) **Celtic** 1 (Forrest 37). Att: 13,055

SECOND LEG

Celtic 3 (Forrest 51, Edouard 61, Christie 76) CFR Cluj 4 (Deac 27, Omrani 74, 80, Tucudean 90+8). Att: 50,964 (CFR Cluj won 5-4 on agg)

ON AGGREGATE

Ajax 5 PAOK Salonika 4; Apoel Nicosia 3 Qarabag 2; Club Bruges 4 Dynamo Kiev 3; Dinamo Zagreb 5 Ferencvaros 1; Krasnodar 3 Porto 3 (Krasnodar won on away goals); Linz 5 Basle 2; Olympiacos 3 Basaksehir 0; Red Star Belgrade 2 Copenhagen 2 (aet, agg 2-2, Red Star Belgrade won 7-6 on pens); Rosenborg 6 Maribor 2

PLAY-OFFS, ON AGGREGATE

Ajax 2 Apoel Nicosia 0; Club Bruges 3 Linz 1; Dinamo Zagreb 3 Rosenborg 1; Olympiacos 6 Krasnodar 1; Red Star Belgrade 3 Young Boys 3 (Red Star Belgrade won on away goals); Slavia Prague 2 CFR Cluj 0

GROUP A

September 18, 2019
Club Bruges 0 **Galatasaray** 0. Att: 26,616
Paris SG 3 (Di Maria 14, 33, Meunier 90+1) **Real Madrid** 0. Att: 46,361

October 1, 2019
Galatasaray 0 **Paris SG** 1 (Icardi 52). Att: 46,532
Real Madrid 2 (Sergio Ramos 55, Casemiro 85) **Club Bruges** 2 (Bonaventure 9, 39).
Att: 65,112

October 22, 2019
Club Bruges 0 **Paris SG** 5 (Icardi 7, 63, Mbappe 61, 79, 83). Att: 26,946
Galatasary 0 **Real Madrid** 1 (Kroos 18). Att: 48,886

November 6, 2019
Paris SG 1 (Icardi 22) **Club Bruges** 0. Att: 47,418
Real Madrid 6 (Rodrygo 4, 7, 90+2, Sergio Ramos 14 pen, Benzema 45, 81) **Galatasaray** 0.
Att: 65,492

November 26, 2019
Galatasaray 1 (Buyuk 11) **Club Bruges** 1 (Diatta 90+2). Att: 34,500
Real Madrid 2 (Benzema 17, 79) **Paris SG** 2 (Mbappe 81, Sarabia 83). Att: 75,534

December 11, 2019
Club Bruges 1 (Vanaken 55) **Real Madrid** 3 (Rodrygo 53, Vinicius Junior 64, Modric 90+1).
Att: 27,306
Paris SG 5 (Icardi 33, Sarabia 35, Neymar 46, Mbappe 63, Cavani 84 pen) **Galatasaray** 0.
Att: 46,509

	P	W	D	L;	F	A	Pts
Paris SG Q	6	5	1	0	17	2	16
Real Madrid Q	6	3	2	1	14	8	11
Club Bruges	6	0	3	3	4	12	3
Galatasaray	6	0	2	4	1	14	2

GROUP B

September 18, 2019
Bayern Munich 3 (Coman 34, Lewandowski 80, Muller 90+1) **Red Star Belgrade** 0. Att: 70,000
Olympiacos 2 (Podence 44, Valbuena 54 pen) **Tottenham** 2 (Kane 26 pen, Lucas Moura 30).
Att: 31,001
Tottenham (4-2-3-1): Lloris, Sanchez, Alderweireld, Vertonghen, Davies, Ndombele (Sissoko 62), Winks, Lucas Moura (Lamela 75), Alli (Son Heung-min 73), Eriksen, Kane. **Booked**: Winks

October 1, 2019
Red Star Belgrade 3 (Vulic 62, Milunovic 87, Boakye 90) **Olympiacos** 1 (Semedo 37). Att: 43,291
Tottenham 2 (Son Heung-min 12, Kane 61 pen) **Bayern Munich** 7 (Kimmich 15, Lewandowski

45, 87, Gnabry 53, 55, 83, 88). Att: 60,127
Tottenham (4-3-1-2): Lloris, Aurier, Vertonghen, Alderweireld, Rose, Ndombele (Eriksen 63), Winks (Lamela 81), Sissoko, Alli (Lucas Moura 70), Kane, Son Heung-min. **Booked**: Ndombele, Kane

October 22, 2019
Olympiacos 2 (El Arabi 23, Guilherme 79) **Bayern Munich** 3 (Lewandowski 34, 62, Tolisso 75). Att: 31,670
Tottenham 5 (Kane 9, 72, Son Heung-min 16, 44, Lamela 57) **Red Star Belgrade** 0. Att: 51,743
Tottenham (4-2-3-1): Gazzaniga, Aurier, Sanchez, Vertonghen (Foyth 73), Davies, Ndombele, Sissoko, Lamela, Alli (Lo Celso 79), Son Heung-min (Dier 68), Kane

November 6, 2019
Bayern Munich 2 (Lewandowski 69, Perisic 89) **Olympiacos** 0. Att: 63,646
Red Star Belgrade 0 **Tottenham** 4 (Lo Celso 34, Son Heung-min 57, 61, Eriksen 85). Att: 42,381
Tottenham (4-2-3-1): Gazzaniga, Foyth, Sanchez, Dier, Rose, Sissoko, Ndombele, Lo Celso (Skipp 86), Alli (Eriksen 62), Son Heung-min (Sessegnon 75), Kane. **Booked**: Dier, Skipp

November 26, 2019
Red Star Belgrade 0 **Bayern Munich** 6 (Goretzka 14, Lewandowski 53 pen, 60, 64, 67, Tolisso 89). Att: 44,118
Tottenham 4 (Alli 45, Kane 50, 77, Aurier 73) **Olympiacos** 2 (El Arabi 6, Semedo 19). Att: 57,024
Tottenham (4-2-3-1): Gazzaniga, Aurier, Sanchez, Alderweireld, Rose, Winks, Dier (Eriksen 29), Lucas Moura (Sissoko 61), Alli (Ndombele 83), Son Heung-min, Kane. **Booked**: Alderweireld

December 11, 2019
Bayern Munich 3 (Coman 14, Muller 45, Coutinho 64) **Tottenham** 1 (Sessegnon 20). Att: 68,353
Tottenham (4-2-3-1): Gazzaniga, Walker-Peters, Foyth, Alderweireld, Rose, Dier (Wanyama 80), Sissoko, Lo Celso (Skipp 55), Eriksen, Sessegnon, Lucas Moura (Son Heung-min 65). **Booked**: Lo Celso
Olympiacos 1 (El Arabi 87 pen) **Red Star Belgrade** 0. Att: 31,896

	P	W	D	L	F	A	Pts
Bayern Munich Q	6	6	0	0	24	5	18
Tottenham Q	6	3	1	2	18	14	10
Olympiacos	6	1	1	4	8	14	4
Red Star Belgrade	6	1	0	5	3	20	3

GROUP C
September 18, 2019
Dinamo Zagreb 4 (Leovac 10, Orsic 31, 42, 68) **Atalanta** 0. Att: 28,863
Shakhtar Donetsk 0 **Manchester City** 3 (Mahrez 24, Gundogan 38, Gabriel Jesus 76). Att: 36,675
Manchester City (4-2-3-1): Ederson, Walker (Cancelo 81), Fernandinho, Otamendi, Zinchenko, Gundogan, Rodri (Mendy 83), Mahrez, De Bruyne (Bernardo Silva 77), Sterling, Gabriel Jesus. **Booked**: Rodri

October 1, 2019
Atalanta 1 (Zapata 28) **Shakhtar Donetsk** 2 (Moraes 41, Solomon 90+5). Att: 26,002
Manchester City 2 (Sterling 66, Foden 90+5) **Dinamo Zagreb** 0. Att: 49,046

Manchester City (4-3-3): Ederson, Cancelo (Sterling 55), Fernandinho, Otamendi, Mendy, Gundogan, Rodri, David Silva (Foden 90+1), Mahrez, Aguero, Bernardo Silva. **Booked**: Cancelo, Fernandinho

October 22, 2019
Manchester City 5 (Aguero 34, 38 pen, Sterling 58, 64, 69) **Atalanta** 1 (Malinovsky 28 pen).
Att: 49,308
Manchester City (4-3-3): Ederson, Walker, Fernandinho, Rodri (Stones 41), Mendy (Cancelo 71), De Bruyne (Otamendi 68), Gundogan, Foden, Mahrez, Aguero, Sterling. **Booked**: Mendy, De Bruyne, Foden, Otamendi. **Sent off**: Foden (82)
Shakhtar Donetsk 2 (Konoplyaka 16, Dodo 75) **Dinamo Zagreb** 2 (Olmo 25, Orsic 60 pen). Att: 21,526

November 6, 2019
Atalanta 1 (Pasalic 49) **Manchester City** 1 (Sterling 7). Att: 32,147
Manchester City (4-4-2): Ederson (Bravo 46), Cancelo, Otamendi, Fernandinho, Mendy, Mahrez (Walker 88), De Bruyne, Gundogan, Sterling, Bernardo Silva, Gabriel Jesus (Aguero 73).
Booked: Fernandinho, Mendy, Bernardo Silva. **Sent off**: Bravo (81)

November 26, 2019
Atalanta 2 (Muriel 27 pen, Gomez 47) **Dinamo Zagreb** 0. Att: 26,496
Manchester City 1 (Gundogan 56) **Shakhtar Donetsk** 1 (Solomon 69). Att: 52,020
Manchester City (4-3-3): Ederson, Cancelo, Otamendi, Fernandinho, Angelino, Gundogan, Rodri (Foden 75), De Bruyne (David Silva 69), Bernardo Silva, Gabriel Jesus, Sterling. **Booked**: Fernandinho

December 11, 2019
Dinamo Zagreb 1 (Olmo 10) **Manchester City** 4 (Gabriel Jesus 34, 50, 54, Foden 84). Att: 29,385
ManchesterCity (4-3-3): Bravo, Cancelo, Garcia, Otamendi (Harwood-Bellis 82), Mendy, Gundogan, Rodri (Sterling 73), Foden, Mahrez, Gabriel Jeses (Zinchenko 66), Bernardo Silva
Shakhtar Donetsk 0 **Atalanta** 3 (Castagne 66, Pasalic 80, Gosens 90+4). Att: 26,536

	P	W	D	L	F	A	Pts
Manchester City Q	6	4	2	0	16	4	14
Atalanta Q	6	2	1	3	8	12	7
Shakhtar Donetsk	6	1	3	2	8	13	6
Dinamo Zagreb	6	1	2	3	10	13	5

GROUP D

September 18, 2019
Atletico Madrid 2 (Savic 70, Herrera 90) **Juventus** 2 (Cuadrado 48, Matuidi 65). Att: 66,283
Bayer Leverkusen 1 (Howedes 25 og) **Lokomotiv Moscow** 2 (Krychowiak 16, Barinov 37). Att: 26,592

October 1, 2019
Juventus 3 (Higuain 17, Bernardeschi 61, Ronaldo 88) **Bayer Leverkusen** 0. Att: 34,525
Lokomotiv Moscow 0 **Atletico Madrid** 2 (Joao Felix 48, Thomas 58). Att: 27,051

October 22, 2019
Atletico Madrid 1 (Morata 78) **Bayer Leverkusen** 0. Att: 56,776
Juventus 2 (Dybala 77, 79) **Lokomotiv Moscow** 1 (Miranchuk 30). Att: 38,547

November 6, 2019
Bayer Leverkusen 2 (Thomas 41 og, Volland 55) **Atletico Madrid** 1 (Morata 90+4). Att: 28,160

Lokomotive Moscow 1 (Miranchuk 12) **Juventus** 2 (Ramsey 3, Douglas Costa 90+3). Att: 26,881

November 26, 2019
Juventus 1 (Dybala 45) **Atletico Madrid** 0. Att: 40,486
Lokomotiv Moscow 0 **Bayer Leverkusen** 2 (Zhemaletdinov 11 og, Bender 54). Att: 25,757

December 11, 2019
Atletico Madrid 2 (Joao Felix 17 pen, Felipe 54) **Lokomotiv Moscow** 0. Att: 58,426
Bayer Leverkusen 0 **Juventus** 2 (Ronaldo 75, Higuain 90+2). Att: 29,542

	P	W	D	L	F	A	Pts
Juventus Q	6	5	1	0	12	4	16
Atletico Madrid Q	6	3	1	2	8	5	10
Bayer Leverkusen	6	2	0	4	5	9	6
Lokomotiv Moscow	6	1	0	5	4	11	3

GROUP E

September 17, 2019
Napoli 2 (Mertens 82 pen, Llorente 90+1) **Liverpool** 0. Att: 38,878
Liverpool (4-3-3): Adrian, Alexander-Arnold, Matip, Van Dijk, Robertson, Henderson (Shaqiri 87), Fabinho, Milner (Wijnaldum 66), Salah, Firmino, Mane. **Booked:** Robertson, Milner
Salzburg 6 (Haaland 2, 34, 45, Hwang 36, Szoboszlai 45, Ulmer 66) **Genk** 2 (Lucumi 40, Samatta 52). Att: 29,520

October 2, 2019
Genk 0 **Napoli** 0. Att: 19,962
Liverpool 4 (Mane 9, Robertson 25, Salah 36, 69) **Salzburg** 3 (Hwang 39, Minamino 56, Haaland 60). Att: 52,243
Liverpool (4-3-3): Adrian, Alexander-Arnold, Gomez, Van Dijk, Robertson, Henderson (Milner 62), Fabinho,Wijnaldum (Origi 64), Salah (Keita 90+1), Firmino, Mane. **Booked:** Fabinho

October 23, 2019
Genk 1 (Odey 88) **Liverpool** 4 (Oxlade-Chamberlain 2, 57, Mane 77, Salah 87). Att: 19,626
Liverpool (4-3-3): Alisson, Milner, Lovren, Van Dijk, Robertson (Gomez 63), Oxlade-Chamberlain (Wijnaldum 74), Fabinho Keita, Salah, Firmino (Origi 80), Mane. **Booked:** Gomez
Salzburg 2 (Haaland 40 pen, 72) **Napoli** 3 (Mertens 17, 64, Insigne 73). Att: 29,520

November 5, 2019
Liverpool 2 (Wijnaldum 14, Oxlade-Chamberlain 53) **Genk** 1 (Samatta 40). Att: 52,611
Liverpool (4-3-3): Alisson, Alexander-Arnold, Gomez, Van Dijk, Milner, Oxlade-Chamberlain (Mane 75), Fabinho, Wijnaldum, Salah, Origi (Firmino 89), Keita (Robertson 75)
Napoli 1 (Lozano 43) **Salzburg** 1 (Haaland 11 pen). Att: 32,862

November 27, 2019
Genk 1 (Samata 85) **Salzburg** 4 (Daka 43, Minamino 45, Hwang 69, Haaland 87). Att: 17,284
Liverpool 1 (Lovren 65) **Napoli** 1 (Mertens 21). Att: 52,128
Liverpool (4-3-3): Alisson, Gomez (Oxlade-Chamberlain 57), Lovren, Van Dijk, Robertson, Henderson, Fabinho (Wijnaldum 19), Milner (Alexander-Arnold 78), Salah, Firmino, Mane.
Booked: Robertson

December 10, 2019
Napoli 4 (Milik 3, 26, 38 pen, Mertens 74 pen) **Genk** 0. Att: 22,265
Salzburg 0 **Liverpool** 2 (Keita 57, Salah 58). Att: 29,520
Liverpool (4-3-3): Alisson, Alexander-Arnold, Lovren (Gomez 53), Van Dijk, Robertson, Henderson, Wijnaldum, Keita (Origi 87), Salah, Firmino (Milner 75), Mane

	P	W	D	L	F	A	Pts
Liverpool Q	6	4	1	1	13	8	13
Napoli Q	6	3	3	0	11	4	12
Salzburg	6	2	1	3	16	13	7
Genk	6	0	1	5	5	20	1

GROUP F

September 17, 2019
Borussia Dortmund 0 **Barcelona** 0. Att: 66,099
Inter Milan 1 (Barella 90+2) **Slavia Prague** 1 (Olayinka 63). Att: 50,128

October 2, 2019
Barcelona 2 (Suarez 58, 84) **Inter Milan** 1 (Martinez 2). Att: 86,141
Slavia Prague 0 **Borussia Dortmund** 2 (Hakimi 35, 89). Att: 19,370

October 23, 2019
Inter Milan 2 (Martinez 22, Candreva 89) **Borussia Dortmund** 0. Att: 65,673
Slavia Prague 1 (Boril 50) **Barcelona** 2 (Messi 3, Olayinka 57 og). Att: 19,170

November 5, 2019
Barcelona 0 **Slavia Prague** 0. Att: 67,023
Borussia Dortmund 3 (Hakimi 51, 77, Brandt 64) **Inter Milan** 2 (Martinez 5, Vecino 40). Att: 66,099

November 27, 2019
Barcelona 3 (Suarez 29, Messi 33, Griezmann 67) **Borussia Dortmund** 1 (Sancho 77). Att: 90,071
Slavia Prague 1 (Soucek 37 pen) **Inter Milan** 3 (Martinez 19, 88, Lukaku 81). Att: 19,370

December 10, 2019
Borussia Dortmund 2 (Sancho 10, Brandt 61) **Slavia Prague** 1 (Soucek 43). Att: 65,079
Inter Milan 1 (Lukaku 44) **Barcelona** 2 (Perez 23, Fati 86). Att: 71,818

	P	W	D	L	F	A	Pts
Barcelona Q	6	4	2	0	9	4	14
Borussia Dortmund Q	6	3	1	2	8	8	10
Inter Milan	6	2	1	3	10	9	7
Slavia Prague	6	0	2	4	4	10	2

GROUP G

September 17, 2019
Benfica 1 (Seferovic 84) **Leipzig** 2 (Werner 69, 78). Att: 46,460
Lyon 1 (Depay 51 pen) **Zenit St Petersburg** 1 (Azmoun 41). Att: 47,201

October 2, 2019
Leipzig 0 **Lyon** 2 (Depay 11, Terrier 65). Att: 42,194
Zenit St Petersburg 3 (Dzyuba 22, Dias 70 og, Azmoun 78) **Benfica** 1 (De Tomas 85). Att: 51,683

October 23, 2019
Benfica 2 (Rafa Silva 4, Pizzi 86) **Lyon** 1 (Depay 70). Att: 53,035
Leipzig 2 (Laimer 49, Sabitzer 59) **Zenit St Petersburg** 1 (Rakitskiy 25). Att: 41,058

November 5, 2019
Lyon 3 (Andersen 4, Depay 33, Traore 89) **Benfica** 1 (Seferovic 76). Att: 51,077
Zenit St Petersburg 0 **Leipzig** 2 (Demme 45, Sabitzer 63). Att: 50,452

November 27, 2019
Leipzig 2 (Forsberg 89 pen, 90+6) **Benfica** 2 (Pizzi 20, Vinicius 59). Att: 38,339
Zenit St Petersburg 2 (Dzyuba 42, Ozdoev 84) **Lyon** 0. Att: 51,183

December 10, 2019
Benfica 3 (Cervi 47, Pizzi 58 pen, Azmoun 79 og) **Zenit St Petersburg** 0. Att: 40,232
Lyon 2 (Aour 50, Depay 82) **Leipzig** 2 (Forsberg 9 pen, Werner 33 pen). Att: 53,228

	P	W	D	L	F	A	Pts
Leipzig Q	6	3	2	1	10	8	11
Lyon Q	6	2	2	2	9	8	8
Benfica	6	2	1	3	10	11	7
Zenit St Petersburg	6	2	1	3	7	9	7

GROUP H

September 17, 2019
Ajax 3 (Promes 18, Alvarez 50, Tagliafico 62) **Lille** 0. Att: 51,441
Chelsea 0 **Valencia** 1 (Rodrigo 74). Att: 39,469
Chelsea (3-4-2-1): Arrizabalaga, Zouma (Giroud 73), Christensen, Tomori, Azpilicueta, Kovacic (Barkley 80), Jorginho, Marcos Alonso, Mount (Pedro 16), Willian, Abraham. **Booked**: Jorginho, Giroud

October 2, 2019
Lille 1 (Osimhen 33) **Chelsea** 2 (Abraham 22, Willian 78). Att: 48,523
Chelsea (3-4-3): Arrizabalaga, Azpilicueta, Zouma, Tomori, James (Hudson-Odoi 67), Kante, Jorginho, Marcos Alonso, Willian (Pedro 85), Abraham, Mount (Kovacic 87). **Booked**: James
Valencia 0 **Ajax** 3 (Ziyech 8, Promes 34, Van de Beek 67). Att: 44,659

October 23, 2019
Ajax 0 **Chelsea** 1 (Batshuayi 86). Att: 52,482
Chelsea (4-3-3): Arrizabalaga, Azpilicueta, Zouma, Tomori, Marcos Alonso, Kovacic, Jorginho, Mount, Willian (Pulisic 66), Abraham (Batshuayi 71), Hudson-Odoi (James 90). **Booked**: Zouma
Lille 1 (Ikone 90+5) **Valencia** 1 (Cheryshev 63). Att: 47,488

November 5, 2019
Chelsea 4 (Jorginho 4 pen, 71 pen, Azpilicueta 63, James 74) **Ajax** 4 (Abraham 2 og, Promes 20, Arrizabalaga 35 og, Van de Beek 55). Att: 39,132
Chelsea (4-2-3-1): Arrizabalaga, Azpilicueta, Zouma, Tomori, Marcos Alonso (James 46), Kovacic (Batshuayi 87), Jorginho, Willian, Mount (Hudson-Odoi 60), Pulisic, Abraham. **Booked**: Tomori, Azpilicueta
Valencia 4 (Parejo 66 pen, Soumaoro 82 og, Kondogbia 84, Torres 90) **Lille** 1 (Osimhen 25). Att: 38,252

November 27, 2019
Lille 0 **Ajax** 2 (Ziyech 2, Promes 59). Att: 48,612
Valencia 2 (Carlos Soler 40, Wass 82) **Chelsea** 2 (Kovacic 41, Pulisic 50). Att: 43,486
Chelsea (4-3-3): Arrizabalaga, James, Christensen, Zouma, Azpilicueta, Jorginho (Emerson 72), Kante, Kovacic, Pulisic, Abraham (Batshuayi 46), Willian (Mount 80). **Booked**: Jorginho, Azpilicueta, Kante, Arrizabalaga

December 10, 2019
Ajax 0 **Valencia** 1 (Rodrigo 24). Att: 53,590
Chelsea 2 (Abraham 19, Azpilicueta 35) **Lille** 1 (Remy 78). Att: 40,016
Chelsea (4-3-2-1): Arrizabalaga, Azpilicueta, Zouma, Rudiger, Emerson, Kante, Kovacic (Mount 81), Jorginho, Willian, Pulisic (Hudson-Odoi 61), Abraham (Batshuayi 71). **Booked**: Zouma

	P	W	D	L	F	A	Pts
Valencia Q	6	3	2	1	9	7	11
Chelsea Q	6	3	2	1	11	9	11
Ajax	6	3	1	2	12	6	10
Lille	6	0	1	5	4	14	1

ROUND OF 16, FIRST LEG

February 18, 2020
Atletico Madrid 1 (Saul 4) **Liverpool** 0. Att: 67,443
Liverpool (4-3-3): Alisson, Alexander-Arnold, Gomez, Van Dijk, Robertson, Henderson (Milner 80), Fabinho, Wijnaldum, Salah (Oxlade-Chamberlain 72), Firmino, Mane (Origi 46). **Booked**: Mane, Gomez
Borussia Dortmund 2 (Haaland 69, 77) **Paris SG** 1 (Neymar 75). Att: 66,099

February 19, 2020
Atalanta 4 (Hateboer 16, 62, Ilicic 42, Freuler 57) **Valencia** 1 (Cheryshev 66). Att: 44,236
Tottenham 0 **Leipzig** 1 (Werner 58 pen). Att: 60,095
Tottenham (4-2-3-1): Lloris, Aurier, Sanchez, Alderweireld, Davies, Winks, Lo Celso, Gedson Fernandes (Lamela 64), Alli (Ndombele 64), Bergwijn, Lucas Moura. **Booked**: Lo Celso, Davies, Lamela

February 25, 2020
Chelsea 0 **Bayern Munich** 3 (Gnabry 51, 54, Lewandowski 76). Att: 36,761
Chelsea (5-4-1): Caballero, James, Azpilicueta, Christensen, Rudiger, Marcos Alonso, Mount, Kovacic, Jorginho, Barkley, Giroud. **Booked**: Jorginho. **Sent off**: Marcos Alonso (83)
Napoli 1 (Mertens 30) **Barcelona** 1 (Griezmann 57. Att: 44,388

February 26, 2020
Lyon 1 (Tousart 31) **Juventus** 0. Att: 57,335
Real Madrid 1 (Isco 60) **Manchester City** 2 (Gabriel Jesus 78, De Bruyne 83 pen). Att: 75,615
Manchester City (4-3-3): Ederson, Walker, Otamendi, Laporte (Fernandinho 33), Mendy, Mahrez, Rodri, Gundogan, Gabriel Jesus, Bernardo Silva (Sterling 73), De Bruyne. **Booked**: Mendy

SECOND LEG

March 10, 2020
Leipzig 3 (Sabitzer 10, 21, Forsberg 87) **Tottenham** 0. Att: 42,146 (Leipzig win 4-0 on agg)
Tottenham (3-4-3): Lloris, Tanganga, Dier, Alderweireld, Aurier (Fagan-Walcott 90), Lo Celso (Gedson Fernandes 80), Winks, Sessegnon, Lamela, Alli, Lucas Moura. **Booked**: Sessegnon, Winks, Alli, Tanganga
Valencia 3 (Gameiro 21, 51, Torres 67) **Atalanta** 4 (Illicic 3 pen, 43 pen, 71, 82). Played behind closed doors (Atalanta won 8-4 on agg)

March 11, 2020
Liverpool 2 (Wijnaldum 43, Firmino 90+4) **Atletico Madrid** 3 (Llorente 97, 105, Morata 120). Att: 52,267 (aet, Atletico Madrid won 4-2 on agg)
Liverpool (4-3-3): Adrian, Alexander-Arnold, Gomez, Van Dijk, Robertson, Henderson (Fabinho 106), Wijnaldum (Origi 106), Oxlade-Chamberlain (Milner 82), Salah, Firmino (Minamino 113), Mane. **Booked**: Alexander-Arnold
Paris SG 2 (Neymar 28, Bernat 45) **Borussia Dortmund** 0. Played behind closed doors (Paris SG won 3-2 on agg)

August 7, 2020
Juventus 2 (Ronaldo 43 pen, 60) **Lyon** 1 (Depay 12 pen) – agg 2-2 Lyon won on away goal. Played behind closed doors

Manchester City 2 (Sterling 9, Gabriel Jesus 68) **Real Madrid** 1 (Benzema 28) - Manchester City won 4-2 on agg. Played behind closed doors
Manchester City (4-3-3): Ederson, Walker, Fernandinho, Laporte, Joao Cancelo, De Bruyne, Rodri (Otamendi 89), Gundogan, Foden (Bernardo Silva 67), Gabriel Jesus, Sterling (David Silva 80). Played behind closed doors

August 8, 2020
Barcelona 3 (Lenglet 10, Messi 23, Suarez 45 pen) **Napoli** 1 (Insigne 45 pen) – Barcelona won 4-2 on agg/ Played behind closed doors
Bayern Munich 4 (Lewandowski 10 pen, 83, Perisic 24, Tolisso 76) **Chelsea** 1 (Abragham 44) – Bayern Munich won 7-1 on agg. Played behind closed doors
Chelsea (4-3-3): Caballero, James, Christensen, Zouma, Emerson, Kante, Kovacic, Barkley, Hudson-Odoi, Abraham (Giroud 81), Mount. **Booked**: Caballero, Emerson

QUARTER-FINALS – ONE MATCH (all in Lisbon – behind closed doors))

August 12, 2020
Atalanta 1 (Pasalic 26) **Paris SG** 2 (Marquinhos 90, Choupo-Moting 90+3)

August 13, 2020
Leipzig 2 (Olmo 50, Adams 88) **Atletico Madrid** 1 (Joao Felix 71 pen)

August 14, 2020
Barcelona 2 (Alaba 7 og, Suarez 57) **Bayern Munich** 8 (Muller 4, 31, Perisic 21, Gnabry 27, Kimmich 63, Lewandowski 82, Coutinho 85, 89)

Aug 15, 2020
Manchester City 1 (De Bruyne 69) **Lyon** 3 (Cornet 24, Dembele 79, 87)
Manchester City (4-3-3): Ederson, Fernandinho (Mahrez 56), Garcia, Laporte, Walker, Rodri (David Silva 84), Gundogan, Cancelo, De Bruyne, Gabriel Jesus, Sterling. **Booked**: Fernandinho, Rodri

SEMI-FINALS – ONE MATCH (both in Lisbon behind closed doors)

August 18, 2020
Leipzig 0 **Paris SG** 3 (Marquinos 13, Di Maria 42, Bernat 56)

August 19, 2020
Lyon 0 **Bayern Munich** 3 (Gnabry 18, 33, Lewandowski 88)

FINAL

PARIS SAINT-GERMAIN 0 BAYERN MUNICH 1 (Coman 59) – behind closed doors
Estadio da Luz, Lisbon, Sunday, August 23, 2020
Paris Saint-Germain (4-3-3): Navas, Kehrer, Thiago Silva (capt), Kimpembe, Bernat (Kurzawa 80), Herrera (Draxler 72), Marquinhos, Paredes (Verratti 65), Di Maria (Choupo-Moting 80), Neymar, Mbappe. **Subs not used**: Bulka, Bakker, Dagba, Diallo, Gueye, Icardi, Rico, Sarabia. **Booked**: Paredes, Neymar, Thiago Silva, Kurzawa. **Coach**: Thomas Tuchel
Bayern Munich (4-2-3-1): Neuer (capt), Kimmich, Boateng (Sule 25), Alaba, Davies; Thiago Alcontara (Tolisso 86), Goretza, Gnabry (Coutinho 68), Muller, Coman (Perisic 68), Lewandowski. **Subs not used**: Ulrich, Cuisance, Hernandez, Hoffmann, Javi Martinez, Odriozola, Pavard, Zirksee. **Booked**: Davies, Gnabry, Sule, Muller. **Coach**: Hans-Dieter Flick
Referee: D Orsato (Italy). **Half-time**: 0-0

Leading scorers: 15 Lewandowski (Bayern Munich); 10 Haaland (Salzburg, Borussia Dortmund); 9 Gnabry (Bayern Munich); 6 Depay (Lyon), Gabriel Jesus (Manchester City), Kane (Tottenham), Mertens (Napoli), Sterling (Manchester City)

EUROPEAN CUP/CHAMPIONS LEAGUE FINALS

1956	Real Madrid 4 Reims 3 (Paris)
1957	Real Madrid 2 Fiorentina 0 (Madrid)
1958†	Real Madrid 3 AC Milan 2 (Brussels)
1959	Real Madrid 2 Reims 0 (Stuttgart)
1960	Real Madrid 7 Eintracht Frankfurt 3 (Glasgow)
1961	Benfica 3 Barcelona 2 (Berne)
1962	Benfica 5 Real Madrid 3 (Amsterdam)
1963	AC Milan 2 Benfica 1 (Wembley)
1964	Inter Milan 3 Real Madrid 1 (Vienna)
1965	Inter Milan 1 Benfica 0 (Milan)
1966	Real Madrid 2 Partizan Belgrade 1 (Brussels)
1967	Celtic 2 Inter Milan 1 (Lisbon)
1968†	Manchester Utd 4 Benfica 1 (Wembley)
1969	AC Milan 4 Ajax 1 (Madrid)
1970†	Feyenoord 2 Celtic 1 (Milan)
1971	Ajax 2 Panathinaikos 0 (Wembley)
1972	Ajax 2 Inter Milan 0 (Rotterdam)
1973	Ajax 1 Juventus 0 (Belgrade)
1974	Bayern Munich 4 Atletico Madrid 0 (replay Brussels after a 1-1 draw Brussels)
1975	Bayern Munich 2 Leeds Utd 0 (Paris)
1976	Bayern Munich 1 St. Etienne 0 (Glasgow)
1977	Liverpool 3 Borussia Moenchengladbach 1 (Rome)
1978	Liverpool 1 Brugge 0 (Wembley)
1979	Nottm Forest 1 Malmo 0 (Munich)
1980	Nottm Forest 1 Hamburg 0 (Madrid)
1981	Liverpool 1 Real Madrid 0 (Paris)
1982	Aston Villa 1 Bayern Munich 0 (Rotterdam)
1983	SV Hamburg 1 Juventus 0 (Athens)
1984†	Liverpool 1 AS Roma 1 (Liverpool won 4-2 on penalties) (Rome)
1985	Juventus 1 Liverpool 0 (Brussels)
1986†	Steaua Bucharest 0 Barcelona 0 (Steaua won 2-0 on penalties) (Seville)
1987	Porto 2 Bayern Munich 1 (Vienna)
1988†	PSV Eindhoven 0 Benfica 0 (PSV won 6-5 on penalties) (Stuttgart)
1989	AC Milan 4 Steaua Bucharest 0 (Barcelona)
1990	AC Milan 1 Benfica 0 (Vienna)
1991†	Red Star Belgrade 0 Marseille 0 (Red Star won 5-3 on penalties) (Bari)
1992	Barcelona 1 Sampdoria 0 (Wembley)
1993	Marseille 1 AC Milan 0 (Munich)
1994	AC Milan 4 Barcelona 0 (Athens)
1995	Ajax 1 AC Milan 0 (Vienna)
1996†	Juventus 1 Ajax 1 (Juventus won 4-2 on penalties) (Rome)
1997	Borussia Dortmund 3 Juventus 1 (Munich)
1998	Real Madrid 1 Juventus 0 (Amsterdam)
1999	Manchester Utd 2 Bayern Munich 1 (Barcelona)
2000	Real Madrid 3 Valencia 0 (Paris)
2001	Bayern Munich 1 Valencia 1 (Bayern Munich won 5-4 on penalties) (Milan)
2002	Real Madrid 2 Bayer Leverkusen 1 (Glasgow)
2003†	AC Milan 0 Juventus 0 (AC Milan won 3-2 on penalties) (Manchester)
2004	FC Porto 3 Monaco 0 (Gelsenkirchen)
2005†	Liverpool 3 AC Milan 3 (Liverpool won 3-2 on penalties) (Istanbul)
2006	Barcelona 2 Arsenal 1 (Paris)
2007	AC Milan 2 Liverpool 1 (Athens)

2008†	Manchester Utd 1 Chelsea 1 (Manchester Utd won 6-5 on penalties) (Moscow)
2009	Barcelona 2 Manchester Utd 0 (Rome)
2010	Inter Milan 2 Bayern Munich 0 (Madrid)
2011	Barcelona 3 Manchester Utd 1 (Wembley)
2012†	Chelsea 1 Bayern Munich 1 (Chelsea won 4-3 on pens) (Munich)
2013	Bayern Munich 2 Borussia Dortmund 1 (Wembley)
2014†	Real Madrid 4 Atletico Madrid 1 (Lisbon)
2015	Barcelona 3 Juventus 1 (Berlin)
2016	Real Madrid 1 Atletico Madrid 1 (Real Madrid won 5-3 on pens) (Milan)
2017	Real Madrid 4 Juventus 1 (Cardiff)
2018	Real Madrid 3 Liverpool 1 (Kiev)† aet
2019	Liverpool 2 Tottenham 0 (Madrid)
2020	Bayern Munich 1 Paris Saint-Germain 0 (Lisbon)

● Champions League since 1993. † after extra time

UEFA EUROPA LEAGUE 2019–20

PRELIMINARY ROUND (selected results)

FIRST LEG
Ballymena 2 (Millar 49, Winchester 56) NSI 0, 2,270. **Barry** 0 **Cliftonville** 0. Att: 2,106. Progres Niederkorn 1 (De Almeida 62) **Cardiff Met** 0. Att: 1,984.

SECOND LEG
Cardiff Met 2 (Lam 2, Rees 67 pen) Progres Niederkorn 1 (De Almeida 73). Att: 1,316 (agg 2-2, Progres Niederkorn won on away goal). **Cliftonville** 4 (McMenamin 25, Gormley 43, McDermott 82, Donnelly 84) **Barry** 0. Att: 1,946 (Cliftonville won 4-0 on agg). NSI 0 **Ballymena** 0. Att: 553 (Ballymena won 2-0 on agg)

FIRST QUALIFYING ROUND (selected results)

FIRST LEG
Aberdeen 2 (McGinn 36, Cosgrove 48) RoPS 1 (Jantii 90+3). Att: 14,377. Brann Bergen 2 (Teniste 12, Berisha 36 pen) **Shamrock Rov** 2 (Ordagic 34 og, Lopes 90+4). Att: 4,560. **Cliftonville** 0 Haugesund 1 (Grindheim 42). Att: 1,342. **Connah's Quay** 1 (Taylor 75 og) **Kilmarnock** 2 (Brophy 82 pen, Findlay 90+2). Att: 1,410. **Cork** 0 Progres Niederkorn 2 (Muratovic 11, De Almeida 21 pen). Att: 3,137
Crusaders 2 (Hegarty 33, Lowry 79) B36 Torshavn 0. Att: 1,112; Malmo 7 (Rosenberg 31, 33, 48, Rakip 44, 74, Brorsson 46, Molins 54) **Ballymena** 0. Att: 8,667. St Joseph's 0 **Rangers** 4 (Jack 50, Ojo 56, Goldson 68, Morelos 77). Att: 2,050. **St Patrick's** 0 Norrkoping 2 (Thern 55, Desmond 85 og). Att: 2,389

SECOND LEG
Ballymena 0 Malmo 4 (Safari 27, Molins 52, Rakip 68, Gall 79 pen). Att: 1,736 (Malmo won 11-0 on agg). B36 Torshavn 2 (Samuelsen 37, Cieslewicz 51) **Crusdaers** 3 (Forsythe 3, Heatley 28, 68). Att: 1,422 (Crusaders won 5-2 on agg). Haugesund 5 (Velde 5, 68, Sandberg 36, Kone 45, Leite 52) **Cliftonville** 1 (McMenamin 17). Att: 2,633 (Haugesund won 6-1 on agg) **Kilmarnock** 0 **Connah's Quay** 2 (Wignall 50, Morris 79 pen). Att: 8,306 (Connah's Quay won 3-2 on agg). Norrkoping 2 (Larsson 37, Holmberg 86) **St Patrick's** 1 (Clifford 72). Att: 5,925 (Norrkoping won 4-1 on agg). Progres Niederkorn 1 (Bah 68) **Cork** 2 (Buckley 3, McCarthy 47). Att: 1,927 (Progres Niederkorn won 3-2 on agg)
Rangers 6 (Aribo 3, Morelos 45, 57 pen, 66, Defoe 77, 86) St Joseph's 0. Att: 45,718 (Rangers won 10-0 on agg). RoPS 1 (Kada 2) **Aberdeen** 2 (Cosgrove 26 pen, Ferguson 90+4). Att: 2,050 (Aberdeen won 4-2 on agg). **Shamrock Rov** 2 (Byrne 76, O'Neil 87) Brann Bergen 1 (Bamba 57). Att: 5,135 (Shamrock Rov won 4-3 on agg)

SECOND QUALIFYING ROUND (selected results)

FIRST LEG

HB Torshavn 2 (Justinussen 37 pen, Petersen 89) **Linfield** 2 (Waterworth 2, 88 pen). Att: 751. Chikhura 1 (Koripadze 41 pen) **Aberdeen** 1 (Cosgrove 68 pen). Att: 3,218. **Connah's Quay** 0 Partizan Belgrade 1 (Scekic 62). Att: 829. **Rangers** 2 (Aribo 20, Ojo 53) Progres Niederkorn 0. Att: 43,629. **Shamrock Rov** 2 (Grace 14, Lopes 58) Apollon Limassol 1 (Papoulis 5). Att: 5,396. **Wolves** 2 (Diogo Jota 37, Ruben Vinagre 90+3) **Crusaders** 0. Att: 29,708

SECOND LEG

Aberdeen 5 (Cosgrove 9, 20, 80, Leigh 58, Wright 65) Chikhura 0. Att: 15,167 (Aberdeen won 6-1 on agg); Apollon Limassol 3 (Zelaya 18, Szalai 64, Sardinero 102) **Shamrock Rov** 1 (Greene 69). Att: 2,987 (aet, Apollon Limassol won 4-3 on agg); **Crusaders** 1 (Bennett 13 og) **Wolves** 4 (Raul Jimenez 15, 45, Bennett 38, Forsyth 77 og). Att: 2,700 (Wolves won 6-1 on agg). **Linfield** 1 (Waterworth 20 pen) HB Torshavn 0. Partial stadium closure – previous crowd trouble (Linfield won 3-2 on agg). Partizan Belgrade 3 (Tosic 54, Ozegovic 69, Stevanovic 72) **Connah's Quay** 0. Att: 8,200 (Partizan Belgrade won 4-0). Progres Niederkorn 0 **Rangers** 0. Att: 3,867 (Rangers won 2-0 on agg)

THIRD QUALIFYING ROUND (selected results)

FIRST LEG

Ludogorets 5 (Harrington 10 og, Tchibota 28, Lukoki 43, Keseru 65, Moti 76) **New Saints** 0. Att: 4,120. Midtjylland 2 (Onyeka 58, Kaba 63) **Rangers** 4 (Morelos 43, Aribo 52, Katic 56, Arfield 70). Att: 9,322. Pyunik 0 **Wolves** 4 (Doherty 29, Raul Jimenez 42, 46, Ruben Neves 90+1 pen). Att: 13,050. Rijeka 2 (Colak 62, Muric 88) **Aberdeen** 0. Att: 6,452. Slovan Bratislava 1 (Holman 86) **Dundalk** 0. Att: 9,980. Sutjeska 1 (Kojasevic 11) **Linfield** 2 (Millar 38, 65). Att: 3,850

SECOND LEG

Aberdeen 0 Rijeka 2 (Loncar 10, Colak 32). Att: 15,246. (Rijeka won 4-0 won agg); **Dundalk** 1 (Duffy 71) Slovan Bratislava 3 (Da Silva 12, Cavric 33, Daniel 90+3). Att: 4,199 (Slovan Bratislava won 4-1 on agg). **Linfield** 3 (Stafford 7, Lavery 18, Clarke 76) Sutjeska 2 (Bozovic 15, 61). Att: 3,639 (Linfield won 5-3 on agg). **New Saints** 0 Ludogorets 4 (Swierczok 36, 77, Lukoki 42, Biton 90+2). Att: 712 (Ludogorets won 9-0 on agg). **Rangers** 3 (Morelos 14, 49, Ojo 39) Midtjylland 1 (Evander 72). Att: 47,184 (Rangers won 7-3 on agg). **Wolves** 4 (Pedro Neto 54, Gibbs-White 58, Ruben Vinagre 64, Diogo Jota 87) Pyunik 0. Att: 29,391 (Wolves won 8-0 on agg)

PLAY-OFFS

FIRST LEG

Celtic 2 (Forrest 48, Edouard 73) AIK 0. Att: 40,885. Legia Warsaw 0 **Rangers** 0. Att: 26,665. **Linfield** 3 (Stafford 40, Lavery 45, 75) Qarabag 2 (Rherras 15, Gueye 90+2 pen). Att: 4,633. Torino 2 (De Silvestri 62, Belotti 89 pen) **Wolves** 3 (Izzo 43 og, Diogo Jota 60, Raul Jimenez 72). Att: 24,091

SECOND LEG

AIK 1 (Larsson 33 pen) **Celtic** 4 (Forrest 17, Johnston 34, Jullien 87, Morgan 90+3). Att: 28,410 (Celtic won 6-1 on agg). Qarabag 2 (Romero 6, Zoubir 88) **Linfield** 1 (Lavery 90+3).Att: 18,349 (agg 4-4, Qarabag won on away goals). **Rangers** 1 (Morelos 90+1) Legia Warsaw 0. Att: 45,463 (Rangers won 1-0 on agg). **Wolves** 2 (Raul Jimenez 31, Dendoncker 59) Torino 1 (Belotti 58). Att: 29,222 (Wolves won 5-3 on agg)

ON AGGREGATE

Astana 3 BATE Borisov 2; AZ Alkmaar 5 Antwerp 2 - aet; Braga 3 Spartak Moscow 1; Copenhagen

3 Riga 2; Dudelange 3 Ararat Armenia 3 (aet, Dudelange won 5-4 on pens); Eintracht Frankfurt 3 Strasbourg 1; Espanyol 5 Zorya 3; Ferencvaros 4 Suduva 2; Feyenoord 3 Hapoel Bee Sheva 0; Gent 3 Rijeka 2; Guimaraes 1 FCSB 0; Ludogorets 2 Maribor 2 (Ludogorets won on away goals); Malmo 4 Bnei Yehuda 0; Partizan Belgrade 3 Molde 2; PSV Eindhoven 7 Apollon Limassol 0; Slovan Bratislava 3 PAOK Salonika 3 (Slovan Bratislava won on away goals); Trabzonspor 3 AEK Athens 3 (Trabzonspor won on away goals)

GROUP A

Match-day 1: Apoel Nicosia 3 (Pavlovic 54, 58, De Vincenti 56 pen) Dudelange 4 (Sinani 36, 82, Bernier 51, Stolz 71). Att: 9,313. Qarabag 0 Sevilla 3 (Hernandez 62, Munir 78, Torres 85). Att: 30,826

Match-day 2: Dudelange 1 (Bernier 90) Qarabag 4 (Zoubir 11, Michel 30, Richard 37 pen, Quintana Sosa 69). Att: 3,005. Sevilla 1 (Hernandez 17) Apoel Nicosia 0. Att: 30,008

Match-day 3: Qarabag 2 (Quintana Sosa 13, Ferreira Silva 58) Apoel Nicosia 2 (Medvedev 29 og, Hallenius 45). Att: 30,824. Sevilla 3 (Vazquez 48, 75, El Haddadi 78) Dudelange 0. Att: 40,972

Match-day 4: Apoel Nicosia 2 (Lucas Souza 59, Ioannou 88) Qarabag 1 (Medvedev 10). Att: 9,432. Dudelange 2 (Sinani 69, 80) Sevilla 5 (Dabbour 17, 36, Munir 27, 33, 66). Att: 2,848

Match-day 5: Dudelange 0 Apoel Nicosia 2 (Matic 12 pen, Merkis 43). Att: 2,912. Sevilla 2 (Gil 61, Dabbour 90+2) Qarabag 0. Att: 19,803

Match-day 6: Apoel Nicosia 1 (Savic 61) Sevilla 0. Att: 5,608. Qarabag 1 (Gueye 90+1) Dudelange 1 (Bougrine 63). Att: 5,823

	P	W	D	L	F	A	Pts
Sevilla Q	6	5	0	1	14	3	15
Apoel Nicosia Q	6	3	1	2	10	8	10
Qarabag	6	1	2	3	8	11	5
Dudelange	6	1	1	4	8	18	4

GROUP B

Match-day 1: Copenhagen 1 (Santos 50) Lugano 0. Att: 18,240. Dynamo Kiev 1 (Buyalsky 84) Malmo 0. Att: 17,159

Match-day 2: Lugano 0 Dynamo Kiev 0. Att: 1,281. Malmo 1 (Rosenberg 55) Copenhagen 1 (Nielsen 45 og). Att: 19,884

Match-day 3: Dynamo Kiev 1 (Shabanov 53) Copenhagen 1 (Sotiriou 2). Att: 21,202. Malmo 2 (Berget 13 pen, Molins 32) Lugano 1 (Gerndt 50). Att: 16,789

Match-day 4: Copenhagen 1 (Stage 4) Dynamo Kiev 1 (Verbic 70). Att: 23,166. Lugano 0 Malmo 0. Att: 1,875

Match-day 5: Lugano 0 Copenhagen 1 (Thomsen 26). Att: 18,240. Malmo 4 (Bengt 2, Rosenberg 48, 90+6, Rakip 57) Dynamo Kiev 2 (Mykolenko 18, Tsygankov 39, Verbic 77). Att: 19,224

Match-day 6: Copenhagen 0 Malmo 1 (Papagiannopoulos 77 og). Att: 32,941. Dynamo Kiev 2 (Tsygankov 90+4) Lugano 1 (Aratore 45). Att: 15,774

	P	W	D	L	F	A	Pts
Malmo Q	6	3	2	1	8	6	11
Copenhagen Q	6	2	3	1	5	4	9
Dynamo Kiev	6	1	4	1	7	7	7
Lugano	6	0	3	3	2	5	3

GROUP C

Match-day 1: Basle 5 (Bua 9, 40, Zuffi 52, Vilhena 54 og, Okafor 79) Krasnodar 0. Att: 14,127. Getafe 1 (Angel 18) Trabzonspor 0. Att: 5,786

Match-day 2: Krasnodar 1 (Ari 69) Getafe 2 (Angel 35, 61). Att: 20,035. Trabzonspor 2 (Parmak 26, Sosa 78) Basle 2 (Widmer 20, Okafor 80). Att: 23,867
Match-day 3: Getafe 0 Basle 1 (Frei 18). Att: 6,213. Trabzonspor 0 Krasnodar 2 (Berg 49, Vilhena 90+2). Att: 26,405
Match-day 4: Basle 2 (Cabral 8, Frei 60) Getafe 1 (Mata 45 pen). Att: 26,298. Krasnodar 3 (Asan 27 og, Manuel Fernandes 35, Ignatjev 90+3) Trabzonspor 1 (Nwakaeme 90+1). Att: 21,669
Match-day 5: Krasnodar 1 (Da Silva Ferreira 72 pen) Basle 0. Att: 22,826. Trabzonspor 0 Getafe 1 (Mata 50). Att: 11,465
Match-day 6: Basle 2 (Widmer 21, Stocker 72) Trabzonspor 0. Att: 17,921. Getafe 3 (Cabrera 76, Molina 78, Kenedy 86) Krasnodar 0. Att: 9,389

	P	W	D	L	F	A	Pts
Basle Q	6	4	1	1	12	4	13
Getafe Q	6	4	0	2	8	4	12
Krasnodar	6	3	0	3	7	11	9
Trabzonspor	6	0	1	5	3	11	1

GROUP D

Match-day 1: LASK 1 (Holland 45) Rosenborg 0. Att: 12,179. PSV Eindhoven 3 (Malen 19, Coates 25 og, Baumgartl 48) Sporting Lisbon 2 (Bruno Fernandes 38 pen, Pedro Mendes 82). Att: 30,000
Match-day 2: Rosenborg 1 (Adegbenro 70) PSV Eindhoven 4 (Rosario 14, Meling 37 og, Malen 41, 78). Att: 10,296. Sporting Lisbon 2 (Luciano Silva 58, Bruno Fernandes 63) LASK 1 (Raguz 16). Att: 31,225
Match-day 3: PSV Eindhoven 0 LASK 0. Att: 29,000. Sporting Lisbon 1 (Bolasie 70) Rosenborg 0. Att: 27,671
Match-day 4: LASK 4 (Ranftl 56, Frieser 60, Klaus 77, 82) PSV Eindhoven 1 (Schwaab 5 pen). Att: 12,658. Rosenborg 0 Sporting Lisbon 2 (Coates 16, Bruno Fernandes 38). Att: 11,018
Match-day 5: Rosenborg 1 (Johnson 45) LASK 2 (Goiginger 20, Frieser 54). Att: 9,775. Sporting Lisbon 4 (Luciano Silva 9, Bruno Fernandes 15, 64 pen, Mathieu 42) PSV Eindhoven 0. Att: 30,146
Match-day 6: LASK 3 (Trauner 23, De Mello 38 pen, Raguz 90+3) Sporting Lisbon 0. Att: 11,627. PSV Eindhoven 1 (Ihattaren 63) Rosenborg 1 (Helland 22). Att: 24,000

	P	W	D	L	F	A	Pts
LASK Q	6	4	1	1	11	4	13
Sporting Lisbon Q	6	4	0	2	11	7	12
PSV Eindhoven	6	2	2	2	9	12	8
Rosenborg	6	0	1	5	3	11	1

GROUP E

Match-day 1: CFR Cluj 2 (Deac 41 pen, Omrani 75) Lazio 1 (Bastos 25). Att: 9,222. Rennes 1 (Niang 38 pen) Celtic 1 (Christie 59 pen). Att: 27,026
Match-day 2: Celtic 2 (Edouard 20, Elyounoussi 59) CFR Cluj 0. Att: 56,172. Lazio 2 (Milinkovic-Savic 63, Immobile 75) Rennes 1 (Morel 55). Att: 13,072
Match-day 3: Celtic 2 (Christie 67, Jullien 89) Lazio 1 (Lazzari 40). Att: 56,172. Rennes 0 CFR Cluj 1 (Deac 9). Att: 27,330
Match-day 4: CFR Cluj 1 (Rondon 87) Rennes 0. Att: 11,067. Lazio 1 (Immobile 7) Celtic 2 (Forrest 38, Ntcham 90+5). Att: 26,155
Match-day 5: Celtic 3 (Morgan 21, Christie 45, Johnston 74) Rennes 1 (Hunou 89). Att:

56,172. Lazio 1 (Correa 24) CFR Cluj 0. Att: 7,604

Match-day 6: CFR Cluj 2 (Burca 48, Djokovic 70) **Celtic** 0. Att: 12,890. Rennes 2 (Gnagnon 30, 87) Lazio 0. Att: 25,082

	P	W	D	L	F	A	Pts
Celtic Q	6	4	1	1	10	6	13
CFR Cluj Q	6	4	0	2	6	4	12
Lazio	6	2	0	4	6	9	6
Rennes	6	1	1	4	5	8	4

GROUP F

Match-day 1: Eintracht Frankfurt 0 **Arsenal** 3 (Willock 38, Saka 85, Aubameyang 87). Att: 47,000. Standard Liege 2 (Hanin 66 og, M'Poku 90+1) Guimaraes 0. Att: 13,477

Match-day 2: **Arsenal** 4 (Martinelli 13, 16, Willock 22, Ceballos 57) Standard Liege 0. Att: 58,725. Guimaraes 0 Eintracht Frankfurt 1 (Ndicka 36). Att: 15,187

Match-day 3: Arsenal 3 (Martinelli 32, Pepe 80, 90+2) Guimaraes 2 (Edwards 8, Duarte 36). Att: 60,195. Eintracht Frankfurt 2 (Abraham 28, Hinteregger 73) Standard Liege 1 (Amallah 82). Att: 47,000

Match-day 4: Guimaraes 1 (Brunto Duarte 90+1) **Arsenal** 1 (Mustafi 80). Att: 17,822. Standard Liege 2 (Vanheusden 56, Lestienne 90+4) Eintracht Frankfurt 1 (Kostic 65). Att: 15,852

Match-day 5: **Arsenal** 1 (Aubameyang 45) Eintracht Frankfurt 2 (Kamada 55, 64). Att: 49,419. Guimaraes 1 (Andre Pereira 45) Standrd Liege 1 (Lestienne 40 pen). Att: 11,221

Match-day 6: Eintracht Frankfurt 2 (Macedo Silva 31 og, Kamada 38) Guimaraes 3 (Costa Rocha 8, El Masrati 85, Edwards 87). Att: 47,000. Standard Liege 2 (Bastien 47, Amallah 69) **Arsenal** 2 (Lacazette 78, Saka 81). Att: 21,797

	P	W	D	L	F	A	Pts
Arsenal Q	6	3	2	1	14	7	11
Eintracht Frankfurt Q	6	3	0	3	8	10	9
Standard Liege	6	2	2	2	8	10	8
Guimaraes	6	1	2	3	7	10	5

GROUP G

Match-day 1: Porto 2 (Tiquinho Soares 8, 29) Young Boys 1 (Nsame 15 pen). Att: 32,929. Rangers 1 (Ojo 23) Feyenoord 0. Att: 46,858

Match-day 2: Feyenoord 2 (Toornstra 49, Karsdorp 80) Porto 0. Att: 41,000. Young Boys 2 (Assale 50, Fassnacht 90+3) **Rangers** 1 (Morelos 44). Att: 26,348

Match-day 3: Porto 1 (Diaz 36) **Rangers** 1 (Morelos 44). Att: 31,307. Young Boys 2 (Assale 14 pen, Nsame 28 pen) Feyenoord 0. Att: 27,641

Match-day 4: Feyenoord 1 (Berghuis 18 pen) Young Boys 1 (Spielmann 71). Att: 45,022. Rangers 2 (Morelos 69, Davis 73) Porto 0. Att: 49,645

Match-day 5: Feyenoord 2 (Toornstra 33, Sinisterra 68) **Rangers** 2 (Morelos 52, 65). Att: 47,500. Young Boys 1 (Fassnacht 6) Porto 2 (Aboubakar 76, 79). Att: 31,120

Match-day 6: Porto 3 (Diaz 4, Malacia 15 og, Dos Santos 33) Feyenoord 2 (Botteghin 19, Larsson 22). Att: 28,507. **Rangers** 1 (Morelos 30) Young Boys 1 (Barisic 89 og). Att: 49,015

	P	W	D	L	F	A	Pts
Porto Q	6	3	1	2	8	9	10
Rangers Q	6	2	3	1	8	6	9
Young Boys	6	2	2	2	8	7	8
Feyenoord	6	1	2	3	7	9	5

GROUP H

Match-day 1: Espanyol 1 (Vargas 60) Ferencvaros 1 (Rios 10 og). Att: 18,125. Ludogorets 5 (Farias 47, Lukoki 50, Keseru 52, 68, 73 pen) CSKA Moscow 1 (Diveev 11). Att: 8,423
Match-day 2: CSKA Moscow 0 Espanyol 2 (Wu 64, Bonilla 90+5). Att: 22,288. Ferencvaros 0 Ludogorets 3 (Lukoki 1, Forster 40, 64). Att: 16,163
Match-day 3: CSKA Moscow 0 Ferencvaros 1 (Varga 86). Att: 18,518. Ludogorets 0 Espanyol 1 (Campuzano 13). Att: 10,334
Match-day 4: Espanyol 6 (Melendo 4, Lopez 19, Vargas 36 pen, Campuzano 52, Pedrosa 73, Ferreyra 76). Ludogorets 0.Att: 13,963. Ferencvaros 0 CSKA Moscow 0. Att: 18,153
Match-day 5: CSKA Moscow 1 (Chalov 75) Ludogorets 1 (Keseru 66). Att: 12,948. Ferencvaros 2 (Siger 23, Shvarkar 90+1 pen) Espanyol 2 (Melendo 31, Darder 90+6). Att: 19,111
Match-day 6: Espanyol 0 CSKA Moscow 1 (Vlasic 84), Att: 10,615. Ludogorets 1 (Lukoki 24) Ferencvaros 1 (Signevich 90+5). Att: 5,528

	P	W	D	L	F	A	Pta
Espanyol Q	6	3	2	1	12	4	11
Ludogorets Q	6	2	2	2	10	10-	8
Ferencvaros	6	1	4	1	5	7	7
CSKA Moscow	6	1	2	3	3	9	5

GROUP I

Match-day 1: Gent 3 (David 2, 43, Perrin 64 og) St Etienne 2 (Khazri 38, Kaminski 74 og). Att: 14,928. Wolfsburg 3 (Arnold 20, Mehmedi 24, Brekalo 67) Oleksandriya 1 (Banada 66). Att: 10,112
Match-day 2: Oleksandriya 1 (Sitalo 61) Gent 1 (Depoitre 6). Att: 7,588. St Etienne 1 (Kolodziejczak 13) Wolfsburg 1 (Furtado 15). Att: 24,815
Match-day 3: Gent 2 (Yaremchuk 41, 90+4) Wolfsburg 2 (Weghorst 3 Santos Sa 24). Att: 15,437. St Etienne 1 (Da Silva 8) Oleksandriya 1 (Da Silva 14 og). Att: 28,573
Match-day 4: Oleksandriya 2 (Bezborodko 84, Zaderaka 90+1) St Etienne 2 (Khazri 24 pen, Camara 72). Att: 6,361. Wolfsburg 1 (Joao Victor 20) Gent 3 (Yaremchuk 50, Depoitre 65, Ngadeu-Ngadjui 76). Att: 11,620
Match-day 5: Oleksandriya 0 Wolfsburg 1 (Weghorst 45 pen). Att: 7,118. St Etienne 0 Gent 0. Att: 25,315
Match-day 6: Gent 2 (Depoitre 7, 16) Oleksandriya 1 (Miroshnichenko 54). Att: 13,156. Wolfsburg 1 (Rosa Silva 52) St Etienne 0. Att: 10,802

	P	W	D	L	F	A	Pts
Gent Q	6	3	3	0	11	7	12
Wolfsburg Q	6	3	2	1	9	7	11
St Etienne	6	0	4	2	6	8	4
Oleksandriya	6	0	3	3	6	10	3

GROUP J

Match-day 1: Borussia Monchengladbach 0 Wolfsberger 4 (Weissman 13, Leitgeb 31, 68, Ritzmaier 41). Att: 34,846. Roma 4 (Caicara 42 og, Dzeko 58, Zaniolo 71, Kluivert 90+3) Basaksehir 0. Att: 21,438
Match-day 2: Basaksehir 1 (Visca 55) Borussia Monchengladbach 1 (Hermann 90+1). Att: 5,646. Wolfsberger 1 (Liendl 51) Roma 1 (Spinazzola 27). Att: 11,169
Match-day 3: Basaksehir 1 (Kahveci 78) Wolfsberger 0. Att: 4,101. Roma 1 (Zaniolo 32) Borussia Monchengladbach 1 (Stindl 90+5 pen). Att: 29,037
Match-day 4: Borussia Monchengladbach 2 (Fazio 35 og, Thuram 90+5) Roma 1 (Fazio 64). Att: 44,570. Wolfsberger 0 Basaksehir 3 (Visca 73 pen, Crivelli 84, 87). Att: 5,286

218

Match-day 5: Basaksehir 0 Roma 3 (Veretout 30 pen, Kluivert 40, Dzeko 45). Att: 12,879. Wolfsberger 0 Borussia Monchengladbach 1 (Stindl 60). Att: 12,073
Match-day 6: Borussia Monchengladbach 1 (Thuram 33) Basaksehir 2 (Kahveci 44, Crivelli 90). Att: 40,046. Roma 2 (Perotti 7 pen, Dzeko 19) Wolfsberger 2 (Florenzi 10 og, Weissman 63). Att: 21,672

	P	W	D	L	F	A	Pts
Basaksehir Q	6	3	1	2	7	9	10
Roma Q	6	2	3	1	12	6	9
Borussia M'gladbach	6	2	2	2	6	9	8
Wolfsberger	6	1	2	3	7	8	5

GROUP K

Match-day 1: Slovan Bratislava 4 (Sporar 14, 58, Ljubicic 90+3, Rharsalla 90+4) Besitkas 2 (Ljajlic 29 pen, Bozhikov 45 og). Att: 5,273. **Wolves** 0 Braga 1 (Ricardo Horta 71). Att: 28,314
Match-day 2: Besitkas 0 **Wolves** 1 (Boly 90+3). Att: 22,670. Braga 2 (Bruno Viana 31, Galeno 63) Slovan Bratislava 2 (Sporar 45, Bruno Viana 87 og). Att: 9,077
Match-day 3: Besitkas 1 (Nayir 71) Braga 2 (Ricardo Horta 38, Wilson Eduardo 80). Att: 20,956. Slovan Bratislava 1 (Sporar 11) **Wolves** 2 (Saiss 58, Raul Jimenez 64 pen). Att: 20,333
Match-day 4: Braga 3 (Paulinho 14, 37, Eduardo 81) Besitkas 1 (Boyd 29). Att: 8,833. **Wolves** 1 (Raul Jimenez 90+2) Slovan Bratislava 0. Att: 29,789
Match-day 5: Besitkas 2 (Roco 75, Ljajlic 90 pen) Slovan Bratislava 1 (Daniel 35). Att: 11,526. Braga 3 (Andre Horta 6, Paulinho 64, Fransergio 79) **Wolves** 3 (Raul Jimenez 13, Doherty 34, Traore 35). Att: 12,058
Match-day 6: Slovan Bratislava 2 (Sporar 42, Rharsalla 70) Braga 4 (Fonte 44, Machado 72, Bozhikov 75 og, Paulinho 90+3). Att: 10,856. **Wolves** 4 (Diogo Jota 57, 63, 68, Dendoncker 67) Besitkas 0. Att: 27,866

	P	W	D	L	F	A	Pts
Braga Q	6	4	2	0	15	9	14
Wolves Q	6	4	1	1	11	5	13
Slovan Bratislava	6	1	1	4	10	13	4
Besitkas	6	1	0	5	6	15	3

GROUP L

Match-day 1: **Manchester Utd** 1 (Greenwood 73) Astana 0. Att: 50,783. Partizan Belgrade 2 (Natcho 42 pen, 61) Alkmaar 2 (Stengs 12, Boadu 67). Att: 22,564
Match-day 2: Alkmaar 0 **Manchester Utd** 0. Att: 13,863. Astana 1 (Sigurjonsson 85) Partizan Belgrade 2 (Umar 28, 73). Att: 20,137
Match-day 3: Alkmaar 6 (Koopmeiners 39 pen, 83 pen, Boadu 43, Stengs 77, Sugawara 85, Idrissi 90) Astana 0. Att: 8,123. Partizan Belgrade 0 **Manchester Utd** 1 (Martial 43 pen). Att: 25,627
Match-day 4: Astana 0 Alkmaar 5 (Boadu 29, 77, Midtsjoe 52, Idrissi 57, Chatzidiakos 76). Att: 11,584. **Manchester Utd** 3 (Greenwood 22, Martial 33, Rashford 49) Partizan Belgrade 0. Att: 62,955
Match-day 5: Alkmaar 2 (Druijf 87, 90+2) Partizan Belgrade 2 (Asano 16, Soumah 27). Att: 9,091. Astana 2 (Shomko 55, Bernard 62 og) **Manchester Utd** 1 (Lingard 10). Att: 28,949
Match-day 6: **Manchester Utd** 4 (Young 53, Greenwood 58, 64, Mata 62 pen) Alkmaar 0. Att: 65,773. Partizan Belgrade 4 (Soumah 4, Sadiq 22, 76, Asano 26) Astana 1 (Pavlovic 79 og). Att: 8,075

	P	W	D	L	F	A	Pts
Manchester Utd Q	6	4	1	1	10	2	13
Alkmaar Q	6	2	3	1	15	8	9
Partizan Belgrade	6	2	2	2	10	10	8
Astana	6	1	0	5	4	19	3

ROUND OF 32, FIRST LEG

Alkmaar 1 (Koopmeiners 86 pen) LASK 1 (Raguz 26). Att: 12,526. Apoel Nicosia 0 Basle 3 (Petretta 16, Stocker 53, Arthur Cabral 66). Att: 8,191. Bayer Leverkusen 2 (Alario 29, Havrtz 29 pen) Porto 1 (Ze Luis 73). Att: 69,694. CFR Cluj 1 (Deac 59 pen) Sevilla 1 (En-Nesyri 82). Att: 14,820

Club Bruges 1 (Bonaventure 15) **Manchester Utd** 1 (Martial 36). Att: 27,006. Copenhagen 1 (N'Doye 52) **Celtic** 1 (Edouard 14). Att: 34,346. Eintracht Frankfurt 4 (Kamada 12, 43, 53, Kostic 56) Salzburg 1 (Hwang 85 pen). At: 47,000. Getafe 2 (Deyverson 37, Kenedy 90+3) Ajax 0. Att: 14,039

Ludogorets 0 Inter Milan 2 (Eriksen 71, Lukaku 90+5 pen). Att: 10,024. Olympiacos 0 **Arsenal** 1 (Lacazette 81). Att: 31,456. **Rangers** 3 (Hagi 67, 82, Aribo 75) Braga 2 (Fransergio 11, Ruiz 59). Att: 49,378. Roma 1 (Perez 13) Gent 0. Att: 28,248

Shakhtar Donetsk 2 (Alan Patrick 56, Kovalenko 72) Benfica 1 (Pizzi 66 pen). Att: 24,429. Sporting Lisbon 3 (Coate 3, Sporar 44, Vietto 51) Basaksehir 1 (Visca 77 pen). Wolfsburg 2 (Brekalo 49, Mehmedi 62) Malmo 1 (Thelin 47 pen). Att: 13,801. **Wolves** 4 (Diogo Jota 15, 67, 81, Ruben Neves 52) Espanyol 0. Att: 30,435

ROUND OF 32, SECOND LEG

Arsenal 1 (Aubameyang 24) Olympiacos 2 (Cisse 53, El Arabi 119). Att: 60,242 (aet, agg 2-2, Olympiacos won on away goals). Ajax 2 (Pereira da Silva 10, Olivera 63 og) Getafe 1 (Mata 5). Att: 51,487 (Getafe won 3-2 on agg). Basaksehir 4 (Skrtel 31, Aleksic 45, Visca 90+1 pen, 119) Sporting Lisbon 1 (Vietto 68). Att: 5,892 (aet, Basaksehir won 5-4 on agg). Basle 1 (Frei 38 pen) Apoel Nicosia 0. Att: 14,428 (Basle won 4-0 on agg).

Benfica 3(Afonso Fernandes 9, Ruben Dias 36, Ferreira Silva 47) Shakhtar Donetsk 3 (Ruben Dias 12 og, Stepanenko 41, Lourenco 71). Att: 48,302 (Shakhtar Donetsk won 5-4 on agg) Braga 0 **Rangers** 1 (Kent 61). Att: 18,113 (Rangers won 4-2 on agg). **Celtic** 1 (Edouard 83 pen) Copenhagen 3 (Santos 51, Mas 85, N'Doye 88). Att: 56,172 (Copenhagen won 4-2 on agg). Espanyol 3 (Calleri 16, 57 pen, 90+1) **Wolves** 2 (Traore 22, Doherty 79). Att: 14,525 (Wolves won 6-3 on agg)

Gent 1 (David 25) Roma 1 (Kluivert 29). Att: 17,557 (Roma won 2-1 on agg). Inter Milan 2 (Biraghi 31, Lukaku 45) Ludogorets 1 (Oliveria Souza 26). Att: 10,024 (Inter Milan .won 4-1 on agg). LASK 2 (Raguz 44 pen, 50) Alkmaar 0. Att: 12,855 (LASK won 3-1 on agg). Malmo 0 Wolfsburg 3 (Brekalo 41, Gerhardt 65, Santos Sa 69). Att: 20,501 (Wolfsburg won 5-1 on agg) **Manchester Utd** 5 (Bruno Fernandes 27 pen, Ighalo 34, McTominay 41, Fred 82, 90+3) Club Bruges 0. Att: 70,397 (Manchester Utd won 6-1 on agg). Porto 1 (Marega 65) Bayer Leverkusen 3 (Alario 10, Demirbay 50, Havertz 57). Att: 30,292 (Bayer Leverkusen won 5-2 on agg). Salzburg 2 (Ulmer 10, Onguene 71) Eintracht Frankfurt 2 (Andre Silva 30, 83). Att: 47,000 (Eintracht Frankfurt won 6-3 on agg). Seville 0 CFR Cluj 0. Att: 31,338 (agg 1-1, Sevilla won on away goal

ROUND OF 16, FIRST LEG

(where no attendance shown, match played behind closed doors)

Basaksehir 1 (Visca 88 pen) Copenhagen 0. Att: 12,205. Eintracht Frankfurt 0 Basle 3 (Campo 27, Bua 73, Frei 85). LASK 0 **Manchester Utd** 5 (Ighalo 28, James 58, Mata 82, Greenwood 90+1, Pereira 90+3). Olympiacos 1 (El Arabi 54) **Wolves** 1 (Pedro Neto 67). **Rangers** 1

(Edmundson 75) Bayer Leverkusen 3 (Havertz 37 pen, Aranguiz 67, Bailley 88). Att: 47,494. Wolfsburg 1 (Brooks 48) Shakhtar Donetsk 2 (Moraes 16, Antonio 73).

SECOND LEG
(played behind closed doors)

Basle 1 (Frei 88) Eintracht Frankfurt –Basle won 4-0 on agg. Bayer Leverkusen 1 (Diaby 51) Rangers 0 – Bayer Leverkusen won 4-1 on agg. Copenhagen 3 (Wind 4, 53 pen, Jensen 62) Basaksehir 0 – Copenhagen won 3-1 on agg. Manchester Utd 2 (Lingard 57, Martial 88) LASK 1 (Wiesinger 55) – Manchester Utd won 7-1 on agg. Shakhtar Donetsk 3 (Moraes 89, 90+3, Solomon 90+1) Wolfsburg 0 – Shakhtar Donetsk won 5-1 on agg). Wolves 1 (Raul Jimenez 8 pen) Olympiacos 0 – Wolves won 2-1 on agg.

ONE-OFF TIES
(played behind closed doors)

Inter Milan 2 (Lukaku 33, Eriksen 83) Getafe 0. Sevilla 2 (Reguilon 22, En-Nesyri 44) Roma 0.

QUARTER-FINALS
(all ties played in Germany behind closed doors and decided on one match)

Inter Milan 2 (Barella 15, Lukaku 21) Bayer Leverkusen 1 (Havertz 24) - Dusseldorf. Manchester Utd 1 (Bruno Fernandes 95 pen) Copenhagen 0 – aet, Cologne. Shakhtar Donetsk 4 (Moraes 2, Taison 22, Patrick 75 pen, Dodo 88) Basle 1 (Van Wolfswinkel 90+2) – Gelsenkirchen. Wolves 0 Sevilla 1 (Ocampos 88) - Duisburg

SEMI-FINALS
(both ties played in Germany behind closed doors and decided on one match)

Inter Milan 5 (Martinez 19, 74, D'Ambrosio 64, Lukaku 78, 83) Shakhtar Donetsk 0 – Dusseldorf. Sevilla 2 (Suso 26, De Jong 78) Manchester Utd 1 (Bruno Fernandes 9 pen) – Cologne

FINAL

SEVILLA 3 (De Jong 12, 33, Lukaku 74 og) INTER MILAN 2 (Lukaku 4 pen, Godin 36)
RheinEnergie Stadion, Cologne, Friday, August 21, 2020
Sevilla (4-3-3): Bono, Navas (capt), Kounde, Diego Carlos (Gudelj 86), Reguilon, Joan Jordan, Fernando, Banega, Suso (Vazquez 78), De Jong (En-Nesyri 85), Ocampos (Munir 70). **Subs not used:** Vaclik, Sergi Gomez, Escudero, Jose Lara, Javi Diaz, Oliver Torres, Genaro Rodriguez, Pabo Perez. **Booked:** Diego Carlos, Banega. **Coach:** Julen Lopetegui
Inter Milan (3-5-2): Handanovic (capt), Godin (Candreva 90), De Vrij, Bastoni, D'Ambrosio (Moses 78), Barella, Brozovic, Gagliardini (Eriksen 78), Young, Lukaku, Lautaro (Sanchez 78). **Subs not used:** Padelli, Sensi, Ranocchia, Borja Valero, Esposito, Pirola, Biraghi, Skriniar. **Booked:** Barella, Bastoni, Gagliardini. **Coach:** Antonio Conte
Referee: D Makkelie (Holland). **Half-time:** 2-2

Leading scorers: 7 Lukaku (Inter Milan); 6 Diogo Jota (Wolves), Kamada (Entracht Frankfurt), Morelos (Rangers), Visca (Basaksehir); 5 Frei (Basle), Greenwood (Manchester Utd), Munir (Sevilla), Raguz (LASK). **Also:** 8 Bruno Fernandes (5 for Sporting Lisbon, 3 for Manchester Utd); 6 Sporar (5 for Slovan Bratislava, 1 for Sporting Lisbon)

FIRMINO AT THE DOUBLE

Roberto Firmino scored two late match-winning goals as Liverpool won FIFA's World Club Cup for the first time in Qatar. The Brazil forward was on the mark in the 91st minute of their semi-final against Monterrey of Mexico after Naby Keita's 12th minute opener was cancelled out three minutes later by Rogelio Funes Mori. In the final against Brazil champions Flamengo, Firmino put an early chance over the bar, then hit a post. Jordan Henderson's 25-yard drive was tipped over before his side's superiority finally paid off in the ninth minute of extra-time. Sadio Mane played in Firmino, who checked, turned inside to create space and finished coolly. Jurgen Klopp had priorised the tournament ahead of the same week's League Cup in which the club's youngest-ever line-up lost 5-0 to Aston Villa in the quarter-finals. It brought Liverpool their first world title after defeats by Flamengo in 1981, Independiente of Argentina in 1984 and Brazil's Sao Paulo in 2005. They joined Manchester United, winners in 1999 and 2008, and became the first to hold this trophy, the Champions League and European Super Cup.

FIRST ROUND

Al Sadd (Qatar) 3 (Bounedjah 26, Hassan 100, Correia 114) Hienghene (New Caledonia) 1 (Roine 46). Att: 7,047 (aet)

SECOND ROUND

Al Hilal (Saudi Arabia) 1 (Gomis 73) Es Tunis (Tunisia) 0. Att: 7,726. Monterrey (Mexico) 3 (Vangioni 23, Funes Mori 45, Rodriguez 77) Al Sadd 2 (Bounedjah 66, Hassan 89). Att: 4,878

SEMI-FINALS

Monterrey 1 (Funes Mori 15) **Liverpool** 2 (Keita 12, Firmino 90+1). Att: 45,416
Liverpool (4-3-3): Alisson, Milner (Alexander-Arnold 75), Gomez, Van Dijk, Robertson, Oxlade-Chamberlain, Lallana, Keita, Salah, Shaqiri (Mane 68), Origi (Firmino 85). **Booked**: Gomez
Flemengo (Brazil) 3 (De Arrascaeta 49, Bruno Henrique 78, Albulayhi 81) Al Hilal 1 (Al Dawsari 18). Att: 21,588

FINAL

LIVERPOOL 1 (Firmino 99) FLAMENGO 0 - aet
Khalifa International Stadium, Doha (45,416) Saturday, December 21, 2019
Liverpool (4-3-3): Alisson, Alexander-Arnold, Gomez, Van Dijk, Robertson, Oxlade-Chamberlain (Lallana 76) Henderson (capt), Keita (Milner 100), Salah, Firmino (Origi 105), Mane. **Subs not used**: Adrian, Lonergan, Van den Berg, Hoever, Williams,Wijnaldum, Jones, Elliott. **Booked** Mane, Salah, Firmino, Milner. **Manager**: Jurgen Klopp
Flamengo (4-2-3-1): Diego Alves, Rodrigo Caio, Kafina, Filipe Luis, Pablo Mari, Willian Arao (Orlandio Berrio 120), Everton Ribeiro (capt), Diego 82), De Arrascaeta (Vitinho 77), Gerson (Lincoln 102), Gabriel Barbosa, Bruno Henrique. **Subs not used**: Gabriel Batista, Cesar, Rodinei, Rene, Thuler, Rhodolfo, Reinier, Robert Piris
Referee: A Al Jassim (Qatar). **Half-time**: 0-0

EUROPEAN SUPER CUP 2019

LIVERPOOL 2 (Mane 48, 95) CHELSEA 2 (Giroud 36, Jorginho 101 pen) – aet, Liverpool won 5-4 on pens)
Vodafone Park, Istanbul (38,434); Wednesday, August 14, 2019
Liverpool (4-3-3): Adrian, Gomez, Matip, Van Dijk, Robertson (Alexander-Arnold 91),

Henderson (capt), Fabinho, Milner (Wijnaldum 64), Salah, Mane (Orighi 103), Oxlade-Chamberlain (Firmino 46). **Booked**: Henderson, Alexander-Arnold. **Manager**: Jurgen Klopp
Chelsea (4-3-2-1): Arrizabalaga, Azpilicueta (capt), Zouma, Christensen (Tomori 85), Emerson, Kante, Jorginho, Kovacic (Barkley 101), Pulisic (Mount 74), Pedro, Giroud (Abraham 74). **Booked**: Azpilicurta. **Manager**: Frank Lampard
Penalty shoot-out: Liverpool – scored: Firmino, Fabinho, Origi, Alexander-Arnold, Salah.
Chelsea – scored: Jorginho, Barkley, Mount, Emerson; saved: Abraham
Referee: Stephanie Frappart (France). **Half-time**: 0-1.

UEFA CUP FINALS

1972	Tottenham beat Wolves 3-2 on agg (2-1a, 1-1h)
1973	Liverpool beat Borussia Moenchengladbach 3-2 on agg (3-0h, 0-2a)
1974	Feyenoord beat Tottenham 4-2 on agg (2-2a, 2-0h)
1975	Borussia Moenchengladbach beat Twente Enschede 5-1 on agg (0-0h, 5-1a)
1976	Liverpool beat Brugge 4-3 on agg (3-2h, 1-1a)
1977	Juventus beat Atletico Bilbao on away goals after 2-2 agg (1-0h, 1-2a)
1978	PSV Eindhoven beat Bastia 3-0 on agg (0-0a, 3-0h)
1979	Borussia Moenchengladbach beat Red Star Belgrade 2-1 on agg (1-1a, 1-0h)
1980	Eintracht Frankfurt beat Borussia Moenchengladbach on away goals after 3-3 agg (2-3a, 1-0h)
1981	Ipswich Town beat AZ 67 Alkmaar 5-4 on agg (3-0h, 2-4a)
1982	IFK Gothenburg beat SV Hamburg 4-0 on agg (1-0h, 3-0a)
1983	Anderlecht beat Benfica 2-1 on agg (1-0h, 1-1a)
1984	Tottenham beat Anderlecht 4-3 on penalties after 2-2 agg (1-1a, 1-1h)
1985	Real Madrid beat Videoton 3-1 on agg (3-0a, 0-1h)
1986	Real Madrid beat Cologne 5-3 on agg (5-1h, 0-2a)
1987	IFK Gothenburg beat Dundee Utd 2-1 on agg (1-0h, 1-1a)
1988	Bayer Leverkusen beat Espanol 3-2 on penalties after 3-3 agg (0-3a, 3-0h)
1989	Napoli beat VfB Stuttgart 5-4 on agg (2-1h, 3-3a)
1990	Juventus beat Fiorentina 3-1 on agg (3-1h, 0-0a)
1991	Inter Milan beat AS Roma 2-1 on agg (2-0h, 0-1a)
1992	Ajax beat Torino on away goals after 2-2 agg (2-2a, 0-0h)
1993	Juventus beat Borussia Dortmund 6-1 on agg (3-1a, 3-0h)
1994	Inter Milan beat Salzburg 2-0 on agg (1-0a, 1-0h)
1995	Parma beat Juventus 2-1 on agg (1-0h, 1-1a)
1996	Bayern Munich beat Bordeaux 5-1 on agg (2-0h, 3-1a)
1997	FC Schalke beat Inter Milan 4-1 on penalties after 1-1 agg (1-0h, 0-1a)
1998	Inter Milan beat Lazio 3-0 (one match) – Paris
1999	Parma beat Marseille 3-0 (one match) – Moscow
2000	Galatasaray beat Arsenal 4-1 on penalties after 0-0 (one match) – Copenhagen
2001	Liverpool beat Alaves 5-4 on golden goal (one match) – Dortmund
2002	Feyenoord beat Borussia Dortmund 3-2 (one match) – Rotterdam
2003	FC Porto beat Celtic 3-2 on silver goal (one match) – Seville
2004	Valencia beat Marseille 2-0 (one match) – Gothenburg
2005	CSKA Moscow beat Sporting Lisbon 3-1 (one match) – Lisbon
2006	Sevilla beat Middlesbrough 4-0 (one match) – Eindhoven
2007	Sevilla beat Espanyol 3-1 on penalties after 2-2 (one match) – Hampden Park
2008	Zenit St Petersburg beat Rangers 2-0 (one match) – City of Manchester Stadium
2009†	Shakhtar Donetsk beat Werder Bremen 2-1 (one match) – Istanbul

EUROPA LEAGUE FINALS

2010†	Atletico Madrid beat Fulham 2-1 (one match) – Hamburg

2011	Porto beat Braga 1-0 (one match) – Dublin
2012	Atletico Madrid beat Athletic Bilbao 3-0 (one match) – Bucharest
2013	Chelsea beat Benfica 2-1 (one match) – Amsterdam
2014	Sevilla beat Benfica 4-2 on penalties after 0-0 (one match) – Turin
2015	Sevilla beat Dnipro 3-2 (one match) – Warsaw
2016	Sevilla beat Liverpool 3-1 (one match) – Basle
2017	Manchester Utd beat Ajax 2-0 (one match) – Stockholm
2018	Atletico Madrid beat Marseille 3-0 (one match) – Lyon
2019	Chelsea beat Arsenal 4-1 (one match) – Baku
2020	Sevilla beat Inter Milan 3-2 (one match) - Cologne

(† After extra-time)

FAIRS CUP FINALS
(As UEFA Cup previously known)

1958	Barcelona beat London 8-2 on agg (2-2a, 6-0h)
1960	Barcelona beat Birmingham 4-1 on agg (0-0a, 4-1h)
1961	AS Roma beat Birmingham City 4-2 on agg (2-2a, 2-0h)
1962	Valencia beat Barcelona 7-3 on agg (6-2h, 1-1a)
1963	Valencia beat Dynamo Zagreb 4-1 on agg (2-1a, 2-0h)
1964	Real Zaragoza beat Valencia 2-1 (Barcelona)
1965	Ferencvaros beat Juventus 1-0 (Turin)
1966	Barcelona beat Real Zaragoza 4-3 on agg (0-1h, 4-2a)
1967	Dinamo Zagreb beat Leeds Utd 2-0 on agg (2-0h, 0-0a)
1968	Leeds Utd beat Ferencvaros 1-0 on agg (1-0h, 0-0a)
1969	Newcastle Utd beat Ujpest Dozsa 6-2 on agg (3-0h, 3-2a)
1970	Arsenal beat Anderlecht 4-3 on agg (1-3a, 3-0h)
1971	Leeds Utd beat Juventus on away goals after 3-3 agg (2-2a, 1-1h)

CUP-WINNERS' CUP FINALS

1961	Fiorentina beat Rangers 4-1 on agg (2-0 Glasgow first leg, 2-1 Florence second leg)
1962	Atletico Madrid beat Fiorentina 3-0 (replay Stuttgart, after a 1-1 draw, Glasgow)
1963	Tottenham beat Atletico Madrid 5-1 (Rotterdam)
1964	Sporting Lisbon beat MTK Budapest 1-0 (replay Antwerp, after a 3-3 draw, Brussels)
1965	West Ham Utd beat Munich 1860 2-0 (Wembley)
1966†	Borussia Dortmund beat Liverpool 2-1 (Glasgow)
1967†	Bayern Munich beat Rangers 1-0 (Nuremberg)
1968	AC Milan beat SV Hamburg 2-0 (Rotterdam)
1969	Slovan Bratislava beat Barcelona 3-2 (Basle)
1970	Manchester City beat Gornik Zabrze 2-1 (Vienna)
1971†	Chelsea beat Real Madrid 2-1 (replay Athens, after a 1-1 draw, Athens)
1972	Rangers beat Moscow Dynamo 3-2 (Barcelona)
1973	AC Milan beat Leeds Utd 1-0 (Salonika)
1974	Magdeburg beat AC Milan 2-0 (Rotterdam)
1975	Dynamo Kiev beat Ferencvaros 3-0 (Basle)
1976	Anderlecht beat West Ham Utd 4-2 (Brussels)
1977	SV Hamburg beat Anderlecht 2-0 (Amsterdam)
1978	Anderlecht beat Austria WAC 4-0 (Paris)
1979†	Barcelona beat Fortuna Dusseldorf 4-3 (Basle)
1980†	Valencia beat Arsenal 5-4 on penalties after a 0-0 draw (Brussels)
1981	Dinamo Tbilisi beat Carl Zeiss Jena 2-1 (Dusseldorf)
1982	Barcelona beat Standard Liege 2-1 (Barcelona)

1983†	Aberdeen beat Real Madrid 2-1 (Gothenburg)
1984	Juventus beat Porto 2-1 (Basle)
1985	Everton beat Rapid Vienna 3-1 (Rotterdam)
1986	Dynamo Kiev beat Atletico Madrid 3-0 (Lyon)
1987	Ajax beat Lokomotiv Leipzig 1-0 (Athens)
1988	Mechelen beat Ajax 1-0 (Strasbourg)
1989	Barcelona beat Sampdoria 2-0 (Berne)
1990	Sampdoria beat Anderlecht 2-0 (Gothenburg)
1991	Manchester Utd beat Barcelona 2-1 (Rotterdam)
1992	Werder Bremen beat Monaco 2-0 (Lisbon)
1993	Parma beat Royal Antwerp 3-1 (Wembley)
1994	Arsenal beat Parma 1-0 (Copenhagen)
1995†	Real Zaragoza beat Arsenal 2-1 (Paris)
1996	Paris St Germain beat Rapid Vienna 1-0 (Brussels)
1997	Barcelona beat Paris St Germain 1-0 (Rotterdam)
1998	Chelsea beat VfB Stuttgart 1-0 (Stockholm)
1999	Lazio beat Real Mallorca 2-1 (Villa Park, Birmingham)

(† After extra time)

EUROPEAN SUPER CUP RESULTS

1972*	Ajax beat Rangers 6-3 on agg (3-1, 3-2)
1973	Ajax beat AC Milan 6-1 on agg (0-1, 6-0)
1974	Bayern Munich and Magdeburg did not play
1975	Dynamo Kiev beat Bayern Munich 3-0 on agg (1-0, 2-0)
1976	Anderlecht beat Bayern Munich 5-3 on agg (1-2, 4-1)
1977	Liverpool beat Hamburg 7-1 on agg (1-1, 6-0)
1978	Anderlecht beat Liverpool 4-3 on agg (3-1, 1-2)
1979	Nottm Forest beat Barcelona 2-1 on agg (1-0, 1-1)
1980	Valencia beat Nottm Forest on away goal after 2-2 agg (1-2, 1-0)
1981	Liverpool and Dinamo Tbilisi did not play
1982	Aston Villa beat Barcelona 3-1 on agg (0-1, 3-0 aet)
1983	Aberdeen beat Hamburg 2-0 on agg (0-0, 2-0)
1984	Juventus beat Liverpool 2-0 – one match (Turin)
1985	Juventus and Everton did not play
1986	Steaua Bucharest beat Dynamo Kiev 1-0 – one match (Monaco)
1987	Porto beat Ajax 2-0 on agg (1-0, 1-0)
1988	Mechelen beat PSV Eindhoven 3-1 on agg (3-0, 0-1)
1989	AC Milan beat Barcelona 2-1 on agg (1-1, 1-0)
1990	AC Milan beat Sampdoria 3-1 on agg (1-1, 2-0)
1991	Manchester Utd beat Red Star Belgrade 1-0 – one match (Old Trafford)
1992	Barcelona beat Werder Bremen 3-2 on agg (1-1, 2-1)
1993	Parma beat AC Milan 2-1 on agg (0-1, 2-0 aet)
1994	AC Milan beat Arsenal 2-0 on agg (0-0, 2-0)
1995	Ajax beat Real Zaragoza 5-1 on agg (1-1, 4-0)
1996	Juventus beat Paris St Germain 9-2 on agg (6-1, 3-1)
1997	Barcelona beat Borussia Dortmund 3-1 on agg (2-0, 1-1)
1998	Chelsea beat Real Madrid 1-0 (Monaco)
1999	Lazio beat Manchester Utd 1-0 (Monaco)
2000	Galatasaray beat Real Madrid 2-1 – aet, golden goal (Monaco)
2001	Liverpool beat Bayern Munich 3-2 (Monaco)
2002	Real Madrid beat Feyenoord 3-1 (Monaco)
2003	AC Milan beat Porto 1-0 (Monaco)

2004	Valencia beat Porto 2-1 (Monaco)
2005	Liverpool beat CSKA Moscow 3-1 – aet (Monaco)
2006	Sevilla beat Barcelona 3-0 (Monaco)
2007	AC Milan beat Sevilla 3-1 (Monaco)
2008	Zenit St Petersburg beat Manchester Utd 2-1 (Monaco)
2009	Barcelona beat Shakhtar Donetsk 1-0 – aet (Monaco)
2010	Atletico Madrid beat Inter Milan 2-0 (Monaco)
2011	Barcelona beat Porto 2-0 (Monaco)
2012	Atletico Madrid beat Chelsea 4-1 (Monaco)
2013	Bayern Munich beat Chelsea 5-4 on pens, aet – 2-2 (Prague)
2014	Real Madrid beat Sevilla 2-0 (Cardiff)
2015	Barcelona beat Sevilla 5-4 – aet (Tbilisi)
2016	Real Madrid beat Sevilla 3-2 – aet (Trondheim)
2017	Real Madrid beat Manchester Utd 2-1 (Skopje)
2018	Atletico Madrid beat Real Madrid 4-2 (Tallinn)
2019	Liverpool beat Chelsea 5-4 on pens, aet – 2-2 (Istanbul)

*not recognised by UEFA; from 1998 one match

INTER-CONTINENTAL CUP

Year	Winners	Runners-up	Score
1960	Real Madrid (Spa)	Penarol (Uru)	0-0 5-1
1961	Penarol (Uru)	Benfica (Por)	0-1 2-1 5-0
1962	Santos (Bra)	Benfica (Por)	3-2 5-2
1963	Santos (Bra)	AC Milan (Ita)	2-4 4-2 1-0
1964	Inter Milan (Ita)	Independiente (Arg)	0-1 2-0 1-0
1965	Inter Milan (Ita)	Independiente (Arg)	3-0 0-0
1966	Penarol (Uru)	Real Madrid (Spa)	2-0 2-0
1967	Racing (Arg)	Celtic	0-1 2-1 1-0
1968	Estudiantes (Arg)	Manchester Utd	1-0 1-1
1969	AC Milan (Ita)	Estudiantes (Arg)	3-0 1-2
1970	Feyenoord (Hol)	Estudiantes (Arg)	2-2 1-0
1971	Nacional (Uru)	Panathanaikos (Gre)	*1-1 2-1
1972	Ajax (Hol)	Independiente (Arg)	1-1 3-0
1973	Independiente (Arg)	Juventus* (Ita)	1-0 #
1974	Atletico Madrid (Spa)*	Independiente (Arg)	0-1 2-0
1975	Not played		
1976	Bayern Munich (WGer)	Cruzeiro (Bra)	2-0 0-0
1977	Boca Juniors (Arg)	Borussia Mönchengladbach* (WGer)	2-2 3-0
1978	Not played		
1979	Olimpia Asuncion (Par)	Malmö* (Swe)	1-0 2-1
1980	Nacional (Arg)	Nott'm Forest	1-0
1981	Flamengo (Bra)	Liverpool	3-0
1982	Penarol (Uru)	Aston Villa	2-0
1983	Porto Alegre (Bra)	SV Hamburg (WGer)	2-1
1984	Independiente (Arg)	Liverpool	1-0
1985	Juventus (Ita)	Argentinos Juniors (Arg)	2-2 (aet)
	(Juventus won 4-2 on penalties)		
1986	River Plate (Arg)	Steaua Bucharest (Rom)	1-0
1987	Porto (Por)	Penarol (Uru)	2-1 (aet)
1988	Nacional (Uru)	PSV Eindhoven (Hol)	1-1 (aet)
	(Nacional won 7-6 on penalties)		
1989	AC Milan (Ita)	Nacional (Col)	1-0 (aet)

1990	AC Milan (Ita)	Olimpia Asuncion (Par)	3-0
1991	Red Star (Yug)	Colo Colo (Chi)	3-0
1992	Sao Paulo (Bra)	Barcelona (Spa)	2-1
1993	Sao Paulo (Bra)	AC Milan (Ita)	3-2
1994	Velez Sarsfield (Arg)	AC Milan (Ita)	2-0
1995	Ajax (Hol)	Gremio (Bra)	0-0 (aet)
	(Ajax won 4-3 on penalties)		
1996	Juventus (Ita)	River Plate (Arg)	1-0
1997	Borussia Dortmund (Ger)	Cruzeiro (Arg)	2-0
1998	Real Madrid (Spa)	Vasco da Gama (Bra)	2-1
1999	Manchester Utd	Palmeiras (Bra)	1-0
2000	Boca Juniors (Arg)	Real Madrid (Spa)	2-1
2001	Bayern Munich (Ger)	Boca Juniors (Arg)	1-0
2002	Real Madrid (Spa)	Olimpia Ascuncion (Par)	2-0
2003	Boca Juniors (Arg)	AC Milan (Ita)	1-1
	(Boca Juniors won 3-1 on penalties)		
2004	FC Porto (Por)	Caldas (Col)	0-0

FC Porto won 8-7 on penalties)
*Played as a single match in Japan since 1980
† European Cup runners-up # One match only
Summary: 43 contests; South America 22 wins, Europe 23 wins

CLUB WORLD CHAMPIONSHIP

2005	Sao Paulo (Bra) beat Liverpool	1-0
2006	Internacional (Bra) beat Barcelona (Spa)	1-0
2007	AC Milan (Ita) beat Boca Juniors (Arg)	4-2

CLUB WORLD CUP

2008	Manchester Utd beat Liga de Quito (Ecu)	1-0
2009	Barcelona beat Estudiantes (Arg)	2-1 (aet)
2010	Inter Milan (Ita) beat TP Mazembe (DR Congo)	3-0
2011	Barcelona beat Santos (Bra)	4-0
2012	Corinthians (Bra) beat Chelsea	1-0
2013	Bayern Munich (Ger) beat Raja Casablanca (Mar)	2-0
2014	Real Madrid (Spa) beat San Lorenzo (Arg)	2-0
2015	Barcelona beat River Plate (Arg)	3-0
2016	Real Madrid beat Kashima Antlers (Jap)	4-2 (aet)
2017	Real Madrid beat Gremio (Bra)	1-0
2018	Real Madrid beat Al AIN (UAE)	4-1
2019	Liverpool beat Flamengo (Bra)	1-0 (aet)

EUROPEAN TABLES 2019–2020

FRANCE – LIGUE 1

	P	W	D	L	F	A	GD	Pts
Paris SG	27	22	2	3	75	24	51	68
Marseille	28	16	8	4	41	29	12	56
Rennes	28	15	5	8	38	24	14	50
Lille	28	15	4	9	35	27	8	49
Reims	28	10	11	7	26	21	5	41
Nice	28	11	8	9	41	38	3	41
Lyon	28	11	7	10	42	27	15	40
Montpellier	28	11	7	10	35	34	1	40
Monaco	28	11	7	10	44	44	0	40
Angers	28	11	6	11	28	33	-5	39
Strasbourg	27	11	5	11	32	32	0	38
Bordeaux	28	9	10	9	40	34	6	37
Nantes	28	11	4	13	28	31	-3	37
Brest	28	8	10	10	34	37	-3	34
Metz	28	8	10	10	27	35	-8	34
Dijon	28	7	9	12	27	37	-10	30
Saint-Etienne	28	8	6	14	29	45	-16	30
Nimes	28	7	6	15	29	44	-15	27
Amiens	28	4	11	13	31	50	-19	23
Toulouse	28	3	4	21	22	58	-36	13

Season abandoned. Paris SG awarded title; Amiens and Toulouse relegated
Leading scorers: 18 Ben Yedder (Monaco), Mbappe (Paris SG); 16 Dembele (Lyon); 13 Neymar (Paris SG), Osimhen (Lille); 12 Diallo (Metz), Icardi (Paris SG); 11 Benedetto (Marseille), Dolberg (Nice); 10 Bouanga (Saint Etienne), Niang (Rennes).
Cup Final: Paris SG 1 (Neymar 14) Saint-Etienne 0

HOLLAND – EREDIVISIE

AAjax	25	18	2	5	68	23	45	56
Alkmaar	25	18	2	5	54	17	37	56
Feyenoord	25	14	8	3	50	35	15	50
PSV Eindhoven	26	14	7	5	54	28	26	49
Willem	26	13	5	8	37	34	3	44
Utrecht	25	12	5	8	50	34	16	41
Vitesse Arnhem	26	12	5	9	45	35	10	41
Heracles	26	10	6	10	40	34	6	36
Groningen	26	10	5	11	27	26	1	35
Heerenveen	26	8	9	9	41	41	0	33
Sparta Rotterdam	26	9	6	11	41	45	-4	33
Emmen	26	9	5	12	32	45	-13	32
Venlo	26	8	4	14	24	51	-27	28
Twente	26	7	6	13	34	46	-12	27
Zwolle	26	7	5	14	37	55	-18	26
Fortuna Sittard	26	6	8	12	29	52	-23	26
Den Haag	26	4	7	15	25	54	-29	19
Waalwijk	26	4	3	19	27	60	-33	15

Season abandoned. No champions or relegation. Cup Final: Feyenoord v Utrecht postponed
Leading scorers: 15 Berghuis (Feyenoord), Dessers (Heracles); 14 Boadu (Alkmaar), Linssen (Vitesse Arnhem); 13 Idrissi (Alkmaar); 12 Matavz (Vitesse Arnhem), Promes (Ajax); 11 Koopmeiners (Alkmaar), Malen (PSV Eindhoven), Pavlidis (Willem), Tadic (Ajax), Vuckic (Twente)

GERMANY – BUNDESLIGA

Bayern Munich	34	24	6	4	88	32	56	78
Borussia Dortmund	34	23	7	4	81	44	37	76
Leipzig	34	19	9	6	63	29	34	66
Bayer Leverkusen	34	18	4	12	69	52	17	58
Borussia M'gladbach	34	16	7	11	55	42	13	55
Wolfsburg	34	16	7	11	62	50	12	55
Eintracht Frankfurt	34	15	9	10	60	48	12	54
Werder Bremen	34	14	11	9	58	49	9	53
Hoffenheim	34	13	12	9	70	52	18	51
Fortuna Dusseldorf	34	13	5	16	49	65	-16	44
Hertha	34	11	10	13	49	57	-8	43
Mainz	34	12	7	15	46	57	-11	43
Freiburg	34	8	12	14	46	61	-15	36
Schalke	34	8	9	17	37	55	-18	33
Augsburg	34	8	8	18	51	71	-20	32
Stuttgart	34	7	7	20	32	70	-38	28
Hannover	34	5	6	23	31	71	-40	21
Nuremberg	34	3	10	21	26	68	-42	19

Leading scorers: 22 Lewandowski (Bayern Munich); 18 Alcacer (Borussia Dortmund); 17 Havertz (Bayer Leverkusen), Jovic (Eintracht Frankfurt), Kramaric (Hoffenheim), Reus (Borussia Dortmund); 16 Belfodil (Hoffenheim), Haller (Eintracht Frankfurt), Poulsen (Leipzig), Werner (Leipzig)

Cup Final: Bayern Munich 3 (Lewandowski 29, 85, Coman 78) Leipzig 0

ITALY – SERIE A

Juventus	38	26	5	7	76	43	33	83
Inter Milan	38	24	10	4	81	36	45	82
Atalanta	38	23	9	6	98	48	50	78
Lazio	38	24	6	8	79	42	37	78
Roma	38	21	7	10	77	51	26	70
AC Milan	38	19	9	10	63	46	17	66
Napoli	38	18	8	12	61	50	11	62
Sassuolo	38	14	9	15	69	63	6	51
Fiorentina	38	12	13	13	51	48	3	49
Parma	38	14	7	17	56	57	-1	49
Verona	38	12	13	13	47	51	-4	49
Bologna	38	12	11	15	52	65	-13	47
Udinese	38	12	9	17	37	51	-14	45
Cagliari	38	11	12	15	52	56	-4	45
Sampdoria	38	12	6	20	48	65	-17	42
Torino	38	11	7	20	46	68	-22	40
Genoa	38	10	9	19	47	73	-26	39
Lecce	38	9	8	21	52	85	-33	35
Brescia	38	6	7	25	35	79	-44	25
SPAL	38	5	5	28	27	77	-50	20

Leading scorers: 36 Immobile (Lazio); 31 Ronaldo (Juventus); 23 Lukaku (Inter Milan); 21 Caputo (Sassuolo); 18 Joao Pedro (Cagliari), Muriel (Atalanta), Zapata (Atalanta); 16 Belotti (Torino), Dzeko (Roma); 15 Ilicic (Atalanta)

Cup Final: Napoli 0 Juventus 1 (Napoli won 4-2 on pens)

PORTUGAL – PRIMEIRA LIGA

Porto	34	26	4	4	74	22	52	82
Benfica	34	24	5	5	71	26	45	77
Sporting Braga	34	18	6	10	61	40	21	60
Sporting Lisbon	34	18	6	10	49	34	15	60
Rio Ave	34	15	10	9	48	36	12	55
Famalicao	34	14	12	8	53	51	2	54
Guimaraes	34	13	11	10	53	38	15	50
Moreirense	34	10	13	11	42	44	-2	43
Santa Clara	34	11	10	13	36	41	-5	43
Gil Vicente	34	11	10	13	40	44	-4	43
Maritimo	34	9	12	13	34	42	-8	39
Boavista	34	10	9	15	28	39	-11	39
Pacos de Ferreira	34	11	6	17	36	52	-16	39
Tondela	34	9	9	16	30	44	-14	36
Belenenses	34	9	8	17	27	54	-27	35
Setubal	34	7	13	14	27	43	-16	34
Portimonense	34	7	12	15	30	45	-15	33
Desportivo	34	5	2	27	24	68	-44	17

Leading scorers: 18 Carlos Vinicius (Benfica), Pizzi (Benfica), Mehdi Taremi (Rio Ave); 17 Paulinho (Sporting Braga); 13 Fabio Abreu (Moreirense); 12 Fabio Martins (Famalicao), Moussa Marega (Porto), Ricardo Horta (Sporting Braga); 11 Alex Telles (Porto); Douglas Tanque (Pacos de Ferreira). Cup Final: Porto 2 (Mbemba 47, 58) Benfica 1 (Carlos Vinicius 84 pen)

SPAIN – LA LIGA

Real Madrid	38	26	9	3	70	25	45	87
Barcelona	38	25	7	6	86	38	48	82
Atletico Madrid	38	18	16	4	51	27	24	70
Sevilla	38	19	13	6	54	34	20	70
Villarreal	38	18	6	14	63	49	14	60
Real Sociedad	38	16	8	14	56	48	8	56
Granada	38	16	8	14	52	45	7	56
Getafe	38	14	12	12	43	37	6	54
Valencia	38	14	11	13	46	53	-7	53
Osasuna	38	13	13	12	46	54	-8	52
Athletic Bilbao	38	13	12	13	41	38	3	51
Levante	38	14	7	17	47	53	-6	49
Real Valladolid	38	9	15	14	32	43	-11	42
Eibar	38	11	9	18	39	56	-17	42
Real Betis	38	10	11	17	48	60	-12	41
Alaves	38	10	9	19	34	59	-25	39
Celta Vigo	38	7	16	15	37	49	-12	37
Leganes	38	8	12	18	30	51	-21	36
Mallorca	38	9	6	23	40	65	-25	33
Espanyol	38	5	10	23	27	58	-31	25

(unbroken line under Celta Vigo)

Leading scorers: 25 Messi (Barcelona); 21 Benzema (Real Madrid); 18 Gerard (Villarreal); 16 Suarez (Barcelona); 15 Garcia (Athletic Bilbao); 14 Aspas (Celta Vigo), Ocampos (Sevilla); 13 Budimir (Mallorca), Morata (Atletico Madrid). Cup Final: Athletic Bilbao v Real Sociedad postponed

BRITISH AND IRISH INTERNATIONALS
2019–20
(*denotes new cap)

EUROPEAN CHAMPIONSHIP
2020 (21) QUALIFYING

ENGLAND 4 (Kane 24, 49 pen, 73 pen, Sterling 55) BULGARIA 0
Wembley (82,605); Saturday, September 7, 2019

England (4-3-3): Pickford, Trippier, Keane, Maguire, Rose, Henderson (*Mount 67), Rice, Barkley, Sterling (Sancho 71), Kane (Oxlade-Chamberlain 77), Rashford. **Booked**: Keane, Rose
Bulgaria (5-4-1): Iliev, S Popov, Bodurov (Dimitrov 65), Sarmov, Bozhikov, Nedyalkov, Ivanov (Mladenov 82), I Popov, Malinov, Wanderson, Marcelinho (Despodov 67). **Booked**: Bodurov
Referee: M Guida (Italy). **Half-time**: 1-0

ENGLAND 5 (Sterling 8, Kane 19, Vojvoda 38 og, Sancho 44, 45) KOSOVO 3 (Berisha 1, 49, Muriqi 55 pen)
St Mary's Stadium, Southampton (30,155); Tuesday, September 10, 2019

England (4-3-3): Pickford, Alexander-Arnold, Keane, Maguire, Chilwell, Henderson, Rice, Barkley, Mount (Rashford 85), Kane, Sterling
Kosovo (4-2-3-1): Muric, Vojvoda, Rrahmani, Aliti, Hadergjonaj, Voca (Rashkaj 59), Halimi, Muslija (Paqarada 46), Celina, Berisha (Hasani 85), Muriqi. **Booked**: Halimi, Paqarada, Aliti, Berisha, Rashkaj
Referee: F Zwayer (Germany). **Half-time**: 5-1

CZECH REPUBLIC 2 (Brabec 9, Ondrasek 85) ENGLAND 1 (Kane 5 pen)
Prague (18,651); Friday, October 11, 2019

Czech Republic (4-2-3-1): Vaclik, Coufal, Celustka, Brabec, Boril, Soucek, Kral, Masopust (Zmrhal 90), Darida, Jankto (Kopic 83), Schick (Ondrasek 65). **Booked**: Jankto
England (4-2-3-1): Pickford, Trippier, Keane, Maguire, Rose, Henderson, Rice (Abraham 88), Sancho (Rashford 73), Mount (Barkley 73), Sterling, Kane. **Booked**: Rose, Sterling, Henderson
Referee: D Skomina (Slovenia). **Half-time**: 1-1

BULGARIA 0 ENGLAND 6 (Rashford 7, Barkley 20, 32, Sterling 45, 69, Kane 85)
Sofia (17,481); Monday, October 14, 2019

Bulgaria (4-1-4-1): Iliev, Pashov, Terziev, Hadzhiev, Zanev, Despodov, Popov, Sarmov (Kraev 46), Kostadinov, Wanderson (Malinov 76), Isa (Ivanov 68)
England (4-3-3): Pickford, Trippier, Maguire, Mings, Chilwell, Henderson, Winks, Barkley (Mount 73), Sterling (Sancho 73), Kane, Rashford (Wilson 76). **Booked**: Henderson
Referee: I Bebek (Croatia). **Half-time**: 0-4

ENGLAND 7 (Oxlade-Chamberlain 11, Kane 18, 24, 37, Rashford 30, Sofranac 66 og, Abraham 84) MONTENEGRO 0
Wembley (77,277);Thursday, November 14, 2019

England (4-3-3): Pickford, Alexander-Arnold, Maguire, Stones, Chilwell, Oxlade-Chamberlain (*Maddison 56), Winks, Mount (Gomez 71), Sancho, Kane (Abraham 57), Rashford
Montenegro (4-3-2-1): Mijatovic, Vesovic, Sofranac, Simic, Radunovic (Raspopovic 46), Hocko, Lagator, Vukcevic, Jovovic (Jankovic 65), Haksabanovic (Boljevic 74), Beqiraj. **Booked**: Vesovic
Referee: A Lahoz Mayeu (Spain). **Half-time**: 5-0
(England's 1000th international)

KOSOVO 0 ENGLAND 4 (Winks 32, Kane 79, Rashford 83, Mount 90)
Pristina (12,326); Sunday, November 17, 2019

Kosovo (4-1-4-1): Muric, Vojvoda, Rrahmani, Aliti, Kololli, Dresevic, Hadergjonaj (Zhegrova 73), Celina, Berisha (Halimi 65), Rashica, Nuhiu (Rashani 82). **Booked:** Kololli
England (4-3-3): Pope, Alexander-Arnold (*Tomori 84), Maguire, Mings, Chilwell, Rice, Winks, Oxlade-Chamberlain (Mount 73), Sterling, Kane, Hudson-Odoi (Rashford 59)
Referee: P Gil (Poland). **Half-time:** 0-1

GROUP C

NORTHERN IRELAND 0 GERMANY 2 (Halstenberg 48, Gnabry 90+2)
Windsor Park (18,104), Monday, September 9, 2019

Northern Ireland (4-5-1): Peacock-Farrell, Dallas, Cathcart, J Evans, Lewis, McGinn (Whyte 59), Saville (Magennis 70), Davis, C Evans, McNair, Washington (Lavery 83). **Booked:** McNair, Saville
Germany (4-2-3-1): Neur, Klostermann, Ginter (Tah 40), Sule, Halstenberg, Kimmich, Kroos, Gnabry, Reus (Emre Can 85), Brandt, Werner (Havertz 68). **Booked:** Gnabry
Referee: D Orsato (Italy). **Half-time:** 0-0

HOLLAND 3 (Depay 80, 90+4, L De Jong 90+1) NORTHERN IRELAND 1 (Magennis 75)
Rotterdam (41,348); Thursday, October 10, 2019

Holland (4-3-3): Cillessen, Dumfries (L De Jong 78), De Light, Van Dijk, Blind, Wijnaldum, De Roon (Van de Beek 66), F De Jong, Bergwijn, Depay, Babel (Mallen 66). **Booked:** Depay
Northern Ireland (4-1-4-1): Peacock-Farrell, Smith, Cathcart, J Evans, Ferguson, C Evans (Flanagan 87), Dallas, McNair, Davis, Saville (Thompson 83), Lafferty (Magennis 67). **Booked:** Peacock-Farrell, J Evans, Smith
Referee: B Bastien (France). **Half-time:** 0-0

NORTHERN IRELAND 0 HOLLAND 0
Windsor Park (18,404); Saturday, November 16, 2019

Northern Ireland (4-2-3-1): Peacock-Farrell, Dallas, Cathcart, J Evans, Lewis (Thompson 81), C Evans (McGinn 70), Davis, Whyte, McNair, Saville (Smith 58), Magennis. **Booked:** Davis, Dallas
Holland (4-3-3): Cillessen, Veltman, De Light, Van Dijk, Blind, De Roon (Propper 37), Van de Beek. F De Jong, Berghuis (L De Jong 65), Babel (Ake 90), Promes. **Booked:** Veltman, De Roon
Referee: S Marciniak (Poland)

GERMANY 6 (Gnabry 19, 47, 60, Goretzka 43, 73, Brandt (90+1) NORTHERN IRELAND 1 (Smith 7)
Frankfurt (42,855); Tuesday, November 19, 2019

Germany (4-2-3-1): ter Stegen, Klostermann (Stark 65), Eme Can, Tah, Hector, Kimmich, Kroos, Goretzka (Serdar 73), Gundogan, Brandt, Gnabry (Amiri 81)
Northern Ireland (4-1-4-1): Peacock-Farrell, Smith, Cathcart, Flanagan, Ferguson, Davis, C Evans (C McLaughlin 65), McNair (Boyce 77), Thompson, Saville, Magennis (Lavery 83)
Referee: C Del Cerro (Spain). **Half-time:** 2-1

GROUP D

REPUBLIC OF IRELAND 1 (McGoldrick 85) SWITZERLAND 1 (Schar 74)
Aviva Stadium (44,111); Thursday, September 5, 2019

Republic of Ireland (4-2-3-1): Randolph, Coleman, Duffy, Keogh, Stevens, Whelan, Hourihane (Hogan 82), Robinson (Judge 58), Hendrick, McClean, McGoldrick (Browne 89). **Booked:** Stevens, Judge, Duffy
Switzerland (5-3-2): Sommer, Mbabu (Fernandes 90+3), Elvedi, Schar, Akanji, Rodriguez,

Zakaria, Xhaka, Freuler (Mehmedi 90), Embolo (Ajeti 86), Seferovic. **Booked:** Mbabu, Schar
Referee: C Del Cerro Grande (Spain). **Half-time:** 0-0

GEORGIA 0 REPUBLIC OF IRELAND 0
Tbilisi (24,385); Saturday, October 12, 2019

Georgia (4-2-3-1): Loria, Kakabadze, Kashia, Grigalava, Tabidze, Kiteishvili (Aburjania 90), Kankava, Okriashvili (Lobjanidze 79) Ananidze, Qazaishvili, Kviliraia (Shengelia 73). **Booked:** Grigalava
Republic of Ireland (4-2-3-1): Randolph, Coleman, Duffy, Egan, Doherty, Whelan Hourihane (D Williams 90+3), Robinson (Browne 73), Hendrick, McClean, Collins (*Connolly 78). **Booked:** Whelan
Referee: M Guida (Italy)

SWITZERLAND 2 (Seferovic 16, Duffy 90+3 og) REPUBLIC OF IRELAND 0
Geneva (24,766); Tuesday, October 15, 2019

Switzerland (3-4-2-1): Sommer, Elvedi, Schar, Akanji, Lichtsteiner (Freuler 70), Xhaka, Zakaria, Rodriguez, Embolo (Steffen 88), Mehmedi (Fernandes 28), Seferovic. **Booked:** Xhaka, Akanji
Republic of Ireland (3-1-4-2): Randolph, Egan, Duffy, Stevens, Whelan, Coleman, Hendrick, Browne, McClean, Connolly (Hogan 70), Collins (O'Dowda 46). **Booked:** Coleman, Browne, Hendrick, Duffy. **Sent off:** Coleman (76)
Referee: S Marciniak (Poland). **Half-time:** 1-0.

REPUBLIC OF IRELAND 1 (Doherty 85) DENMARK 1 (Braithwaite 73)
Aviva Stadium (51,700); Monday, November 18, 2019

Republic of Ireland (4-2-3-1): Randolph, Doherty, Duffy, Egan (Clark 46), Stevens, Whelan (Maguire 82), Hourihane (Robinson 68), Browne, Hendrick, McClean, McGoldrick. **Booked:** Whelan, McClean
Denmark (4-2-3-1): Schmeichel, Dalsgaard, Jorgensen, Kjaer, Stryger, Schone (Christensen 84), Delaney (Hojbjerg 13), Poulsen, Eriksen, Braithwaite, Cornelius (Dolberg 33). **Booked:** Schone
Referee: F Brych (Germany). **Half-time:** 0-0

GROUP E

WALES 2 (Pashaev 26 og, Bale 84) AZERBAIJAN 1 (Emreli 58)
Cardiff City Stadium (28,385); Friday, September 6, 2019

Wales (4-2-3-1): Hennessey C Roberts, Mepham, *Rodon, Taylor (B Davies 80), Ampadu (Vokes 75), Allen, Bale, Wilson (J Williams 63), James, T Lawrence. **Booked:** Mepham, Allen
Azerbaijan (4-2-3-1): Agayev, Pashayev, Medveded, Mustafazade, Krivotsuyk, Qarayev, Almeida (Eyubov 68), Emreli, Nazarov (Ramazanov 86), Rahimov (Khalilzade 73), Sheydaev. **Booked:** Nazarov, Almeida, Krivotsuyk
Referee: T Farrugia Cann (Malta). **Half-time:** 1-0

SLOVAKIA 1 (Kucka 53) WALES 1 (Moore 25)
Trnava (18,071); Thursday, October 10, 2019

Slovakia (4-3-3): Dubravka, Pekarik, Gyomber, Skriniar, Hancko, Kucka, Lobotka, Hamsik, Rusnak, Bozenik (Safranko 86), Mak (Haraslin 79). **Booked:** Gyomber. **Sent off:** Gyomber (88)
Wales (4-2-3-1): Hennessey, C Roberts, Lockyer, Rodon, B Davies, Ampadu (Morrell 57), Allen, Bale, J Williams (Wilson 66), James, Moore. **Booked:** Bale, Ampadu, J Williams, James
Referee: C Del Cerro (Spain). **Half-time:** 0-1

WALES 1 (Bale 45) CROATIA 1 (Vlasic 9)
Cardiff City Stadium (31,745); Sunday, October 13, 2019

Wales (4-2-3-1): Hennessey, C Roberts, Lockyer, Rodon, B Davies, Ampadu (Morrell 49),

Allen, Bale, J Williams (Wilson 68), James, Moore (T Roberts 86). **Booked**: Moore, Allen, James
Croatia (4-2-3-1): Livakovic, Jedvaj, Lovren, Vida, Barisic, Modric (Badelj 89), Kovacic (Rakitic 46), Perisic, Vlasic, Brekalo, Petkovic (Rebic 63). **Booked**: Vida, Lovren, Petkovic, Rakitic, Modric
Referee: B Kuipers (Holland). **Half-time**: 1-1

AZERBAIJAN 0 WALES 2 (Moore 10, Wilson 34)
Baku (8,622): Saturday, November 16
Azerbaijan (4-5-1): Balayev, Pashayev, Mustafazade, B Huseynov, Krivosyuk (Khalilzade 46), Abdullayev (Ramazanov 64), Nazarov (C Huseynov 82), Qarayev, Almeida, Rahimov, Seyadev. **Booked**: Nazarov, Seyadev, Rahimov, C Huseynov
Wales (4-2-3-1): Hennessey, C Roberts, Lockyer, Mepham, B Davies, Ampadu (Vaulks 87), Morrell, Bale (Ramsey 59), Wilson, James (Matondo 82), Moore. **Booked**: Ampadu, Morrell, Wilson, Matondo
Referee: D Aytekin (Germany). **Half-time**: 0-2

WALES 2 (Ramsey 15, 47) HUNGARY 0
Cardiff City Stadium (31,762);Tuesday, November 19, 2019
Wales (4-2-3-1): Hennessey, C Roberts, Lockyer, Mepham, B Davies, Allen Morrell (Ampadu 50), Bale (Wilson 88), Ramsey, James, Moore. **Booked**: Lockyer, James
Hungary (4-2-3-1): Gulacsi, Lovrncsics, Barath, Lang, Z Nagy, A Nagy (Kovacs 60), Patkai, Dzsudzsak (Varga 72), Szobosziai, Sallai (Holender 83), Szalai. **Booked**: Patkai, Kovacs
Referee: O Hategan (Romania). **Half-time**: 1-0

GROUP I

SCOTLAND 1 (McGinn 10) RUSSIA 2 (Dzyuba 40, O'Donnell 59 og)
Hampden Park (32,432); Friday, September 6, 2019
Scotland (4-3-3): Marshall, O'Donnell, Mulgrew, *Cooper, Robertson, McTominay (Phillips 78), McGinn (Christie 62), C McGregor, Forrest (McLean 62), McBurnie, Fraser. **Booked**: Cooper, McLean
Russia (4-2-3-1): Guilherme, Fernandes, Semenov, Dzhikija, Kudryashov, Ozdoev, Zobnin (Barinov 66), Ionov (Erokhin 80), Golovin (Akhmetov 89), Zhirkov, Dzyuba. **Booked**: Zobnin, Barinov, Akhmetov
Referee: A Sidiropoulos (Greece). **Half-time**: 1-1

SCOTLAND 0 BELGIUM 4 (Lukaku 9, Vermaelen 24, Alderweireld 32, De Bruyne 82)
Hampden Park (25,524); Monday, September 9, 2019
Scotland (4-4-2): Marshall, O'Donnell, Mulgrew, Cooper, Robertson, Snodgrass, McLean, McTominay, C McGregor (Armstrong 68), Christie (McGinn 86), Phillips (Russell 77). **Booked**: O'Donnell, McTominay
Belgium (3-4-2-1): Courtois, Alderweireld, Vermaelen, Vertonghen, Meunier (Raman 90), Dendoncker, Tielemans (Verschaeren 86), Chadli (Carrasco 78), De Bruyne, Mertens, Lukaku. **Booked**: Vermaelen
Referee: P Gil (Poland). **Half-time**: 0-3

RUSSIA 4 (Dzyuba 57, 70, Ozdoev 60, Golovin 84) SCOTLAND 0
Moscow (65,703); Thursday, October 10, 2019
Russia (4-2-3-1): Guilherme, Fernandes, Semenov, Dzhikija, Kudryashov, Ozdoev, Barinov, Ionov (Akhmetov 79), Golovin, Zhirkov (Cheryshev 66), Dzyuba (Komlichenko 86).
Scotland (4-2-3-1): Marshall, Palmer, *Devlin, Mulgrew, Robertson, C McGregor, *Fleck (Armstrong 81), Fraser (Christie 68), McGinn, Snodgrass, Burke (*Shankland 46). **Booked**: Fleck
Referee: J Kehlet (Denmark). **Half-time**: 0-0

SCOTLAND 6 (McGinn 12, 27, 45, Shankland 65, Findlay 67, Armstrong 86) **SAN MARINO 0**
Hampden Park (20,699); Sunday, October 13, 2019
Scotland (4-2-3-1): McLaughlin, Palmer, Devlin, *Findlay, Robertson, McTominay, C McGregor (Russell 67), Christie, McGinn (Armstrong 67), Forrest, Shankland. **Booked:** McTominay
San Marino (4-2-3-1): Simoncini, Battistini, Censoni, Brolli, D'Addario (Grandoni 46), Mularoni, Golinucci, Gasperoni, Berardi (Ceccaroli 80), Giardi (Hirsch 46), Nanni. **Booked:** Giardi, Golinucci
Referee: J Brisard (France). **Half-time:** 3-0

CYPRUS 1 (Efrem 47) **SCOTLAND 2** (Christie 12, McGinn 53)
Nicosia (7,595): Saturday, November 16, 2019
Cyprus (5-4-1): Pardo, Demetriou, Karo (Kastanos 42) Merkis, Kousoulos, Ioannou, Kosti. Papoulis, Kyriakou (Theodorou 77), Efrem (Spoljaric 72), Sotiriou
Scotland (4-2-3-1): Marshall, Palmer, *Gallagher, McKenna, Taylor, Jack, C McGregor, Christie (Devlin 90+2), McGinn, Forrest (Burke 71), Naismith (McBurnie 62). **Booked:** C McGregor, McKenna. McGinn, Taylor, Palmer
Referee: H Lechner (Austria). **Half-time:** 0-1

SCOTLAND 3 (McGinn 48, 90+1, Naismith 64) **KAZAKHSTAN 1** (Zainutdinov 34)
Hampden Park (19,515); Tuesday, November 19, 2019
Scotland (4-2-3-1): Marshall, Palmer, Gallagher, McKenna, Taylor, Jack, C McGregor, Christie (Fleck 83), McGinn (Armstrong 90+2), Forrest, Naismith (Burke 77). **Booked:** Gallagher
Kazakhstan (3-4-2-1): Nepogodov, Marochkin, Maliy. Logvinenko, Suyumbayev, Pertsukh (Kuat 74), Abiken, Shomko, Zainutdinov, Islamkhan (Fedin 74), Shchetkin (Aymbetov 83). **Booked:** Islamkhan, Abiken, Marochkin, Kuat
Referee: B Nijhuis (Holland): **Half-time:** 0-1

QUALIFYING TABLES

GROUP A

	P	W	D	L	F	A	Pts
England Q	8	7	0	1	37	6	21
Czech Republic Q	8	5	0	3	13	11	15
Kosovo	8	3	2	3	13	16	11
Bulgaria	8	1	3	4	6	17	6
Montenegro	8	0	3	5	3	22	3

GROUP B

Ukraine Q	8	6	2	0	17	4	20
Portugal Q	8	5	2	1	22	6	17
Serbia	8	4	2	2	17	17	14
Luxembourg	8	1	1	6	7	16	4
Lithuania	8	0	1	7	5	25	1

GROUP C

Germany Q	8	7	0	1	30	7	21
Holland Q	8	6	1	1	24	7	19
Northern Ireland	8	4	1	3	9	13	13
Belarus	8	1	1	6	4	16	4
Estonia	8	0	1	7	2	26	1

GROUP D

Switzerland Q	8	5	2	1	19	6	17
Denmark Q	8	4	4	0	23	6	16
Republic of Ireland	8	3	4	1	7	5	13

Georgia	8	2	2	4	7	11	8
Gibraltar	8	0	0	8	3	31	0

GROUP E

Croatia Q	8	5	2	1	17	7	17
Wales Q	8	4	2	2	10	6	14
Slovakia	8	4	1	3	13	11	13
Hungary	8	4	0	4	8	11	12
Azerbaijan	8	0	1	7	5	18	1

GROUP F

Spain Q	10	8	2	0	31	5	26
Sweden Q	10	6	3	1	23	9	21
Norway	10	4	5	1	19	11	17
Romania	10	4	2	4	17	15	14
Faroe Islands	10	1	0	9	4	30	3
Malta	10	1	0	89	3	27	3

GROUP G

Poland Q	10	8	1	1	18	5	25
Austria Q	10	6	1	3	19	9	19
N Macedonia	10	4	2	4	12	13	14
Slovenia	10	4	2	4	16	11	14
Israel	10	3	2	5	16	18	11
Latvia	10	1	0	9	3	28	3

GROUP H

France Q	10	8	1	1	25	6	25
Turkey Q	10	7	2	1	18	3	23
Iceland	10	6	1	3	14	11	19
Albania	10	4	1	5	16	14	13
Andorra	10	1	1	8	3	20	4
Moldova	10	1	0	9	4	26	3

GROUP I

Belgium Q	10	10	0	0	40	3	30
Russia Q	10	8	0	2	33	8	24
Scotland	10	5	0	5	16	19	15
Cyprus	10	3	1	6	15	20	10
Kazakhstan	10	3	1	6	13	17	10
San Marino	10	0	0	10	1	51	0

GROUP J

Italy Q	10	10	0	0	37	4	30
Finland Q	10	6	0	4	16	10	18
Greece	10	4	2	4	12	14	14
Bosnia-Herz	10	4	1	5	20	17	13
Armenia	10	3	1	6	14	25	10
Liechtenstein	10	0	2	8	2	31	2

Play-offs:
Path A: Iceland v Romania; *Bulgaria v Hungary. **Path B**: *Bosnia-Herzegovina v Northern Ireland; Slovakia v Republic of Ireland. **Path C**: Scotland v Israel; *Norway v Serbia. **Path** D: *Georgia v Belarus; North Macedonia v Kosovo
*Winners to host final

FRIENDLY INTERNATIONALS

NORTHERN IRELAND 1 (Malget 37 og) LUXEMBOURG 0
Windsor Park (14,108); Thursday, September 5, 2019
Northern Ireland (4-3-3): Peacock-Farrell (McGovern 67), C McLaughlin, Flanagan, *Brown, Ferguson, C Evans (Donnelly 67), Thompson (Davis 88), Saville (*McCalmont 60), Whyte (*Galbraith 89), Magennis, Lafferty (Lavery 59). **Booked**: Magennis, Flanagan
Luxembourg (4-4-2): Moris (Schon 46), Jans, Malget (Hall 46), Gerson, Carlson, Sinani (Da Mota 74), Barreiro (Philipps 73), V Thill (Bohnert 86), Rodrigues, Deville (Turpel 60).
Booked: Hall, Da Mota
Referee: B Markham-Jones (Wales). **Half-time**: 1-0

WALES 1 (James 17) BELARUS 0
Cardiff City Stadium (7,666); Monday, September 9, 2019
Wales (4-2-3-1): Ward, C Roberts, Mepham (Lockyer 76), Rodon, B Davies (Gunter 90+1), Allen, *Morrell, Wilson (Vaulks 88), J Williams, James (Bale 50), *Moore (Vokes 75)
Belarus (4-2-3-1): Plotnikov, Zolotov, Volkov, Politevich, Polyakov, Yablonski (Maevski 46), Baga (Dragun 70), Kovalev (Ngome 46), Bakhar (Klimovich 85), Skavysh (Pechenin 76), Signevich (Stasevich 70). **Booked**: Zolotov
Referee: W Collum (Scotland). **Half-time**: 1-0

REPUBLIC OF IRELAND 3 (Browne 56, K Long 83, Collins 86) BULGARIA 1 (I Popov 67 pen)
Aviva Stadium (18,259); Tuesday, September 10, 2019
Republic of Ireland (4-3-3): *Travers (*O'Hara 75), Christie, Egan, K Long, Hourihane (McClean 68), Browne, Judge (*Byrne 58), *Cullen, O'Dowda (Stevens 76), Hogan (*Collins 59), Curtis (Hendrick 76). **Booked**: Collins
Bulgaria (5-4-1): Ivanov, Pashov, K Dimitrov (Panayotov 80), Slavchev, Nedyalkov (Bozhikov 59), Goranov, N Dimitrov (Wanderson 59), G Milanov (I Popov 46), K Malinov (Terziev 80), Mladenov (Despodov 68), Kraev
Referee: T Welz (Germany). **Half-time**: 0-0

CZECH REPUBLIC 2 (Darida 67, Kral 68) NORTHERN IRELAND 3 (McNair 9, 40, J Evans 23)
Prague (9,139); Monday, October 14, 2019
Czech Republic (4-2-3-1): Pavlenka, Reznik, Simic (Celustka 46), Kudela, Krejci (Masopust 75), Husbauer (Schick 65), Kalvach (Darida 46), Zrmhal (Boril 46), Kral, Kopic, Krmencik (Ondrasek 46). **Booked**: Ondrasek
Northern Ireland (3-5-2): McGovern, Cathcart, J Evans, Flanagan, C McLaughlin, McNair, Davis (C Evans 65), Thompson (Saville 65), Dallas, Boyce (Magennis 71), Whyte (McGinn 87).
Booked: McGovern
Referee: I Kruzlaik (Slovakia). **Half-time**: 0-3

REPUBLIC OF IRELAND 3 (Williams 45, Maguire 52, Robinson 75) NEW ZEALAND 1 (McCowatt 30)
Aviva Stadium (18,728); Thursday, November 14, 2019
Republic of Ireland (4-2-3-1): O'Hara (Travers 65), *O'Connor, K Long, Clark, D Williams (O'Dowda 56), Browne (Hourihane 64), Cullen, Brady, Byrne (Judge 63), Maguire (Collins 74), *Parrott (Robinson 63)
New Zealand (4-3-3): Marinovic, Roux (Payne 90+2), Reid (Tuiloma 46), Boxall (Smith 74), Cacace, Singh, Bell, Thomas (McGlinchey 74), McCowatt (Collier 85), Wood (De Jong 76), Just
Referee: R Jenkins (Wales). **Half-time**: 1-1

OTHER BRITISH & IRISH INTERNATIONAL RESULTS

ENGLAND

v ALBANIA

1989	Tirana (WC)	2	0
1989	Wembley (WC)	5	0
2001	Tirana (WC)	3	1
2001	Newcastle (WC)	2	0

v ALGERIA

2010	Cape Town (WC)	0	0

v ANDORRA

2006	Old Trafford (EC)	5	0
2007	Barcelona (EC)	3	0
2008	Barcelona (WC)	2	0
2009	Wembley (WC)	6	0

v ARGENTINA

1951	Wembley	2	1
1953*	Buenos Aires	0	0
1962	Rancagua (WC)	3	1
1964	Rio de Janeiro	0	1
1966	Wembley (WC)	1	0
1974	Wembley	2	2
1977	Buenos Aires	1	1
1980	Wembley	3	1
1986	Mexico City (WC)	1	2
1991	Wembley	2	2
1998†	St Etienne (WC)	2	2
2000	Wembley	0	0
2002	Sapporo (WC)	1	0
2005	Geneva	3	2

(*Abandoned after 21 mins – rain)
(† England lost 3-4 on pens)

v AUSTRALIA

1980	Sydney	2	1
1983	Sydney	0	0
1983	Brisbane	1	0
1983	Melbourne	1	1
1991	Sydney	1	0
2003	West Ham	1	3
2016	Sunderland	2	1

v AUSTRIA

1908	Vienna	6	1
1908	Vienna	11	1
1909	Vienna	8	1
1930	Vienna	0	0
1932	Stamford Bridge	4	3
1936	Vienna	1	2
1951	Wembley	2	2
1952	Vienna	3	2
1958	Boras (WC)	2	2
1961	Vienna	1	3
1962	Wembley	3	1
1965	Wembley	2	3
1967	Vienna	1	0
1973	Wembley	7	0
1979	Vienna	3	4
2004	Vienna (WC)	2	2
2005	Old Trafford (WC)	1	0
2007	Vienna	1	0

v AZERBAIJAN

2004	Baku (WC)	1	0
2005	Newcastle (WC)	2	0

v BELARUS

2008	Minsk (WC)	3	1
2009	Wembley (WC)	3	0

v BELGIUM

1921	Brussels	2	0
1923	Highbury	6	1
1923	Antwerp	2	2
1924	West Bromwich	4	0
1926	Antwerp	5	3
1927	Brussels	9	1
1928	Antwerp	3	1
1929	Brussels	5	1
1931	Brussels	4	1
1936	Brussels	2	3
1947	Brussels	5	2
1950	Brussels	4	1
1952	Wembley	5	0
1954	Basle (WC)	4	4
1964	Wembley	2	2
1970	Brussels	3	1
1980	Turin (EC)	1	1
1990	Bologna (WC)	1	0
1998*	Casablanca	0	0
1999	Sunderland	2	1
2012	Wembley	1	0
2018	Kaliningrad (WC)	0	1
2018	St Petersburg (WC)	0	2

(*England lost 3-4 on pens)

v BOHEMIA

1908	Prague	4	0

v BRAZIL

Year	Venue		
1956	Wembley	4	2
1958	Gothenburg (WC)	0	0
1959	Rio de Janeiro	0	2
1962	Vina del Mar (WC)	1	3
1963	Wembley	1	1
1964	Rio de Janeiro	1	5
1969	Rio de Janeiro	1	2
1970	Guadalajara (WC)	0	1
1976	Los Angeles	0	1
1977	Rio de Janeiro	0	0
1978	Wembley	1	1
1981	Wembley	0	1
1984	Rio de Janeiro	2	0
1987	Wembley	1	1
1990	Wembley	1	0
1992	Wembley	1	1
1993	Washington	1	1
1995	Wembley	1	3
1997	Paris (TF)	0	1
2000	Wembley	1	1
2002	Shizuoka (WC)	1	2
2007	Wembley	1	1
2009	Doha	0	1
2013	Wembley	2	1
2013	Rio de Janeiro	2	2
2017	Wembley	0	0

v BULGARIA

Year	Venue		
1962	Rancagua (WC)	0	0
1968	Wembley	1	1
1974	Sofia	1	0
1979	Sofia (EC)	3	0
1979	Wembley (EC)	2	0
1996	Wembley	1	0
1998	Wembley (EC)	0	0
1999	Sofia (EC)	1	1
2010	Wembley (EC)	4	0
2011	Sofia (EC)	3	0
2019	Wembley (EC)	4	0
2019	Sofia (EC)	6	0

v CAMEROON

Year	Venue		
1990	Naples (WC)	3	2
1991	Wembley	2	0
1997	Wembley	2	0
2002	Kobe (Japan)	2	2

v CANADA

Year	Venue		
1986	Vancouver	1	0

v CHILE

Year	Venue		
1950	Rio de Janeiro (WC)	2	0

1953	Santiago	2	1
1984	Santiago	0	0
1989	Wembley	0	0
1998	Wembley	0	2
2013	Wembley	0	2

v CHINA

Year	Venue		
1996	Beijing	3	0

v CIS
(formerly Soviet Union)

Year	Venue		
1992	Moscow	2	2

v COLOMBIA

Year	Venue		
1970	Bogota	4	0
1988	Wembley	1	1
1995	Wembley	0	0
1998	Lens (WC)	2	0
2005	New York	3	2
2018†	Moscow (WC)	1	1

(† England won 4-3 on pens)

v COSTA RICA

Year	Venue		
2014	Belo Horizonte (WC)	0	0
2018	Leeds	2	0

v CROATIA

Year	Venue		
1995	Wembley	0	0
2003	Ipswich	3	1
2004	Lisbon (EC)	4	2
2006	Zagreb (EC)	0	2
2007	Wembley (EC)	2	3
2008	Zagreb (WC)	4	1
2009	Wembley (WC)	5	1
2018	Moscow (WC)	1	2
2018	Rijeka (NL)	0	0
2018	Wembley (NL)	2	1

v CYPRUS

Year	Venue		
1975	Wembley (EC)	5	0
1975	Limassol (EC)	1	0

v CZECH REPUBLIC

Year	Venue		
1998	Wembley	2	0
2008	Wembley	2	2
2019	Wembley (EC)	5	0
2019	Prague (EC)	1	2

v CZECHOSLOVAKIA

Year	Venue		
1934	Prague	1	2
1937	White Hart Lane	5	4
1963	Bratislava	4	2
1966	Wembley	0	0

1970	Guadalajara (WC)	1	0
1973	Prague	1	1
1974	Wembley (EC)	3	0
1975*	Bratislava (EC)	1	2
1978	Wembley (EC)	1	0
1982	Bilbao (WC)	2	0
1990	Wembley	4	2
1992	Prague	2	2

(* Aband 0-0, 17 mins prev day – fog)

v DENMARK

1948	Copenhagen	0	0
1955	Copenhagen	5	1
1956	W'hampton (WC)	5	2
1957	Copenhagen (WC)	4	1
1966	Copenhagen	2	0
1978	Copenhagen (EC)	4	3
1979	Wembley (EC)	1	0
1982	Copenhagen (EC)	2	2
1983	Wembley (EC)	0	1
1988	Wembley	1	0
1989	Copenhagen	1	1
1990	Wembley	1	0
1992	Malmo (EC)	0	0
1994	Wembley	1	0
2002	Niigata (WC)	3	0
2003	Old Trafford	2	3
2005	Copenhagen	1	4
2011	Copenhagen	2	1
2014	Wembley	1	0

v EAST GERMANY

1963	Leipzig	2	1
1970	Wembley	3	1
1974	Leipzig	1	1
1984	Wembley	1	0

v ECUADOR

1970	Quito	2	0
2006	Stuttgart (WC)	1	0
2014	Miami	2	2

v EGYPT

1986	Cairo	4	0
1990	Cagliari (WC)	1	0
2010	Wembley	3	1

v ESTONIA

2007	Tallinn (EC)	3	0
2007	Wembley (EC)	3	0
2014	Tallinn (EC)	1	0
2015	Wembley (EC)	2	0

v FIFA

1938	Highbury	3	0
1953	Wembley	4	4
1963	Wembley	2	1

v FINLAND

1937	Helsinki	8	0
1956	Helsinki	5	1
1966	Helsinki	3	0
1976	Helsinki (WC)	4	1
1976	Wembley (WC)	2	1
1982	Helsinki	4	1
1984	Wembley (WC)	5	0
1985	Helsinki (WC)	1	1
1992	Helsinki	2	1
2000	Helsinki (WC)	0	0
2001	Liverpool (WC)	2	1

v FRANCE

1923	Paris	4	1
1924	Paris	3	1
1925	Paris	3	2
1927	Paris	6	0
1928	Paris	5	1
1929	Paris	4	1
1931	Paris	2	5
1933	White Hart Lane	4	1
1938	Paris	4	2
1947	Highbury	3	0
1949	Paris	3	1
1951	Highbury	2	2
1955	Paris	0	1
1957	Wembley	4	0
1962	Hillsborough (EC)	1	1
1963	Paris (EC)	2	5
1966	Wembley (WC)	2	0
1969	Wembley	5	0
1982	Bilbao (WC)	3	1
1984	Paris	0	2
1992	Wembley	2	0
1992	Malmo (EC)	0	0
1997	Montpellier (TF)	1	0
1999	Wembley	0	2
2000	Paris	1	1
2004	Lisbon (EC)	1	2
2008	Paris	0	1
2010	Wembley	1	2
2012	Donetsk (EC)	1	1
2015	Wembley	2	0
2017	Paris	2	3

v GEORGIA

| 1996 | Tbilisi (WC) | 2 | 0 |
| 1997 | Wembley (WC) | 2 | 0 |

v GERMANY/WEST GERMANY

Year	Venue		
1930	Berlin	3	3
1935	White Hart Lane	3	0
1938	Berlin	6	3
1954	Wembley	3	1
1956	Berlin	3	1
1965	Nuremberg	1	0
1966	Wembley	1	0
1966	Wembley (WCF)	4	2
1968	Hanover	0	1
1970	Leon (WC)	2	3
1972	Wembley (EC)	1	3
1972	Berlin (EC)	0	0
1975	Wembley	2	0
1978	Munich	1	2
1982	Madrid (WC)	0	0
1982	Wembley	1	2
1985	Mexico City	3	0
1987	Dusseldorf	1	3
1990*	Turin (WC)	1	1
1991	Wembley	0	1
1993	Detroit	1	2
1996†	Wembley (EC)	1	1
2000	Charleroi (EC)	1	0
2000	Wembley (WC)	0	1
2001	Munich (WC)	5	1
2007	Wembley	1	2
2008	Berlin	2	1
2010	Bloemfontein (WC)	1	4
2012	Donetsk (EC)	1	1
2013	Wembley	0	1
2016	Berlin	3	2
2017	Dortmund	0	1
2017	Wembley	0	0

(*England lost 3-4 on pens)
(† England lost 5-6 on pens)

v GHANA

2011	Wembley	1	1

v GREECE

1971	Wembley (EC)	3	0
1971	Athens (EC)	2	0
1982	Salonika (EC)	3	0
1983	Wembley (EC)	0	0
1989	Athens	2	1
1994	Wembley	5	0
2001	Athens (WC)	2	0
2001	Old Trafford (WC)	2	2
2006	Old Trafford	4	0

v HOLLAND

1935	Amsterdam	1	0
1946	Huddersfield	8	2
1964	Amsterdam	1	1
1969	Amsterdam	1	0
1970	Wembley	0	0
1977	Wembley	0	2
1982	Wembley	2	0
1988	Wembley	2	2
1988	Dusseldorf (EC)	1	3
1990	Cagliari (WC)	0	0
1993	Wembley (WC)	2	2
1993	Rotterdam (WC)	0	2
1996	Wembley (EC)	4	1
2001	White Hart Lane	0	2
2002	Amsterdam	1	1
2005	Villa Park	0	0
2006	Amsterdam	1	1
2009	Amsterdam	2	2
2012	Wembley	2	3
2016	Wembley	1	2
2018	Amsterdam	1	0
2019	Guimaraes (NL)	1	3

v HONDURAS

2014	Miami	0	0

v HUNGARY

1908	Budapest	7	0
1909	Budapest	4	2
1909	Budapest	8	2
1934	Budapest	1	2
1936	Highbury	6	2
1953	Wembley	3	6
1954	Budapest	1	7
1960	Budapest	0	2
1962	Rancagua (WC)	1	2
1965	Wembley	1	0
1978	Wembley	4	1
1981	Budapest (WC)	3	1
1981	Wembley (WC)	1	0
1983	Wembley (EC)	2	0
1983	Budapest (EC)	3	0
1988	Budapest	0	0
1990	Wembley	1	0
1992	Budapest	1	0
1996	Wembley	3	0
1999	Budapest	1	1
2006	Old Trafford	3	1
2010	Wembley	2	1

v ICELAND

1982	Reykjavik	1	1
2004	City of Manchester	6	1
2016	Nice (EC)	1	2

241

v ISRAEL

1986	Tel Aviv	2	1
1988	Tel Aviv	0	0
2006	Tel Aviv (EC)	0	0
2007	Wembley (EC)	3	0

v ITALY

1933	Rome	1	1
1934	Highbury	3	2
1939	Milan	2	2
1948	Turin	4	0
1949	White Hart Lane	2	0
1952	Florence	1	1
1959	Wembley	2	2
1961	Rome	3	2
1973	Turin	0	2
1973	Wembley	0	1
1976	New York	3	2
1976	Rome (WC)	0	2
1977	Wembley (WC)	2	0
1980	Turin (EC)	0	1
1985	Mexico City	1	2
1989	Wembley	0	0
1990	Bari (WC)	1	2
1996	Wembley (WC)	0	1
1997	Nantes (TF)	2	0
1997	Rome (WC)	0	0
2000	Turin	0	1
2002	Leeds	1	2
2012*	Kiev (EC)	0	0
2012	Berne	2	1
2014	Manaus (WC)	1	2
2015	Turin	1	1
2018	Wembley	1	1
(*England lost 2-4 on pens)			

v JAMAICA

2006	Old Trafford	6	0

v JAPAN

1995	Wembley	2	1
2004	City of Manchester	1	1
2010	Graz	2	1

v KAZAKHSTAN

2008	Wembley (WC)	5	1
2009	Almaty (WC)	4	0

v KOSOVO

2019	Southampton (EC)	5	3
2019	Pristina (EC)	4	0

v KUWAIT

1982	Bilbao (WC)	1	0

v LIECHTENSTEIN

2003	Vaduz (EC)	2	0
2003	Old Trafford (EC)	2	0

v LITHUANIA

2015	Wembley (EC)	4	0
2015	Vilnius (EC)	3	0
2017	Wembley (WC)	2	0
2017	Vilnius (WC)	1	0

v LUXEMBOURG

1927	Luxembourg	5	2
1960	Luxembourg (WC)	9	0
1961	Highbury (WC)	4	1
1977	Wembley (WC)	5	0
1977	Luxembourg (WC)	2	0
1982	Wembley (EC)	9	0
1983	Luxembourg (EC)	4	0
1998	Luxembourg (EC)	3	0
1999	Wembley (EC)	6	0

v MACEDONIA

2002	Southampton (EC)	2	2
2003	Skopje (EC)	2	1
2006	Skopje (EC)	1	0
2006	Old Trafford (EC)	0	0

v MALAYSIA

1991	Kuala Lumpur	4	2

v MALTA

1971	Valletta (EC)	1	0
1971	Wembley (EC)	5	0
2000	Valletta	2	1
2016	Wembley (WC)	2	0
2017	Ta'Qali (WC)	4	0

v MEXICO

1959	Mexico City	1	2
1961	Wembley	8	0
1966	Wembley (WC)	2	0
1969	Mexico City	0	0
1985	Mexico City	0	1
1986	Los Angeles	3	0
1997	Wembley	2	0
2001	Derby	4	0
2010	Wembley	3	1

v MOLDOVA

1996	Kishinev	3	0
1997	Wembley (WC)	4	0
2012	Chisinu (WC)	5	0
2013	Wembley (WC)	4	0

v MONTENEGRO

2010	Wembley (EC)	0	0
2011	Podgorica (EC)	2	2
2013	Podgorica (WC)	1	1
2013	Wembley (WC)	4	1
2019	Podgorica (EC)	5	1
2019	Wembley (EC)	7	0
(England's 1,000th international)			

v MOROCCO

1986	Monterrey (WC)	0	0
1998	Casablanca	1	0

v NEW ZEALAND

1991	Auckland	1	0
1991	Wellington	2	0

v NIGERIA

1994	Wembley	1	0
2002	Osaka (WC)	0	0
2018	Wembley	2	1

v NORWAY

1937	Oslo	6	0
1938	Newcastle	4	0
1949	Oslo	4	1
1966	Oslo	6	1
1980	Wembley (WC)	4	0
1981	Oslo (WC)	1	2
1992	Wembley (WC)	1	1
1993	Oslo (WC)	0	2
1994	Wembley	0	0
1995	Oslo	0	0
2012	Oslo	1	0
2014	Wembley	1	0

v PANAMA

2018	Nizhny Novgorod (WC)	6	1

v PARAGUAY

1986	Mexico City (WC)	3	0
2002	Anfield	4	0
2006	Frankfurt (WC)	1	0

v PERU

1959	Lima	1	4
1961	Lima	4	0

2014	Wembley	3	0

v POLAND

1966	Goodison Park	1	1
1966	Chorzow	1	0
1973	Chorzow (WC)	0	2
1973	Wembley (WC)	1	1
1986	Monterrey (WC)	3	0
1989	Wembley (WC)	3	0
1989	Katowice (WC)	0	0
1990	Wembley (EC)	2	0
1991	Poznan (EC)	1	1
1993	Chorzow (WC)	1	1
1993	Wembley (WC)	3	0
1996	Wembley (WC)	2	1
1997	Katowice (WC)	2	0
1999	Wembley (EC)	3	1
1999	Warsaw (EC)	0	0
2004	Katowice (WC)	2	1
2005	Old Trafford (WC)	2	1
2012	Warsaw (WC)	1	1
2013	Wembley (WC)	2	0

v PORTUGAL

1947	Lisbon	10	0
1950	Lisbon	5	3
1951	Goodison Park	5	2
1955	Oporto	1	3
1958	Wembley	2	1
1961	Lisbon (WC)	1	1
1961	Wembley (WC)	2	0
1964	Lisbon	4	3
1964	Sao Paulo	1	1
1966	Wembley (WC)	2	1
1969	Wembley	1	0
1974	Lisbon	0	0
1974	Wembley (EC)	0	0
1975	Lisbon (EC)	1	1
1986	Monterrey (WC)	0	1
1995	Wembley	1	1
1998	Wembley	3	0
2000	Eindhoven (EC)	2	3
2002	Villa Park	1	1
2004	Faro	1	1
2004*	Lisbon (EC)	2	2
2006†	Gelsenkirchen (WC)	0	0
2016	Wembley	1	0
(† England lost 1–3 on pens)			
(*England lost 5–6 on pens)			

v REPUBLIC OF IRELAND

1946	Dublin	1	0
1949	Goodison Park	0	2
1957	Wembley (WC)	5	1

1957	Dublin (WC)	1	1
1964	Dublin	3	1
1977	Wembley	1	1
1978	Dublin (EC)	1	1
1980	Wembley (EC)	2	0
1985	Wembley	2	1
1988	Stuttgart (EC)	0	1
1990	Cagliari (WC)	1	1
1990	Dublin (EC)	1	1
1991	Wembley (EC)	1	1
1995*	Dublin	0	1
2013	Wembley	1	1
2015	Dublin	0	0

(*Abandoned 27 mins – crowd riot)

v ROMANIA

1939	Bucharest	2	0
1968	Bucharest	0	0
1969	Wembley	1	1
1970	Guadalajara (WC)	1	0
1980	Bucharest (WC)	1	2
1981	Wembley (WC)	0	0
1985	Bucharest (WC)	0	0
1985	Wembley (WC)	1	1
1994	Wembley	1	1
1998	Toulouse (WC)	1	2
2000	Charleroi (EC)	2	3

v RUSSIA

2007	Wembley (EC)	3	0
2007	Moscow (EC)	1	2
2016	Marseille (EC)	1	1

v SAN MARINO

1992	Wembley (WC)	6	0
1993	Bologna (WC)	7	1
2012	Wembley (WC)	5	0
2013	Serravalle (WC)	8	0
2014	Wembley (EC)	5	0
2015	Serravalle (EC)	6	0

v SAUDI ARABIA

| 1988 | Riyadh | 1 | 1 |
| 1998 | Wembley | 0 | 0 |

v SERBIA-MONTENEGRO

| 2003 | Leicester | 2 | 1 |

v SLOVAKIA

2002	Bratislava (EC)	2	1
2003	Middlesbrough (EC)	2	1
2009	Wembley	4	0
2016	St Etienne (EC)	0	0

| 2016 | Trnava (WC) | 1 | 0 |
| 2017 | Wembley (WC) | 2 | 1 |

v SLOVENIA

2009	Wembley	2	1
2010	Port Elizabeth (WC)	1	0
2014	Wembley (EC)	3	1
2015	Ljubljana (EC)	3	2
2016	Ljubljana (WC)	0	0
2017	Wembley (WC)	1	0

v SOUTH AFRICA

| 1997 | Old Trafford | 2 | 1 |
| 2003 | Durban | 2 | 1 |

v SOUTH KOREA

| 2002 | Seoguipo | 1 | 1 |

v SOVIET UNION (see also CIS)

1958	Moscow	1	1
1958	Gothenburg (WC)	2	2
1958	Gothenburg (WC)	0	1
1958	Wembley	5	0
1967	Wembley	2	2
1968	Rome (EC)	2	0
1973	Moscow	2	1
1984	Wembley	0	2
1986	Tbilisi	1	0
1988	Frankfurt (EC)	1	3
1991	Wembley	3	1

v SPAIN

1929	Madrid	3	4
1931	Highbury	7	1
1950	Rio de Janeiro (WC)	0	1
1955	Madrid	1	1
1955	Wembley	4	1
1960	Madrid	0	3
1960	Wembley	4	2
1965	Madrid	2	0
1967	Wembley	2	0
1968	Wembley (EC)	1	0
1968	Madrid (EC)	2	1
1980	Barcelona	2	0
1980	Naples (EC)	2	1
1981	Wembley	1	2
1982	Madrid (WC)	0	0
1987	Madrid	4	2
1992	Santander	0	1
1996*	Wembley (EC)	0	0
2001	Villa Park	3	0
2004	Madrid	0	1
2007	Old Trafford	0	1

2009	Seville	0	2
2011	Wembley	1	0
2015	Alicante	0	2
2016	Wembley	2	2
(*England won 4-2 on pens)			
2018	Wembley (NL)	1	2
2018	Seville (NL)	3	2

v SWEDEN

1923	Stockholm	4	2
1923	Stockholm	3	1
1937	Stockholm	4	0
1948	Highbury	4	2
1949	Stockholm	1	3
1956	Stockholm	0	0
1959	Wembley	2	3
1965	Gothenburg	2	1
1968	Wembley	3	1
1979	Stockholm	0	0
1986	Stockholm	0	1
1988	Wembley (WC)	0	0
1989	Stockholm (WC)	0	0
1992	Stockholm (EC)	1	2
1995	Leeds	3	3
1998	Stockholm (EC)	1	2
1999	Wembley (EC)	0	0
2001	Old Trafford	1	1
2002	Saitama (WC)	1	1
2004	Gothenburg	0	1
2006	Cologne (WC)	2	2
2011	Wembley	1	0
2012	Kiev (EC)	3	2
2012	Stockholm	2	4
2018	Samara (WC)	2	0

v SWITZERLAND

1933	Berne	4	0
1938	Zurich	1	2
1947	Zurich	0	1
1949	Highbury	6	0
1952	Zurich	3	0
1954	Berne (WC)	2	0
1962	Wembley	3	1
1963	Basle	8	1
1971	Basle (EC)	3	2
1971	Wembley (EC)	1	1
1975	Basle	2	1
1977	Wembley	0	0
1980	Wembley (WC)	2	1
1981	Basle (WC)	1	2
1988	Lausanne	1	0
1995	Wembley	3	1
1996	Wembley (EC)	1	1
1998	Berne	1	1

2004	Coimbra (EC)	3	0
2008	Wembley	2	1
2010	Basle (EC)	3	1
2011	Wembley (EC)	2	2
2014	Basle (EC)	2	0
2015	Wembley (EC)	2	0
2018	Leicester	1	0
2019*	Guimaraes (NL)	0	0
(* England won 6-5 on pens)			

v TRINIDAD & TOBAGO

2006	Nuremberg (WC)	2	0
2008	Port of Spain	3	0

v TUNISIA

1990	Tunis	1	1
1998	Marseille (WC)	2	0
2018	Volgograd (WC)	2	1

v TURKEY

1984	Istanbul (WC)	8	0
1985	Wembley (WC)	5	0
1987	Izmir (EC)	0	0
1987	Wembley (EC)	8	0
1991	Izmir (EC)	1	0
1991	Wembley (EC)	1	0
1992	Wembley (WC)	4	0
1993	Izmir (WC)	2	0
2003	Sunderland (EC)	2	0
2003	Istanbul (EC)	0	0
2016	Etihad Stadium	2	1

v UKRAINE

2000	Wembley	2	0
2004	Newcastle	3	0
2009	Wembley (WC)	2	1
2009	Dnipropetrovski (WC)	0	1
2012	Donetsk (EC)	1	0
2012	Wembley (WC)	1	1
2013	Kiev (WC)	0	0

v URUGUAY

1953	Montevideo	1	2
1954	Basle (WC)	2	4
1964	Wembley	2	1
1966	Wembley (WC)	0	0
1969	Montevideo	2	1
1977	Montevideo	0	0
1984	Montevideo	0	2
1990	Wembley	1	2
1995	Wembley	0	0
2006	Anfield	2	1
2014	Sao Paulo (WC)	1	2

v USA

1950	Belo Horizonte (WC)	0	1
1953	New York	6	3
1959	Los Angeles	8	1
1964	New York	10	0
1985	Los Angeles	5	0
1993	Boston	0	2
1994	Wembley	2	0
2005	Chicago	2	1
2008	Wembley	2	0
2010	Rustenburg (WC)	1	1
2018	Wembley	3	0

v YUGOSLAVIA

1939	Belgrade	1	2
1950	Highbury	2	2
1954	Belgrade	0	1
1956	Wembley	3	0
1958	Belgrade	0	5
1960	Wembley	3	3
1965	Belgrade	1	1
1966	Wembley	2	0
1968	Florence (EC)	0	1
1972	Wembley	1	1
1974	Belgrade	2	2
1986	Wembley (EC)	2	0
1987	Belgrade (EC)	4	1
1989	Wembley	2	1

ENGLAND'S RECORD England's first international was a 0-0 draw against Scotland in Glasgow, on the West of Scotland cricket ground, Partick, on November 30, 1872 The 1,000th was a 7-0 win over Montenegro at Wembley on November 14, 2019. Their complete record at the start of 2020–21 is:

P	W	D	L	F	A
1001	570	241	190	2199	984

ENGLAND B

1937	Stockholm	4	0
1948	Highbury	4	2
1949	Stockholm	1	3
1956	Stockholm	0	0
1959	Wembley	2	3
1965	Gothenburg	2	1
1968	Wembley	3	1
1979	Stockholm	0	0
1986	Stockholm	0	1
1988	Wembley (WC)	0	0
1989	Stockholm (WC)	0	0
1992	Stockholm (EC)	1	2
1995	Leeds	3	3
1998	Stockholm (EC)	1	2
1999	Wembley (EC)	0	0
2001	Old Trafford	1	1
2002	Saitama (WC)	1	1
2004	Gothenburg	0	1
2006	Cologne (WC)	2	2
1949	Finland (A)	4	0
1949	Holland (A)	4	0
1950	Italy (A)	0	5
1950	Holland (H)	1	0
1950	Holland (A)	0	3
1950	Luxembourg (A)	2	1
1950	Switzerland (H)	5	0
1952	Holland (A)	1	0
1952	France (A)	1	7
1953	Scotland (A)	2	2
1954	Scotland (H)	1	1
1954	Germany (A)	4	0
1954	Yugoslavia (A)	1	2
1954	Switzerland (A)	0	2
1955	Germany (H)	1	1
1955	Yugoslavia (H)	5	1
1956	Switzerland (H)	4	1
1956	Scotland (A)	2	2
1957	Scotland (H)	4	1
1978	W Germany (A)	2	1
1978	Czechoslovakia (A)	1	0
1978	Singapore (A)	8	0
1978	Malaysia (A)	1	1
1978	N Zealand (A)	4	0
1978	N Zealand (A)	3	1
1978	N Zealand (A)	4	0
1979	Austria (A)	1	0
1979	N Zealand (A)	4	1
1980	USA (H)	1	0
1980	Spain (H)	1	0
1980	Australia (H)	1	0
1981	Spain (A)	2	3
1984	N Zealand (A)	2	0
1987	Malta (A)	2	0
1989	Switzerland (A)	2	0
1989	Iceland (A)	2	0
1989	Norway (A)	1	0
1989	Italy (H)	1	1
1989	Yugoslavia (H)	2	1
1990	Rep of Ireland (A)	1	4
1990	Czechoslovakia (H)	2	0
1990	Algeria (A)	0	0
1991	Wales (A)	1	0
1991	Iceland (H)	1	0
1991	Switzerland (H)	2	1

1991	Spanish XI (A)	1	0
1992	France (H)	3	0
1992	Czechoslovakia (A)	1	0
1992	CIS (A)	1	1
1994	N Ireland (H)	4	2
1995	Rep of Ireland (H)	2	0
1998	Chile (H)	1	2
1998	Russia (H)	4	1
2006	Belarus (H)	1	2
2007	Albania	3	1

GB v REST OF EUROPE

| 1947 | at Glsagow | 6-1 |
| 1955 | at Belfast | 1-4 |

SCOTLAND

v ALBANIA
| 2018 | Glasgow (NL) | 2 | 0 |
| 2018 | Shkoder (NL) | 4 | 0 |

v ARGENTINA
1977	Buenos Aires	1	1
1979	Glasgow	1	3
1990	Glasgow	1	0
2008	Glasgow	0	1

v AUSTRALIA
1985*	Glasgow (WC)	2	0
1985*	Melbourne (WC)	0	0
1996	Glasgow	1	0
2000	Glasgow	0	2
2012	Edinburgh	3	1
(* World Cup play-off)

v AUSTRIA
1931	Vienna	0	5
1933	Glasgow	2	2
1937	Vienna	1	1
1950	Glasgow	0	1
1951	Vienna	0	4
1954	Zurich (WC)	0	1
1955	Vienna	4	1
1956	Glasgow	1	1
1960	Vienna	1	4
1963*	Glasgow	4	1
1968	Glasgow (WC)	2	1
1969	Vienna (WC)	0	2
1978	Vienna (EC)	2	3
1979	Glasgow (EC)	1	1
1994	Vienna	2	1
1996	Vienna (WC)	0	0
1997	Glasgow (WC)	2	0

(* Abandoned after 79 minutes)
2003	Glasgow	0	2
2005	Graz	2	2
2007	Vienna	1	0

v BELARUS
1997	Minsk (WC)	1	0
1997	Aberdeen (WC)	4	1
2005	Minsk (WC)	0	0
2005	Glasgow (WC)	0	1

v BELGIUM
1947	Brussels	1	2
1948	Glasgow	2	0
1951	Brussels	5	0
1971	Liege (EC)	0	3
1971	Aberdeen (EC)	1	0
1974	Brugge	1	2
1979	Brussels (EC)	0	2
1979	Glasgow (EC)	1	3
1982	Brussels (EC)	2	3
1983	Glasgow (EC)	1	1
1987	Brussels (EC)	1	4
1987	Glasgow (EC)	2	0
2001	Glasgow (WC)	2	2
2001	Brussels (WC)	0	2
2012	Brussels (WC)	0	2
2013	Glasgow (WC)	0	2
2018	Glasgow	0	4
2019	Brussels (EC)	0	3
2019	Glasgow (EC)	0	4

v BOSNIA
| 1999 | Sarajevo (EC) | 2 | 1 |
| 1999 | Glasgow (EC) | 1 | 0 |

v BRAZIL
1966	Glasgow	1	1
1972	Rio de Janeiro	0	1
1973	Glasgow	0	1
1974	Frankfurt (WC)	0	0
1977	Rio de Janeiro	0	2
1982	Seville (WC)	1	4
1987	Glasgow	0	2
1990	Turin (WC)	0	1
1998	St Denis (WC)	1	2
2011	Arsenal	0	2

v BULGARIA
1978	Glasgow	2	1
1986	Glasgow (EC)	0	0
1987	Sofia (EC)	1	0
1990	Sofia (EC)	1	1

1991	Glasgow (EC)	1	1
2006	Kobe	5	1

v CANADA
1983	Vancouver	2	0
1983	Edmonton	3	0
1983	Toronto	2	0
1992	Toronto	3	1
2002	Edinburgh	3	1
2017	Edinburgh	1	1

v CHILE
1977	Santiago	4	2
1989	Glasgow	2	0

v CIS (formerly Soviet Union)
1992	Norrkoping (EC)	3	0

v COLOMBIA
1988	Glasgow	0	0
1996	Miami	0	1
1998	New York	2	2

v COSTA RICA
1990	Genoa (WC)	0	1
2018	Glasgow	0	1

v CROATIA
2000	Zagreb (WC)	1	1
2001	Glasgow (WC)	0	0
2008	Glasgow	1	1
2013	Zagreb (WC)	1	0
2013	Glasgow (WC)	2	0

v CYPRUS
1968	Nicosia (WC)	5	0
1969	Glasgow (WC)	8	0
1989	Limassol (WC)	3	2
1989	Glasgow (WC)	2	1
2011	Larnaca	2	1
2019	Glasgow (EC)	2	1
2019	Nicosia (EC)	2	1

v CZECH REPUBLIC
1999	Glasgow (EC)	1	2
1999	Prague (EC)	2	3
2008	Prague	1	3
2010	Glasgow	1	0
2010	Prague (EC)	0	1
2011	Glasgow (EC)	2	2
2016	Prague	1	0

v CZECHOSLOVAKIA
1937	Prague	3	1
1937	Glasgow	5	0
1961	Bratislava (WC)	0	4
1961	Glasgow (WC)	3	2
1961*	Brussels (WC)	2	4
1972	Porto Alegre	0	0
1973	Glasgow (WC)	2	1
1973	Bratislava (WC)	0	1
1976	Prague (WC)	0	2
1977	Glasgow (WC)	3	1

(*World Cup play-off)

v DENMARK
1951	Glasgow	3	1
1952	Copenhagen	2	1
1968	Copenhagen	1	0
1970	Glasgow (EC)	1	0
1971	Copenhagen (EC)	0	1
1972	Copenhagen (WC)	4	1
1972	Glasgow (WC)	2	0
1975	Copenhagen (EC)	1	0
1975	Glasgow (EC)	3	1
1986	Neza (WC)	0	1
1996	Copenhagen	0	2
1998	Glasgow	0	1
2002	Glasgow	0	1
2004	Copenhagen	0	1
2011	Glasgow	2	1
2016	Glasgow	1	0

v EAST GERMANY
1974	Glasgow	3	0
1977	East Berlin	0	1
1982	Glasgow (EC)	2	0
1983	Halle (EC)	1	2
1986	Glasgow	0	0
1990	Glasgow	0	1

v ECUADOR
1995	Toyama, Japan	2	1

v EGYPT
1990	Aberdeen	1	3

v ESTONIA
1993	Tallinn (WC)	3	0
1993	Aberdeen	3	1
1996	Tallinn (WC)		
*No result			
1997	Monaco (WC)	0	0
1997	Kilmarnock (WC)	2	0
1998	Edinburgh (EC)	3	2

1999	Tallinn (EC)	0	0
(* Estonia absent)			
2004	Tallinn	1	0
2013	Aberdeen	1	0

v FAROE ISLANDS

1994	Glasgow (EC)	5	1
1995	Toftir (EC)	2	0
1998	Aberdeen (EC)	2	1
1999	Toftir (EC)	1	1
2002	Toftir (EC)	2	2
2003	Glasgow (EC)	3	1
2006	Glasgow (EC)	6	0
2007	Toftir (EC)	2	0
2010	Aberdeen	3	0

v FINLAND

1954	Helsinki	2	1
1964	Glasgow (WC)	3	1
1965	Helsinki (WC)	2	1
1976	Glasgow	6	0
1992	Glasgow	1	1
1994	Helsinki (EC)	2	0
1995	Glasgow (EC)	1	0
1998	Edinburgh	1	1

v FRANCE

1930	Paris	2	0
1932	Paris	3	1
1948	Paris	0	3
1949	Glasgow	2	0
1950	Paris	1	0
1951	Glasgow	1	0
1958	Orebro (WC)	1	2
1984	Marseilles	0	2
1989	Glasgow (WC)	2	0
1990	Paris (WC)	0	3
1997	St Etienne	1	2
2000	Glasgow	0	2
2002	Paris	0	5
2006	Glasgow (EC)	1	0
2007	Paris (EC)	1	0
2016	Metz	0	3

v GEORGIA

2007	Glasgow (EC)	2	1
2007	Tbilisi (EC)	0	2
2014	Glasgow (EC)	1	0
2015	Tbilisi (EC)	0	1

v GERMANY/WEST GERMANY

1929	Berlin	1	1
1936	Glasgow	2	0
1957	Stuttgart	3	1
1959	Glasgow	3	2
1964	Hanover	2	2
1969	Glasgow (WC)	1	1
1969	Hamburg (WC)	2	3
1973	Glasgow	1	1
1974	Frankfurt	1	2
1986	Queretaro (WC)	1	2
1992	Norrkoping (EC)	0	2
1993	Glasgow	0	1
1999	Bremen	1	0
2003	Glasgow (EC)	1	1
2003	Dortmund (EC)	1	2
2014	Dortmund (EC)	1	2
2015	Glasgow (EC)	2	3

v GIBRALTAR

| 2015 | Glasgow (EC) | 6 | 1 |
| 2015 | Faro (EC) | 6 | 0 |

v GREECE

| 1994 | Athens (EC) | 0 | 1 |
| 1995 | Glasgow | 1 | 0 |

v HOLLAND

1929	Amsterdam	2	0
1938	Amsterdam	3	1
1959	Amsterdam	2	1
1966	Glasgow	0	3
1968	Amsterdam	0	0
1971	Amsterdam	1	2
1978	Mendoza (WC)	3	2
1982	Glasgow	2	1
1986	Eindhoven	0	0
1992	Gothenburg (EC)	0	1
1994	Glasgow	0	1
1994	Utrecht	1	3
1996	Birmingham (EC)	0	0
2000	Arnhem	0	0
2003*	Glasgow (EC)	1	0
2003*	Amsterdam (EC)	0	6
2009	Amsterdam (WC)	0	3
2009	Glasgow (WC)	0	1
2017	Aberdeen	0	1
(*Qual Round play-off)			

v HUNGARY

1938	Glasgow	3	1
1955	Glasgow	2	4
1955	Budapest	1	3
1958	Glasgow	1	1
1960	Budapest	3	3
1980	Budapest	1	3
1987	Glasgow	2	0

| 2004 | Glasgow | 0 | 3 |
| 2018 | Budapest | 1 | 0 |

v ICELAND

1984	Glasgow (WC)	3	0
1985	Reykjavik (WC)	1	0
2002	Reykjavik (EC)	2	0
2003	Glasgow (EC)	2	1
2008	Reykjavik (WC)	2	1
2009	Glasgow (WC)	2	1

v IRAN

| 1978 | Cordoba (WC) | 1 | 1 |

v ISRAEL

1981	Tel Aviv (WC)	1	0
1981	Glasgow (WC)	3	1
1986	Tel Aviv	1	0
2018	Haifa (NL)	1	2
2018	Glasgow (NL)	3	2

v ITALY

1931	Rome	0	3
1965	Glasgow (WC)	1	0
1965	Naples (WC)	0	3
1988	Perugia	0	2
1992	Glasgow (WC)	0	0
1993	Rome (WC)	1	3
2005	Milan (WC)	0	2
2005	Glasgow (WC)	1	1
2007	Bari (EC)	0	2
2007	Glasgow (EC)	1	2
2016	Ta'Qali	0	1

v JAPAN

1995	Hiroshima	0	0
2006	Saitama	0	0
2009	Yokohama	0	2

v KAZAKHSTAN

| 2019 | Astana (EC) | 0 | 3 |
| 2019 | Glasgow (EC) | 3 | 1 |

v LATVIA

1996	Riga (WC)	2	0
1997	Glasgow (WC)	2	0
2000	Riga (WC)	1	0
2001	Glasgow (WC)	2	1

v LIECHTENSTEIN

| 2010 | Glasgow (EC) | 2 | 1 |
| 2011 | Vaduz (EC) | 1 | 0 |

v LITHUANIA

1998	Vilnius (EC)	0	0
1999	Glasgow (EC)	3	0
2003	Kaunus (EC)	0	1
2003	Glasgow (EC)	1	0
2006	Kaunas (EC)	2	1
2007	Glasgow (EC)	3	1
2010	Kaunas (EC)	0	0
2011	Glasgow (EC)	1	0
2016	Glasgow (WC)	1	1
2017	Vilnius (WC)	3	0

v LUXEMBOURG

1947	Luxembourg	6	0
1986	Glasgow (EC)	3	0
1987	Esch (EC)	0	0
2012	Josy Barthel	2	1`

v MACEDONIA

2008	Skopje (WC)	0	1
2009	Glasgow (WC)	2	0
2012	Glasgow (WC)	1	1
2013	Skopje (WC)	2	1

v MALTA

1988	Valletta	1	1
1990	Valletta	2	1
1993	Glasgow (WC)	3	0
1993	Valletta (WC)	2	0
1997	Valletta	3	2
2016	Ta'Qali (WC)	5	1
2017	Glasgow (WC)	2	0

v MEXICO

| 2018 | Mexico City | 0 | 1 |

v MOLDOVA

| 2004 | Chisinau (WC) | 1 | 1 |
| 2005 | Glasgow (WC) | 2 | 0 |

v MOROCCO

| 1998 | St Etienne (WC) | 0 | 3 |

v NEW ZEALAND

| 1982 | Malaga (WC) | 5 | 2 |
| 2003 | Edinburgh | 1 | 1 |

v NIGERIA

| 2002 | Aberdeen | 1 | 2 |
| 2014 | Fulham | 2 | 2 |

v NORWAY

| 1929 | Bergen | 7 | 3 |

1954	Glasgow	1	0
1954	Oslo	1	1
1963	Bergen	3	4
1963	Glasgow	6	1
1974	Oslo	2	1
1978	Glasgow (EC)	3	2
1979	Oslo (EC)	4	0
1988	Oslo (WC)	2	1
1989	Glasgow (WC)	1	1
1992	Oslo	0	0
1998	Bordeaux (WC)	1	1
2003	Oslo	0	0
2004	Glasgow (WC)	0	1
2005	Oslo (WC)	2	1
2008	Glasgow (WC)	0	0
2009	Oslo (WC)	0	4
2013	Molde	1	0

v PARAGUAY

1958	Norrkoping (WC)	2	3

v PERU

1972	Glasgow	2	0
1978	Cordoba (WC)	1	3
1979	Glasgow	1	1
2018	Lima	0	2

v POLAND

1958	Warsaw	2	1
1960	Glasgow	2	3
1965	Chorzow (WC)	1	1
1965	Glasgow (WC)	1	2
1980	Poznan	0	1
1990	Glasgow	1	1
2001	Bydgoszcz	1	1
2014	Warsaw	1	0
2014	Warsaw (EC)	2	2
2015	Glasgow (EC)	2	2

v PORTUGAL

1950	Lisbon	2	2
1955	Glasgow	3	0
1959	Lisbon	0	1
1966	Glasgow	0	1
1971	Lisbon (EC)	0	2
1971	Glasgow (EC)	2	1
1975	Glasgow	1	0
1978	Lisbon (EC)	0	1
1980	Glasgow (EC)	4	1
1980	Glasgow (WC)	0	0
1981	Lisbon (WC)	1	2
1992	Glasgow (WC)	0	0
1993	Lisbon (WC)	0	5
2002	Braga	0	2
2018	Glasgow	1	3

v QATAR

2015	Edinburgh	1	0

v REPUBLIC OF IRELAND

1961	Glasgow (WC)	4	1
1961	Dublin (WC)	3	0
1963	Dublin	0	1
1969	Dublin	1	1
1986	Dublin (EC)	0	0
1987	Glasgow (EC)	0	1
2000	Dublin	2	1
2003	Glasgow (EC)	0	2
2011	Dublin (CC)	0	1
2014	Glasgow (EC)	1	0
2015	Dublin (EC)	1	1

v ROMANIA

1975	Bucharest (EC)	1	1
1975	Glasgow (EC)	1	1
1986	Glasgow	3	0
1990	Glasgow (EC)	2	1
1991	Bucharest (EC)	0	1
2004	Glasgow	1	2

v RUSSIA

1994	Glasgow (EC)	1	1
1995	Moscow (EC)	0	0
2019	Glasgow (EC)	1	2
2019	Moscow (EC)	0	4

v SAN MARINO

1991	Serravalle (EC)	2	0
1991	Serravalle (EC)	4	0
1995	Serravalle (EC)	2	0
1995	Glasgow (EC)	5	0
2000	Serravalle (WC)	2	0
2001	Glasgow (WC)	4	0
2019	Serravalle (EC)	2	0
2019	Glasgow (EC)	6	0

v SAUDI ARABIA

1988	Riyadh	2	2

v SERBIA

2012	Glasgow (WC)	0	0
2013	Novi Sad (WC)	0	2

v SLOVAKIA

2016	Trnava (WC)	0	3
2017	Glasgow (WC)	1	0

v SLOVENIA

2004	Glasgow (WC)	0	0

2005	Celje (WC)	3	0
2012	Koper	1	1
2017	Glasgow (WC)	1	0
2017	Ljubljana (WC)	2	2

v SOUTH AFRICA

| 2002 | Hong Kong | 0 | 2 |
| 2007 | Aberdeen | 1 | 0 |

v SOUTH KOREA

| 2002 | Busan | 1 | 4 |

v SOVIET UNION (see also CIS and RUSSIA)

1967	Glasgow	0	2
1971	Moscow	0	1
1982	Malaga (WC)	2	2
1991	Glasgow	0	1

v SPAIN

1957	Glasgow (WC)	4	2
1957	Madrid (WC)	1	4
1963	Madrid	6	2
1965	Glasgow	0	0
1975	Glasgow (EC)	1	2
1975	Valencia (EC)	1	1
1982	Valencia	0	3
1985	Glasgow (WC)	3	1
1985	Seville (WC)	0	1
1988	Madrid	0	0
2004*	Valencia	1	1
(*Abandoned after 59 mins – floodlight failure)			
2010	Glasgow (EC)	2	3
2011	Alicante (EC)	1	3

v SWEDEN

1952	Stockholm	1	3
1953	Glasgow	1	2
1975	Gothenburg	1	1
1977	Glasgow	3	1
1980	Stockholm (WC)	1	0
1981	Glasgow (WC)	2	0
1990	Genoa (WC)	2	1
1995	Solna	0	2
1996	Glasgow (WC)	1	0
1997	Gothenburg (WC)	1	2
2004	Edinburgh	1	4
2010	Stockholm	0	3

v SWITZERLAND

| 1931 | Geneva | 3 | 2 |
| 1948 | Berne | 1 | 2 |

1950	Glasgow	3	1
1957	Basle (WC)	2	1
1957	Glasgow (WC)	3	2
1973	Berne	0	1
1976	Glasgow	1	0
1982	Berne (EC)	0	2
1983	Glasgow (EC)	2	2
1990	Glasgow (EC)	2	1
1991	Berne (EC)	2	2
1992	Berne (WC)	1	3
1993	Aberdeen (WC)	1	1
1996	Birmingham (EC)	1	0
2006	Glasgow	1	3

v TRINIDAD & TOBAGO

| 2004 | Hibernian | 4 | 1 |

v TURKEY

| 1960 | Ankara | 2 | 4 |

v UKRAINE

| 2006 | Kiev (EC) | 0 | 2 |
| 2007 | Glasgow (EC) | 3 | 1 |

v USA

1952	Glasgow	6	0
1992	Denver	1	0
1996	New Britain, Conn	1	2
1998	Washington	0	0
2005	Glasgow	1	1
2012	Jacksonville	1	5
2013	Glasgow	0	0

v URUGUAY

1954	Basle (WC)	0	7
1962	Glasgow	2	3
1983	Glasgow	2	0
1986	Neza (WC)	0	0

v YUGOSLAVIA

1955	Belgrade	2	2
1956	Glasgow	2	0
1958	Vaasteras (WC)	1	1
1972	Belo Horizonte	2	2
1974	Frankfurt (WC)	1	1
1984	Glasgow	6	1
1988	Glasgow (WC)	1	1
1989	Zagreb (WC)	1	3

v ZAIRE

| 1974 | Dortmund (WC) | 2 | 0 |

WALES

v ALBANIA
1994	Cardiff (EC)	2	0
1995	Tirana (EC)	1	1
2018	Elbasan	0	1

v ANDORRA
2014	La Vella (EC)	2	1
2015	Cardiff (EC)	2	0

v ARGENTINA
1992	Gifu (Japan)	0	1
2002	Cardiff	1	1

v ARMENIA
2001	Yerevan (WC)	2	2
2001	Cardiff (WC)	0	0

v AUSTRALIA
2011	Cardiff	1	2

v AUSTRIA
1954	Vienna	0	2
1955	Wrexham	1	2
1975	Vienna (EC)	1	2
1975	Wrexham (EC)	1	0
1992	Vienna	1	1
2005	Cardiff	0	2
2005	Vienna	0	1
2013	Swansea	2	1
2016	Vienna (WC)	2	2
2017	Cardiff (WC)	1	0

v AZERBAIJAN
2002	Baku (EC)	2	0
2003	Cardiff (EC)	4	0
2004	Baku (WC)	1	1
2005	Cardiff (WC)	2	0
2008	Cardiff (WC)	1	0
2009	Baku (WC)	1	0
2019	Cardiff (EC)	2	1
2019	Baku (EC)	2	0

v BELARUS
1998	Cardiff (EC)	3	2
1999	Minsk (EC)	2	1
2000	Minsk (WC)	1	2
2001	Cardiff (WC)	1	0
2019	Cardiff	1	0

v BELGIUM
1949	Liege	1	3

1949	Cardiff	5	1
1990	Cardiff (EC)	3	1
1991	Brussels (EC)	1	1
1992	Brussels (WC)	0	2
1993	Cardiff (WC)	2	0
1997	Cardiff (WC)	1	2
1997	Brussels (WC)	2	3
2012	Cardiff (WC)	0	2
2013	Brussels (WC)	1	1
2014	Brussels (EC)	0	0
2015	Cardiff (EC)	1	0
2016	Lille (EC)	3	1

v BOSNIA-HERZEGOVINA
2003	Cardiff	2	2
2012	Llanelli	0	2
2014	Cardiff (EC)	0	0
2015	Zenica (EC)	0	2

v BRAZIL
1958	Gothenburg (WC)	0	1
1962	Rio de Janeiro	1	3
1962	Sao Paulo	1	3
1966	Rio de Janeiro	1	3
1966	Belo Horizonte	0	1
1983	Cardiff	1	1
1991	Cardiff	1	0
1997	Brasilia	0	3
2000	Cardiff	0	3
2006	White Hart Lane	0	2

v BULGARIA
1983	Wrexham (EC)	1	0
1983	Sofia (EC)	0	1
1994	Cardiff (EC)	0	3
1995	Sofia (EC)	1	3
2006	Swansea	0	0
2007	Bourgas	1	0
2010	Cardiff (EC)	0	1
2011	Sofia (EC)	1	0

v CANADA
1986	Toronto	0	2
1986	Vancouver	3	0
2004	Wrexham	1	0

v CHILE
1966	Santiago	0	2

v CHINA
2018	Nanning	6	0

v COSTA RICA
1990	Cardiff	1	0
2012	Cardiff	0	1

v CROATIA

2002	Varazdin	1	1
2010	Osijek	0	2
2012	Osijek (WC)	0	2
2013	Swansea (WC)	1	2
2019	Osijek (EC)	1	2
2019	Cardiff (EC)	1	1

v CYPRUS

1992	Limassol (WC)	1	0
1993	Cardiff (WC)	2	0
2005	Limassol	0	1
2006	Cardiff (EC)	3	1
2007	Nicosia (EC)	1	3
2014	Cardiff (EC)	2	1
2015	Nicosia	1	0

v CZECHOSLOVAKIA (see also RCS)

1957	Cardiff (WC)	1	0
1957	Prague (WC)	0	2
1971	Swansea (EC)	1	3
1971	Prague (EC)	0	1
1977	Wrexham (WC)	3	0
1977	Prague (WC)	0	1
1980	Cardiff (WC)	1	0
1981	Prague (WC)	0	2
1987	Wrexham (EC)	1	1
1987	Prague (EC)	0	2

v CZECH REPUBLIC

2002	Cardiff	0	0
2006	Teplice (EC)	1	2
2007	Cardiff (EC)	0	0

v DENMARK

1964	Copenhagen (WC)	0	1
1965	Wrexham (WC)	4	2
1987	Cardiff (EC)	1	0
1987	Copenhagen (EC)	0	1
1990	Copenhagen	0	1
1998	Copenhagen (EC)	2	1
1999	Anfield (EC)	0	2
2008	Copenhagen	1	0
2018	Aarhus (NL)	0	2
2018	Cardiff (NL)	1	2

v EAST GERMANY

1957	Leipzig (WC)	1	2
1957	Cardiff (WC)	4	1
1969	Dresden (WC)	1	2
1969	Cardiff (WC)	1	3

v ESTONIA

1994	Tallinn	2	1
2009	Llanelli	1	0

v FAROE ISLANDS

1992	Cardiff (WC)	6	0
1993	Toftir (WC)	3	0

v FINLAND

1971	Helsinki (EC)	1	0
1971	Swansea (EC)	3	0
1986	Helsinki (EC)	1	1
1987	Wrexham (EC)	4	0
1988	Swansea (WC)	2	2
1989	Helsinki (WC)	0	1
2000	Cardiff	1	2
2002	Helsinki (EC)	2	0
2003	Cardiff (EC)	1	1
2009	Cardiff (WC)	0	2
2009	Helsinki (WC)	1	2
2013	Cardiff	1	1

v FRANCE

1933	Paris	1	1
1939	Paris	1	2
1953	Paris	1	6
1982	Toulouse	1	0
2017	Paris	0	2

v GEORGIA

1994	Tbilisi (EC)	0	5
1995	Cardiff (EC)	0	1
2008	Swansea	1	2
2016	Cardiff (WC)	1	1
2017	Tbilisi (WC)	1	0

v GERMANY/WEST GERMANY

1968	Cardiff	1	1
1969	Frankfurt	1	1
1977	Cardiff	0	2
1977	Dortmund	1	1
1979	Wrexham (EC)	0	2
1979	Cologne (EC)	1	5
1989	Cardiff (WC)	0	0
1989	Cologne (WC)	1	2
1991	Cardiff (EC)	1	0
1991	Nuremberg (EC)	1	4
1995	Dusseldorf (EC)	1	1
1995	Cardiff (EC)	1	2
2002	Cardiff	1	0
2007	Cardiff (EC)	0	2
2007	Frankfurt (EC)	0	0
2008	Moenchengladbach (WC)	0	1
2009	Cardiff (WC)	0	2

v GREECE
1964	Athens (WC)	0	2
1965	Cardiff (WC)	4	1

v HOLLAND
1988	Amsterdam (WC)	0	1
1989	Wrexham (WC)	1	2
1992	Utrecht	0	4
1996	Cardiff (WC)	1	3
1996	Eindhoven (WC)	1	7
2008	Rotterdam	0	2
2014	Amsterdam	0	2
2015	Cardiff	2	3

v HUNGARY
1958	Sanviken (WC)	1	1
1958	Stockholm (WC)	2	1
1961	Budapest	2	3
1963	Budapest (EC)	1	3
1963	Cardiff (EC)	1	1
1974	Cardiff (EC)	2	0
1975	Budapest (EC)	2	1
1986	Cardiff	0	3
2004	Budapest	2	1
2005	Cardiff	2	0
2019	Budapest (EC)	0	1
2019	Cardiff (EC)	2	0

v ICELAND
1980	Reykjavik (WC)	4	0
1981	Swansea (WC)	2	2
1984	Reykjavik (WC)	0	1
1984	Cardiff (WC)	2	1
1991	Cardiff	1	0
2008	Reykjavik	1	0
2014	Cardiff	3	1

v IRAN
1978	Tehran	1	0

v ISRAEL
1958	Tel Aviv (WC)	2	0
1958	Cardiff (WC)	2	0
1984	Tel Aviv	0	0
1989	Tel Aviv	3	3
2015	Haifa (EC)	3	0
2015	Cardiff (EC)	0	0

v ITALY
1965	Florence	1	4
1968	Cardiff (WC)	0	1
1969	Rome (WC)	1	4
1988	Brescia	1	0

1996	Terni	0	3
1998	Anfield (EC)	0	2
1999	Bologna (EC)	0	4
2002	Cardiff (EC)	2	1
2003	Milan (EC)	0	4

v JAMAICA
1998	Cardiff	0	0

v JAPAN
1992	Matsuyama	1	0

v KUWAIT
1977	Wrexham	0	0
1977	Kuwait City	0	0

v LATVIA
2004	Riga	2	0

v LIECHTENSTEIN
2006	Wrexham	4	0
2008	Cardiff (WC)	2	0
2009	Vaduz (WC)	2	0

v LUXEMBOURG
1974	Swansea (EC)	5	0
1975	Luxembourg (EC)	3	1
1990	Luxembourg (EC)	1	0
1991	Luxembourg (EC)	1	0
2008	Luxembourg	2	0
2010	Llanelli	5	1

v MACEDONIA
2013	Skopje (WC)	1	2
2013	Cardiff (WC)	1	0

v MALTA
1978	Wrexham (EC)	7	0
1979	Valletta (EC)	2	0
1988	Valletta	3	2
1998	Valletta	3	0

v MEXICO
1958	Stockholm (WC)	1	1
1962	Mexico City	1	2
2012	New York	0	2
2018	Pasadena	0	0

v MOLDOVA
1994	Kishinev (EC)	2	3
1995	Cardiff (EC)	1	0
2016	Cardiff (WC)	4	0
2017	Chisinau (WC)	2	0

v MONTENEGRO
2009	Podgorica	1	2
2010	Podgorica (EC)	0	0
2011	Cardiff (EC)	2	1

v NEW ZEALAND
2007	Wrexham	2	2

v NORWAY
1982	Swansea (EC)	1	0
1983	Oslo (EC)	0	0
1984	Trondheim	0	1
1985	Wrexham	1	1
1985	Bergen	2	4
1994	Cardiff	1	3
2000	Cardiff (WC)	1	1
2001	Oslo (WC)	2	3
2004	Oslo	0	0
2008	Wrexham	3	0
2011	Cardiff	4	1

v PANAMA
2017	Cardiff	1	1

v PARAGUAY
2006	Cardiff	0	0

v POLAND
1973	Cardiff (WC)	2	0
1973	Katowice (WC)	0	3
1991	Radom	0	0
2000	Warsaw (WC)	0	0
2001	Cardiff (WC)	1	2
2004	Cardiff (WC)	2	3
2005	Warsaw (WC)	0	1
2009	Vila-Real (Por)	0	1

v PORTUGAL
1949	Lisbon	2	3
1951	Cardiff	2	1
2000	Chaves	0	3
2016	Lyon (EC)	0	2

v QATAR
2000	Doha	1	0

v RCS (formerly Czechoslovakia)
1993	Ostrava (WC)	1	1
1993	Cardiff (WC)	2	2

v REPUBLIC OF IRELAND
1960	Dublin	3	2
1979	Swansea	2	1
1981	Dublin	3	1
1986	Dublin	1	0
1990	Dublin	0	1
1991	Wrexham	0	3
1992	Dublin	1	0
1993	Dublin	1	2
1997	Cardiff	0	0
2007	Dublin (EC)	0	1
2007	Cardiff (EC)	2	2
2011	Dublin (CC)	0	3
2013	Cardiff	0	0
2017	Dublin (WC)	0	0
2017	Cardiff (WC)	0	1
2018	Cardiff (NL)	4	1
2018	Dublin (NL)	1	0

v REST OF UNITED KINGDOM
1951	Cardiff	3	2
1969	Cardiff	0	1

v ROMANIA
1970	Cardiff (EC)	0	0
1971	Bucharest (EC)	0	2
1983	Wrexham	5	0
1992	Bucharest (WC)	1	5
1993	Cardiff (WC)	1	2

v RUSSIA (See also Soviet Union)
2003*	Moscow (EC)	0	0
2003*	Cardiff (EC)	0	1
2008	Moscow (WC)	1	2
2009	Cardiff (WC)	1	3
2016	Toulouse (EC)	3	0
(*Qual Round play-offs)			

v SAN MARINO
1996	Serravalle (WC)	5	0
1996	Cardiff (WC)	6	0
2007	Cardiff (EC)	3	0
2007	Serravalle (EC)	2	1

v SAUDI ARABIA
1986	Dahran	2	1

v SERBIA
2012	Novi Sad (WC)	1	6
2013	Cardiff (WC)	0	3
2016	Cardiff (WC)	1	1
2017	Belgrade (WC)	1	1

v SERBIA & MONTENEGRO

2003	Belgrade (EC)	0	1
2003	Cardiff (EC)	2	3

v SLOVAKIA

2006	Cardiff (EC)	1	5
2007	Trnava (EC)	5	2
2016	Bordeaux (EC)	2	1
2019	Cardiff (EC)	1	0
2019	Trnava (EC)	1	1

v SLOVENIA

2005	Swansea	0	0

v SOVIET UNION (See also Russia)

1965	Moscow (WC)	1	2
1965	Cardiff (WC)	2	1
1981	Wrexham (WC)	0	0
1981	Tbilisi (WC)	0	3
1987	Swansea	0	0

v SPAIN

1961	Cardiff (WC)	1	2
1961	Madrid (WC)	1	1
1982	Valencia	1	1
1984	Seville (WC)	0	3
1985	Wrexham (WC)	3	0
2018	Cardiff	1	4

v SWEDEN

1958	Stockholm (WC)	0	0
1988	Stockholm	1	4
1989	Wrexham	0	2
1990	Stockholm	2	4
1994	Wrexham	0	2
2010	Swansea	0	1
2016	Stockholm	0	3

v SWITZERLAND

1949	Berne	0	4
1951	Wrexham	3	2
1996	Lugano	0	2
1999	Zurich (EC)	0	2
1999	Wrexham (EC)	0	2
2010	Basle (EC)	1	4
2011	Swansea (EC)	2	0

v TRINIDAD & TOBAGO

2006	Graz	2	1
2019	Wrexham	1	0

v TUNISIA

1998	Tunis	0	4

v TURKEY

1978	Wrexham (EC)	1	0
1979	Izmir (EC)	0	1
1980	Cardiff (WC)	4	0
1981	Ankara (WC)	1	0
1996	Cardiff (WC)	0	0
1997	Istanbul (WC)	4	6

v UKRAINE

2001	Cardiff (WC)	1	1
2001	Kiev (WC)	1	1
2015	Kiev	0	1

v URUGUAY

1986	Wrexham	0	0
2018	Nanning	0	1

v USA

2003	San Jose	0	2

v YUGOSLAVIA

1953	Belgrade	2	5
1954	Cardiff	1	3
1976	Zagreb (EC)	0	2
1976	Cardiff (EC)	1	1
1982	Titograd (EC)	4	4
1983	Cardiff (EC)	1	1
1988	Swansea	1	2

NORTHERN IRELAND

v ALBANIA

1965	Belfast (WC)	4	1
1965	Tirana (WC)	1	1
1983	Tirana (EC)	0	0
1983	Belfast (EC)	1	0
1992	Belfast (WC)	3	0
1993	Tirana (WC)	2	1
1996	Belfast (WC)	2	0
1997	Zurich (WC)	0	1
2010	Tirana	0	1

v ALGERIA

1986	Guadalajara (WC)	1	1

v ARGENTINA

1958	Halmstad (WC)	1	3

v ARMENIA

1996	Belfast (WC)	1	1
1997	Yerevan (WC)	0	0
2003	Yerevan (EC)	0	1
2003	Belfast (EC)	0	1

v AUSTRALIA
1980	Sydney	2	1
1980	Melbourne	1	1
1980	Adelaide	2	1

v AUSTRIA
1982	Madrid (WC)	2	2
1982	Vienna (EC)	0	2
1983	Belfast (EC)	3	1
1990	Vienna (EC)	0	0
1991	Belfast (EC)	2	1
1994	Vienna (EC)	2	1
1995	Belfast (EC)	5	3
2004	Belfast (WC)	3	3
2005	Vienna (WC)	0	2
2018	Vienna (NL)	0	1
2018	Belfast(NL)	1	2

v AZERBAIJAN
2004	Baku (WC)	0	0
2005	Belfast (WC)	2	0
2012	Belfast (WC)	1	1
2013	Baku (WC)	0	2
2016	Belfast (WC)	4	0
2017	Baku (WC)	1	0

v BARBADOS
2004	Bridgetown	1	1

v BELARUS
2016	Belfast	3	0
2019	Belfast (EC)	2	1
2019	Borisov (EC)	1	0

v BELGIUM
1976	Liege (WC)	0	2
1977	Belfast (WC)	3	0
1997	Belfast	3	0

v BOSNIA-HERZEGOVINA
2018	Belfast (NL)	1	2
2018	Sarajevo (NL)	0	2

v BRAZIL
1986	Guadalajara (WC)	0	3

v BULGARIA
1972	Sofia (WC)	0	3
1973	Sheffield (WC)	0	0
1978	Sofia (EC)	2	0
1979	Belfast (EC)	2	0
2001	Sofia (WC)	3	4
2001	Belfast (WC)	0	1
2008	Belfast	0	1

v CANADA
1995	Edmonton	0	2
1999	Belfast	1	1
2005	Belfast	0	1

v CHILE
1989	Belfast	0	1
1995	Edmonton, Canada	0	2
2010	Chillan	0	1
2014	Valparaiso	0	2

v COLOMBIA
1994	Boston, USA	0	2

v COSTA RICA
2018	San Jose	0	3

v CROATIA
2016	Belfast	0	3

v CYPRUS
1971	Nicosia (EC)	3	0
1971	Belfast (EC)	5	0
1973	Nicosia (WC)	0	1
1973	Fulham (WC)	3	0
2002	Belfast	0	0
2014	Nicosia	0	0

v CZECHOSLOVAKIA/CZECH REP
1958	Halmstad (WC)	1	0
1958	Malmo (WC)	2	1
2001	Belfast (WC)	0	1
2001	Teplice (WC)	1	3
2008	Belfast (WC)	0	0
2009	Prague (WC)	0	0
2016	Prague (WC)	0	0
2017	Belfast (WC)	2	0
2019	Prague	3	2

v DENMARK
1978	Belfast (EC)	2	1
1979	Copenhagen (EC)	0	4
1986	Belfast	1	1
1990	Belfast (EC)	1	1
1991	Odense (EC)	1	2
1992	Belfast (WC)	0	1
1993	Copenhagen (WC)	0	1
2000	Belfast (WC)	1	1
2001	Copenhagen (WC)	1	1
2006	Copenhagen (EC)	0	0
2007	Belfast (EC)	2	1

v ESTONIA

Year	Venue		
2004	Tallinn	1	0
2006	Belfast	1	0
2011	Tallinn (EC)	1	4
2011	Belfast (EC)	1	2
2019	Belfast (EC)	2	0
2019	Tallinn (EC)	2	1

v FAROE ISLANDS

Year	Venue		
1991	Belfast (EC)	1	1
1991	Landskrona, Sw (EC)	5	0
2010	Toftir (EC)	1	1
2011	Belfast (EC)	4	0
2014	Belfast (EC)	2	0
2015	Torshavn (EC)	3	1

v FINLAND

Year	Venue		
1984	Pori (WC)	0	1
1984	Belfast (WC)	2	1
1998	Belfast (EC)	1	0
1999	Helsinki (EC)	1	4
2003	Belfast	0	1
2006	Helsinki	2	1
2012	Belfast	3	3
2015	Belfast (EC)	2	1
2015	Helsinki (EC)	1	1

v FRANCE

Year	Venue		
1951	Belfast	2	2
1952	Paris	1	3
1958	Norrkoping (WC)	0	4
1982	Paris	0	4
1982	Madrid (WC)	1	4
1986	Paris	0	0
1988	Belfast	0	0
1999	Belfast	0	1

v GEORGIA

Year	Venue		
2008	Belfast	4	1

v GERMANY/WEST GERMANY

Year	Venue		
1958	Malmo (WC)	2	2
1960	Belfast (WC)	3	4
1961	Berlin (WC)	1	2
1966	Belfast	0	2
1977	Cologne	0	5
1982	Belfast (EC)	1	0
1983	Hamburg (EC)	1	0
1992	Bremen	1	1
1996	Belfast	1	1
1997	Nuremberg (WC)	1	1
1997	Belfast (WC)	1	3
1999	Belfast (EC)	0	3
1999	Dortmund (EC)	0	4
2005	Belfast	1	4
2016	Paris (EC)	0	1
2016	Hannover (WC)	0	2
2017	Belfast (WC)	1	3
2019	Belfast (EC)	0	2
2019	Frankfurt (EC)	1	6

v GREECE

Year	Venue		
1961	Athens (WC)	1	2
1961	Belfast (WC)	2	0
1988	Athens	2	3
2003	Belfast (EC)	0	2
2003	Athens (EC)	0	1
2014	Piraeus (EC)	2	0
2015	Belfast (EC)	3	1

v HOLLAND

Year	Venue		
1962	Rotterdam	0	4
1965	Belfast (WC)	2	1
1965	Rotterdam (WC)	0	0
1976	Rotterdam (WC)	2	2
1977	Belfast (WC)	0	1
2012	Amsterdam	0	6
2019	Rotterdam (EC)	1	3
2019	Belfast (EC)	0	0

v HONDURAS

Year	Venue		
1982	Zaragoza (WC)	1	1

v HUNGARY

Year	Venue		
1988	Budapest (WC)	0	1
1989	Belfast (WC)	1	2
2000	Belfast	0	1
2008	Belfast	0	2
2014	Budapest (EC)	2	1
2015	Belfast (EC)	1	1

v ICELAND

Year	Venue		
1977	Reykjavik (WC)	0	1
1977	Belfast (WC)	2	0
2000	Reykjavik (WC)	0	1
2001	Belfast (WC)	3	0
2006	Belfast (EC)	0	3
2007	Reykjavik (EC)	1	2

v ISRAEL

Year	Venue		
1968	Jaffa	3	2
1976	Tel Aviv	1	1
1980	Tel Aviv (WC)	0	0
1981	Belfast (WC)	1	0
1984	Belfast	3	0
1987	Tel Aviv	1	1

2009	Belfast	1	1
2013	Belfast (WC)	0	2
2013	Ramat Gan (WC)	1	1
2018	Belfast	3	0

v ITALY

1957	Rome (WC)	0	1
1957	Belfast	2	2
1958	Belfast (WC)	2	1
1961	Bologna	2	3
1997	Palermo	0	2
2003	Campobasso	0	2
2009	Pisa	0	3
2010	Belfast (EC)	0	0
2011	Pescara (EC)	0	3

v LATVIA

1993	Riga (WC)	2	1
1993	Belfast (WC)	2	0
1995	Riga (EC)	1	0
1995	Belfast (EC)	1	2
2006	Belfast (EC)	1	0
2007	Riga (EC)	0	1
2015	Belfast	1	0

v LIECHTENSTEIN

1994	Belfast (EC)	4	1
1995	Eschen (EC)	4	0
2002	Vaduz	0	0
2007	Vaduz (EC)	4	1
2007	Belfast (EC)	3	1

v LITHUANIA

1992	Belfast (WC)	2	2

v LUXEMBOURG

2000	Luxembourg	3	1
2012	Belfast (WC)	1	1
2013	Luxembourg (WC)	2	3
2019	Belfast	1	0

v MALTA

1988	Belfast (WC)	3	0
1989	Valletta (WC)	2	0
2000	Ta'Qali	3	0
2000	Belfast (WC)	1	0
2001	Valletta (WC)	1	0
2005	Valletta	1	1
2013	Ta'Qali	0	0

v MEXICO

1966	Belfast	4	1
1994	Miami	0	3

v MOLDOVA

1998	Belfast (EC)	2	2
1999	Kishinev (EC)	0	0

v MONTENEGRO

2010	Podgorica	0	2

v MOROCCO

1986	Belfast	2	1
2010	Belfast	1	1

v NEW ZEALAND

2017	Belfast	1	0

v NORWAY

1974	Oslo (EC)	1	2
1975	Belfast (EC)	3	0
1990	Belfast	2	3
1996	Belfast	0	2
2001	Belfast	0	4
2004	Belfast	1	4
2012	Belfast	0	3
2017	Belfast (WC)	2	0
2017	Oslo (WC)	0	1

v PANAMA

2018	Panama City	0	0

v POLAND

1962	Katowice (EC)	2	0
1962	Belfast (EC)	2	0
1988	Belfast	1	1
1991	Belfast	3	1
2002	Limassol (Cyprus)	1	4
2004	Belfast (WC)	0	3
2005	Warsaw (WC)	0	1
2009	Belfast (WC)	3	2
2009	Chorzow (WC)	1	1
2016	Nice (EC)	0	1

v PORTUGAL

1957	Lisbon (WC)	1	1
1957	Belfast (WC)	3	0
1973	Coventry (WC)	1	1
1973	Lisbon (WC)	1	1
1980	Lisbon (WC)	0	1
1981	Belfast (WC)	1	0
1994	Belfast (EC)	1	2
1995	Oporto (EC)	1	1
1997	Belfast (WC)	0	0
1997	Lisbon (WC)	0	1
2005	Belfast	1	1
2012	Porto (WC)	1	1
2013	Belfast (WC)	2	4

v QATAR

2015	Crewe	1	1

v REPUBLIC OF IRELAND

1978	Dublin (EC)	0	0
1979	Belfast (EC)	1	0
1988	Belfast (WC)	0	0
1989	Dublin (WC)	0	3
1993	Dublin (WC)	0	3
1993	Belfast (WC)	1	1
1994	Belfast (EC)	0	4
1995	Dublin (EC)	1	1
1999	Dublin	1	0
2011	Dublin (CC)	0	5
2018	Dublin	0	0

v ROMANIA

1984	Belfast (WC)	3	2
1985	Bucharest (WC)	1	0
1994	Belfast	2	0
2006	Chicago	0	2
2014	Bucharest (EC)	0	2
2015	Belfast (EC)	0	0

v RUSSIA

2012	Moscow (WC)	0	2
2013	Belfast (WC)	1	0

v SAN MARINO

2008	Belfast (WC)	4	0
2009	Serravalle (WC)	3	0
2016	Belfast (WC)	4	0
2017	Serravalle (WC)	3	0

v SERBIA & MONTENEGRO

2004	Belfast	1	1

v SERBIA

2009	Belfast	0	1
2011	Belgrade (EC)	1	2
2011	Belfast (EC)	0	1

v SLOVAKIA

1998	Belfast	1	0
2008	Bratislava (WC)	1	2
2009	Belfast (WC)	0	2
2016	Trnava	0	0

v SLOVENIA

2008	Maribor (WC)	0	2
2009	Belfast (WC)	1	0
2010	Maribor (EC)	1	0
2011	Belfast (EC)	0	0
2016	Belfast	1	0

v SOUTH KOREA

2018	Belfast	2	1

v SOVIET UNION

1969	Belfast (WC)	0	0
1969	Moscow (WC)	0	2
1971	Moscow (EC)	0	1
1971	Belfast (EC)	1	1

v SPAIN

1958	Madrid	2	6
1963	Bilbao	1	1
1963	Belfast	0	1
1970	Seville (EC)	0	3
1972	Hull (EC)	1	1
1982	Valencia (WC)	1	0
1985	Palma, Majorca	0	0
1986	Guadalajara (WC)	1	2
1988	Seville (WC)	0	4
1989	Belfast (WC)	0	2
1992	Belfast (WC)	0	0
1993	Seville (WC)	1	3
1998	Santander	1	4
2002	Belfast	0	5
2002	Albacete (EC)	0	3
2003	Belfast (EC)	0	0
2006	Belfast (EC)	3	2
2007	Las Palmas (EC)	0	1

v ST KITTS & NEVIS

2004	Basseterre	2	0

v SWEDEN

1974	Solna (EC)	2	0
1975	Belfast (EC)	1	2
1980	Belfast (WC)	3	0
1981	Stockholm (WC)	0	1
1996	Belfast	1	2
2007	Belfast (EC)	2	1
2007	Stockholm (EC)	1	1

v SWITZERLAND

1964	Belfast (WC)	1	0
1964	Lausanne (WC)	1	2
1998	Belfast	1	0
2004	Zurich	0	0
2010	Basle (EC)	1	4
2017	Belfast (WC)	0	1
2017	Basle (WC)	0	0

v THAILAND

1997	Bangkok	0	0

v TRINIDAD & TOBAGO
2004	Port of Spain	3	0

v TURKEY
1968	Belfast (WC)	4	1
1968	Istanbul (WC)	3	0
1983	Belfast (EC)	2	1
1983	Ankara (EC)	0	1
1985	Belfast (WC)	2	0
1985	Izmir (WC)	0	0
1986	Izmir (EC)	0	0
1987	Belfast (EC)	1	0
1998	Istanbul (EC)	0	3
1999	Belfast (EC)	0	3
2010	Connecticut	0	2
2013	Adana	0	1

v UKRAINE
1996	Belfast (WC)	0	1
1997	Kiev (WC)	1	2
2002	Belfast (EC)	0	0
2003	Donetsk (EC)	0	0
2016	Lyon (EC)	2	0

v URUGUAY
1964	Belfast	3	0
1990	Belfast	1	0
2006	New Jersey	0	1
2014	Montevideo	0	1

v YUGOSLAVIA
1975	Belfast (EC)	1	0
1975	Belgrade (EC)	0	1
1982	Zaragoza (WC)	0	0
1987	Belfast (EC)	1	2
1987	Sarajevo (EC)	0	3
1990	Belfast (EC)	0	2
1991	Belgrade (EC)	1	4
2000	Belfast	1	2

REPUBLIC OF IRELAND

v ALBANIA
1992	Dublin (WC)	2	0
1993	Tirana (WC)	2	1
2003	Tirana (EC)	0	0
2003	Dublin (EC)	2	1

v ALGERIA
1982	Algiers	0	2
2010	Dublin	3	0

v ANDORRA
2001	Barcelona (WC)	3	0

2001	Dublin (WC)	3	1
2010	Dublin (EC)	3	1
2011	La Vella (EC)	2	0

v ARGENTINA
1951	Dublin	0	1
1979*	Dublin	0	0
1980	Dublin	0	1
1998	Dublin	0	2
2010	Dublin	0	1
(*Not regarded as full Int)			

v ARMENIA
2010	Yerevan (EC)	1	0
2011	Dublin (EC)	2	1

v AUSTRALIA
2003	Dublin	2	1
2009	Limerick	0	3

v AUSTRIA
1952	Vienna	0	6
1953	Dublin	4	0
1958	Vienna	1	3
1962	Dublin	2	3
1963	Vienna (EC)	0	0
1963	Dublin (EC)	3	2
1966	Vienna	0	1
1968	Dublin	2	2
1971	Dublin (EC)	1	4
1971	Linz (EC)	0	6
1995	Dublin (EC)	1	3
1995	Vienna (EC)	1	3
2013	Dublin (WC)	2	2
2013	Vienna (WC)	0	1
2016	Vienna (WC)	1	0
2017	Dublin (WC	1	1

v BELARUS
2016	Cork	1	2

v BELGIUM
1928	Liege	4	2
1929	Dublin	4	0
1930	Brussels	3	1
1934	Dublin (WC)	4	4
1949	Dublin	0	2
1950	Brussels	1	5
1965	Dublin	0	2
1966	Liege	3	2
1980	Dublin (WC)	1	1
1981	Brussels (WC)	0	1
1986	Brussels (EC)	2	2

1987	Dublin (EC)	0	0
1997*	Dublin (WC)	1	1
1997*	Brussels (WC)	1	2
2016	Bordeaux (EC)	0	3
(*World Cup play-off)			

v BOLIVIA
1994	Dublin	1	0
1996	East Rutherford, NJ	3	0
2007	Boston	1	1

v BOSNIA HERZEGOVINA
2012	Dublin	1	0
2015	Zenica (EC)	1	1
2015	Dublin (EC)	2	0

v BRAZIL
1974	Rio de Janeiro	1	2
1982	Uberlandia	0	7
1987	Dublin	1	0
2004	Dublin	0	0
2008	Dublin	0	1
2010	Arsenal	0	2

v BULGARIA
1977	Sofia (WC)	1	2
1977	Dublin (WC)	0	0
1979	Sofia (EC)	0	1
1979	Dublin (EC)	3	0
1987	Sofia (EC)	1	2
1987	Dublin (EC)	2	0
2004	Dublin	1	1
2009	Dublin (WC)	1	1
2009	Sofia (WC)	1	1
2019	Dublin	3	1

v CAMEROON
| 2002 | Niigata (WC) | 1 | 1 |

v CANADA
| 2003 | Dublin | 3 | 0 |

v CHILE
1960	Dublin	2	0
1972	Recife	1	2
1974	Santiago	2	1
1982	Santiago	0	1
1991	Dublin	1	1
2006	Dublin	0	1

v CHINA
| 1984 | Sapporo | 1 | 0 |
| 2005 | Dublin | 1 | 0 |

v COLOMBIA
| 2008 | Fulham | 1 | 0 |

v COSTA RICA
| 2014 | Chester, USA | 1 | 1 |

v CROATIA
1996	Dublin	2	2
1998	Dublin (EC)	2	0
1999	Zagreb (EC)	0	1
2001	Dublin	2	2
2004	Dublin	1	0
2011	Dublin	0	0
2012	Poznan (EC)	1	3

v CYPRUS
1980	Nicosia (WC)	3	2
1980	Dublin (WC)	6	0
2001	Nicosia (WC)	4	0
2001	Dublin (WC)	4	0
2004	Dublin (WC)	3	0
2005	Nicosia (WC)	1	0
2006	Nicosia (EC)	2	5
2007	Dublin (EC)	1	1
2008	Dublin (WC)	1	0
2009	Nicosia (WC)	2	1

v CZECHOSLOVAKIA/CZECH REP
1938	Prague	2	2
1959	Dublin (EC)	2	0
1959	Bratislava (EC)	0	4
1961	Dublin (WC)	1	3
1961	Prague (WC)	1	7
1967	Dublin (EC)	0	2
1967	Prague (EC)	2	1
1969	Dublin (WC)	1	2
1969	Prague (WC)	0	3
1979	Prague	1	4
1981	Dublin	3	1
1986	Reykjavik	1	0
1994	Dublin	1	3
1996	Prague	0	2
1998	Olomouc	1	2
2000	Dublin	3	2
2004	Dublin	2	1
2006	Dublin (EC)	1	1
2007	Prague (EC)	0	1
2012	Dublin	1	1

v DENMARK
1956	Dublin (WC)	2	1
1957	Copenhagen (WC)	2	0
1968*	Dublin (WC)	1	1
1969	Copenhagen (WC)	0	2

1969	Dublin (WC)	1	1
1978	Copenhagen (EC)	3	3
1979	Dublin (EC)	2	0
1984	Copenhagen (WC)	0	3
1985	Dublin (WC)	1	4
1992	Copenhagen (WC)	0	0
1993	Dublin (WC)	1	1
2002	Dublin	3	0

(*Abandoned after 51 mins – fog)

2007	Aarhus	4	0
2017	Copenhagen (WC)	0	0
2017	Dublin (WC)	1	5
2018	Dublin (NL)	0	0
2018	Aarhus (NL)	0	0
2019	Copenhagen (EC)	1	1
2019	Dublin (EC)	1	1

v ECUADOR

| 2007 | New York | 1 | 1 |

v EGYPT

| 1990 | Palermo (WC) | 0 | 0 |

v ESTONIA

2000	Dublin (WC)	2	0
2001	Tallinn (WC)	2	0
2011	Tallinn (EC)	4	0
2011	Dublin (EC)	1	1

v FAROE ISLANDS

2004	Dublin (WC)	2	0
2005	Torshavn (WC)	2	0
2012	Torshavn (WC)	4	1
2013	Dublin (WC)	3	0

v FINLAND

1949	Dublin (WC)	3	0
1949	Helsinki (WC)	1	1
1990	Dublin	1	1
2000	Dublin	3	0
2002	Helsinki	3	0

v FRANCE

1937	Paris	2	0
1952	Dublin	1	1
1953	Dublin (WC)	3	5
1953	Paris (WC)	0	1
1972	Dublin (WC)	2	1
1973	Paris (WC)	1	1
1976	Paris (WC)	0	2
1977	Dublin (WC)	1	0
1980	Paris (WC)	0	2
1981	Dublin (WC)	3	2

1989	Dublin	0	0
2004	Paris (WC)	0	0
2005	Dublin (WC)	0	1
2009	Dublin (WC)	0	1
2009	Paris (WC)	1	1
2016	Lyon (EC)	1	2
2018	Paris	0	2

v GEORGIA

2002	Tbilisi (EC)	2	1
2003	Dublin (EC)	2	0
2008	Mainz (WC)	2	1
2009	Dublin (WC)	2	1
2013	Dublin	4	0
2014	Tbilisi (EC)	2	1
2015	Dublin (EC)	1	0
2016	Dublin (WC)	1	0
2017	Tbilisi (WC)	1	1
2019	Dublin (EC)	1	0
2019	Tbilisi (EC)	0	0

v GERMANY/WEST GERMANY

1935	Dortmund	1	3
1936	Dublin	5	2
1939	Bremen	1	1
1951	Dublin	3	2
1952	Cologne	0	3
1955	Hamburg	1	2
1956	Dublin	3	0
1960	Dusseldorf	1	0
1966	Dublin	0	4
1970	Berlin	1	2
1975*	Dublin	1	0
1979	Dublin	1	3
1981	Bremen	0	3
1989	Dublin	1	1
1994	Hanover	2	0
2002	Ibaraki (WC)	1	1
2006	Stuttgart (EC)	0	1
2007	Dublin (EC)	0	0
2012	Dublin (WC)	1	6
2013	Cologne (WC)	0	3
2014	Gelsenkirchen (EC)	1	1
2015	Dublin (EC)	1	0

(*v W Germany 'B')

v GIBRALTAR

2014	Dublin (EC)	7	0
2015	Faro (EC)	4	0
2019	Victoria (EC)	1	0
2019	Dublin (EC)	2	0

v GREECE
2000	Dublin	0	1
2002	Athens	0	0
2012	Dublin	0	1

v HOLLAND
1932	Amsterdam	2	0
1934	Amsterdam	2	5
1935	Dublin	3	5
1955	Dublin	1	0
1956	Rotterdam	4	1
1980	Dublin (WC)	2	1
1981	Rotterdam (WC)	2	2
1982	Rotterdam (EC)	1	2
1983	Dublin (EC)	2	3
1988	Gelsenkirchen (EC)	0	1
1990	Palermo (WC)	1	1
1994	Tilburg	1	0
1994	Orlando (WC)	0	2
1995*	Liverpool (EC)	0	2
1996	Rotterdam	1	3

(*Qual Round play-off)

2000	Amsterdam (WC)	2	2
2001	Dublin (WC)	1	0
2004	Amsterdam	1	0
2006	Dublin	0	4
2016	Dublin	1	1

v HUNGARY
1934	Dublin	2	4
1936	Budapest	3	3
1936	Dublin	2	3
1939	Cork	2	2
1939	Budapest	2	2
1969	Dublin (WC)	1	2
1969	Budapest (WC)	0	4
1989	Budapest (WC)	0	0
1989	Dublin (WC)	2	0
1992	Gyor	2	1
2012	Budapest	0	0

v ICELAND
1962	Dublin (EC)	4	2
1962	Reykjavik (EC)	1	1
1982	Dublin (EC)	2	0
1983	Reykjavik (EC)	3	0
1986	Reykjavik	2	1
1996	Dublin (WC)	0	0
1997	Reykjavik (WC)	4	2
2017	Dublin	0	1

v IRAN
1972	Recife	2	1

2001*	Dublin (WC)	2	0
2001*	Tehran (WC)	0	1

(*Qual Round play-off)

v ISRAEL
1984	Tel Aviv	0	3
1985	Tel Aviv	0	0
1987	Dublin	5	0
2005	Tel Aviv (WC)	1	1
2005	Dublin (WC)	2	2

v ITALY
1926	Turin	0	3
1927	Dublin	1	2
1970	Florence (EC)	0	3
1971	Dublin (EC)	1	2
1985	Dublin	1	2
1990	Rome (WC)	0	1
1992	Boston, USA	0	2
1994	New York (WC)	1	0
2005	Dublin	1	2
2009	Bari (WC)	1	1
2009	Dublin (WC)	2	2
2011	Liege	2	0
2012	Poznan (EC)	0	2
2014	Fulham	0	0
2016	Lille (EC)	1	0

v JAMAICA
2004	Charlton	1	0

v KAZAKHSTAN
2012	Astana (WC)	2	1
2013	Dublin (WC)	3	1

v LATVIA
1992	Dublin (WC)	4	0
1993	Riga (WC)	2	0
1994	Riga (EC)	3	0
1995	Dublin (EC)	2	1
2013	Dublin	3	0

v LIECHTENSTEIN
1994	Dublin (EC)	4	0
1995	Eschen (EC)	0	0
1996	Eschen (WC)	5	0
1997	Dublin (WC)	5	0

v LITHUANIA
1993	Vilnius (WC)	1	0
1993	Dublin (WC)	2	0
1997	Dublin (WC)	0	0
1997	Zalgiris (WC)	2	1

v LUXEMBOURG
1936	Luxembourg	5	1
1953	Dublin (WC)	4	0
1954	Luxembourg (WC)	1	0
1987	Luxembourg (EC)	2	0
1987	Luxembourg (EC)	2	1

v MACEDONIA
1996	Dublin (WC)	3	0
1997	Skopje (WC)	2	3
1999	Dublin (EC)	1	0
1999	Skopje (EC)	1	1
2011	Dublin (EC)	2	1
2011	Skopje (EC)	2	0

v MALTA
1983	Valletta (EC)	1	0
1983	Dublin (EC)	8	0
1989	Dublin (WC)	2	0
1989	Valletta (WC)	2	0
1990	Valletta	3	0
1998	Dublin (EC)	1	0
1999	Valletta (EC)	3	2

v MEXICO
1984	Dublin	0	0
1994	Orlando (WC)	1	2
1996	New Jersey	2	2
1998	Dublin	0	0
2000	Chicago	2	2
2017	New Jersey	1	3

v MOLDOVA
2016	Chisinau (WC)	3	1
2017	Dublin (WC)	2	0

v MONTENEGRO
2008	Podgorica (WC)	0	0
2009	Dublin (WC)	0	0

v MOROCCO
1990	Dublin	1	0

v NEW ZEALAND
2019	Dublin	3	1

v NIGERIA
2002	Dublin	1	2
2004	Charlton	0	3
2009	Fulham	1	1

v NORWAY
1937	Oslo (WC)	2	3
1937	Dublin (WC)	3	3
1950	Dublin	2	2
1951	Oslo	3	2
1954	Dublin	2	1
1955	Oslo	3	1
1960	Dublin	3	1
1964	Oslo	4	1
1973	Oslo	1	1
1976	Dublin	3	0
1978	Oslo	0	0
1984	Oslo (WC)	0	1
1985	Dublin (WC)	0	0
1988	Oslo	0	0
1994	New York (WC)	0	0
2003	Dublin	1	0
2008	Oslo	1	1
2010	Dublin	1	2

v OMAN
2012	Fulham	4	1
2014	Dublin	2	0
2016	Dublin	4	0

v PARAGUAY
1999	Dublin	2	0
2010	Dublin	2	1

v POLAND
1938	Warsaw	0	6
1938	Dublin	3	2
1958	Katowice	2	2
1958	Dublin	2	2
1964	Cracow	1	3
1964	Dublin	3	2
1968	Dublin	2	2
1968	Katowice	0	1
1970	Dublin	1	2
1970	Poznan	0	2
1973	Wroclaw	0	2
1973	Dublin	1	0
1976	Poznan	2	0
1977	Dublin	0	0
1978	Lodz	0	3
1981	Bydgoszcz	0	3
1984	Dublin	0	0
1986	Warsaw	0	1
1988	Dublin	3	1
1991	Dublin (EC)	0	0
1991	Poznan (EC)	3	3
2004	Bydgoszcz	0	0
2008	Dublin	2	3
2013	Dublin	2	0
2013	Poznan	0	0

2015	Dublin (EC)	1	1
2015	Warsaw (EC)	1	2
2018	Wroclaw	1	1

v PORTUGAL
1946	Lisbon	1	3
1947	Dublin	0	2
1948	Lisbon	0	2
1949	Dublin	1	0
1972	Recife	1	2
1992	Boston, USA	2	0
1995	Dublin (EC)	1	0
1995	Lisbon (EC)	0	3
1996	Dublin	0	1
2000	Lisbon (WC)	1	1
2001	Dublin (WC)	1	1
2005	Dublin	1	0
2014	East Rutherford, USA	1	5

v ROMANIA
1988	Dublin	2	0
1990*	Genoa	0	0
1997	Bucharest (WC)	0	1
1997	Dublin (WC)	1	1
2004	Dublin	1	0
(*Rep won 5-4 on pens)			

v RUSSIA (See also Soviet Union)
1994	Dublin	0	0
1996	Dublin	0	2
2002	Dublin	2	0
2002	Moscow (EC)	2	4
2003	Dublin (EC)	1	1
2010	Dublin (EC)	2	3
2011	Moscow (EC)	0	0

v SAN MARINO
| 2006 | Dublin (EC) | 5 | 0 |
| 2007 | Rimini (EC) | 2 | 1 |

v SAUDI ARABIA
| 2002 | Yokohama (WC) | 3 | 0 |

v SERBIA
2008	Dublin	1	1
2012	Belgrade	0	0
2014	Dublin	1	2
2016	Belgrade (WC)	2	2
2017	Dublin (WC)	0	1

v SLOVAKIA
| 2007 | Dublin (EC) | 1 | 0 |
| 2007 | Bratislava (EC) | 2 | 2 |

2010	Zilina (EC)	1	1
2011	Dublin (EC)	0	0
2016	Dublin	2	2

v SOUTH AFRICA
| 2000 | New Jersey | 2 | 1 |
| 2009 | Limerick | 1 | 0 |

v SOVIET UNION (See also Russia)
1972	Dublin (WC)	1	2
1973	Moscow (WC)	0	1
1974	Dublin (EC)	3	0
1975	Kiev (EC)	1	2
1984	Dublin (WC)	1	0
1985	Moscow (WC)	0	2
1988	Hanover (EC)	1	1
1990	Dublin	1	0

v SPAIN
1931	Barcelona	1	1
1931	Dublin	0	5
1946	Madrid	1	0
1947	Dublin	3	2
1948	Barcelona	1	2
1949	Dublin	1	4
1952	Madrid	0	6
1955	Dublin	2	2
1964	Seville (EC)	1	5
1964	Dublin (EC)	0	2
1965	Dublin (WC)	1	0
1965	Seville (WC)	1	4
1965	Paris (WC)	0	1
1966	Dublin (EC)	0	0
1966	Valencia (EC)	0	2
1977	Dublin	0	1
1982	Dublin (EC)	3	3
1983	Zaragoza (EC)	0	2
1985	Cork	0	0
1988	Seville (WC)	0	2
1989	Dublin (WC)	1	0
1992	Seville (WC)	0	0
1993	Dublin (WC)	1	3
2002*	Suwon (WC)	1	1
(*Rep lost 3-2 on pens)			
2012	Gdansk (EC)	0	4
2013	New York	0	2

v SWEDEN
1949	Stockholm (WC)	1	3
1949	Dublin (WC)	1	3
1959	Dublin	3	2
1960	Malmo	1	4
1970	Dublin (EC)	1	1

1970	Malmo (EC)	0	1
1999	Dublin	2	0
2006	Dublin	3	0
2013	Stockholm (WC)	0	0
2013	Dublin (WC)	1	2
2016	Paris (EC)	1	1

v SWITZERLAND

1935	Basle	0	1
1936	Dublin	1	0
1937	Berne	1	0
1938	Dublin	4	0
1948	Dublin	0	1
1975	Dublin (EC)	2	1
1975	Berne (EC)	0	1
1980	Dublin	2	0
1985	Dublin (WC)	3	0
1985	Berne (WC)	0	0
1992	Dublin	2	1
2002	Dublin (EC)	1	2
2003	Basle (EC)	0	2
2004	Basle (WC)	1	1
2005	Dublin (WC)	0	0
2016	Dublin	1	0
2019	Dublin (EC)	1	1
2019	Geneva (EC)	0	2

v TRINIDAD & TOBAGO

| 1982 | Port of Spain | 1 | 2 |

v TUNISIA

| 1988 | Dublin | 4 | 0 |

v TURKEY

| 1966 | Dublin (EC) | 2 | 1 |
| 1967 | Ankara (EC) | 1 | 2 |

1974	Izmir (EC)	1	1
1975	Dublin (EC)	4	0
1976	Ankara	3	3
1978	Dublin	4	2
1990	Izmir	0	0
1990	Dublin (EC)	5	0
1991	Istanbul (EC)	3	1
1999	Dublin (EC)	1	1
1999	Bursa (EC)	0	0
2003	Dublin	2	2
2014	Dublin	1	2
2018	Antalya	0	1

v URUGUAY

1974	Montevideo	0	2
1986	Dublin	1	1
2011	Dublin	2	3
2017	Dublin	3	1

v USA

1979	Dublin	3	2
1991	Boston	1	1
1992	Dublin	4	1
1992	Washington	1	3
1996	Boston	1	2
2000	Foxboro	1	1
2002	Dublin	2	1
2014	Dublin	4	1
2018	Dublin	2	1

v YUGOSLAVIA

1955	Dublin	1	4
1988	Dublin	2	0
1998	Belgrade (EC)	0	1
1999	Dublin (EC)	2	1

BRITISH AND IRISH INTERNATIONAL
APPEARANCES SINCE THE WAR (1946–2020)

(As start of season 2020–21; in year shown 2020 = season 2019-20. *Also a pre-War international player.
Totals include appearances as substitute)

ENGLAND

Agbonlahor G (Aston Villa, 2009–10)	3
Abraham T (Chelsea, 2018 – 20)	4
A'Court A (Liverpool, 1958–59)	5
Adams T (Arsenal, 1987–2001)	66
Alexander-Arnold T (Liverpool, 2018 – 20)	9
Alli D (Tottenham, 2016–18)	37
Allen A (Stoke, 1960)	3
Allen C (QPR, Tottenham, 1984–88)	5
Allen R (WBA, 1952–55)	5
Anderson S (Sunderland, 1962)	2
Anderson V (Nottm Forest, Arsenal, Manchester Utd, 1979–88)	30
Anderton D (Tottenham, 1994–2002)	30
Angus J (Burnley, 1961)	1
Armfield J (Blackpool, 1959–66)	43
Armstrong D (Middlesbrough, Southampton, 1980–4)	3
Armstrong K (Chelsea, 1955)	1
Ashton D (West Ham, 2008)	1
Astall G (Birmingham, 1956)	2
Astle J (WBA, 1969–70)	5
Aston J (Manchester Utd, 1949–51)	17
Atyeo J (Bristol City, 1956–57)	6
Bailey G (Manchester Utd, 1985)	2
Bailey M (Charlton, 1964–5)	2
Baily E (Tottenham, 1950–3)	9
Baines L (Everton, 2010–15)	30
Baker J (Hibernian, Arsenal, 1960–6)	8
Ball A (Blackpool, Everton, Arsenal, 1965–75)	72
Ball M (Everton, 2001)	1
Banks G (Leicester, Stoke, 1963–72)	73
Banks T (Bolton, 1958–59)	6
Bardsley D (QPR, 1993)	2
Barham M (Norwich, 1983)	2
Barkley R (Everton, Chelsea, 2014–20)	33
Barlow R (WBA, 1955)	1
Barmby N (Tottenham, Middlesbrough, Everton, Liverpool, 1995–2002)	23
Barnes J (Watford, Liverpool, 1983–96)	79
Barnes P (Manchester City, WBA, Leeds, 1978–82)	22
Barrass M (Bolton, 1952–53)	3
Barrett E (Oldham, Aston Villa, 1991–93)	3
Barry G (Aston Villa, Manchester City, 2000–12)	53
Barton J (Manchester City, 2007)	1
Barton W (Wimbledon, Newcastle, 1995)	3
Batty D (Leeds, Blackburn, Newcastle, Leeds, 1991–2000)	42
Baynham R (Luton, 1956)	3
Beardsley P (Newcastle, Liverpool, Newcastle, 1986–96)	59
Beasant D (Chelsea, 1990)	2

Beattie J (Southampton, 2003–04)	5
Beattie K (Ipswich, 1975–58)	9
Beckham D (Manchester Utd, Real Madrid, LA Galaxy, AC Milan 1997–2010)	115
Bell C (Manchester City, 1968–76)	48
Bent D (Charlton, Tottenham Sunderland, Aston Villa, 2006–12)	13
Bentley D (Blackburn, 2008–09)	7
Bentley R (Chelsea, 1949–55)	12
Berry J (Manchester Utd, 1953–56)	4
Bertrand R (Chelsea, Southampton, 2013–18)	19
Birtles G (Nottm Forest, 1980–81)	3
Blissett L (Watford, AC Milan, 1983–84)	14
Blockley J (Arsenal, 1973)	1
Blunstone F (Chelsea, 1955–57)	5
Bonetti P (Chelsea, 1966–70)	7
Bothroyd J (Cardiff, 2011)	1
Bould S (Arsenal, 1994)	2
Bowles S (QPR, 1974–77)	5
Bowyer L (Leeds, 2003)	1
Boyer P (Norwich, 1976)	1
Brabrook P (Chelsea, 1958–60)	3
Bracewell P (Everton, 1985–86)	3
Bradford G (Bristol Rov, 1956)	1
Bradley W (Manchester Utd, 1959)	3
Bridge W (Southampton, Chelsea, Manchester City 2002–10)	36
Bridges B (Chelsea, 1965–66)	4
Broadbent P (Wolves, 1958–60)	7
Broadis I (Manchester City, Newcastle, 1952–54)	14
Brooking T (West Ham, 1974–82)	47
Brooks J (Tottenham, 1957)	3
Brown A (WBA, 1971)	1
Brown K (West Ham, 1960)	1
Brown W (Manchester Utd, 1999–2010)	23
Bull S (Wolves, 1989–91)	13
Butcher T (Ipswich, Rangers, 1980–90)	77
Butland J (Birmingham, Stoke, 2013–19)	9
Butt N (Manchester Utd, Newcastle, 1997–2005)	39
Byrne G (Liverpool, 1963–66)	2
Byrne J (Crystal Palace, West Ham, 1962–65)	11
Byrne R (Manchester Utd, 1954–58)	33
Cahill G (Bolton, Chelsea, 2011–18)	61
Callaghan I (Liverpool, 1966–78)	4
Campbell F (Sunderland, 2012)	1
Campbell S (Tottenham, Arsenal, Portsmouth, 1996–2008)	73
Carragher J (Liverpool, 1999–2010)	38
Carrick M (West Ham, Tottenham, Manchester Utd, 2001–16)	34
Carroll A (Newcastle, Liverpool 2011– 13)	9
Carson S (Liverpool, Aston Villa WBA, Bursaspor 2008–12)	4

*Carter H (Derby, 1947) 7
Caulker S (Tottenham, 2013) 1
Chamberlain M (Stoke, 1983–85) 8
Chalobah N (Watford, 2019) 1
Chambers C (Arsenal, 2015) 3
Channon M (Southampton, Manchester
  City, 1973–78) 46
Charles G (Nottm Forest, 1991) 2
Charlton, J (Leeds, 1965–70) 35
Charlton, R (Manchester Utd, 1958–70) 106
Charnley R (Blackpool, 1963) 1
Cherry T (Leeds, 1976–80) 27
Chilton A (Manchester Utd, 1951–52) 2
Chilwell B (Leicester, 2019–20) 11
Chivers M (Tottenham, 1971–74) 24
Clamp E (Wolves, 1958) 4
Clapton D (Arsenal, 1959) 1
Clarke A (Leeds, 1970–6) 19
Clarke H (Tottenham, 1954) 1
Clayton R (Blackburn, 1956–60) 35
Clemence R (Liverpool, Tottenham, 1973–84) 61
Clement D (QPR, 1976–7) 5
Cleverley T (Manchester Utd, 2013–14) 13
Clough B (Middlesbrough, 1960) 2
Clough N (Nottm Forest, Liverpool, 1989–93) 14
Clyne N (Southampton, Liverpool, 2015–17) 14
Coates R (Burnley, Tottenham, 1970–71) 4
Cockburn H (Manchester Utd, 1947–52) 13
Cohen G (Fulham, 1964–68) 37
Cole Andy (Manchester Utd, 1995–2002) 15
Cole Ashley (Arsenal, Chelsea, 2001–14) 107
Cole C (West Ham, 2009–10) 7
Cole J (West Ham, Chelsea, 2001–10) 56
Collymore S (Nottm Forest, Aston Villa, 1995–97) 3
Compton L (Arsenal, 1951) 2
Connelly J (Burnley, Manchester Utd,1960–66) 20
Cook L (Bournemouth, 2018) 1
Cooper C (Nottm Forest, 1995) 2
Cooper T (Leeds, 1969–75) 20
Coppell S (Manchester Utd, 1978–83) 42
Cork J (Burnley 2018) 1
Corrigan J (Manchester City, 1976–82) 9
Cottee T (West Ham, Everton, 1987–89) 7
Cowans G (Aston Villa, Bari, Aston Villa,
  1983–91) 10
Crawford R (Ipswich, 1962) 2
Cresswell A (West Ham, 2017–18) 3
Crouch P (Southampton, Liverpool,
  Portsmouth, Tottenham, 2005–11) 42
Crowe C (Wolves, 1963) 1
Cunningham L (WBA, Real Madrid, 1979–81) 6
Curle K (Manchester City, 1992) 3
Currie A (Sheffield Utd, Leeds, 1972–79) 17

Daley T (Aston Villa, 1992) 7
Davenport P (Nottm Forest, 1985) 1
Davies K (Bolton, 2011) 1
Dawson M (Tottenham 2011) 4
Deane B (Sheffield Utd, 1991–93) 3
Deeley N (Wolves, 1959) 2
Defoe J (Tottenham, Portsmouth, Tottenham,
  Sunderland, 2004–17) 57

Delph F (Aston Villa, Manchester City, 2015–19) 20
Devonshire A (West Ham, 1980–84) 8
Dickinson J (Portsmouth, 1949–57) 48
Dier E (Tottenham, 2016–19) 40
Ditchburn E (Tottenham, 1949–57) 6
Dixon K (Chelsea, 1985–87) 8
Dixon L (Arsenal, 1990–99) 22
Dobson M (Burnley, Everton, 1974–75) 5
Dorigo T (Chelsea, Leeds, 1990–94) 15
Douglas B (Blackburn, 1959–63) 36
Downing S (Middlesbrough, Aston Villa,
  Liverpool, West Ham, 2005–15) 35
Doyle M (Manchester City, 1976–77) 5
Drinkwater D (Leicester, 2016) 3
Dublin D (Coventry, Aston Villa, 1998–99) 4
Dunk L (Brighton, 2019) 1
Dunn D (Blackburn, 2003) 1
Duxbury, M (Manchester Utd, 1984–85) 10
Dyer K (Newcastle, West Ham, 2000–08) 33

Eastham G (Arsenal, 1963–66) 19
Eckersley W (Blackburn, 1950–54) 17
Edwards, D (Manchester Utd, 1955–58) 18
Ehiogu U (Aston Villa, Middlesbrough,
  1996–2002) 4
Ellerington W (Southampton, 1949) 2
Elliott W (Burnley, 1952–53) 5

Fantham J (Sheffield Wed, 1962) 1
Fashanu J (Wimbledon, 1989) 2
Fenwick T (QPR, 1984–88) 20
Ferdinand L (QPR, Newcastle,
  Tottenham, 1993–98) 17
Ferdinand R (West Ham, Leeds,
  Manchester Utd, 1997–2011) 81
Finney T (Preston, 1947–59) 76
Flanagan J (Liverpool, 2014) 1
Flowers R (Wolves, 1955–66) 49
Flowers T (Southampton, Blackburn,
  1993–98) 11
Forster F (Celtic, Southampton, 2014–16) 6
Foster B (Manchester Utd,
  Birmingham, WBA, 2007–14) 8
Foster S (Brighton, 1982) 3
Foulkes W (Manchester Utd, 1955) 1
Fowler R (Liverpool, Leeds, 1996–2002) 26
Francis G (QPR, 1975–76) 12
Francis T (Birmingham, Nottm Forest,
  Man City, Sampdoria, 1977–86) 52
Franklin N (Stoke, 1947–50) 27
Froggatt J (Portsmouth, 1950–53) 13
Froggatt R (Sheffield Wed, 1953) 4

Gardner A (Tottenham, 2004) 1
Garrett T (Blackpool, 1952–54) 3
Gascoigne P (Tottenham, Lazio,
  Rangers, Middlesbrough, 1989–98) 57
Gates E (Ipswich, 1981) 2
George C (Derby, 1977) 1
Gerrard S (Liverpool, 2000–14) 114
Gibbs K (Arsenal, 2011–16) 10
Gidman J (Aston Villa, 1977) 1

Gillard I (QPR, 1975–76) 3
Goddard P (West Ham, 1982) 1
Gomez J (Liverpool, 2018–20) 8
Grainger C (Sheffield Utd, Sunderland,
 1956–57) 7
Gray A (Crystal Palace, 1992) 1
Gray M (Sunderland, 1999) 3
Greaves J (Chelsea, Tottenham, 1959–67) 57
Green R (Norwich, West Ham 2005–12) 12
Greenhoff B (Manchester Utd, Leeds, 1976–80) 18
Gregory J (QPR, 1983–84) 6
Guppy S (Leicester, 2000) 1

Hagan J (Sheffield Utd, 1949) 1
Haines J (WBA, 1949) 1
Hall J (Birmingham, 1956–57) 17
Hancocks J (Wolves, 1949–50) 3
Hardwick G (Middlesbrough, 1947–48) 13
Harford M (Luton, 1988–89) 2
Hargreaves O (Bayern Munich,
 Manchester Utd, 2002–08) 42
Harris G (Burnley, 1966) 1
Harris P (Portsmouth, 1950–54) 2
Hart J (Manchester City, 2010–18) 75
Harvey C (Everton, 1971) 1
Hassall H (Huddersfield, Bolton, 1951–54) 5
Hateley M (Portsmouth, AC Milan, Monaco,
 Rangers, 1984–92) 32
Haynes J (Fulham, 1955–62) 56
Heaton T (Burnley, 2016–17) 3
Hector K (Derby, 1974) . 2
Hellawell M (Birmingham, 1963) 2
Henderson J (Sunderland, Liverpool, 2011–20) 55
Hendrie L (Aston Villa, 1999) 1
Henry R (Tottenham, 1963) 1
Heskey E (Leicester, Liverpool, Birmingham,
 Wigan, Aston Villa 1999–2010) 62
Hill F (Bolton, 1963) 2
Hill G (Manchester Utd, 1976–78) 6
Hill R (Luton, 1983–86) 3
Hinchcliffe A (Everton, Sheffield Wed, 1997–99) 3
Hinton A (Wolves, Nottm Forest, 1963–65) 3
Hirst D (Sheffield Wed, 1991–92) 3
Hitchens G (Aston Villa, Inter Milan, 1961–62) 7
Hoddle G (Tottenham, Monaco, 1980–88) 53
Hodge S (Aston Villa, Tottenham,
 Nottm Forest, 1986–91) 24
Hodgkinson A (Sheffield Utd, 1957–61) 5
Holden D (Bolton, 1959) 5
Holliday E (Middlesbrough, 1960) 3
Hollins J (Chelsea, 1967) 1
Hopkinson E (Bolton, 1958–60) 14
Howe D (WBA, 1958–60) 23
Howe J (Derby, 1948–49) 3
Howey S (Newcastle, 1995–96) 4
Huddlestone T (Tottenham, 2010–13) 4
Hudson A (Stoke, 1975) 2
Hudson–Odoi C (Chelsea, 2019–20) 3
Hughes E (Liverpool, Wolves, 1970–80) 62
Hughes L (Liverpool, 1950) 3
Hunt R (Liverpool, 1962–69) 34
Hunt S (WBA, 1984) 2

Hunter N (Leeds, 1966–75) 28
Hurst G (West Ham, 1966–72) 49
Ince P (Manchester Utd, Inter Milan,
 Liver-ool, Middlesbrough, 1993–2000) 53
Ings D (Liverpool 2016) 1
Jagielka P (Everton, 2008–17) 40
James D (Liverpool, Aston Villa, West Ham,
 Manchester City, Portsmouth,
 1997–2010) 53
Jarvis M (Wolves, 2011) 1
Jeffers F (Arsenal, 2003) 1
Jenas J (Newcastle, Tottenham, 2003–10) 21
Jenkinson C (Arsenal, 2013) 1
Jezzard B (Fulham, 1954–56) 2
Johnson A (Crystal Palace, Everton,
 2005–08) 8
Johnson A (Manchester City, 2010–13) 12
Johnson D (Ipswich, Liverpool, 1975–80) 8
Johnson G (Chelsea,
 Portsmouth, Liverpool, 2004–14) 54
Johnson S (Derby, 2001) 1
Johnston H (Blackpool, 1947–54) 10
Jones M (Leeds, Sheffield Utd, 1965–70) 3
Jones P (Manchester Utd, 2012–18) 27
Jones R (Liverpool, 1992–95) 8
Jones W H (Liverpool, 1950) 2

Kane H (Tottenham, 2015–20) 45
Kay A (Everton, 1963) 1
Keane M (Burnley, Everton, 2017–20) 10
Keegan K (Liverpool, Hamburg,
 Southampton, 1973–82) 63
Kelly, M (Liverpool, 2012) 1
Kennedy A (Liverpool, 1984) 2
Kennedy R (Liverpool, 1976–80) 17
Keown M (Everton, Arsenal,
 1992–2002) 43
Kevan D (WBA, 1957–61) 14
Kidd B (Manchester Utd, 1970) 2
King L (Tottenham, 2002–10) 21
Kirkland C (Liverpool, 2007) 1
Knight Z (Fulham, 2005) 2
Knowles C (Tottenham, 1968) 4
Konchesky P (Charlton, 2003–06) 2

Labone B (Everton, 1963–70) 26
Lallana A (Southampton, Liverpool, 2014–18) 34
Lambert R (Southampton, Liverpool, 2014–15) 11
Lampard F Snr (West Ham, 1973–80) 2
Lampard F Jnr (West Ham, Chelsea, 2000–14) 106
Langley J (Fulham, 1958) 3
Langton R (Blackburn, Preston,
 Bolton, 1947–51) 11
Latchford R (Everton, 1978–9) 12
Lawler C (Liverpool, 1971–72) 4
*Lawton T (Chelsea, Notts Co, 1947–49) 15
Lee F (Manchester City, 1969–72) 27
Lee J (Derby, 1951) 1
Lee R (Newcastle, 1995–99) 21
Lee S (Liverpool, 1983–84) 14
Lennon A (Tottenham, 2006–13) 21
Le Saux G (Blackburn, Chelsea, 1994–2001) 36

271

Lescott J (Everton, Manchester City, 2008–13)	26
Le Tissier M (Southampton, 1994–97)	8
Lindsay A (Liverpool, 1974)	4
Lineker G (Leicester, Everton, Barcelona, Tottenham, 1985–92)	80
Lingard J (Manchester Utd, 2017–19)	24
Little B (Aston Villa, 1975)	1
Livermore J (Tottenham, WBA, 2013–18)	7
Lloyd L (Liverpool, Nottm Forest, 1971–80)	4
Lofthouse N (Bolton, 1951–59)	33
Loftus-Cheek R (Chelsea, 2018–19)	10
Lowe E (Aston Villa, 1947)	3
Mabbutt G (Tottenham, 1983–92)	16
Macdonald M (Newcastle, 1972–76)	14
Madeley P (Leeds, 1971–77)	24
Maddison J (Leicester, 2020)	1
Maguire H (Leicester, Manchester Utd, 2018–20)	26
Mannion W (Middlesbrough, 1947–52)	26
Mariner P (Ipswich, Arsenal, 1977–85)	35
Marsh R (QPR, Manchester City, 1972–73)	9
Mason R (Tottenham, 2015)	1
Martin A (West Ham, 1981–87)	17
Martyn N (Crystal Palace, Leeds, 1992–2002)	23
Marwood B (Arsenal, 1989)	1
Matthews R (Coventry, 1956–57)	5
*Matthews S (Stoke, Blackpool, 1947–57)	37
McCann G (Sunderland, 2001)	1
McCarthy A (Southampton, 2019)	1
McDermott T (Liverpool, 1978–82)	25
McDonald C (Burnley, 1958–59)	8
McFarland R (Derby, 1971–77)	28
McGarry W (Huddersfield, 1954–56)	4
McGuinness W (Manchester Utd, 1959)	2
McMahon S (Liverpool, 1988–91)	17
McManaman S (Liverpool, Real Madrid, 1995–2002)	37
McNab R (Arsenal, 1969)	4
McNeil M (Middlesbrough, 1961–62)	9
Meadows J (Manchester City, 1955)	1
Medley L (Tottenham, 1951–52)	6
Melia J (Liverpool, 1963)	2
Merrick G (Birmingham, 1952–54)	23
Merson P (Arsenal, Middlesbrough, Aston Villa, 1992–99)	21
Metcalfe V (Huddersfield, 1951)	2
Milburn J (Newcastle, 1949–56)	13
Miller B (Burnley, 1961)	1
Mills D (Leeds, 2001–04)	19
Mills M (Ipswich, 1973–82)	42
Milne G (Liverpool, 1963–65)	14
Milner J (Aston Villa, Manchester City, Liverpool, 2010–16)	61
Milton A (Arsenal, 1952)	1
Mings T (Aston Villa, 2020)	2
Moore R (West Ham, 1962–74)	108
Morley A (Aston Villa, 1982–83)	6
Morris J (Derby, 1949–50)	3
Mortensen S (Blackpool, 1947–54)	25
Mount M (Chelsea, 2020)	6
Mozley B (Derby, 1950)	3
Mullen J (Wolves, 1947–54)	12

Mullery A (Tottenham, 1965–72)	35
Murphy D (Liverpool, 2002–04)	9
Neal P (Liverpool, 1976–84)	50
Neville G (Manchester Utd, 1995–2009)	85
Neville P (Manchester Utd, Everton, 1996–2008)	59
Newton K (Blackburn, Everton, 1966–70)	27
Nicholls J (WBA, 1954)	2
Nicholson W (Tottenham, 1951)	1
Nish D (Derby, 1973–74)	5
Norman M (Tottenham, 1962–5)	23
Nugent D (Preston, 2007)	1
O'Grady M (Huddersfield, Leeds, 1963–9)	2
Osgood P (Chelsea, 1970–74)	4
Osman L (Everton, 2013)	2
Osman R (Ipswich, 1980–84)	11
Owen M (Liverpool, Real Madrid, Newcastle, 1998–2008)	89
Owen S (Luton, 1954)	3
Oxlade-Chamberlain A (Arsenal, Liverpool, 2012–20)	35
Paine T (Southampton, 1963–66)	19
Pallister G (Middlesbrough, Manchester Utd 1988–97)	22
Palmer C (Sheffield Wed, 1992–94)	18
Parker P (QPR, Manchester Utd, 1989–94)	19
Parker S (Charlton, Chelsea, Newcastle, West Ham, Tottenham, 2004–13)	18
Parkes P (QPR, 1974)	1
Parlour R (Arsenal, 1999–2001)	10
Parry R (Bolton, 1960)	2
Peacock A (Middlesbrough, Leeds, 1962–66)	6
Pearce S (Nottm Forest, West Ham, 1987–2000)	78
Pearson Stan (Manchester Utd, 1948–52)	8
Pearson Stuart (Manchester Utd, 1976–78)	15
Pegg D (Manchester Utd, 1957)	1
Pejic M (Stoke, 1974)	4
Perry W (Blackpool, 1956)	3
Perryman S (Tottenham, 1982)	1
Peters M (West Ham, Tottenham, 1966–74)	67
Phelan M (Manchester Utd, 1990)	1
Phillips K (Sunderland, 1999–2002)	8
Phillips L (Portsmouth, 1952–55)	3
Pickering F (Everton, 1964–65)	3
Pickering N (Sunderland, 1983)	1
Pickford J (Everton, 2018–20)	24
Pilkington B (Burnley, 1955)	1
Platt D (Aston Villa, Bari, Juventus, Sampdoria, Arsenal, 1990–96)	62
Pointer R (Burnley, 1962)	3
Pope N (Burnley, 2018–20)	2
Powell C (Charlton, 2001–02)	5
Pye J (Wolves, 1950)	1
Quixall A (Sheffield Wed, 1954–55)	5
Radford J (Arsenal, 1969–72)	2

Ramsey A (Southampton, Tottenham, 1949–54) 32
Rashford M (Manchester Utd, 2016–20) 38
Reaney P (Leeds, 1969–71) 3
Redknapp J (Liverpool, 1996–2000) 17
Redmond N (Southampton 2017) 1
Reeves K (Norwich, Manchester City, 1980) 2
Regis C (WBA, Coventry, 1982–88) 5
Reid P (Everton, 1985–88) 13
Revie D (Manchester City, 1955–57) 6
Rice D (West Ham, 2019–20) 7
Richards, J (Wolves, 1973) 1
Richards M (Manchester City, 2007–12) 13
Richardson K (Aston Villa, 1994) 1
Richardson K (Manchester Utd, 2005–07) 8
Rickaby S (WBA, 1954) 1
Ricketts M (Bolton, 2002) 1
Rimmer J (Arsenal, 1976) 1
Ripley S (Blackburn, 1994–97) 2
Rix G (Arsenal, 1981–84) 17
Robb G (Tottenham, 1954) 1
Roberts G (Tottenham, 1983–84) 6
Robinson P (Leeds, Tottenham, 2003–08) 41
Robson B (WBA, Manchester Utd, 1980–92) 90
Robson R (WBA, 1958–62) 20
Rocastle D (Arsenal, 1989–92) 14
Rodriguez J (Southampton, 2014) 1
Rodwell J (Everton, Manchester City, 2012–13) 3
Rooney W (Everton, Manchester Utd, DC United, 2003–19) 120
Rose D (Tottenham, 2016–20) 29
Rowley J (Manchester Utd, 1949–52) 6
Royle J (Everton, Manchester City, 1971–77) 6
Ruddock N (Liverpool, 1995) 1
Ruddy J (Norwich, 2013) 1

Sadler D (Manchester Utd, 1968–71) 4
Salako J (Crystal Palace, 1991–92) 5
Sancho J (Borussia Dortmund, 2019–20) 11
Sansom K (Crystal Palace, Arsenal, 1979–88) 86
Scales J (Liverpool, 1995) 3
Scholes P (Manchester Utd, 1997–2004) 66
Scott L (Arsenal, 1947–49) 17
Seaman D (QPR, Arsenal, 1989–2003) 75
Sewell J (Sheffield Wed, 1952–54) 6
Shackleton L (Sunderland, 1949–55) 5
Sharpe L (Manchester Utd, 1991–94) 8
Shaw G (Sheffield Utd, 1959–63) 5
Shaw L (Southampton, Manchester Utd, 2014–19) 8
Shawcross, N (Stoke, 2013) 1
Shearer A (Southampton, Blackburn, Newcastle, 1992–2000) 63
Shellito K (Chelsea, 1963) 1
Shelvey J (Liverpool, Swansea, 2013–16) 6
Sheringham E (Tottenham, Manchester Utd, Tottenham, 1993–2002) 51
Sherwood T (Tottenham, 1999) 3
Shilton P (Leicester, Stoke, Nottm Forest, Southampton, Derby, 1971–90) 125
Shimwell E (Blackpool, 1949) 1
Shorey N (Reading, 2007) 1
Sillett P (Chelsea, 1955) 3

Sinclair T (West Ham, Manchester City, 2002–04) 12
Sinton A (QPR, Sheffield Wed, 1992–94) 12
Slater W (Wolves, 1955–60) 12
Smalling C (Manchester Utd, 2012–17) 31
Smith A (Arsenal, 1989–92) 13
Smith A (Leeds, Manchester Utd, Newcastle, 2001–08) 19
Smith L (Arsenal, 1951–53) 6
Smith R (Tottenham, 1961–64) 15
Smith T (Birmingham, 1960) 2
Smith T (Liverpool, 1971) 1
Solanke D (Liverpool, 2018) 1
Southgate G (Aston Villa, Middlesbrough, 1996–2004) 57
Spink N (Aston Villa, 1983) 1
Springett R (Sheffield Wed, 1960–66) 33
Staniforth R (Huddersfield, 1954–55) 8
Statham D (WBA, 1983) 3
Stein B (Luton, 1984) 1
Stepney A (Manchester Utd, 1968) 1
Sterland M (Sheffield Wed, 1989) 1
Sterling R (Liverpool, Manchester City, 2013–20) 56
Steven T (Everton, Rangers, Marseille, 1985–92) 36
Stevens G (Everton, Rangers, 1985–92) 46
Stevens G (Tottenham, 1985–86) 7
Stewart P (Tottenham, 1992) 3
Stiles N (Manchester Utd, 1965–70) 28
Stone S (Nottm Forest, 1996) 9
Stones J (Everton, Manchester City, 2014–20) 39
Storey P (Arsenal, 1971–73) 19
Storey–Moore I (Nottm Forest, 1970) 1
Streten B (Luton, 1950) 1
Sturridge D (Chelsea, Liverpool, 2012–18) 26
Summerbee M (Manchester City, 1968–73) 8
Sunderland, A (Arsenal, 1980) 1
Sutton C (Blackburn, 1997) 1
Swan P (Sheffield Wed, 1960–62) 19
Swift F (Manchester City, 1947–79) 19

Talbot B (Ipswich, Arsenal, 1977–80) 6
Tambling R (Chelsea, 1963–66) 3
Tarkowski J (Burnley, 2018–19) 2
Taylor E (Blackpool, 1954) 1
Taylor J (Fulham, 1951) 1
Taylor P (Liverpool, 1948) 3
Taylor P (Crystal Palace, 1976) 4
Taylor T (Manchester Utd, 1953–58) 19
Temple D (Everton, 1965) 1
Terry J (Chelsea, 2003–12) 78
Thomas D (QPR, 1975–76) 8
Thomas D (Coventry, 1983) 2
Thomas G (Crystal Palace, 1991–92) 9
Thomas M (Arsenal, 1989–90) 2
Thompson A (Celtic, 2004) 1
Thompson Peter (Liverpool, 1964–70) 16
Thompson Phil (Liverpool, 1976–83) 42
Thompson T (Aston Villa, Preston, 1952–57) 2
Thomson R (Wolves, 1964–65) 8
Todd C (Derby, 1972–77) 27

273

Tomori F (Chelsea, 2020) 1
Towers A (Sunderland, 1978) 3
Townsend A (Tottenham, Newcastle,
Crystal Palace, 2014–17) 13
Trippier K (Tottenham, Atletico Madrid, 2017–20) 19
Tueart D (Manchester City, 1975–77) 6

Ufton D (Charlton, 1954) 1
Unsworth D (Everton, 1995) 1
Upson M (Birmingham, West Ham, 2003–10) 21

Vardy (Leicester, 2015–18) 26
Vassell D (Aston Villa, 2002–04) 22
Venables T (Chelsea, 1965) 2
Venison B (Newcastle, 1995) 2
Viljoen C (Ipswich, 1975) 2
Viollet D (Manchester Utd, 1960) 2

Waddle C (Newcastle, Tottenham,
Marseille, 1985–92) 62
Waiters A (Blackpool, 1964–65) 5
Walcott T (Arsenal, 2006–17) 47
Walker D (Nottm Forest, Sampdoria,
Sheffield Wed, 1989–94) 59
Walker I (Tottenham, Leicester,
1996–2004) 48
Walker K (Tottenham, Manchester City,
2012–19) 48
Wallace D (Southampton, 1986) 1
Walsh P (Luton, 1983–4) 5
Walters M (Rangers, 1991) 1
Ward P (Brighton, 1980) 1
Ward T (Derby, 1948) 2
Ward-Prowse J (Southampton, 2017–19) 2
Warnock S (Blackburn, Aston Villa, 2008–11) 2
Watson D (Sunderland, Manchester City,
Werder Bremen, Southampton, Stoke, 1974–82) 65
Watson D (Norwich, Everton, 1984–8) 12
Watson W (Sunderland, 1950–1) 4
Webb N (Nottm Forest, Manchester
Utd, 1988–92) 26
Welbeck D (Manchester Utd, Arsenal, 2011–19) 42
Weller K (Leicester, 1974) 4
West G (Everton, 1969) 3
Wheeler J (Bolton, 1955) 1
White D (Manchester City, 1993) 1
Whitworth S (Leicester, 1975–76) 7
Whymark T (Ipswich, 1978) 1
Wignall F (Nottm Forest, 1965) 2
Wilcox J (Blackburn, Leeds, 1996–2000) 3
Wilkins R (Chelsea, Manchester Utd,
AC Milan, 1976–87) 84
Williams B (Wolves, 1949–56) 24
Williams S (Southampton, 1983–85) 6
Willis A (Tottenham, 1952) 1
Wilshaw D (Wolves, 1954–57) 12
Wilshere J (Arsenal, 2011–16) 34
Wilson C (Bournemouth, 2019–20) 4
Wilson R (Huddersfield, Everton, 1960–8) 63
Winks H (Tottenham, 2018–20) 6
Winterburn N (Arsenal, 1990–93) 2
Wise D (Chelsea, 1991–2001) 21

Withe P (Aston Villa, 1981–85) 11
Wood R (Manchester Utd, 1955–56) 3
Woodcock A (Nottm Forest, Cologne,
Arsenal, 1977–86) 42
Woodgate J (Leeds, Newcastle, Middlesbrough,
Tottenham, 1999–2008) 8
Woods C (Norwich, Rangers,
Sheffield Wed, 1984–93) 43
Worthington F (Leicester, 1974–75) 8
Wright I (Crystal Palace, Arsenal, West Ham,
1991–99) 33
Wright M (Southampton, Derby,
Liverpool, 1984–96) 45
Wright R (Ipswich, Arsenal, 2000–02) 2
Wright T (Everton, 1968–70) 11
Wright W (Wolves, 1947–59) 105
Wright-Phillips S (Manchester City,
Chelsea, Manchester City, 2005–11) 36

Young A (Aston Villa, Manchester Utd, 2008–18) 39
Young G (Sheffield Wed, 1965) 1
Young L (Charlton, 2005) 7

SCOTLAND

Zaha W (Manchester Utd, 2013–14) 2
Zamora R (Fulham, 2011–12) 2
Adam C (Rangers, Blackpool, Liverpool,
Stoke, 2007–15) 26
Aird J (Burnley, 1954) 4
Aitken G (East Fife, 1949–54) 8
Aitken R (Celtic, Newcastle, St Mirren,
1980–92) 57
Albiston A (Manchester Utd, 1982–6) 14
Alexander G (Preston, Burnley, 2002–10) 40
Alexander N (Cardiff, 2006) 2
Allan T (Dundee, 1974) 2
Anderson J (Leicester, 1954) 1
Anderson R (Aberdeen, Sunderland, 2003–08) 11
Anya I (Watford, Derby, 2014–18) 29
Archer J (Millwall, 2018) 1
Archibald S (Aberdeen, Tottenham,
Barcelona, 1980–86) 27
Armstrong S (Celtic, Southampton, 2017–20) 19
Auld B (Celtic, 1959–60) 3

Bain S (Celtic, 2018–19) 3
Baird H (Airdrie, 1956) 1
Baird S (Rangers, 1957–58) 7
Bannan B (Aston Villa, Crystal Palace,
Sheffield Wed, 2011–18) 27
Bannon E (Dundee Utd, 1980–86) 11
Bardsley P (Sunderland, 2011–14) 13
Barr D (Falkirk, 2009) 1
Bauld W (Hearts, 1950) 3
Baxter J (Rangers, Sunderland, 1961–68) 34
Beattie C (Celtic, WBA, 2006–08) 7
Bell C (Kilmarnock, 2011) 1
Bell W (Leeds, 1966) 2
Bernard P (Oldham, 1995) 2
Berra C (Hearts, Wolves, Ipswich,
Hearts, 2008–18) 41

Bett J (Rangers, Lokeren, Aberdeen, 1982–90) 26
Black E (Metz, 1988) 2
Black I (Southampton, 1948) 1
Black I (Rangers, 2013) 1
Blacklaw A (Burnley, 1963–66) 3
Blackley J (Hibernian, 1974–77) 7
Blair J (Blackpool, 1947) 1
Blyth J (Coventry, 1978) 2
Bone J (Norwich, 1972–73) 2
Booth S (Aberdeen, Borussia Dortmund, Twente Enschede 1993–2002) 22
Bowman D (Dundee Utd, 1992–94) 6
Boyd G (Peterborough, Hull, 2013–14) 2
Boyd K (Rangers, Middlesbrough, 2006–11) 18
Boyd T (Motherwell, Chelsea, Celtic, 1991–2002) 72
Brand R (Rangers, 1961–62) 8
Brazil A (Ipswich, Tottenham, 1980–83) 13
Bremner D (Hibernian, 1976) 1
Bremner W (Leeds, 1965–76) 54
Brennan F (Newcastle, 1947–54) 7
Bridcutt L (Brighton, Sunderland, 2013–16) 2
Broadfoot K (Rangers, 2009–11) 4
Brogan J (Celtic, 1971) 4
Brophy E (Kilmarnock, 2019) 1
Brown A (East Fife, Blackpool, 1950–54) 13
Brown H (Partick, 1947) 3
Brown J (Sheffield Utd, 1975) 1
Brown R (Rangers, 1947–52) 5
Brown S (Hibernian, Celtic, 2007–18) 55
Brown W (Dundee, Tottenham, 1958–66) 28
Brownlie J (Hibernian, 1971–76) 7
Bryson C (Kilmarnock, Derby, 2011–16) 3
Buchan M (Aberdeen, Manchester Utd, 1972–8) 34
Buckley P (Aberdeen, 1954–55) 3
Burchill M (Celtic, 2000) 6
Burke C (Rangers, Birmingham, 2006–14) 7
Burke O (Nottm Forest, Leipzig, WBA, 2016–20) 11
Burley C (Chelsea, Celtic, Derby, 1995–2003) 46
Burley G (Ipswich, 1979–82) 11
Burns F (Manchester Utd, 1970) 1
Burns K (Birmingham, Nottm Forest, 1974–81) 20
Burns T (Celtic, 1981–88) 8

Cadden C (Motherwell, 2018) 2
Caddis P (Birmingham, 2016) 1
Calderwood C (Tottenham, Aston Villa, 1995–2000) 36
Caldow E (Rangers, 1957–63) 40
Cairney T (Fulham, 2017–18) 2
Caldwell G (Newcastle, Sunderland, Hibernian, Wigan, 2002–13) 55
Caldwell S (Newcastle, Sunderland, Celtic, Wigan, 2001–11) 12
Callaghan T (Dunfermline, 1970) 2
Cameron C (Hearts, Wolves, 1999–2005) 28
Campbell R (Falkirk, Chelsea, 1947–50) 5
Campbell W (Morton, 1947–48) 5
Canero P (Leicester, 2004) 1
Carr W (Coventry, 1970–73) 6
Chalmers S (Celtic, 1965–67) 5

Christie R (Celtic, 2018–20) 11
Clark J (Celtic, 1966–67) 4
Clark R (Aberdeen, 1968–73) 17
Clarke S (Chelsea, 1988–94) 6
Clarkson D (Motherwell, 2008–09) 2
Collins J (Hibernian, Celtic, Monaco, Everton, 1988–2000) 58
Collins R (Celtic, Everton, Leeds, 1951–65) 31
Colquhoun E (Sheffield Utd, 1972–73) 9
Colquhoun J (Hearts, 1988) 2
Combe J (Hibernian, 1948) 3
Commons K (Derby, Celtic, 2009–13) 12
Conn A (Hearts, 1956) 1
Conn A (Tottenham, 1975) 2
Connachan E (Dunfermline, 1962) 2
Connelly G (Celtic, 1974) 2
Connolly J (Everton, 1973) 1
Connor R (Dundee, Aberdeen, 1986–91) 4
Conway C (Dundee Utd, Cardiff, 2010–14) 7
Cooke C (Dundee, Chelsea, 1966–75) 16
Cooper D (Rangers, Motherwell, 1980–90) 22
Cooper L (Leeds, 2020) 2
Cormack P (Hibernian, 1966–72) 9
Cowan J (Morton, 1948–52) 25
Cowie D (Dundee, 1953–58) 20
Cowie D (Watford, 2010–12) 10
Cox C (Hearts, 1948) 1
Cox S (Rangers, 1948–54) 25
Craig JP (Celtic, 1968) 1
Craig J (Celtic, 1977) 1
Craig T (Newcastle, 1976) 1
Crainey S (Celtic, Southampton, Blackpool, 2002–12) 12
Crawford S (Raith, Dunfermline, Plymouth Argyle, 1995–2005) 25
Crerand P (Celtic, Manchester Utd, 1961–66) 16
Cropley A (Hibernian, 1972) 2
Cruickshank J (Hearts, 1964–76) 6
Cullen M (Luton, 1956) 1
Cumming J (Hearts, 1955–60) 9
Cummings J (Nottm Forest, 2018) 2
Cummings W (Chelsea, 2002) 1
Cunningham W (Preston, 1954–55) 8
Curran H (Wolves, 1970–71) 5

Dailly C (Derby, Blackburn, West Ham, 1997–2008) 67
Dalglish K (Celtic, Liverpool, 1972–87) 102
Davidson C (Blackburn, Leicester, Preston, 1999–2010) 19
Davidson M (St Johnstone, 2013) 1`
Davidson J (Partick, 1954–55) 8
Dawson A (Rangers, 1980–83) 5
Deans J (Celtic, 1975) 2
*Delaney J (Manchester Utd, 1947–48) 4
Devlin M (Aberdeen, 2020) 3
Devlin P (Birmingham, 2003–04) 10
Dick J (West Ham, 1959) 1
Dickov P (Manchester City, Leicester, Blackburn, 2001–05) 10

Dickson W (Kilmarnock, 1970–71) 5
Dixon P (Huddersfield, 2013) 3
Dobie S (WBA, 2002–03) 6
Docherty T (Preston, Arsenal, 1952–59) 25
Dodds D (Dundee Utd, 1984) 2
Dodds W (Aberdeen, Dundee Utd,
  Rangers, 1997–2002) 26
Donachie W (Manchester City, 1972–79) 35
Donnelly S (Celtic, 1997–99) 10
Dorrans G (WBA, Norwich, 2010–16) 12
Dougall C (Birmingham, 1947) 1
Dougan R (Hearts, 1950) 1
Douglas B (Wolves, 2018) 1
Douglas R (Celtic, Leicester, 2002–06) 19
Doyle J (Ayr, 1976) 1
Duncan A (Hibernian, 1975–76) 6
Duncan D (East Fife, 1948) 3
Duncanson J (Rangers, 1947) 1
Durie G (Chelsea, Tottenham, Rangers,
  1988–98) 43
Durrant I (Rangers, Kilmarnock, 1988–2000) 20

Elliott M (Leicester, 1997–2002) 18
Evans A (Aston Villa, 1982) 4
Evans R (Celtic, Chelsea, 1949–60) 48
Ewing T (Partick, 1958) 2

Farm G (Blackpool, 1953–59) 10
Ferguson B (Rangers, Blackburn,
  Rangers, 1999–2009) 45
Ferguson D (Dundee Utd, Everton, 1992–97) 7
Ferguson D (Rangers, 1988) 2
Ferguson I (Rangers, 1989–97) 9
Ferguson R (Kilmarnock, 1966–67) 7
Fernie W (Celtic, 1954–58) 12
Findlay S (Kilmarnock, 2020) 1
Flavell R (Airdrie, 1947) 2
Fleck J (Sheffield Utd, 2020) 2
Fleck R (Norwich, 1990–91) 4
Fleming C (East Fife, 1954) 1
Fletcher D (Manchester Utd, WBA, 2004–18) 80
Fletcher S (Hibernian, Burnley, Wolves,
  Sunderland, Sheffield Wed, 2008–19) 33
Forbes A (Sheffield Utd, Arsenal, 1947–52) 14
Ford D (Hearts, 1974) 3
Forrest J (Motherwell, 1958) 1
Forrest J (Rangers, Aberdeen, 1966–71) 5
Forrest J (Celtic, 2011–20) 34
Forsyth A (Partick, Manchester Utd,
  1972–76) 10
Forsyth C (Kilmarnock, 1964) 4
Forsyth C (Derby, 2014–15) 4
Forsyth T (Motherwell, Rangers, 1971–78) 22
Fox D (Burnley, Southampton, 2010–13) 4
Fraser D (WBA, 1968–69) 2
Fraser R (Bournemouth, 2017–20) 11
Fraser W (Sunderland, 1955) 1
Freedman D (Crystal Palace, 2002) 2

Gabriel J (Everton, 1961–64) 2
Gallacher K (Dundee Utd, Coventry,
  Blackburn, Newcastle, 1988–2001) 53

Gallacher P (Dundee Utd, 2003–04) 8
Gallagher D (Motherwell, 2020) 2
Gallagher P (Blackburn, 2004) 1
Galloway M (Celtic, 1992) 1
Gardiner I (Motherwell, 1958) 1
Gemmell T (St Mirren, 1955) 2
Gemmell T (Celtic, 1966–71) 18
Gemmill A (Derby, Nottm Forest,
  Birmingham, 1971–81) 43
Gemmill S (Nottm Forest, Everton,
  1995–2003) 26
Gibson D (Leicester, 1963–65) 7
Gilks M (Blackpool, 2013–14) 3
Gillespie G (Liverpool, 1988–91) 13
Gilzean A (Dundee, Tottenham, 1964–71) 22
Glass S (Newcastle Utd 1999) 1
Glavin R (Celtic, 1977) 1
Glen A (Aberdeen, 1956) 2
Goodwillie D (Dundee Utd, Blackburn,
  2011–12) 3
Goram A (Oldham, Hibernian,
  Rangers, 1986–98) 43
Gordon C (Hearts, Sunderland, Celtic, 2004–19) 54
Gough R (Dundee Utd, Tottenham,
  Rangers, 1983–93) 61
Gould J (Celtic, 2000–01) 2
Govan J (Hibernian, 1948–49) 6
Graham A (Leeds, 1978–81) 10
Graham G (Arsenal, Manchester Utd,
  1972–73) 12
Gray A (Aston Villa, Wolves, Everton,
  1976–85) 20
Gray A (Bradford City, 2003) 2
Gray E (Leeds, 1969–77) 12
Gray F (Leeds, Nottm Forest, 1976–83) 32
Grant J (Hibernian, 1958) 2
Grant P (Celtic, 1989) 2
Green A (Blackpool, Newcastle, 1971–72) 6
Greer R (Brighton, 2014–16) 11
Greig J (Rangers, 1964–76) 44
Griffiths L (Wolves, Celtic, 2013–19) 19
Gunn B (Norwich, 1990–94) 6

Haddock H (Clyde, 1955–58) 6
Haffey F (Celtic, 1960–61) 2
Hamilton A (Dundee, 1962–66) 24
Hamilton G (Aberdeen, 1947–54) 5
Hamilton W (Hibernian, 1965) 1
Hammell S (Motherwell, 2005) 1
Hanley G (Blackburn, Newcastle,
  Norwich, 2011–18) 29
Hansen A (Liverpool, 1979–87) 26
Hansen J (Partick, 1972) 2
Harper J (Aberdeen, Hibernian, 1973–78) 4
Hartford A (WBA, Manchester City,
  Everton, 1972–82) 50
Hartley P (Hearts, Celtic, Bristol City,
  2005–10) 25
Harvey D (Leeds, 1973–77) 16
Haughney M (Celtic, 1954) 1
Hay D (Celtic, 1970–74) 27
Hegarty P (Dundee Utd, 1979–83) 8

Henderson J (Portsmouth, Arsenal, 1953–59) — 7
Henderson W (Rangers, 1963–71) — 29
Hendry C (Blackburn, Rangers, Coventry, Bolton, 1994–2001) — 51
Hendry J (Celtic, 2018–19) — 3
Herd D (Arsenal, 1959–61) — 5
Herd G (Clyde, 1958–61) — 5
Herriot J (Birmingham, 1969–70) — 8
Hewie J (Charlton, 1956–60) — 19
Holt D (Hearts, 1963–64) — 5
Holt G (Kilmarnock, Norwich, 2001–05) — 10
Holton J (Manchester Utd, 1973–75) — 15
Hope R (WBA, 1968–69) — 2
Hopkin D (Crystal Palace, Leeds, 1997–2000) — 7
Houliston W (Queen of the South, 1949) — 3
Houston S (Manchester Utd, 1976) — 1
Howie H (Hibernian, 1949) — 1
Hughes J (Celtic, 1965–70) — 8
Hughes R (Portsmouth, 2004–06) — 5
Hughes S (Norwich, 2010) — 1
Hughes W (Sunderland, 1975) — 1
Humphries W (Motherwell, 1952) — 1
Hunter A (Kilmarnock, Celtic, 1972–74) — 4
Hunter W (Motherwell, 1960–61) — 3
Husband J (Partick, 1947) — 1
Hutchison D (Everton, Sunderland, West Ham, 1999–2004) — 26
Hutchison T (Coventry, 1974–76) — 17
Hutton A (Rangers, Tottenham, Aston Villa, 2007–16) — 50

Imlach S (Nottm Forest, 1958) — 4
Irvine B (Aberdeen, 1991–94) — 9
Iwelumo C (Wolves, Burnley, 2009–11) — 4

Jack R (Rangers, 2018–20) — 4
Jackson C (Rangers, 1975–77) — 8
Jackson D (Hibernian, Celtic, 1995–99) — 28
Jardine A (Rangers, 1971–80) — 38
Jarvie A (Airdrie, 1971) — 3
Jess E (Aberdeen, Coventry, Aberdeen, 1993–99) — 18
Johnston A (Sunderland, Rangers, Middlesbrough, 1999–2003) — 18
Johnston L (Clyde, 1948) — 2
Johnston M (Watford, Celtic, Nantes, Rangers, 1984–92) — 38
Johnston W (Rangers, WBA, 1966–78) — 21
Johnstone D (Rangers, 1973–80) — 14
Johnstone J (Celtic, 1965–75) — 23
Johnstone R (Hibernian, Manchester City, 1951–56) — 17
Jordan J (Leeds, Manchester Utd, AC Milan, 1973–82) — 52

Kelly H (Blackpool, 1952) — 1
Kelly J (Barnsley, 1949) — 2
Kelly L (Kilmarnock, 2013) — 1
Kennedy J (Celtic, 1964–65) — 6
Kennedy J (Celtic, 2004) — 1
Kennedy S (Rangers, 1975) — 5
Kennedy S (Aberdeen, 1978–82) — 8

Kenneth G (Dundee Utd, 2011) — 2
Kerr A (Partick, 1955) — 2
Kerr B (Newcastle, 2003–04) — 3
Kingsley S (Swansea, 2016) — 1
Kyle K (Sunderland, Kilmarnock, 2002–10) — 10
Lambert P (Motherwell, Borussia Dortmund, Celtic, 1995–2003) — 40
Law D (Huddersfield, Manchester City, Torino, Manchester Utd, 1959–74) — 55
Lawrence T (Liverpool, 1963–69) — 3
Leggat G (Aberdeen, Fulham, 1956–60) — 18
Leighton J (Aberdeen, Manchester Utd, Hibernian, Aberdeen, 1983–99) — 91
Lennox R (Celtic, 1967–70) — 10
Leslie L (Airdrie, 1961) — 5
Levein C (Hearts, 1990–95) — 16
Liddell W (Liverpool, 1947–55) — 28
Linwood A (Clyde, 1950) — 1
Little R (Rangers, 1953) — 1
Logie J (Arsenal, 1953) — 1
Long H (Clyde, 1947) — 1
Lorimer P (Leeds, 1970–76) — 21

Macari L (Celtic, Manchester Utd, 1972–78) — 24
Macaulay A (Brentford, Arsenal, 1947–48) — 7
MacDonald A (Rangers, 1976) — 1
MacDougall E (Norwich, 1975–76) — 7
Mackail-Smith C (Peterborough, Brighton 2011–12) — 7
MacKay D (Celtic, 1959–62) — 14
Mackay D (Hearts, Tottenham, 1957–66) — 22
Mackay G (Hearts, 1988) — 4
Mackay M (Norwich, 2004–05) — 5
Mackay-Steven G (Dundee Utd, 2014) — 2
MacKenzie J (Partick, 1954–56) — 9
Mackie J (QPR, 2011–13) — 9
MacLeod J (Hibernian, 1961) — 4
MacLeod M (Celtic, Borussia Dortmund, Hibernian, 1985–91) — 20
Maguire C (Aberdeen, 2011) — 2
Maloney S (Celtic, Aston Villa, Celtic, Wigan, Chicago, Hull, 2006–16) — 47
Malpas M (Dundee Utd, 1984–93) — 55
Marshall D (Celtic, Cardiff, Hull, 2005–20) — 34
Marshall G (Celtic, 1992) — 1
Martin B (Motherwell, 1995) — 2
Martin C (Derby, 2014–18) — 17
Martin F (Aberdeen, 1954–55) — 6
Martin N (Hibernian, Sunderland, 1965–66) — 3
Martin R (Norwich, 2011–17) — 29
Martis J (Motherwell, 1961) — 1
Mason J (Third Lanark 1949–51) — 7
Masson D (QPR, Derby, 1976–78) — 17
Mathers D (Partick, 1954) — 1
Matteo D (Leeds, 2001–02) — 6
May S (Sheffield Wed, 2015) — 1
McAllister B (Wimbledon, 1997) — 3
McAllister G (Leicester, Leeds, Coventry, 1990–99) — 57
McAllister J (Livingston, 2004) — 1
McArthur J (Wigan, Crystal Palace, 2011–18) — 32
McAvennie F (West Ham, Celtic, 1986–88) — 5

McBride J (Celtic, 1967) 2
McBurnie O (Swansea, Sheffield Utd, 2018–20) 9
McCall S (Everton, Rangers, 1990–98) 40
McCalliog J (Sheffield Wed, Wolves, 1967–71) 5
McCann N (Hearts, Rangers,
Southampton, 1999–2006) 26
McCann R (Motherwell, 1959–61) 5
McClair B (Celtic, Manchester Utd,
1987–93) 30
McCloy P (Rangers, 1973) 4
McCoist A (Rangers, Kilmarnock,
1986–99) 61
McColl I (Rangers, 1950–58) 14
McCormack R (Motherwell, Cardiff,
Leeds, Fulham, 2008–16) 13
McCreadie E (Chelsea, 1965–9) 23
McCulloch L (Wigan, Rangers, 2005–11) 18
McDonald J (Sunderland, 1956) 2
McDonald K (Fulham, 2018–19) 5
McEveley, J (Derby, 2008) 3
McFadden J (Motherwell, Everton,
Birmingham, 2002–11) 48
McFarlane W (Hearts, 1947) 1
McGarr E (Aberdeen, 1970) 2
McGarvey F (Liverpool, Celtic, 1979–84) 7
McGeouch D (Hibernian, 2018) 2
McGhee M (Aberdeen, 1983–84) 4
McGinlay J (Bolton, 1995–97) 13
McGinn J (Hibernian, Aston Villa, 2016–20) 21
McGrain D (Celtic, 1973–82) 62
McGregor A (Rangers, Besiktas, Hull,
Rangers, 2007–19) 42
McGregor C (Celtic 2018–20) 19
McGrory J (Kilmarnock, 1965–66) 3
McInally A (Aston Villa, Bayern Munich,
1989–90) 8
McInally J (Dundee Utd, 1987–93) 10
McInnes D (WBA, 2003) 2
McKay B (Rangers, 2016) 1
Mackay–Steven D (Dundee Utd,
Aberdeen, 2014–19) 2
McKean R (Rangers, 1976) 1
McKenna S (Aberdeen, 2018–20) 14
McKimmie S (Aberdeen, 1989–96) 40
McKinlay T (Celtic, 1996–98) 22
McKinlay W (Dundee Utd, Blackburn,
1994–99) 29
McKinnon R (Rangers, 1966–71) 28
McKinnon R (Motherwell, 1994–95) 3
McLaren A (Preston, 1947–48) 4
McLaren A (Hearts, Rangers, 1992–96) 24
McLaren A (Kilmarnock, 2001) 1
McLaughlin J (Hearts, Sunderland, 2018–20) 2
McLean G (Dundee, 1968) 1
McLean K (Aberdeen, Norwich, 2016–20) 10
McLean T (Kilmarnock, Rangers,1969–71) 6
McLeish A (Aberdeen, 1980–93) 77
McLintock F (Leicester, Arsenal,1963–71) 9
McManus S (Celtic, Middlesbrough,2007–11) 26
McMillan I (Airdrie, 1952–61) 6
McNamara J (Celtic, Wolves,1997–2006) 33
McNamee D (Livingston, 2004–06) 4

McNaught W (Raith, 1951–55) 5
McNaughton K (Aberdeen, Cardiff, 2002–08) 4
McNeill W (Celtic, 1961–72) 29
McNulty M (Reading, 2019) 2
McPhail J (Celtic, 1950–54) 5
McPherson D (Hearts, Rangers, 1989–93) 27
McQueen G (Leeds, Manchester Utd, 1974–81) 30
McStay P (Celtic, 1984–97) 76
McSwegan G (Hearts, 2000) 2
McTominay S (Manchester Utd, 2018–20) 12
Millar J (Rangers, 1963) 2
Miller C (Dundee Utd, 2001) 1
Miller K (Rangers, Wolves, Celtic, Derby,
Rangers, Bursaspor, Cardiff,
Vancouver, 2001–14) 69
Miller L (Dundee Utd, Aberdeen 2006–10) 3
Miller W (Celtic, 1946–47) 6
Miller W (Aberdeen, 1975–90) 65
Mitchell J (Aberdeen, 1951) 2
Mochan N (Celtic, 1954) 3
Moir W (Bolton, 1950) 1
Moncur R (Newcastle, 1968–72) 16
Morgan L (Celtic, 2018) 2
Morgan W (Burnley, Manchester Utd,
1968–74) 21
Morris H (East Fife, 1950) 1
Morrison J (WBA, 2008–18) 46
Mudie J (Blackpool, 1957–58) 17
Mulgrew C (Celtic, Blackburn, 2012–20) 44
Mulhall G (Aberdeen, Sunderland, 1960–64) 3
Munro F (Wolves, 1971–75) 9
Munro I (St Mirren, 1979–80) 7
Murdoch R (Celtic, 1966–70) 12
Murphy J (Brighton, 2018) 2
Murray I (Hibernian, Rangers, 2003–06) 6
Murray J (Hearts, 1958) 5
Murray S (Aberdeen, 1972) 1
Murty G (Reading, 2004–08) 4

Naismith S (Kilmarnock, Rangers, Everton,
Norwich, Hearts, 2007–20) 51
Narey D (Dundee Utd, 1977–89) 35
Naysmith G (Hearts, Everton, Sheffield Utd,
2000–09) 46
Neilson R (Hearts, 2007) 1
Nevin P (Chelsea, Everton, Tranmere,
1987–96) 28
Nicholas C (Celtic, Arsenal, Aberdeen,
1983–89) 20
Nicholson B (Dunfermline, 2001–05) 3
Nicol S (Liverpool, 1985–92) 27

O'Connor G (Hibernian, Lokomotiv Moscow,
Birmingham, 2002–10) 16
O'Donnell P (Motherwell, 1994) 1
O'Donnell S (Kilmarnock, 2018–20) 11
O'Hare J (Derby, 1970–72) 13
O'Neil B (Celtic, VfL Wolfsburg, Derby,
Preston, 1996–2006) 7
O'Neil J (Hibernian, 2001) 1
Ormond W (Hibernian, 1954–59) 6
Orr T (Morton, 1952) 2

Parker A (Falkirk, Everton, 1955–56)	15
Parlane D (Rangers, 1973–77)	12
Palmer L (Sheffield Wed, 2019–20)	5
Paterson C (Hearts, Cardiff, 2016–19)	12
Paton A (Motherwell, 1952)	2
Pearson S (Motherwell, Celtic, Derby, 2004–07)	10
Pearson T (Newcastle, 1947)	2
Penman A (Dundee, 1966)	1
Pettigrew W (Motherwell, 1976–77)	5
Phillips M (Blackpool, QPR, WBA, 2012–20)	16
Plenderleith J (Manchester City, 1961)	1
Pressley S (Hearts, 2000–07)	32
Provan D (Rangers, 1964–66)	5
Provan D (Celtic, 1980–82)	10
Quashie N (Portsmouth, Southampton, WBA, 2004–07)	14
Quinn P (Motherwell, 1961–62)	4
Rae G (Dundee, Rangers, Cardiff, 2001–09)	14
Redpath W (Motherwell, 1949–52)	9
Reilly L (Hibernian, 1949–57)	38
Rhodes J (Huddersfield, Blackburn, Sheffield Wed, 2012–17)	14
Ring T (Clyde, 1953–58)	12
Rioch B (Derby, Everton, 1975–78)	24
Riordan D (Hibernian, 2006–10)	3
Ritchie M (Bournemouth, Newcastle, 2015–18)	16
Ritchie P (Hearts, Bolton, 1999–2000)	7
Ritchie W (Rangers, 1962)	1
Robb D (Aberdeen, 1971)	5
Robertson A (Clyde, 1955)	5
Robertson A (Dundee Utd, Hull, Liverpool, 2014–20)	34
Robertson D (Rangers, 1992–94)	3
Robertson H (Dundee, 1962)	1
Robertson J (Tottenham, 1964)	1
Robertson J (Nottm Forest, Derby, 1978–84)	28
Robertson J (Hearts, 1991–96)	16
Robertson S (Dundee Utd, 2009–11)	2
Robinson R (Dundee, 1974–75)	4
Robson B (Celtic, Middlesbrough, 2008–11)	17
Ross M (Rangers, 2002–04)	13
Rough A (Partick, Hibernian, 1976–86)	53
Rougvie D (Aberdeen, 1984)	1
Russell J (Derby, Kansas, 2015–20)	14
Rutherford E (Rangers, 1948)	1
Saunders S (Motherwell, 2011)	1
Schaedler E (Hibernian, 1974)	1
Scott A (Rangers, Everton, 1957–66)	16
Scott J (Hibernian, 1966)	1
Scott J (Dundee, 1971)	2
Scoular J (Portsmouth, 1951–53)	9
Severin S (Hearts, Aberdeen, 2002–07)	15
Shankland L (Dundee Utd, 2020)	2
Sharp G (Everton, 1985–88)	12
Shaw D (Hibernian, 1947–49)	8
Shaw J (Rangers, 1947)	4
Shearer D (Aberdeen, 1994–96)	7
Shearer R (Rangers, 1961)	4

Shinnie A (Inverness, 2013)	1
Shinnie G (Aberdeen, 2018–19)	6
Simpson N (Aberdeen, 1983–88)	5
Simpson R (Celtic, 1967–69)	5
Sinclair J (Leicester, 1966)	1
Smith D (Aberdeen, Rangers, 1966–68)	2
Smith G (Hibernian, 1947–57)	18
Smith H (Hearts, 1988–92)	3
Smith JE (Celtic, 1959)	2
Smith J (Aberdeen, Newcastle, 1968–74)	4
Smith J (Celtic, 2003)	2
Snodgrass R (Leeds, Norwich, West Ham, 2011–20)	28
Souness G (Middlesbrough, Liverpool, Sampdoria, Rangers, 1975–86)	54
Souttar J (Hearts, 2019)	3
Speedie D (Chelsea, Coventry, 1985–89)	10
Spencer J (Chelsea, QPR, 1995–97)	14
Stanton P (Hibernian, 1966–74)	16
Steel W (Morton, Derby, Dundee, 1947–53)	30
Stein C (Rangers, Coventry, 1969–73)	21
Stephen J (Bradford Park Avenue, 1947–48)	2
Stevenson L (Hibernian, 2018)	1
Stewart D (Leeds, 1978)	1
Stewart J (Kilmarnock, Middlesbrough, 1977–79)	2
Stewart M (Manchester Utd, Hearts 2002–09)	4
Stewart R (West Ham, 1981–7)	10
St John I (Motherwell, Liverpool, 1959–65)	21
Stockdale R (Middlesbrough, 2002–03)	5
Strachan G (Aberdeen, Manchester Utd, Leeds, 1980–92)	50
Sturrock P (Dundee Utd, 1981–87)	20
Sullivan N (Wimbledon, Tottenham, 1997–2003)	28
Taylor G (Kilmarnock, Celtic, 2019–20)	3
Teale G (Wigan, Derby, 2006–09)	13
Telfer P (Coventry, 2000)	1
Telfer W (St Mirren, 1954)	1
Thomson K (Rangers, Middlesbrough, 2009–11)	3
Thompson S (Dundee Utd, Rangers, 2002–05)	16
Thomson W (St Mirren, 1980–84)	7
Thornton W (Rangers, 1947–52)	7
Tierney K (Celtic, 2016–19)	12
Toner W (Kilmarnock, 1959)	2
Turnbull E (Hibernian, 1948–58)	8
Ure I (Dundee, Arsenal, 1962–68)	11
Waddell W (Rangers, 1947–55)	17
Walker A (Celtic, 1988–95)	3
Walker N (Hearts, 1993–96)	2
Wallace I (Coventry, 1978–79)	3
Wallace L (Hearts, Rangers, 2010–17)	10
Wallace R (Preston, 2010)	1
Wallace W (Hearts, Celtic, 1965–69)	7
Wardhaugh J (Hearts, 1955–57)	2
Wark J (Ipswich, Liverpool, 1979–85)	29
Watson J (Motherwell, Huddersfield, 1948–54)	2
Watson R (Motherwell, 1971)	1

Williams A (Stockport, Swansea, Everton, 2008–19) 86
Williams A (Reading, Wolves, Reading, 1994–2003) 13
Williams A (Southampton, 1997–98) 2
Williams D (Norwich, 1986–87) 5
Williams G (Cardiff, 1951) 1
Williams G (Derby, Ipswich, 1988–96) 13
Williams G (West Ham, 2006) 2
Williams G (Fulham, 2014–16) 7
Williams GE (WBA, 1960–69) 26
Williams GG (Swansea, 1961–62) 5
Williams HJ (Swansea, 1965–72) 3
Williams HT (Newport, Leeds, 1949–50) 4
Williams J (Crystal Palace, Charlton, 2013–20) 22
Williams S (WBA, Southampton, 1954–66) 43
Wilson H (Liverpool, 2014–20) 17
Wilson J (Bristol City, 2014) 1
Witcomb D (WBA, Sheffield Wed, 1947) 3
Woosnam P (Leyton Orient, West Ham, Aston Villa, 1959–63) 17
Woodburn B (Liverpool, 2018–19) 10

Yorath T (Leeds, Coventry, Tottenham, Vancouver Whitecaps 1970–81) 59
Young E (Wimbledon, Crystal Palace, Wolves, 1990–96) 21

NORTHERN IRELAND

Aherne T (Belfast Celtic, Luton, 1947–50) 4
Anderson T (Manchester Utd, Swindon, Peterborough, 1973–79) 22
Armstrong G (Tottenham, Watford, Real Mallorca, WBA, 1977–86) 63

Baird C (Southampton, Fulham, Burnley, WBA, Derby, 2003–16) 79
Barr H (Linfield, Coventry, 1962–63) 3
Barton A (Preston, 2011) 1
Best G (Manchester Utd, Fulham, 1964–77) 37
Bingham W (Sunderland, Luton, Everton, Port Vale, 1951–64) 56
Black K (Luton, Nottm Forest, 1988–94) 30
Blair R (Oldham, 1975–76) 5
Blanchflower RD (Barnsley, Aston Villa, Tottenham, 1950–63) 56
Blanchflower J (Manchester Utd, 1954–58) 12
Blayney A (Doncaster, Linfield, 2006–11) 5
Bowler G (Hull, 1950) 3
Boyce L (Werder Bremen, Ross Co, Burton, 2011–20) 21
Braithwaite R (Linfield, Middlesbrough, 1962–65) 10
Braniff K (Portadown, 2010) 2
Brennan R (Luton, Birmingham, Fulham, 1949–51) 5
Briggs W (Manchester Utd, Swansea, 1962–65) 2
Brotherston N (Blackburn, 1980–85) 27
Brown C (Cardiff, 2020) 1
Bruce A (Hull, 2013–14) 2

Bruce W (Glentoran, 1961–67) 2
Brunt C (Sheffield Wed, WBA, 2005–18) 65
Bryan, M (Watford, 2010) 2

Camp L (Nottm Forest, 2011–13) 9
Campbell D (Nottm Forest, Charlton, 1987–88) 10
Campbell J (Fulham, 1951) 2
Campbell R (Crusaders, 1963–65) 2
Campbell R (Bradford City, 1982) 2
Campbell W (Dundee, 1968–70) 6
Capaldi A (Plymouth Argyle, Cardiff, 2004–08) 22
Carey J (Manchester Utd, 1947–49) 7
Carroll R (Wigan, Manchester Utd, West Ham, Olympiacos, Notts Co, Linfield; 1997–2017) 45
Carson J (Ipswich, 2011–13) 4
Carson S (Coleraine, 2009) 1
Carson T (Motherwell, 2018–19) 5
Casey N (Newcastle, Portsmouth, 1955–59) 12
Casement C (Ipswich, 2009) 1
Caskey W (Derby, Tulsa, Roughnecks, 1979–82) 7
Cassidy T (Newcastle, Burnley, 1971–82) 24
Cathcart C (Blackpool, Watford, 2011–2020) 50
Caughey M (Linfield, 1986) 2
Clarke C (Bournemouth, Southampton, QPR, Portsmouth, 1986–93) 38
Cleary J (Glentoran, 1982–85) 5
Clements D (Coventry, Sheffield Wed, Everton, New York Cosmos, 1965–76) 48
Clingan S (Nottm Forest, Norwich, Coventry, Kilmarnock, 2006–15) 39
Clyde, M (Wolves, 2005) 3
Coates C (Crusaders, 2009–11) 6
Cochrane A (Coleraine, Burnley, Middlesbrough, Gillingham, 1976–84) 26
Cochrane D (Leeds, 1947–50) 10
Connell T (Coleraine, 1978) 1
Coote A (Norwich, 1999–2000) 6
Cowan J (Newcastle, 1970) 1
Coyle F (Coleraine, Nottm Forest, 1956–58) 4
Coyle L (Derry City, 1989) 1
Coyle R (Sheffield Wed, 1973–74) 5
Craig D (Newcastle, 1967–75) 25
Craigan S (Partick, Motherwell, 2003–11) 54
Crossan E (Blackburn, 1950–55) 3
Crossan J (Sparta Rotterdam, Sunderland, Manchester City, Middlesbrough, 1960–68) 24
Cunningham W (St Mirren, Leicester, Dunfermline, 1951–62) 30
Cush W (Glenavon, Leeds, Portadown, 1951–62) 26

Dallas S (Crusaders, Brentford, Leeds, 2011–20) 44
D'Arcy S (Chelsea, Brentford, 1952–53) 5
Davis S (Aston Villa, Fulham, Rangers, Southampton, Rangers, 2005–20) 117
Davison A (Bolton, Bradford City, Grimsby, 1996–97) 3
Dennison R (Wolves, 1988–97) 18

Kelly P (Barnsley, 1950) 1
Kennedy P (Watford, Wigan, 1999–2004) 20
Kirk A (Hearts, Boston, Northampton,
   Dunfermline, 2000–10) 11

Lafferty D (Burnley, 2012–16) 13
Lafferty K (Burnley, Rangers, Sion, Palermo,
   Norwich, Hearts, Rangers, Sarpsborg, 2006–20)75
Lavery S (Everton, Linfield, 2018–20) 4
Lawrie J (Port Vale, 2009–10) 3
Lawther W (Sunderland, Blackburn, 1960–62) 4
Lennon N (Crewe, Leicester, Celtic, 1994–2002) 40
Lewis J (Norwich, 2018–20) 12
Little A (Rangers, 2009–13) 9
Lockhart N (Linfield, Coventry,
   Aston Villa, 1947–56) 8
Lomas S (Manchester City, West Ham,
   1994–2003) 45
Lund M (Rochdale, 2017) 3
Lutton B (Wolves, West Ham, 1970–4) 6

Magennis J (Cardiff, Aberdeen, Kilmarnock,
   Charlton, Bolton, Hull, 2010–2020) 50
Magill E (Arsenal, Brighton, 1962–66) 26
Magilton J (Oxford Utd, Southampton,
   Sheffield Wed, Ipswich, 1991–2002) 52
Mannus A (Linfield, St Johnstone, 2004–17) 9
Martin C (Glentoran, Leeds, Aston Villa,
   1947–50) 6
McAdams W (Manchester City, Bolton,
   Leeds, 1954–62) 15
*McAlinden J (Portsmouth, Southend, 1947–49) 2
McArdle R (Rochdale, Aberdeen,
   Bradford, 2010–14) 7
McAuley G (Lincoln, Leicester, Ipswich,
   WBA, Rangers, 2010–19) 80
McBride S (Glenavon, 1991–92) 4
McCabe J (Leeds, 1949–54) 6
McCalmont A (Leeds, 2020) 1
McCann G (West Ham, Cheltenham, Barnsley,
   Scunthorpe, Peterborough, 2002–12) 39
McCartan S (Accrington, Bradford, 2017–18) 2
McCarthy J (Port Vale, Birmingham, 1996–2001) 18
McCartney G (Sunderland, West Ham,
   Sunderland 2002–10) 34
McCavana T (Coleraine, 1954–55) 3
McCleary J (Cliftonville, 1955) 1
McClelland J (Arsenal, Fulham, 1961–67) 6
McClelland J (Mansfield, Rangers,
   Watford, Leeds, 1980–90) 53
McCourt F (Manchester City, 1952–53) 6
McCourt P (Rochdale, Celtic, Barnsley,
   Brighton, Luton, 2002–16) 18
McCoy R (Coleraine, 1987) 1
McCreery D (Manchester Utd, QPR,
   Tulsa, Newcastle, 1976–90) 67
McCrory S (Southend, 1958) 1
McCullough L (Doncaster, 2014–18) 6
   McCullough W (Arsenal, Millwall,1961–67) 10
McCurdy C (Linfield, 1980) 1
McDonald A (QPR, 1986–96) 52
McElhinney G (Bolton, 1984–85) 6

McEvilly L (Rochdale, 2002) 1
McFaul W (Linfield, Newcastle, 1967–74) 6
McGarry J (Cliftonville, 1951) 3
McGaughey M (Linfield, 1985) 1
McGibbon P (Manchester Utd, Wigan,
   1995–2000) 7
McGinn N (Derry, Celtic, Aberdeen, 2009–20) 60
McGivern R (Manchester City, Hibernian,
   Port Vale, Shrewsbury, 2009–17) 24
McGovern M (Ross Co, Hamilton,
   Norwich, 2010–20) 31
McGrath C (Tottenham, Manchester Utd
   1974–79) 21
McIlroy J (Burnley, Stoke, 1952–66) 55
McIlroy S (Manchester Utd, Stoke,
   Manchester City, 1972–87) 88
McKay W (Inverness, Wigan, 2013–16) 11
McKeag W (Glentoran, 1968) 2
McKenna J (Huddersfield, 1950–52) 7
McKenzie R (Airdrie, 1967) 1
McKinney W (Falkirk, 1966) 1
McKnight A (Celtic, West Ham, 1988–89) 10
McLaughlin C (Preston, Fleetwood,
   Millwall, Sunderland, 2012–20) 37
McLaughlin J (Shrewsbury, Swansea,
   1962–66) 12
McLaughlin R (Liverpool, Oldham, 2014–18) 5
McLean B (Motherwell, 2006) 1
McMahon G (Tottenham, Stoke,
   1995–98) 17
McMichael A (Newcastle, 1950–60) 40
McMillan S (Manchester Utd, 1963) 2
McMordie A (Middlesbrough, 1969–73) 21
McMorran E (Belfast Celtic, Barnsley,
   Doncaster, 1947–57) 15
McNair P (Manchester Utd, Sunderland,
   Middlesbrough, 2015–20) 34
McNally B (Shrewsbury, 1987–88) 5
McPake J (Coventry, 2012) 1
McParland P (Aston Villa, Wolves, 1954–62) 34
McQuoid J (Millwall, 2011–12) 5
McVeigh P (Tottenham, Norwich,
   1999–2005) 20
Montgomery F (Coleraine, 1955) 1
Moore C (Glentoran, 1949) 1
Moreland V (Derby, 1979–80) 6
Morgan S (Port Vale, Aston Villa,
   Brighton, Sparta Rotterdam, 1972–99) 18
Morrow S (Arsenal, QPR, 1990–2000) 39
Mulgrew J (Linfield, 2010) 2
Mullan G (Glentoran, 1983) 4
Mulryne P (Manchester Utd,
   Norwich, 1997–2005) 27
Murdock C (Preston, Hibernian, Crewe,
   Rotherham, 2000–06) 34

Napier R (Bolton, 1966) 1
Neill T (Arsenal, Hull, 1961–73) 59
Nelson S (Arsenal, Brighton, 1970–82) 51
Nicholl C (Aston Villa, Southampton,
   Grimsby, 1975–83) 51
Nicholl J (Manchester Utd, Toronto,

Williams P (WBA, 1991) 1
Wilson D (Brighton, Luton,
Sheffield Wed, 1987–92) 24
Wilson K (Ipswich, Chelsea, Notts Co,
Walsall, 1987–95) 42
Wilson S (Glenavon, Falkirk, Dundee,
1962–68) 12
Winchester C (Oldham, 2011) 1
Wood T (Walsall, 1996) 1
Worthington N (Sheffield Wed, Leeds,
Stoke, 1984–97) 66
Wright T (Newcastle, Nottm Forest, Reading,
Manchester City, 1989–2000) 31

REPUBLIC OF IRELAND

Aherne T (Belfast Celtic, Luton, 1946–54) 16
Aldridge J (Oxford Utd, Liverpool, Real
Sociedad, Tranmere, 1986–97) 69
Ambrose P (Shamrock R, 1955–64) 5
Anderson J (Preston, Newcastle, 1980–89) 16
Andrews K (Blackburn, WBA, 2009–13) 35
Arter H (Bournemouth, 2015–19) 16

Babb P (Coventry, Liverpool, Sunderland,
1994–2003) 35
Bailham E (Shamrock R, 1964) 1
Barber E (Bohemians, Birmingham, 1966) 2
Barrett G (Arsenal, Coventry, 2003–05) 6
Beglin J (Liverpool, 1984–87) 15
Bennett A (Reading, 2007) 2
Best L (Coventry, 2009–10) 7
Braddish S (Dundalk, 1978) 2
Branagan K (Bolton, 1997) 1
Bonner P (Celtic, 1981–96) 80
Boyle A (Preston, 2017) 1
Brady L (Arsenal, Juventus, Sampdoria,
Inter–Milan, Ascoli, West Ham, 1975–90) 72
Brady R (QPR, 1964) 6
Brady R (Manchester Utd, Hull,
Burnley, 2013–20) 46
Breen G (Birmingham, Coventry, West Ham,
Sunderland, 1996–2006) 63
*Breen T (Shamrock R, 1947) 3
Brennan F (Drumcondra, 1965) 1
Brennan S (Manchester Utd, Waterford,
1965–71) 19
Browne A (Preston, 2017–20) 9
Browne W (Bohemians, 1964) 3
Bruce A (Ipswich, 2007–09) 2
Buckley L (Shamrock R, Waregem, 1984–85) 2
Burke F (Cork Ath, 1952) 1
Burke G (Shamrock Rov, Preston 2018–19) 3
Butler P (Sunderland, 2000) 1
Butler T (Sunderland, 2003) 2
Byrne A (Southampton, 1970–74) 14
Byrne J (Shelbourne, 2004–06) 2
Byrne J (QPR, Le Havre, Brighton,
Sunderland, Millwall, 1985–93) 23
Byrne J (Shamrock, 2020) 2
Byrne P (Shamrock R, 1984–86) 8

Campbell A (Santander, 1985) 3
Campbell N (St Patrick's Ath,
Fortuna Cologne, 1971–77) 11
Cantwell N (West Ham, Manchester Utd,
1954–67) 36
Carey B (Manchester Utd, Leicester,
1992–94) 3
*Carey J (Manchester Utd, 1946–53) 21
Carolan J (Manchester Utd, 1960) 2
Carr S (Tottenham, Newcastle, 1999–2008) 43
Carroll B (Shelbourne, 1949–50) 2
Carroll T (Ipswich, 1968–73) 17
Carsley L (Derby, Blackburn, Coventry,
Everton, 1997–2008) 39
Cascarino A (Gillingham, Millwall,
Aston Villa, Chelsea, Marseille, Nancy,
1986–2000) 88
Chandler J (Leeds, 1980) 2
Christie C (Derby, Middlesbrough,
Fulham, 2015–20) 24
Clark C (Aston Villa, Newcastle, 2011–20) 34
Clarke C (Stoke, 2004) 2
Clarke J (Drogheda, 1978) 1
Clarke K (Drumcondra, 1948) 2
Clarke M (Shamrock R, 1950) 1
Clinton T (Everton, 1951–54) 3
Coad P (Shamrock R, 1947–52) 11
Coffey T (Drumcondra, 1950) 1
Colfer M (Shelbourne, 1950–51) 2
Coleman S (Everton 2011–20) 56
Colgan N (Hibernian, 2002–07) 9
Collins J (Luton, 2020) 4
Conmy O (Peterborough, 1965–70) 5
Connolly A (Brighton, 2020) 2
Connolly D (Watford, Feyenoord, Excelsior
Feenoord, Wimbledon, West Ham,
Wigan, 1996–2006) 41
Conroy G (Stoke, 1970–77) 27
Conway J (Fulham, Manchester City,
1967–77) 20
Corr P (Everton, 1949–50) 4
Courtney E (Cork Utd, 1946) 1
Cox S (WBA, Nottm Forest, 2011–14) 30
Coyle O (Bolton, 1994) 1
Coyne T (Celtic, Tranmere,
Motherwell, 1992–98) 22
Crowe G (Bohemians, 2003) 2
Cullen J (West Ham, 2020) 2
Cummins G (Luton, 1954–61) 19
Cuneen T (Limerick, 1951) 1
Cunningham G (Man City, Bristol City, 2010–13) 4
Cunningham K (Wimbledon,
Birmingham, 1996–2006) 72
Curtis D (Shelbourne, Bristol City,
Ipswich, Exeter, 1956–63) 17
Curtis R (Portsmouth, 2019) 2
Cusack S (Limerick, 1953) 1

Daish L (Cambridge Utd, Coventry, 1992–96) 5
Daly G (Manchester Utd, Derby, Coventry,
Birmingham, Shrewsbury, 1973–87) 48
Daly M (Wolves, 1978) 2

Daly P (Shamrock R, 1950)   1
Deacy E (Aston Villa, 1982)   4
Delaney D (QPR, Ipswich, Crystal Palace, 2008–14)   9
Delap R (Derby, Southampton, 1998–2004)   11
De Mange K (Liverpool, Hull, 1987–89)   2
Dempsey J (Fulham, Chelsea, 1967–72)   19
Dennehy J (Cork Hibernian, Nottm Forest, Walsall, 1972–77)   11
Desmond P (Middlesbrough, 1950)   4
Devine J (Arsenal, 1980–85)   13
Doherty G (Tottenham, Norwich, 2000–06)   34
Doherty M (Wolves, 2018–20)   9
Donovan D (Everton, 1955–57)   5
Donovan T (Aston Villa, 1980)   2
Douglas J (Blackburn, Leeds, 2004–08)   8
Doyle C (Shelbourne, 1959)   1
Doyle C (Birmingham, Bradford, 2007–18)   4
Doyle K (Reading Wolves, Colorado, 2006–17)   63
Doyle M (Coventry, 2004)   1
Duff D (Blackburn, Chelsea, Newcastle, Fulham, 1998–2012)   100
Duffy B (Shamrock R, 1950)   1
Duffy S (Everton, Blackburn, Brighton, 2014–20)   33
Dunne A (Manchester Utd, Bolton,1962–76)   33
Dunne J (Fulham, 1971)   1
Dunne P (Manchester Utd, 1965–67)   5
Dunne R (Everton, Manchester City, Aston Villa, 2000–14)   80
Dunne S (Luton, 1953–60)   15
Dunne T (St Patrick's, 1956–57)   3
Dunning P (Shelbourne, 1971)   2
Dunphy E (York, Millwall, 1966–71)   23
Dwyer N (West Ham, Swansea, 1960–65)   14

Eccles P (Shamrock R, 1986)   1
Egan J (Brentford, Sheffield Utd, 2017–20)   8
Eglington T (Shamrock R, Everton, 1946–56)   24
Elliot R (Newcastle, 2014–16)   4
Elliott S (Sunderland, 2005–07)   9
Evans M (Southampton, 1997)   1

Fagan E (Shamrock R, 1973)   1
Fagan F (Manchester City, Derby, 1955–61)   8
Fahey K (Birmingham, 2010–13)   16
Fairclough M (Dundalk, 1982)   2
Fallon S (Celtic, 1951–55)   8
Farrell P (Shamrock R, Everton, 1946–57)   28
Farrelly G (Aston Villa, Everton, Bolton, 1996–2000)   6
Finnan S (Fulham, Liverpool, Espanyol 2000–09)   53
Finucane A (Limerick, 1967–72)   11
Fitzgerald F (Waterford, 1955–6)   2
Fitzgerald P (Leeds, 1961–2)   5
Fitzpatrick K (Limerick, 1970)   1
Fitzsimons A (Middlesbrough, Lincoln, 1950–59)   26
Fleming C (Middlesbrough, 1996–8)   10
Fogarty A (Sunderland, Hartlepool Utd, 1960–64)   11

Folan C (Hull, 2009–10)   7
Foley D (Watford, 2000–01)   6
Foley K (Wolves, 2009–11)   8
Foley T (Northampton, 1964–67)   9
Fullam J (Preston, Shamrock R, 1961–70)   11
Forde D (Millwall, 2011–16)   24
Fullam J (Preston, Shamrock, 1961–70)   11

Gallagher C (Celtic, 1967)   2
Gallagher M (Hibernian, 1954)   1
Galvin A (Tottenham, Sheffield Wed, Swindon, 1983–90)   29
Gamble J (Cork City, 2007)   2
Gannon E (Notts Co, Sheffield Wed, Shelbourne, 1949–55)   14
Gannon M (Shelbourne, 1972)   1
Gavin J (Norwich, Tottenham, Norwich, 1950–57)   7
Gibbons A (St Patrick's Ath, 1952–56)   4
Gibson D (Manchester Utd, Everton, 2008–16)   27
Gilbert R (Shamrock R, 1966)   1
Giles C (Doncaster, 1951)   1
Giles J (Manchester Utd, Leeds, WBA, Shamrock R, 1960–79)   59
Given S (Blackburn, Newcastle, Manchester City, Aston Villa, Stoke, 1996–2016)   134
Givens D (Manchester Utd, Luton, QPR, Birmingham, Neuchatel, 1969–82)   56
Gleeson S (Wolves, Birmingham, 2007–17)   4
Glynn D (Drumcondra, 1952–55)   2
Godwin T (Shamrock R, Leicester, Bournemouth, 1949–58)   13
Goodman J (Wimbledon, 1997)   4
Goodwin J (Stockport, 2003)   1
*Gorman W (Brentford, 1947)   2
Grealish A (Orient Luton, Brighton, WBA, 1976–86)   45
Green P (Derby, Leeds, 2010–14)   22
Gregg E (Bohemians, 1978–80)   8
Grimes A (Manchester Utd, Coventry, Luton, 1978–88)   18

Hale A (Aston Villa, Doncaster, Waterford, 1962–72)   14
Hamilton T (Shamrock R, 1959)   2
Hand E (Portsmouth, 1969–76)   20
Harte I (Leeds, Levante, 1996–2007)   64
Hartnett J (Middlesbrough, 1949–54)   2
Haverty J (Arsenal, Blackburn, Millwall, Celtic, Bristol Rov, Shelbourne, 1956–67)   32
Hayes A (Southampton, 1979)   1
Hayes J (Aberdeen, 2016–17)   4
*Hayes W (Huddersfield, 1947)   2
Hayes W (Limerick, 1949)   1
Healey R (Cardiff, 1977–80)   2
Healy C (Celtic, Sunderland, 2002–04)   13
Heighway S (Liverpool, Minnesota, 1971–82)   34
Henderson B (Drumcondra, 1948)   2
Henderson W (Brighton, Preston, 2006–08)   6
Hendrick J (Derby, Burnley, 2013–20)   54

Hennessy J (Shelbourne, St Patrick's Ath, 1956–69) 5

Herrick J (Cork Hibernian, Shamrock R, 1972–73) 3

Higgins J (Birmingham, 1951) 1

Hogan S (Aston Villa, 2018–20) 8

Holland M (Ipswich, Charlton, 2000–06) 49

Holmes J (Coventry, Tottenham, Vancouver W'caps, 1971–81) 30

Hoolahan W (Blackpool, Norwich, 2008–18) 43

Horgan D (Preston, Hibernian, 2017–19) 6

Houghton R (Oxford Utd, Liverpool, Aston Villa, Crystal Palace, Reading, 1986–97) 73

Hourihane C (Aston Villa, 2017–20) 17

Howlett G (Brighton, 1984) 1

Hughton C (Tottenham, West Ham, 1980–92) 53

Hunt N (Reading, 2009) 2

Hunt S (Reading, Hull, Wolves, 2007–12) 39

Hurley C (Millwall, Sunderland, Bolton, 1957–69) 40

Ireland S (Manchester City, 2006–08) 6

Irwin D (Manchester Utd, 1991–2000) 56

Judge A (Brentford, Ipswich, 2016–20) 9

Kavanagh G (Stoke, Cardiff, Wigan, 1998–2007) 16

Keane, R (Wolves, Coventry, Inter Milan, Leeds Tottenham, Liverpool, LA Galaxy, 1998–2017) 146

Keane R (Nottm Forest, Manchester Utd, 1991–2006) 67

Keane T (Swansea, 1949) 4

Kearin M (Shamrock R, 1972) 1

Kearns F (West Ham, 1954) 1

Kearns M (Oxford Utd, Walsall, Wolves, 1970–80) 18

Kelly A (Sheffield Utd, Blackburn, 1993–2002) 34

Kelly D (Walsall, West Ham, Leicester, Newcastle, Wolves, Sunderland, Tranmere, 1988–98) 26

Kelly G (Leeds, 1994–2003) 52

Kelly JA (Drumcondra, Preston, 1957–73) 47

Kelly M (Portsmouth, 1988–91) 4

Kelly N (Nottm Forest, 1954) 1

Kelly P (Wolves, 1961–62) 1

Kelly S (Tottenham, Birmingham, Fulham, Reading, 2006–14) 39

Kenna J (Blackburn, 1995–2000) 27

Kennedy M (Portsmouth, 1986) 2

Kennedy M (Liverpool, Wimbledon, Manchester City, Wolves, 1996–2004) 35

Kenny P (Sheffield Utd, 2004–07) 7

Keogh A (Wolves, Millwall, 2007–14) 30

Keogh J (Shamrock R, 1966) 1

Keogh R (Derby, 2013–20) 26

Keogh S (Shamrock R, 1959) 1

Kernaghan A (Middlesbrough, Manchester City, 1993–96) 22

Kiely D (Charlton, WBA, 2000–09) 11

Kiernan F (Shamrock R, Southampton, 1951–2) 5

Kilbane K (WBA, Sunderland, Everton, Wigan, Hull, 1997–2011) 110

Kinnear J (Tottenham, Brighton, 1967–76) 26

Kinsella M (Charlton, Aston Villa, WBA, 1998–2004) 48

Langan D (Derby, Birmingham, Oxford Utd, 1978–88) 26

Lapira J (Notre Dame, 2007) 1

Lawler R (Fulham, 1953–56) 8

Lawlor J (Drumcondra, Doncaster, 1949–51) 3

Lawlor M (Shamrock R, 1971–73) 5

Lawrence L (Stoke, Portsmouth, 2009–11) 15

Lawrenson M (Preston, Brighton, Liverpool, 1977–88) 39

Lee A (Rotherham, Cardiff, Ipswich, 2003–07) 10

Leech M (Shamrock R, 1969–73) 8

Lenihan D (Blackburn, 2018–19) 2

Long K (Burnley, 2017–20) 13

Long S (Reading WBA, Hull, Southampton, 2007–19) 82

Lowry D (St Patrick's Ath, 1962) 1

McAlinden J (Portsmouth, 1946) 2

McAteer J (Bolton, Liverpool, Blackburn, Sunderland, 1994–2004) 52

McCann J (Shamrock R, 1957) 1

McCarthy J (Wigan, Everton, 2011–17) 41

McCarthy M (Manchester City, Celtic, Lyon, Millwall, 1984–92) 57

McClean J (Sunderland, Wigan, WBA, Stoke, 2012–20) 72

McConville T (Dundalk, Waterford, 1972–73) 6

McDonagh J (Everton, Bolton, Sunderland, Notts Co, 1981–86) 25

McDonagh J (Shamrock R, 1984–85) 3

McEvoy A (Blackburn, 1961–67) 17

McGeady A (Celtic, Spartak Moscow, Everton, Sunderland, 2004–18) 93

McGee P (QPR, Preston, 1978–81) 15

McGoldrick E (Crystal Palace, Arsenal, 1992–95) 15

McGoldrick D (Ipswich, Sheffield Utd, 2015–20) 12

McGowan D (West Ham, 1949) 3

McGowan J (Cork Utd, 1947) 1

McGrath M (Blackburn, Bradford PA, 1958–66) 22

McGrath P (Manchester Utd, Aston Villa, Derby, 1985–97) 83

Macken J (Manchester City, 2005) 1

Mackey G (Shamrock R, 1957) 3

McLoughlin A (Swindon, Southampton, Portsmouth, 1990–2000) 42

McMillan W (Belfast Celtic, 1946) 2

McNally B (Luton, 1959–63) 3

McPhail S (Leeds, 2000–04) 10

McShane P (WBA, Sunderland, Hull, Reading, 2006–16) 33

Macken A (Derby, 1977) 1

Madden P (Yeovil, 2014) 1
Maguire S (Preston, 2018–20) 8
Mahon A (Tranmere, 2000) 2
Malone G (Shelbourne, 1949) 1
Mancini T (QPR, Arsenal, 1974–75) 5
Martin C (Glentoran, Leeds, Aston Villa, 1946–56) 30
Martin M (Bohemians, Manchester Utd, 1972–83) 52
Maybury, A (Leeds, Hearts, Leicester, 1998–2005) 10
Meagan M (Everton, Huddersfield, Drogheda, 1961–70) 17
Meyler D (Sunderland, Hull, 2013–19) 26
Miller L (Celtic, Manchester Utd, Sunderland, QPR 2004–10) 21
Milligan M (Oldham, 1992) 1
Mooney J (Shamrock R, 1965) 2
Moore A (Middlesbrough, 1996–97) 8
Moran K (Manchester Utd, Sporting Gijon, Blackburn, 1980–94) 71
Moroney J (West Ham, 1948–54) 12
Morris C (Celtic, Middlesbrough, 1988–93) 35
Morrison C (Crystal Palace, Birmingham, Crystal Palace, 2002–07) 36
Moulson G (Lincoln, 1948–49) 3
Mucklan C (Drogheda, 1978) 1
Mulligan P (Shamrock R, Chelsea, Crystal Palace, WBA, Shamrock R, 1969–80) 50
Munroe L (Shamrock R, 1954) 1
Murphy A (Clyde, 1956) 1
Murphy B (Bohemians, 1986) 1
Murphy D (Sunderland, Ipswich, Newcastle, Nottm Forest, 2007–18) 33
Murphy J (Crystal Palace, 1980) 3
Murphy J (Scunthorpe, 2009–10) 2
Murphy J (WBA, 2004) 1
Murphy P (Carlisle, 2007) 1
Murray T (Dundalk, 1950) 1

Newman W (Shelbourne, 1969) 1
Nolan E (Preston, 2009–10) 3
Nolan R (Shamrock R, 1957–63) 10

Obafemi M (Southampton, 2019) 1
O'Brien Alan (Newcastle, 2007) 5
O'Brien Aiden (Millwall, 2018–19) 4
O'Brien Andy (Newcastle, Portsmouth, 2001–07) 26
O'Brien F (Philadelphia Forest, 1980) 3
O'Brien J (Bolton, West Ham, 2006–13) 5
O'Brien L (Shamrock R, Manchester Utd, Newcastle, Tranmere, 1986–97) 16
O'Brien R (Notts Co, 1976–77) 5
O'Byrne L (Shamrock R, 1949) 1
O'Callaghan B (Stoke, 1979–82) 6
O'Callaghan K (Ipswich, Portsmouth, 1981–87) 21
O'Cearuill J (Arsenal, 2007) 2
O'Connell A (Dundalk, Bohemians, 1967–71) 2
O'Connor L (Celtic, 2020) 1
O'Connor T (Shamrock R, 1950) 4

O'Connor T (Fulham, Dundalk, Bohemians, 1968–73) 7
O'Dowda C (Oxford, Bristol City, 2016–20) 18
O'Dea D (Celtic, Toronto, Metalurh Donetsk, 2010–14) 20
O'Driscoll J (Swansea, 1949) 3
O'Driscoll S (Fulham, 1982) 3
O'Farrell F (West Ham, Preston, 1952–59) 9
*O'Flanagan Dr K (Arsenal, 1947) 3
O'Flanagan M (Bohemians, 1947) 1
O'Halloran S (Aston Villa, 2007) 2
O'Hanlon K (Rotherham, 1988) 1
O'Hara K (Manchester Utd, 2020) 2
O'Kane E (Bournemouth, Leeds, 2016–17) 7
O'Keefe E (Everton, Port Vale, 1981–85) 5
O'Leary D (Arsenal, 1977–93) 68
O'Leary P (Shamrock R, 1980–1) 7
O'Neill F (Shamrock R, 1962–72) 20
O'Neill J (Everton, 1952–59) 17
O'Neill J (Preston, 1961) 1
O'Neill K (Norwich, Middlesbrough, 1996–2000) 13
O'Regan K (Brighton, 1984–85) 4
O'Reilly J (Cork Utd, 1946) 2
O'Shea J (Manchester Utd, Sunderland, 2002–18) 118

Parrott T (Tottenham, 2020) 1
Pearce A (Reading, Derby, 2013–17) 9
Peyton G (Fulham, Bournemouth, Everton, 1977–92) 33
Peyton N (Shamrock R, Leeds, 1957–61) 6
Phelan T (Wimbledon, Manchester City, Chelsea, Everton, Fulham, 1992–2000) 42
Pilkington A (Norwich, Cardiff, 2014–16) 9
Potter D (Wolves, 2007–08) 5

Quinn A (Sheffield Wed, Sheffield Utd, 2003–07) 7
Quinn B (Coventry, 2000) 4
Quinn N (Arsenal, Manchester City, Sunderland, 1986–2002) 92
Quinn S (Hull, Reading, 2013–17) 18

Randolph D (Motherwell, West Ham, Middlesbrough, 2013–19) 42
Reid A (Nottm Forest, Tottenham, Charlton, Sunderland, Nottm Forest, 2004–14) 29
Reid S (Millwall, Blackburn, 2002–09) 23
Rice D (West Ham, 2018) 3
Richardson D (Shamrock R, Gillingham, 1972–80) 3
Ringstead A (Sheffield Utd, 1951–59) 20
Robinson C (Preston, Sheffield Utd, 2018–20) 12
Robinson M (Brighton, Liverpool, QPR, 1981–86) 24
Roche P (Shelbourne, Manchester Utd, 1972–76) 8
Rogers E (Blackburn, Charlton, 1968–73) 19
Rowlands M (QPR, 2004–10) 5
Ryan G (Derby, Brighton, 1978–85) 18
Ryan R (WBA, Derby, 1950–56) 16

Sadlier R (Millwall, 2002)	1
Sammon C (Derby, 2013–14)	9
Savage D (Millwall, 1996)	5
Saward P (Millwall, Aston Villa, Huddersfield, 1954–63)	18
Scannell T (Southend, 1954)	1
Scully P (Arsenal, 1989)	1
Sheedy K (Everton, Newcastle, 1984–93)	46
Sheridan C (Celtic, CSKA Sofia, 2010–11)	3
Sheridan J (Leeds, Sheffield Wed, 1988–96)	34
Slaven B (Middlesbrough, 1990–93)	7
Sloan P (Arsenal, 1946)	2
Smyth M (Shamrock R, 1969)	1
St Ledger S (Preston, Leicester, 2009–14)	37
Stapleton F (Arsenal, Manchester Utd, Ajax Derby, Le Havre, Blackburn, 1977–90)	71
Staunton S (Liverpool, Aston Villa, Liverpool, Crystal Palace, Aston Villa, 1989–2002)	102
Stevens E (Sheffield Utd, 2018–20)	14
*Stevenson A (Everton, 1947–49)	6
Stokes A (Sunderland, Celtic, 2007–15)	9
Strahan F (Shelbourne, 1964–65)	5
Swan M (Drumcondra, 1960)	1
Synnott N (Shamrock R, 1978–79)	3
Taylor T (Waterford, 1959)	1
Thomas P (Waterford, 1974)	2
Thompson J (Nottm Forest, 2004)	1
Townsend A (Norwich, Chelsea, Aston Villa, Middlesbrough, 1989–97)	70
Traynor T (Southampton, 1954–64)	8
Treacy K (Preston, Burnley 2011–12)	6
Treacy R (WBA, Charlton, Swindon, Preston, Shamrock R, 1966–80)	42
Travers M (Bournemouth, 2020)	2
Tuohy L (Shamrock R, Newcastle, Shamrock R, 1956–65)	8
Turner A (Celtic, 1963)	2
Vernon J (Belfast Celtic, 1946)	2
Waddock G (QPR, Millwall, 1980–90)	21
Walsh D (WBA, Aston Villa, 1946–54)	20
Walsh J (Limerick, 1982)	1
Walsh M (Blackpool, Everton, QPR, Porto, 1976–85)	21
Walsh M (Everton, Norwich, 1982–83)	4
Walsh W (Manchester City, 1947–50)	9
Walters J (Stoke, Burnley, 2011–19)	54
Ward S (Wolves, Burnley, 2011–19)	50
Waters J (Grimsby, 1977–80)	2
Westwood K (Coventry, Sunderland, Sheffield Wed, 2009–17)	21
Whelan G (Stoke, Aston Villa, 2009–20)	91
Whelan R (St Patrick's Ath, 1964)	2
Whelan R (Liverpool, Southend, 1981–95)	53
Whelan R (Manchester Utd, 1956–57)	4
Whittaker R (Chelsea, 1959)	1
Williams D (Blackburn, 2018)	3
Williams S (Millwall, 2018–19)	3
Wilson M (Stoke, Bournemouth, 2011–17)	25

INTERNATIONAL GOALSCORERS 1946–2020

(start of season 2020–21)

ENGLAND

Rooney	53	Hunt R	18	Rashford	10
Charlton R	49	Beckham	17	Wilshaw	10
Lineker	48	Lawton	16	Beardsley	9
Greaves	44	Taylor T	16	Bell	9
Owen	40	Woodcock	16	Bentley	9
Kane	32	Welbeck	16	Hateley	9
Finney	30	Scholes	14	Wright I	9
Lofthouse	30	Chivers	13	Ball	8
Shearer	30	Mariner	13	Broadis	8
Lampard Frank jnr	29	Smith R	13	Byrne J	8
Platt	27	Francis T	12	Hoddle	8
Robson B	26	Sterling	12	Kevan	8
Hurst	24	Barnes J	11	Sturridge	8
Mortensen	23	Douglas	11	Walcott	8
Crouch	22	Mannion	11	Anderton	7
Channon	21	Sheringham	11	Connelly	7
Gerrard	21	Clarke A	10	Coppell	7
Keegan	21	Cole J	10	Fowler	7
Defoe	20	Flowers R	10	Heskey	7
Peters	20	Gascoigne	10	Oxlade-Chamberlain	7
Haynes	18	Lee F	10	Paine	7
		Milburn	10	Vardy	7

SCOTLAND

MacKenzie	1	
McAvennie	1	
McCall	1	
McCalliog	1	
McCulloch	1	
McKimmie	1	
McKinnon	1	
McLean K	1	
McLean T	1	
McLintock	1	
McSwegan	1	
Miller W	1	
Mitchell	1	
Morgan	1	
Mulhall	1	
Murray J	1	
Narey	1	
Naysmith	1	
Orr	1	
Parlane	1	
Phillips	1	
Provan D (1980–82)	1	
Quashie	1	
Ritchie P	1	
Russell	1	
Sharp	1	
Shankland	1	
Stewart R	1	
Thornton	1	
Wallace I	1	
Webster	1	
Weir A	1	
Weir D	1	
Wilkie	1	
Wilson Danny	1	

WALES

Bale	33
Rush	28
Allchurch I	23
Ford	23
Saunders	22
Bellamy	19
Earnshaw	16
Hughes M	16
Jones C	16
Ramsey	16
Charles John	15
Hartson	14
Toshack	13
Giggs	12
Vokes	11
James L	10
Koumas	10
Davies RT	9
Vernon	8
Flynn	7
James R	7
Speed	7

Walsh I	7
Charles M	6
Curtis A	6
Davies RW	6
Davies S	6
Griffiths A	6
Medwin	6
Pembridge	6
Clarke R	5
Leek	5
Blake	4
Coleman	4
Deacy	4
Eastwood	4
Edwards I	4
England	4
Ledley	4
Robson-Kanu	4
Tapscott	4
Thomas M	4
Allen M	3
Bodin	3
Bowen M	3
Church	3
Collins J	3
Edwards D	3
Lawrence T	3
Melville	3
Palmer D	3
Rees R	3
Robinson J	3
Wilson H	3
Woosnam	3
Allen J	2
Cotterill	2
Davies G	2
Durban A	2
Dwyer	2
Edwards G	2
Evans C	2
Giles D	2
Godfrey	2
Griffiths M	2
Hodges	2
Horne	2
James D	2
Jones Barrie	2
Jones Bryn	2
King	2
Lowrie	2
Moore K	2
Nicholas	2
Phillips D	2
Reece G	2
Savage	2
Slatter	2
Symons	2
Taylor N	2
Williams Ashley	2

Woodburn	2
Yorath	2
Barnes	1
Blackmore	1
Blake	1
Bowen D	1
Boyle T	1
Brooks	1
Burgess R	1
Charles Jeremy	1
Evans I	1
Fletcher	1
Foulkes	1
Harris C	1
Hewitt R	1
Hockey	1
Huws	1
Jones A	1
Jones D	1
Jones J	1
Krzywicki	1
Llewellyn	1
Lovell	1
Mahoney	1
Moore G	1
Morison	1
O'Sullivan	1
Parry	1
Paul	1
Powell A	1
Powell D	1
Price P	1
Roberts C	1
Roberts P	1
Robinson C	1
Smallman	1
Vaughan	1
Williams Adrian	1
Williams GE	1
Williams GG	1
Young	1

N IRELAND

Healy	36
Lafferty K	20
Clarke	13
Armstrong	12
Davis	12
Dowie	12
Quinn JM	12
Bingham	10
Crossan J	10
McIlroy J	10
McParland	10
Best	9
McAuley	9
Whiteside	9
Dougan	8
Irvine W	8

Andrews	3	Hurley	2	Hunt S	1
Carey J	3	Kelly G	2	Judge	1
Coad	3	Keogh A	2	Kavanagh	1
Conway	3	Lawrence	2	Keogh R	1
Duffy	3	Leech	2	Kernaghan	1
Fahey	3	McCarthy	2	Long K	1
Farrell	3	McLoughlin	2	Mancini	1
Fogarty	3	O'Connor (1968–73	2	McCann	1
Haverty	3	O'Farrell	2	Maguire	1
Hoolahan	3	Pearce	2	McGoldrick	1
Kennedy Mark	3	Reid S	2	McPhail	1
Kinsella	3	Whelan G	2	Miller	1
McAteer	3	Ambrose	1	Mooney	1
Murphy D	3	Anderson	1	Moroney	1
O'Shea	3	Browne A	1	Mulligan	1
Ryan R	3	Burke G	1	O'Brien Aiden	1
St Ledger S	3	Carroll	1	O'Brien Andy	1
Waddock	3	Coleman	1	O'Dea	1
Walsh M	3	Collins	1	O'Callaghan K	1
Ward	3	Dempsey	1	O'Keefe	1
Whelan R	3	Doherty M	1	O'Leary	1
Barrett	2	Elliott	1	O'Neill F	1
Clark	2	Fitzgerald F	1	O'Reilly J	1
Conroy	2	Fullam	1	Pilkington	1
Christie	2	Galvin	1	Robinson C	1
Dennehy	2	Gibson	1	Ryan G	1
Eglington	2	Gleeson	1	Slaven	1
Fallon	2	Glynn	1	Sloan	1
Finnan	2	Gibson	1	Strahan	1
Fitzgerald P	2	Green	1	Waters	1
Foley	2	Grimes	1	Williams D	1
Gavin	2	Healy	1	Williams S	1
Hale	2	Holmes	1	Wilson	1
Hand	2	Hourihane	1		
Hendrick	2	Hughton	1		

HOME INTERNATIONAL RESULTS

Note: In the results that follow, WC = World Cup, EC = European Championship, CC = Carling Cup
TF = Tournoi de France For Northern Ireland read Ireland before 1921

ENGLAND V SCOTLAND
Played 114; England won 48; Scotland 41; drawn 25 Goals: England 203, Scotland 174

		E	S				
1872	Glasgow	0	0	1890	Glasgow	1	1
1873	The Oval	4	2	1891	Blackburn	2	1
1874	Glasgow	1	2	1892	Glasgow	4	1
1875	The Oval	2	2	1893	Richmond	5	2
1876	Glasgow	0	3	1894	Glasgow	2	2
1877	The Oval	1	3	1895	Goodison Park	3	0
1878	Glasgow	2	7	1896	Glasgow	1	2
1879	The Oval	5	4	1897	Crystal Palace	1	2
1880	Glasgow	4	5	1898	Glasgow	3	1
1881	The Oval	1	6	1899	Birmingham	2	1
1882	Glasgow	1	5	1900	Glasgow	1	4
1883	Sheffield	2	3	1901	Crystal Palace	2	2
1884	Glasgow	0	1	1902	Birmingham	2	2
1885	The Oval	1	1	1903	Sheffield	1	2
1886	Glasgow	1	1	1904	Glasgow	1	0
1887	Blackburn	2	3	1905	Crystal Palace	1	0
1888	Glasgow	5	0	1906	Glasgow	1	2
1889	The Oval	2	3	1907	Newcastle	1	1
				1908	Glasgow	1	1

Year	Venue			Year	Venue		
1909	Crystal Palace	2	0	1960	Glasgow	1	1
1910	Glasgow	0	2	1961	Wembley	9	3
1911	Goodison Park	1	1	1962	Glasgow	0	2
1912	Glasgow	1	1	1963	Wembley	1	2
1913	Stamford Bridge	1	0	1964	Glasgow	0	1
1914	Glasgow	1	3	1965	Wembley	2	2
1920	Sheffield	5	4	1966	Glasgow	4	3
1921	Glasgow	0	3	1967	Wembley (EC)	2	3
1922	Birmingham	0	1	1968	Glasgow (EC)	1	1
1923	Glasgow	2	2	1969	Wembley	4	1
1924	Wembley	1	1	1970	Glasgow	0	0
1925	Glasgow	0	2	1971	Wembley	3	1
1926	Manchester	0	1	1972	Glasgow	1	0
1927	Glasgow	2	1	1973	Glasgow	5	0
1928	Wembley	1	5	1973	Wembley	1	0
1929	Glasgow	0	1	1974	Glasgow	0	2
1930	Wembley	5	2	1975	Wembley	5	1
1931	Glasgow	0	2	1976	Glasgow	1	2
1932	Wembley	3	0	1977	Wembley	1	2
1933	Glasgow	1	2	1978	Glasgow	1	0
1934	Wembley	3	0	1979	Wembley	3	1
1935	Glasgow	0	2	1980	Glasgow	2	0
1936	Wembley	1	1	1981	Wembley	0	1
1937	Glasgow	1	3	1982	Glasgow	1	0
1938	Wembley	0	1	1983	Wembley	2	0
1939	Glasgow	2	1	1984	Glasgow	1	1
1947	Wembley	1	1	1985	Glasgow	0	1
1948	Glasgow	2	0	1986	Wembley	2	1
1949	Wembley	1	3	1987	Glasgow	0	0
1950	Glasgow (WC)	1	0	1988	Wembley	1	0
1951	Wembley	2	3	1989	Glasgow	2	0
1952	Glasgow	2	1	1996	Wembley (EC)	2	0
1953	Wembley	2	2	1999	Glasgow (EC)	2	0
1954	Glasgow (WC)	4	2	1999	Wembley (EC)	0	1
1955	Wembley	7	2	2013	Wembley	3	2
1956	Glasgow	1	1	2014	Glasgow	3	1
1957	Wembley	2	1	2016	Wembley (WC)	3	0
1958	Glasgow	4	0	2017	Glasgow (WC)	2	2
1959	Wembley	1	0				

ENGLAND v WALES

Played 102; England won 67; Wales 14; drawn 21; Goals: England 247 Wales 91

Year	Venue	E	W	Year	Venue		
1879	The Oval	2	1	1898	Wrexham	3	0
1880	Wrexham	3	2	1899	Bristol	4	0
1881	Blackburn	0	1	1900	Cardiff	1	1
1882	Wrexham	3	5	1901	Newcastle	6	0
1883	The Oval	5	0	1902	Wrexham	0	0
1884	Wrexham	4	0	1903	Portsmouth	2	1
1885	Blackburn	1	1	1904	Wrexham	2	2
1886	Wrexham	3	1	1905	Anfield	3	1
1887	The Oval	4	0	1906	Cardiff	1	0
1888	Crewe	5	1	1907	Fulham	1	1
1889	Stoke	4	1	1908	Wrexham	7	1
1890	Wrexham	3	1	1909	Nottingham	2	0
1891	Sunderland	4	1	1910	Cardiff	1	0
1892	Wrexham	2	0	1911	Millwall	3	0
1893	Stoke	6	0	1912	Wrexham	2	0
1894	Wrexham	5	1	1913	Bristol	4	3
1895	Queens Club, London	1	1	1914	Cardiff	2	0
1896	Cardiff	9	1	1920	Highbury	1	2
1897	Bramall Lane	4	0	1921	Cardiff	0	0
				1922	Anfield	1	0

1923	Cardiff	2	2		1961	Cardiff	1	1
1924	Blackburn	1	2		1962	Wembley	4	0
1925	Swansea	2	1		1963	Cardiff	4	0
1926	Selhurst Park	1	3		1964	Wembley	2	1
1927	Wrexham	3	3		1965	Cardiff	0	0
1927	Burnley	1	2		1966	Wembley (EC)	5	1
1928	Swansea	3	2		1967	Cardiff (EC)	3	0
1929	Stamford Bridge	6	0		1969	Wembley	2	1
1930	Wrexham	4	0		1970	Cardiff	1	1
1931	Anfield	3	1		1971	Wembley	0	0
1932	Wrexham	0	0		1972	Cardiff	3	0
1933	Newcastle	1	2		1972	Cardiff (WC)	1	0
1934	Cardiff	4	0		1973	Wembley (WC)	1	1
1935	Wolverhampton	1	2		1973	Wembley	3	0
1936	Cardiff	1	2		1974	Cardiff	2	0
1937	Middlesbrough	2	1		1975	Wembley	2	2
1938	Cardiff	2	4		1976	Wrexham	2	1
1946	Maine Road	3	0		1976	Cardiff	1	0
1947	Cardiff	3	0		1977	Wembley	0	1
1948	Villa Park	1	0		1978	Cardiff	3	1
1949	Cardiff (WC)	4	1		1979	Wembley	0	0
1950	Sunderland	4	2		1980	Wrexham	1	4
1951	Cardiff	1	1		1981	Wembley	0	0
1952	Wembley	5	2		1982	Cardiff	1	0
1953	Cardiff (WC)	4	1		1983	Wembley	2	1
1954	Wembley	3	2		1984	Wrexham	0	1
1955	Cardiff	1	2		2004	Old Trafford (WC)	2	0
1956	Wembley	3	1		2005	Cardiff (WC)	1	0
1957	Cardiff	4	0		2011	Cardiff (EC)	2	0
1958	Villa Park	2	2		2011	Wembley (EC)	1	0
1959	Cardiff	1	1		2016	Lens (EC)	2	1
1960	Wembley	5	1					

ENGLAND v N IRELAND

Played 98; England won 75; Ireland 7; drawn 16 Goals: England 323, Ireland 81

		E	I				E	I
1882	Belfast	13	0		1907	Goodison Park	1	0
1883	Aigburth, Liverpool	7	0		1908	Belfast	3	1
1884	Belfast	8	1		1909	Bradford PA	4	0
1885	Whalley Range	4	0		1910	Belfast	1	1
1886	Belfast	6	1		1911	Derby	2	1
1887	Bramall Lane	7	0		1912	Dublin	6	1
1888	Belfast	5	1		1913	Belfast	1	2
1889	Goodison Park	6	1		1914	Middlesbrough	0	3
1890	Belfast	9	1		1919	Belfast	1	1
1891	Wolverhampton	6	1		1920	Sunderland	2	0
1892	Belfast	2	0		1921	Belfast	1	1
1893	Perry Barr	6	1		1922	West Bromwich	2	0
1894	Belfast	2	2		1923	Belfast	1	2
1895	Derby	9	0		1924	Goodison Park	3	1
1896	Belfast	2	0		1925	Belfast	0	0
1897	Nottingham	6	0		1926	Anfield	3	3
1898	Belfast	3	2		1927	Belfast	0	2
1899	Sunderland	13	2		1928	Goodison Park	2	1
1900	Dublin	2	0		1929	Belfast	3	0
1901	Southampton	3	0		1930	Bramall Lane	5	1
1902	Belfast	1	0		1931	Belfast	6	2
1903	Wolverhampton	4	0		1932	Blackpool	1	0
1904	Belfast	3	1		1933	Belfast	3	0
1905	Middlesbrough	1	1		1935	Goodison Park	2	1
1906	Belfast	5	0		1935	Belfast	3	1
					1936	Stoke	3	1

Year	Venue		
1937	Belfast	5	1
1938	Old Trafford	7	0
1946	Belfast	7	2
1947	Goodison Park	2	2
1948	Belfast	6	2
1949	Maine Road (WC)	9	2
1950	Belfast	4	1
1951	Villa Park	2	0
1952	Belfast	2	2
1953	Goodison Park (WC)	3	1
1954	Belfast	2	0
1955	Wembley	3	0
1956	Belfast	1	1
1957	Wembley	2	3
1958	Belfast	3	3
1959	Wembley	2	1
1960	Belfast	5	2
1961	Wembley	1	1
1962	Belfast	3	1
1963	Wembley	8	3
1964	Belfast	4	3
1965	Wembley	2	1
1966	Belfast (EC)	2	0
1967	Wembley (EC)	2	0
1969	Belfast	3	1
1970	Wembley	3	1
1971	Belfast	1	0
1972	Wembley	0	1
1973	*Goodison Park	2	1
1974	Wembley	1	0
1975	Belfast	0	0
1976	Wembley	4	0
1977	Belfast	2	1
1978	Wembley	1	0
1979	Wembley (EC)	4	0
1979	Belfast	2	0
1979	Belfast (EC)	5	1
1980	Wembley	1	1
1982	Wembley	4	0
1983	Belfast	0	0
1984	Wembley	1	0
1985	Belfast (WC)	1	0
1985	Wembley (WC)	0	0
1986	Wembley (EC)	3	0
1987	Belfast (EC)	2	0
2005	Old Trafford (WC)	4	0
2005	Belfast (WC)	0	1

(*Switched from Belfast because of political situation)

SCOTLAND v WALES

Played 107; Scotland won 61; Wales 23; drawn 23; Goals: Scotland 243, Wales 124

Year	Venue	s	w
1876	Glasgow	4	0
1877	Wrexham	2	0
1878	Glasgow	9	0
1879	Wrexham	3	0
1880	Glasgow	5	1
1881	Wrexham	5	1
1882	Glasgow	5	0
1883	Wrexham	3	0
1884	Glasgow	4	1
1885	Wrexham	8	1
1886	Glasgow	4	1
1887	Wrexham	2	0
1888	Edinburgh	5	1
1889	Wrexham	0	0
1890	Paisley	5	0
1891	Wrexham	4	3
1892	Edinburgh	6	1
1893	Wrexham	8	0
1894	Kilmarnock	5	2
1895	Wrexham	2	2
1896	Dundee	4	0
1897	Wrexham	2	2
1898	Motherwell	5	2
1899	Wrexham	6	0
1900	Aberdeen	5	2
1901	Wrexham	1	1
1902	Greenock	5	1
1903	Cardiff	1	0
1904	Dundee	1	1
1905	Wrexham	1	3
1906	Edinburgh	0	2
1907	Wrexham	0	1
1908	Dundee	2	1
1909	Wrexham	2	3
1910	Kilmarnock	1	0
1911	Cardiff	2	2
1912	Tynecastle	1	0
1913	Wrexham	0	0
1914	Glasgow	0	0
1920	Cardiff	1	1
1921	Aberdeen	2	1
1922	Wrexham	1	2
1923	Paisley	2	0
1924	Cardiff	0	2
1925	Tynecastle	3	1
1926	Cardiff	3	0
1927	Glasgow	3	0
1928	Wrexham	2	2
1929	Glasgow	4	2
1930	Cardiff	4	2
1931	Glasgow	1	1
1932	Wrexham	3	2
1933	Edinburgh	2	5
1934	Cardiff	2	3
1935	Aberdeen	3	2
1936	Cardiff	1	1
1937	Dundee	1	2
1938	Cardiff	1	2
1939	Edinburgh	3	2
1946	Wrexham	1	3
1947	Glasgow	1	2
1948	Cardiff (WC)	3	1
1949	Glasgow	2	0
1950	Cardiff	3	1
1951	Glasgow	0	1
1952	Cardiff (WC)	2	1
1953	Glasgow	3	3
1954	Cardiff	1	0
1955	Glasgow	2	0
1956	Cardiff	2	2
1957	Glasgow	1	1
1958	Cardiff	3	0
1959	Glasgow	1	1

Year	Venue	S	I		Year	Venue	S	I
1960	Cardiff	0	2		1977	Wrexham	0	0
1961	Glasgow	2	0		1977	Anfield (WC)	2	0
1962	Cardiff	3	2		1978	Glasgow	1	1
1963	Glasgow	2	1		1979	Cardiff	0	3
1964	Cardiff	2	3		1980	Glasgow	1	0
1965	Glasgow (EC)	4	1		1981	Swansea	0	2
1966	Cardiff (EC)	1	1		1982	Glasgow	1	0
1967	Glasgow	3	2		1983	Cardiff	2	0
1969	Wrexham	5	3		1984	Glasgow	2	1
1970	Glasgow	0	0		1985	Glasgow (WC)	0	1
1971	Cardiff	0	0		1985	Cardiff (WC)	1	1
1972	Glasgow	1	0		1997	Kilmarnock	0	1
1973	Wrexham	2	0		2004	Cardiff	0	4
1974	Glasgow	2	0		2009	Cardiff	0	3
1975	Cardiff	2	2		2011	Dublin (CC)	3	1
1976	Glasgow	3	1		2012	Cardiff (WC)	1	2
1977	Glasgow (WC)	1	0		2013	Glasgow (WC)	1	2

SCOTLAND v NORTHERN IRELAND

Played 96; Scotland won 64; Northern Ireland 15; drawn 17; Goals: Scotland 258, Northern Ireland 80

Year	Venue	S	I		Year	Venue	S	I
1884	Belfast	5	0		1930	Glasgow	3	1
1885	Glasgow	8	2		1931	Belfast	0	0
1886	Belfast	7	2		1932	Glasgow	3	1
1887	Belfast	4	1		1933	Belfast	4	0
1888	Belfast	10	2		1934	Glasgow	1	2
1889	Glasgow	7	0		1935	Belfast	1	2
1890	Belfast	4	1		1936	Edinburgh	2	1
1891	Glasgow	2	1		1937	Belfast	3	1
1892	Belfast	3	2		1938	Aberdeen	1	1
1893	Glasgow	6	1		1939	Belfast	2	0
1894	Belfast	2	1		1946	Glasgow	0	0
1895	Glasgow	3	1		1947	Belfast	0	2
1896	Belfast	3	3		1948	Glasgow	3	2
1897	Glasgow	5	1		1949	Belfast	8	2
1898	Belfast	3	0		1950	Glasgow	6	1
1899	Glasgow	9	1		1951	Belfast	3	0
1900	Belfast	3	0		1952	Glasgow	1	1
1901	Glasgow	11	0		1953	Belfast	3	1
1902	Belfast	5	1		1954	Glasgow	2	2
1902	Belfast	3	0		1955	Belfast	1	2
1903	Glasgow	0	2		1956	Glasgow	1	0
1904	Dublin	1	1		1957	Belfast	1	1
1905	Glasgow	4	0		1958	Glasgow	2	2
1906	Dublin	1	0		1959	Belfast	4	0
1907	Glasgow	3	0		1960	Glasgow	5	1
1908	Dublin	5	0		1961	Belfast	6	1
1909	Glasgow	5	0		1962	Glasgow	5	1
1910	Belfast	0	1		1963	Belfast	1	2
1911	Glasgow	2	0		1964	Glasgow	3	2
1912	Belfast	4	1		1965	Belfast	2	3
1913	Dublin	2	1		1966	Glasgow	2	1
1914	Belfast	1	1		1967	Belfast	0	1
1920	Glasgow	3	0		1969	Glasgow	1	1
1921	Belfast	2	0		1970	Belfast	1	0
1922	Glasgow	2	1		1971	Glasgow	0	1
1923	Belfast	1	0		1972	Glasgow	2	0
1924	Glasgow	2	0		1973	Glasgow	1	2
1925	Belfast	3	0		1974	Glasgow	0	1
1926	Glasgow	4	0		1975	Glasgow	3	0
1927	Belfast	2	0		1976	Glasgow	3	0
1928	Glasgow	0	1		1977	Glasgow	3	0
1929	Belfast	7	3		1978	Glasgow	1	1
					1979	Glasgow	1	0

1980	Belfast	0	1
1981	Glasgow (WC)	1	1
1981	Glasgow	2	0
1981	Belfast (WC)	0	0
1982	Belfast	1	1
1983	Glasgow	0	0

1984	Belfast	0	2
1992	Glasgow	1	0
2008	Glasgow	0	0
2011	Dublin (CC)	3	0
2015	Glasgow	1	0

WALES v NORTHERN IRELAND
Played 97; Wales won 45; Northern Ireland won 27; drawn 25; Goals: Wales 191 Northern Ireland 132

		W	I
1882	Wrexham	7	1
1883	Belfast	1	1
1884	Wrexham	6	0
1885	Belfast	8	2
1886	Wrexham	5	0
1887	Belfast	1	4
1888	Wrexham	11	0
1889	Belfast	3	1
1890	Shrewsbury	5	2
1891	Belfast	2	7
1892	Bangor	1	1
1893	Belfast	3	4
1894	Swansea	4	1
1895	Belfast	2	2
1896	Wrexham	6	1
1897	Belfast	3	4
1898	Llandudno	0	1
1899	Belfast	0	1
1900	Llandudno	2	0
1901	Belfast	1	0
1902	Cardiff	0	3
1903	Belfast	0	2
1904	Bangor	0	1
1905	Belfast	2	2
1906	Wrexham	4	4
1907	Belfast	3	2
1908	Aberdare	0	1
1909	Belfast	3	2
1910	Wrexham	4	1
1911	Belfast	2	1
1912	Cardiff	2	3
1913	Belfast	1	0
1914	Wrexham	1	2
1920	Belfast	2	2
1921	Swansea	2	1
1922	Belfast	1	1
1923	Wrexham	0	3
1924	Belfast	1	0
1925	Wrexham	0	0
1926	Belfast	0	3
1927	Cardiff	2	2
1928	Belfast	2	1
1929	Wrexham	2	2
1930	Belfast	0	7
1931	Wrexham	3	2
1932	Belfast	0	4
1933	Wrexham	4	1
1934	Belfast	1	1
1935	Wrexham	3	1
1936	Belfast	2	3
1937	Wrexham	4	1
1938	Belfast	0	1
1939	Wrexham	3	1
1947	Belfast	1	2
1948	Wrexham	2	0
1949	Belfast	2	0
1950	Wrexham (WC)	0	0
1951	Belfast	2	1
1952	Swansea	3	0
1953	Belfast	3	2
1954	Wrexham (WC)	1	2
1955	Belfast	3	2
1956	Cardiff	1	1
1957	Belfast	0	0
1958	Cardiff	1	1
1959	Belfast	1	4
1960	Wrexham	3	2
1961	Belfast	5	1
1962	Cardiff	4	0
1963	Belfast	4	1
1964	Swansea	2	3
1965	Belfast	5	0
1966	Cardiff	1	4
1967	Belfast (EC)	0	0
1968	Wrexham (EC)	2	0
1969	Belfast	0	0
1970	Swansea	1	0
1971	Belfast	0	1
1972	Wrexham	0	0
1973	*Goodison Park	0	1
1974	Wrexham	1	0
1975	Belfast	0	1
1976	Swansea	1	0
1977	Belfast	1	1
1978	Wrexham	1	0
1979	Belfast	1	1
1980	Cardiff	0	1
1982	Wrexham	3	0
1983	Belfast	1	0
1984	Swansea	1	1
2004	Cardiff (WC)	2	2
2005	Belfast (WC)	3	2
2007	Belfast	0	0
2008	Glasgow	0	0
2011	Dublin (CC)	2	0
2016	Cardiff	1	1
2016	Paris (EC)	1	0

(*Switched from Belfast because of political situation)

WORLD CUP SUMMARIES 1930–2018

1930 – URUGUAY

WINNERS: Uruguay RUNNERS-UP: Argentina THIRD: USA FOURTH: Yugoslavia
Other countries taking part: Belgium, Bolivia, Brazil, Chile, France, Mexico, Paraguay, Peru, Romania. **Total entries:** 13
Venue: All matches played in Montevideo
Top scorer: Stabile (Argentina) 8 goals
Final (30/7/30): **Uruguay 4** (Dorado 12, Cea 55, Iriarte 64, Castro 89) **Argentina 2** (Peucelle 29, Stabile 35). **Att:** 90,000
Uruguay: Ballesteros; Nasazzi (capt), Mascheroni, Andrade, Fernandez, Gestido, Dorado, Scarone, Castro, Cea, Iriarte. **Argentina:** Botasso; Della Torre, Paternoster, J Evaristo, Monti, Suarez, Peucelle, Varallo, Stabile, Ferreira (capt), M Evaristo
Referee: Langenus (Belgium). **Half-time:** 1-2

1934 – ITALY

WINNERS: Italy RUNNERS-UP: Czechoslovakia THIRD: Germany FOURTH: Austria
Other countries in finals: Argentina, Belgium, Brazil, Egypt, France, Holland, Hungary, Romania, Spain, Sweden, Switzerland, USA. **Total entries:** 29 (16 qualifiers)
Venues: Bologna, Florence, Genoa, Milan, Naples, Rome, Trieste, Turin
Top scorers: Conen (Germany), Nejedly (Czechoslovakia), Schiavio (Italy), each 4 goals. **Final** (Rome, 10/6/34): **Italy 2** (Orsi 82, Schiavio 97) **Czechoslovakia 1** (Puc 70) after extra-time. **Att:** 50,000
Italy: Combi (capt); Monzeglio, Allemandi, Ferraris, Monti, Bertolini, Guaita, Meazza, Schiavio, Ferrari, Orsi. **Czechoslovakia:** Planicka (capt); Zenisek, Ctyroky, Kostalek, Cambal, Krcil, Junek, Svoboda, Sobotka, Nejedly, Puc
Referee: Eklind (Sweden). **Half-time:** 0-0 (90 mins: 1-1)

1938 – FRANCE

WINNERS: Italy RUNNERS-UP: Hungary THIRD: Brazil FOURTH: Sweden
Other countries in finals: Belgium, Cuba, Czechoslovakia, Dutch East Indies, France, Germany, Holland, Norway, Poland, Romania, Switzerland. **Total entries:** 25 (15 qualifiers)
Venues: Antibes, Bordeaux, Le Havre, Lille, Marseille, Paris, Reims, Strasbourg, Toulouse
Top scorer: Leonidas (Brazil) 8 goals
Final (Paris, 19/6/38): **Italy 4** (Colaussi 6, 36, Piola 15, 81) **Hungary 2** (Titkos 7, Sarosi 65). **Att:** 45,000
Italy: Olivieri; Foni, Rava, Serantoni, Andreolo, Locatelli, Biavati, Meazza (capt), Piola, Ferrari, Colaussi. **Hungary:** Szabo; Polgar, Biro, Szalay, Szucs, Lazar, Sas, Vincze, Sarosi (capt), Szengeller, Titkos
Referee: Capdeville (France). **Half-time:** 3-1

1950 – BRAZIL

WINNERS: Uruguay RUNNERS-UP: Brazil THIRD: Sweden FOURTH: Spain
Other countries in finals: Bolivia, Chile, England, Italy, Mexico, Paraguay, Switzerland, USA, Yugoslavia. **Total entries:** 29 (13 qualifiers)
Venues: Belo Horizonte, Curitiba, Porto Alegre, Recife, Rio de Janeiro, Sao Paulo
Top scorer: Ademir (Brazil) 9 goals
Deciding Match (Rio de Janeiro, 16/7/50): **Uruguay 2** (Schiaffino 64, Ghiggia 79) **Brazil 1** (Friaca 47). **Att:** 199,850
(For the only time, the World Cup was decided on a final pool system, in which the winners of the four qualifying groups met in a six-match series So, unlike previous and subsequent tournaments, there was no official final as such, but Uruguay v Brazil was the deciding match in the final pool)
Uruguay: Maspoli; Gonzales, Tejera, Gambetta, Varela (capt), Andrade, Ghiggia, Perez, Miguez, Schiaffino, Moran

Brazil: Barbosa; Augusto (capt), Juvenal, Bauer, Danilo, Bigode, Friaca, Zizinho, Ademir, Jair, Chico
Referee: Reader (England). **Half-time:** 0-0

1954 – SWITZERLAND

WINNERS: West Germany RUNNERS-UP: Hungary THIRD: Austria FOURTH: Uruguay
Other countries in finals: Belgium, Brazil, Czechoslovakia, England, France, Italy, Korea, Mexico, Scotland, Switzerland, Turkey, Yugoslavia. **Total entries:** 35 (16 qualifiers)
Venues: Basle, Berne, Geneva, Lausanne, Lugano, Zurich
Top scorer: Kocsis (Hungary) 11 goals
Final (Berne, 4/7/54): **West Germany 3** (Morlock 12, Rahn 17, 84) **Hungary 2** (Puskas 4, Czibor 9). **Att:** 60,000
West Germany: Turek; Posipal, Kohlmeyer, Eckel, Liebrich, Mai, Rahn, Morlock, O Walter, F Walter (capt), Schaefer. **Hungary:** Grosics; Buzansky, Lantos, Bozsik, Lorant, Zakarias, Czibor, Kocsis, Hidegkuti, Puskas (capt), J Toth
Referee: Ling (England). **Half-time:** 2-2

1958 – SWEDEN

WINNERS: Brazil RUNNERS-UP: Sweden THIRD: France FOURTH: West Germany
Other countries in finals: Argentina, Austria, Czechoslovakia, England, Hungary, Mexico, Northern Ireland, Paraguay, Scotland, Soviet Union, Wales, Yugoslavia. **Total entries:** 47 (16 qualifiers)
Venues: Boras, Eskilstuna, Gothenburg, Halmstad, Helsingborgs, Malmo, Norrkoping, Orebro, Sandviken, Stockholm, Vasteras
Top scorer: Fontaine (France) 13 goals
Final (Stockholm, 29/6/58): **Brazil 5** (Vava 10, 32, Pele 55, 88, Zagalo 76) **Sweden 2** (Liedholm 4, Simonsson 83). **Att:** 49,737
Brazil: Gilmar; D Santos, N Santos, Zito, Bellini (capt), Orlando, Garrincha, Didi, Vava, Pele, Zagallo. **Sweden:** Svensson; Bergmark, Axbom, Boerjesson, Gustavsson, Parling, Hamrin, Gren, Simonsson, Liedholm (capt), Skoglund
Referee: Guigue (France). **Half-time:** 2-1

1962 – CHILE

WINNERS: Brazil RUNNERS-UP: Czechoslovakia THIRD: Chile FOURTH: Yugoslavia
Other countries in finals: Argentina, Bulgaria, Colombia, England, Hungary, Italy, Mexico, Soviet Union, Spain, Switzerland, Uruguay, West Germany. **Total entries:** 53 (16 qualifiers)
Venues: Arica, Rancagua, Santiago, Vina del Mar
Top scorer: Jerkovic (Yugoslavia) 5 goals
Final (Santiago, 17/6/62): **Brazil 3** (Amarildo 17, Zito 69, Vava 77) **Czechoslovakia 1** (Masopust 16). **Att:** 68,679
Brazil: Gilmar; D Santos, Mauro (capt), Zozimo, N Santos, Zito, Didi, Garrincha, Vava, Amarildo, Zagallo. **Czechoslovakia:** Schroiff; Tichy, Novak, Pluskal, Popluhar, Masopust (capt), Pospichal, Scherer, Kvasnak, Kadraba, Jelinek
Referee: Latychev (Soviet Union). **Half-time:** 1-1

1966 – ENGLAND

WINNERS: England RUNNERS-UP: West Germany THIRD: Portugal FOURTH: USSR
Other countries in finals: Argentina, Brazil, Bulgaria, Chile, France, Hungary, Italy, Mexico, North Korea, Spain, Switzerland, Uruguay. **Total entries:** 53 (16 qualifiers)
Venues: Birmingham (Villa Park), Liverpool (Goodison Park), London (Wembley and White City), Manchester (Old Trafford), Middlesbrough (Ayresome Park), Sheffield (Hillsborough), Sunderland (Roker Park)
Top scorer: Eusebio (Portugal) 9 goals
Final (Wembley, 30/7/66): **England 4** (Hurst 19, 100, 120, Peters 78) **West Germany 2** (Haller 13, Weber 89) after extra-time. **Att:** 93,802

England: Banks; Cohen, Wilson, Stiles, J Charlton, Moore (capt), Ball, Hurst, Hunt, R Charlton, Peters. **West Germany:** Tilkowski; Hottges, Schnellinger, Beckenbauer, Schulz, Weber, Haller, Held, Seeler (capt), Overath, Emmerich
Referee: Dienst (Switzerland). **Half-time:** 1-1 (90 mins: 2-2)

1970 – MEXICO

WINNERS: Brazil RUNNERS-UP: Italy THIRD: West Germany FOURTH: Uruguay
Other countries in finals: Belgium, Bulgaria, Czechoslovakia, El Salvador, England, Israel, Mexico, Morocco, Peru, Romania, Soviet Union, Sweden. Total entries: 68 (16 qualifiers)
Venues: Guadalajara, Leon, Mexico City, Puebla, Toluca
Top scorer: Muller (West Germany) 10 goals
Final (Mexico City, 21/6/70): **Brazil** 4 (Pele 18, Gerson 66, Jairzinho 71, Carlos Alberto 87) **Italy** 1 (Boninsegna 38). **Att:** 107,412
Brazil: Felix; Carlos Alberto (capt), Brito, Piazza, Everaldo, Clodoaldo, Gerson, Jairzinho, Tostao, Pele, Rivelino. **Italy:** Albertosi; Burgnich, Facchetti (capt), Cera, Rosato, Bertini (Juliano 72), Domenghini, De Sisti, Mazzola, Boninsegna (Rivera 84), Riva
Referee: Glockner (East Germany). **Half-time:** 1-1

1974 – WEST GERMANY

WINNERS: West Germany RUNNERS-UP: Holland THIRD: Poland FOURTH: Brazil
Other countries in finals: Argentina, Australia, Bulgaria, Chile, East Germany, Haiti, Italy, Scotland, Sweden, Uruguay, Yugoslavia, Zaire. **Total entries:** 98 (16 qualifiers)
Venues: Berlin, Dortmund, Dusseldorf, Frankfurt, Gelsenkirchen, Hamburg, Hanover, Munich, Stuttgart
Top scorer: Lato (Poland) 7 goals
Final (Munich, 7/7/74): **West Germany** 2 (Breitner 25 pen, Muller 43) **Holland** 1 (Neeskens 2 pen). **Att:** 77,833
West Germany: Maier; Vogts, Schwarzenbeck, Beckenbauer (capt), Breitner, Bonhof, Hoeness, Overath, Grabowski, Muller, Holzenbein. **Holland:** Jongbloed; Suurbier, Rijsbergen (De Jong 69), Haan, Krol, Jansen, Van Hanegem, Neeskens, Rep, Cruyff (capt), Rensenbrink (R Van der Kerkhof 46)
Referee: Taylor (England). **Half-time:** 2-1

1978 – ARGENTINA

WINNERS: Argentina RUNNERS-UP: Holland THIRD: Brazil FOURTH: Italy
Other countries in finals: Austria, France, Hungary, Iran, Mexico, Peru, Poland, Scotland, Spain, Sweden, Tunisia, West Germany. **Total entries:** 102 (16 qualifiers)
Venues: Buenos Aires, Cordoba, Mar del Plata, Mendoza, Rosario
Top scorer: Kempes (Argentina) 6 goals
Final (Buenos Aires, 25/6/78): **Argentina** 3 (Kempes 38, 104, Bertoni 115) **Holland** 1 (Nanninga 82) after extra-time. **Att:** 77,000 .
Argentina: Fillol; Passarella (capt), Olguin, Galvan, Tarantini, Ardiles (Larrosa 66), Gallego, Ortiz (Houseman 74), Bertoni, Luque, Kempes. **Holland:** Jongbloed; Krol (capt), Poortvliet, Brandts, Jansen (Suurbier 73), Haan, Neeskens, W Van der Kerkhof, Rep (Nanninga 58), R Van der Kerkhof, Rensenbrink
Referee: Gonella (Italy). **Half-time:** 1-0 (90 mins: 1-1)

1982 – SPAIN

WINNERS: Italy RUNNERS-UP: West Germany THIRD: Poland FOURTH: France
Other countries in finals: Algeria, Argentina, Austria, Belgium, Brazil, Cameroon, Chile, Czechoslovakia, El Salvador, England, Honduras, Hungary, Kuwait, New Zealand, Northern Ireland, Peru, Scotland, Soviet Union, Spain, Yugoslavia. **Total entries:** 109 (24 qualifiers)
Venues: Alicante, Barcelona, Bilbao, Coruna, Elche, Gijon, Madrid, Malaga, Oviedo, Seville, Valencia, Valladolid, Vigo, Zaragoza

Top scorer: Rossi (Italy) 6 goals

Final (Madrid, 11/7/82): **Italy** 3 (Rossi 57, Tardelli 69, Altobelli 81) **West Germany** 1 (Breitner 84). **Att:** 90,089

Italy: Zoff (capt); Bergomi, Scirea, Collovati, Cabrini, Oriali, Gentile, Tardelli, Conti, Rossi, Graziani (Altobelli 18 – Causio 88). **West Germany:** Schumacher; Kaltz, Stielike, K-H Forster, B Forster, Dremmler (Hrubesch 63), Breitner, Briegel, Rummenigge (capt) (Muller 70), Fischer, Littbarski
Referee: Coelho (Brazil). **Half-time:** 0-0

1986 – MEXICO

WINNERS: Argentina RUNNERS-UP: West Germany THIRD: France FOURTH: Belgium
Other countries in finals: Algeria, Brazil, Bulgaria, Canada, Denmark, England, Hungary, Iraq, Italy, Mexico, Morocco, Northern Ireland, Paraguay, Poland, Portugal, Scotland, South Korea, Soviet Union, Spain, Uruguay. **Total entries:** 118 (24 qualifiers)
Venues: Guadalajara, Irapuato, Leon, Mexico City, Monterrey, Nezahualcoyotl, Puebla, Queretaro, Toluca
Top scorer: Lineker (England) 6 goals
Final (Mexico City, 29/6/86): **Argentina** 3 (Brown 23, Valdano 56, Burruchaga 85) **West Germany** 2 (Rummenigge 74, Voller 82). **Att:** 115,026
Argentina: Pumpido; Cuciuffo, Brown, Ruggeri, Olarticoechea, Batista, Giusti, Maradona (capt), Burruchaga (Trobbiani 89), Enrique, Valdano. **West Germany:** Schumacher; Berthold, K-H Forster, Jakobs, Brehme, Briegel, Eder, Matthaus, Magath (Hoeness 62), Allofs (Voller 45), Rummenigge (capt)
Referee: Filho (Brazil). **Half-time:** 1-0

1990 – ITALY

WINNERS: West Germany RUNNERS-UP: Argentina THIRD: Italy FOURTH: England
Other countries in finals: Austria, Belgium, Brazil, Cameroon, Colombia, Costa Rica, Czechoslovakia, Egypt, Holland, Republic of Ireland, Romania, Scotland, Spain, South Korea, Soviet Union, Sweden, United Arab Emirates, USA, Uruguay, Yugoslavia. **Total entries:** 103 (24 qualifiers)
Venues: Bari, Bologna, Cagliari, Florence, Genoa, Milan, Naples, Palermo, Rome, Turin, Udine, Verona
Top scorer: Schillaci (Italy) 6 goals
Final (Rome, 8/7/90): **Argentina** 0 **West Germany** 1 (Brehme 85 pen). **Att:** 73,603
Argentina: Goycochea; Ruggeri (Monzon 45), Simon, Serrizuela, Lorenzo, Basualdo, Troglio, Burruchaga (Calderon 53), Sensini, Maradona (capt), Dezotti **Sent-off:** Monzon (65), Dezotti (86) – first players ever to be sent off in World Cup Final. **West Germany:** Illgner; Berthold (Reuter 75), Buchwald, Augenthaler, Kohler, Brehme, Matthaus (capt), Littbarski, Hassler, Klinsmann, Voller
Referee: Codesal (Mexico). **Half-time:** 0-0

1994 – USA

WINNERS: Brazil RUNNERS-UP: Italy THIRD: Sweden FOURTH: Bulgaria
Other countries in finals: Argentina, Belgium, Bolivia, Cameroon, Colombia, Germany, Greece, Holland, Mexico, Morocco, Nigeria, Norway, Republic of Ireland, Romania, Russia, Saudi Arabia, South Korea, Spain, Switzerland, USA. **Total entries:** 144 (24 qualifiers)
Venues: Boston, Chicago, Dallas, Detroit, Los Angeles, New York City, Orlando, San Francisco, Washington
Top scorers: Salenko (Russia), Stoichkov (Bulgaria), each 6 goals
Final (Los Angeles, 17/7/94): **Brazil** 0 **Italy** 0 after extra-time; Brazil won 3-2 on pens
Att: 94,194
Brazil: Taffarel; Jorginho (Cafu 21), Aldair, Marcio Santos, Branco, Mazinho, Mauro Silva, Dunga (capt), Zinho (Viola 105), Romario, Bebeto. **Italy:** Pagliuca; Mussi (Apolloni 35), Baresi (capt), Maldini, Benarrivo, Berti, Albertini,
D Baggio (Evani 95), Donadoni, R Baggio, Massaro
Referee: Puhl (Hungary)

Shoot-out: Baresi missed, Marco Santos saved, Albertini 1-0, Romario 1-1, Evani 2-1, Branco 2-2, Massaro saved, Dunga 2-3, R Baggio missed

1998 – FRANCE

WINNERS: France RUNNERS-UP: Brazil THIRD: Croatia FOURTH: Holland
Other countries in finals: Argentina, Austria, Belgium, Bulgaria, Cameroon, Chile, Colombia, Denmark, England, Germany, Iran, Italy, Jamaica, Japan, Mexico, Morocco, Nigeria, Norway, Paraguay, Romania, Saudi Arabia, Scotland, South Africa, South Korea, Spain, Tunisia, USA, Yugoslavia. **Total entries:** 172 (32 qualifiers)
Venues: Bordeaux, Lens, Lyon, Marseille, Montpellier, Nantes, Paris (St Denis, Parc des Princes), Saint-Etienne, Toulouse
Top scorer: Davor Suker (Croatia) 6 goals
Final (Paris St Denis, 12/7/98): **Brazil** 0 **France** 3 (Zidane 27, 45, Petit 90). **Att:** 75,000
Brazil: Taffarel; Cafu, Junior Baiano, Aldair, Roberto Carlos; Dunga (capt), Leonardo (Denilson 46), Cesar Sampaio (Edmundo 74), Rivaldo; Bebeto, Ronaldo. **France:** Barthez; Thuram, Leboeuf, Desailly, Lizarazu; Karembeu (Boghossian 56), Deschamps (capt), Petit, Zidane, Djorkaeff (Viera 75); Guivarc'h (Dugarry 66) **Sent-off:** Desailly (68)
Referee: Belqola (Morocco). **Half-time:** 0-2

2002 – JAPAN/SOUTH KOREA

WINNERS: Brazil RUNNERS-UP: Germany THIRD: Turkey FOURTH: South Korea
Other countries in finals: Argentina, Belgium, Cameroon, China, Costa Rica, Croatia, Denmark, Ecuador, England, France, Italy, Japan, Mexico, Nigeria, Paraguay, Poland, Portugal, Republic of Ireland, Russia, Saudi Arabia, Senegal, Slovenia, South Africa, Spain, Sweden, Tunisia, USA, Uruguay. **Total entries:** 195 (32 qualifiers)
Venues: Japan – Ibaraki, Kobe, Miyagi, Niigata, Oita, Osaka, Saitama, Sapporo, Shizuoka, Yokohama. **South Korea** – Daegu, Daejeon, Gwangju, Incheon, Jeonju, Busan, Seogwipo, Seoul, Suwon Ulsan
Top scorer: Ronaldo (Brazil) 8 goals
Final (Yokohama, 30/6/02): **Germany** 0, **Brazil** 2 (Ronaldo 67, 79). **Att:** 69,029
Germany: Kahn (capt), Linke, Ramelow, Metzelder, Frings, Jeremies (Asamoah 77), Hamann, Schneider, Bode (Zeige 84), Klose (Bierhoff 74), Neuville. **Brazil:** Marcos, Lucio, Edmilson, Roque Junior, Cafu (capt) Kleberson, Gilberto Silva, Roberto Carlos, Ronaldinho (Juninho 85), Rivaldo, Ronaldo (Denilson 90)
Referee: Collina (Italy). **Half-time:** 0-0

2006 – GERMANY

WINNERS: Italy RUNNERS-UP: France THIRD: Germany FOURTH: Portugal
Other countries in finals: Angola, Argentina, Australia, Brazil, Costa Rica, Croatia, Czech Republic, Ecuador, England, Ghana, Holland, Iran, Ivory Coast, Japan, Mexico, Paraguay, Poland, Saudi Arabia, Serbia & Montenegro, South Korea, Spain, Sweden, Switzerland, Trinidad & Tobago, Togo, Tunisia, Ukraine, USA. **Total entries:** 198 (32 qualifiers)
Venues: Berlin, Cologne, Dortmund, Frankfurt, Gelsenkirchen, Hamburg, Hanover, Kaiserslautern, Leipzig, Munich, Nuremberg, Stuttgart
Top scorer: Klose (Germany) 5 goals
Final (Berlin, 9/7/06): **Italy** 1 (Materazzi 19) **France** 1 (Zidane 7 pen) after extra-time: Italy won 5-3 on pens. **Att:** 69,000
Italy: Buffon; Zambrotta, Cannavaro (capt), Materazzi, Grosso, Perrotta (De Rossi 61), Pirlo, Gattuso, Camoranesi (Del Piero 86), Totti (Iaquinta 61), Toni. **France:** Barthez; Sagnol, Thuram, Gallas, Abidal, Makelele, Vieira (Diarra 56), Ribery (Trezeguet 100), Malouda, Zidane (capt), Henry (Wiltord 107) **Sent-off:** Zidane (110)
Referee: Elizondo (Argentina). **Half-time:** 1-1 90 mins: 1-1
Shoot-out: Pirlo 1-0, Wiltord 1-1, Materazzi 2-1, Trezeguet missed, De Rossi 3-1, Abidal 3-2, Del Piero 4-2, Sagnol 4-3, Grosso 5-3

2010 – SOUTH AFRICA

WINNERS: Spain RUNNERS-UP: Holland THIRD: Germany FOURTH: Uruguay
Other countries in finals: Algeria, Argentina, Australia, Brazil, Cameroon, Chile, Denmark, England, France, Ghana, Greece, Honduras, Italy, Ivory Coast, Japan, Mexico, New Zealand, Nigeria, North Korea, Paraguay, Portugal, Serbia, Slovakia, Slovenia, South Africa, South Korea, Switzerland, USA. **Total entries:** 204 (32 qualifiers)
Venues: Bloemfontein, Cape Town, Durban, Johannesburg (Ellis Park), Johannesburg (Soccer City), Nelspruit, Polokwane, Port Elizabeth, Pretoria, Rustenburg
Top scorers: Forlan (Uruguay), Muller (Germany), Sneijder (Holland), Villa (Spain) 5 goals
Final (Johannesburg, Soccer City, 11/7/10): **Holland** 0 **Spain** 1 (Iniesta 116) after extra-time; **Att:** 84,490
Holland: Stekelenburg; Van der Wiel, Heitinga, Mathijsen, Van Bronckhorst (capt) (Braafheid 105), Van Bommel, De Jong (Van der Vaart 99), Robben, Sneijder, Kuyt (Elia 71), Van Persie.
Sent off: Heitinga (109). **Spain:** Casillas (capt); Sergio Ramos, Puyol, Piquet, Capdevila, Busquets, Xabi Alonso (Fabregas 87), Iniesta, Xavi, Pedro (Jesus Navas 60), Villa (Torres 106)
Referee: Webb (England). **Half-time:** 0-0

2014 – BRAZIL

WINNERS: Germany RUNNERS-UP: Argentina THIRD: Holland FOURTH: Brazil
Other countries in finals: Algeria, Argentina, Australia, Belgium, Bosnia-Herzegovina, Brazil, Cameroon, Chile, Colombia, Costa Rica, Croatia, Ecuador, England, France, Germany, Ghana, Greece, Holland, Honduras, Iran, Italy, Ivory Coast, Japan, Mexico, Nigeria, Portugal, Russia, South Korea, Spain, Switzerland, Uruguay, USA. **Total entries:** 204 (32 qualifiers)
Venues: Belo Horizonte, Brasilia, Cuiaba, Curitiba, Fortaleza, Manaus, Natal, Porto Alegre, Recife, Rio de Janeiro, Salvador, Sao Paulo
Top scorer: Rodriguez (Colombia) 6 goals
Final (Rio de Janeiro, 13/7/14): **Germany** 1 (Gotze 113) **Argentina** 0 after extra-time; **Att:** 74,738
Germany: Neuer; Lahm (capt), Boateng, Hummels, Howedes, Kramer (Schurrle 32), Schweinsteiger, Muller, Kroos, Ozil (Mertesacker 120), Klose (Gotze 88). **Argentina:** Romero; Zabaleta, Demichelis, Garay, Rojo, Biglia, Mascherano, Perez (Gago 86), Messi (capt), Lavezzi (Aguero 46), Higuain (Palacio 78)
Referee: Rizzoli (Italy). **Half-time:** 0-0

2018 – RUSSIA

WINNERS: France RUNNERS-UP: Croatia THIRD: Belgium FOURTH: England
Other countries in finals: Argentina, Australia, Brazil, Colombia, Costa Rica, Denmark, Egypt, Germany, Iceland, Iran, Japan, Mexico, Morocco, Nigeria, Panama, Peru, Poland, Portugal, Russia, Saudi Arabia, Senegal, Serbia, Spain, South Korea, Sweden, Switzerland, Tunisia, Uruguay. **Total entries:** 209 (32 qualifiers)
Venues: Ekaterinburg, Kaliningrad, Kazan, Moscow Luzhniki, Moscow Spartak, Nizhny Novgorod, Rostov, Samara, Saransk, Sochi, St Petersburg, Volgograd
Top scorer: Kane (England) 6 goals
Final (Moscow Luzhniki, 15/7/18): **France** 4 (Mandzukic 18 og, Griezmann 38 pen, Pogba 59, Mbappe 65) **Croatia** 2 (Perisic 28, Mandzukic 69). **Att:** 78,011
France: Lloris (capt), Pavard, Varane, Umtiti, Hernandez, Pogba, Kante (Nzonzi 55), Mbappe, Griezmann, Matuidi (Tolisso 73), Giroud (Fekir 81). **Croatia:** Subasic, Vrsaljko, Lovren, Vida, Strinic (Pjaca 81), Brozovic, Rebic (Kramaric 71), Modric (capt), Rakitic, Perisic, Mandzukic
Referee: Pitana (Argentina). **Half-time:** 2-1

BRITISH AND IRISH UNDER-21
INTERNATIONALS 2019–20
EUROPEAN CHAMPIONSHIP 2022
QUALIFYING

GROUP ONE

REPUBLIC OF IRELAND 3 LUXEMBOURG 0
Tallaght Stadium, Dublin (4,772); March 24, 2019

Republic of Ireland: Kelleher, L O'Connor, Masterson, O'Shea, Leahy, Molumby (Lennon 78), Coventry, Elbouzedi (M O'Connor 90+1), Ronan (Mandroiu 86), Farrugia (Drinan (90+2), Idah (Kavanagh 90+1). **Booked**: Masterson, O'Shea
Scorers – Republic of Ireland: Idah (34, 68), Farrugia (38). **Half-time**: 2-0

REPUBLIC OF IRELAND 1 ARMENIA 0
Tallaght Stadium, Dublin (3,658); September 6, 2019

Republic of Ireland: Kelleher, L O'Connor, Masterson, O'Shea, Leahy, Molumby, Coventry, Kilkenny (Elbouzedi 65), Parrott (Afolabi 82), Connolly (Knight 89), Idah (Mandroiu 66). **Booked**: Coventry
Scorer – Republic of Ireland: Parrott (31). **Half-time**: 1-0

SWEDEN 1 REPUBLIC OF IRELAND 3
Kalmar (4,078); September 10, 2019

Republic of Ireland: Kelleher, L O'Connor, Masterson, O'Shea, Leahy, Mandroiu (Parrott 51), Coventry, Molumby, Elbouzedi (Kilkenny 73), Connolly, Afolaba (Idah 82). **Booked**: Molumby, Parrott
Scorers – Sweden: Svanberg (19). **Republic of Ireland**: Parrott (69, 90+2), Masterson (87). **Half-time**: 1-0

REPUBLIC OF IRELAND 0 ITALY 0
Tallaght Stadium, Dublin (7,231 – record); October 10, 2019

Republic of Ireland: Kelleher, Masterson, O'Shea, Scales, L O'Connor, Ronan (Knight 62), Coventry, Molumby (Kilkenny 85), Elbouzedi (Obafemi 68), Parrott, Idah. **Booked**: Parrott, Molumby, Ronan, Coventry, Idah. **Sent off**: Parrott (64)

ICELAND 1 REPUBLIC OF IRELAND 0
Reykjavik (228); October 15, 2019

Republic of Ireland: Kelleher, L O'Connor, Masterson, O'Shea, Ledwidge, Mandroiu (Drinan 86), Coventry, Molumby, Elbouzedi, Obafemi (Kilkenny 75), Idah. **Booked**: L O'Connor. **Sent off**: L O'Connor (89)
Scorer – Iceland: Gudjohnsen (29 pen). **Half-time**: 1-0

ARMENIA 0 REPUBLIC OF IRELAND 1
Yerevan (270); November 14, 2019

Republic of Ireland: Bazunu, T O'Connor, O'Shea, Elbouzedi, Knight, Coventry, McNamara, Kilkenny (Taylor 81), Idah (Keeena 86). Ronan (Scales 77). **Booked**: Knight. **Sent off**: O'Shea (76)
Scorer – Republic of Ireland: Elbouzedi (63). **Half-time**: 0-0

REPUBLIC OF IRELAND 4 SWEDEN 1
Tallaght Stadium, Dublin (2,760); November 19, 2019

Republic of Ireland: Bazunu, Masterson (Scales 46), Collins, T O'Connor, L O'Connor, Knight

(Taylor 90+2). Molumby (Ronan 46), Coventry, Elbouzedi, Parrott (Kilkenny 86), Idah (Keena 90+2). **Booked**: Collins
Scorers – Republic of Ireland: L O'Connor (50), Idah (63), Parrott (73), Elbouzedi (87).
Sweden: Gyokeres (18). **Half-time**: 0-1

	P	W	D	L	F	A	Pts
Republic of Ireland	7	5	1	1	12	3	16
Italy	5	4	1	0	15	0	13
Iceland	5	3	0	2	10	9	9
Sweden	4	2	0	2	10	7	6
Armenia	6	1	0	5	3	15	3
Luxembourg	5	0	0	5	0	16	0

GROUP THREE

TURKEY 2 ENGLAND 3
Kocaeli (14,955); September 6, 2019
England: Ramsdale, Aarons, Guehi, Chalobah, Panzo, Sessegnon (Greenwood 59), Gibbs-White (Godfrey 81), Davies, Foden, Nketiah, Nelson (Brewster 79). **Booked**: Davies, Aarons
Scorers – Turkey: Sinik (25), Mulder (51). **England**: Nketiah (4, 74), Nelson (75). **Half-time**: 1-1

ENGLAND 2 KOSOVO 0
KCOM Stadium, Hull (15,258); September 9 2019
England: Ramsdale, Guehi, Chalobah, Godfrey, Aarons (Justin 80), Gibbs-White (Cantwell 61), Davies, Foden, Sessegnon, Nketiah (Brewster 76), Nelson (Greenwood 61). **Booked**: Godfrey
Scorer – England: Foden (25, 90+3). **Half-time**: 1-0

ENGLAND 5 AUSTRIA 1
Stadium MK, Milton Keynes (11,772); October 15, 2019
England: Ramsdale, Justin, Guehi, Kelly, Aarons (Sessegnon 60), Willock (Skipp 74), Davies, Foden, McNeil (Brewster 61), Nketiah (Surridge 86), Hudson-Odoi (Gallagher 86). **Booked**: Justin
Scorers – England: Hudson-Odoi (12, 45), Nketiah (28, 39, 79). **Austria**: Baumgartner (66). **Half-time**: 4-0

ALBANIA 0 ENGLAND 3
Shkoder (1,050); November 15, 2019
England: Ramsdale, James, Guehi, Godfrey, Panzo (Justin 64), Davies, Foden (Eze 81), Willock (Nelson 64), Gallagher, Greenwood, Brewster (Sessegnon 72)
Scorers – England: Foden (22 pen), Gallagher (43), Nelson (90+3). **Half-time**: 0-2

	P	W	D	L	F	A	Pts
England	4	4	0	0	13	3	12
Austria	5	4	0	1	15	6	12
Kosovo	5	2	0	3	8	9	6
Albania	6	1	2	3	7	14	5
Andorra	4	1	1	2	5	9	4
Turkey	6	1	1	4	7	14	4

GROUP FOUR

SCOTLAND 2 SAN MARINO 0
St Mirren Park (1,542); September 6, 2019
Scotland: Robby McCrorie, Reading (Harvie 87), Johnston, Campbell, Magennis, Gilmour (Maguire 88), Middleton (McAllister 72), Holsgrove, McLennan (Smith 64), Ferguson (Scott 72), Ross McCrorie. **Booked**: Middleton

Scorers – Scotland: Tosi (20 og), Middleton (27). Half-time: 2-0

CROATIA 1 SCOTLAND 2
Sibenik (2,134); September 10, 2019
Scotland: Doohan, Reading (Middleton 78) Harvie, Porteous, Johnston (Maguire 84), Ross McCrorie, Campbell, Magennis, Holsgrove, Ferguson (McLennan 78), Hornby. Booked: Porteous

Scorers – Croatia: Kulenovic (10). Scotland: McLennan (81, 89). Half-time: 1-0

SCOTLAND 0 LITHUANIA 0
Tynecastle Park, Edinburgh (1,084); October 10, 2019
Scotland: Doohan, Harvie, Porteous. Johnston, Campbell (Henderson 87), Magennis (Kelly 64), Gilmour, Hornby, Middleton, Ferguson (McLennan 58), Ross McCrorie. Booked: Porteous, Hornby, Ferguson

CZECH REPUBLIC 0 SCOTLAND 0
Uherske Hradiste (5,187); October 14, 2019
Scotland: Robby McCrorie, Reading, Harvie, Porteous, Johnston, Campbell, Ross McCrorie, Magennis, Gilmour, Middleton (Maguire 63), Hornby. Booked: Johnston, Magennis, Campbell

SCOTLAND 0 GREECE 1
Tynecastle Park, Edinburgh (1,284); November 15, 2019
Scotland: Doohan, Harvie, Brandon, Maguire, Johnston, Campbell, Holsgrove (McLennan 85), Ferguson, Kelly (Middleton 70), Gilmour, Hornby. Booked: Campbell, Holsgrove

Scorer – Greece: Nikolaou (90+1). Half-time: 0-0

	P	W	D	L	F	A	Pts
Czech Republic	5	3	2	0	11	2	11
Greece	4	3	1	0	8	1	10
Scotland	5	2	2	1	4	2	8
Croatia	4	2	0	2	12	5	6
Lithuania	5	1	1	3	4	6	4
San Marino	5	0	0	5	0	23	0

GROUP EIGHT

NORTHERN IRELAND 0 MALTA 0
Showgrounds, Ballymena (3,824); September 6, 2019
Northern Ireland: Hazard, Burns, Toal, Thompson, Balmer, Gordon (Palmer 71), McClean (McCann 78), Dunwoody, McCalmont (Galbraith 71), Parkhouse, Boyd Munce (Gallagher 88). Booked: Balmer

FINLAND 1 NORTHERN IRELAND 1
Oulu (3,666); September 10, 2019
Northern Ireland: Hazard, Burns (Marron 90+3), Toal, Thompson (McClean 46), Balmer, Gordon (Scott 70), Dunwoody, McCalmont, Galbraith, Boyd Munce (Palmer 70), L McCann (Ferris 76). Booked: Palmer, McCalmont

Scorers – Finland: Valakari (4). Northern Ireland: Thompson (35). Half-time: 1-1

DENMARK 2 NORTHERN IRELAND 1
Aalborg (647); October 10, 2019
Northern Ireland: Hazard, Toal, Thompson, Balmer, Dunwoody (Galbraith 88), McCalmont, Parkhouse (L McCann 71), Gordon (O'Mahoney 88), Marron (Palmer 78), Boyd Munce (McClean 71), A McCann. Booked: Toal, Marron

Scorers – Denmark: Poulsen (30), Odgaard (86). Northern Ireland: Dunwoody (56). Half-time: 1-0

ROMANIA 3 NORTHERN IRELAND 0
Voluntari (4,067); October 14, 2019
Northern Ireland: Hazard, Balmer, Toal, Brown, Graham (Thompson 75), McCalmont (Parkhouse 74), McCann, Gordon (Boyd-Munce 74), Dunwoody (Palmer 61), Galbraith (Hughes 38), Lavery. **Sent off:** Hazard (38)
Scorers – Romania: Baluta (48), Mihaila (59), Ciobanu (67). **Half-time:** 0-0

NORTHERN IRELAND 0 ROMANIA 0
Showgrounds, Ballymena (1,641): November 19, 2019
Northern Ireland: Gartside, Toal, Burns, Balmer, Marron, Dunwoody (Galbraith 84), McCalmont, Boyd Munce (Thompson 84), Parkhouse, Gordon (Palmer 30), McCann. **Booked:** Balmer, McCann, McCalmont

	P	W	D	L	F	A	Pts
Denmark	5	5	0	0	13	5	15
Romania	5	3	1	1	11	3	10
Finland	5	2	1	2	8	6	7
Ukraine	4	1	0	3	6	8	3
Northern Ireland	5	0	3	2	2	6	3
Malta	4	0	1	3	1	13	1

GROUP NINE

WALES 1 BELGIUM 0
Racecourse Ground, Wrexham (304); September 6, 2019
Wales: Ratcliffe, Coxe, Cabango, Poole, Norrington-Davies, J Evans (Stirk 86), Burton, Mooney (Cooper 76), Harris, Johnson, Cullen. **Booked:** Norrington-Davies, Cullen, J Evans, Harris
Scorer – Wales: Johnson (3). **Half-time:** 1-0

WALES 1 GERMANY 5
Racecourse Ground, Wrexham (841); September 10, 2019
Wales: Ratcliffe, Coxe, Cabango, Poole, Norrington-Davies, J Evans (Stirk 66), Burton, Mooney (Cooper 86), Harris, Johnson (Clifton 76), Cullen (Lewis 66). **Booked:** Burton
Scorers – Wales: Harris (48 pen). **Germany:** Hack (19, 24, 29), Eggestein (41), Fein (50).
Half-time: 0-4

MOLDOVA 2 WALES 1
Orhei (350); October 11, 2019
Wales: Pryzbek, Coxe (Lewis 67), Norrington-Davies, J Evans, Cooper, Cabango, Burton (K Evans 67), Harris (Vale 85), Johnson, Broadhead, Levitt. **Booked:** J Evans, Cooper, Johnson
Scorers – Moldova: Belousov (41, 47). **Wales:** Broadhead (24). **Half-time:** 1-1

WALES 1 BOSNIA-HERZEGOVINA 0
Racecourse Ground, Wrexham (1,282); November 19, 2019
Wales: Ratcliffe, Lewis, Cabango, Cooper, Norrington-Davies, Burton (Stirk 73), J Evans, Cullen, Johnson (Mooney 60), Broadhead, Harris. **Booked:** Burton, Stirk, Cabango, Mooney, Harris
Scorer – Wales: Cullen (71). **Half-time:** 0-0

	P	W	D	L	F	A	Pts
Belgium	4	2	1	1	7	4	7
Germany	3	2	0	1	9	4	6
Wales	4	2	0	2	4	7	6
Bosnia-Herz	4	1	1	2	4	3	4
Moldova	3	1	0	2	3	9	3

FRIENDLY INTERNATIONALS

SLOVENIA 2 ENGLAND 2
Maribor; October 11, 2019

England: Ramsdale, Guehi, Panzo, Kelly (Richards 63), Aarons (Wilmot 46), Willock (Gallagher 63), Davies, Foden (Skipp 63), McNeil (Justin 46), Hudson-Odoi (Brewster 46), Nketiah (Surridge 46). **Booked**: Panzo, Skipp, Surridge
Scorers – Slovenia: Petrovic (82), Pisek (90+4). **England**: Nketiah (39 pen), Surridge (70). **Half-time**: 0-1

HOLLAND 2 ENGLAND 1
Doetincham; November 19, 2019

England: Ramsdale, Chalobah, Guehi, Justin, Aarons (James 62), Diangana (Sessegnon 76), Foden (Willock 79), Gallagher (McNeil 62), Skipp, Eze (Nelson 62), Brewster (Greenwood 62)
Scorers – Holland: Sierhuis (23), Dilrosun (90+2). **England**: Greenwood (75). **Half-time**: 1-0

THE THINGS THEY SAY...

'It's like going to a fight with a gun without bullets' – **Jose Mourinho**, Tottenham manager, after losing Harry Kane and Son Heung-min to injuries at a crucial point in the season.

'Sergio didn't read the script' – **Ole GunnarSolskjaer**, Manchester United manager, after his goalkeeper Sergio Romero twice saved free-kicks from Derby's Wayne Rooney in the FA Cup tie against his former club.

'I've been in the game for 60 years and this is the biggest disappointment I've ever had' – **Barry Fry**, Peterborough's director of football, after his team are overtaken for a League One play-off place by Wycombe on a points-per-game basis.

'Finally, I can leave the stadium, look at (Sir Bobby Robson) Mr Robson's statue and laugh with him, because every time I have come here before I have left and looked at him with a sad face' – **Jose Mourinho**, Tottenham manager, after his first Premier League win at Newcastle.

'We're stood there at the sideline thinking "is this ever going to stop"'? – **Grant McCann**, Hull manager, after his side conceded seven goals in the first 45 minutes against Wigan.

TRANSFER TRAIL

Player	From	To	Date	£
Philippe Coutinho	Liverpool	Barcelona	1/18	142,000,000
Paul Pogba	Juventus	Manchester Utd	8/16	89,300,000
Eden Hazard	Chelsea	Real Madrid	6/19	89,000,000
Gareth Bale	Tottenham	Real Madrid	8/13	85,300,000
Cristiano Ronaldo	Manchester Utd	Real Madrid	7/09	80,000,000
Harry Maguire	Leicester	Manchester Utd	8/19	80,000,000
Romelu Lukaku	Everton	Manchester Utd	7/17	75,000,000
Virgil van Dijk	Southampton	Liverpool	1/18	75,000,000
Romelu Lukaku	Manchester Utd	Inter Milan	8/19	74,000,000
Nicolas Pepe	Lille	Arsenal	8/19	72,000,000
Kepa Arrizabalaga	Athletic Bilbao	Chelsea	8/18	71,600,000
Luis Suarez	Liverpool	Barcelona	7/14	65,000,000
Alisson	Roma	Liverpool	7/18	65,000,000
Rodri	Atletico Madrid	Manchester City	7/19	62,800,000
Riyad Mahrez	Leicester	Manchester City	7/18	60,000,000
Joao Cancelo	Juventus	Manchester City	8/19	60,000,000
Angel di Maria	Real Madrid	Manchester Utd	8/14	59,700,000
Christian Pulisic	Borussia Dortmund	Chelsea	7/19	58,000,000
Alvaro Morata	Real Madrid	Chelsea	7/17	57,200,000
Diego Costa	Chelsea	Atletico Madrid	1/18	57,000,000
Aymeric Laporte	Athletic Bilbao	Manchester City	1/18	57,000,000
Pierre-Emerick Aubameyang	Borussia Dortmund	Arsenal	1/18	56,000,000
Kevin De Bruyne	Wolfsburg	Manchester City	8/15	54,500,000
Tanguy Ndombele	Lyon	Tottenham	7/19	53,800,000
Oscar	Chelsea	Shanghai Shenhua	1/17	52,000,000
Benjamin Mendy	Monaco	Manchester City	7/17	52,000,000
Fred	Shaktar Donetsk	Manchester Utd	6/18	52,000,000
Fernando Torres	Liverpool	Chelsea	1/11	50,000,000
David Luiz	Chelsea	Paris SG	6/14	50,000,000
Jorginho	Napoli	Chelsea	7/18	50,000,000
Aaron Wan-Bissaka	Crystal Palace	Manchester Utd	6/19	50,000,000
Raheem Sterling	Liverpool	Manchester City	7/15	49,000,000
Naby Keita	Leipzig	Liverpool	7/18	48,000,000
John Stones	Everton	Manchester City	8/16	47,500,000
Alexandre Lacazette	Lyon	Arsenal	7/17	46,500,000
Bruno Fernandes	Sporting Lisbon	Manchester Utd	1/20	47,000,000
Gylfi Sigurdsson	Swansea	Everton	8/17	45,000,000
Kyle Walker	Tottenham	Manchester City	7/17	45,000,000
Sebastien Haller	Eintracht Frankfurt	West Ham	7/19	45,000,000
Leroy Sane	Manchester City	Bayern Munich	7/20	44,700,000
Angel di Maria	Manchester Utd	Paris SG	8/15	44,300,000
Fabinho	Monaco	Liverpool	5/8	43,700,000
Bernardo Silva	Monaco	Manchester City	6/17	43,000,000
Mesut Ozil	Real Madrid	Arsenal	9/13	42,400,000
Davinson Sanchez	Ajax	Tottenham	8/17	42,000,000
Nemanja Matic	Chelsea	Manchester Utd	7/17	40,000,000
Richarlison	Watford	Everton	7/18	40,000,000
Youri Tielemans	Monaco	Leicester	7/19	40,000,000
Mateo Kovacic	Real Madrid	Chelsea	7/19	40,000,000
Nathan Ake	Bournemouth	Manchester City	8/20	40,000,000

Joelinton	Hoffenheim	Newcastle	7/19	40,000,000
Tiemoue Bakayoko	Monaco	Chelsea	7/17	39,700,000
Sergio Aguero	Atletico Madrid	Manchester City	7/11	38,500,000
Thibaut Courtois	Chelsea	Real Madrid	8/18	38,000,000
Hakim Ziyech	Ajax	Chelsea	6/00	37,800,000
Juan Mata	Chelsea	Manchester Utd	1/14	37,100,000
Leroy Sane	Schalke	Manchester City	7/16	37,000,000
Anthony Martial	Monaco	Manchester Utd	9/15	36,000,000
Felipe Anderson	Lazio	West Ham	7/18	36,000,000
Andy Carroll	Newcastle	Liverpool	1/11	35,000,000
Cesc Fabregas	Arsenal	Barcelona	8/11	35,000,000
Alexis Sanchez	Barcelona	Arsenal	7/14	35,000,000
Granit Xhaka	Borussia M'gladbach	Arsenal	6/16	35,000,000
Shkodran Mustafi	Valencia	Arsenal	8/16	35,000,000
Alex Oxlade-Chamberlain	Arsenal	Liverpool	8/17	35,000,000
Danny Drinkwater	Leicester	Chelsea	8/17	35,000,000
Ederson	Benfica	Manchester City	6/17	34,900,000
Mohamed Salah	Roma	Liverpool	7/17	34,300,000
Danilo	Manchester City	Juventus	8/19	34,100,000
Sadio Mane	Southampton	Liverpool	6/16	34,000,000
Michy Batshuayi	Marseille	Chelsea	7/16	33,000,000
Robinho	Real Madrid	Manchester City	9/08	32,500,000
Christian Benteke	Aston Villa	Liverpool	7/15	32,500,000
Eden Hazard	Lille	Chelsea	6/12	32,000,000
Diego Costa	Atletico Madrid	Chelsea	7/14	32,000,000
N'Golo Kante	Leicester	Chelsea	7/16	32,000,000
David Luiz	Paris SG	Chelsea	8/16	32,000,000
Eliaquim Mangala	Porto	Manchester City	8/14	31,900,000
Ismaila Sarr	Rennes	Watford	8/19	31,000,000
Dimitar Berbatov	Tottenham	Manchester Utd	9/08	30,750,000
Victor Lindelof	Benfica	Manchester Utd	6/17	30,700,000
Andriy Shevchenko	AC Milan	Chelsea	5/06	30,800,000
Xabi Alonso	Liverpool	Real Madrid	8/09	30,000,000
Fernandinho	Shakhtar Donetsk	Manchester City	6/13	30,000,000
Willian	Anzhi Makhachkala	Chelsea	8/13	30,000,000
Erik Lamela	Roma	Tottenham	8/13	30,000,000
Luke Shaw	Southampton	Manchester Utd	6/14	30,000,000
Eric Bailly	Villarreal	Manchester Utd	6/16	30,000,000
Moussa Sissoko	Newcastle	Tottenham,	8/16	30,000,000
Ayoze Perez	Newcastle	Leicester	7/19	30,000,000
Idrissa Gueye	Everton	Paris SG	7/19	30,000,000
Islam Slimani	Sporting Lisbon	Leicester	8/16	29,700,000
Rio Ferdinand	Leeds	Manchester Utd	7/02	29,100,000
Antonio Rudiger	Roma	Chelsea	7/17	29,000,000
Ander Herrera	Athletic Bilbao	Manchester Utd	6/14	28,800,000
Nicolas Otamendi	Valencia	Manchester City	8/15	28,500,000
Juan Sebastian Veron	Lazio	Manchester Utd	7/01	28,100,000
Yaya Toure	Barcelona	Manchester City	7/10	28,000,000
Romelu Lukaku	Chelsea	Everton	7/14	28,000,000
Wilfried Bony	Swansea	Manchester City	1/15	28,000,000
Roberto Firmino	Hoffenheim	Liverpool	6/15	28,000,000
Marouane Fellaini	Everton	Manchester Utd	9/13	27,500,000
Wayne Rooney	Everton	Manchester Utd	8/04	27,000,000
Yerry Mina	Barcelona	Everton	8/18	27,200,000

Edin Dzeko	Wolfsburg	Manchester City	1/11	27,000,000
Luka Modric	Tottenham	Real Madrid	8/12	27,000,000
Cesc Fabregas	Barcelona	Chelsea	6/14	27,000,000
Gabriel Jesus	Palmeiras	Manchester City	7/16	27,000,000
Christian Benteke	Liverpool	Crystal Palace	8/16	27,000,000
Cenk Tosun	Besiktas	Everton	1/18	27,000,000
William Saliba	Saint-Etienne	Arsenal	7/19	27,000,000
Steven Bergwijn	PSV Eindhoven	Tottenham	1/20	27,000,000
Giovani Lo Celso	Real Betis	Tottenham	1/20	27,000,000
Danilo	Real Madrid	Manchester City	7/17	26,500,000
Roberto Soldado	Valencia	Tottenham	8/13	26,000,000
Henrikh Mkhitaryan	Borussua Dortmund	Manchester Utd	7/16	26,000,000
Mamadou Sakho	Liverpool	Crystal Palace	8/17	26,000,000
Lucas Torreira	Sampdoria	Arsenal	7/18	26,000,000
Marc Overmars	Arsenal	Barcelona	7/00	25,000,000
Carlos Tevez	Manchester Utd	Manchester City	7/09	25,000,000
Emmanuel Adebayor	Arsenal	Manchester City	7/09	25,000,000
Samir Nasri	Arsenal	Manchester City	8/11	25,000,000
Oscar	Internacional	Chelsea	7/12	25,000,000
Adam Lallana	Southampton	Liverpool	7/14	25,000,000
Memphis Depay	PSV Eindhoven	Manchester Utd	6/15	25,000,000
Morgan Schneiderlin	Southampton	Manchester Utd	7/15	25,000,000
Ramires	Chelsea	Jiangsu Suning	2/16	25,000,000
Georginio Wijnaldum	Newcastle	Liverpool	7/16	25,000,000
Yannick Bolasie	Crystal Palace	Everton	8/16	25,000,000
Jordan Pickford	Sunderland	Everton	6/17	25,000,000
Michael Keane	Burnley	Everton	7/17	25,000,000
Kelechi Iheanacho	Manchester City	Leicester	7/17	25,000,000
Theo Walcott	Arsenal	Everton	1/18	25,000,000
Davide Zappacosta	Torino	Chelsea	8/17	25,000,000
Jean Michael Seri	Nice	Fulham	7/18	25,000,000
Jefferson Lerma	Levante	Bournemouth	8/18	25,000,000
Jean-Philippe Gbamin	Mainz	Everton	8/19	25,000,000
Ryan Sessegnon	Fulham	Tottenham	8/19	25,000,000
Kieran Tierney	Celtic	Arsenal	8/19	25,000,000
Jude Bellingham	Birmingham	Borussia Dortmund	7/20	25,000,000
Arjen Robben	Chelsea	Real Madrid	8/07	24,500,000
Michael Essien	Lyon	Chelsea	8/05	24,400,000
David Silva	Valencia	Manchester City	7/10	24,000,000
James Milner	Aston Villa	Manchester City	8/10	24,000,000
Mario Balotelli	Inter Milan	Manchester City	8/10	24,000,000
Robin van Persie	Arsenal	Manchester Utd	8/12	24,000,000
Marko Arnautovic	Stoke	West Ham	7/17	24,000,000
Pablo Fornals	Villarreal	West Ham	6/19	24,000,000
Alvaro Negredo	Manchester City	Valencia	7/15	23,800,000
Davy Klaassen	Ajax	Everton	6/17	23,600,000
Juan Mata	Valencia	Chelsea	8/11	23,500,000
David Beckham	Manchester Utd	Real Madrid	7/03	23,300,000
Juan Cuadrado	Fiorentina	Chelsea	2/15	23,300,000
Didier Drogba	Marseille	Chelsea	7/04	23,200,000
Andre Schurrle	Chelsea	Wolfsburg	2/15	23,000,000
Marcos Alonso	Fiorentina	Chelsea	8/16	23,000,000
Serge Aurier	Paris SG	Tottenham	8/17	23,000,000
Lucas Moura	Paris SG	Tottenham	1/18	23,000,000

Luis Suarez	Ajax	Liverpool	1/11	22,700,000
Ademola Lookman	Everton	Leipzig	7/19	22,500,000
Nicolas Anelka	Arsenal	Real Madrid	8/99	22,300,000
Andre-Frank Anguissa	Marseille	Fulham	8/18	22,300,000
Wesley	Club Bruges	Aston Villa	6/19	22,200,000
Fernando Torres	Atletico Madrid	Liverpool	7/07	22,000,000
Joleon Lescott	Everton	Manchester City	8/09	22,000,000
Stevan Jovetic	Fiorentina	Manchester City	7/13	22,000,000
Adrien Silva	Sporting Lisbon	Leicester	1/18	22,000,000
Issa Diop	Toulouse	West Ham	6/18	22,000,000
Wesley	Club Bruges	Aston Villa	6/19	22,000,000
James Maddison	Norwich	Leicester	6/18	22,000,000
Son Heung-min	Bayer Leverkusen	Tottenham	8/15	21,900,000
Baba Rahman	Augsburg	Chelsea	8/15	21,700,000
David Luiz	Benfica	Chelsea	1/11	21,300,000
Shaun Wright-Phillips	Manchester City	Chelsea	7/05	21,000,000
Nemanja Matic	Benfica	Chelsea	01/14	21,000,000
Pedro	Barcelona	Chelsea	8/15	21,000,000
Ilkay Gundogan	Borussia Dortmund	Manchester City	6/16	21,000,000

BRITISH RECORD TRANSFERS FROM FIRST £1,000 DEAL

Player	From	To	Date	£
Alf Common	Sunderland	Middlesbrough	2/1905	1,000
Syd Puddefoot	West Ham	Falkirk	2/22	5,000
Warney Cresswell	South Shields	Sunderland	3/22	5,500
Bob Kelly	Burnley	Sunderland	12/25	6,500
David Jack	Bolton	Arsenal	10/28	10,890
Bryn Jones	Wolves	Arsenal	8/38	14,500
Billy Steel	Morton	Derby	9/47	15,000
Tommy Lawton	Chelsea	Notts Co	11/47	20,000
Len Shackleton	Newcastle	Sunderland	2/48	20,500
Johnny Morris	Manchester Utd	Derby	2/49	24,000
Eddie Quigley	Sheffield Wed	Preston	12/49	26,500
Trevor Ford	Aston Villa	Sunderland	10/50	30,000
Jackie Sewell	Notts Co	Sheffield Wed	3/51	34,500
Eddie Firmani	Charlton	Sampdoria	7/55	35,000
John Charles	Leeds	Juventus	4/57	65,000
Denis Law	Manchester City	Torino	6/61	100,000
Denis Law	Torino	Manchester Utd	7/62	115,000
Allan Clarke	Fulham	Leicester	6/68	150,000
Allan Clarke	Leicester	Leeds	6/69	165,000
Martin Peters	West Ham	Tottenham	3/70	200,000
Alan Ball	Everton	Arsenal	12/71	220,000
David Nish	Leicester	Derby	8/72	250,000
Bob Latchford	Birmingham	Everton	2/74	350,000
Graeme Souness	Middlesbrough	Liverpool	1/78	352,000
Kevin Keegan	Liverpool	Hamburg	6/77	500,000
David Mills	Middlesbrough	WBA	1/79	516,000
Trevor Francis	Birmingham	Nottm Forest	2/79	1,180,000
Steve Daley	Wolves	Manchester City	9/79	1,450,000
Andy Gray	Aston Villa	Wolves	9/79	1,469,000
Bryan Robson	WBA	Manchester Utd	10/81	1,500,000
Ray Wilkins	Manchester Utd	AC Milan	5/84	1,500,000

Mark Hughes	Manchester Utd	Barcelona	5/86	2,300,000
Ian Rush	Liverpool	Juventus	6/87	3,200,000
Chris Waddle	Tottenham	Marseille	7/89	4,250,000
David Platt	Aston Villa	Bari	7/91	5,500,000
Paul Gascoigne	Tottenham	Lazio	6/92	5,500,000
Andy Cole	Newcastle	Manchester Utd	1/95	7,000,000
Dennis Bergkamp	Inter Milan	Arsenal	6/95	7,500,000
Stan Collymore	Nottm Forest	Liverpool	6/95	8,500,000
Alan Shearer	Blackburn	Newcastle	7/96	15,000,000
Nicolas Anelka	Arsenal	Real Madrid	8/99	22,500,000
Juan Sebastian Veron	Lazio	Manchester Utd	7/01	28,100,000
Rio Ferdinand	Leeds	Manchester Utd	7/02	29,100,000
Andriy Shevchenko	AC Milan	Chelsea	5/06	30,800,000
Robinho	Real Madrid	Manchester City	9/08	32,500,000
Cristiano Ronaldo	Manchester Utd	Real Madrid	7/09	80,000,000
Gareth Bale	Tottenham	Real Madrid	9/13	85,300,000
Paul Pogba	Juventus	Manchester Utd	8/16	89.300,000
Philippe Coutinho	Liverpool	Barcelona	1/18	142,000,000

• World's first £1m transfer: GuiseppeSavoldi, Bologna to Napoli, July 1975

TOP FOREIGN SIGNINGS

Player	From	To	Date	£
Neymar	Barcelona	Paris SG	8/17	198,000,000
Kylian Mbappe	Monaco	Paris SG	8/17	165,700,000
Ousmane Dembele	Borussia Dortmund	Barcelona	8/17	134,000,000
Joao Felix	Benfica	Atletico Madrid	7/19	113,000,000
Antoine Griezmann	Atletico Madrid	Barcelona	7/19	107,000,000
Cristiano Ronaldo	Real Madrid	Juventus	7/18	99,200,000
Gonzalo Higuain	Napoli	Juventus	7/16	75,300,000
Lucas Hernandez	Atletico Madrid	Bayern Munich	7/19	68,000,000
Matthijs de Ligt	Ajax	Juventus	7/19	67,500,000
Frenkie de Jong	Ajax	Barcelona	1/19	65,000,000
Luka Jovic	Eintracht Frankfurt	Real Madrid	6/19	62,000,000
Zlatan Ibrahimovic	Inter Milan	Barcelona	7/09	60,300,000
James Rodriguez	Monaco	Real Madrid	7/14	60,000,000
Kaka AC	Milan	Real Madrid	6/08	56,000,000
Miralem Pjanic	Juventus	Barcelona	6/20	54,900,000
Edinson Cavani	Napoli	Paris SG	7/13	53,000,000
Thomas Lemar	Monaco	Atletico Madrid	6/18	52,700,000
Radamel Falcao	Atletico Madrid	Monaco	6/13	51,000,000
Neymar	Santos	Barcelona	6/13	48,600,000
Zinedine Zidane	Juventus	Real Madrid	7/01	47,200,000
Ferland Mendy	Lyon	Real Madrid	6/19	47,100,000
Hulk	Zenit St Petersburg	Shanghai SIPG	7/16	46,100,000
Eder Militao	Porto	Real Madrid	3/19	42,700,000
Vinicius Junior	Flamengo	Real Madrid	7/18	39,600,000
James Rodriguez	Porto	Monaco	5/13	38,500,000
Alex Teixeira	Shakhtar Donetsk	Jiangsu Suning	2/16	38,400,000
Joao Mario	Sporting Lisbon	Inter Milan	8/16	38,400,000
Luis Figo	Barcelona	Real Madrid	7/00	37,200,000
Javier Pastore	Palermo	Paris SG	8/11	36,600,000
Corentin Tolisso	Lyon	Bayern Munich	6/17	36,500,000
Malcom	Bordeaux	Barcelona	7/18	36,500,000

Malcom	Barcelona	Zenit St Petersburg	8/19	36,500,000
Joao Cancelo	Valencia	Juventus	7/18	36,300,000
Rodrygo	Santos	Real Madrid	6/18	36,000,000
Goncalo Guedes	Paris SG	Valencia	8/18	36,000,000
Karim Benzema	Lyon	Real Madrid	7/09	35,800,000
Julian Draxler	Wolfsburg	Paris SG	1/17	35,500,000
Arthur	Gremio	Barcelona	7/18	35,500,000
Douglas Costa	Bayern Munich	Juventus	6/18	35,200,000
Hernan Crespo	Parma	Lazio	7/00	35,000,000
Radamel Falcao	Porto	Atletico Madrid	8/11	34,700,000
Gonzalo Higuain	Real Madrid	Napoli	7/13	34,500,000
David Villa	Valencia	Barcelona	5/10	34,000,000
Thiago Silva	AC Milan	Paris SG	7/12	34,000,000
Lucas Moura	Sao Paulo	Paris SG	1/13	34,000,000
Asier Illarramendi	Real Sociedad	Real Madrid	7/13	34,000,000
Ronaldo	Inter Milan	Real Madrid	8/02	33,000,000
Thilo Kehrer	Schalke	Paris SG	8/18	33,000,000
Gianluigi Buffon	Parma	Juventus	7/01	32,600,000
Axel Witsel	Benfica	Zenit St Petersburg	8/12	32,500,000
Hulk	Porto	Zenit St Petersburg	8/12	32,000,000
Javi Martinez	Athletic Bilbao	Bayern Munich	8/12	31,600,000
Krzysztof Piatek	Genoa	AC Milan	1/19	30,900,000
Mario Gotze	Borussia Dortmund	Bayern Munich	6/13	31,500,000
Christian Vieri	Lazio	Inter Milan	6/99	31,000,000
Jackson Martinez	Atletico Madrid	Guangzhou Evergrande	2/16	31,000,000
Alessandro Nesta	Lazio	AC Milan	8/02	30,200,000

WORLD'S MOST EXPENSIVE TEENAGER

£165,700,000: Kylian Mbappe, 19, Monaco to Paris SG, August 2017

WORLD RECORD FOR 16-YEAR-OLD

£39,600,000: Vinicius Junior, Flamengo to Real Madrid, July 2018

RECORD TRIBUNAL FEE

£6.5m: Danny Ings, Burnley to Liverpool, Jun 2016

RECORD FEE BETWEEN SCOTTISH CLUBS

£4.4m: Scott Brown, Hibernian to Celtic, May 2007

RECORD NON-LEAGUE FEE

£1m: Jamie Vardy, Fleetwood to Leicester, May 2012

RECORD FEE BETWEEN NON-LEAGUE CLUBS

£275,000: Richard Brodie, York to Crawley, Aug 2010

MILESTONES

1848: First code of rules compiled at Cambridge University.
1857: Sheffield FC, world's oldest football club, formed.
1862: Notts Co (oldest League club) formed.
1863: Football Association founded – their first rules of game agreed.
1871: FA Cup introduced.
1872: First official International: Scotland 0 England 0. Corner-kick introduced.
1873: Scottish FA formed; Scottish Cup introduced.
1874: Shinguards introduced.
1875: Crossbar introduced (replacing tape).
1876: FA of Wales formed.
1877: Welsh Cup introduced.
1878: Referee's whistle first used.
1880: Irish FA founded; Irish Cup introduced.
1883: Two-handed throw-in introduced.
1885: Record first-class score (Arbroath 36 Bon Accord 0 – Scottish Cup). Professionalism legalised.
1886: International Board formed.
1887: Record FA Cup score (Preston 26 Hyde 0).
1888: Football League founded by William McGregor. First matches on Sept 8.
1889 Preston win Cup and League (first club to complete Double).
1890: Scottish League and Irish League formed.
1891: Goal-nets introduced. Penalty-kick introduced.
1892: Inter-League games began. Football League Second Division formed.
1893: FA Amateur Cup launched.
1894: Southern League formed.
1895: FA Cup stolen from Birmingham shop window – never recovered.
1897: First Players' Union formed. Aston Villa win Cup and League.
1898: Promotion and relegation introduced.
1901: Maximum wage rule in force (£4 a week). Tottenham first professional club to take FA Cup south. First six-figure attendance (110,802) at FA Cup Final.
1902: Ibrox Park disaster (25 killed). Welsh League formed.
1904: FIFA founded (7 member countries).
1905: First £1,000 transfer (Alf Common, Sunderland to Middlesbrough).
1907: Players' Union revived.
1908: Transfer fee limit (£350) fixed in January and withdrawn in April.
1911: New FA Cup trophy – in use to 1991. Transfer deadline introduced.
1914: King George V first reigning monarch to attend FA Cup Final.
1916: Entertainment Tax introduced.
1919: League extended to 44 clubs.
1920: Third Division (South) formed.
1921: Third Division (North) formed.
1922: Scottish League (Div II) introduced.
1923: Beginning of football pools. First Wembley Cup Final.
1924: First International at Wembley (England 1 Scotland 1). Rule change allows goals to be scored direct from corner-kicks.
1925: New offside law.
1926: Huddersfield complete first League Championship hat-trick.
1927: First League match broadcast (radio): Arsenal v Sheffield United. First radio broadcast of Cup Final (winners Cardiff City). Charles Clegg, president of FA, becomes first knight of football.
1928: First £10,000 transfer – David Jack (Bolton to Arsenal). WR ('Dixie') Dean (Everton)

creates League record – 60 goals in season. Britain withdraws from FIFA

1930: Uruguay first winners of World Cup.

1931: WBA win Cup and promotion.

1933: Players numbered for first time in Cup Final (1-22).

1934: Sir Frederick Wall retires as FA secretary; successor Stanley Rous. Death of Herbert Chapman (Arsenal manager).

1935: Arsenal equal Huddersfield's Championship hat-trick record. Official two-referee trials.

1936: Joe Payne's 10-goal League record (Luton 12 Bristol Rov 0).

1937: British record attendance: 149,547 at Scotland v England match.

1938: First live TV transmission of FA Cup Final. Football League 50th Jubilee. New pitch marking – arc on edge of penalty-area. Laws of Game re-drafted by Stanley Rous. Arsenal pay record £14,500 fee for Bryn Jones (Wolves).

1939: Compulsory numbering of players in Football League. First six-figure attendance for League match (Rangers v Celtic 118,567). All normal competitions suspended for duration of Second World War.

1945: Scottish League Cup introduced.

1946: British associations rejoin FIFA. Bolton disaster (33 killed) during FA Cup tie with Stoke. Walter Winterbottom appointed England's first director of coaching.

1947: Great Britain beat Rest of Europe 6-1 at Hampden Park, Glasgow. First £20,000 transfer – Tommy Lawton, Chelsea to Notts Co

1949: Stanley Rous, secretary FA, knighted. England's first home defeat outside British Champ. (0-2 v Eire).

1950: Football League extended from 88 to 92 clubs. World record crowd (203,500) at World Cup Final, Brazil v Uruguay, in Rio. Scotland's first home defeat by foreign team (0-1 v Austria).

1951: White ball comes into official use.

1952: Newcastle first club to win FA Cup at Wembley in successive seasons.

1953: England's first Wembley defeat by foreign opponents (3-6 v Hungary).

1954: Hungary beat England 7-1 in Budapest.

1955: First FA Cup match under floodlights (prelim round replay): Kidderminster v Brierley Hill Alliance.

1956: First FA Cup ties under floodlights in competition proper. First League match by floodlight (Portsmouth v Newcastle). Real Madrid win the first European Cup.

1957: Last full Football League programme on Christmas Day. Entertainment Tax withdrawn.

1958: Manchester United air crash at Munich. League re-structured into four divisions.

1960: Record transfer fee: £55,000 for Denis Law (Huddersfield to Manchester City). Wolves win Cup, miss Double and Championship hat-trick by one goal. For fifth time in ten years FA Cup Final team reduced to ten men by injury. FA recognise Sunday football. Football League Cup launched.

1961: Tottenham complete the first Championship–FA Cup double this century. Maximum wage (£20 a week) abolished in High Court challenge by George Eastham. First British £100-a-week wage paid (by Fulham to Johnny Haynes). First £100,000 British transfer – Denis Law, Manchester City to Torino. Sir Stanley Rous elected president of FIFA

1962: Manchester United raise record British transfer fee to £115,000 for Denis Law.

1963: FA Centenary. Season extended to end of May due to severe winter. First pools panel. English "retain and transfer" system ruled illegal in High Court test case.

1964: Rangers' second great hat-trick – Scottish Cup, League Cup and League. Football League and Scottish League guaranteed £500,000 a year in new fixtures copyright agreement with Pools. First televised 'Match of the Day' (BBC2): Liverpool 3 Arsenal 2.

1965: Bribes scandal – ten players jailed (and banned for life by FA) for match-fixing 1960–63. Stanley Matthews knighted in farewell season. Arthur Rowley (Shrewsbury) retires with record of 434 League goals. Substitutes allowed for injured players in Football League matches (one per team).

1966: England win World Cup (Wembley).

1967: Alf Ramsey, England manager, knighted; OBE for captain Bobby Moore. Celtic become first British team to win European Cup. First substitutes allowed in FA Cup Final (Tottenham v Chelsea) but not used. Football League permit loan transfers (two per club).

1968: First FA Cup Final televised live in colour (BBC2 – WBA v Everton). Manchester United first English club to win European Cup.

1970: FIFA/UEFA approve penalty shoot-out in deadlocked ties.

1971: Arsenal win League Championship and FA Cup. Sixty-six supporters die in the Ibrox Stadium disaster.

1973: Football League introduce 3-up, 3-down promotion/relegation between Divisions 1, 2 and 3 and 4-up, 4-down between Divisions 3 and 4.

1974: First FA Cup ties played on Sunday. League football played on Sunday for first time. Last FA Amateur Cup Final. Joao Havelange (Brazil) succeeds Sir Stanley Rous as FIFA president.

1975: Scottish Premier Division introduced.

1976: Football League introduce goal difference (replacing goal average) and red/yellow cards.

1977: Liverpool achieve the double of League Championship and European Cup. Don Revie defects to United Arab Emirates when England manager – successor Ron Greenwood.

1978: Freedom of contract for players accepted by Football League. PFA lifts ban on foreign players in English football. Football League introduce Transfer Tribunal. Viv Anderson (Nottm Forest) first black player to win a full England cap. Willie Johnston (Scotland) sent home from World Cup Finals in Argentina after failing dope test.

1979: First all-British £500,000 transfer – David Mills, Middlesbrough to WBA. First British million pound transfer (Trevor Francis – Birmingham to Nottm Forest). Andy Gray moves from Aston Villa to Wolves for a record £1,469,000 fee.

1981: Tottenham win 100th FA Cup Final. Liverpool first British side to win European Cup three times. Three points for a win introduced by Football League. QPR install Football League's first artificial pitch. Death of Bill Shankly, manager–legend of Liverpool 1959–74. Record British transfer – Bryan Robson (WBA to Manchester United), £1,500,000.

1982: Aston Villa become sixth consecutive English winners of European Cup. Tottenham retain FA Cup – first club to do so since Tottenham 1961 and 1962. Football League Cup becomes the (sponsored) Milk Cup.

1983: Liverpool complete League Championship–Milk Cup double for second year running. Manager Bob Paisley retires. Aberdeen first club to do Cup-Winners' Cup and domestic Cup double. Football League clubs vote to keep own match receipts. Football League sponsored by Canon, Japanese camera and business equipment manufacturers – 3-year agreement starting 1983–4. Football League agree two-year contract for live TV coverage of ten matches per season (5 Friday night, BBC, 5 Sunday afternoon, ITV).

1984: One FA Cup tie in rounds 3, 4, 5 and 6 shown live on TV (Friday or Sunday). Aberdeen take Scottish Cup for third successive season, win Scottish Championship, too. Tottenham win UEFA Cup on penalty shoot-out. Liverpool win European Cup on penalty shoot-out to complete unique treble with Milk Cup and League title (as well as Championship hat-trick). N Ireland win the final British Championship. France win European Championship – their first honour. FA National Soccer School opens at Lilleshall. Britain's biggest score this century: Stirling Alb 20 Selkirk 0 (Scottish Cup).

1985: Bradford City fire disaster – 56 killed. First £1m receipts from match in Britain (FA Cup Final). Kevin Moran (Manchester United) first player to be sent off in FA Cup Final. Celtic win 100th Scottish FA Cup Final. European Cup Final horror (Liverpool v Juventus, riot in Brussels) 39 die. UEFA ban all English clubs indefinitely from European competitions. No TV coverage at start of League season – first time since 1963 (resumption delayed until January 1986). Sept: first ground-sharing in League history – Charlton Athletic move from The Valley to Selhurst Park (Crystal Palace).

1986: Liverpool complete League and Cup double in player-manager Kenny Dalglish's first season in charge. Swindon (4th Div Champions) set League points record (102). League approve reduction of First Division to 20 clubs by 1988. Everton chairman Philip Carter elected president of Football League. Death of Sir Stanley Rous (91). 100th edition of News of the World Football Annual. League Cup sponsored for next three years by Littlewoods (£2m). Football League voting majority (for rule changes) reduced from three-quarters to two-thirds. Wales move HQ from Wrexham to Cardiff after 110 years. Two substitutes in FA Cup and League (Littlewoods) Cup. Two-season League/TV deal (£6.2m):- BBC and ITV each show seven live League matches per season, League Cup semi-finals and Final. Football League sponsored by Today newspaper. Luton first club to ban all visiting supporters; as sequel are themselves banned from League Cup. Oldham and Preston install artificial pitches, making four in Football League (following QPR and Luton).

1987: League introduce play-off matches to decide final promotion/relegation places in all divisions. Re-election abolished – bottom club in Div 4 replaced by winners of GM Vauxhall Conference. Two substitutes approved for Football League 1987–8. Red and yellow disciplinary cards (scrapped 1981) re-introduced by League and FA Football League sponsored by Barclays. First Div reduced to 21 clubs.

1988: Football League Centenary. First Division reduced to 20 clubs.

1989: Soccer gets £74m TV deal: £44m over 4 years, ITV; £30m over 5 years, BBC/BSB. But it costs Philip Carter the League Presidency. Ted Croker retires as FA chief executive; successor Graham Kelly, from Football League. Hillsborough disaster: 95 die at FA Cup semi-final (Liverpool v Nottm Forest). Arsenal win closest-ever Championship with last kick. Peter Shilton sets England record with 109 caps.

1990: Nottm Forest win last Littlewoods Cup Final. Both FA Cup semi-finals played on Sunday and televised live. Play-off finals move to Wembley; Swindon win place in Div 1, then relegated back to Div 2 (breach of financial regulations) – Sunderland promoted instead. England reach World Cup semi-final in Italy and win FIFA Fair Play Award. Peter Shilton retires as England goalkeeper with 125 caps (world record). Graham Taylor (Aston Villa) succeeds Bobby Robson as England manager. International Board amend offside law (player 'level' no longer offside). FIFA make "professional foul" a sending-off offence. English clubs back in Europe (Manchester United and Aston Villa) after 5-year exile.

1991: First FA Cup semi-final at Wembley (Tottenham 3 Arsenal 1). Bert Millichip (FA chairman) and Philip Carter (Everton chairman) knighted. End of artificial pitches in Div 1 (Luton, Oldham). Scottish League reverts to 12-12-14 format (as in 1987–8). Penalty shoot-out introduced to decide FA Cup ties level after one replay.

1992: FA launch Premier League (22 clubs). Football League reduced to three divisions (71 clubs). Record TV-sport deal: BSkyB/BBC to pay £304m for 5-year coverage of Premier League. ITV do £40m, 4-year deal with Football League. Channel 4 show Italian football live (Sundays). FIFA approve new back-pass rule (goalkeeper must not handle ball kicked to him by team-mate). New League of Wales formed. Record all-British transfer, £3.3m: Alan Shearer (Southampton to Blackburn). Charlton return to The Valley after 7-year absence.

1993: Barclays end 6-year sponsorship of Football League. For first time both FA Cup semi-finals at Wembley (Sat, Sun). Arsenal first club to complete League Cup/FA Cup double. Rangers pull off Scotland's domestic treble for fifth time. FA in record British sports sponsorship deal (£12m over 4 years) with brewers Bass for FA Carling Premiership, from Aug. Brian Clough retires after 18 years as Nottm Forest manager; as does Jim McLean (21 years manager of Dundee Utd). Football League agree 3-year, £3m sponsorship with Endsleigh Insurance. Premier League introduce squad numbers with players' names on shirts. Record British transfer: Duncan Ferguson, Dundee Utd to Rangers (£4m). Record English-club signing: Roy Keane, Nottm Forest to Manchester United (£3.75m). Graham Taylor resigns as England manager after World Cup exit (Nov). Death of Bobby Moore (51), England World Cup winning captain 1966.

1994: Death of Sir Matt Busby. Terry Venables appointed England coach. Manchester United complete the Double. Last artificial pitch in English football goes – Preston revert to grass, summer 1994. Bobby Charlton knighted. Scottish League format changes to four divisions of ten clubs. Record British transfer: Chris Sutton, Norwich to Blackburn (£5m). FA announce first sponsorship of FA Cup – Littlewoods Pools (4-year, £14m deal, plus £6m for Charity Shield). Death of Billy Wright.

1995: New record British transfer: Andy Cole, Newcastle to Manchester United (£7m). First England match abandoned through crowd trouble (v Republic of Ireland, Dublin). Blackburn Champions for first time since 1914. Premiership reduced to 20 clubs. British transfer record broken again: Stan Collymore, Nottm Forest to Liverpool (£8.5m). Starting season 1995–6, teams allowed to use 3 substitutes per match, not necessarily including a goalkeeper. European Court of Justice upholds Bosman ruling, barring transfer fees for players out of contract and removing limit on number of foreign players clubs can field.

1996: Death of Bob Paisley (77), ex-Liverpool, most successful manager in English Football. FA appoint Chelsea manager Glenn Hoddle to succeed Terry Venables as England coach after Euro 96. Manchester United first English club to achieve Double twice (and in 3 seasons). Football League completes £125m, 5-year TV deal with BSkyB starting 1996–7. England stage European Championship, reach semi-finals, lose on pens to tournament winners Germany. Keith Wiseman succeeds Sir Bert Millichip as FA Chairman. Linesmen become known as 'referees' assistants'. Alan Shearer football's first £15m player (Blackburn to Newcastle). Nigeria first African country to win Olympic soccer. Nationwide Building Society sponsor Football League in initial 3-year deal worth £5.25m Peter Shilton first player to make 1000 League appearances.

1997: Howard Wilkinson appointed English football's first technical director. England's first home defeat in World Cup (0–1 v Italy). Ruud Gullit (Chelsea) first foreign coach to win FA Cup. Rangers equal Celtic's record of 9 successive League titles. Manchester United win Premier League for fourth time in 5 seasons. New record World Cup score: Iran 17, Maldives 0 (qualifying round). Season 1997–8 starts Premiership's record £36m, 4-year sponsorship extension with brewers Bass (Carling).

1998: In French manager Arsene Wenger's second season at Highbury, Arsenal become second English club to complete the Double twice. Chelsea also win two trophies under new player-manager Gianluca Vialli (Coca-Cola Cup, Cup Winners' Cup). In breakaway from Scottish League, top ten clubs form new Premiership under SFA, starting season 1998–9. Football League celebrates its 100th season, 1998–9. New FA Cup sponsors – French insurance giants AXA (25m, 4-year deal). League Cup becomes Worthington Cup in £23m, 5-year contract with brewers Bass. Nationwide Building Society's sponsorship of Football League extended to season 2000–1.

1999: FA buy Wembley Stadium (£103m) for £320m, plan rebuilding (Aug 2000–March 2003) as new national stadium (Lottery Sports fund contributes £110m) Scotland's new Premier League takes 3-week mid-season break in January. Sky screen Oxford Utd v Sunderland (Div 1) as first pay-per-view match on TV. FA sack England coach Glenn Hoddle; Fulham's Kevin Keegan replaces him at £1m a year until 2003. Sir Alf Ramsey, England's World Cup-winning manager, dies aged 79. With effect 1999, FA Cup Final to be decided on day (via penalties, if necessary). Hampden Park re-opens for Scottish Cup Final after £63m refit. Alex Ferguson knighted after Manchester United complete Premiership, FA Cup, European Cup treble. Starting season 1999–2000, UEFA increase Champions League from 24 to 32 clubs. End of Cup-Winners' Cup (merged into 121-club UEFA Cup). FA allow holders Manchester United to withdraw from FA Cup to participate in FIFA's inaugural World Club Championship in Brazil in January. Chelsea first British club to field an all-foreign line-up – at Southampton (Prem). FA vote in favour of streamlined 14-man board of directors to replace its 92-member council.

2000: Scot Adam Crozier takes over as FA chief executive. Wales move to Cardiff's £125m Millennium Stadium (v Finland). Brent Council approve plans for new £475m Wembley Stadium (completion target spring 2003); demolition of old stadium to begin after England v Germany (World Cup qual.). Fulham Ladies become Britain's first female professional team. FA Premiership and Nationwide League to introduce (season 2000–01) rule whereby referees advance free-kick by 10 yards and caution player who shows dissent, delays kick or fails to retreat 10 yards. Scottish football increased to 42 League clubs in 2000–01 (12 in Premier League and 3 divisions of ten; Peterhead and Elgin elected from Highland League). France win European Championship – first time a major international tournament has been jointly hosted (Holland/ Belgium). England's £10m bid to stage 2006 World Cup fails; vote goes to Germany. England manager Kevin Keegan resigns after 1-0 World Cup defeat by Germany in Wembley's last International. Lazio's Swedish coach Sven-Goran Eriksson agrees to become England head coach.

2001: Scottish Premier League experiment with split into two 5-game mini leagues (6 clubs in each) after 33 matches completed. New transfer system agreed by FIFA/UEFA is ratified. Barclaycard begin £48m, 3-year sponsorship of the Premiership, and Nationwide's contract with the Football League is extended by a further 3 years (£12m). ITV, after winning auction against BBC's Match of the Day, begin £183m, 3-season contract for highlights of Premiership matches; BSkyB's live coverage (66 matches per season) for next 3 years will cost £1.1bn. BBC and BSkyB pay £400m (3-year contract) for live coverage of FA Cup and England home matches. ITV and Ondigital pay £315m to screen Nationwide League and Worthington Cup matches. In new charter for referees, top men can earn up to £60,000 a season in Premiership. Real Madrid break world transfer record, buying Zinedine Zidane from Juventus for £47.2m. FA introduce prize money, round by round, in FA Cup.

2002: Scotland appoint their first foreign manager, Germany's former national coach Bertie Vogts replacing Craig Brown. Collapse of ITV Digital deal, with Football League owed £178m, threatens lower-division clubs. Arsenal complete Premiership/FA Cup Double for second time in 5 seasons, third time in all. Newcastle manager Bobby Robson knighted in Queen's Jubilee Honours. New record British transfer and world record for defender, £29.1m Rio Ferdinand (Leeds to Manchester United). Transfer window introduced to British football. FA Charity Shield renamed FA Community Shield. After 2-year delay, demolition of Wembley Stadium begins. October: Adam Crozier, FA chief executive, resigns.

2003: FA Cup draw (from 4th Round) reverts to Monday lunchtime. Scottish Premier League decide to end mid-winter shut-down. Mark Palios appointed FA chief executive. For first time, two Football League clubs demoted (replaced by two from Conference). Ban lifted on loan transfers between Premiership clubs. July: David Beckham becomes record British export (Manchester United to Real Madrid, £23.3m). Biggest takeover in British football history – Russian oil magnate Roman Abramovich buys control of Chelsea for £150m Wimbledon leave rented home at Selhurst Park, become England's first franchised club in 68-mile move to Milton Keynes.

2004: Arsenal first club to win Premiership with unbeaten record and only the third in English football history to stay undefeated through League season. Trevor Brooking knighted in Queen's Birthday Honours. Wimbledon change name to Milton Keynes Dons. Greece beat hosts Portugal to win European Championship as biggest outsiders (80-1 at start) ever to succeed in major international tournament. New contracts – Premiership in £57m deal with Barclays, seasons 2004–07. Coca-Cola replace Nationwide as Football League sponsors (£15m over 3 years), rebranding Div 1 as Football League Championship, with 2nd and 3rd Divisions, becoming Leagues 1 and 2. All-time League record of 49 unbeaten Premiership matches set by Arsenal. Under new League rule, Wrexham forfeit 10 points for going into administration.

2005: Brian Barwick, controller of ITV Sport, becomes FA chief executive. Foreign managers take all major trophies for English clubs: Chelsea, in Centenary year, win Premiership (record 95 points) and League Cup in Jose Mourinho's first season; Arsene Wenger's Arsenal win FA Cup in Final's first penalty shoot-out; under new manager Rafael Benitez, Liverpool lift European Cup on penalties after trailing 0-3 in Champions League Final. Wigan, a League club only since 1978, promoted to Premiership. In new record

British-club take-over, American tycoon Malcolm Glazer buys Manchester United for £790m Tributes are paid world-wide to George Best, who dies aged 59.

2006: Steve Staunton succeeds Brian Kerr as Republic of Ireland manager. Chelsea post record losses of £140m. Sven-Goran Eriksson agrees a settlement to step down as England coach. Steve McClaren replaces him. The Premier League announce a new 3-year TV deal worth £1.7 billion under which Sky lose their monopoly of coverage. Chelsea smash the British transfer record, paying £30.8m for Andriy Shevchenko. Clydesdale Bank replace Bank of Scotland as sponsor of the SPL.

2007: Michel Platini becomes the new president of UEFA. Walter Smith resigns as Scotland manager to return to Rangers and is replaced by Alex McLeish. The new £800m Wembley Stadium is finally completed. The BBC and Sky lose TV rights for England's home matches and FA Cup ties to ITV and Setanta. World Cup-winner Alan Ball dies aged 61. Lawrie Sanchez resigns as Northern Ireland manager to take over at Fulham. Nigel Worthington succeeds him. Lord Stevens names five clubs in his final report into alleged transfer irregularities. Steve McClaren is sacked after England fail to qualify for the European Championship Finals and is replaced by Fabio Capello. The Republic of Ireland's Steve Staunton also goes. Scotland's Alex McLeish resigns to become Birmingham manager.

2008: The Republic of Ireland follow England's lead in appointing an Italian coach – Giovanni Trapattoni. George Burley leaves Southampton to become Scotland manager. Manchester United beat Chelsea in the first all-English Champions League Final. Manchester City smash the British transfer record when signing Robinho from Real Madrid for £32.5m.

2009: Sky secure the rights to five of the six Premier League packages from 2010–13 with a bid of £1.6bn. Reading's David Beckham breaks Bobby Moore's record number of caps for an England outfield player with his 109th appearance. A British league record for not conceding a goal ends on 1,311 minutes for Manchester United's Edwin van der Sar. AC Milan's Kaka moves to Real Madrid for a world record fee of £56m. Nine days later, Manchester United agree to sell Cristiano Ronaldo to Real for £80m. Sir Bobby Robson dies aged 76 after a long battle with cancer. Shay Given and Kevin Kilbane win their 100th caps for the Republic of Ireland. The Premier League vote for clubs to have eight home-grown players in their squads. George Burley is sacked as Scotland manager and replaced by Craig Levein.

2010: npower succeed Coca-Cola as sponsors of the Football League. Portsmouth become the first Premier League club to go into administration. Chelsea achieve the club's first League and FA Cup double. Lord Triesman resigns as chairman of the FA and of England's 2018 World Cup bid. John Toshack resigns as Wales manager and is replaced by former captain Gary Speed. England are humiliated in the vote for the 2018 World Cup which goes to Russia, with the 2022 tournament awarded to Qatar.

2011: Seven club managers are sacked in a week. The transfer record between Britsh clubs is broken twice in a day, with Liverpool buying Newcastle's Andy Carroll for £35m and selling Fernando Torres to Chelsea for £50m. Vauxhall replace Nationwide as sponsors of England and the other home nations. John Terry is restored as England captain. Football League clubs vote to reduce the number of substitutes from seven to five. Nigel Worthington steps down as Northern Ireland manager and is succeeded by Michael O'Neill. Sir Alex Ferguson completes 25 years as Manchester United manager. Manchester City post record annual losses of nearly £195m. Huddersfield set a Football League record of 43 successive unbeaten league games. Football mourns Gary Speed after the Wales manager is found dead at his home.

2012: Chris Coleman is appointed the new Wales manager. Fabio Capello resigns as manager after John Terry is stripped of the England captaincy for the second time. Roy Hodgson takes over. Rangers are forced into liquidation by crippling debts and a newly-formed club are demoted from the Scottish Premier League to Division Three. Manchester City become champions for the first time since 1968 after the tightest finish to a Premier League season. Chelsea win a penalty shoot-out against Bayern Munich in the Champions League Final. Capital One replace Carling as League Cup sponsors. Steven Gerrard

(England) and Damien Duff (Republic of Ireland) win their 100th caps. The FA's new £120m National Football Centre at Burton upon Trent is opened. Scotland manager Craig Levein is sacked.

2013: Gordon Strachan is appointed Scotland manager. FIFA and the Premier League announce the introduction of goal-line technology. Energy company npower end their sponsorship of the Football League and are succeeded by Sky Bet. Sir Alex Ferguson announces he is retiring after 26 years as Manchester United manager. Wigan become the first club to lift the FA Cup and be relegated in the same season. Chelsea win the Europa League. Ashley Cole and Frank Lampard win their 100th England caps. Robbie Keane becomes the most capped player in the British Isles on his 126th appearance for the Republic of Ireland. Scottish Football League clubs agree to merge with the Scottish Premier League. Greg Dyke succeeds David Bernstein as FA chairman. Real Madrid sign Tottenham's Gareth Bale for a world record £85.3m. Giovanni Trapatonni is replaced as Republic of Ireland manager by Martin O'Neill.

2014: Sir Tom Finney, one of the finest British players of all-time, dies aged 91. England experience their worst-ever World Cup, finishing bottom the group with a single point. Germany deliver one of the most remarkable scorelines in World Cup history – 7-1 against Brazil in the semi-finals. Manchester United announce a world-record kit sponsorship with adidas worth £750m. United break the incoming British transfer record by paying £59.7m for Real Madrid's Angel di Maria, part of a record £835m spending by Premier League clubs in the summer transfer window. England's Wayne Rooney and the Republic of Ireland's John O'Shea win their 100th caps.

2015: The Premier League sell live TV rights for 2016-19 to Sky and BT for a record £5.13bn. Bournemouth, a club on the brink of folding in 2008, win promotion to the Premier League. FIFA president Sepp Blatter resigns as a bribery and corruption scandal engulfs the world governing body. Blatter and suspended UEFA president Michel Platini are banned for eight years, reduced on appeal to six years.

2016: An inquest jury rules that the 96 Liverpool fans who died in the Hillsborough disaster of 1989 were unlawfully killed. Leicester, 5,000-1 outsiders become Premier League champions in one of the game's biggest-ever surprises. Aaron Hughes wins his 100th cap for Northern Ireland. FA Cup quarter-final replays are scrapped. England manager Roy Hodgson resigns. He is replaced by Sam Allardyce, who is forced out after one match for 'inappropriate conduct' and succeeded by Gareth Southgate. Manchester United sign Paul Pogba for a world record £89.3m.

2017 Paris Saint-Germain sign Barcelona's Neymar for a world record £198m. Managers Gordon Strachan (Scotland) and Chris Coleman (Wales) resign. Steven Davis reaches a century of Northern Ireland caps. Manchester United win the Europa League. Celtic are champions without losing a game. Arsenal win a record 13th FA Cup, Arsene Wenger for a record seventh time. Wayne Rooney retires from international football as England's record scorer with 53 goals.

2018 Manchester City become the first English champions to total 100 points. Celtic are the first in Scotland to win back-to-back domestic trebles. Alex McLeish (Scotland) and Ryan Giggs (Wales) are appointed. Arsene Wenger leaves Arsenal after 22 years as manager. A helicopter crash outside Leicester's King Power Stadium claims the lives of club owner Vichai Srivaddhanaprabha, the pilot and three others on board. Martin O'Neill is sacked as Republic of Ireland manager and replaced by Mick McCarthy, his second time in charge.

2019 Gordon Banks, England's World Cup-winning goalkeeper in 1966, dies aged 81. Tottenham open their new £1bn stadium. Manchester City achieve an unprecedented domestic treble. Celtic also make history with a third successive Scottish treble. Scotland manager Alex McLeish is sacked and replaced by Kilmarnock's Steve Clarke. For the first time, English clubs occupy all four places in the European finals - Liverpool defeating Tottenham in the Champions League and Chelsea beating Arsenal to win the Europa League.

FINAL WHISTLE – OBITUARIES 2019–20

JULY 2019

SAMMY CHAPMAN, 81, had two spells as manager of Wolves. He first took over on an interim basis after Tommy Docherty was dismissed in the summer of 1985. Later that year, he replaced Bill McGarry, whose return to the club lasted just 61 days. Chapman was unable to prevent Wolves dropping into the fourth tier for the first time in their history and left the club in August 1986 – succeeded by Brian Little. His playing career as a winger included spells at Portsmouth and Mansfield and a place in Northern Ireland's squad for the 1958 World Cup in Sweden. It ended after a second spell at Mansfield when he was jailed and banned for involvement in the 1960's betting scandal which rocked football.

STEVE TALBOYS, 52, made 31 appearances for Wimbledon, then in the Premier League, following an £11,000 move from Gloucester in 1992. The midfielder moved to Second Division Watford in 1996 before returning to non-league football.

PETER MCCONNELL, 82, captained Carlisle to successive promotions – second place in Division Four in 1963–64, then the club's first league title the following season. The wing-half, who started his career with Leeds, made nearly 300 appearances for the club before joining Bradford City in 1969.

KEVIN STONEHOUSE, 59, scored 29 goals in 91 apperances for Blackburn between 1979–83. The forward left to join Huddersfield and later played for Blackpool, Darlington, where he led the club's Football in the Community scheme, Carlisle and Rochdale.

BERNARD EVANS, 82, was a centre-forward who scored 27 seconds into his debut as a 17-year-old for Wexham against Bradford City in 1954. He gained a Welsh Cup winners' medal with the club before moving to Queens Park Rangers, then had spells with Football League newcomers Oxford United, Tranmere and Crewe.

BOBBY PARK, 72, helped Wrexham to promotion from Division Four, as runners-up to Chesterfield, in season 1969–70. The wing-half started his career with Aston Villa and later played for Peterborough, Northampton and Hartlepool.

JOE RAYMENT, 84, played in the match which attracted Darlington's record crowd of 21,023 at Feethams – a League Cup third round tie against Bolton in 1960. The right-winger spent six years at the club after spells with Hartlepool and Middlesbrough.

RON HUGHES, 89, joined Chester as an amateur in 1947, turned professional three years later and made 399 league appearances for the club, second only to his contemporary, Ray Gill (406). The full-back played in four Welsh Cup Finals, without a victory.

BRIAN CARTER, 80, was a wing-half who joined Portsmouth from Weymouth in 1956 and had four years at Fratton Park. He then played for Bristol Rovers and Bath.

AUGUST 2019

JUNIOR AGOGO, 40, was a much-travelled striker who played for 15 clubs and made 27 international appearances for Ghana. His career included promotion with Nottingham Forest from League One in season 2007–08 when he was top scorer with 13 goals. There were spells at Sheffield Wednesday, Queens Park Rangers, Barnet and Bristol Rovers, along with loans at Oldham, Chester, Chesterfield and Lincoln. He also played for Chicago, Colorado and San Jose in the United States and teams in Egypt and Cyprus. Among his 12 international goals were three at the 2008 Africa Cup of Nations. Agogo finished at Hibernian in 2012. He suffered a stroke in 2015 and struggled with his speech afterwards.

JOHN LOWEY, 61, was part of Sheffield Wednesday's Third Division promotion-winning squad under Jack Charlton in 1979–80. The previous season, he scored in the club's marathon FA Cup third round tie which stretched to five games before Arsenal won it 2-0. Lowey, a midfielder, also played for Blackburn, Port Vale, Wigan, Chesterfield. York, Preston and Chester, as well as for clubs in the United States and Australia.

DOUG CLARKE, 85, joined Hull from Bury in 1955, scored on his debut against West Ham and made 411 appearances in a decade at the club. They included the 1958–59 season when Hull won promotion back to the old Second Division as runners-up to Plymouth. The right-winger ended his career at Torquay.

STEVE PARR, 92, had to wait three years for his first-team debut after signing for Liverpool in 1948. The full-back, who could play on both flanks, was restricted to 20 appearances because of strong competition at the club. He moved on to Exeter and finished his career with Rochdale.

JOHN DILLON, 76, made his debut for Sunderland aged 17 against Middlesbrough in 1960. All but one of his 23 appearances came in that season, including the club's first League Cup tie. The winger moved to Brighton in 1962, then played for Crewe before spells in Scotland with Albion, Queen of the South, Stranraer and Hamilton.

SEPTEMBER 2019

FERNANDO RICKSEN, 43, spent six trophy-laden seasons with Rangers after joining the club from Alkmaar for £3.75m in 2000. He won two league titles, two Scottish Cups and three League Cups, as well as sharing the PFA Player of the Year award with Celtic's John Hartson in 2005. Ricksen, who played at right-back and in midfield, was reunited with manager Dick Advocaat after leaving Ibrox for Zenit St Petersburg. There, he won the Russian title and was an unused substitute in the club's 2-0 UEFA Cup Final victory over Rangers in 2008. After that, he returned to his first club, Fortuna Sittard. Ricksen, capped 12 times by Holland, died after a six-year battle with motor neurone disease, having had a benefit match in 2015, watched by a 41,000 crowd at Ibrox.

PETER DOWNSBOROUGH, 76, was Swindon's goalkeeper in their famous 3-1 victory over Arsenal after extra-time in the 1969 League Cup Final. He made 320 appearances in eight seasons at the club after starting his career with home-town team Halifax. After a short spell at Brighton, Downsborough played 225 games for Bradford City, who reached the FA Cup quarter-finals in 1976 and won promotion from Division Four the following season.

DENNIS EDWARDS, 82, was an England amateur international who turned professional with Wycombe in 1957, then scored 66 goals in 187 appearances for Charlton. The centre-forward, later played for Portsmouth, Brentford and Aldershot.

BOBBY PRENTICE, 65, was an under 23 international winger who made 240 appearances for his boyhood club Hearts in the 1970s. They included the 1976 Scottish Cup Final, which his side lost 3-1 to Rangers, and promotion back to the Premier Division two years later. He later played for Toronto in the Northern American League and Baltimore and Buffalo in the indoor league.

KENNY MITCHELL, 62, made his debut for Newcastle against Manchester City in 1977 and made 73 appearances for the club. The utility player then had spells with Darlington and Workington and helped the Finnish club Kuusysi become league champions.

OCTOBER 2019

BERT MOZLEY, 96, was the oldest surviving England international. The full-back played three times in 1949 – the first a 2-0 loss to the Republic of Ireland at Goodison Park in which he conceded a penalty for the first goal. It was England's first home defeat by a team from outside Britain. His other caps were against Wales (4-1) and Northern Ireland (9-2). Mozley spent his entire club career with home-town Derby, making his league debut against Preston at the Baseball Ground in 1946 during the first post-war season, and accumulating 321 appearances through to 1955. Derby were FA Cup semi-finalists in 1947–48 and finished third behind Portsmouth and Manchester United in the old First Division the following season.

DUNCAN FORBES, 78, captained Norwich to promotion to the top division for the first time in season 1971–72 when they finished champions, a point ahead of Birmingham. The central defender also led his side into two League Cup Finals, losing 1-0 to Tottenham in 1973 and 1-0 to Aston Villa two years later. Forbes made 357 appearances over 13 years after joining the club in 1968 from Colchester, for whom he played nearly 300 games, including the 1965–66 Division Four promotion-winning campaign.

STUART TAYLOR, 72, made a record 546 league appearances over 13 years for Bristol Rovers. The 6ft 5in central defender broke into team alongside Larry Lloyd in 1965 and served the club throughout his playing career. It included promotion from Division Three as runners-up to Oldham in 1974. Taylor later managed Bath City.

FRED MOLYNEUX, 75, joined Liverpool in 1962, spent three years at Anfield without breaking into the senior team, then started and finished a league career with Southport. In between, the central defender played for Plymouth, Exeter and Tranmere.

JOHN FLEMING, 62, was the Scottish FA's head of referee operations, spending eight years in the role. He had a long career as a referee and linesman, including Euro 96, served as an observer for UEFA and was on the technical advisory panel of the International FA Board.

NOVEMBER 2019

SEAN HASLEGRAVE, 68, played for six clubs in a career spanning nearly 20 years and 599 matches. He started in 1970 with home-town side Stoke, who under Tony Waddington twice finished fifth in the old First Division. Brian Clough took the midfielder to Nottingham Forest, he then won promotion from Division Three under Nobby Stiles at Preston in season 1977–78 and was part of York's Fourth Division title-winning team with a record 101 points in 1983–84. Haslegrave also had spells at Crewe and Torquay.

CYRIL ROBINSON, 90, was the last surviving member of Blackpool's 1953 FA Cup-winning team. He played left-half in one of the most famous of all finals in which his side retrieved a 3-1 deficit to defeat Bolton 4-3 through the magic of Stanley Matthews and a hat-trick from Stan Mortensen Robinson joined the club from Mansfield and later played for Bradford Park Avenue, Southport and Newcastle Croatia in Australia.

JOHNNY WHEELER, 91, was the oldest surviving Liverpool captain. He joined the club for a fee of £9,000 in 1956 and in his first season scored a hat-trick in four minutes (81, 82, 85) in a 4-1 Division Two win over Port Vale. The wing-half previously played for Bolton in the 1953 FA Cup Final against Blackpool, which his side lost 4-3, and won one England cap, against Northern Ireland. He began his career with Tranmere and played his final game for Liverpool in 1961.

LES CAMPBELL, 84, was a team-mate of two famous England wingers. He spent much of his time at Preston (1953–60) as understudy to Tom Finney, then played alongside Stanley Matthews at Blackpool. The 5ft 2in outside-left also had a spell with Tranmere before returning his first club, non-league Wigan.

LORD BRIAN MAWHINNEY, 79, was chairman of the Football League from 2003–10 and introduced the fit and proper persons test for prospective club directors. In a long political career he served in John Major's Cabinet and was chairman of the Conservative Party.

DECEMBER 2019

MARTIN PETERS, 76, went from fledgling England international to World Cup winner in just three months. The gifted midfielder, nicknamed 'The Ghost' for his ability to drift unnoticed into scoring positions, impressed Alf Ramsey on his debut, a 2-0 win over Yugoslavia in the build-up to the tournament. It was rewarded with a place in the squad for the finals, where he became a key part of the manager's new 'wingless wonders' line-up after missing out on the opening goalless group match against Uruguay. Peters played in wins over Mexico and France, then delivered the cross for Geoff Hurst to head the only goal of the quarter-final against Argentina. He scored their second in the 4-2 Wembley win over West Germany which crowned England world champions, having made such an impact that Ramsey would later describe him as 'ten years ahead of his time.' More success beckoned four years later in Mexico after he put England 2-0 ahead in the quarter-finals. Instead, he was substituted, along with Bobby Charlton, and the Germans turned the tables to win 3-2 in extra-time. England failed to qualify for the next World Cup after a 1-1 draw against Poland, with Peters captain that night. His 67th and final appearance for his country came in a 2-0 defeat by Scotland in May 1974, having scored 20 goals and led the side four times. He became the fifth player from that Wembley triumph to be lost – after captain Bobby Moore, Alan Ball, Ray Wilson and Gordon Banks. Peters also had a distinguished club career, embracing 882 appearances and 220 goals. At West Ham, alongside Moore and Hurst, he won the 1965 European Cup-Winners' Cup (2-0 v Munich 1860 at Wembley). At Tottenham, after becoming Britain's first £200,000 player – with Jimmy Greaves going the other way – he won the League Cup in 1971 (2-0 v Aston Villa) and 1973 (1-0 Norwich), along with the inaugural UEFA Cup in 1972 (3-2 on aggregate v Wolves). After that he was at Norwich, played for and managed Sheffield United and finished in defence for Gorleston in the Eastern Counties League. Peters, awarded an MBE in1978, returned to Tottenham as a non-executive director and also did hospitality work for West Ham. He died after three years battling Alzheimer's disease.

RON SAUNDERS, 87, enjoyed a free-scoring career as a combative centre-forward, but it was as a steely, disciplinarian manager over 20 years that he made an indelible mark on the game. Most notably, he led Aston Villa to their first League title for 71 years in season 1980–1981, four points ahead of runners-up Ipswich and seven clear of third-place Arsenal. Remarkably, it was achieved by a squad of just 14 players, seven of whom featured in all 42 games. Saunders took three different teams to successive League Cup Finals in the 1970's –Norwich (0-1 v Tottenham), Manchester City (1-2 v Wolves) and Villa (1-0 v Norwich). He was also the only man to manage all three west Midlands clubs – Villa, Birmingham and West Bromwich Albion. But he turned his back on the ultimate prize – the European Cup – walking out with Villa in the quarter-finals in 1982 over a contract dispute. With his assistant Tony Barton taking over, Villa went on to defeat Bayern Munich 1-0 in the final in Rotterdam. Saunders had been in charge for eight years, winning a second League Cup, 3-2 against Everton after two drawn matches in the final. Previously, he took Norwich to the top division as champions after beginning his managerial career at Yeovil, then Oxford United. As a player with Everton, Gillingham, Portsmouth, Watford and Charlton, he scored 234 goals in 425 appearances.

JIM SMITH, 79, had a 38-year career in management spanning more than 1,400 matches with nine clubs. Two of his five promotions took Oxford into the old First Division in 1985 after back-to-back title wins. But he never got to manage them in the top-flight, resigning over a contract dispute with owner Robert Maxwell. Ironically, his next club, Queens Park Rangers, met Oxford in the following season's League Cup Final, losing 3-0. Smith eventually made it after taking a break in 1995 to become chief executive of the League Managers' Association. Returning to the dug-out, the man known throughout the game as the 'Bald Eagle' led Derby into the Premier League and remained there for six years – his longest spell at one club. Smith also managed Colchester and Birmingham – gaining promotion with both – Boston, Blackburn, Newcastle and Portsmouth. After No 2 jobs at Coventry, then Portsmouth and Southampton alongside Harry Redknapp, he finished off back at Oxford in 2007. His playing career as a wing-half included spells at Sheffield United, Aldershot, Halifax and Lincoln.

BILLY HUGHES, 70, played a key role in Sunderland's 1973 FA Cup triumph. He scored twice in a fifth round replay against Manchester City, netted the winner against Arsenal in the semi-final, then delivered the corner which fellow Scot Ian Porterfield converted for their Wembley victory over hot favourites Leeds. Hughes was the Second Division club's top scorer that season with 19 of the 81 goals accumulated in 335 appearances spanning 11 years. There was also one international cap, against Sweden. He left for Derby in 1977, followed by time at Leicester and Carlisle and brief spells in Canada and America.

ALAN HARRINGTON, 86, helped Wales reach their first major tournament – the 1958 World Cup. He featured in both play-off matches against Israel (2-0, 2-0), but missed the finals in Sweden with a dislocated shoulder. Harrington, who played at half-back or inside-forward, won 11 caps. He spent his entire 15-year club career at Cardiff, making more than 400 appearances before retiring with a broken leg in 1966.

IAN YOUNG, 76, was part of the Celtic side that ended an era of under-achievement to become the dominant force in Scottish football under Jock Stein.The right-back featured in their 3-2 win over Dunfermline in the 1965 Scottish Cup Final, the 2-1 League Cup success against Rangers later that year and the first of the club's nine successive league titles in 1966. After seven years at Parkhead, Young joined St Mirren, where his career was cut short at 27 by a cruciate ligament injury.

ROY CHEETHAM, 79, spent a decade at Manchester City and was the club's first substitute, coming on against Wolves in 1965 when Mike Summerbee sustained a cut head. The wing-half did not make sufficient appearances during the 1967–68 season when City became League champions under Joe Mercer and Malcom Allison. He later played for Chester and for Detroit in the United States. In 1999, Cheetham met his boyhood hero, Ferenc Puskas, in Budapest. In 2006, he represented City at the Hungary legend's funeral.

JOHN SHUKER, 77, made a record number of Football League appearances for Oxford United during 17 years at the club. He joined as an amateur in 1960 and turned professional two years later on their election to the league. Shuker made his debut at centre-forward, developed into an outstanding left-half, then switched to left back, succeeding Ron Atkinson as captain. He played 529 games and won two promotions – Division Four in 1964–65 and Division Three as champions three seasons later.

TOM WHITE, 80, played for four Scottish clubs – Raith, St Mirren, Hearts and Aberdeen – from 1959–66 before continuing his career in English football. The inside-forward had spells at Crystal Palace, Blackpool, Bury and Crewe, retiring in 1972. He also played in a testimonial match between Tottenham and a Scotland X1after his brother, Spurs star John White, was killed in a lightning strike on a golf course in 1964. Tom later served Blackpool as caretaker-manager and on the board of directors.

BRIAN SPARROW, 57, was a full-back who came through the youth ranks at Arsenal. He was restricted to two league appearances, spending most of the time on loan at Wimbledon, Millwall and Gillingham, before signing for Crystal Palace. Sparrow then coached at Brentford and in China and managed Crawley before the club's promotion to the Football League.

DUNCAN MACKAY, 82, was an early exponent of the attacking full-back-role during nine years at Celtic. He made his debut in a League Cup tie against Clyde in 1958 and was appointed captain three years later before passing on the armband to Billy McNeill. Mackay, capped 14 times by Scotland, later played for Third Lanark and in Australia with Melbourne and Perth.

GARY TALBOT, 82, combined a career as a prolific scorer for Chester with his work as a press photographer. He was spotted playing in a charity match and in 1964 delivered one of the FA Cup's fastest-ever hat-tricks – two minutes and fifty seven seconds in a 5-0 first round win over Crewe. That same season, when Chester totalled 119 goals in Division Four and all five forwards netted more than 20, he led the way with 28. Talbot then helped Crewe to promotion from Division Four before returning for a second spell with Chester.

TOMMY FORGAN, 90, was the last surviving member of the York side from Division Three North that reached the semi-finals of the FA Cup in season 1954–55, beating Tottenham on the way before losing to Newcastle in a replay. The goalkeeper's 120 clean sheets remains a club record. He signed from Hull in 1954 and made 428 appearances in 11 years at Bootham Crescent.

DUDLEY KERNICK, 98, was an inside-forward who played war-time football for Birmingham, then had spells at Torquay, Northampton and Shrewsbury. He worked as a youth coach for

Jimmy Hill at Coventry and later became Stoke's commercial manager.

JANUARY 2020

BOBBY BROWN, 96, had a trophy-laden career with Rangers as a goalkeeper, then became Scotland's first full-time manager. He was appointed in 1967, after nearly nine years in charge of St Johnstone, and made a notable start with a 3-2 win over world champions England at Wembley. The national side failed narrowly to qualify for the 1970 World Cup and Brown stepped down the following year after 28 matches, frustrated at the reluctance of some club managers to release players for international duty. He briefly managed Hull and scouted for Plymouth. As part of the 'Iron Curtain' defence at Rangers, Brown won three league titles, three Scottish Cups and two League Cups, including the first-ever treble in season 1948–49. Between August 1946 and April 1952 he made 179 successive league starts, while combining football with a job as a schoolmaster. Brown, who started out at Queen's Park, made 296 appearances in a decade at Ibrox. He finished at Falkirk and was the last amateur to play for his country, gaining five caps.

CHRIS BARKER, 39, made more than 500 appearances for seven teams in a 17-year career. He joined Cardiff from his first club Barnsley in a £500,000 transfer, was part of the Division Two promotion-winning side, via the play-offs, in 2002–03 and was their Player of the Year two seasons later. The full back then had spells with Stoke and Colchester on loan, Queens Park Rangers, Plymouth and Southend, where he received another Player of the Year award. Barker also played non-league for Aldershot and Hereford, retiring in 2017. He joined Forest Green as under-18 team manager following the club's promotion to the Football League and played a leading role in developing the club's Academy. A coroner ruled he had taken his own life.

HANS TILKOWSKI, 84, was West Germany's goalkeeper in the 1966 World Cup Final which England won 4-2 at Wembley with a hat-trick from Geoff Hurst. Tilkowski maintained that Hurst's second goal, awarded after the ball bounced down off the crossbar, should not have been allowed. Subsequently, the two players continued to disagree, on friendly terms, whenever their paths crossed. Tilkowski did achieve one victory over an English team that season when Borussia Dortmund defeated Bill Shankly's Liverpool 2-1 after extra-time in the European Cup Winners' Cup Final at Hampden Park. He also played club football for Eintracht Frankfurt and went on to coach 1860 Munich, Nuremberg, Werder Bremen and AEK Athens. He made 39 appearances for his country and was second-choice goalkeeper at the 1962 World Cup in Chile.

DALE JASPER, 56, made his debut in central defence for Chelsea during the Division Two title winning season of 1983–84 under John Neal when they pipped Sheffield Wednesday on goal difference after both sides finished with 88 points. He rarely featured when John Hollins succeeded Neal as manager, joining Brighton for first-team football and sharing promotion from Division Three in 1987–88. Jasper, who also played in midfield, then helped Crewe go up from the Fourth Division the following season. He also had a spell with non-league Crawley.

ERIC BROOKES, 75, signed for home-town Barnsley in 1959 and made his first-team debut at 16 – then the youngest to play for the club. Showing a maturity beyond his years, the England youth international left-back made 35 appearances in his first season, including a key role in Barnsley reaching the sixth round of the FA Cup. He went on to play 377 games before joining Northampton for £8,000 in 1969. Two years at the County Ground included an 8-2 FA Cup fifth round defeat by Manchester United, with George Best scoring six goals. Brookes also served Peterborough before retiring through injury.

JIMMY SHIELDS, 88, failed to find first-team football at Sunderland after a move from the Irish club Crusaders, but quickly made an impact at his next port of call, Southampton in 1956. The centre-forward scored on his debut and netted 14 times in 24 league matches by Boxing Day. He finished with 18, alongside his one cap for Northern Ireland, against Scotland. A broken leg ruined the following season and Shields eventually signed for Southern League

Headington, shortly before the club became Oxford United.

MICK VINTER, 65, gained promotion at three Football League clubs after starting out with home-town team Boston United under Jim Smith. The striker went up from Division Three with Notts County in 1973, won that divisional title ten years later, after being reunited with Smith at Oxford, and helped Mansfield go up from the Fourth Division in 1986. He also played for Wrexham, after a £150,000 move from Notts County, and latterly Newport before finishing in non-league football.

BRIAN CLIFTON, 85, was a key player in Southampton's Third Division title-winning side of season 1959–60. They finished two points ahead of Norwich in second place, with Clifton's match-winning header against Reading on Easter Monday effectively sealing promotion. The wing-half played for the club for five years before moving on to captain Grimsby, then going part-time at Boston after suffering shin-splints.

RAY BYROM, 85, started in 1953 in the youth ranks at his home-town club Blackburn. The left-winger moved to Accrington, then followed manager Walter Galbraith to Bradford Park Avenue, where his career was cut short by a broken leg sustained against Crewe in 1961.

JORDAN SINNOTT, 25, followed in the footsteps of his father Lee by playing for Huddersfield. He came through the youth ranks, made his senior debut in an FA Cup tie against Leicester in 2013 and had his first league outing the following month against Nottingham Forest. The midfielder later had spells at Bury and Chesterfield and played non-league under his father, who was manager at Altrincham. Lee Sinnott's career included an FA Cup Final appearance for Watford, against Everton, in 1984. His son died of injuries sustained in an assault. He was on loan at Matlock from Alfreton.

FEBRUARY 2020

HARRY GREGG, 87, had no trophies to show from a distinguished goalkeeping career, yet achieved hero status which remained undiminished for the rest of his life after the 1958 Munich air disaster. Eight Manchester United team-mates were among 23 victims of the tragedy when their plane crashed on take-off after refuelling on the way back from a European Cup tie in Belgrade. The toll would have been higher had Gregg not pulled three other players, Bobby Charlton, Jackie Blanchflower and Dennis Viollet, manager Matt Busby and a mother and her baby from the burning plane. Remarkably, Gregg was back playing 13 days later when a makeshift United team of reserve and loaned players, defeated Sheffield Wednesday in an FA Cup fifth round tie. Further victories over West Bromwich Albion and Fulham took them to the final at Wembley, where Gregg, Charlton, Viollet and another survivor, Bill Foulkes, were in the side managed by Busby's assistant Jimmy Murphy. They lost 2-0 to two goals by Nat Lofthouse, the second allowed to stand when he bundled goalkeeper and ball into the net. Gregg was not selected for the 1963 Wembley win over Leicester, having just returned from a shoulder injury, missed too many games to qualify for a First Division championship medal in 1965 and was sold to Stoke during the first part of the club's title-winning campaign two years later. His one career honour was being chosen the best goalkeeper at the 1958 World Cup in Sweden when Northern Ireland reached the quarter-finals. Gregg, who won 25 international caps, made 247 appearances in nine years for United after signing from Doncaster for £23,500, then a world record for a goalkeeper. He retired in 1967 after half a season at Stoke, then managed Shrewsbury, Swansea, Crewe and Carlisle, while also returning to Old Trafford for a spell as goalkeeping coach under Dave Sexton. Later, Gregg had a testimonial match between United and an Irish League select at Windsor Park and established the Harry Gregg Foundation for young people. He was made an MBE in 1995 and received an OBE in 2019.

BRIAN PILKINGTON, 86, was a key player in Burnley's Football League championship-winning side of season 1959–60 when they finished a point ahead of Wolves and two clear of Tottenham. The outside-left missed only one game and scored 11 goals, including the first in a 2-1 win over Manchester City which clinched the title. He made 340 appearances and netted 77 goals in a decade at the club after signing in 1951. His last two came in a European Cup tie against Hamburg at Turf Moor. Pilkington, who won one England cap when replacing the injured Tom Finney for a Home International against Northern Ireland, spent three years at Bolton, then had spells with Bury and Barrow. In 2018, the Lancashire FA named a stand after him at the County Ground in Leyland.

JIMMY CONWAY, 73, was part of Fulham's FA Cup marathon of 1975. He played in ten of their 12 ties which involved two replays against Hull in round three, three replays against Nottingham Forest in round four and one in the semi-final against Birmingham. Conway was part of the team, captained by Alan Mullery and including Bobby Moore, beaten 2-0 in the final by West Ham. Signed from the Irish club Bohemians, he spent ten years at Craven Cottage, through successive relegations from Division One to Division Three, making 360 appearances and scoring 76 goals from positions at half-back and on the right-wing. He was offered a testimonial, but turned it down, maintaining that Fulham supporters had spent enough money watching him. Conway, who won 20 caps with the Republic of Ireland, eventually joined Manchester City for £40,000 and was part of the team beaten by one point to the Division One tile by Liverpool in 1977. He ended his career in the United States with Portland.

JIMMY WHEELER, 86, made 453 appearances for Reading and scored 168 goals, second to Trevor Senior in their all-time list of marksmen. The inside-forward signed amateur forms with his home-town club in 1952, turned professional a year and was a fixture in the team for more than a decade. His most productive season was 1960–61 with 31 goals in 40 Third Division matches. Wheeler netted all four in a 4-2 win over Southend in 1964, but a broken leg the following campaign ended his Football League career. He was appointed Reading's assistant manager under Roy Bentley, while coaching and captaining the reserves from full-back. After they won the Football Combination's Second Division title in 1966, he was named the club's Player of the Season. Wheeler became manager of Bradford City in 1968, winning their first promotion in 40 years with a fourth-place finish in Division Four on the back of a club-record unbeaten run of 21 games. He spent two more seasons at Valley Parade before resigning.

JIMMY MORAN, 84, was part of the Norwich squad that reached the FA Cup semi-finals in season 1958–59. Then in the Third Division, they defeated Manchester United, Tottenham and Sheffield United on the way to the last four before losing 1-0 to Luton in a replay. Moran, an inside-forward, had three seasons at the club after signing from Leicester. He went on to play for Northampton, Darlington and Workington, then coached and managed non-league sides in East Anglia.

MALCOLM PYKE, 81, was a Second Division title winner with West Ham in season 1957–58. The wing-half, who joined the club as a schoolboy, played in ten of the final 17 matches as his team overhauled Blackburn, Charlton and Liverpool to return to the top-flight under manager Ted Fenton. They finished a point ahead of Blackburn after winning 3-1 at Middlesbrough on the final day. With strong competition for places the following season, including from a young Bobby Moore, Pyke's opportunities were limited and he moved to Crystal Palace, then into non-league with Dartford.

BRIAN JACKSON, 86, made a scoring debut for Liverpool against Bolton in 1951. He made 133 appearances in six years there after starting his career as an amateur with Arsenal, then playing for Leyton Orient. The outside-right left Anfield a year before Bill Shankly arrived to revolutionise the club, helping Port Vale become Division Four champions in season 1958–59, then serving Peterborough, Lincoln Burton and Boston.

PETER MCCALL, 83, sustained a broken ankle in his second game for Bristol City's colts team after joining the club in 1952. The wing-half had to bide his time in the reserves before finally making his debut for the senior side in 1958. Increased competition for places led to a move to Oldham, where he helped win promotion from Division Four as runners-up to Brentford in season 1962–63. McCall then played for Southern League Hereford.

ALAN BASS, 90, was the doctor for England's 1966 World Cup-winning team. The former Harley

Street consultant and head of FIFA's medical committee, was seated next to manager Alf Ramsey at the 4-2 win over West Germany in the final at Wembley. He was also England doctor at the 1970 World Cup in Mexico.

MARCH 2020

PETER WHITTINGHAM, 35, joined the ranks of Cardiff's most famous players of all-time during a decade at the club. A stylish, left-footed playmaker and marksman, he made 459 appearances and scored 98 goals, many of them with spectacular long-range shots. They earned him a place in the Football League's team of the decade for 2005–15 and, three times, selection for the PFA Championship team of the year. The England under 21 international, a £350,000 signing from Aston Villa where he won the FA Youth Cup, was an influential figure in Cardiff's promotion, as champions, to the Premier League in season 2012–13. He helped them reach the 2008 FA Cup Final against Portsmouth (0-1) and the 2012 League Cup Final which Liverpool won on penalties. Whittingham also had spells on loan at Burnley and Derby and finished his career with Blackburn. He died in hospital following a fall.

JOHN HASELDEN, 76, was Mick Buxton's right-hand man as Huddersfield won two promotions to become a force to be reckoned with in football's second tier. His coaching and physiotherapy skills were influential as they became Division Four champions in 1980 and won promotion from the Third Division three years later. Haselden later had spells with Reading, Nottingham Forest, Aston Villa and Notts County. His playing career as a centre-half embraced Rotherham, home-town club Doncaster who won Division Four in season 1968–69, then Mansfield.

MICK MORRIS, 77, played in two Division Four promotion-winning teams. The winger helped Oxford go up in season 1964–65 and was in Port Vale's team elevated in the 1969–70 campaign. Moving on, he helped non-league Stafford reach round four of the FA Cup in 1975 and the following year was in the side beaten 3-2 by Scarborough in the FA Trophy Final.

FREDDIE SMITH, 77, spent more than a decade at Burnley. The full-back made his senior debut in 1963, played in their Inter-Cities Fairs Cup campaign of 1966–67 and had his best season in 1968–69 with 29 league and cup appearances. But over the years he struggled to hold down a regular place because of the consistency of John Angus, eventually moving on to Portsmouth, then playing for Halifax.

ARTHUR MARSH, 72, worked through the ranks after joining Bolton as an apprentice, making his senior debut in season 1966–67 in a 3-1 win at Preston delivered by a Francis Lee hat-trick. He played for four years at full-back or centre-back, then moved to Rochdale and later Darlington.

MICKEY HOLIFIELD, 71, made 566 appearances for Wycombe in their non-league days. The midfield player helped the club to three Isthmian League titles in four years and featured in their run to the third round of the FA Cup in 1975 when they took Jack Charlton's Middlesbrough to a replay before losing 1-0.

APRIL 2020

NORMAN HUNTER, 76, played a key role in the wide-ranging success enjoyed by Leeds over a decade under Don Revie from the mid-1960s. Hunter, who partnered Jack Charlton at the heart of their defence, was told by the manager to win the ball and present it to 'those who can play' – the likes of Billy Bremner, Johnny Giles and Eddie Gray. He carried out the instruction to a tee, earning the nickname 'bites yer legs' and contributing to Revie's side being labelled cynical and intimidating in their pursuit of trophies. One infamous incident involved Derby's Francis Lee, with both players sent off for a punch-up at the Baseball Ground. Yet Hunter was also a skilful and visionary left-footed player, qualities reflected in him becoming the first recipient of the PFA Player of the Year award. Leeds twice become champions of England, heading Liverpool each time, and were runners-up five times. They defeated Arsenal to win the FA Cup, in addition to losing three more finals, and overcame the same opponents to lift the League Cup. There were two successful seasons in the Inter-Cities Fairs Cup, forerunner of the UEFA Cup, with victories in two-leg ties against Ferencvaros, then Juventus. Leeds also reached a European Cup Final, losing to Bayern Munich a year after Revie left to manage England, and a Cup Winners' Cup decider against AC Milan in which Hunter was sent off by Greek referee Christos Michas, who was later banned for match fixing. Hunter won 28 England caps and was member of the 1966 World Cup-winning squad in which team-mate Charlton and Bobby Moore were the first-choice central defensive pair. Four years later in Mexico, he made a brief appearance from the bench in England's quarter-final defeat by West Germany. The qualifying campaign for 1974 brought the worst moment of his career – a mistake which contributed to Alf Ramsey's side conceding a goal to Poland at Wembley and failing to qualify for the finals in West Germany. After 726 appearances for Leeds, a club he joined at 15, Hunter had three years at Bristol City, led Barnsley to promotion from Division Three in his first season as manager and also managed Rotherham. He later coached at West Bromwich Albion and Bradford City. He died in hospital after contracting the COVID-19.

PETER BONETTI, 78, had neither the height nor the build normally associated with a top-class goalkeeper, but compensated with great agility, anticipation and bravery during a distinguished 19-year career with Chelsea which earned him the nickname 'The Cat.' It spanned 729 matches and embraced domestic and European honours which offset the one bitter disappointment experienced while playing for England. Bonetti's first trophy was the FA Youth Cup; the second the 1965 League Cup, achieved with a 3-2 aggregate victory over Leicester, who had Gordon Banks in goal. Arguably his finest moments came in the 1970 FA Cup Final against Leeds, with brilliant saves earning a 2-2 draw at Wembley, followed by a repeat performance in the 2-1 replay victory at Old Trafford, despite a wrenched knee sustained in the first few minutes. That same year, Banks was laid low by food poisoning and Bonetti came in for England's World Cup quarter-final against West Germany in the searing Mexican heat of Leon. They led 2-0 before a mistake, which he freely admitted, allowed Franz Beckenbauer to pull back a goal which changed the course of the game. He was also blamed for Uwe Seeler's equaliser and the eventual 3-2 defeat for Sir Alf Ramsey's side was Bonetti's seventh and final appearance for the national side, five of which were clean sheets. The following year he was a winner again as Chelsea defeated Real Madrid 2-1 in a replay in Athens to lift the European Cup Winners' Cup. There was to be one more final, the League Cup in 1972, which his side lost 2-1 to Stoke, with Banks once more in the opposite goal. Bonetti left Stamford Bridge on a free transfer for St Louis in the United States in 1975, but was back the following year to help former team-mate Eddie McCreadie's young side regain a place in the top flight. His final appearance came against Arsenal in April 1979 when only Ron Harris (795) had played more times for the club. And it was not until 2014 that his record of 208 clean sheets was overtaken by Petr Cech. He came out of retirement briefly with Dundee United, then, at 45, with non-league Woking. After that there were spells as goalkeeping coach back at Chelsea, Newcastle, Fulham, Manchester City and England. His last medal came in 2009 when the non-playing members of England's World Cup-winning squad of 1966, were at last recognised.

TREVOR CHERRY, 72, had a distinguished career for club and country, beginning with home-town Huddersfield, where he won the Second Division title in season 1969–70 and attracted the attention of Leeds manager Don Revie, who saw him as the long-term replacement for Jack Charlton. A £100,000 move took him to Elland Road, where he covered for the injured Terry Cooper at full-back before forging a partnership at the heart of the defence with Norman Hunter. It helped deliver the 1973–74 League Championship when Leeds finished five points ahead of Liverpool. There was an FA Cup Final in which Cherry's header produced the first of two remarkable saves from Jim Montgomery in Sunderland's against-the-odds victory. Another 1-0 defeat came against AC Milan in that year's Cup Winners' Cup Final. Two years later, he played a key role in the European Cup semi-final win over Barcelona by marking Johan Cruyff effectively in both legs. But it was followed by a major disappointment when Jimmy Armfield left him out of the side beaten 2-0 by Bayern Munich in the final. Cherry, given the captaincy after Billy Bremner's departure, made 486 appearances in a decade at the club and won 27 England caps, the first against Wales, the last against Spain in a European Championship group match. He left to become player-manager at Bradford City, leading the club to the 1984–85 Division Three title – a success which turned to tragedy on the final day of the season when, approaching half-time of the match against Lincoln, fire broke out destroying the main stand and 56 people died. Cherry was heavily involved in supporting families of the victims, attending funerals and visiting survivors in hospital. City were struggling when they returned to Valley Parade 19 months later, having played home games at other grounds, He was sacked soon after – a decision which provoked demonstrations by supporters against the board. He died 19 days after Norman Hunter passed away.

MICHAEL ROBINSON, 61, was a treble winner in his one full season with Liverpool, a frustrated onlooker with Brighton at Wembley and a successful broadcaster abroad during an eventful career on and off the pitch. The striker made 24 league appearances as the club he supported as a boy claimed a third successive title in 1983–84, three points clear of Southampton and six ahead of Nottingham Forest. He came off the bench during their League Cup success against Everton and replaced Kenny Dalglish as Joe Fagan's side overcame Roma on penalties in the European Cup Final. Robinson previously played for Preston and Manchester City, then scored an FA Cup semi-final winner for Brighton against Sheffield Wednesday. In the final, he presented Gordon Smith with the chance of a late winner, but saw his team-mate denied by goalkeeper Gary Bailey, whose save earned Manchester United a replay which they won easily. After leaving Liverpool for regular first-team football, the Republic of Ireland international, capped 24 times, returned to Wembley with Queens Park Rangers, who lost to Oxford in the League Cup. He finished playing in La Liga with Osasuna, learning the language there and becoming an influential voice in Spanish football. Robinson, who was diagnosed with skin cancer in 2018, continued working to the end, with Liverpool's Champions League tie against Atletico Madrid his final game.

RON WYLIE, 86, was an influential figure in Midlands football with nearly 700 appearances over nearly two decades after first making his mark as a Scottish schoolboy international. The inside-forward followed eight years at Notts County with a move to Aston Villa in 1958, helping the club return to the top flight as Division Two champions and to lift the inaugural League Cup with a 3-2 aggregate win over Rotherham in the final. He had five years at Birmingham from 1965, retiring at the age of 37 and becoming assistant manager under Gordon Milne at Coventry. Wylie coached in Cyprus and Hong Kong, had 19 months as manager of West Bromwich Albion after succeeding Ronnie Allen and resumed his affinity with Villa as reserve team manager, scout and community liaison officer.

RADDY ANTIC, 71, achieved hero status at Luton with the goal which preserved the club's place in the top flight at the end of season 1982–83. They were on the verge of an immediate return to the old Second Division when the Yugoslav midfielder's volley from the edge of the penalty box five minutes from the end delivered 1-0 win at Maine Road which relegated Manchester City instead. Manager David Pleat also won a place in Luton folklore by dancing a jig of delight across the pitch at the final whistle. Antic, who previously played for Partizan Belgrade, Fenerbahce and Real Zaragoza, had another year at the club before becoming the only coach to take charge of Real Madrid, Atletico Madrid and Barcelona. Highspot was the league and cup double with Atletico in 1996. Antic also led Serbia into the 2010 World Cup in South Africa.

RAY HIRON, 76, spent 11 years as a free-scoring centre forward with Portsmouth after being spotted playing non-league football for Fareham. At the time he also worked in the city's dockyard and hitched a lift on a friend's motorbike to sign professional forms at Fratton Park during his lunch break in 1964. Hiron scored 117 goals in 364 appearances, four of them in a 5-2 win over Norwich in the old Second Division. He also netted both goals in victory over Southampton in his testimonial match. Hiron then captained Reading to promotion from Division Four in his first season with the club.

PETER MADDEN, 85, attracted the attention of Liverpool manager Bill Shankly with his ability to play in several positions. Rotherham turned down two bids and also rejected an approach from Fulham for a player who operated at left-back, inside-left and centre-forward before settling in central defence. Madden made 353 appearances in a decade at the club, including the 1960–61 season when they were close to lifting their first major trophy, beating Aston Villa 2-0 in the first leg of the inaugural League Cup Final, then losing the return 3-0. He returned to his home town to play for Bradford Park Avenue and ended his career at Aldershot. After that, he managed Darlington and Rochdale for three years each.

JIMMY GOODFELLOW, 76, won the FA Amateur Cup with Crook Town after being released by Newcastle at 17, scoring the equaliser in their 2-1 win over Enfield in the 1964 final at Wembley. In the professional ranks, he helped Rotherham to promotion from Division Four in season 1974–75 and to within goal difference of another move up two years later. The inside-forward also played for Port Vale, Workington and Stockport, then had a long association with Cardiff as manager, coach, trainer and physio which earned him a testimonial against Manchester United.

ALF WOOD, 74, developed into a free-scoring centre-forward after Shrewsbury manager Harry Gregg switched him from central defence. He netted 40 goals in all competitions in season 1971–72, including five in a 7-1 win over Blackburn, leading to a £45,000 move to Millwall. Wood, who started his career at Manchester City, moved on to Hull for a club-record £75,000 then played for Middlesbrough and Walsall. He finished his career with both goals for Stafford in their 1979 FA Trophy Final win over Kettering.

CYRIL LAWRENCE, 99, was Blackpool's oldest surviving player. He died six weeks before turning 100 after contracting the coronavirus. Prior to the outbreak of war in 1939, with the club top of the First Division, the promising inside-forward was close to breaking into their senior squad. When the conflict ended, he joined joined Rochdale, then played for Wrexham before a knee injury ended his career at the age of 31.

JOHN COLLINS, 71, came through the youth ranks at Tottenham and made his Football League debut against Sunderland in 1966. Amid strong competition for places at full-back, he made only one further senior appearance, moved on to Portsmouth, then played for Dallas in the United States, Halifax and Sheffield Wednesday. The Wales under-23 international finished his league career at Barnsley, where he was an ever-present in the side promoted from Division Four in season 1978–79.

DAVE BACUZZI, 79, was an England youth international full-back who helped Manchester City to the Second Division title in season 1965–66 after joining from Arsenal. Bacuzzi, whose father Joe played for Fulham, moved on to Reading, then became player-manager of Cork Hibernians, leading the club to championship and cup success in the League of Ireland in the early 1970s.

SID BISHOP, 86, twice won promotion during 13 years with Leyton Orient. The centre-half played in the Third Division South title-winning side of season 1955–56 and was an ever-present as Orient reached the old First Division as runners-up to Liverpool in the 1961–62 campaign. Bishop made 323 appearances for the club up to 1965 when he became player-manager of Southern League Hastings.

DICKIE DOWSETT, 88, started his career at Tottenham, scoring against Aston Villa on his only senior appearance for the club in 1954. The centre-forward moved on to Southend, then played for Southampton, Crystal Palace and Bournemouth, where he was top scorer in three successive seasons, including 1961–62 when his team came close to promotion from Division Three. He later became commercial manager and was instrumental in changing the club's name from Bournemouth and Boscombe Athletic to AFC Bournemouth.

SHAY KEOGH, 85, was a Republic of Ireland international centre-half who won three league titles and the FAI Cup with Shamrock Rovers in the 1950s. He also played for Dundalk and was player-manager at St Patrick's. His one cap came against Poland in 1958.

PETER PHOENIX, 83, experienced Stockport's bitter-sweet season of 1964–65. The club finished bottom of the old Fourth Division and had to apply – successfully – for re-election to the Football League. In the FA Cup, however, they reached the fourth round and held Liverpool 1-1 at Anfield before losing the replay 2-0. Phoenix, a left-winger previously played for Southport, Exeter, Rochdale and Oldham.

JOHN ROWLANDS, 73, played for eight Football League clubs and for teams in the United States and South Africa, either at centre-forward or in the defence. He began a 13-year career at Mansfield in 1967, then had spells with Torquay, Exeter, Stockport, Barrow, Workington, Crewe and Hartlepool. Abroad, he played for Seattle, San Jose, Oakland, Tulsa and Cape Town.

BILLY WRIGHT, 89, spent five years with home-town club Blackpool, playing the majority of his games in the reserves but also deputising when needed on the right-wing for Stanley Matthews. He moved to Leicester in 1955, then served Newcastle, Plymouth and Millwall.

DON WOAN, 92, made his debut for Liverpool at Derby in 1951 and played again the following week against Everton at Anfield. They were his only two senior appearances. He moved on to Leyton Orient and also had spells at Bradford City, Tranmere and Yeovil.

JOHN MURPHY, 77, made a record 459 league appearance for Ayr United between 1963–78. When the left-back was inducted into the club's Hall of Fame, Sir Alex Ferguson, who ended his playing career at the club, sent a video tribute to his former team-mate.

DAVE CORBETT, 79, was a right-winger who played for Swindon between 1958–62, then had five years at Plymouth before injuries forced him to retire at 26.

RICKY MOIR, 74, joined Shrewsbury from Scottish junior football and spent five years at the club. The inside-forward then played for Halifax before a hip injury ended his career.

IAN STOTT, 86, was chairman of Oldham from 1982–98, overseeing some of club's best years. Under Joe Royle they were promoted as Second Division champions in 1991 and spent two seasons in the top flight, including the inaugural Premier League campaign. Oldham also reached the 1990 League Cup Final, losing 1-0 to Nottingham Forest, and the FA Cup semi-finals four years later. Stott served on the board of the FA and Football League management committee.

BRIAN ARROWSMITH, 79, made 580 appearances for Barrow in two spells between 1961–77. The right-back's first included promotion from the Fourth Division. His second, after a spell with Northern Premier Netherfield, came as player-manager, with his home-town club having been voted out of the Football League in 1972. In 2017, Arrowsmith had the main stand named after him at the Holker Street ground.

ALLAN GAUDEN, 75, was part of Grimsby's Fourth Division title-winning side under Lawrie McMenemy in season 1971–72. The winger previously played for Darlington and Sunderland and later had spells with Hartlepool and Gillingham.

MAY 2020

GLYN PARDOE, 73, became Manchester City's younger-ever player when making his debut against Birmingham, aged 15 years and 314 days, in 1962. He went on to win domestic and European trophies under Joe Mercer and Malcolm Allison, beginning with the League title in 1968 when his side finished two points ahead of Manchester United and three clear of Liverpool. Pardoe, a versatile, right-footed left-back who was able to fill other positions, lifted the FA Cup the following year when City defeated Leicester 1-0. He scored the extra-time winner when they beat West Bromwich Albion 2-1 in the 1970 League Cup Final, followed by victory by the same scoreline against Polish team Gornik Zabrze in the Cup-Winners' Cup Final in Vienna. There was another Wembley appearance in 1974, this time in the side beaten 2-1 by Wolves in the League Cup. The England under-23 international, who was rated unlucky never to win a full cap, made 380 appearances for the club, retiring in 1976 having spent nearly two years recovering from a broken leg sustained in a tackle with George Best in a Manchester derby. He later joined City's coaching staff. Pardoe's grandson, 18-year-old midfielder Tommy Doyle, played his first game for the club in a League Cup tie against Southampton in October 2019.

JOHN OGILVIE, 91, played a key role in Hibernian's Scottish title win in season 1950–51 when they finished ten points ahead of Rangers. But he sustained a career-changing double leg break in a Scottish Cup semi-final against Motherwell, took two years to recover and made only one more appearance for the club. The left-back joined Leicester, helping the club return to the top flight as Second Division champions ahead of Nottingham Forest and Liverpool in the 1956–57 campaign, then had a spell with Mansfield.

JOHN RIDLEY, 67, made 310 appearances in two spells with Port Vale. The first included a Player of the Year award and led to a then club-record £55,000 move in 1978 to Leicester, where he played in Gary Lineker's debut match. Ridley, at home in central defence or midfield, returned to Vale Park after a spell with Chesterfield and was part of the Fourth Division promotion-winning side of 1982-83. He was then player-coach at Stafford.

CHRISTIAN MBULU, 23, signed professional forms with Millwall in 2015 and had three seasons at the club. The defender moved on to Motherwell and Crewe, then joined Morecambe in the 2020 winter transfer window and made three appearances before the League Two season was abandoned.

PAUL SHRUBB, 64, was a utility player who featured in two Division Four promotion-winning teams. He went up with Brentford in season 1977–78 and play-off winners Aldershot, who defeated Wolves in the 1986–87 final. Shrubb, who started his career at Fulham, then had a spell in South Africa with Hellenic, returned to the new, non-league Aldershot Town club in 1992 and also scouted for Charlton, AFC Wimbledon and Plymouth.

JUNE 2020

TONY DUNNE, 78, won domestic and European honours during a distinguished 13-year career at left-back with Manchester United. Matt Busby signed him in 1960 after the Irishman helped Shelbourne lift the FAI Cup. Dunne was an FA Cup winner against Leicester (3-1) in 1963 and part of two League championship sides – in 1964-65 when United headed Leeds on goal average and two seasons later when they were four points clear of Nottingham Forest. He also played a key role in United becoming the first English team to win the European Cup when beating Benfica 4-1 at Wembley in 1968. Dunne, capped 33 times by the Republic of Ireland, four as captain, was given a free transfer after 535 appearances. He spent the next five years with Bolton, winning the Second Division title in 1978, and finished in the United States near Detroit. There were two years as Bolton's assistant manager, along with a spell in charge of the Norwegian club Steinkjer, where he took over from former United team-mate Bill Foulkes.

THEO FOLEY, 83, served ten league clubs as player, manager, coach and scout in a career spanning nearly half a century. Pride of place was his role as George Graham's assistant in Arsenal's dramatic title triumph in season 1988–89 when they beat Liverpool 2-0 at Anfield in the final match to finish top on goals scored after both clubs had identical records. The pair were previously at Millwall and towards the end of his career Foley was reunited with Graham in backroom roles at Leeds and Tottenham. In between, the Irishman coached at Queens Park Rangers, Fulham and Southend, as well as managing Northampton, the club where he won two promotions as a player on their rise from the Fourth to the First Division. Foley, a full-back, also had spells at Exeter and Charlton after starting out at the Dublin club Home Farm. He won nine Republic of Ireland caps.

JIM FRYATT, 79, was a much-travelled centre-forward credited with scoring the Football League's fastest-ever goal. It came after four seconds of Bradford Park Avenue's Fourth Division match against Tranmere in April 1965. Referee Bob Simons was quoted as saying afterwards: 'I blew my whistle for the start and still had my stopwatch in my hand when the ball entered the net.' Another scoring feat was a ten-minute hat-trick for Southport against Darlington in their Fourth Division title-winning season of 1972–73. The player nicknamed 'Pancho' because of his swarthy looks, had two spells at the club, along with two at Torquay and Stockport. He also played for Charlton, Southend, Blackburn and Oldham. In a an 18-year career starting in 1957, Fryatt scored 187 league goals in 498 appearances, alongside helping Philadelphia win the North American Soccer League in 1973.

RON THOMPSON, 88, made 406 appearances for home-town club Carlisle between 1951–64 – a record for an outfield player. They included the Fourth Division promotion-winning season of 1963-64 when his side finished level on 60 points with Gillingham, who became champions with a superior goal average. The wing-half's career was ended the following season by an achilles injury.

RALPH WRIGHT, 72, played for six Football League clubs, including Bolton where he helped Jimmy Armfield's side win the Third Division title in season 1972–73. He also had spells with Norwich, Bradford Park Avenue, Hartlepool, Stockport and Southport. Wright, a winger, finished his career in the United States – at New York Cosmos alongside Pele, Miami and Dallas.

HARRY PENK, 85, was part of Plymouth's Division Three title-winning team of season 1958–59, scoring in a 1-1 draw at Accrington which ensured promotion. The right-winger started out at home-town club Wigan, in their non-league days, had First Division football with Portsmouth, then after leaving Plymouth played for Southampton.

JULY 2020

JACK CHARLTON, 85, had a simple footballing philosophy. 'Unlike my brother Bobby, I can't play,' he said. 'He's creative. My job is the stop other people playing. There is a place in the game for both types.' Throughout his career, the 6ft 2in centre-half did what he did best to great effect for club and country, reaching the pinnacle in the 1966 World Cup Final against West Germany. It was captured by the iconic images of Jack joyfully dropping to the Wembley turf on his knees and Bobby shedding tears after Geoff Hurst's goal sealed a 4-2 win for England. Charlton won his first cap a year earlier, aged 29, and went on to play for his country 35 times, a perfect foil alongside the classy Bobby Moore at the heart of the defence. In 1967, he followed his brother as the footballer writers' Footballer of the Year. Charlton made a record-equalling 773 appearances, the same as Billy Bremner, in a 21-year career with Leeds, his only club. They were Second Division champions in 1963-64 and won the top-flight title in 1968-69, ahead of Liverpool and Everton. His other successes came in the 1968 League Cup and 1972 FA Cup, with 1-0 wins against Arsenal in both finals, alongside Fairs Cup victories over Ferencvaros (1968) and Juventus (1971). Leeds fell just short on numerous other occasions – title runners-up five times, FA Cup beaten finalists twice, and Fairs Cup once. After retiring in 1973, he led Middlesbrough and Sheffield Wednesday to promotion and also managed Newcastle. Then, he was hailed for 'changing Irish football forever' by taking the Republic to their first major finals at Euro 88 and to the quarter-finals of the World Cup in Italia 90. Charlton, who won an OBE, was the sixth member of England's 1966 team to pass away after Moore, Alan Ball, Ray Wilson, Gordon Banks and Martin Peters. In recent months, Leeds also lost Norman Hunter and Trevor Cherry.

ALEX DAWSON, 80, played a key role in Manchester United's team rebuilding after the 1958 Munich air crash which claimed the lives of eight players returning from a European Cup tie in Belgrade. The centre-forward, who was not selected for that ill-fated trip, lined up alongside two of the survivors, goalkeeper Harry Gregg and defender Bill Foulkes, for the club's first match following the tragedy. He scored in a 3-0 win over Sheffield Wednesday and netted a hat-trick in that season's 5-3 FA Cup semi-final victory over Fulham at Highbury. Dawson, who played in the final which Bolton won 2-0, came through the club's youth ranks under Matt Busby, scored on his senior debut against Burnley and was part of the League championship-winning team of season 1956–57. He scored 54 goals in 93 appearances for United and had another impressive tally in six years spent with Preston – 114 goals in 197 matches. One came in the 1964 FA Cup Final when he was again on the losing side – 2-3 against West Ham. Dawson later had spells with Bury, Brighton and Brentford before retiring in 1973.

GERRY HARRIS, 84, won two League titles and the FA Cup during Wolves's glory days. The tough-tackling left-back was a key member of Stan Cullis's team that finished five points ahead of Preston in 1957–58 and six clear of Manchester United the following season. He was part of the 3-0 Wembley success against Blackburn in 1960 and played in all their European Cup matches. Harris made 270 appearances in a decade in the first-team, leaving the club in 1966 for Walsall, where injury ended his career.

PAT QUINN, 84, featured in one of Hibernian's finest performances in Europe – overturning a 4-1 first-leg deficit against Napoli in the 1967-68 Fairs Cup, forerunner of the UEFA Cup. They won the return match 5-0, with Quinn scoring the second goal on the way a third round tie against Leeds, who won it 2-1 on aggregate. The following season, his side reached the League Cup final, losing 6-2 to Celtic. Previously, the inside-forward won four Scotland caps with Motherwell, then joined Blackpool in a £34,000 move. He also had spells with Albion and East Fife.

ALAN GARNER, 69, joined Luton from Millwall and played a major role in winning promotion to the old First Division as runners-up to Middlesbrough in season 1973–74. Their stay in the top-flight lasted a single season and the defender was sold to Watford, where he won a player-of-the-year award during five seasons at the club. Garner finished his career at Portsmouth.

DAVID HAGEN, 47, started his career with Rangers and was part of the squad that achieved a domestic treble in season 1992–93. The Scotland under-21 midfielder moved on to Hearts, then played for Falkirk in the 1997 Scottish Cup Final which his side lost 1-0 to Kilmarnock. In that same season, he scored the only goal of the Challenge Cup Final against Queen of the South. Hagen, who was diagnosed with motor neurone disease, won the First Division title with Livingston and with Clyde scored the fastest goal of the 2001–02 season, after 16 seconds, against Raith. His last senior club was Peterhead.

DON TOWNSEND, 89, father of former Republic of Ireland midfielder Andy Townsend, made 249 league appearances in eight years with Charlton. The left-back then helped Crystal Palace to promotion from Division Three, as runners-up to Coventry, in season 1963–64.

JOHN TALBUT, 79, won the FA Cup with West Bromwich Albion, who defeated Everton 1-0 after extra-time at Wembley in 1968 with a goal from Jeff Astle. He was back there two years later for the League Cup Final against Manchester City which his side lost 2-1. That came at the end of his time with the club when he handed over the centre-half position to a young John Wile and became player-manager of the Belgian club Mechelen. Talbut joined Albion in a £30,000 move from Burnley, where he was close to selection for Alf Ramsey's England team until an injury sustained while playing for the under-23 side ruled him out of their summer tour of 1964.

DANNY CAMPBELL, 76, was a long-standing understudy to John Talbut and Stan Jones at The Hawthorns. He came in for the 1966 League Cup Final against West Ham, when Talbut was cup-tied, and played in both legs which Albion won 5-3 on aggregate against a team featuring Bobby Moore, Geoff Hurst and Martin Peters. Campbell left the following year for Los Angeles, returning for spells with Stockport and Bradford Park Avenue, then building a new life in South Africa, where he played for Port Elizabeth.

TOM FORSYTH, 71, joined Rangers after five years at Motherwell and marked his first season with the winner in the 1973 Scottish Cup Final against Celtic (3-2) watched by a crowd of 122,000 at Hampden Park. It was the start of a trophy-laden ten years at Ibrox for the central defender, who shared three League titles, four Scottish Cups and two League Cups. Forsyth also collected 22 international caps and played in all three of Scotland's group matches at the 1978 World Cup in Argentina against Peru, Iran and Holland. He made 326 appearances for Rangers, then managed Dunfermline before spells as former team-mate Tommy McLean's assistant at Morton, Motherwell and Hearts. They included Motherwell's 4-3 victory, after extra-time, against Dundee United in the 1991 Scottish Cup Final.

KEITH PONTIN, 64, won the first of two Wales caps in their first home win over England for 25 years. Under Mike England, they defeated Ron Greenwood's side 4-1 in a Home International match at the Racecourse Ground, Wrexham in 1980. Pontin made his second appearance four days later in a 1-0 defeat by Scotland. The central defender came through the youth ranks at Cardiff, making his senior debut on the opening day of season 1976–77 against Charlton. He made 40 appearances in 1981–82, more than anyone else, but was unable to prevent Cardiff being relegated from the old Second Division and left the club for Merthyr Tydfil after falling out with manager Len Ashurst.

TOMMY CARROLL, 77 was a Republic of Ireland international who helped Ipswich win the Second Division title in season 1967–68, one point ahead of Queens Park Rangers and Blackpool. He also played for Birmingham and Cambridge City before returning to Shelbourne, where he previously had league and cup success. Carroll, who won 17 caps, also managed the Irish club.

WILLIE HUNTER, 80, scored on his debut for Scotland – a 3-3 draw against Hungary in 1960. The inside-forward won two further caps, against Turkey and Wales, during a decade at Motherwell. Hunter made nearly 300 appearances there and was regarded as one of the club's finest players. He also served Hibernian, along with spells at Detroit in the United States and Hellenic and Cape Town in South Africa. Later, he managed Queen of the South and the old Inverness Caledonian and was assistant to former team-mate Ian St John at Portsmouth.

ERNIE PHYTHIAN, 78, was an England youth international who played for Hartlepool during Brian Clough's first spell as a manger between 1965–67. The centre-forward, who joined the club after spells with Bolton and Wrexham, scored 51 goals in124 games before falling out with Clough's successor, Gus McLean, and moving to South Africa where he played for Southern Suburbs.

MIKE TINDALL, 79, was an England youth international who played alongside Bobby Moore for England at the 1958 World Youth Cup. The inside-forward spent nine years at his boyhood club Aston Villa, then played for Walsall.

JACKIE WREN, 84, spent four years at the start of his career with Hibernian, where his chances were limited because of the form of future Scotland goalkeeper Lawrie Leslie. After brief spells in England with Southend and Rotherham, he returned to Scotland to serve Stirling, Falkirk, Dundee United and Berwick, then moved to South Africa to play for Hellenic and Cape Town.

COLIN PARRY, 79, missed only one game in Rochdale's first promotion season when they finished third in the old Fourth Division in 1968–69. The centre-half was also involved, although to a lesser extent, in home-town Stockport's title win in that division two years earlier, restricted to a handful of appearances because of strong competition for places. Parry had a loan spell at Bradford City and finished his career with non-league Macclesfield and Morecambe.

RECORDS SECTION

GOALSCORING
(†Football League pre-1992–93)

Highest: Arbroath 36 Bon Accord (Aberdeen) 0 in Scottish Cup 1, Sep 12, 1885. On same day, also in Scottish Cup 1, Dundee Harp beat Aberdeen Rov 35-0.

Internationals: France 0 England 15 in Paris, 1906 (Amateur); Ireland 0 England 13 in Belfast Feb 18, 1882 (record in UK); England 9 Scotland 3 at Wembley, Apr 15, 1961; Biggest England win at Wembley: 9-0 v Luxembourg (Euro Champ), Dec 15, 1982.

Other record wins: Scotland: 11-0 v Ireland (Glasgow, Feb 23, 1901); **Northern Ireland:** 7-0 v Wales (Belfast, Feb 1, 1930); **Wales:** 11-0 v Ireland (Wrexham, Mar 3, 1888); **Rep of Ireland:** 8-0 v Malta (Euro Champ, Dublin, Nov 16, 1983).

Record international defeats: England: 1-7 v Hungary (Budapest, May 23, 1954); **Scotland:** 3-9 v England (Wembley, Apr 15, 1961); **Ireland:** 0-13 v England (Belfast, Feb 18, 1882); **Wales:** 0-9 v Scotland (Glasgow, Mar 23, 1878); **Rep of Ireland:** 0-7 v Brazil (Uberlandia, May 27, 1982).

World Cup: Qualifying round – Australia 31 American Samoa 0, world record international score (Apr 11, 2001); Australia 22 Tonga 0 (Apr 9, 2001); Iran 19 Guam 0 (Nov 25, 2000); Maldives 0 Iran 17 (Jun 2, 1997). **Finals – highest scores:** Hungary 10 El Salvador 1 (Spain, Jun 15, 1982); Hungary 9 S Korea 0 (Switzerland, Jun 17, 1954); Yugoslavia 9 Zaire 0 (W Germany, Jun 18, 1974).

European Championship: Qualifying round – highest scorers: San Marino 0 Germany 13 (Serravalle, Sep 6, 2006). **Finals – highest score:** Holland 6 Yugoslavia 1 (quarter-final, Rotterdam, Jun 25, 2000).

Biggest England U-21 win: 9-0 v San Marino (Shrewsbury, Nov 19, 2013).

FA Cup: Preston 26 Hyde 0 1st round, Oct 15, 1887.

League Cup: West Ham 10 Bury 0 (2nd round, 2nd leg, Oct 25, 1983); Liverpool 10 Fulham 0 (2nd round, 1st leg, Sep 23, 1986). **Record aggregates:** Liverpool 13 Fulham 2 (10-0h, 3-2a), Sep 23, Oct 7, 1986; West Ham 12 Bury 1 (2-1a, 10-0h), Oct 4, 25, 1983; Liverpool 11 Exeter 0 (5-0h, 6-0a), Oct 7, 28, 1981.

League Cup – most goals in one match: 12 Reading 5 Arsenal 7 aet (4th round, Oct 30, 2012). Dagenham & Redbridge 6 Brentford 6 aet (Brentford won 4-2 on pens; 1st round, Aug 12, 2014

Premier League (beginning 1992–93): Manchester Utd 9 Ipswich 0, Mar 4, 1995. **Record away win:** Southampton 0 Leicester 9, Oct 25, 2019.

Highest aggregate scores in Premier League – 11: Portsmouth 7 Reading 4, Sep 29, 2007; **10:** Tottenham 6 Reading 4, Dec 29, 2007; Tottenham 9 Wigan 1, Nov 22, 2009; Manchester Utd 8 Arsenal 2, Aug 28, 2011; Arsenal 7 Newcastle 3, Dec 29, 2012; WBA 5 Manchester Utd 5, May 19, 2013.

Big back-to-back wins: Manchester City became the first Premier League team to score five or more goals in three successive matches in the same season – beating Liverpool 5-0, Watford 6-0 and Crystal Palace 5-0 in September 2017. Chelsea also scored heavily in the last game of the 2009-10 season (Wigan 8-0) and in the first two fixtures of the following campaign (WBA 6-0, Wigan 6-0).

†**Football League (First Division):** Aston Villa 12 Accrington 2, Mar 12, 1892; Tottenham 10 Everton 4, Oct 11, 1958 (highest Div 1 aggregate that century); WBA 12 Darwen 0, Apr 4, 1892; Nottm Forest 12 Leicester Fosse 0, Apr 21, 1909. **Record away win:** Newcastle 1 Sunderland 9, Dec 5, 1908; Cardiff 1 Wolves 9, Sep 3, 1955; Wolves 0 WBA 8, Dec 27, 1893.

New First Division (beginning 1992–93): Bolton 7 Swindon 0, Mar 8, 1997; Sunderland 7 Oxford Utd 0, Sep 19, 1998. **Record away win:** Stoke 0 Birmingham 7, Jan 10, 1998; Oxford Utd 0 Birmingham 7, Dec 12, 1998. **Record aggregate:** Grimsby 6 Burnley 5, Oct 29, 2002; Burnley 4 Watford 7, Apr 5, 2003.

Championship (beginning 2004–05): Birmingham 0 Bournemouth 8, Oct 25, 2014. **Record away win:** Birmingham 0 Bournemouth 8, Oct 25, 2014. **Record aggregate:** Leeds 3 Preston 6, Sep 29, 2010; Leeds 3 Nottm Forest 7, Mar 20, 2012; Bristol City 5 Hull 5, Apr 21, 2018. Aston Villa 5 Nottm Forest 5, Nov 28, 2018.

†**Second Division:** Newcastle 13 Newport Co 0, Oct 5, 1946; Small Heath 12 Walsall Town Swifts 0, Dec 17, 1892; Darwen 12 Walsall 0, Dec 26, 1896; Woolwich Arsenal 12 Loughborough 0, Mar 12, 1900; Small Heath 12 Doncaster 0, Apr 11, 1903. **Record away win:** *Burslem Port Vale 0 Sheffield Utd 10, Dec 10, 1892. **Record aggregate:** Manchester City 11 Lincoln 3, Mar 23, 1895.

New Second Division (beginning 1992–93): Hartlepool 1 Plymouth Argyle 8, May 7, 1994; Hartlepool 8 Grimsby 1, Sep 12, 2003.

New League 1 (beginning 2004–05): MK Dons 7 Oldham 0, Dec 20, 2014; Oxford 0 Wigan 7, Dec 23, 2017. **Record aggregate:** Hartlepool 4 Wrexham 6, Mar 5, 2005; Wolves 6 Rotherham 4, Apr 18, 2014; Bristol City 8 Walsall 2, May 3, 2015.

†**Third Division:** Gillingham 10 Chesterfield 0, Sep 5, 1987; Tranmere 9 Accrington 0, Apr 18, 1959; Brentford 9 Wrexham 0, Oct 15, 1963. **Record away win:** Halifax 0 Fulham 8, Sep 16, 1969. **Record aggregate:** Doncaster 7 Reading 5, Sep 25, 1982.

New Third Division (beginning 1992–93): Barnet 1 Peterborough 9, Sep 5, 1998. **Record aggregate:** Hull 7 Swansea 4, Aug 30, 1997.

New League 2 (beginning 2004–05): Peterborough 7 Brentford 0, Nov 24, 2007 Shrewsbury 7 Gillingham 0, Sep 13, 2008; Crewe 7 Barnet 0, Aug 21, 2010; Crewe 8 Cheltenham 1, Apr 2, 2011; Cambridge 7 Morecambe 0, Apr 19, 2016; Luton 7 Cambridge 0, Nov 18, 2017. **Record away win:** Boston 0 Grimsby 6, Feb 3, 2007; Macclesfield 0 Darlington 6, Aug 30, 2008; Lincoln 0 Rotherham 6, Mar 25, 2011; Accrington 7 Gillingham 4, Oct 2, 2010. **Record aggregate:** Burton 5 Cheltenham 6, Mar 13, 2010; Accrington 7 Gillingham 4, Oct 2, 2010.

†**Third Division (North):** Stockport 13 Halifax 0 (still joint biggest win in Football League – see Div 2) Jan 6, 1934; Tranmere 13 Oldham 4, Dec 26, 1935. (17 is highest Football League aggregate score). **Record away win:** Accrington 0 Barnsley 9, Feb 3, 1934.

†**Third Division (South):** Luton 12 Bristol Rov 0, Apr 13, 1936; Bristol City 9 Gillingham 4, Jan 15, 1927; Gillingham 9 Exeter 4, Jan 7, 1951. **Record away win:** Northampton 0 Walsall 8, Apr 8, 1947.

†**Fourth Division:** Oldham 11 Southport 0, Dec 26, 1962. **Record away win:** Crewe 1 Rotherham 8, Sep 8, 1973. **Record aggregate:** Hartlepool 10 Barrow 1, Apr 4, 1959; Crystal Palace 9 Accrington 2, Aug 20, 1960; Wrexham 10 Hartlepool 1, Mar 3, 1962; Oldham 11 Southport 0, Dec 26, 1962; Torquay 8 Newport 3, Oct 19, 1963; Shrewsbury 7 Doncaster 4, Feb 1, 1975; Barnet 4 Crewe 7, Aug 17, 1991.

Scottish Premier – Highest aggregate: 12: Motherwell 6 Hibernian 6, May 5, 2010; **11:** Celtic 8 Hamilton 3, Jan 3, 1987; Motherwell 5 Aberdeen 6, Oct 20, 1999. **Other highest team scores:** Aberdeen 8 Motherwell 0 (Mar 26, 1979); Hamilton 0 Celtic 8 (Nov 5, 1988); Celtic 9 Aberdeen 0 (Nov 6, 2010).

Scottish League Div 1: Celtic 11 Dundee 0, Oct 26, 1895. **Record away win:** Hibs 11 *Airdrie 1, Oct 24, 1959.

Scottish League Div 2: Airdrieonians 15 Dundee Wanderers 1, Dec 1, 1894 (biggest win in history of League football in Britain).

Record modern Scottish League aggregate: 12 – Brechin 5 Cowdenbeath 7, Div 2, Jan 18, 2003.

Record British score since 1900: Stirling 20 Selkirk 0 (Scottish Cup 1, Dec 8, 1984). Winger Davie Thompson (7 goals) was one of 9 Stirling players to score.

LEAGUE GOALS – BEST IN SEASON (Before restructure in 1992)

Div		Goals	Games
1	WR (Dixie) Dean, Everton, 1927–28	60	39
2	George Camsell, Middlesbrough, 1926–27	59	37
3(S)	Joe Payne, Luton, 1936–37	55	39
3(N)	Ted Harston, Mansfield, 1936–37	55	41
3	Derek Reeves, Southampton, 1959–60	39	46
4	Terry Bly, Peterborough, 1960–61	52	46

(Since restructure in 1992)

Div		Goals	Games
1	Guy Whittingham, Portsmouth, 1992–93	42	46
2	Jordan RhodesHuddersfield 2011-12	36	40
3	Andy Morrell, Wrexham, 2002–03	34	45

Premier League – BEST IN SEASON

Andy Cole **34 goals** (Newcastle – 40 games, 1993–94); Alan Shearer **34 goals** (Blackburn – 42 games, 1994–95).

FOOTBALL LEAGUE – BEST MATCH HAULS

(Before restructure in 1992)

Div	Goals	
1	Ted Drake (Arsenal), away to Aston Villa, Dec 14, 1935	7
	James Ross (Preston) v Stoke, Oct 6, 1888	7
2	*Neville (Tim) Coleman (Stoke) v Lincoln, Feb 23, 1957	7
	Tommy Briggs (Blackburn) v Bristol Rov, Feb 5, 1955	7
3(S)	Joe Payne (Luton) v Bristol Rov, Apr 13, 1936	10
3(N)	Robert ('Bunny') Bell (Tranmere) v Oldham, Dec 26, 1935 he also missed a penalty	9
3	Barrie Thomas (Scunthorpe) v Luton, Apr 24, 1965	5
	Keith East (Swindon) v Mansfield, Nov 20, 1965	5
	Steve Earle (Fulham) v Halifax, Sep 16, 1969	5
	Alf Wood (Shrewsbury) v Blackburn, Oct 2, 1971	5
	Tony Caldwell (Bolton) v Walsall, Sep 10, 1983	5
	Andy Jones (Port Vale) v Newport Co., May 4, 1987	5
4	Bert Lister (Oldham) v Southport, Dec 26, 1962	6
	*Scored from the wing	

(Since restructure in 1992)

Div Goals

1   **4** in match – John Durnin (Oxford Utd v Luton, 1992–93); Guy Whittingham (Portsmouth v Bristol Rov 1992–93); Craig Russell (Sunderland v Millwall, 1995–96); David Connolly (Wolves at Bristol City 1998–99); Darren Byfield (Rotherham at Millwall, 2002–03); David Connolly (Wimbledon at Bradford City, 2002–03); Marlon Harewood (Nottm Forest v Stoke, 2002–03); Michael Chopra (Watford at Burnley, 2002–03); Robert Earnshaw (Cardiff v Gillingham, 2003–04). **25** in match – Paul Barnes (Burnley v Stockport, 1996–97); Robert Taylor (all 5, Gillingham at Burnley, 1998–99); Lee Jones (all 5, Wrexham v Cambridge Utd, 2001–02).

3   **5** in match – Tony Naylor (Crewe v Colchester, 1992–93); Steve Butler (Cambridge Utd v Exeter, 1993–4); Guiliano Grazioli (Peterborough at Barnet, 1998–99).

Champ **4** in match – Garath McCleary (Nottm Forest at Leeds 2011–12); Nikola Zigic (Birmingham at Leeds 2011–12); Craig Davies (Barnsley at Birmingham 2012–13); Ross McCormack (Leeds at Charlton 2013–14); Jesse Lingard (Birmingham v Sheffield Wed 2013–14); Odion Ighalo (Watford v Blackpool, 2014-15); Leon Clarke (all 4, Sheffield Utd v Hull, 2017–18); Tammy Abraham (Aston Villa v Nottm Forest, 2018–19); Yakou Meite (Reading at Luton, 2019–20).

Lge 1 **4** in match – Jordan Rhodes (all 4, Huddersfield at Sheffield Wed, 2011–12); Ellis
Harrison (Bristol Rov v Northampton, 2016–17); James Vaughan (Bury v Peterborough,
2016–17).
5 in match – Juan Ugarte (Wrexham at Hartlepool, 2004–05); Jordan Rhodes
(Huddersfield at Wycombe, 2011–12).
Last player to score 6 in English League match: Geoff Hurst (West Ham 8 Sunderland 0, Div 1
Oct 19,1968.

PREMIER LEAGUE – BEST MATCH HAULS

5 goals in match: Andy Cole (Manchester Utd v Ipswich, Mar 4, 1995); Alan Shearer
(Newcastle v Sheffield Wed, Sep 19, 1999); Jermain Defoe (Tottenham v Wigan, Nov 22,
2009); Dimitar Berbatov (Manchester Utd v Blackburn, Nov 27, 2010), Sergio Aguero
(Manchester City v Newcastle, Oct 3, 2015).

SCOTTISH LEAGUE

Div		Goals
Prem	Gary Hooper (Celtic) v Hearts, May 13, 2012	5
	Kris Boyd (Rangers) v Dundee Utd, Dec 30, 2009	5
	Kris Boyd (Kilmarnock) v Dundee Utd, Sep 25, 2004	5
	Kenny Miller (Rangers) v St Mirren, Nov 4, 2000	5
	Marco Negri (Rangers) v Dundee Utd, Aug. 23, 1997	5
	Paul Sturrock (Dundee Utd) v Morton, Nov 17, 1984	5
1	Jimmy McGrory (Celtic) v Dunfermline, Jan 14, 1928	8
1	Owen McNally (Arthurlie) v Armadale, Oct 1, 1927	8
2	Jim Dyet (King's Park) v Forfar, Jan 2, 1930	
	on his debut for the club	8
2	John Calder (Morton) v Raith, Apr 18, 1936	8
2	Norman Haywood (Raith) v Brechin, Aug. 20, 1937	8

SCOTTISH LEAGUE – BEST IN SEASON

Prem	Brian McClair (Celtic, 1986–87)	35
	Henrik Larsson (Celtic, 2000–01)	35
1	William McFadyen (Motherwell, 1931–32)	53
2	*Jimmy Smith (Ayr, 1927–28 – 38 appearances)	66
	(*British record)	

CUP FOOTBALL

Scottish Cup: John Petrie (Arbroath) v Bon Accord, at Arbroath, 1st round,
Sep 12, 1885 — **13**
FA Cup: Ted MacDougall (Bournemouth) v Margate, 1st round, Nov 20,1971 — **9**
FA Cup Final: Billy Townley (Blackburn) v Sheffield Wed, at Kennington
Oval, 1890; Jimmy Logan (Notts Co) v Bolton, at Everton, 1894;
Stan Mortensen (Blackpool) v Bolton, at Wembley, 1953 — **3**
League Cup: Frank Bunn (Oldham) v Scarborough (3rd round), Oct 25, 1989 — **6**
Scottish League Cup: Willie Penman (Raith) v Stirling, Sep 18, 1948 — **6**
Scottish Cup: Most goals in match since war: 10 by **Gerry Baker** (St Mirren) in 15-0 win (1st
round) v Glasgow Univ, Jan 30, 1960; 9 by his brother **Joe Baker** (Hibernian) in 15-1 win
(2nd round) v Peebles, Feb 11, 1961.

AGGREGATE LEAGUE SCORING RECORDS

	Goals
*Arthur Rowley (1947–65, WBA, Fulham, Leicester, Shrewsbury)	**434**
†Jimmy McGrory (1922–38, Celtic, Clydebank)	**410**
Hughie Gallacher (1921–39, Airdrieonians, Newcastle, Chelsea, Derby,	
Notts Co, Grimsby, Gateshead)	**387**

William ('Dixie') Dean (1923–37, Tranmere, Everton, Notts Co) **379**
Hugh Ferguson (1916–30, Motherwell, Cardiff, Dundee) **362**
• Jimmy Greaves (1957–71, Chelsea, Tottenham, West Ham) **357**
Steve Bloomer (1892–1914, Derby, Middlesbrough, Derby) **352**
George Camsell (1923–39, Durham City, Middlesbrough) **348**
Dave Halliday (1920–35, St Mirren, Dundee, Sunderland, Arsenal,
    Manchester City, Clapton Orient) **338**
John Aldridge (1979–98, Newport, Oxford Utd, Liverpool, Tranmere) **329**
Harry Bedford (1919–34, Nottm Forest, Blackpool, Derby, Newcastle,
    Sunderland, Bradford PA, Chesterfield) **326**
John Atyeo (1951–66, Bristol City) **315**
Joe Smith (1908–29, Bolton, Stockport) **315**
Victor Watson (1920–36, West Ham, Southampton) **312**
Harry Johnson (1919–36, Sheffield Utd, Mansfield) **309**
Bob McPhail (1923–1939, Airdrie, Rangers) **306**

(***Rowley** scored 4 for WBA, 27 for Fulham, 251 for Leicester, 152 for Shrewsbury.

• **Greaves'** 357 is record top-division total (he also scored 9 League goals for AC Milan). **Aldridge** also scored 33 League goals for Real Sociedad. †**McGrory** scored 397 for Celtic, 13 for Clydebank).

Most League goals for one club: 349 – Dixie Dean (Everton 1925–37); **326 – George Camsell** (Middlesbrough 1925–39); **315 – John Atyeo** (Bristol City 1951–66); **306 – Vic Watson** (West Ham 1920–35); **291 – Steve Bloomer** (Derby 1892–1906, 1910–14); **259 – Arthur Chandler** (Leicester 1923–35); **255 – Nat Lofthouse** (Bolton 1946–61); **251 – Arthur Rowley** (Leicester 1950–58).

More than 500 goals: Jimmy McGrory (Celtic, Clydebank and Scotland) scored a total of **550** goals in his first-class career (1922–38).

More than 1,000 goals: Brazil's **Pele** is reputedly the game's all-time highest scorer with **1,283** goals in 1,365 matches (1956–77), but many of them were scored in friendlies for his club, Santos. He scored his 1,000th goal, a penalty, against Vasco da Gama in the Maracana Stadium, Rio, on Nov 19, 1969. • Pele (born Oct 23, 1940) played regularly for Santos from the age of 16. During his career, he was sent off only once. He played 95 'A' internationals for Brazil and in their World Cup-winning teams in 1958 and 1970. † Pele (Edson Arantes do Nascimento) was subsequently Brazil's Minister for Sport. He never played at Wembley, apart from being filmed there scoring a goal for a commercial. Aged 57, Pele received an 'honorary knighthood' (Knight Commander of the British Empire) from the Queen at Buckingham Palace on Dec 3, 1997.

Romario (retired Apr, 2008, aged 42) scored more than 1,000 goals for Vasco da Gama, Barcelona, PSV Eindhoven, Valencia and Brazil (56 in 73 internationals).

MOST LEAGUE GOALS IN SEASON: DEAN'S 60

WR ('Dixie') Dean, Everton centre-forward, created a League scoring record in 1927–28 with 60 in 39 First Division matches. He also scored three in FA Cup ties, and 19 in representative games, totalling 82 for the season.

George Camsell, of Middlesbrough, previously held the record with 59 goals in 37 Second Division matches in 1926–27, his total for the season being 75.

SHEARER'S RECORD 'FIRST'

Alan Shearer (Blackburn) is the only player to score more than 30 top-division goals in 3 successive seasons since the War: 31 in 1993–94, 34 in 1994–95, 31 in 1995–96.

Thierry Henry (Arsenal) is the first player to score more than 20 Premier League goals in five consecutive seasons (2002–06). **David Halliday** (Sunderland) topped 30 First Division goals in 4 consecutive seasons with totals of 38, 36, 36 and 49 from 1925–26 to 1928–29.

MOST GOALS IN A MATCH

Sep 12, 1885: John Petrie set the all-time British individual record for a first-class match when, in Arbroath's 36-0 win against Bon Accord (Scottish Cup 1), he scored **13**.

Apr 13, 1936: Joe Payne set the still-existing individual record on his debut as a centre-forward, for Luton v Bristol Rov (Div 3 South). In a 12-0 win he scored **10**.

ROWLEY'S ALL-TIME RECORD

Arthur Rowley is English football's top club scorer with a total of 464 goals for WBA, Fulham, Leicester and Shrewsbury (1947–65). There were 434 in the League, 26 FA Cup, 4 League Cup.

Jimmy Greaves is second with a total of 420 goals for Chelsea, AC Milan, Tottenham and West Ham, made up of 366 League, 35 FA Cup, 10 League Cup and 9 in Europe. He also scored nine goals for AC Milan.

John Aldridge retired as a player at the end of season 1997–98 with a career total of 329 League goals for Newport, Oxford Utd, Liverpool and Tranmere (1979–98). In all competitions for those clubs he scored 410 in 737 appearances. He also scored 45 in 63 games for Real Sociedad.

MOST GOALS IN INTERNATIONAL MATCHES

13 by **Archie Thompson** for Australia v American Samoa in World Cup (Oceania Group qualifier) at Coff's Harbour, New South Wales, Apr 11, 2001. Result: 31-0.

7 by **Stanley Harris** for England v France in Amateur International in Paris, Nov 1, 1906. Result: 15-0.

6 by **Nat Lofthouse** for Football League v Irish League, at Wolverhampton, Sep 24, 1952. Result: 7-1.

    Joe Bambrick for Northern Ireland against Wales (7-0) in Belfast, Feb 1, 1930 – a record for a Home Nations International.

    WC Jordan in Amateur International for England v France, at Park Royal, Mar 23, 1908. Result: 12-0.

    Vivian Woodward for England v Holland in Amateur International, at Chelsea, Dec 11,1909. Result: 9-1.

5 by **Howard Vaughton** for England v Ireland (Belfast) Feb 18, 1882. Result: 13-0.

    Steve Bloomer for England v Wales (Cardiff) Mar 16, 1896. Result: 9-1.

    Hughie Gallacher for Scotland against Ireland (Belfast), Feb 23, 1929. Result: 7-3.

    Willie Hall for England v Northern Ireland, at Old Trafford, Nov 16, 1938. Five in succession (first three in 3'5 mins – fastest international hat-trick). Result: 7-0.

    Malcolm Macdonald for England v Cyprus (Wembley) Apr 16, 1975. Result: 5-0.

    Hughie Gallacher for Scottish League against Irish League (Belfast) Nov 11, 1925. Result: 7-3.

    Barney Battles for Scottish League against Irish League (Firhill Park, Glasgow) Oct 31, 1928. Result: 8-2.

    Bobby Flavell for Scottish League against Irish League (Belfast) Apr 30, 1947. Result: 7-4.

    Joe Bradford for Football League v Irish League (Everton) Sep 25, 1929. Result: 7-2.

    Albert Stubbins for Football League v Irish League (Blackpool) Oct 18, 1950. Result: 6-3.

    Brian Clough for Football League v Irish League (Belfast) Sep 23, 1959. Result: 5-0.

LAST ENGLAND PLAYER TO SCORE ...

3 goals: Harry Kane v Bulgaria (4-0) Euro Champ qual, Wembley, Sept 7, 2019; Harry Kane v Montenegro (7-0) Euro Champ qual, Wembley, Nov 14. 2019 (England's 1,000th international).

4 goals: Ian Wright v San Marino (7-1), World Cup qual, Bologna, Nov 17, 1993.

5 goals: Malcolm Macdonald v Cyprus (5-0), Euro Champ qual, Wembley, Apr 16, 1975.

INTERNATIONAL TOP SHOTS

		Goals	Games
England	Wayne Rooney (2003–2019)	53	120

N Ireland	David Healy (2000–13)	36	95
Scotland	Denis Law (1958–74)	30	55
	Kenny Dalglish (1971–86)	30	102
Wales	Gareth Bale (2006–20)	33	83
Rep of Ire	Robbie Keane (1998–2017)	68	146

ENGLAND'S TOP MARKSMEN

(As at start of season 2020–21)

	Goals	Games
Wayne Rooney (2003–17)	53	120
Bobby Charlton (1958–70)	49	106
Gary Lineker (1984–92)	48	80
Jimmy Greaves (1959–67)	44	57
Michael Owen (1998–2008)	40	89
Tom Finney (1946–58)	30	76
Nat Lofthouse (1950–58)	30	33
Alan Shearer (1992–2000)	30	63
Vivian Woodward (1903–11)	29	23
Frank Lampard (2003–14)	29	106
Steve Bloomer (1895–1907)	28	23
David Platt (1989–96)	27	62
Bryan Robson (1979–91)	26	90
Geoff Hurst (1966–72)	24	49
Stan Mortensen (1947–53)	23	25
Harry Kane (2015–2020)	32	45
Tommy Lawton (1938–48)	22	23
Peter Crouch (2005–11)	22	42
Mike Channon (1972–77)	21	46
Steven Gerrard (2000–14)	21	114
Kevin Keegan (1972–82)	21	63

ROONEY'S ENGLAND RECORD

Wayne Rooney reached 50 international goals with a penalty against Switzerland at Wembley on September 8, 2015 to become England's record scorer, surpassing Bobby Charlton's mark. Charlton's record was set in 106 games, Rooney's tally in 107.

CONSECUTIVE GOALS FOR ENGLAND

Steve Bloomer scored in 10 consecutive appearances (19 goals) between Mar 1895 and Mar 1899.
Jimmy Greaves scored 11 goals in five consecutive matches from the start of season 1960–61.

ENGLAND'S TOP FINAL SERIES MARKSMEN

Gary Lineker with 6 goals at 1986 World Cup in Mexico.
Harry Kane with 6 goals at 2018 World Cup in Russia.

ENGLAND TOP SCORERS IN COMPETITIVE INTERNATIONALS

Harry Kane 27 goals in 35 matches; **Michael Owen** 26 in 53; **Gary Lineker** 22 in 40; **Alan Shearer** 21 in 31.

MOST ENGLAND GOALS IN SEASON

13 – **Jimmy Greaves** (1960–61 in 9 matches); **12** – Dixie Dean (1926–27 in 6 matches); 11 – Harry Kane (2017-18 in 11 matches); **10** – Gary Lineker (1990–91 in 10 matches); 10 – Wayne Rooney – (2008–09 in 9 matches); **Harry Kane** (2019–20 in six matches).

MOST ENGLAND HAT-TRICKS

Jimmy Greaves 6; **Gary Lineker** 5, **Bobby Charlton** 4, **Vivian Woodward** 4, **Stan Mortensen** 3; **Harry Kane** 3.

MOST GOALS FOR ENGLAND U-21s

13 – Alan Shearer (11 apps) Francis Jeffers (13 apps).

GOLDEN GOAL DECIDERS

The Football League, in an experiment to avoid penalty shoot-outs, introduced a new golden goal system in the 1994–95 **Auto Windscreens Shield** to decide matches in the knock-out stages of the competition in which scores were level after 90 minutes. The first goal scored in overtime ended play.

Iain Dunn (Huddersfield) became the first player in British football to settle a match by this sudden-death method. His 107th-minute goal beat Lincoln 3-2 on Nov 30, 1994, and to mark his 'moment in history' he was presented with a golden football trophy.

The AWS Final of 1995 was decided when Paul Tait headed the only goal for Birmingham against Carlisle 13 minutes into overtime – the first time a match at Wembley had been decided by the 'golden goal' formula.

First major international tournament match to be decided by sudden death was the Final of the **1996 European Championship** at Wembley in which Germany beat Czech Rep 2-1 by **Oliver Bierhoff's** goal in the 95th minute.

In the **1998 World Cup Finals** (2nd round), host country France beat Paraguay 1-0 with **Laurent Blanc's** goal (114).

France won the **2000 European Championship** with golden goals in the semi-final, 2-1 v Portugal (Zinedine Zidane pen, 117), and in the Final, 2-1 v Italy (David Trezeguet, 103).

Galatasaray (Turkey) won the **European Super Cup** 2-1 against Real Madrid (Monaco, Aug 25, 2000) with a 103rd minute golden goal, a penalty.

Liverpool won the **UEFA Cup** 5-4 against Alaves with a 117th-min golden goal, an own goal, in the Final in Dortmund (May 19, 2001).

In the **2002 World Cup Finals**, 3 matches were decided by Golden Goals: in the 2nd round Senegal beat Sweden 2-1 (Henri Camara, 104) and South Korea beat Italy 2-1 (Ahn Jung-hwan, 117); in the quarter-final, Turkey beat Senegal 1-0 (Ilhan Mansiz, 94).

France won the 2003 **FIFA Confederations Cup Final** against Cameroon (Paris, Jun 29) with a 97th-minute golden goal by Thierry Henry.

Doncaster won promotion to Football League with a 110th-minute golden goal winner (3-2) in the Conference Play-off Final against Dagenham at Stoke (May 10, 2003).

Germany won the **Women's World Cup Final** 2-1 v Sweden (Los Angeles, Oct 12, 2003) with a 98th-minute golden goal.

GOLD TURNS TO SILVER

Starting with the 2003 Finals of the UEFA Cup and Champions League/European Cup, UEFA introduced a new rule by which a silver goal could decide the winners if the scores were level after 90 minutes.

Team leading after 15 minutes' extra time win match. If sides level, a second period of 15 minutes to be played. If still no winner, result to be decided by penalty shoot-out.

UEFA said the change was made because the golden goal put too much pressure on referees and prompted teams to play negative football.

Although both 2003 European Finals went to extra-time, neither was decided by a silver goal. The new rule applied in the 2004 European Championship Finals, and Greece won their semi-final against the Czech Republic in the 105th minute.

The **International Board** decided (Feb 28 2004) that the golden/silver goal rule was 'unfair' and that from July 1 competitive international matches level after extra-time would, when necessary, be settled on penalties.

PREMIER LEAGUE TOP SHOTS (1992–2020)

Alan Shearer	260	Nicolas Anelka	125
Wayne Rooney	208	Dwight Yorke	123
Andy Cole	187	Steven Gerrard	120
Sergio Aguero	180	Romelu Lukaku	113
Frank Lampard	177	Ian Wright	113
Thierry Henry	175	Dion Dublin	111
Robbie Fowler	163	Emile Heskey	110
Jermain Defoe	162	Ryan Giggs	109
Michael Owen	150	Peter Crouch	108
Les Ferdinand	149	Paul Scholes	107
Teddy Sheringham	146	Darren Bent	106
Robin van Persie	144	Didier Drogba	104
Harry Kane	143	Jamie Vardy	103
Jimmy Floyd Hasselbaink	127	Matt Le Tissier	100
Robbie Keane	126		

LEAGUE GOAL RECORDS

The highest goal-scoring aggregates in the Football League, Premier and Scottish League are:

For

	Goals	Games	Club	Season
Prem	106	38	Manchester City	2017–18
Div 1	128	42	Aston Villa	1930–31
New Div 1	108	46	Manchester City	2001–02
New Champ	99	46	Reading	2005–06
Div 2	122	42	Middlesbrough	1926–27
New Div 2	89	46	Millwall	2000–01
New Lge 1	106	46	Peterborough	2010–11
Div 3(S)	127	42	Millwall	1927–28
Div 3(N)	128	42	Bradford City	1928–29
Div 3	111	46	QPR	1961–62
New Div 3	96	46	Luton	2001–02
New Lge 2	96	46	Notts Co	2009–10
Div 4	134	46	Peterborough	1960–61
Scot Prem	105	38	Celtic	2003–04
Scot L 1	132	34	Hearts	1957–58
Scot L 2	142	34	Raith Rov	1937–38
Scot L 3 (Modern)	130	36	Gretna	2004–05

Against

	Goals	Games	Club	Season
Prem	100	42	Swindon	1993–94
Div 1	125	42	Blackpool	1930–31
New Div 1	102	46	Stockport	2001–02
New Champ	86	46	Crewe	2004–05
Div 2	141	34	Darwen	1898–99
New Div 2	102	46	Chester	1992–93
New Lge 1	98	46	Stockport	2004–05
Div 3(S)	135	42	Merthyr T	1929–30
Div 3(N)	136	42	Nelson	1927–28
Div 3	123	46	Accrington Stanley	1959–60
New Div 3	113	46	Doncaster	1997–98
New Lge 2	96	46	Stockport	2010–11
Div 4	109	46	Hartlepool Utd	1959–60
Scot Prem	100	36	Morton	1984–85

Scot Prem	100	44	Morton	1987–88
Scot L 1	137	38	Leith A	1931–32
Scot L 2	146	38	Edinburgh City	1931–32
Scot L 3 (Modern)	118	36	East Stirling	2003–04

BEST DEFENSIVE RECORDS

Denotes under old offside law

Div	Goals Agst	Games	Club	Season
Prem	15	38	Chelsea	2004–05
1	16	42	Liverpool	1978–79
1	*15	22	Preston	1888–89
New Div 1	28	46	Sunderland	1998–99
New Champ	30	46	Preston	2005–06
2	18	28	Liverpool	1893–94
2	*22	34	Sheffield Wed	1899–1900
2	24	42	Birmingham	1947–48
2	24	42	Crystal Palace	1978–79
New Div 2	25	46	Wigan	2002–03
New Lge 1	32	46	Nottm Forest	2007–08
3(S)	*21	42	Southampton	1921–22
3(S)	30	42	Cardiff	1946–47
3(N)	*21	38	Stockport	1921–22
3(N)	21	46	Port Vale	1953–54
3	30	46	Middlesbrough	1986–87
New Div 3	20	46	Gillingham	1995–96
New Lge 2	31	46	Notts Co	2009–10
4	25	46	Lincoln	1980–81

SCOTTISH LEAGUE

Div	Goals Agst	Games	Club	Season
Prem	17	38	Celtic	2014–15
1	*12	22	Dundee	1902–03
1	*14	38	Celtic	1913–14
2	20	38	Morton	1966–67
2	*29	38	Clydebank	1922–23
2	29	36	East Fife	1995–96
New Div 3	21	36	Brechin	1995–96

TOP SCORERS (LEAGUE ONLY)

		Goals	Div
2019–20	Aleksandar Mitrovic (Fulham)	26	Champ
2018–19	Teemu Pukki (Norwich)	29	Champ
	James Norwood (Tranmere)	29	Lge s2
2017–18	Mohamed Salah (Liverpool)	32	Prem
2016–17	Billy Sharp (Sheffield Utd)	30	Lge 1
2015–16	Matt Taylor (Bristol Rov)	27	Lge 2
2014–15	Daryl Murphy (Ipswich)	27	Champ
2013–14	Luis Suarez (Liverpool)	31	Prem
2012–13	Tom Pope (Port Vale)	31	Lge 2
2011–12	Jordan Rhodes (Huddersfield)	36	Lge 1
2010–11	Clayton Donaldson (Crewe)	28	Lge 2
2009–10	Rickie Lambert (Southampton)	31	Lge 1
2008– 09	Simon Cox (Swindon)		
	Rickie Lambert (Bristol Rov)	29	Lge 1
2007–08	Cristiano Ronaldo (Manchester Utd)	31	Prem

2006–07	Billy Sharp (Scunthorpe)	30	Lge 1
2005–06	Thierry Henry (Arsenal)	27	Prem
2004–05	Stuart Elliott (Hull)	27	1
	Phil Jevons (Yeovil)	27	2
	Dean Windass (Bradford City)	27	1
2003–04	Thierry Henry (Arsenal)	30	Prem
2002–03	Andy Morrell (Wrexham)	34	3
2001–02	Shaun Goater (Manchester City)	28	1
	Bobby Zamora (Brighton)	28	2
2000–01	Bobby Zamora (Brighton)	28	3
1999–00	Kevin Phillips (Sunderland)	30	Prem
1998–99	Lee Hughes (WBA)	31	1
1997–98	Pierre van Hooijdonk (Nottm Forest)	29	1
	Kevin Phillips (Sunderland)	29	1
1996–97	Graeme Jones (Wigan)	31	3
1995–96	Alan Shearer (Blackburn)	31	Prem
1994–95	Alan Shearer (Blackburn)	34	Prem
1993–94	Jimmy Quinn (Reading)	35	2
1992–93	Guy Whittingham (Portsmouth)	42	1
1991–92	Ian Wright (Crystal Palace 5, Arsenal 24)	29	1
1990–91	Teddy Sheringham (Millwall)	33	2
1989–90	Mick Quinn (Newcastle)	32	2
1988–89	Steve Bull (Wolves)	37	3
1987–88	Steve Bull (Wolves)	34	4
1986–87	Clive Allen (Tottenham)	33	1
1985–86	Gary Lineker (Everton)	30	1
1984–85	Tommy Tynan (Plymouth Argyle)	31	3
	John Clayton (Tranmere)	31	4
1983–84	Trevor Senior (Reading)	36	4
1982–83	Luther Blissett (Watford)	27	1
1981–82	Keith Edwards (Hull 1, Sheffield Utd 35)	36	4
1980–81	Tony Kellow (Exeter)	25	3
1979–80	Clive Allen (Queens Park Rangers)	28	2
1978–79	Ross Jenkins (Watford)	29	3
1977–78	Steve Phillips (Brentford)	32	4
	Alan Curtis (Swansea City)	32	4
1976–77	Peter Ward (Brighton)	32	3
1975–76	Dixie McNeil (Hereford)	35	3
1974–75	Dixie McNeil (Hereford)	31	3
1973–74	Brian Yeo (Gillingham)	31	4
1972–73	Bryan (Pop) Robson (West Ham)	28	1
1971–72	Ted MacDougall (Bournemouth)	35	3
1970–71	Ted MacDougall (Bournemouth)	42	4
1969–70	Albert Kinsey (Wrexham)	27	4
1968–69	Jimmy Greaves (Tottenham)	27	1
1967–68	George Best (Manchester Utd)	28	1
	Ron Davies (Southampton)	28	1
1966–67	Ron Davies (Southampton)	37	1
1965–66	Kevin Hector (Bradford PA)	44	4
1964–65	Alick Jeffrey (Doncaster)	36	4
1963–64	Hugh McIlmoyle (Carlisle)	39	4
1962–63	Jimmy Greaves (Tottenham)	37	1
1961–62	Roger Hunt (Liverpool)	41	2
1960–61	Terry Bly (Peterborough)	52	4

100 LEAGUE GOALS IN SEASON

Manchester City, First Div Champions in 2001–02, scored 108 goals.

Bolton, First Div Champions in 1996–97, reached 100 goals, the first side to complete a century in League football since 103 by **Northampton** (Div 4 Champions) in 1986–87.

Last League Champions to reach 100 League goals: **Manchester City** (106 in 2017–18). Last century of goals in the top division: 111 by runners-up **Tottenham** in 1962–63.

Clubs to score a century of Premier League goals in season: **Manchester City** 106 in 2017–18, **Chelsea** 103 in 2009–10, Manchester City (102) and Liverpool (101) in 2013–14.

Wolves topped 100 goals in four successive First Division seasons (1957–58, 1958–59, 1959–60, 1960–61).

In **1930–31,** the top three all scored a century of League goals: 1 Arsenal (127), 2 Aston Villa (128), 3 Sheffield Wed (102).

Latest team to score a century of League goals: Peterborough with 106 in 2010–11 (Lge 1).

100 GOALS AGAINST

Swindon, relegated with 100 goals against in 1993–94, were the first top-division club to concede a century of League goals since **Ipswich** (121) went down in 1964. Most goals conceded in the top division: 125 by **Blackpool** in 1930–31, but they avoided relegation.

MOST LEAGUE GOALS ON ONE DAY

A record of 209 goals in the four divisions of the Football League (43 matches) was set on **Jan 2, 1932:** 56 in Div 1, 53 in Div 2, 57 in Div 3 South and 43 in Div 3 North.

There were two 10-goal aggregates: Bradford City 9, Barnsley 1 in Div 2 and Coventry City 5, Fulham 5 in Div 3 South.

That total of 209 League goals on one day was equalled on **Feb 1, 1936** (44 matches): 46 in Div 1, 46 in Div 2, 49 in Div 3 South and 69 in Div 3 North. Two matches in the Northern Section produced 23 of the goals: Chester 12, York 0 and Crewe 5, Chesterfield 6.

MOST GOALS IN TOP DIV ON ONE DAY

This record has stood since **Dec 26, 1963,** when 66 goals were scored in the ten First Division matches played.

MOST PREMIER LEAGUE GOALS ON ONE DAY

47, in nine matches on **May 8, 1993** (last day of season). For the first time, all 20 clubs scored in the Premier League programme over the weekend of Nov 27-28, 2010.

FEWEST PREMIER LEAGUE GOALS IN ONE WEEK-END

10, in **10** matches on **Nov 24/25, 2001.**

FEWEST FIRST DIV GOALS ON ONE DAY

For full/near full programme: **Ten goals,** all by home clubs, in ten matches on Apr 28, 1923 (day of Wembley's first FA Cup Final).

SCORER OF LEAGUE'S FIRST GOAL

Kenny Davenport (2 mins) for Bolton v Derby, Sep 8, 1888.

VARDY'S RECORD

Jamie Vardy set a Premier League record by scoring in 11 consecutive matches for Leicester (Aug-Nov 2015). The all-time top division record of scoring in 12 successive games was set by **Jimmy Dunne** for Sheffield Utd in the old First Division in season 1931-32. **Stan Mortensen** scored in 15 successive matches for Blackpool (First Division) in season 1950-51, but that sequence included two injury breaks.

LUTON GOAL FEAST

Luton set a Football League record in season 2017–18 by scoring seven or more goals in three games before Christmas – beating Yeovil 8-2 on the opening day of the season, Stevenage 7-1 and Cambridge 7-0.

SCORERS FOR 7 PREMIER LEAGUE CLUBS

Craig Bellamy (Coventry, Newcastle, Blackburn, Liverpool, West Ham, Manchester City, Cardiff).

SCORERS FOR 6 PREMIER LEAGUE CLUBS

Les Ferdinand (QPR, Newcastle, Tottenham, West Ham, Leicester, Bolton); **Andy Cole** (Newcastle, Manchester Utd, Blackburn, Fulham, Manchester City, Portsmouth); **Marcus Bent** (Crystal Palace, Ipswich, Leicester, Everton, Charlton, Wigan); **Nick Barmby** (Tottenham, Middlesbrough, Everton, Liverpool, Leeds, Hull); **Peter Crouch** (Tottenham, Aston Villa, Southampton, Liverpool, Portsmouth, Stoke); **Robbie Keane** (Coventry, Leeds, Tottenham, Liverpool, West Ham, Aston Villa); **Nicolas Anelka** (Arsenal, Liverpool, Manchester City, Bolton, Chelsea, WBA); **Darren Bent** (Ipswich, Charlton, Tottenham, Sunderland, Aston Villa, Fulham).

SCORERS FOR 5 PREMIER LEAGUE CLUBS

Stan Collymore (Nottm Forest, Liverpool, Aston Villa, Leicester, Bradford); **Mark Hughes** (Manchester Utd, Chelsea, Southampton, Everton, Blackburn); **Benito Carbone** (Sheffield Wed, Aston Villa, Bradford, Derby, Middlesbrough); **Ashley Ward** (Norwich, Derby, Barnsley, Blackburn Bradford); **Teddy Sheringham** (Nottm Forest, Tottenham, Manchester Utd, Portsmouth, West Ham); **Chris Sutton** (Norwich, Blackburn, Chelsea, Birmingham, Aston Villa).

SCORERS IN MOST CONSECUTIVE LEAGUE MATCHES

Arsenal broke the record by scoring in 55 successive Premier League fixtures: the last match in season 2000–01, then all 38 games in winning the title in 2001–02, and the first 16 in season 2002–03. The sequence ended with a 2-0 defeat away to Manchester Utd on December 7, 2002.
Chesterfield previously held the record, having scored in 46 consecutive matches in Div 3 (North), starting on Christmas Day, 1929 and ending on December 27, 1930.

SIX-OUT-OF-SIX HEADERS

When **Oxford Utd** beat Shrewsbury 6-0 (Div 2) on Apr 23, 1996, all six goals were headers.

ALL–ROUND MARKSMEN

Alan Cork scored in four divisions of the Football League and in the Premier League in his 18-season career with Wimbledon, Sheffield Utd and Fulham (1977–95).
Brett Ormerod scored in all four divisions (2, 1, Champ and Prem Lge) for Blackpool in two spells (1997–2002, 2008–11). **Grant Holt** (Sheffield Wed, Rochdale, Nottm Forest, Shrewsbury, Norwich) has scored in four Football League divisions and in the Premier League.

CROUCH AHEAD OF THE GAME

Peter Crouch holds the record for most headed goals in the Premier League with a total of 53, ahead of Alan Shearer (46) and Dion Dublin (45).

MOST CUP GOALS

FA Cup – most goals in one season: 20 by Jimmy Ross (Preston, runners-up 1887–88); 15 by **Alex (Sandy) Brown** (Tottenham, winners 1900–01).
Most FA Cup goals in individual careers: 49 by Harry Cursham (Notts Co 1877–89); 20th century: **44** by **Ian Rush** (39 for Liverpool, 4 for Chester, 1 for Newcastle 1979–98). **Denis Law** was the previous highest FA Cup scorer in the 20th century with 41 goals for Huddersfield Town, Manchester City and Manchester Utd (1957–74).
Most FA Cup Final goals by individual: 5 by **Ian Rush** for Liverpool (2 in 1986, 2 in 1989, 1 in 1992).

HOTTEST CUP HOT-SHOT

Geoff Hurst scored 21 cup goals in season 1965–66: 11 League Cup, 4 FA Cup and 2 Cup-Winners' Cup for West Ham, and 4 in the World Cup for England.

SCORERS IN EVERY ROUND

Twelve players have scored in every round of the FA Cup in one season, from opening to Final inclusive: **Archie Hunter** (Aston Villa, winners 1887); **Sandy Brown** (Tottenham, winners 1901); **Harry Hampton** (Aston Villa, winners 1905); **Harold Blackmore** (Bolton, winners 1929); **Ellis Rimmer** (Sheffield Wed, winners 1935); **Frank O'Donnell** (Preston, beaten 1937); **Stan Mortensen** (Blackpool, beaten 1948); **Jackie Milburn** (Newcastle, winners 1951); **Nat Lofthouse** (Bolton, beaten 1953); **Charlie Wayman** (Preston, beaten 1954); **Jeff Astle** (WBA, winners 1968); **Peter Osgood** (Chelsea, winners 1970).

Blackmore and the next seven completed their 'set' in the Final at Wembley; Osgood did so in the Final replay at Old Trafford.

Only player to score in every **Football League Cup** round possible in one season: **Tony Brown** for WBA, winners 1965–66, with 9 goals in 10 games (after bye in Round 1).

TEN IN A ROW

Dixie McNeill scored for Wrexham in ten successive FA Cup rounds (18 goals): 11 in Rounds 1-6, 1977–78; 3 in Rounds 3-4, 1978–79; 4 in Rounds 3-4, 1979–80.

Stan Mortensen (Blackpool) scored 25 goals in 16 FA Cup rounds out of 17 (1946–51).

TOP MATCH HAULS IN FA CUP

Ted MacDougall scored nine goals, a record for the competition proper, in the FA Cup first round on Nov 20, 1971, when Bournemouth beat Margate 11-0. On Nov 23, 1970 he had scored six in an 8-1 first round replay against Oxford City.

Other six-goal FA Cup scorers include **George Hilsdon** (Chelsea v Worksop, 9-1, 1907–08), **Ronnie Rooke** (Fulham v Bury, 6-0, 1938–39), **Harold Atkinson** (Tranmere v Ashington, 8-1, 1952–53), **George Best** (Manchester Utd v Northampton 1969–70, 8-2 away), **Duane Darby** (Hull v Whitby, 8-4, 1996–97).

Denis Law scored all six for Manchester City at Luton (6-2) in an FA Cup 4th round tie on Jan 28, 1961, but none of them counted – the match was abandoned (69 mins) because of a waterlogged pitch. He also scored City's goal when the match was played again, but they lost 3-1.

Tony PhillIskirk scored **five** when Peterborough beat Kingstonià̀n 9-1 in an FA Cup 1st round replay on Nov 25, 1992, but had them wiped from the records.

With the score at 3-0, the Kingstonian goalkeeper was concussed by a coin thrown from the crowd and unable to play on. The FA ordered the match to be replayed at Peterborough behind closed doors, and Kingstonian lost 1-0.

● Two players have scored **ten goals** in FA Cup preliminary round matches: **Chris Marron** for South Shields against Radcliffe in Sep 1947; **Paul Jackson** when Sheffield-based club Stocksbridge Park Steels beat Oldham Town 17-1 on Aug 31, 2002. He scored 5 in each half and all ten with his feet – goal times 6, 10, 22, 30, 34, 68, 73, 75, 79, 84 mins.

QUICKEST GOALS AND RAPID SCORING

A goal in **4 sec** was claimed by **Jim Fryatt**, for Bradford PA v Tranmere (Div 4, Apr 25, 1965), and by **Gerry Allen** for Whitstable v Danson (Kent League, Mar 3,1989). **Damian Mori** scored in **4 sec** for Adelaide v Sydney (Australian National League, December 6, 1995).

Goals after **6 sec** – **Albert Mundy** for Aldershot v Hartlepool, Oct 25, 1958; **Barrie Jones** for Notts Co v Torquay, Mar 31, 1962; **Keith Smith** for Crystal Palace v Derby, Dec 12, 1964.

9.6 sec by **John Hewitt** for Aberdeen at Motherwell, 3rd round, Jan 23, 1982 (fastest goal in Scottish Cup history).

Colin Cowperthwaite reputedly scored in **3.5 sec** for Barrow v Kettering (Alliance Premier League) on Dec 8, 1979, but the timing was unofficial.

Phil Starbuck for Huddersfield **3 sec** after entering the field as 54th min substitute at home to Wigan (Div 2) on Easter Monday, Apr 12, 1993. Corner was delayed, awaiting his arrival and he scored with a header.

Malcolm Macdonald after **5 sec** (officially timed) in Newcastle's 7-3 win in a pre-season friendly at St Johnstone on Jul 29, 1972.

World's fastest goal: 2.8 sec, direct from kick-off, Argentinian **Ricardo Olivera** for Rio Negro v Soriano (Uruguayan League), December 26, 1998.

Fastest international goal: 7 sec, Christian Benteke for Belgium v Gibraltar (World Cup qual, Faro), Oct 10, 2016.

Fastest England goals: 17 sec, Tommy Lawton v Portugal in Lisbon, May 25, 1947. **27 sec, Bryan Robson** v France in World Cup at Bilbao, Spain on Jun 16, 1982; **37 sec, Gareth Southgate** v South Africa in Durban, May 22, 2003; **30 sec, Jack Cock** v Ireland, Belfast, Oct 25, 1919; **30 sec, Bill Nicholson** v Portugal at Goodison Park, May 19, 1951. **38 sec, Bryan Robson** v Yugoslavia at Wembley, Dec 13, 1989; **42 sec, Gary Lineker** v Malaysia in Kuala Lumpur, Jun 12, 1991.

Fastest international goal by substitute: 5 sec, John Jensen for Denmark v Belgium (Euro Champ), Oct 12, 1994.

Fastest goal by England substitute: 10 sec, Teddy Sheringham v Greece (World Cup qualifier) at Old Trafford, Oct 6, 2001.

Fastest FA Cup goal: 4 sec, Gareth Morris (Ashton Utd) v Skelmersdale, 1st qual round, Sep 15, 2001.

Fastest FA Cup goal (comp proper): 9.7 sec, Jimmy Kebe for Reading v WBA, 5th Round, Feb 13, 2010.

Fastest FA Cup Final goal: 25 sec, Louis Saha for Everton v Chelsea at Wembley, May 30, 2009.

Fastest goal by substitute in FA Cup Final: 96 sec, Teddy Sheringham for Manchester Utd v Newcastle at Wembley, May 22, 1999.

Fastest League Cup Final goal: 45 sec, John Arne Riise for Liverpool v Chelsea, 2005.

Fastest goal on full League debut: 7.7 sec, Freddy Eastwood for Southend v Swansea (Lge 2), Oct 16, 2004. He went on to score hat-trick in 4-2 win.

Fastest goal in cup final: 4.07 sec, 14-year-old Owen Price for Ernest Bevin College, Tooting, beaten 3-1 by Barking Abbey in Heinz Ketchup Cup Final at Arsenal on May 18, 2000. Owen, on Tottenham's books, scored from inside his own half when the ball was played back to him from kick-off.

Fastest Premier League goals: 7.69 sec, Shane Long for Southampton v Watford, Apr 23, 2019 **9.82 sec, Ledley King** for Tottenham away to Bradford, Dec 9, 2000; **10.52 sec, Alan Shearer for** Newcastle v Manchester City, Jan 18, 2003; **10.54 sec Christian Eriksen** for Tottenham v Manchester Utd, Jan 31, 2018; **11.9 sec, Mark Viduka** for Leeds v Charlton, Mar 17, 2001, **11.90 sec. James Beattie** for Southampton at Chelsea, Aug 28, 2004; **13 sec, Chris Sutton** for Blackburn at Everton, Apr 1, 1995; **13 sec, Dwight Yorke** for Aston Villa at Coventry, Sep 30, 1995; **13 sec Asmir Begovic** (goalkeeper) for Stoke v Southampton, Nov 2, 2013; **13 sec Jay Rodriguez** for Southampton at Chelsea, Dec 1, 2013.

Fastest top-division goal: 7 sec, Bobby Langton for Preston v Manchester City (Div 1), Aug 25, 1948.

Fastest goal in Champions League: 10 sec, Roy Makaay for Bayern Munich v Real Madrid (1st ko rd), Mar 7, 2007.

Fastest Premier League goal by substitute: 9 sec, Shaun Goater, Manchester City's equaliser away to Manchester Utd (1-1), Feb 9, 2003. In Dec, 2011, Wigan's **Ben Watson** was brought off the bench to take a penalty against Stoke and scored.

Fastest goal on Premier League debut: 36 sec, Thievy Bifouma on as sub for WBA away to Crystal Palace, Feb 8, 2014.

Fastest Scottish Premiership goal: 10 sec, Kris Boyd for Kilmarnock v Ross Co, Jan 28, 2017.

Fastest-ever hat-trick: 90 sec, credited to 18-year-old **Tommy Ross** playing in a Highland match for Ross County against Nairn County on Nov 28, 1964.

Fastest goal by goalkeeper in professional football: 13 sec, Asmir Begovic for Stoke v Southampton (Prem Lge), Nov 2, 2013.

Fastest goal in Olympic Games: 14 sec, Neymar for Brazil in semi-finals v Honduras, Aug 17,

2016, Rio de Janeiro.

Fastest goal in women's football: 7 sec, Angie Harriott for Launton v Thame (Southern League, Prem Div), season 1998–99.

Fastest hat-trick in League history: 2 min 20 sec, Bournemouth's 84th-minute substitute **James Hayter** in 6-0 home win v Wrexham (Div 2) on Feb 24, 2004 (goal times 86, 87, 88 mins).

Fastest First Division hat-tricks since war: Graham Leggat, 3 goals in 3 minutes (first half) when Fulham beat Ipswich 10-1 on Boxing Day, 1963; **Nigel Clough,** 3 goals in **4 minutes** (81, 82, 85 pen) when Nottm Forest beat QPR 4-0 on Dec 13, 1987.

Fastest Premier League hat-trick: 2 min 56 sec (13, 14, 16) by **Sadio Mane** in Southampton 6, Aston Villa 1 on May 16, 2015.

Fastest international hat-trick: 2 min 35 sec, Abdul Hamid Bassiouny for Egypt in 8-2 win over Namibia in Abdallah, Libya, (African World Cup qual), Jul 13, 2001.

Fastest international hat-trick in British matches: 3.5 min, Willie Hall for England v N Ireland at Old Trafford, Manchester, Nov 16, 1938. (Hall scored 5 in 7-0 win); **3min 30 sec, Arif Erdem** for Turkey v N Ireland, European Championship qualifier, at Windsor Park, Belfast, on Sep 4, 1999.

Fastest FA Cup hat-tricks: In 3 min, Billy Best for Southend v Brentford (2nd round, Dec 7, 1968); **2 min 20 sec, Andy Locke** for Nantwich v Droylsden (1st Qual round, Sep 9, 1995).

Fastest Scottish hat-trick: 2 min 30 sec, Ian St John for Motherwell away to Hibernian (Scottish League Cup), Aug 15, 1959.

Fastest hat-trick of headers: Dixie Dean's 5 goals in Everton's 7-2 win at home to Chelsea (Div 1) on Nov 14, 1931 included 3 headers between **5th** and **15th-min.**

Scored first kick: Billy Foulkes (Newcastle) for Wales v England at Cardiff, Oct 20, 1951, in his first international match.

Preston scored six goals in **7 min** in record 26-0 FA Cup 1st round win v Hyde, Oct 15, 1887.

Notts Co scored six second-half goals in **12 min** (Tommy Lawton 3, Jackie Sewell 3) when beating Exeter 9-0 (Div 3 South) at Meadow Lane on Oct 16, 1948.

Arsenal scored six in **18 min** (71-89 mins) in 7-1 home win (Div 1) v Sheffield Wed, Feb 15, 1992.

Tranmere scored six in first **19 min** when beating Oldham 13-4 (Div 3 North), December 26, 1935.

Sunderland scored eight in **28 min** at Newcastle (9-1 Div 1), December 5, 1908. Newcastle went on to win the title.

Southend scored all seven goals in **29 min** in 7-0 win at home to Torquay (Leyland Daf Cup, Southern quarter-final), Feb 26, 1991. Score was 0-0 until 55th minute.

Plymouth scored five in first **18 min** in 7-0 home win v Chesterfield (Div 2), Jan 3, 2004.

Five in 20 min: Frank Keetley in Lincoln's 9-1 win over Halifax in Div 3 (North), Jan 16, 1932; **Brian Dear** for West Ham v WBA (6-1, Div 1) Apr 16, 1965. **Kevin Hector** for Bradford PA v Barnsley (7-2, Div 4), Nov 20, 1965.

Four in 5 min: John McIntyre for Blackburn v Everton (Div 1), Sep 16, 1922; **WG (Billy) Richardson** for WBA v West Ham (Div 1), Nov 7, 1931.

Three in 2'5 min: Jimmy Scarth for Gillingham v Leyton Orient (Div 3S), Nov 1, 1952.

Three in three minutes: Billy Lane for Watford v Clapton Orient (Div 3S), December 20, 1933; **Johnny Hartburn** for Leyton Orient v Shrewsbury (Div 3S), Jan 22, 1955; **Gary Roberts** for Brentford v Newport, (Freight Rover Trophy, South Final), May 17, 1985; **Gary Shaw** for Shrewsbury v Bradford City (Div 3), December 22, 1990.

Two in 9 sec: Jamie Bates with last kick of first half, **Jermaine McSporran** 9 sec into second half when Wycombe beat Peterborough 2-0 at home (Div 2) on Sep 23, 2000.

Premier League – fastest scoring: Four goals in 4 min 44 sec, Tottenham home to Southampton on Sunday, Feb 7, 1993.

Premier League – fast scoring away: When **Aston Villa** won 5-0 at Leicester (Jan 31, 2004), all goals scored in **18 second-half min** (50-68).

Four in 13 min by Premier League sub: Ole Gunnar Solskjaer for Manchester Utd away to Nottm Forest, Feb 6, 1999.

Five in 9 mins by substitute: Robert Lewandowski for Bayern Munich v Wolfsburg (5-1, Bundesliga), Sep 22, 2015.

FASTEST GOALS IN WORLD CUP FINAL SERIES

10.8 sec, Hakan Sukur for Turkey against South Korea in 3rd/4th-place match at Taegu, Jun 29, 2002; **15 sec, Vaclav Masek** for Czechoslovakia v Mexico (in Vina, Chile, 1962); **27 sec, Bryan Robson** for England v France (in Bilbao, Spain, 1982).

TOP MATCH SCORES SINCE WAR

By English clubs: 13-0 by Newcastle v Newport (Div 2, Oct 1946); 13-2 by Tottenham v Crewe (FA Cup 4th. Rd replay, Feb 1960); 13-0 by Chelsea v Jeunesse Hautcharage, Lux. (Cup-Winners' Cup 1st round, 2nd leg, Sep 1971).
By Scottish club: 20-0 by Stirling v Selkirk (E. of Scotland League) in Scottish Cup 1st round. (Dec 1984). That is the highest score in British first-class football since Preston beat Hyde 26-0 in FA Cup, Oct 1887.

MOST GOALS IN CALENDAR YEAR

91 by **Lionel Messi** in 2012 (79 Barcelona, 12 Argentina).

ROONEY'S DOUBLE TOP

Wayne Rooney ended season 2016–17 as top scorer for England (53) and Manchester Utd (253).

PREMIER LEAGUE LONGEST-RANGE GOALS BY OUTFIELD PLAYERS

66 yards: Charlie Adam (Stoke at Chelsea, Apr 4, 2015)
64 yards: Xabi Alonso (Liverpool v Newcastle, Sep 20, 2006)
62 yards: Maynor Figueroa (Wigan at Stoke, Dec 12, 2009)
60 yards: Wayne Rooney (Everton v West Ham, Nov 29, 2017)
59 yards: David Beckham (Manchester Utd at Wimbledon, Aug 17, 1996)
55 yards: Wayne Rooney (Manchester Utd at West Ham, Mar 22, 2014)

GOALS BY GOALKEEPERS

(Long clearances unless stated)
Pat Jennings for Tottenham v Manchester Utd (goalkeeper Alex Stepney), Aug 12, 1967 (FA Charity Shield).
Peter Shilton for Leicester v Southampton (Campbell Forsyth), Oct 14, 1967 (Div 1).
Ray Cashley for Bristol City v Hull (Jeff Wealands), Sep 18, 1973 (Div 2).
Steve Sherwood for Watford v Coventry (Raddy Avramovic), Jan 14, 1984 (Div 1).
Steve Ogrizovic for Coventry v Sheffield Wed (Martin Hodge), Oct 25, 1986 (Div 1).
Andy Goram for Hibernian v Morton (David Wylie), May 7, 1988 (Scot Prem Div)
Andy McLean, on Irish League debut, for Cliftonville v Linfield (George Dunlop), Aug 20, 1988.
Alan Paterson for Glentoran v Linfield (George Dunlop), Nov 30, 1988 (Irish League Cup Final – only instance of goalkeeper scoring winner in a senior cup final in UK).
Ray Charles for East Fife v Stranraer (Bernard Duffy), Feb 28, 1990 (Scot Div 2).
Iain Hesford for Maidstone v Hereford (Tony Elliott), Nov 2, 1991 (Div 4).
Chris Mackenzie for Hereford v Barnet (Mark Taylor), Aug 12, 1995 (Div 3).
Peter Schmeichel for Manchester Utd v Rotor Volgograd, Sep 26, 1995 (header, UEFA Cup 1).
Mark Bosnich (Aston Villa) for Australia v Solomon Islands, Jun 11, 1997 (penalty in World Cup qual – 13-0).
Peter Keen for Carlisle away to Blackpool (goalkeeper John Kennedy), Oct 24, 2000 (Div 3).
Steve Mildenhall for Notts Co v Mansfield (Kevin Pilkington), Aug 21, 2001 (free-kick inside own half, League Cup 1).
Peter Schmeichel for Aston Villa v Everton (Paul Gerrard), Oct 20, 2001 (volley, first goalkeeper to score in Premier League).
Mart Poom for Sunderland v Derby (Andy Oakes), Sep 20, 2003 (header, Div 1).
Brad Friedel for Blackburn v Charlton (Dean Kiely), Feb 21, 2004 (shot, Prem).
Paul Robinson for Leeds v Swindon (Rhys Evans), Sep 24, 2003 (header, League Cup 2).
Andy Lonergan for Preston v Leicester (Kevin Pressman), Oct 2, 2004 (Champ).

Matt Glennon for St Johnstone away to Ross Co (Joe Malin), Mar 11, 2006 (shot, Scot Div 1).
Gavin Ward for Tranmere v Leyton Orient (Glenn Morris), Sep 2, 2006 (free-kick Lge 1).
Mark Crossley for Sheffield Wed v Southampton (Kelvin Davis), Dec 23, 2006 (header, Champ).
Paul Robinson for Tottenham v Watford (Ben Foster), Mar 17, 2007 (Prem).
Adam Federici for Reading v Cardiff (Peter Enckelman), Dec 28, 2008 (shot, Champ).
Chris Weale for Yeovil v Hereford (Peter Gulacsi), Apr 21, 2009 (header, Lge 1).
Scott Flinders for Hartlepool v Bournemouth (Shwan Jalal), Apr 30, 2011 (header, Lge 1).
Iain Turner for Preston v Notts Co (Stuart Nelson), Aug 27 2011 (shot, Lge 1).
Andy Leishman for Auchinleck v Threave (Vinnie Parker), Oct 22, 2011 (Scot Cup 2).
Tim Howard for Everton v Bolton (Adam Bogdan), Jan 4, 2012 (Prem).
Asmir Begovic for Stoke v Southampton (Artur Boruc), Nov 2, 2013 (Prem).
Mark Oxley for Hibernian v Livingston (Darren Jamieson), May 9, 2014 (Scot Champ).
Jesse Joronen for Stevenage v Wycombe (Matt Ingram), Oct 17, 2015 (Lge 2).
Barry Roche for Morecambe v Portsmouth (Ryan Fulton), Feb 2, 2016 (header, Lge 2).
Lewis McMinn for Brechin v Stirling (Blair Currie), Dec 7, 2019 (Scot Lge 2).

MORE GOALKEEPING HEADLINES

Arthur Wilkie, sustained a hand injury in Reading's Div 3 match against Halifax on Aug 31, 1962, then played as a forward and scored twice in a 4-2 win.

Alex Stepney was Manchester Utd's joint top scorer for two months in season 1973–74 with two penalties.

Dundee Utd goalkeeper Hamish McAlpine scored three penalties in a ten-month period between 1976–77, two against Hibernian, home and away, and one against Rangers at Ibrox.

Alan Fettis scored twice for Hull in 1994–95 Div 2 season, as a substitute in 3-1 home win over Oxford Utd (Dec 17) and, when selected outfield, with last-minute winner (2-1) against Blackpool on May 6.

Roger Freestone scored for Swansea with a penalty at Oxford Utd (Div 2, Apr 30, 1995) and twice from the spot the following season against Shrewsbury (Aug 12) and Chesterfield (Aug 26).

Jimmy Glass, on loan from Swindon, kept Carlisle in the Football League on May 8, 1999. With ten seconds of stoppage-time left, he went upfield for a corner and scored the winner against Plymouth that sent Scarborough down to the Conference instead.

Paul Smith, Nottm Forest goalkeeper, was allowed to run through Leicester's defence unchallenged and score direct from the kick-off of a Carling Cup second round second match on Sep 18, 2007. It replicated the 1-0 score by which Forest had led at half-time when the original match was abandoned after Leicester defender Clive Clarke suffered a heart attack. Leicester won the tie 3-2.

Tony Roberts (Dagenham), is the only known goalkeeper to score from open play in the FA Cup, his last-minute goal at Basingstoke in the fourth qualifying round on Oct 27, 2001 earning a 2-2 draw. Dagenham won the replay 3-0 and went on to reach the third round proper.

The only known instance in first-class football in Britain of a goalkeeper scoring direct from a goal-kick was in a First Division match at Roker Park on Apr 14, 1900. The kick by Manchester City's **Charlie Williams** was caught in a strong wind and Sunderland keeper J. E Doig fumbled the ball over his line.

Jose Luis Chilavert, Paraguay's international goalkeeper, scored a hat-trick of penalties when his club Velez Sarsfield beat Ferro Carril Oeste 6-1 in the Argentine League on Nov 28, 1999. In all, he scored 8 goals in 72 internationals. He also scored with a free-kick from just inside his own half for Velez Sarsfield against River Plate on Sep 20, 2000.

Most goals by a goalkeeper in a League season: 5 (all penalties) by **Arthur Birch** for Chesterfield (Div 3 North), 1923–24.

When Brazilian goalkeeper **Rogerio Ceni** (37) converted a free-kick for Sao Paulo's winner (2-1) v Corinthians in a championship match on Mar 27, 2011, it was his 100th goal (56 free-kicks, 44 pens) in a 20-season career.

OWN GOALS

Most by player in one season: 5 by **Robert Stuart** (Middlesbrough) in 1934–35.

Three in match by one team: Sheffield Wed's **Vince Kenny**, **Norman Curtis** and **Eddie Gannon** in 5-4 defeat at home to WBA (Div 1) on Dec 26, 1952; Rochdale's **George Underwood**, **Kenny Boyle** and **Danny Murphy** in 7-2 defeat at Carlisle (Div 3 North), Dec 25, 1954; Sunderland's **Stephen Wright** and **Michael Proctor** (2) at home to Charlton (1-3, Prem), Feb 1, 2003; Brighton's **Liam Bridcutt** (2) and **Lewis Dunk** in 6-1 FA Cup 5th rd defeat at Liverpool, Feb 19, 2012.; Sunderland's **Santiago Vergini**, **Liam Bridcutt** and **Patrick van Aanholt** in 8-0 defeat at Southampton (Prem), Oct 18, 2014.

One-man show: Chris Nicholl (Aston Villa) scored all four goals in 2-2 draw away to Leicester (Div 1), Mar 20, 1976 – two for his own side and two own goals.

Fastest own goals: 8 sec by **Pat Kruse** of Torquay, for Cambridge Utd (Div 4), Jan 3, 1977; in First Division, **16 sec** by **Steve Bould** (Arsenal) away to Sheffield Wed, Feb 17, 1990.

Late own-goal man: Frank Sinclair (Leicester) put through his own goal in the 90th minute of Premier League matches away to Arsenal (L1-2) and at home to Chelsea (2-2) in Aug 1999.

Half an own goal each: Chelsea's second goal in a 3-1 home win against Leicester on December 18, 1954 was uniquely recorded as 'shared own goal'. Leicester defenders **Stan Milburn** and **Jack Froggatt**, both lunging at the ball in an attempt to clear, connected simultaneously and sent it rocketing into the net.

Match of 149 own goals: When Adama, Champions of Malagasy (formerly Madagascar) won a League match 149-0 on Oct 31, 2002, all 149 were own goals scored by opponents Stade Olympique De L'Emryne. They repeatedly put the ball in their own net in protest at a refereeing decision.

MOST SCORERS IN MATCH

Liverpool set a Football League record with **eight** scorers when beating Crystal Palace 9-0 (Div 1) on Sep 12, 1989. Marksmen were: Steve Nicol (7 and 88 mins), Steve McMahon (16), Ian Rush (45), Gary Gillespie (56), Peter Beardsley (61), John Aldridge (67 pen), John Barnes (79), Glenn Hysen (82).

Fifteen years earlier, **Liverpool** had gone one better with **nine** different scorers when they achieved their record win, 11-0 at home to Stromsgodset (Norway) in the Cup-Winners' Cup 1st round, 1st leg on Sep 17, 1974.

Eight players scored for **Swansea** when they beat Sliema, Malta, 12-0 in the Cup-Winners' Cup 1st round, 1st leg on Sep 15, 1982.

Nine Stirling players scored in the 20-0 win against Selkirk in the Scottish Cup 1st Round on December 8, 1984.

Premier League record: **Seven** Chelsea scorers in 8-0 home win over Aston Villa, Dec 23, 2012. An eighth player missed a penalty.

LONG SCORING RUNS

Tom Phillipson scored in 13 consecutive matches for Wolves (Div 2) in season 1926–27, which is still an English League record. In the same season, **George Camsell** scored in 12 consecutive matches for Middlesbrough (Div 2). **Bill Prendergast** scored in 13 successive League and Cup appearances for Chester (Div 3 North) in season 1938–39.

Dixie Dean scored in 12 consecutive games (23 goals) for Everton in Div 2 in 1930–31.

Danish striker **Finn Dossing** scored in 15 consecutive matches (Scottish record) for Dundee Utd (Div 1) in 1964–65.

50-GOAL PLAYERS

With **52** goals for **Wolves** in 1987–78 (34 League, 12 Sherpa Van Trophy, 3 Littlewoods Cup, 3 FA Cup), **Steve Bull** became the first player to score 50 in a season for a League club since **Terry Bly** for Div 4 newcomers Peterborough in 1960–61. Bly's 54 comprised 52 League goals and 2 in the FA Cup, and included 7 hat-tricks, still a post-war League record. Bull was again the country's top scorer with 50 goals in season 1988–89: 37 League, 2 Littlewoods Cup and

11 Sherpa Van Trophy. Between Bly and Bull, the highest individual scoring total for a season was 49 by two players: **Ted MacDougall** (Bournemouth 1970–71, 42 League, 7 FA Cup) and **Clive Allen** (Tottenham 1986–87, 33 League, 12 Littlewoods Cup, 4 FA Cup).

HOT SHOTS

Jimmy Greaves was top Div 1 scorer (League goals) six times in 11 seasons: 32 for Chelsea (1958–59), 41 for Chelsea (1960–61) and, for Tottenham, 37 in 1962–63, 35 in 1963–64, 29 in 1964–65 (joint top) and 27 in 1968–69.

Brian Clough (Middlesbrough) was leading scorer in Div 2 in three successive seasons: 40 goals in 1957–58, 42 in 1958–59 and 39 in 1959–60.

John Hickton (Middlesbrough) was top Div 2 scorer three times in four seasons: 24 goals in 1967–68, 24 in 1969–70 and 25 in 1970–71.

MOST HAT-TRICKS

Nine by George Camsell (Middlesbrough) in Div 2, 1926–27, is the record for one season. Most League hat-tricks in career: 37 by **Dixie Dean** for Tranmere and Everton (1924–38).

Most top division hat-tricks in a season since last War: six by **Jimmy Greaves** for Chelsea (1960–61). **Alan Shearer** scored five hat-tricks for Blackburn in the Premier League, season 1995–96.

Frank Osborne (Tottenham) scored three consecutive hat-tricks in Div 1 in Oct–Nov 1925, against Liverpool, Leicester (away) and West Ham.

Tom Jennings (Leeds) scored hat-tricks in three successive Div 1 matches (Sep–Oct, 1926): 3 goals v Arsenal, 4 at Liverpool, 3 v Blackburn. Leeds were relegated that season.

Jack Balmer (Liverpool) scored his three hat-tricks in a 17-year career in successive Div 1 matches (Nov 1946): 3 v Portsmouth, 4 at Derby, 3 v Arsenal. No other Liverpool player scored during that 10-goal sequence by Balmer.

Gilbert Alsop scored hat-tricks in three successive matches for Walsall in Div 3 South in Apr 1939: 3 at Swindon, 3 v Bristol City and 4 v Swindon.

Alf Lythgoe scored hat-tricks in three successive games for Stockport (Div 3 North) in Mar 1934: 3 v Darlington, 3 at Southport and 4 v Wrexham.

TRIPLE HAT-TRICKS

There have been at least three **instances of 3 hat-tricks being scored for one team in a Football League match:**

Apr 21, 1909: Enoch West, Billy Hooper and **Alfred Spouncer** for Nottm Forest (12-0 v Leicester Fosse, Div 1).

Mar 3, 1962: Ron Barnes, Wyn Davies and **Roy Ambler** in Wrexham's 10-1 win against Hartlepool (Div 4).

Nov 7, 1987: Tony Adcock, Paul Stewart and **David White** for Manchester City in 10-1 win at home to Huddersfield (Div 2).

For the first time in the Premier League, **three** hat-tricks were completed on one day (Sep 23, 1995): **Tony Yeboah** for Leeds at Wimbledon; **Alan Shearer** for Blackburn v Coventry; **Robbie Fowler** with 4 goals for Liverpool v Bolton.

In the FA Cup, **Jack Carr, George Elliott** and **Walter Tinsley** each scored 3 in Middlesbrough's 9-3 first round win against Goole in Jan, 1915. **Les Allen** scored 5, **Bobby Smith** 4 and **Cliff Jones** 3 when Tottenham beat Crewe 13-2 in a fourth-round replay in Feb 1960.

HAT-TRICKS v THREE 'KEEPERS

When West Ham beat Newcastle 8-1 (Div 1) on Apr 21, 1986 **Alvin Martin** scored 3 goals against different goalkeepers: Martin Thomas injured a shoulder and was replaced, in turn, by outfield players Chris Hedworth and Peter Beardsley.

Jock Dodds of Lincoln had done the same against West Ham on Dec 18, 1948, scoring past Ernie Gregory, Tommy Moroney and George Dick in 4-3 win.

David Herd (Manchester Utd) scored against Sunderland's Jim Montgomery, Charlie Hurley and Johnny Parke in 5-0 First Division home win on Nov 26, 1966.

Brian Clark, of Bournemouth, scored against Rotherham's Jim McDonagh, Conal Gilbert and Michael Leng twice in 7-2 win (Div 3) on Oct 10, 1972.

On Oct 16, 1993 (Div 3) **Chris Pike** (Hereford) scored a hat-trick in 5-0 win over Colchester, who became the first team in league history to have two keepers sent off in the same game.

On Dec 18, 2004 (Lge 1), in 6-1 defeat at Hull, Tranmere used **John Achterberg** and **Russell Howarth,** both retired injured, and defender **Theo Whitmore.**

On Mar 9, 2008, Manchester Utd had three keepers in their 0-1 FA Cup quarter-final defeat by Portsmouth. **Tomasz Kuszczak** came on at half-time for **Edwin van der Sar** but was sent off when conceding a penalty. **Rio Ferdinand** went in goal and was beaten by Sulley Muntari's spot-kick.

Derby used three keepers in a 4-1 defeat at Reading (Mar 10, 2010, Champ). **Saul Deeney,** who took over when **Stephen Bywater** was injured, was sent off for a foul and **Robbie Savage** replaced him.

EIGHT-DAY HAT-TRICK TREBLE

Joe Bradford, of Birmingham, scored three hat-tricks in eight days in Sep 1929–30 v Newcastle (won 5-1) on the 21st, 5 for the Football League v Irish League (7-2) on the 25th, and 3 in his club's 5-7 defeat away to Blackburn on the 28th.

PREMIER LEAGUE DOUBLE HAT-TRICK

Robert Pires and **Jermaine Pennant** each scored 3 goals in Arsenal's 6-1 win at home to Southampton (May 7, 2003).

TON UP – BOTH ENDS

Manchester City are the only club to score and concede a century of League goals in the same season. When finishing fifth in the 1957–58 season, they scored 104 and gave away 100.

TOURNAMENT TOP SHOTS

Most individual goals in a World Cup Final series: 13 by **Just Fontaine** for France, in Sweden 1958. Most in European Championship Finals: 9 by **Michel Platini** for France, in France 1984.

MOST GOALS ON CLUB DEBUT

Jim Dyet scored eight in King's Park's 12-2 win against Forfar (Scottish Div 2, Jan 2, 1930). **Len Shackleton** scored six times in Newcastle's 13-0 win v Newport (Div 2, Oct 5, 1946) in the week he joined them from Bradford Park Avenue.

MOST GOALS ON LEAGUE DEBUT

Five by **George Hilsdon,** for Chelsea (9-2) v Glossop, Div 2, Sep 1, 1906. **Alan Shearer,** with three goals for Southampton (4-2) v Arsenal, Apr 9, 1988, became, at 17, the youngest player to score a First Division hat-trick on his full debut.

FOUR-GOAL SUBSTITUTE

James Collins (Swindon), sub from 60th minute, scored 4 in 5-0 home win v Portsmouth (Lge 1) on Jan 1, 2013.

CLEAN-SHEET RECORDS

On the way to promotion from Div 3 in season 1995–96, Gillingham's ever-present goalkeeper **Jim Stannard** set a clean-sheet record. In 46 matches. He achieved 29 shut-outs (17 at home, 12 away), beating the 28 by **Ray Clemence** for Liverpool (42 matches in Div 1, 1978–79) and the previous best in a 46-match programme of 28 by Port Vale (Div 3 North, 1953–54). In conceding only 20 League goals in 1995–96, Gillingham created a defensive record for the lower divisions.

Chris Woods, Rangers' England goalkeeper, set a British record in season 1986–87 by going 1,196 minutes without conceding a goal. The sequence began in the UEFA Cup match against

Borussia Moenchengladbach on Nov 26, 1986 and ended when Rangers were sensationally beaten 1-0 at home by Hamilton in the Scottish Cup 3rd round on Jan 31, 1987 with a 70th-minute goal by **Adrian Sprott**. The previous British record of 1,156 minutes without a goal conceded was held by Aberdeen goalkeeper **Bobby Clark** (season 1970–01).

Manchester Utd set a new Premier League clean-sheet record of 1,333 minutes (including 14 successive match shut-outs) in season 2008–09 (Nov 15–Feb 21). **Edwin van der Sar's** personal British league record of 1,311 minutes without conceding ended when United won 2-1 at Newcastle on Mar 4, 2009.

Most clean sheets in season in top English division: **28** by **Liverpool** (42 matches) in 1978–79; **25** by **Chelsea** (38 matches) in 2004–05.

There have been three instances of clubs keeping 11 consecutive clean sheets in the Football League: **Millwall** (Div 3 South, 1925–26), **York** (Div 3, 1973–74) and **Reading** (Div 4, 1978–79). In his sequence, Reading goalkeeper **Steve Death** set the existing League shut-out record of 1,103 minutes.

Sasa Ilic remained unbeaten for over 14 hours with 9 successive shut-outs (7 in Div 1, 2 in play-offs) to equal a Charlton club record in Apr/May 1998. He had 12 clean sheets in 17 first team games after winning promotion from the reserves with 6 successive clean sheets.

Sebastiano Rossi kept a clean sheet in 8 successive away matches for AC Milan (Nov 1993–Apr 1994).

A world record of 1,275 minutes without conceding a goal was set in 1990–01 by **Abel Resino**, the Atletico Madrid goalkeeper. He was finally beaten by Sporting Gijon's Enrique in Atletico's 3-1 win on Mar 19, 1991.

In international football, the record is held by **Dino Zoff** with a shut-out for Italy (Sep 1972 to Jun 1974) lasting 1,142 minutes.

LOW SCORING

Fewest goals by any club in season in Football League: 18 by **Loughborough** (Div 2, 34 matches, 1899–1900); in 38 matches 20 by **Derby** (Prem Lge, 2007–08); in 42 matches, 24 by **Watford** (Div 2, 1971–72) and by **Stoke** (Div 1, 1984–85)); in 46-match programme, 27 by **Stockport** (Div 3, 1969–70).

Arsenal were the lowest Premier League scorers in its opening season (1992–93) with 40 goals in 42 matches, but won both domestic cup competitions. In subsequent seasons the lowest Premier League scorers were **Ipswich** (35) in 1993–94, **Crystal Palace** (34) in 1994–95, **Manchester City** (33) in 1995–96 and **Leeds** (28) in 1996–97 until **Sunderland** set the Premier League's new fewest-goals record with only 21 in 2002–03. Then, in 2007–08, **Derby** scored just 20.

LONG TIME NO SCORE

The world international non-scoring record was set by **Northern Ireland** when they played 13 matches and 1,298 minutes without a goal. The sequence began against Poland on Feb 13, 2002 and ended 2 years and 5 days later when David Healy scored against Norway (1-4) in Belfast on Feb 18, 2004.

Longest non-scoring sequences in Football League: 11 matches by **Coventry** in 1919–20 (Div 2); 11 matches in 1992–93 (Div 2) by **Hartlepool**, who after beating Crystal Palace 1-0 in the FA Cup 3rd round on Jan 2, went 13 games and 2 months without scoring (11 League, 1 FA Cup, 1 Autoglass Trophy). The sequence ended after 1,227 blank minutes with a 1-1 draw at Blackpool (League) on Mar 6.

In the Premier League (Oct–Jan season 1994–95) **Crystal Palace** failed to score in nine consecutive matches.

The British non-scoring club record is held by **Stirling**: 14 consecutive matches (13 League, 1 Scottish Cup) and 1,292 minutes play, from Jan 31 1981 until Aug 8, 1981 (when they lost 4-1 to Falkirk in the League Cup).

In season 1971–72, **Mansfield** did not score in any of their first nine home games in Div 3. They were relegated on goal difference of minus two.

FA CUP CLEAN SHEETS

Most consecutive FA Cup matches without conceding a goal: 11 by **Bradford City**. The sequence spanned 8 rounds, from 3rd in 1910–11 to 4th. Round replay in 1911–12, and included winning the Cup in 1911.

GOALS THAT WERE WRONGLY GIVEN

Tottenham's last-minute winner at home to Huddersfield (Div 1) on Apr 2, 1952: Eddie Baily's corner-kick struck referee WR Barnes in the back, and the ball rebounded to Baily, who crossed for Len Duquemin to head into the net. Baily had infringed the Laws by playing the ball twice, but the result (1-0) stood. Those two points helped Spurs to finish Championship runners-up; Huddersfield were relegated.

The second goal (66 mins) in **Chelsea's** 2-1 home win v Ipswich (Div 1) on Sep 26, 1970: Alan Hudson's shot hit the stanchion on the outside of goal and the ball rebounded on to the pitch. But instead of the goal-kick, referee Roy Capey gave a goal, on a linesman's confirmation. TV pictures proved otherwise. The Football League quoted from the Laws of the Game: 'The referee's decision on all matters is final.'

When **Watford's** John Eustace and **Reading's** Noel Hunt challenged for a 13th minute corner at Vicarage Road on Sep 20, 2008, the ball was clearly diverted wide. But referee Stuart Attwell signalled for a goal on the instruction to his assistant and it went down officially as a Eustace own goal. The Championship match ended 2-2.

Sunderland's 1-0 Premier League win over **Liverpool** on Oct 17, 2009 was decided by one of the most bizarre goals in football history when Darren Bent's shot struck a red beach ball thrown from the crowd and wrong-footed goalkeeper Jose Reina. Referee Mike Jones wrongly allowed it to stand. The Laws of the Game state: 'An outside agent interfering with play should result in play being stopped and restarted with a drop ball.'

Blackburn's 59th minute equaliser (2-2) in 3-3 draw away to Wigan (Prem) on Nov 19, 2011 was illegal. Morten Gamst Pedersen played the ball to himself from a corner and crossed for Junior Hoilett to net.

The Republic of Ireland were deprived of the chance of a World Cup place in the second leg of their play-off with France on Nov 18, 2009. They were leading 1-0 in Paris when Thierry Henry blatantly handled before setting up William Gallas to equalise in extra-time time and give his side a 2-1 aggregate victory. The FA of Ireland's call for a replay was rejected by FIFA.

• The most notorious goal in World Cup history was fisted in by Diego Maradona in **Argentina's** 2-1 quarter-final win over England in Mexico City on Jun 22, 1986.

ATTENDANCES

GREATEST WORLD CROWDS

World Cup, Maracana Stadium, Rio de Janeiro, Jul 16, 1950. Final match (Brazil v Uruguay) attendance 199,850; receipts £125,000.

Total attendance in three matches (including play-off) between Santos (Brazil) and AC Milan for the Inter-Continental Cup (World Club Championship) 1963, exceeded 375,000.

BRITISH RECORD CROWDS

Most to pay: 149,547, Scotland v England, at Hampden Park, Glasgow, Apr 17, 1937. This was the first all-ticket match in Scotland (receipts £24,000).

At Scottish FA Cup Final: 146,433, Celtic v Aberdeen, at Hampden Park, Apr 24, 1937. Estimated another 20,000 shut out.

For British club match (apart from a Cup Final): 143,470, Rangers v Hibernian, at Hampden Park, Mar 27, 1948 (Scottish Cup semi-final).

FA Cup Final: 126,047, Bolton v West Ham, Apr 28, 1923. Estimated 150,000 in ground at opening of Wembley Stadium.

New Wembley: 89,874, FA Cup Final, Cardiff v Portsmouth, May 17, 2008.

World Cup Qualifying ties: 120,000, Cameroon v Morocco, Yaounde, Nov 29, 1981; 107,580, Scotland v Poland, Hampden Park, Oct 13, 1965.

European Cup: 135,826, Celtic v Leeds (semi-final, 2nd leg) at Hampden Park, Apr 15, 1970.

European Cup Final: 127,621, Real Madrid v Eintracht Frankfurt, at Hampden Park, May 18, 1960.

European Cup-Winners' Cup Final: 100,000, West Ham v TSV Munich, at Wembley, May 19, 1965.

Scottish League: 118,567, Rangers v Celtic, Jan 2, 1939.

Scottish League Cup Final: 107,609, Celtic v Rangers, at Hampden Park, Oct 23, 1965.

Football League old format: First Div: 83,260, Manchester Utd v Arsenal, Jan 17, 1948 (at Maine Road); **Div 2** 70,302 Tottenham v Southampton, Feb 25, 1950; **Div 3S:** 51,621, Cardiff v Bristol City, Apr 7, 1947; **Div 3N:** 49,655, Hull v Rotherham, Dec 25, 1948; **Div 3:** 49,309, Sheffield Wed v Sheffield Utd, Dec 26, 1979; **Div 4:** 37,774, Crystal Palace v Millwall, Mar 31, 1961.

Premier League: 83,222, Tottenham v Arsenal (Wembley), Feb 10, 2018

Football League – New Div 1: 41,214, Sunderland v Stoke, Apr 25, 1998; **New Div 2:** 32,471, Manchester City v York, May 8, 1999; **New Div 3:** 22,319, Hull v Hartlepool Utd, Dec 26, 2002. **New Champs:** 52,181, Newcastle v Ipswich, Apr 24, 2010; **New Lge 1:** 46,039, Sunderland v Bradford, Dec 26, 2018; **New Lge 2:** 28,343, Coventry v Accrington, Feb 10, 2018.

In English Provinces: 84,569, Manchester City v Stoke (FA Cup 6), Mar 3, 1934.

Record for Under-21 International: 55,700, England v Italy, first match at New Wembley, Mar 24, 2007.

Record for friendly match: 104,679, Rangers v Eintracht Frankfurt, at Hampden Park, Glasgow, Oct 17, 1961.

FA Youth Cup: 38,187, Arsenal v Manchester Utd, at Emirates Stadium, Mar 14, 2007.

Record Football League aggregate (season): 41,271,414 (1948–49) – 88 clubs.

Record Football League aggregate (single day): 1,269,934, December 27, 1949, previous day, 1,226,098.

Record average home League attendance for season: 75,691 by Manchester Utd in 2007–08.

Long-ago League attendance aggregates: 10,929,000 in 1906–07 (40 clubs); 28,132,933 in 1937–38 (88 clubs).

Last 1m crowd aggregate, League (single day): 1,007,200, December 27, 1971.

Record Amateur match attendance: 100,000 for FA Amateur Cup Final, Pegasus v Harwich & Parkeston at Wembley, Apr 11, 1953.

Record Cup-tie aggregate: 265,199, at two matches between Rangers and Morton, in Scottish Cup Final, 1947–48.

Abandoned match attendance records: In England – 63,480 at Newcastle v Swansea City FA Cup 3rd round, Jan 10, 1953, abandoned 8 mins (0-0), fog.

In Scotland: 94,596 at Scotland v Austria (4-1), Hampden Park, May 8, 1963. Referee Jim Finney ended play (79 minutes) after Austria had two players sent off and one carried off.

Colchester's record crowd (19,072) was for the FA Cup 1st round tie v Reading on Nov 27, 1948, abandoned 35 minutes (0-0), fog.

SMALLEST CROWDS

Smallest League attendances: 450 Rochdale v Cambridge Utd (Div 3, Feb 5, 1974); 469, Thames v Luton (Div 3 South, December 6, 1930).

Only 13 people paid to watch Stockport v Leicester (Div 2, May 7, 1921) at Old Trafford, but up to 2,000 stayed behind after Manchester Utd v Derby earlier in the day. Stockport's ground was closed.

Lowest Premier League crowd: 3,039 for Wimbledon v Everton, Jan 26, 1993 (smallest top-division attendance since War).

Lowest Saturday post-war top-division crowd: 3,231 for Wimbledon v Luton, Sep 7, 1991 (Div 1).

Lowest Football League crowds, new format – Div 1: 849 for Wimbledon v Rotherham, (Div 1) Oct 29, 2002 (smallest attendance in top two divisions since War); 1,054 Wimbledon v Wigan (Div 1), Sep 13, 2003 in club's last home match when sharing Selhurst Park; **Div 2:** 1,077, Hartlepool Utd v Cardiff, Mar 22, 1994; **Div 3:** 739, Doncaster v Barnet, Mar 3, 1998.

Lowest top-division crowd at a major ground since the war: 4,554 for Arsenal v Leeds (May 5, 1966) – fixture clashed with live TV coverage of Cup-Winners' Cup Final (Liverpool v Borussia Dortmund).

Smallest League Cup attendances: 612, Halifax v Tranmere (1st round, 2nd leg) Sep 6, 2000; 664, Wimbledon v Rotherham (3rd round), Nov 5, 2002.

Smallest League Cup attendance at top-division ground: 1,987 for Wimbledon v Bolton (2nd Round, 2nd Leg) Oct 6, 1992.

Smallest Wembley crowds for England matches: 15,628 v Chile (Rous Cup, May 23, 1989 – affected by Tube strike); 20,038 v Colombia (Friendly, Sep 6, 1995); 21,432 v Czech. (Friendly, Apr 25, 1990); 21,142 v Japan (Umbro Cup, Jun 3, 1995); 23,600 v Wales (British Championship, Feb 23, 1983); 23,659 v Greece (Friendly, May 17, 1994); 23,951 v East Germany (Friendly, Sep 12, 1984); 24,000 v N Ireland (British Championship, Apr 4, 1984); 25,756 v Colombia (Rous Cup, May 24, 1988); 25,837 v Denmark (Friendly, Sep 14, 1988).

Smallest international modern crowds: 221 for Poland v N Ireland (4-1, friendly) at Limassol, Cyprus, on Feb 13, 2002. Played at neutral venue at Poland's World Cup training base. 265 (all from N Ireland) at their Euro Champ qual against Serbia in Belgrade on Mar 25, 2011. Serbia ordered by UEFA to play behind closed doors because of previous crowd trouble.

Smallest international modern crowds at home: N Ireland: 2,500 v Chile (Belfast, May 26, 1989 – clashed with ITV live screening of Liverpool v Arsenal Championship decider); Scotland: 7,843 v N Ireland (Hampden Park, May 6, 1969); Wales: 2,315 v N Ireland (Wrexham, May 27, 1982).

Smallest attendance for post-war England match: 2,378 v San Marino (World Cup) at Bologna (Nov 17, 1993). Tie clashed with Italy v Portugal (World Cup) shown live on Italian TV.

Lowest England attendance at New Wembley: 40,181 v Norway (friendly), Sep 3, 2014

Smallest paid attendance for British first-class match: 29 for Clydebank v East Stirling, CIS Scottish League Cup 1st round, Jul 31, 1999. Played at Morton's Cappielow Park ground, shared by Clydebank. Match clashed with the Tall Ships Race which attracted 200,000 to the area.

FA CUP CROWD RECORD (OUTSIDE FINAL)

The first FA Cup-tie shown on closed-circuit TV (5th round, Saturday, Mar 11, 1967, kick-off 7pm) drew a total of 105,000 spectators to Goodison Park and Anfield. At Goodison, 64,851 watched the match 'for real', while 40,149 saw the TV version on eight giant screens at Anfield. Everton beat Liverpool 1-0.

LOWEST SEMI-FINAL CROWD

The smallest FA Cup semi-final attendance since the War was 17,987 for the Manchester Utd– Crystal Palace replay at Villa Park on Apr 12, 1995. Palace supporters largely boycotted tie after a fan died in car-park clash outside pub in Walsall before first match.

Previous lowest: 25,963 for Wimbledon v Luton, at Tottenham on Apr 9, 1988.

Lowest quarter-final crowd since the war: 8,735 for Chesterfield v Wrexham on Mar 9, 1997.

Smallest FA Cup 3rd round attendances for matches between League clubs: 1,833 for Chester v Bournemouth (at Macclesfield) Jan 5, 1991; 1,966 for Aldershot v Oxford Utd, Jan 10, 1987.

PRE-WEMBLEY CUP FINAL CROWDS

AT CRYSTAL PALACE

1895	42,560	1902	48,036	1908	74,967
1896	48,036	Replay	33,050	1909	67,651
1897	65,891	1903	64,000	1910	76,980
1898	62,017	1904	61,734	1911	69,098
1899	73,833	1905	101,117	1912	54,434
1900	68,945	1906	75,609	1913	120,028
1901	110,802	1907	84,584	1914	72,778

AT OLD TRAFFORD

1915   50,000

AT STAMFORD BRIDGE

1920	50,018	1921	72,805	1922	53,000

England women's record crowd: 77,768 v Germany, 1-2 (Wembley, Nov 9, 2019).

INTERNATIONAL RECORDS

MOST APPEARANCES

Peter Shilton, England goalkeeper, then aged 40, retired from international football after the 1990 World Cup Finals with the European record number of caps – 125. Previous record (119) was set by **Pat Jennings,** Northern Ireland's goalkeeper from 1964–86, who retired on his 41st birthday during the 1986 World Cup in Mexico. Shilton's England career spanned 20 seasons from his debut against East Germany at Wembley on Nov 25, 1970.

Nine players have completed a century of appearances in full international matches for England. **Billy Wright** of Wolves, was the first, retiring in 1959 with a total of 105 caps. **Bobby Charlton,** of Manchester Utd, beat Wright's record in the World Cup match against West Germany in Leon, Mexico, in Jun 1970 and **Bobby Moore,** of West Ham, overtook Charlton's 106 caps against Italy in Turin, in Jun 1973. Moore played 108 times for England, a record that stood until **Shilton** reached 109 against Denmark in Copenhagen (Jun 7, 1989). In season 2008–09, **David Beckham** (LA Galaxy/AC Milan) overtook Moore as England's most-capped outfield player. In the vastly different selection processes of their eras, Moore played 108 full games for his country, whereas Beckham's total of 115 to the end of season 2009–10, included 58 part matches, 14 as substitute and 44 times substituted. **Steven Gerrard** won his 100th cap against Sweden in Stockholm on Nov 14, 2012 and **Ashley Cole** reached 100 appearances against Brazil at Wembley on Feb 6, 2013. **Frank Lampard** played his 100th game against Ukraine in Kiev (World Cup qual) on Sep 10, 2013. **Wayne Rooney's** 100th appearance was against Slovenia at Wembley (Euro Champ qual) on Nov 15, 2014.

Robbie Keane won his 126th Republic of Ireland cap, overtaking Shay Given's record, In a World Cup qualifier against the Faroe Islands on Jun 7, 2013. Keane scored all his team's three goals in a 3-0 win.

Kenny Dalglish became Scotland's first 100-cap international v Romania (Hampden Park, Mar 26, 1986).

World's most-capped player: Ahmed Hassan, 184 for Egypt (1995–2012).

Most-capped European player: Vitalijs Astafjevs, 167 for Latvia (1992–2010).

Most-capped European goalkeeper: Thomas Ravelli, 143 Internationals for Sweden (1981–97).

BRITAIN'S MOST-CAPPED PLAYERS

(As at start of season 2020–21)

England		Alex McLeish	77	Northern Ireland	
Peter Shilton	125	Paul McStay	76	Pat Jennings	119
Wayne Rooney	120	Tommy Boyd	72	Steven Davis	117
David Beckham	115			Aaron Hughes	112
Steven Gerrard	114	**Wales**		David Healy	95
Bobby Moore	108	Chris Gunter	96	Mal Donaghy	91
Ashley Cole	107	Neville Southall	92	Sammy McIlroy	88
Bobby Charlton	106	Wayne Hennessey	89	Maik Taylor	88
Frank Lampard	106	Ashley Williams	86		
Billy Wright	105	Gary Speed	85	**Republic of Ireland**	
		Gareth Bale	83	Robbie Keane	146
Scotland		Craig Bellamy	78	Shay Given	134
Kenny Dalglish	102	Joe Ledley	77	John O'Shea	118
Jim Leighton	91			Kevin Kilbane	110
Darren Fletcher	80			Steve Staunton	102
				Damien Duff	100

ENGLAND'S MOST-CAPPED PLAYER (either gender)

Fara Williams (Reading midfielder) with 171 appearances for England women's team to end of season 2019–20.

MOST ENGLAND CAPS IN ROW

Most consecutive international appearances: 70 by **Billy Wright,** for England from Oct 1951 to May 1959. He played 105 of England's first 108 post-war matches.

England captains most times: Billy Wright and Bobby Moore, 90 each.

England captains – 4 in match (v Serbia & Montenegro at Leicester Jun 3, 2003): **Michael Owen** was captain for the first half and after the interval the armband passed to **Emile Heskey** (for 15 minutes), **Phil Neville** (26 minutes) and substitute **Jamie Carragher** (9 minutes, including time added).

MOST SUCCESSIVE ENGLAND WINS

10 (Jun 1908–Jun 1909. Modern: 8 (Oct 2005–Jun 2006).

ENGLAND'S LONGEST UNBEATEN RUN

19 matches (16 wins, 3 draws), Nov 1965–Nov 1966.

ENGLAND'S TALLEST

At **6ft 7in,** Peter Crouch became England's tallest-ever international when he made his debut against Colombia in New Jersey, USA on May 31, 2005.

MOST PLAYERS FROM ONE CLUB IN ENGLAND SIDES

Arsenal supplied seven men (a record) to the England team v Italy at Highbury on Nov 14, 1934. They were: Frank Moss, George Male, Eddie Hapgood, Wilf Copping, Ray Bowden, Ted Drake and Cliff Bastin. In addition, Arsenal's Tom Whittaker was England's trainer.

Since then until 2001, the most players from one club in an England team was six from **Liverpool** against Switzerland at Wembley in Sep 1977. The side also included a Liverpool old boy, Kevin Keegan (Hamburg).

Seven **Arsenal** men took part in the England – France (0-2) match at Wembley on Feb 10, 1999. Goalkeeper David Seaman and defenders Lee Dixon, Tony Adams and Martin Keown lined up for England. Nicolas Anelka (2 goals) and Emmanuel Petit started the match for France and Patrick Vieira replaced Anelka.

Manchester Utd equalled Arsenal's 1934 record by providing England with seven players in the World Cup qualifier away to Albania on Mar 28, 2001. Five started the match – David Beckham (captain), Gary Neville, Paul Scholes, Nicky Butt and Andy Cole – and two went on as substitutes: Wes Brown and Teddy Sheringham.

INTERNATIONAL SUBS RECORDS

Malta substituted all 11 players in their 1-2 home defeat against England on Jun 3, 2000. Six substitutes by England took the total replacements in the match to 17, then an international record.

Most substitutions in match by **England:** 11 in second half by Sven-Goran Eriksson against Holland at Tottenham on Aug 15, 2001; 11 against Italy at Leeds on Mar 27, 2002; Italy sent on 8 players from the bench – the total of 19 substitutions was then a record for an international match; 11 against Australia at Upton Park on Feb 12, 2003 (entire England team changed at half-time); 11 against Iceland at City of Manchester Stadium on Jun 5, 2004.

Forty three players, a record for an England match, were used in the international against Serbia & Montenegro at Leicester on Jun 3, 2003. England sent on 10 substitutes in the second half and their opponents changed all 11 players.

The **Republic of Ireland** sent on 12 second-half substitutes, using 23 players in all, when they beat Russia 2-0 in a friendly international in Dublin on Feb 13, 2002.

First England substitute: Wolves winger **Jimmy Mullen** replaced injured Jackie Milburn (15 mins) away to Belgium on May 18, 1950. He scored in a 4-1 win.

ENGLAND'S WORLD CUP-WINNERS

At Wembley, Jul 30, 1966, 4-2 v West Germany (2-2 after 90 mins), scorers Hurst 3, Peters. Team: Banks; Cohen, Wilson, Stiles, Jack Charlton, Moore (capt), Ball, Hurst, Bobby Charlton, Hunt, Peters. Manager **Alf Ramsey** fielded that same eleven in six successive matches (an

England record): the World Cup quarter-final, semi-final and Final, and the first three games of the following season. England wore red shirts in the Final and The Queen presented the Cup to Bobby Moore. The players each received a £1,000 bonus, plus £60 World Cup Final appearance money, all less tax, and Ramsey a £6,000 bonus from the FA The match was shown live on TV (in black and white).

England's non-playing 'reserves' – there were no substitutes – also received the £1,000 bonus, but no medals. That remained the case until FIFA finally decided that non-playing members and staff of World Cup-winning squads should be given replica medals. England's 'forgotten heroes' received theirs at a reception in Downing Street on June 10, 2009 and were later guests of honour at the World Cup qualifier against Andorra at Wembley. The 11 'reserves' were: Springett, Bonetti, Armfield, Byrne, Flowers, Hunter, Paine, Connelly, Callaghan, Greaves, Eastham. Jimmy Greaves played in all three group games, against Uruguay, Mexico and France. John Connelly was in the team against Uruguay, Terry Paine against Mexico and Ian Callaghan against France.

BRAZIL'S RECORD RUN

Brazil hold the record for the longest unbeaten sequence in international football: 45 matches from 1993–97. The previous record of 31 was held by Hungary between Jun 1950 and Jul 1954.

ENGLAND MATCHES ABANDONED

May 17, 1953 v **Argentina** (Friendly, Buenos Aires) after 23 mins (0-0) – rain.
Oct 29, 1975 v **Czechoslovakia** (Euro Champ qual, Bratislava) after 17 mins (0-0) – fog. Played next day.
Feb 15, 1995 v **Rep of Ireland** (Friendly, Dublin) after 27 mins (1-0) – crowd disturbance.

ENGLAND POSTPONEMENTS

Nov 21, 1979 v **Bulgaria** (Euro Champ qual, Wembley, postponed for 24 hours – fog; Aug 10, 2011 v **Holland** (friendly), Wembley, postponed after rioting in London.
Oct 16, 2012 v **Poland** (World Cup qual, Warsaw) postponed to next day – pitch waterlogged.
The friendly against **Honduras** (Miami, Jun 7, 2014) was suspended midway through the first half for 44 minutes – thunderstorm.

ENGLAND UNDER COVER

England played indoors for the first time when they beat Argentina 1-0 in the World Cup at the Sapporo Dome, Japan, on Jun 7, 2002.

ALL-SEATED INTERNATIONALS

The first **all-seated crowd** (30,000) for a full international in Britain saw **Wales** and **West Germany** draw 0-0 at Cardiff Arms Park on May 31, 1989. The terraces were closed.
England's first all-seated international at Wembley was against Yugoslavia (2-1) on December 13, 1989 (attendance 34,796). The terracing behind the goals was closed for conversion to seating.
The first **full-house all-seated** international at Wembley was for England v Brazil (1-0) on Mar 28, 1990, when a capacity 80,000 crowd paid record British receipts of £1,200,000.

MOST NEW CAPS IN ENGLAND TEAM

6, by Sir Alf Ramsey (v Portugal, Apr 3, 1974) and **by Sven-Goran Eriksson** (v Australia, Feb 12, 2003; 5 at half-time when 11 changes made).

PLAYED FOR MORE THAN ONE COUNTRY

Multi-nationals in senior international football include: **Johnny Carey** (1938–53) – caps Rep of Ireland 29, N Ireland 7; **Ferenc Puskas** (1945–62) – caps Hungary 84, Spain 4; **Alfredo di Stefano** (1950–56) – caps Argentina 7, Spain 31; **Ladislav Kubala** (1948–58) – caps, Hungary 3, Czechoslovakia 11, Spain 19, only player to win full international honours with 3 countries. Kubala also played in a fourth international team, scoring twice for FIFA v England at Wembley in 1953. Eleven players, including **Carey**, appeared for both N Ireland and the Republic of Ireland in seasons directly after the last war.

Cecil Moore, capped by N Ireland in 1949 when with Glentoran, played for USA v England in 1953.

Hawley Edwards played for England v Scotland in 1874 and for Wales v Scotland in 1876.

Jack Reynolds (Distillery and WBA) played for both Ireland (5 times) and England (8) in the 1890s.

Bobby Evans (Sheffield Utd) had played 10 times for Wales when capped for England, in 1910–11. He was born in Chester of Welsh parents.

In recent years, several players have represented USSR and one or other of the breakaway republics. The same applies to Yugoslavia and its component states. **Josip Weber** played for Croatia in 1992 and made a 5-goal debut for Belgium in 1994.

THREE-GENERATION INTERNATIONAL FAMILY

When Bournemouth striker **Warren Feeney** was capped away to Liechtenstein on Mar 27, 2002, he became the third generation of his family to play for Northern Ireland. He followed in the footsteps of his grandfather James (capped twice in 1950) and father Warren snr. (1 in 1976).

FATHERS & SONS CAPPED BY ENGLAND

George Eastham senior (pre-war) and **George Eastham junior**; **Brian Clough** and **Nigel Clough**; **Frank Lampard snr** and **Frank Lampard jnr**; **Mark Chamberlain** and **Alex Oxlade-Chamberlain**.

FATHER & SON SAME-DAY CAPS

Iceland made father-and-son international history when they beat Estonia 3-0 in Tallin on Apr 24, 1996. **Arnor Gudjohnsen** (35) started the match and was replaced (62 mins) by his 17-year-old son **Eidur**.

LONGEST UNBEATEN START TO ENGLAND CAREER

Steven Gerrard, 21 matches (W16, D5) 2000–03.

SUCCESSIVE ENGLAND HAT-TRICKS

The last player to score a hat-trick in consecutive England matches was **Dixie Dean** on the summer tour in May 1927, against Belgium (9-1) and Luxembourg (5-2).

MOST GOALS BY PLAYER v ENGLAND

4 by **Zlatan Ibrahimovic** (Sweden 4 England 2, Stockholm, Nov 14, 2012).

POST-WAR HAT-TRICKS v ENGLAND

Nov 25, 1953, **Nandor Hidegkuti** (England 3, Hungary 6, Wembley); May 11, 1958, **Aleksandar Petakovic** (Yugoslavia 5, England 0, Belgrade); May 17, 1959, **Juan Seminario** (Peru 4, England 1, Lima); Jun 15, 1988, **Marco van Basten** (Holland 3, England 1, European Championship, Dusseldorf). Six other players scored hat-tricks against England (1878–1930).

NO-SAVE GOALKEEPERS

Chris Woods did not have one save to make when England beat San Marino 6-0 (World Cup) at Wembley on Feb 17, 1993. He touched the ball only six times.

Gordon Banks had a similar no-save experience when England beat Malta 5-0 (European Championship) at Wembley on May 12, 1971. Malta did not force a goal-kick or corner, and the four times Banks touched the ball were all from back passes.

Robert Green was also idle in the 6-0 World Cup qualifying win over Andorra at Wembley on Jun 10, 2009.

Joe Hart was untroubled in England's 5-0 win over San Marino in a World Cup qualifier at Wembley on Oct 12, 2012.

WORLD/EURO MEMBERS

FIFA has 211 member countries, **UEFA** 55

NEW FIFA PRESIDENT

The 18-year reign of FIFA president **Sepp Blatter** ended in December 2015 amid widespread allegations of corruption. He was replaced in February 2016 by Gianni Infantino, a 45-year-old Swiss-Italian lawyer, who was previously general secretary of UEFA. Under new rules, he will serve four years.

FIFA WORLD YOUTH CUP (UNDER-20)

Finals: 1977 (Tunis) Soviet Union 2 Mexico 2 (Soviet won 9-8 on pens.); 1979 (Tokyo) Argentina 3 Soviet Union 1; 1981 (Sydney) W Germany 4 Qatar 0; 1983 (Mexico City) Brazil 1 Argentina 0; 1985 (Moscow) Brazil 1 Spain 0; 1987 (Santiago) Yugoslavia 1 W Germany 1 (Yugoslavia won 5-4 on pens.); 1989 (Riyadh) Portugal 2 Nigeria 0; 1991 (Lisbon) Portugal 0 Brazil 0 (Portugal won 4-2 on pens.); 1993 (Sydney) Brazil 2 Ghana 1; 1995 (Qatar) Argentina 2 Brazil 0; 1997 (Kuala Lumpur) Argentina 2 Uruguay 1; 1999 (Lagos) Spain 4 Japan 0; 2001 (Buenos Aires) Argentina 3 Ghana 0; 2003 (Dubai) Brazil 1 Spain 0; 2005 (Utrecht) Argentina 2 Nigeria 1; 2007 (Toronto) Argentina 2 Czech Republic 1; 2009 (Cairo) Ghana 0 Brazil 0 (aet, Ghana won 4-3 on pens); 2011 (Bogota) Brazil 3 Portugal 2 (aet); 2013 (Istanbul) France 0 Uruguay 0 (aet, France won 4-1 on pens); 2015 (Auckland) Serbia 2 Brazil 1 (aet); 2017 (Suwon) England 1 Venezuela 0; 2019 (Lodz) Ukraine 3 South Korea 1.

FAMOUS CLUB FEATS

Manchester City won the 2017–18 Premier League title under Pep Guardiola in record style. They became England's first champions to total 100 points and had the longest winning streak, 18 matches, in top-flight history. There were other new Premier League marks for goals scored (106), goal difference (79), overall wins (32), away victories (16), and for a 19-point gap to second-place. In season 2018–19, City made history with a domestic treble, winning the Premier League, FA Cup and League Cup.

Arsenal created an all-time English League record sequence of 49 unbeaten Premier League matches (W36, D13), spanning 3 seasons, from May 7, 2003 until losing 2-0 away to Manchester Utd on Oct 24, 2004. It included all 38 games in season 2003–04.

The Double: There have been 11 instances of a club winning the Football League/Premier League title and the FA Cup in the same season. Preston 1888–89; Aston Villa 1896–97; Tottenham 1960–61; **Arsenal** 1970–71, 1997–98, 2001–02; Liverpool 1985–86; Manchester Utd 1993–94, 1995–96, 1998–99; Chelsea 2009–10.

The Treble: Liverpool were the first English club to win three major competitions in one season when in 1983–84, Joe Fagan's first season as manager, they were League Champions, League Cup winners and European Cup winners.

Sir Alex Ferguson's **Manchester Utd** achieved an even more prestigious treble in 1998–99, completing the domestic double of Premier League and FA Cup and then winning the European Cup. In season 2008–09, they completed another major triple success – Premier League, Carling Cup and World Club Cup.

Liverpool completed a unique treble by an English club with three cup successes under Gerard Houllier in season 2000–01: the League Cup, FA Cup and UEFA Cup.

Liverpool the first English club to win five major trophies in one calendar year (Feb– Aug 2001): League Cup, FA Cup, UEFA Cup, Charity Shield, UEFA Super Cup.

As Champions in season 2001–02, **Arsenal** set a Premier League record by winning the last 13 matches. They were the first top-division club since Preston in the League's inaugural season (1888–89) to maintain an unbeaten away record.

(See Scottish section for treble feats by Rangers and Celtic).

Record Home Runs: Liverpool went 85 consecutive first-team games unbeaten at home between losing 2-3 to Birmingham on Jan 21, 1978 and 1-2 to Leicester on Jan 31, 1981. They comprised 63 in the League, 9 League Cup, 7 in European competition and 6 FA Cup.

Chelsea hold the record unbeaten home League sequence of 86 matches (W62, D24) between losing 1-2 to Arsenal, Feb 21, 2004, and 0-1 to Liverpool, Oct 26, 2008.

Third to First: Charlton, in 1936, became the first club to advance from the Third to First Division in successive seasons. **Queens Park Rangers** were the second club to achieve the feat in 1968, and **Oxford Utd** did it in 1984 and 1985 as Champions of each division. Subsequently, **Derby** (1987), **Middlesbrough** (1988), **Sheffield Utd** (1990) and **Notts Co** (1991) climbed from Third Division to First in consecutive seasons.

Watford won successive promotions from the modern Second Division to the Premier League in 1997–98, 1998–99. **Manchester City** equalled the feat in 1998–99, 1999–2000. **Norwich** climbed from League 1 to the Premier League in seasons 2009–10, 2010–11. **Southampton** did the same in 2010–11 and 2011–12.

Fourth to First: Northampton , in 1965 became the first club to rise from the Fourth to the First Division. **Swansea** climbed from the Fourth Division to the First (three promotions in four seasons), 1977–78 to 1980–81. **Wimbledon** repeated the feat, 1982–83 to 1985–86. **Watford** did it in five seasons, 1977–8 to 1981–82. **Carlisle** climbed from Fourth Division to First, 1964–74.

Non-League to First: When **Wimbledon** finished third in the Second Division in 1986, they completed the phenomenal rise from non-League football (Southern League) to the First Division in nine years. Two years later they won the FA Cup.

Tottenham, in 1960–61, not only carried off the First Division Championship and the FA Cup for the first time that century but set up other records by opening with 11 successive wins, registering most First Division wins (31), most away wins in the League's history (16), and equalling Arsenal's First Division records of 66 points and 33 away points. They already held the Second Division record of 70 points (1919–20).

Arsenal, in 1993, became the first club to win both English domestic cup competitions (FA Cup and League Cup) in the same season. **Liverpool** repeated the feat in 2001. **Chelsea** did it in 2007.

Chelsea achieved the FA Cup/Champions League double in May 2012.

Preston, in season 1888–89, won the first League Championship without losing a match and the FA Cup without having a goal scored against them. Only other English clubs to remain unbeaten through a League season were **Liverpool** (Div 2 Champions in 1893–94) and **Arsenal** (Premier League Champions 2003–04).

Bury, in 1903, also won the FA Cup without conceding a goal.

Everton won Div 2, Div 1 and the FA Cup in successive seasons, 1930–31, 1931–32, 1932–33.

Wolves won the League Championship in 1958 and 1959 and the FA Cup in 1960.

Liverpool won the title in 1964, the FA Cup in 1965 and the title again in 1966. In 1978 they became the first British club to win the European Cup in successive seasons. Nottm Forest repeated the feat in 1979 and 1980.

Liverpool won the League Championship six times in eight seasons (1976–83) under **Bob Paisley's** management.

Sir Alex Ferguson's **Manchester Utd** won the Premier League in 13 of its 21 seasons (1992–2013). They were runners-up five times and third three times.

FA CUP/PROMOTION DOUBLE

WBA are the only club to achieve this feat in the same season (1930–31).

COVENTRY UNIQUE

Coventry are the only club to have played in the Premier League, all four previous divisions of the Football League, in both sections (North and South) of the old Third Division and in the modern Championship.

FAMOUS UPS & DOWNS

Sunderland: Relegated in 1958 after maintaining First Division status since their election to the Football League in 1890. They dropped into Division 3 for the first time in 1987.

Aston Villa: Relegated with Preston to the Third Division in 1970.

Arsenal up: When the League was extended in 1919, Woolwich Arsenal (sixth in Division Two in 1914–15, last season before the war) were elected to Division One. Arsenal have been in the top division ever since.

Tottenham down: At that same meeting in 1919 Chelsea (due for relegation) retained their place in Division One but the bottom club (Tottenham) had to go down to Division Two.

Preston and Burnley down: Preston, the first League Champions in season 1888–89, dropped into the Fourth Division in 1985. So did Burnley, also among the League's original members in 1888. In 1986, Preston had to apply for re-election.

Wolves' fall: Wolves, another of the Football League's original members, completed the fall from First Division to Fourth in successive seasons (1984–85–86).

Lincoln out: Lincoln became the first club to suffer automatic demotion from the Football League when they finished bottom of Div 4, on goal difference, in season 1986–87. They were replaced by Scarborough, champions of the GM Vauxhall Conference. Lincoln regained their place a year later.

Swindon up and down: In the 1990 play-offs, Swindon won promotion to the First Division for the first time, but remained in the Second Division because of financial irregularities.

MOST CHAMPIONSHIP WINS

Manchester Utd have been champions of England a record 20 times (7 Football League, 13 Premier League).

LONGEST CURRENT MEMBERS OF TOP DIVISION

Arsenal (since 1919), **Everton** (1954), **Liverpool** (1962), **Manchester Utd** (1975).

CHAMPIONS: FEWEST PLAYERS

Liverpool used only **14** players (five ever-present) when they won the League Championship in season 1965–66. **Aston Villa** also called on no more than 14 players to win the title in 1980–81, with seven ever-present.

UNBEATEN CHAMPIONS

Only two clubs have become Champions of England with an unbeaten record: **Preston** as the Football League's first winners in 1888–89 (22 matches) and **Arsenal**, Premier League winners in 2003–04 (38 matches).

LEAGUE HAT-TRICKS

Huddersfield created a record in 1924–25–26 by winning the League Championship three years in succession.

Arsenal equalled this hat-trick in 1933–34–35, **Liverpool** in 1982–83–84 and **Manchester Utd** in 1999–2000–01. Sir Alex Ferguson's side became the first to complete two hat-tricks (2007–08–09).

'SUPER DOUBLE' WINNERS

Since the War, there have been three instances of players appearing in and then managing FA Cup and Championship-winning teams:

Joe Mercer: Player in Arsenal Championship teams 1948, 1953 and in their 1950 FA Cup side; manager of Manchester City when they won Championship 1968, FA Cup 1969.

Kenny Dalglish: Player in Liverpool Championship-winning teams 1979, 1980, 1982, 1983, 1984, player-manager 1986, 1988, 1990: player-manager when Liverpool won FA Cup (to complete Double) 1986; manager of Blackburn, Champions 1995.

George Graham: Played in Arsenal's Double-winning team in 1971, and as manager took them to Championship success in 1989 and 1991 and the FA Cup – League Cup double in 1993.

ORIGINAL TWELVE

The original 12 members of the Football League (formed in 1888) were: **Accrington, Aston Villa, Blackburn, Bolton, Burnley, Derby, Everton, Notts Co, Preston, Stoke, WBA** and **Wolves.** Results on the opening day (Sep 8, 1888): Bolton 3, Derby 6; Everton 2, Accrington 1; Preston 5, Burnley 2; Stoke 0, WBA 2; Wolves 1, Aston Villa 1. Preston had the biggest first-day crowd: 6,000. Blackburn and Notts Co did not play that day. They kicked off a week later (Sep 15) – Blackburn 5, Accrington 5; Everton 2, Notts Co 1.

Accrington FC resigned from the league in 1893 and later folded. A new club, Accrington Stanley, were members of the league from 1921 until 1962 when financial problems forced their demise. The current Accrington Stanley were formed in 1968 and gained league status in 2007.

FASTEST CLIMBS

Three promotions in four seasons by two clubs – **Swansea City:** 1978 third in Div 4; 1979 third in Div 3; 1981 third in Div 2; **Wimbledon:** 1983 Champions of Div 4; 1984 second in Div 3; 1986 third in Div 2.

MERSEYSIDE RECORD

Liverpool is the only city to have staged top-division football – through Everton and/or Liverpool – **in every season** since League football began in 1888.

EARLIEST PROMOTIONS TO TOP DIVISION POST-WAR

Mar 23, 1974, **Middlesbrough;** Mar 25, 2006, **Reading.**

EARLIEST RELEGATIONS POST-WAR

From top division: **QPR** went down from the old First Division on Mar 29, 1969; **Derby** went down from the Premier League on Mar 29, 2008, with 6 matches still to play. From modern First Division: **Stockport** on Mar 16, 2002, with 7 matches still to play; **Wimbledon** on Apr 6, 2004, with 7 matches to play.

LEAGUE RECORDS

CHAMPIONS OF ENGLAND 1888–2020

Football League and Premier league

Manchester Utd 20, Liverpool 19, Arsenal 13, Everton 9, Aston Villa 7, Chelsea 6, Manchester City 6, Sunderland 6, Newcastle 4, Sheffield Wed 4, Blackburn 3, Huddersfield 3, Leeds 3, Wolves 3, Burnley 2, Derby 2, Portsmouth 2, Preston 2, Tottenham 2, Ipswich 1, Leicester 1, Nottm Forest 1, Sheffield Utd 1, WBA 1

DOUBLE CHAMPIONS

Nine men have played in and managed League Championship-winning teams:

Ted Drake Player – Arsenal 1934, 1935, 1938. Manager – Chelsea 1955.
Bill Nicholson Player – Tottenham 1951. Manager – Tottenham 1961.
Alf Ramsey Player – Tottenham 1951. Manager – Ipswich 1962.
Joe Mercer Player – Everton 1939, Arsenal 1948, 1953. Manager – Manchester City 1968.
Dave Mackay Player – Tottenham 1961. Manager – Derby 1975.
Bob Paisley Player – Liverpool 1947. Manager – Liverpool 1976, 1977, 1979, 1980, 1982, 1983.
Howard Kendall Player – Everton 1970. Manager – Everton 1985, 1987.
Kenny Dalglish Player – Liverpool 1979, 1980, 1982, 1983, 1984. Player-manager – Liverpool 1986, 1988, 1990. Manager – Blackburn 1995.
George Graham Player – Arsenal 1971. Manager – Arsenal 1989, 1991.

CANTONA'S FOUR-TIMER

Eric Cantona played in four successive Championship-winning teams: Marseille 1990–01, Leeds 1991–92, Manchester Utd 1992–93 and 1993–94.

ARRIVALS AND DEPARTURES

The following are the Football League arrivals and departures since 1923:

Year	In	Out
1923	Doncaster	Stalybridge Celtic
	New Brighton	

1927	Torquay	Aberdare Athletic
1928	Carlisle	Durham
1929	York	Ashington
1930	Thames	Merthyr Tydfil
1931	Mansfield	Newport Co
	Chester	Nelson
1932	Aldershot	Thames
	Newport Co	Wigan Borough
1938	Ipswich	Gillingham
1950	Colchester, Gillingham	
	Scunthorpe, Shrewsbury	
1951	Workington	New Brighton
1960	Peterborough	Gateshead
1962	Oxford Utd	Accrington (resigned)
1970	Cambridge Utd	Bradford PA
1972	Hereford	Barrow
1977	Wimbledon	Workington
1978	Wigan	Southport
1987	Scarborough	Lincoln
1988	Lincoln	Newport Co
1989	Maidstone	Darlington
1990	Darlington	Colchester
1991	Barnet	
1992	Colchester	Aldershot, Maidstone (resigned)
1993	Wycombe	Halifax
1997	Macclesfield	Hereford
1998	Halifax	Doncaster
1999	Cheltenham	Scarborough
2000	Kidderminster	Chester
2001	Rushden	Barnet
2002	Boston	Halifax
2003	Yeovil, Doncaster	Exeter, Shrewsbury
2004	Chester, Shrewsbury	Carlisle, York
2005	Barnet, Carlisle	Kidderminster, Cambridge Utd
2006	Accrington, Hereford	Oxford Utd, Rushden & Diamonds
2007	Dagenham, Morecambe	Torquay, Boston
2008	Aldershot, Exeter	Wrexham, Mansfield
2009	Burton, Torquay	Chester, Luton
2010	Stevenage, Oxford Utd	Grimsby, Darlington
2011	Crawley, AFC Wimbledon	Lincoln, Stockport
2012	Fleetwood, York	Hereford, Macclesfield
2013	Mansfield, Newport	Barnet, Aldershot
2014	Luton, Cambridge Utd	Bristol Rov, Torquay
2015	Barnet, Bristol Rov	Cheltenham, Tranmere
2016	Cheltenham, Grimsby	Dagenham & Redbridge, York
2017	Lincoln, Forest Green	Hartlepool, Leyton Orient
2018	Macclesfield, Tranmere	Barnet, Chesterfield
2019	Leyton Orient, Salford	Notts Co Yeovil
2020	Barrow, Harrogate	Macclesfield

Leeds City were expelled from Div 2 in Oct, 1919; Port Vale took over their fixtures.

EXTENSIONS TO FOOTBALL LEAGUE

Clubs	Season	Clubs	Season
12 to 14	1891–92	44 to 66†	1920–21
14 to 28*	1892–93	66 to 86†	1921–22

28 to 31	1893–94	86 to 88	1923–24
31 to 32	1894–95	88 to 92	1950–51
32 to 36	1898–99	92 to 93	1991–92
36 to 40	1905–06	(Reverted to 92 when Aldershot closed, Mar 1992)

*Second Division formed. † Third Division (South) formed from Southern League clubs.
†Third Division (North) formed.
Football League reduced to 70 clubs and three divisions on the formation of the FA Premier League in 1992; increased to 72 season 1994–95, when Premier League reduced to 20 clubs.

RECORD RUNS

Arsenal hold the record unbeaten sequence in the English League – 49 Premier League matches (36 wins, 13 draws) from May 7, 2003 until Oct 24, 2004 when beaten 2-0 away to Manchester Utd. The record previously belonged to **Nottm Forest** – 42 First Division matches (21 wins, 21 draws) from Nov 19, 1977 until beaten 2-0 at Liverpool on December 9, 1978.

Huddersfield set a new Football League record of 43 League 1 matches unbeaten from Jan 1, 2011 until Nov 28, 2011 when losing 2-0 at Charlton.

Best debuts: Ipswich won the First Division at their first attempt in 1961–62.

Peterborough in their first season in the Football League (1960–01) not only won the Fourth Division but set the all-time scoring record for the League of 134 goals. **Hereford** were promoted from the Fourth Division in their first League season, 1972–73.

Wycombe were promoted from the Third Division (via the play-offs) in their first League season, 1993–94. **Stevenage** were promoted from League 2 (via the play-offs) in their first League season, 2010–11. **Crawley** gained automatic promotion in their first season in 2011–12.

Record winning sequence in a season: 18 consecutive League victories by Manchester City, 2017-18, and Liverpool, 2019-20, longest in English top-flight.

Best winning start to League season: 13 successive victories in Div 3 by **Reading**, season 1985–86.

Best starts in 'old' First Division: 11 consecutive victories by **Tottenham** in 1960–61; 10 by **Manchester Utd** in 1985–86. In 'new' First Division, 11 consecutive wins by **Newcastle** in 1992–93 and by **Fulham** in 2000–01.

Longest unbeaten sequence (all competitions): 40 by **Nottm Forest**, Mar–December 1978. It comprised 21 wins, 19 draws (in 29 League matches, 6 League Cup, 4 European Cup, 1 Charity Shield).

Longest unbeaten starts to League season: 38 matches (26 wins, 12 draws) in **Arsenal's** undefeated Premier League season, 2003–04; 29 matches – **Leeds**, Div 1 1973–74 (19 wins, 10 draws); **Liverpool**, Div 1 1987–88 (22 wins, 7 draws).

Most consecutive League matches unbeaten in a season: 38 **Arsenal** Premier League season 2003–04 (see above); 33 **Reading** (25 wins, 8 draws) 2005–06.

Longest winning sequence in Div 1: 13 matches by **Tottenham** – last two of season 1959–60, first 11 of 1960–61.

Longest unbeaten home League sequence in top division: 86 matches (62 wins, 24 draws) by **Chelsea** (Mar 2004–Oct 2008).

League's longest winning sequence with clean sheets: 9 matches by **Stockport** (Lge 2, 2006–07 season).

Premier League – best starts to season: Arsenal, 38 games, 2003–04; **Manchester City**, 14 games, 2011–12.

Best winning start to Premier League season: 9 consecutive victories by **Chelsea** in 2005–06.

Premier League – most consecutive home wins: 20 by **Manchester City** (last 5 season 2010–11, first 15 season 2011–12).

Most consecutive away League wins in top flight: 11 by **Chelsea** (3 at end 2007–08 season, 8 in 2008–09).

Premier League – longest unbeaten away run: 27 matches (W17, D10) by **Arsenal** (Apr 5, 2003–Sep 25, 2004).

Record home-win sequences: Bradford Park Avenue won 25 successive home games in Div 3 North – the last 18 in 1926–27 and the first 7 the following season. Longest run of home wins

in the top division is 21 by **Liverpool** – the last 9 of 1971–72 and the first 12 of 1972–73.
British record for successive League wins: 25 by **Celtic** (Scottish Premier League), 2003–04.

WORST SEQUENCES

Derby experienced the longest run without a win in League history in season 2007–08 – 32 games from Sep 22 to the end of the campaign (25 lost, 7 drawn). They finished bottom by a 24-pt margin. The sequence increased to 36 matches (28 lost, 8 drawn) at the start of the following season. Macclesfield also went 36 games without winning – 23 up to the end of the club's relegation season of 2011–12 and 13 after returning to League Two in 2018–19.

Cambridge Utd had the previous worst of 31 in 1983–84 (21 lost, 10 drawn). They were bottom of Div 2.

Longest sequence without home win: Sunderland, in the Championship, went an English record 21 games in all competitions without a victory in front of their own supporters (Dec 2016-Nov 2017).

Worst losing start to a League season : 12 consecutive defeats by **Manchester Utd** (Div 1), 1930–31.

Worst Premier League start: QPR 16 matches without win (7 draws, 9 defeats), 2012–13.

Premier League – most consecutive defeats: 20 **Sunderland** last 15 matches, 2002–03, first five matches 2005–06.

Longest non-winning start to League season: 25 matches (4 draws, 21 defeats) by **Newport,** Div 4. Worst no-win League starts since then: 16 matches by **Burnley** (9 draws, 7 defeats in Div 2, 1979–80); 16 by **Hull** (10 draws, 6 defeats in Div 2, 1989–90); 16 by **Sheffield Utd** (4 draws, 12 defeats in Div 1, 1990–91).

Most home League defeats in a season: 18 by Cambridge Utd (Div 3, 1984–85) and by Leyton Orient (Lg 2, 2016–17).

Fewest League wins in season: 1 by **Loughborough** (Div 2, season 1899–1900). They lost 27, drew 6, goals 18-100 and dropped out of the League. (See also Scottish section). 1 by **Derby** (Prem Lge, 2007–08). They lost 29, drew 8, goals 20-89.

Most consecutive League defeats in season: 18 by Darwen (Div 1, 1898–99); 17 by Rochdale (Div 3 North, 1931–32).

Fewest home League wins in season: 1 by Loughborough (Div 2, 1899–1900), **Notts Co** (Div 1, 1904–05), Woolwich Arsenal (Div 1, 1912–13), Blackpool (Div 1, 1966–67), Rochdale (Div 3, 1973–74), Sunderland (Prem Lge, 2005–06); **Derby** (Prem Lge, 2007–08).

Away League defeats record: 24 in row by Crewe (Div 2) – all 15 in 1894–95 followed by 9 in 1895–96; by **Nelson** (Div 3 North) – 3 in Apr 1930 followed by all 21 in season 1930–31. They then dropped out of the League.

Biggest defeat in Champions' season: During Newcastle's title-winning season in 1908–09, they were beaten 9-1 at home by Sunderland on December 5.

WORST START BY EVENTUAL CHAMPIONS

Sunderland took only 2 points from their first 7 matches in season 1912–13 (2 draws, 5 defeats). They won 25 of the remaining 31 games to clinch their fifth League title.

DISMAL DERBY

Derby were relegated in season 2007–08 as the worst-ever team in the Premier League: fewest wins (1), fewest points (11); fewest goals (20), first club to go down in March (29th).

UNBEATEN LEAGUE SEASON

Only three clubs have completed an English League season unbeaten: **Preston** (22 matches in 1888–89, the League's first season), **Liverpool** (28 matches in Div 2, 1893–94) and **Arsenal** (38 matches in Premier League, 2003–04).

100 PER CENT HOME RECORDS

Six clubs have won every home League match in a season: **Sunderland** (13 matches)' in 1891–92 and four teams in the old Second Division: **Liverpool** (14) in 1893–94, **Bury** (15) in 1894–95, **Sheffield Wed** (17) in 1899–1900 and **Small Heath,** subsequently **Birmingham**

(17) in 1902–03. The last club to do it, **Brentford,** won all 21 home games in Div 3 South in 1929–30. **Rotherham** just failed to equal that record in 1946–47. They won their first 20 home matches in Div 3 North, then drew the last 3-3 v Rochdale.

BEST HOME LEAGUE RECORDS IN TOP FLIGHT

Sunderland, 1891–92 (P13, W13); **Newcastle,** 1906–07 (P19, W18, D1); **Chelsea,** 2005–06 (P19, W18, D1); **Manchester Utd,** 2010–11 (P19, W18, D1); **Manchester City,** 2011–12 (P19, W18, D1); **Liverpool,** 2019-20 (P19, W18, D1)

MOST CONSECUTIVE CLEAN SHEETS

Premier League – 14: Manchester Utd (2008–09); **Football League** – 11: Millwall (Div 3 South 1925–26); **York** (Div 3 1973–74); **Reading** (Div 4, 1978–79).

WORST HOME RUNS

Most consecutive home League defeats: 14 **Rochdale** (Div 3 North) seasons 1931–32 and 1932–33; 10 **Birmingham** (Div 1) 1985–86; 9 **Darwen** (Div 2) 1897–98; 9 **Watford** (Div 2) 1971–72.

Between Nov 1958 and Oct 1959 **Portsmouth** drew 2 and lost 14 out of 16 consecutive home games.

West Ham did not win in the Premier League at Upton Park in season 2002–03 until the 13th home match on Jan 29.

MOST AWAY WINS IN SEASON

Doncaster won 18 of their 21 away League fixtures when winning Div 3 North in 1946–47.

AWAY WINS RECORD

Most consecutive away League wins: 11 **Chelsea** (Prem Lge) – 8 at start of 2008–09 after ending previous season with 3.

100 PER CENT HOME WINS ON ONE DAY

Div 1 – All 11 home teams won on Feb 13, 1926 and on Dec 10, 1955. **Div 2** – All 12 home teams won on Nov 26, 1988. **Div 3**, all 12 home teams won in the week-end programme of Oct 18–19, 1968.

NO HOME WINS IN DIV ON ONE DAY

Div 1 – 8 away wins, 3 draws in 11 matches on Sep 6, 1986. **Div 2** – 7 away wins, 4 draws in 11 matches on Dec 26, 1987. **Premier League** – 6 away wins, 5 draws in 11 matches on Dec 26, 1994.

The weekend **Premier League** programme on Dec 7–8–9, 1996 produced no home win in the ten games (4 aways, 6 draws). There was again no home victory (3 away wins, 7 draws) in the week-end **Premier League** fixtures on Sep 23–24, 2000.

MOST DRAWS IN A SEASON (FOOTBALL LEAGUE)

23 by **Norwich** (Div 1, 1978–79), **Exeter** (Div 4, 1986–87). **Cardiff** and **Hartlepool** (both Div 3, 1997–98). **Norwich** played 42 matches, the others 46.

MOST DRAWS IN PREMIER LEAGUE SEASON

18 (in 42 matches) by **Manchester City** (1993–94), **Sheffield Utd** (1993–94), **Southampton** (1994–95).

MOST DRAWS IN ONE DIV ON ONE DAY

On Sep 18, 1948 **nine** out of 11 First Division matches were drawn.

MOST DRAWS IN PREMIER DIV PROGRAMME

Over the week-ends of December 2–3–4, 1995, and Sep 23–24, 2000, **seven** out of the ten matches finished level.

FEWEST DRAWS IN SEASON

In 46 matches: 3 by **Reading** (Div 3 South, 1951–52); **Bradford Park Avenue** (Div 3 North, 1956–57); **Tranmere** (Div 4, 1984–85); **Southend** (Div 3, 2002–03); in 42 matches: 2 by **Reading** (Div 3 South, 1935–36); **Stockport** (Div 3 North, 1946–47); in 38 matches: 2 by **Sunderland** (Div 1, 1908–09).

HIGHEST-SCORING DRAWS IN LEAGUE

Leicester 6, **Arsenal** 6 (Div 1 Apr 21, 1930); **Charlton** 6, **Middlesbrough** 6 (Div 2. Oct 22, 1960)
Latest **6-6** draw in first-class football was between **Tranmere** and **Newcastle** in the Zenith Data Systems Cup 1st round on Oct 1, 1991. The score went from 3-3 at 90 minutes to 6-6 after extra time, and Tranmere won 3-2 on penalties. In Scotland: **Queen of the South** 6, **Falkirk** 6 (Div 1, Sep 20, 1947).
Most recent **5-5** draws in top division: **Southampton** v **Coventry** (Div 1, May 4, 1982); **QPR** v **Newcastle** (Div 1, Sep 22, 1984); **WBA** v **Manchester Utd** (Prem Lge, May 19, 2013).

DRAWS RECORDS

Most consecutive drawn matches in Football League: 8 by **Torquay** (Div 3, 1969–70), **Middlesbrough** (Div 2, 1970–71), **Peterborough** (Div 4, 1971–72), **Birmingham** (Div 3 (1990–91), **Southampton** (Champ, 2005–06), **Chesterfield** (Lge 1, 2005–06), **Swansea** (Champ, 2008–09).
Longest sequence of draws by the same score: six 1-1 results by **QPR** in season 1957–58. **Tranmere** became the first club to play **five consecutive 0-0 League draws**, in season 1997–98. Relegated **Chesterfield** drew nine successive National League games in season 2018–19.

IDENTICAL RECORDS

There is only **one instance** of two clubs in one division finishing a season with identical records. In 1907–08, **Blackburn** and **Woolwich Arsenal** were bracketed equal 14th in the First Division with these figures: P38, W12, D12, L14, Goals 51-63, Pts. 36.
The total of **1195 goals** scored in the Premier League in season 1993–94 was repeated in 1994–95.

DEAD LEVEL

Millwall's record in Division Two in season 1973–74 was P42, W14, D14, L14, F51, A51, Pts 42.

CHAMPIONS OF ALL DIVISIONS

Wolves, Burnley and **Preston** are the only clubs to have won titles in the old Divisions 1, 2, 3 and 4. Wolves also won the Third Division North and the new Championship.

POINTS DEDUCTIONS

2000–01: Chesterfield 9 for breach of transfer regulations and falsifying gate receipts.
2002–03: Boston 4 for contractual irregularities.
2004–05: Wrexham, Cambridge Utd 10 for administration.
2005–06: Rotherham 10 for administration.
2006–07: Leeds, Boston 10 for administration; **Bury** 1 for unregistered player.
2007–08: Leeds 15 over insolvency rules; **Bournemouth, Luton, Rotherham** 10 for administration.
2008–09: Luton 20 for failing Insolvency rules, 10 over payments to agents; **Bournemouth, Rotherham** 17 for breaking administration rules; **Southampton, Stockport** 10 for administration – **Southampton** with effect from season 2009–10 **Crystal Palace** 1 for ineligible player.

2009–10: Portsmouth 9, **Crystal Palace** 10 for administration; **Hartlepool** 3 for ineligible player.
2010–11: Plymouth 10 for administration; **Hereford** 3, **Torquay** 1, each for ineligible player
2011–12: Portsmouth and **Port Vale** both 10 for administration – Portsmouth from following season.
2013–14: Coventry 10 for administration; **AFC Wimbledon** 3 for ineligible player.
2014–15: Rotherham 3 for ineligible player.
2015–16: Bury 3 for ineligible player.
2018–19: Birmingham 9 for financial irregularities; **Bolton** 12 for administration, triggered in season 2019–20.

Among previous points penalties imposed:

Nov 1990: Arsenal 2, **Manchester Utd** 1 following mass players' brawl at Old Trafford.
Dec 1996: Brighton 2 for pitch invasions by fans.
Jan 1997: Middlesbrough 3 for refusing to play Premier League match at Blackburn because of injuries and illness.
Jun 1994: Tottenham 12 (reduced to 6) and banned from following season's FA Cup for making illegal payments to players. On appeal, points deduction annulled and club re-instated in Cup.
2019–20: Bury 12 for insolvency (club later expelled); **Wigan** 12 into administration; **Macclesfield** 17 for breaches of regulations; 12 **Sheffield Wed** for breaking spending rules, triggered in season 2020–21.

NIGHTMARE STARTS

Most goals conceded by a goalkeeper on League debut: 13 by **Steve Milton** when Halifax lost 13-0 at Stockport (Div 3 North) on Jan 6, 1934.
Post-war: 11 by Crewe's new goalkeeper **Dennis Murray** (Div 3 North) on Sep 29, 1951, when Lincoln won 11-1.

RELEGATION ODD SPOTS

None of the Barclays Premier League relegation places in season 2004–05 were decided until the last day (Sunday, May 15). **WBA** (bottom at kick-off) survived with a 2-0 home win against Portsmouth, and the three relegated clubs were **Southampton** (1-2 v Manchester Utd), **Norwich** (0-6 at Fulham) and **Crystal Palace** (2-2 at Charlton).

In season 1937–38, **Manchester City** were the highest-scoring team in the First Division with 80 goals (3 more than Champions Arsenal), but they finished in 21st place and were relegated – a year after winning the title. They scored more goals than they conceded (77).

That season produced the **closest relegation battle** in top-division history, with only 4 points spanning the bottom 11 clubs in Div 1. **WBA** went down with **Manchester City**.

Twelve years earlier, in 1925–26, City went down to Division 2 despite totalling 89 goals – still the most scored in any division by a relegated team. Manchester City also scored 31 FA Cup goals that season, but lost the Final 1-0 to Bolton Wanderers.

Cardiff were relegated from Div 1 in season 1928–29, despite conceding fewest goals in the division (59). They also scored fewest (43).

On their way to relegation from the First Division in season 1984–85, **Stoke** twice lost ten matches in a row.

RELEGATION TREBLES

Two Football League clubs have been relegated three seasons in succession. **Bristol City** fell from First Division to Fourth in 1980–81–82 and **Wolves** did the same in 1984–85–86.

OLDEST CLUBS

Oldest Association Football Club is **Sheffield FC** (formed in 1857). The oldest Football League clubs are **Nottm Forest,** 1865; and **Sheffield Wed,** 1866.

NOTTS COUNTY RELEGATED

Notts County, formed in 1862 and the world's oldest professional club, were relegated from the Football League for the first time in season 2018–19.

FOUR DIVISIONS

In **May, 1957**, the Football League decided to re-group the two sections of the Third Division into Third and Fourth Divisions in **season 1958–59**.

The Football League was reduced to three divisions on the formation of the Premier League in **1992**.

In season 2004–05, under new sponsors Coca-Cola, the titles of First, Second and Third Divisions were changed to League Championship, League One and League Two.

THREE UP – THREE DOWN

The Football League annual general meeting of Jun 1973 agreed to adopt the promotion and relegation system of three up and three down.

The **new system** came into effect in **season 1973–74** and applied only to the first three divisions; four clubs were still relegated from the Third and four promoted from the Fourth.

It was the first change in the promotion and relegation system for the top two divisions in 81 years.

MOST LEAGUE APPEARANCES

Players with more than 700 English League apps (as at end of season 2019–20)

1005   Peter Shilton 1966–97 (286 Leicester, 202 Stoke, 202 Nottm Forest, 188 Southampton, 175 Derby, 34 Plymouth Argyle, 1 Bolton, 9 Leyton Orient).

931   Tony Ford 1975–2002 (423 Grimsby, 9 Sunderland, 112 Stoke, 114 WBA, 5 Bradford City, 76 Scunthorpe, 103 Mansfield, 89 Rochdale).

840   Graham Alexander 1991–2012 (159 Scunthorpe, 152 Luton, 372 Preston, 157 Burnley)

824   Terry Paine 1956–77 (713 Southampton, 111 Hereford).

795   Tommy Hutchison 1968–91 (165 Blackpool, 314 Coventry City, 46 Manchester City, 92 Burnley, 178 Swansea). In addition, 68 Scottish League apps for Alloa 1965–68, giving career League app total of 863.

791   David James 1988–2013 (89 Watford, 217 Liverpool, 67 Aston Villa, 91 West Ham, 93 Manchester City, 134 Portsmouth, 81 Bristol City, 19 Bournemouth).

790   Neil Redfearn 1982–2004 (35 Bolton, 100 Lincoln, 46 Doncaster, 57 Crystal Palace, 24 Watford, 62 Oldham, 292 Barnsley, 30 Charlton, 17 Bradford City, 22 Wigan, 42 Halifax, 54 Boston, 9 Rochdale).

782   Robbie James 1973–94 (484 Swansea, 48 Stoke, 87 QPR, 23 Leicester, 89 Bradford City, 51 Cardiff).

777   Alan Oakes 1959–84 (565 Manchester City, 211 Chester, 1 Port Vale).

773   Dave Beasant 1980–2003 (340 Wimbledon, 20 Newcastle, 6 Grimsby, 4 Wolves, 133 Chelsea, 88 Southampton, 139 Nottm F, 27 Portsmouth, 16 Brighton).

770   John Trollope 1960–80 (all for Swindon, record total for one club).

764   Jimmy Dickinson 1946–65 (all for Portsmouth).

761   Roy Sproson 1950–72 (all for Port Vale).

760   Mick Tait 1974–97 (64 Oxford Utd, 106 Carlisle, 33 Hull, 240 Portsmouth, 99 Reading, 79 Darlington, 139 Hartlepool Utd).

758   Billy Bonds 1964–88 (95 Charlton, 663 West Ham).

758   Ray Clemence 1966–88 (48 Scunthorpe, 470 Liverpool, 240 Tottenham).

757   Pat Jennings 1963–86 (48 Watford, 472 Tottenham, 237 Arsenal).

757   Frank Worthington 1966–88 (171 Huddersfield Town, 210 Leicester, 84 Bolton, 75 Birmingham, 32 Leeds, 19 Sunderland, 34 Southampton, 31 Brighton, 59 Tranmere, 23 Preston, 19 Stockport).

755   Wayne Allison 1986–2008 (84 Halifax, 7 Watford, 195 Bristol City, 103 Swindon, 76 Huddersfield, 102 Tranmere, 73 Sheffield Utd, 115 Chesterfield).

749   Ernie Moss 1968–88 (469 Chesterfield, 35 Peterborough, 57 Mansfield, 74 Port Vale, 11 Lincoln, 44 Doncaster, 26 Stockport, 23 Scarborough, 10 Rochdale).

746   Les Chapman 1966–88 (263 Oldham, 133 Huddersfield Town, 70 Stockport, 139 Bradford City, 88 Rochdale, 53 Preston).

744   Asa Hartford 1967–90 (214 WBA, 260 Manchester City, 3 Nottm Forest, 81 Everton,

28 Norwich, 81 Bolton, 45 Stockport, 7 Oldham, 25 Shrewsbury).

743 Alan Ball 1963–84 (146 Blackpool, 208 Everton, 177 Arsenal, 195 Southampton, 17 Bristol Rov).

743 John Hollins 1963–84 (465 Chelsea, 151 QPR, 127 Arsenal).

743 Phil Parkes 1968–91 (52 Walsall, 344 QPR, 344 West Ham, 3 Ipswich).

737 Steve Bruce 1979–99 (205 Gillingham, 141 Norwich, 309 Manchester Utd 72 Birmingham, 10 Sheffield Utd).

734 Teddy Sheringham 1983–2007 (220 Millwall, 5 Aldershot, 42 Nottm Forest, 104 Manchester Utd, 236 Tottenham, 32 Portsmouth, 76 West Ham, 19 Colchester)

732 Mick Mills 1966–88 (591 Ipswich, 103 Southampton, 38 Stoke).

731 Ian Callaghan 1959–81 (640 Liverpool, 76 Swansea, 15 Crewe).

731 David Seaman 1982–2003 (91 Peterborough, 75 Birmingham, 141 QPR, 405 Arsenal, 19 Manchester City).

725 Steve Perryman 1969–90 (655 Tottenham, 17 Oxford Utd, 53 Brentford).

722 Martin Peters 1961–81 (302 West Ham, 189 Tottenham, 207 Norwich, 24 Sheffield Utd).

718 Mike Channon 1966–86 (511 Southampton, 72 Manchester City, 4 Newcastle, 9 Bristol Rov, 88 Norwich, 34 Portsmouth).

716 Ron Harris 1961–83 (655 Chelsea, 61 Brentford).

716 Mike Summerbee 1959–79 (218 Swindon, 357 Manchester City, 51 Burnley, 3 Blackpool, 87 Stockport).

714 Glenn Cockerill 1976–98 (186 Lincoln, 26 Swindon, 62 Sheffield Utd, 387 Southampton, 90 Leyton Orient, 40 Fulham, 23 Brentford).

705 Keith Curle 1981–2003 (32 Bristol Rov, 16 Torquay, 121 Bristol City, 40 Reading, 93 Wimbledon, 171 Manchester City, 150 Wolves, 57 Sheffield Utd, 11 Barnsley, 14 Mansfield).

705 Phil Neal 1968–89 (186 Northampton, 455 Liverpool, 64 Bolton).

705 John Wile 1968–86 (205 Peterborough, 500 WBA).

703 Rob Lee 1983-2006 (298 Charlton, 303 Newcastle, 48 Derby, 16 West Ham, 38 Wycombe).

703 Andy Melville 1986-2005 (175 Swansea, 135 Oxford, 204 Sunderland, 6 Bradford City, 153 Fulham, 17 West Ham, 13 Nottm F).

701 Neville Southall 1980–2000 (39 Bury, 578 Everton, 9 Port Vale, 9 Southend, 12 Stoke, 53 Torquay, 1 Bradford City).

- **Stanley Matthews** made 701 League apps 1932–65 (322 Stoke, 379 Blackpool), incl. 3 for Stoke at start of 1939–40 before season abandoned (war).
- Goalkeeper **John Burridge** made a total of 771 League appearances in a 28-season career in English and Scottish football (1968–96). He played 691 games for 15 English clubs (Workington, Blackpool, Aston Villa, Southend, Crystal Palace, QPR, Wolves, Derby, Sheffield Utd, Southampton, Newcastle, Scarborough, Lincoln, Manchester City and Darlington) and 80 for 5 Scottish clubs (Hibernian, Aberdeen, Dumbarton, Falkirk and Queen of the South).

LONGEST LEAGUE APPEARANCE SEQUENCE

Harold Bell, centre-half of Tranmere, was ever-present for the first nine post-war seasons (1946–55), achieving a League record of 401 consecutive matches. Counting FA Cup and other games, his run of successive appearances totalled 459.

The longest League sequence since Bell's was 394 appearances by goalkeeper **Dave Beasant** for Wimbledon, Newcastle and Chelsea. His nine-year run began on Aug 29, 1981 and was ended by a broken finger sustained in Chelsea's League Cup-tie against Portsmouth on Oct 31, 1990. Beasant's 394 consecutive League games comprised 304 for Wimbledon (1981–88), 20 for Newcastle (1988–89) and 70 for Chelsea (1989–90).

Phil Neal made 366 consecutive First Division appearances for Liverpool between December 1974 and Sep 1983, a remarkable sequence for an outfield player in top-division football.

MOST CONSECUTIVE PREMIER LEAGUE APPEARANCES

310 by goalkeeper **Brad Friedel** (152 Blackburn, 114 Aston Villa, 44 Tottenham, May 2004–Oct 2012). He played in 8 **ever-present seasons** (2004–12, Blackburn 4, Villa 3, Tottenham 1).

EVER-PRESENT DEFENCE

The **entire defence** of **Huddersfield** played in all 42 Second Division matches in season 1952–53, namely, Bill Wheeler (goal), Ron Staniforth and Laurie Kelly (full-backs), Bill McGarry, Don McEvoy and Len Quested (half-backs). In addition, Vic Metcalfe played in all 42 League matches at outside-left.

FIRST SUBSTITUTE USED IN LEAGUE

Keith Peacock (Charlton), away to Bolton (Div 2) on Aug 21, 1965.

FROM PROMOTION TO CHAMPIONS

Clubs who have become Champions of England a year after winning promotion: **Liverpool** 1905, 1906; **Everton** 1931, 1932; **Tottenham** 1950, 1951; **Ipswich** 1961, 1962; **Nottm Forest** 1977, 1978. The first four were placed top in both seasons: Forest finished third and first.

PREMIER LEAGUE'S FIRST MULTI-NATIONAL LINE-UP

Chelsea made history on December 26, 1999 when starting their Premier League match at Southampton without a single British player in the side.

Fulham's Unique XI: In the Worthington Cup 3rd round at home to Bury on Nov 6, 2002, Fulham fielded 11 players of 11 different nationalities. Ten were full Internationals, with Lee Clark an England U–21 cap.

On Feb 14, 2005 **Arsenal** became the first English club to select an all-foreign match squad when Arsene Wenger named 16 non-British players at home to Crystal Palace (Premier League).

Fifteen nations were represented at Fratton Park on Dec 30, 2009 (Portsmouth 1 Arsenal 4) when, for the first time in Premier League history, not one Englishman started the match. The line-up comprised seven Frenchmen, two Algerians and one from each of 13 other countries.

Players from 22 nationalities (subs included) were involved in the Blackburn–WBA match at Ewood Park on Jan 23, 2011.

PREMIER LEAGUE'S FIRST ALL-ENGLAND LINE-UP

On Feb 27, 1999 **Aston Villa** (at home to Coventry) fielded the first all-English line up seen in the Premier League (starting 11 plus 3 subs).

ENTIRE HOME-GROWN TEAM

Crewe Alexandra's starting 11 in the 2-0 home win against Walsall (Lge 1) on Apr 27, 2013 all graduated from the club's academy.

THREE-NATION CHAMPIONS

David Beckham won a title in four countries: with Manchester Utd six times (1996–97–99–2000–01–03), Real Madrid (2007), LA Galaxy (2011 and Paris St Germain (2013).

Trevor Steven earned eight Championship medals in three countries: two with Everton (1985, 1987); five with Rangers (1990, 1991, 1993, 1994, 1995) and one with Marseille in 1992.

LEEDS NO WIN AWAY

Leeds, in 1992–93, provided the first instance of a club failing to win an away League match as reigning Champions.

PIONEERS IN 1888 AND 1992

Three clubs among the twelve who formed the Football League in 1888 were also founder members of the Premier League: **Aston Villa, Blackburn** and **Everton**.

CHAMPIONS (MODERN) WITH TWO CLUBS – PLAYERS

Francis Lee (Manchester City 1968, Derby 1975); **Ray Kennedy** (Arsenal 1971, Liverpool 1979, 1980, 1982); **Archie Gemmill** (Derby 1972, 1975, Nottm Forest 1978); **John McGovern** (Derby 1972, Nottm Forest 1978) **Larry Lloyd** (Liverpool 1973, Nottm Forest 1978); **Peter Withe** (Nottm Forest 1978, Aston Villa 1981); **John Lukic** (Arsenal 1989, Leeds 1992); **Kevin Richardson** (Everton 1985, Arsenal 1989); **Eric Cantona** (Leeds 1992, Manchester Utd 1993, 1994, 1996, 1997); **David Batty** (Leeds 1992, Blackburn 1995), **Bobby Mimms** (Everton 1987, Blackburn 1995), **Henning Berg** (Blackburn 1995, Manchester Utd 1999, 2000); **Nicolas Anelka** (Arsenal 1998, Chelsea 2010); **Ashley Cole** (Arsenal 2002, 2004, Chelsea 2010); **Gael Clichy** (Arsenal 2004, Manchester City 2012); **Robert Huth** (Chelsea 2005, 2006, Leicester 2016); **Kolo Toure** (Arsenal 2004, Manchester City 2012); **Carlos Tevez** (Manchester Utd 2008, 2009, Manchester City 2012, James Milner (Manchester City 2012, 2014, Liverpool 2020); **N'Golo Kante** (Leicester 2016, Chelsea 2017); **Riyad Mahrez** (Leicester 2016, Manchester City 2019).

TITLE TURNABOUTS

In Jan 1996, **Newcastle** led the Premier League by 13 points. They finished runners-up to Manchester Utd.

At Christmas 1997, **Arsenal** were 13 points behind leaders Manchester Utd and still 11 points behind at the beginning of Mar 1998. But a run of 10 wins took the title to Highbury.

On Mar 2, 2003, **Arsenal**, with 9 games left, went 8 points clear of Manchester Utd, who had a match in hand. United won the Championship by 5 points.

In Mar 2002, **Wolves** were in second (automatic promotion) place in Nationwide Div 1, 11 points ahead of WBA, who had 2 games in hand. They were overtaken by Albion on the run-in, finished third, then failed in the play-offs. A year later they won promotion to the Premier League via the play-offs.

CLUB CLOSURES

Five clubs have left the Football League in mid-season: **Leeds City** (expelled Oct 1919); **Wigan Borough** (Oct 1931, debts of £20,000); **Accrington Stanley** (Mar 1962, debts £62,000); **Aldershot** (Mar 1992, debts £1.2m). **Maidstone**, with debts of £650,000, closed Aug 1992, on the eve of the season; **Bury** (expelled Aug 2019, financial mismanagement).

FOUR-DIVISION MEN

In season 1986–87, goalkeeper **Eric Nixon**, became the first player to appear in **all four divisions** of the Football League **in one season**. He served two clubs in Div 1: Manchester City (5 League games) and Southampton (4); in Div 2 Bradford City (3); in Div 3 Carlisle (16); and in Div 4 Wolves (16). Total appearances: 44.

Harvey McCreadie, a teenage forward, played in four divisions over two seasons inside a calendar year – from Accrington (Div 3) to Luton (Div 1) in Jan 1960, to Div 2 with Luton later that season and to Wrexham (Div 4) in Nov.

Tony Cottee played in all four divisions in season 2000–01, for Leicester (Premier League), Norwich (Div 1), Barnet (Div 3, player-manager) and Millwall (Div 2).

FATHERS AND SONS

When player-manager **Ian** (39) and **Gary** (18) **Bowyer** appeared together in the **Hereford** side at Scunthorpe (Div 4, Apr 21, 1990), they provided the first instance of father and son playing in the same team in a Football League match for 39 years. Ian played as substitute, and Gary scored Hereford's injury-time equaliser in a 3-3 draw.

Alec (39) and **David** (17) **Herd** were among previous father-and-son duos in league football – for Stockport, 2-0 winners at Hartlepool (Div 3 North) on May 5, 1951.

When Preston won 2-1 at Bury in Div 3 on Jan 13, 1990, the opposing goalkeepers were brothers: **Alan Kelly** (21) for Preston and **Gary** (23) for Bury. Their father, **Alan** (who kept goal for Preston in the 1964 FA Cup Final and won 47 Rep of Ireland caps) flew from America to watch the sons he taught to keep goal line up on opposite sides.

Other examples: **Bill Dodgin Snr** (manager, Bristol Rov) faced son **Bill Jnr** (manager of Fulham) four times between 1969 and 1971. On Apr 16, 2013 (Lge 1), Oldham, under **Lee Johnson,** won 1-0 at home to Yeovil, managed by his father **Gary.**

George Eastham Snr (manager) and son **George Eastham Jnr** were inside-forward partners for Ards in the Irish League in season 1954–55.

FATHER AND SON REFEREE PLAY-OFF FINALS

Father and son refereed two of the 2009 Play-off Finals. **Clive Oliver,** 46, took charge of Shrewsbury v Gillingham (Lge 2) and **Michael Oliver,** 26, refereed Millwall v Scunthorpe (Lge 1) the following day.

FATHER AND SON BOTH CHAMPIONS

John Aston snr won a Championship medal with Manchester Utd in 1952 and **John Aston jnr** did so with the club in 1967. **Ian Wright** won the Premier League title with Arsenal in 1998 and **Shaun Wright-Phillips** won with Chelsea in 2006.

FATHER AND SON RIVAL MANAGERS

When **Bill Dodgin snr** took Bristol Rov to Fulham for an FA Cup 1st Round tie in Nov 1971, the opposing manager was his son, **Bill jnr.** Rovers won 2-1. Oldham's new manager, **Lee Johnson,** faced his father **Gary's** Yeovil in a Lge 1 match in April, 2013. Oldham won 1-0.

FATHER AND SON ON OPPOSITE SIDES

It happened for the first time in FA Cup history (1st Qual Round on Sep 14, 1996) when 21-year-old **Nick Scaife** (Bishop Auckland) faced his father **Bobby** (41), who played for Pickering. Both were in midfield. Home side Bishops won 3-1.

THREE BROTHERS IN SAME SIDE

Southampton provided the first instance for 65 years of three brothers appearing together in a Div 1 side when **Danny Wallace** (24) and his 19-year-old twin brothers **Rodney** and **Ray** played against Sheffield Wed on Oct 22, 1988. In all, they made 25 appearances together for Southampton until Sep 1989.

A previous instance in Div 1 was provided by the Middlesbrough trio, **William, John** and **George Carr** with 24 League appearances together from Jan 1920 to Oct 1923.

The **Tonner** brothers, **Sam, James** and **Jack,** played together in 13 Second Division matches for Clapton Orient in season 1919–20.

Brothers **David, Donald** and **Robert Jack** played together in Plymouth's League side in 1920.

TWIN TEAM-MATES (see also Wallace twins above)

Twin brothers **David** and **Peter Jackson** played together for three League clubs (Wrexham, Bradford City and Tranmere) from 1954–62. The **Morgan** twins, **Ian** and **Roger,** played regularly in the QPR forward line from 1964–68. WBA's **Adam** and **James Chambers,** 18, were the first twins to represent England (v Cameroon in World Youth Championship, Apr 1999). They first played together in Albion's senior team, aged 19, in the League Cup 2nd. Round against Derby in Sep 2000. Brazilian identical twins **Rafael** and **Fabio Da Silva** (18) made first team debuts at full-back for Manchester Utd in season 2008– 09. Swedish twins **Martin** and **Marcus Olsson** played together for Blackburn in season 2011–12. **Josh** and **Jacob Murphy,** 19, played for Norwich in season 2013–2014.

SIR TOM DOES THE HONOURS

Sir Tom Finney, England and Preston legend, opened the Football League's new headquarters on their return to Preston on Feb 23, 1999. Preston had been the League's original base for 70 years before the move to Lytham St Annes in 1959.

SHORTENED MATCHES

The 0-0 score in the **Bradford City v Lincoln** Third Division fixture on May 11, 1985, abandoned through fire after 40 minutes, was subsequently confirmed as a result. It is the shortest officially- completed League match on record, and was the fourth of only five instances in Football League history of the score of an unfinished match being allowed to stand.

The other occasions: **Middlesbrough 4, Oldham 1** (Div 1, Apr 3, 1915), abandoned after 55 minutes when Oldham defender Billy Cook refused to leave the field after being sent off; **Barrow 7, Gillingham 0** (Div 4, Oct 9, 1961), abandoned after 75 minutes because of bad light, the match having started late because of Gillingham's delayed arrival.

A crucial **Manchester** derby (Div 1) was abandoned after 85 minutes, and the result stood, on Apr 27, 1974, when a pitch invasion at Old Trafford followed the only goal, scored for City by Denis Law, which relegated United, Law's former club.

The only instance of a first-class match in England being abandoned **'through shortage of players'** occurred in the First Division at Bramall Lane on Mar 16, 2002. Referee Eddie Wolstenholme halted play after 82 minutes because **Sheffield Utd** were reduced to 6 players against **WBA**. They had had 3 men sent off (goalkeeper and 2 substitutes), and with all 3 substitutes used and 2 players injured, were left with fewer than the required minimum of 7 on the field. Promotion contenders WBA were leading 3-0, and the League ordered the result to stand.

The last 60 seconds of **Birmingham v Stoke** (Div 3, 1-1, on Feb 29, 1992) were played behind locked doors. The ground had been cleared after a pitch invasion.

A First Division fixture, **Sheffield Wed v Aston Villa** (Nov 26, 1898), was abandoned through bad light after 79 mins with Wednesday leading 3-1. The Football League ruled that the match should be completed, and the remaining 10.5 minutes were played four months later (Mar 13, 1899), when Wednesday added another goal to make the result 4-1.

FIVE TRANSFER RECORDS

Promoted Sheffield Utd broke their transfer record four times during the 2019 summer window, signing Luke Freeman (£5m), Callum Robinson (£8m), Lys Mousset £10m) and Oliver McBurnie (£20m). They broke the record again in the 2020 winter window, paying £22m for Sander Berge

FA CUP RECORDS
(See also Goalscoring section)

CHIEF WINNERS

14 Arsenal; **12** Manchester Utd; **8** Tottenham, Chelsea; **7** Aston Villa, Liverpool; **6** Blackburn, Manchester City, Newcastle.

Three times in succession: The Wanderers (1876–77–78) and Blackburn (1884–85–86).

Trophy handed back: The FA Cup became the Wanderers' absolute property in 1878, but they handed it back to the Association on condition that it was not to be won outright by any club.

In successive years by professional clubs: Blackburn (1890 and 1891); Newcastle (1951 and 1952); Tottenham (1961 and 1962); Tottenham (1981 and 1982); Arsenal (2002 and 2003); Chelsea (2009 and 2010); Arsenal (2014 and 2015).

Record Final-tie score: Bury 6, Derby 0 (1903); Manchester City 6 Watford 0 (2019)

Most FA Cup Final wins at Wembley: Arsenal 11, Manchester Utd 10, Chelsea 7, Tottenham 6, Liverpool 5, Manchester City 5, Newcastle 5.

SECOND DIVISION WINNERS

Notts Co (1894), **Wolves** (1908), **Barnsley** (1912), **WBA** (1931), **Sunderland** (1973), **Southampton** (1976), **West Ham** (1980). When **Tottenham** won the Cup in 1901 they were a Southern League club.

'OUTSIDE' SEMI-FINALISTS

Sheffield Utd, in 2014, became the ninth team from outside the top two divisions to reach the semi-finals, following **Millwall** (1937), **Port Vale** (1954), **York** (1955), **Norwich** (1959),

Crystal Palace (1976), **Plymouth** (1984), **Chesterfield** (1997) and **Wycombe** (2001). None reached the Final.

FOURTH DIVISION QUARTER-FINALISTS

Oxford Utd (1964), **Colchester** (1971), **Bradford City** (1976), **Cambridge Utd** (1990).

FOURTH ROUND – NO REPLAYS

No replays were necessary in the 16 fourth round ties in January 2008 (7 home wins, 9 away). This had not happened for 51 years, since 8 home and 8 away wins in season 1956–57.

FIVE TROPHIES

The trophy which Arsenal won in 2014 was the fifth in FA Cup history. These were its predecessors:
1872–95: First Cup stolen from shop in Birmingham while held by Aston Villa. Never seen again.
1910: Second trophy presented to Lord Kinnaird on completing 21 years as FA president.
1911–91: Third trophy used until replaced ('battered and fragile') after 80 years' service.
1992–2013 Fourth FA Cup lasted 21 years – now retained at FA headquarters at Wembley Stadium.
Traditionally, the Cup stays with the holders until returned to the FA in March.

FINALISTS RELEGATED

Six clubs have reached the FA Cup Final and been relegated. The first five all lost at Wembley – **Manchester City** 1926, **Leicester** 1969, **Brighton** 1983, **Middlesbrough** 1997 and **Portsmouth** 2010. **Wigan**, Cup winners for the first time in 2013, were relegated from the Premier League three days later.

FA CUP – TOP SHOCKS

(2019 = season 2019–20; rounds shown in brackets; R = replay)

1922 (1)	Everton	0	Crystal Palace	6
1933 (3)	Walsall	2	Arsenal	0
1939 (F)	Portsmouth	4	Wolves	1
1948 (3)	Arsenal	0	Bradford PA	1
1948 (3)	Colchester	1	Huddersfield	0
1949 (4)	Yeovil	2	Sunderland	1
1954 (4)	Arsenal	1	Norwich	2
1955 (5)	York	2	Tottenham	1
1957 (4)	Wolves	0	Bournemouth	1
1957 (5)	Bournemouth	3	Tottenham	1
1958 (4)	Newcastle	1	Scunthorpe	3
1959 (3)	Norwich	3	Manchester Utd	0
1959 (3)	Worcester	2	Liverpool	1
1961 (3)	Chelsea	1	Crewe	2
1964 (3)	Newcastle	1	Bedford	2
1965 (4)	Peterborough	2	Arsenal	1
1971 (5)	Colchester	3	Leeds	2
1972 (3)	Hereford	2	Newcastle	1R
1973 (F)	Sunderland	1	Leeds	0
1975 (3)	Burnley	0	Wimbledon	1
1976 (F)	Southampton	1	Manchester Utd	0
1978 (F)	Ipswich	1	Arsenal	0
1980 (3)	Chelsea	0	Wigan	1
1980 (3)	Halifax	1	Manchester City	0
1980 (F)	West Ham	1	Arsenal	0
1981 (4)	Exeter	4	Newcastle	0R
1984 (3)	Bournemouth	2	Manchester Utd	0

1985 (4)	York	1	Arsenal	0
1986 (3)	Birmingham	1	Altrincham	2
1988 (F)	Wimbledon	1	Liverpool	0
1989 (3)	Sutton	2	Coventry	1
1991 (3)	WBA	2	Woking	4
1992 (3)	Wrexham	2	Arsenal	1
1994 (3)	Liverpool	0	Bristol City	1R
1994 (3)	Birmingham	1	Kidderminster	2
1997 (5)	Chesterfield	1	Nottm Forest	0
2001 (4)	Everton	0	Tranmere	3
2003 (3)	Shrewsbury	2	Everton	1
2005 (3)	Oldham	1	Manchester City	0
2008 (6)	Barnsley	1	Chelsea	0
2009 (2)	Histon	1	Leeds	0
2010 (4)	Liverpool	1	Reading	2R
2011 (3)	Stevenage	3	Newcastle	1
2012 (3)	Macclesfield	2	Cardiff	1
2013 (4)	Norwich	0	Luton	1
2013 (4)	Oldham	3	Liverpool	2
2013 (F)	Wigan	1	Manchester City	0
2014 (3)	Rochdale	2	Leeds	0
2015 (4)	Chelsea	2	Bradford City	4
2015 (5)	Bradford City	2	Sunderland	0
2016 (3)	Oxford	3	Swansea	2
2017 (5)	Burnley	0	Lincoln	1
2018 (5)	Wigan	1	Manchester City	0
2019 (3)	Fulham	1	Oldham	2
2019 (3)	Gillingham	1	Cardiff	0
2019 (3)	Newport	2	Leicester	1
2019 (3)	Sheffield Utd	0	Barnet	1
2019 (4)	AFC Wimbledon	4	West Ham	2
2020 (3)	Tranmere	2	Watford	1R

YEOVIL TOP GIANT-KILLERS

Yeovil's victories over Colchester and Blackpool in season 2000–01 gave them a total of 20 FA Cup wins against League opponents. They set another non-League record by reaching the third round 13 times.

This was Yeovil's triumphant (non-League) Cup record against League clubs: 1924–25 Bournemouth 3-2; 1934–35 Crystal Palace 3-0, Exeter 4-1; 1938–39 Brighton 2-1; 1948–49 Bury 3-1, Sunderland 2-1; 1958–59 Southend 1-0; 1960–61 Walsall 1-0; 1963–64 Southend 1-0, Crystal Palace 3-1; 1970–71 Bournemouth 1-0; 1972–73 Brentford 2-1; 1987–88 Cambridge Utd 1-0; 1991–92 Walsall 1-0; 1992–93 Torquay 5-2, Hereford 2-1; 1993–94 Fulham 1-0; 1998–99 Northampton 2-0; 2000–01 Colchester 5-1, Blackpool 1-0.

NON-LEAGUE BEST

Since League football began in 1888, three non-League clubs have reached the FA Cup Final. **Sheffield Wed** (Football Alliance) were runners-up in 1890, as were **Southampton** (Southern League) in 1900 and 1902. **Tottenham** won the Cup as a Southern League team in 1901.

Lincoln won 1-0 at Burnley on Feb 18, 2017, to become the first non-league club to reach the last eight in 103 years. Two non-league sides – **Lincoln** and **Sutton** – had reached the last 16 for the first time.

Otherwise, the furthest progress by non-League clubs has been to the 5th round on 7 occasions: **Colchester** 1948, **Yeovil** 1949, **Blyth** 1978, **Telford** 1985, **Kidderminster** 1994, **Crawley** 2011, **Luton** 2013.

Greatest number of non-League sides to reach the **3rd round** is **8** in 2009: **Barrow, Blyth, Eastwood, Forest Green, Histon, Kettering, Kidderminster** and **Torquay**.

Most to reach **Round 4: 3** in 1957 (**Rhyl, New Brighton, Peterborough**) and 1975 (**Leatherhead, Stafford** and **Wimbledon**).

Five non-League clubs reaching **round 3** in 2001 was a Conference record. They were **Chester, Yeovil, Dagenham, Morecambe** and **Kingstonian**.

In season 2002–03, **Team Bath** became the first University-based side to reach the FA Cup 1st Round since **Oxford University** (Finalists in 1880).

NON-LEAGUE 'LAST TIMES'

Last time no non-League club reached round 3: 1951. Last time only one did so: 1969 (**Kettering**).

TOP-DIVISION SCALPS

Victories in FA Cup by non-League clubs over top-division teams since 1900 include: 1900–01 (Final, replay): Tottenham 3 Sheffield Utd 1 (Tottenham then in Southern League); 1919–20 **Cardiff** 2, Oldham 0; Sheffield Wed 0, **Darlington** 2; 1923–24 **Corinthians** 1, Blackburn 0; 1947–48 **Colchester** 1, Huddersfield 0; 1948–9 **Yeovil** 2, Sunderland 1; 1971–72 **Hereford** 2, Newcastle 1; 1974–75 Burnley 0, **Wimbledon** 1; 1985–86 Birmingham 1, **Altrincham** 2; 1988–89 **Sutton** 2, Coventry 1; 2012–13 Norwich 0, **Luton** 1, 2016–17 Burnley 0 **Lincoln** 1.

MOST WINNING MEDALS

Ashley Cole has won the trophy seven times, with (Arsenal 2002–03–05) and Chelsea (2007–09–10–12). **The Hon Arthur Kinnaird** (The Wanderers and Old Etonians), **Charles Wollaston** (The Wanderers) and **Jimmy Forrest** (Blackburn) each earned five winners' medals. Kinnaird, later president of the FA, played in nine of the first 12 FA Cup Finals, and was on the winning side three times for The Wanderers, in 1873 (captain), 1877, 1878 (captain), and twice as captain of Old Etonians (1879, 1882).

MANAGERS' MEDALS BACKDATED

In 2010, the FA agreed to award Cup Final medals to all living managers who took their teams to the Final before 1996 (when medals were first given to Wembley team bosses). Lawrie McMenemy had campaigned for the award since Southampton's victory in 1976.

MOST WINNERS' MEDALS AT WEMBLEY

4 – **Mark Hughes** (3 for Manchester Utd, 1 for Chelsea), **Petr Cech, Frank Lampard, John Terry, Didier Drogba, Ashley Cole** (all Chelsea), **Olivier Giroud** (3 for Arsenal, 1 for Chelsea).

3 – **Dick Pym** (3 clean sheets in Finals), **Bob Haworth, Jimmy Seddon, Harry Nuttall, Billy Butler** (all Bolton); **David Jack** (2 Bolton, 1 Arsenal); **Bob Cowell, Jack Milburn, Bobby Mitchell** (all Newcastle); **Dave Mackay** (Tottenham); **Frank Stapleton** (1 Arsenal, 2 Manchester Utd); **Bryan Robson** (3 times winning captain), **Arthur Albiston, Gary Pallister** (all Manchester Utd); **Bruce Grobbelaar, Steve Nicol, Ian Rush** (all Liverpool); **Roy Keane, Peter Schmeichel, Ryan Giggs** (all Manchester Utd); **Dennis Wise** (1 Wimbledon, 2 Chelsea).

Arsenal's **David Seaman** and **Ray Parlour** have each earned 4 winners' medals (2 at Wembley, 2 at Cardiff) as have Manchester Utd's **Roy Keane** and **Ryan Giggs** (3 at Wembley, 1 at Cardiff).

MOST WEMBLEY FINALS

Nine players appeared in five FA Cup Finals at Wembley, replays excluded:
- **Joe Hulme** (Arsenal: 1927 lost, 1930 won, 1932 lost, 1936 won; Huddersfield: 1938 lost).
- **Johnny Giles** (Manchester Utd: 1963 won; Leeds: 1965 lost, 1970 drew at Wembley, lost replay at Old Trafford, 1972 won, 1973 lost).
- **Pat Rice** (all for Arsenal: 1971 won, 1972 lost, 1978 lost, 1979 won, 1980 lost).
- **Frank Stapleton** (Arsenal: 1978 lost, 1979 won, 1980 lost; Manchester Utd; 1983 won, 1985 won).
- **Ray Clemence** (Liverpool: 1971 lost, 1974 won, 1977 lost; Tottenham: 1982 won, 1987 lost).

- **Mark Hughes** (Manchester Utd: 1985 won, 1990 won, 1994 won, 1995 lost; Chelsea: 1997 won).
- **John Barnes** (Watford: 1984 lost; Liverpool: 1988 lost, 1989 won, 1996 lost; Newcastle: 1998 sub, lost): – first player to lose Wembley FA Cup Finals with three different clubs.
- **Roy Keane** (Nottm Forest: 1991 lost; Manchester Utd: 1994 won, 1995 lost, 1996 won, 1999 won).
- **Ryan Giggs** (Manchester Utd: 1994 won, 1995 lost, 1996 won, 1999 won, 2007 lost).
- Clemence, Hughes and Stapleton also played in a replay, making six actual FA Cup Final appearances for each of them.
- **Glenn Hoddle** also made six appearances at Wembley: 5 for Tottenham (incl. 2 replays), in 1981 lost, 1982 won and 1987 lost, and 1 for Chelsea as sub in 1994 lost.
- **Paul Bracewell** played in four FA Cup Finals without being on the winning side – for Everton 1985, 1986, 1989, Sunderland 1992.

MOST WEMBLEY/CARDIFF FINAL APPEARANCES

8 by **Ashley Cole** (Arsenal: 2001 lost; 2002 won; 2003 won; 2005 won; Chelsea: 2007 won; 2009 won; 2010 won, 2012 won).

7 by **Roy Keane** (Nottm Forest: 1991 lost; Manchester Utd: 1994 won; 1995 lost; 1996 won; 1999 won; 2004 won; 2005 lost).

7 by **Ryan Giggs** (Manchester Utd): 1994 won; 1995 lost; 1996 won; 1999 won; 2004 won; 2005 lost; 2007 lost.

6 by **Paul Scholes** (Manchester Utd): 1995 lost; 1996 won; 1999 won; 2004 won; 2005 lost; 2007 lost.

5 by **David Seaman** and **Ray Parlour** (Arsenal): 1993 won; 1998 won; 2001 lost; 2002 won; 2003 won; **Dennis Wise** (Wimbledon 1988 won; Chelsea 1994 lost; 1997 won; 2000 lost; Millwall 2004 lost); Patrick Vieira (Arsenal): 1998 won; 2001 lost; 2002 won; 2005 won; (Manchester City) 2011 won.

BIGGEST FA CUP SCORE AT WEMBLEY

6-0 by Manchester City v Watford (final, May 18, 2019).

WINNING GOALKEEPER-CAPTAINS

1988 **Dave Beasant** (Wimbledon); 2003 **David Seaman** (Arsenal).

MOST WINNING MANAGERS

7 **Arsene Wenger** (Arsenal) 1998, 2002, 2003, 2005, 2014, 2015, 2017; **6 George Ramsay** (Aston Villa) 1887, 1895, 1897, 1905, 1913, 1920; **5 Sir Alex Ferguson** (Manchester Utd) 1990, 1994, 1996, 1999, 2004.

PLAYER-MANAGERS IN FINAL

Kenny Dalglish (Liverpool, 1986); **Glenn Hoddle** (Chelsea, 1994); **Dennis Wise** (Millwall, 2004).

DEBUTS IN FINAL

Alan Davies (Manchester Utd v Brighton, 1983); **Chris Baird** (Southampton v Arsenal, 2003); **Curtis Weston** (Millwall sub v Manchester Utd, 2004).

SEMI-FINALS AT WEMBLEY

1991 Tottenham 3 Arsenal 1; **1993** Sheffield Wed 2 Sheffield Utd 1, Arsenal 1 Tottenham 0; **1994** Chelsea 2 Luton 0, Manchester Utd 1 Oldham 1; **2000** Aston Villa beat Bolton 4-1 on pens (after 0-0), Chelsea 2 Newcastle 1; **2008** Portsmouth 1 WBA 0, Cardiff 1 Barnsley 0; **2009** Chelsea 2 Arsenal 1, Everton beat Manchester Utd 4-2 on pens (after 0-0); **2010** Chelsea 3 Aston Villa 0, Portsmouth 2 Tottenham 0; **2011** Manchester City 1 Manchester Utd 0, Stoke 5 Bolton 0; **2012** Liverpool 2 Everton 1, Chelsea 5 Tottenham 1; **2013** Wigan 2 Millwall 0, Manchester City 2 Chelsea 1; **2014** Arsenal beat Wigan 4-2 on pens (after

1-1), Hull 5 Sheffield Utd 3; **2015** Arsenal 2 Reading 1, Aston Villa 2 Liverpool 1; **2016** Manchester Utd 2 Everton 1, Crystal Palace 2 Watford 1; **2017** Arsenal 2 Manchester City 1, Chelsea 4 Tottenham 2; **2018** Chelsea 2 Southampton 0, Manchester Utd 2 Tottenham 1; **2019** Manchester City 1 Brighton 0, Watford 3 Wolves 2; **2020** Arsenal 2 Manchester City 0, Chelsea 3 Manchester Utd 1

CHELSEA'S FA CUP MILESTONES

Their victory over Liverpool in the 2012 Final set the following records:

Captain **John Terry** first player to lift the trophy four times for one club; **Didier Drogba** first to score in four Finals; **Ashley Cole** first to earn seven winner's medals (Arsenal 3, Chelsea 4); **Roberto Di Matteo** first to score for and manage the same winning club (player for Chelsea 1997, 2000, interim manager 2012).

Chelsea's four triumphs in six seasons (2007–12) the best winning sequence since Wanderers won five of the first seven competitions (1872–78) and Blackburn won five out of eight (1884–91).

FIRST ENTRANTS (1871–72)

Barnes, Civil Service, Crystal Palace, Clapham Rov, Donnington School (Spalding), Hampstead Heathens, Harrow Chequers, Hitchin, Maidenhead, Marlow, Queen's Park (Glasgow), Reigate Priory, Royal Engineers, Upton Park and Wanderers. Total 15.

LAST ALL-ENGLISH WINNERS

Manchester City, in 1969, were the last club to win the final with a team of all English players.

FA CUP FIRSTS

Out of country: Cardiff, by defeating Arsenal 1-0 in the 1927 Final at Wembley, became the first and only club to take the FA Cup out of England.

All-English Winning XI: First club to win the FA Cup with all-English XI: Blackburn Olympic in 1883. Others since: WBA in 1888 and 1931, Bolton (1958), Manchester City (1969), West Ham (1964 and 1975).

Non-English Winning XI: Liverpool in 1986 (Mark Lawrenson, born Preston, was a Rep of Ireland player).

Won both Cups: Old Carthusians won the FA Cup in 1881 and the FA Amateur Cup in 1894 and 1897. Wimbledon won Amateur Cup in 1963, FA Cup in 1988.

MOST GAMES NEEDED TO WIN

Barnsley played a record 12 matches (20 hours' football) to win the FA Cup in season 1911–12. All six replays (one in round 1, three in round 4 and one in each of semi-final and Final) were brought about by goalless draws.

Arsenal played 11 FA Cup games when winning the trophy in 1979. Five of them were in the 3rd round against Sheffield Wed.

LONGEST TIES

6 matches: (11 hours): Alvechurch v Oxford City (4th qual round, 1971–72). Alvechurch won 1-0.

5 matches: (9 hours, 22 mins – record for competition proper): Stoke v Bury (3rd round, 1954–55). Stoke won 3-2.

5 matches: Chelsea v Burnley (4th round, 1955–56). Chelsea won 2-0.

5 matches: Hull v Darlington (2nd round, 1960–61). Hull won 3-0.

5 matches: Arsenal v Sheffield Wed (3rd round, 1978–79). Arsenal won 2-0.

Other marathons (qualifying comp, all 5 matches, 9 hours): Barrow v Gillingham (last qual round, 1924–25) – winners Barrow; Leyton v Ilford (1924–25) – winners Leyton; Falmouth v Bideford (3rd qual round, 1973–74) – winners Bideford.

End of Cup Final replays: The FA decided that, with effect from 1999, there would be no Cup Final replays. In the event of a draw after extra-time, the match would be decided on penalties. This happened for the first time in 2005, when Arsenal beat Manchester Utd 5-4 on penalties after a 0-0 draw. A year later, Liverpool beat West Ham 3-1 on penalties after a 3-3 draw.

FA Cup marathons ended in season 1991–92, when the penalty shoot-out was introduced to decide ties still level after one replay and extra-time.

In 1932–33 **Brighton** (Div 3 South) played 11 FA Cup games, including replays, and scored 43 goals, without getting past round 5. They forgot to claim exemption and had to play from 1st qual round.

LONGEST ROUND

The longest round in FA Cup history was the **3rd round** in **1962–63**. It took 66 days to complete, lasting from Jan 5 to Mar 11, and included 261 postponements because of bad weather.

LONGEST UNBEATEN RUN

23 matches by Blackburn In winning the Cup in three consecutive years (1884–05–06), they won 21 ties (one in a replay), and their first Cup defeat in four seasons was in a first round replay of the next competition.

RE-STAGED TIES

Sixth round, Mar 9, 1974: Newcastle 4, Nottm Forest 3. Match declared void by FA and ordered to be replayed following a pitch invasion after Newcastle had a player sent off. Forest claimed the hold-up caused the game to change its pattern. The tie went to two further matches at Goodison Park (0-0, then 1-0 to Newcastle).

Third round, Jan 5, 1985: Burton 1, Leicester 6 (at Derby). Burton goalkeeper Paul Evans was hit on the head by a missile thrown from the crowd and continued in a daze. The FA ordered the tie to be played again, behind closed doors at Coventry (Leicester won 1-0).

First round replay, Nov 25, 1992: Peterborough 9 (Tony Philliskirk 5), Kingstonian 1. Match expunged from records because, at 3-0 after 57 mins, Kingstonian were reduced to ten men when goalkeeper Adrian Blake was concussed by a 50 pence coin thrown from the crowd. The tie was re-staged on the same ground behind closed doors (Peterborough won 1-0).

Fifth round: Within an hour of holders Arsenal beating Sheffield Utd 2-1 at Highbury on Feb 13, 1999, the FA took the unprecedented step of declaring the match void because an unwritten rule of sportsmanship had been broken. With United's Lee Morris lying injured, their goalkeeper Alan Kelly kicked the ball into touch. Play resumed with Arsenal's Ray Parlour throwing it in the direction of Kelly, but Nwankwo Kanu took possession and centred for Marc Overmars to score the 'winning' goal. After four minutes of protests by manager Steve Bruce and his players, referee Peter Jones confirmed the goal. Both managers absolved Kanu of cheating but Arsenal's Arsene Wenger offered to replay the match. With the FA immediately approving, it was re-staged at Highbury ten days later (ticket prices halved) and Arsenal again won 2-1.

PRIZE FUND

The makeover of the FA Cup competition took off in 2001–02 with the introduction of round-by-round prize-money.

FA CUP FOLLIES

1999–2000 The FA broke with tradition by deciding the 3rd round be moved from its regular Jan date and staged before Christmas. Criticism was strong, gates poor and the 3rd round in 2000–01 reverted to the New Year. By allowing the holders Manchester Utd to withdraw from the 1999–2000 competition in order to play in FIFA's inaugural World Club Championship in Brazil in Jan, the FA were left with an odd number of clubs in the 3rd round. Their solution was a 'lucky losers' draw among clubs knocked out in round 2. Darlington, beaten at Gillingham, won it to re-enter the competition, then lost 2-1 away to Aston Villa.

HAT-TRICKS IN FINAL

There have been three in the history of the competition: **Billy Townley** (Blackburn, 1890), **Jimmy Logan** (Notts Co, 1894) and **Stan Mortensen** (Blackpool, 1953).

MOST APPEARANCES

88 by **Ian Callaghan** (79 for Liverpool, 7 for Swansea City, 2 for Crewe); **87** by **John Barnes** (31 for Watford, **51** for Liverpool, 5 for Newcastle); **86** by **Stanley Matthews** (37 for Stoke, 49 for Blackpool); **84** by **Bobby Charlton** (80 for Manchester Utd, 4 for Preston); **84** by **Pat Jennings** (3 for Watford, 43 for Tottenham, 38 for Arsenal); **84** by **Peter Shilton** for seven clubs (30 for Leicester, 7 for Stoke, **18** for Nottm Forest, 17 for Southampton, 10 for Derby, 1 for Plymouth Argyle, 1 for Leyton Orient); **82** by **David Seaman** (5 for Peterborough, 5 for Birmingham, 17 for QPR, 54 for Arsenal, 1 for Manchester City).

THREE-CLUB FINALISTS

Five players have appeared in the FA Cup Final for three clubs: **Harold Halse** for Manchester Utd (1909), Aston Villa (1913) and Chelsea (1915); **Ernie Taylor** for Newcastle (1951), Blackpool (1953) and Manchester Utd (1958); **John Barnes** for Watford (1984), Liverpool (1988, 1989, 1996) and Newcastle (1998); **Dennis Wise** for Wimbledon (1988), Chelsea (1994, 1997, 2000), Millwall (2004); **David James** for Liverpool (1996), Aston Villa (2000) and Portsmouth (2008, 2010).

CUP MAN WITH TWO CLUBS IN SAME SEASON

Stan Crowther, who played for Aston Villa against Manchester Utd in the 1957 FA Cup Final, appeared for both Villa and United in the 1957–58 competition. United signed him directly after the Munich air crash and, in the circumstances, he was given dispensation to play for them in the Cup, including the Final.

CAPTAIN'S CUP DOUBLE

Martin Buchan is the only player to have captained Scottish and English FA Cup-winning teams – Aberdeen in 1970 and Manchester Utd in 1977.

MEDALS BEFORE AND AFTER

Two players appeared in FA Cup Final teams before and after the Second World War: **Raich Carter** was twice a winner (Sunderland 1937, Derby 1946) and **Willie Fagan** twice on the losing side (Preston 1937, Liverpool 1950).

DELANEY'S COLLECTION

Scotland winger **Jimmy Delaney** uniquely earned Scottish, English, Northern Ireland and Republic of Ireland Cup medals. He was a winner with Celtic (1937), Manchester Utd (1948) and Derry City (1954) and a runner-up with Cork City (1956).

STARS WHO MISSED OUT

Internationals who never won an FA Cup winner's medal include: Tommy Lawton, Tom Finney, Johnny Haynes, Gordon Banks, George Best, Terry Butcher, Peter Shilton, Martin Peters, Nobby Stiles, Alan Ball, Malcolm Macdonald, Alan Shearer, Matthew Le Tissier, Stuart Pearce, Des Walker, Phil Neal, Ledley King.

CUP WINNERS AT NO COST

Not one member of **Bolton**'s 1958 FA Cup-winning team cost the club a transfer fee. Each joined the club for a £10 signing-on fee.

11-NATIONS LINE-UP

Liverpool fielded a team of 11 different nationalities in the FA Cup 3rd round at Yeovil on Jan 4, 2004.

HIGH-SCORING SEMI-FINALS

The **record team score** in FA Cup semi-finals is **6**: 1891–92 WBA 6, Nottm Forest 2; 1907–08 Newcastle 6, Fulham 0; 1933–34 Manchester City 6, Aston Villa 1.
Most goals in semi-finals (aggregate): 17 in 1892 (4 matches) and 1899 (5 matches). In modern times: 15 in 1958 (3 matches, including Manchester Utd 5, Fulham 3 – highest-scoring

semi-final since last war); 16 in 1989–90 (Crystal Palace 4, Liverpool 3; Manchester Utd v Oldham 3-3, 2-1. All **16 goals** in those three matches were scored by **different players**.

Stoke's win against Bolton at Wembley in 2011 was the first 5-0 semi-final result since Wolves beat Grimsby at Old Trafford in 1939. In 2014, Hull defeated Sheffield Utd 5-3.

Last hat-trick in an FA Cup semi-final was scored by **Alex Dawson** for Manchester Utd in 5-3 replay win against Fulham at Highbury in 1958.

SEMI-FINAL VENUES

Villa Park has staged more such matches (55 including replays) than any other ground. Next is Hillsborough (33).

ONE IN A HUNDRED

The 2008 semi-finals included only one top-division club, Portsmouth, for the first time in 100 years – since Newcastle in 1908.

FOUR SPECIAL AWAYS

For the only time in FA Cup history, **all four quarter-finals** in season 1986–87 were won by the away team.

DRAWS RECORD

In season 1985–86, **seven** of the eight 5th round ties went to replays – a record for that stage of the competition.

SHOCK FOR TOP CLUBS

The fourth round on Jan 24, 2015 produced an astonishing set of home defeats for leading clubs. The top three in the Premier League, Chelsea, Manchester City and Southampton were all knocked out and sixth-place Tottenham also lost at home. Odds against this happening were put at 3825-1.

LUCK OF THE DRAW

In the FA Cup on Jan 11, 1947, eight of **London**'s ten Football League clubs involved in the 3rd round were drawn at home (including Chelsea v Arsenal). Only Crystal Palace played outside the capital (at Newcastle).

In the 3rd round in Jan 1992, Charlton were the only London club drawn at home (against Barnet), but the venue of the Farnborough v West Ham tie was reversed on police instruction. So Upton Park staged Cup ties on successive days, with West Ham at home on the Saturday and Charlton (who shared the ground) on Sunday.

Arsenal were drawn away in every round on the way to reaching the Finals of 1971 and 1972. **Manchester Utd** won the Cup in 1990 without playing once at home.

The 1999 finalists, **Manchester Utd** and **Newcastle,** were both drawn at home every time in Rounds 3–6.

On their way to the semi-finals of both domestic Cup competitions in season 2002–03, **Sheffield Utd** were drawn at home ten times out of ten and won all ten matches – six in the League's Worthington Cup and four in the FA Cup.

On their way to winning the Cup in 2014, **Arsenal** did not play once outside London. Home draws in rounds 3, 4, 5 and 6 were followed by the semi-final at Wembley.

ALL TOP-DIVISION VICTIMS

The only instance of an FA Cup-winning club meeting top-division opponents in every round was provided by Manchester Utd in 1947–48. They beat Aston Villa, Liverpool, Charlton, Preston, then Derby in the semi-final and Blackpool in the Final.

In contrast, these clubs have reached the Final without playing top-division opponents on the way: West Ham (1923), Bolton (1926), Blackpool (1948), Bolton (1953), Millwall (2004).

WON CUP WITHOUT CONCEDING GOAL

1873 **The Wanderers** (1 match; as holders, exempt until Final); 1889 **Preston** (5 matches); 1903

Bury (5 matches). In 1966 **Everton** reached Final without conceding a goal (7 matches), then beat Sheffield Wed 3-2 at Wembley.

HOME ADVANTAGE

For the first time in FA Cup history, all eight ties in the 1992–93 5th round were won (no replays) by the **clubs drawn at home.** Only other instance of eight home wins at the last 16 stage was in 1889–90, in what was then the 2nd round.

NORTH-EAST WIPE-OUT

For the first time in 54 years, since the 4th round in Jan, 1957, the North-East's 'big three' were knocked out on the same date, Jan 8, 2011 (3rd round). All lost to lower-division opponents – **Newcastle** 3-1 at Stevenage, **Sunderland** 2-1 at home to Notts County and **Middlesbrough** 2-1 at Burton.

FEWEST TOP-DIVISION CLUBS IN LAST 16 (5th ROUND)

5 in 1958; **6** in 1927, 1970, 1982; **7** in 1994, 2003; **8** in 2002, 2004.

SIXTH-ROUND ELITE

For the first time in FA Cup 6th round history, dating from 1926 when the format of the competition changed, all **eight quarter-finalists** in 1995–96 were from the top division.

SEMI-FINAL – DOUBLE DERBIES

There have been three instances of both FA Cup semi-finals in the same year being local derbies: **1950** Liverpool beat Everton 2-0 (Maine Road), Arsenal beat Chelsea 1-0 after 2-2 draw (both at Tottenham); **1993** Arsenal beat Tottenham 1-0 (Wembley), Sheffield Wed beat Sheffield Utd 2-1 (Wembley); **2012** Liverpool beat Everton 2-1 (Wembley), Chelsea beat Tottenham 5-1 (Wembley).

TOP CLUB DISTINCTION

Since the Football League began in 1888, there has never been an FA Cup Final in which **neither club** represented the top division.

CLUBS THROWN OUT

Bury expelled (Dec 2006) for fielding an ineligible player in 3-1 2nd rd replay win at Chester. **Droylsden** expelled for fielding a suspended player in 2-1 2nd rd replay win at home to Chesterfield (Dec 2008).

SPURS OUT – AND IN

Tottenham were banned, pre-season, from the 1994–95 competition because of financial irregularities, but were re-admitted on appeal and reached the semi-finals.

FATHER & SON FA CUP WINNERS

Peter Boyle (Sheffield Utd 1899, 1902) and **Tommy Boyle** (Sheffield Utd 1925); **Harry Johnson Snr** (Sheffield Utd 1899, 1902) and **Harry Johnson Jnr** (Sheffield Utd 1925); **Jimmy Dunn Snr** (Everton 1933) and **Jimmy Dunn Jnr** (Wolves 1949); **Alec Herd** (Manchester City 1934) and **David Herd** (Manchester Utd 1963); **Frank Lampard Snr** (West Ham 1975, 1980) and **Frank Lampard Jnr** (Chelsea 2007, 2009, 2010, 2012).

BROTHERS IN FA CUP FINAL TEAMS (modern times)

1950 **Denis and Leslie Compton** (Arsenal); 1952 **George and Ted Robledo** (Newcastle); 1967 **Ron and Allan Harris** (Chelsea); 1977 **Jimmy and Brian Greenhoff** (Manchester Utd); 1996 and 1999 **Gary and Phil Neville** (Manchester Utd).

FA CUP SPONSORS

Littlewoods Pools became the first sponsors of the FA Cup in season 1994–95 in a £14m, 4-year deal. French insurance giants **AXA** took over (season 1998–99) in a sponsorship worth £25m over 4 years. German energy company **E.ON** agreed a 4-year deal worth £32m from season 2006–07 and extended it for a year to 2011. American beer company **Budweiser** began a three-year sponsorship worth £24m in season 2011–12. The **Emirates** airline became the first title sponsor (2015-18) in a reported £30m deal with the FA. This sponsorship was extended for a further three years.

FIRST GOALKEEPER-SUBSTITUTE IN FINAL
Paul Jones (Southampton), who replaced injured Antti Niemi against Arsenal in 2003.

LEAGUE CUP RECORDS
(See also Goalscoring section)

Most winning managers: 4 Brian Clough (Nottm Forest), Sir Alex Ferguson (Manchester Utd), Jose Mourinho (3 Chelsea, 1 Manchester Utd).

Highest scores: West Ham 10-0 v Bury (2nd round, 2nd leg 1983–84; agg 12-1); Liverpool 10-0 v Fulham (2nd round, 1st leg 1986–87; agg 13-2).

Most League Cup goals (career): 49 Geoff Hurst (43 West Ham, 6 Stoke, 1960–75); 49 Ian Rush (48 Liverpool, 1 Newcastle, 1981–98).

Highest scorer (season): 12 Clive Allen (Tottenham 1986–87 in 9 apps).

Most goals in match: 6 Frank Bunn (Oldham v Scarborough, 3rd round, 1989–90).

Most winners' medals: 5 Ian Rush (Liverpool).

Most appearances in Final: 6 Kenny Dalglish (Liverpool 1978–87), Ian Rush (Liverpool 1981–95). Emile Heskey (Leicester 1997, 1999, 2000), Liverpool (2001, 2003), Aston Villa (2010)

Biggest Final win: Swansea City 5 Bradford City 0 (2013).

League Cup sponsors: Milk Cup 1981–86, Littlewoods Cup 1987–90, Rumbelows Cup 1991–92, Coca-Cola Cup 1993–98. Worthington Cup 1999–2003, Carling Cup 2003–12; Capital One Cup from season 2012–16; Carabao 2017–22.

Up for the cup, then down: In 2011, Birmingham became only the second club to win a major trophy (the Carling Cup) and be relegated from the top division. It previously happened to Norwich in 1985 when they went down from the old First Division after winning the Milk Cup.

Liverpool's League Cup records: Winners a record 8 times. **Ian Rush** only player to win 5 times. Rush also first to play in 8 winning teams in Cup Finals **at Wembley**, all with Liverpool (FA Cup 1986–89–92; League Cup 1981–82–83–84–95).

Britain's first under-cover Cup Final: Worthington Cup Final between Blackburn and Tottenham at Cardiff's Millennium Stadium on Sunday, Feb 24, 2002. With rain forecast, the retractable roof was closed on the morning of the match.

Record penalty shoot-out: Liverpool beat Middlesbrough 14-13 (3rd round, Sep 23, 2014) after 2-2. Derby beat Carlisle 14-13 (2nd round, Aug 23, 2016) after 1-1.

DISCIPLINE

SENDINGS-OFF
Season 2003–04 set an **all-time record** of 504 players sent off in English domestic football competitions. There were 58 in the Premier League, 390 Nationwide League, 28 FA Cup (excluding non-League dismissals), 22 League Cup, 2 in Nationwide play-offs, 4 in LDV Vans Trophy.

Most sendings-off in Premier League programme (10 matches): 9 (8 Sat, 1 Sun, Oct 31–Nov 1, 2009).

The 58 Premier League red cards was 13 fewer than the record English **top-division** total of 71 in 2002–03. **Bolton** were the only club in the English divisions without a player sent off in any first-team competition that season.

Worst day for dismissals in English football was Boxing Day, 2007, with **20 red cards** (5 Premier League and 15 Coca-Cola League). Three players, Chelsea's Ashley Cole and Ricardo Carvalho and Aston Villa's Zat Knight were sent off in a 4-4 draw at Stamford Bridge. Luton had three men dismissed in their game at Bristol Rov, but still managed a 1-1 draw.

Previous worst day was Dec 13, 2003, with **19 red cards** (2 Premier League and the 17 Nationwide League).

In the entire first season of post-war League football (1946–47) only 12 players were sent off, followed by 14 in 1949–50, and the total League dismissals for the first nine seasons after the War was 104.

The worst pre-War total was 28 in each of seasons 1921–22 and 1922–23.

ENGLAND SENDINGS-OFF

In a total of 15 England dismissals, David Beckham and Wayne Rooney have been red-carded twice. Beckham and Steven Gerrard are the only England captains to be sent off and Robert Green the only goalkeeper.

Jun 5, 1968	**Alan Mullery**	v Yugoslavia (Florence, Euro Champ)
Jun 6, 1973	**Alan Ball**	v Poland (Chorzow, World Cup qual)
Jun 12, 1977	**Trevor Cherry**	v Argentina (Buenos Aires, friendly)
Jun 6, 1986	**Ray Wilkins**	v Morocco (Monterrey, World Cup Finals)
Jun 30, 1998	**David Beckham**	v Argentina (St Etienne, World Cup Finals)
Sep 5, 1998	**Paul Ince**	v Sweden (Stockholm, Euro Champ qual)
Jun 5, 1999	**Paul Scholes**	v Sweden (Wembley, Euro Champ qual)
Sep 8, 1999	**David Batty**	v Poland (Warsaw, Euro Champ qual)
Oct 16, 2002	**Alan Smith**	v Macedonia (Southampton, Euro Champ qual)
Oct 8, 2005	**David Beckham**	v Austria (Old Trafford, World Cup qual)
Jul 1, 2006	**Wayne Rooney**	v Portugal (Gelsenkirchen, World Cup Finals)
Oct 10, 2009	**Robert Green**	v Ukraine (Dnipropetrovsk, World Cup qual)
Oct 7, 2011	**Wayne Rooney**	v Montenegro (Podgorica, Euro Champ qual)
Sep 11, 2012	**Steven Gerrard**	v Ukraine (Wembley, World Cup qual)
Jun 4, 2014	**Raheem Sterling**	v Ecuador (Miami, friendly)

Other countries: Most recent sendings-off of players representing other Home Countries:

N Ireland – Chris Baird (European Champ qual v Hungary, Belfast, Sep 7, 2015).

Scotland – John Souttar (Nations Lge v Israel, Haifa, Oct 11, 2018).

Wales – Neil Taylor (World Cup qual v Republic of Ireland, Dublin, Mar 24, 2017).

Rep of Ireland – Seamus Coleman (Euro Champ v Switzerland, Geneva, Oct 15, 2019).

England dismissals at other levels:

U-23: Stan Anderson (v Bulgaria, Sofia, May 19, 1957); **Alan Ball** (v Austria, Vienna, Jun 2, 1965); **Kevin Keegan** (v E Germany, Magdeburg, Jun 1, 1972); **Steve Perryman** (v Portugal, Lisbon, Nov 19, 1974).

U-21: Sammy Lee (v Hungary, Keszthely, Jun 5, 1981); **Mark Hateley** (v Scotland, Hampden Park, Apr 19, 1982); **Paul Elliott** (v Denmark, Maine Road, Manchester, Mar 26, 1986); **Tony Cottee** (v W Germany, Ludenscheid, Sep 8, 1987); **Julian Dicks** (v Mexico, Toulon, France, Jun 12, 1988); **Jason Dodd** (v Mexico, Toulon, May 29, 1991; 3 Mexico players also sent off in that match); **Matthew Jackson** (v France, Toulon, May 28, 1992); **Robbie Fowler** (v Austria, Kafkenberg, Oct 11, 1994); **Alan Thompson** (v Portugal, Oporto, Sep 2, 1995); **Terry Cooke** (v Portugal, Toulon, May 30, 1996); **Ben Thatcher** (v Italy, Rieti, Oct 10, 1997); **John Curtis** (v Greece, Heraklion, Nov 13, 1997); **Jody Morris** (v Luxembourg, Grevenmacher, Oct 13, 1998); **Stephen Wright** (v Germany, Derby, Oct 6, 2000); **Alan Smith** (v Finland, Valkeakoski, Oct 10, 2000); **Luke Young** and **John Terry** (v Greece, Athens, Jun 5, 2001); **Shola Ameobi** (v Portugal, Rio Maior, Mar 28, 2003); **Jermaine Pennant** (v Croatia, Upton Park, Aug 19, 2003); **Glen Johnson** (v Turkey, Istanbul, Oct 10, 2003); **Nigel Reo-Coker** (v Azerbaijan, Baku, Oct 12, 2004); **Glen Johnson** (v Spain, Henares, Nov 16, 2004); **Steven Taylor** (v Germany, Leverkusen, Oct 10, 2006); **Tom Huddlestone** (v Serbia & Montenegro, Nijmegen, Jun 17, 2007); **Tom Huddlestone** (v Wales, Villa Park, Oct 14, 2008); **Michael Mancienne** (v Finland, Halmstad, Jun 15, 2009); **Fraizer Campbell** (v Sweden, Gothenburg, Jun 26, 2009); **Ben Mee** (v Italy, Empoli, Feb 8, 2011); **Danny Rose** (v Serbia, Krusevac, Oct 16, 2012); **Andre Wisdom** (v Finland, Tampere, Sep 9, 2013); **Jack Stephens** (v Bosnia-Herz, Sarajevo,

Nov 12, 2015; **Jordon Ibe** (vSwitzerland, Thun, Mar 26, 2016).
England 'B' (1): **Neil Webb** (v Algeria, Algiers, Dec 11, 1990).

MOST DISMISSALS IN INTERNATIONAL MATCHES

19 (10 Chile, 9 Uruguay), Jun 25, 1975; **6** (2 Mexico, 4 Argentina), 1956; **6** (5 Ecuador, 1 Uruguay), Jan 4, 1977 (4 Ecuadorians sent off in 78th min, match abandoned, 1-1); **5** (Holland 3, Brazil 2), Jun 6, 1999 in Goianio, Brazil.

INTERNATIONAL STOPPED THROUGH DEPLETED SIDE

Portugal v Angola (5-1), friendly international in Lisbon on Nov 14, 2001, abandoned (68 mins) because Angola were down to 6 players (4 sent off, 1 carried off, no substitutes left).

MOST 'CARDS' IN WORLD CUP FINALS MATCH

20 in Portugal v Holland quarter-final, Nuremberg, Jun 25, 2006 (9 yellow, 2 red, Portugal; 7 yellow, 2 red, Holland).

FIVE OFF IN ONE MATCH

For the first time since League football began in 1888, five players were sent off in one match (two Chesterfield, three Plymouth) in Div 2 at Saltergate on **Feb 22, 1997**. Four were dismissed (two from each side) in a goalmouth brawl in the last minute. Five were sent off on Dec 2, 1997 (4 Bristol Rov, 1 Wigan) in Div 2 match at Wigan, four in the 45th minute. The third instance occurred at Exeter on **Nov 23, 2002** in Div 3 (three Exeter, two Cambridge United) all in the last minute. On **Mar 27, 2012** (Lge 2) three Bradford players and two from Crawley were shown red cards in the dressing rooms after a brawl at the final whistle at Valley Parade.

Matches with **four** Football League club players being sent off in one match:

Jan 8, 1955: Crewe v Bradford City (Div 3 North), two players from each side.

Dec 13, 1986: Sheffield Utd (1 player) v Portsmouth (3) in Div 2.

Aug 18, 1987: Port Vale v Northampton (Littlewoods Cup 1st Round, 1st Leg), two players from each side.

Dec 12, 1987: Brentford v Mansfield (Div 3), two players from each side.

Sep 6, 1992: First instance in British first-class football of four players from one side being sent off in one match. Hereford's seven survivors, away to Northampton (Div 3), held out for a 1-1 draw.

Mar 1, 1977: Norwich v Huddersfield (Div 1), two from each side.

Oct 4, 1977: Shrewsbury (1 player), Rotherham (3) in Div 3.

Aug 22, 1998: Gillingham v Bristol Rov (Div 2), two players from each side, all after injury-time brawl.

Mar 16, 2001: Bristol City v Millwall (Div 2), two from each side.

Aug 17, 2002: Lincoln (1 player), Carlisle (3) in Div 3.

Aug 26, 2002: Wycombe v QPR (Div 2), two from each side.

Nov 1, 2005: Burnley (1 player) v Millwall (3) in Championship.

Nov 24, 2007: Swindon v Bristol Rov (Lge 1), two from each side.

Mar 4, 2008: Hull v Burnley (Champ) two from each side.

Four Stranraer players were sent off away to Airdrie (Scottish Div 1) on Dec 3, 1994, and that Scottish record was equalled when four Hearts men were ordered off away to Rangers (Prem Div) on Sep 14, 1996. Albion had four players sent off (3 in last 8 mins) away to Queen's Park (Scottish Div 3) on Aug 23, 1997.

In the **Island Games** in Guernsey (Jul 2003), five players (all from Rhodes) were sent off against Guernsey for violent conduct and the match was abandoned by referee Wendy Toms.

Most dismissals one team, one match: Five players of America Tres Rios in first ten minutes after disputed goal by opponents Itaperuna in Brazilian cup match in Rio de Janeiro on Nov 23, 1991. Tie then abandoned and awarded to Itaperuna.

Eight dismissals in one match: Four on each side in South American Super Cup quarter-final (Gremio, Brazil v Penarol, Uruguay) in Oct 1993.

Five dismissals in one season – Dave Caldwell (2 with Chesterfield, 3 with Torquay) in 1987–88.

First instance of four dismissals in Scottish match: three Rangers players (all English – Terry Hurlock, Mark Walters, Mark Hateley) and Celtic's Peter Grant in Scottish Cup quarter-final at Parkhead on Mar 17, 1991 (Celtic won 2-0).

Four players (3 Hamilton, 1 Airdrie) were sent off in Scottish Div 1 match on Oct 30, 1993.

Four players (3 Ayr, 1 Stranraer) were sent off in Scottish Div 1 match on Aug 27, 1994.

In Scottish Cup first round replays on Dec 16, 1996, there were two instances of three players of one side sent off: Albion Rov (away to Forfar) and Huntly (away to Clyde).

FASTEST SENDINGS-OFF

World record – 10 sec: Giuseppe Lorenzo (Bologna) for striking opponent in Italian League match v Parma, Dec 9, 1990. Goalkeeper **Preston Edwards** (Ebbsfleet) for bringing down opponent and conceding penalty in Blue Square Premier League South match v Farnborough, Feb 5, 2011.

World record (non-professional) – 3 sec: David Pratt (Chippenham) at Bashley (British Gas Southern Premier League, Dec 27, 2008).

Domestic – 13 sec: Kevin Pressman (Sheffield Wed goalkeeper at Wolves, Div 1, Sunday, Aug 14, 2000); **15 sec: Simon Rea** (Peterborough at Cardiff, Div 2, Nov 2, 2002). **19 sec: Mark Smith** (Crewe goalkeeper at Darlington, Div 3, Mar 12, 1994). **Premier League – 72 sec: Tim Flowers** (Blackburn goalkeeper v Leeds Utd, Feb 1, 1995).

In World Cup – 55 sec: Jose Batista (Uruguay v Scotland at Neza, Mexico, Jun 13, 1986).

In European competition – 90 sec: Sergei Dirkach (Dynamo Moscow v Ghent UEFA Cup 3rd round, 2nd leg, Dec 11, 1991).

Fastest FA Cup dismissal – 52 sec: Ian Culverhouse (Swindon defender, deliberate hand-ball on goal-line, away to Everton, 3rd Round, Sunday Jan 5, 1997).

Fastest League Cup dismissal – 33 sec: Jason Crowe (Arsenal substitute v Birmingham, 3rd Round, Oct 14, 1997). Also fastest sending off on debut.

Fastest Sending-off of substitute – 0 sec: Walter Boyd (Swansea City) for striking opponent before ball in play after he went on (83 mins) at home to Darlington, Div 3, Nov 23, 1999. **15 secs: Keith Gillespie** (Sheffield Utd) for striking an opponent at Reading (Premier League), Jan 20, 2007. **90 sec: Andreas Johansson** (Wigan), without kicking a ball, for shirt-pulling (penalty) away to Arsenal (Premier League), May 7, 2006.

MOST SENDINGS-OFF IN CAREER

21	**Willie Johnston**, 1964–82 (Rangers 7, WBA 6, Vancouver Whitecaps 4, Hearts 3, Scotland 1)
21	**Roy McDonough**, 1980–95 (13 in Football League – Birmingham, Walsall, Chelsea, Colchester, Southend, Exeter, Cambridge Utd plus 8 non-league)
13	**Steve Walsh** (Wigan, Leicester, Norwich, Coventry)
13	**Martin Keown** (Arsenal, Aston Villa, Everton)
13	**Alan Smith** (Leeds, Manchester Utd, Newcastle, England U–21, England)
12	**Dennis Wise** (Wimbledon, Chelsea, Leicester, Millwall)
12	**Vinnie Jones** (Wimbledon, Leeds, Sheffield Utd, Chelsea, QPR)
12	**Mark Dennis** (Birmingham, Southampton, QPR)
12	**Roy Keane** (Manchester Utd, Rep of Ireland)
10	**Patrick Vieira** (Arsenal)
10	**Paul Scholes** (Manchester Utd, England)

Most Premier League sendings-off: Patrick Vieira 9, Duncan Ferguson 8, Richard Dunne 8, Vinnie Jones 7, Roy Keane 7, Alan Smith 7. Lee Cattermole 7.

● **Carlton Palmer** holds the unique record of having been sent off with each of his five Premier League clubs: Sheffield Wed, Leeds, Southampton, Nottm Forest and Coventry.

FA CUP FINAL SENDINGS-OFF

Kevin Moran (Manchester Utd) v Everton, Wembley, 1985; **Jose Antonio Reyes** (Arsenal) v Manchester Utd, Cardiff, 2005; **Pablo Zabaleta** (Manchester City) v Wigan, Wembley 2013; **Chris Smalling** (Manchester Utd) v Crystal Palace, Wembley, 2016; **Victor Moses** (Chelsea) v Arsenal, Wembley, 2017. **Mateo Kovacic** (Chelsea) v Arsenal, Wembley 2020.

WEMBLEY SENDINGS-OFF

Aug 1948	**Branko Stankovic** (Yugoslavia) v Sweden, Olympic Games

Aug 1948   **Branko Stankovic** (Yugoslavia) v Sweden, Olympic Games
Jul 1966   **Antonio Rattin** (Argentina captain) v England, World cup quarter-final
Aug 1974   **Billy Bremner** (Leeds) and **Kevin Keegan** (Liverpool), Charity Shield
Mar 1977   **Gilbert Dresch** (Luxembourg) v England, World Cup
May 1985   **Kevin Moran** (Manchester Utd) v Everton, FA Cup Final
Apr 1993   **Lee Dixon** (Arsenal) v Tottenham, FA Cup semi-final
May 1993   **Peter Swan** (Port Vale) v WBA, Div 2 Play-off Final
Mar 1994   **Andrei Kanchelskis** (Manchester Utd) v Aston Villa, League Cup Final
May 1994   **Mike Wallace, Chris Beaumont** (Stockport) v Burnley, Div 2 Play-off Final
Jun 1995   **Tetsuji Hashiratani** (Japan) v England, Umbro Cup
May 1997   **Brian Statham** (Brentford) v Crewe, Div 2 Play-off Final
Apr 1998   **Capucho** (Portugal) v England, friendly
Nov 1998   **Ray Parlour** (Arsenal) and **Tony Vareilles** (Lens), Champions League
Mar 1999   **Justin Edinburgh** (Tottenham) v Leicester, League Cup Final
Jun 1999   **Paul Scholes** (England) v Sweden, European Championship qual
Feb 2000   **Clint Hill** (Tranmere) v Leicester, League Cup Final
Apr 2000   **Mark Delaney** (Aston Villa) v Bolton, FA Cup semi-final
May 2000   **Kevin Sharp** (Wigan) v Gillingham, Div 2 Play-off Final
Aug 2000   **Roy Keane** (Manchester Utd captain) v Chelsea, Charity Shield
May 2007   **Marc Tierney** (Shrewsbury) v Bristol Rov, Lge 2 Play-off Final
May 2007   **Matt Gill** (Exeter) v Morecambe, Conf Play-off Final
May 2009   **Jamie Ward** (Sheffield Utd) and **Lee Hendrie** (Sheffield Utd) v Burnley, Champ
            Play-off Final (Hendrie after final whistle)
May 2009   **Phil Bolland** (Cambridge Utd) v Torquay, Blue Square Prem Lge Play-off Final
May 2010   **Robin Hulbert** (Barrow) and **David Bridges** (Stevenage), FA Trophy Final
Apr 2011   **Paul Scholes** (Manchester Utd) v Manchester City, FA Cup semi-final
Apr 2011   **Toumani Diagouraga** (Brentford) v Carlisle, Johnstone's Paint Trophy Final
Sep 2012   **Steven Gerrard** (England) v Ukraine, World Cup qual
Feb 2013   **Matt Duke** (Bradford) v Swansea, League Cup Final
May 2013   **Pablo Zabaleta** (Manchester City) v Wigan, FA Cup Final
Mar 2014   **Joe Newell** (Peterborough) v Chesterfield, Johnstone's Paint Trophy Final
May 2014   **Gary O'Neil** (QPR) v Derby, Champ Play-off Final
May 2016   **Chris Smalling** (Manchester Utd) v Crystal Palace, FA Cup Final
May 2017   **Victor Moses** (Chelsea) v Arsenal, FA Cup Final
Aug 2017   **Pedro** (Chelsea) v Arsenal, Community Shield
Sep 2017   **Jan Vertonghen** (Tottenham) v Borussia Dortmund, Champions League
May 2018   **Liam Ridehalgh** (Tranmere) v Boreham Wood, National League Play-off Final –
            after 48 secs
May 2018   **Denis Odoi** (Fulham) v Aston Villa, Championship Play-off Final
May 2019   **Mark O'Brien** (Newport) v Tranmere, Lge 2 Play-off Final
Jun 2020   **Dean Moxey** (Exeter) v Northampton, Lge 2 Play-off Final
Aug 2020   **Mateo Kovacic** (Chelsea) v Arsenal, FA Cup Final

WEMBLEY'S SUSPENDED CAPTAINS

Suspension prevented four **club captains** playing at Wembley in modern finals, in successive years. Three were in FA Cup Finals – **Glenn Roeder** (QPR, 1982), **Steve Foster** (Brighton, 1983), **Wilf Rostron** (Watford, 1984). Sunderland's **Shaun Elliott** was banned from the 1985 Milk Cup Final. Roeder was banned from QPR's 1982 Cup Final replay against Tottenham, and Foster was ruled out of the first match in Brighton's 1983 Final against Manchester Utd.

RED CARD FOR KICKING BALL-BOY

Chelsea's **Eden Hazard** was sent off (80 mins) in the League Cup semi-final, second leg at Swansea on Jan 23, 2013 for kicking a 17-year-old ball-boy who refused to hand over the ball that had gone out of play. The FA suspended Hazard for three matches.

BOOKINGS RECORDS

Most players of one Football League club booked in one match is **TEN** – members of the Mansfield team away to Crystal Palace in FA Cup third round, Jan 1963. Most yellow cards for one team in Premier League match – **9** for Tottenham away to Chelsea, May 2, 2016.

Fastest bookings – 3 seconds after kick-off, **Vinnie Jones** (Chelsea, home to Sheffield Utd, FA Cup fifth round, Feb 15, 1992); 5 seconds after kick-off: **Vinnie Jones** (Sheffield Utd, away to Manchester City, Div 1, Jan 19, 1991). He was sent-off (54 mins) for second bookable offence.

FIGHTING TEAM-MATES

Charlton's **Mike Flanagan** and **Derek Hales** were sent off for fighting each other five minutes from end of FA Cup 3rd round tie at home to Southern League Maidstone on Jan 9, 1979.

Bradford City's **Andy Myers** and **Stuart McCall** had a fight during the 1-6 Premier League defeat at Leeds on Sunday, May 13, 2001.

On Sep 28, 1994 the Scottish FA suspended Hearts players **Graeme Hogg** and **Craig Levein** for ten matches for fighting each other in a pre-season 'friendly' v Raith.

Blackburn's England players **Graeme Le Saux** and **David Batty** clashed away to Spartak Moscow (Champions League) on Nov 22, 1995. Neither was sent off.

Newcastle United's England Internationals **Lee Bowyer** and **Kieron Dyer** were sent off for fighting each other at home to Aston Villa (Premier League on Apr 2, 2005).

Arsenal's **Emmanuel Adebayor** and **Nicklas Bendtner** clashed during the 5-1 Carling Cup semi-final 2nd leg defeat at Tottenham on Jan 22, 2008. Neither was sent off; each fined by their club.

Stoke's **Ricardo Fuller** was sent off for slapping his captain, Andy Griffin, at West Ham in the Premier League on Dec 28, 2008.

Preston's **Jermaine Beckford** and **Eoin Doyle** clashed in the Championship game against Sheffield Wednesday on Dec 3, 2016, and were sent off.

St Johnstone's **Richard Foster** and **Danny Swanson** were dismissed for brawling in the Scottish Premier League match with Hamilton on Apr 1, 2017.

FOOTBALL'S FIRST BETTING SCANDAL

A Football League investigation into the First Division match which ended Manchester Utd 2, Liverpool 0 at Old Trafford on Good Friday, Apr 2, 1915 proved that the result had been 'squared' by certain players betting on the outcome. Four members of each team were suspended for life, but some of the bans were lifted when League football resumed in 1919 in recognition of the players' war service.

PLAYERS JAILED

Ten professional footballers found guilty of conspiracy to fraud by 'fixing' matches for betting purposes were given prison sentences at Nottingham Assizes on Jan 26, 1965.

Jimmy Gauld (Mansfield), described as the central figure, was given four years. Among the others sentenced, **Tony Kay** (Sheffield Wed, Everton & England), **Peter Swan** (Sheffield Wed & England) and **David 'Bronco' Layne** (Sheffield Wed) were suspended from football for life by the FA.

DRUGS BANS

Abel Xavier (Middlesbrough) was the first Premier League player found to have taken a performance-enchancing drug. He was banned by UEFA for 18 months in Nov 2005 after testing positive for an anabolic steroid. The ban was reduced to a year in Jul 2006 by the Court of Arbitration for Sport. **Paddy Kenny** (Sheffield Utd goalkeeper) was suspended by an FA commission for 9 months from July, 2009 for failing a drugs test the previous May. Kolo Toure (Manchester City) received a 6-month ban in May 2011 for a doping offence. It was backdated to Mar 2.

LONG SUSPENSIONS

The longest suspension (8 months) in modern times for a player in British football was imposed on two Manchester Utd players. First was **Eric Cantona** following his attack on a spectator as he left the pitch after being sent off at Crystal Palace (Prem League) on Jan 25, 1995. The club immediately suspended him to the end of the season and fined him 2 weeks' wages (est £20,000). Then, on a disrepute charge, the FA fined him £10,000 (Feb 1995) and extended the ban to Sep 30 (which FIFA confirmed as world-wide). A subsequent 2-weeks' jail sentence on Cantona for assault was altered, on appeal, to 120 hours' community service, which took the form of coaching schoolboys in the Manchester area.

On **Dec 19, 2003** an FA Commission, held at Bolton, suspended **Rio Ferdinand** from football for 8 months (plus £50,000 fine) for failing to take a random drug test at the club's training ground on Sep 23. The ban operated from Jan 12, 2004.

Aug 1974: Kevin Keegan (Liverpool) and **Billy Bremner** (Leeds) both suspended for 10 matches and fined £500 after being sent off in FA Charity Shield at Wembley.

Jan 1988: Mark Dennis (QPR) given 8-match ban after 11th sending-off of his career.

Oct 1988: Paul Davis (Arsenal) banned for 9 matches for breaking the jaw of Southampton's Glenn Cockerill.

Oct 1998: Paolo Di Canio (Sheff Wed) banned for 11 matches and fined £10,000 for pushing referee Paul Alcock after being sent off at home to Arsenal (Prem), Sep 26.

Mar 2005: David Prutton (Southampton) banned for 10 matches (plus 1 for red card) and fined £6,000 by FA for shoving referee Alan Wiley when sent off at home to Arsenal (Prem), Feb 26.

Aug 2006: Ben Thatcher (Manchester City) banned for 8 matches for elbowing Pedro Mendes (Portsmouth).

Sep 2008: Joey Barton (Newcastle) banned for 12 matches (6 suspended) and fined £25,000 by FA for training ground assault on former Manchester City team-mate Ousmane Dabo.

May 2012: Joey Barton (QPR) suspended for 12 matches and fined £75,000 for violent conduct when sent off against Manchester City on final day of Premier League season.

Mar 2014: Joss Labadie (Torquay) banned for 10 matches and fined £2,000 for biting Chesterfield's Ollie Banks (Lge 2) on Feb 15, 2014.

Seven-month ban: Frank Barson, 37-year-old Watford centre-half, sent off at home to Fulham (Div 3 South) on Sep 29, 1928, was suspended by the FA for the remainder of the season.

Twelve-month ban: Oldham full-back **Billy Cook** was given a 12-month suspension for refusing to leave the field when sent off at Middlesbrough (Div 1), on Apr 3, 1915. The referee abandoned the match with 35 minutes still to play, and the score (4-1 to Middlesbrough) was ordered to stand.

Long Scottish bans: Sep 1954: Willie Woodburn, Rangers and Scotland centre-half, suspended for rest of career after fifth sending-off in 6 years.

Billy McLafferty, Stenhousemuir striker, was banned (Apr 14) for 8 and a half months, to Jan 1, 1993, and fined £250 for failing to appear at a disciplinary hearing after being sent off against Arbroath on Feb 1.

Twelve-match ban: On May 12, 1994 Scottish FA suspended Rangers forward **Duncan Ferguson** for 12 matches for violent conduct v Raith on Apr 16. On Oct 11, 1995, Ferguson (then with Everton) sent to jail for 3 months for the assault (served 44 days); Feb 1, 1996 Scottish judge quashed 7 matches that remained of SFA ban on Ferguson.

On Sep 29, 2001 the SFA imposed a **17-match suspension** on Forfar's former Scottish international **Dave Bowman** for persistent foul and abusive language when sent off against Stranraer on Sep 22. As his misconduct continued, he was shown **5 red cards** by the referee.

On Apr 3, 2009, captain **Barry Ferguson** and goalkeeper **Allan McGregor** were banned for life from playing for Scotland for gestures towards photographers while on the bench for a World Cup qualifier against Iceland.

On Dec 20, 2011 Liverpool and Uruguay striker **Luis Suarez** was given an 8-match ban and fined £40,000 by the FA for making 'racially offensive comments' to Patrice Evra of Manchester Utd (Prem Lge, Oct 15).

On Apr 25, 2013 **Luis Suarez** was given a 10-match suspension by the FA for 'violent conduct' – biting Chelsea defender Branislav Ivanovic, Prem Lge, Apr 21. The Liverpool player was also fined £200,000 by Liverpool. His ban covered the last 4 games of that season and the first 6 of 2013-14. On Jun 26, 2014, Suarez, while still a Liverpool player, received the most severe punishment in World Cup history – a four-month ban from 'all football activities' and £66,000 fine from FIFA for biting Giorgio Chiellini during Uruguay's group game against Italy.

On Nov 4, 2016 Rochdale's **Calvin Andrew** was banned by the FA for 12 matches – reduced to 9 on appeal – for elbowing Peter Clarke (Oldham) in the face.

On Apr 16, 2017 **Joey Barton** was banned by the FA for 18 months and fined £30,000 for breaching betting rules. The Burnley player admitted placing 1,260 bets on matches.

TWO-YEAR EUROPEAN BAN OVERTURNED

Manchester City received a two-season European ban and £25m fine in February 2020 after being charged with breaking UEFA's Financial Fair Play rules. The club lodged an appeal with the Court of Arbitration for Sport and the ban was quashed in July 2020. The fine, for not co-operating with UEFA, was reduced to £9m.

TOP FINES

Clubs: £49,000,000 (World record) Manchester City: May 2014 for breaking UEFA Financial Fair Play rules (**£32,600,000** suspended subject to City meeting certain conditions over two seasons). **£42m** settlement Queens Park Rangers: Jul 2018, breaching Financial Fair Play rules; **£7.6m** Bournemouth: May 2016, for breaking Financial Fair Play rules; **£5,500,000** West Ham: Apr 2007, for breaches of regulations involving 'dishonesty and deceit' over Argentine signings Carlos Tevez and Javier Mascherano; **£3.95m**: Watford: Aug 2017, forged banking letter; **£1,500,000** (increased from original £600,000) Tottenham: Dec 1994, financial irregularities; **£875,000** QPR: May 2011 for breaching rules when signing Argentine Alejandro Faurlin; **£500,000** (plus 2-year academy signings ban) Everton: Nov 2018, breaking recruitment rules; **£460,000** plus signings ban in two transfer windows (reduced on appeal to £230,000 and one transfer window) Chelsea: breaching rules relating to under-18 foreign players; **£390,000** FA: Feb 2019, failing to police recruitment of young players; **£375,000** (reduced to £290,000 on appeal) Chelsea: May 2016, players brawl v Tottenham; **£315,000** Manchester City: Aug 2019, breaching rules on signing youth players; **£300,000** (reduced to £75,000 on appeal) Chelsea: Jun 2005, illegal approach to Arsenal's Ashley Cole; **£300,000** (plus 2-year ban on signing academy players, part suspended) Manchester City: May 2017, approaching young players; **£225,000** (reduced to £175,000 on appeal) Tottenham: May 2016, players brawl v Chelsea; **£200,000** Aston Villa: May 2015 for fans' pitch invasion after FA Cup quarter-final v WBA; **£200,000** Leeds: Feb 2019, spying on other clubs' training sessions; **£200,000** (half suspended): Liverpool: Oct 2019, ineligible player, League Cup v MK Dons; **£175,000** Arsenal: Oct 2003, players' brawl v Manchester Utd; **£150,000** Leeds: Mar 2000, players' brawl v Tottenham; **£150,000** Tottenham: Mar 2000, players brawl v Leeds; **£145,000** Hull: Feb 2015, breaching Financial Fair Play rules; **£115,000** West Ham: Aug 2009, crowd misconduct at Carling Cup; v Millwall; **£105,000** Chelsea: Jan 1991, irregular payments; **£100,000** Boston Utd: Jul 2002, contract irregularities; **£100,000** Arsenal and Chelsea: Mar 2007 for mass brawl after Carling Cup Final; **£100,000** (including suspended fine) Blackburn: Aug 2007, poor disciplinary record; **£100,000** Sunderland: May 2014, breaching agents' regulations; **£100,000** Reading: Aug 2015, pitch invasion, FA Cup tie v Bradford (reduced to £40,000 on appeal); **£100,000** Chelsea: Dec 2016, players brawl v Manchester City; **£100,000** (plus 2-year ban on signing academy players, part suspended) Liverpool: Apr 2017, approaching young players; **£100,000** West Ham: Jan 2019, pitch invasions v Burnley; **£90,000** Brighton: Feb 2015, breaching rules on agents; **£71,000** West Ham: Feb 2015 for playing Diafra Sakho in FA Cup 4th round tie against Bristol City after declaring him unfit for Senegal's Africa Cup of Nations squad; **£65,000** Chelsea: Jan 2016, players brawl v WBA; **£62,000** Macclesfield: Dec 2005, funding of a stand at club's ground.

Players: £220,000 (plus 4-match ban) John Terry (Chelsea): Sep 2012, racially abusing Anton Ferdinand (QPR); **£150,000** Roy Keane (Manchester Utd): Oct 2002, disrepute offence over autobiography; **£150,000** plus 4-month ban (increased from £75,000 and two-week ban after appeal by FA) Daniel Sturridge (ex-Liverpool): Mar 2020, breaching betting rules; **£100,000** (reduced to £75,000 on appeal) Ashley Cole (Arsenal): Jun 2005, illegal approach by Chelsea; **£100,000 (plus 5-match ban)** Jonjo Shelvey (Newcastle): Dec 2016, racially abusing Romain Saiss (Wolves); **£90,000** Ashley Cole (Chelsea): Oct 2012, offensive Tweet against FA; **£80,000 (plus 5-match ban)** Nicolas Anelka (WBA): Feb 2014, celebrating goal at West Ham with racially-offensive 'quenelle' gesture; **£75,000 (plus 12-match ban)** Joey Barton (QPR): May 2012, violent conduct v Manchester City; **£60,000 (plus 3-match ban)** John Obi Mikel (Chelsea): Dec 2012, abusing referee Mark Clattenburg after Prem Lge v Manchester Utd); **£60,000** Dexter Blackstock (Nottm Forest): May 2014, breaching betting rules; **£60,000 (plus 8-match ban)** Kiko Casilla (Leeds): Feb 2020, racially abusing Jonathan Leko (Charlton);**£50,000** Cameron Jerome (Stoke): Aug 2013, breaching FA betting rules; **£50,000** Benoit Assou-Ekotto (Tottenham): Sep 2014, publicly backing Nicolas Anelka's controversial 'quenelle' gesture; **£50,000 (plus 1-match ban)** Bernardo Silva (Manchester City): Nov 2019, offensive social media message to team-mate Benjamin Mendy; **£50,000 (plus 1-match ban)** Dele Alli (Tottenham): Jun 2020, offensive social media post; **£45,000** Patrick Vieira (Arsenal): Oct 1999, tunnel incidents v West Ham; **£45,000** Rio Ferdinand (Manchester Utd): Aug 2012, improper comments about Ashley Cole on Twitter; **£40,000** Lauren (Arsenal): Oct 2003, players' fracas v Manchester Utd; **£40,000 (plus 8-match ban)** Luis Suarez (Liverpool): Dec 2011, racially abusing Patrice Evra (Manchester Utd); **£40,000 (plus 3-match ban)** Dani Osvaldo (Southampton): Jan 2014, violent conduct, touchline Newcastle; **£40,000** Bacary Sagna (Manchester City): Jan 2017, questioning integrity of referee Lee Mason; **£40,000 (plus 4-match ban)** Eric Dier (Tottenham): Jul 2020, confronting spectator in the stand.

*In eight seasons with Arsenal (1996–2004) **Patrick Vieira** was fined a total of £122,000 by the FA for disciplinary offences.

Managers: £200,000 (reduced to £75,000 on appeal) Jose Mourinho (Chelsea): Jun 2005, illegal approach to Arsenal's Ashley Cole; **£60,000 (plus 7-match ban)** Alan Pardew (Newcastle): head-butting Hull player David Meyler (also fined £100,000 by club); **£60,000** Rafael Benitez (Newcastle): Oct 2018, talking about match referee ahead of fixture; **£60,000** Rafael Benitez (Newcastle): Oct 2018, talking about match referee ahead of fixture; **£58,000** Jose Mourinho (Manchester Utd): Nov 2016, misconduct involving referees Mark Clattenburg and Anthony Taylor; **£50,000** Jose Mourinho (Chelsea): Oct 2015, accusing referees of bias; **£45,000** Jurgen Klopp (Liverpool): Feb 2019, questioning integrity of referee Kevin Friend; **£40,000 (plus 1 match stadium ban)** Jose Mourinho (Chelsea): Nov 2015, abusive behaviour towards referee Jon Moss v West Ham; **£40,000 (plus 3-match Euro ban)** Arsene Wenger (Arsenal): Jan 2018, abuse towards referee Mike Dean v WBA; **£33,000 (plus 3-match Euro ban)** Arsene Wenger: Mar 2012, criticising referee after Champions League defeat by AC Milan; **£30,000** Sir Alex Ferguson (Manchester Utd): Mar 2011 criticising referee Martin Atkinson v Chelsea; **£30,000 (plus 6-match ban ((plus 6-match ban reduced to 4 on appeal)** Rui Faria (Chelsea assistant): May 2014, confronting match officials v Sunderland.

• Jonathan Barnett, Ashley Cole's agent was fined **£100,000** in Sep 2006 for his role in the 'tapping up' affair involving the player and Chelsea.

• Gillingham and club chairman Paul Scally each fined £75,000 in Jul 2015 for 'racial victimisation' towards player Mark McCammon. Club fine reduced to £50,000 on appeal.

• Leyton Orient owner Francesco Becchetti fined £40,000 and given six-match stadium ban in Jan 2016 for violent conduct towards assistant manager Andy Hessenthaler.

***£68,000** FA: May 2003, pitch invasions and racist chanting by fans during England v Turkey, Sunderland.

£50,000 FA: Dec 2014, for Wigan owner-chairman Dave Whelan, plus six-week ban from all football activity, for remarks about Jewish and Chinese people in newspaper interview.

***£250,000** FA: Dec 2016, for Leeds owner Massimo Cellino, plus 18-month ban, for breaking agent regulations (reduced to £100,000 and one year on appeal). Club fined £250,000 (reduced to £200,000 on appeal). Agent Derek Day fined £75,000 and banned for 18 months (11 months suspended).

MANAGERS

INTERNATIONAL RECORDS
(As at start of season 2020–2021

	P	W	D	L	F	A
Gareth Southgate (England appointed Sep 2016	41	24	9	8	87	33
Steve Clarke (Scotland – appointed May 2019)	8	4	0	4	14	16
Ryan Giggs (Wales – appointed Jan 2018)	19	9	3	7	25	17
Ian Baraclough (Northern Ireland – appointed Jun 2020)	–					
Stephen Kenny (Republic of Ireland – appointed Apr 2020)	–					

COMPLETED RECORDS

	P	W	D	L	F	A
Michael O'Neill (Northern Ireland)	72	26	18	28	75	83
Mick McCarthy (Republic of Ireland)	10	5	4	1	13	7

ENGLAND MANAGERS

		P	W	D	L
1946–62	**Walter Winterbottom**	139	78	33	28
1963–74	**Sir Alf Ramsey**	113	69	27	17
1974	**Joe Mercer**, caretaker	7	3	3	1
1974–77	**Don Revie**	29	14	8	7
1977–82	**Ron Greenwood**	55	33	12	10
1982–90	**Bobby Robson**	95	47	30	18
1990–93	**Graham Taylor**	38	18	13	7
1994–96	**Terry Venables**	23	11	11	1
1996–99	**Glenn Hoddle**	28	17	6	5
1999	**Howard Wilkinson**, caretaker	1	0	0	1
1999–2000	**Kevin Keegan**	18	7	7	4
2000	**Howard Wilkinson**, caretaker	1	0	1	0
2000	**Peter Taylor**, caretaker	1	0	0	1
2001–06	**Sven–Goran Eriksson**	67	40	17	10
2006–07	**Steve McClaren**	18	9	4	5
2007–12	**Fabio Capello**	42	28	8	6
2012	**Stuart Pearce**, caretaker	1	0	0	1
2012–16	**Roy Hodgson**	56	33	15	8
2016	**Sam Allardyce**	1	1	0	0

INTERNATIONAL MANAGER CHANGES

England: Walter Winterbottom 1946–62 (initially coach); **Alf Ramsey** (Feb 1963–May 1974); **Joe Mercer** (caretaker May 1974); **Don Revie** (Jul 1974–Jul 1977); **Ron Greenwood** (Aug 1977–Jul 1982); **Bobby Robson** (Jul 1982–Jul 1990); **Graham Taylor** (Jul 1990–Nov 1993); **Terry Venables**, coach (Jan 1994–Jun 1996); **Glenn Hoddle**, coach (Jun 1996–Feb 1999); **Howard Wilkinson** (caretaker Feb 1999); **Kevin Keegan** coach (Feb 1999–Oct 2000); **Howard Wilkinson** (caretaker Oct 2000); **Peter Taylor** (caretaker Nov 2000); **Sven–Goran Eriksson** (Jan 2001–Aug 2006); **Steve McClaren** (Aug 2006–Nov 2007); **Fabio Capello** (Dec 2007–Feb 2012); **Roy Hodgson** (May 2012– Jun 2016); **Sam Allardyce** (Jul–Sep 2016); **Gareth Southgate** (Sep-Nov 2016 interim, then permanent appointment).

Scotland (modern): Bobby Brown (Feb 1967–Jul 1971); **Tommy Docherty** (Sep 1971–Dec 1972); **Willie Ormond** (Jan 1973–May 1977); **Ally MacLeod** (May 1977–Sep 1978); **Jock Stein** (Oct 1978–Sep 1985); **Alex Ferguson** (caretaker Oct 1985–Jun 1986); **Andy Roxburgh**, coach (Jul 1986–Sep 1993); **Craig Brown** (Sep 1993–Oct 2001); **Berti Vogts** (Feb 2002–Oct 2004); **Walter Smith** (Dec 2004–Jan 2007); **Alex McLeish** (Jan 2007–Nov 2007); **George Burley** (Jan 2008–Nov 2009); **Craig Levein** (Dec 2009–Nov 2012); **Billy Stark** (caretaker Nov–Dec 2012); **Gordon Strachan** (Jan 2013-Oct 2017); **Malky Mackay**, (caretaker Nov

2017); **Alex McLeish** (Feb 2018–Apr 2019; **Steve Clarke** (since May 2019).

Northern Ireland (modern): Peter Doherty (1951–62); **Bertie Peacock** (1962–67); **Billy Bingham** (1967–Aug 1971); **Terry Neill** (Aug 1971–Mar 1975); **Dave Clements** (player–manager Mar 1975–1976); **Danny Blanchflower** (Jun 1976–Nov 1979); **Billy Bingham** (Feb 1980–Nov 1993); **Bryan Hamilton** Feb 1994–Feb 1998); **Lawrie McMenemy** (Feb 1998–Nov 1999); **Sammy McIlroy** (Jan 2000–Oct 2003); **Lawrie Sanchez** (Jan 2004–May 2007); **Nigel Worthington** (May 2007–Oct 2011); **Michael O'Neill** (Oct 2011–Apr 2020); **Ian Baraclough** (since Jun 2020).

Wales (modern): Mike Smith (Jul 1974–Dec 1979); **Mike England** (Mar 1980–Feb 1988); **David Williams** (caretaker Mar 1988); **Terry Yorath** (Apr 1988–Nov 1993); **John Toshack** (Mar 1994, one match); **Mike Smith** (Mar 1994–Jun 1995); **Bobby Gould** (Aug 1995–Jun 1999); **Mark Hughes** (Aug 1999 – Oct 2004); **John Toshack** (Nov 2004–Sep 2010); **Brian Flynn** (caretaker Sep–Dec 2010); **Gary Speed** (Dec 2010–Nov 2011); **Chris Coleman** (Jan 2012-Nov 2017); **Ryan Giggs** (since Jan 2018).

Republic of Ireland (modern): Liam Tuohy (Sep 1971–Nov 1972); **Johnny Giles** (Oct 1973– Apr 1980, initially player–manager); **Eoin Hand** (Jun 1980–Nov 1985); **Jack Charlton** (Feb 1986–Dec 1995); **Mick McCarthy** (Feb 1996–Oct 2002); **Brian Kerr** (Jan 2003–Oct 2005); **Steve Staunton** (Jan 2006–Oct 2007); **Giovanni Trapattoni** (May 2008–Sep 2013); **Martin O'Neill** (Nov 2013–Nov 2018); **Mick McCarthy** (Nov 2018–Apr 2020); **Stephen Kenny** (since Apr 2020).

WORLD CUP-WINNING MANAGERS

1930 Uruguay (Alberto Suppici); 1934 and 1938 Italy (Vittorio Pozzo); 1950 Uruguay (Juan Lopez Fontana); 1954 West Germany (Sepp Herberger); 1958 Brazil (Vicente Feola); 1962 Brazil (Aymore Moreira); 1966 England (Sir Alf Ramsey); 1970 Brazil (Mario Zagallo); 1974 West Germany (Helmut Schon); 1978 Argentina (Cesar Luis Menotti); 1982 Italy (Enzo Bearzot); 1986 Argentina (Carlos Bilardo); 1990 West Germany (Franz Beckenbauer); 1994 Brazil (Carlos Alberto Parreira); 1998 France (Aimee Etienne Jacquet); 2002 Brazil (Luiz Felipe Scolari); 2006 Italy (Marcello Lippi); 2010 Spain (Vicente Del Bosque); 2014 Germany (Joachim Low); 2018 France (Didier Deschamps).

Each of the 21 winning teams had a manager/coach of that country's nationality.

YOUNGEST LEAGUE MANAGERS

Ivor Broadis, 23, appointed player-manager of Carlisle, Aug 1946; **Chris Brass**, 27, appointed player-manager of York, Jun 2003; **Terry Neill**, 28, appointed player manager of Hull, Jun 1970; **Graham Taylor**, 28, appointed manager of Lincoln, Dec 1972.

LONGEST-SERVING LEAGUE MANAGERS – ONE CLUB

Fred Everiss, secretary–manager of WBA for 46 years (1902–48); **George Ramsay**, secretary– manager of Aston Villa for 42 years (1884–1926); **John Addenbrooke**, Wolves, for 37 years (1885–1922). Since last war: **Sir Alex Ferguson** at Manchester Utd for 27 seasons (1986– 2013); **Sir Matt Busby**, in charge of Manchester Utd for 25 seasons (1945–69, 1970–71); **Dario Gradi** at Crewe for 26 years (1983–2007, 2009–11); **Jimmy Seed** at Charlton for 23 years (1933–56); **Brian Clough** at Nottm Forest for 18 years (1975–93); **Arsene Wenger** at Arsenal for 22 years (1996-2018).

LAST ENGLISH MANAGER TO WIN CHAMPIONSHIP

Howard Wilkinson (Leeds), season 1991–92.

MANAGERS WITH MORE THAN 1000 MATCHES

Sir Alex Ferguson, Sir Bobby Robson, Sir Matt Busby, Arsene Wenger, Roy Hodgson, Harry Redknapp, Alec Stock, Brian Clough, Jim Smith, Graham Taylor, Dario Gradi, Tony Pulis, Dave Bassett, Lennie Lawrence, Alan Buckley, Denis Smith, Joe Royle, Ron Atkinson, Brian Horton, Neil Warnock, Len Ashurst, Lawrie McMenemy, Graham Turner, Steve Coppell, John

Toshack, Rafael Benitez, Sven-Goran Eriksson, Claudio Ranieri and Carlo Ancelotti, Sam Allardyce, Danny Wilson.

SHORT-TERM MANAGERS

Departed

3 days	Bill Lambton (Scunthorpe)	Apr 1959
6 days	Tommy McLean (Raith Rov)	Sep 1996
7 days	Tim Ward (Exeter)	Mar 1953
7 days	Kevin Cullis (Swansea City)	Feb 1996
8 days	Billy McKinlay (Watford)	Oct 2014
10 days	Dave Cowling (Doncaster)	Oct 1997
10 days	Peter Cormack (Cowdenbeath)	Dec 2000
13 days	Johnny Cochrane (Reading)	Apr 1939
13 days	Micky Adams (Swansea City)	Oct 1997
16 days	Jimmy McIlroy (Bolton)	Nov 1970
19 days	Martin Allen (Barnet)	Apr 2011
20 days	Paul Went (Leyton Orient)	Oct 1981
27 days	Malcolm Crosby (Oxford Utd)	Jan 1998
27 days	Oscar Garcia (Watford)	Sep 2014
28 days	Tommy Docherty (QPR)	Dec 1968
28 days	Paul Hart (QPR)	Jan 2010
29 days	Carl Fletcher (Leyton Orient)	Nov 2019
31 days	Paul Scholes (Oldham)	Mar 2019
32 days	Steve Coppell (Manchester City)	Nov 1996
32 days	Darko Milanic (Leeds)	Oct 2014
34 days	Niall Quinn (Sunderland)	Aug 2006
36 days	Steve Claridge (Millwall)	Jul 2005
39 days	Paul Gascoigne (Kettering)	Dec 2005
39 days	Kenny Jackett (Rotherham)	Nov 2016
40 days	Alex McLeish (Nottm Forest)	Feb 2013
41 days	Steve Wicks (Lincoln)	Oct 1995
41 days	Les Reed (Charlton)	Dec 2006
43 days	Mauro Milanese (Leyton Orient)	Dec 2014
44 days	Brian Clough (Leeds)	Sep 1974
44 days	Jock Stein (Leeds)	Oct 1978
45 days	Paul Murray (Hartlepool)	Dec 2014
48 days	John Toshack (Wales)	Mar 1994
48 days	David Platt (Sampdoria coach)	Feb 1999
49 days	Brian Little (Wolves)	Oct 1986
49 days	Terry Fenwick (Northampton)	Feb 2003
52 days	Alberto Cavasin (Leyton Orient)	Nov 2016
54 days	Craig Levein (Raith Rov)	Oct 1996
54 days	Chris Lucketti (Bury)	Jan 2018
56 days	Martin Ling (Swindon)	Dec 2015
57 days	Henning Berg (Blackburn)	Dec 2012
59 days	Kevin Nugent (Barnet)	Apr 2017
61 days	Bill McGarry (Wolves)	Nov 1985
63 days	Graham Westley (Stevenage)	Feb 2020

- In May 1984, Crystal Palace named **Dave Bassett** as manager, but he changed his mind four days later, without signing the contract, and returned to Wimbledon.
- In May 2007, **Leroy Rosenior** was reportedly appointed manager of Torquay after relegation and sacked ten minutes later when the club came under new ownership.
- **Brian Laws** lost his job at Scunthorpe on Mar 25, 2004 and was reinstated three weeks later.

- In an angry outburst after a play-off defeat in May 1992, Barnet chairman Stan Flashman sacked manager **Barry Fry** and re-instated him a day later.

EARLY-SEASON MANAGER SACKINGS

2012: Andy Thorn (Coventry) 8 days; John Sheridan (Chesterfield) 10 days; **2011:** Jim Jefferies (Hearts) 9 days; **2010** Kevin Blackwell (Sheffield Utd) 8 days; **2009** Bryan Gunn (Norwich) 6 days; **2007:** Neil McDonald (Carlisle) 2 days; Martin Allen (Leicester) 18 days; **2004:** Paul Sturrock (Southampton) 9 days; **2004:** Sir Bobby Robson (Newcastle) 16 days; **2003:** Glenn Roeder (West Ham) 15 days; **2000:** Alan Buckley (Grimsby) 10 days; **1997:** Kerry Dixon (Doncaster) 12 days; **1996:** Sammy Chung (Doncaster) on morning of season's opening League match; **1996:** Alan Ball (Manchester City) 12 days; **1994:** Kenny Hibbitt (Walsall) and Kenny Swain (Wigan) 20 days; **1993:** Peter Reid (Manchester City) 12 days; **1991:** Don Mackay (Blackburn) 14 days; **1989:** Mick Jones (Peterborough) 12 days; **1980:** Bill McGarry (Newcastle) 13 days; **1979:** Dennis Butler (Port Vale) 12 days; **1977:** George Petchey (Leyton O) 13 days; **1977:** Willie Bell (Birmingham) 16 days; **1971:** Len Richley (Darlington) 12 days; **2019** Jan Siewert (Huddersfield) 14 days

DOUBLE DISMISSAL

Mark Hughes became the first manager to be sacked by two Premier League clubs in the same calendar year (2018) – Stoke in January and Southampton in December.

FOUR GAMES AND OUT

Frank de Boer was sacked as Crystal Palace manager after his first four Premier League matches at the start of the 2017–18 season – the competition's shortest reign in terms of games.

BRUCE'S FOUR-TIMER

Steve Bruce is the only manager to win four promotions to the Premier League – with Birmingham in 2002 and 2007 and with Hull in 2013 and 2016.

RECORD START FOR MANAGER

Russ Wilcox, appointed by Scunthorpe in Nov 2013, remained unbeaten in his first 28 league matches (14 won, 14 drawn) and took the club to promotion from League Two. It was the most successful start to a managerial career In English football, beating the record of 23 unbeaten games by Preston's William Sudell in 1889.

RECORD TOP DIVISION START

Arsenal were unbeaten in 17 league matches from the start of season 1947-48 under new manager **Tom Whittaker**.

SACKED, REINSTATED, FINISHED

Brian McDermott was sacked as Leeds manager on Jan 31, 2014. The following day, he was reinstated. At the end of the season, with the club under new ownership, he left by 'mutual consent.'

CARETAKER SUPREME

As Chelsea's season collapsed, Andre Villas-Boas was sacked in March 2012 after eight months as manager, 2012. Roberto Di Matteo was appointed caretaker and by the season's end his team had won the FA Cup and the Champions League.

MANAGER DOUBLES

Four managers have won the League Championship with different clubs: **Tom Watson**, secretary–manager with Sunderland (1892–93–95) and **Liverpool** (1901); **Herbert Chapman** with Huddersfield (1923–24, 1924–25) and Arsenal (1930–31, 1932–33); **Brian Clough** with Derby (1971–72) and Nottm Forest (1977–78); **Kenny Dalglish** with Liverpool (1985–86, 1987–88, 1989–90) and Blackburn (1994–95).

Managers to win the FA Cup with different clubs: **Billy Walker** (Sheffield Wed 1935, Nottm Forest 1959); **Herbert Chapman** (Huddersfield 1922, Arsenal 1930).

Kenny Dalglish (Liverpool) and **George Graham** (Arsenal) completed the Championship/FA Cup double as both player and manager with a single club. **Joe Mercer** won the title as a player with Everton, the title twice and FA Cup as a player with Arsenal and both competitions as manager of Manchester City.

CHAIRMAN–MANAGER

On Dec 20, 1988, after two years on the board, Dundee Utd manager **Jim McLean** was elected chairman, too. McLean, Scotland's longest-serving manager (appointed on Nov 24, 1971), resigned at end of season 1992–93 (remained chairman).

Ron Noades was chairman-manager of Brentford from Jul 1998–Mar 2001. **John Reames** did both jobs at Lincoln from Nov 1998–Apr 2000)

Niall Quinn did both jobs for five weeks in 2006 before appointing Roy Keane as manager of Sunderland.

TOP DIVISION PLAYER–MANAGERS

Les Allen (QPR 1968–69); **Johnny Giles** (WBA 1976–77); **Howard Kendall** (Everton 1981–82); **Kenny Dalglish** (Liverpool, 1985–90); **Trevor Francis** (QPR, 1988–89); **Terry Butcher** (Coventry, 1990–91), **Peter Reid** (Manchester City, 1990–93), **Trevor Francis** (Sheffield Wed, 1991–94), **Glenn Hoddle**, (Chelsea, 1993–95), **Bryan Robson** (Middlesbrough, 1994–97), **Ray Wilkins** (QPR, 1994–96), **Ruud Gullit** (Chelsea, 1996–98), **Gianluca Vialli** (Chelsea, 1998–2000).

FIRST FOREIGN MANAGER IN ENGLISH LEAGUE

Uruguayan **Danny Bergara** (Rochdale 1988–89).

COACHING KINGS OF EUROPE

Five coaches have won the European Cup/Champions League with two different clubs: **Ernst Happel** with Feyenoord (1970) and Hamburg (1983); **Ottmar Hitzfeld** with Borussia Dortmund (1997) and Bayern Munich (2001); **Jose Mourinho** with Porto (2004) and Inter Milan (2010); **Jupp Heynckes** with Real Madrid (1998) and Bayern Munich (2013); **Carlo Ancelotti** with AC Milan (2003, 2007) and Real Madrid (2014).

FOREIGN TRIUMPH

Former Dutch star **Ruud Gullit** became the first foreign manager to win a major English competition when Chelsea took the FA Cup in 1997.

Arsene Wenger and **Gerard Houllier** became the first foreign managers to receive recognition when they were awarded honorary OBEs in the Queen's Birthday Honours in Jun 2003 'for their contribution to English football and Franco–British relations'.

MANAGERS OF POST-WAR CHAMPIONS (*Double winners)

1947 George Kay (Liverpool); **1948** Tom Whittaker (Arsenal); **1949** Bob Jackson (Portsmouth).
1950 Bob Jackson (Portsmouth); **1951** Arthur Rowe (Tottenham); **1952** Matt Busby (Manchester Utd); **1953** Tom Whittaker (Arsenal); **1954** Stan Cullis (Wolves); **1955** Ted Drake (Chelsea); **1956** Matt Busby (Manchester Utd); **1957** Matt Busby (Manchester Utd); **1958** Stan Cullis (Wolves); **1959** Stan Cullis (Wolves).
1960 Harry Potts (Burnley); **1961** *Bill Nicholson (Tottenham); **1962** Alf Ramsey (Ipswich); **1963** Harry Catterick (Everton); **1964** Bill Shankly (Liverpool); **1965** Matt Busby (Manchester Utd); **1966** Bill Shankly (Liverpool); **1967** Matt Busby (Manchester Utd); **1968** Joe Mercer (Manchester City); **1969** Don Revie (Leeds).
1970 Harry Catterick (Everton); **1971** *Bertie Mee (Arsenal); **1972** Brian Clough (Derby); **1973** Bill Shankly (Liverpool); **1974** Don Revie (Leeds); **1975** Dave Mackay (Derby); **1976** Bob Paisley (Liverpool); **1977** Bob Paisley (Liverpool); **1978** Brian Clough (Nottm Forest); **1979** Bob Paisley (Liverpool).
1980 Bob Paisley (Liverpool); **1981** Ron Saunders (Aston Villa); **1982** Bob Paisley (Liverpool);

1983 Bob Paisley (Liverpool); 1984 Joe Fagan (Liverpool); 1985 Howard Kendall (Everton); 1986 *Kenny Dalglish (Liverpool – player/manager); 1987 Howard Kendall (Everton); 1988 Kenny Dalglish (Liverpool – player/manager); 1989 George Graham (Arsenal).
1990 Kenny Dalglish (Liverpool); 1991 George Graham (Arsenal); 1992 Howard Wilkinson (Leeds); 1993 Alex Ferguson (Manchester Utd); 1994 *Alex Ferguson (Manchester Utd); 1995 Kenny Dalglish (Blackburn); 1996 *Alex Ferguson (Manchester Utd); 1997 Alex Ferguson (Manchester Utd); 1998 *Arsene Wenger (Arsenal); 1999 *Alex Ferguson (Manchester Utd).
2000 Sir Alex Ferguson (Manchester Utd); 2001 Sir Alex Ferguson (Manchester Utd); 2002 *Arsene Wenger (Arsenal); 2003 Sir Alex Ferguson (Manchester Utd); 2004 Arsene Wenger (Arsenal); 2005 Jose Mourinho (Chelsea); 2006 Jose Mourinho (Chelsea); 2007 Sir Alex Ferguson (Manchester Utd); 2008 Sir Alex Ferguson (Manchester Utd); 2009 Sir Alex Ferguson (Manchester Utd); 2010 *Carlo Ancelotti (Chelsea); 2011 Sir Alex Ferguson (Manchester Utd); 2012 Roberto Mancini (Manchester City); 2013 Sir Alex Ferguson (Manchester Utd); 2014 Manuel Pellegrini (Manchester City); 2015 Jose Mourinho (Chelsea); 2016 Claudio Ranieri (Leicester); 2017 Antonio Conte (Chelsea); 2018 Pep Guardiola (Manchester City); 2019 Pep Guardiola (Manchester City); 2020 Jurgen Klopp (Liverpool).

WORLD NO 1 MANAGER

When **Sir Alex Ferguson**, 71, retired in May 2013, he ended the most successful managerial career in the game's history. He took Manchester United to a total of 38 prizes – 13 Premier League titles, 5 FA Cup triumphs, 4 League Cups, 10 Charity/Community Shields (1 shared), 2 Champions League wins, 1 Cup-Winners' Cup, 1 FIFA Club World Cup, 1 Inter-Continental Cup and 1 UEFA Super Cup. Having played centre-forward for Rangers, the Glaswegian managed 3 Scottish clubs, East Stirling, St Mirren and then Aberdeen, where he broke the Celtic/Rangers duopoly with 9 successes: 3 League Championships, 4 Scottish Cups, 1 League Cup and 1 UEFA Cup. Appointed at Old Trafford in November 1986, when replacing Ron Atkinson, he did not win a prize there until his fourth season (FA Cup 1990), but thereafter the club's trophy cabinet glittered with silverware. His total of 1,500 matches in charge ended with a 5-5 draw away to West Bromwich Albion. The longest-serving manager in the club's history, he constructed 4 triumphant teams. Sir Alex was knighted in 1999 and in 2012 he received the FIFA award for services to football. On retirement from management, he became a director and club ambassador. United maintained the dynasty of long-serving Scottish managers (Sir Matt Busby for 24 seasons) by appointing David Moyes, who had been in charge at Everton for 11 years.

WENGER'S LEGACY

Arsene Wenger was a virtually unknown French manager when taking over Arsenal in 1996. He left 22 years later as the most successful in the club's history. Wenger led them to three Premier League titles, including the unbeaten season in 2003-04 achieved by the team known as the 'Invincibles.' There were seven FA Cup successes, one in 2002 when Arsenal completed the Double. He was also closely involved in planning the move from Highbury to the Emirates Stadium in 2006.

THE PROMOTION MAN

Neil Warnock set a record of eight promotions when he took Cardiff back to the Premier League in 2018. In 38 years as a manager, he was also successful with Scarborough, Notts County twice, Plymouth, Huddersfield, Sheffield United and Queens Park Rangers. Warnock's achievements were marked by a special award from the League Managers' Association.

MANAGERS' EURO TREBLES

Two managers have won the European Cup/Champions League three times. **Bob Paisley** did it with Liverpool (1977,78, 81).
Carlo Ancelotti's successes were with AC Milan in 2003 and 2007 and with Real Madrid in 2014.

WINNER MOURINHO

In winning the Premier League and League Cup in 2015, Jose Mourinho embellished his reputation as Chelsea's most successful manager. Those achievements took his total of honours in two spells at the club to 8: 3 Premier League, 3 League Cup, 1 FA Cup, 1 Community Shield. Joining from Portuguese champions Porto, Mourinho was initially with Chelsea from June 2004 to September 2007. He then successfully coached Inter Milan and Real Madrid before returning to Stamford Bridge in June 2013. His Premier League triumph in 2015 was his eighth title In 11 years in four countries (England 3, Portugal 2, Italy 2, Spain 1). In his first season with Manchester Utd (2016–17), he won three trophies – League Cup, Europa League and Community Shield.

WENGER'S CUP AGAIN

Arsenal's win against Aston Villa in the 2015 Final was a record 12th success for them in the FA Cup and a sixth triumph in the competition for manager Arsene Wenger, equalling the record of George Ramsay for Villa (1887-1920). With his sixth victory in seven Finals, Wenger made history as the first manager to win the Cup in successive seasons twice (previously In 2002 and 2003). He won it for a record seventh time – in eight finals – in 2017.

RECORD MANAGER FEE

Chelsea paid Porto a record £13.25m compensation when they appointed **Andre Villas-Boas** as manager in June 2011. He lasted less than nine months at Stamford Bridge.

FATHER AND SON MANAGERS WITH SAME CLUB

Fulham: Bill Dodgin Snr 1949–53; Bill Dodgin Jnr 1968–72. **Brentford:** Bill Dodgin Snr 1953–57; Bill Dodgin Jnr 1976–80. **Bournemouth:** John Bond 1970–73; Kevin Bond 2006–08. **Derby:** Brian Clough 1967–73; Nigel Clough 2009–2013. **Bristol City:** Gary Johnson 2005–10; Lee Johnson 2016-present.

SIR BOBBY'S HAT-TRICK

Sir Bobby Robson, born and brought up in County Durham, achieved a unique hat-trick when he received the Freedom of Durham in Dec 2008. He had already been awarded the Freedom of Ipswich and Newcastle. He died in July 2009 and had an express loco named after him on the East Coast to London line.

MANAGERS WITH MOST FA CUP SUCCESSES

7 Arsene Wenger (Arsenal); **6 George Ramsay** (Aston Villa); **5 Sir Alex Ferguson** (Manchester Utd); **3 Charles Foweraker** (Bolton), **John Nicholson** (Sheffield Utd), **Bill Nicholson** (Tottenham).

RELEGATION 'DOUBLES'

Managers associated with two clubs relegated in same season: **John Bond** in 1985–86 (Swansea City and Birmingham); **Ron Saunders** in 1985–86 (WBA – and their reserve team – and Birmingham); **Bob Stokoe** in 1986–87 (Carlisle and Sunderland); **Billy McNeill** in 1986–87 (Manchester City and Aston Villa); **Dave Bassett** in 1987–88 (Watford and Sheffield Utd); **Mick Mills** in 1989–90 (Stoke and Colchester); **Gary Johnson** in 2014-15 (Yeovil and Cheltenham)

THREE FA CUP DEFEATS IN ONE SEASON

Manager **Michael Appleton** suffered three FA Cup defeats in season 2012-13, with Portsmouth (v Notts Co, 1st rd); Blackpool (v Fulham, 3rd rd); Blackburn (v Millwall, 6th rd).

WEMBLEY STADIUM

NEW WEMBLEY

A new era for English football began in March 2007 with the completion of the new national stadium. The 90,000-seater arena was hailed as one of the world's finest – but came at a price. Costs soared, the project fell well behind schedule and disputes involving the FA, builders Multiplex and the Government were rife. The old stadium, opened in 1923, cost £750,000.

The new one, originally priced at £326m in 2000, ended up at around £800m. The first international after completion was an Under-21 match between England and Italy. The FA Cup Final returned to its spiritual home after being staged at the Millennium Stadium in Cardiff for six seasons. Then, England's senior team were back for a friendly against Brazil.

DROGBA'S WEMBLEY RECORD

Didier Drogba's FA Cup goal for Chelsea against Liverpool in May 2012 meant that he had scored in all his 8 competitive appearances for the club at Wembley. (7 wins, 1 defeat). They came in: 2007 FA Cup Final (1-0 v Manchester Utd); 2008 League Cup Final (1-2 v Tottenham); 2009 FA Cup semi-final (2-1 v Arsenal); 2009 FA Cup Final (2-1 v Everton); 2010 FA Cup semi-final (3-0 v Aston Villa); 2010 FA Cup Final (1-0 v Portsmouth); 2012 FA Cup semi-final (5-1 v Tottenham); 2012 FA Cup Final (2-1 v Liverpool).

INVASION DAY

Memorable scenes were witnessed at the first **FA Cup Final at Wembley**, Apr 28, 1923, between **Bolton** and **West Ham**. An accurate return of the attendance could not be made owing to thousands breaking in, but there were probably more than 200,000 spectators present. The match was delayed for 40 minutes by the crowd invading the pitch. Official attendance was 126,047. Gate receipts totalled £27,776. The two clubs and the FA each received £6,365 and the FA refunded £2,797 to ticket-holders who were unable to get to their seats. Cup Final admission has since been by ticket only.

REDUCED CAPACITY

Capacity of the all-seated Wembley Stadium was 78,000. The last 100,000 attendance was for the 1985 FA Cup Final between Manchester Utd and Everton. Crowd record for New Wembley: 89,874 for 2008 FA Cup Final (Portsmouth v Cardiff).

WEMBLEY'S FIRST UNDER LIGHTS

Nov 30, 1955 (England 4, Spain 1), when the floodlights were switched on after 73 minutes (afternoon match played in damp, foggy conditions).
First Wembley international played throughout under lights: England 8, N Ireland 3 on evening of Nov 20, 1963 (att: 55,000).

MOST WEMBLEY APPEARANCES

59 by **Tony Adams** (35 England, 24 Arsenal); 57 by **Peter Shilton** (52 England, 3 Nottm Forest, 1 Leicester, 1 Football League X1).

WEMBLEY HAT-TRICKS

Three players have scored hat-tricks in major finals at Wembley: **Stan Mortensen** for Blackpool v Bolton (FA Cup Final, 1953), **Geoff Hurst** for England v West Germany (World Cup Final, 1966) and **David Speedie** for Chelsea v Manchester City (Full Members Cup, 1985).

ENGLAND'S WEMBLEY DEFEATS

England have lost 25 matches to foreign opponents at Wembley:

Nov 1953	3-6 v Hungary		Jun 1995	1-3 v Brazil
Oct 1959	2-3 v Sweden		Feb 1997	0-1 v Italy
Oct 1965	2-3 v Austria		Feb 1998	0-2 v Chile
Apr 1972	1-3 v W Germany		Feb 1999	0-2 v France
Nov 1973	0-1 v Italy		Oct 2000	0-1 v Germany
Feb 1977	0-2 v Holland		Aug 2007	1-2 v Germany
Mar 1981	1-2 v Spain		Nov 2007	2-3 v Croatia
May 1981	0-1 v Brazil		Nov 2010	1-2 v France
Oct 1982	1-2 v W Germany		Feb 2012	2-3 v Holland
Sep 1983	0-1 v Denmark		Nov 2013	0-2 v Chile

Jun 1984	0-2 v Russia	**Nov 2013**	0-1 v Germany
May 1990	1-2 v Uruguay	**Mar 2016**	1-2 v Holland
Sep 1991	0-1 v Germany		

A further defeat came in **Euro 96**. After drawing the semi-final with Germany 1-1, England went out 6-5 on penalties.

FASTEST GOALS AT WEMBLEY

In first-class matches: **25 sec** by **Louis Saha** for Everton in 2009 FA Cup Final against Chelsea; **38 sec** by **Bryan Robson** for England's against Yugoslavia in 1989; **42 sec** by **Roberto Di Matteo** for Chelsea in 1997 FA Cup Final v Middlesbrough; **44 sec** by **Bryan Robson** for England v Northern Ireland in 1982.

Fastest goal in **any** match at Wembley: **20 sec** by **Maurice Cox** for Cambridge University against Oxford in 1979.

FOUR WEMBLEY HEADERS

When **Wimbledon** beat Sutton 4-2 in the FA Amateur Cup Final at Wembley on May 4, 1963, Irish centre-forward **Eddie Reynolds** headed all four goals.

WEMBLEY ONE-SEASON DOUBLES

In 1989, **Nottm Forest** became the first club to win two Wembley Finals in the same season (Littlewoods Cup and Simod Cup).

In 1993, **Arsenal** made history there as the first club to win the League (Coca-Cola) Cup and the FA Cup in the same season. They beat Sheffield Wed 2-1 in both finals.

In 2012, **York** won twice at Wembley in nine days at the end of the season, beating Newport 2-0 in the FA Trophy Final and Luton 2-1 in the Conference Play-off Final to return to the Football League.

SUDDEN-DEATH DECIDERS

First Wembley Final decided on sudden death (first goal scored in overtime): Apr 23, 1995 – **Birmingham** beat Carlisle (1-0, Paul Tait 103 mins) to win Auto Windscreens Shield.

First instance of a golden goal deciding a major international tournament was at Wembley on Jun 30, 1996, when **Germany** beat the Czech Republic 2-1 in the European Championship Final with Oliver Bierhoff's goal in the 95th minute.

WEMBLEY'S MOST ONE-SIDED FINAL (in major domestic cups)

Manchester City 6 Watford 0 (FA Cup, May 18,2019).

FOOTBALL TRAGEDIES

DAYS OF TRAGEDY – CLUBS

Season 1988–89 brought the worst disaster in the history of British sport, with the death of 96 Liverpool supporters (200 injured) at the **FA Cup semi-final** against Nottm Forest at **Hillsborough, Sheffield**, on Saturday, Apr 15. The tragedy built up in the minutes preceding kick-off, when thousands surged into the ground at the Leppings Lane end. Many were crushed in the tunnel between entrance and terracing, but most of the victims were trapped inside the perimeter fencing behind the goal. The match was abandoned without score after six minutes' play. The dead included seven women and girls, two teenage sisters and two teenage brothers. The youngest victim was a boy of ten, the oldest 67-year-old Gerard Baron, whose brother Kevin played for Liverpool in the 1950 Cup Final. (*Total became 96 in Mar 1993, when Tony Bland died after being in a coma for nearly four years). A two-year inquest at Warrington ended on April 26, 2016 with the verdict that the 96 were 'unlawfully killed.' It cleared Liverpool fans of any blame and ruled that South Yorkshire Police and South Yorkshire Ambulance Service 'caused or contributed' to the loss of life.

The two worst disasters in one season in British soccer history occurred at the end of 1984–

85. On May 11, the last Saturday of the League season, 56 people (two of them visiting supporters) were burned to death – and more than 200 taken to hospital – when fire destroyed the main stand at the **Bradford City–Lincoln** match at Valley Parade.

The wooden, 77-year-old stand was full for City's last fixture before which, amid scenes of celebration, the club had been presented with the Third Division Championship trophy. The fire broke out just before half-time and, within five minutes, the entire stand was engulfed.

Heysel Tragedy

Eighteen days later, on May 29, at the European Cup Final between **Liverpool** and **Juventus** at the Heysel Stadium, Brussels, 39 spectators (31 of them Italian) were crushed or trampled to death and 437 injured. The disaster occurred an hour before the scheduled kick-off when Liverpool supporters charged a Juventus section of the crowd at one end of the stadium, and a retaining wall collapsed. The sequel was a 5-year ban by UEFA on English clubs generally in European competition, with a 6-year ban on Liverpool.

On May 26 1985 ten people were trampled to death and 29 seriously injured in a crowd panic on the way into the **Olympic Stadium, Mexico City** for the Mexican Cup Final between local clubs National University and America.

More than 100 people died and 300 were injured in a football disaster at **Nepal's national stadium** in Katmandu in Mar 1988. There was a stampede when a violent hailstorm broke over the capital. Spectators rushed for cover, but the stadium exits were locked, and hundreds were trampled in the crush.

In South Africa, on Jan 13 1991 40 black fans were trampled to death (50 injured) as they tried to escape fighting that broke out at a match in the gold-mining town of Orkney, 80 miles from Johannesburg. The friendly, between top teams **Kaiser Chiefs** and **Orlando Pirates**, attracted a packed crowd of 20,000. Violence erupted after the referee allowed Kaiser Chiefs a disputed second-half goal to lead 1-0.

Disaster struck at the French Cup semi-final (May 5, 1992), with the death of 15 spectators and 1,300 injured when a temporary metal stand collapsed in the Corsican town of Bastia. The tie between Second Division **Bastia** and French Champions **Marseille** was cancelled. Monaco, who won the other semi-final, were allowed to compete in the next season's Cup-Winners' Cup.

A total of 318 died and 500 were seriously injured when the crowd rioted over a disallowed goal at the National Stadium in Lima, Peru, on May 24, 1964. **Peru** and **Argentina** were competing to play in the Olympic Games in Tokyo.

That remained **sport's heaviest death** toll until Oct 20, 1982, when (it was revealed only in Jul 1989) 340 Soviet fans were killed in Moscow's Lenin Stadium at the UEFA Cup second round first leg match between **Moscow Spartak** and **Haarlem** (Holland). They were crushed on an open stairway when a last-minute Spartak goal sent departing spectators surging back into the ground.

Among other crowd disasters abroad: Jun, 1968 – 74 died in Argentina. Panic broke out at the end of a goalless match between River Plate and Boca Juniors at Nunez, Buenos Aires, when Boca supporters threw lighted newspaper torches on to fans in the tiers below.

Feb 1974 – 49 killed in **Egypt** in crush of fans clamouring to see Zamalek play Dukla Prague.

Sep 1971 – 44 died in **Turkey**, when fighting among spectators over a disallowed goal (Kayseri v Siwas) led to a platform collapsing.

The then worst disaster in the history of British football, in terms of loss of life, occurred at Glasgow Rangers' ground at **Ibrox Park**, Jan 2 1971. Sixty-six people were trampled to death (100 injured) as they tumbled down Stairway 13 just before the end of the **Rangers v Celtic** New Year's match. That disaster led to the 1975 Safety of Sports Grounds legislation.

The Ibrox tragedy eclipsed even the Bolton disaster in which 33 were killed and about 500 injured when a wall and crowd barriers collapsed near a corner-flag at the **Bolton v Stoke** FA Cup sixth round tie on Mar 9 1946. The match was completed after half an hour's stoppage.

In a previous crowd disaster at **Ibrox** on Apr 5, 1902, part of the terracing collapsed during the Scotland v England international and 25 people were killed. The match, held up for 20 minutes, ended 1-1, but was never counted as an official international.

Eight leading players and three officials of **Manchester Utd** and eight newspaper representatives were among the 23 who perished in the air crash at **Munich** on Feb 6, 1958, during take-off following a European Cup-tie in Belgrade. The players were Roger Byrne, Geoffrey Bent, Eddie Colman, Duncan Edwards, Mark Jones, David Pegg, Tommy Taylor and Liam Whelan, and the officials were Walter Crickmer (secretary), Tom Curry (trainer) and Herbert Whalley (coach). The newspaper representatives were Alf Clarke, Don Davies, George Follows, Tom Jackson, Archie Ledbrooke, Henry Rose, Eric Thompson and Frank Swift (former England goalkeeper of Manchester City).

On May 14, 1949, the entire team of Italian Champions **Torino**, 8 of them Internationals, were killed when the aircraft taking them home from a match against Benfica in Lisbon crashed at Superga, near Turin. The total death toll of 28 included all the club's reserve players, the manager, trainer and coach.

On Feb 8, 1981, 24 spectators died and more than 100 were injured at a match in **Greece**. They were trampled as thousands of the 40,000 crowd tried to rush out of the stadium at Piraeus after Olympiacos beat AEK Athens 6-0.

On Nov 17, 1982, 24 people (12 of them children) were killed and 250 injured when fans stampeded at the end of a match at the Pascual Guerrero stadium in **Cali, Colombia**. Drunken spectators hurled fire crackers and broken bottles from the higher stands on to people below and started a rush to the exits.

On Dec 9, 1987, the 18-strong team squad of **Alianza Lima**, one of Peru's top clubs, were wiped out, together with 8 officials and several youth players, when a military aircraft taking them home from Puccalpa crashed into the sea off Ventillana, ten miles from Lima. The only survivor among 43 on board was a member of the crew.

On Apr 28, 1993, 18 members of **Zambia's international squad** and 5 ZFA officials died when the aircraft carrying them to a World Cup qualifying tie against Senegal crashed into the Atlantic soon after take-off from Libreville, Gabon.

On Oct 16 1996, 81 fans were crushed to death and 147 seriously injured in the '**Guatemala Disaster**' at the World Cup qualifier against Costa Rica in Mateo Flores stadium. The tragedy happened an hour before kick-off, allegedly caused by ticket forgery and overcrowding – 60,000 were reported in the 45,000-capacity ground – and safety problems related to perimeter fencing.

On Jul 9, 1996, 8 people died, 39 injured in riot after derby match between **Libya's two top clubs** in Tripoli. Al-Ahli had beaten Al-Ittihad 1-0 by a controversial goal.

On Apr 6, 1997, 5 spectators were crushed to death at **Nigeria's national stadium** in Lagos after the 2-1 World Cup qualifying victory over Guinea. Only two of five gates were reported open as the 40,000 crowd tried to leave the ground.

It was reported from the **Congo** (Oct 29, 1998) that a bolt of lightning struck a village match, killing all 11 members of the home team Benatshadi, but leaving the opposing players from Basangana unscathed. It was believed the surviving team wore better-insulated boots.

On Jan 10, 1999, eight fans died and 13 were injured in a stampede at **Egypt's Alexandria Stadium**. Some 25,000 spectators had pushed into the ground. Despite the tragedy, the cup-tie between Al-Ittihad and Al-Koroum was completed.

Three people suffocated and several were seriously injured when thousands of fans forced their way into **Liberia's national stadium** in Monrovia at a goalless World Cup qualifying match against Chad on Apr 23, 2000. The stadium (capacity 33,000) was reported 'heavily overcrowded'.

On Jul 9, 2000, 12 spectators died from crush injuries when police fired tear gas into the 50,000 crowd after South Africa scored their second goal in a World Cup group qualifier against Zimbabwe in **Harare**. A stampede broke out as fans scrambled to leave the national stadium. Players of both teams lay face down on the pitch as fumes swept over them. FIFA launched an investigation and decided that the result would stand, with South Africa leading 2-0 at the time of the 84th-minute abandonment.

On Apr 11, 2001, at one of the biggest matches of the South African season, 43 died and 155 were injured in a crush at **Ellis Park, Johannesburg**. After tearing down a fence, thousands of fans surged into a stadium already packed to its 60,000 capacity for the Premiership derby between top Soweto teams Kaizer Chiefs and Orlando Pirates. The match was abandoned at 1-1 after 33 minutes. In Jan 1991, 40 died in a crowd crush at a friendly between the same clubs at Orkney, 80 miles from Johannesburg.

On Apr 29, 2001, seven people were trampled to death and 51 injured when a riot broke out at a match between two of Congo's biggest clubs, Lupopo and Mazembe at **Lubumbashi**, southern Congo.

On May 6, 2001, two spectators were killed in Iran and hundreds were injured when a glass fibre roof collapsed at the over-crowded Mottaqi Stadium at Sari for the match between Pirouzi and Shemshak Noshahr.

On May 9, 2001, in Africa's worst football disaster, 123 died and 93 were injured in a stampede at the national stadium in **Accra, Ghana**. Home team Hearts of Oak were leading 2-1 against Asante Kotoko five minutes from time, when Asanti fans started hurling bottles on to the pitch. Police fired tear gas into the stands, and the crowd panicked in a rush for the exits, which were locked. It took the death toll at three big matches in Africa in Apr/May to 173.

On Aug 12, 2001, two players were killed by lightning and ten severely burned at a **Guatemala** Third Division match between Deportivo Culquimulilla and Pueblo Nuevo Vinas.

On Nov 1, 2002, two players died from injuries after lightning struck Deportivo Cali's training ground in **Colombia**.

On Mar 12 2004, five people were killed and more than 100 injured when spectators stampeded shortly before the Syrian Championship fixture between Al-Jihad and Al-Fatwa in **Qameshli**, Northern Syria. The match was cancelled.

On Oct 10, 2004, three spectators died in a crush at the African Zone World Cup qualifier between **Guinea** and **Morocco** (1-1) at Conakry, Guinea.

On Mar 25, 2005, five were killed as 100,000 left the Azadi Stadium, **Tehran**, after Iran's World Cup qualifying win (2-1) against Japan.

On Jun 2, 2007, 12 spectators were killed and 46 injured in a crush at the Chillabombwe Stadium, **Zambia**, after an African Nations Cup qualifier against Congo.

On Mar 29, 2009, 19 people died and 139 were injured after a wall collapsed at the Ivory Coast stadium in **Abidjan** before a World Cup qualifier against Malawi. The match went ahead, Ivory Coast winning 5-0 with two goals from Chelsea's Didier Drogba. The tragedy meant that, in 13 years, crowd disasters at club and internationals at ten different grounds across Africa had claimed the lives of 283 people.

On Jan 8, 2010, terrorists at **Cabinda**, Angola machine-gunned the Togo team buses travelling to the Africa Cup of Nations. They killed a driver, an assistant coach and a media officer and injured several players. The team were ordered by their Government to withdraw from the tournament.

On Oct 23, 2010, seven fans were trampled to death when thousands tried to force their way into the Nyayo National Stadium in **Nairobi** at a Kenya Premier League match between the Gor Mahia and AFC Leopards clubs.

On Feb 1, 2012, 74 died and nearly 250 were injured in a crowd riot at the end of the Al-Masry v Al-Ahly match in **Port Said** – the worst disaster in Egyptian sport.

On Nov 28, 2016, 71 died in the worst air crash in world football history when a charter flight carrying players, officials and staff of leading Brazilian club Chapecoense from **Bolivia** to **Colombia** hit a mountain ridge at 8,500 feet. The victims included 65 people from the club.

On Feb 8, 2019, ten young players died when fire engulfed a dormitory at the youth team training centre of one of Brazil's biggest clubs, Flamengo in Rio de Janeiro.

DAYS OF TRAGEDY – PERSONAL

Sam Wynne, Bury right-back, collapsed five minutes before half-time in the First Division match away to Sheffield Utd on Apr 30, 1927, and died in the dressing-room.

John Thomson, Celtic and Scotland goalkeeper, sustained a fractured skull when diving at an opponent's feet in the Rangers v Celtic League match on Sep 5, 1931, and died the same evening.

Sim Raleigh (Gillingham), injured in a clash of heads at home to Brighton (Div 3 South) on Dec 1, 1934, continued to play but collapsed in second half and died in hospital the same night.

James Thorpe, Sunderland goalkeeper, was injured during the First Division match at home to Chelsea on Feb 1, 1936 and died in a diabetic coma three days later.

Derek Dooley, Sheffield Wed centre-forward and top scorer in 1951–52 in the Football League with 46 goals in 30 matches, broke a leg in the League match at Preston on Feb 14, 1953, and, after complications set in, had to lose the limb by amputation.

John White, Tottenham's Scottish international forward, was killed by lightning on a golf course at Enfield, North London in Jul, 1964.

Tony Allden, Highgate centre-half, was struck by lightning during an Amateur Cup quarter-final with Enfield on Feb 25, 1967. He died the following day. Four other players were also struck but recovered.

Roy Harper died while refereeing the York v Halifax (Div 4) match on May 5, 1969.

Jim Finn collapsed and died from a heart attack while refereeing Exeter v Stockport (Div 4) on Sep 16, 1972.

Scotland manager **Jock Stein**, 62, collapsed and died at the end of the Wales-Scotland World Cup qualifying match (1-1) at Ninian Park, Cardiff on Sep 10, 1985.

David Longhurst, York forward, died after being carried off two minutes before half-time in the Fourth Division fixture at home to Lincoln on Sep 8, 1990. The match was abandoned (0-0). The inquest revealed that Longhurst suffered from a rare heart condition.

Mike North collapsed while refereeing Southend v Mansfield (Div 3) on Apr 16, 2001 and died shortly afterwards. The match was abandoned and re-staged on May 8, with the receipts donated to his family.

Marc-Vivien Foe, on his 63rd appearance in Cameroon's midfield, collapsed unchallenged in the centre circle after 72 minutes of the FIFA Confederations Cup semi-final against Colombia in Lyon, France, on Jun 26, 2003, and despite the efforts of the stadium medical staff he could not be revived. He had been on loan to Manchester City from Olympique Lyonnais in season 2002–03, and poignantly scored the club's last goal at Maine Road.

Paul Sykes, Folkestone Invicta (Ryman League) striker, died on the pitch during the Kent Senior Cup semi-final against Margate on Apr 12, 2005. He collapsed after an innocuous off-the-ball incident.

Craig Gowans, Falkirk apprentice, was killed at the club's training ground on Jul 8, 2005 when he came into contact with power lines.

Peter Wilson, Mansfield goalkeeping coach, died of a heart attack after collapsing during the warm-up of the League Two game away to Shrewsbury on Nov 19, 2005.

Matt Gadsby, Hinckley defender, collapsed and died while playing in a Conference North match at Harrogate on Sep 9, 2006.

Phil O'Donnell, 35-year-old Motherwell captain and Scotland midfield player, collapsed when about to be substituted near the end of the SPL home game against Dundee Utd on Dec 29, 2007 and died shortly afterwards in hospital.

Vichai Srivaddhanaprabha, Leicester owner, died in a helicopter crash following the club's Premier League match against West Ham. The pilot and three others on board also died in the crash outside the King Power Stadium, seconds after the helicopter's take-off from the pitch on Oct 27, 2018.

Emiliano Sala, Argentine striker, died in a plane crash in the English Channel on Jan 21, 2019 two days after signing for Cardiff from Nantes. The pilot of the light aircraft also died.

Justin Edinburgh, Leyton Orient manager, suffered a cardiac arrest and died five days later on Apr 8, 2019

GREAT SERVICE

'For services to Association Football', **Stanley Matthews** (Stoke, Blackpool and England), already a CBE, became the first professional footballer to receive a knighthood. This was bestowed in 1965, his last season. Before he retired and five days after his 50th birthday, he played for Stoke to set a record as the oldest First Division footballer (v Fulham, Feb 6, 1965).

Over a brilliant span of 33 years, he played in 886 first-class matches, including 54 full Internationals (plus 31 in war time), 701 League games (including 3 at start of season 1939–40, which was abandoned on the outbreak of war) and 86 FA Cup-ties, and scored 95 goals. He was never booked in his career.

Sir Stanley died on Feb 23, 2000, three weeks after his 85th birthday. His ashes were buried under the centre circle of Stoke's Britannia Stadium. After spending a number of years in Toronto, he made his home back in the Potteries in 1989, having previously returned to his home town, Hanley in Oct, 1987 to unveil a life-size bronze statue of himself. The inscription reads: 'Sir Stanley Matthews, CBE. Born Hanley, 1 Feb 1915.

His name is symbolic of the beauty of the game, his fame timeless and international, his sportsmanship and modesty universally acclaimed. A magical player, of the people, for the people.' On his home-coming in 1989, Sir Stanley was made President of Stoke, the club he joined as a boy of 15 and served as a player for 20 years between 1931 and 1965, on either side of his spell with Blackpool.

In Jul 1992 FIFA honoured him with their 'Gold merit award' for outstanding services to the game.

Former England goalkeeper **Peter Shilton** has made more first-class appearances (1,387) than any other footballer in British history. He played his 1,000th. League game in Leyton Orient's 2-0 home win against Brighton on Dec 22, 1996 and made 9 appearances for Orient in his final season. He retired from international football after the 1990 World Cup in Italy with 125 caps, then a world record. Shilton kept a record 60 clean sheets for England.

Shilton's career spanned 32 seasons, 20 of them on the international stage. He made his League debut for Leicester in May 1966, two months before England won the World Cup.

His 1,387 first-class appearances comprise a record 1,005 in the Football League, 125 Internationals, 102 League Cup, 86 FA Cup, 13 for England U-23s, 4 for the Football League and 52 other matches (European Cup, UEFA Cup, World Club Championship, Charity Shield, European Super Cup, Full Members' Cup, Play-offs, Screen Sports Super Cup, Anglo-Italian Cup, Texaco Cup, Simod Cup, Zenith Data Systems Cup and Autoglass Trophy).

Shilton appeared 57 times at Wembley, 52 for England, 2 League Cup Finals, 1 FA Cup Final, 1 Charity Shield match, and 1 for the Football League. He passed a century of League appearances with each of his first five clubs: Leicester (286), Stoke (110), Nottm Forest (202), Southampton (188) and Derby (175) and subsequently played for Plymouth, Bolton and Leyton Orient.

He was awarded the MBE and OBE for services to football. At the Football League Awards ceremony in March 2013, he received the League's Contribution award.

Six other British footballers have made more than 1,000 first-class appearances:

Ray Clemence, formerly with Tottenham, Liverpool and England, retired through injury in season 1987–88 after a goalkeeping career of 1,119 matches starting in 1965–66.

Clemence played 50 times for his first club, Scunthorpe; 665 for Liverpool; 337 for Tottenham; his 67 representative games included 61 England caps.

A third great British goalkeeper, **Pat Jennings**, ended his career (1963–86) with a total of 1,098 first-class matches for Watford, Tottenham, Arsenal and N Ireland. They were made up of 757 in the Football League, 119 full Internationals, 84 FA Cup appearances, 72 League/ Milk Cup, 55 European club matches, 2 Charity Shield, 3 Other Internationals, 1 Under-23 cap, 2 Texaco Cup, 2 Anglo-Italian Cup and 1 Super Cup. Jennings played his 119th and final international on his 41st birthday, Jun 12, 1986, against Brazil in Guadalajara in the Mexico World Cup.

Yet another outstanding 'keeper, **David Seaman**, passed the 1,000 appearances milestone for clubs and country in season 2002–03, reaching 1,004 when aged 39, he captained Arsenal to FA Cup triumph against Southampton.

With Arsenal, Seaman won 3 Championship medals, the FA Cup 4 times, the Double twice, the League Cup and Cup-Winners' Cup once each. After 13 seasons at Highbury, he joined Manchester City (Jun 2003) on a free transfer. He played 26 matches for City before a shoulder injury forced his retirement in Jan 2004, aged 40.

Seaman's 22-season career composed 1,046 first-class matches: 955 club apps (Peterborough 106, Birmingham 84, QPR 175, Arsenal 564, Manchester City 26); 75 senior caps for England, 6 'B' caps and 10 at U-21 level.

Defender **Graeme Armstrong**, 42-year-old commercial manager for an Edinburgh whisky company and part-time assistant-manager and captain of Scottish Third Division club Stenhousemuir, made the 1000th first team appearance of his career in the Scottish Cup 3rd Round against Rangers at Ibrox on Jan 23, 1999. He was presented with the Man of the Match award before kick-off.

Against East Stirling on Boxing Day, he had played his 864th League game, breaking the British record for an outfield player set by another Scot, Tommy Hutchison, with Alloa, Blackpool, Coventry, Manchester City, Burnley and Swansea City.

Armstrong's 24-year career, spent in the lower divisions of the Scottish League, began as a 1-match trialist with Meadowbank Thistle in 1975 and continued via Stirling Albion, Berwick Rangers, Meadowbank and, from 1992, Stenhousemuir.

Tony Ford became the first English outfield player to reach 1000 senior appearances in Rochdale's 1-0 win at Carlisle (Auto Windscreens Shield) on Mar 7, 2000. Grimsby-born, he began his 26-season midfield career with Grimsby and played for 7 other League clubs: Sunderland (loan), Stoke, WBA, Bradford City (loan), Scunthorpe, Mansfield and Rochdale. He retired, aged 42, in 2001 with a career record of 1072 appearances (121 goals) and his total of 931 League games is exceeded only by Peter Shilton's 1005.

On Apr 16, 2011, **Graham Alexander** reached 1,000 appearances when he came on as a sub for Burnley at home to Swansea. Alexander, 40, ended a 22-year career with the equaliser for Preston against Charlton (2-2, Lge 1) on Apr 28, 2012 – his 1,023rd appearance. He also played for Luton and Scunthorpe and was capped 40 times by Scotland.

RECORD FOR BARRY

Gareth Barry surpassed Ryan Giggs's record of 632 Premier League appearances in West Bromwich Albion's 2-0 defeat by Arsenal in the 2017–18 season.

GIGGS RECORD COLLECTION

Ryan Giggs (Manchester Utd) has collected the most individual honours in English football with a total of 34 prizes. They comprise: 13 Premier League titles, 4 FA Cups, 3 League Cups, 2 European Cups, 1 UEFA Super Cup, 1 Inter-Continental Cup, 1 World Club Cup, 9 Charity Shields/Community Shields. One-club man Giggs played 24 seasons for United, making a record 963 appearances. He won 64 Wales caps and on retiring as a player, aged 40, in May 2014, became the club's assistant manager. He ended a 29-year association with the club in June 2016.

KNIGHTS OF SOCCER

Players, managers and administrators who have been honoured for their services to football: **Charles Clegg** (1927), **Stanley Rous** (1949), **Stanley Matthews** (1965), **Alf Ramsey** (1967), **Matt Busby** (1968), **Walter Winterbottom** (1978) **Bert Millichip** (1991), **Bobby Charlton** (1994), **Tom Finney** (1998), **Geoff Hurst** (1998), **Alex Ferguson** (1999), **Bobby Robson** (2002), **Trevor Brooking** (2004), **Dave Richards** (2006), **Doug Ellis** (2011), **Kenny Dalglish** (2018).

● On Nov 6, 2014, **Karren Brady**, vice-chairman of West Ham, was elevated to the Lords as Karren, Baroness Brady, OBE, of Knightsbridge, life peer

PENALTIES

The **penalty-kick** was introduced to the game, following a proposal to the Irish FA in 1890 by William McCrum, son of the High Sheriff for Co Omagh, and approved by the International Football Board on Jun 2, 1891.

First penalty scored in a first-class match in England was by John Heath, for Wolves v Accrington Stanley (5-0 in Div 1, Sep 14, 1891).

The greatest influence of the penalty has come since the 1970s, with the introduction of the shoot-out to settle deadlocked ties in various competitions.

Manchester Utd were the first club to win a competitive match in British football via a shoot-out (4-3 away to Hull, Watney Cup semi-final, Aug 5, 1970); in that penalty contest, George Best was the first player to score, Denis Law the first to miss.

The shoot-out was adopted by FIFA and UEFA the same year (1970).
In season 1991–92, penalty shoot-outs were introduced to decide FA Cup ties still level after one replay and extra time.
Wembley saw its first penalty contest in the 1974 Charity Shield. Since then many major matches across the world have been settled in this way, including:

1976	**European Championship Final (Belgrade):** Czechoslovakia beat West Germany 5-3 (after 2-2)	
1980	**Cup-Winners' Cup Final (Brussels):** Valencia beat Arsenal 5-4 (after 0-0)	
1984	**European Cup Final (Rome):** Liverpool beat Roma 4-2 (after 1-1)	
1984	**UEFA Cup Final:** Tottenham (home) beat Anderlecht 4-3 (2-2 agg)	
1986	**European Cup Final (Seville):** Steaua Bucharest beat Barcelona 2-0 (after 0-0).	
1987	**Freight Rover Trophy Final (Wembley):** Mansfield beat Bristol City 5-4 (after 1-1)	
1987	**Scottish League Cup Final (Hampden Park):** Rangers beat Aberdeen 5-3 (after 3-3)	
1988	**European Cup Final (Stuttgart):** PSV Eindhoven beat Benfica 6-5 (after 0-0)	
1988	**UEFA Cup Final:** Bayer Leverkusen (home) beat Espanyol 3-2 after 3-3 (0-3a, 3-0h)	
1990	**Scottish Cup Final (Hampden Park):** Aberdeen beat Celtic 9-8 (after 0-0)	
1991	**European Cup Final (Bari):** Red Star Belgrade beat Marseille 5-3 (after 0-0)	
1991	**Div 4 Play-off Final (Wembley):** Torquay beat Blackpool 5-4 (after 2-2)	
1992	**Div 4 Play-off Final (Wembley):** Blackpool beat Scunthorpe 4-3 (after 1-1)	
1993	**Div 3 Play-off Final(Wembley):** York beat Crewe 5-3 (after 1-1)	
1994	**Autoglass Trophy Final (Wembley):** Swansea City beat Huddersfield 3-1 (after 1-1)	
1994	**World Cup Final (Los Angeles):** Brazil beat Italy 3-2 (after 0-0)	
1994	**Scottish League Cup Final (Ibrox Park):** Raith beat Celtic 6-5 (after 2-2)	
1995	**Copa America Final (Montevideo):** Uruguay beat Brazil 5-3 (after 1-1)	
1996	**European Cup Final (Rome):** Juventus beat Ajax 4-2 (after 1-1)	
1996	**European U-21 Champ Final (Barcelona):** Italy beat Spain 4-2 (after 1-1)	
1997	**Auto Windscreens Shield Final (Wembley):** Carlisle beat Colchester 4-3 (after 0-0)	
1997	**UEFA Cup Final:** FC Schalke beat Inter Milan 4-1 (after 1-1 agg)	
1998	**Div 1 Play-off Final (Wembley):** Charlton beat Sunderland 7-6 (after 4-4)	
1999	**Div 2 Play-off Final (Wembley):** Manchester City beat Gillingham 3-1 (after 2-2)	
1999	**Women's World Cup Final (Pasedena):** USA beat China 5-4 (after 0-0)	
2000	**African Nations Cup Final (Lagos):** Cameroon beat Nigeria 4-3 (after 0-0)	
2000	**UEFA Cup Final (Copenhagen):** Galatasaray beat Arsenal 4-1 (after 0-0)	
2000	**Olympic Final (Sydney):** Cameroon beat Spain 5-3 (after 2-2)	
2001	**League Cup Final (Millennium Stadium):** Liverpool beat Birmingham 5-4 (after 1-1)	
2001	**Champions League Final (Milan):** Bayern Munich beat Valencia 5-4 (after 1-1)	
2002	**Euro U-21 Champ Final (Basle):** Czech Republic beat France 3-1 (after 0-0)	
2002	**Div 1 Play-off Final (Millennium Stadium):** Birmingham beat Norwich 4-2 (after 1-1)	
2003	**Champions League Final (Old Trafford):** AC Milan beat Juventus 3-2 (after 0-0)	
2004	**Div 3 Play-off Final (Millennium Stadium):** Huddersfield beat Mansfield 4-1 (after 0-0)	
2004	**Copa America Final (Lima):** Brazil beat Argentina 4-2 (after 2-2)	
2005	**FA Cup Final (Millennium Stadium):** Arsenal beat Manchester Utd 5-4 (after 0-0)	
2005	**Champions League Final (Istanbul):** Liverpool beat AC Milan 3-2 (after 3-3)	
2006	**African Cup of Nations Final (Cairo):** Egypt beat Ivory Coast 4-2 (after 0-0)	
2006	**FA Cup Final (Millennium Stadium):** Liverpool beat West Ham 3-1 (after 3-3)	
2006	**Scottish Cup Final (Hampden Park):** Hearts beat Gretna 4-2 (after 1-1)	
2006	**Lge 1 Play-off Final (Millennium Stadium):** Barnsley beat Swansea City 4-3 (after 2-2)	
2006	**World Cup Final (Berlin):** Italy beat France 5-3 (after 1-1)	
2007	**UEFA Cup Final (Hampden Park):** Sevilla beat Espanyol 3-1 (after 2-2)	
2008	**Champions League Final (Moscow):** Manchester Utd beat Chelsea 6-5 (after 1-1)	
2008	**Scottish League Cup Final (Hampden Park):** Rangers beat Dundee Utd 3-2 (after 2-2)	
2009	**League Cup Final (Wembley):** Manchester Utd beat Tottenham 4-1 (after 0-0)	

2011	**Women's World Cup Final (Frankfurt):** Japan beat USA 3-1 (after 2-2)
2012	**League Cup Final (Wembley):** Liverpool beat Cardiff 3-2 (after 2-2)
2012	**Champions League Final (Munich):** Chelsea beat Bayern Munich 4-3 (after 1-1)
2012	**Lge 1 Play-off Final (Wembley):** Huddersfield beat Sheffield Utd 8-7 (after 0-0)
2012	**Africa Cup of Nations Final (Gabon):** Zambia beat Ivory Coast 8-7 (after 0-0)
2013	**FA Trophy Final (Wembley):** Wrexham beat Grimsby 4-1 (after 1-1)
2013	**European Super Cup (Prague):** Bayern Munich beat Chelsea 5-4 (after 2-2)
2014	**Scottish League Cup Final (Celtic Park):** Aberdeen beat Inverness 4-2 (after 0-0)
2014	**Lge 1 Play-off Final (Wembley):** Rotherheam beat Leyton Orient 4-3 (after 2-2)
2014	**Europa Lge Final (Turin):** Sevilla beat Benfica 4-2 (after 0-0)
2015	**Africa Cup of Nations Final (Equ Guinea):** Ivory Coast beat Ghana 9-8 (after 0-0)
2015	**Conference Play-off Final (Wembley):** Bristol Rov beat Grimsby 5-3 (after 1-1)
2015	**Lge 2 Play-off Final (Wembley):** Southend beat Wycombe 7-6 (after 1-1)
2015	**FA Trophy Final (Wembley):** North Ferriby beat Wrexham 5-4 (after3-3)
2015	**Euro U-21 Champ Final (Prague):** Sweden beat Portugal 4-3 (after 0-0)
2015	**Copa America Final (Santiago):** Chile beat Argentina 4-1 (after 0-0)
2016	**League Cup Final (Wembley):** Manchester City beat Liverpool 3-1 (after 1-1)
2016	**Champions League Final (Milan):** Real Madrid beat Atletico Madrid 5-3 (after 1-1)
2016	**Olympic Men's Final (Rio de Janeiro):** Brazil beat Germany 5-4 (after 1-1)
2017	**Champ Play-off Final (Wembley):** Huddersfield beat Reading 4-3 (after 0-0)
2017	**Community Shield (Wembley):** Arsenal beat Chelsea 4-1 (after 1-1)
2019	**League Cup Final (Wembley):** Manchester City beat Chelsea 4-3 (after 0-0)
2019	**Football League Trophy Final (Wembley):** Portsmouth beat Sunderland 5-4 (after 2-2)
2019	**Community Shield (Wembley):** Manchester City beat Liverpool 5-4 (after 2-2)

bIn South America in 1992, in a 26-shot competition, **Newell's Old Boys** beat America 11-10 in the Copa Libertadores.

Longest-recorded penalty contest in first-class matches was in Argentina in 1988 – from 44 shots, **Argentinos Juniors** beat Racing Club 20-19. Genclerbirligi beat Galatasaray 17-16 in a Turkish Cup-tie in 1996. Only one penalty was missed.

Highest-scoring shoot-outs in international football: **North Korea** beat Hong Kong 11-10 (after 3-3 draw) in an Asian Cup match in 1975; and **Ivory Coast** beat Ghana 11-10 (after 0-0 draw) in African Nations Cup Final, 1992.

Most penalties needed to settle an adult game in Britain: **44** in Norfolk Primary Cup 4th round replay, Dec 2000. Aston Villa side **Freethorpe** beat Foulsham 20-19 (5 kicks missed). All 22 players took 2 penalties each, watched by a crowd of 20. The sides had drawn 2-2, 4-4 in a tie of 51 goals.

Penalty that took 24 days: That was how long elapsed between the award and the taking of a penalty in an Argentine Second Division match between **Atalanta** and Defensores in 2003. A riot ended the original match with 5 minutes left. The game resumed behind closed doors with the penalty that caused the abandonment. Lucas Ferreiro scored it to give Atalanta a 1-0 win.

INTERNATIONAL PENALTIES, MISSED

Four penalties out of five were missed when **Colombia** beat Argentina 3-0 in a Copa America group tie in Paraguay in Jul 1999. Martin Palmermo missed three for Argentina and Colombia's Hamilton Ricard had one spot-kick saved.

In the European Championship semi-final against Italy in Amsterdam on Jun 29, 2000, **Holland** missed five penalties – two in normal time, three in the penalty contest which Italy won 3-1 (after 0-0). Dutch captain Frank de Boer missed twice from the spot.

ENGLAND'S SHOOT-OUT RECORD

England have been beaten in eight out of 11 penalty shoot-outs in major tournaments:
1990	(World Cup semi-final, Turin) 3-4 v West Germany after 1-1.
1996	(Euro Champ quarter-final, Wembley) 4-2 v Spain after 0-0.
1996	(Euro Champ semi-final, Wembley) 5-6 v Germany after 1-1.
1998	(World Cup 2nd round., St Etienne) 3-4 v Argentina after 2-2.

2004 (Euro Champ quarter-final, Lisbon) 5-6 v Portugal after 2-2.
2006 (World Cup quarter-final, Gelsenkirchen) 1-3 v Portugal after 0-0.
2007 (Euro U-21 Champ semi-final, Heerenveen) 12-13 v Holland after 1-1.
2009 (Euro U-21 Champ semi-final, Gothenburg) 5-4 v Sweden after 3-3.
2012 (Euro Champ quarter-final, Kiev) 2-4 v Italy after 0-0.
2017 (Euro-21 Champ semi-final, Tychy) 3-4 v Germany after 2-2.
2018 (World Cup round of 16, Moscow) 4-3 v Colombia after 1-1.
2019 (Nations Lge, third-place play-off, Guimaraes) 6-5 v Switzerland after 0-0

FA CUP SHOOT-OUTS

First penalty contest in the FA Cup took place in 1972. In the days of the play-off for third place, the match was delayed until the eve of the following season when losing semi-finalists Birmingham and Stoke met at St Andrew's on Aug 5. The score was 0-0 and Birmingham won 4-3 on penalties.

Highest-scoring: Preliminary round replay (Aug 30, 2005): Tunbridge Wells beat Littlehampton 16-15 after 40 spot-kicks (9 missed).

Competition proper: Scunthorpe beat Worcester 14-13 in 2nd round replay (Dec 17, 2014) after 1-1 (32 kicks).

Shoot-out abandoned: The FA Cup 1st round replay between Oxford City and Wycombe at Wycombe on Nov 9, 1999 was abandoned (1-1) after extra-time. As the penalty shoot-out was about to begin, a fire broke out under a stand. Wycombe won the second replay 1-0 at Oxford Utd's ground.

First FA Cup Final to be decided by shoot-out was in 2005 (May 21), when Arsenal beat Manchester Utd 5-4 on penalties at Cardiff's Millennium Stadium (0-0 after extra time). A year later (May 13) Liverpool beat West Ham 3-1 (3-3 after extra-time).

ENGLISH RECORD SHOOT-OUT

Total of 34 spot-kicks: Football League Trophy group match, Nov 8, 2016, won 13-12 by Chelsea under-23 v Oxford United. Also: Southern League Challenge Cup 2nd rd, Nov 20, 2019, won 12-11 by Taunton v Truro.

SHOOT-OUT RECORD WINNERS AND LOSERS

When **Bradford** beat Arsenal 3-2 on penalties in a League Cup fifth round tie, it was the club's ninth successive shoot-out victory in FA Cup, League Cup and Johnstone's Paint Trophy ties between Oct 2009 and Dec 2012.

Tottenham's 4-1 spot-kick failure against Basel in the last 16 of the Europa League was their seventh successive defeat in shoot-outs from Mar 1996 to Apr 2013 (FA Cup, League Cup, UEFA Cup, Europa League)

MISSED CUP FINAL PENALTIES

John Aldridge (Liverpool) became the first player to miss a penalty in an FA Cup Final at Wembley when Dave Beasant saved his shot in 1988 to help Wimbledon to a shock 1-0 win. Seven penalties before had been scored in the Final at Wembley.

Previously, **Charlie Wallace**, of Aston Villa, had failed from the spot in the 1913 Final against Sunderland at Crystal Palace, which his team won 1-0

Gary Lineker (Tottenham) had his penalty saved by Nottm Forest's Mark Crossley in the 1991 FA Cup Final.

For the first time, two spot-kicks were missed in an FA Cup Final. In 2010, Petr Cech saved from Portsmouth's **Kevin-Prince Boateng** while Chelsea's **Frank Lampard** put his kick wide.

Another miss at Wembley was by Arsenal's **Nigel Winterburn**, Luton's Andy Dibble saving his spot-kick in the 1988 Littlewoods Cup Final, when a goal would have put Arsenal 3-1 ahead. Instead, they lost 3-2.

Winterburn was the third player to fail with a League Cup Final penalty at Wembley, following **Ray Graydon** (Aston Villa) against Norwich in 1975 and **Clive Walker** (Sunderland), who shot wide in the 1985 Milk Cup Final, also against Norwich who won 1-0. Graydon had his penalty saved by Kevin Keelan, but scored from the rebound and won the cup for Aston Villa (1-0).

Derby's Martin Taylor saved a penalty from **Eligio Nicolini** in the Anglo-Italian Cup Final at Wembley on Mar 27, 1993, but Cremonese won 3-1.

LEAGUE PENALTIES RECORD

Most penalties in Football League match: Five – 4 to Crystal Palace (3 missed), 1 to Brighton (scored) in Div 2 match at Selhurst Park on Mar 27 (Easter Monday), 1989. Crystal Palace won 2-1. Three of the penalties were awarded in a 5-minute spell. The match also produced 5 bookings and a sending-off. Other teams missing 3 penalties in a match: Burnley v Grimsby (Div 2), Feb 13, 1909; Manchester City v Newcastle (Div 1), Jan 17, 1912.

HOTTEST MODERN SPOT-SHOTS

Matthew Le Tissier ended his career in season 2001–02 with the distinction of having netted 48 out of 49 first-team penalties for Southampton. He scored the last 27 after his only miss when Nottm Forest keeper Mark Crossley saved in a Premier League match at The Dell on Mar 24, 1993.

Graham Alexander scored 78 out of 84 penalties in a 22-year career (Scunthorpe, Luton, Preston twice and Burnley) which ended in 2012.

SPOT-KICK HAT-TRICKS

Right-back **Joe Willetts** scored three penalties when Hartlepool beat Darlington 6-1 (Div 3N) on Good Friday 1951.

Danish international **Jan Molby**'s only hat-trick in English football, for Liverpool in a 3-1 win at home to Coventry (Littlewoods Cup, 4th round replay, Nov 26, 1986) comprised three goals from the penalty spot.

It was the first such hat-trick in a major match for two years – since **Andy Blair** scored three penalties for Sheffield Wed against Luton (Milk Cup 4th round, Nov 20 1984).

Portsmouth's **Kevin Dillon** scored a penalty hat-trick in the Full Members Cup (2nd round) at home to Millwall (3-2) on Nov 4, 1986.

Alan Slough scored a hat-trick of penalties in an away game, but was on the losing side, when Peterborough were beaten 4-3 at Chester (Div 3, Apr 29, 1978).

Josh Wright's three penalties in the space of 11 minutes enabled Gillingham to come from 2-0 down to defeat his former club Scunthorpe 3-2 in League One on Mar 11, 2017

Penalty hat-tricks in **international football:** Dimitris Saravakos (in 9 mins) for Greece v Egypt in 1990. He scored 5 goals in match. **Henrik Larsson**, among his 4 goals in Sweden's 6-0 home win v Moldova in World Cup qualifying match, Jun 6, 2001.

MOST PENALTY GOALS (LEAGUE) IN SEASON

13 out of 13 by **Francis Lee** for Manchester City (Div 1) in 1971–72. His goal total for the season was 33. In season 1988–89, **Graham Roberts** scored 12 League penalties for Second Division Champions Chelsea. In season 2004–05, **Andrew Johnson** scored 11 Premier League penalties for Crystal Palace, who were relegated.

PENALTY-SAVE SEQUENCES

Ipswich goalkeeper **Paul Cooper** saved eight of the ten penalties he faced in 1979–80. **Roy Brown** (Notts Co) saved six in a row in season 1972–73.

Andy Lomas, goalkeeper for Chesham (Diadora League) claimed a record eighth **consecutive** penalty saves – three at the end of season 1991–92 and five in 1992–93.

Mark Bosnich (Aston Villa) saved five in two consecutive matches in 1993–94: three in Coca-Cola Cup semi-final penalty shoot–out v Tranmere (Feb 26), then two in Premier League at Tottenham (Mar 2).

MISSED PENALTIES SEQUENCE

Against Wolves in Div 2 on Sep 28, 1991, **Southend** missed their seventh successive penalty (five of them the previous season).

RANGERS SPOT-ON

Rangers were awarded four penalties in their 4-0 win Scottish Premiership win over St Mirren on Feb 2, 2019, converting three of them.

SCOTTISH RECORDS

(See also under 'Goals' & 'Discipline')

CELTIC SUPREME

In winning the Treble for the fourth time in 2016–17, **Celtic** rewrote the Scottish records. In the first season under **Brendan Rodgers**, previously Liverpool manager, they did not lose a domestic match, the first to stay unbeaten in the league since Rangers in 1899. They set new records for points (106), goals (106), victories (34) and for a 30-point winning margin. In 2017–18, Celtic became the first in Scotland to win back-to-back domestic trebles and stretched an unbeaten run to a British record 69 games in domestic competitions. Their 25 consecutive victories in season 2003–04 also represents a British best, while the 1966–67 record was the most successful by a British side in one season. They won the Treble and became the first to win the European Cup. Under Jock Stein, there were nine titles in a row (1966–74). In season 2018–19, Celtic completed a third successive domestic treble, this one under **Brendan Rodgers** and **Neil Lennon**, who took over when Rodgers left to become Leicester manager in late February. After a ninth straight title in the curtailed 2019–20 season Celtic set their sights on a record tenth in the new campaign.

RANGERS' MANY RECORDS

Rangers' record-breaking feats include:

League Champions: 54 times (once joint holders) – world record.

Winning every match in Scottish League (18 games, 1898–99 season).

Major hat-tricks: Rangers have completed the domestic treble (League Championship, League Cup and Scottish FA Cup) a record seven times (1948–49, 1963–64, 1975–76, 1977–78, 1992–93, 1998–99, 2002–03).

League & Cup double: 17 times.

Nine successive Championships (1989–97). Four men played in all nine sides: Richard Gough, Ally McCoist, Ian Ferguson and Ian Durrant.

115 major trophies: Championships 54, Scottish Cup 33, League Cup 27, Cup-Winners' Cup 1.

UNBEATEN SCOTTISH CHAMPIONS

Celtic and **Rangers** have each won the Scottish Championship with an unbeaten record: Celtic in 1897–98 (P18, W15, D3), Rangers in 1898–99 (P18, W18).

FORSTER'S SHUT-OUT RECORD

Celtic goalkeeper **Fraser Forster** set a record in Scottish top-flight football by not conceding a goal for 1,256 consecutive minutes in season 2013–14.

TRIO OF TOP CLUBS MISSING

Three of Scotland's leading clubs were missing from the 2014–15 Premiership season. With **Hearts** finishing bottom and **Rangers** still working their way back through the divisions after being demoted, they were joined in the second tier by **Hibernian**, who lost the play-off final on penalties to Hamilton.

SCOTTISH CUP HAT-TRICKS

Aberdeen's feat of winning the Scottish FA Cup in 1982–83–84 made them only the third club to achieve that particular hat-trick. **Queen's Park** did it twice (1874–75–76 and 1880–81–82), and **Rangers** have won the Scottish Cup three years in succession on three occasions: 1934–35–36, 1948–49–50 and 1962–63–64.

SCOTTISH CUP FINAL DISMISSALS

Five players have been sent off in the Scottish FA Cup Final: **Jock Buchanan** (Rangers v Kilmarnock, 1929); **Roy Aitken** (Celtic v Aberdeen, 1984); **Walter Kidd** (Hearts captain v Aberdeen, 1986); **Paul Hartley** (Hearts v Gretna, 2006); **Pa Kujabi** (Hibernian v Hearts, 2012); **Carl Tremarco** (Inverness v Falkirk, 2015).

HIGHEST-SCORING SHOOT-OUT

In Scottish football's highest-scoring penalty shoot-out, **Stirling Albion** beat junior club Hurlford 13-12 after 28 spot-kicks in a third round replay. The tie, on Nov 8, 2014, had ended 2-2 after extra-time.

RECORD SEQUENCES

Celtic hold Britain's League record of 62 matches undefeated, from Nov 13, 1915 to Apr 21, 1917, when Kilmarnock won 2-0 at Parkhead. They won 49, drew 13 (111 points) and scored 126 goals to 26.

Greenock Morton in 1963–64 accumulated 67 points out of 72 and scored 135 goals.

Queen's Park did not have a goal scored against them during the first seven seasons of their existence (1867–74, before the Scottish League was formed).

EARLIEST PROMOTIONS IN SCOTLAND

Dundee promoted from Div 2, Feb 1, 1947; **Greenock Morton** promoted from Div 2, Mar 2, 1964; **Gretna** promoted from Div 3, Mar 5, 2005; **Hearts** promoted from Championship, Mar 21, 2015.

WORST HOME SEQUENCE

After gaining promotion to Div 1 in 1992, **Cowdenbeath** went a record 38 consecutive home League matches without a win. They ended the sequence (drew 8, lost 30) when beating Arbroath 1-0 on Apr 2, 1994, watched by a crowd of 225.

ALLY'S RECORDS

Ally McCoist became the first player to complete 200 goals in the Premier Division when he scored Rangers' winner (2-1) at Falkirk on Dec 12, 1992. His first was against Celtic in Sep 1983, and he reached 100 against Dundee on Boxing Day 1987.

When McCoist scored twice at home to Hibernian (4-3) on Dec 7, 1996, he became Scotland's record post-war League marksman, beating Gordon Wallace's 264.

Originally with St Johnstone (1978–81), he spent two seasons with Sunderland (1981–83), then joined Rangers for £200,000 in Jun 1983.

In 15 seasons at Ibrox, he scored 355 goals for Rangers (250 League), and helped them win 10 Championships (9 in succession), 3 Scottish Cups and earned a record 9 League Cup winner's medals. He won the European Golden Boot in consecutive seasons (1991–92, 1992–93).

His 9 Premier League goals in three seasons for Kilmarnock gave him a career total of 281 Scottish League goals when he retired at the end of 2000–01. McCoist succeeded Walter Smith as manager of Rangers in May 2011.

SCOTLAND'S MOST SUCCESSFUL MANAGER

Bill Struth, 30 trophies for Rangers, 1920–54 (18 Championships, 10 Scottish Cups, 2 League Cups).

SMITH'S IBROX HONOURS

Walter Smith, who retired in May, 2011, won a total of 21 trophies in two spells as Rangers manager (10 League titles, 5 Scottish Cups, 6 League Cups).

RANGERS PUNISHED

In April 2012, **Rangers** (in administration) were fined £160,000 by the Scottish FA and given a

12-month transfer ban on charges relating to their finances. The ban was later overturned in court. The club had debts estimated at around £135m and on June 12, 2012 were forced into liquidation. A new company emerged, but Rangers were voted out of the Scottish Premier League and demoted to Division Three for the start of the 2012-13 season. They returned to the top division in 2016 via three promotions in four seasons.

FIVE IN A MATCH

Paul Sturrock set an individual scoring record for the Scottish Premier Division with 5 goals in Dundee Utd's 7-0 win at home to Morton on Nov 17, 1984. **Marco Negri** equalled the feat with all 5 when Rangers beat Dundee Utd 5-1 at Ibrox (Premier Division) on Aug 23, 1997, and **Kenny Miller** scored 5 in Rangers' 7-1 win at home to St Mirren on Nov 4, 2000. **Kris Boyd** scored all Kilmarnock's goals in a 5-2 SPL win at home to Dundee Utd on Sep 25, 2004. **Boyd** scored another 5 when Rangers beat Dundee Utd 7-1 on Dec 30, 2009. That took his total of SPL goals to a record 160. **Gary Hooper** netted all Celtic's goals in 5-0 SPL win against Hearts on May 13, 2012

NEGRI'S TEN-TIMER

Marco Negri scored in Rangers' first ten League matches (23 goals) in season 1997–98, a Premier Division record. The previous best was 8 by **Ally MacLeod** for Hibernian in 1978.

DOUBLE SCOTTISH FINAL

Rangers v Celtic drew **129,643** and **120,073** people to the Scottish Cup Final and replay at Hampden Park, Glasgow, in 1963. Receipts for the two matches totalled £50,500.

MOST SCOTTISH CHAMPIONSHIP MEDALS

13 by **Sandy Archibald** (Rangers, 1918–34). Post-war record: 10 by **Bobby Lennox** (Celtic, 1966–79).

Alan Morton won **nine** Scottish Championship medals with Rangers in 1921–23–24–25–27–28–29–30–31. **Ally McCoist** played in the Rangers side that won nine successive League titles (1989–97).

Between 1927 and 1939 **Bob McPhail** helped Rangers win nine Championships, finish second twice and third once. He scored 236 League goals but was never top scorer in a single season.

TOP SCOTTISH LEAGUE SCORERS IN SEASON

Raith Rovers (Div 2) 142 goals in 1937–38; **Morton** (Div 2) 135 goals in 1963–64; **Hearts** (Div 1) 132 goals in 1957–58; **Falkirk** (Div 2) 132 goals in 1935–36; **Gretna** (Div 3) 130 goals in 2004–05.

SCOTTISH CUP – NO DECISION

The **Scottish FA** withheld their Cup and medals in 1908–09 after Rangers and Celtic played two drawn games in the Final. Spectators rioted.

FEWEST LEAGUE WINS IN SEASON

In modern times: 1 win by **Ayr** (34 matches, Div 1, 1966–67); **Forfar** (38 matches, Div 2, 1973–74); **Clydebank** (36 matches, Div 1, 1999–2000).

Vale of Leven provided the only instance of a British team failing to win a single match in a league season (Div 1, 18 games, 1891–92).

HAMPDEN'S £63M REDEVELOPMENT

On completion of redevelopment costing £63m **Hampden Park**, home of Scottish football and the oldest first-class stadium in the world, was re-opened full scale for the Rangers-Celtic Cup Final on May 29, 1999.

Work on the 'new Hampden' (capacity 52,000) began in 1992. The North and East stands were restructured (£12m); a new South stand and improved West stand cost £51m. The Millennium Commission contributed £23m and the Lottery Sports Fund provided a grant of £3.75m.

FIRST FOR INVERNESS

Inverness Caledonian Thistle won the Scottish Cup for the Highlands for the first time when beating Falkirk 2-1 in the Final on May 30, 2015.

FASTEST GOALS IN SPL

10.4 sec by **Kris Boyd** for Kilmarnock in 3-2 win over Ross Co, Jan 28, 2017; 12.1 sec by **Kris Commons** for Celtic in 4-3 win over Aberdeen, Mar 16, 2013; 12.4 sec by **Anthony Stokes** for Hibernian in 4-1 home defeat by Rangers, Dec 27, 2009.

YOUNGEST SCORER IN SPL

Fraser Fyvie, aged 16 years and 306 days, for Aberdeen v Hearts (3-0) on Jan 27, 2010.

12 GOALS SHARED

There was a record aggregate score for the SPL on May 5, 2010, when **Motherwell** came from 6-2 down to draw 6-6 with **Hibernian**.

25-POINT DEDUCTION

Dundee were deducted 25 points by the Scottish Football League in November 2010 for going into administration for the second time. It left the club on minus 11 points, but they still managed to finish in mid-table in Division One.

GREAT SCOTS

In Feb 1988, the Scottish FA launched a national **Hall of Fame**, initially comprising the first 11 Scots to make 50 international appearances, to be joined by all future players to reach that number of caps. Each member receives a gold medal, invitation for life at all Scotland's home matches, and has his portrait hung at Scottish FA headquarters in Glasgow.

MORE CLUBS IN 2000

The **Scottish Premier League** increased from 10 to 12 clubs in season 2000–01. The **Scottish Football League** admitted two new clubs – Peterhead and Elgin City from the Highland League – to provide three divisions of 10 in 2000–01.

FIRST FOR EDINBURGH CITY

In May 2016, **Edinburgh City** became the first club to be promoted to Scottish League Two through the pyramid system with a 2-1 aggregate play-off aggregate win over East Stirling, whose 61 years in senior football came to an end.

NOTABLE SCOTTISH 'FIRSTS'

- The father of League football was a Scot, **William McGregor**, a draper in Birmingham. The 12-club Football League kicked off in Sep 1888, and McGregor was its first president.
- **Hibernian** were the first British club to play in the European Cup, by invitation. They reached the semi-final when it began in 1955–56.
- Celtic were Britain's first winners of the European Cup, in 1967.
- Scotland's First Division became the **Premier Division** in season 1975–76.
- Football's **first international** was staged at the West of Scotland cricket ground, Partick, on Nov 30, 1872: Scotland 0, England 0.
- Scotland introduced its **League Cup** in 1945–46, the first season after the war. It was another 15 years before the Football League Cup was launched.
- Scotland pioneered the use in British football of **two subs** per team in League and Cup matches.
- The world's **record football score** belongs to Scotland: Arbroath 36, Bon Accord 0 (Scottish Cup 1st rd) on Sep 12, 1885.
- The Scottish FA introduced the penalty **shoot-out** to their Cup Final in 1990.
- On Jan 22, 1994 all six matches in the **Scottish Premier Division** ended as draws.
- Scotland's new Premier League introduced a **3-week shut-down** in Jan 1999 – first instance

of British football adopting the winter break system that operates in a number of European countries. The SPL ended its New Year closure after 2003. The break returned from season 2016–17.
- **Rangers** made history at home to St Johnstone (Premier League, 0-0, Mar 4, 2000) when fielding a team entirely without Scottish players.
- **John Fleck**, aged 16 years, 274 days, became the youngest player in a Scottish FA Cup Final when he came on as a substitute for Rangers in their 3-2 win over Queen of the South at Hampden Park on May 24, 2008

SCOTTISH CUP SHOCK RESULTS

1885–86	(1)	Arbroath 36 Bon Accord 0
1921–22	(F)	Morton 1 Rangers 0
1937–38	(F)	East Fife 4 Kilmarnock 2 (replay, after 1-1)
1960–61	(F)	Dunfermline 2 Celtic 0 (replay, after 0-0)
1966–67	(1)	Berwick 1 Rangers 0
1979–80	(3)	Hamilton 2 Keith 3
1984–85	(1)	Stirling 20 Selkirk 0
1984–85	(3)	Inverness 3 Kilmarnock 0
1986–87	(3)	Rangers 0 Hamilton 1
1994–95	(4)	Stenhousemuir 2 Aberdeen 0
1998–99	(3)	Aberdeen 0 Livingston 1
1999–2000	(3)	Celtic 1 Inverness 3
2003–04	(5)	Inverness 1 Celtic 0
2005–06	(3)	Clyde 2 Celtic 1
2008–09	(6)	St Mirren 1 Celtic 0
2009–10	(SF)	Ross Co 2 Celtic 0
2013–14	(4)	Albion 1 Motherwell 0

Scottish League (Coca-Cola) Cup Final
1994–95	Raith 2, Celtic 2 (Raith won 6-5 on pens)

Europa League first qualifying round
2017–18	Progres Niederkorn (Luxembourg) 2 Rangers 1 (on agg)
2019–20	Connah's Quay (Wales) 3 Kilmarnock 2 (on agg)

MISCELLANEOUS

NATIONAL ASSOCIATIONS FORMED

FA	**1863**
FA of Wales	**1876**
Scottish FA	**1873**
Irish FA	**1904**
Federation of International Football Associations (FIFA)	**1904**

NATIONAL & INTERNATIONAL COMPETITIONS LAUNCHED

FA Cup	**1871**
Welsh Cup	**1877**
Scottish Cup	**1873**
Irish Cup	**1880**
Football League	**1888**
Premier League	**1992**
Scottish League	**1890**
Scottish Premier League	**1998**

Scottish League Cup	1945
Football League Cup	1960
Home International Championship	1883–84
World Cup	1930
European Championship	1958
European Cup	1955
Fairs/UEFA Cup	1955
Cup-Winners' Cup	1960
European Champions League	1992
Olympic Games Tournament, at Shepherd's Bush	1908

INNOVATIONS

Size of Ball: Fixed in **1872**.

Shinguards: Introduced and registered by Sam Weller Widdowson (Nottm Forest & England) in **1874**.

Referee's whistle: First used on Nottm Forest's ground in **1878**.

Professionalism: Legalised in England in the summer of **1885** as a result of agitation by Lancashire clubs.

Goal-nets: Invented and patented in **1890** by Mr JA Brodie of Liverpool. They were first used in the North v South match in Jan, **1891**.

Referees and linesmen: Replaced umpires and referees in Jan, **1891**.

Penalty-kick: Introduced at Irish FA's request in the season **1891–92**. The penalty law ordering the goalkeeper to remain on the goal-line came into force in Sep, **1905**, and the order to stand on his goal-line until the ball is kicked arrived in **1929–30**.

White ball: First came into official use in **1951**.

Floodlighting: First FA Cup-tie (replay), Kidderminster Harriers v Brierley Hill Alliance, **1955**. First Football League match: Portsmouth v Newcastle (Div 1), **1956**.

Heated pitch to beat frost tried by Everton at Goodison Park in **1958**.

First soccer closed-circuit TV: At Coventry ground in Oct **1965** (10,000 fans saw their team win at Cardiff, 120 miles away).

Substitutes (one per team) were first allowed in Football League matches at the start of season **1965–66**. Three substitutes (one a goalkeeper) allowed, two of which could be used, in Premier League matches, **1992–93**. The Football League introduced three substitutes for **1993–94**.

Three points for a win: Introduced by the Football League in **1981–82**, by FIFA in World Cup games in **1994**, and by the Scottish League in the same year.

Offside law amended, player 'level' no longer offside, and 'professional foul' made sending-off offence, **1990**.

Penalty shoot-outs introduced to decide FA Cup ties level after one replay and extra time, **1991–92**.

New back-pass rule: goalkeeper must not handle ball kicked to him by team-mate, **1992**.

Linesmen became 'referees' assistants', **1998**.

Goalkeepers not to hold ball longer than 6 seconds, **2000**.

Free-kicks advanced by ten yards against opponents failing to retreat, **2000**. This experimental rule in England was scrapped in 2005).

YOUNGEST AND OLDEST

Youngest Caps

Harry Wilson (Wales v Belgium, Oct 15, 2013)	**16 years 207 days**
Norman Whiteside (N Ireland v Yugoslavia, Jun 17, 1982)	**17 years 41 days**
Theo Walcott (England v Hungary, May 30, 2006)	**17 years 75 days**
Johnny Lambie (Scotland v Ireland, Mar 20, 1886)	**17 years 92 days**
Jimmy Holmes (Rep of Ireland v Austria, May 30, 1971)	**17 years 200 days**

Youngest England scorer: Wayne Rooney (17 years, 317 days) v Macedonia, Skopje, Sep 6, 2003.

Youngest scorer on England debut: Marcus Rashford (18 years, 208 days) v Australia,

Sunderland, May 27, 2016.

Youngest England hat-trick scorer: Theo Walcott (19 years, 178 days) v Croatia, Zagreb, Sep 10, 2008.

Youngest England captains: Bobby Moore (v Czech., Bratislava, May 29, 1963), 22 years, 47 days; Michael Owen (v Paraguay, Anfield, Apr 17, 2002), 22 years, 117 days.

Youngest England goalkeeper: Jack Butland (19 years, 158 days) v Italy, Bern, Aug 15, 2012

Youngest England players to reach 50 caps: Michael Owen (23 years, 6 months) v Slovakia at Middlesbrough, Jun 11, 2003; Bobby Moore (25 years, 7 months) v Wales at Wembley, Nov 16, 1966.

Youngest player in World Cup Final: Pele (Brazil) aged 17 years, 237 days v Sweden in Stockholm, Jun 12, 1958.

Youngest player to appear in World Cup Finals: Norman Whiteside (N Ireland v Yugoslavia in Spain – Jun 17, 1982, age 17 years and 42 days.

Youngest First Division player: Derek Forster (Sunderland goalkeeper v Leicester, Aug 22, 1964) aged 15 years, 185 days.

Youngest First Division scorer: At 16 years and 57 days, schoolboy Jason Dozzell (substitute after 30 minutes for Ipswich at home to Coventry on Feb 4, 1984). Ipswich won 3-1 and Dozzell scored their third goal.

Youngest Premier League player: Harvey Elliott (Fulham on loan from Liverpool, sub away to Wolves, May 4, 2019), 16 years and 30 days.

Youngest Premier League scorer: James Vaughan (Everton, home to Crystal Palace, Apr 10, 2005), 16 years, 271 days.

Youngest Premier League captain: Lee Cattermole (Middlesbrough away to Fulham, May 7, 2006) aged 18 years, 47 days.

Youngest player sent off in Premier League: Wayne Rooney (Everton, away to Birmingham, Dec 26, 2002) aged 17 years, 59 days.

Youngest First Division hat-trick scorer: Alan Shearer, aged 17 years, 240 days, in Southampton's 4-2 home win v Arsenal (Apr 9, 1988) on his full debut. Previously, Jimmy Greaves (17 years, 309 days) with 4 goals for Chelsea at home to Portsmouth (7-4), Christmas Day, 1957.

Youngest to complete 100 Football League goals: Jimmy Greaves (20 years, 261 days) when he did so for Chelsea v Manchester City, Nov 19, 1960.

Youngest players in Football League: Reuben Noble-Lazarus (Barnsley 84th minute sub at Ipswich, Sep 30, 2008, Champ) aged 15 years, 45 days; Mason Bennett (Derby at Middlesbrough, Champ, Oct 22, 2011) aged 15 years, 99 days; Albert Geldard (Bradford PA v Millwall, Div 2, Sep 16, 1929) aged 15 years, 158 days; Ken Roberts (Wrexham v Bradford Park Avenue, Div 3 North, Sep 1, 1951) also 15 years, 158 days.

Youngest Football League scorer: Ronnie Dix (for Bristol Rov v Norwich, Div 3 South, Mar 3, 1928) aged 15 years, 180 days.

Youngest player in Scottish League: Goalkeeper Ronnie Simpson (Queens Park) aged 15 in 1946.

Youngest player in FA Cup: Andy Awford, Worcester City's England Schoolboy defender, aged 15 years, 88 days when he substituted in second half away to Boreham Wood (3rd qual round) on Oct 10, 1987.

Youngest player in FA Cup proper: Luke Freeman, Gillingham substitute striker (15 years, 233 days) away to Barnet in 1st round, Nov 10, 2007.

Youngest FA Cup scorer: Sean Cato (16 years, 25 days), second half sub in Barrow Town's 7-2 win away to Rothwell Town (prelim rd), Sep 3, 2011.

Youngest Wembley Cup Final captain: Barry Venison (Sunderland v Norwich, Milk Cup Final, Mar 24, 1985 – replacing suspended captain Shaun Elliott) – aged 20 years, 220 days.

Youngest FA Cup-winning captain: Bobby Moore (West Ham, 1964, v Preston), aged 23 years, 20 days.

Youngest FA Cup Final captain: David Nish aged 21 years and 212 days old when he captained Leicester against Manchester City at Wembley on Apr 26, 1969.

Youngest FA Cup Final player: Curtis Weston (Millwall sub last 3 mins v Manchester Utd, 2004) aged 17 years, 119 days.

Youngest FA Cup Final scorer: Norman Whiteside (Manchester Utd v Brighton, 1983 replay,

Wembley), aged 18 years, 19 days.

Youngest FA Cup Final managers: Stan Cullis, Wolves (32) v Leicester, 1949; Steve Coppell, Crystal Palace (34) v Manchester Utd, 1990; Ruud Gullit, Chelsea (34) v Middlesbrough, 1997.

Youngest player in Football League Cup: Chris Coward (Stockport) sub v Sheffield Wed, 2nd Round, Aug 23, 2005, aged 16 years and 31 days.

Youngest Wembley scorer: Norman Whiteside (Manchester Utd v Liverpool, Milk Cup Final, Mar 26, 1983) aged 17 years, 324 days.

Youngest Wembley Cup Final goalkeeper: Chris Woods (18 years, 125 days) for Nottm Forest v Liverpool, League Cup Final on Mar 18, 1978.

Youngest Wembley FA Cup Final goalkeeper: Peter Shilton (19 years, 219 days) for Leicester v Manchester City, Apr 26, 1969.

Youngest senior international at Wembley: Salomon Olembe (sub for Cameroon v England, Nov 15, 1997), aged 16 years, 342 days.

Youngest winning manager at Wembley: Stan Cullis, aged 32 years, 187 days, as manager of Wolves, FA Cup winners on April 30 1949.

Youngest scorer in full international: Mohamed Kallon (Sierra Leone v Congo, African Nations Cup, Apr 22, 1995), reported as aged 15 years, 192 days.

Youngest English player to start a Champions League game: Phil Foden (Manchester City v Shakhtar Donetsk, Dec 6, 2017) aged 17 years, 192 days

Youngest English scorer in Champions League: Alex Oxlade-Chamberlain (Arsenal v Olympiacos, Sep 28, 2011) aged 18 years 1 month, 13 days

Youngest player sent off in World Cup Final series: Rigobert Song (Cameroon v Brazil, in USA, Jun 1994) aged 17 years, 358 days.

Youngest FA Cup Final referee: Kevin Howley, of Middlesbrough, aged 35 when in charge of Wolves v Blackburn, 1960.

Youngest player in England U-23 team: Duncan Edwards (v Italy, Bologna, Jan 20, 1954), aged 17 years, 112 days.

Youngest player in England U-21 team: Theo Walcott (v Moldova, Ipswich, Aug 15, 2006), aged 17 years, 152 days.

Youngest player in Scotland U-21 team: Christian Dailly (v Romania, Hampden Park, Sep 11, 1990), aged 16 years, 330 days.

Youngest player in senior football: Cameron Campbell Buchanan, Scottish-born outside right, aged 14 years, 57 days when he played for Wolves v WBA in War-time League match, Sep 26, 1942.

Youngest player in peace-time senior match: Eamon Collins (Blackpool v Kilmarnock, Anglo-Scottish Cup quarter-final 1st leg, Sep 9, 1980) aged 14 years, 323 days.

World's youngest player in top division match: Centre-forward Fernando Rafael Garcia, aged 13, played for 23 minutes for Peruvian club Juan Aurich in 3-1 win against Estudiantes on May 19, 2001.

Oldest player to appear in Football League: New Brighton manager Neil McBain (51 years, 120 days) as emergency goalkeeper away to Hartlepool (Div 3 North, Mar 15, 1947).

Other oldest post-war League players: Sir Stanley Matthews (Stoke, 1965, 50 years, 5 days); Peter Shilton (Leyton Orient 1997, 47 years, 126 days); Kevin Poole (Burton, 2010, 46 years, 291 days); Dave Beasant (Brighton 2003, 44 years, 46 days); Alf Wood (Coventry, 1958, 43 years, 199 days); Tommy Hutchison (Swansea City, 1991, 43 years, 172 days).

Oldest Football League debutant: Andy Cunningham, for Newcastle at Leicester (Div 1) on Feb 2, 1929, aged 38 years, 2 days.

Oldest post-war debut in English League: Defender David Donaldson (35 years, 7 months, 23 days) for Wimbledon on entry to Football League (Div 4) away to Halifax, Aug 20, 1977.

Oldest player to appear in First Division: Sir Stanley Matthews (Stoke v Fulham, Feb 6, 1965), aged 50 years, 5 days – on that his last League appearance, the only 50-year-old ever to play in the top division.

Oldest players in Premier League: Goalkeepers John Burridge (Manchester City v QPR, May 14, 1995), 43 years, 5 months, 11 days; Alec Chamberlain (Watford v Newcastle, May 13, 2007) 42 years, 11 months, 23 days; Steve Ogrizovic (Coventry v Sheffield Wed, May 6, 2000), 42 years, 7 months, 24 days; Brad Friedel (Tottenham v Newcastle, Nov 10, 2013) 42 years, 4 months, 22 days; Neville Southall (Bradford City v Leeds, Mar 12, 2000), 41 years, 5 months, 26 days. Outfield: Teddy Sheringham (West Ham v Manchester City, Dec 30, 2006), 40 years, 8 months, 28 days; Ryan Giggs (Manchester Utd v Hull, May 6, 2014), 40 years, 5 months, 7 days; Gordon Strachan (Coventry City v Derby, May 3, 1997), 40 years, 2 months, 24 days.

Oldest player for British professional club: John Ryan (owner-chairman of Conference club Doncaster, played as substitute for last minute in 4-2 win at Hereford on Apr 26, 2003), aged 52 years, 11 months, 3 weeks.

Oldest FA Cup Final player: Walter (Billy) Hampson (Newcastle v Aston Villa on Apr 26, 1924), aged 41 years, 257 days.

Oldest captain and goalkeeper in FA Cup Final: David James (Portsmouth v Chelsea, May 15, 2010) aged 39 years, 287 days.

Oldest FA Cup Final scorers: Bert Turner (Charlton v Derby, Apr 27, 1946) aged 36 years, 312 days. Scored for both sides. Teddy Sheringham (West Ham v Liverpool, May 13, 2006) aged 40 years, 41 days. Scored in penalty shoot-out.

Oldest FA Cup-winning team: Arsenal 1950 (average age 31 years, 2 months). Eight of the players were over 30, with the three oldest centre-half Leslie Compton 37, and skipper Joe Mercer and goalkeeper George Swindin, both 35.

Oldest World Cup-winning captain: Dino Zoff, Italy's goalkeeper v W Germany in 1982 Final, aged 40 years, 92 days.

Oldest player capped by England: Stanley Matthews (v Denmark, Copenhagen, May 15, 1957), aged 42 years, 103 days.

Oldest England scorer: Stanley Matthews (v N Ireland, Belfast, Oct 6, 1956), aged 41 years, 248 days.

Oldest British international player: Billy Meredith (Wales v England at Highbury, Mar 15, 1920), aged 45 years, 229 days.

Oldest 'new caps': Goalkeeper Alexander Morten, aged 41 years, 113 days when earning his only England Cap against Scotland on Mar 8, 1873; Arsenal centre-half Leslie Compton, at 38 years, 64 days when he made his England debut in 4-2 win against Wales at Sunderland on Nov 15, 1950. **For Scotland:** Goalkeeper Ronnie Simpson (Celtic) at 36 years, 186 days v England at Wembley, Apr 15, 1967.

Oldest scorer in Wembley Final: Chris Swailes, 45, for Morpeth in 4-1 win over Hereford (FA Vase), May 22, 2016.

Longest Football League career: This spanned 32 years and 10 months, by Stanley Matthews (Stoke, Blackpool, Stoke) from Mar 19, 1932 until Feb 6, 1965.

Shortest FA Cup-winning captain: 5ft 4in – Bobby Kerr (Sunderland v Leeds, 1973).

KANTE'S PEAK

N'Golo Kante became the first player in English football to win back-to-back titles with different clubs while playing a full season with each – Leicester (2015-16), Chelsea (2016–17).

EURO FIRST FOR REFEREE

Liverpool's defeat of Chelsea on penalties in the Super Cup on Aug 14, 2019, was refereed by Stephanie Frappart, of France, who became the first woman to take charge of a major European men's match.

SHIRT NUMBERING

Numbering players in Football League matches was made compulsory in 1939. Players wore numbered shirts (1-22) in the FA Cup Final as an experiment in 1933 (Everton 1-11 v Manchester City 12-22).

Squad numbers for players were introduced by the Premier League at the start of season 1993–94. They were optional in the Football League until made compulsory in 1999–2000.

Names on shirts: For first time, players wore names as well as numbers on shirts in League Cup and FA Cup Finals, 1993.

SUBSTITUTES

In **1965**, the Football League, by 39 votes to 10, agreed that **one substitute** be allowed for an injured player at any time during a League match. First substitute used in Football League: Keith Peacock (Charlton), away to Bolton in Div 2, Aug 21, 1965.

Two substitutes per team were approved for the League (Littlewoods) Cup and FA Cup in season 1986–87 and two were permitted in the Football League for the first time in 1987–88.

Three substitutes (one a goalkeeper), two of which could be used, introduced by the Premier League for 1992–93. The Football League followed suit for 1993–94.

Three substitutes (one a goalkeeper) were allowed at the World Cup Finals for the first time at US '94.

Three substitutes (any position) introduced by Premier League and Football League in 1995–96.

Five named substitutes (three of which could be used) introduced in Premier League in 1996–97, in FA Cup in 1997–98, League Cup in 1998–99 and Football League in 1999–2000.

Seven named substitutes for Premier League, FA Cup and League Cup in 2008–09. Still only three to be used. Football League adopted this rule for 2009–10, reverted to five in 2011–12 and went back to seven for the 2012–13 season.

First substitute to score in FA Cup Final: Eddie Kelly (Arsenal v Liverpool, 1971). The **first recorded use** of a substitute was in 1889 (Wales v Scotland at Wrexham on Apr 15) when Sam Gillam arrived late – although he was a Wrexham player – and Allen Pugh (Rhostellyn) was allowed to keep goal until he turned up. The match ended 0–0.

When **Dickie Roose**, the Welsh goalkeeper, was injured against England at Wrexham, Mar 16, 1908, **Dai Davies** (Bolton) was allowed to take his place as substitute. Thus Wales used 12 players. England won 7–1.

END OF WAGE LIMIT

Freedom from the maximum wage system – in force since the formation of the Football League in 1888 – was secured by the Professional Footballers' Association in 1961. About this time Italian clubs renewed overtures for the transfer of British stars and Fulham's **Johnny Haynes** became the first British player to earn £100 a week.

THE BOSMAN RULING

On Dec 15, 1995 the **European Court of Justice** ruled that clubs had no right to transfer fees for out-of-contract players, and the outcome of the 'Bosman case' irrevocably changed football's player-club relationship. It began in 1990, when the contract of 26-year-old **Jean-Marc Bosman**, a midfield player with FC Liege, Belgium, expired. French club Dunkirk wanted him but were unwilling to pay the £500,000 transfer fee, so Bosman was compelled to remain with Liege. He responded with a lawsuit against his club and UEFA on the grounds of 'restriction of trade', and after five years at various court levels the European Court of Justice ruled not only in favour of Bosman but of all professional footballers.

The end of restrictive labour practices revolutionised the system. It led to a proliferation of transfers, rocketed the salaries of elite players who, backed by an increasing army of agents, found themselves in a vastly improved bargaining position as they moved from team to team, league to league, nation to nation. Removing the limit on the number of foreigners clubs could field brought an increasing ratio of such signings, not least in England and Scotland.

Bosman's one-man stand opened the way for footballers to become millionaires, but ended his own career. All he received for his legal conflict was 16 million Belgian francs (£312,000) in compensation, a testimonial of poor reward and martyrdom as the man who did most to change the face of football.

By 2011, he was living on Belgian state benefits, saying: 'I have made the world of football rich and shifted the power from clubs to players. Now I find myself with nothing.'

INTERNATIONAL SHOCK RESULTS

| 1950 | USA 1 England 0 (World Cup). |
| 1953 | England 3 Hungary 6 (friendly). |

1954	Hungary 7 England 1 (friendly)
1966	North Korea 1 Italy 0 (World Cup).
1982	Spain 0, Northern Ireland 1; Algeria 2, West Germany 1 (World Cup).
1990	Cameroon 1 Argentina 0; Scotland 0 Costa Rica 1; Sweden 1 Costa Rica 2 (World Cup).
1990	Faroe Islands 1 Austria 0 (European Champ qual).
1992	Denmark 2 Germany 0 (European Champ Final).
1993	USA 2 England 0 (US tournament).
1993	Argentina 0 Colombia 5 (World Cup qual).
1993	France 2 Israel 3 (World Cup qual).
1994	Bulgaria 2 Germany 1 (World Cup).
1994	Moldova 3 Wales 2; Georgia 5 Wales 0 (European Champ qual).
1995	Belarus 1 Holland 0 (European Champ qual).
1996	Nigeria 4 Brazil 3 (Olympics).
1998	USA 1 Brazil 0 (Concacaf Gold Cup).
1998	Croatia 3 Germany 0 (World Cup).
2000	Scotland 0 Australia 2 (friendly).
2001	Australia 1 France 0; Australia 1, Brazil 0 (Confederations Cup).
2001	Honduras 2 Brazil 0 (Copa America).
2001	Germany 1 England 5 (World Cup qual).
2002	France 0 Senegal 1; South Korea 2 Italy 1 (World Cup).
2003:	England 1 Australia 3 (friendly)
2004:	Portugal 0 Greece 1 (European Champ Final).
2005:	Northern Ireland 1 England 0 (World Cup qual).
2014:	Holland 5 Spain 1 (World Cup).
2014:	Brazil 1 Germany 7 (World Cup).
2016	England 1 Iceland 2 (European Champ)
2018	South Korea 2 Germany 0 (World Cup)

GREAT RECOVERIES – DOMESTIC FOOTBALL

On Dec 21, 1957, **Charlton** were losing 5-1 against Huddersfield (Div 2) at The Valley with only 28 minutes left, and from the 15th minute, had been reduced to ten men by injury, but they won 7-6, with left-winger Johnny Summers scoring five goals. **Huddersfield** (managed by Bill Shankly) remain the only team to score six times in a League match and lose. On Boxing Day, 1927 in Div 3 South, **Northampton** won 6-5 at home to Luton after being 1-5 down at half-time.

Season 2010–11 produced a Premier League record for **Newcastle**, who came from 4-0 down at home to Arsenal to draw 4-4. Previous instance of a team retrieving a four-goal deficit in the top division to draw was in 1984 when Newcastle trailed at QPR in a game which ended 5-5.

In the 2012-13 League Cup, **Arsenal** were 0-4 down in a fourth round tie at Reading, levelled at 4-4 and went on to win 7-5 in extra-time.

MATCHES OFF

Worst day for postponements: Feb 9, 1963, when 57 League fixtures in England and Scotland were frozen off. Only 7 Football League matches took place, and the entire Scottish programme was wiped out.

Other weather-hit days:

Jan 12, 1963 and Feb 2, 1963 – on both those Saturdays, only 4 out of 44 Football League matches were played.

Jan 1, 1979 – 43 out of 46 Football League fixtures postponed.

Jan 17, 1987 – 37 of 45 scheduled Football League fixtures postponed; only 2 Scottish matches survived.

Feb 8–9, 1991 – only 4 of the week-end's 44 Barclays League matches survived the freeze-up (4 of the postponements were on Friday night). In addition, 11 Scottish League matches were off.

Jan 27, 1996 – 44 Cup and League matches in England and Scotland were frozen off.

On the weekend of Jan 9, 10, 11, 2010, 46 League and Cup matches in England and Scotland were victims of the weather. On the weekend of Dec 18-21, 2010, 49 matches were frozen off in England and Scotland.

Fewest matches left on one day by postponements was during the Second World War – Feb 3, 1940 when, because of snow, ice and fog only one out of 56 regional league fixtures took place. It resulted Plymouth Argyle 10, Bristol City 3.

The Scottish Cup second round tie between Inverness Thistle and Falkirk in season 1978–79 was **postponed 29 times** because of snow and ice. First put off on Jan 6, it was eventually played on Feb 22. Falkirk won 4–0.

Pools Panel's busiest days: Jan 17, 1987 and Feb 9, 1991 – on both dates they gave their verdict on 48 postponed coupon matches.

FEWEST 'GAMES OFF'

Season 1947–48 was the best since the war for English League fixtures being played to schedule. Only six were postponed.

LONGEST SEASON

The latest that League football has been played in a season was **Jun 7, 1947** (six weeks after the FA Cup Final). The season was extended because of mass postponements caused by bad weather in mid-winter.

The latest the FA Cup competition has been completed was in season 2014–15 when Arsenal beat Aston Villa 4–0 in the Final on May 30, kick-off 5.30pm

Worst winter hold-up was in season 1962–63. The Big Freeze began on Boxing Day and lasted until Mar, with nearly 500 first-class matches postponed. The FA Cup 3rd round was the longest on record – it began with only three out of 32 ties playable on Jan 5 and ended 66 days and 261 postponements later on Mar 11. The Lincoln–Coventry tie was put off 15 times. The Pools Panel was launched that winter, on Jan 26, 1963.

HOTTEST DAYS

The Nationwide League kicked off season 2003–04 on Aug 9 with pitch temperatures of 102 degrees recorded at Luton v Rushden and Bradford v Norwich. On the following day, there was a pitch temperature of 100 degrees for the Community Shield match between Manchester Utd and Arsenal at Cardiff's Millennium Stadium. Wembley's pitch-side thermometer registered 107 degrees for the 2009 Chelsea–Everton FA Cup Final.

FOOTBALL LEAGUE NAME CHANGE

From the start of the 2016-17 season, the Football League was renamed the English Football League, as part of a corporate and competition rebranding.

FOOTBALL ASSOCIATION SECRETARIES/CHIEF EXECUTIVES

1863–66 Ebenezer Morley; 1866–68 **Robert Willis**; 1868–70 RG **Graham**; 1870–95 **Charles Alcock** (paid from 1887); 1895–1934 **Sir Frederick Wall**; 1934–62 **Sir Stanley Rous**; 1962–73 **Denis Follows**; 1973–89 **Ted Croker** (latterly chief executive); 1989–99 **Graham Kelly** (chief executive); 2000–02 **Adam Crozier** (chief executive); 2003–04 **Mark Palios** (chief executive); 2005–08: **Brian Barwick** (chief executive); 2009–10 **Ian Watmore** (chief executive); 2010-15 **Alex Horne** (chief executive); 2015–19 **Martin Glenn** (chief executive); 2019 **Mark Bullingham** (chief executive).

FOOTBALL'S SPONSORS

Football League: Canon 1983–86; Today Newspaper 1986–87; Barclays 1987–93; Endsleigh Insurance 1993–96; Nationwide Building Society 1996–2004; Coca-Cola 2004–10; npower 2010–14; Sky Bet from 2014.

League Cup: Milk Cup 1982–86; Littlewoods 1987–90; Rumbelows 1991–92; Coca-Cola 1993–98; Worthington 1998–2003; Carling 2003–12; Capital One 2012–16; Carabao from 2017.

Premier League: Carling 1993–2001; Barclaycard 2001–04; Barclays 2004–16.

FA Cup: Littlewoods 1994–98; AXA 1998–2002; E.ON 2006–11; Budweiser 2011–15; Emirates (title sponsor) from 2015.

NEW HOMES FOR CLUBS

Newly-constructed League grounds in England since the war: 1946 Hull (Boothferry Park); 1950 Port Vale (Vale Park); 1955 Southend (Roots Hall); 1988 Scunthorpe (Glanford Park); 1990 Walsall (Bescot Stadium); 1990 Wycombe (Adams Park); 1992 Chester (Deva Stadium); 1993 Millwall (New Den); 1994 Huddersfield (McAlpine Stadium); 1994 Northampton (Sixfields Stadium); 1995 Middlesbrough (Riverside Stadium); 1997 Bolton (Reebok Stadium); 1997 Derby (Pride Park); 1997 Stoke (Britannia Stadium); 1997 Sunderland (Stadium of Light); 1998 Reading (Madejski Stadium); 1999 Wigan (JJB Stadium); 2001 Southampton (St Mary's Stadium); 2001 Oxford Utd (Kassam Stadium); 2002 Leicester (Walkers Stadium); 2002 Hull (Kingston Communications Stadium); 2003 Manchester City (City of Manchester Stadium); 2003 Darlington (New Stadium); 2005 Coventry (Ricoh Arena); Swansea (Stadium of Swansea, Morfa); 2006 Arsenal (Emirates Stadium); 2007 Milton Keynes Dons (Stadium: MK); Shrewsbury (New Meadow); Doncaster (Keepmoat Stadium); 2008 Colchester (Community Stadium); 2009 Cardiff City Stadium); 2010 Chesterfield (b2net Stadium), Morecambe (Globe Arena); 2011 Brighton (American Express Stadium); 2012 Rotherham (New York Stadium). 2016 West Ham (Olympic Stadium); 2020 Brentford (Community Stadium).

NATIONAL FOOTBALL CENTRE

The FA's new £120m centre at St George's Park, Burton upon Trent, was opened on Oct 9, 20012 by the Duke of Cambridge, president of the FA. The site covers 330 acres, has 12 full-size pitches (5 with undersoil heating and floodlighting). There are 5 gyms, a 90-seat lecture theatre, a hydrotherapy unit with swimming pool for the treatment of injuries and two hotels. It is the base for England teams, men and women, at all levels.

GROUND-SHARING

Manchester Utd played their home matches at Manchester City's Maine Road ground for 8 years after Old Trafford was bomb-damaged in Aug 1941. Crystal Palace and Charlton shared Selhurst Park (1985–91); Bristol Rov and Bath City (Twerton Park, Bath, 1986–96); Partick Thistle and Clyde (Firhill Park, Glasgow, 1986–91; in seasons 1990–01, 1991–92 Chester shared Macclesfield's ground (Moss Rose).

Crystal Palace and Wimbledon shared Selhurst Park, from season 1991–92, when Charlton (tenants) moved to rent Upton Park from West Ham, until 2003 when Wimbledon relocated to Milton Keynes. Clyde moved to Douglas Park, Hamilton Academical's home, in 1991–92. Stirling Albion shared Stenhousemuir's ground, Ochilview Park, in 1992–93. In 1993–94, Clyde shared Partick's home until moving to Cumbernauld. In 1994–95, Celtic shared Hampden Park with Queen's Park (while Celtic Park was redeveloped); Hamilton shared Partick's ground. Airdrie shared Clyde's Broadwood Stadium. Bristol Rov left Bath City's ground at the start of season 1996–97, sharing Bristol Rugby Club's Memorial Ground. Clydebank shared Dumbarton's Boghead Park from 1996–97 until renting Greenock Morton's Cappielow Park in season 1999–2000. Brighton shared Gillingham's ground in seasons 1997–98, 1998–99. Fulham shared QPR's home at Loftus Road in seasons 2002–03, 2003–04, returning to Craven Cottage in Aug 2004. Coventry played home fixtures at Northampton in season 2013–14, returning to their own ground, the Ricoh Arena, in Sept 2014 Coventry were unable to agree terms to play at the Ricoh Arena in season 2019–20 and moved home games to Birmingham's St Andrew's Stadium.

Inverness Caledonian Thistle moved to share Aberdeen's Pittodrie Stadium in 2004–05 after being promoted to the SPL; Gretna's home matches on arrival in the SPL in 2007–08 were held at Motherwell and Livingston. Stenhousemuir (owners) share Ochilview with East Stirling (tenants).

ARTIFICIAL TURF

QPR were the first British club to install an artificial pitch, in 1981. They were followed by Luton in 1985, and Oldham and Preston in 1986. QPR reverted to grass in 1988, as did Luton and promoted Oldham in season 1991–92 (when artificial pitches were banned in Div 1). **Preston** were the last Football League club playing 'on plastic' in 1993–94, and their Deepdale ground was restored to grass for the start of 1994–95.

Stirling were the **first Scottish club** to play on plastic, in season 1987–88.

DOUBLE RUNNERS-UP

There have been nine instances of clubs finishing runner-up in **both the League Championship** and **FA Cup** in the same season: 1928 Huddersfield; 1932 Arsenal; 1939 Wolves; 1962 Burnley; 1965 and 1970 Leeds; 1986 Everton; 1995 Manchester Utd; 2001 Arsenal.

CORNER-KICK RECORDS

Not a single corner-kick was recorded when **Newcastle** drew 0-0 at home to **Portsmouth** (Div 1) on Dec 5, 1931.

The record for **most corners** in a match for one side is believed to be **Sheffield Utd's 28** to **West Ham's 1** in Div 2 at Bramall Lane on Oct 14, 1989. For all their pressure, Sheffield Utd lost 2-0.

Nottm Forest led **Southampton** 22-2 on corners (Premier League, Nov 28, 1992) but lost the match 1-2.

Tommy Higginson (Brentford, 1960s) once passed back to his own goalkeeper from a corner kick.

When **Wigan** won 4-0 at home to Cardiff (Div 2) on Feb 16, 2002, all four goals were headed in from corners taken by N Ireland international **Peter Kennedy**.

Steve Staunton (Rep of Ireland) is believed to be the only player to score direct from a corner in **two** Internationals.

In the 2012 Champions League Final, **Bayern Munich** forced 20 corners without scoring, while **Chelsea** scored from their only one.

SACKED AT HALF-TIME

Leyton Orient sacked **Terry Howard** on his 397th appearance for the club – at half-time in a Second Division home defeat against Blackpool (Feb 7, 1995) for 'an unacceptable performance'. He was fined two weeks' wages, given a free transfer and moved to Wycombe.

Bobby Gould resigned as **Peterborough**'s head coach at half-time in their 1-0 defeat in the LDV Vans Trophy 1st round at Bristol City on Sep 29, 2004.

Harald Schumacher, former Germany goalkeeper, was sacked as Fortuna Koln coach when they were two down at half-time against Waldhof Mannheim (Dec 15, 1999). They lost 5-1.

MOST GAMES BY 'KEEPER FOR ONE CLUB

Alan Knight made 683 League appearances for Portsmouth, over 23 seasons (1978–2000), a record for a goalkeeper at one club. The previous holder was Peter Bonetti with 600 League games for Chelsea (20 seasons, 1960–79).

PLAYED TWO GAMES ON SAME DAY

Jack Kelsey played full-length matches for both club and country on Wednesday Nov 26, 1958. In the afternoon he kept goal for Wales in a 2-2 draw against England at Villa Park, and he then drove to Highbury to help Arsenal win 3-1 in a prestigious floodlit friendly against Juventus.

On the same day, winger **Danny Clapton** played for England (against Wales and Kelsey) and then in part of Arsenal's match against Juventus.

On Nov 11, 1987, **Mark Hughes** played for Wales against Czechoslovakia (European Championship) in Prague, then flew to Munich and went on as substitute that night in a winning Bayern Munich team, to whom he was on loan from Barcelona.

On Feb 16, 1993 goalkeeper **Scott Howie** played in Scotland's 3-0 U-21 win v Malta at Tannadice Park, Dundee (ko 1.30pm) and the same evening played in Clyde's 2-1 home win v Queen of South (Div 2).

Ryman League **Hornchurch**, faced by end-of-season fixture congestion, played **two matches** on the same night (May 1, 2001). They lost 2-1 at home to Ware and drew 2-2 at Clapton.

RECORD LOSS

Manchester City made a record loss of £194.9m in the 2010–11 financial year.

FIRST 'MATCH OF THE DAY'

BBC TV (recorded highlights): Liverpool 3, Arsenal 2 on Aug 22, 1964. **First complete match to be televised:** Arsenal 3, Everton 2 on Aug 29, 1936. **First League match televised in colour:** Liverpool 2, West Ham 0 on Nov 15, 1969.

'MATCH OF THE DAY' – BIGGEST SCORES

Football League: Tottenham 9, Bristol Rov 0 (Div 2, 1977–78). **Premier League:** Nottm Forest 1, Manchester Utd 8 (1998–99); Portsmouth 7 Reading 4 (2007–08).

FIRST COMMENTARY ON RADIO

Arsenal 1 Sheffield Utd 1 (Div 1) broadcast on BBC, Jan 22, 1927.

OLYMPIC FOOTBALL WINNERS

1908 Great Britain (in London); **1912** Great Britain (Stockholm); **1920** Belgium (Antwerp); **1924** Uruguay (Paris); **1928** Uruguay (Amsterdam); **1932** No soccer in Los Angeles Olympics; **1936** Italy (Berlin); **1948** Sweden (London); **1952** Hungary (Helsinki); **1956** USSR (Melbourne); **1960** Yugoslavia (Rome); **1964** Hungary (Tokyo); **1968** Hungary (Mexico City); **1972** Poland (Munich); **1976** E Germany (Montreal); **1980** Czechoslovakia (Moscow); **1984** France (Los Angeles); **1988** USSR (Seoul); **1992** Spain (Barcelona); **1996** Nigeria (Atlanta); **2000** Cameroon (Sydney); **2004** Argentina (Athens); **2008** Argentina (Beijing); **2012** Mexico (Wembley); **2016** Brazil (Rio de Janeiro).

Highest scorer in Final tournament: Ferenc Bene (Hungary) 12 goals, 1964.
Record crowd for Olympic Soccer Final: 108,800 (France v Brazil, Los Angeles 1984).

MOST AMATEUR CUP WINS

Bishop Auckland set the FA Amateur Cup record with 10 wins, and in 1957 became the only club to carry off the trophy in three successive seasons. The competition was discontinued after the Final on Apr 20, 1974. (Bishop's Stortford 4, Ilford 1, at Wembley).

FOOTBALL FOUNDATION

This was formed (May 2000) to replace the **Football Trust**, which had been in existence since 1975 as an initiative of the Pools companies to provide financial support at all levels, from schools football to safety and ground improvement work throughout the game.

SEVEN-FIGURE TESTIMONIALS

The first was **Sir Alex Ferguson**'s at Old Trafford on Oct 11, 1999, when a full-house of 54,842 saw a Rest of the World team beat Manchester Utd 4-2. United's manager pledged that a large percentage of the estimated £1m receipts would go to charity.

Estimated receipts of £1m and over came from testimonials for **Denis Irwin** (Manchester Utd) against Manchester City at Old Trafford on Aug 16, 2000 (45,158); **Tom Boyd** (Celtic) against Manchester Utd at Celtic Park on May 15, 2001 (57,000) and **Ryan Giggs** (Manchester Utd) against Celtic on Aug 1, 2001 (66,967).

Tony Adams' second testimonial (1-1 v Celtic on May 13, 2002) two nights after Arsenal completed the Double, was watched by 38,021 spectators at Highbury. Of £1m receipts, he donated £500,000 to Sporting Chance, the charity that helps sportsmen/women with drink, drug, gambling problems.

Sunderland and a Republic of Ireland XI drew 0-0 in front of 35,702 at the Stadium of Light on May 14, 2002. The beneficiary, **Niall Quinn**, donated his testimonial proceeds, estimated at £1m, to children's hospitals in Sunderland and Dublin, and to homeless children in Africa and Asia.

A record testimonial crowd of 69,591 for **Roy Keane** at Old Trafford on May 9, 2006 netted more than £2m for charities in Dublin, Cork and Manchester. Manchester Utd beat Celtic 1-0, with Keane playing for both teams.

Alan Shearer's testimonial on May 11, 2006, watched by a crowd of 52,275 at St James' Park, raised more than £1m. The club's record scorer, in his farewell match, came off the bench in stoppage time to score the penalty that gave Newcastle a 3-2 win over Celtic. Total proceeds from his testimonial events, £1.64m, were donated to 14 charities in the north-east.

Ole Gunnar Solskjaer, who retired after 12 years as a Manchester Utd player, had a crowd of 68,868, for his testimonial on Aug 2, 2008 (United 1 Espanyol 0). He donated the estimated receipts of £2m to charity, including the opening of a dozen schools In Africa.

Liverpool's **Jamie Carragher** had his testimonial against Everton (4-1) on Sep 4, 2010. It was watched by a crowd of 35,631 and raised an estimated £1m for his foundation, which supports community projects on Merseyside.

Gary Neville donated receipts of around £1m from his testimonial against Juventus (2-1) in front of 42,000 on May 24, 2011, to charities and building a Supporters' Centre near Old Trafford.

Paul Scholes had a crowd of 75,000 for his testimonial, Manchester United against New York Cosmos, on Aug 5, 2011. Receipts were £1.5m.

Steven Gerrard, Liverpool captain, donated £500,000 from his testimonial to the local Alder Hey Children's Hospital after a match against Olympiacos was watched by a crowd of 44,362 on Aug 3, 2013. Gerrard chose the Greek champions because he scored a special goal against them in the season Liverpool won the 2005 Champions League.

Wayne Rooney's match against Everton on Aug 3, 2016, raised £1.2m, which the Manchester United captain donated to local children's charities.

WHAT IT USED TO COST

Minimum admission to League football was one shilling in 1939 After the war, it was increased to 1s 3d in 1946; 1s 6d in 1951; 1s 9d in 1952; 2s in 1955; 2s 6d; in 1960; 4s in 1965; 5s in 1968; 6s in 1970; and 8s (40p) in 1972 After that, the fixed minimum charge was dropped.

Wembley's first Cup Final programme in 1923 cost three pence (1¼p in today's money). The programme for the 'farewell' FA Cup Final in May, 2000 was priced £10.

FA Cup Final ticket prices in 2011 reached record levels – £115, £85, £65 and £45.

WHAT THEY USED TO EARN

In the 1930s, First Division players were on £8 a week (£6 in close season) plus bonuses of £2 win, £1 draw. The maximum wage went up to £12 when football resumed post-war in 1946 and had reached £20 by the time the limit was abolished in 1961.

EUROPEAN TROPHY WINNERS

European Cup/Champions League: 13 Real Madrid; **7** AC Milan; **6** Liverpool, Bayern Munich; **5** Barcelona; **4** Ajax; **3** Inter Milan, Manchester Utd; **2** Benfica, Juventus, Nottm Forest, Porto; **1** Aston Villa, Borussia Dortmund, Celtic, Chelsea, Feyenoord, Hamburg, Marseille, PSV Eindhoven, Red Star Belgrade, Steaua Bucharest

Cup-Winners' Cup: 4 Barcelona; **2** Anderlecht, Chelsea, Dynamo Kiev, AC Milan; **1** Aberdeen, Ajax, Arsenal, Atletico Madrid, Bayern Munich, Borussia Dortmund, Dynamo Tbilisi, Everton, Fiorentina, Hamburg, Juventus, Lazio, Magdeburg, Manchester City, Manchester Utd, Mechelen, Paris St Germain, Parma, Rangers, Real Zaragoza, Sampdoria, Slovan Bratislava, Sporting Lisbon, Tottenham, Valencia, Werder Bremen, West Ham.

UEFA Cup: 3 Barcelona, Inter Milan, Juventus, Liverpool, Valencia; **2** Borussia Moenchengladbach, Feyenoord, Gothenburg, Leeds, Parma, Real Madrid, Sevilla, Tottenham; **1** Anderlecht, Ajax, Arsenal, Bayer Leverkusen, Bayern Munich, CSKA Moscow, Dynamo Zagreb, Eintracht Frankfurt, Ferencvaros, Galatasaray, Ipswich, Napoli, Newcastle, Porto, PSV Eindhoven, Real Zaragoza, Roma, Schalke, Shakhtar Donetsk, Zenit St Petersburg.

Europa League: 4 Sevilla; **3** Atletico Madrid; **2** Chelsea; **1** Manchester Utd, Porto.

● The Champions League was introduced into the European Cup in 1992–93 to counter the threat of a European Super League. The UEFA Cup became the Europa League, with a new format, in season 2009–10.

BRITAIN'S 37 TROPHIES IN EUROPE

Euro Cup/Champs Lge (14)	Cup-Winners' Cup (10)	Fairs/UEFA Cup/Europa Lge (13)
1967 Celtic	1963 Tottenham	1968 Leeds
1968 Manchester Utd	1965 West Ham	1969 Newcastle
1977 Liverpool	1970 Manchester City	1970 Arsenal
1978 Liverpool	1971 Chelsea	1971 Leeds
1979 Nottm Forest	1972 Rangers	1972 Tottenham
1980 Nottm Forest	1983 Aberdeen	1973 Liverpool
1981 Liverpool	1985 Everton	1976 Liverpool
1982 Aston Villa	1991 Manchester Utd	1981 Ipswich
1984 Liverpool	1994 Arsenal	1984 Tottenham
1999 Manchester Utd	1998 Chelsea	2001 Liverpool
2005 Liverpool		2013 Chelsea
2008 Manchester Utd		2017 Manchester Utd
2012 Chelsea		2019 Chelsea
2019 Liverpool		

ENGLAND'S EUROPEAN RECORD

England had an unprecedented clean sweep of finalists in the two European club competitions in season 2018–19, with Liverpool defeating Tottenham in the Champions League and Chelsea beating Arsenal in the Europa League.

END OF CUP-WINNERS' CUP

The **European Cup-Winners' Cup**, inaugurated in 1960–61, terminated with the 1999 Final. The competition merged into a revamped **UEFA Cup**.

From its inception in 1955, the **European Cup** comprised only championship-winning clubs until 1998–99, when selected runners-up were introduced. Further expansion came in 1999–2000 with the inclusion of clubs finishing third in certain leagues and fourth in 2002.

EUROPEAN CLUB COMPETITIONS – SCORING RECORDS

European Cup – record aggregate: 18-0 by Benfica v Dudelange (Lux) (8-0a, 10-0h), prelim rd, 1965–66.

Record single-match score: 11-0 by Dinamo Bucharest v Crusaders (rd 1, 2nd leg, 1973-74 (agg 12-0).

Champions League – record single-match score: Liverpool 8-0 v Besiktas, Group A qual (Nov 6, 2007).

Highest match aggregate: 13 – Bayern Munich 12 Sporting Lisbon 1 (5-0 away, 7-1 at home, 1st ko rd, 2008–09)

Cup-Winners' Cup – *record aggregate: 21-0 by Chelsea v Jeunesse Hautcharage (Lux) (8-0a, 13-0h), 1st rd, 1971–72.

Record single-match score: 16-1 by Sporting Lisbon v Apoel Nicosia, 2nd round, 1st leg, 1963–64 (aggregate was 18-1).

UEFA Cup (prev Fairs Cup) – *Record aggregate: 21-0 by Feyenoord v US Rumelange (Lux) (9-0h, 12-0a), 1st round, 1972–73.

Record single-match score: 14-0 by Ajax Amsterdam v Red Boys (Lux) 1st rd, 2nd leg, 1984–85 (aggregate also 14-0).

Record British score in Europe: 13-0 by **Chelsea** at home to Jeunesse Hautcharage (Lux) in Cup-Winners' Cup 1st round, 2nd leg, 1971–72. Chelsea's overall 21-0 win in that tie is highest aggregate by British club in Europe.

Individual scoring record for European tie (over two legs): 10 goals (6 home, 4 away) by **Kiril Milanov** for Levski Spartak in 19-3 agg win Cup-Winners' Cup 1st round v Lahden Reipas, 1976–77. Next highest: **8 goals** by **Jose Altafini** for AC Milan v US Luxembourg (European Cup, prelim round, 1962–63, agg 14-0) and by **Peter Osgood** for Chelsea v Jeunesse Hautcharage (Cup-Winners' Cup, 1st round 1971–72, agg 21-0). Altafini and Osgood each scored 5 goals at home, 3 away.

Individual single-match scoring record in European competition: **6** by **Mascarenhas** for Sporting Lisbon in 16-1 Cup-Winner's Cup 2nd round, 1st leg win v Apoel, 1963–64; and by **Lothar Emmerich** for Borussia Dortmund in 8-0 CWC 1st round, 2nd leg win v Floriana 1965–66; and by **Kiril Milanov** for Levski Spartak in 12-2 CWC 1st round, 1st leg win v Lahden Reipas, 1976–77.

Most goals in single European campaign: 15 by **Jurgen Klinsmann** for Bayern Munich (UEFA Cup 1995–96).

Most goals by British player in European competition: 30 by **Peter Lorimer** (Leeds, in 9 campaigns).

Most individual goals in Champions League match: 5 by **Lionel Messi** (Barcelona) in 7-1 win at home to Bayer Leverkusen in round of 16 second leg, 2011–12.

Most European Cup goals by individual player: 49 by **Alfredo di Stefano** in 58 apps for Real Madrid (1955–64).

(*Joint record European aggregate)

First European treble: Clarence Seedorf became the first player to win the European Cup with three clubs: Ajax in 1995, Real Madrid in 1998 and AC Milan in 2003.

EUROPEAN FOOTBALL – BIG RECOVERIES

In the most astonishing Final in the history of the European Cup/Champions League, **Liverpool** became the first club to win it from a 3-0 deficit when they beat AC Milan 3-2 on penalties after a 3-3 draw in Istanbul on May 25, 2005. Liverpool's fifth triumph in the competition meant that they would keep the trophy.

The following season, **Middlesbrough** twice recovered from three-goal aggregate deficits in the **UEFA Cup**, beating Basel 4-3 in the quarter finals and Steaua Bucharest by the same scoreline in the semi-finals. In 2010, **Fulham** beat Juventus 5-4 after trailing 1-4 on aggregate in the second leg of their Europa League, Round of 16 match at Craven Cottage.

Two Scottish clubs have won a European tie from a 3-goal, first leg deficit: **Kilmarnock** 0-3, 5-1 v Eintracht Frankfurt (Fairs Cup 1st round, 1964–65); **Hibernian** 1-4, 5-0 v Napoli (Fairs Cup 2nd Round, 1967–68).

English clubs have three times gone out of the **UEFA Cup** after leading 3-0 from the first leg: 1975–76 (2nd Rd) **Ipswich** lost 3-4 on agg to Bruges; 1976–77 (quarter-final) **QPR** lost on penalties to AEK Athens after 3-3 agg; 1977–78 (3rd round) **Ipswich** lost on penalties to Barcelona after 3-3 agg.

On Oct 16, 2012, Sweden recovered from 0-4 down to draw 4-4 with Germany (World Cup qual) in Berlin.

● In the **1966 World Cup quarter-final** (Jul 23) at Goodison Park, North Korea led Portugal 3-0, but Eusebio scored 4 times to give **Portugal** a 5-3 win.

RONALDO'S EURO CENTURY

Cristiano Ronaldo became the first player to reach a century of goals in European club competitions when scoring twice for Real Madrid away to Bayern Munich on Apr 12, 2017. He reached the hundred in 143 matches (84 for Real, 16 for Manchester Utd) in the Champions League (97), UEFA Super Cup (2) and Champions League qualifying round (1).

RECORD COMEBACK

The greatest turnaround in Champions League history took place in a round of 16 match on Mar 8, 2017. **Barcelona**, 0-4 down to Paris St Germain, won the return leg 6-1, scoring three goals in the last seven minutes.

HEAVIEST ENGLISH-CLUB DEFEATS IN EUROPE

(Single-leg scores)

Champions League: Porto 5 Leicester 0 (group, Dec 6, 2016); Tottenham 2 Bayern Munich 7 (group, Oct 1, 2019)

European Cup: Artmedia Bratislava 5, **Celtic** 0 (2nd qual round), Jul 2005 (agg 5-4); Ajax 5, **Liverpool** 1 (2nd round), Dec 1966 (agg 7-3); Real Madrid 5, **Derby** 1 (2nd round), Nov 1975 (agg 6-5).

Cup-Winners' Cup: Sporting Lisbon 5, **Manchester Utd** 0 (quarter-final), Mar 1964 (agg 6-4).

Fairs/UEFA Cup: Bayern Munich 6, **Coventry** 1 (2nd round), Oct 1970 (agg 7-3). **Combined London** team lost 6-0 (agg 8-2) in first Fairs Cup Final in 1958. Barcelona 5, **Chelsea** 0 in Fairs Cup semi-final play-off, 1966, in Barcelona (after 2-2 agg).

SHOCK ENGLISH CLUB DEFEATS

1968–69 (Eur Cup, 1st round): **Manchester City** beaten by Fenerbahce, 1-2 agg.
1971–72 (CWC, 2nd round): **Chelsea** beaten by Atvidaberg on away goals.
1993–94 (Eur Cup, 2nd round): **Manchester Utd** beaten by Galatasaray on away goals.
1994–95 (UEFA Cup, 1st round): **Blackburn** beaten by Trelleborgs, 2-3 agg.
2000–01 (UEFA Cup, 1st round): **Chelsea** beaten by St Gallen, Switz 1-2 agg.

PFA FAIR PLAY AWARD (Bobby Moore Trophy from 1993)

1988	Liverpool	2003	Crewe
1989	Liverpool	2004	Crewe
1990	Liverpool	2005	Crewe
1991	Nottm Forest	2006	Crewe
1992	Portsmouth	2007	Crewe
1993	Norwich	2008	Crewe
1994	Crewe	2009	Stockport
1995	Crewe	2010	Rochdale
1996	Crewe	2011	Rochdale
1997	Crewe	2012	Chesterfield
1998	Cambridge Utd	2013	Crewe
1999	Grimsby	2014	Exeter
2000	Crewe	2015	Exeter
2001	Hull	2016	Walsall
2002	Crewe	2017	Bradford City

RECORD MEDAL SALES

At Sotherby's in London on Nov 11, 2014, the FA Cup winner's medal which **Sir Stanley Matthews** earned with Blackpool in 1953 was sold for £220,000 – the most expensive medal in British sporting history. At the same auction, **Ray Wilson's** 1966 World Cup winner's medal fetched £136,000, while **Jimmy Greaves**, who was left out of the winning England team, received £44,000 for the medal the FA belatedly awarded him in 2009

West Ham bought (Jun 2000) the late **Bobby Moore**'s collection of medals and trophies for £1.8m at Christie's auction. It was put up for sale by his first wife Tina and included his World Cup-winner's medal.

A No. 6 duplicate red shirt made for England captain **Bobby Moore** for the 1966 World Cup Final fetched £44,000 at an auction at Wolves' ground in Sep, 1999. Moore kept the shirt he wore in that Final and gave the replica to England physio Harold Shepherdson.

Sir Geoff Hurst's 1966 World Cup-winning shirt fetched a record £91,750 at Christie's in Sep, 2000. His World Cup Final cap fetched £37,600 and his Man of the Match trophy £18,800. Proceeds totalling £274,410 from the 129 lots went to Hurst's three daughters and charities of his choice, including the Bobby Moore Imperial Cancer Research Fund.

In Aug, 2001, Sir Geoff sold his World Cup-winner's medal to his former club West Ham Utd (for their museum) at a reported £150,000.

'The **Billy Wright** Collection' – caps, medals and other memorabilia from his illustrious career – fetched over £100,000 at Christie's in Nov, 1996.

At the sale in Oct 1993, trophies, caps and medals earned by **Ray Kennedy**, former England, Arsenal and Liverpool player, fetched a then record total of £88,407. Kennedy, suffering from Parkinson's Disease, received £73,000 after commission. The PFA paid £31,080 for a total of 60 lots – including a record £16,000 for his 1977 European Cup winner's medal – to be exhibited at their Manchester museum. An anonymous English collector paid £17,000 for the medal and plaque commemorating Kennedy's part in the Arsenal Double in 1971.

Previous record for one player's medals, shirts etc collection: £30,000 (**Bill Foulkes**, Manchester Utd in 1992). The sale of **Dixie Dean**'s medals etc in 1991 realised £28,000.

In Mar, 2001, **Gordon Banks**' 1966 World Cup-winner's medal fetched a new record £124,750. TV's Nick Hancock, a Stoke fan, paid £23,500 for **Sir Stanley Matthews**'s 1953 FA Cup-winner's medal. He also bought one of Matthews's England caps for £3,525 and paid £2,350 for a Stoke Div 2 Championship medal (1963).

Dave Mackay's 1961 League Championship and FA Cup winner's medals sold for £18,000 at Sotherby's. Tottenham bought them for their museum.

A selection of England World Cup-winning manager **Sir Alf Ramsey**'s memorabilia – England caps, championship medals with Ipswich etc. – fetched more than £80,000 at Christie's. They were offered for sale by his family, and his former clubs Tottenham and Ipswich were among the buyers.

Ray Wilson's 1966 England World Cup-winning shirt fetched £80,750. Also in Mar, 2002, the No. 10 shirt worn by **Pele** in Brazil's World Cup triumph in 1970 was sold for a record £157,750 at Christies. It went to an anonymous telephone bidder.

In Oct, 2003, **George Best**'s European Footballer of the Year (1968) trophy was sold to an anonymous British bidder for £167,250 at Bonham's. It was the then most expensive item of sporting memorabilia ever auctioned in Britain.

England captain **Bobby Moore**'s 1970 World Cup shirt, which he swapped with Pele after Brazil's 1-0 win in Mexico, was sold for £60,000 at Christie's in Mar, 2004.

Sep, 2004: England shirt worn by tearful **Paul Gascoigne** in 1990 World Cup semi-final v Germany sold at Christie's for £28,680. At same auction, shirt worn by Brazil's **Pele** in 1958 World Cup Final in Sweden sold for £70,505.

May, 2005: The **second FA Cup** (which was presented to winning teams from 1896 to 1909) was bought for £420,000 at Christie's by Birmingham chairman David Gold, a world record for an item of football memorabilia. It was presented to the National Football Museum, Preston. At the same auction, the World Cup-winner's medal earned by England's **Alan Ball** in 1966 was sold for £164,800.

Oct, 2005: At auction at Bonham's, the medals and other memorabilia of Hungary and Real Madrid legend **Ferenc Puskas** were sold for £85,000 to help pay for hospital treatment.

Nov, 2006: A ball used in the 2006 World Cup Final and signed by the winning **Italy** team was sold for £1.2m (a world record for football memorabilia) at a charity auction in Qatar. It was bought by the Qatar Sports Academy.

Feb, 2010: A pair of boots worn by **Sir Stanley Matthews** in the 1953 FA Cup Final was sold at Bonham's for £38,400.

Oct, 2010: Trophies and memorabilia belonging to **George Best** were sold at Bonham's for £193,440. His 1968 European Cup winner's medal fetched £156,000.

Oct–Nov 2010: **Nobby Stiles** sold his 1966 World Cup winner's medal at an Edinburgh auction for a record £188,200. His old club, Manchester Utd, also paid £48,300 for his 1968 European Cup medal to go to the club's museum at Old Trafford. In London, the shirt worn by Stiles in the 1966 World Cup Final went for £75,000. A total of 45 items netted £424,438. **George Cohen** and **Martin Peters** had previously sold their medals from 1966.

Oct 2011: **Terry Paine** (who did not play in the Final) sold his 1966 World Cup medal for £27,500 at auction.

Mar 2013: **Norman Hunter** (Leeds and England) sold his honours' collection on line for nearly £100,000

Nov 2013: A collection of **Nat Lofthouse**'s career memorabilia was sold at auction for £100,000. Bolton Council paid £75,000 for items including his 1958 FA Cup winner's medal to go on show at the local museum.

LONGEST UNBEATEN CUP RUN

Liverpool established the longest unbeaten Cup sequence by a Football League club: 25 successive rounds in the League/Milk Cup between semi-final defeat by Nottm Forest (1-2 agg) in 1980 and defeat at Tottenham (0-1) in the third round on Oct 31, 1984. During this period Liverpool won the tournament in four successive seasons, a feat no other Football League club has achieved in any competition.

BIG HALF-TIME SCORES

Tottenham 10, Crewe 1 (FA Cup 4th round replay, Feb 3, 1960; result 13-2); Tranmere 8, Oldham 1 (Div 3N., Dec 26, 1935; result 13-4); **Chester City 8, York 0** (Div 3N., Feb 1, 1936; result 12-0; believed to be record half-time scores in League football).

Nine goals were scored in the first half – **Burnley 4, Watford 5** in Div 1 on Apr 5, 2003. Result: 4-7.

Stirling Albion led Selkirk 15-0 at half-time (result 20-0) in the Scottish Cup 1st round, Dec 8, 1984.

World record half-time score: **16-0** when **Australia** beat **American Samoa** 31-0 (another world record) in the World Cup Oceania qualifying group at Coff's Harbour, New South Wales, on Apr 11 2001.

- On Mar 4 1933 **Coventry** beat QPR (Div 3 South) 7-0, having led by that score at half-time. This repeated the half-time situation in Bristol City's 7-0 win over Grimsby on Dec 26, 1914.

TOP SECOND-HALF TEAM

Most goals scored by a team in one half of a League match is **11. Stockport** led Halifax 2-0 at half-time in Div 3 North on Jan 6 1934 and won 13-0.

FIVE NOT ENOUGH

Last team to score **5** in League match and lose: **Burton**, beaten 6-5 by Cheltenham (Lge 2, Mar 13, 2010).

LONG SERVICE WITH ONE CLUB

Bill Nicholson, OBE, was associated with Tottenham for 67 years – as a wing-half (1938–55), then the club's most successful manager (1958–74) with 8 major prizes, subsequently chief advisor and scout. He became club president, and an honorary freeman of the borough, had an executive suite named after him at the club, and the stretch of roadway from Tottenham High Road to the main gates has the nameplate Bill Nicholson Way. He died, aged 85, in Oct 2004.

Ted Bates, the Grand Old Man of Southampton with 66 years of unbroken service to the club, was awarded the Freedom of the City in Apr, 2001. He joined Saints as an inside-forward from Norwich in 1937, made 260 peace-time appearances for the club, became reserve-team trainer in 1953 and manager at The Dell for 18 years (1955–73), taking Southampton into the top division in 1966. He was subsequently chief executive, director and club president. He died in Oct 2003, aged 85.

Bob Paisley was associated with Liverpool for 57 years from 1939, when he joined them from Bishop Auckland, until he died in Feb 1996. He served as player, trainer, coach, assistant-manager, manager, director and vice-president. He was Liverpool's most successful manager, winning 13 major trophies for the club (1974–83).

Dario Gradi, MBE, stepped down after completing 24 seasons and more than 1,000 matches as manager of Crewe (appointed Jun 1983). Never a League player, he previously managed Wimbledon and Crystal Palace. At Crewe, his policy of finding and grooming young talent has earned the club more than £20m in transfer fees. He stayed with Crewe as technical director, and twice took charge of team affairs again following the departure of the managers who succeeded him, Steve Holland and Gudjon Thordarson.

Ronnie Moran, who joined Liverpool in as a player 1952, retired from the Anfield coaching staff in season 1998–99.

Ernie Gregory served West Ham for 52 years as goalkeeper and coach. He joined them as boy of 14 from school in 1935, retired in May 1987.

Ryan Giggs played 24 seasons for Manchester Utd (1990-2014), then became assistant manager under Louis van Gaal.

Ted Sagar, Everton goalkeeper, 23 years at Goodison Park (1929–52, but only 16 League seasons because of war).

Alan Knight, goalkeeper, played 23 seasons (1977–2000) for his only club, Portsmouth.

Sam Bartram was recognised as one of the finest goalkeepers never to play for England, apart from unofficial wartime games. He was with Charlton from 1934–56

Jack Charlton, England World Cup winner, served Leeds from 1952–73.
Roy Sproson, defender, played 21 League seasons for his only club, Port Vale (1950–71).
John Terry had a 22-year association with Chelsea from 1994–2017.

TIGHT AT HOME

Fewest home goals conceded in League season (modern times): 4 by **Liverpool** (Div 1, 1978–9);
4 by **Manchester Utd** (Premier League, 1994–95) – both in 21 matches.

VARSITY MATCH

First played in 1873, this is the game's second oldest contest (after the FA Cup). Played 135,
Oxford 53 wins, Cambridge 50, draws 32. Goals: Oxford 218, Cambridge 208. The latest
match, at The Hive, Barnet, was drawn 1-1, with Cambridge winning 5-3 on penalties.

TRANSFER WINDOW

This was introduced to Britain in Sep 2002 via FIFA regulations to bring uniformity across
Europe (the rule previously applied in a number of other countries).
The transfer of contracted players is restricted to two periods: Jun 1–Aug 31 and Jan 1–31).
On appeal, Football League clubs continued to sign/sell players (excluding deals with Premier
League clubs).

PROGRAMME PIONEERS

Chelsea pioneered football's magazine-style programme by introducing a 16-page issue for the First
Division match against Portsmouth on Christmas Day 1948. It cost sixpence (2.5p). A penny
programme from the 1909 FA Cup Final fetched £23,500 at a London auction in May, 2012.

FOOTBALL POOLS

Littlewoods launched them in 1923 with capital of £100. Coupons (4,000 of them) were first
issued outside Manchester United's ground, the original 35 investors staking a total of £4 7s
6d (pay-out £2 12s). Vernons joined Littlewoods as leading promoters. The Treble Chance,
leading to bonanza dividends, was introduced in 1946 and the Pools Panel began in January
1963 to counter mass fixture postponements caused by the Big Freeze winter.
But business was hard hit by the launch of the National Lottery in 1994. Dividends slumped,
the work-force was cut severely and in June 2000 the Liverpool-based Moores family sold
Littlewoods Pools in a £161m deal. After 85 years, the name Littlewoods disappeared from
Pools betting in August 2008. The New Football Pools was formed. Vernons and Zetters
continued to operate in their own name under the ownership of Sportech. The record prize
remains the £2,924,622 paid to a syndicate in Worsley, Manchester, in November 1994.

WORLD'S OLDEST FOOTBALL ANNUAL

Now in its 134th edition, this publication began as the 16-page Athletic News Football
Supplement & Club Directory in 1887. From the long-established Athletic News, it became the
Sunday Chronicle Annual in 1946, the Empire News in 1956, the News of the World & Empire
News in 1961 and the News of the World Annual from 1965 until becoming the Nationwide
Annual in 2008.

PREMIER LEAGUE CLUB DETAILS AND SQUADS 2020–21

(at time of going to press)

ARSENAL

Ground: Emirates Stadium, Highbury, London, N5 IBU
Telephone: 0207 619 5003. **Club nickname:** Gunners
Capacity: 60,260. **Colours:** Red and white. **Shirt sponsor:** Emirates
Record transfer fee: £72m to Lille for Nicolas Pepe, Aug 2019
Record fee received: £35m from Barcelona for Cesc Fabregas, Aug 2011; £35m from Liverpool for Alex Oxlade-Chamberlain, 8/17
Record attendance: Highbury: 73,295 v Sunderland (Div 1) Mar 9,1935. Emirates Stadium: 60,161 v Manchester Utd (Prem Lge) Nov 3,2007. Wembley: 73,707 v Lens (Champ Lge) Nov 25,1998
League Championship: Winners 1930–31, 1932–33, 1933–34, 1934–35, 1937–38, 1947–48, 1952–53, 1970–71, 1988–89, 1990–91, 1997–98, 2001–02, 2003–04
FA Cup: Winners 1930, 1936, 1950, 1971, 1979, 1993, 1998, 2002, 2003, 2005, 2014, 2015, 2017
League Cup: Winners 1987, 1993
Finishing positions in Premier League: 1992–93 10th, 1993–94 4th, 1994–95 12th, 1995–96 5th, 1996–97 3rd, 1997–98 1st, 1998–99 2nd, 1999–2000 2nd, 2000–01 2nd, 2001–02 1st, 2002–03 2nd, 2003–04 1st, 2004–05 2nd, 2005–06 4th, 2006–07 4th, 2007–08 3rd, 2008–09 4th, 2009–10 3rd, 2010–11 4th, 2011–12 3rd, 2012–13 4th, 2013–14 4th, 2014–15 3rd, 2015–16 2nd, 2016–17 5th, 2017–18 6th, 2018–19 5th, 2019–20 8th
Biggest win: 12-0 v Loughborough (Div 2) Mar 12, 1900
Biggest defeat: 0-8 v Loughborough (Div 2) Dec 12, 1896
Highest League scorer in a season: Ted Drake 42 (1934–35)
Most League goals in aggregate: Thierry Henry 175 (1999–2007) (2012)
Longest unbeaten League sequence: 49 matches (2003–04)
Longest sequence without a League win: 23 matches (1912–13)
Most capped player: Thierry Henry (France) 81

Name	Ht ft in	Previous club	Birthplace	Birthdate
Goalkeepers				
Leno, Bernd	6.3	Bayer Leverkusen	Bietighem-Bissingen, Ger	04.03.92
Macey, Matt	6.7	Bristol Rov	Bath	09.09.94
Martinez, Damian	6.4	Independiente	Mar del Plata, Arg	02.09.92
Defenders				
Bellerin, Hector	5.10	Barcelona	Barcelona, Sp	19.03.95
Chambers, Calum	6.0	Southampton	Petersfield	20.01.95
Holding, Rob	6.0	Bolton	Tameside	12.09.95
Kolasinac, Sead	6.0	Schalke	Karlsruhe, Ger	20.06.93
Koscielny, Laurent	6.1	Lorient	Tulle, Fr	10.09.85
Luiz, David	6.2	Chelsea	Diadema, Br	22.04.87
Mari, Pablo	6.4	Flamengo	Valencia	31.08.93
Mustafi, Shkodran	6.1	Valencia	Bad Hersfeld, Ger	17.04.92
Saliba, William	6.4	Saint-Etienne	Bondy, Fr	24.03.01
Soares, Cedric	5.8	Southampton	Singen, Ger	31.08.91
Sokratis	6.1	Borussia Dortmund	Kalamata, Gre	09.06.88
Tierney, Kieran	5.10	Celtic	Douglas, IOM	05.06.97
Midfielders				
Ceballos, Dani	5.10	Real Madrid (loan)	Utrera, Sp	07.08.96

Guendouzi, Matteo	6.1	Lorient	Poissy, Fr	14.04.99
Maitland-Niles, Ainsley	5.10	–	Goodmayes	29.08.97
Ozil, Mesut	5.11	Real Madrid	Gelsenkirchen, Ger	15.10.88
Smith Rowe, Emile	6.0	–	Croydon	28.07.00
Torreira, Lucas	5.6	Sampdoria	Fray Bentos, Uru	11.02.96
Xhaka, Granit	6.1	Borussia M'gladbach	Basle, Swi	27.09.92
Willian	5.9	Chelsea	Ribeirao Pires, Br	09.08.88
Willock, Joe	5.10	–	Waltham Foret	20.08.99
Forwards				
Aubameyang, Pierre-Emerick	6.2	Borussia Dortmund	Laval, Fr	18.06.89
Lacazette, Alexandre	5.9	Lyon	Lyon, Fr	28.05.91
Nelson, Reiss	5.9	–	Elephant and Castle	10.12.99
Nketiah, Eddie	5.9	–	Lewisham	30.05.99
Pepe, Nicolas	6.0	Lille	Mantes-la-Jolie, Fr	29.05.95
Saka, Bukayo	5.10	–	Ealing	05.09.01

ASTON VILLA

Ground: Villa Park, Trinity Road, Birmingham, B6 6HE
Telephone: 0333 323 1874. **Club nickname:** Villans
Capacity: 42,682. **Colours:** Claret and blue. **Shirt sponsor:** Cazoo
Record transfer fee: £22m to Club Bruges for Wesley, Jun 2019
Record fee received: £32.5m from Liverpool for Christian Benteke, Jul 2015
Record attendance: 76,588 v Derby (FA Cup 6) Mar 2, 1946
League Championship: Winners 1893–94, 1895–96, 1896–97, 1898–99, 1899–1900, 1909–10, 1980–81
FA Cup: Winners 1887, 1895, 1897, 1905, 1913, 1920, 1957
League Cup: Winners 1961, 1975, 1977, 1994, 1996
European competitions: Winners European Cup 1981–82; European Super Cup 1982
Finishing positions in Premier League: 1992–93 2nd, 1993–94 10th, 1994–95 18th, 1995–96 4th, 1996–97 5th, 1997–98 7th, 1998–99 6th, 1999–2000 6th, 2000–01 8th, 2001–02 8th, 2002–03 16th, 2003–04 6th, 2004–05 10th, 2005–06 16th, 2006–07 11th, 2007–08 6th, 2008–09 6th, 2009–10 6th, 2010–11 9th, 2011–12 16th, 2012–13th 15th, 2013–14 15th, 2014–15 17th, 2015–16 20th, 2019–20 17th
Biggest win: 12-2 v Accrington (Div 1) Mar 12, 1892; 11-1 v Charlton (Div 2) Nov 24, 1959; 10-0 v Sheffield Wed (Div 1) Oct 5, 1912, v Burnley (Div 1) Aug 29, 1925. Also: 13-0 v Wednesbury (FA Cup 1) Oct 30, 1886
Biggest defeat: 0-8 v Chelsea (Prem Lge) Dec 23, 2012
Highest League scorer in a season: 'Pongo' Waring 49 (1930–31)
Most League goals in aggregate: Harry Hampton 215 (1904–15)
Longest unbeaten League sequence: 15 matches (1897, 1909–10 and 1949
Longest sequence without a League win: 19 matches (2015–16)
Most capped player: Steve Staunton (Republic of Ireland) 64

Goalkeepers

Heaton, Tom	6.1	Burnley	Chester	15.04.86
Nyland, Orjan	6.3	Ingolstadt	Kristiansund, Nor	10.09.90
Steer, Jed	6.3	Norwich	Norwich	23.09.92
Defenders				
Bree, James	5.10	Barnsley	Wakefield	11.10.97
Engels, Bjorn	6.4	Reims	Kaprijke, Bel	15.09.94
Guilbert, Frederic	5.10	Caen	Valognes, Fr	24.12.94
Hause, Kortney	6.3	Wolves	Goodmayes	16.07.95
Konsa, Ezri	6.0	Brentford	Newham	23.10.97
Mings, Tyrone	6.3	Bournemouth	Bath	13.03.93

Taylor, Neil	5.9	Swansea	St Asaph	07.02.89
Midfielders				
Douglas Luiz	5.9	Manchester City	Rio de Janeiro, Br	09.05.98
El Ghazi, Anwar	6.2	Lille	Barendrecht, Hol	03.05.95
Elmohamady, Ahmed	5.11	Hull	Basyoun, Egy	09.09.87
Grealish, Jack	5.9	–	Solihull	10.09.95
Hourihane, Conor	6.0	Barnsley	Cork, Ire	02.02.91
Jota	5.11	Birmingham	Pobra do Caraminal, Sp	16.06.91
Lansbury, Henri	6.0	Nottm Forest	Enfield	12.10.90
Marvelous Nakamba	5.10	Club Bruges	Hwange, Zim	19.01.94
McGinn, John	5.10	Hibernian	Glasgow	18.10.94
Targett, Matt	6.0	Southampton	Eastleigh	18.09.95
Trezeguet	5.11	Kasimpasa	Kafr El Sheikh, Egy	01.10.94
Forwards				
Borja Baston	6.3	Swansea	Madrid, Sp	25.08.92
Davis, Keinan	6.3	–	Stevenage	13.02.98
Gelhardt, Joe	5.10	Wigan	Liverpool	04.05.02
Hogan, Scott	5.11	Brentford	Salford	13.04.92
Samatta, Mbwana	6.0	Genk	Dar es SalaAm, Tanz	23.12.92
Vassilev, Indiana	5.8	–	Savannah, US	16.02.01
Wesley	6.2	Club Bruges	Juiz de Fora, Br	26.11.96

BRIGHTON AND HOVE ALBION

Ground: American Express Community Stadium, Village Way, Brighton BN1 9BL
Telephone: 0344 324 6282. **Club nickname:** Seagulls
Capacity: 30,666. **Colours:** Blue and white. **Shirt sponsor:** American Express
Record transfer fee: £20m to Bristol City for Adam Webster, Aug 2019 and to Brentford for Neal Maupay Aug 2019
Record fee received: £15m from Fulham for Anthony Knockaert, Jul 2020
Record attendance: Goldstone Ground: 36,747 v Fulham (Div 2) Dec 27, 1958; Withdean Stadium: 8,729 v Manchester City (League Cup 2) Sep 24, 2008; Amex Stadium: 30,634 v Liverpool (Prem Lge) Dec 2, 2017
League Championship: 13th 1981–82
FA Cup: Runners-up 1983
League Cup: Fifth round 1979
Finishing position in Premier League: 2017–18 15th, 2018–19 17th, 2019–2015th
Biggest win: 10-1 v Wisbech (FA Cup 1) Nov 13, 1965
Biggest defeat: 0-9 v Middlesbrough (Div 2) Aug 23, 1958
Highest League scorer in a season: Peter Ward 32 (1976–77)
Most League goals in aggregate: Tommy Cook 114 (1922–29)
Longest unbeaten League sequence: 22 matches (2015)
Longest sequence without a League win: 15 matches (1972–73)
Most capped player: Shane Duffy (Republic of Ireland) 28

Goalkeepers				
Button, David	6.3	Fulham	Stevenage	27.02.89
Ryan, Mathew	6.1	Valencia	Plumpton, Aus	08.04.92
Steele, Jason	6.2	Sunderland	Newton Aycliffe	18.08.90
Defenders				
Bernardo	6.1	Leipzig	Sao Paulo, Br	14.05.95
Burn, Dan	6.7	Wigan	Blyth	09.05.92
Duffy, Shane	6.4	Blackburn	Derry	01.01.92
Dunk, Lewis	6.4	–	Brighton	1.11.91
Lamptey, Tariq	5.5	Chelsea	Hillingdon	30.09.00

Montoya, Martin	5.9	Valencia	Barcelona, Sp	04.04.91
Schelotto, Ezequiel	6.2	Sporting CP	Buenos Aires, Arg	23.05.89
Veltman, Joel	6.0	Ajax	Ijmuiden, Hol	15.01.92
Webster, Adam	6.3	Bristol City	West Wittering	04.01.95
Midfielders				
Alzate, Steven	5.11	Leyton Orient	Camden	08.09.98
Bissouma, Yves	6.0	Lille	Issia, Iv C	30.08.96
Gross, Pascal	6.0	Ingolstadt	Mannheim, Ger	15.06.91
Izquierdo, Jose	5.8	Club Bruges	Pereira, Col	07.07.92
Lallana, Adam	5.10	Liverpool	Bournemouth	10.05.88
MacAllister, Alexis	5.9	Argentinos	La Pampa, Arg	24.12.98
March, Solly	5.11	–	Eastbourne	20.07.94
Maupay, Neal	5.7	Brentford	Versailles, Fr	14.08.96
Mooy, Aaron	5.11	Huddersfield	Sydney, Aus	15.09.90
Propper, Davy	6.1	PSV Eindhoven	Arnhem, Hol	02.09.91
Stephens, Dale	5.7	Charlton	Bolton	12.06.89
Forwards				
Andone, Florin	5.11	Dep La Coruna	Botosani, Rom	11.04.93
Connolly, Aaron	5.10	Mervue	Galway, Ire	28.01.00
Jahanbakhsh, Alireza	5.11	Alkmaar	Jirandeh, Ira	11.08.93
Locadia, Jurgen	6.1	PSV Eindhoven	Emmen, Hol	07.11.93
Murray, Glenn	6.1	Bournemouth	Maryport	25.09.83
Trossard, Leandro	5.8	Genk	Waterschei, Bel	04.12.94

BURNLEY

Ground: Turf Moor, Harry Potts Way, Burnley BB10 4BX
Telephone: 0871 221 1882. **Club nickname:** Clarets
Capacity: 21,944. **Colours:** Claret and blue. **Shirt sponsor:** LoveBet
Record transfer fee: £15m to Leeds for Chris Wood, Aug 2017, £15m to Middlesbrough for Ben Gibson, Aug 2018
Record fee received: £25m from Everton for Michael Keane, Jul 2017
Record attendance: 54,775 v Huddersfield (FA Cup 3) Feb 23, 1924
League Championship: Winners 1920–21, 1959–60
FA Cup: Winners 1914
League Cup: Semi-finals 1961, 1969, 1983, 2009
European competitions: European Cup quarter-finals 1960–61
Finishing positions in Premier League: 2014–15 19th, 2016–17 16th, 2017–18 7th, 2018–19 15th, 2019–20 10th
Biggest win: 9-0 v Darwen (Div 1) Jan 9, 1892, v Crystal Palace (FA Cup 2) Feb 10, 1909, v New Brighton (FA up 4) Jan 26, 1957, v Penrith (FA Cup 1) Nov 17, 1984
Biggest defeat: 0-10 v Aston Villa (Div 1) Aug 29, 1925, v Sheffield Utd (Div 1) Jan 19, 1929
Highest League scorer in a season: George Beel 35 (1927–28)
Highest League scorer in aggregate: George Beel 178 (1923–32)
Longest unbeaten League sequence: 30 matches (1920–21)
Longest sequence without a League win: 24 matches (1979)
Most capped player: Jimmy McIlroy (Northern Ireland) 51

Goalkeepers				
Norris, Will	6.4	Wolves	Watford	12.08.93
Peacock-Farrell, Bailey	6.4	Leeds	Darlington	29.10.96
Pope, Nick	6.3	Charlton	Cambridge	19.04.92
Defenders				
Bardsley, Phil	5.11	Stoke	Salford	28.06.85
Gibson, Ben	6.1	Middlesbrough	Nunthorpe	05.01.93

Long, Kevin	6.2	Cork	Cork, Ire	18.08.90
Lowton, Matthew	5.11	Aston Villa	Chesterfield	09.06.89
Mee, Ben	5.11	Manchester City	Sale	23.09.89
Pieters, Erik	6.1	Stoke	Tiel, Hol	07.08.88
Tarkowski, James	6.1	Brentford	Manchester	19.11.92
Taylor, Charlie	5.9	Leeds	York	18.09.93
Midfielders				
Brady, Robbie	5.10	Norwich	Dublin, Ire	14.01.92
Brownhill, Josh	5.10	Bristol City	Warrington	19.12.95
Cork, Jack	6.1	Swansea	Carshalton	25.06.89
Gudmundsson, Johann	6.1	Charlton	Reykjavik, Ice	27.10.90
Hendrick, Jeff	6.1	Derby	Dublin, Ire	31.01.92
McNeil, Dwight	6.1	–	Rochdale	22.11.99
Westwood, Ashley	5.7	Aston Villa	Nantwich	01.04.90
Forwards				
Barnes, Ashley	6.0	Brighton	Bath	31.10.89
Rodriguez, Jay	6.1	WBA	Burnley	29.07.89
Thompson, Max	6.0	Everton	Macclesfield	09.02.02
Wood, Chris	6.3	Leeds	Auckland, NZ	07.12.91
Vydra, Matej	5.11	Derby	Chotebor, Cz	01.05.92

CHELSEA

Ground: Stamford Bridge Stadium, London SW6 1HS
Telephone: 0371 811 1955. **Club nickname:** Blues
Capacity: 40,853. **Colours:** Blue. **Shirt sponsor:** Three
Record transfer fee: £71.6m to Athletic Bilbao for Kepa Arrizabalaga, Aug 2018
Record fee received: £88.5m from Real Madrid for Eden Hazard, Jun 2019
Record attendance: 82,905 v Arsenal (Div 1) Oct 12, 1935
League Championship: Winners 1954–55, 2004–05, 2005–06, 2009–10, 2014–15, 2016–17
FA Cup: Winners 1970, 1997, 2000, 2007, 2009, 2010, 2012, 2018
League Cup: Winners 1965, 1998, 2005, 2007, 2015
European competitions: Winners Champions League 2011–12; Cup-Winners' Cup 1970–71, 1997–98; Europa League 2012–13, 2018–19; European Super Cup 1998
Finishing positions in Premier League: 1992–93 11th, 1993–94 14th, 1994–95 11th, 1995–96 11th, 1996–97 6th, 1997–98 4th, 1998–99 3rd, 1999–2000 5th, 2000–01 6th, 2001–02 6th, 2002–03 4th, 2003–04 2nd, 2004–05 1st, 2005–06 1st, 2006–07 2nd, 2007–08 2nd, 2008–09 3rd, 2009–10 1st, 2010–11 2nd, 2011–12 6th, 2012–13 3rd, 2013–14 3rd, 2014–15 1st, 2015–16 10th, 2016–17 1st, 2017–18 5th, 2018–19 3rd, 2019–20 4th
Biggest win: 8-0 v Aston Villa (Prem Lge) Dec 23, 2012. Also: 13-0 v Jeunesse Hautcharage, (Cup-Winners' Cup 1) Sep 29, 1971
Biggest defeat: 1-8 v Wolves (Div 1) Sep 26, 1953; 0-7 v Leeds (Div 1) Oct 7, 1967, v Nottm Forest (Div 1) Apr 20, 1991
Highest League scorer in a season: Jimmy Greaves 41 (1960–61)
Most League goals in aggregate: Bobby Tambling 164 (1958–70)
Longest unbeaten League sequence: 40 matches (2004–05)
Longest sequence without a League win: 21 matches (1987–88)
Most capped player: Frank Lampard (England) 104

Goalkeepers				
Arrizabalaga, Kepa	6.2	Athletic Bilbao	Ondarroa, Sp	03.10.94
Caballero, Willy	6.1	Manchester City	Santa Elena, Arg	28.09.81
Defenders				
Azpilicueta, Cesar	5.10	Marseille	Pamplona, Sp	28.08.89

Christensen, Andreas	6.2	Brondby	Lillerod, Den	10.04.96
Emerson	5.9	Roma	Santos, Br	03.08.94
James, Reece	6.0	–	Redbridge	08.12.99
Marcos Alonso	6.2	Fiorentina	Madrid, Sp	28.12.90
Rudiger, Antonio	6.3	Roma	Berlin, Ger	03.03.93
Tomori, Fikayo	6.1	–	Calgary, Can	19.12.97
Zouma, Kurt	6.3	St Etienne	Lyon, Fr	27.10.94
Midfielders				
Anjorin, Faustino	6.1	–	Poole	23.11.01
Barkley, Ross	6.2	Everton	Liverpool	05.12.93
Gilmour, Billy	5.6	Rangers	Glasgow	11.06.01
Jorginho	5.11	Napoli	Imbituba, Bra	20.12.91
Kante, N'Golo	5.7	Leicester	Paris, Fr	29.03.91
Kovacic, Mateo	5.10	Real Madrid	Linz, Aut	06.05.94
Loftus-Cheek, Ruben	6.3	–	Lewisham	23.01.96
Mount, Mason	5.10	–	Portsmouth	10.01.99
Pulisic, Christian	5.8	Borussia Dortmund	Hershey, US	18.09.98
Ziyech, Hakim	5.11	Ajax	Dronten, Hol	19.03.93
Forwards				
Abraham, Tammy	6.3	–	Camberwell	02.10.97
Batshuayi, Michy	6.0	Marseille	Brussels, Bel	02.10.93
Giroud, Olivier	6.4	Arsenal	Chambery, Fr	30.09.86
Hudson-Odoi, Callum	6.0	–	Wandsworth	07.11.00
Werner, Timo	5.11	Leipzig	Stuttgart, Ger	06.03.96

CRYSTAL PALACE

Ground: Selhurst Park, Whitehorse Lane, London SE25, 6PU
Telephone: 0208 768 6000. **Club nickname:** Eagles
Capacity: 25,486. **Colours:** Red and blue. **Shirt sponsor:** W888
Record transfer fee: £27m to Liverpool for Christian Benteke, Aug 2016
Record fee received: £50m from Manchester Utd for Aaron Wan-Bissaka, Jun 2019
Record attendance: 51,482 v Burnley (Div 2), May 11, 1979
League Championship: 3rd 1990–91
FA Cup: Runners-up 1990, 2016
League Cup: Semi-finals 1993, 1995, 2001, 2012
Finishing positions in Premier League: 1992–93 20th, 1994–95 19th, 1997–98 20th, 2004–05 18th, 2013–14 11th, 2014–15 10th, 2015–16 15th, 2016–17 14th, 2017–18 11th, 2018–19 12th, 2019–20 14th
Biggest win: 9-0 v Barrow (Div 4) Oct 10, 1959
Biggest defeat: 0-9 v Liverpool (Div 1) Sep 12, 1989. Also: 0-9 v Burnley (FA Cup 2 rep) Feb 10, 1909
Highest League scorer in a season: Peter Simpson 46 (1930–31)
Most League goals in aggregate: Peter Simpson 153 (1930–36)
Longest unbeaten League sequence: 18 matches (1969)
Longest sequence with a League win: 20 matches (1962)
Most capped player: Wayne Hennessey (Wales) 48

Goalkeepers				
Guaita, Vicente	6.3	Getafe	Torrente, Sp	10.01.87
Henderson, Stephen	6.3	Nottm Forest	Dublin, Ire	02.05.88
Hennessey, Wayne	6.5	Wolves	Bangor, Wal	24.01.87
Defenders				
Cahill, Gary	6.4	Chelsea	Sheffield	19.12.85
Dann, Scott	6.2	Blackburn	Liverpool	14.02.87

Ferguson, Nathan	5.11	WBA	Birmingham	06.10.00
Kelly, Martin	6.3	Liverpool	Whiston	27.04.90
Kouyate, Cheikhou	6.4	West Ham	Dakar, Sen	21.12.89
Mitchell, Tyrick	5.9	–	Brent	01.09.99
Riedewald, Jairo	6.0	Ajax	Haarlem, Hol	09.09.96
Sakho, Mamadou	6.2	Liverpool	Paris, Fr	13.02.90
Schlupp, Jeffrey	5.8	Leicester	Hamburg, Ger	23.12.92
Tomkins, James	6.3	West Ham	Basildon	29.03.89
Van Aanholt, Patrick	5.9	Sunderland	Hertogenbosch, Hol	29.08.90
Ward, Joel	6.2	Portsmouth	Emsworth	29.10.89
Midfielders				
McArthur, James	5.7	Wigan	Glasgow	07.10.87
McCarthy, James	5.11	Everton	Glasgow	12.11.90
Meyer, Max	5.8	Schalke	Oberhausen, Ger	18.09.95
Milivojevic, Luka	6.0	Olympiacos	Kragujevac, Serb	07.04.91
Pierrick, Brandon	6.0	–	Lambeth	10.12.01
Townsend, Andros	6.0	Newcastle	Leytonstone	16.07.91
Forwards				
Ayew, Jordan	6.0	Swansea	Marseille, Fr	11.09.91
Benteke, Christian	6.3	Liverpool	Kinshasa, DR Cong	03.12.90
Sorloth, Alexander	6.4	Midtjylland	Trondheim, Nor	05.12.95
Wickham, Connor	6.3	Sunderland	Colchester	31.03.93
Zaha, Wilfried	5.10	Manchester Utd	Abidjan, Iv C	10.11.92

EVERTON

Ground: Goodison Park, Liverpool L4 4EL
Telephone: 0151 556 1878. **Club nickname:** Toffees
Capacity: 39,221. **Colours:** Blue and white. **Shirt sponsor:** Cazoo
Record transfer fee: £45m to Swansea for Gylfi Sigurdsson, Aug 2017
Record fee received: £75m from Manchester Utd for Romelu Lukaku, Jul 2017
Record attendance: 78,299 v Liverpool (Div 1) Sep 18, 1948
League Championship: Winners 1890–91, 1914–15, 1927–28, 1931–31, 1938–39, 1962–63, 1969–70, 1984–85, 1986–87
FA Cup: Winners 1906, 1933, 1966, 1984, 1995
League Cup: Runners-up 1977, 1984
European competitions: Winners Cup-Winners' Cup 1984–85
Finishing positions in Premier League: 1992–93 13th, 1993–94 17th, 1994–95 15th, 1995–96 6th 1996–97 15th 1997–98 17th 1998–99 14th, 1999–2000 13th, 2000–01 16th, 2001–02 15th, 2002–03 7th, 2003–04 17th, 2004–05 4th, 2005–06 11th, 2006–07 6th, 2007–08 5th, 2008–09 5th, 2009–10 8th, 20010–11 7th, 2011–12 7th, 2012–13 6th, 2013–14 5th, 2014–15 11th, 2015–16 11th, 2016–17 7th, 2017–18 8th, 2018–19 8th, 2019–20 12th
Biggest win: 9-1 v Manchester City (Div 1) Sep 3, 1906, v Plymouth (Div 2) Dec 27, 1930. Also: 11-2 v Derby (FA Cup 1) Jan 18, 1890
Biggest defeat: 0-7 v Portsmouth (Div 1) Sep 10, 1949, v Arsenal (Prem Lge) May 11, 2005
Highest League scorer in a season: Ralph 'Dixie' Dean 60 (1927–28)
Most League goals in aggregate: Ralph 'Dixie' Dean 349 (1925–37)
Longest unbeaten League sequence: 20 matches (1978)
Longest sequence without a League win: 14 matches (1937)
Most capped player: Neville Southall (Wales) 92

Goalkeepers

| Lossl, Jonas | 6.5 | Huddersfield | Kolding, Den | 01.02.89 |
| Pickford, Jordan | 6.1 | Sunderland | Washington, Co Dur | 07.03.94 |

| Virginia, Joao | 6.3 | Arsenal | Faro, Por | 10.10.99 |

Defenders

Branthwaite, Jarrad	6.2	Carlisle	Carlisle	27.06.02
Coleman, Seamus	5.10	Sligo	Donegal, Ire	11.10.88
Digne, Lucas	5.10	Barcelona	Meaux, Fr	20.07.93
Holgate, Mason	5.11	Barnsley	Doncaster	22.10.96
Keane, Michael	6.3	Burnley	Stockport	11.01.93
Kenny, Jonjoe	5.11	–	Liverpool	15.03.97
Nkounkou, Niels	5.11	Marseille	Pontoise, Fr	01.11.00
Mina, Yerry	6.4	Barcelona	Guachene, Col	23.09.94

Midfielders

Adeniran, Dennis	5.11	Fulham	Southwark	02.01.99
Baningime, Beni	5.10	–	Kinshase, DR Cong	09.09.98
Bernard	5.5	Shakhtar Donetsk	Belo Horizonte, Br	08.09.92
Davies, Tom	5.11	–	Liverpool	30.06.98
Delph, Fabian	5.9	Manchester City	Bradford	21.11.89
Gbamin, Jean-Philippe	6.1	Mainz	San Pedro, Iv C	25.09.95
Gomes, Andre	6.2	Barcelona	Grijo, Por	30.07.93
Sigurdsson, Gylfi	6.1	Swansea	Hafnarfjordur, Ice	08.09.89

Forwards

Calvert-Lewin, Dominic	6.2	Sheffield Utd	Sheffield	16.03.97
Gordon, Anthony	5.10	–	Liverpool	24.02.01
Iwobi, Alex	5.11	Arsenal	Lagos, Nig	03.05.96
Kean, Moise	6.0	Juventus	Vercelli, It	28.02.00
Richarlison	5.10	Watford	Nova Venecia, Br	10.05.97
Cenk Tosun	6.0	Besiktas	Wetzlar, Ger	07.06.91
Walcott, Theo	5.8	Arsenal	Newbury	16.03.89

FULHAM

Ground: Craven Cottage, Stevenage Road, Lndon SW6 6HH
Telephone: 0843 208 1222. **Club nickname:** Cottagers
Capacity: 20,000 (during Riverside stand development). **Colours:** White and black. **Shirt sponsor:** tbc
Record transfer fee: £25m to Nice for Jean Michael Seri, Jul 2018
Record fee received: £25m from Tottenham for Ryan Sessegnon, Aug 2019
League Championship: 7th 2008–09
FA Cup: Runners-up 1975
League Cup: 5th rd 1968, 1971, 2000
European competitions: Runners-up Europa League 2009-10
Finishing positions in Premier League: 2001–02 13th, 2002–03 14th, 2003–04 9th, 2004–05 13th, 2005–06 12th, 2006–07 16th, 2007–08 17th, 2008–09 7th, 2009–10 12th, 2010–11 8th, 2011–12 9th, 2012–13 12th, 2013–14 19th, 2018–19 19th
Biggest win: 10-1 v Ipswich (Div 1) Dec 26, 1963
Biggest defeat: 0-10 v Liverpool (League Cup 2), Sep 23, 1986
Highest League scorer in a season: Frank Newton 43 (1931–32)
Most League goals in aggregate: Gordon Davies 159 (1978–84 and 1986–91)
Longest unbeaten League sequence: 23 matches (2017–18)
Longest sequence without a League win: 15 matches (1950)
Most capped player: Johnny Haynes (England) 56

Goalkeepers

| Bettinelli, Marcus | 6.4 | Simpeleen | Camberwell | 24.05.92 |
| Rodak, Marek | 6.5 | – | Kosice, Slovak | 13.12.96 |

Defenders

Bryan, Joe	5.7	Bristol City	Bristol	17.09.93
Christie, Cyrus	6.2	Middlesbrough	Coventry	30.09.92
Hector, Michael	6.4	Chelsea	East Ham	19.07.92
Le Marchand, Maxime	5.11	Nice	Saint-Malo, Fr	11.10.89
Mawson, Alfie	6.2	Swansea	Hillingdon	19.01.94
Odoi, Denis	5.10	Lokeren	Leuven, Bel	27.05.88
Ream, Tim	6.1	Bolton	St Louis, US	05.10.87
Robinson, Antonee	6.0	Wigan	Milton Keynes	08.08.97
Sessegnon, Steve	5.9	–	Roehampton	18.05.00

Midfielders

Cairney, Tom	6.0	Blackburn	Nottingham	20.01.91
Johansen, Stefan	6.0	Celtic	Vardo, Nor	08.01.91
Kebano, Neeskens	5.11	Genk	Montereau, Fr	10.03.92
Knockaert, Anthony	5.8	Brighton	Roubaix, Fr	20.11.91
McDonald, Kevin	6.2	Wolves	Carnoustie	04.11.88
Onomah, Josh	5.11	Tottenham	Enfield	27.04.97

Forwards

Ivan Cavaleiro,	5.9	Wolves	Vila Franca de Xira, Por	18.10.93
Kamara, Aboubakar	5.10	Amiens	Gonesse, Fr	07.03.95
Mitrovic, Aleksandar	6.3	Newcastle	Smederevo, Serb	16.09.94
Reid, Bobby	5.7	Cardiff	Bristol	02.02.93

LEEDS UNITED

Ground: Elland Road, Leeds S11 OES
Telephone: 0871 334 1919. **Club nickname:** Whites
Capacity: 37,890. **Colours:** White. **Shirt Sponsor:** Sbotop
Record transfer fee: £18m to West Ham for Rio Ferdinand, Nov 2000
Record fee received: £29.1m from Manchester Utd for Rio Ferdinand, Jul 2002
Record attendance: 57,892 v Sunderland (FA Cup 5 rep) Mar 15, 1967
League Championship: Winners 1968–69, 1973–74, 1991–92
FA Cup: Winners 1972
League Cup: Winners 1968
European competitions: Winners Fairs Cup 1967–68, 1970–71
Finishing positions in Premier League: 1992–93 17th, 1993–94 5th, 1994–95 5th, 1995–96 13th, 1996–97 11th, 1997–98 5th, 1998–99 4th, 1999–2000 3rd, 2000–01 4th, 2001–02 5th, 2002–03 15th, 2003–04 19th
Biggest win: 8-0 v Leicester (Div 1) Apr 7, 1934
Biggest defeat: 1-8 v Stoke (Div 1) Aug 27, 1934
Highest League scorer in a season: John Charles 43 (1953–54)
Most League goals in aggregate: Peter Lorimer 168 (1965–79, 1983–86)
Longest unbeaten League sequence: 34 matches (1968–69)
Longest sequence without a League win: 17 matches (1947)
Most capped player: Billy Bremner (Scotland) 54

Goalkeepers

Casilla, Kiko	6.3	Real Madrid	Alcover, Sp	02.10.86
Meslier, Illan	6.5	Lorient	Lorient, Fr	02.03.00

Defenders

Ayling, Luke	6.1	Bristol City	Lambeth	25.08.91
Berardi, Gaetano	5.11	Sampdoria	Sorengo, Swi	21.08.88
Cooper, Liam	6.0	Chesterfield	Hull	30.08.91
Douglas, Barry	5.9	Wolves	Glasgow	04.09.89
Drameh, Cody	5.8	Fulham	London	08.12.01

Struijk, Pascal	6.3	Ajax	Deurne, Bel	11.08.99
Midfielders				
Alioski, Ezgjan	5.8	Lugano	Prilep, Maced	12.02.92
Dallas, Stuart	6.0	Brentford	Cookstown	19.04.91
Forshaw, Adam	6.1	Middlesbrough	Liverpool	08.10.91
Harrison, Jack	5.9	Manchester City (loan)	Stoke	20.11.96
Hernandez, Pablo	5.8	Al-Arabi	Castellon, Sp	11.04.85
Klich, Mateusz	6.0	FC Twente	Tarnow, Pol	13.06.90
Phillips, Kalvin	5.10	–	Leeds	02.12.95
Poveda, Ian	5.6	Manchester City	Southwark	09.02.00
Shackleton, Jamie	5.7	–	Leeds	08.10.99
Forwards				
Bamford, Patrick	6.1	Middlesbrough	Grantham	05.09.93
Gelhardt, Joe	5.10	Wigan	Liverpool	04.05.92
Helder Costa	5.10	Wolves	Luandra, Ang	12.01.94
Roberts, Tyler	5.11	WBA	Gloucester	12.01.99

LEICESTER CITY

Ground: King Power Stadium, Filbert Way, Leicester, LE2 7FL
Telephone: 0344 815 5000. **Club nickname:** Foxes
Capacity: 32,273. **Colours:** Blue and white. **Shirt sponsor:** Thailand
Record transfer fee: £40m to Monaco for Youri Tielemans, Jul 2019
Record fee received: £60m from Manchester City for Riyad Mahrez, Jul 2018
Record attendance: Filbert Street: 47,298 v. Tottenham (FA Cup 5) Feb 18, 1928; King Power Stadium: 32,148 v Newcastle (Prem Lge) Dec 26, 2003. Also: 32,188 v Real Madrid (friendly) Jul 30, 2011
League Championship: Winners 2015–16
FA Cup: Runners-up 1949, 1961, 1963, 1969
League Cup: Winners 1964, 1997, 2000
European competitions: Champions League quarter-finals 2016–17
Finishing positions in Premier League: 1994–95 21st, 1996–97 9th, 1997–98 10th, 1998–99 10th, 1999–2000 8th, 2000–01 13th, 2001–02 20th, 2003–04 18th, 2014–15 14th, 2015–16 1st, 2016–17 12th, 2017–18 9th, 2018–19 9th, 2019–20 5th
Biggest win: 10-0 v Portsmouth (Div 1) Oct 20, 1928. Also: 13-0 v Notts Olympic (FA Cup) Oct 13, 1894
Biggest defeat (while Leicester Fosse): 0-12 v Nottm Forest (Div 1) Apr 21, 1909
Highest League scorer in a season: Arthur Rowley 44 (1956–57)
Most League goals in aggregate: Arthur Chandler 259 (1923–35)
Longest unbeaten League sequence: 23 matches (2008–09)
Longest sequence without a League win: 19 matches (1975)
Most capped player: Andy King (Wales) 50

Goalkeepers				
Jakupovic, Eldin	6.3	Hull	Sarajevo, Bos	02.10.84
Schmeichel, Kasper	6.0	Leeds	Copenhagen, Den	05.11.86
Ward, Danny	6.4	Liverpool	Wrexham	22.06.93
Defenders				
Caglar Soyuncu	6.1	Freiburg	Izmir, Tur	23.05.96
Chilwell, Ben	5.10	–	Milton Keynes	21.12.96
Evans, Jonny	6.2	WBA	Belfast	02.01.88
Fuchs, Christian	6.1	Schalke	Neunkirchen, Aut	07.04.86
Justin, James	6.3	Luton	Luton	11.07.97
Morgan, Wes	6.1	Nottm Forest	Nottingham	21.01.84
Ricardo Pereira	5.9	Porto	Lisbon, Por	06.10.93
Midfielders				

Adrien Silva	5.9	Sporting Lisbon	Angouleme, Fr	15.03.89
Albrighton, Mark	6.1	Aston Villa	Tamworth	18.11.89
Amartey, Daniel	6.0	Copenhagen	Accra, Gh	01.12.94
Choudhury, Hamza	5.10	–	Loughborough	01.10.97
Ghezzal, Rachid	6.0	Monaco	Decines, Fr	09.05.92
Gray, Demarai	5.10	Birmingham	Birmingham	28.06.96
James, Matty	5.11	Manchester Utd	Bacup	22.07.91
Maddison, James	5.10	Norwich	Coventry	23.11.96
Mendy, Nampalys	5.6	Nice	La Seyne, Fr	23.06.92
Ndidi, Wilfred	6.0	Genk	Lagos, Nig	16.12.96
Praet, Dennis	5.11	Sampdoria	Leuven, Bel	14.05.94
Tielemans, Youri	5.9	Monaco	Sint-Pieters-Leeuw, Bel	07.05.97
Forwards				
Ayoze Perez	5.11	Newcastle	Santa Cruz, Ten	23.07.93
Barnes, Harvey	5.9	–	Burnley	09.12.97
Iheanacho, Kelechi	6.2	Manchester City	Owerri, Nig	03.10.96
Vardy, Jamie	5.10	Fleetwood	Sheffield	11.01.87

LIVERPOOL

Ground: Anfield, Liverpool L4 OTH
Telephone: 0151 263 2361. **Club nickname:** Reds or Pool
Capacity: 53,394. **Colours:** Red. **Shirt sponsor:** Standard Chartered
Record transfer fee: £75m to Southampton for Virgil van Dijk Jan 2018
Record fee received: £142m from Barcelona for Philippe Coutinho, Jan 2018
Record attendance: 61,905 v Wolves, (FA Cup 4), Feb 2, 1952
League Championship: Winners 1900–01, 1905–06, 1921–22, 1922–23, 1946–47, 1963–64, 1965–66, 1972–73, 1975–76, 1976–77, 1978–79, 1979–80, 1981–82, 1982–83, 1983–84, 1985–86, 1987–88, 1989–90, 2019–20
FA Cup: Winners 1965, 1974, 1986, 1989, 1992, 2001, 2006
League Cup: Winners 1981, 1982, 1983, 1984, 1995, 2001, 2003, 2012
European competitions: Winners European Cup/Champions League 1976–77, 1977–78, 1980–81, 1983–84, 2004–05, 2018–19; UEFA Cup 1972–73, 1975–76, 2000–01; European Super Cup 1977, 2001, 2005
World Club Cup: Winners 2019
Finishing positions in Premier League: 1992–93 6th, 1993–94 8th, 1994–95 4th, 1995–96 3rd, 1996–97 4th, 1997–98 3rd, 1998–99 7th, 1999–2000 4th, 2000–01 3rd, 2001–02 2nd, 2002–03 5th, 2003–04 4th, 2004–05 5th, 2005–06 3rd, 2006–07 3rd, 2007–08 4th, 2008–09 2nd, 2009–10 7th, 2010–11 6th, 2011–12 8th, 2012–13 7th, 2013–14 2nd, 2014–15 6th, 2015–16 8th, 2016–17 4th, 2017–18 4th, 2018–19 2nd, 2019–20, 1st
Biggest win: 10-1 v Rotherham (Div 2) Feb 18, 1896. Also: 11-0 v Stromsgodset (Cup-Winners' Cup 1) Sep 17, 1974
Biggest defeat: 1-9 v Birmingham (Div 2) Dec 11, 1954
Highest League scorer in a season: Roger Hunt 41 (1961–62)
Most League goals in aggregate: Roger Hunt 245 (1959–69)
31 matches (1987–88))
Longest sequence without a League win: 14 matches (1953–54))
Most capped player: Steven Gerrard (England) 114

Goalkeepers
Adrian	6.3	West Ham	Seville, Sp	03.01.87
Alisson	6.4	Roma	Novo Hamburgo, Bra	02.10.92
Karius, Loris	6.2	Mainz	Biberach, Ger	22.06.93
Defenders				
Alexander-Arnold, Trent	5.10	–	Liverpool	07.10.98

Gomez, Joe	6.1	Charlton	Catford	23.05.97
Tsimikas, Kostas	5.10	Olympiacos	Thessaloniki, Gre	12.05.96
Matip, Joel	6.5	Schalke	Bochum, Ger	08.08.91
Robertson, Andrew	5.10	Hull	Glasgow	11.03.94
Van Dijk, Virgil	6.4	Southampton	Breda, Hol	08.07.91
Williams, Neco	6.0	–	Wrexham	13.04.01
Midfielders				
Elliott, Harvey	5.7	Fulham	Chertsey	04.04.03
Fabinho	6.2	Monaco	Campinas, Br	23.10.93
Ferran Torres	6.0	Valencia	Foios, Sp	29.02.00
Henderson, Jordan	5.10	Sunderland	Sunderland	17.06.90
Jones, Curtis	6.1	–	Liverpool	30.01.01
Keita, Naby	5.8	Leipzig	Conakry, Guin	10.02.95
Milner, James	5.11	Manchester City	Leeds	04.01.86
Oxlade-Chamberlain, Alex	5.11	Arsenal	Portsmouth	15.08.93
Shaqiri, Xherdan	5.7	Stoke	Gjilan, Kos	10.10.91
Wijnaldum, Georginio	5.9	Newcastle	Rotterdam, Hol	11.11.90
Forwards				
Firmino, Roberto	6.0	Hoffenheim	Maceio, Br	02.10.91
Mane, Sadio	5.9	Southampton	Sedhiou, Sen	10.04.92
Minamino, Takumi	5.9	Salzburg	Osaka, Jap	16.01.95
Origi, Divock	6.1	Lille	Ostend, Bel	18.04.95
Salah, Mohamed	5.9	Roma	Basyoun, Egy	15.06.92

MANCHESTER CITY

Ground: Etihad Stadium, Etihad Campus, Manchester M11 3FF
Telephone: 0161 444 1894. **Club nickname:** City
Capacity: 55,017. **Colours:** Sky blue and white. **Shirt sponsor:** Etihad
Record transfer fee: £62.8m to Atletico Madrid for Rodri, Jul 2019
Record fee received: £25m from Leicester for Kelechi Iheanacho, Jul 2017
Record attendance: Maine Road: 84,569 v Stoke (FA Cup 6) Mar 3, 1934 (British record for any game outside London or Glasgow). Etihad Stadium: 54,693 v Leicester (Prem Lge) February 6, 2016
League Championship: Winners 1936–37, 1967–68, 2011–12, 2013–14, 2017–18, 2018–19
FA Cup: Winners 1904, 1934, 1956, 1969, 2011, 2019
League Cup: Winners 1970, 1976, 2014, 2016, 2018, 2019, 2020
European competitions: Winners Cup-Winners' Cup 1969–70
Finishing positions in Premier League: 1992–93 9th, 1993–94 16th, 1994–95 17th, 1995–96 18th, 2000–01: 18th, 2002–03 9th, 2003–04 16th, 2004–05 8th, 2005–06 15th, 2006–07 14th, 2007–08 9th, 2008–09 10th, 2009–10 5th, 2010–11 3rd, 2011–12 1st, 2012–13 2nd, 2013–14 1st, 2014–15 2nd, 2015–16 4th, 2016–17 3rd, 2017–18 1st, 2018–19 1 st, 2019–20 2nd
Biggest win: 10-1 v Huddersfield (Div 2) Nov 7, 1987. Also: 10-1 v Swindon (FA Cup 4) Jan 29, 1930
Biggest defeat: 1-9 v Everton (Div 1) Sep 3, 1906
Highest League scorer in a season: Tommy Johnson 38 (1928–29)
Most League goals in aggregate: Tommy Johnson, 158 (1919–30)
Longest unbeaten League sequence: 22 matches (1946–47) and (2017–18)
Longest sequence without a League win: 17 matches (1979–80)
Most capped player: Joe Hart (England) 63

Goalkeepers

Ederson	6.2	Benfica	Osasco, Br	17.08.93
Muric, Arijanet	6.6	Grasshoppers	Schlieren, Switz	07.11.98

Defenders

Ake, Nathan	5.11	Bournemouth	The Hague, Hol	18.02.95
Garcia, Eric	6.0	Barcelona	Barcelona, Sp	09.01.01
Joao Cancelo	6.0	Juventus	Barreiro, Por	27.05.94
Laporte, Aymeric	6.3	Athletic Bilbao	Agen, Fr	27.05.94
Mendy, Benjamin	6.0	Monaco	Longjumeau, Fr	17.07.94
Otamendi, Nicolas	6.0	Valencia	Buenos Aires, Arg	12.02.88
Stones, John	6.2	Everton	Barnsley	28.05.94
Walker, Kyle	6.0	Tottenham	Sheffield	28.05.90
Zinchenko, Oleksandr	5.9	FC Ufa	Radomyshl, Ukr	15.12.96

Midfielders

Bernardo Silva	5.8	Monaco	Lisbon, Por	10.08.94
De Bruyne, Kevin	5.11	Wolfsburg	Drongen, Bel	28.06.91
Fernandinho	5.10	Shakhtar Donetsk	Londrina, Br	04.05.85
Foden, Phil	5.7	–	Stockport	28.05.00
Gundogan, Ilkay	5.11	Borussia Dortmund	Gelsenkirchen, Ger	24.10.90
Mahrez, Riyad	5.10	Leicester	Sarcelles, Fr	21.02.91
Rodri	6.3	Atletico Madrid	Madrid, Sp	23.06.96

Forwards

Aguero, Sergio	5.8	Atletico Madrid	Quilmes, Arg	02.06.88
Gabriel Jesus	5.9	Palmeiras	Sao Paulo, Br	03.04.97
Sterling, Raheem	5.7	Liverpool	Kingston, Jam	08.12.94

MANCHESTER UNITED

Ground: Old Trafford Stadium, Sir Matt Busby Way, Manchester, M16 0RA
Telephone: 0161 868 8000. **Club nickname:** Red Devils
Capacity: 74,879. **Colours:** Red and white. **Shirt sponsor:** Chevrolet
Record transfer fee: £89.3m to Juventus for Paul Pogba, Aug 2016
Record fee received: £80m from Real Madrid for Cristiano Ronaldo, Jun 2009
Record attendance: 75,811 v Blackburn (Prem Lge), Mar 31, 2007. Also: 76,962 Wolves v Grimsby (FA Cup semi-final) Mar 25, 1939. Crowd of 83,260 saw Manchester Utd v Arsenal (Div 1) Jan 17, 1948 at Maine Road – Old Trafford out of action through bomb damage
League Championship: Winners 1907–08, 1910–11, 1951–52, 1955–56, 1956–7, 1964–65, 1966–67, 1992–93, 1993–94, 1995–96, 1996–97, 1998–99, 1999–2000, 2000–01, 2002–03, 2006–07, 2007–08, 2008–09, 2010–11, 2012–13
FA Cup: Winners 1909, 1948, 1963, 1977, 1983, 1985, 1990, 1994, 1996, 1999, 2004, 2016
League Cup: Winners 1992, 2006, 2009, 2010, 2017
European competitions: Winners European Cup/Champions League 1967–68, 1998–99, 2007–08; Cup-Winners' Cup 1990–91; European Super Cup 1991; Europa League 2016–17
World Club Cup: Winners 2008
Finishing positions in Premier League: 1992–93 1st, 1993–94 1st, 1994–95 2nd, 1995–96 1st, 1996–97 1st, 1997–98 2nd, 1998–99 1st, 1999–2000 1st, 2000–01 1st, 2001–02 3rd, 2002–03 1st, 2003–04 3rd, 2004–05 3rd, 2005–06 2nd, 2006–07 1st, 2007–08 1st, 2000–09 1st, 2009–10 2nd, 2010–11 1st, 2011–12 2nd, 2012–13 1st, 2013–14 7th, 2014–15 4th, 2015–16 5th, 2016–17 6th, 2017–18 2nd, 2018–19 6th, 2019–20 3rd
Biggest win: As Newton Heath: 10-1 v Wolves (Div 1) Oct 15, 1892. As Manchester Utd: 9-0 v Ipswich (Prem Lge), Mar 4, 1995. Also: 10-0 v Anderleht (European Cup prelim rd) Sep 26, 1956
Biggest defeat: 0-7 v Blackburn (Div 1) Apr 10, 1926, v Aston Villa (Div 1) Dec 27, 1930, v Wolves (Div 2) 26 Dec, 1931
Highest League scorer in a season: Dennis Viollet 32 (1959–60)
Most League goals in aggregate: Bobby Charlton 199 (1956–73)
Longest unbeaten League sequence: 29 matches (1998–99)

Longest sequence without a League win: 16 matches (1930)
Most capped player: Sir Bobby Charlton (England) 106

Goalkeepers

Bishop, Nathan	6.1	Southend	Hillingdon	15.10.99
De Gea, David	6.4	Atletico Madrid	Madrid, Sp	07.11.90
Romero, Sergio	6.4	Sampdoria	Bernardo, Arg	22.02.87

Defenders

Bailly, Eric	6.1	Villarreal	Bingerville, Iv C	12.04.94
Dalot, Diogo	6.1	Porto	Braga, Port	18.03.99
Jones, Phil	5.11	Blackburn	Blackburn	21.02.92
Lindelof, Victor	6.2	Benfica	Vasteras, Swe	17.07.94
Maguire, Harry	6.2	Leicester	Sheffield	05.03.93
Rojo, Marcos	6.2	Sporting Lisbon	La Plata, Arg	20.03.90
Shaw, Luke	6.1	Southamptonn	Kingston upon Thames	12.07.95
Tuanzebe, Axel	6.1	–	Bunia, Dr Cong	14.11.97
Wan-Bissaka, Aaron	6.0	Crystal Palace	Croydon	26.11.97
Williams, Brandon	5.7	–	Manchester	03.09.00

Midfielders

Bruno Fernandes	5.8	Sporting Lisbon	Maia, Port	08.09.94
Fred	5.7	Shakhtar Donetsk	Belo Horizonte, Bra	05.03.93
James, Daniel	5.8	Swansea	Beverley	10.11.97
Mata, Juan	5.7	Chelsea	Burgos, Sp	28.04.88
Matic, Nemanja	6.4	Chelsea	Sabac, Serb	01.08.88
McTominay, Scott	6.4	–	Lancaster	08.12.96
Pereira, Andreas	5.10	PSV Eindhoven	Duffel, Bel	01.01.96
Pogba, Paul	6.3	Juventus	Lagny-sur-Marne, Fr	15.03.93

Forwards

Greenwood, Mason	5.11	–	Bradford	01.10.01
Lingard, Jesse	6.2	–	Warrington	15.12.92
Martial, Anthony	5.11	Monaco	Massy, Fr	05.12.95
Rashford, Marcus	6.0	–	Wythensawe	31.10.97
Ighalo, Odion	5.11	Shanghai Shenhua (loan)	Lagos, Nig	16.06.89

NEWCASTLE UNITED

Ground: St James' Park, Newcastle-upon-Tyne, NE1 4ST
Telephone: 0844 372 1892. **Club nickname:** Magpies
Capacity: 52,305. **Colours:** Black and white. **Shirt sponsor:** Fun88
Record attendance: 68,386 v Chelsea (Div 1) Sep 3, 1930
Record transfer fee: £40m to Hoffenheim for Joelinton, Jul 2019
Record fee received: £35m from Liverpool for Andy Carroll, Jan 2011
League Championship: Winners 1904–05, 1906–07, 1908–09, 1926–27
FA Cup: Winners: 1910, 1924, 1932, 1951, 1952, 1955
League Cup: Runners-up 1976
European competitions: Winners Fairs Cup 1968–69; Anglo-Italian Cup 1972–73
Finishing positions in Premier League: 1993–94 3rd, 1994–95 6th, 1995–96 2nd, 1996–97 2nd, 1997–98 13th, 1998–99 13th, 1999–2000 11th, 2000–01 11th, 2001–02 4th, 2002–03 3rd, 2003–04 5th, 2004–05 14th, 2005–06 7th, 2006–07 13th, 2007–08 12th, 2008–09 18th, 2010–11 12th, 2011–12 5th, 2012–13 16th, 2013–14 10th, 2014–15 15th, 2015–16 18th, 2017–18 10th, 2018–19 13th, 2019–20 13th
Biggest win: 13-0 v Newport (Div 2) Oct 5, 1946
Biggest defeat: 0-9 v Burton (Div 2) Apr 15, 1895
Highest League scorer in a season: Hughie Gallacher 36 (1926–27)
Most League goals in aggregate: Jackie Milburn 177 (1946–57)

Longest unbeaten League sequence: 14 matches (1950)
Longest sequence without a League win: 21 matches (1978)
Most capped player: Shay Given (Republic of Ireland) 83

Goalkeepers

Darlow, Karl	6.1	Nottm Forest	Northampton	08.10.90
Dubravka, Martin	6.3	Sparta Prague	Zilina, Slovak	15.01.89
Gillespie, Mark	6.3	Motherwell	Newcastle	27.03.92

Defenders

Clark, Ciaran	6.2	Aston Villa	Harrow	26.09.89
Dummett, Paul	6.0	–	Newcastle	26.09.91
Fernandez, Federico	6.3	Swansea	Tres Algarrobos, Arg	21.02.89
Krafth, Emil	6.0	Amiens	Ljungby, Swe	02.08.94
Lascelles, Jamaal	6.2	Nottm Forest	Derby	11.11.93
Lejeune, Florian	6.3	Eibar	Paris, Fr	20.05.91
Manquillo, Javier	6.0	Atletico Madrid	Madrid, Sp	05.05.94
Schar, Fabian	6.2	Dep La Coruna	Wil, Switz	20.12.91
Yedlin, DeAndre	5.9	Tottenham	Seattle, US	09.07.93

Midfielders

Almiron, Miguel	5.9	Atlanta	Asuncion, Par	10.02.94
Atsu, Christian	5.8	Chelsea	Ada Foah, Gh	10.01.92
Hayden, Isaac	6.1	Arsenal	Chelmsford	22.03.95
Longstaff, Matty	5.7	–	Rotherham	21.03.00
Longstaff, Sean	5.11	–	North Shields	30.10.97
Murphy, Jacob	5.10	Norwich	Wembley	24.02.95
Ritchie, Matt	5.8	Bournemouth	Gosport	10.09.89
Shelvey, Jonjo	6.0	Swansea	Romford	27.02.92

Forwards

Carroll, Andy	6.4	West Ham	Gateshead	06.01.89
Gayle, Dwight	5.10	Crystal Palace	Walthamstow	20.10.90
Joelinton	6.1	Hoffenheim	Alianca, Br	14.08.96
Muto, Yoshinori	5.10	Mainz	Tokyo, Jap	15.07.92
Saint-Maximin, Allan		Nice	Chatenay-Malabry, Fr	12.03.97

SHEFFIELD UNITED

Ground: Bramall Lane, Sheffield S2 4SU
Telephone: 0114 253 7200. **Club nickname:** Blades
Capacity: 32,702. **Colours:** Red and white, **Shirt sponsor:** Union Standard Group
Record attendance: 68,287 v Leeds (FA Cup 5) Feb 15, 1936
Record transfer fee: £22m to Genk for Sander Berge, Jan 2020
Record fee received: £11.1m from Bournemouth for David Brooks, Jul 2018
League Championship: Winners 1897-98
FA Cup: Winners 1899, 1902, 1915, 1925
League Cup: Semi-finals 2003, 2015
Finishing positions in Premier League: 1992–93 14th, 1993–94 20th, 2006–07 18th, 2019–20 9th
Biggest win: 10-0 v Burslem Port Vale (Div 2) Dec 10, 1892
Biggest defeat: 0-13 v Bolton (FA Cup 2) Feb 1, 1890
Highest League scorer in a season: Jimmy Dunne 41 (1930–31)
Most League goals in aggregate: Harry Johnson 205 (1919–30)
Longest unbeaten League sequence: 22 matches (1899–1900)
Longest sequence without a League win: 19 matches (1975–76)
Most capped player: Billy Gillespie (Northern Ireland) 25

Goalkeepers

Foderingham, Wes	6.1	Rangers	Hammersmith	14.01.91
Moore, Simon	6.3	Cardiff	Sandown, IOW	19.05.90
Ramsdale, Aaron	6.2	Bournemouth	Stoke	14.05.98

Defenders

Baldock, George	5.9	MK Dons	Buckingham	09.03.93
Basham, Chris	5.11	Blackpool	Hebburn	18.02.88
Egan, John	6.2	Brentford	Cork, Ire	20.10.92
Freeman, Kieron	6.1	Derby	Bestwood	21.03.92
Jagielka, Phil	5.11	Everton	Manchester	17.08.82
Lundstram, John	5.11	Oxford	Liverpool	18.02.94
O'Connell, Jack	6.3	Brentford	Liverpool	29.03.94
Robinson, Jack	5.7	Nottm Forest	Warrington	01.09.93
Stevens, Enda	6.0	Portsmouth	Dublin, Ire	09.07.90

Midfielders

Berge, Sander	6.4	Genk	Baerum, Nor	14.02.98
Fleck, John	5.7	Coventry	Glasgow	24.08.91
Freeman, Luke	5.10	QPR	Dartford	22.03.92
Norwood, Oliver	5.11	Brighton	Burnley	12.04.91
Osborn, Ben	5.9	Nottm Forest	Derby	05.08.94
Rodwell, Jack	6.2	Blackburn	Southport	11.03.91

Forwards

Clarke, Leon	6.2	Bury	Birmingham	10.02.85
McBurnie, Oliver	6.2	Swansea	Leeds	04.06.96
McGoldrick, David	6.1	Ipswich	Nottingham	29.11.87
Mousset, Lys	6.0	Bournemouth	Montivilliers, Fr	08.12.96
Sharp, Billy	5.9	Leeds	Sheffield	05.02.86

SOUTHAMPTON

Ground: St Mary's Stadium, Britannia Road, Southampton, SO14 5FP
Telephone: 0845 688 9448. **Club nickname:** Saints
Capacity: 32,384. **Colours:** Red and white. **Shirt sponsor:** LD Sports
Record transfer fee: £20m to Liverpool for Danny Ings, Jul 2019
Record fee received: £75m from Liverpool for Virgil van Dijk, Jan 2018
Record attendance: The Dell: 31,044 v Manchester Utd (Div 1) Oct 8, 1969. St Mary's: 32,363 v Coventry (Champ) Apr 28, 2012
League Championship: Runners-up 1983–84
FA Cup: Winners 1976
League Cup: Runners-up 1979, 2017
European competitions: Fairs Cup rd 3 1969–70; Cup-Winners' Cup rd 3 1976–77
Finishing positions in Premier League: 1992–93 18th, 1993–94 18th, 1994–5 10th, 1995–96 17th, 1996–97 16th, 1997–98 12th, 1998–99 17th, 1999–200 15th, 2000–01 10th, 2001–02 11th, 2002–03 8th, 2003–04 12th, 2004–05 20th, 2012–13 14th, 2013–14 8th, 2014–15 7th, 2015–16 6th, 2016–17 8th, 2017–18 17th, 2018–19 16th, 2019–20 11th
Biggest win: 8-0 v Northampton (Div 3S) Dec 24, 1921, v Sunderland (Prem Lge) Oct 18, 2014
Biggest defeat: 0-9 v Leicester(Prem Lge) Oct 25, 2019
Highest League scorer in a season: Derek Reeves 39 (1959–60)
Most League goals in aggregate: Mick Channon 185 (1966–82)
Longest unbeaten League sequence: 19 matches (1921)
Longest unbeaten League sequence: 20 matches (1969)
Most capped player: Steven Davis (Northern Ireland)) 65

Goalkeepers

Gunn, Angus	6.5	Manchester City	Norwich	22.01.96

| McCarthy, Alex | 6.4 | Crystal Palace | Guildford | 03.12.89 |

Defenders

Bednarek, Jan	6.2	Lech Poznan	Slupca, Pol	12.04.96
Bertrand, Ryan	5.10	Chelsea	Southwark	05.08.89
Hoedt, Wesley	6.2	Lazio	Alkmaar, Hol	06.03.94
Salisu, Mohammed	6.3	Real Valladolid	Accra, Gha	17.04.99
Stephens, Jack	6.1	Plymouth	Torpoint	27.01.94
Valery, Yan	5.11	Rennes	Champigny, Fr	22.02.99
Vestergaard, Jannik	6.6	Borussia M'gladbach	Copenhagen, Den	03.08.92
Vokins, Jake	5.11	–	Oxford	17, 03.00
Walker-Peters, Kyle	5.8	Tottenham	Edmonton	13.04.97

Midfielders

Armstrong, Stuart	6.0	Celtic	Inverness	30.03.92
Boufal, Sofiane	5.7	Lille	Paris, Fr	17.09.93
Djenepo, Moussa	5.10	Standard Liege	Bamako, Mali	15.06.98
Lemina, Mario	6.1	Juventus	Libreville, Gab	01.09.93
Redmond, Nathan	5.8	Norwich	Birmingham	06.03.94
Romeu, Oriol	6.0	Chelsea	Ulldecona, Sp	24.09.91
Sims, Joshua	5.9	–	Yeovil	28.03.97
Smallbone, William	5.8	–	Basingstoke	21.02.00
Ward-Prowse, James	5.8	–	Portsmouth	01.11.94

Forwards

Adams, Che	5.10	Birmingham	Leicester	13.07.96
Ings, Danny	5.10	Liverpool	Winchester	16.03.92
Long, Shane	5.10	Hull	Gortnahoe, Ire	22.01.87
Obafemi, Michael	5.7	–	Dublin, Ire	06.07.00

TOTTENHAM HOTSPUR

Ground: Tottenham Hotspur Stadium, High Road , Tottenham N17 OBX
Telephone: 0344 499 5000. **Club nickname:** Spurs
Capacity: 62,062 Or 62,303. **Colours:** White. **Shirt sponsor:** AIA
Record transfer fee: £54m to Lyon for Tanguy Ndombele, Jul 2019
Record fee received: £85.3m from Real Madrid for Gareth Bale, Aug 2013
Record attendance: White Hart Lane: 75,038 v Sunderland (FA Cup 6) Mar 5, 1938. Wembley: 85,512 v Bayer Leverkusen (Champs Lge group) Nov 2, 2016. Tottenham Hotspur Stadium: 60,243 v Ajax (Champs Lge semi-final) Apr 29, 2019
League Championship: Winners 1950–51, 1960–61
FA Cup: Winners 1901, 1921, 1961, 1962, 1967, 1981, 1982, 1991
League Cup: Winners 1971, 1973, 1999, 2008
European competitions: Winners Cup-Winners' Cup 1962–63; UEFA Cup 1971–72, 1983–84
Finishing positions in Premier League: 1992–93 8th, 1993–94 15th, 1994–95 7th, 1995–96 8th, 1996–97 10th, 1997–98 14th, 1998–99 11th, 1999–2000 10th, 2000–01 12th, 2001–02 9th, 2002–03 10th, 2003–04 14th, 2004–05 9th, 2005–06 5th, 2006–07 5th, 2007–08 11th, 2008–09 8th, 2009–10 4th, 2010–11 5th, 2011–12 4th, 2012–13 5th, 2013–14 6th, 2014–15 5th, 2015–16 3rd, 2016–17 2nd, 2017–18 3rd, 2018–19 4th, 2019–20 6th
Biggest win: 9-0 v Bristol Rov (Div 2) Oct 22, 1977. Also: 13-2 v Crewe (FA Cup 4 replay) Feb 3, 1960
Biggest defeat: 0-7 v Liverpool (Div 1) Sep 2, 1979. Also: 0-8 v Cologne (Inter Toto Cup) Jul 22, 1995
Highest League scorer in a season: Jimmy Greaves 37 (1962–63)
Most League goals in aggregate: Jimmy Greaves 220 (1961–70)
Longest unbeaten League sequence: 22 matches (1949)
Longest sequence without a League win: 16 matches (1934–35)
Most capped player: Pat Jennings (Northern Ireland) 74

Goalkeepers

Gazzaniga, Paulo	6.5	Southampton	Murphy, Arg	02.01.92
Hart, Joe	6.3	Burnley	Shrewsbury	19.04.87
Lloris, Hugo	6.2	Lyon	Nice, Fr	26.12.86

Defenders

Alderweireld, Toby	6.2	Atletico Madrid	Antwerp, Bel	02.03.89
Aurier, Serge	5.9	Paris SG	Ouragahio, Iv C	24.12.92
Davies, Ben	5.6	Swansea	Neath	24.04.93
Dier, Eric	6.2	Sporting Lisbon	Cheltenham	15.01.94
Foyth, Juan	5.10	Estudiantes	La Plata, Arg	12.01.98
Rose, Danny	5.8	Leeds	Doncaster	02.07.90
Sanchez, Davinson	6.2	Ajax	Caloto, Col	12.06.96
Tanganga, Japhet	6.1	–	Hackney	31.03.99

Midfielders

Alli, Dele	6.1	MK Dons	Milton Keynes	11.04.96
Dembele, Mousa	6.1	Fulham	Wilrijk, Bel	16.07.87
Hojbjerg, Pierre-Emile	6.1	Southampton	Copenhagen, Den	05.08.95
Lamela, Erik	6.0	Roma	Buenos Aires, Arg	04.03.92
Lo Celso, Giovani	5.10	Real Betis	Rosario, Arg	09.04.96
Lucas Moura	5.8	Paris SG	Sao Paulo, Br	13.08.92
Ndombele, Tanguy	5.11	Lyon	Longjumeau, Fr	28.12.96
Sessegnon, Ryan	5.10	Fulham	Roehampton	18.05.00
Sissoko, Moussa	6.2	Newcastle	Le Blanc-Mesnil, Fr	16.08.89
Winks, Harry	5.10	–	Hemel Hempstead	02.02.96

Forwards

Bergwijn, Steven	5.10	PSV Eindhoven	Amsterdam, Hol	08.10.97
Kane, Harry	6.2	–	Walthamstow	28.07.93
Son Heung-Min	6.1	Bayer Leverkusen	Chuncheon, S Kor	08.07.92

WEST BROMWICH ALBION

Ground: The Hawthorns, Halfords Lane, West Bromwich B71 4LF
Telephone: 0871 271 1100. **Club nickname:** Baggies
Capacity: 26,688. **Colours:** Blue and white. **Shirt Sponsor:** Ideal Boilers
Record transfer fee: £13m to Tottenham for Nacer Chadli, Aug 2016
Record fee received: £11.m from Stoke for Saido Berahino, Jan 2017
Record attendance: 64,815 v Arsenal (FA Cup 6) Mar 6, 1937
League Championship: Winners 1919–20
FA Cup: Winners 1888, 1892, 1931, 1954, 1968
League Cup: Winners 1966
European competitions: Cup-Winners' Cup quarter-finals 1968–69; UEFA Cup quarter-finals 1978–79
Finishing positions in Premier League: 2002–03 19th, 2004–05 17th, 2005–06 19th, 2008–09 20th, 2010–11 11th, 2011–12 10th 2012–13 8th, 2013–14 17th, 2014–15 13th, 2015–16 14th, 2016–17 10th, 2017–18 20th
Biggest win: 12-0 v Darwen (Div 1) Apr 4, 1892
Biggest defeat: 3-10 v Stoke (Div 1) Feb 4, 1937
Highest League scorer in a season: William Richardson 39 (1935–36)
Most League goals in aggregate: Tony Brown 218 (1963–79)
Longest unbeaten League sequence: 17 matches (1957)
Longest sequence without a League win: 14 matches (1995)
Most capped player : Chris Brunt (Northern Ireland 48 caps

Goalkeepers

Johnstone, Sam	6.4	Manchester Utd	Preston	25.03.93

Defenders

Ajayi, Semi	6.4	Rotherham	Crayford	09.11.93
Bartley, Kyle	6.1	Swansea	Stockport	22.05.91
Furlong, Darnell	6.1	QPR	Luton	31.10.95
Gibbs, Kieran	5.10	Arsenal	Lambeth	26.09.89
Hegazi, Ahmed	6.4	Al Ahly	Ismailia, Egy	25.01.91
O'Shea, Dara	6.2	–	Dublin, Ire	04.03.99
Townsend, Conor	5.6	Scunthorpe	Hessle	04.03.93

Midfielders

Burke, Oliver	6.2	Leipzig	Kircaldy	07.04.97
Field, Sam	5.11	–	Stourbridge	08.05.98
Grosicki, Kamil	5.11	Hull	Szczecin, Pol	08.06.88
Harper, Rekeem	6.0	–	Birmingham	08.03.00
Leko, Jonathan	6.0	–	Kinshasa, DR Cong	24.04.99
Livermore, Jake	6.0	Hull	Enfield	14.11.89
Pereira, Matheus	5.9	Sporting Lisbon	Belo Horizonte, Br	05.05.96
Phillips, Matt	6.0	QPR	Aylesbury	13.03.91
Sawyers, Romaine	5.9	Brentford	Birmingham	01.11.91

Forwards

Austin, Charlie	6.2	Southampton	Hungerford	05.07.89
Edwards, Kyle	5.9	–	Dudley	17.02.98
Robson-Kanu, Hal	6.0	Reading	Acton	21.05.89
Zohore, Kenneth	6.2	Cardiff	Copenhagen, Den	31.01.94

WEST HAM UNITED

Ground: Queen Elizabeth Olympic Park, London E20 2ST
Telephone: 0208 548 2748. **Club nickname:** Hammers
Capacity: 60,000. **Colours:** Claret and blue. **Shirt sponsor:** Betway
Record transfer fee: £45m to Eintracht Frankfurt for Sebastien Haller, Jul 2019
Record fee received: £25m from Marseille for Dimitri Payet, Jan 2017
Record attendance: Upton Park: 43,322 v Tottenham (Div 1) Oct 17, 1970. Olympic Stadium: 59,988 v Everton (Prem Lge) Mar 30, 2019
League Championship: 3rd 1985–86
FA Cup: Winners 1964, 1975, 1980
League Cup: Runners-up 1966, 1981
European competitions: Winners Cup-Winners' Cup 1964–65
Finishing positions in Premier League: 1993–94 13th, 1994–95 14th, 1995–96 10th, 1996–97 14th, 1997–98 8th, 1998–99 5th, 1999–2000 9th, 2000–01 15th, 2001–02 7th, 2002–03 18th, 2005–06 9th, 2006–07 15th, 2007–08 10th, 2008–09: 9th, 2009 10th, 2010–11 20th, 2012–13 10th, 2013–14 13th, 2014–15 12th, 2015–16 7th, 2016–17 11th, 2017–18 13th, 2018–19 10th, 2019–20 16th
Biggest win: 8-0 v Rotherham (Div 2) Mar 8, 1958, v Sunderland (Div 1) Oct 19, 1968. Also: 10-0 v Bury (League Cup 2) Oct 25, 1983
Biggest defeat: 0-7 v Barnsley (Div 2) Sep 1, 1919, v Everton (Div 1) Oct 22, 1927, v Sheffield Wed (Div 1) Nov 28, 1959
Highest League scorer in a season: Vic Watson 42 (1929–30)
Most League goals in aggregate: Vic Watson 298 (1920–35)
Longest unbeaten League sequence: 27 matches (1980–81)
Longest sequence without a League win: 17 matches (1976)
Most capped player: Bobby Moore (England) 108

Goalkeepers

Fabianski, Lukasz	6.3	Swansea	Kostrzyn, Pol	18.04.85
Martin, David	6.2	Millwall	Romford	22.01.86

Randolph, Darren	6.1	Middlesbrough	Bray, Ire	12.05.87
Defenders				
Balbuena, Fabian	6.2	Corinthians	Ciudad del Este, Par	23.08.91
Cresswell, Aaron	5.7	Ipswich	Liverpool	15.12.89
Diop, Issa	6.4	Toulouse	Toulouse	09.01.97
Fredericks, Ryan	5.8	Fulham	Potters Bar	10.10.92
Johnson, Ben	5.9	–	Waltham Forrest	24.01.00
Masuaku, Arthur	5.11	Olympiacos	Lille, Fr	07.11.93
Ogbonna, Angelo	6.3	Juventus	Cassino, It	23.05.88
Rice, Declan	6.1	–	London	14.01.99
Midfielders				
Antonio, Michail	5.11	Nottm Forest	Wandsworth	28.03.90
Cullen, Josh	5.9	–	Westcliff-on-Sea	07.04.96
Diangana, Grady	5.11	–	DR Congo	19.04.98
Felipe Anderson	5.10	Lazio	Santa Maria, Br	15.04.93
Fornals, Pablo	5.10	Villarreal	Castellon, Sp	22.02.96
Holland, Nathan	5.10	Everton	Wythenshawe	19.06.98
Lanzini, Manuel	5.6	Al Jazira	Ituzaingo, Arg	15.02.93
Noble, Mark	5.11	–	West Ham	08.05.87
Snodgrass, Robert	6.0	Hull	Glasgow	07.09.87
Soucek, Tomas	6.3	Slavia Prague	Havlicku Brod, Cz	27.02.95
Wilshere, Jack	5.8	Arsenal	Stevenage	01.01.92
Forwards				
Bowen, Jarrod	5.9	Hull	Leominster	20.12.96
Haller, Sebastien	6.3	Eintracht Frankfurt	Ris Orangis, Fr	22.06.94
Hugill, Jordan	6.0	Preston	Middlesbrough	04.06.92
Xande Silva	5.10	Guimaraes	Porto, Port	16.03.97
Yarmolenko, Andriy	6.2	Borussia Dortmund	St Petersburg, Rus	23.10.89

WOLVERHAMPTON WANDERERS

Ground: Molineux Stadium, Waterloo Road, Wolverhampton WV1 4QR
Telephone: 0871 222 1877. **Club nickname:** Wolves
Capacity: 32,050. **Colours:** Yellow and black. **Shirt sponsor:** ManBetX
Record attendance: 61, 315 v Liverpool (FA Cup 5) Feb 11, 1939
Record transfer fee: £30m to Benfica for Raul Jimenez, Apr 2019
Record fee received: £14m from Sunderland for Steven Fletcher, Aug 2012
Record attendance: 61,315 v Liverpool (FA Cup 5), Feb 11, 1935
League Championship: Winners 1953–54, 1957–58, 1958–59
FA Cup: Winners 1893, 1908, 1949, 1960
League Cup: Winners 1974, 1980
European competitions: UEFA Cup runners-up 1971–72
Finishing positions in Premier League: 2003–04 20th, 2009–10 15th, 2003–04 20th, 2011–12 20th, 2018–19 7th, 2019–20 7th
Biggest win: 10-1 v Leicester (Div 2) Apr 15, 1938. Also: 14-0 v Crosswell's Brewery (FA Cup 2) Nov 13, 1886
Biggest defeat: 1-10 v Newton Heath (Div 1) Oct 15, 1892
Highest League scorer in a season: Dennis Westcott 38 (1946–47)
Most League goals in aggregate: Steve Bull 250 (1986–90)
Longest unbeaten League sequence: 20 matches (1923–24) (1984–85)
Longest sequence without a League win: 19 matches (1984–85)
Most capped player: Billy Wright (England) 105

Goalkeepers

Rui Patricio	6.2	Sporting Lisbon	Marrazes, Port	15.02.88

Ruddy, John	6.4	Norwich	St Ives, Camb	24.10.86
Defenders				
Bennett, Ryan	6.2	Norwich	Orsett	06.03.90
Boly, Willy	6.2	Porto	Melun, Fr	03.02.91
Coady, Conor	6.1	Huddersfield	St Helens	25.02.93
Doherty, Matt	5.11	–	Dublin, Ire	16.01.92
Jonny	5.9	Atletico Madrid	Vigo, Sp	03.03.94
Ruben Vinagre	5.9	Monaco	Charneca, Port	09.04.99
Midfielders				
Bruno Jordao	5.11	Braga	Marinha Grande, Por	12.10.98
Dendoncker, Leander	6.2	Anderlecht	Passendale, Bel	15.04.95
Diogo Jota	5.10	Atletico Madrid	Porto	04.12.96
Gibbs-White, Morgan	5.11	–	Stafford	27.01.00
Joao Moutinho	5.7	Monaco	Portimao, Port	08.09.86
Kilman, Max	5.10	Maidenhead	Kensington	23.05.97
Podence, Daniel	5.6	Olympiacos	Oeiras, Por	21.10.95
Ruben Neves	6.0	Porto	Mozelos, Port	13.03.97
Saiss, Romain	6.3	Angers	Bourg-de-Peage, Fr	26.03.90
Forwards				
Bonatini, Leo	6.1	Al-Hilal	Belo Horizonte, Br	28.03.94
Mir, Rafael	6.1	Valencia	Murcia, Sp	18.06.97
Pedro Neto	5.8	Braga	Viana do Castelo, Por	09.03.00
Raul Jimenez	6.2	Benfica	Tepeji del Rio, Mex	05.05.91
Traore, Adama	5.10	Middlesbrough	L'Hospitalet, Sp	25.01.96

ENGLISH FOOTBALL LEAGUE

(At time of going to press)

CHAMPIONSHIP

BARNSLEY

Ground: Oakwell Stadium, Barnsley S71 1ET
Telephone: 01226 211211. **Club nickname:** Tykes
Colours: Red and white. **Capacity:** 23,009
Record attendance: 40,255 v Stoke (FA Cup 5) Feb 15, 1936

Goalkeepers				
Collins, Brad	6.0	Chelsea	Southampton	18.02.97
Walton, Jack	6.1	–	Bury	23.04.98
Defenders				
Andersen, Mads	6.4	Horsens	Albertsund, Den	27.12.97
Diaby, Bambo	6.1	Lokeren	Mataro, Sp	17.12.97
Halme, Aapo	6.5	Leeds	Helsinki, Fin	22.05.98
Ludewig, Kilian	5.9	Salzburg	Germany	05.03.00
Oduor, Clarke	5.10	Leeds	Siaya, Ken	25.06.99
Sollbauer, Michael	6.2	Wolfsberger	St Veit, Aut	15.05.90
Williams, Ben	5.10	Blackburn	–	31.03.99
Williams, Jordan	5.10	Huddersfield	Huddersfield	22.10.99
Midfielders				
Bahre, Mike	5.10	Hannover	Garbsen, Ger	10.08.95
Frieser, Dominik	5.9	LASK	Graz, Aut	09.09.93
Mowatt, Alex	5.10	Leeds	Doncaster	13.02.95

Ritzmaier, Marcel	5.10	Wolfsberger	Knittelfeld, Aut	22.04.93
Simoes, Elliot	5.9	FC United	Portugal	20.12.99
Styles, Callum		Burnley	Bury	28.03.00
Thomas, Luke	5.8	Derby	Soudley	19.02.99
Forwards				
Brown, Jacob	5.10	–	Halifax	10.04.98
Chaplin, Conor	5.7	Coventry	Worthing	16.02.97
Schmidt, Patrick	5.10	Admira Wacker	Eisenstadt, Aut	22.07.98
Woodrow, Cauley	6.1	Fulham	Hemel Hempstead	02.12.94

BIRMINGHAM CITY

Ground: St Andrew's Trillion Trophy Stadium, Birmingham B9 4NH
Telephone: 0844 557 1875. **Club nickname:** Blues
Colours: Blue and white. **Capacity:** 30,016
Record attendance: 66,844 v Everton (FA Cup 5) Feb 11, 1939

Goalkeepers				
Camp, Lee	6.1	Cardiff	Derby	22.08.84
Defenders				
Bajrami, Geraldo	6.2	–	Birmingham	24.09.99
Burke, Ryan	5.11	St Patrick's	Dublin, Ire	23.11.00
Colin, Maxime	5.11	Brentford	Arras, Fr	15.11.91
Dean, Harlee	5.10	Brentford	Basingstoke	26.07.91
Friend, George	6.0	Middlesbrough	Barnstaple	19.10.87
Pedersen, Kristian	6.2	Union Berlin	Ringsted, Den	04.08.94
Roberts, Marc	6.0	Barnsley	Wakefield	26.07.90
Midfielders				
Crowley, Dan	5.9	Willem	Coventry	03.08.97
Davis, David	5.9	Wolve	Smethwick	20.02.91
Gardner, Gary	6.2	Aston Villa	Solihull	29.06.92
Kieftenbeld, Maikel	5.11	Groningen	Lemelerveld, Hol	26.06.90
McEachran, Josh	5.10	Brentford	Oxford	01.03.93
Sunjic, Ivan	6.0	Dinamo Zagreb	Zenica, Bos	09.10.96
Forwards				
Bela, Jeremie	5.8	Albacete	Melun, Fr	08.04.93
Boyd-Munce, Caolan	5.10	Glentoran	Belfast	26.01.00
Jutkiewicz, Lukas	6.1	Burnley	Southampton	20.03.89

BLACKBURN ROVERS

Ground: Ewood Park, Blackburn BB2 4JF
Telephone: 0871 702 1875. **Nickname:** Rovers
Colours: Blue and white. **Capacity:** 31,367
Record attendance: 62,522 v Bolton (FA Cup 6) Mar 2, 1929

Goalkeepers				
Fisher, Andrew	6.0	–	Wigan	12.02.98
Defenders				
Bell, Amari'i	5.11	Fleetwood	Burton	05.05.94
Carter, Hayden	6.2	Manchester City	–	17.12.99
Lenihan, Darragh	5.10	Belvedere	Dunboyne, Ire	16.03.94
Mulgrew, Charlie	6.3	Celtic	Glasgow	06.03.86
Nyambe, Ryan	6.0	–	Katima, Nam	04.12.97
Travis, Lewis	6.0	Liverpool	Whiston	16.10.97

Platt, Matty	6.0	–	Knowsley	03.0.97
Wharton, Scott	–	–	Blackburn	03.10.97
Williams, Derrick	6.2	Bristol City	Waterford, Ire	17.01.93
Midfielders				
Bennett, Elliott	5.10	Norwich	Telford	18.12.88
Buckley, John	5.8	–	Manchester	13.10.99
Dack, Bradley	5.8	Gillingham	Greenwich	31.12.93
Davenport, Jacob	5.10	Manchester City	–	28.12.98
Evans, Corry	5.11	Hull	Belfast	30.07.90
Holtby, Lewis	5.10	Hamburger	Erkelenz, Ger	18.09.90
Johnson, Bradley	5.10	Derby	Hackney	28.04.87
Rankin-Costello, Joe	6.0	Manhester Utd	–	26.07.99
Rothwell, Joe	6.1	Oxford	Manchester	11.01.95
Forwards				
Armstrong, Adam	5.8	Newcastle	Newcastle	10.02.97
Brereton, Ben	6.0	Nottm Forest	Blythe Bridge	18.04.99
Chapman, Harry	5.10	Middlesbrough	Hartlepool	15.11.97
Gallagher, Sam	6.4	Southampton	Crediton	15.09.95
Nuttall, Joe	6.0	Aberdeen	Bury	27.11.97

BOURNEMOUTH

Ground: Vitality Stadium, Dean Court, Bournemouth BH7 7AF
Telephone: 0344 576 1910. **Club nickname:** Cherries
Colours: Red and black. **Capacity:** 11,329
Record attendance: 28,799 v Manchester Utd (FA Cup 6) Mar 2, 1957

Goalkeepers				
Dennis, Will	6.2	Watford	–	10.07.00
Travers, Mark	6.3	–	Maynooth, Ire	18.05.99
Defenders				
Cook, Steve	6.1	Brighton	Hastings	19.04.91
Kelly, Lloyd	5.10	Bristol City	Bristol	01.10.98
Mepham, Chris	6.3	Brentford	Hammersmith	05.11.97
Rico, Diego	6.0	Leganes	Burgos, Sp	23.02.93
Simpson, Jack	5.10	–	Weymouth	08.01.97
Smith, Adam	5.11	Tottenham	Leystonstone	29.04.91
Stanislas, Junior	6.0	Burnley	Eltham	26.11.89
Stanislas, Junior	6.0	Burnley	Eltham	26.11.89
Stacey, Jack	5.11	Luton	Bracknell	06.04.96
Midfielders				
Arter, Harry	5.9	Woking	Eltham	28.12.89
Brooks, David	5.8	Sheffield Utd	Warrington	08.07.97
Cook, Lewis	5.9	Leeds	Leeds	03.02.97
Danjuma, Arnaut	5.10	Club Bruges	Lagos, Nig	31.01.97
Gosling, Dan	5.10	Newcastle	Brixham	02.02.90
Ibe, Jordon	5.7	Liverpool	Bermondsey	08.12.95
Lerma, Jefferson	5.10	Levante	Cerrito, Col	25.10.94
Forwards				
King, Josh	5.11	Blackburn	Oslo, Nor	15.01.92
Solanke, Dominic	6.1	Liverpool	Reading	14.09.97
Surridge, Sam	6.3	–	Slough	28.07.98
Wilson, Callum	5.11	Coventry	Coventry	27.02.92

BRENTFORD

Ground: Community Stadium, Lionel Road, Brentford TW8
Telephone: tbc. **Club nickname:** Bees
Colours: Red, white and black. **Capacity:** 17,250
Record attendance: Griffin Park 38,678 v Leicester (FA Cup 6) Feb 26, 1949

Goalkeepers

Daniels, Luke	6.4	Scunthorpe	Bolton	05.01.88
Raya, David	6.0	Blackburn	Barcelona, Sp	15.09.95

Defenders

Dalsgaard, Henrik	6.3	Zulte Waregem	Roum, Den	27.07.89
Goode, Charlie	6.5	Northampton	Watford	03.08.95
Henry, Rico	5.8	Walsall	Birmingham	08.07.97
Jansson, Pontus	6.4	Leeds	Arlov, Swe	13.02.91
Jeanvier, Julian	6.0	Reims	Clichy, Fr	31.03.92
Pinnock, Ethan	6.2	Barnsley	Lambeth	29.05.93
Roersley, Mads	6.0	FC Copenhagen	Copenhagen, Den	24.06.99
Sorensen, Mads	6.2	AC Horsens	Horsens, Den	07.01.99

Midfielders

Baptiste, Shandon	5.10	Oxford	Grenada	08.04.98
Jensen, Mathias	5.8	Celta	Jersley, Den	01.01.96
Josh Dasilva	6.0	Arsenal	Ilford	23.10.98
Marcondes, Emiliano	6.0	Nordsjaelland	Hvidovre, Den	09.03.95
Mbeumo, Bryan	5.7	Troyes	Avallon, Fr	07.08.99
Norgaard, Christian	6.1	Fiorentina	Copenhagen, Den	10.03.94
Valencia, Joel	5.6	Gliwice	Quininde, Ec	16.11.94

Forwards

Benrahma, Said	5.8	Nice	Temouchent, Alg	10.08.95
Canos, Sergi	5.9	Norwich	Nules, Sp	02.02.97
Forss, Marcus	6.0	–	Turku, Fin	18.06.99
Dervisoglu, Halil	6.0	Sparta Rotterdam	Rotterdam, Hol	08.12.99
Watkins, Ollie	5.10	Exeter	Torbay	30.12.95

BRISTOL CITY

Ground: Ashton Gate, Bristol BS3 2EJ
Telephone: 0871 222 6666. **Club nickname:** Robins
Colours: Red and white. **Capacity:** 27, 000
Record attendance: 43, 335 v Preston (FA Cup 5) Feb 16, 1935

Goalkeepers

Bentley, Daniel	6.2	Brentford	Basildon	13.07.93
Maenpaa, Niki	6.3	Brighton	Espoo, Fin	23.01.85

Defenders

Baker, Nathan	6.3	Aston Villa	Worcester	23.04.91
Dasilva, Jay	5.7	Chelsea	Luton	22.04.98
Hunt, Jack	5.9	Sheffield Wed	Rothwell	06.12.90
Kalas, Tomas	6.0	Chelsea	Olomouc, Cz	15.05.93
Moore, Taylor	6.1	Lens	Walthamstow	12.05.97
Vyner, Zak	6.2	–	London	14.05.97
Williams, Ashley	6.0	Everton	Wolverhampton	23.08.84

Midfielders

Adelakun, Hakeeb	6.0	Scunthorpe	Hackney	11.06.96
Eliasson, Niclas	5.9	Norrkoping	Sweden	07.12.95

Massengo, Han-Noah	5.9	Monaco	Villepinte, Fr	07.07.01
Nagy, Adam	5.10	Bologna	Budapest, Hun	17.06.95
O'Dowda, Callum	5.11	Oxford	Oxford	23.04.95
Rowe, Tommy	5.11	Doncaster	Manchester	01.05.89
Szmodics, Sammie	5.7	Colchester	Colchester	24.09.95
Walsh, Liam	5.8	Everton	Huyton	15.09.97
Williams, Joe	5.10	Wigan	Liverpool	08.12.96
Forwards				
Diedhiou, Famara	6.2	Angers	Saint-Louis, Sen	15.12.92
Paterson, Jamie	5.9	Nottm Forest	Coventry	20.12.91
Weimann, Andreas	6.2	Derby	Vienna, Aut	05.08.91
Wells, Nahki	5.7	Burnley	Hamilton, Berm	01.06.90

CARDIFF CITY

Ground: Cardiff City Stadium, Leckwith Road, Cardiff CF11 8AZ
Telephone: 0845 365 1115. **Club nickname:** Bluebirds
Colours: Blue. **Capacity:** 33,300
Record attendance: Ninian Park: 62,634 Wales v England, Oct 17, 1959; Club: 57,893 v Arsenal (Div 1) Apr 22, 1953, Cardiff City Stadium: 33,280 (Wales v Belgium) Jun 12, 2015. Club: 33,082 v Liverpool (Prem Lge) Apr 21, 2019

Goalkeepers				
Etheridge, Neil	6.3	Walsall	Enfield	07.02.90
Smithies, Alex	6.3	QPR	Huddersfield	05.03.90
Defenders				
Bamba, Sol	6.3	Leeds	Ivry-sur-Seine, Fr	13.01.85
Bennett, Joe	5.10	Aston Villa	Rochdale	28.03.90
Flint, Adan	6.5	Middlesbrough	Pinxton	11.07.89
Morrison, Sean	6.1	Reading	Plymouth	08.01.91
Nelson, Curtis	6.0	Oxford	Newcastle-under-Lyme	21.05.93
Midfielders				
Bacuna, Leandro	6.2	Reading	Groningen, Hol	21.08.91
Hoilett, Junior	5.8	QPR	Brampton, Can	05.06.90
Mendez-Laing, Nathaniel	5.10	Rochdale	Birmingham	15.04.92
Murphy, Josh	5.9	Norwich	Wembley	24.02.95
Pack, Marlon	6.2	Bristol City	Portsmouth	25.03.91
Ralls, Joe	6.0	–	Aldershot	13.10.93
Vaulks, Will	5.11	Rotherham	Wirral	13.09.93
Whyte, Gavin	5.7	Oxford	Belfast	31.01.96
Forwards				
Glatzel, Robert	6.4	Heidenheim	Munich, Ger	08.01.94
Moore, Kieffer	6.4	Wigan	Torquay	08.08.92
Paterson, Callum	6.0	Hearts	London	13.10.94
Tomlin, Lee	5.11	Bristol City	Leicester	12.01.89
Vassell, Isaac	6.0	Birmingham	Newquay	09.09.93

COVENTRY CITY

Ground: St Andrew's, Birmingham B9 4NH (ground sharing).
Telephone: 02476 992326. **Club nickname:** Sky Blues
Colours: Sky blue. **Capacity:** 32,500
Record attendance: Highfield Road: 51,455 v Wolves (Div 2) Apr 29, 1967. Ricoh Arena: 31,407 v Chelsea (FA Cup 6), Mar 7, 2009

Goalkeepers				
Marosi, Marko	6.3	Doncaster	Slovakia	23.10.93
Wilson, Ben	6.1	Bradford	Stanley	09.08.92
Defenders				
Dabo, Fankaty	5.11	Chelsea	Southwark	11.10.95
Dacosta, Julien	6.0	Niort	Marseille	29.05.96
Drysdale, Declan	6.2	Tranmere	Birkenhead	14.11.99
Hyam, Dom	6.2	Reading	Dundee	20.12.95
Mason, Brandon	5.9	Watford	Westminster	30.09.97
McFadzean, Kyle	6.1	Burton	Sheffield	28.02.87
Pask, Josh	6.2	West Ham	Waltham Forest	01.11.97
Rose, Michael	5.11	Ayr	Aberdeen	11.10.95
Midfielders				
Allen, Jamie	5.11	Burton	Rochdale	29.01.95
Eccles, Josh	6.0	–	Coventry	02.04.00
Giles, Ryan	5.11	Wolves (loan)	Telford	26.01.00
Hamer, Gustavo	5.7	Zwolle	Itajai, Br	24.06.97
Hilssner, Marcel	6.0	Paderborn	Leipzig, Ger	30.01.96
Jobello, Wesley	5.10	Ajaccio	Gennevilliers, Mart	23.01.94
Kelly, Liam	5.10	Leyton Orient	Milton Keynes	10.02.90
O'Hare, Callum	5.9	–	Solihull	01.05.8
Shipley, Jordan	6.0	–	Leamington Spa	26.09.97
Forwards				
Bakayoko, Amadou	6.3	Walsall	Sierra Leone	01.01.96
Biamou, Maxime	6.1	Sutton	Creteil, Fr	13.11.90
Godden, Matt	6.1	Peterborough	Canterbury	29.07.71
Kastaneer, Gervane	6.2	Breda	Rotterdam, Hol	09.06.96
Ponticelli, Jordan	5.11	–	Nuneaton	10.09.98

DERBY COUNTY

Ground: Pride Park, Derby DE24 8XL
Telephone: 0871 472 1884. **Club nickname:** Rams
Colours: White and black. **Capacity:** 33,597
Record attendance: Baseball Ground: 41,826 v Tottenham (Div 1) Sep 20, 1969; Pride Park: 33,597 (England v Mexico) May 25, 2011; Club: 33,475 v Rangers (Ted McMinn testimonial) May 1, 2006

Goalkeepers				
Marshall, David	6.3	Wigan	Glasgow	05.03.85
Roos, Kelle	6.5	Nuneaton	Rijkevoort, Hol	31.05.92
Defenders				
Bielik, Kystian	6.2	Arsenal	Konin, Pol	04.01.98
Bogle, Jayden	5.10	Swindon	Reading	27.07.00
Davies, Curtis	6.2	Hull	Waltham Forest	15.03.85
Forsyth, Craig	6.0	Watford	Carnoustie	24.02.89
Lowe, Max	5.9	Birmingham	11.05.97	
Te Wierik, Mike	6.3	Groningen	Hengevelde, Hol	08.06.92
Wisdom, Andre	6.1	Liverpool	Leeds	09.05.93
Midfielders				
Bird, Max	6.0	–	Burton	08.09.00
Brown, Jordan	5.11	–	Stoke	21.06.01
Evans, George	6.1	Reading	Cheadle	13.12.94
Holmes, Duane	5.6	Scunthoprpe	Columbus, US	06.11.94
Knight, Jason	5.9	Cabinteely	Dublin, Ire	13.02.01

Rooney, Wayne	5.9	DC United	Croxteth	24.10.85
Shinnie, Graeme	5.9	Aberdee,	Aberdeen	04.08.91
Sibley, Louie	5.11	–	Birmingham	13.09.01
Forwards				
Bennett, Mason	5.10	–	Shirebrook	15.07.96
Jozefzoon, Florian	5.9	Brentford	Saint-Laurent, Fr Gui	09.01.91
Lawrence, Tom	5.10	Leicester	Wrexham	13.01.94
Marriott, Jack	5.9	Peterborough	Beverley	09.09.84
Martin, Chris	5.10	Norwich	Beccles	04.11.88
Waghorn, Martyn	5.10	Ipswich	South Shields	23.01.93

HUDDERSFIELD TOWN

Ground: John Smith's Stadium, Huddersfield HD1 6PX
Telephone: 0870 444 4677. **Club nickname:** Terriers.
Colours: Blue and white. **Capacity:** 24,169.
Record attendance: Leeds Road: 67,037 v Arsenal (FA Cup 6) Feb 27, 1932; John Smith's Stadium: 24,426 v Manchester Utd (Prem Lge), Oct 21, 2017

Goalkeepers				
Hamer, Ben	6.4	Leicester	Chard	20.11.87
Schofield, Ryan	6.3	–	Huddersfield	11.12.99
Defenders				
Brown, Jaden	5.9	Tottenham	Lewisham	24.01.99
Duhaney, Demaco	5.11	Manchester City	Manchester	13.10.98
Edmonds-Green, Rarmani	6.0	–	Peckham	14.04.00
Elphick, Tommy	5.11	Aston Villa	Brighton	07.09.87
Hadergjonaj, Florent	6.0	Ingolstadt	Langnau, Switz	31.07.94
Kongolo, Terence	6.2	Monaco	Fribourg, Switz	14.02.94
Schindler, Christopher	6.2	1860 Munich	Munich, Ger	29.04.90
Stearman, Richard	6.2	Sheffield Utd	Wolverhampton	19.08.87
Toffolo, Harry	6.0	Lincoln	Welwyn Garden City	19.08.95
Midfielders				
Bacuna, Juninho	5.10	Groningen	Groningen, Hol	07.08.97
Daly, Matty	5.10	Everton	Stckport	10.03.01
Diakhaby, Adama	6.1	Monaco	Ajaccio, Fr	05.07.96
Hogg, Jonathan	5.7	Watford	Middlesbrough	06.12.88
O'Brien, Lewis	5.8	–	Colchester	14.10.98
Pritchard, Alex	5.8	Norwich	Orsett	03.05.93
Sobhi, Ramadan	6.0	Stoke	Cairo, Egy	23.01.97
Forwards				
Campbell, Fraizer	5.9	Hull	Huddersfield	13.09.87
Grant, Karlan	6.0	Charlton	Greenwich	19.12.97
Harratt, Kian	5.11	Leeds	Barnsley	21.06.02
Koroma, Josh	5.10	Leyton Orient	Southwark	09.11.98
Mbenza, Isaac	6.2	Montpellier	Saint-Dennis, Fr	08.03.96
Mounie, Steve	6.3	Montpellier	Parakin, Benin	29.09.94

LUTON TOWN

Ground: Kenilworth Road, Maple Road, Luton LU4 8AW
Telephone: 01582 411622. **Club nickname:** Hatters
Colours: Orange and black. **Capacity:** 10,226
Record attendance: 30,069 v Blackpool (FA Cup 6) Mar 4, 1959

Goalkeepers

Shea, James	5.11	AFC Wimbledon	Islington	16.06.91
Sluga, Simon	6.1	Rijeka	Porec, Cro	17.03.93

Defenders

Bradley, Sonny	6.4	Plymouth	Hull	13.09.91
Cranie, Martin	6.0	Sheffield Utd	Yeovil	26.09.86
Galloway, Brendan	6.1	Everton	Harare, Zim	17.03.96
Pearson, Matty	6.3	Barnsley	Keighley	03.08.93
Potts, Dan	5.8	West Ham	Romford	13.04.94
Rea, Glen	6.1	Brighton	Brighton	03.09.94

Midfielders

Berry, Luke	5.9	Cambridge	Cambridge	12.07.92
Clark, Jordan	6.0	Accrington	Hoyland	22.09.93
Moncur, George	5.9	Barnsley	Swindon	18.08.93
Shinnie, Andrew	5.11	Birmingham	Aberdeen	17.07.89
Tunnicliffe, Ryan	6.0	Millwall	Heywood	30.12.92

Forwards

Collins, James	6.2	Crawley	Coventry	01.12.90
Cornick, Harry	5.11	Bournemouth	Poole	06.03.95
Hylton, Danny	6.0	Oxford	Camden	25.02.89
Lee, Elliot	5.11	Barnsley	Durham	16.12.94
LuaLua Kazenga	5.11	Sunderland	Kinshasa, DR Cong	10.12.90

MIDDLESBROUGH

Ground: Riverside Stadium, Middlesbrough, TS3 6RS
Telephone: 0844 499 6789. **Club nickname:** Boro
Capacity: 35,100. **Colours:** Red
Record attendance: Ayresome Park: 53,596 v Newcastle (Div 1) Dec 27, 1949; Riverside Stadium: 35,000 (England v Slovakia) Jun 11, 2003. Club: 34,836 v Norwich (Prem Lge) Dec 28, 2004

Goalkeepers

Pears, Aynsley	6.1	–	Durham	23.04.98
Stojanovic, Dejan	6.5	St Gallen	Fieldkirch, Aut	19.07.93

Defenders

Bola, Marc	6.1	Blackpool	Greenwich	09.12.97
Coulson, Hayden	5.11	–	Gateshead	17.06.98
Dijksteel, Anfernee	6.0	Charlton	Amsterdam, Hol	27.10.96
Fry, Dael	6.0	–	Middlesbrough	30.08.97
Hall, Grant	6.4	QPR	Brightonm	29.10.91
Spence, Djed	6.1	Fulham	London	09.08.0
Wood, Nathan	6.2	–	Ingleby-Barwick	31.05.02

Midfielders

Browne, Marcus	5.10	West Ham	London	18.12.97
Howson, Jonny	5.11	Norwich	Leeds	21.05.88
Johnson, Marvin	5.10	Oxford	Birmingham	01.12.90
Liddle, Ben	5.7	–	Durham	21.09.98
McNair, Paddy	6.0	Sunderland	Ballyclare	27.04.95
Saville, George	5.10	Millwall	Camberley	01.06.93
Tavernier, Marcus	5.10	Newcastle	Leeds	22.03.99
Walker, Stephen	5.11	–	Middlesbrough	11.10.00
Wing, Lewis	6.1	Shildon	Newton Aycliffe	23.05.95

Forwards

Assombalonga, Britt	5.10	Nottm Forest	Kinshasa, DR Cong	06.12.92

| Fletcher, Ashley | 6.1 | West Ham | Keighley | 02.10.95 |
| O'Neill, Tyrone | 6.1 | – | Grangetown | 12.10.99 |

MILLWALL

Ground: The Den, Zampa Road, London SE16 3LN
Telephone: 0207 232 1222. **Club nickname:** Lions
Colours: Blue. **Capacity:** 20,146
Record attendance: The Den: 48,672 v Derby (FA Cup 5) Feb 20, 1937. New Den: 20,093 v Arsenal (FA Cup 3) Jan 10, 1994

Goalkeepers

| Bialkowski, Bartosz | 6.0 | Ipswich | Braniewo, Pol | 06.07.87 |
| Fielding, Frank | 6.0 | Bristol City | Blackburn | 04.04.88 |

Defenders

Brown, James	6.1	–	Dover	12.01.98
Cooper, Jake	6.4	Reading	Bracknell	03.02.95
Hutchinson, Shaun	6.2	Fulham	Newcastle	23.11.90
McCarthy, Jason	6.1	Wycombe	Southampton	07.11.95
Meredith, James	6.1	Bradford	Albury, Aus	04.04.88
Pearce, Alex	6.2	Derby	Wallingford	09.11.88
Romeo, Mahlon	5.10	Gillingham	Westminster	19.09.95
Wallace, Murray	6.2	Scunthorpe	Glasgow	10.01.93

Midfielders

Burey, Tyler	6.2	AFC Wimbledon	–	09.01.01
Ferguson, Shane	5.11	Newcastle	Derry	12.07.91
Leonard, Ryan	6.1	Sheffield Utd	Plymouth	24.05.92
Mitchell, Billy	5.9	–	Orpington	07.04.01
Connor Mahoney	5.9	Blackburn	Blackburn	12.02.97
Skalak, Jiri	5.9	Brighton	Pardubice, Cz	12.03.92
Thompson, Ben	5.10	–	Sidcup	03.10.95
Wallace, Jed	5.10	Wolves	Reading	26.03.94
Williams, Shaun	6.0	MK Dons	Dublin, Ire	19.09.86
Woods, Ryan	5.8	Stoke (loan)	Norton Canes	13.12.93

Forwards

Bodvarsson, Jon Dadi	6.2	Reading	Slfoss, Ice	25.05.92
Bradshaw, Tom	5.10	Barnsley	Shrewsbury	27.07.92
Smith, Matt	6.6	QPR	Birmingham	07.06.89
Parrott, Troy	6.1	Tottenham (loan)	Dublin, Ire	04.02.02\z

NORWICH CITY

Ground: Carrow Road, Norwich NR1 1JE
Telephone: 01603 760760. **Club nickname:** Canaries
Colours: Yellow and green. **Capacity:** 27,244
Record attendance: 43,984 v Leicester (FA Cup 6), Mar 30, 1963

Goalkeepers

Fahrmann, Ralf	6.5	Schalke (loan)	Chemnitz, Ger	27.09.88
Krul, Tim	6.3	Brighton	Den Haag, Hol	03.04.88
McGovern, Michael	6.3	Hamilton	Enniskillen	12.07.84

Defenders

Aarons, Max	5.10	Luton	Hammersmith	04.01.00
Byram, Sam	5.11	West Ham	Thurrock	16.09.93
Godfrey, Ben	6.0	Middlesbrough	York	1501.98

Hanley, Grant	6.2	Newcastle	Dumfries	20.11.91
Klose, Timm	6.4	Wolfsburg	Frankfurt, Ger	09.05.88
Lewis, Jamal	5.10	–	Luton	25.01.98
McCallum, Sam	5.10	Coventry	Canterbury	02.09.00
Xavi Quintilla	5.10	Villarreal (loan)	Lleida, Sp	23.08.96
Zimmermann, Christoph	6.4	Borussia Dortmund	Dusseldorf, Ger	12.01.93
Midfielders				
Adshead, Daniel	5.7	Rochdale	Manchester	02.09.01
Buendia, Emiliano	5.8	Getafe	Mar del Plata, Arg	25.12.96
Cantwell, Todd	6.0	–	Dereham	27.02.98
Dowell, Kieran	6.0	Everton	Ormskirk	10.10.97
Hernandez, Onel	5.8	Braunschweig	Moron, Cub	01.12.93
Leitner, Moritz	5.9	Augsburg	Munchen, Ger	08.12.92
McLean, Kenny	6.0	Aberdeen	Rutherglen	08.01.92
Rupp, Lukas	5.10	Hoffenheim	Heidelberg, Ger	08.01.91
Skipp, Oliver	5.9	Tottenham (loan)	Welwyn Garden City	16.09.00
Sinani, Danel	6.1	Dudelange	Belgrade, Serb	05.04.97
Sorensen, Jacob	6.0	Esbjerg	Esbjerg, Den	03.03.98
Stiepermann, Marco	6.3	Bochum	Dortmund, Ger	09.02.91
Tettey, Alexander	5.11	Rennes	Accra, Gh	04.04.86
Trybull, Tom	5.11	Den Haag	Berlin, Ger	09.03.93
Vrancic, Mario	6.1	Darmstadt	Slavonski Brod, Croa	23.05.89
Forwards				
Drmic, Josip	6.0	Borussia M'gladbach	Freienbach, Switz	08.08.92
Idah, Adam	6.3	Corinthians	Cork, Ire	11.02.01
Pukki, Teemu	5.11	Brondby	Kotka, Fin	29.03.90
Srbeny, Dennis	6.3	Paderborn	Berlin, Ger	05.05.94

NOTTINGHAM FOREST

Ground: City Ground, Pavilion Road, Nottingham NG2 5FJ
Telephone: 0115 982 4444. **Club nickname:** Forest
Colours: Red and white. **Capacity:** 30,576
Record attendance: 49,946 v Manchester Utd (Div 1) Oct 28, 1967

Goalkeepers				
Samba, Brice	6.1	Caen	Linzolo, Rep Cong	25.04.94
Smith, Jordan	6.1	–	South Normanton	08.12.94
Defenders				
Benalouane, Yohan	6.2	Leicester	Bagnols-sur-Ceze, Fr	28.03.87
Blackett, Tyler	6.1	Reading	Manchester	02.04.94
Bong, Gaetan	6.2	Brighton	Sakbayeme, Cam	25.04.88
Dawson, Michael	6.2	Hull	Northallerton	18.11.83
Figueiredo, Tobias	6.2	Sporting CP	Satao, Port	02.02.94
Jenkinson, Carl	6.1	Arsenal	Harlow	08.02.92
Ribeiro, Yuri	5.11	Benfica	Vieira do Minho, Por	24.01.97
Worrall, Joe	6.4	–	Hucknall	10.01.97
Midfielders				
Adomah, Albert	6.1	Aston Villa	Lambeth	13.12.87
Ameobi, Sammy	6.4	Bolton	Newcastle	01.05.92
Cash, Matty	6.1	–	Slough	07.08.97
Colback, Jack	5.10	Newcastle	Killingworth	24.10.89
Joao Carvalho	5.8	Benfica	Castanheira, Port	09.03.97
Mighten, Alex	5.9	–	Nottingham	11.04.02
Samba Sow	6.1	Dynamo Moscow	Bamako	29.04.89

Tiago Silva	5.8	Feirense	Lisbon, Port	02.06.93
Watson, Ben	5.10	Watford	Camberwell	09.07.85
Yates, Ryan	6.3	–	Lincoln	21.11.97
Forwards				
Grabban, Lewis	6.0	Bournemouth	Croydon	12.01.88
Lolley, Joe	5.10	Huddersfield	Redditch	25.08.92
Taylor, Lyle	6.2	Charlton	Greenwich	29.03.90
Walker, Tyler	5.11	–	Nottingham	17.10.96

PRESTON NORTH END

Ground: Deepdale, Sir Tom Finney Way, Preston PR1 6RU
Telephone: 0844 856 1964. **Club nickname:** Lilywhites
Colours: White and navy. **Capacity:** 23,404
Record attendance: 42,684 v Arsenal (Div 1) Apr 23, 1938

Goalkeepers				
Ripley, Connor	6.3	Middlesbrough	Middlesbrough	13.02.93
Rudd, Declan	6.3	Norwich	Diss	16.01.91
Defenders				
Bauer, Patrick	6.4	Charlton	Backnang, Ger	28.10.92
Davies, Ben	5.11	–	Barrow	11.08.95
Earl, Josh	6.4	–	Southport	24.10.98
Fisher, Darnell	5.9	Rotherham	Reading	04.04.94
Hughes, Andrew	5.11	Peterborough	Cardiff	05.06.92
Huntington, Paul	6.2	Yeovil	Carlisle	17.09.87
Rafferty, Joe	6.0	Rochdale	Liverpool	06.10.93
Storey, Jordan	6.2	Exeter	Yeovil	02.09.97
Midfielders				
Browne, Alan	5.8	Cork	Cork, Ire	15.04.95
Ginnelly, Josh	5.8	Walsall	Coventry	
Harrop, Josh	5.9	Manchester Utd	Stockport	15.12.95
Johnson, Daniel	5.8	Aston Villa	Kingston, Jam	08.10.92
Ledson, Ryan	5.9	Oxford	Liverpool	19.08.97
Pearson, Ben	5.5	Manchester Utd	Oldham	04.01.95
Potts, Brad	6.2	Barnsley	Hexham	07.03.94
Sinclair, Scott	5.8	Celtic	Bath	25.03.89
Forwards				
Barkhuizen, Tom	5.11	Preston	Blackpool	04.07.93
Bodin, Billy	5.11	Bristol Rov	Swindon	24.03.92
Gallagher, Paul	6.0	Leicester	Glasgow	09.08.84
Maguire, Sean	5.9	Cork	Luton	01.05.94
Moult, Louis	6.0	Motherwell	Stoke	14.05.92
Nugent, David	5.11	Derby	Huyton	02.05.85
Robinson, Callum	5.10	Aston Villa	Northampton	02.02.95
Stockley, Jayden	6.3	Exeter	Poole	15.09.93

QUEENS PARK RANGERS

Ground: Kiyan Prince Foundation Stadium, South Africa Road, London W12 7PA
Telephone: 0208 743 0262. **Club nickname:** Hoops
Colours: Blue and white. **Capacity:** 18,360
Record attendance: 35,353 v Leeds (Div 1) 27 Apr, 1974

Goalkeepers

Kelly, Liam	6.3	Livingston	Glasgow	23.01.96
Lumley, Joe	6.4	Tottenham	Harlow	15.02.95

Defenders

Ball, Dominic	6.1	Rotherham	Welwyn Garden City	02.08.95
Barbet, Yoann	62	Brentford	Libourne, Fr	10.05.93
Furlong, Darnell	5.11	–	Luton	31.10.95
Kakay, Osman	5.11	–	Westminster	25.08.97
Leistner, Toni	6.3	Union Berlin	Dresden, Ger	19.08.90
Masterson, Conor	6.1	Liverpool	Cellbridge, Ire	08.09.98
Rangel, Angel	5.11	Swansea	Tortosa, Sp	28.10.82
Wallace, Lee	6.1	Rangers	Edinburgh	01.08.87

Midfielders

Amos, Luke	5.10	Tottenham	Welwyn Garden City	23.02.97
Bettache, Faysal	6.1	Watford	Westminster	07.07.00
Cameron, Geoff	6.3	Stoke	Attleboro, US	11.07.85
Chair, Ilias	5.4	Lierse	Belgium	30.10.97
Manning, Ryan	5.11	Galway	Galway, Ire	14.06.96
Osayi-Samuel, Bright	5.9	Blackpool	Okija, Nig	01.02.97
Shodipo, Olamide	5.10	–	Leixlip, Ire	05.07.97
Thomas, George	5.8	Leicester	Leicester	24.03.97

Forwards

Dykes, Lyndon	6.2	Livingston	Gold Coast, Aus	07.10.95
Eze, Eberechi	5.8	Millwall	Greenwich	29.06.98
Oteh, Aramide	5.9	Tottenham	Lewisham	10.09.98

READING

Ground: Madejski Stadium, Junction 11 M4, Reading RG2 0FL
Telephone: 0118 968 1100. **Club nickname:** Royals
Colours: Blue and white. **Capacity:** 24,200
Record attendance: Elm Park: 33,042 v Brentford (FA Cup 5) Feb 19, 1927; Madejski Stadium: 24,184 v Everton (Prem Lge) Nov 17, 2012

Goalkeepers

Rafael Cabral	6.1	Sampdoria	Sorocabo, Br	20.05.90
Walker, Sam	6.6	Colchester	Gravesend	02.10.91

Defenders

Gunter, Chris	5.11	Nottm Forest	Newport	21.07.89
McIntyre, Tom	6.1	–	Reading	06.11.98
Moore, Liam	6.1	Leicester	Leicester	31.01.93
Morrison, Michael	6.0	Birmingham	Bury St Edmunds	
Obita, Jordan	5.11	–	Oxford	08.12.93
Osho, Gabriel	6.1	–	Reading	14.08.98
Richards, Omar	–	Fulham	Lewisham	15.02.98
Yiadom, Andy	5.11	Barnsley	Holloway	02.12.91

Midfielders

Adam, Charlie	6.1	Stoke	Dunee	10.12.85
Felipe Araruna	5.9	Sao Paulo	Porto Alegre, Br	12.03.96
Laurent, Josh	6.2	Shrewsbury	Leystonstone	06.05.95
McCleary, Garath	5.11	Nottm Forest	Bromley	15.05.87
Meyler, David	6.2	Hull	Cork, Ire	29.05.89
Olise, Michael	6.2	–	–	12.12.01
Rinomhota, Andy	5.9	Portchester	Leeds	21.04.97
Swift, John	6.0	Chelsea	Portsmouth	23.06.95

Forwards

Baldock, Sam	5.8	Brighton	Bedford	15.03.89
Lucas Joao	6.4	Sheffield Wed	Lisbon, Por	04.09.93
Masika, Ayub	5.7	Beijing Ranhe	Nairobi, Ken	10.09.92
Meite, Yakou	6.1	Paris SG	Paris, Fr	11.02.96
Puscas, George	6.2	Palermo	Marghita, Rom	08.04.96

ROTHERHAM UNITED

Ground: New York Stadium, New York Way, Rotherham S60 1AH
Telephone: 08444 140733. **Club nickname:** Millers
Colours: Red and white. **Capacity:** 12,021
Record attendance: Millmoor: 25,170 v Sheffield Wed (Div 2) Jan 26, 1952 and v Sheffield Wed (Div 2) Dec 13, 1952; Don Valley Stadium: 7,082 v Aldershot (Lge 2 play-off semi-final, 2nd leg) May 19, 2010; New York Stadium: 11,758 v Sheffield Utd (Lge 1) Sep 7, 2013

Goalkeepers

Price, Lewis	6.3	Sheffield Wed	Bournemouth	19.07.84

Defenders

Clarke, Trevor	5.9	Shamrock Rov	Dublin, Ire	26.03.98
Harding, Wes	5.11	Birmingham	Leicester	20.10.96
Ihiekwe, Michael	6.1	Tranmere	Liverpool	29.11.92
Jones, Billy	5.11	Sunderland	Shrewsbury	24.03.87
MacDonald, Angus	6.2	Hull	Winchester	15.10.92
Mattock, Joe	6.0	Sheffield Wed	Leicester	15.05.90
Olosunde, Matthew	6.1	Manchester Utd	Philadelphia, US	07.03.98
Robertson, Clark	6.2	Blackpool	Aberdeen	05.09.93
Thompson, Adam	6.1	Bury	Harlow	28.09.92
Tilt, Curtis	6.4	Blackpool	Walsall	04.08.91
Wood, Richard	6.3	Charlton	Ossett	05.07.85

Midfielders

Crooks, Matt	6.1	Northampton	Leeds	20.01.94
Lindsay, Jamie	6.0	Ross Co	Rutherglen	11.10.95
MacDonald, Shaun	6.1	Wigan	Swansea	17.06.88
Sadlier, Kieran	6.0	Doncaster	Haywards Heath	14.09.94
Wiles, Ben	5.8	–	Rotherham	17.04.99

Forwards

Ladapo, Freddie	6.0	Plymouth	Romford	01.02.93
Miller, Mickel	5.8	Hamilton	Croydon	02.12.95
Ogbene, Chiedozie	5.11	Brentford	Lagos, Nig	01.05.97
Proctor, Jamie	6.2	Bolton	Preston	25.03.92
Smith, Michael	6.4	Bury	Wallsend	17.10.91
Vassell, Kyle	6.0	Blackpool	Milton Keynes	07.02.93

SHEFFIELD WEDNESDAY

Ground: Hillsborough, Sheffield, S6 1SW
Telephone: 0871 995 1867. **Club nickname:** Owls
Colours: Blue and white. **Capacity:** 39,812
Record attendance: 72,841 v Manchester City (FA Cup 5) Feb 17, 1934

Goalkeepers

Dawson, Cameron	6.0	Sheffield Utd	Sheffield	07.07.95
Westwood, Keiren	6.1	Sunderland	Manchester	23.10.84

Defenders

Borner, Julian	6.2	Arminia Bielefeld	Weimar, Ger	21.01.91

Dunkley, Chey	6.2	Wigan	Wolverhampton	13.02.92
Hunt, Alex	5.9	–	Sheffield	29.05.00
Iorfa, Dominic	6.4	Wolves	Southend	24.06.95
Lees, Tom	6.1	Leeds	Warwick	18.11.90
Palmer, Liam	6.2	–	Worksop	19.09.91
Midfielders				
Bannan, Barry	5.11	Crystal Palace	Airdrie	01.12.89
Brown, Izzy	6.0	Chelsea (loan)	Peterborough	07.01.97
Dele-Bashiru, Fisayo	5.11	Manchester City	Hamburg, Ger	06.02.01
Harris, Kadeem	5.9	Cardiff	Westminster	08.06.93
Luongo, Massimo	5.9	QPR	Sydney, Aus	25.09.92
Pelupessy, Joel	5.11	Heracles	Nijverdal, Hol	15.05.93
Reach, Adam	6.1	Middlesbrough	Gateshead	03.02.93
Forwards				
Nuhiu, Atdhe	6.6	Rapid Vienna	Prishtina, Kos	29.07.89
Rhodes, Jordan	6.1	Middlesbrough	Oldham	05.02.90

STOKE CITY

Ground: bet365 Stadium, Stanley Matthews Way, Stoke-on-Trent ST4 7EG
Telephone: 01782 367598. **Club nickname:** Potters
Colours: Red and white. **Capacity:** 30,183
Record attendance: Victoria Ground: 51,380 v Arsenal (Div 1) Mar 29, 1937. bet365 Stadium:
30,022 v Everton (Prem Lge) Mar 17, 2018

Goalkeepers				
Butland, Jack	6.4	Birmingham	Bristol	10.03.93
Davies, Adam	6.1	Barnsley	Rintein, Ger	17.07.92
Defenders				
Batth, Danny	6.3	Wolves	Brierley Hill	21.09.90
Collins, Nathan	6.4	Cherry Orchard	Leixlip, Ire	30.04.01
Edwards, Tom	5.9	–	Stafford	22.01.99
Fox, Morgan	6.1	Sheffield Wed	Chelmsford	21.09.93
Lindsay, Liam	6.3	Barnsley	Paisley	12.10.95
Martins Indi, Bruno	6.1	Porto	Barreiro, Port	08.02.92
Shawcross, Ryan	6.3	Manchester Utd	Chester	04.10.87
Smith, Tom	6.1	Huddersfield	Warrington	14.04.92
Tymon, Josh	5.10	Hull	Hull	22.05.99
Midfielders				
Allen, Joe	5.7	Liverpool	Carmarthen	14.03.90
Chester, James	5.11	Aston Villa	Warrington	23.01.89
Clucas, Sam	5.10	Swansea	Lincoln	25.09.90
Cousins, Jordan	5.10	QPR	Greenwich	06.03.94
Imbula, Giannelli	6.1	Porto	Vilvoorde, Bel	12.09.92
Ince, Tom	5.10	Huddersfield	Stockport	30.01.92
McClean, James	5.11	WBA	Derry	22.04.89
Oakley-Boothe, Tashan	6.0	Tottenham	Lambeth	14.02.00
Obi, John Mikel	6.2	Trabzonspor	Jos, Nig	22.04.87
Ndiaye, Badou	5.11	Galatasaray	Dakar, Sen	27.10.90
Powell, Nick	6.0	Wigan	Crewe	23.03.94
Sorenson, Lasse	6.1	Esbjerg	Vejen, Den	21.10.99
Thompson, Jordan	5.9	Blackpool	Belfast	03.01.97
Verlinden, Thibaud	5.8	Standard Liege	Brussels, Bel	09.07.99
Forwards				
Afobe, Benik	6.0	Wolves	Waltham Forest	12.02.93

Campbell, Tyrese	6.0	Manchester City	Cheadle Hulme	28.12.99
Fletcher, Steven	6.1	Sheffield Wed	Shrewsbury	26.03.87
Gregory, Lee	6.2	Millwall	Sheffield	26.08.88
Vokes, Sam	5.11	Burnley	Lymington	21.10.89

SWANSEA CITY

Ground: Liberty Stadium, Morfa, Swansea SA1 2FA
Telephone: 01792 616600. **Club nickname:** Swans
Colours: White. **Capacity:** 20,972.
Record attendance: Vetch Field: 32, 796 v Arsenal (FA Cup 4) Feb 17, 1968. Liberty Stadium: 20, 972 v Liverpool (Prem Lge) May 1, 2016

Goalkeepers

| Benda, Steven | 6.3 | 1860 Munich | Stuttgart, Ger | 01.10.98 |
| Woodman, Freddie | 6.2 | Newcastle (loan) | Croydon | 04.03.97 |

Defenders

Bidwell, Jake	6.1	QPR	Southport	21.03.93
Cabango, Ben	6.1	Newport	Cardiff	30.05.00
John, Declan	5.10	Rangers	Merthyr Tydfil	30.06.95
Naughton, Kyle	5.10	Tottenham	Sheffield	11.11.88
Roberts, Connor	5.10	–	Neath	23.09.95
Rodon, Joe	6.4	–	Llangyfelach	22.10.97

Midfielders

Byers, George	5.11	Watford	Ilford	29.05.96
Celina, Bersant	5.11	Manchester City	Prizren, Kos	09.09.96
Dhanda, Yan	5.8	Liverpool	Birmingham	14.12.98
Dyer, Nathan	5.10	Southampton	Trowbridge	29.11.87
Fulton, Jay	5.10	Falkirk	Bolton	04.04.94
Grimes, Matt	5.10	Exeter	Exeter	15.07.95
McKay, Barrie	5.9	Nottm Forest	Paisley	30.12.94

Forwards

| Ayew, Andre | 5.10 | West Ham | Seclin, Fr | 17.12.89 |
| Cullen, Liam | 5.10 | – | Tenby | 23.04.99 |

WATFORD

Ground: Vicarage Road Stadium, Vicarage Road, Watford WD18 OER
Telephone: 01923 496000. **Club nickname:** Hornets
Colours: Yellow and black. **Capacity:** 21,000
Record attendance: 34,099 v Manchester Utd (FA Cup 4 rep) Feb 3, 1969

Goalkeepers

| Bachmann, Daniel | 6.3 | Stoke | Vienna, Aut | 09.07.94 |
| Foster, Ben | 6.2 | WBA | Leamington | 03.04.83 |

Defenders

Cathcart, Craig	6.2	Blackpool	Belfast	06.02.89
Dawson, Craig	6.2	WBA	Rochdale	06.05.90
Femenia, Kiko	5.9	Alaves	Sanet Negrals, Sp	02.02.91
Janmaat, Daryl	6.1	Newcastle	Leidschendam, Hol	22.07.89
Kabasele, Christian	6.1	Genk	Lubumbashi, DR Cong	24.02.91
Masina, Adam	6.2	Bologna	Khouribga, Mor	02.01.94
Ngakia, Jeremy	6.1	West Ham	Lewisham	07.09.00
Prodl, Sebastian	6.4	Werder Bremen	Graz, Aut	21.06.87

Midfielders

| Capoue, Etienne | 6.2 | Tottenham | Niort, Fr | 11.07.88 |

Chalobah, Nathaniel	6.1	Chelsea	Freetown, SLeone	12.12.94
Cleverley, Tom	5.10	Everton	Basingstoke	12.08.89
Doucoure, Abdoulaye	6.0	Rennes	Meulan, Fr	01.01.93
Hughes, Will	6.1	Derby	Weybridge	07.04.95
Pereyra, Roberto	6.0	Juventus	San Miguel, Arg	07.01.91
Pussetto, Ignacio	5.11	Udinese	Canada Rosquin, Arg	21.12.95
Quina, Domingos	5.10	West Ham	Bissau, Guin-Biss	18.11.99
Forwards				
Deeney, Troy	6.0	Walsall	Birmingham	29.06.88
Deulofeu, Gerard	5.10	Barcelona	Riudarenes, Sp	13.03.94
Gray, Andre	5.10	Burnley	Wolverhampton	26.06.91
Sarr, Ismaila	6.1	Rennes	Saint-Louis, Sen	25.02.98
Success, Isaac	6.0	Granada	Benin City, Nig	07.01.96
Welbeck, Danny	6.1	Arsenal	Manchester	26.11.90

WYCOMBE WANDERERS

Ground: Adams Park, Hillbottom Road, High Wycombe HP12 4HJ
Telephone: 01494 472100. **Club nickname:** Chairboys
Colours: Light and dark blue. **Capacity:** 10,300
Record attendance: 10,000 v Chelsea (friendly) July 13, 2005

Goalkeepers				
Allsop, Ryan	6.3	Bournemouth	Birmingham	17.06.92
Yates, Cameron	6.0	Leicester	Edinburgh	14.02.99
Defenders				
Charles, Darius	6.1	AFC Wimbledon	Ealing	10.12.87
Grimmer, Jack	–	Coventry	Aberdeen	25.01.94
Jacobson, Joe	5.11	Shrewsbury	Cardiff	17.11.86
Phillips, Giles	6.3	QPR	Chicago, US	22.06.97
Stewart, Anthony	6.0	Crewe	Lambeth	18.09.92
Midfielders				
Bloomfield, Matt	5.8	Ipswich	Felixstowe	08.02.84
Freeman, Nick	5.11	Biggleswade	Stevenage	07.11.95
Gape, Dominic	5.11	Southampton	Burton Bradstock	09.09.94
Onyedinma, Fred		Millwall	Lagos, Nig	24.11.96
Pattison, Alex	5.8	Middlesbrough	Darlington	06.09.97
Wheeler, David	5.11	QPR	Brighton	04.10.90
Thompson, Curtis	5.7	Notts Co	Nottingham	02.09.93
Forwards				
Akinfenwa, Adebayo	6.0	Wimbledon	Islington	10.05.82
Ikpeazu, Uche	6.2	Hearts	Harrow	28.02.95
Kashket, Scott	5.9	Leyton Orient	Chigwell	25.02.96
Parker, Josh	5.11	Charlton	Slough	01.12.90
Samuel; Alex	5.9	Stevenage	Neath	20.09.95

LEAGUE ONE

ACCRINGTON STANLEY

Ground: Wham Stadium, Livingstone Road, Accrington BB5 5BX
Telephone: 0871 434 1968. **Club nickname:** Stanley
Colours: Red and white. **Capacity:** 5,500
Record attendance: 5,397 v Derby (FA Cup 4) Jan 26, 2019

Goalkeepers

Savin, Toby	6.4	Crewe	–	26.05.00

Defenders

Barclay, Ben	6.2	Brighton	Altrincham	07.10.96
Burgess, Cameron	6.4	Scunthorpe	Aberdeen	21.10.95
Conneely, Seamus	6.1	Sligo	Lambeth	09.07.88
Hughes, Mark	6.3	Stevenage	Kirkby	09.12.86
Callum Johnson	–	Middlesbrough	Yarm	23.10.96
Maguire, Joe	5.10	Fleetwood	Manchester	18.01.96
Ogle, Reaagan	5.8	–	Wollongong, Aus	29.03.99
Mohammed, Zehn	5.11	–	Blackburn	28.01.00
Rodgers, Harvey	5.11	Fleetwood	York	20.10.96
Sykes, Ross	6.5	–	Burnley	26.03.99

Midfielders

Cassidy, Ryan	5.9	Watford (loan)	Ireland	02.03.01
Finley, Sam	5.8	Fylde	Liverpool	04.08.92
McConville, Sean	5.11	Chester	Burscough	06.03.89
Pritchard, Joe	5.8	Bolton	Watford	10.09.96
Sherif, Lamine	5.10	Leicester	Conakry, Guin	27.01.99

Forwards

Allan, Tom	5.11	Newcastle	Newcastle	23.09.99
Bishop, Colby	5.11	Leamington	Nottingham	04.11.96
Charles, Dion	6.0	Southport	Preton	07.10.95

AFC WIMBLEDON

Ground: Kingsmeadow, Kingston Road, Kingston upon Thames KT1 3PB
Telephone: 0208 547 3528. **Club nickname:** Dons
Colours: Blue. Capacity: 4,850
Record attendance: 4,870 v Accrington (Lge 2 play-off semi-final 1st leg) May 14, 2016

Goalkeepers

Trueman, Connal	6.1	Birmingham (loan)	Birmingham	26.03.96
Tzanev, Nik	6.5	Brentford	Wellington, NZ	23.12.96

Defenders

Guinness-Walker, Nesta	5.11	Met Police	London	14.09.99
Kalambay, Paul	6.0	–	Dulwich	09.07.99
Madelin, Jack	6.1	–	London	19.04.02
Nightingale, Will	6.1	–	Wandsworth	02.08.95
Oksanen, Jaakko	6.0	Brentford (loan)	Helsinki, Fin	07.11.00
Osew, Paul	5.7	Brentford	London	25.11.00
O'Neill, Luke	6.0	Gillingham	Slough	20.08.91
Thomas, Terell	6.0	Wigan	Redbridge	13.10.97

Midfielders

Chislett, Ethan	5.10	Aldershot	Guldford	22.02.00
Hartigan, Anthony	5.10	–	Kingston upon Thames	27.01.00
McLoughlin, Shane	5.9	Ipswich	Castleisland, Ire	01.03.97
Reilly, Callum	6.1	Gillingham	Warrington	03.10.93
Woodyard, Alex	5.9	Peterborough	Gravesend	03.05.93

Forwards

Palmer, Ollie	6.6	Crawley	Epsom	21.01.92
Pigott, Joe	6.2	Maidstone	Maidstone	24.11.93

BLACKPOOL

Ground: Bloomfield Road, Blackpool FY1 6JJ
Telephone: 0871 622 1953. **Club nickname:** Seasiders
Colours: Tangerine and white. **Capacity:** 17,338
Record attendance: 38,098 v Wolves (Div 1) Sep 17, 1955

Goalkeepers

Maxwell, Chris	6.1	Preston	St Asaph	30.07.90
Sims, Jack	6.0	–	Southend	27.01.99

Defenders

Ekpiteta, Marvin	6.4	Leyton Orient	Enfield	26.08.95
Howe, Teddy	5.11	Reading	Oxford	09.10.98
Husband, James	5.11	Norwich	Leeds	03.01.94
Nottingham, Michael	6.4	Salford	Birmingham	14.04.89
Thorniley, Jordan	5.11	Sheffield Wed	Warrington	24.11.96
Turton, Ollie	5.11	Crewe	Manchester	06.12.92

Midfielders

Antwi, Cameron	6.0	Fulham	London	07.10.01
Devitt, Jamie	5.10	Carlisle	Dublin, Ire	06.07.90
Feeney, Liam	6.0	Blackburn	Hammersmith	21.01.87
Kaikai, Sullay	6.0	Breda	Southwark	26.08.95
Robson, Ethan	6.0	Sunderland	Houghton-le-Spring	25.10.96
Virtue, Matty	5.10	Liverpool	Epsom	02.05.97
Ward, Grant	5.10	Ipswich	Lewisham	05.12.94

Forwards

Anderson, Keshi	5.9	Swindon	Luton	06.04.95
Hamilton CJ	5.7	Mansfield	Harrow	23.03.95
Madine, Gary	6.3	Cardiff	Gateshead	24.08.90
Nuttall, Joe	6.0	Blackburn	Bury	27.01.97
Sarkic, Oliver	6.0	Burton	Grimsby	23.07.97
Yates, Jerry	5.10	Rotherham	Doncaster	10.11.96
Yussuf, Adi	6.1	Solihull	Zanzibar, Tanz	20.02.92

BRISTOL ROVERS

Ground: Memorial Stadium, Filton Avenue, Horfield, Bristol BS7 0BF
Telephone: 0117 909 6648. **Club nickname:** Pirates
Colours: Blue and white. **Capacity:** 12,011
Record attendance: Eastville: 38,472 v Preston (FA Cup 4) Jan 30, 1960. Memorial Stadium: 12,011 v WBA (FA Cup 6) Mar 9, 2008

Goalkeepers

Jaakkola, Anssi	6.5	Reading	Kemi, Fin	13.03.87
Van Stappershoef, Jordi	6.0	Volendam	Amsterdam, Hol	10.03.96

Defenders

Baldwin, Jack	6.1	Sunderland	Barking	30.06.93
Davies, Tom	5.11	Coventry	Warrington	18.04.92
Ehmer, Max	6.2	Gillingham	Frankfurt, Ger	03.02.92
Grant, Josh	6.1	Chelsea	Brixton	11.10.98
Hare, Josh	6.0	Eastleigh	Canterbury	12.08.94
Harries, Cian	6.1	Swansea	Birmingham	01.04.97
Kelly, Michael	5.11	Leicester	Kilmarnock	03.11.97
Kilgour, Alfie	5.10	–	Bath	18.05.98
Leahy, Luke	5.10	Walsall	Coventry	19.11.92

| Little, Mark | 6.1 | Bolton | Worcester | 20.08.88 |
| Westbrooke, Zain | 5.11 | Coventry | Chertsey | 28.10.96 |

Midfielders

Barrett, Josh	5.11	Reading	Oxford	21.06.98
Bennett, Kyle	5.5	Portsmouth	Telford	09.09.90
Hargreaves, Cameron	5.10	Exeter	Plymouth	01.12.98
Mitchell-Lawson, Jayden	5.6	Derby (loan)	–	17.09.99
Nicholson, Sam	5.10	Colorado	Edinburgh	20.01.95
Ogogo, Abu	5.9	Coventry	Epsom	03.11.89
Upson, Ed	5.10	MK Dons	Bury St Edmunds	21.11.89

Forwards

Ayunga, Jonah	6.1	Havant	Beaminster	24.04.97
Clarke-Harris, Jonson	6.0	Coventry	Leicester	20.07.94
Daly, James	5.11	Crystal Palace	Brighton	12.01.00
Rodman, Alex	6.2	Shrewsbury	Sutton Coldfield	15.12.87

BURTON ALBION

Ground: Pirelli Stadium, Princess Way, Burton upon Trent DE13 AR
Telephone: 01283 565938. **Club nickname:** Brewers
Colours: Yellow and black. **Capacity:** 6,912
Record attendance: 6,746 v Derby (Champ), Aug 26, 2016

Goalkeepers

| Garratt, Ben | 6.1 | Crewe | Market Drayton | 25.04.94 |
| Hawkins, Callum | 6.2 | – | Rotherham | 12.12.99 |

Defenders

Anderson, Jevan	6.1	Formartine	Aberdeen-	03.03.00
Bostwick, Michael	6.3	Lincoln	Eltham	17.05.88
Brayford, John	5.8	Sheffield Utd	Stoke	29.12.87
Buxton, Jake	5.11	Wigan	Sutton-in-Ashfield	04.03.85
Daniel, Colin	5.11	Peterboroughl	Nottingham	15.02.88
Eardley, Neal	5.11	Lincoln	Llandudno	06.11.88
Hutchinson, Reece	5.8	–	Birmingham	14.04.00
Wallace, Kieran	6.1	Matlock	Nottingham	26.01.95

Midfielders

Edwards, Ryan	5.9	Hearts	Singapore	17.11.93
Fox, Ben	5.11	–	Burton	01.02.98
Lawless, Steven	5.7	Livingston	Glasgow	12.04.91
O'Toole, John-Joe	6.2	Northampton	Harrow	30.09.88
Powell, Joe	5.11	West Ham	Newham,	30.10.98
Quinn, Stephen	5.6	Reading	Dublin, Ire	01.04.86

Forwards

Akins, Lucas	6.0	Stevenage	Huddersfield	25.02.89
Hemmings, Kane	6.1	Dundee	Burton	08.04.91
Varney, Luke	5.11	Cheltenham	Burton	28.09.82
Vernam, Charles	5.9	Derby	Lincoln	08.10.96

CHARLTON ATHLETIC

Ground: The Valley, Floyd Road, London SE7 8BL
Telephone: 0208 333 4000. **Club nickname:** Addicks
Colours: Red and white. **Capacity:** 27,111
Record attendance: 75,031 v Aston Villa (FA Cup 5) Feb 12, 1938

Goalkeepers

Amos, Ben	6.4	Bolton	Macclesfield	10.04.90
Phillips, Dillon	6.2	–	Hornchurch	11.06.95

Defenders

Lockyer, Tom	6.1	Bristol Rov	Cardiff	03.12.94
Matthews, Adam	5.10	Sunderland	Swansea	13.01.92
Oshilaja, Deji	6.0	AFC Wimbledon	Bermondsey	16.07.93
Pearce, Jason	5.11	Wigan	Hillingdon	06.12.87
Purrington, Ben	5.9	Rotherham	Exeter	05.05.96
Sarr, Naby	6.5	Sporting Lisbon	Marseille, Fr	13.08.93

Midfielders

Doughty, Alfie	6.0	–	London	21.12.99
Forster-Caskey, Jake	5.10	Brighton	Southend	05.04.94
Gilbey, Alex	6.0	MK Dons	Dagenham	09.12.94
Lapslie, George	5.9	–	Waltham Forest	05.09.97
Morgan, Albie	5.11	–	Rochester	02.02.00
Pratley, Darren	6.0	Bolton	Barking	22.04.85
Vennings, James	5.8	–	–	24.05.00
Williams, Jonathan	5.7	Crystal Palace	Pembury	09.10.93

Forwards

Aneke, Chuks	6.3	MK Dons	Newham	03.07.93
Bonne, Macauley	5.11	Leyton Orient	Ipswich	26.10.95
Hemed, Tomer	6.0	Brighton	Kioryat Tiv'on, Isr	02.05.87
Washington, Conor		Hearts	Chatham	18.05.92

CREWE ALEXANDRA

Ground: Alexandra Stadium, Gresty Road, Crewe CW2 6EB
Telephone: 01270 213014. **Club nickname:** Railwaymen
Colours: Red and white. **Capacity:** 10,066
Record attendance: 20,000 v Tottenham (FA Cup 4) Jan 30, 1960

Goalkeepers

Jaaskelainen, Will	6.0	Bolton	Bolton	25.07.98
Richards, David	6.0	Bristol City	Abergavenny	31.12.93

Defenders

Adebisi, Rio	5.10	–	Croydon	27.09.00
Johnson, Travis	6.3	–	Stoke	28.08.00
Lancashire, Olly	6.1	Swindon	Basingstoke	13.12.88
Ng, Perry	5.11	–	Liverpool	27.04.96
Nolan, Eddie	6.0	Blackpool	Waterford, Ire	05.08.88
Offord, Luke	5.7	–	Chichester	19.11.99

Midfielders

Ainley, Callum	5.8	–	Middlewich	02.11.97
Dale, Owen	5.9	–	Warrington	01.11.98
Finney, Oliver	5.7	–	Stoke	15.12.97
Griffiths, Regan	5.11	–	Liverpool	01.05.00
Kirk, Charlie	5.7	–	Winsford	24.12.97
Lowery, Tom	–	–	Holmes Chapel	31.12.97
Lundstram, Josh	5.9	–	Stoke	19.02.99
Pickering, Harry	–	–	Chester	29.12.98
Powell, Daniel	6.2	Northampton	Luton	12.03.91
Wintle, Ryan	5.6	Alsager	Newcastle-under-Lyme	13.06.97

Forwards

Mandron, Mikael	6.3	Gillingham	Boulogne, Fr	11.01.94

| Porter, Chris | 6.1 | Colchester | Wigan | 12.12.83 |
| Zanzala, Offrande | 6.1 | Accrington | Brazzaville, Rep Cong | 08.11.96 |

DONCASTER ROVERS

Ground: Keepmoat Stadium, Stadium Way, Doncaster DN4 5JW
Telephone: 01302 764664. **Club nickname:** Rovers
Colours: Red and white. **Capacity:** 15,231
Record attendance: Belle Vue: 37,149 v Hull (Div 3 N) Oct 2, 1948. Keepmoat Stadium: 15,001 v Leeds (Lge 1) Apr 1, 2008

Goalkeepers
| Bursik, Josef | 6.2 | Stoke (loan) | Lambeth | 12.07.00 |
| Jones, Louis | 6.1 | – | Doncaster | 12.10.98 |

Defenders
Anderson, Tom	6.3	Burnley	Burnley	02.09.93
James, Reece	6.0	Sunderland	Bacup	07.11.93
Wright, Joe	6.4	Huddersfield	Monk Fryston	26.02.95

Midfielders
Amos, Danny	5.11	–	Sheffield	22.12.99
Blair, Matty	5.10	Mansfield	Warwick	30.11.87
Coppinger, James	5.7	Exeter	Middlesbrough	10.01.81
Crawford, Ali	5.8	Hamilton	Lanark	30.07.91
Halliday, Brad	5.11	Cambridge	Redcar	10.07.95
Lokilo, Jason	5.9	Crystal Palace	Brussels, Bel	17.09.98
Madger Gomes	5.10	Istra NK	Alicante, Sp	01.02.92
Whiteman, Ben	6.0	Sheffield Utd	Rochdale	17.06.96

Forwards
| Okenabirhie, Fejiri | 5.10 | Shrewsbury | Hendon | 25.02.96 |
| Taylor, Jon | 5.11 | Rotherham | Liverpool | 20.07.92 |

FLEETWOOD TOWN

Ground: Highbury Stadium, Park Avenue, Fleetwod FY7 6TX
Telephone: 01253 775080. **Club nickname:** Fishermen
Colours: Red and white. **Capacity:** 5,311
Record attendance: 5,194 v York (Lge 2 play-off semi-final, 2nd leg) May 16, 2014

Goalkeepers
| Cairns, Alex | 6.0 | Rotherham | Doncaster | 04.01.93 |
| Coleman, Joel | 6.4 | Huddersfield | Bolton | 06.09.95 |

Defenders
| Andrew, Danny | 5.11 | Doncaster | Holbeach | 23.12.90 |
| Boyes, Morgan | 5.11 | Liverpool (loan) | Chester | 22.04.01 |

Midfielders
Camps, Callum	5.11	Rochdale	Stockport	14.03.96
Coutts, Paul	6.1	Sheffield Utd	Aberdeen	22.07.88
Morris, Josh	5, 0	Scunthorpe	Preston	30.09.91
Rossiter, Jordan	5.10	Rangers	Liverpool	24.03.97
Sowerby, Jack	5.9	–	Preston	23.03.95
Wallace, James	5.11	Tranmere	Liverpool	19.12.91
Whelan, Glenn	5.11	Hearts	Dublin, Ire	13.01.84

Forwards
| Biggins, Harrison | 5.11 | Stocksbridge | Sheffield | 15.03.96 |
| Burns, Wes | 5.8 | Bristol City | Cardiff | 23.11.94 |

| Evans, Ched | 6.0 | Sheffield Utd | Rhyl | 28.12.88 |
| Madden, Paddy | 6.0 | Scunthorpe | Dublin, Ire | 04.03.90 |

GILLINGHAM

Ground: Mems Priestfield Stadium, Redfern Avenue, Gillingham ME7 4DD
Telephone: 01634 300000. **Club nickname:** Gills
Colours: Blue and white. **Capacity:** 11,582
Record attendance: 23,002 v QPR. (FA Cup 3) Jan 10, 1948

Goalkeepers

| Bonham, Jack | 6.4 | Brentford | Stevenage | 14.09.93 |
| Walsh, Joe | 6.2 | – | Medway | 01.04.02 |

Defenders

Fuller, Barry	5.10	AFC Wimbledon	Ashford, Kent	25.09.84
Graham, Jordan	6.0	Wolves	Coventry	05.03.95
Hodson, Lee	5.11	Rangers	Boreham Wood	02.10.91
Jackson, Ryan	5.9	Colchester	Streatham	31.07.90
McKenzie, Robbie	6.1	Hull	Hull	25.09.98
Medley, Zech	6.5	Arsenal (loan)	Greenwich	09.07.00
Ogilvie, Connor	6.1	Tottenham	Waltham Abbey	14.02.96
Tucker, Jack	6.2	–	Whitstable	12.11.99

Midfielders

Coyle, Trae	5.10	Arsenal (loan)	London	11.01.01
Dempsey, Kyle	5.10	Fleetwood	Whitehaven	17.09.95
MacDonald, Alex	5.7	Mansfield	Nottingham	14.04.90
Mellis, Jacob	5.11	Bolton	Nottingham	08.01.91
O'Keefe, Stuart	5.8	Cardiff	Norwich	04.03.91
Willock, Matty	5.8	Manchester Utd	Waltham Forest	20.08.96

Forwards

Akinde, John	6.2	Lincoln	Gravesend	08.07.89
Hanlan, Brandon	6.0	Charlton	Chelsea	31.05.97
Oliver, Vadaine	6.1	Northampton	Sheffield	21.10.91

HULL CITY

Ground: KCOM Stadium, Anlaby Road, Hull, HU3 6HU
Telephone: 01482 504 600. **Club nickname:** Tigers
Colours: Amber and black. **Capacity:** 25,404
Record attendance: Boothferry Park: 55,019 v Manchester Utd (FA Cup 6) Feb 26, 1949. KC Stadium: 25,030 v Liverpool (Prem Lge) May 9, 2010. Also: 25,280 (England U21 v Holland) Feb 17, 2004

Goalkeepers

| Ingram, Matt | 6.3 | QPR | High Wycombe | 18.12.93 |
| Long, George | 6.4 | Sheffield Utd | Sheffield | 05.11.93 |

Defenders

Arthur, Festus	6.2	Stockport	Hamburg, Ger	27.02.00
Burke, Reece	6.2	West Ham	Newham	02.09.96
Coyle, Lewie	5.8	Fleetwood	Hull	15.10.95
Elder, Callum	5.11	Leicester	Sydney, Aus	27.01.95
Emmanuel, Josh	6.0	Bolton	London	18.08.97
De Wijs, Jordy	6.2	PSV Eindhoven	Kortrijk, Bel	08.01.95
Fleming, Brandon	5.10	–	Dewsbury	03.12.99
McLoughlin, Sean	6.3	Cork City	Cork, Iree	13.11.96
Tafazolli, Ryan	6.5	Peterborough	Sutton	28.09.91

Midfielders

Batty, Daniel	5.11	–	Pontefract	10.12.97
Docherty, Greg	5.8	Rangers	Milngavie	10.09.96
Honeyman, George	5.8	Sunderland	Prudhoe	08.09.94
Leonardo Da Silva	5.7	Wigan	Lisbon, Por	30.11.98
Milinkovic, David	5.11	Genoa	Antibes, Fr	20.05.94
Samuelsen, Martin	6.2	West Ham	Haugesund, Nor	17.04.97
Sheaf, Max	5.10	–	Gravesend	10.03.0
Smallwood, Richie	5.11	Blackburn	Redcar	29.12.90

Forwards

Lewis-Potter, Keane	5.11	–	Hull	22.02.0
Magennis, Josh	6.2	Bolton	Bangor, NI	15.08.90
Scott, James	6.2	Motherwell	Glasgow	30.08.00
Wilks, Mallik	5.11	Barnsley	Leeds	15.12.98

IPSWICH TOWN

Ground: Portman Road, Ipswich IP1 2DA
Telephone: 01473 400500. **Club nickname:** Blues/Town
Colours: Blue and white. **Capacity:** 30,300
Record attendance: 38,010 v Leeds (FA Cup 6) Mar 8, 1975

Goalkeepers

| Cornell, David | 6.2 | Northampton | Waunarlwydd | 28.03.91 |
| Holy, Tomas | 6.9 | Gillingham | Rychnov, Cz | 10.12.91 |

Defenders

Chambers, Luke	5.11	Nottm Forest	Kettering	29.08.85
Donacien, Janoi	6.0	Accrington	Castries, St Luc	03.11.93
Kenlock, Myles	6.1	–	Croydon	29.11.96
Nsiala, Toto	6.4	Shrewsbury	Kinshasa, DR Cong	25.03.92
Nydam, Tristan	5.8	–	Harare, Zim	06.11.99
Vincent-Young, Kane	5.11	Colchester	Camden	15.03.96
Ward, Stephen	5.11	Stoke	Dublin, Ire	20.08.85
Wilson, James	6.3	Lincoln	Newpoprt	26.12.89
Woolfenden, Luke	6.1	–	Ipswich	21.10.98

Midfielders

Bishop, Teddy	5.11	–	Cambridge	15.07.96
Downes, Flynn	5.10	–	Brentwood	20.01.99
Dozzell, Andre	5.10	–	Ipswich	02.05.99
Edwards, Gwion	5.9	Peterborough	Lampeter	01.03.93
El Mizouni, Idris	5.10	–	Paris, Fr	26.09.00
Huws, Emyr	5.10	Cardiff	Llanelli	30.09.93
Judge, Alan	6.0	Brentford	Dublin, Ire	11.11.88
Nolan, Jon	5.10	Shrewsbury	Huyton	22.04.92
Skuse, Cole	5.9	Bristol City	Bristol	29.03.86

Forwards

Hawkins, Oli	6.4	Portsmouth	Ealing	08.04.92
Jackson, Kayden	5.11	Accrington	Bradford	22.02.94
Norwood, James	5.10	Tranmere	Eastbourne	05.09.90
Sears, Freddie	5.10	Colchester	Hornchurch	27.11.89

LINCOLN CITY

Ground: Sincil Bank Stadium, Lincoln LN5 8LD
Telephone: 01522 880011. **Club nickname:** Imps

Colours: Red and white. **Capacity:** 10,130
Record attendance: 23,196 v Derby (League Cup 4) Nov 15, 1967

Goalkeepers

Ross, Ethan	6.3	Colchester	Ashington	06.03.97

Defenders

Eyoma, Timothy	6.0	Tottenham (loan)	Hackney	29.01.00
Jackson, Adam	6.2	Hibernian	Darlington	18.05.94
Lewis, Aaron	6.0	Swansea	Swansea	26.06.98
Melbourne, Max	5.10	WBA	Solihull	24.10.98
Montsma, Lewis	6.3	Dordrecht	Amsterdam, Hol	25.04.98

Midfielders

Anderson, Harry	5.7	Peterborough	Slough	09.01.97
Bradley, Alex	5.11	WBA	Worcester	27.01.99
Bridcutt, Liam	5.9	Nottm Forest	Reading	08.05.89
Chapman, Ellis	6.1	–	Lincoln	08.01.01
Jones, Jamie	5.9	Crewe	Winsford	01.02.96
Elbouzedi, Zack	6.1	Waterford	Dublin, Ire	05.04.98
Grant, Jorge	5.10	Nottm Forest	Banbury	19.12.94
McGrandles, Conor	6.0	MK Dons	Falkirk	24.09.95
Payne, Jack	5.6	Huddersfield	Tower Hamlets	25.10.94
Tayo Edun	5.10	Fulham	Islington	14.05.98
Walsh, Joe	5.11	MK Dons	Cardiff	13.05.92

Forwards

Adebayo-Smith, Jordan	6.1	–	California, US	11.01.01
Scully, Anthony	5.9	West Ham	London	19.04.99
Hopper, Tom	6.1	Southend	Boston	14.12.93

MILTON KEYNES DONS

Ground: stadiummk, Stadium Way West, Milton Keynes MK1 1ST
Telephone: 01908 622922. **Club nickname:** Dons
Colours: White. **Capacity:** 30,500
Record attendance: Record attendance: 28,521 v Liverpool (League Cup 3) Sep 25, 2019

Goalkeepers

Nicholls, Lee	6.3	Wigan	Huyton	05.10.92

Defenders

Brittain, Callum	5.10	–	Bedford	12.03.98
Cargill, Baily	6.2	Bournemouth	Winchester	05.07.95
Harvie, Daniel	6.0	Ayr	Glasgow	14.07.98
Keogh, Richard	6.2	Derby	Harlow	11.08.86
Lewington, Dean	5.11	Wimbledon	Kingston upon Thames	18.05.84
O'Hora, Warren	6.2	Brighton (loan)	Dublin, Ire	19.04.99
Sorinola, Matthew	5.9	Fulham	Lambeth	19.12.01
Williams, George	5.9	Barnsley	Hillingdon	14.04.93

Midfielders

Boateng, Hiram	6.0	Exeter	Wandsworth	08.01.96
Houghton, Jordan	6.0	Chelsea	Chertsey	09.11.95
Kasumu, David	5.11	–	Lambert	05.10.99
Poole, Regan	5.10	Manchester Utd	Cardiff	18.06.98
Thompson, Louis	5.11	Norwich (loan)	Bristol	19.12.94

Forwards

Agard, Kieran	5.10	Bristol City	Newham	10.10.89
Bird, Jay	6.0	–	Milton Keynes	13.09.00

Healey, Rhys	5.11	Cardiff	Manchester	06.12.94
Morris, Carlton	6.2	Norwich (loan)	Cambridge	16.12.95
Nombe, Sam	5.11	–	Croydon	22.10.98

NORTHAMPTON TOWN

Ground: PTS Academy Stadium, Upton Way, Northampton NN5 5QA
Telephone: 01604 683700. **Club nickname:** Cobblers
Colours: Claret and white. **Capacity:** 7,795
Record attendance: County Ground: 24,523 v Fulham (Div 1) Apr 23, 1966. Sixfields Stadium/
PTS Academy Stadium: 7,798 v Manchester Utd (Lge Cup 3) Sep 21, 2016

Goalkeepers
| Arnold, Steve | 6.1 | Shrewsbury | Welham Green | 22.08.89 |
| Mitchell, Jonathan | 6.2 | Derby (loan) | Hartlepool | 24.11.94 |

Defenders
Barnett, Leon	6.1	Bury	Luton	30.11.85
Bolger, Cian	6.4	Lincoln	Cellbridge, Ire	12.03.92
Harriman, Michael	5.7	Wycombe	Chichester	23.10.92
Horsfall, Fraser	6.3	Macclesfield	Huddersfield	12.11.96
Martin, Joe	6.0	Stevenage	Dagenham	29.11.88
Mills, Joseph	5.9	Forest Green	Swindon	30.10.89
Racic, Luka	6.2	Brentford (loan)	Greve, Den	08.05.99

Midfielders
Adams, Nicky	5.10	Bury	Bolton	16.10.83
Lines, Chris	6.2	Bristol Rov	Bristol	30.11.85
Marshall, Mark	6.3	Gillingham	Manchester, Jam	05.05.87
Missilou, Christopher	5.11	Oldham	Auxerre, Fr	18.07.92
Pollock, Scott	5.10	–	Northampton	12.03.01
Roberts, Morgan	5.10	–	Northampton	20.12.00
Watson, Ryan	6.1	MK Dons	Crewe	07.07.93

Forwards
Hoskins, Sam	5.8	Yeovil	Dorchester	04.02.93
Morias, Junior	5.8	Peterborough	Kingston, Jam	04.07.95
Smith, Harry	6.5	Macclesfield	Chatham	18.05.95
Warburton, Matt	5.9	Stockport	Manchester	24.05.92

OXFORD UNITED

Ground: Kassam Stadium, Grenoble Road, Oxford OX4 4XP
Telephone: 01865 337500. **Club nickname:** U's
Colours: Yellow. **Capacity:** 12,500
Record attendance: Manor Ground: 22,750 v Preston (FA Cup 6) Feb 29, 1964. Kassam
Stadium: 12,243 v Leyton Orient (Lge 2) May 6, 2006

Goalkeepers
| Eastwood, Simon | 6.2 | Blackburn | Luton | 26.06.89 |
| Stevens, Jack | 6.2 | – | Ealing | 02.08.97 |

Defenders
Atkinson, Rob	6.4	Eastleigh	Chesterfield	13.07.98
Dickie, Rob	6.3	Reading	Wokingham	03.03.96
Long, Sam	5.10	–	Oxford	16.01.95
Moore, Elliott	6.5	Leicester	Coalville	16.03.97
Mousinho, John	6.1	Burton	Isleworth	30.04.86
Sykes, Mark	6.0	Glenavon	Belfast	04.08.97

Midfielders

Brannagan, Cameron	5.11	Liverpool	Manchester	09.05.96
Clare, Sean	6.3	Hearts	Hackney	18.09.96
Cooper, Joel	5.11	Linfield	Northern Ireland	29.02.96
Forde, Anthony	6.1	Rotherham	Ballingarry, Ire	16.11.93
Gorrin, Alex	6.0	Motherwell	Tenerife	01.08.93
Hanson, Jamie	6.3	Derby	Burton upon Trent	10.11.95
Kelly, Liam	5.4	Feyenoord (loan)	Basingstoke	22.11.95
McGuane, Marcus	5.10	Nottm Forest (loan)	Greenwich	02.02.99
Osei, Derick	6.2	Brest	Toulouse, Fr	10.09.98
Ruffels, Josh	5.10	Coventry	Oxford	23.10.93
Thorne, George	6.2	Derby	Chatham	04.01.93

Forwards

Agyei, Dan	6.0	Burnley	Kingston upon Thames	01.06.97
Asonganyi, Dylan	5.10	MK Dons	Sheffield	10.12.00
Hall, Rob	6.2	Bolton	Aylesbury	20.10.93
Henry, James	6.1	Wolves	Reading	10.06.89
Taylor, Matty	5.9	Bristol City	Oxford	30.03/90

PETERBOROUGH UNITED

Ground: Weston Homes Stadium, London Road, Peterborough PE2 8AL
Telephone: 01733 563947. **Club nickname:** Posh
Colours: Blue and white. **Capacity:** 14,319
Record attendance: 30,096 v Swansea (FA Cup 5) Feb 20, 1965

Goalkeepers

Gyollai, Daniel	6.5	Wigan	Bekescsaba, Hun	07.04/97
Pym, Christy	5.11	Exeter	Exeter	24.04.95

Defenders

Beevers, Mark	6.4	Bolton	Barnsley	21.11.89
Blake-Tracy, Frazer	6.0	King's Lynn	Dereham	10.09.95
Butler, Dan	5.9	Newport	Cowes	26.08.94
Kent, Frankie	6.2	Colchester	Romford	21.11.95
Mason, Niall	5.11	Doncaster	Bromley	10.01.97
Thompson, Nathan	5.10	Portsmouth	Chester	09.11.90

Midfielders

Boyd, George	6.1	Sheffield Wed	Chatham	02.10.85
Burrows, Harrison	5.10	–	Murrow	12.01.02
Dembele, Siriki	5.8	Grimsby	Ivory Coast	07.09.96
Hamilton, Ethan	6.2	Manchester Utd	Edinburgh	18.10.98
Jade-Jones, Ricky	6.0	–	Peterborogh	08.11.02
Reed, Louis	5.8	Sheffield Utd	Barnsley	25.07.97
Tasdemir, Serhat	5.11	Fylde	Blackburn	21.07.00
Taylor, Jack	6.1	Barnet	Hammersmih	23.06.98
Ward, Joe	5.6	Woking	Chelmsford	22.08.95

Forwards

Eisa, Mo	6.0	Bristol City	Khartoum, Sud	12.07.94
Kanu, Idris	6.0	Aldershot	London	05.12.99
Toney, Ivan	5.10	Newcastle	Northampton	16.03.96

PLYMOUTH ARGYLE

Ground: Home Park, Plymouth PL2 3DQ
Telephone: 01752 562561. **Club nickname:** Pilgrims

Colours: Green and white. **Capacity:** 16,388
Record attendance: 43,596 v Aston Villa (Div 2) Oct 10, 1936

Goalkeepers

Cooper, Mikel	6.1	–	Exeter	08.10.99
McCormick, Luke	6.0	Swindon	Coventry	15.08.83

Defenders

Aimson, Will	5.10	Bury	Christchurch	01.01.94
Canavan, Niall	6.3	Rochdale	Leeds	11.04.91
Sawyer, Gary	6.0	Leyton Orient	Bideford	05.07.85
Wootton, Scott	6.2	MK Dons	Birkenhead	12.09.91

Midfielders

Edwards, Joe	5.9	Walsall	Gloucester	31.10.90
Grant, Conor	5.9	Everton	Fazakerley	18.04.95
Jephcott, Luke	5.10	–	Truro	26.01.00
Mayor, Danny	6.0	Bury	Leyland	18.10.90
Macleod, Lewis	5.9	Wigan	Wishaw	16.06.94
McFadzean, Callum	5.11	Bury	Sheffield	16.01.94
Randell, Adam	5.9	–	Plymouth	01.10.00

Forwards

Camara, Panutche	6.1	Crawley	Guin-Bass	28.02.97
Hardie, Ryan	6.2	Blackpool (loan)	Stranraer	17.03.97
Moore, Byron	6.0	Bury	Stoke	24.08.88
Nouble, Frank	6.3	Colchester	Lewisham	24.09.91
Telford, Dom	5.7	Bury	Burnley	05.12.96

PORTSMOUTH

Ground: Fratton Park, Frogmore Road, Portsmouth, PO4 8RA
Telephone: 0239 273 1204. **Club nickname:** Pompey
Colours: Blue and white. **Capacity:** 20,700
Record attendance: 51,385 v Derby (FA Cup 6) Feb 26, 1949

Goalkeepers

Bass, Alex	6.2	–	Southampton	01.04.98
MacGillivray, Craig	6.2	Shrewsbury	Harrogate	12.01.93

Defenders

Bolton, James	6.0	Shrewsbury	Stone	13.08.94
Brown, Lee	6.0	Bristol Rov	Farnborough	10.08.90
Downing, Paul	6.1	Blackburn	Taunton	26.10.91
Naylor, Tom	6.0	Burton	Sutton-in-Ashfield	28.06.91
Raggett, Sean	6.5	Norwich	Gillingham	25.01.94
Whatmough, Jack	6.0	–	Gosport	19.08.96

Midfielders

Cannon, Andy	5.9	Rochdale	Tameside	14.03.96
Close, Ben	5.9	–	Portsmouth	08.08.96
Curtis, Ronan	6.0	Derry	Donegal	29.03.96
Evans, Gareth	6.0	Fleetwood	Macclesfield	26.04.88
Harness, Marcus	6.0	Burton	Coventry	24.02.96
Morris, Bryn	6.0	Shrewsbury	Hartlepool	25.04.96
Williams, Ryan	5.8	Rotherham	Perth, Aus	28.10.93

Forwards

Hackett-Fairchild, Reeco	6.3	Bromley	Redbridge	09.01.98
Harrison, Ellis	5.11	Ipswich	Newport	29.01.94
Marquis, John	6.1	Doncaster	Leisham	16.05.92

ROCHDALE

Ground: Crown Oil Arena, Wilbutts Lane, Rochdale OL11 5DS
Telephone: 01706 644648. **Club nickname:** Dale
Colours: Blue and black. **Capacity:** 10,249
Record attendance: 24,231 v Notts Co (FA Cup 2) Dec 10, 1949

Goalkeepers

Lynch, Jay	6.2	AFC Fylde	Salford	31.03.93

Defenders

McNulty, Jim	6.0	Bury	Liverpool	13.02.85
McShane, Paul	6.0	Reading	Wicklow, Ire	06.01.86
Norrington-Davies Rhys	5.11	Sheffield Utd (loan)	Riyadh	22.04.99
O'Connell, Eoghan	6.2	Bury	Cork, Ire	13.08.95

Midfielders

Bradley, Lewis	5.10	–	Stockport	29.05.01
Dooley, Stephen	5.11	Coleraine	Ballymoney	19.10.91
Hopper, Harrison	5.9	–	Camden	24.12.00
Keohane, Jimmy	5.11	Cork	Aylesbury	22.01.91
Lund, Matty	6.0	Scunthorpe	Manchester	21.11.90
Morley, Aaron		–	Bury	27.02.00
Newby, Alex	5.9	Chorley	Barrow	21.11.95
Rathbone, Oliver	5.11	Manchester Utd	Blackburn	10.10.96
Ryan, Jimmy	5.11	Blackpool	Liverpool	06.09.88

Forwards

Done, Matt	5.10	Sheffield Utd	Oswestry	22.07.88
Tavares, Fabio	5.11	–	Rochdale	22.01.01

SHREWSBURY TOWN

Ground: Montgomery Waters Meadow, Oteley Road, Shrewsbury SY2 6ST
Telephone: 01743 289177. **Club nickname:** Shrews
Colours: Blue and yellow. **Capacity:** 9,875
Record attendance: Gay Meadow: 18,917 v Walsall (Div 3) Apr 26, 1961. Greenhous Meadow: 10,210 v Chelsea (Lge Cup 4) Oct 28, 2014

Goalkeepers

Burgoyne, Harry	6.4	Wolves	Ludlow	28.12.96
Gregory, Cameron	6.3	–	Sutton Coldfield	20.01.00

Defenders

Beckles, Omar	6.3	Accrington	Kettering	19.10.91
Ebanks-Landell, Ethan	6.2	Wolves	West Bromwich	16.12.92
Golbourne, Scott	5.8	Bristol City	Bristol	29.02.88
Love, Donald	5.10	Sunderland	Rochdale	02.12.94
Pierre, Aaron	6.1	Northampton	Southall	17.02.93
Sears, Ryan	5.11	–	Newtown	30.12.98
Williams, Ro-Shaun	6.0	Manchester Utd	Manchester	03.09.98

Midfielders

Barnett, Ryan	5.11	–	Shrewsbury	23.09.99
Daniels, Josh	5.10	Glenavon	Derry	22.02.96
Edwards, Dave	5.11	Reading	Pontesbury	03.02.85
Goss, Sean	5.10	QPR	Wegberg, Ger	01.10.95
High, Scott	5.10	Huddersfield (loan)	Dewsbury	15.02.01
Norburn, Ollie	6.1	Tranmere	Bolton	26.10.92
Rowland, James	5.6	WBA	Walsall	03.12.01
Vela, Josh	5.11	Hibernian	Salford	14.12.93

Walker, Brad	6.1	Crewel	Billingham	25.04.96
Forwards				
Cummings, Jason	5.11	Nottm Forest	Edinburgh	01.08.95
Pyke, Rekeil	6.2	Huddersfield	Leeds	01.09.97
Udoh, Daniel	6.1	AFC Telord	Lagos, Nig	30.08.96
Whalley, Shaun	5.9	Luton	Whiston	07.08.87

SUNDERLAND

Ground: Stadium of Light, Sunderland SR5 1SU
Telephone: 0871 911 1200. **Club nickname:** Black Cats
Capacity: 48,707. **Colours:** Red and white
Record attendance: Roker Park: 75,118 v Derby (FA Cup 6 rep) Mar 8, 1933. Stadium of Light: 48,353 v Liverpool (Prem Lge) Apr 13, 2002

Goalkeepers				
Burge, Lee	6.0	Coventry	Hereford	09.01.93
Matthews, Remi	6.0	Bolton	Gorleston	10.02.94
Defenders				
Feeney, Morgan	6.3	Everton	Bootle	08.02.99
Flanagan, Tom	6.2	Burton	Hammersmith	21.10.91
Hume, Denver	5.10	–	Newbiggin	11.08.98
McLaughlin, Conor	6.0	Millwall	Belfast	26.07.91
Willis, Jordan	5.11	Coventry	Coventry	24.08.94
Wright, Bailey	5.10	Bristol City	Melbourne, Aus	28.07.92
Midfielders				
Dobson, George	5.11	Walsall	Harold Wood	15.11.97
Embleton, Elliot	5.8	–	Durham	02.04.99
Gooch, Lynden	5.8	–	Santa Cruz, US	24.12.95
Leadbitter, Grant	5.9	Middlesbrough	Chester-le-Street	07.01.86
Maguire, Chris	5.8	Bury	Bellshill	16.01.89
McGeady, Aiden	5.11	Everton	Paisley	04.04.86
O'Nien, Luke	5.9	Wycombe	Hemel Hempstead	21.11.94
Power, Max	5.11	Wigan	Birkenhead	27.07.93
Scowen, Josh	5.10	QPR	Enfield	28.03.93
Forwards				
Grigg, Will	5.11	Wigan	Solihull	03.07.91
Kimpioka, Benji	6.0	–	Knivsta, Swe	21.02.00
O'Brien, Aiden	5.9	Millwall	Islington	04.10.93
Wyke, Charlie	5.11	Bradford	Middlesbrough	06.12.92

SWINDON TOWN

Ground: Energy Check County Ground, County Road, Swindon SN1 2ED
Telephone: 0871 423 6433. **Club nickname:** Robins
Colours: Red and white. **Capacity:** 15,728
Record attendance: 32,000 v Arsenal (FA Cup 3) Jan 15, 1972

Goalkeepers				
Matthews, Archie	6.1	-	Bath	02.08.01
Defenders				
Baudry, Mathieu	6.2	MK Dons	Le Havre, Fr	24.02.88
Broadbent, Tom	6.3	Bristol Rov	Basingstoke	15.02.92
Caddis, Paul	5.7	Bradford	Irvine	19.04.88
Conroy, Dion	6.2	Chelsea	Redhill	11.12.95

Curran, Taylor	6.0	Southend	Redbridge	07.07.00
Fryers, Zeki	6.0	Barnsley	Manchester	09.09.92
Hunt, Rob	5.8	Oldham	Dagenham	07.07.95
Odimayo, Akin	6.0	Reading	Camden	28.11.99
Reid, Tyler	5.11	Swansea	Luton	02.09.97

Midfielders

Doughty, Michael	6.1	Peterborough	Westminster	20.11.92
Grant, Anthony	5.10	Shrewsbury	Lambeth	04.06.87
Isgrove, Lloyd	5.10	Barnsley	Yeovil	12.01.93
Jaiyesimi, Diallang	6.0	Norwich	Southwark	07.05.98
Lyden, Jordan	6.0	Aston Villa	Perth, Aus	30.01.96
McGilp, Cameron	5.11	Birmingham	Glasgow	08.02.98
Palmer, Matt	5.10	Rotherham	Derby	01.08.93
Rose, Danny	5.8	Portsmouth	Bristol	21.02.88
Smith, Matt	5.9	Arsenal (loan)	Harlow	05.10.00

Forwards

Hope, Hallam	5.11	Carlisle	Manchester	17.03.94
Iandolo, Ellis	5.10	–	Chatham	22.08.97
Twine, Scott	5.9	–	Swindon	14.07.99
Woolery, Kaiyne	5.10	Wigan	Hackney	11.01.95

WIGAN ATHLETIC

Ground: DW Stadium, Robin Park, Wigan WN5 0UZ
Telephone: 01942 774000. Club nickname: Latics
Colours: Blue and white. **Capacity:** 25,023
Record attendance: Springfield Park: 27,526 v Hereford (FA Cup 2) Dec 12, 1953; DW Stadium: 25,133 v Manchester Utd (Prem Lge) May 11, 2008

Goalkeepers

| Jones, Jamie | 6.2 | Stevenage | Kirkby | 18.02.89 |

Defenders

Byrne, Nathan	5.11	Wolves	St Albans	05.06.92`
Fox, Danny	6.0	Nottm Forest	Winsford	29.05.86
Kipre, Cedric	6.3	Motherwell	Paris, Fr	09.12.96
Pearce, Tom	6.1	Leeds	Ormskirk	12.04.98

Midfielders

Evans, Lee	6.1	Sheffield Utd	Newport	24.07.94
Jacobs, Michael	5.9	Wolves	Rothwell	04.11.91
Lowe, Jamal	6.0	Portsmouth	Harrow	21.07.94
Massey, Gavin	5.10	Leyton Orient	Watford	14.10.92
Morsy, Sam	5.9	Chesterfield	Wolverhampton	10.09.91
Naismith, Kai	6.1	Portsmouth	Glasgow	18.02.92
Pilkington, Anthony	6.0	Cardiff	Blackburn	06.06.88
Roberts, Gary	5.10	Portsmouth	Chester	18.03.84

Forwards

| Garner, Joe | 5.10 | Ipswich | Blackburn | 12.04.88 |
| Windass, Josh | 5.9 | Rangers | Hull | 09.01.94 |

LEAGUE TWO

BARROW

Ground: Progressionb Solicitoprs Stadium, Wilkie Road, Barrow LA14 5UW
Telephone: 01229 666010. **Club nickname:** Bluebirds
Colours; Blue and white. **Capacity:** 5,045
Record attendance: 16,874 v Swansea (FA Cup 3) Jan 9, 1954

Goalkeepers

Dixon, Joel	6.4	Sunderland	Middlesbrough	09.12.93

Defenders

Beadling, Tom	6.1	Dunfermline	Barrow	16.01.96
Barry, Brad	6.0	Chesterfield	Hastings	13.02.95
Brough, Patrick	6.3	Falkirk	Carlisle	20.02.96
Brown, Connor	5.9	York	Sheffield	02.10.91
Burns, Bobby	5.9	Hearts	Antrim	07.10.99
Hird, Sam	6.0	Alfreton	Doncaster	07.09.87
Jones, James	6.4	Altrincham	Wrexham	13.03.97
Platt, Matty	6.0	Blackburn	Knowsley	03.10.97

Midfielders

Gribbin, Callum	5.10	Sheffield Utd	Salford	19.12.98
Hardcastle, Lewis	5.9	Blackburn	Atherton	04.07.98
James, Luke	5.11	Hartlepool	Amble	04.01.94
Jones, Mike	6.0	Carlisle	Birkenhead	15.08.87
Kay, Josh	6.0	Chesterfield	Blackpool	30.01.97
Taylor, Jason	6.1	Eastleigh	Droylsden	28.01.87

Forwards

Angus, Dior	6.0	Port Vale	Coventry	18.01.94
Hindle, Jack	5.11	Colwyn Bay	Warrington	29.10.93
Penfold, Morgan	6.1	Peterborough	Whittlesey	03.12.98
Quigley, Scott	6.4	Blackpool	Shrewsbury	02.09.92

BOLTON WANDERERS

Ground: University of Bolton Stadium, Burnden Way, Lostock, Bolton BL6 6JW
Telephone: 0844 871 2932. **Club nickname:** Trotters
Colours: White and navy. **Capacity:** 28,723
Record attendance: Burnden Park: 69,912 v Manchester City (FA Cup 5) Feb 18, 1933.
Macron Stadium: 28,353 v Leicester (Prem Lge) Dec 28, 2003

Goalkeepers

Alexander, Matt		Newcastle	Newcastle	07.05.02
Crellin, Billy	6.1	Fleetwood (loan)	Blackpool	30.06.00

Defenders

Baptiste, Alex	5.11	Doncaster	Sutton-in-Ashfield	31.01.86
Brockbank, Harry	5.11	–	Bolton	26.09.98
Delaney, Ryan	6.0	Rochdale	Wexford, Ire	06.09.96
Gordon, Liam	6.1	Dagenham	Croydon	15.05.99
Greenidge, Reiss	6.6	Arendal	Enfield	08.02.96
Hickman, Jak	5.9	Coventry	Sandwell	11.09.98
Jones, Gethin	5.10	Carlisle	Perth, Aus	13.10.95
Santos, Ricardo	6.6	Barnet	Almada, Por	18.06.95
Seniotm, Adam	6.0	–	Bolton	20.01.02
Taft, George	6.3	Cambridge	Leicester	29.07.93

Midfielders

Comley, Brandon	5.11	Colchester	Islington	18.11.95
Crawford, Ali	5.8	Doncaster	Lanark	30.07.91
Graham, Sonny	6.1	Longridge	Morecambe	12.01.02
Politic, Dennis	5.10	Manchester Utd	Brasov, Rom	05.03.00
Sarcevic, Antoni	6.0	Plymouth	Manchester	13.03.92
White, Tom White	5.11	Blackburn (loan)	–	09.05.97

Forwards

Delfouneso, Nathan	6.1	Blackpool	Birmingham	02.02.91
Doyle, Eoin	6.0	Swindon	Dublin, Ire	12.03.88
Faal, Muhammadu	6.4	Enfield	Hackney	01.07.97

BRADFORD CITY

Ground: Utilita Energy Stadium, Valley Parade, Bradford BD8 7DY
Telephone: 01274 773355. **Club nickname:** Bantams
Colours: Yellow and claret. **Capacity:** 25,136
Record attendance: 39,146 v Burnley (FA Cup 4) Mar 11, 1911

Goalkeepers

O'Donnell, Richard	6.2	Northampton	Sheffield	12.09.88

Defenders

Cooke, Callum	5.8	Peterborough	Peterles	21.02.97
French, Tyler	6.3	Sudbury	Bury St Edmunds	12.02.99
Longridge, Jackson	6.0	Dunfermline	Glasgow	12.04.95
O'Connor, Anthony	6.2	Aberdeen	Cork, Ire	25.10.92
O'Connor, Paudie	6.3	Leeds	Limerick, Ire	14.07.97
Richards-Everton, Ben	6.4	Accrington	Birmingham	17.10.91
Staunton, Reece	6.0	–	Bradford	10.12.01	
Wood, Connor	5.10	Leicester	Harlow	17.07.96

Midfielders

Ismail, Zeli	5.9	Walsall	Kukes, Alb	12.12.93
Mottley-Henry, Dylan	5.10	Barnsley	Leeds	02.08.97
Pritchard, Harry	5.9	Blackpool	High Wycombe	14.09.92
Robinson, Tyrell	5.9	Arsenal	Basildon	16.09.97
Sutton, Levi	5.11	Scunthorpe	Scunthorpe	24.03.96
Watt, Elliot	5.11	Wolves	Preston	11.03.00

Forwards

Clarke, Billy	5.7	Grimsby	Cork, Ire	13.12.87
Donaldson, Clayton	6.1	Bolton	Bradford	07.02.84
Guthrie, Kurtis	6.3	Stevenage	Jersey	21.04.93
Novak, Lee	6.0	Scunthorpe	Newcastle	28.09, 88

CAMBRIDGE UNITED

Ground: Abbey Stadium, Newmarket Road, Cambridge CB5 8LN
Telephone: 01223 566500. **Club nickname:** U's
Colours: Yellow and black. **Capacity:** 9,617
Record attendance: 14,000 v Chelsea (friendly) May 1, 1970

Goalkeepers

Burton, Callum	6.2	Hull	Newport, Salop	15.08.96
Mitov, Dimitar	6.2	Charlton	–	22.01.97

Defenders

Cundy, Robbie	6.2	Bristol City (loan)	Oxford	30.05.97

Darling, Harry	5.11	–	Cambridge	08.08.99
Davies, Leon	5.11	–	Cambridge	22.11.99
Iredale, Jack	6.1	Carlisle	Greenock	02.05.96
Knoyle, Kyle	5.10	Swindon	Newham	24.09.96
Taylor, Greg	6.1	Luton	Bedford	15.01.90
Midfielders				
Digby, Paul	6.3	Stevenage	Sheffield	02.02.95
Dunk, Harrison	6.0	Bromley	London	25.10.90
Hannant, Luke	5.11	Port Vale	Great Yarmouth	04.11.93
Hoolahan, Wes	5.7	Newcastle Jets	Dublin, Ire	20.05.82
Knowles, Tom	6.0	–	Cambridge	27.09.98
O'Neil, Liam	5.11	Chesterfield	Cambridge	31.07.93
Worman, Ben	5.8	–	Cambridge	30.08.01
Forwards				
Dallas, Andrew	5.10	Rangers	–	22.07.99
Ironside, Joe	5.11	Macclesfield	Middlesbrough	16.10.93
Knibbs, Harvey	5.10	Aston Villa	Bristol	26.04.99
Mullin, Paul	5.10	Tranmere	Liverpool	06.11.94

CARLISLE UNITED

Ground: Brunton Park, Warwick Road, Carlisle CA1 1LL
Telephone: 01228 526237. **Club nickname:** Cumbrians
Colours: Blue and white. **Capacity:** 17,949
Record attendance: 27,500 v Birmingham City (FA Cup 3) Jan 5, 1957, v Middlesbrough (FA Cup 5) Jan 7, 1970

Goalkeepers				
Farman, Paul	6.5	Stevenage	North Shields	02.11.89
Norman, Magnus	6.4	Fulham	London	19.01.97
Defenders				
Anderton, Nick	6.2	Blackpool	Preston	22.04.96
Armer, Jack	6.1	Preston	Preston	16.04.01
Hayden, Aaron	6.1	Wolves	Croydon	16.01.97
Hunt, Max				01.05.99
McDonald, Rod	6.3	AFC Wimbledon	Crewe	11.04.92
Mellish, Jon	6.2	Gateshead	South Shields	19.09.97
Tanner, George	5.11	Manchester Utd	Blackpool	16.11.99
Webster, Byron	6.4	Scunthorpe	Sherburn	31.03.87
Midfielders				
Bridge, Jack	5.10	Northampton	Southend	21.09.95
Charters, Taylor			Whitehavern	02.10.01
Devine Danny	5.11	Bradford	Bradford	04.09.97
Dickenson, Brennan	6.0	Exeter	Ferndown	26.02.93
Dixon, Josh	5.11	–	–	07.02.01
Guy, Callum	5.10	Blackpool	Nottingham	25.11.96
Riley, Joe	5.10	Bradford	Blackpool	06.12.96
Forwards				
Alessandra, Lewis	5.10	Morecambe	Heywood	08.02.89
Kayode, Josh	6.3	Rotherham (loan)	Lagos, Nig	04.05.00
Patrick, Omari	6.1	Bradford	Slough	24.05.96
Reilly, Gavin	5.11	Bristol Rov	Dumfries	10.05.93
Toure, Gime	6.3	Hartlepool	France	07.05.94

CHELTENHAM TOWN

Ground: Jonny-Rocks Stadium, Whaddon Road, Cheltenham GL52 5NA
Telephone: 01242 573558. Robins
Colours: Red and black. **Capacity:** 7,066
Record attendance: 8,326 v Reading (FA Cup 1) Nov 17, 1956

Goalkeepers

Flinders, Scott	6.4	Macclesfield	Rotherham	12.06.86
Griffiths, Josh	6.1	WBA (loan)	Hereford	05.09.01

Defenders

Bowry, Dan	6.0	Charlton	London	29.04.98
Boyle, Will	6.2	Huddersfield	Garforth	01.09.95
Freestone, Lewis	5.9	Brighton	King's Lynn	26.10.99
Hussey, Chris	6.0	Sheffield Utd	Hammersmith	02.01.89
Long, Sean	5.10	Lincoln	Dublin	02.05.95
Raglan, Charlie	6.0	Oxford	Wythenshawe	28.04.93

Midfielders

Addai Alex	5.10	Merstham	Stepney	20.12.93
Bonds, Elliot	5.10	Hull (loan)	Brent	23.03.00
Broom, Ryan	5.10	Bristol Rov	Newport	04.09.96
Clements, Chris	5.9	Grimsby	Birmingham	06.02.90
Sercombe, Liam	5.10	Bristol Rov	Exeter	25.04.90
Thomas, Conor	6.1	ATK	Coventry	29.10.93
Tozer, Ben	6.1	Newport	Plymouth	01.03.90

Forwards

Campbell, Tahvon	5.8	Forest Green	Birmingham	10.01.97
Lloyd, George	5.8	–	Gloucester	11.02.00
May, Alfie	5.10	Doncaster	Gravesend	02.07.93
Reid, Reuben	6.0	Forest Green	Bristol	26.07.88
Williams, Andy	5.10	Northampton	Hereford	14.08.86

COLCHESTER UNITED

Ground: JobServe Community Stadium, United Way, Colchester CO4 5HE
Telephone: 01206 755100. **Club nickname:** U's
Colours: Blue and white. **Capacity:** 10,105
Record attendance: Layer Road: 19,072 v Reading (FA Cup 1) Nov 27, 1948. Community Stadium: 10,064 v Norwich (Lge 1) Jan 16, 2010

Goalkeepers

Gerken, Dean	6.0	Ipswich	Rochford	22.05.85

Defenders

Bramall, Cohen	5.9	Arsenal	Crewe	02.04.96
Clampin, Ryan	5.11	–	Colchester	29.01.99
Eastman, Tom	6.3	Ipswich	Colchester	21.10.91
Kensdale, Ollie	6.2	–	Colchester	20.04.00
Sowunmi, Omar	6.6	Yeovil	Colchester	07.11.95
Welch-Hayes, Miles	5.11	Macclesfield	Oxford	25.10.96

Midfielders

Brown, Jevani	5.9	Cambridge	Letchworth	16.10.94
Gambin, Luke	5.7	Luton	Sutton	16.03.93
Hasanally, Andrer	5.10	–	Waltham Forest	10.02.02
Lapslie, Tom	5.6	–	Waltham Forest	05.10.95
Pell, Harry	6.4	Cheltenham	Tilbury	21.10.91

Poku, Kwame	5.9	Worthing	Croydon	11.08.01
Senior, Courtney	5.9	Brentford	Croydon	11.02.98
Stevenson, Ben	6.0	Wolves	Leicester	23.03.97
Forwards				
Cowan-Hall, Paris	5.8	Wycombe	Hillingdon	05.10.90
Harriott, Callum	5.6	Reading	Norbury	04.03.94
Norris, Luke	6.1	Swindon	Stevenage	03.06.93

CRAWLEY TOWN

Ground: People's Pension Stadium, Winfield Way, Crawley RH11 9RX
Telephone: 01293 410000. **Club nickname:** Reds
Colours: Red. **Capacity:** 6,134
Record attendance: 5,880 v Reading (FA Cup 3) Jan 5, 2013

Goalkeepers				
Jones, Alfie	6.0	MK Dons	–	02.10.00
Morris, Glenn	6.0	Gillingham	Woolwich	20.12.83
Defenders				
Craig, Tony	6.0	Bristol Rov	Greenwich	20.04.85
Dallison, Tom	6.1	Falkirk	Romford	02.02.96
Doherty, Josh	5.10	Ards	Newtonards	15.03.96
McNerney, Joe	6.4	Woking	Chertsey	24.01.90
Sesay, David	6.1	Watford	Brent	18.09.98
Tunnicliffe, Jordan	6.1	AFC Fylde	Nuneaton	13.10.93
Young, Lewis	5.9	Bury	Stevenage	27.09.89
Midfielders				
Al-Hussaini, Zaid	5.11	Hampton	London	07.06.00
Allarakhia, Tarryn	5.10	–	Redbridge	17.10.97
Bulman, Dannie	5.8	AFC Wimbledon	Ashford, Surrey	24.01.79
Ferguson, Nathan	5.10	Dulwich Hamlet	Walthamstow	12.10.95
Francomb, George	6.0	AFC Wimbledon	Hackney	08.09.91
Mathews, Sam	5.10	Bristol Rov	Poole	01.03.97
Morais, Filipe	5.9	Bolton	Benavente, Por	21.11.85
Nathaniel-George, Ashley	5.10	Hendon	London	14.06.95
Forwards				
Ashford, Sam	5.11	Hemel Hempstead	Chelmsford	21.12.95
Galach, Brian	5.9	Aldershot	Poland	16.05.01
German, Ricky	5.11	Hendon	Harlesden	13.01.99
Grego-Cox, Reece	5.7	Woking	Hammersmith	02.11.96
Lubula, Beryly	5.10	Birmingham	DR Congo	08.01.98
Nadesan, Ashley	6.2	Fleetwood	Redhill	09.09.94

EXETER CITY

Ground: St James Park, Stadium Way, Exeter EX4 6PX
Telephone: 01392 411243. **Club nickname:** Grecians
Colours: Red and white. **Capacity:** 8 830
Record attendance: 20,984 v Sunderland (FA Cup 6 replay) Mar 4, 1931

Goalkeepers				
Maxted, Jonny	6.0	Accrington	Tadcaster	26.10.93
Ward, Lewis	6.5	Reading	–	05.03.97
Defenders				
Caprice, Jake	5.11	Tranmere	Lambeth	11.11.92

| McArdle, Rory | 6.1 | Scunthorpe | Sheffield | 01.05.87 |
| Sweeney, Pierce | 5.11 | Reading | Dublin, Ire | 11.09.94 |

Midfielders

Atangana, Nigel	6.2	Cheltenham	Corbeil-Essonnes, Fr	09.09.89
Collins, Archie	5.9	–	Taunton	31.08.99
Law, Nicky	5.10	Bradford	Plymouth	29.03.88
Parkes, Tom	6.3	Carlisle	Sutton-in-Ashfield	15.01.92
Randall, Joel	5.10	–	Salisbury	01.11.99
Sparkes, Jack	5.9	–	Exeter	29.09.00
Taylor, Jake	5.10	Reading	Ascot	01.12.91
Williams, Randell	5.9	Watford	Lambeth	30.12.96

Forwards

Ajose, Nicky	5.7	Charlton	Bury	07.10.91
Bowman, Ryan	6.2	Motherwell	Carlisle	30.11.91
Fisher, Alex	6.3	Yeovil	Westminster	30.06.90
Jay, Matt	5.10	–	Torbay	27.02.96
Seymour, Ben	6.0	–	Watford	16.04.99

FOREST GREEN ROVERS

Ground: New Lawn, Another Way, Nailsworth GL6 OFG
Telephone: 01453 835291. **Club nickname:** Green Devils
Colours: Green. **Capacity:** 5,140
Record attendance: 4,836 v Derby (FA Cup 3, Jan 3, 2009)

Goalkeepers

| McGee, Luke | 6.2 | Portsmouth | Edgware | 02.09.95 |
| Thomas, Lewis | 6.1 | Swan sea | Swansea | 20.09.97 |

Defenders

Bernard, Dominic	5.11	Birmingham	Gloucester	29.03.97
Kitching, Liam	6.0	Leeds	Harrogate	01.10.99
Moore-Taylor, Jordan	5.10	MK Dons	Exeter	21.01.94
Stokes, Chris	6.1	Stevenage	Trowbridge	08.03.91
Udoka Godwin-Malife	5.11	Oxford City	–	09.05.00
Wilson, Kane	5.10	WBA	Birmingham	11.03.00

Midfielders

Adams, Ebou	5.11	Ebbsfleet	Greenwich	15.01.96
Bunker, Harvey	5.11	Southampton	Portsmouth	15.04.03
Cadden, Nicky	5.10	Morton	Bellshill	19.09.96
Covil, Vaughn	5.10	Southampton	San Diego, US	26.07.03
Sweeney, Dan	6.3	Barnet	Kingston upon Thames	25.04.94
Whitehouse, Elliott	5.11	Grimsby	Worksop	27.10.93
Winchester, Carl	6.0	Cheltenham	Belfast	12.04.93

Forwards

Collins, Aaron	6.1	Morecambe	Newport	27.05.97
March, Josh	5.10	Leamington	–	18.03.97
Matt, Jamille	6.1	Newport	Jamaica	20.10.89
Stevens, Matty	5.11	Peterborough	Guldford	12.02.98
Young, Jake	5.11	Sheffield Utd	Huddersfield	22.07.02

GRIMSBY TOWN

Ground: Blundell Park, Cleethorpes DN35 7PY
Telephone: 01472 605050. **Club nickname:** Mariners
Colours: Black and white: **Capacity:** 9,052
Record attendance: 31,651 v Wolves (FA Cup 5) 20 February, 1937

Goalkeepers

McKeown, James	6.1	Peterborough	Birmingham	24.07.89
Russell, Sam	6.0	Forest Green	Middlesbrough	04.10.82

Defenders

Hendrie, Luke	6.2	Shrewsbury	Leeds	27.08.94
Hewitt, Elliott	5.11	Notts Co	Bodelwyddan	30.05.94
Mohsni, Bilel	6.3	Dundee Utd	Paris, Fr	21.07.87
Ohman, Ludvig	6.3	Brommapojkarna	Umea, Swe	10.09.91
Pollock, Matthew	6.3	Leeds	Redhill	21.09.00
Waterfall, Luke	6.2	Shrewsbury	Sheffield	30.07.90

Midfielders

Clifton, Harry	5.11	–	Grimsby	12.06.98
Tilley, James	5.9	Brighton	Billingshurst	13.06.98
Wright, Max	5.8	–	Grimsby	06.04.98

Forwards

Gibson, Montel	5.11	Halesowen	Birmingham	15.12.97
Green, Matt	6.1	Salford	Bath	02.01.87
Hanson, James	6.4	AFC Wimbledon	Bradford	09.11.87
Williams, George	5.9	Forest Green	Milton Keynes	07.09.95

HARROGATE TOWN

Ground: CNG Stadium, Wetherby Road, Harrogate, HG2 7SA,
Telephone: 01423 210600. **Club nickname**: Town
Colours: Yellow and black. **Capacity**: 4,108
Record attendance: 4,280 v Harrogate Railway (Whitworth Cup Final), 1949-50

Goalkeepers

Belshaw, James	6.3	Tamworth	Nottingham	12.10.90
Cracknell, Joe	6.0	Bradford	Hull	28.09.94

Defenders

Burrell, Warren	6.1	Buxton	Sheffield	03.06.90
Fallowfield, Ryan	5.9	North Ferriby	Hull	03.01.96
Hall, Connor	6.4	Brackley	–	23.05.93
Lawlor, Jake	6.4	Wrexham	Halifax	08.04.91
Lokko, Kevin	6.2	Dover	Whitechapel	03.11.95
Smith, Will	6.1	Barnsley	Leeds	04.11.98

Midfielders

Agnew, Liam	5.10	Boston	Sunderand	11.04.95
Brown, Scott	5.10	Accrington	Chester	08.05.85
Emmett, Jack	5.9	–	Harrogate	22.10.93
Falkingham, Josh	5.7	Darlington	Leeds	25.08.90
Kerry, Lloyd	5.6	Tamworth	Chesterfield	22.07.88
Kiernan, Brendan	5.9	Welling	Lambeth	10.11.92
Kirby, Connor	5.10	Sheffield Wed	Barnsley	10.09.98
Leesley, Joe	6.0	Alfreton	Sheffield	29.03.94
Thomson, George	5.9	FC United	Sheffield	19.05.92
Walker, Tom	6.0	AFC Fylde	Salford	12.12.95

Forwards

Beck, Mark	6.5	Darlington	Sunderland	02.02.94
Martin, Aaron	6.0	Guiseley	Sheffield	06.07.91
Muldoon, Jack	5.10	AFC Fylde	Scunthorpe	19.05.89
Stead, Jon	6.3	Notts Co	Huddersfield	07.04.83

LEYTON ORIENT

Ground: Breyer Group Stadium, Brisbane Road, London E10 5NF
Telephone: 0208 926 1111. **Club nickname:** O's
Colours: Red. **Capacity:** 9,217
Record attendance: 34,345 v West Ham (FA Cup 4) Jan 25, 1964

Goalkeepers				
Sargeant, Sam	6.0	–	Greenwich	23.09.97
Vigouroux, Lawrence	6.4	Everton de Vina	Camden	19.11.93
Defenders				
Coulson, Josh	6.3	Cambridge Utd	Cambridge	28.01.89
Happe, Dan	–	–	Tower Hamlets	28.09.98
Judd, Myles	5.10	–	Redbridge	03.02.99
Ling, Sam	5.9	Dagenham	Broxbourne	17.12.96
Turley, Jamie	6.0	Notts Co	Reading	07.04.90
Widdowson, Joe	6.0	Dagenham	Forest Gate	29.03.89
Midfielders				
Brophy, James	5.10	Swindon	Brent	25.07.94
Cisse, Ousseynou	–	Gillingham	Suresnes, Fr	07.04.91
Clay, Craig	5.11	Motherwell	Nottingham	05.05.92
Dayton, James	5.8	Cheltenham	Enfield	12.12.88
Kyprianou, Hector	6.1	Tottenham	Enfield	27.05.01
Maguire-Drew, Jordan	5.11	Brighton	Crawley	19.09.97
McAnuff, Jobi	5.11	Stevenage	Edmonton	09.11.81
Wright, Josh	6.0	Bradford	Bethnal Green	06.11.89
Forwards				
Angol, Lee	6.2	Shrewsbury	Sutton	04.08.94
Dennis, Louis	6.1	Portsmouth	Hendon	09.10.92
Johnson, Danny	5.10	Dundee	Middlesbrough	28.02.93
Sotiriou, Ruel	–		Edmonton	24.08.00
Wilkinson, Conor	6.3	Dagenham	Croydon	23.01.95

MANSFIELD TOWN

Ground: One Call Stadium, Quarry Lane, Mansfield NG18 5DA
Telephone: 01623 482482. **Club nickname:** Stags
Colours: Amber and blue. **Capacity:** 10,000
Record attendance: 24,467 v Nottm Forest (FA Cup 3) Jan 10, 1953

Goalkeepers				
Stech, Marek	6.5	Luton	Prague, Cz	28.01.90
Stone, Aiden	6.1	Burnley	Stafford	20.07.99
Defenders				
Benning, Malvind	5.10	Walsall	Sandwell	02.11.93
Clarke, James	6.0	Burnley	Birkenhead	02.04.00
Menayesse, Rollin	6.3	Bristol Rov	Kinshasa, DR Con	04.12.97
O'Driscoll, Aaron	6.2	Southampton	Dublin, Ire	04.04.99
O'Keeffe, Corey	6.0	Birmingham	Birmingham,	05.06.98
Perch, James	6.0	Scunthorpe	Mansfield	28.09.85
Rawson, Farrend	6.2	Forest Green	Nottingham	11.07.96
Riley, Joe	6.0	Plymouth	Salford	13.10.91
Sweeney, Ryan	6.5	Stoke	Kingston upon Thames	15.04.97
White, Hayden	6.1	Peterborough	Greenwich	15.04.95

Midfielders

Charsley, Harry	5.10	Everton	Birkenhead	01.11.96
Clarke, Ollie	5.11	Bristol Rov	Bristol	29.06.92
Gordon, Kellan	5.11	Derby		25.12.97
Smith, Alistair	6.2	Hull	Beverley	19.05.99
Tomlinson, Willem	5.11	Blackburn	Burnley	27.01.98

Forwards

Bowery, Jordan	6.1	MK Dons	Nottingham	02.07.91
Cook, Andy	6.1	Walsall	Bishop Auckland	18.10.90
Knowles, Jimmy	6.0	Nottm Forest	Sutton-in-Ashfield	27.02.01
Law, Jason	5.10	Carlton	Nottingham	26.04.99
Maris, George	5.11	Cambridge	Sheffield	06.03.96
Maynard, Nicky	5.11	Bury	Winsford	11.12.86
Rose, Danny	5.10	Bury	Barnsley	10.12.93

MORECAMBE

Ground: Globe Arena, Christie Way, Westgate, Morecambe LA4 4TB
Telephone: 01524 411797. **Club nickname:** Shrimps
Colours: Red and white. **Capacity:** 6,476
Record attendance: Christie Park: 9,234 v Weymouth (FA Cup 3) Jan 6, 1962. Globe Arena: 5,003 v Burnley (League Cup 2) Aug 24, 2010

Goalkeepers

Halstead, Mark	6.3	Southport	Blackpool	17.09.90
Turner, Jake	6.4	Newcastle (loan)	Wilmslow	25.02.99

Defenders

Conlan, Luke	5.11	Burnley	Portaferry	31.10.94
Cooney, Ryan	5.10	Burnley (loan)	Manchester	26.02.00
Davis, Harry	6.2	Grimsby	Burnlry	24.09.91
Hendrie, Stephen	5.10	West Ham	Glasgow	08.01.95
Knight-Percival, Nat	6.0	Carlisle	Cambridge	31.03.87
Lavelle, Sam	6.0	Bolton	Blackpool	03.10.96
Mellor, Kelvin	6.2	Bradford	Crewe	25.01.91

Midfielders

Diagouraga, Toumani	6.2	Swindon	Paris, Fr	10.06.87
Kenyon, Alex	6.0	Stockport	Euxton	17.07.92
O'Sullivan, John	5.11	Blackpool	Dublin, Ire	18.09.93
Phillips, Adam	5.11	Burnley (loan)	Garstang	15.01.98
Pringle, Ben	5.9	Gillingham	Whitley Bay	25.07.88
Wildig, Aaron	5.9	Shrewsbury	Hereford	15.04.92

Forwards

Leitch-Smith AJ	5.11	Shrewsbury	Crewe	06.03.90
McAlinden, Liam	6.1	Stockport	Cannock	26.09.93
Mendes Gomes, Carlos	5.10	Atletico Madtrid	Yeumbeul, Sen	14.11.98
Slew, Jordan	6.3	Ashton	Sheffield	07.09.92
Stockton, Cole	6.1	Tranmere	Huyton	13.03.94

NEWPORT COUNTY

Ground: Rodney Parade, Newport NP19 OUU
Telephone: 01633 670690. **Club nickname:** Exiles
Colours: Amber and black. **Capacity:** 7,850
Record attendance: Somerton Park: 24,268 v Cardiff (Div 3S) Oct 16, 1937. Rodney Parade: 9,836 v Tottenham (FA Cup 4) Jan 27, 2018

Goalkeepers

King, Tom	6.1	Millwall	Plymouth	09.03.95
Townsend, Nick	5.11	Barnsley	Solihull	01.11.94

Defenders

Baker, Ashley	5.10	Sheffield Wed	Bridgend	30.10.96
Bennett, Scott	5.10	Notts Co	Newquay	30.11.90
Demetriou, Mickey	6.2	Shrewsbury	Dorrington	12.03.90
Haynes, Ryan	6.1	Shrewsbury	Northampton	27.09.95
Howkins, Kyle	6.4	WBA	Walsall	04.05.96
Leadbitter, Daniel	6.1	Newcastle	Newcastle upon Tyne	07.10.90

Midfielders

Collins, Lewis	5.10	–	Newport	09.05.01
Dolan, Matt	5.9	Yeovil	Hartlepool	11.02.93
Labadie, Joss	6.3	Dagenham	Croydon	30.08.90
Sheehan, Josh	6.0	Swansea	Pembrey	30.03.95
Willmott, Robbie	5.9	Chelmsford	Harlow	16.05.90

Forwards

Abrahams, Tristan	5.10	Norwich	Lewisham	29.12.98
Amond, Padraig	5.11	Hartlepool	Carlow, Ire	15.04.88
Whitely, Corey	5.10	Ebbsfleet	Enfield	11.07.91

OLDHAM ATHLETIC

Ground: Boundary Park, Oldham OL1 2PA
Telephone: 0161 624 4972. **Club nickname:** Latics
Colours: Blue and white. **Capacity:** 13,500
Record attendance: 47,761 v Sheffield Wed (FA Cup 4) Jan 25, 1930

Goalkeepers

Lawlor, Ian	6.4	Doncaster (loan)	Dublin, Ire	27.10.94
Woods, Gary	6.0	Hamilton	Kettering	01.10.90
Zeus de la Paz	6.2	Cincinnati	Nijmegen, Hol	11.03.95

Defenders

Borthwick-Jackson, Carmeron	6.0	Manchester Utd	Manchester	02.02.97
Egert, Thomas	6.4	Burton	Prague, Cz	01.08.94
Hamer, Tom	6.2	–	Bolton	16.11.99
Jombati, Sido	6.1	Wycombe	Lisbon, Por	20.08.87
Piergianni, Carl	6.1	Salford	Peterborough	03.05.92
Wheater, David	6.5	Bolton	Redcar	14.02.87

Midfielders

Dearnley, Zak	5.11	Manchester Utd	Sheffield	28.09.98
Fage, Dylan	5.10	Auxerre	France	18.03.99
Grant, Bobby	5.11	Wrexham (loan)	Liverpool	01.07.90
Keillor-Dunn, Davis	5.11	Wrexham	Sunderland	02.11.97
Maouche, Mohamed	5.11	Tours	Ambilly, Fr	10.01.93

Forwards

Branger, Johan	6.0	Dieppe	Sens, Fr	05.07.93
McAleny, Conor	5.10	Fleetwood	Liverpool	12.08.92
Rowe, Danny	6.1	AFC Fylde	Blackpool	29.01.90

PORT VALE

Ground: Vale Park, Hamil Road, Burslem, Stoke-on-Trent ST6 1AW
Telephone: 01782 655800. **Club nickname:** Valiants
Colours: Black and white. **Capacity:** 18,947
Record attendance: 49,768 v Aston Villa (FA Cup 5) Feb 20, 1960

Goalkeepers

Brown, Scott	6.1	Wycombe	Wolverhampton	26.04.85

Defenders

Brisley, Shaun	6.4	Notts Co	Macclesfield	06.05.90
Campbell-Godon, Ryan	5.11	–	Nottingham	02.05.01
Crookes, Adam	6.0	Nottm Forest	Lincoln	18.11.97
Gibbons, James	5.9	–	Stoke	16.03.98
Legge, Leon	6.1	Cambridge	Hastings	28.04.85
Mills, Zak	5.10	Oldham	Peterborough	28.05.92
Smith, Nathan	6.0	–	Madeley	03.04.96

Midfielders

Amoo, David	5.10	Cambridge	Southwark	13.04.91
Browne, Rhys	5.10	Yeovil	Romford	16.11.95
Burgess, Scott	5.10	Bury	Warrington	12.08.97
Conlon, Tom	5.9	Stevenage	Stoke	03.02.96
Hurst, Alex	5.8	Bradford PA	–	06.10.99
Joyce, Luke	5.11	Carlisle	Bolton	09.07.87
Montano, Cristian	5.11	Bristol Rov	Cali, Col	11.12.91
Oyeleke, Manny	5.9	Aldershot	Wandsworth	24.12.92
Whitehead, Danny	5.10	Salford	Manchester	23.10.93
Worrall, David	6.0	Millwall	Manchester	12.06.90

Forwards

Cullen, Mark	5.9	Blackpool	Stakeford	21.04.92
Miller, Ricky	6.2	Peterborough	Hatfield	13.03.89
Pope, Tom	6.3	Bury	Stoke	27.08.85
Rodney, Devante	5.10	Salford	Manchester	19.05.98

SALFORD CITY

Ground: Peninsula Stadium, Moor Lane, Salford M7 3PZ
Telephone: 0161 792 6287. **Club nickname:** Ammies
Colours: Red and white. **Capacity:** 5,106

Goalkeepers

Hladky, Vaclav	6.2	St Mirren	Bron, Cz	14.11.90

Defenders

Clarke, Tom	5.11	Preston	Halifax	21.12.87
Eastham, Ashley	6.3	Fleetwood	Preston	22.03.91
Jones, Dan	6.0	Barrow	Bishop Auckland	14.12.94
Threlkeld, Oscar	6.0	Beveren	Radcliffe	15.12.94
Touray, Ibou	5.10	Nantwich	Liverpool	24.12.94
Turnbull, Jordan	6.1	Northampton	Trowbridge	30.10.94

Midfielders

Gibson, Darron	6.0	Wigan	Derry	25.10.87
Lloyd, Danny	5.8	Peterborough	Liverpool	03.12.91
Lowe, Jason	5.10	Bolton	Wigan	02.09.91
Jones, Joey	6.1	Eastleigh	Kingston	15.04.94
Smith, Martin	5.10	Swindon	Sunderland	02.10.95
Towell, Richie	5.8	Brighton	Dublin, Ire	17.07.91

Forwards

Armstrong, Luke	6.1	Middlesbrough	Durham	02.07.96
Bruno Andrade	5.9	Lincoln	Viseu, Port	02.10.93
Dieseruvwe, Emmanuel	6.5	Kidderminster	Leeds	20.02.95
Elliott, Tom	6.4	Millwall	Leeds	09.11.90
Henderson, Ian	5.10	Rochdale	Thetford	24.01.85

Hunter, Ashley	5.10	Fleetwood	Derby	29.09.95
Thomas-Asante, Brandon	5.11	Ebbsfleet	Milton Keynes	29.12.98
Wilson, James	6.1	Aberdeen	Biddulph	01.12.95

SCUNTHORPE UNITED

Ground: Sands Venue Stadium, Doncaster Road, Scunthorpe DN15 8TD
Telephone: 0871 221 1899. **Club nickname:** Iron
Colours: Claret and blue. **Capacity:** 9,183
Record attendance: Old Show Ground: 23,935 v Portsmouth (FA Cup 4) Jan 30, 1954. Glanford Park: 8,921 v Newcastle (Champ) Oct 20, 2009

Goalkeepers

Kelsey, Adam	6.2	Hull	–	12.11.99
Watson, Rory	6.3	Hull	York	05.02.96
Defenders				
Bedeau, Jacob	6.1	Aston Villa	Waltham Forest	24.12.99
Butroid, Lewis	5.9	–	Gainsborough	17.09.98
Clarke, Jordan	6.0	Coventry	Coventry	19.11.91
Cordner, Tyler	6.1	Bournemouth (loan)	Southampton	04.12.98
McGahey, Harrison	6.1	Rochdale	Preston	26.09.95
Onariase, Manny	6.2	Dagenham	Croydon	21.10.96
Rowe, Jai	5.11	Barwell	Nuneaton	08.08.01
Midfielders				
Colclough, Ryan	6.0	Wigan	Burslem	27.12.94
Dales, Andy	5.11	Dundee	Derby	13.11.94
Hallam, Jordan	5.8	Sheffield Utd	Sheffield	06.10.98
Gillieard, Alex	6.0	Shrewsbury	Shotley Bridge	11.02.96
Spence, Lewis	6.0	Ross Co	Kirkcaldy	28.01.96
Forwards				
Beestin, Alfie	5.10	Doncaster	Leeds	01.10.97
Eisa, Abo	5.11	Shrewsbury	Khartoum, Sud	05.01.96
Green, Devarn	5.8	Southport	Sandwell	26.08.96
Jarvis, Aaron	6.2	Luton	Basingstoke	24.01.98
McAtee, John	5.11	Shrewsbury	Salford	23.07.99
Mooney, Kelsey	5.11	Hereford	–	05.02.99
Olomola, Olufela	5.8	Southampton	London	05.09/97
Van Veen, Kevin	6.0	Northampton	Eindhovern, Hol	01.06.91

SOUTHEND UNITED

Ground: Roots Hall, Victoria Avenue, Southend SS2 6NQ
Telephone: 01702 304050. **Club nickname:** Shrimpers
Colours: Blue and white. **Capacity:** 12,392
Record attendance: 31,090 v Liverpool (FA Cup 3) Jan 10, 1979

Goalkeepers

Oxley, Mark	6.2	Hibernian	Sheffield	28.09.90
Seaden, Harry	6.3	–	Southend	23.04.01
Defenders				
Bwomono, Elvis	5.11	QPR	Uganda	29.11.98
Demetriou, Jason	5.11	Walsall	Newham	18.11.87
Kyprianou, Harry	6.0	Watford	Enfield	16.03.97
Lennon, Harry	6.3	Charlton	Romford	16.12.94
Ralph, Nathan	5.9	Dundee	Dunmow	14.01.93
White, John	6.0	Colchester	Colchester	25.07.86

Midfielders

Barratt, Sam	5.11	Maidenhead	–	22.08.95
Dieng, Timothee	6.2	Bradford	Grenoble, Fr	09.04.92
Egbri, Terell	5.9	–		21.06.01
Green, Jordan	5.6	Barnsley (loan)	New Cross	22.02.95
Hutchinson, Isaac	6.1	–	Eastbourne	10.04.00
McLaughlin, Stephen	5.10	Nottm Forest	Donegal, Ire	14.06.90
Phillips, Harry	5.10	–	Wickford	19.09.97

Forwards

Goodship, Brandon	6.2	Weymouth	Poole	22.09.94
Humphrys, Stephen	6.1	Fulham	Oldham	15.09.97
Kelman, Charlie	5.11	–	Basildon	02.11.01

STEVENAGE

Ground: Lamex Stadium, Broadhall Way, Stevenage SG2 8RH
Telephone: 01438 223223. **Club nickname:** Boro
Colours: White and red. **Capacity:** 6,920
Record attendance: 8,040 v Newcastle (FA Cup 4) January 25, 1998

Goalkeepers

Cumming, Jamie	6.1	Chelsea (loan)	Winchester	04.09.99
Johnson, Billy	6.1	Norwich	–	25.09.99

Defenders

Coker, Ben	5.11	Lincoln (loan)	Hatfield	17.06.89
Cuthbert, Scott	6.2	Luton	Alexandria, Scot	15.06.87
Fernandez, Luis	6.4	–	Enfield	28.09.01
Fielding, Jamie	6.1	Hastings	–	18.08.99
Marshall, Ross	6.1	Maidstone	–	09.10.99
Prosser, Luke	6.3	Colchester	Enfield	28.05.88
Vancooten, Terence	6.1	Reading	Kingston upon Thames	29.12.97
Vincelot, Romain	5.10	Shrewsbuey	Poitiers, Fr	29.10.85
Wildin, Luther	5.10	Nuneaton	Leicester	03.12.97

Midfielders

Carter, Charlie	6.1	Chesterfield	London	25.10.96
Iontton, Arthur	6.0	–	Enfield	16.12.00
List, Elliott	5.10	Gillingham	Camberwell	12.05.97
Osborne, Elliot	6.0	Stockport	Stoke	12.05.96

Forwards

Akinwande, Femi	5.10	Billericay	–	01.05.96
Effiong, Inih	6.4	Dover	Brent	02.03.91
Dinanga, Marcus	5.11	AFC Telford	–	30.06.97
Marsh, Tyrone	5.11	Boreham Wood	Bedford	24.12.93
Newton, Dan	5.10	Tamworth	Liverpool	01.02.98

TRANMERE ROVERS

Ground: Prenton Park, Prenton Road, West Birkenhead CH42 9PY
Telephone: 0871 221 2001. **Club nickname:** Rovers
Colours: White. **Capacity:** 16,567
Record attendance: 24,424 v Stoke (FA Cup 4) Feb 5, 1972

Goalkeepers

Davies, Scott	6.0	Fleetwood	Blackpool	27.02.87
Murphy, Joe	6.2	Shrewsbury	Dublin, Ire	21.08.81

Defenders

Clarke, Peter	6.0	Fleetwood	Southport	03.01.82
Khan, Otis	5.9	Mansfield	Ashton-under-Lyne	05.09.95
Monthe, Manny	6.1	Forest Green	Cameroon	26.01.95
Nelson, Sid	6.1	Millwall	Lewisham	01.01.96
O'Connor, Lee	5.10	Celtic (loan)	Waterford, Ire	28.07.00
Ray, George	6.0	Crewe	Warrington	03.10.93
Ridehalgh, Liam	5.10	Huddersfield	Halifax	20.04.91

Midfielders

Blackett-Taylor, Corey	5.8	Aston Villa	Erdington	23.09.97
Gilmour, Harvey	5.11	Sheffield Utd	Sheffield	15.12.98
Lewis, Paul	6.1	Cambridge	Liverpool	17.12.94
Morris, Kieron	5.10	Walsall	Hereford	03.06.94
Spearing, Jay	5.7	Blackpool	Wallasey	25.11.88

Forwards

Payne, Stefan	5.10	Bristol Rov	Lambeth	10.08.91
Vaughan, James	5.11	Bradford	Birmingham	14.07.88

WALSALL

Ground: Banks's Stadium, Bescot Crescent, Walsall WS1 4SA
Telephone: 01922 622791. **Club nickname:** Saddlers
Colours: Red and white. **Capacity:** 11,300
Record attendance: Fellows Park: 25,453 v Newcastle (Div 2) Aug 29, 1961. Banks's
Stadium: 11,049 v Rotherham (Div 1) May 10, 2004

Goalkeepers

Roberts, Liam	6.0	–	Walsall	24.11.94

Defenders

Clarke, James	6.0	Bristol Rov	Aylesbury	17.11.89
Cockerill-Mollett, Callum	5.10	–	Leicester	15.01.99
Jules, Zak	6.3	Macclesfield	Islington	02.07.97
Norman, Cameron	6.2	Oxford	Norwich	12.10.95
Sadler, Mat	5.11	Shrewsbury	Birmingham	26.02.85
Scarr, Dan	6.2	Birmingham	Bromsgrove	24.12.94

Midfielders

Bates, Alfie	5.7	Birmingham	Coventry	03.05.01
Guthrie, Danny	5.9	Mitra Kukar	Shrewsbury	18.04.87
Kiersey, Jack	5.10	Everton	Manchester	26.09.98
Kinsella, Liam	5.9	–	Colchester	23.02.96
McDonald, Wes		Yeovil	London	04.05.97
Nolan, Jack	5.11	Reading	–	25.05.01
Sinclair, Stuart	5.8	Bristol Rov	Houghton Conquest	09.11.87

Forwards

Adebayo, Elijah	6.4	Fulham	Brent	07.01.98
Holden, Rory	5.6	Bristol City	Derry	23.08.97
Lavery, Caolan	5.11	Sheffield Utd	Alberta, Can	22.10.92
Gordon, Josh	5.10	Leicester	Stoke	19.01.95

SCOTTISH PREMIERSHIP SQUADS
2020–2021

(at time of going to press)

ABERDEEN

Ground: Pittodrie Stadium, Pittodrie Street, Aberdeen AB24 5QH. **Capacity:** 22, 199.
Telephone: 01224 650400. **Manager:** Derek McInnes. **Colours:** Red and white. **Nickname:**
Dons
Goalkeepers: Joe Lewis, Tomas Cerny
Defenders: Andrew Considine, Michael Devlin, Ronald Hernandez, Jonny Hayes, Tommie
Hoban, Shaleum Logan, Ross McCrorie (loan),Scott McKenna, Ash Taylor
Midfielders: Craig Bryson, Dean Campbell, Lewis Ferguson, Ryan Hedges, Matty Kennedy,
Dylan McGeouch, Niall McGinn, Connor McLennan, Funso Ojo, Ethan Ross, Miko Virtanen
Forwards: Bruce Anderson, Sam Cosgrove, Ryan Edmondson (loan), Curtis Main, Marley
Watkins, Scott Wright

CELTIC

Ground: Celtic Park, Glasgow G40 3RE. **Capacity:** 60, 832. **Telephone:** 0871 226 1888
Manager: Neil Lennon. **Colours:** Green and white. **Nickname:** Bhoys
Goalkeepers: Scott Bain, Vasilis Barkas, Conor Hazard
Defenders: Kristoffer Ajer, Boli Bolingoli, Luca Connell, Jeremie Frimpong, Christopher Jullien,
Anthony Ralston
Midfielders: Nir Bitton, Scott Brown, Ryan Christie, Karamoko Dembele, Mohamed Elyounoussi
(loan), James Forrest, Ewan Henderson, Mikey Johnston, Callum McGregor, Olivier Ntcham,
Scott Robertson, Tom Rogic, Ismaila Soro, Greg Taylor
Forwards: Albian Ajeti, Odsonne Edouard. Leigh Griffiths, Patryk Klimala

DUNDEE UNITED

Ground: Tannadice Park, Tannadice Street, Dundee DD3 7JW. **Capacity:** 14, 209
Telephone: 01382 833166
Manager: Micky Mellon. **Colours:** Tangerine and black. **Nickname:** Terrors
Goalkeepers: Deniz Mehmet, Jack Newman, Benjamin Siegrist
Defenders: Mark Connolly, Nathan Cooney, Jake Davidson, Ryan Edwards, Kieran Freeman,
Ross Graham, Mark Reynolds, Jamie Robson, Liam Smith, Adrian Sporle
Midfielders: Louis Appere, Luke Bolton, Calum Butcher, Declan Glass, Ian Harkes, Adam King,
Paul McMullan, Archie Meekison, Chris Mochrie, Lewis Neilson, Peter Pawlett, Dillon Powers
Forwards: Logan Chalmers. Nicky Clark, Lawrence Shankland, Cammy Smith

HAMILTON ACADEMICAL

Ground: New Douglas Park, Hamilton ML3 0FT. **Capacity:** 6, 000. **Telephone:** 01698 368652.
Manager: Brian Rice. **Colours:** Red and white. **Nickname:** Accies
Goalkeepers: Ryan Fulton, Owain Kyle Gourlay, Jamie Smith
Defenders: Brian Easton, Markus Fjortoft, Jamie Hamilton, Lee Hodson (loan),
Ciaran McKenna, Scott McMann, Hakeem Odoffin, George Stanger, Shaun Want
Midfielders: Ross Callachan, Will Collar, Ronan Hughes, Justin Johnson, Scott Martin, Reegan
Mimnaugh, Lewis Smith, Charlie Trafford
Forwards: Ross Cunningham, David Moyo, Marios Ogkmpoe, Callum Smith, David Templeton,
Andy Winter

HIBERNIAN

Ground: Easter Road Stadium, Albion Place, Edinburgh EH7 5QG. **Capacity:** 20, 451.
Telephone: 0131 661 2159. **Manager:** Jack Ross. **Colours:** Green and white. **Nickname:** Hibees
Goalkeepers: Kevin Dabrowski, Ofir Marciano
Defenders: Alex Gogic, David Gray, Paul Hanlon, Tom James, Sean Mackie, Paul McGinn, Darren McGregor, Ryan Porteous, Lewis Stevenson, Ben Stirling
Midfielders: Scott Allan, Melker Hallberg, Daryl Horgan, Stevie Mallan, Fraser Murray, Joe Newell, Drey Wright
Forwards: Martin Boyle, Christian Doidge, Jamie Gullan, Florian Kamberi, Kevin Nisbet

KILMARNOCK

Ground: Rugby Park, Kilmarnock KA 1 2DP. **Capacity:** 18, 128. **Telephone:** 01563 545300
Manager: Alex Dyer. **Colours:** Blue and white. **Nickname:** Killie
Goalkeepers: Jake Eastwood (loan), Curtis Lyle, Danny Rogers
Defenders: Kirk Broadfoot, Stuart Findlay, Brandon Haunstrup, Aaron McGowan, Ross Millen, Zeno Rossi (loan), Ally Taylor, Calum Waters
Midfielders: Chris Burke, Kyle Connell, Gary Dicker, Mohamed El Makrini, Mitch Pinnock, Alan Power, Aaron Tshibola
Forwards: Eamonn Brophy, Innes Cameron, Nicke Kabamba, Greg Kiltie, Rory McKenzie, Danny Whitehall

LIVINGSTON

Ground: Tony Macaroni Arena, Alderstone Road, Livingston EH54 7DN. **Capacity:** 10, 000
Telephone: 01506 417000. **Manager:** Gary Holt. **Colours:** Gold and black. **Nickname:** Livvy's Lions
Goalkeepers: Gary Maley, Robby McCrorie (loan), Max Stryjek
Defenders: Efe Ambrose, Ciaron Brown (loan), Nicky Devlin, Jack Fitzwater, Jon Guthrie, Steve Lawson, Alan Lithgow, Jack McMillan, Cece Pepe, Julien Serrano (loan), Aaron Taylor-Sinclair
Midfielders: Marvin Bartley, Robbie Crawford, Rafaele De Vita, Alan Forrest, Jason Holt, Keaghan Jacobs, Steve Lawson, Carlo Pignatiello, Scott Pittman, Scott Robinson, Craig Sibbald, Scott Tiffoney
Forwards: Jack Hamilton, Salim Kouider-Aissa, Lars Lokotsch, Matej Poplatnik, Aymen Souda

MOTHERWELL

Ground: Fir Park, Firpark Street, Motherwell ML1 2QN. **Capacity:** 13, 742. **Telephone:** 01698 333333. **Manager:** Stephen Robinson. **Colours:** Claret and amber. **Nickname:** Well
Goalkeepers: Trevor Carson, Scott Fox, Peter Morrison
Defenders: Jake Carroll, Liam Donnelly, Charles Dunne, Declan Gallagher, Liam Grimshaw, Yusuf Hussain, Ricki Lamie, Barry Maguire, Nathan McGinley, Bevis Mugabi
Midfielders: Allan Campbell, Callum Lang (loan), Ross McIver, Mark O'Hara, Liam Polworth, Harry Robinson, David Turnbull
Forwards: Jermaine Hylton, Callum Lang, Chris Long, Sherwin Seedorf, Tony Watt, Jordan White

RANGERS

Ground: Ibrox Park, Edmison Drive, Glasgow G51 2XD. **Capacity:** 50, 411
Telephone: 0871 702 1972. **Manager:** Steven Gerrard. **Colours:** Blue. **Nickname:** Gers
Goalkeepers: Andy Firth, Allan McGregor, Jon McLaughlin
Defenders: Leon Balogun, Borna Barisic, Calvin Bassey, George Edmundson, Connor Goldson, Nikola Katic, James Tavernier, Aidan Wilson
Midfielders: Scott Arfield, Joe Aribo, Steven Davis, Ianis Hagi, Ryan Jack, Jordan Jones, Glen

Kamara, Charlie Lindsay

Forwards: Jermain Defoe, James Graham, Cedric Itte, Alfredo Morelos, Jamie Murphy, Kemar Roofe, Greg Stewart

ROSS COUNTY

Ground: Global Energy Stadium, Victoria Park, Jubilee Road, Dingwall IV15 9QZ. 10, 673
Telephone: 01738 459090. **Manager:** Stuart Kettlewell. **Colours:** Blue and white. **Nickname:** Staggies
Goalkeepers: Ross Doohan (loan), Ross Laidlaw, Ross Munro
Defenders: Regan Charles-Cook, Coll Donaldson, Liam Fontaine, Tom Grivosti, Alex Iacovitti, Callum Morris, Connor Randall, Josh Reid, Carl Tremarco, Keith Watson
Midfielders: Joe Chalmers, Ross Draper, Michael Gardyne, Stephen Kelly (loan), Josh Mullin, Harry Paton, Blair Spittal, Jordan Tillson, Iain Vigurs
Forwards: Lee Erwin, Billy McKay, Oli Shaw, Ross Stewart, Matthew Wright

ST JOHNSTONE

Ground: McDiarmid Park, Crieff Road, Perth PH1 2SJ. **Capacity:** 10, 673. **Telephone:** 01738 459090. **Manager:** Callum Davidson. **Colours:** Blue and white. **Nickname:** Saints
Goalkeepers: Zander Clark, Eliot Parish, Ross Sinclair
Defenders: Cammy Ballantyne, Callum Booth, Craig Conway Wallace Duffy, Liam Gordon, Jason Kerr, Jamie McCart, Danny McNamara (loan), Shaun Rooney Scott Tanser
Midfielders: Liam Craig, Murray Davidson, Oliver Hamilton, Ali McCann, David Wotherspoon
Forwards: Callum Hendry, Chris Kane, Stevie May, Michael O'Halloran, Isaac Olaofe (loan). John Robertson

ST MIRREN

Ground: Simple Digital Arena Greenhill Road, Paisley PA3 IRU. **Capacity:** 8, 023
Telephone: 0141 889 2558. **Manager:** Jim Goodwin. **Colours:** Black and white. Nickname: Buddies
Goalkeepers: Jack Alnwick, Dean Lyness, Peter Urminsky
Defenders: Jack Baird, Marcus Fraser, Nick McAllister, Conor McCarthy, Joe Shaughnessy, Nathan Sheron (loan), Richard Tait
Midfielders: Cameron Breadner, Ilkay Durmus, Ethan Erhahon, Ryan Flynn, Sam Foley, Cameron MacPherson, Kyle Magennis, Kyle McAllister, Isak Thorvaldsson (loan)
Forwards: Lewis Jamieson, Kristian Dennis, Junior Morias, Jamie McGrath, Jonathan Obika

ENGLISH FIXTURES 2020–2021
Premier League and Football League

Saturday 12 September
Premier League
Burnley v Man Utd
Crystal Palace v Southampton
Fulham v Arsenal
Liverpool v Leeds
Man City v Aston Villa
Tottenham v Everton
WBA v Leicester
West Ham v Newcastle

Championship
Barnsley v Luton
Birmingham v Brentford
Bournemouth v Blackburn
Bristol City v Coventry
Cardiff v Sheff Wed
Derby v Reading
Huddersfield v Norwich
Millwall v Stoke
Preston v Swansea
QPR v Nottm Forest
Watford v Middlesbrough
Wycombe v Rotherham

League One
Accrington v Peterborough
Crewe v Charlton
Doncaster v MK Dons
Fleetwood v Burton
Gillingham v Hull
Ipswich v Wigan
Lincoln v Oxford
Northampton v AFC Wimbledon
Plymouth v Blackpool
Portsmouth v Shrewsbury
Sunderland v Bristol Rov
Swindon v Rochdale

League Two
Barrow v Stevenage
Bolton v Forest Green
Bradford v Colchester
Cambridge v Carlisle
Cheltenham v Morecambe
Mansfield v Tranmere
Oldham v Leyton Orient
Port Vale v Crawley
Salford v Exeter
Scunthorpe v Newport
Southend v Harrogate
Walsall v Grimsby

Monday 14 September
Premier League
Brighton v Chelsea
Sheff Utd v Wolves

Saturday 19 September
Premier League
Arsenal v West Ham
Aston Villa v Sheff Utd
Chelsea v Liverpool
Everton v WBA
Leeds v Fulham
Leicester v Burnley
Man Utd v Crystal Palacee
Newcastle v Brighton
Southampton v Tottenham
Wolves v Man City

Championship
Blackburn v Wycombe
Brentford v Huddersfield
Coventry v QPR
Luton v Derby
Middlesbrough v Bournemouth
Norwich v Preston
Nottm Forest v Cardiff
Reading v Barnsley
Rotherham v Millwall
Sheff Wed v Watford
Stoke v Bristol City
Swansea v Birmingham

League One
AFC Wimbledon v Plymouth
Blackpool v Swindon
Bristol Rov v Ipswich
Burton v Accrington
Charlton v Doncaster
Hull v Crewe
MK Dons v Lincoln
Oxford v Sunderland
Peterborough v Fleetwood
Rochdale v Portsmouth
Shrewsbury v Northampton
Wigan v Gillingham

League Two
Carlisle v Southend
Colchester v Bolton
Crawley v Scunthorpe
Exeter v Port Vale
Forest Green v Bradford
Grimsby v Salford
Harrogate v Walsall
Leyton Orient v Mansfield

Morecambe v Cambridge
Newport v Barrow
Stevenage v Oldham
Tranmere v Cheltenham

Saturday 26 September
Premier League
Brighton v Man Utd
Burnley v Southampton
Crystal Palace v Everton
Fulham v Aston Villa
Liverpool v Arsenal
Man City v Leicester
Sheff Utd v Leeds
Tottenham v Newcastle
WBA v Chelsea
West Ham v Wolves

Championship
Barnsley v Coventry
Birmingham v Rotherham
Bournemouth v Norwich
Bristol City v Sheff Wed
Cardiff v Reading
Derby v Blackburn
Huddersfield v Nottm Forest
Millwall v Brentford
Preston v Stoke
QPR v Middlesbrough
Watford v Luton
Wycombe v Swansea

League One
Accrington v Oxford
Crewe v MK Dons
Doncaster v Bristol Rov
Fleetwood v AFC Wimbledon
Gillingham v Blackpool
Ipswich v Rochdale
Lincoln v Charlton
Northampton v Hull
Plymouth v Shrewsbury
Portsmouth v Wigan
Sunderland v Peterborough
Swindon v Burton

League Two
Barrow v Colchester
Bolton v Newport
Bradford v Stevenage
Cambridge v Tranmere
Cheltenham v Grimsby
Mansfield v Exeter
Oldham v Crawley
Port Vale v Harrogate
Salford v Forest Green
Scunthorpe v Carlisle
Southend v Morecambe
Walsall v Leyton Orient

Saturday 3 October
Premier League
Arsenal v Sheff Utd
Aston Villa v Liverpool
Chelsea v Crystal Palace
Everton v Brighton
Leeds v Man City
Leicester v West Ham
Man Utd v Tottenham
Newcastle v Burnley
Southampton v WBA
Wolves v Fulham

Championship
Blackburn v Cardiff
Brentford v Preston
Coventry v Bournemouth
Luton v Wycombe
Middlesbrough v Barnsley
Norwich v Derby
Nottm Forest v Bristol City
Reading v Watford
Rotherham v Huddersfield
Sheff Wed v QPR
Stoke v Birmingham
Swansea v Millwall

League One
AFC Wimbledon v Accrington
Blackpool v Lincoln
Bristol Rov v Northampton
Burton v Portsmouth
Charlton v Sunderland
Hull v Plymouth
MK Dons v Ipswich
Oxford v Crewe
Peterborough v Swindon
Rochdale v Fleetwood
Shrewsbury v Gillingham
Wigan v Doncaster

League Two
Carlisle v Barrow
Colchester v Oldham
Crawley v Southend
Exeter v Cambridge
Forest Green v Walsall
Grimsby v Bradford
Harrogate v Bolton
Leyton Orient v Cheltenham
Morecambe v Port Vale
Newport v Mansfield
Stevenage v Salford
Tranmere v Scunthorpe

Saturday 10 October
League Two
Barrow v Leyton Orient

Bolton v Grimsby
Bradford v Harrogate
Cambridge v Newport
Cheltenham v Crawley
Mansfield v Stevenage
Oldham v Morecambe
Port Vale v Carlisle
Salford v Tranmere
Scunthorpe v Forest Green
Southend v Exeter
Walsall v Colchester

League One
Accrington v Rochdale
Crewe v Wigan
Doncaster v Shrewsbury
Fleetwood v Hull
Gillingham v Oxford
Ipswich v Charlton
Lincoln v Bristol Rov
Northampton v Peterborough
Plymouth v Burton
Portsmouth v MK Dons
Sunderland v Blackpool
Swindon v AFC Wimbledon

Saturday 17 October
Premier League
Chelsea v Southampton
Crystal Palace v Brighton
Everton v Liverpool
Leeds v Wolves
Leicester v Aston Villa
Man City v Arsenal
Newcastle v Man Utd
Sheff Utd v Fulham
Tottenham v West Ham
WBA v Burnley

Championship
Barnsley v Bristol City
Birmingham v Sheff Wed
Blackburn v Nottm Forest
Bournemouth v QPR
Brentford v Coventry
Derby v Watford
Luton v Stoke
Middlesbrough v Reading
Preston v Cardiff
Rotherham v Norwich
Swansea v Huddersfield
Wycombe v Millwall

League One
AFC Wimbledon v Shrewsbury
Bristol Rov v Burton
Charlton v Wigan
Crewe v Blackpool

Fleetwood v Lincoln
Ipswich v Accrington
MK Dons v Gillingham
Peterborough v Oxford
Plymouth v Northampton
Portsmouth v Doncaster
Rochdale v Hull
Swindon v Sunderland

League Two
Bolton v Oldham
Carlisle v Colchester
Crawley v Morecambe
Forest Green v Stevenage
Harrogate v Barrow
Leyton Orient v Grimsby
Mansfield v Bradford
Newport v Tranmere
Port Vale v Salford
Scunthorpe v Cambridge
Southend v Cheltenham
Walsall v Exeter

Tuesday 20 October
Championship
Bristol City v Middlesbrough
Coventry v Swansea
Millwall v Luton
Norwich v Birmingham
Nottm Forest v Rotherham
Reading v Wycombe

League One
Accrington v Fleetwood
Blackpool v Charlton
Burton v Rochdale
Gillingham v Portsmouth
Hull v AFC Wimbledon
Lincoln v Plymouth
Northampton v Swindon
Oxford v MK Dons
Shrewsbury v Bristol Rov
Sunderland v Crewe
Wigan v Peterborough
Doncaster v Ipswich

League Two
Barrow v Bolton
Bradford v Walsall
Cambridge v Port Vale
Cheltenham v Scunthorpe
Colchester v Forest Green
Exeter v Crawley
Grimsby v Harrogate
Morecambe v Mansfield
Oldham v Carlisle
Salford v Southend
Stevenage v Newport
Tranmere v Leyton Orient

Wednesday 21 October

Championship
Cardiff v Bournemouth
Huddersfield v Derby
QPR v Preston
Sheff Wed v Brentford
Stoke v Barnsley
Watford v Blackburn

Saturday 24 October

Premier League
Arsenal v Leicester
Aston Villa v Leeds
Brighton v WBA
Burnley v Tottenham
Fulham v Crystal Palace
Liverpool v Sheff Utd
Man Utd v Chelsea
Southampton v Everton
West Ham v Man City
Wolves v Newcastle

Championship
Bristol City v Swansea
Cardiff v Middlesbrough
Coventry v Blackburn
Huddersfield v Preston
Millwall v Barnsley
Norwich v Wycombe
Nottm Forest v Derby
QPR v Birmingham
Reading v Rotherham
Sheff Wed v Luton
Stoke v Brentford
Watford v Bournemouth

League One
Accrington v Bristol Rov
Blackpool v MK Dons
Burton v AFC Wimbledon
Doncaster v Crewe
Gillingham v Fleetwood
Hull v Peterborough
Lincoln v Ipswich
Northampton v Charlton
Oxford v Swindon
Shrewsbury v Rochdale
Sunderland v Portsmouth
Wigan v Plymouth

League Two
Barrow v Walsall
Bradford v Newport
Cambridge v Bolton
Cheltenham v Mansfield
Colchester v Harrogate
Exeter v Scunthorpe
Grimsby v Carlisle

Morecambe v Forest Green
Oldham v Port Vale
Salford v Crawley
Stevenage v Leyton Orient
Tranmere v Southend

Tuesday 27 October

Championship
Barnsley v QPR
Blackburn v Reading
Brentford v Norwich
Middlesbrough v Coventry
Swansea v Stoke
Wycombe v Watford

League One
AFC Wimbledon v Blackpool
Bristol Rov v Hull
Charlton v Oxford
Crewe v Lincoln
Fleetwood v Shrewsbury
Ipswich v Gillingham
MK Dons v Wigan
Peterborough v Burton
Plymouth v Doncaster
Portsmouth v Northampton
Rochdale v Sunderland
Swindon v Accrington

League Two
Carlisle v Morecambe
Crawley v Tranmere
Forest Green v Grimsby
Harrogate v Stevenage
Leyton Orient v Exeter
Mansfield v Barrow
Newport v Colchester
Port Vale v Cheltenham
Scunthorpe v Salford
Southend v Oldham
Walsall v Cambridge
Bolton v Bradford

Wednesday 28 October

Championship
Birmingham v Huddersfield
Bournemouth v Bristol City
Derby v Cardiff
Luton v Nottm Forest
Preston v Millwall
Rotherham v Sheff Wed

Saturday 31 October

Premier League
Aston Villa v Southampton
Burnley v Chelsea
Fulham v WBA
Leeds v Leicester
Liverpool v West Ham

Man Utd v Arsenal
Newcastle v Everton
Sheff Utd v Man City
Tottenham v Brighton
Wolves v Crystal Palace

Championship
Barnsley v Watford
Bournemouth v Derby
Bristol City v Norwich
Coventry v Reading
Luton v Brentford
Middlesbrough v Nottm Forest
Millwall v Huddersfield
Preston v Birmingham
QPR v Cardiff
Stoke v Rotherham
Swansea v Blackburn
Wycombe v Sheff Wed

League One
Accrington v Plymouth
Burton v Blackpool
Doncaster v Lincoln
Fleetwood v Oxford
Gillingham v Sunderland
Ipswich v Crewe
MK Dons v AFC Wimbledon
Peterborough v Shrewsbury
Portsmouth v Charlton
Rochdale v Bristol Rov
Swindon v Hull
Wigan v Northampton

League Two
Barrow v Bradford
Cheltenham v Forest Green
Crawley v Cambridge
Exeter v Carlisle
Leyton Orient v Bolton
Mansfield v Walsall
Newport v Harrogate
Salford v Oldham
Scunthorpe v Colchester
Southend v Port Vale
Stevenage v Grimsby
Tranmere v Morecambe
November 2020

Tuesday 3 November
Championship
Blackburn v Middlesbrough
Brentford v Swansea
Cardiff v Barnsley
Huddersfield v Bristol City
Norwich v Millwall
Sheff Wed v Bournemouth

League One
AFC Wimbledon v Doncaster
Blackpool v Wigan
Bristol Rov v Peterborough
Charlton v Fleetwood
Crewe v Gillingham
Hull v Accrington
Lincoln v Portsmouth
Northampton v MK Dons
Oxford v Rochdale
Plymouth v Swindon
Shrewsbury v Burton
Sunderland v Ipswich

League Two
Bradford v Southend
Cambridge v Salford
Carlisle v Newport
Colchester v Stevenage
Forest Green v Leyton Orient
Grimsby v Barrow
Harrogate v Tranmere
Morecambe v Exeter
Oldham v Cheltenham
Port Vale v Scunthorpe
Walsall v Crawley
Bolton v Mansfield

Wednesday 4 November
Championship
Birmingham v Wycombe
Derby v QPR
Nottm Forest v Coventry
Reading v Preston
Rotherham v Luton
Watford v Stoke

Saturday 7 November
Premier League
Arsenal v Aston Villa
Brighton v Burnley
Chelsea v Sheff Utd
Crystal Palace v Leeds
Everton v Man Utd
Leicester v Wolves
Man City v Liverpool
Southampton v Newcastle
WBA v Tottenham
West Ham v Fulham

Championship
Birmingham v Bournemouth
Blackburn v QPR
Brentford v Middlesbrough
Cardiff v Bristol City
Derby v Barnsley
Huddersfield v Luton
Norwich v Swansea

Nottm Forest v Wycombe
Reading v Stoke
Rotherham v Preston
Sheff Wed v Millwall
Watford v Coventry

Saturday 14 November
League One
AFC Wimbledon v Wigan
Blackpool v Ipswich
Bristol Rov v Fleetwood
Charlton v Rochdale
Crewe v Peterborough
Hull v Burton
Lincoln v Gillingham
Northampton v Accrington
Oxford v Doncaster
Plymouth v Portsmouth
Shrewsbury v Swindon
Sunderland v MK Dons

League Two
Bolton v Salford
Bradford v Exeter
Cambridge v Barrow
Carlisle v Cheltenham
Colchester v Leyton Orient
Forest Green v Mansfield
Grimsby v Newport
Harrogate v Crawley
Morecambe v Stevenage
Oldham v Scunthorpe
Port Vale v Tranmere
Walsall v Southend

Saturday 21 November
Premier League
Aston Villa v Brighton
Burnley v Crystal Palace
Fulham v Everton
Leeds v Arsenal
Liverpool v Leicester
Man Utd v WBA
Newcastle v Chelsea
Sheff Utd v West Ham
Tottenham v Man City
Wolves v Southampton

Championship
Barnsley v Nottm Forest
Bournemouth v Reading
Bristol City v Derby
Coventry v Birmingham
Luton v Blackburn
Middlesbrough v Norwich
Millwall v Cardiff
Preston v Sheff Wed
QPR v Watford

Stoke v Huddersfield
Swansea v Rotherham
Wycombe v Brentford

League One
Accrington v Lincoln
Burton v Northampton
Doncaster v Sunderland
Fleetwood v Plymouth
Gillingham v Charlton
Ipswich v Shrewsbury
MK Dons v Hull
Peterborough v Blackpool
Portsmouth v Crewe
Rochdale v AFC Wimbledon
Swindon v Bristol Rov
Wigan v Oxford

League Two
Barrow v Forest Green
Cheltenham v Walsall
Crawley v Carlisle
Exeter v Oldham
Leyton Orient v Harrogate
Mansfield v Colchester
Newport v Port Vale
Salford v Bradford
Scunthorpe v Morecambe
Southend v Cambridge
Stevenage v Bolton
Tranmere v Grimsby

Tuesday 24 November
Championship
Barnsley v Brentford
Bournemouth v Nottm Forest
Luton v Birmingham
Preston v Blackburn
QPR v Rotherham
Stoke v Norwich

League One
Accrington v Crewe
Burton v Charlton
Fleetwood v Sunderland
Gillingham v AFC Wimbledon
Ipswich v Hull
MK Dons v Shrewsbury
Peterborough v Plymouth
Portsmouth v Oxford
Rochdale v Northampton
Swindon v Lincoln
Wigan v Bristol Rov
Doncaster v Blackpool

League Two
Barrow v Oldham
Cheltenham v Cambridge
Crawley v Grimsby

521

Exeter v Colchester
Leyton Orient v Bradford
Mansfield v Harrogate
Newport v Walsall
Salford v Morecambe
Scunthorpe v Bolton
Southend v Forest Green
Stevenage v Port Vale
Tranmere v Carlisle

Wednesday 25 November
Championship
Bristol City v Watford
Coventry v Cardiff
Middlesbrough v Derby
Millwall v Reading
Swansea v Sheff Wed
Wycombe v Huddersfield

Saturday 28 November
Premier League
Arsenal v Wolves
Brighton v Liverpool
Chelsea v Tottenham
Crystal Palace v Newcastle
Everton v Leeds
Leicester v Fulham
Man City v Burnley
Southampton v Man Utd
WBA v Sheff Utd
West Ham v Aston Villa

Championship
Birmingham v Millwall
Blackburn v Barnsley
Brentford v QPR
Cardiff v Luton
Derby v Wycombe
Huddersfield v Middlesbrough
Norwich v Coventry
Nottm Forest v Swansea
Reading v Bristol City
Rotherham v Bournemouth
Sheff Wed v Stoke
Watford v Preston

Tuesday 1 December
Championship
Birmingham v Barnsley
Bournemouth v Preston
Cardiff v Huddersfield
Derby v Coventry
QPR v Bristol City
Rotherham v Brentford

League One
AFC Wimbledon v Peterborough
Blackpool v Portsmouth
Bristol Rov v Gillingham

Charlton v MK Dons
Crewe v Swindon
Hull v Doncaster
Lincoln v Wigan
Northampton v Fleetwood
Oxford v Ipswich
Plymouth v Rochdale
Shrewsbury v Accrington
Sunderland v Burton

League Two
Bradford v Cheltenham
Cambridge v Mansfield
Carlisle v Salford
Colchester v Crawley
Forest Green v Newport
Grimsby v Exeter
Harrogate v Scunthorpe
Morecambe v Barrow
Oldham v Tranmere
Port Vale v Leyton Orient
Walsall v Stevenage
Bolton v Southend

Wednesday 2 December
Championship
Blackburn v Millwall
Luton v Norwich
Middlesbrough v Swansea
Nottm Forest v Watford
Sheff Wed v Reading
Wycombe v Stoke

Saturday 5 December
Premier League
Aston Villa v Newcastle
Brighton v Southampton
Burnley v Everton
Chelsea v Leeds
Liverpool v Wolves
Man City v Fulham
Sheff Utd v Leicester
Tottenham v Arsenal
WBA v Crystal Palace
West Ham v Man Utd

Championship
Barnsley v Bournemouth
Brentford v Blackburn
Bristol City v Birmingham
Coventry v Rotherham
Huddersfield v QPR
Millwall v Derby
Norwich v Sheff Wed
Preston v Wycombe
Reading v Nottm Forest
Stoke v Middlesbrough
Swansea v Luton
Watford v Cardiff

League One

AFC Wimbledon v Bristol Rov
Accrington v MK Dons
Burton v Crewe
Fleetwood v Blackpool
Gillingham v Swindon
Northampton v Doncaster
Oxford v Hull
Plymouth v Ipswich
Portsmouth v Peterborough
Rochdale v Lincoln
Shrewsbury v Charlton
Sunderland v Wigan

League Two

Barrow v Salford
Bolton v Port Vale
Bradford v Carlisle
Cambridge v Oldham
Cheltenham v Exeter
Colchester v Grimsby
Harrogate v Forest Green
Mansfield v Crawley
Newport v Morecambe
Scunthorpe v Leyton Orient
Stevenage v Southend
Tranmere v Walsall

Tuesday 8 December

Championship

Coventry v Luton
Huddersfield v Sheff Wed
Millwall v QPR
Stoke v Cardiff
Swansea v Bournemouth
Watford v Rotherham

Wednesday 9 December

Championship

Barnsley v Wycombe
Brentford v Derby
Bristol City v Blackburn
Norwich v Nottm Forest
Preston v Middlesbrough
Reading v Birmingham

Saturday 12 December

Premier League

Arsenal v Burnley
Crystal Palace v Tottenham
Everton v Chelsea
Fulham v Liverpool
Leeds v West Ham
Leicester v Brighton
Man Utd v Man City
Newcastle v WBA
Southampton v Sheff Utd
Wolves v Aston Villa

Championship

Birmingham v Watford
Blackburn v Norwich
Bournemouth v Huddersfield
Cardiff v Swansea
Derby v Stoke
Luton v Preston
Middlesbrough v Millwall
Nottm Forest v Brentford
QPR v Reading
Rotherham v Bristol City
Sheff Wed v Barnsley
Wycombe v Coventry

League One

Blackpool v Oxford
Bristol Rov v Plymouth
Charlton v AFC Wimbledon
Crewe v Northampton
Doncaster v Gillingham
Hull v Shrewsbury
Ipswich v Portsmouth
Lincoln v Sunderland
MK Dons v Burton
Peterborough v Rochdale
Swindon v Fleetwood
Wigan v Accrington

League Two

Carlisle v Stevenage
Crawley v Barrow
Exeter v Tranmere
Forest Green v Cambridge
Grimsby v Mansfield
Leyton Orient v Newport
Morecambe v Harrogate
Oldham v Bradford
Port Vale v Colchester
Salford v Cheltenham
Southend v Scunthorpe
Walsall v Bolton

Tuesday 15 December

Premier League

Arsenal v Southampton
Aston Villa v Burnley
Fulham v Brighton
Leeds v Newcastle
Leicester v Everton
Sheff Utd v Man Utd
West Ham v Crystal Palace
Wolves v Chelsea

Championship

Barnsley v Preston
Bournemouth v Wycombe
Bristol City v Millwall
Nottm Forest v Sheff Wed

QPR v Stoke
Watford v Brentford

League One
Blackpool v Hull
Charlton v Bristol Rov
Crewe v Plymouth
Gillingham v Accrington
Ipswich v Burton
Lincoln v Shrewsbury
MK Dons v Peterborough
Oxford v Northampton
Portsmouth v Fleetwood
Sunderland v AFC Wimbledon
Wigan v Rochdale
Doncaster v Swindon

League Two
Cambridge v Colchester
Carlisle v Mansfield
Cheltenham v Bolton
Crawley v Bradford
Exeter v Harrogate
Morecambe v Leyton Orient
Oldham v Walsall
Port Vale v Forest Green
Salford v Newport
Scunthorpe v Barrow
Southend v Grimsby
Tranmere v Stevenage

Wednesday 16 December
Premier League
Liverpool v Tottenham
Man City v WBA

Championship
Blackburn v Rotherham
Cardiff v Birmingham
Coventry v Huddersfield
Derby v Swansea
Middlesbrough v Luton
Reading v Norwich

Saturday 19 December
Premier League
Brighton v Sheff Utd
Burnley v Wolves
Chelsea v West Ham
Crystal Palace v Liverpool
Everton v Arsenal
Man Utd v Leeds
Newcastle v Fulham
Southampton v Man City
Tottenham v Leicester
WBA v Aston Villa

Championship
Birmingham v Middlesbrough

Brentford v Reading
Huddersfield v Watford
Luton v Bournemouth
Millwall v Nottm Forest
Norwich v Cardiff
Preston v Bristol City
Rotherham v Derby
Sheff Wed v Coventry
Stoke v Blackburn
Swansea v Barnsley
Wycombe v QPR

League One
AFC Wimbledon v Crewe
Accrington v Blackpool
Bristol Rov v Oxford
Burton v Doncaster
Fleetwood v Wigan
Hull v Portsmouth
Northampton v Lincoln
Peterborough v Ipswich
Plymouth v MK Dons
Rochdale v Gillingham
Shrewsbury v Sunderland
Swindon v Charlton

League Two
Barrow v Cheltenham
Bolton v Tranmere
Bradford v Cambridge
Colchester v Morecambe
Forest Green v Carlisle
Grimsby v Scunthorpe
Harrogate v Salford
Leyton Orient v Crawley
Mansfield v Southend
Newport v Oldham
Stevenage v Exeter
Walsall v Port Vale

Saturday 26 December
Premier League
Arsenal v Chelsea
Aston Villa v Crystal Palace
Fulham v Southampton
Leeds v Burnley
Leicester v Man Utd
Liverpool v WBA
Man City v Newcastle
Sheff Utd v Everton
West Ham v Brighton
Wolves v Tottenham

Championship
Barnsley v Huddersfield
Blackburn v Sheff Wed
Bournemouth v Millwall
Bristol City v Wycombe

Cardiff v Brentford
Coventry v Stoke
Derby v Preston
Middlesbrough v Rotherham
Nottm Forest v Birmingham
QPR v Swansea
Reading v Luton
Watford v Norwich

League One
Blackpool v Rochdale
Charlton v Plymouth
Crewe v Fleetwood
Doncaster v Accrington
Gillingham v Peterborough
Ipswich v Northampton
Lincoln v Burton
MK Dons v Bristol Rov
Oxford v AFC Wimbledon
Portsmouth v Swindon
Sunderland v Hull
Wigan v Shrewsbury

League Two
Cambridge v Leyton Orient
Carlisle v Bolton
Cheltenham v Stevenage
Crawley v Newport
Exeter v Forest Green
Morecambe v Grimsby
Oldham v Harrogate
Port Vale v Barrow
Salford v Walsall
Scunthorpe v Mansfield
Southend v Colchester
Tranmere v Bradford

Monday 28 December
Premier League
Brighton v Arsenal
Burnley v Sheff Utd
Chelsea v Aston Villa
Crystal Palace v Leicester
Everton v Man City
Man Utd v Wolves
Newcastle v Liverpool
Southampton v West Ham
Tottenham v Fulham
WBA v Leeds

Tuesday 29 December
Championship
Birmingham v Derby
Brentford v Bournemouth
Huddersfield v Blackburn
Luton v Bristol City
Millwall v Watford
Norwich v QPR

Preston v Coventry
Rotherham v Barnsley
Sheff Wed v Middlesbrough
Stoke v Nottm Forest
Swansea v Reading
Wycombe v Cardiff

League One
AFC Wimbledon v Ipswich
Accrington v Sunderland
Bristol Rov v Portsmouth
Burton v Wigan
Fleetwood v Doncaster
Hull v Lincoln
Northampton v Gillingham
Peterborough v Charlton
Plymouth v Oxford
Rochdale v Crewe
Shrewsbury v Blackpool
Swindon v MK Dons
January 2021

League Two
Barrow v Tranmere
Bradford v Port Vale
Colchester v Cheltenham
Forest Green v Crawley
Grimsby v Oldham
Harrogate v Carlisle
Leyton Orient v Southend
Mansfield v Salford
Newport v Exeter
Stevenage v Cambridge
Walsall v Scunthorpe
Bolton v Morecambe

Saturday 2 January
Premier League
Brighton v Wolves
Burnley v Fulham
Chelsea v Man City
Crystal Palace v Sheff Utd
Everton v West Ham
Man Utd v Aston Villa
Newcastle v Leicester
Southampton v Liverpool
Tottenham v Leeds
WBA v Arsenal

Championship
Birmingham v Blackburn
Brentford v Bristol City
Huddersfield v Reading
Luton v QPR
Millwall v Coventry
Norwich v Barnsley
Preston v Nottm Forest
Rotherham v Cardiff

Sheff Wed v Derby
Stoke v Bournemouth
Swansea v Watford
Wycombe v Middlesbrough

League One
AFC Wimbledon v Lincoln
Accrington v Portsmouth
Bristol Rov v Blackpool
Burton v Oxford
Fleetwood v Ipswich
Hull v Charlton
Northampton v Sunderland
Peterborough v Doncaster
Plymouth v Gillingham
Rochdale v MK Dons
Shrewsbury v Crewe
Swindon v Wigan

League Two
Barrow v Exeter
Bolton v Crawley
Bradford v Morecambe
Colchester v Tranmere
Forest Green v Oldham
Grimsby v Cambridge
Harrogate v Cheltenham
Leyton Orient v Salford
Mansfield v Port Vale
Newport v Southend
Stevenage v Scunthorpe
Walsall v Carlisle

Saturday 9 January
League One
Blackpool v Northampton
Charlton v Accrington
Crewe v Bristol Rov
Doncaster v Rochdale
Gillingham v Burton
Ipswich v Swindon
Lincoln v Peterborough
MK Dons v Fleetwood
Oxford v Shrewsbury
Portsmouth v AFC Wimbledon
Sunderland v Plymouth
Wigan v Hull

Tuesday 12 January
Premier League
Arsenal v Crystal Palace
Aston Villa v Tottenham
Fulham v Man Utd
Leeds v Southampton
Leicester v Chelsea
Sheff Utd v Newcastle
West Ham v WBA
Wolves v Everton

League Two
Cambridge v Harrogate
Carlisle v Leyton Orient
Cheltenham v Newport
Crawley v Stevenage
Exeter v Bolton
Morecambe v Walsall
Oldham v Mansfield
Port Vale v Grimsby
Salford v Colchester
Scunthorpe v Bradford
Southend v Barrow
Tranmere v Forest Green

Wednesday 13 January
Premier League
Liverpool v Burnley
Man City v Brighton

Saturday 16 January
Premier League
Arsenal v Newcastle
Aston Villa v Everton
Fulham v Chelsea
Leeds v Brighton
Leicester v Southampton
Liverpool v Man Utd
Man City v Crystal Palace
Sheff Utd v Tottenham
West Ham v Burnley
Wolves v WBA

Championship
Barnsley v Swansea
Blackburn v Stoke
Bournemouth v Luton
Bristol City v Preston
Cardiff v Norwich
Coventry v Sheff Wed
Derby v Rotherham
Middlesbrough v Birmingham
Nottm Forest v Millwall
QPR v Wycombe
Reading v Brentford
Watford v Huddersfield

League One
AFC Wimbledon v Sunderland
Accrington v Gillingham
Bristol Rov v Charlton
Burton v Ipswich
Fleetwood v Portsmouth
Hull v Blackpool
Northampton v Oxford
Peterborough v MK Dons
Plymouth v Crewe
Rochdale v Wigan
Shrewsbury v Lincoln
Swindon v Doncaster

League Two
Barrow v Scunthorpe
Bolton v Cheltenham
Bradford v Crawley
Colchester v Cambridge
Forest Green v Port Vale
Grimsby v Southend
Harrogate v Exeter
Leyton Orient v Morecambe
Mansfield v Carlisle
Newport v Salford
Stevenage v Tranmere
Walsall v Oldham

Tuesday 19 January
Championship
Blackburn v Swansea
Derby v Bournemouth
Reading v Coventry
Rotherham v Stoke
Sheff Wed v Wycombe
Watford v Barnsley

Wednesday 20 January
Championship
Birmingham v Preston
Brentford v Luton
Cardiff v QPR
Huddersfield v Millwall
Norwich v Bristol City
Nottm Forest v Middlesbrough

Saturday 23 January
Championship
Barnsley v Cardiff
Bournemouth v Sheff Wed
Bristol City v Huddersfield
Coventry v Nottm Forest
Luton v Rotherham
Middlesbrough v Blackburn
Millwall v Norwich
Preston v Reading
QPR v Derby
Stoke v Watford
Swansea v Brentford
Wycombe v Birmingham

League One
Blackpool v Accrington
Charlton v Swindon
Crewe v AFC Wimbledon
Doncaster v Burton
Gillingham v Rochdale
Ipswich v Peterborough
Lincoln v Northampton
MK Dons v Plymouth
Oxford v Bristol Rov
Portsmouth v Hull

Sunderland v Shrewsbury
Wigan v Fleetwood

League Two
Cambridge v Bradford
Carlisle v Forest Green
Cheltenham v Barrow
Crawley v Leyton Orient
Exeter v Stevenage
Morecambe v Colchester
Oldham v Newport
Port Vale v Walsall
Salford v Harrogate
Scunthorpe v Grimsby
Southend v Mansfield
Tranmere v Bolton

Tuesday 26 January
Premier League
Brighton v Fulham
Burnley v Aston Villa
Everton v Leicester
Man Utd v Sheff Utd
WBA v Man City

League One
Accrington v Hull
Burton v Shrewsbury
Fleetwood v Northampton
Gillingham v Crewe
Ipswich v Sunderland
MK Dons v Charlton
Peterborough v Bristol Rov
Portsmouth v Lincoln
Rochdale v Oxford
Swindon v Plymouth
Wigan v Blackpool
Doncaster v AFC Wimbledon

League Two
Barrow v Grimsby
Cheltenham v Oldham
Crawley v Walsall
Exeter v Morecambe
Leyton Orient v Forest Green
Mansfield v Bolton
Newport v Carlisle
Salford v Cambridge
Scunthorpe v Port Vale
Southend v Bradford
Stevenage v Colchester
Tranmere v Harrogate

Wednesday 27 January
Premier League
Chelsea v Wolves
Newcastle v Leeds
Southampton v Arsenal

Tottenham v Liverpool
Crystal Palace v West Ham

Saturday 30 January
Premier League
Arsenal v Man Utd
Brighton v Tottenham
Chelsea v Burnley
Crystal Palace v Wolves
Everton v Newcastle
Leicester v Leeds
Man City v Sheff Utd
Southampton v Aston Villa
WBA v Fulham
West Ham v Liverpool

Championship
Birmingham v Coventry
Blackburn v Luton
Brentford v Wycombe
Cardiff v Millwall
Derby v Bristol City
Huddersfield v Stoke
Norwich v Middlesbrough
Nottm Forest v Barnsley
Reading v Bournemouth
Rotherham v Swansea
Sheff Wed v Preston
Watford v QPR

League One
AFC Wimbledon v MK Dons
Blackpool v Burton
Bristol Rov v Rochdale
Charlton v Portsmouth
Crewe v Ipswich
Hull v Swindon
Lincoln v Doncaster
Northampton v Wigan
Oxford v Fleetwood
Plymouth v Accrington
Shrewsbury v Peterborough
Sunderland v Gillingham
February 2021

League Two
Bolton v Leyton Orient
Bradford v Barrow
Cambridge v Crawley
Carlisle v Exeter
Colchester v Scunthorpe
Forest Green v Cheltenham
Grimsby v Stevenage
Harrogate v Newport
Morecambe v Tranmere
Oldham v Salford
Port Vale v Southend
Walsall v Mansfield

Tuesday 2 February
Premier League
Aston Villa v West Ham
Burnley v Man City
Fulham v Leicester
Leeds v Everton
Sheff Utd v WBA
Wolves v Arsenal
Man Utd v Southampton

Wednesday 3 February
Premier League
Newcastle v Crystal Palace
Tottenham v Chelsea
Liverpool v Brighton

Saturday 6 February
Premier League
Aston Villa v Arsenal
Burnley v Brighton
Fulham v West Ham
Leeds v Crystal Palace
Liverpool v Man City
Man Utd v Everton
Newcastle v Southampton
Sheff Utd v Chelsea
Tottenham v WBA
Wolves v Leicester

Championship
Barnsley v Derby
Bournemouth v Birmingham
Bristol City v Cardiff
Coventry v Watford
Luton v Huddersfield
Middlesbrough v Brentford
Millwall v Sheff Wed
Preston v Rotherham
QPR v Blackburn
Stoke v Reading
Swansea v Norwich
Wycombe v Nottm Forest

League One
Accrington v Northampton
Burton v Hull
Doncaster v Oxford
Fleetwood v Bristol Rov
Gillingham v Lincoln
Ipswich v Blackpool
MK Dons v Sunderland
Peterborough v Crewe
Portsmouth v Plymouth
Rochdale v Charlton
Swindon v Shrewsbury
Wigan v AFC Wimbledon

League Two
Barrow v Cambridge
Cheltenham v Carlisle
Crawley v Harrogate
Exeter v Bradford
Leyton Orient v Colchester
Mansfield v Forest Green
Newport v Grimsby
Salford v Bolton
Scunthorpe v Oldham
Southend v Walsall
Stevenage v Morecambe
Tranmere v Port Vale

Saturday 13 February
Premier League
Arsenal v Leeds
Brighton v Aston Villa
Chelsea v Newcastle
Crystal Palace v Burnley
Everton v Fulham
Leicester v Liverpool
Man City v Tottenham
Southampton v Wolves
WBA v Man Utd
West Ham v Sheff Utd

Championship
Birmingham v Luton
Blackburn v Preston
Brentford v Barnsley
Cardiff v Coventry
Derby v Middlesbrough
Huddersfield v Wycombe
Norwich v Stoke
Nottm Forest v Bournemouth
Reading v Millwall
Rotherham v QPR
Sheff Wed v Swansea
Watford v Bristol City

League One
AFC Wimbledon v Rochdale
Blackpool v Peterborough
Bristol Rov v Swindon
Charlton v Gillingham
Crewe v Portsmouth
Hull v MK Dons
Lincoln v Accrington
Northampton v Burton
Oxford v Wigan
Plymouth v Fleetwood
Shrewsbury v Ipswich
Sunderland v Doncaster

League Two
Bolton v Stevenage
Bradford v Salford

Cambridge v Southend
Carlisle v Crawley
Colchester v Mansfield
Forest Green v Barrow
Grimsby v Tranmere
Harrogate v Leyton Orient
Morecambe v Scunthorpe
Oldham v Exeter
Port Vale v Newport
Walsall v Cheltenham

Tuesday 16 February
Championship
Bristol City v Reading
Luton v Cardiff
Middlesbrough v Huddersfield
Preston v Watford
Stoke v Sheff Wed
Wycombe v Derby

Wednesday 17 February
Championship
Barnsley v Blackburn
Bournemouth v Rotherham
Coventry v Norwich
Millwall v Birmingham
QPR v Brentford
Swansea v Nottm Forest

Saturday 20 February
Premier League
Arsenal v Man City
Aston Villa v Leicester
Brighton v Crystal Palace
Burnley v WBA
Fulham v Sheff Utd
Liverpool v Everton
Man Utd v Newcastle
Southampton v Chelsea
West Ham v Tottenham
Wolves v Leeds

Championship
Bristol City v Barnsley
Cardiff v Preston
Coventry v Brentford
Huddersfield v Swansea
Millwall v Wycombe
Norwich v Rotherham
Nottm Forest v Blackburn
QPR v Bournemouth
Reading v Middlesbrough
Sheff Wed v Birmingham
Stoke v Luton
Watford v Derby

League One
Accrington v Shrewsbury

Burton v Sunderland
Doncaster v Hull
Fleetwood v Charlton
Gillingham v Bristol Rov
Ipswich v Oxford
MK Dons v Northampton
Peterborough v AFC Wimbledon
Portsmouth v Blackpool
Rochdale v Plymouth
Swindon v Crewe
Wigan v Lincoln

League Two
Barrow v Morecambe
Cheltenham v Bradford
Crawley v Colchester
Exeter v Grimsby
Leyton Orient v Port Vale
Mansfield v Cambridge
Newport v Forest Green
Salford v Carlisle
Scunthorpe v Harrogate
Southend v Bolton
Stevenage v Walsall
Tranmere v Oldham

Tuesday 23 February
Championship
Birmingham v Norwich
Derby v Huddersfield
Luton v Millwall
Middlesbrough v Bristol City
Rotherham v Nottm Forest
Wycombe v Reading

League One
AFC Wimbledon v Gillingham
Blackpool v Doncaster
Bristol Rov v Wigan
Charlton v Burton
Crewe v Accrington
Hull v Ipswich
Lincoln v Swindon
Northampton v Rochdale
Oxford v Portsmouth
Plymouth v Peterborough
Shrewsbury v MK Dons
Sunderland v Fleetwood

League Two
Bradford v Leyton Orient
Cambridge v Cheltenham
Carlisle v Tranmere
Colchester v Exeter
Forest Green v Southend
Grimsby v Crawley
Harrogate v Mansfield
Morecambe v Salford

Oldham v Barrow
Port Vale v Stevenage
Walsall v Newport
Bolton v Scunthorpe

Wednesday 24 February
Championship
Barnsley v Stoke
Blackburn v Watford
Bournemouth v Cardiff
Brentford v Sheff Wed
Preston v QPR
Swansea v Coventry

Saturday 27 February
Premier League
Chelsea v Man Utd
Crystal Palace v Fulham
Everton v Southampton
Leeds v Aston Villa
Leicester v Arsenal
Man City v West Ham
Newcastle v Wolves
Sheff Utd v Liverpool
Tottenham v Burnley
WBA v Brighton

Championship
Barnsley v Millwall
Birmingham v QPR
Blackburn v Coventry
Bournemouth v Watford
Brentford v Stoke
Derby v Nottm Forest
Luton v Sheff Wed
Middlesbrough v Cardiff
Preston v Huddersfield
Rotherham v Reading
Swansea v Bristol City
Wycombe v Norwich

League One
AFC Wimbledon v Hull
Bristol Rov v Shrewsbury
Charlton v Blackpool
Crewe v Sunderland
Fleetwood v Accrington
Ipswich v Doncaster
MK Dons v Oxford
Peterborough v Wigan
Plymouth v Lincoln
Portsmouth v Gillingham
Rochdale v Burton
Swindon v Northampton

League Two
Bolton v Barrow
Carlisle v Oldham
Crawley v Exeter

Forest Green v Colchester
Harrogate v Grimsby
Leyton Orient v Tranmere
Mansfield v Morecambe
Newport v Stevenage
Port Vale v Cambridge
Scunthorpe v Cheltenham
Southend v Salford
Walsall v Bradford

Tuesday 2 March
Championship
Cardiff v Derby
Coventry v Middlesbrough
Huddersfield v Birmingham
Millwall v Preston
Nottm Forest v Luton
Reading v Blackburn

League One
Accrington v Ipswich
Blackpool v Crewe
Burton v Bristol Rov
Gillingham v MK Dons
Hull v Rochdale
Lincoln v Fleetwood
Northampton v Plymouth
Oxford v Peterborough
Shrewsbury v AFC Wimbledon
Sunderland v Swindon
Wigan v Charlton
Doncaster v Portsmouth

League Two
Barrow v Harrogate
Bradford v Mansfield
Cambridge v Scunthorpe
Cheltenham v Southend
Colchester v Carlisle
Exeter v Walsall
Grimsby v Leyton Orient
Morecambe v Crawley
Oldham v Bolton
Salford v Port Vale
Stevenage v Forest Green
Tranmere v Newport

Wednesday 3 March
Championship
Bristol City v Bournemouth
Norwich v Brentford
QPR v Barnsley
Sheff Wed v Rotherham
Stoke v Swansea
Watford v Wycombe

Saturday 6 March
Premier League
Aston Villa v Wolves

Brighton v Leicester
Burnley v Arsenal
Chelsea v Everton
Liverpool v Fulham
Man City v Man Utd
Sheff Utd v Southampton
Tottenham v Crystal Palace
WBA v Newcastle
West Ham v Leeds

Championship
Barnsley v Birmingham
Brentford v Rotherham
Bristol City v QPR
Coventry v Derby
Huddersfield v Cardiff
Millwall v Blackburn
Norwich v Luton
Preston v Bournemouth
Reading v Sheff Wed
Stoke v Wycombe
Swansea v Middlesbrough
Watford v Nottm Forest

League One
Accrington v Swindon
Blackpool v AFC Wimbledon
Burton v Peterborough
Doncaster v Plymouth
Gillingham v Ipswich
Hull v Bristol Rov
Lincoln v Crewe
Northampton v Portsmouth
Oxford v Charlton
Shrewsbury v Fleetwood
Sunderland v Rochdale
Wigan v MK Dons

League Two
Barrow v Mansfield
Bradford v Bolton
Cambridge v Walsall
Cheltenham v Port Vale
Colchester v Newport
Exeter v Leyton Orient
Grimsby v Forest Green
Morecambe v Carlisle
Oldham v Southend
Salford v Scunthorpe
Stevenage v Harrogate
Tranmere v Crawley

Tuesday 9 March
League One
AFC Wimbledon v Burton
Bristol Rov v Accrington
Charlton v Northampton
Crewe v Doncaster

Fleetwood v Gillingham
Ipswich v Lincoln
MK Dons v Blackpool
Peterborough v Hull
Plymouth v Wigan
Portsmouth v Sunderland
Rochdale v Shrewsbury
Swindon v Oxford

League Two
Carlisle v Grimsby
Crawley v Salford
Forest Green v Morecambe
Harrogate v Colchester
Leyton Orient v Stevenage
Mansfield v Cheltenham
Newport v Bradford
Port Vale v Oldham
Scunthorpe v Exeter
Southend v Tranmere
Walsall v Barrow
Bolton v Cambridge

Saturday 13 March
Premier League
Arsenal v Tottenham
Crystal Palace v WBA
Everton v Burnley
Fulham v Man City
Leeds v Chelsea
Leicester v Sheff Utd
Man Utd v West Ham
Newcastle v Aston Villa
Southampton v Brighton
Wolves v Liverpool

Championship
Birmingham v Bristol City
Blackburn v Brentford
Bournemouth v Barnsley
Cardiff v Watford
Derby v Millwall
Luton v Swansea
Middlesbrough v Stoke
Nottm Forest v Reading
QPR v Huddersfield
Rotherham v Coventry
Sheff Wed v Norwich
Wycombe v Preston

League One
Blackpool v Fleetwood
Bristol Rov v AFC Wimbledon
Charlton v Shrewsbury
Crewe v Burton
Doncaster v Northampton
Hull v Oxford
Ipswich v Plymouth

Lincoln v Rochdale
MK Dons v Accrington
Peterborough v Portsmouth
Swindon v Gillingham
Wigan v Sunderland

League Two
Carlisle v Bradford
Crawley v Mansfield
Exeter v Cheltenham
Forest Green v Harrogate
Grimsby v Colchester
Leyton Orient v Scunthorpe
Morecambe v Newport
Oldham v Cambridge
Port Vale v Bolton
Salford v Barrow
Southend v Stevenage
Walsall v Tranmere

Tuesday 16 March
Championship
Bournemouth v Swansea
Cardiff v Stoke
Derby v Brentford
Luton v Coventry
Middlesbrough v Preston
Rotherham v Watford

Wednesday 17 March
Championship
Birmingham v Reading
Blackburn v Bristol City
Nottm Forest v Norwich
QPR v Millwall
Sheff Wed v Huddersfield
Wycombe v Barnsley

Saturday 20 March
Premier League
Brighton v Newcastle
Burnley v Leicester
Crystal Palace v Man Utd
Fulham v Leeds
Liverpool v Chelsea
Man City v Wolves
Sheff Utd v Aston Villa
Tottenham v Southampton
WBA v Everton
West Ham v Arsenal

Championship
Barnsley v Sheff Wed
Brentford v Nottm Forest
Bristol City v Rotherham
Coventry v Wycombe
Huddersfield v Bournemouth
Millwall v Middlesbrough
Norwich v Blackburn

Preston v Luton
Reading v QPR
Stoke v Derby
Swansea v Cardiff
Watford v Birmingham

League One
AFC Wimbledon v Charlton
Accrington v Wigan
Burton v MK Dons
Fleetwood v Swindon
Gillingham v Doncaster
Northampton v Crewe
Oxford v Blackpool
Plymouth v Bristol Rov
Portsmouth v Ipswich
Rochdale v Peterborough
Shrewsbury v Hull
Sunderland v Lincoln

League Two
Barrow v Crawley
Bolton v Walsall
Bradford v Oldham
Cambridge v Forest Green
Cheltenham v Salford
Colchester v Port Vale
Harrogate v Morecambe
Mansfield v Grimsby
Newport v Leyton Orient
Scunthorpe v Southend
Stevenage v Carlisle
Tranmere v Exeter

Saturday 27 March
League One
AFC Wimbledon v Northampton
Blackpool v Plymouth
Bristol Rov v Sunderland
Burton v Fleetwood
Charlton v Crewe
Hull v Gillingham
MK Dons v Doncaster
Oxford v Lincoln
Peterborough v Accrington
Rochdale v Swindon
Shrewsbury v Portsmouth
Wigan v Ipswich

League Two
Carlisle v Cambridge
Colchester v Bradford
Crawley v Port Vale
Exeter v Salford
Forest Green v Bolton
Grimsby v Walsall
Harrogate v Southend
Leyton Orient v Oldham

Morecambe v Cheltenham
Newport v Scunthorpe
Stevenage v Barrow
Tranmere v Mansfield

Friday 2 April
Championship
Barnsley v Reading
Birmingham v Swansea
Bournemouth v Middlesbrough
Bristol City v Stoke
Cardiff v Nottm Forest
Derby v Luton
Huddersfield v Brentford
Millwall v Rotherham
Preston v Norwich
QPR v Coventry
Watford v Sheff Wed
Wycombe v Blackburn

League One
Accrington v Burton
Crewe v Hull
Doncaster v Charlton
Fleetwood v Peterborough
Gillingham v Wigan
Ipswich v Bristol Rov
Lincoln v MK Dons
Northampton v Shrewsbury
Plymouth v AFC Wimbledon
Portsmouth v Rochdale
Sunderland v Oxford
Swindon v Blackpool

League Two
Barrow v Newport
Bolton v Colchester
Bradford v Forest Green
Cambridge v Morecambe
Cheltenham v Tranmere
Mansfield v Leyton Orient
Oldham v Stevenage
Port Vale v Exeter
Salford v Grimsby
Scunthorpe v Crawley
Southend v Carlisle
Walsall v Harrogate

Saturday 3 April
Premier League
Arsenal v Liverpool
Aston Villa v Fulham
Chelsea v WBA
Everton v Crystal Palace
Leeds v Sheff Utd
Leicester v Man City
Man Utd v Brighton
Newcastle v Tottenham

Southampton v Burnley
Wolves v West Ham

Monday 5 April
Championship
Blackburn v Bournemouth
Brentford v Birmingham
Coventry v Bristol City
Luton v Barnsley
Middlesbrough v Watford
Norwich v Huddersfield
Nottm Forest v QPR
Reading v Derby
Rotherham v Wycombe
Sheff Wed v Cardiff
Stoke v Millwall
Swansea v Preston

League One
AFC Wimbledon v Fleetwood
Blackpool v Gillingham
Bristol Rov v Doncaster
Burton v Swindon
Charlton v Lincoln
Hull v Northampton
MK Dons v Crewe
Oxford v Accrington
Peterborough v Sunderland
Rochdale v Ipswich
Shrewsbury v Plymouth
Wigan v Portsmouth

League Two
Carlisle v Scunthorpe
Colchester v Barrow
Crawley v Oldham
Exeter v Mansfield
Forest Green v Salford
Grimsby v Cheltenham
Harrogate v Port Vale
Leyton Orient v Walsall
Morecambe v Southend
Newport v Bolton
Stevenage v Bradford
Tranmere v Cambridge

Saturday 10 April
Premier League
Brighton v Everton
Burnley v Newcastle
Crystal Palace v Chelsea
Fulham v Wolves
Liverpool v Aston Villa
Man City v Leeds
Sheff Utd v Arsenal
Tottenham v Man Utd
WBA v Southampton
West Ham v Leicester

Championship
Barnsley v Middlesbrough
Birmingham v Stoke
Bournemouth v Coventry
Bristol City v Nottm Forest
Cardiff v Blackburn
Derby v Norwich
Huddersfield v Rotherham
Millwall v Swansea
Preston v Brentford
QPR v Sheff Wed
Watford v Reading
Wycombe v Luton

League One
Accrington v AFC Wimbledon
Crewe v Oxford
Doncaster v Wigan
Fleetwood v Rochdale
Gillingham v Shrewsbury
Ipswich v MK Dons
Lincoln v Blackpool
Northampton v Bristol Rov
Plymouth v Hull
Portsmouth v Burton
Sunderland v Charlton
Swindon v Peterborough

League Two
Barrow v Carlisle
Bolton v Harrogate
Bradford v Grimsby
Cambridge v Exeter
Cheltenham v Leyton Orient
Mansfield v Newport
Oldham v Colchester
Port Vale v Morecambe
Salford v Stevenage
Scunthorpe v Tranmere
Southend v Crawley
Walsall v Forest Green

Saturday 17 April
Premier League
Arsenal v Fulham
Aston Villa v Man City
Chelsea v Brighton
Everton v Tottenham
Leeds v Liverpool
Leicester v WBA
Man Utd v Burnley
Newcastle v West Ham
Southampton v Crystal Palace
Wolves v Sheff Utd

Championship
Blackburn v Derby
Brentford v Millwall

Coventry v Barnsley
Luton v Watford
Middlesbrough v QPR
Norwich v Bournemouth
Nottm Forest v Huddersfield
Reading v Cardiff
Rotherham v Birmingham
Sheff Wed v Bristol City
Stoke v Preston
Swansea v Wycombe

League One
AFC Wimbledon v Swindon
Blackpool v Sunderland
Bristol Rov v Lincoln
Burton v Plymouth
Charlton v Ipswich
Hull v Fleetwood
MK Dons v Portsmouth
Oxford v Gillingham
Peterborough v Northampton
Rochdale v Accrington
Shrewsbury v Doncaster
Wigan v Crewe

League Two
Carlisle v Port Vale
Colchester v Walsall
Crawley v Cheltenham
Exeter v Southend
Forest Green v Scunthorpe
Grimsby v Bolton
Harrogate v Bradford
Leyton Orient v Barrow
Morecambe v Oldham
Newport v Cambridge
Stevenage v Mansfield
Tranmere v Salford

Tuesday 20 April
Championship
Birmingham v Nottm Forest
Brentford v Cardiff
Norwich v Watford
Preston v Derby
Sheff Wed v Blackburn
Swansea v QPR

League One
AFC Wimbledon v Oxford
Accrington v Doncaster
Bristol Rov v MK Dons
Burton v Lincoln
Fleetwood v Crewe
Hull v Sunderland
Northampton v Ipswich
Peterborough v Gillingham
Plymouth v Charlton

Rochdale v Blackpool
Shrewsbury v Wigan
Swindon v Portsmouth

League Two
Barrow v Port Vale
Bradford v Tranmere
Colchester v Southend
Forest Green v Exeter
Grimsby v Morecambe
Harrogate v Oldham
Leyton Orient v Cambridge
Mansfield v Scunthorpe
Newport v Crawley
Stevenage v Cheltenham
Walsall v Salford
Bolton v Carlisle

Wednesday 21 April
Championship
Huddersfield v Barnsley
Luton v Reading
Millwall v Bournemouth
Rotherham v Middlesbrough
Stoke v Coventry
Wycombe v Bristol City

Saturday 24 April
Premier League
Arsenal v Everton
Aston Villa v WBA
Fulham v Tottenham
Leeds v Man Utd
Leicester v Crystal Palace
Liverpool v Newcastle
Man City v Southampton
Sheff Utd v Brighton
West Ham v Chelsea
Wolves v Burnley

Championship
Barnsley v Rotherham
Blackburn v Huddersfield
Bournemouth v Brentford
Bristol City v Luton
Cardiff v Wycombe
Coventry v Preston
Derby v Birmingham
Middlesbrough v Sheff Wed
Nottm Forest v Stoke
QPR v Norwich
Reading v Swansea
Watford v Millwall

League One
Blackpool v Shrewsbury
Charlton v Peterborough
Crewe v Rochdale
Doncaster v Fleetwood

Gillingham v Northampton
Ipswich v AFC Wimbledon
Lincoln v Hull
MK Dons v Swindon
Oxford v Plymouth
Portsmouth v Bristol Rov
Sunderland v Accrington
Wigan v Burton

League Two
Cambridge v Stevenage
Carlisle v Harrogate
Cheltenham v Colchester
Crawley v Forest Green
Exeter v Newport
Morecambe v Bolton
Oldham v Grimsby
Port Vale v Bradford
Salford v Mansfield
Scunthorpe v Walsall
Southend v Leyton Orient
Tranmere v Barrow

Saturday 1 May
Premier League
Brighton v Leeds
Burnley v West Ham
Chelsea v Fulham
Crystal Palace v Man City
Everton v Aston Villa
Man Utd v Liverpool
Newcastle v Arsenal
Southampton v Leicester
Tottenham v Sheff Utd
WBA v Wolves

Championship
Birmingham v Cardiff
Brentford v Watford
Huddersfield v Coventry
Luton v Middlesbrough
Millwall v Bristol City
Norwich v Reading
Preston v Barnsley
Rotherham v Blackburn
Sheff Wed v Nottm Forest
Stoke v QPR
Swansea v Derby
Wycombe v Bournemouth

League One
AFC Wimbledon v Portsmouth
Accrington v Charlton
Bristol Rov v Crewe
Burton v Gillingham
Fleetwood v MK Dons
Hull v Wigan
Northampton v Blackpool
Peterborough v Lincoln

Plymouth v Sunderland
Rochdale v Doncaster
Shrewsbury v Oxford
Swindon v Ipswich

League Two
Barrow v Southend
Bolton v Exeter
Bradford v Scunthorpe
Colchester v Salford
Forest Green v Tranmere
Grimsby v Port Vale
Harrogate v Cambridge
Leyton Orient v Carlisle
Mansfield v Oldham
Newport v Cheltenham
Stevenage v Crawley
Walsall v Morecambe

Saturday 8 May
Premier League
Arsenal v WBA
Aston Villa v Man Utd
Fulham v Burnley
Leeds v Tottenham
Leicester v Newcastle
Liverpool v Southampton
Man City v Chelsea
Sheff Utd v Crystal Palace
West Ham v Everton
Wolves v Brighton

Championship
Barnsley v Norwich
Blackburn v Birmingham
Bournemouth v Stoke
Bristol City v Brentford
Cardiff v Rotherham
Coventry v Millwall
Derby v Sheff Wed
Middlesbrough v Wycombe
Nottm Forest v Preston
QPR v Luton
Reading v Huddersfield
Watford v Swansea

League One
Blackpool v Bristol Rov
Charlton v Hull
Crewe v Shrewsbury
Doncaster v Peterborough
Gillingham v Plymouth
Ipswich v Fleetwood
Lincoln v AFC Wimbledon
MK Dons v Rochdale
Oxford v Burton
Portsmouth v Accrington
Sunderland v Northampton
Wigan v Swindon

League Two
Cambridge v Grimsby
Carlisle v Walsall
Cheltenham v Harrogate
Crawley v Bolton
Exeter v Barrow
Morecambe v Bradford
Oldham v Forest Green
Port Vale v Mansfield
Salford v Leyton Orient
Scunthorpe v Stevenage
Southend v Newport
Tranmere v Colchester

Tuesday 11 May
Premier League
Brighton v West Ham
Burnley v Leeds
Everton v Sheff Utd
Man Utd v Leicester
WBA v Liverpool

Wednesday 12 May
Premier League
Chelsea v Arsenal
Newcastle v Man City
Southampton v Fulham
Tottenham v Wolves
Crystal Palace v Aston Villa

Saturday 15 May
Premier League
Brighton v Man City
Burnley v Liverpool
Chelsea v Leicester
Crystal Palace v Arsenal
Everton v Wolves
Man Utd v Fulham
Newcastle v Sheff Utd
Southampton v Leeds
Tottenham v Aston Villa
WBA v West Ham

Sunday 23 May
Premier League
Arsenal v Brighton
Aston Villa v Chelsea
Fulham v Newcastle
Leeds v WBA
Leicester v Tottenham
Liverpool v Crystal Palace
Man City v Everton
Sheff Utd v Burnley
West Ham v Southampton
Wolves v Man Utd

SCOTTISH FIXTURES 2020–2021
Premiership Championship League One and League Two

Saturday 1 August
Premiership
Aberdeen v Rangers
Dundee Utd v St Johnstone
Hibernian v Kilmarnock
St Mirren v Livingston

Sunday 2 August
Premiership
Celtic v Hamilton

Monday 3 August
Premiership
Ross Co v Motherwell
Saturday 8 August
Premiership
Hamilton v Ross Co
Livingston v Hibernian
Motherwell v Dundee Utd
St Johnstone v Aberdeen pp

Sunday 9 August
Premiership

Rangers v St Mirren
Kilmarnock v Celtic

Tuesday 11 August
Premiership
Dundee Utd v Hibernian

Wednesday 12 August
Premiership
Aberdeen v Hamilton pp
Motherwell v Livingston
Rangers v St Johnstone
Ross Co v Kilmarnock
St Mirren v Celtic pp

Saturday 15 August
Premiership
Celtic v Aberdeen pp
Hamilton v St Mirren
Kilmarnock v St Johnstone
Ross Co v Dundee Utd
Hibernian v Motherwell

Sunday 16 August
Premiership
Livingston v Rangers
St Johnstone v Aberdeen

Saturday 22 August
Premiership
Aberdeen v Livingston
Motherwell v Hamilton
Rangers v Kilmarnock
St Mirren v Ross Co
Dundee Utd v Celtic

Sunday 23 August
Premiership
Aberdeen v Livingston
St Johnstone v Hibernian

Saturday 29 August
Premiership
Kilmarnock v Dundee Utd
Livingston v Ross Co
St Johnstone v St Mirren
Hamilton v Rangers

Sunday 30 August
Premiership
Celtic v Motherwell
Hibernian v Aberdeen

Saturday 12 September
Premiership
Aberdeen v Kilmarnock
Livingston v Hamilton
Motherwell v St Johnstone
Rangers v Dundee Utd
Ross Co v Celtic
St Mirren v Hibernian

Saturday 19 September
Premiership
Aberdeen v Motherwell
Celtic v Livingston
Dundee Utd v St Mirren
Hibernian v Rangers
Kilmarnock v Hamilton
St Johnstone v Ross Co

Saturday 26 September
Premiership
Celtic v Hibernian
Hamilton v Dundee Utd
Livingston v St Johnstone
Motherwell v Rangers
Ross Co v Aberdeen
St Mirren v Kilmarnock

Friday 2 October
Premiership

Aberdeen v St Mirren
Dundee Utd v Livingston
Hibernian v Hamilton
Kilmarnock v Motherwell
Rangers v Ross Co
St Johnstone v Celtic

Saturday 17 October
Premiership
Celtic v Rangers
Dundee Utd v Aberdeen
Hamilton v St Johnstone
Livingston v Kilmarnock
Ross Co v Hibernian
St Mirren v Motherwell

Championship
Ayr v Queen of South
Dunfermline v Inverness
Hearts v Dundee
Morton v Alloa
Raith v Arbroath

League One
Airdrieonians v Peterhead
Clyde v Partick
Cove v East Fife
Forfar v Dumbarton
Montrose v Falkirk

League Two
Albion Rovers v Stenhousemuir
Brechin v Edinburgh City
Cowdenbeath v Annan
Stirling v Queen's Park
Stranraer v Elgin

Saturday 24 October
Premiership
Aberdeen v Celtic
Kilmarnock v Hibernian
Motherwell v Ross Co
Rangers v Livingston
St Johnstone v Dundee Utd
St Mirren v Hamilton

Championship
Alloa v Dunfermline
Arbroath v Hearts
Dundee v Morton
Inverness v Ayr
Queen of South v Raith

League One
Dumbarton v Clyde
East Fife v Montrose
Falkirk v Forfar
Partick v Airdrieonians
Peterhead v Cove

League Two
Annan v Stranraer
Edinburgh City v Cowdenbeath
Elgin v Brechin
Queen's Park v Albion Rovers
Stenhousemuir v Stirling

Saturday 31 October
Premiership
Dundee Utd v Ross Co
Kilmarnock v Rangers
Livingston v Motherwell

Championship
Dundee v Raith
Dunfermline v Queen of South
Inverness v Arbroath
Morton v Ayr

League One
Clyde v Peterhead
Cove v Partick
Dumbarton v Airdrieonians
Falkirk v East Fife
Forfar v Montrose

League Two
Albion Rovers v Brechin
Cowdenbeath v Stenhousemuir
Edinburgh City v Elgin
Stirling v Annan
Stranraer v Queen's Park

Friday 6 November
Premiership
Aberdeen v Hibernian
Motherwell v Celtic
Rangers v Hamilton
Ross Co v Livingston
St Johnstone v Kilmarnock
St Mirren v Dundee Utd

Saturday 7 November
Championship
Alloa v Dundee
Arbroath v Queen of South
Ayr v Dunfermline
Hearts v Inverness
Raith v Morton

League One
Airdrieonians v Clyde
Cove v Forfar
East Fife v Dumbarton
Montrose v Peterhead
Partick v Falkirk

League Two
Annan v Albion Rovers
Brechin v Stirling

Elgin v Queen's Park
Stenhousemuir v Edinburgh City
Stranraer v Cowdenbeath

Saturday 21 November
Premiership
Dundee Utd v Hamilton
Hibernian v Celtic
Kilmarnock v Ross Co
Livingston v St Mirren
Rangers v Aberdeen
St Johnstone v Motherwell

Championship
Arbroath v Morton
Ayr v Dundee
Dunfermline v Hearts
Inverness v Raith
Queen of South v Alloa

League One
Clyde v Montrose
Falkirk v Cove
Forfar v Airdrieonians
Partick v East Fife
Peterhead v Dumbarton

League Two
Cowdenbeath v Albion Rovers
Edinburgh City v Stranraer
Queen's Park v Brechin
Stenhousemuir v Annan
Stirling v Elgin

Saturday 28 November
League One
Airdrieonians v Cove
Dumbarton v Falkirk
East Fife v Clyde
Montrose v Partick
Peterhead v Forfar

League Two
Albion Rovers v Stirling
Annan v Edinburgh City
Brechin v Stranraer
Elgin v Cowdenbeath
Queen's Park v Stenhousemuir

Saturday 5 December
Premiership
Celtic v St Johnstone
Hamilton v Kilmarnock
Livingston v Dundee Utd
Motherwell v Hibernian
Ross Co v Rangers
St Mirren v Aberdeen

Championship
Alloa v Ayr

Dundee v Arbroath
Morton v Hearts
Queen of South v Inverness
Raith v Dunfermline

League One
Clyde v Forfar
Cove v Montrose
East Fife v Airdrieonians
Falkirk v Peterhead
Partick v Dumbarton

League Two
Cowdenbeath v Queen's Park
Edinburgh City v Albion Rovers
Elgin v Annan
Stenhousemuir v Brechin
Stranraer v Stirling

Saturday 12 December
Premiership
Aberdeen v Ross Co
Celtic v Kilmarnock
Dundee Utd v Rangers
Hamilton v Hibernian
Motherwell v St Mirren
St Johnstone v Livingston

Championship
Arbroath v Alloa
Ayr v Raith
Dunfermline v Morton
Hearts v Queen of South
Inverness v Dundee

League One
Airdrieonians v Montrose
Clyde v Falkirk
Dumbarton v Cove
Forfar v Partick
Peterhead v East Fife

League Two
Albion Rovers v Elgin
Brechin v Annan
Queen's Park v Edinburgh City
Stenhousemuir v Stranraer
Stirling v Cowdenbeath

Saturday 19 December
Premiership
Hibernian v Dundee Utd
Kilmarnock v Aberdeen
Livingston v Celtic
Rangers v Motherwell
Ross Co v Hamilton
St Mirren v St Johnstone

Championship
Alloa v Inverness
Arbroath v Ayr

Dundee v Dunfermline
Morton v Queen of South
Raith v Hearts

League One
Cove v Clyde
East Fife v Forfar
Falkirk v Airdrieonians
Montrose v Dumbarton
Partick v Peterhead

League Two
Annan v Queen's Park
Cowdenbeath v Brechin
Edinburgh City v Stirling
Elgin v Stenhousemuir
Stranraer v Albion Rovers

Wednesday 23 December
Premiership
Celtic v Ross Co
Dundee Utd v Kilmarnock
Hamilton v Livingston
Hibernian v St Mirren
Motherwell v Aberdeen
St Johnstone v Rangers

Saturday 26 December
Premiership
Aberdeen v St Johnstone
Dundee Utd v Motherwell
Hamilton v Celtic
Kilmarnock v Livingston
Rangers v Hibernian
Ross Co v St Mirren

Championship
Alloa v Raith
Dunfermline v Arbroath
Hearts v Ayr
Morton v Inverness
Queen of South v Dundee

League One
Clyde v Airdrieonians
Dumbarton v East Fife
Falkirk v Partick
Forfar v Cove
Peterhead v Montrose

Tuesday 29 December
Championship
Ayr v Morton
Dundee v Alloa
Hearts v Arbroath
Inverness v Dunfermline
Raith v Queen of South

Wednesday 30 December
Premiership

Celtic v Dundee Utd
Hibernian v Ross Co
Livingston v Aberdeen
Motherwell v Kilmarnock
St Johnstone v Hamilton
St Mirren v Rangers

Saturday 2 January
Premiership
Aberdeen v Dundee Utd
Hamilton v Motherwell
Hibernian v Livingston
Kilmarnock v St Mirren
Rangers v Celtic
Ross Co v St Johnstone

Championship
Alloa v Morton
Arbroath v Inverness
Dundee v Hearts
Dunfermline v Raith
Queen of South v Ayr

League One
Airdrieonians v Dumbarton
Cove v Peterhead
East Fife v Falkirk
Montrose v Forfar
Partick v Clyde

League Two
Albion Rovers v Queen's Park
Brechin v Elgin
Cowdenbeath v Edinburgh City
Stirling v Stenhousemuir
Stranraer v Annan

Saturday 9 January
Premiership
Aberdeen v Rangers
Celtic v Hibernian
Dundee Utd v St Johnstone
Kilmarnock v Hamilton
Livingston v Ross Co
St Mirren v Motherwell

Championship
Ayr v Alloa
Hearts v Dunfermline
Inverness v Queen of South
Morton v Arbroath
Raith v Dundee

Saturday 16 January
Premiership
Celtic v Livingston
Hamilton v Dundee Utd
Hibernian v Kilmarnock
Motherwell v Rangers
Ross Co v Aberdeen
St Johnstone v St Mirren

Championship
Alloa v Hearts
Dundee v Ayr
Morton v Dunfermline
Queen of South v Arbroath
Raith v Inverness

League One
Clyde v East Fife
Dumbarton v Forfar
Falkirk v Montrose
Partick v Cove
Peterhead v Airdrieonians

League Two
Annan v Cowdenbeath
Elgin v Edinburgh City
Queen's Park v Stranraer
Stenhousemuir v Albion Rovers
Stirling v Brechin

Saturday 23 January
Premiership
Aberdeen v Motherwell
Dundee Utd v Hibernian
Kilmarnock v St Johnstone
Livingston v Hamilton
Rangers v Ross Co
St Mirren v Celtic

Championship
Arbroath v Dundee
Dunfermline v Ayr
Hearts v Raith
Inverness v Alloa
Queen of South v Morton

League One
Airdrieonians v Partick
Dumbarton v Peterhead
East Fife v Cove
Forfar v Falkirk
Montrose v Clyde

League Two
Albion Rovers v Annan
Brechin v Queen's Park
Cowdenbeath v Stranraer
Edinburgh City v Stenhousemuir
Elgin v Stirling

Wednesday 27 January
Premiership
Celtic v Hamilton
Dundee Utd v St Mirren
Hibernian v Rangers
Livingston v Kilmarnock
Ross Co v Motherwell
St Johnstone v Aberdeen

Saturday 30 January

League Two
Albion Rovers v Edinburgh City
Annan v Elgin
Queen's Park v Stirling
Stenhousemuir v Cowdenbeath
Stranraer v Brechin

Wednesday 3 February

Premiership
Aberdeen v Livingston
Hamilton v Ross Co
Kilmarnock v Celtic
Motherwell v Dundee Utd
Rangers v St Johnstone
St Mirren v Hibernian

Saturday 6 February

Premiership
Celtic v Motherwell
Hamilton v Rangers
Hibernian v Aberdeen
Livingston v St Johnstone
Ross Co v Dundee Utd
St Mirren v Kilmarnock

Championship
Alloa v Queen of South
Arbroath v Dunfermline
Ayr v Hearts
Dundee v Inverness
Morton v Raith

League One
Cove v Airdrieonians
Falkirk v Dumbarton
Montrose v East Fife
Partick v Forfar
Peterhead v Clyde

League Two
Brechin v Stenhousemuir
Edinburgh City v Annan
Elgin v Stranraer
Queen's Park v Cowdenbeath
Stirling v Albion Rovers

Saturday 13 February

Premiership
Aberdeen v St Mirren
Dundee Utd v Livingston
Motherwell v Hamilton
Rangers v Kilmarnock
Ross Co v Hibernian
St Johnstone v Celtic

Championship
Alloa v Arbroath
Dunfermline v Dundee
Inverness v Morton

Queen of South v Hearts
Raith v Ayr

League One
Airdrieonians v Falkirk
Clyde v Cove
Dumbarton v Montrose
East Fife v Partick
Forfar v Peterhead

League Two
Annan v Stirling
Brechin v Albion Rovers
Cowdenbeath v Elgin
Stenhousemuir v Queen's Park
Stranraer v Edinburgh City

Saturday 20 February

Championship
Arbroath v Raith
Ayr v Inverness
Dundee v Queen of South
Dunfermline v Alloa
Hearts v Morton

League One
Cove v Dumbarton
Falkirk v Clyde
Forfar v East Fife
Montrose v Airdrieonians
Peterhead v Partick

League Two
Albion Rovers v Cowdenbeath
Edinburgh City v Brechin
Queen's Park v Annan
Stenhousemuir v Elgin
Stirling v Stranraer

Saturday 27 February

Premiership
Celtic v Aberdeen
Hamilton v St Johnstone
Hibernian v Motherwell
Kilmarnock v Dundee Utd
Livingston v Rangers
St Mirren v Ross Co

Championship
Ayr v Arbroath
Inverness v Hearts
Morton v Dundee
Queen of South v Dunfermline
Raith v Alloa

League One
Airdrieonians v Forfar
Clyde v Dumbarton
Cove v Falkirk
East Fife v Peterhead
Partick v Montrose

League Two
Annan v Brechin
Cowdenbeath v Stirling
Edinburgh City v Queen's Park
Elgin v Albion Rovers
Stranraer v Stenhousemuir

Saturday 6 March
Premiership
Aberdeen v Hamilton
Dundee Utd v Celtic
Motherwell v Livingston
Rangers v St Mirren
Ross Co v Kilmarnock
St Johnstone v Hibernian

Championship
Alloa v Inverness
Arbroath v Queen of South
Hearts v Dundee
Morton v Ayr
Raith v Dunfermline

League One
Airdrieonians v East Fife
Dumbarton v Partick
Forfar v Clyde
Montrose v Cove
Peterhead v Falkirk

League Two
Albion Rovers v Stranraer
Annan v Stenhousemuir
Brechin v Cowdenbeath
Queen's Park v Elgin
Stirling v Edinburgh City

Saturday 13 March
Championship
Dundee v Arbroath
Dunfermline v Morton
Hearts v Ayr
Inverness v Raith
Queen of South v Alloa

League One
Clyde v Montrose
East Fife v Dumbarton
Falkirk v Forfar
Partick v Airdrieonians
Peterhead v Cove

League Two
Edinburgh City v Albion Rovers
Elgin v Annan
Queen's Park v Brechin
Stenhousemuir v Stirling
Stranraer v Cowdenbeath

Saturday 20 March
Premiership
Celtic v Rangers

Dundee Utd v Aberdeen
Hamilton v St Mirren
Kilmarnock v Motherwell
Livingston v Hibernian
St Johnstone v Ross Co

Championship
Alloa v Dundee
Arbroath v Hearts
Ayr v Raith
Dunfermline v Inverness
Morton v Queen of South

League One
Clyde v Peterhead
Cove v Partick
Dumbarton v Airdrieonians
Falkirk v East Fife
Forfar v Montrose

League Two
Annan v Albion Rovers
Brechin v Stranraer
Cowdenbeath v Stenhousemuir
Edinburgh City v Elgin
Stirling v Queen's Park

Saturday 27 March
Championship
Alloa v Ayr
Dundee v Dunfermline
Hearts v Queen of South
Inverness v Arbroath
Raith v Morton

League One
Airdrieonians v Peterhead
Cove v Forfar
East Fife v Clyde
Montrose v Dumbarton
Partick v Falkirk

League Two
Albion Rovers v Brechin
Elgin v Cowdenbeath
Stenhousemuir v Edinburgh City
Stirling v Annan
Stranraer v Queen's Park

Saturday 3 April
Premiership
Aberdeen v Kilmarnock
Hibernian v Hamilton
Motherwell v St Johnstone
Rangers v Dundee Utd
Ross Co v Celtic
St Mirren v Livingston

Championship
Arbroath v Alloa
Ayr v Dundee

Dunfermline v Hearts
Morton v Inverness
Queen of South v Raith

League One
Clyde v Partick
Dumbarton v Cove
East Fife v Montrose
Falkirk v Airdrieonians
Peterhead v Forfar

League Two
Brechin v Stirling
Cowdenbeath v Annan
Edinburgh City v Stranraer
Elgin v Stenhousemuir
Queen's Park v Albion Rovers

Saturday 10 April
Championship
Ayr v Dunfermline
Dundee v Morton
Hearts v Alloa
Queen of South v Inverness
Raith v Arbroath

League One
Airdrieonians v Clyde
Cove v East Fife
Forfar v Dumbarton
Montrose v Falkirk
Partick v Peterhead

League Two
Albion Rovers v Stirling
Annan v Edinburgh City
Cowdenbeath v Queen's Park
Stenhousemuir v Brechin
Stranraer v Elgin

Saturday 17 April
Championship
Alloa v Raith
Arbroath v Ayr
Dunfermline v Queen of South
Inverness v Dundee
Morton v Hearts

League One
Airdrieonians v Montrose
Clyde v Forfar
Falkirk v Cove
Partick v Dumbarton
Peterhead v East Fife

League Two
Albion Rovers v Elgin
Annan v Stranraer
Brechin v Edinburgh City
Queen's Park v Stenhousemuir
Stirling v Cowdenbeath

Tuesday 20 April
League One
Cove v Clyde
Dumbarton v Falkirk
East Fife v Airdrieonians
Forfar v Partick
Montrose v Peterhead

League Two
Stenhousemuir19:30Annan
Stranraer19:30Albion Rovers
Cowdenbeath v Brechin
Edinburgh City v Stirling
Elgin v Queen's Park

Saturday 24 April
Championship
Ayr v Queen of South
Dundee v Raith
Dunfermline v Arbroath
Hearts v Inverness
Morton v Alloa

League One
Airdrieonians v Cove
Clyde v Falkirk
East Fife v Forfar
Montrose v Partick
Peterhead v Dumbarton

League Two
Brechin v Annan
Cowdenbeath v Albion Rovers
Queen's Park v Edinburgh City
Stenhousemuir v Stranraer
Stirling v Elgin

Friday 30 April
Championship
Alloa v Dunfermline
Arbroath v Morton
Inverness v Ayr
Queen of South v Dundee
Raith v Hearts

Saturday 1 May
League One
Cove v Montrose
Dumbarton v Clyde
Falkirk v Peterhead
Forfar v Airdrieonians
Partick v East Fife

League Two
Albion Rovers v Stenhousemuir
Annan v Queen's Park
Edinburgh City v Cowdenbeath
Elgin v Brechin
Stranraer v Stirling